East Asia

A Cultural, Social, and Political History

PATRICIA BUCKLEY EBREY
University of Washington–Seattle

ANNE WALTHALL
University of California–Irvine

JAMES B. PALAIS
University of Washington–Seattle

HOUGHTON MIFFLIN COMPANY
Boston   New York

HEILONGJIANG

•Harbin

HOKKAIDO

•Changchun   JILIN

Sea of
Japan

NEI MENGGU

•Vladivostok

•Sendai

•Ulaanbaatar

•Hohhot

Yellow

Shenyang•
LIAONING

Datong•

Beijing• BEIJING
Tianjin•
HEBEI TIANJIN

Bay of
Bohai

NORTH
KOREA
•Pyongyang

HONSHU

Tokyo⊛

NINGXIA

Taiyuan•

Shijiazhuang•

SHANXI
SHANDONG

•Jinan

•Qufu

Seoul•

SOUTH
KOREA

Nagoya•

Kyoto•
Osaka•

JAPAN

SHIKOKU

yuan

Luoyang• •Zhengzhou

Pusan•

Wei
•Xi'an

SHAANXI   HENAN

JIANGSU

KYUSHU

Yellow Sea

Huai

ANHUI

Nagasaki•

du

Hun

•Suizhou

•Hefei

Nanjing•
Suzhou• Shanghai•
Lake
Tai SHANGHAI

Jialing

HUBEI

Hankou•

Yangzi

Hangzhou•

Fuchun

RYUKYU ISLANDS

•Ningbo

Chongqing•

CHONGQING

Dongting
Lake

Poyang
Lake
Nanchang•

ZHEJIANG

East
China
Sea

PACIFIC

•Chongqing

Yuan

Changsha•

JIANGXI

Gan

HUNAN

Xiao Xiang

Guiyang•

GUIZHOU

Fuzhou•

OCEAN

FUJIAN

Taipei•

GUANGXI

Xiamen•

TAIWAN

Nanning•

GUANGDONG

Xi

Xijiang

Guangzhou•

Xianggang
HONG KONG

South China Sea

⊛

Haikou•

|||| Modern Grand Canal

HAINAN

wwww Great Wall

Province boundaries in China

PHILIPPINES

North China Plain

Area of major loess deposits

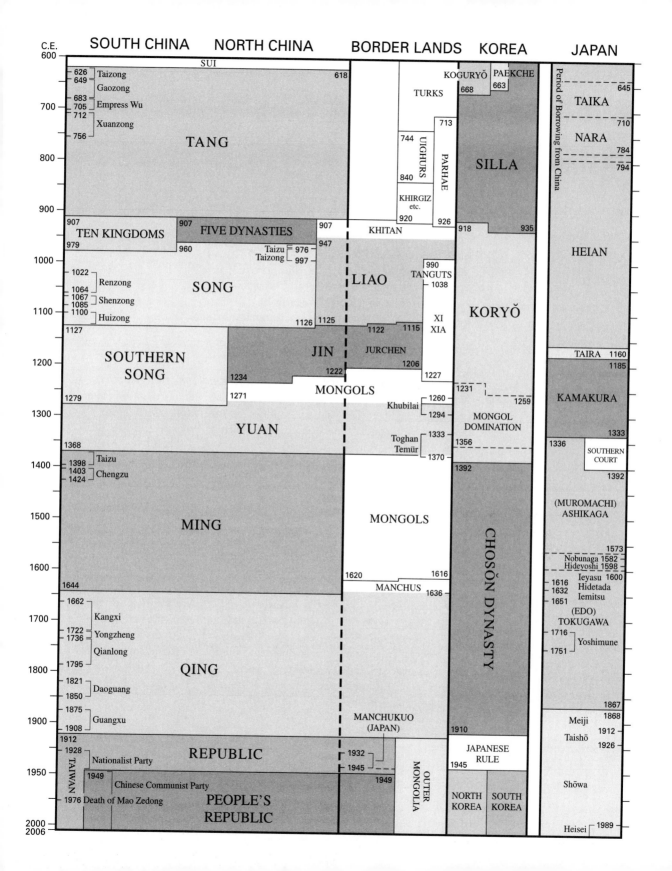

Publisher: Charles Hartford
Senior Sponsoring Editor: Nancy Blaine
Senior Development Editor: Julie Swasey
Senior Project Editor: Jane Lee
Editorial Assistant: Kristen Truncellito
Senior Art and Design Coordinator: Jill Haber
Senior Photo Editor: Jennifer Meyer Dare
Composition Buyer/Manufacturing Coordinator: Chuck Dutton
Senior Marketing Manager: Sandra McGuire
Marketing Assistant: Molly Parke

Cover image: Caption: *Portrait of Yinti, Prince Xun (1688–1755) and His Wife,* second half of the 18th century, Qing dynasty, ink and paint on paper. Credit: Arthur M. Sackler Gallery, Smithsonian Institution, Washington, D.C.: Purchase–Smithsonian Collections Acquisition Program and partial gift of Richard G. Pritzlaff, S1991.88.

Text credits appear on page 625.

Printed in the U.S.A.

Library of Congress Control Number: 2001133244

ISBN: 0-618-13384-4

123456789-MP-09 08 07 06 05

CONTENTS

MAPS AND FIGURES

PREFACE

THERE ARE MANY REASONS TO LEARN about East Asia. A fifth of the world's population lives there. Every day newspapers carry articles on the rapid transformations of the world economy that make China, Japan, and Korea a growing presence in our lives. Globalization means that not only are people crossing the Pacific in ever increasing numbers, but also that American popular culture draws from many sources in East Asia, from Korean martial arts to Japanese anime and Chinese films.

But why approach East Asia through its history, rather than, say, its economy or contemporary culture? Many reasons can be offered. One cannot gain an adequate understanding of modern phenomena without knowing the stages and processes that led up to them. Moreover, all of the countries of East Asia are strongly historically-minded. To a much greater extent than in the United States, people know and identify with people and events of a thousand or more years ago. In all three countries, people still read for pleasure *The Three Kingdoms*, a novel written in fourteenth century China about the leaders of three contending states in third century China. Historical consciousness also underlies the strong sense of separate identities among the people of China, Korea, and Japan. The fact that time and again Korea was able to protect its independence despite the attempts of both China and Japan to conquer it is a central part of Korean identity today. Yet another reason to learn about East Asia in the past is its comparative value. As a region that developed nearly independently of the West, East Asia sheds light on other ways human beings have found meaning, formed communities, and governed themselves, expanding our understanding of the human condition.

When the three authors of this volume were students themselves (in the 1960s and 1970s), the fullest and most up-to-date textbook on East Asia was the two-volume set published in 1960 and 1965 by Houghton Mifflin, *East Asia: The Great Tradition* and *East Asia: The Modern Transformation*, written by Edwin O. Reischauer, John K. Fairbank and Albert M. Craig. Not only did we learn the basic political chronology from these books, but they introduced us to such central issues as the dynastic cycle, the interplay of the Chinese and "barbarians," the ways Korea and Japan adapted features of the Chinese model, the challenge posed by the West in the nineteenth century, and modern revolutionary movements. When it came time for us to develop our own research agendas, these books still cast a shadow as we pursued questions that they did not pose or delved more deeply into topics that they covered only superficially.

It was because we respected these books that we were willing to listen when Nancy Blaine of Houghton Mifflin approached us about doing a new history of East Asia for the current generation of students. We knew that the task would be daunting. Could we take into account the wealth of scholarship that had been published in the forty-odd years since the original *East Asia* books and yet produce the leaner, more visual book wanted by students and teachers today? As we discussed how to meet these challenges, we came up with a plan for this book.

COMPARABLE COVERAGE OF KOREA

The growth of Korean studies over the last quarter century now makes it possible to give

Korea comparable coverage to China and Japan (we ended up giving China about 50 percent of the space, Japan 30 percent, and Korea 20 percent). We know that many teachers have been frustrated in their attempts to cover Korea in their East Asia courses for lack of suitable materials and hope that our efforts prove useful to both them and their students.

A BROAD FOCUS: *CONNECTIONS* CHAPTERS

A second key decision we made was to search for ways to keep in mind the larger whole as we told the separate stories of China, Korea, and Japan. Our solution was to periodically zoom out to look at the wider region from a global or world-historical perspective. Thus, every few chapters we have inserted a mini-chapter on developments that link the societies of East Asia both to each other and to the larger global context. We have labeled these mini-chapters "Connections" because they put their emphasis on the many ways each society was connected to what went on outside it. For instance, the origins and spread of Buddhism are of great importance to all of the societies of East Asia, but much of the story can be told as a common story that connects East Asia with the rest of Asia. Similarly, many books write about World War II in East Asia in entirely different ways in their China and Japan chapters. By stepping back and writing about the war from a more global perspective, we can help students see the larger picture.

BALANCED CULTURAL, SOCIAL, AND POLITICAL HISTORY

Even though the volume of scholarship on East Asia has increased many-fold since the original *East Asia* set was written, we decided to honor its example of striving for balanced coverage of the different strands of history. A basic political narrative is essential to give students a firm sense of chronology and to let them think about issues of change. Moreover, there is no denying that the creation of state structures has much to do with how people lived their lives. Even the fact that people think of themselves as "Chinese," "Korean," or "Japanese" is largely a by-product of political history.

We also believed that students should gain an understanding of the philosophies and religions of East Asia. Confucianism and Buddhism have both been of great importance throughout the region, but in very diverse ways, as the historical context has continually changed. Other elements of high culture also deserve coverage, such as the arts of poetry and calligraphy.

Yet we did not want to neglect topics in social, cultural, and economic history, where much of our own work has been concentrated. Even if the state is important to understanding how people lived, so were families, villages, and religious sects. We also wanted to bring in the results of scholarship on those who had been marginalized in the traditional histories, from laborers and minorities to women at all social levels.

A NARROW FOCUS: BIOGRAPHIES, DOCUMENTS, AND MATERIAL CULTURE

The danger of trying to cover so much is that we would have to stay at a high level of generalization. To keep our readers engaged and bring our story down to earth, we decided to devote three or four pages per chapter to closer looks at specific people, documents, and material objects.

Biographies

Many chapters have a one-page biography, about someone who would not normally be mentioned in a history book. Although we found few truly ordinary people to write about for the earlier periods, we still ended up with a diverse set of individuals. The people sketched range from the most accomplished (such as the eminent Chinese poet Du Fu and the Korean philosopher Yi

Chehyŏn) to remarkably ordinary people (such as a woman whose job was to mind the neighborhood telephone). Three military men are portrayed; others were physicians, entrepreneurs, and founders of religious sects. We also have included some agitators and revolutionaries, and even a winning volleyball coach.

Documents

In our chapters we frequently cite short passages from primary sources, but thought that students would also benefit from texts long enough for them to get a sense of the genre, the author's point of view, and the circumstances described. A few of those we have included were written by famous writers, such as Fukuzawa Yūkichi and Lu Xun. Some are excerpted from well-known pieces of literature, such as the play, *The Peony Pavilion*. Others will be less familiar to teachers and students alike. Legal documents have been selected for what they reveal of ordinary people's lives. Religious texts of several sorts were chosen to help us see religion and popular beliefs in action. Many authors are utterly serious, complaining bitterly of war or corruption, for instance; others have well-developed senses of humor. All of the documents selected prompt active involvement and critical interpretation as they get readers to listen to the concerns of people of the past.

Material Culture

Texts are not our only sources for reconstructing the past; there is much to be discovered from material remains of many sorts. To give focus to this dimension of history, for each chapter we have selected one element of material culture to describe in some detail. These range from the most mundane—food, drink, clothing, houses, and means of transportation—to objects of art, including specific paintings, sculptures, or performing arts. Many of the objects discussed have economic significance, for example, fertilizers, periodic markets, and the Grand Canal. Others are examples of ingenuity, such as the Korean

water clock. Most of the features for the late nineteenth or twentieth century bring out ways material culture has changed along with so much else in modern times—from changes in the food people eat, to streetcars and political posters.

THINKING LIKE A HISTORIAN

The "Documents" and "Material Culture" features challenge students to draw inferences from primary materials much the way historians do. Another way we have tried to help students learn to think like historians is to present history as a set of questions more than a set of answers. What historians are able to say about a period or topic depends not only on the sources available, but also the questions asked. To help students see this, we begin each chapter with a brief discussion of the sorts of questions that motivate contemporary historians to do research on the time period. Most of these questions have no easy answers—these are not questions students will be able to answer simply by reading the chapter. Rather they are real questions, ones interesting enough to motivate historians to sift through recalcitrant evidence in their efforts to find answers. The earliest chapter on Korea, for instance, poses the question of how the three states on the Korean peninsula were able to survive in the face of Chinese power. The chapter on early nineteenth century Japan points out that historians have studied the period for clues to the causes of the Meiji Restoration, wanting to know the relative weight to assign to foreign pressure and domestic unrest. For the chapter dealing with China under the Nationalists, readers are told that the desire to explain the Communist victory in 1949 has motivated historians to ponder such questions as why May Fourth Liberalism lost its appeal and whether the economic politics of the Nationalists could have brought prosperity to China if Japan had not invaded. We hope that posing these questions at the beginning of each chapter will help readers see the significance of the topics and issues presented in the chapter.

USING THIS TEXT IN CLASS

East Asian history is taught many ways, as a one-semester or one-year course, or as linked courses on China and Japan (and sometimes also Korea). To fit the needs of these different approaches, this text is available in three formats: comprehensive, divided by country, and divided chronologically. Since those who divide chronologically might prefer to break either at the end of Part Three (1600) or at the end of Part Four (1800), Part Four appears in both of the chronologically-divided volumes. Similarly, the separate volumes on China and Japan each include all of the Connections mini-chapters.

Those who wish to supplement this text with other readings will find many suggestions at the end of each chapter.

ACKNOWLEDGMENTS

Many people have contributed to the shaping of this book. The three authors have been teaching about the societies of East Asia for two or three decades, and the ways they approach their subjects owe much to questions from their students, conversations with their colleagues, and the outpouring of scholarship in their fields. As we worked on this text, we received much advice from others, from early suggestions of possible collaborators, to critiques of our original proposal and reviews of the drafts of our chapters. The reviewers' reports prompted us to rethink some generalizations, urged us not to weigh the book down with too much detail, and saved us from a number of embarrassing errors. We appreciate the time and attention the following reviewers gave to helping us produce a better book:

James Anderson, University of North Carolina at Greensboro; R. David Arkush, University of Iowa; Craig N. Canning, College of William and Mary; Sue Fawn Chung, University of Nevada, Las Vegas; Anthony DeBlasi, University of Albany; Ronald G. Dimberg, University of Virginia; Franklin M. Doeringer, Lawrence University; Alexis Dudden, Connecticut College; Karl Friday, University of Georgia; Karl Gerth, University of South Carolina; Andrew Goble, University of Oregon; John B. Henderson, Louisiana State University; Jeff Hornibrook, SUNY Plattsburgh; William Johnston, Wesleyan University; Fujiya Kawashima, Bowling Green State University; Ari Daniel Levine, University of Georgia; Huaiyin Li, University of Missouri-Columbia; Angelene Naw, Judson College; Steve Phillips, Towson University; Jonathan Porter, University of New Mexico; Wesley Sasaki-Uemura, University of Utah; S. A. Thornton, Arizona State University; Lu Yan, University of New Hampshire; Ka-che Yip, University of Maryland, Baltimore County; Theodore Jun Yoo, University of Hawaii at Manoa.

We also are grateful for all the work put into this book by the editorial staff at Houghton Mifflin: Nancy Blaine originally convinced us to take on this job; Julie Swasey went through all of our drafts, arranged the reviews, and made numerous suggestions; Linda Sykes secured the photos; Penny Peters handled the art; and Jane Lee managed the production details.

The division of work among the three authors was primarily by country of specialization, with Patricia Ebrey writing the parts on China, Anne Walthall those on Japan, and James Palais those on Korea. The Connections chapters we divided among ourselves chronologically, with Patricia Ebrey taking the early ones (on prehistory, Buddhism, Cultural Contact Across Eurasia, and the Mongols), Anne Walthall taking the early modern and modern ones (on Europe Enters the Scene, Western Imperialism, and World War II), and James Palais doing the final one on East Asia in the Twenty-First Century.

CONVENTIONS

Throughout this book names are given in East Asian order, with family name preceding personal name. Thus Mao Zedong was from the Mao family, Ashikaga Takauji from the Ashikaga family, and Yi Sŏnggye from the Yi family.

Both Japanese and Korean have phonetic scripts (Japanese a syllabary, Korean an alphabet), though Japanese additionally makes extensive use of Chinese characters. There are standard ways to transcribe these scripts into our alphabet (the Hepburn system for Japanese and the McCune-Reischauer for Korean with a few modifications, primarily placing priority on pronunciation rather than orthography). Chinese does not have a phonetic script, and more than one system of transcribing it has been commonly used. The romanization system used here is the pinyin system.

The basic vowels, *a, e, i, o,* and *u* in all three languages are pronounced as in Italian, German, and Spanish.

a as in f*a*ther

e as in *e*nd

i as the first *e* in *e*ve (in Chinese often like the *e* in sh*e*)

o as in *o*ld (shorter in length and with less of the *ou* sound of English)

u as in r*u*de (shorter in length than English)

Diacritical marks over vowels change the pronunciations:

ŏ in Korean is like the *o* in r*o*t, except shorter in length than English

ŭ in Korean is something like he *oo* in f*oo*t

The macron over the *ō* or *ū* in Japanese indicates that the vowel is "long," taking twice as long to say, as though it were doubled. Macrons have been omitted from common place names

well known without them, such as Tokyo and Kyoto.

ü in Chinese (used only after *l* or *n*) is like the German *ü*

The three languages are not so similar when one vowel follows another. In the case of Japanese, each vowel is pronounced as a separate syllable. In Chinese, they create a (one syllable) diphthong (e.g., *mei,* which is pronounced like may). In Korean, two vowels also form diphthongs, but with some special pronunciations; *ae* is like the *a* in *a*dd; *oe* like the *ö* of German; and *ŭi* like the *uee* in q*uee*r.

Consonants for Japanese romanization are close enough to English to give readers little difficulty. In the case of Korean, voiced consonants (*j, g, b, d*) are like English. However, aspirated consonants (*ch', k', p', t'*) marked by a marked exhalation of air, and unaspirated consonants (*ch, k, p, t*) are like English but without any aspiration at all. In the Chinese case, divergence between how an English speaker would guess a pronunciation and how the word is actually pronounced is even greater. The most confusing consonants are listed below:

c   ts in tsar

z   dz in adze

zh j in jack

q   ch in chin

x   sh

In the case of Chinese, the romanization system does not convey tones, which are also an important element in pronunciation. Another complication is that pinyin has only become the standard system of romanization in recent decades. Some earlier spellings were based on dialects other than Mandarin (Peking, Canton, Sun Yat-sen). More often the Wade-Giles system of romanization was employed. From context, if nothing else, most readers have inferred that Mao Zedong is the same person whose name used to be spelled Mao Tse-tung, or that Wang Anshi is the pinyin form of Wang An-shih. Two older spellings have been retained in this book because they are so widely known (Sun Yatsen and Chiang Kaishek). Charts for converting pinyin to Wade-Giles and vice versa are widely available on the Internet, should anyone want verification of their guesses (see, for instance, http://www.loc.gov/catdir/pinyin/romcover.html; http://www.library.ucla.edu/libraries/eastasian/ctable2.htm; or http://oclccjk.lib.uci.edu/wgtopy.htm).

PART ONE

The Foundations of East Asian Civilization in China

The Prehistory of East Asia

THINKING ABOUT THE WHOLE OF EAST Asia before the invention of writing helps to remind us that East Asia has always been a part of Eurasia and did not develop in isolation. During the Pleistocene geological era (the last great Ice Age), plants and animals spread across Eurasia as far as Japan, then connected to the mainland. In later times, peoples, crops, and inventions traveled in many directions.

Early human beings *(Homo erectus)* appeared in East Asia over 1 million years ago, having gradually spread from Africa and West Asia during the Pleistocene. Peking Man, discovered in the 1920s, is one of the best-documented examples of *H. erectus,* with skeletal remains of some forty individuals found in a single cave complex. Peking Man could stand erect, hunt, make fire, and use chipped stones as tools. In recent decades, even earlier examples of *H. erectus* have been found in south China.

Modern human beings *(Homo sapiens)* appeared in East Asia around 100,000 years ago. The dominant theory in the West, supported by studies of the mitochondrial DNA of modern people, is that *H. sapiens* also spread out of Africa and displaced *H. erectus,* which became extinct. Chinese archaeologists have given more credence to the theory that *H. erectus* evolved into *H. sapiens* independently in many parts of the world, making Peking Man the ancestor of modern Chinese. They can point to similarities between Peking Man and modern Chinese, such as the shape of certain teeth.

During the period from 100,000 to 10,000 B.C.E., East Asia was home to numerous groups of Paleolithic hunters, gatherers, and fishermen. Many of these people were on the move, following the wild animals they hunted or searching for new environments to exploit. This was the period that saw the movement of people from northeast Asia to the Americas and also from south China and Southeast Asia to the Pacific and Australia.

During this long period, humans began to speak, and so the affinities of modern languages offer a rough clue to the spread of peoples in early times. In East Asia, three large language families can be identified. Korean and Japanese are related to each other and more distantly to other North Asian languages such as Turkic and Mongolian (the Ural-Altaic languages). Chinese has distant ties to Tibetan and Burman (the Sino-Tibetan-Burman languages). Many of the languages spoken by minorities in south China belong to a large group found widely in mainland and insular Southeast Asia (the Austro-Asiatic languages). Language affinities suggest at least three migratory routes through East Asia: from North Asia into Mongolia, Manchuria, Korea, and Japan; from China into Tibet and Southeast Asia; and from south China to both Southeast Asia and the islands of the Philippines and Indonesia. Other evidence suggests additional routes, for instance, from Southeast Asia and Micronesia to Japan.

All through Eurasia, much greater advance came after the end of the last Ice Age around 10,000 B.C.E. (see Map C1.1). Soon after this date, people in Japan began making pottery, some of the earliest in the world. Pottery is of great value for holding water and storing food. In China and Korea, the earliest pottery finds are somewhat later, but pottery was apparently in use by 6000 B.C.E. Throughout East Asia,

Map C1.1   Neolithic Sites in East Asia

early pottery was commonly imprinted on its surface to give it texture. In Japan this period is referred to as Jōmon and dated from about 10,000 to 300 B.C.E. The comparable period in Korea is called Chulmun and dated from about 8000 to 700 B.C.E. These cultures share many features. From shell mounds found in many places in both Korea and Japan, it is evident that sites were occupied for long periods, that shellfish were collected onshore, and that fish were caught from both rivers and the ocean. Other food sources were animals such as deer and wild boar, which were hunted. Dogs seem to have been domesticated, perhaps used as hunting animals.

China in the millennia after the last Ice Age followed more closely the pattern seen in western Eurasia involving crop agriculture, domesti-

cation of animals for food and work, pottery, textiles, and villages. Agriculture is a crucial change because cultivating crops allows denser and more permanent settlements. Because tending crops, weaving, and fashioning pots require different sorts of technical and social skills than hunting and gathering, it is likely that skilled elders began to vie with hunters and warriors for leadership.

The dozen or more distinct Neolithic cultures that have been identified in China can be roughly divided by latitude into the southern rice zone and the northern millet zone and by longitude into the eastern jade zone and the western painted pottery zone. Dogs and pigs were found in both areas as early as 5000 B.C.E. By 3000 B.C.E. sheep and cattle had become important in the north, water buffalo and cattle in the south.

Whether rice was independently domesticated in China or spread there from Southeast Asia is not yet certain. The earliest finds in China date to about 8000 B.C.E. At Hemudu, a site south of Shanghai and dating to about 5000 B.C.E., Neolithic villagers grew rice in wet fields and supplemented their diet with fish and water plants such as lotus and water chestnut. Hemudu villagers built wooden houses on piles, wove baskets, and made hoes, spears, mallets, paddles, and other tools of wood. They decorated their pottery and lacquered bowls with incised geometrical designs or pictures of birds, fish, or trees.

Millet, a crop domesticated in China, became the foundation of agriculture in north China. Nanzhuangtou, the earliest site found so far, is in southern Hebei and dates to about 8000 B.C.E. At Cishan, a site in Hebei dating to about 5500 B.C.E., millet was cut with stone sickles and stored in cord-marked pottery bowls, jars, and tripods (three-legged pots). Besides growing millet, the local people hunted deer and collected clams, snails, and turtles.

The east-west divide among Chinese Neolithic cultures in terms of expressive culture may well have had connections to less tangible elements of culture such as language and religion. In the west (Shaanxi and Gansu provinces especially), pottery decorated with painted geometrical designs was commonly produced from about 5000 to 3000 B.C.E. In the fully developed Yangshao style, grain jars were exuberantly painted in red and black with spirals, diamonds, and other geometrical patterns.

In the east, from Liaodong near Korea in the north to near Shanghai in the south, early pottery was rarely painted, but more elaborate forms appeared very early, with the finest wares formed on potters' wheels. Some had exceptionally thin walls polished to an almost metallic appearance. Many forms were constructed by adding parts, such as legs, spouts, handles, or lids. The many ewers and goblets found in eastern sites were probably used for rituals of feasting or sacrifice. Eastern cultures were also marked by progressively more elaborate burials.

Jade Plaque. This small plaque (6.2 by 8.3 cm, or 2.5 by 3.25 in) is incised to depict a human figure who merges into a monster mask. The lower part could be interpreted as his arms and legs, but at the same time resembles a monster mask with bulging eyes, prominent nostrils, and a large mouth. *(Zhejiang Provincial Institute of Archaeology/Cultural Relics Publishing House)*

At Dawenkou in Shandong (ca. 5000–2500 B.C.E.), not only were wooden coffins used, but even wooden burial chambers were occasionally constructed. The richest burials had over a hundred objects placed in them, including jade, stone, or pottery necklaces and bracelets. Some of those buried there had their upper lateral incisors extracted, a practice Chinese authors in much later times considered "barbarian," and which is also seen in some Japanese sites.

Even more distinctive of the eastern Neolithic cultures is the use of jade. Because jade does not crack, shaping it requires slow grinding with abrasive sand. The most spectacular discoveries of Neolithic jades have been made in Liaodong near Korea (Hongshan culture, ca. 3500 B.C.E.) and south of Shanghai (Liangzhu culture, ca. 2500 B.C.E.)—areas that literate Chinese in ca. 500 B.C.E. considered barbarian. In the Hongshan culture area, jade was made into small sculptures of turtles, birds, and strange coiled "pig dragons." In the Liangzhu area, jade was fashioned into objects with no obvious utilitarian purpose and which are therefore considered ritual objects. Most common are disks and notched columns.

In China, the late Neolithic period (ca. 3000–2000 B.C.E.) was a time of increased contact and cultural borrowing between these regional cultures. Cooking tripods, for instance, spread west, while painted pottery spread east. This period must also have been one of increased conflict between communities, since people began building defensive walls around settlements out of rammed earth, sometimes as large as 20 feet high and 30 feet thick. Enclosing a settlement with such a wall required chiefs able to command men and resources on a large scale. Another sign of the increasing power of religious or military elites is human sacrifice, probably of captives. The earliest examples, dating to about 2000 B.C.E., involved human remains placed under the foundations of buildings. At about the same time, metal began to be used on a small scale for weapons. These trends in Neolithic sites on the north China plain link it closely to the early stages of the Bronze Age civilization there, discussed in Chapter 1.

For China, prehistory conventionally stops soon after 2000 B.C.E. It is true that in the Chinese subcontinent outside the core of Shang territories, subsistence technology continued in the Neolithic pattern for many more centuries. In Korea and Japan, the period before writing lasted longer, but during the first millennium B.C.E., technologies from China began to have an impact.

To understand the links between early China and its East Asian neighbors, we must briefly consider the wider Eurasian context, especially the northern steppe region. In terms of contemporary countries, the steppe extends from southern Russia past the Caspian and Aral seas, through the Central Asian republics, into Mongolia and farther east. Horses were domesticated on the southern Russian steppe by about 4000 B.C.E. but spread only slowly to other regions. Chariots spread first, then riding on horseback. A fourteenth-century B.C.E. Hittite

text on horsemanship discusses the training of chariot horses; within a century or so, chariots appeared in Shang China. The Scythians appeared as mounted archers in the tenth or ninth century B.C.E. East of them, the Karasuk, with a similar culture, dominated the region from western Mongolia into south Siberia. The Scythians and the Karasuk lived in felt tents, traveled in covered carts, and had bronze technology, including the bronze bit that made possible horseback riding. By the seventh century B.C.E. in the Altai region of Mongolia, there were two distinct groups of nomadic pastoralists: those who buried the dead under mounds and those who buried the dead in stone boxes. Their bronze implements, however, were much the same.

South of these groups on the steppe, but in contact with them, were pastoral-agricultural cultures in China's Northern Zone, stretching in terms of modern provinces from Gansu through northern Shaanxi, northern Shanxi, and northern Hebei, into Liaoning (southern Manchuria). During the late second millennium B.C.E., this zone was settled by a variety of cultures with distinct pottery and burial customs but bronze knives much like those of the steppe to the north. In the early first millennium B.C.E., warrior elites emerged in many of these cultures, and animal raising became more central to their economy, perhaps in response to a climate that was becoming colder and drier. From 600 to 300 B.C.E., evidence of horses becomes more and more common, as does riding astride. Some of these cultures adopted nomadic pastoralism, moving with their herds to new pastures. These cultures also adopted the art styles common on the steppe, such as bronze and gold animal plaques. They made increasing use of iron, which may have spread to them from the Central Asian steppe rather than from China, which was also beginning to use iron in this period. These Northern Zone cultures were in contact with the Chinese states, however, and early Chinese coins have been found at some sites.

The eastern end of this Northern Zone was directly north of Korea. Archaeologists have

Figure C1.1   **Dolmens.** Burial structures capped with large stones, called dolmens, have been found in both the Korean peninsula and nearby parts of Japan. The two shown on the left were found in northern and southern Korea, respectively. The one on the right, which also shows the arrangement of the bones beneath the capstone, was found in Kyushu, across the Korean Strait.

identified a culture there that lasted eight centuries, from the eleventh to the fourth centuries B.C.E., called Upper Xiajiadian culture. Finds include an ancient mine, along with distinctive bronze knives, helmets, mirrors, and horse fittings. The faces of the dead were covered with a cloth decorated with bronze buttons. During the next phase there was such a radical change in burial practices that archaeologists suspect that a different, and militarily superior, horse-riding group entered the area. This new group used both wooden and stone-cist coffins. A cist burial is one with a burial chamber built of stones to form a box, with a flagstone or similar large, flat stone to cover it. By the third century B.C.E., the cultures of the Northern Zone became

increasingly homogeneous in material culture and rituals, with similar warrior elites and ornamental art.

These societies came into contact with people settled farther south in the Korean peninsula. As mentioned previously, after the end of the last Ice Age, the Korean peninsula was home to the fishing and foraging Chulmun peoples. By the middle of the first millennium B.C.E., a new culture, called Mumun (from the name of its pottery), became established. Mumun sites, in contrast to the earlier Chulmun seaside ones, were on hillsides or hilltops. Grain production became more important, and metalworking was adopted. Bronze began to be used in Korea about 700 B.C.E. and iron by about 400 B.C.E. Mumun farmers grew barley, millet, sorghum, and short-grained rice, a similar mix of crops to north China. Another distinctive feature of this culture, the use of stone cist burials, links it to the Northern Zone. A fifth-century B.C.E. site in west-central Korea has a stone cist burial, twenty-one pit buildings, red burnished pottery, a pottery kiln, a stone mold for casting bronze implements, whetstones for sharpening blades, bronze daggers and swords, and a bronze dagger of the type found farther north in the Northern Zone. Soon, however, Korea was producing its own distinctive metalwork, such as finely decorated mirrors. A new burial form also emerged: large above-ground stone vaults called dolmens.

The shift from Chulmun to Mumun probably reflects the same movement of people seen in southern Manchuria. Without textual evidence, however, it is impossible to decide whether the local Chulmun quickly adopted the superior technology of the Mumun people or whether the Mumun moved into the area in large numbers, gradually pushing out those who were already there. Some scholars speculate that the newcomers were the speakers of languages that were the ancestors of the Korean and Japanese languages.

Another important technology that made its way to Korea and Japan before writing was rice cultivation. Studies based on stone reaping knives suggest that rice spread north along the China seaboard, reaching Korea and Japan by about 300 B.C.E. In the case of Japan, rice seems to have been grown by the end of the Jōmon period, but is more strongly associated with the next stage, called the Yayoi period. The Yayoi period is marked by distinctive pottery, found earliest in Kyushu, then spreading east through Honshu, though farther north more of the Jōmon style is retained in Yayoi pieces. Rice cultivation too was more thoroughly adopted in western Japan, with the marine-based way of life retaining more of its hold in northern Japan. Iron tools such as hoes and shovels also spread through Japan in this period, as did silk and associated spinning and weaving technology.

It is likely that the shift to Yayoi-style pottery and associated technologies was the result of an influx of people from Korea. Archaeologists have identified two distinct skeleton types in Yayoi period sites in western Japan, which they interpret as the indigenous Jōmon people and the new immigrants from Korea. The Jōmon type were shorter and more round-faced. The influx of the immigrants seems to have been greatest in Kyushu and western Honshu. Some scholars speculate that the Ainu, who survived into modern times only on the northern island of Hokkaido, are of relatively pure Jōmon stock.

Another sign that the influx of Yayoi people was not so great in eastern Japan is that bronze implements did not become important in the east, nor did easterners adopt the western Yayoi style of burying the whole body in a jar, a coffin, or a pit. Rather, in the east, reburial of the bones in a jar predominated. Because contact between southern Korea and western Japan continued through this period and because new technologies entered through this route, western Japan in this period was relatively more advanced than eastern Japan.

As we can see from this review of prehistory, contact among the societies of East Asia did not lead to identical developmental sequences. In China a millennium passed between the introduction of bronze technology and that of iron, in Korea only three centuries, and in Japan they were acquired together. Geography has much to do with the fact that Korea's direct neighbors frequently were not Chinese but nomadic pastoralists with distinctive cultures. Geography also dictates that passage from Korea to Japan was shorter and easier than crossing from China, giving Korea more direct influence on Japan than China had.

In Chapters 6 and 7, when we pick up the story of Korea and Japan again, it will be evident that as we move into the historical period, not only is the prehistoric period of continuing significance, but many of the same cultural processes continued to be at work.

SUGGESTED READING

The best book for the archaeology of East Asia as a whole is G. Barnes, *China, Korea, and Japan: The Rise of Civilization in East Asia* (1993). For early China, see also K. C. Chang, *The Archaeology of Ancient China,* 4th ed. (1986), and D. Keightley, ed., *The Origins of Chinese Civilization* (1983). On the Northern Zone, see N. di Cosmo, *Ancient China and Its Enemies: The Rise of Nomadic Power in East Asian History* (2002), and V. Mair, ed., *The Bronze Age and Early Iron Age Peoples of Eastern Central Asia* (1998). On Korea, see S. Nelson, *The Archaeology of Korea* (1993), and for Japan, see R. Pearson, *Ancient Japan* (1992) and K. Imamura, *Prehistoric Japan: New Perspective on Insular East Asia* (1996).

CHAPTER ONE

China in the Bronze Age: The Shang and Western Zhou Dynasties (ca. 1500–771 B.C.E.)

China's Bronze Age began soon after 2000 B.C.E., and by 1200 B.C.E. there were bronze-based civilizations in several regions of China. The best known of these was centered on Anyang in north-central China, where the Shang Dynasty developed a complex state with writing and large settlements. The inscribed oracle bones found at Anyang confirm traditions about Shang rulers passed down in early texts.

In 1045 B.C.E. the Shang Dynasty was overthrown by an erstwhile ally-vassal, the state of Zhou. The early Zhou Dynasty is known not only from archaeological evidence, but also from transmitted texts, which provide the Zhou version of their righteous victory over the decadent Shang. The Zhou rulers sent out vassals to establish settlements in distant regions, creating a feudal-like system.

The issues that engage archaeologists, paleographers, and historians of China's bronze age remain the basic ones: Can we reconcile texts that talk of a sequence of dynasties with the archaeological evidence of distinct cultural centers? What were the consequences of the invention of writing? What can be inferred about Shang society and culture from surviving material artifacts such as bronze vessels? Is there any way to tell if cultures outside the core regions of the Shang and Zhou spoke the same language or considered themselves part of the same culture? How significant in political and cultural terms was the transition from Shang to Zhou? Was anything significant learned from other parts of Eurasia in this period, or were all advances locally generated?

Map 1.1   **Political Map of China Showing Modern Province Boundaries**

THE GEOGRAPHY OF THE CHINESE SUBCONTINENT

The term *China* as it is used in this book does not refer to the same geographical entity at all points in history. The historical China, also called China proper, was smaller than present-day China and changed in size over time. It can be thought of as the area settled by Chinese speakers or controlled by a Chinese state, or both. (To simplify complex issues of identity radically, references here to "the Chinese" can be taken to mean speakers of the Chinese language, a group that can also be referred to as the Han Chinese.) The contemporary People's Republic of China includes territories like Tibet, Inner Mongolia, Turkestan, and Manchuria that were the traditional homes of other peoples and not incorporated into Chinese states until relatively late in their histories. In this book, to indicate the location of historically significant places within China, modern province names are used for convenience (see Map 1.1).

The geographical context in which Chinese civilization developed changed slowly over time: rivers and coastlines have shifted, forests have been cleared, and climates have warmed and cooled. The human geography has undergone even more extensive changes as the area occupied by speakers of Chinese has expanded and they have faced different neighbors.

China proper, by the nineteenth century about a thousand miles north to south and east to west, occupies much of the temperate zone of East Asia. The northern part, drained by the Yellow River, is colder, flatter, and more arid than the south. Rainfall in many northern areas is less than 20 inches a year, making it best suited to crops like wheat and millet. The dominant soil is loess—fine wind-driven earth that is fertile and easy to work even with primitive tools. Much of the loess soil ends up as silt in the Yellow River, causing the river bed to rise over time. Once people began to dike the river, it became flood prone, since when the dikes break, huge floods result. Drought is another perennial problem for farmers in the north.

The Yangzi River is the dominant feature of the warmer, wetter, and more lush south, a region well suited to rice cultivation and to growing two crops a year. The Yangzi and many of its tributaries are navigable, so boats were traditionally the preferred means of transportation in the south.

Mountains, deserts, and grasslands separated China proper from the sites of other early civilizations. Between China and India lay Tibet, with its vast mountain ranges and high plateaus. North of Tibet are great expanses of desert where nothing grows except in rare oases, and north of them grasslands stretch from the Ukraine to eastern Siberia. Until modern times, Chinese civilization did not spread into these Inner Asian regions because they were not suited to crop agriculture. The northern grasslands, where raising animals is a more productive use of land than planting crops, was the heartland of China's traditional enemies, such as the Xiongnu and the Mongols.

THE SHANG DYNASTY
(CA. 1500–1045 B.C.E.)

China's Neolithic Age has been discussed in **Connections: The Prehistory of East Asia.** China had agriculture from about 10,000 B.C.E.; by 4000 B.C.E. distinct regional cultures are evident; by 2500 B.C.E. settlements were sometimes walled and burials give evidence of increasing

social differentiation. It was from these roots that China's first civilization emerged.

After 2000 B.C.E. a Bronze Age civilization appeared in north China. Early Chinese texts refer to the first dynasty as the Xia Dynasty and give the names of its kings. The earliest Bronze Age sites may have some connection to Xia, but they contain no texts to prove or disprove this supposition. The Shang dynasty, however, is documented in both excavated and transmitted texts, and no one today doubts that it existed. The key excavated texts are the oracle bone inscriptions found in and near the Shang settlement at Anyang, in modern Henan province. Although these inscribed cattle bones and turtle shells had been unearthed from time to time, it was only after 1898 that scholars connected them to Shang kings. Since then, rubbings of some 48,000 bone fragments have been published, giving paleographers much to study.

Pronouncing Chinese	
Pinyin	English
c	ts in *tsar*
z	dz in *adze*
zh	j in *jack*
q	ch in *chin*
x	sh
ui	*way*

According to tradition, Shang kings ruled from five successive cities. The best known is the last, Anyang, first excavated between 1928 and 1937. The Shang kings ruled there from approximately 1200 B.C.E. to 1045 B.C.E. At the center of Anyang were large palaces, temples, and altars which were constructed on rammed earth foundations (see **Material Culture: Rammed Earth**).

The Shang kings were military chieftains who regularly sent out armies of three thousand to five thousand men on campaigns, and when they were not at war would go on hunts lasting months. Their armies fought rebellious vassals

MATERIAL CULTURE

Rammed Earth

From the late Neolithic period on, pounded or rammed earth was used in north China to build foundations and walls. In fact, in areas of loess soil, rammed earth is still used as a building material, primarily for the walls around houses or farmyards. The method used today begins with dumping loose soil into wooden frames, then pounding it into thin layers with wooden logs. At archaeological sites, the impressions of the pounders are often still visible on the top layer of the wall. Ancient rammed earth can be nearly as hard as concrete.

The most massive rammed earth structure of Shang date excavated so far is the wall surrounding the city of Zhengzhou (Henan province). It is about 1,800 meters on each side and about 9 meters tall. The base of the wall was as much as 20 meters thick. Chinese archaeologists have estimated that it contained 870,000 cubic meters of rammed earth, which would have required a labor force of 10,000 men working for eight years to dig the soil, transport it to the site, and pound it into a wall.

Earthen Walls. Walls are still constructed today of rammed earth. A frame of logs is constructed, the earth is pounded into place, and after it is dry, the frame is removed. *(Ronald G. Knapp)*

and foreign tribes, but the situation constantly changed as vassals became enemies and enemies accepted offers of alliance. War booty, espe-cially the war captives who could be enslaved or sacrificed, was an important source of the king's revenue.

Bronze technology gave Shang warriors improved weapons: bronze-tipped spears and dagger-axes (blades mounted at right angles to the shaft), used for hacking and stabbing. Bronze was also used for the fittings of the spoke-wheeled chariots that came into use around 1200 B.C.E. There is no evidence of animal traction in China before the chariot or of the use of wheels, spoked or solid disk, leading to the conclusion that the chariot was introduced to China by diffusion across Asia. Shang chariots were pulled by two or four horses and provided commanders with a mobile station from which they could supervise their troops; chariots also gave archers and soldiers armed with battleaxes increased mobility.

Shang power did not rest solely on military supremacy. The oracle bone texts show that the Shang king also acted as the high priest, the one best qualified to offer sacrifices to the royal ancestors and the high god, Di, who could command rain, thunder, and wind. The king also made offerings to an array of nature gods, such as the spirits of the sun and moon, the Yellow River, the winds of the four directions, and specific mountains.

Royal ancestors were viewed as able to intervene with the remote Di. They also could send curses on their own, produce dreams, assist the king in battle, and so on. The king addressed his ancestors in prayers and made offerings to them of millet wine, cattle, sheep, grain, and human victims. He discerned his ancestors' wishes and responses by interpreting the cracks made on the oracle bones when they were heated. When King Wu Ding (ca. 1200 B.C.E.) had a toothache, he had his diviner ask whether it was his father who was causing it. Before building a new settlement, he asked if the high god Di would cause problems. Di or the ancestors were also asked about rain, the harvest, military expeditions, dreams, floods, tribute payments, sacrifices, and other matters of importance. It was common to verify the result of a divination by repeating the question in negative form, such as, "Di approves the king," followed by, "Di does not approve the king." Probably as a form of record keeping, these questions were often inscribed on the bones. Scholars of the oracle bone inscriptions have noticed that the style of the calligraphy decreased in size over time and the questions posed became more routinized and more focused on ritual matters.

Contents of Fu Hao's Tomb, ca. 1200 B.C.E.	
468 bronze objects	including
	195 ritual vessels
	130 weapons
	23 bells
	27 knives
	4 mirrors
	4 tigers or tiger heads
755 jade objects	
63 stone objects	
5 ivory objects	
564 bone objects	including nearly 500 bone hairpins and over 20 bone arrowheads
11 pottery objects	
6,900 pieces of cowrie shell	
16 retainers	male and female, adults and children

Shang palaces were undoubtedly splendid, but they were constructed of perishable material like wood, and nothing remains of them today. What has survived are the lavish underground tombs built for Shang kings and their consorts. The one royal tomb not to have been robbed before it was excavated was for Lady Hao, one of the many wives of King Wu Ding. Although it was one of the smaller royal tombs (about 13 by 18 feet at the mouth and about 25 feet deep) and not in the main royal cemetery, it was nonetheless filled with an extraordinary array of valuable goods. The hundreds of bronze objects in the tomb weighed 1.6 metric tons (see the listing of its contents in the table). About sixty of the bronze vessels had Lady Hao's name inscribed on them. The weapons found in this tomb show that Lady Hao took an interest in military affairs. From inscribed bones found elsewhere at Anyang, we know that she led several military campaigns, once with thirteen thousand troops against the Qiang tribes to the west. Some of the objects in her tomb appear to be tribute sent to Anyang from distant places. These include both bronze vessels from the south and knives and mirrors from the Northern Zone (occupied by non-Han peoples, discussed below).

In addition to objects of symbolic value or practical use, the Shang interred human beings, sometimes dozens of them, in royal tombs. Why did they do this? From oracle bone texts, it seems that captives not needed as slaves often ended up as sacrificial victims. Other people buried with the king had chosen their fate; that is, his spouses, retainers, or servants could decide to accompany him in death. Those who voluntarily followed their king to the grave generally had their own ornaments and might also have coffins and grave goods such as weapons. Early Shang graves rarely had more than three victims or followers accompanying the main occupant, but the practice grew over time. A late Shang king's tomb contained the remains of ninety followers plus seventy-four human sacrifices, twelve horses, and eleven dogs. Archaelogists often can identify sacrificial victims because they were decapitated or cut in two at the waist.

Human sacrifice occurred not only at burials. Divination texts refer to ceremonies where from three to four hundred captives were sacrificed. In 1976, twelve hundred victims were found in 191 pits near the royal tombs, apparently representing successive sacrifices of a few dozen victims. Animals were also frequently offered in sacrifice. Thus, a central part of being a Shang king was taking the lives of others and offering the victims up on the altars.

What about those in Shang society who were not buried in well-furnished tombs? The Shang nobility lived in large houses built on platforms of rammed earth (see **Material Culture: Rammed Earth**). Those lower down on the social scale often lived in homes built partly below ground level, probably as a way to conserve heat. Ani-

mal husbandry was a major element in the Shang economy. The bone workshops at Anyang made use of the leg bones of cattle, sheep, pigs, deer, dogs, and horses. Divinations proposed the sacrifice of one hundred, two hundred, or three hundred cattle, sheep, pigs, or dogs.

In the urban centers, substantial numbers of craftsmen worked in stone, bone, bronze, and clay. Their workshops, concentrated in certain sections of the city, were often quite specialized. Some workshops specialized in hairpins, others arrowheads, others ritual vessels. Another important product was silk, made from the cocoons of the silkworm, which fed on the leaves of mulberry trees. Silk from Shang China has recently been discovered in an Egyptian tomb, evidence that its importance as an item of east-west trade began very early.

At the level of technology, the life of Shang farmers was not very different from that of their Neolithic ancestors. They lived in small, compact villages, surrounded by fields that they worked with stone tools. Millet continued to be the basic grain, but some new crops became common in Shang times, most notably wheat, which had spread from West Asia.

The primary difference between Shang farmers and their Neolithic predecessors is the huge gulf that separated them from the most powerful in their society. Shang rulers could command the labor of thousands of men for long periods of time. Huge work forces were mobilized to build the rammed earth city walls, dig the great tombs, open new lands, and fight in war. Some scholars assume that those laboring for the king were slaves, perhaps acquired through warfare. Others speculate that these laborers also included conscripts, called up as needed from among the serf-like farmers. Whatever the status of the workers, coercion, backed by violence, was an essential element of the Shang state.

Writing

The inscribed oracle bones demonstrate that writing was already a major element in Chinese culture by 1200 B.C.E. Writing must have been

Oracle Bone. The thousands of inscribed bones that survive from Shang sites are our best source for early Chinese writing. The questions they record were usually addressed to the king's ancestors. *(Institute of History and Philogy. Academia Sinica/Laurie Platt Winfrey, Inc.)*

invented earlier, but the early stages of its development cannot be traced, probably because writing was done on perishable materials like wood, bamboo, or silk. Late Neolithic pots sometimes have marks on them that some scholars speculate are early forms of writing. Not until the oracle bones from late Shang, however, is there evidence of full sentences.

What impact did writing have? Literacy is an ally of political control, facilitating communication across an expanding realm. From the oracle bones, we know that Shang kept records of enemy slain, booty taken, animals bagged in hunts, and other information, using lunar months and ten-day and sixty-day cycles to record dates.

Although only about 40 percent of the five thousand or so characters used on Shang divination texts have been deciphered, there is no longer any doubt that the language and the writing system of the Shang are directly ancestral to both the language and the writing systems of later Chinese. This script was logographic, like ancient Egyptian and Sumerian, meaning that each word was represented by a single graph (character). In the Chinese case, some of these graphs began as pictures, but for the names of abstract concepts, other methods were adopted to represent the word. Sometimes the graph for a different word was borrowed because the two words were pronounced alike. As in later times, sometimes two different graphs were combined; for instance, to represent different types of trees, the graph for tree could be combined with the graph for another word that sounded like the name of a kind of tree. More than half of the characters found on oracle bones combine components in these ways.

In western Eurasia, logographic scripts were eventually modified or replaced by phonetic scripts, but that never happened in China (though, because of changes in the spoken language, many words today are represented by two or three characters rather than a single one). Basic literacy requires knowing the characters for two or three thousand common words, and well-educated people learn a couple of thousand more. Because characters are composed of a couple of hundred components, this task is not as daunting as it may seem at first, but it still takes much longer than learning to read a phonetic script. Thus, because China retained its logographic writing system, it took many years of study for a person to master reading and writing.

Why did China retain a logographic writing system even after encounters with phonetic ones? Although phonetic systems make learning to read easier, there are costs to abandoning a logographic system. Those who learned to read Chinese could communicate with a wider range of people than those who read scripts based on speech. Since Chinese characters remained recognizable after the passage of many centuries, despite phonological change, educated Chinese could read texts written centuries earlier without the need for them to be translated. More-over, as the Chinese language developed mutu-ally unintelligible regional variants, readers of Chinese could read books and letters by con-temporaries whose oral language they could not comprehend. Thus, the Chinese script played a large role in holding China together and foster-ing a sense of connection with the past.

For the history of East Asia, the Chinese script has a further significance. Korea, Japan, and Vietnam all began writing by adopting the Chinese script. For several centuries, reading and writing in these countries was done in a for-eign language, Chinese. Since most available books had been written in Chinese, learning meant learning through a Chinese lens. In time, however, Chinese characters were used for their meaning or their sound to record the local lan-guages. Those used for their meaning are much like Arabic numerals whose names are pro-nounced differently depending on the reader's language.

Metalworking

As in Egypt, Mesopotamia, and India, the devel-opment of more complex forms of social organ-ization in Shang China coincided with the mastery of metalworking, specifically bronze. Beginning about 2000 B.C.E., people learned to prospect metals, remove them from their ores, and fashion them into tools or ornaments. The next stage, reached about 1500 B.C.E., involved large-scale production.

In Shang times, bronze was used more for rit-ual than for war. Most surviving Shang bronze objects are vessels such as cups, goblets, steam-ers, and cauldrons, which originally would have been used to hold food and wine offered to the ancestors or gods during sacrificial ceremonies. Both kings and nobles owned bronze vessels, but the kings had many more.

When compared to bronze objects made in other early societies, Chinese bronzes stand out for their quantity, their decoration, and the ways they were manufactured. Shang bronze making required a large labor force to mine,

Figure 1.1   **Mold for Bronze Casting.** Shang bronze vessels were made with ceramic molds. After the molten bronze hardened, the pieces of the mold could be removed.

refine, and transport copper, tin, and lead ores and to produce and transport charcoal. To achieve the high degree of precision and stan-dardization evident from surviving bronze ves-sels, there must have been considerable division of labor. Technically skilled artisans were needed to make clay models, construct ceramic piece molds, and assemble and finish each ves-sel. There also would have had to be managers overseeing the entire process. It has been esti-mated that two to three hundred craftsmen were needed to make the largest surviving Shang bronze vessel, which weighs 875 kilograms.

The technique used to make bronze vessels began with a clay model. After it hardened, soft clay was pressed against it, taking on the nega-tive impression of its shape and decoration. These clay pieces were removed in sections to form the piece molds. The model was then shaved down to become the core (the walls of

Front View of a Shang Bronze Vessel. This rectangular covered vessel, about 10 inches (25 cm) tall, dates from the twelfth century B.C.E.. At the base and the top register are opposed dragons. Between them are stylized mask (*taotie*) designs, with eyes, eyebrows, ears, horns, mouth, and front paws all floating free. The designs on the sides are compressed versions of the designs on the front. *(The Metropolitan Museum of Art, Purchase, Arthur M. Sackler Gift, 1974 [1974.268.2ab])*

the bronze vessel would exactly equal the thickness of this shaved-off layer). After the piece molds were reassembled around the core, molten bronze would be poured into the space between the mold and the core. After cooling, the piece molds were removed.

Scholars have not reached a consensus on the meaning of the decoration on Shang bronzes. In the art of ancient Egypt, Assyria, and Babylonia, images of domesticated plants and animals match our understanding of the importance of agriculture in those societies, much as depictions of social hierarchy (kings, priests, scribes, and slaves) match our understandings of their social

and political development. Why then did images of wild animals predominate in Shang China? The symbolic meaning of some animals is easy to guess. Cicadas, which spend years underground before emerging, probably evoked rebirth in the realm of ancestral spirits. Birds similarly suggest to many the idea of messengers who can reach realms in the sky. More problematic is the most common image, the stylized animal face called the *taotie*. To some it is a monster—a fearsome image that would scare away evil forces. Some hypothesize that it reflects masks used in rituals. Others associate it with animal sacrifices, totemism, or shamanism. Still others see these images as hardly more than designs. Scholars' inability to reach a consensus on something so basic as the meaning of the decoration on Shang bronzes reminds us of the huge gaps in our understanding of Shang culture.

DEVELOPMENTS OUTSIDE THE SHANG CORE

The Shang were constantly at war with other groups, tribes, or states, and the area in which the Shang king could safely travel was confined to northern Henan and western Shandong provinces. Key elements of their culture, however, such as their bronze technology, spread well beyond the area they controlled. In the middle Yangzi region, many bronzes have been found that share Shang technology but differ in design, some even using human faces in place of the *taotie*. Bells are particularly common in the Yangzi region, and at one site they were buried in groups in the side of a mountain. The profusion of objects in some tombs in Jiangxi province shows that the elites of this region were able to amass wealth on a scale similar to Shang elites. Their bronze vessels often have tigers on their handles, a style distinctive to the region. Whether this region should be considered a provincial version of Shang civilization or a different culture that borrowed extensively from Shang technology is still not certain. Without written documents like the divination texts of Anyang, there is no way to know if Chinese was the language used in this region.

As discussed in **Connections: The Prehistory of East Asia,** a more independent bronze culture existed north of the Shang core, where people grew millet and raised pigs, sheep, and cattle. Knives, axes, and mirrors are common finds there, but their bronze technology resembles that of Central Asia and Siberia more than the Shang core. Their practice of oracle bone divination, however, links them to Shang civilization. These finds could be evidence of the people who brought chariots to the Shang.

Another strong case for a distinct culture can be made for the civilization discovered at Sanxingdui in the western province of Sichuan. In 1986 two pits of Shang date were found packed with objects never found in Shang sites, including elephant tusks and huge masks, some covered in gold foil (see the table). Both pits were filled in layers, with small objects on the bottom, then the larger ones, then the elephant tusks, then rammed earth. (See Color Plate 1.)

Contents of the Pits at Sanxingdui, ca. 1200 B.C.E.	
Pit 1	**Pit 2**
13 elephant tusks	67 elephant tusks
107 bronze rings	20 bronze masks
13 bronze heads	40 bronze heads
44 bronze dagger-axe blades	bronze statue
4 gold items	bronze trees
60 stone tools	4,600 cowrie shells
70 stone or jade blades	almost 500 small beads or
40 pottery vessels	tubes of jade, stone, or ivory
burned animal bones	burned animal bones

Why were these objects placed in the pits? Many of those in pit 1 had been burned before being deposited, and others had been purposely broken. Thus, one possibility is that these objects are the remnants of a huge sacrifice. Unlike major Shang sacrifices, however, there is no sign of human sacrifice. Some scholars spec-

ulate that the bronze figures of humans were being used to replace humans in a sacrificial ceremony. The heads most likely were originally attached to wood or clay statues and could have represented gods or ancestors. Thus, it is also possible that the statues with the bronze heads represented gods and the local people had for some reason decided that those gods or the representations of them had to be burned and buried.

Further archaeological exploration has revealed that the pits lay within a large walled city, nearly 2 kilometers square. Foundations of fifty or so buildings have been found, most rectangular but some round. Five other pits have been found, but they contained no bronze artifacts, only jade and stone ones. Perhaps because of flooding, the city was abandoned around 1000 B.C.E. No sites for later stages of this culture have been found, and there are no nearby sites from succeeding centuries that give evidence of comparable wealth. Perhaps whatever led to the abandonment of Sanxingdui also led to the collapse of the civilization.

The existence of sites like Sanxingdui has forced archaeologists to reconsider the political landscape during the centuries when the Shang ruled at Anyang. Shang rulers wished to see their own polity as the central one, but since we lack written records from sites of other cultures, there is no reason to assume that elites in other places had less self-centered notions of themselves.

THE WESTERN ZHOU DYNASTY (1045–771 B.C.E.)

Outside the Shang domains were the domains of allied and rival polities. To the west were the fierce Qiang, who probably spoke an early form of Tibetan. Between the Shang capital and the Qiang was a frontier state called Zhou, which shared most of the material culture of the Shang. In 1045 B.C.E., this state rose against the Shang and defeated it. The first part of the Zhou Dynasty is called the Western Zhou period (1045–771 B.C.E.) because its capital was in the west near modern Xi'an in Shaanxi province (to distinguish it from the Eastern Zhou, after the capital was moved to near modern Luoyang in Henan province).

In early written traditions, three Zhou rulers are given credit for the Zhou conquest of the Shang. They are King Wen (*wen* means "cultured" or "lettered"), who expanded the Zhou domain; his son King Wu (*wu* means "martial"), who conquered the Shang; and Wu's brother, the duke of Zhou, who consolidated the conquest and served as regent for Wu's heir.

These rulers and their age are portrayed in the earliest transmitted text, the *Book of Documents* (see **Documents: The Announcement of Shao**). The speeches, pronouncements, and reports in this book depict the Zhou conquest as the victory of just and noble warriors, supported by Heaven, over the decadent Shang court led by an evil king. Bronze inscriptions provide another important source for the early Zhou period. Court scribes would prepare written documents on bamboo or wooden strips to specify appointments to offices or fiefs. Later, during a court ceremony, an official would read the document on behalf of the king. A copy of the document would be handed over to the grantee, who then later had it reproduced in bronze so that it could be passed down in his family.

The early Zhou period did not mark an abrupt break with Shang culture, but some Shang practices declined. Divining by heating oracle bones became less common, as did sacrifices of human victims. Interring followers in tombs continued, though their numbers gradually declined.

The Mandate of Heaven

Like the Shang kings, the Zhou kings sacrificed to their ancestors, but they also sacrificed to the divine force called Sky or Heaven. The *Book of Documents* assumes a close relationship between Heaven and the king, who was called the "Son of Heaven." Heaven gives the king a mandate to rule only as long as he rules in the interests of the people. Because the theory of the Mandate of Heaven does not seem to have had any place in Shang cosmology, some scholars think it was elaborated by the early Zhou rulers as propaganda to win over the conquered subjects of the Shang. Whatever its origins, it remained a central feature of Chinese political ideology from the early Zhou period on.

The Zhou Political Structure

At the center of the Western Zhou political structure was the Zhou king, who was simultaneously ritual head of the royal lineage and supreme lord of the nobility. Rather than attempt to rule all of their territories directly, the early Zhou rulers sent out relatives and trusted subordinates to establish walled garrisons in the conquered territories, creating a decentralized, quasi-feudal system. The king's authority was maintained by rituals of ancestor worship and court visits. For instance, in 806 B.C.E., a younger son of King You was made a duke and sent east to establish the state of Zheng in a swampy area that needed to be drained. This duke and his successors nevertheless spent much of their time at the Zhou court, serving as high ministers.

Zhou vassals were generally able to pass their positions on to a son, so that in time the domains became hereditary fiefs. By 800 B.C.E., there were about two hundred lords with domains large and small, of which only about twenty-five were large enough to matter much in interstate politics. Each lord appointed officers to serve him in ritual, administrative, or military capacities. These posts and their associated titles tended to become hereditary as well. Each domain thus came to have noble families with patrimonies in offices and associated lands.

Some Zhou bronzes record benefactions from the king and mention the services that had earned the king's favor. One inscription, for instance, recorded the rewards given to Yu for obeying the king's command to repel attacks of the Southern Huai barbarians. After his successful return, the

DOCUMENTS

The Announcement of Shao

Several texts in the Book of Documents *record speeches and pronouncements of the early Zhou rulers. Scholars used to distrust the early attributions of these texts, but with the discovery and study of more and more inscriptions on early Zhou bronzes, scholars now believe that many of them were in fact written in the first century of Zhou rule. The "Announcement of Shao" records a speech by the duke of Zhou or his brother, the duke of Shao, in which the duke explains the Mandate of Heaven to the newly subjugated people of Shang.*

Ah! August Heaven, High God, has changed his principal son and has revoked the Mandate of this great state of Shang. When a king receives the Mandate, without limit is the grace thereof, but also without limit is the anxiety of it. Ah! How can he fail to be reverently careful!

Heaven has rejected and ended the Mandate of this great state of Shang. Thus, although Shang has many former wise kings in Heaven, when their successor kings and successor people undertook their Mandate, in the end wise and good men lived in misery. Knowing that they must care for and sustain their wives and children, they then called out in anguish to Heaven and fled to places where they could not be caught. Ah! Heaven too grieved for the people of all the lands, wanting, with affection, in giving its Mandate to employ those who are deeply committed. The king should have reverent care of his virtue.

Look at the former peoples of ancient times, the Xia. Heaven guided, indulged, and cherished them, so that they would strive to understand what Heaven favors, but by this time they have let their Mandate fall to the ground. Now look at the Shang; Heaven guided them, stayed near them, nourished them, so that they would strive to comprehend what Heaven favors; but now they have let their Mandate fall to the ground.

Now a young son succeeds to the throne; let him not, then, neglect the aged and experienced. Not only do they comprehend the virtue of our men of old—nay, more, they are sometimes able to comprehend counsels that come from Heaven.

Ah! Even though it be that the king is young, he is [Heaven's] principal son. Let him be grandly able to be in harmony with the little people. In the present time of grace, the king must not dare to be slow, but should be prudently apprehensive about what the people say. . . .

Those above and below being zealous and careful, let them say, "As we receive Heaven's Mandate, let it grandly be like the long years enjoyed by the Xia, and not fail of the years enjoyed by the Shang"—in order that [as one would wish] the king, through the little people, may receive Heaven's enduring Mandate.

Translated by David S. Nivison in *Sources of Chinese Tradition*, 2nd ed., comp. Wm. Theodore de Bary and Irene Bloom (New York: Columbia University Press, 1999), pp. 35–37, slightly modified.

king brought Yu into the ancestral temple, where he conferred on him two bronze ritual vessels, fifty strands of cowrie shells, and one hundred fields as reward for bringing back one hundred heads and forty manacled prisoners. The inscription concludes, "Yu dares in response to extol the

Chariot Burial. The type of chariot found in this Western Zhou burial pit, with large, many-spoked wheels, spread across Asia around 1200 B.C.E. *(Institute of Archaeology, Beijing)*

Son of Heaven's beneficence, herewith making this offertory tureen; may Yu for 10,000 years have sons' sons and grandsons' grandsons eternally treasure and use it."[1]

As in Shang times, there continued to be groups viewed as alien living in the same general region as the Zhou states as well as beyond its borders. Various groups of Yi ("eastern barbarians"), for instance, lived interspersed through the east, as did different groups of Rong ("northern barbarians") in the north and west. These groups spoke distinct languages, though they were not necessarily more primitive than the Zhou people in technology. Over the course of the nearly three centuries of Western Zhou

rule, the Zhou kings drew many of these groups into the Zhou political order by recognizing their chiefs as the lords of their domains. To participate in this order, they had to use the Chinese writing system for matters of state.

Ties of loyalty and kinship linking the Zhou vassals to the king weakened over time, and in 771 B.C.E. the Zhou king was killed by an alliance of Rong tribesmen and Zhou vassals. Zhou nobles fleeing this attack buried their bronze vessels, expecting to unearth them after they returned. One such hoard discovered in 1976 contained 103 vessels belonging to Earl Xing of Wei cast by several generations of his family. Instead of returning, however, the Zhou royal house and nobles moved east to the area of modern Luoyang, just south of the Yellow River in the heart of the central plains. Eastern Zhou never fully regained control over its vassals, and China entered a prolonged period without a strong central authority, which will be discussed in Chapter 2.

Western Zhou Society and Culture

Western Zhou society was highly aristocratic. Inherited ranks placed people in a hierarchy ranging from the king, to the rulers of states with titles like duke and marquis, the hereditary great officials of these lords, and the lower ranks of the aristocracy called *shi*, men who could serve in either military or civil capacities. At the bottom were ordinary subjects. Patrilineal family ties were very important throughout this society, and at the upper reaches at least, sacrifices to ancestors were one of the key rituals used to forge social ties.

Land in this system was held on feudal tenures, and the economy was a manorial one. When the Zhou king bestowed land on a relative or subordinate, he generally also gave him people to work it. These farmers were treated as serfs, obliged to provide food and labor for the lord, who was expected in turn to look after their welfare.

Glimpses of what life was like at various social levels in the early Zhou period can be

---

1. Edward L. Shaughnessy, "Western Zhou History," in M. Loewe and E. Shaughnessy, eds., *The Cambridge History of Ancient China: From the Origins of Civilization to 221 B.C.* (New York: Cambridge University Press, 1999), p. 331.

found in the *Book of Poetry,* which contains the earliest Chinese songs and poems. Many of the folk songs are love songs. Others depict the farming life, which involved not merely the cultivation of crops like millet, hemp (for cloth), beans, and vegetables, but also hunting small animals and collecting grasses and rushes to make rope and baskets. The seasons set the pace for rural life, and poems contain many references to seasonal changes such as the appearance of grasshoppers and crickets.

The *Book of Poetry* also offers glimpses of court life and its ceremonies. Besides congratulatory court odes were ones with a critical edge. In the following stanza, the ancestors are rebuked for not providing aid to their descendants in distress:

> The drought has become so severe
> That it cannot be stopped.
> Glowing and burning,
> We have no place.
> The great mandate is about at an end,
> Nothing to look ahead to or back upon.
> The host of dukes and past rulers
> Does not help us.
> As for father and mother and the
>   ancestors,
> How can they bear to treat us so?[2]

Men and women had very different roles at court, and one poem shows that these differences were marked from birth:

> A male child is born.
> He is made to sleep on a bed.
> He is made to wear a skirt.
> He is made to play with a scepter.
> His crying is loud.
> His red knee-covers are august.
> He is the hall and household's lord and
>   king.

> A female child is born.
> She is made to sleep on the floor.
> She is made to wear a wrap-cloth.
> She is made to play with pottery.
> She has no wrong and right.
> Only wine and food are for her to talk
>   about.
> May she not send her father and mother
>   any troubles.[3]

SUMMARY

How different was China at the end of the Western Zhou period in 771 B.C.E. compared to China at the beginning of the Bronze Age in 2000 B.C.E.? Differences in technology were pervasive. At the beginning of this period, China was just beginning to fashion objects of metal; by the end, bronze workers had centuries of experience in casting all sorts of objects, and bronze was used not only for ritual vessels but also for helmets, swords, knives, axes, and other tools. Horses had been domesticated and trained to pull chariots. Writing had become a central feature in the life of the political elite, and a substantial body of literature was in circulation. Some elements of culture and organization had already undergone major transformations. Divination by oracle bones had largely disappeared, as had the practice of making offerings of human victims, except at the burial of rulers, where it continued somewhat sporadically. Previously alien groups were incorporated into the Zhou political order, and more and more of them participated in the culture associated with the Chinese written language. Thus, in all likelihood there were more people we can call Chinese by the end of this period.

---

2. Ode 258, in Shaughnessy, "Western Zhou History," p. 336.

3. Ode 189, in Paul Rakita Goldin, *The Culture of Sex in Ancient China* (Honolulu: University of Hawaii Press, 2002), p. 24.

SUGGESTED READING

For early China, the most authoritative volume is M. Loewe and E. Shaughnessy, *The Cambridge History of Ancient China: From the Origins of Civilization to 221 B.C.* (1999). The journal *Early China* often reports on important new archaeological finds. On the archaeology of early China, see K. C. Chang, *The Archeology of Ancient China*, 4th ed. (1986); *Shang Civilization* (1986); and *Art, Myth, and Ritual: The Path to Political Authority in Ancient China* (1983). For the development of the Chinese writing system, see W. Boltz, *The Origin and Early Development of the Chinese Writing System* (1994). S. Allan examines Shang cosmology and Zhou myths in *The Shape of the Turtle: Myth, Art, and Cosmology in Early China* (1991). For the Western Zhou period, see M. Lewis, *Sanctioned Violence in Early China* (1990), and C. Hsu and K. Linduff, *Western Chou Civilization* (1988). For a translation of the earliest Chinese history of the Shang and Western Zhou periods, dating to the first century B.C.E., see W. Nienhauser et al., *The Grand Scribes Records*, vol. 1 (1994).

Two attractive volumes on ancient art and technology are X. Yang, ed., *The Golden Age of Chinese Archaeology: Celebrated Discoveries from the People's Republic of China* (1999), and W. Fong, *Great Bronze Age of China* (1980). L. Ledderose, *Ten Thousand Things: Module and Mass Production in Chinese Art* (2000) offers fresh perspectives on both the Chinese script and the production of bronze vessels, among other subjects. Other good introductions to early Chinese art are J. Rawson, ed., *The British Museum Book of Chinese Art* (1992), and R. Thorp and R. Vinograd, *Chinese Art and Culture* (2001). On the discoveries in Sichuan, see R. Bagley, ed., *Ancient Sichuan: Treasures from a Lost Civilization* (2001).

Philosophers and Warring States During the Eastern Zhou Period (770–256 B.C.E.)

The foundations of Chinese thought were established in the five centuries that followed the transfer of the Zhou court to Luoyang in 770 B.C.E. In this period, the old Zhou fiefs came to function more and more like independent states, linked to each other in a multistate system. Gradually, warfare between the states intensified, and social, political, and cultural change also quickened. By the third century B.C.E., only seven important states remained. Over the course of these centuries, hereditary ranks meant less and less, and rulers made more use of the *shi*, the lower ranks of the old aristocratic order. As these *shi* competed to offer advice to rulers, they advanced the art of argument and set in motion a tremendous intellectual flowering. China entered one of its most creative periods, when the ideas underlying Confucian, Daoist, and Legalist traditions were developed.

Historians of ideas, warfare, and social and political change have all found the Eastern Zhou a fascinating period to study. Archaeological evidence remains fundamental to enlarging our understanding of this period and has been particularly valuable for showing the richness of the culture of the south, the region of the state of Chu. Few of the philosophical texts of this period were written by a single known author, so scholars have devoted much of their energy to distinguishing the earlier and later layers of texts. Knowing the importance of the strong, centralized state in later periods of Chinese history, historians have also drawn attention to the advances in statecraft of this period and the connections between the ideas articulated in this period and the social and political situation. Would comparable ideas have emerged if China had not been politically divided? How significant was the emergence of the *shi* to the intellectual history of this period? Is it more than coincidental that China's first intellectual flowering occurred in roughly the same centuries as that of ancient India, Greece, Persia, and Israel?

THE MULTISTATE SYSTEM OF THE EASTERN ZHOU

The Eastern Zhou Dynasty is conventionally divided into two periods named after books that recorded events of the time: the Spring and Autumn period, to 479 B.C.E., and the Warring States period after it. The history of the Eastern Zhou Dynasty is better documented than the history of the Western Zhou because of advances in the art of political narrative. For the Spring and Autumn period, the most important chronicle is the *Zuo zhuan,* a narrative covering the years 722 to 463 B.C.E., traditionally treated as a commentary to the much briefer *Spring and Autumn Annals.* For the Warring States period, *The Intrigues of the Warring States* presents lengthy narratives, arranged by state rather than chronologically. A third work, the *Discourses of the States,* also arranged by state, concentrates on speeches and covers both periods. The authorship and dating of all three of these works are uncertain, but at a minimum they contain Zhou material.

Although the Zhou kings were still considered the supreme monarchs, they no longer had the military might to force obedience. Sometimes supposed vassals would even attack the Zhou king. In this period, the ruler of one state would sometimes be recognized as the hegemon, the leader of the alliance of Zhou states (see **Biography: Guan Zhong**). These hegemons periodically called meetings of the allied states where rulers or leading ministers would swear to uphold the Zhou feudal structure. At a meeting in 657 B.C.E., the states

Map **2.1**   **Zhou States in the Sixth Century** B.C.E.

swore not to dam irrigation waters, withhold sales of grain, replace heirs apparent, promote concubines to wives, or let women interfere in state affairs. The principal states of the early Warring States period are shown on Map 2.1.

Succession disputes were a common pretext for war between states. Rulers regularly had concubines in addition to a wife and thus would have children by several women. In theory, succession went to the eldest son of the wife, then younger sons by her, and only in their absence sons of concubines. In actual practice, however, the ruler of a state or head of a powerful ministerial family could select a son of a concubine to be his heir if he wished. During his lifetime, this led to much scheming for favor among the various sons and their mothers and the common perception that women were incapable of taking a disinterested view of the larger good. Sons who felt unfairly excluded often journeyed to other states in search of allies. Since rulers regularly took their wives from the ruling families of other states, a contender could try the state that his mother or grandmother had come from or the states his

BIOGRAPHY Guan Zhong

By the time of Confucius, the success of states was often credited more to the lord's astute advisers than to the lords themselves. To Confucius, the most praiseworthy political advisor was Guan Zhong (ca. 720–645 B.C.E.), the genius behind the rise of the state of Qi in eastern China.

The earliest historical sources that recount Guan Zhong's accomplishments are the commentaries compiled in the Warring States period to elaborate on the dry chronicle known as the *Spring and Autumn Annals*. The *Zuo zhuan,* for instance, tells us that in 660 B.C.E., Guan Zhong advised Duke Huan to aid the small state of Xing, then under attack by the non-Chinese Rong tribes: "The Rong and the Di are wolves who cannot be satiated. The Xia [Chinese] states are kin who should not be abandoned." In 652, it tells us, Guan Zhong urged the duke to maintain the respect of the other states by refusing the request for an alliance by a ruler's son who wished to depose his father. Because the duke regularly listened to Guan Zhong's sound advice, Qi brought the other states under its sway, and the duke came to be recognized as the first hegemon, or leader of the alliance of states.

Guan Zhong was also credited with strengthening the duke's internal administration. He encouraged the employment of officials on the basis of their moral character and ability rather than their birth. He introduced a system of drafting commoners for military service. In the history of China written by Sima Qian in about 100 B.C.E., Guan Zhong is also given credit for enriching Qi by promoting trade, issuing coins, and standardizing merchants' scales. He was credited with the statement that "when the granaries are full, the people will understand ritual and moderation. When they have enough food and clothing, they will understand honor and disgrace."

Sima Qian's biography of Guan Zhong emphasized his early poverty and the key role played by a friend, Bao Shuya, who recognized his worth. As young men, both Bao and Guan Zhong served brothers of the duke of Qi. When this duke was killed and a messy succession struggle followed, Bao's patron won out and became the next duke, while Guan Zhong's patron had to flee and in the end was killed. Bao, however, recommended Guan Zhong to the new duke, Duke Huan, and Guan Zhong took up a post under him.

In the *Analects,* one of Confucius's disciples thought this lack of loyalty to his first lord made Guan Zhong a man unworthy of respect: "When Duke Huan killed his brother Jiu, Guan Zhong was unable to die with Jiu but rather became chancellor to Duke Huan." Confucius disagreed: "Guan Zhong became chancellor to Duke Huan and made him hegemon among the lords, uniting and reforming all under heaven. The people, down to the present, continued to receive benefits from this. Were it not for Guan Zhong our hair would hang unbound and we would fold our robes on the left [that is, live as barbarians]" (*Analects* 14.18).

A book of the teachings associated with Guan Zhong, the *Guanzi,* was in circulation by the late Warring States period. Although today it is not thought to reflect the teachings of the historical Guan Zhong, the fact that later statecraft thinkers would borrow his name is an indication of his fame as a great statesman.

sisters or aunts had married into. The rulers of these states were often happy to see someone indebted to them on the throne of a neighboring state and would lend armies to help oust rivals.

There were, of course, other reasons for warfare. States tried to maintain a balance of power and prevent any one state from becoming too strong. States on the periphery had the advantage, as they could expand outward. Thus, the four states to gain the most over the course of the Spring and Autumn period were Qin in the west, Jin in the north, Qi in the east, and Chu in the south. As Chu expanded from its base in the south, Qi organized other states to resist it. Sometimes the states in the middle, weary of being caught in the fighting between the larger powers, organized peace conferences.

Another common reason for the hegemon to bring troops to the aid of a state was to help it fend off attack by various forces from beyond the Zhou world. But those labeled with the non-Chinese ethnic terms Di, Rong, or Yi were not always in a position of enmity to the Chinese states. For instance, Jin often enlisted Rong or Di polities to join it in fighting Qin. Moreover, some Rong and Di leaders were versed in Chinese literature. There was also intermarriage between the ruling class of Zhou states and the Rong and Di elites. Duke Wen of Jin's mother was a Rong, his wife a Di. The only written language in this world, however, was Chinese, which worked toward making Chinese the common language. In the south, the states of Wu and Yue emerged from outside the Zhou sphere but adopted Zhou cultural patterns; Yue, in fact, claimed to be descended from the Xia Dynasty, making it more ancient than the Zhou Dynasty.

Archaeological evidence confirms steady cultural exchange between Zhou and non-Zhou elements in this period. The rulers of the state of Zhongshan in the northeast were recognized as descended from White Di, who had been driven by other tribes from Shaanxi into Hebei in the sixth century. With help from the state of Wei, they established their own city there. Although Zhongshan was a very minor state, its rulers decided to call themselves kings when other states' rulers did. The tomb of King Cuo of Zhongshan, who died around 308 B.C.E., included inscribed bronzes that record historical events in typically Confucian language, full of stock phrases from the classics.

Rulers continued to be buried with followers in this period. Duke Mu of Qin had 177 people accompany him in death after he died in 621 B.C.E., and nearly a century later, in 537 B.C.E., Duke Jin was buried with 166. By this period, there were people who disapproved of the practice. In the state of Qin, the practice was outlawed in 383 B.C.E. Moreover, the sacrificing of war captives in ceremonies unrelated to burials no longer seems to have been practiced. Remnants of this practice could still be seen in the use of the blood of captives to consecrate newly cast war drums and the ritual of presenting captives at the ancestral temple or other altar.

WARFARE AND ITS CONSEQUENCES

The purpose and conduct of war changed dramatically in the Eastern Zhou period. In the Spring and Autumn period, a large army would have up to ten thousand soldiers, the chariot remained central to warfare, and states were ranked by how many hundreds of chariots they could deploy. A code of chivalrous conduct regulated warfare between the states. The two sides would agree on the time and place for a battle, and each would perform divination and sacrifices before initiating hostilities. One state would not attack another while it was in mourning for its ruler. Ruling houses were not wiped out so that a successor could continue to sacrifice to their ancestors. Battle narratives in the *Zuo zhuan* give the impression that commanders cared as much about proving their honor as about winning. In 638 B.C.E. the duke of the small state of Song felt compelled to fight a much stronger state. Because his forces were greatly outnumbered, his minister of war urged him to attack the enemy while they were fording a river, but the duke refused. The *Zuo zhuan* reports that he explained his behavior this way: "The gentleman does not inflict a second wound, nor does he capture those with gray hair. On campaigns the ancients did not obstruct those in a narrow pass. Even though I am but the remnant of a destroyed state, I will not drum an attack when the other side has not yet drawn up its ranks."[1] When combat was hedged with these ceremonial restrictions, war was less deadly—a wound ended the victim's combat status but not necessarily his life.

By the Warring States period, such niceties were being abandoned as advances in military technology changed the nature of warfare. Large, well-drilled infantry armies were becoming a potent military force, able to withstand and defeat chariot-led forces. By the late Warring States period military obligations were nearly universal for men. For Qin's campaign against Zhao in 260 B.C.E., it mobilized all men over age fifteen. By 300 B.C.E. states were sending out armies of a couple hundred thousand drafted foot soldiers, usually accompanied by horsemen. Conscripts with a year or two of training would not have the martial skills of aristocratic warriors who trained for years and tested their skills in hunts. But infantry armies won out through standardization, organization, discipline, and sheer size.

Adding to the effectiveness of armies of drafted foot soldiers was the crossbow, invented in the southern state of Chu. The trigger of a crossbow is an intricate bronze mechanism that allowed a foot soldier to shoot farther than a horseman carrying a light bow. One text of the period claimed that a skilled soldier with a powerful crossbow and a sharp sword was the match for a hundred ordinary men. To defend against crossbows, soldiers began wearing armor and helmets. Most of the armor was made of leather strips tied with cords. Helmets were sometimes made of iron.

Although most soldiers were drafted peasants, it became common to select and train elite corps of crack troops. The elite troops in the state of Wei had to wear heavy armor and helmets, shoulder a crossbow and fifty arrows, strap a spear to their backs and a sword by their waists, carry three days' supply of food, and march about fifty kilometers in a single day. Those meeting this standard earned their household exemption from all taxes and labor service obligations.

The development of infantry armies created the need for a new type of general, as rulers became less willing to let men lead troops merely because of aristocratic birth. Treatises on the art of war described the ideal general as a master of maneuver, illusion, and deception, ruthless in searching for the advantage that would lead to victory. He also had to be an organizer, able to integrate the efforts of the units under him.

Because cities were walled, attacks on them resulted in prolonged sieges, and generals were eager to try new ways to attack and defend walls. Portable ladders were brought to scale the walls. When attackers dug tunnels under the walls, defenders would use large bellows of the sort common in smelting iron to pump smoke into the tunnels and suffocate the attackers.

City walls were not the only defensive structure important to warfare of the period. States began building chains of watch stations and forts, often connecting them with long defensive walls. Permanent garrisons were left at strategic points to prevent the passage of armies. Barriers also allowed states to check those who entered or left their territories and to collect transit taxes from merchants.

The introduction of cavalry struck another blow at the chariot-riding aristocracy. Shooting bows and arrows from horseback was first perfected by non-Chinese peoples to the north of China proper, who at that time were making the transition to a nomadic pastoral economy. As the northern states expanded northward, absorbing non-Chinese communities of mixed shepherds and farmers, they came into direct contact with the horse riders of the steppe. In 307 B.C.E. the king of the northern state of Jin

---

1. Duke Xi, 22nd year. Translations cited by the traditional sections are by the author.

ordered his troops to adopt the nomads' trousers and practice mounted archery (see **Documents: The King of Zhao Persuades His Uncle to Wear Barbarian Dress**). Soon Zhao was using cavalry against other Chinese states, which then had to master the new technology to defend themselves. Larger infantry armies of 100,000 or 200,000 men would be supported by a few hundred mounted warriors. Cavalry were considered especially valuable for reconnaissance, pursuing fleeing soldiers, cutting supply lines, and pillaging the countryside. From this time on, acquiring and pasturing horses was a key component of Chinese military preparedness (see Color Plate 2).

As a result of all these developments in the art of war, conflicts came to be waged with greater intensity and on a much larger scale than ever before. Whereas Spring and Autumn period campaigns had lasted no longer than a season and battles no longer than a day or two, some campaigns in the Warring States period lasted for years, with separate armies operating independently on several fronts. Qin's defeat of Zhao in 260 B.C.E. came after a campaign that lasted three years and involved hundreds of thousands of soldiers on each side deadlocked across a front that stretched more than a hundred miles.

Because these developments in the art of war made commoners and craftsmen crucial, rulers of the warring states tried to find ways to increase their populations. To increase agricultural output, they brought new land into cultivation, drained marshes, and dug irrigation channels. By the sixth century B.C.E. some rulers were surveying their land and beginning to try to levy taxes on farmers. They wanted to undermine the power of lords over their subjects in order to get direct access to peasants' labor power. Serfdom thus gradually declined. Registering populations led to the extension of family names to commoners at an earlier date than anywhere else in the world.

The development of iron technology in the early Zhou period also promoted economic expansion. Iron was cast from the beginning, unlike in the west, where iron was wrought long before it was cast. By the fifth century B.C.E., iron was being widely used for both farm tools and weapons. By the third century B.C.E., the largest smelters employed two hundred or more workmen.

The economic growth of the late Zhou period is evident in the appearance of cities all over north China. In addition to the thick earthen walls built around the palaces and ancestral temples of the ruler and other aristocrats, outer walls were added to protect the artisans, merchants, and farmers living in the surrounding area. Another sign of economic growth is the emergence of a new powerful group in society: the rich, who had acquired their wealth through trade or industry rather than inheritance or political favor. Late Zhou texts frequently mention cross-regional trade in objects such as furs, copper, dyes, hemp, salt, and horses. To promote trade, rulers began casting coins, at first in the shape of miniature spades.

In the fourth century B.C.E., rulers of states started calling themselves kings, a step that amounted to announcing their intent to conquer all the other states. Rulers strengthened their control by dispatching their own officials rather than delegating authority to hereditary lesser lords. Rulers controlled these officials from a distance through the transmission of documents and could dismiss them if they proved unsatisfactory. For the *shi*, serving a ruler in this way offered new opportunities for advancement. There were plenty of *shi* eager for these opportunities because every time a state was destroyed, its old nobility sunk in status to *shi*. Although many *shi* did not have military skills by this period, they retained knightly values such as a sense of honor and an ideal of loyal service.

THE HUNDRED SCHOOLS OF THOUGHT

The late Zhou was a period when all sorts of ideas were proposed, debated, written down, and put to use, leading Chinese to refer to it as

DOCUMENTS

The King of Zhao Convinces His Uncle to Wear Barbarian Dress

The Intrigues of the Warring States is a collection of late Zhou historical anecdotes and fables about the political ploys adopted by the various competing states. The book, full of speeches by kings and court advisers, has been appreciated as a work of literature, even by those who were dismayed by its morality. In this passage, the king of Zhao has decided to adopt the trousers of the northern nomads, the Hu (also called Xiongnu), but he worried that others would make fun of him. He sent a messenger to ask his uncle, Gongzi Cheng, to join him in changing his dress. We begin here with the uncle's response.

[The uncle] Gongzi Cheng bowed twice: "I had, of course, heard of the king's Hu clothing but having been ill abed I had not yet gone to him to present my opinions. Since the king now sends me these orders, I must now make my clumsy gesture of loyalty.

"I have heard the Middle Kingdoms described as the home of all wisdom and learning, the place where all things needful of life are found, where saints and sages taught, where humanity and justice prevail, where the *Book of Poetry* and *Book of Documents* and *Canons of Ritual* and *Music* are used; a country where extraordinary skills and uncommon intelligence are given hearing, a land looked up to from afar, and a model of behavior for the barbarian. But now the king would discard all this and wear the habit of foreign regions. Let him think carefully, for he is changing the teachings of our ancients, turning from the ways of former times, going counter to the desires of his people, offending scholars, and ceasing to be part of the Middle Kingdoms."

When [the messenger] Wangsun Xie had reported, the king said merely, "I knew, of course, that he had been ill." Then, going in person to the home of Gongzi Cheng, the king urged his support: "Clothes exist to be useful and manners respond to conditions. Therefore the sage was guided by what was right and proper for each locality and encouraged behavior related to its conditions: always they sought to profit the peo-ple and strengthen their states," said the king. "To crop the hair, decorate the body, rub pigment into arms and fasten garments on the left side are the ways of the Ba and Yue [southern barbarians]. In the country of Daiwu the habit is to blacken teeth, scar cheeks, and wear caps of sheepskin stitched crudely with an awl. Their costumes and customs differ but each derives benefit from his own. . . .

"From Changshan to Dai and Shangdang, we border Yan and the Eastern Hu in the east, and Loufan, Qin, and Han in the west. Along this line we have not a single mounted archer. . . . I change our garments and mount archers to guard our borders with Yan, the Eastern Hu, Loufan, Qin, and Han. . . . With my men dressed as mounted archers I can today prepare for Shangdang nearby and exact vengeance upon Zhongshan at a distance. . . ."

Gongzi Cheng made deepest obeisance twice: "Such has been my stupidity that I had not even conceived of these arguments, your majesty. I had instead the temerity to mouth platitudes. But now that I too wish to carry out the hopes of Kings Jian and Xiang, the ambitions of our ancestral rulers, what choice have I but to make obeisance and obey your order?"

He was given the Hu garments.

Source: J. I. Crump, trans., *Chan-kuo Ts'e*, rev. ed. (Ann Arbor: University of Michigan Center for Chinese Studies, 1996), pp. 288–292, modified.

a period "when a hundred schools of thought bloomed." The political rivalry and constant warfare of the period helped rather than hindered intellectual creativity. Rulers turned to men of ideas for both solutions to the disorder around them and the prestige of attracting to their court wise and able men from across the country. Political strategists would travel from state to state urging rulers to form alliances. Lively debate often resulted as strategists proposed policies and challengers critiqued them. Successful men of ideas attracted followers, who took to recording their teacher's ideas on the rolls of silk and tied together strips of wood or bamboo that functioned as books.

Historians of later periods, beginning with Sima Qian in about 100 B.C.E., grouped these thinkers into schools, using labels that have survived until today, such as Confucianism, Daoism, and Legalism, which may give the mistaken impression that people of the time thought in those terms. Even the books we have today are not identical to the books that first circulated, as the works of an author were added to, subtracted from, and rearranged after his death, usually by his followers. Scholars today try to distinguish the different layers of texts to analyze the development of ideas and emphasize the extensive interchange of ideas among diverse teachers and thinkers.

Confucius and the *Analects*

Confucius (who early historians dated to 551–479 B.C.E.) was the first and most important of the men of ideas seeking to influence the rulers of the day. As a young man, Confucius served in the court of his home state of Lu without gaining much influence. After leaving Lu, he wandered through neighboring states with a small group of students, searching for a ruler who would follow his advice.

Confucius's ideas are known to us primarily through the sayings recorded by his disciples in the *Analects*. The thrust of his thought was ethical rather than theoretical or metaphysical. He talked repeatedly of an ideal age in the early

Zhou, which he conceived of as a perfect society in which all people devoted themselves to fulfilling their roles: superiors looked after those dependent on them, inferiors devoted themselves to the service of their superiors, and parents and children, husbands and wives, all wholeheartedly did what was expected of them.

Confucius saw much of value in family ties. He extolled filial piety, which to him encompassed reverent obedience of children toward their parents and performance of the expected rituals, such as mourning them when they died and making sacrifices to them afterward. If one's parents were about to make a major mistake, the filial child should try to dissuade them as tactfully as possible but should try not to anger them. The relationship between father and son was one of the five cardinal relations stressed by Confucius. The others were between ruler and subject, husband and wife, elder and younger brother, and between friends. Mutual obligations of a hierarchal sort underlay the first four of these relationships: the senior leads and protects, the junior supports and obeys. The exception was the relationship between friends, which was conceived in terms of the mutual obligations between equals.

Confucian Virtues	
ren	humanity, benevolence
xiao	filial piety
yi	integrity, righteousness
zhong	loyalty, constancy
xin	honesty
jing	reverence, respect
li	propriety, ritual decorum

Confucius urged his followers to aspire to become true gentlemen (*junzi*, literally "son of a lord"), a term that he redefined to mean men of moral cultivation rather than men of noble birth. He contrasted gentlemen of integrity to petty men seeking personal gain. The gentleman, he said, "feels bad when his capabilities fall short of the task. He does not feel bad when people fail to recognize him" (15.18).

The Confucian gentleman should advise his ruler on the best way to govern. Much of the *Analects* consequently concerns how to govern well:

> The Master said, "Lead the people by means of government policies and regulate them through punishments, and they will be evasive and have no sense of shame. Lead them by means of virtue and regulate them through rituals and they will have a sense of shame and moreover have standards." (2.3)

To Confucius, the ultimate virtue was *ren,* a term that has been translated as humanity, perfect goodness, benevolence, human-heartedness, and nobility. A person of humanity cares about others and acts accordingly:

> Zhonggong asked about humanity. The Master said, "When you go out, treat everyone as if you were welcoming a great guest. Employ people as though you were conducting a great sacrifice. Do not do unto others what you would not have them do unto you. Then neither in your country nor in your family will there be complaints against you." (12.2)

Treating people as though they were guests and employing them as though participating in a great sacrifice is another way of saying that they should be treated according to *li* (ritual, manners, propriety, good form). In other passages as well, Confucius stressed the importance of disciplining one's behavior through adherence to ritual: "Respect without ritual is tiresome; caution without ritual is timidity; boldness without ritual is insubordination; straightforwardness without ritual is rudeness" (8.2). But ritual must not be empty form: "Ritual performed without reverence and mourning performed without grief are things I cannot bear" (3.26).

In the Confucian tradition, studying texts came to be valued over speculation, meditation, and mystical identification with deities. Confucius encouraged the men who came to study with him to master the poetry, rituals, and historical traditions that we know today as the Confucian classics. Many passages in the *Analects* reveal Confucius's confidence in the power of study:

> The Master said, "I am not someone who was born wise. I am someone who loves the ancients and tries to learn from them." (7.19)
>
> The Master said, "I once spent a whole day without eating and a whole night without sleeping in order to think. It was of no use. It is better to study." (15.30)

Confucius talked mostly about the social and political realms rather than the world of gods, ghosts, or ancestral spirits. Moreover, although he is portrayed as deeply committed to ritual, he was said to have performed sacrifices as though the spirits were present, leaving open the possibility that he was not convinced that ancestors or other spirits were actually aided by the offerings people made to them.

Mozi

Not long after Confucius died, his ideas were challenged by Mozi (ca. 480–390 B.C.E.), a man who came not from the aristocracy but from among the master craftsmen. He was, however, well read and like Confucius quoted from the *Book of Documents* and *Book of Poetry.* Unlike Confucius, though, he did not talk of the distinction between gentlemen and vulgar "petty men," but rather of "concern for everyone," sometimes translated as "universal love." He put forward the idea that conflict could be eliminated if everyone gave other people's families and other people's states the same concern he gave his own. Mozi contended that all people recognize the validity of this idea because if they have to leave their family in someone else's care, they choose someone who accepts this ideal. To counter the argument that impartiality is not easy to achieve, Mozi said the sage kings of old had practiced it, proving its feasibility. Mozi also argued strongly for the merit principle, asserting that rulers should choose their advisers on the basis of their ability, not their birth.

The book ascribed to Mozi (called *Mozi*) proposes that every idea be evaluated on the basis of its utility: Does it benefit the people and the state? Using this standard, Mozi rejected many of the rituals emphasized by Confucius's followers, especially mourning parents for three years, which Mozi noted interrupts work, injures health, and thus impoverishes the people and weakens the state. Music, too, Mozi saw as a wasteful extravagance of no utility.

Mozi made a similar case against aggressive war, seeing no glory in expansion for its own sake. He pointed to the huge losses in weapons, horses, and human lives it causes. The capture of a city, he argued, is not worth the loss of thousands of men. But Mozi was for strong government and obedience toward superiors. He argued that disorder could be eliminated if everyone conformed his beliefs to those of his superior, the king conforming to Heaven.

Mozi had many followers over the next couple of centuries, and they organized themselves into tight groups. Because they saw offensive warfare as evil, these Mohists, as they are called, considered it their duty to come to the aid of cities under attack. They became experts in defending against sieges, teaching, for instance, that each soldier on the city walls should be held responsible for the two soldiers on his immediate left and right, a form of group responsibility later picked up by the Legalists.

After a few centuries, however, Mozi's school declined and eventually lost its distinct identity. Certain ideas, such as support for the merit principle and criticism of extravagance, were absorbed into Confucian thought in later centuries. Mencius, who lived a century after Mozi, borrowed his arguments against military aggression, and like him would often try to persuade rulers that they had not correctly identified where their advantage lay. Confucians, however, never accepted Mohist ideas about treating everyone equally, unnatural in their minds, or of applying rigidly utilitarian tests to ritual and music, whose value they saw in very different terms.

Mencius

Among the followers of Confucius eager to defend his teachings against Mozi's attacks, Mencius stands out. We know of Mencius (ca. 370–ca. 300 B.C.E.) largely from the book that bears his name, which Mencius may have written in large part himself. Mencius came from the small and unimportant state of Zou, next to Confucius's home state of Lu. He was born too late to have studied with Confucius himself, but he quotes Confucius approvingly and was said to have studied Confucian teachings with a student of Confucius's grandson.

The first two of the seven parts of the *Mencius* record conversations that took place from 320 to 314 B.C.E. between Mencius and a king of Qi and two successive kings of Wei. The opening passage in the *Mencius* records one such encounter:

> *Mencius had an audience with King Hui of Liang [Wei]. The king said, "Sir, you did not consider a thousand* li *too far to come. You must have some ideas about how to benefit my state."*
>
> *Mencius replied, "Why must Your Majesty use the word 'benefit'? All I am concerned with are the benevolent and the right. If Your Majesty says, 'How can I benefit my state?' your officials will say, 'How can I benefit my family,' and officers and common people will say, 'How can I benefit myself.' Once superiors and inferiors are competing for benefit, the state will be in danger." (1A.1)*

Like Confucius, Mencius traveled around offering advice to rulers of various states. He tried repeatedly to convert them to the view that the ruler able to win over the people through benevolent government would succeed in unifying "all under Heaven." Mencius proposed concrete political and financial measures for easing tax burdens and otherwise improving the people's lot. He also tried to get rulers to give up seeking military victories. To seek military domination will backfire, he argued, for it will turn the world against you, whereas those who are benevolent will have no enemies.

Men willing to serve an unworthy ruler earned Mencius's contempt, especially when they worked hard to fill his coffers or expand his territory. He pointed out that Confucius broke off his relationship with his disciple Ran Qiu when he doubled the tax collection but did not do anything to reform the ruler's character.

Although the bulk of the *Mencius* concerns issues of governing, Mencius also discussed issues in moral philosophy. He argued strongly, for instance, that human nature was fundamentally good, as everyone is born with the capacity to recognize what is right. He gave the example of the person who automatically grabs a baby about to fall into a well: "It would not be because he wanted to improve his relations with the child's parents, nor because he wanted a good reputation among his friends and neighbors, nor because he disliked hearing the child cry" (2A.6). Rather it was due to his inborn feelings of commiseration and sense of right and wrong.

Mencius quotes some conversations with a contemporary philosopher who disagreed with his interpretation of human nature:

> Gaozi said, "Human nature is like whirling water. When an outlet is opened to the east, it flows east; when an outlet is opened to the west, it flows west. Human nature is no more inclined to good or bad than water is inclined to east or west."
>
> Mencius responded, "Water, it is true, is not inclined to either east or west, but does it have no preference for high or low? Goodness is to human nature like flowing downward is to water. There are no people who are not good and no water that does not flow down. Still, water, if splashed, can go higher than your head; if forced, it can be brought up a hill. This isn't the nature of water; it is the specific circumstances. Although people can be made to be bad, their natures are not changed." (6A.2)

Sometimes Mencius related men's moral nature to Heaven. Heaven wants men to be moral and operates in history through men's

choices. Heaven validates a ruler's authority through the people's acceptance of him. But Mencius did not think all rulers had been validated by Heaven; true kings tended to appear only about every five hundred years.

Xunzi

The *Xunzi* was written in large part by Xunzi (ca. 310–ca. 215 B.C.E.), who lived a half-century after Mencius and was Mencius's rival as an interpreter of Confucius's legacy. Xunzi explicitly opposed Mencius's view on human nature, arguing that people are born selfish and that it is only through education and ritual that they learn to put moral principle above their own interest. Much of what is desirable is not inborn, he said, but must be taught:

> When a son yields to his father, or a younger brother yields to his elder brother, or when a son takes on the work for his father or a younger brother for his elder brother, their actions go against their natures and run counter to their feelings. And yet these are the way of the filial son and the principles of ritual and morality. (13)

Neither Confucius nor Mencius had had much actual political or administrative experience. By contrast, Xunzi worked for many years in the governments of several of the states. Not surprisingly, he showed more consideration than either Confucius or Mencius for the difficulties a ruler might face in trying to rule through ritual and virtue. He strongly supported the view, earlier articulated by Mozi, that the worthy should be promoted even if they were descendants of commoners. In response to a question on how to govern, Xunzi said the ruler should promote the worthy and capable and dismiss the incompetent, and punish the evil without bothering to try to reform them. Xunzi, like Mencius, supported the basic message of the Mandate of Heaven: "The ruler is the boat, the common people are the water. It is the water that bears up the boat but also the water that capsizes it" (9).

Xunzi was a more rigorous thinker than his predecessors and developed the philosophical foundations of many ideas that Confucius or Mencius had merely outlined. Confucius, for instance, had declined to discuss gods, portents, and anomalies and had spoken of sacrificing as if the spirits were present. Xunzi went further and explicitly argued that Heaven does not intervene in human affairs. Praying to Heaven or to gods, he asserted, does not induce them to act. "Why does it rain after a prayer for rain? In my opinion, for no reason. It is the same as raining when you had not prayed" (17).

Although he did not think praying could bring rain or other benefits from Heaven, Xunzi did not propose abandoning traditional rituals. In contrast to Daoists and Mohists, who saw rituals as unnatural or extravagant, Xunzi saw in ritual an efficient way to attain order in society. Rulers and educated men should continue traditional ritual practices such as complex funeral protocols because the rites themselves have positive effects on performers and observers. Not only do they let people express feelings and satisfy desires in an orderly way, but by specifying graduated ways to perform the rites according to social rank, ritual traditions sustain the social hierarchy. Xunzi compared and contrasted ritual and music: music shapes people's emotions and creates feelings of solidarity, while ritual shapes people's sense of duty and creates social differentiation.

Daoism and the *Laozi* and *Zhuangzi*

Confucius and his followers believed in moral and political effort. They thought men of virtue should devote themselves to making the government work to the benefit of the people. Those who later came to be labeled Daoists disagreed. The authors of the *Laozi* and *Zhuangzi* thought striving to make things better generally makes them worse. They defended private life and wanted the rulers to leave the people alone. They sought to go beyond everyday concerns and let their minds wander freely. Rather than making human beings and human actions the

center of concern, they focused on the larger scheme of things, the whole natural order identified as the Way or Dao.

Both the *Laozi* and the *Zhuangzi* date to the third century B.C.E. Master Lao, the putative author of the *Laozi,* may not be a historical figure, but the text ascribed to him has been of enduring importance. A recurrent theme in this brief, aphoristic text is the mystical superiority of yielding over assertion and silence over words. "The Way that can be discussed is not the constant Way" (1). The highest good is like water: "Water benefits all creatures but does not compete. It occupies the places people disdain and thus comes near to the Way" (8).

Because purposeful action is counterproductive, the ruler should let people return to a natural state of ignorance and contentment:

> Do not honor the worthy,
> And the people will not compete.
> Do not value rare treasures,
> And the people will not steal.
> Do not display what others want,
> And the people will not have their hearts
>   confused.
> A sage governs this way:
> He empties people's minds and fills their
>   bellies.
> He weakens their wills and strengthens
>   their bones.
> Keep the people always without knowledge
>   and without desires,
> For then the clever will not dare act.
> Engage in no action and order will
>   prevail. (3)

In the philosophy of the *Laozi*, the people would be better off if they knew less, gave up tools, renounced writing, stopped envying their neighbors, and lost their desire to travel or wage war.

Zhuangzi (369–286 B.C.E.), the author of the book of the same name, was a historical figure who shared many of the central ideas of the

Laozi, such as the usefulness of the useless and the relativity of ordinary distinctions. He was proud of his disinterest in politics. In one of his many anecdotes, he reported that the King of Chu once sent an envoy to invite him to take over the government of his realm. In response, Zhuangzi asked the envoy whether a tortoise that had been held as sacred for three thousand years would prefer to be dead with its bones venerated or alive with its tail dragging in the mud. When the envoy agreed that life was preferable, Zhuangzi told the envoy to leave, as he would rather drag his tail in the mud.

The *Zhuangzi* is filled with parables, flights of fancy, and fictional encounters between historical figures, including Confucius and his disciples. Yet the book also deals with serious issues, including death. Zhuangzi questioned whether we can be sure life is better than death. People fear what they do not know, the same way a captive girl will be terrified when she learns she is to become the king's concubine. Perhaps people will discover that death has as many delights as life in the palace. When a friend expressed shock that Zhuangzi was not weeping at his wife's death, Zhuangzi explained that he had at first, but then began thinking back to before she had life or form or vital energy. "In this confused amorphous realm, something changed and vital energy appeared; when the vital energy was changed, form appeared; with changes in form, life began. Now there is another change bringing death. This is like the progression of the four seasons of spring and fall, winter and summer" (18). Once he had realized this, he stopped sobbing.

Zhuangzi was similarly iconoclastic in his political ideas. In one parable, a wheelwright insolently tells a duke that books are useless since all they contain are the dregs of men long dead. The duke, insulted, threatened to execute him if he could not give an adequate explanation of his remark. The wheelwright then explained that he could feel in his hand how to chisel but could not describe it in words. "I cannot teach it to my son, and my son cannot learn it from me. So I have gone on for seventy years,

growing old chiseling wheels. The men of old died in possession of what they could not transmit. So it follows that what you are reading are their dregs" (13). Zhuangzi here questions the validity of verbal reasoning and the sorts of knowledge conveyed through words.

The ideas of the *Laozi* and *Zhuangzi* can be seen as a response to Confucianism, a rejection of many of its basic premises. Nevertheless, over the course of Chinese history, many people felt the pull of both Confucian and Daoist ideas and studied the writings of both schools. Even Confucian scholars who devoted much of their life to public service might find the teachings of Laozi or Zhuangzi helped them put their frustrations in perspective. Whereas Confucianism often seems sternly masculine, Daoism was more accepting of feminine principles (yin of the yin-yang pair) and even celebrated passivity and yielding. Those drawn to the arts were also often drawn to Daoism, with its validation of spontaneity and freedom. Rulers too saw merit in the Daoist notion of the ruler who can have great power simply by being himself without instituting anything.

Legalism

Over the course of the fourth and third centuries B.C.E., as one small state after another was conquered, rulers fearful that their state might be next were ready to listen to political theorists who claimed expertise in the accumulation of power. These theorists, labeled Legalists because of their emphasis on the need for rigorous laws, argued that strong government depended not on the moral qualities of the ruler and his officials, as Confucians claimed, but on establishing effective laws and procedures.

In the fourth century B.C.E., the state of Qin, under the leadership of its chancellor, Lord Shang (d. 338 B.C.E.), adopted many Legalist policies. Instead of an aristocracy with inherited titles, social distinctions were based on military ranks determined by the objective criterion of the number of enemy heads cut off in battle. In the place of the old fiefs, Qin divided the country into counties and appointed officials to administer them according to the laws decreed at court. To increase the population, migrants were recruited from other states with offers of land. To encourage farmers to work hard and improve their land, they were allowed to buy and sell it. Ordinary farmers were thus freed from serf-like obligations to the local nobility. Nevertheless, direct control by the state could be even more onerous, as taxes and labor service obligations were heavy.

In the third century B.C.E., Legalism found its greatest exponent in Han Feizi (d. 233 B.C.E.), who had studied with the Confucian master Xunzi but had little interest in Confucian virtues. Alarmed at the weakness of his own state of Han, Han Feizi wrote to warn rulers of the political pitfalls awaiting them. They had to be careful where they placed their trust, for "when the ruler trusts someone, he falls under that person's control" (17). This was true even of wives and concubines, who think of the interests of their sons. Given subordinates' propensities to pursue their own selfish interests, the ruler should keep them ignorant of his intentions and control them by manipulating competition among them. Warmth, affection, or candor should have no place in his relationships with others.

Han Feizi saw the Confucian notion that government could be based on virtue as naive. Even parents calculate their long-term advantage in favoring sons over daughters. One cannot expect rulers to be more selfless than parents. If rulers would make the laws and prohibitions clear and the rewards and punishments automatic, then the officials and common people would be easy to govern. Uniform laws get people to do things they would not otherwise be inclined to do, such as work hard and fight wars, essential to the goal of establishing hegemony over all the other states.

The laws of the Legalists were designed as much to constrain officials as to regulate the common people. The third century B.C.E. tomb of a Qin official has yielded statutes detailing the rules for keeping accounts, supervising sub-

ordinates, managing penal labor, conducting investigations, and many other responsibilities. Those who violated these statutes were fined.

Legalism saw no value in intellectual debate or private opinion. The ruler should not allow others to undermine his laws by questioning them. Rulers of several states adopted some Legalist ideas, but only the state of Qin systematically followed them. The extraordinary but brief success Qin had with these policies is discussed in Chapter 3.

Other Schools of Thought and Types of Learning

The thinkers and books discussed here had the greatest long-term impact on Chinese civilization, but the late Zhou "Hundred Schools of Thought" also included much else. There were logicians, hedonists, utopians, hermits, and agriculturalists who argued that no one should eat who does not farm. There were natural philosophers who drew lessons from their study of such fields as astronomy, medicine, music, and calendrical calculations. The concepts of yin and yang were particularly important to natural philosophy. Yin is the feminine, dark, receptive, yielding, negative, and weak; yang is the masculine, bright, assertive, creative, positive, and strong. Yin and yang are complementary poles rather than distinct entities or opposing forces. The movement of yin and yang accounts for the transition from day to night and from summer to winter. They are also involved in health and illness. The *Zuo zhuan* quotes Physician He on the six qi (vapors, forms of energy), which he defines as yin and yang, wind and rain, dark and bright. These six qi divide to make the four seasons, radiate to make the five colors and five sounds, and when they go to excess produce the six illnesses. Numerology of the sort apparent here is another feature of late Zhou natural philosophy.

Another important strand of thought of this period concerns military strategy. Sunzi's *Art of War*, dating probably to the third century B.C.E., warns against bravado. Since warfare causes loss of life and property, it is better to win without expending resources. "One hundred victories in one hundred battles is not skillful; what is skillful is subjugating the opponent's army without battle" (Chap. 3). Great generals are not those who charge up hills against overwhelming odds but those who advance when they know they can win. Heroism is a useless virtue that leads to needless deaths. Discipline, however, is essential, and Sunzi insisted that the entire army had to be trained to follow the orders of its commanders without questioning them. Spying on and manipulating the enemy are tactics worth learning, as is doing things the enemy will not anticipate. Often phrases in the *Art of War* echo ones from the *Laozi*: "The form of the military is like water. Water in its movements avoids the high and hastens to the low. The military in its victory avoids the solid and strikes the empty. Thus water determines its movement in accordance with the earth. The military determines victory in accordance with the enemy."[2]

The development of rationalistic and naturalistic ways of thinking does not mean that people no longer took an interest in the world of spirits. The records of divination found in the tomb of an official who died in 316 B.C.E. show that illness was seen as the result of unsatisfied spirits or malevolent demons, best dealt with through exorcisms or sacrifices to the astral deity Taiyi (Grand One). Some texts give incantations that could be used to exorcise offending demons. There were also ceremonies that could offer protection from evil spirits. To escape trouble on a trip, travelers were encouraged to perform a ceremony at the threshold of the gate to the city. They would call on the sage-king Yu to clear the road for them, draw five lines on the ground, then pick up some of the soil by the lines, and put it in the folds of their robe by their

bosom. Texts on these occult and magico-religious subjects that have been found in excavation of late Warring States tombs have shown that traditions in these fields were transmitted in writing much as those of the philosophers were.

WARRING STATES LITERATURE AND ART: THE CASE OF CHU

Despite political division, all through the Eastern Zhou Dynasty, peoples on the periphery of the Zhou world were drawn into it. This does not mean, however, that all cultural differences were eliminated. As discussed in Chapter 1, the bronzes found south of the Yangzi River during the Shang Dynasty employed the same technology used at Anyang yet often featured highly distinctive decoration. For the Zhou period, because of the much greater survival of texts and an abundance of archaeological finds, it is possible to trace how the south steadily became a more integral part of the Zhou world and the ways it maintained a distinctive style.

The dominant state in the south was Chu. From Western Zhou times on, Chu gradually expanded, absorbing fifty or more small states as it pushed its borders northward and eastward. In the Eastern Zhou period, Chu became one of the strongest and most innovative states. In 548 B.C.E. it conducted a survey of its population to assess tax and military duties. Chu also was the first to form counties (*xian*) out of newly annexed land and to dispatch officials to administer them (instead of conferring the land on hereditary lords). In 334 B.C.E. Chu conquered the state of Yue, gaining control of the Lower Yangzi region. By the third century, Chu was a full participant in the alliances designed to maintain a balance of power. This does not mean those in the central regions no longer put it down as a primitive or barbarian region. Mencius chastised a man for following a teacher who came from Chu, saying, "I have heard of men using Chinese ways to transform the barbarians but not of being transformed by the barbarians" (*Mencius* 3A.4).

---

2. Translation by Kidder Smith in Wm. Theodore de Bary and Irene Bloom, eds., *Sources of Chinese Tradition*, rev. ed. (New York: Columbia University Press, 1999), p. 221.

MATERIAL CULTURE

Lacquer

Lacquer is made from the sap of a tree native to south and central China. When it is heated and purified, the sap makes a light, strong, smooth, and waterproof material highly resistant to decay. By Eastern Zhou times, craftsmen were using lacquer on furniture, coffins, bowls, cups, musical instruments, and sculpture. In most cases, many layers of lacquer were applied over a wooden core. Lacquer objects could be decorated with pictures or designs, using lacquer colored with pigments such as cinnabar for red and carbon for black.

Illustrated here is a small cup from Tomb 1 at Mashan, Jiangling, Hubei Province, decorated with images of two large birds. See also Color Plate 3, which shows the design painted in lacquer on a coffin from the late fourth century B.C.E. at Baoshan, Jingmen, Hubei province. It is covered with intertwining dragons and mythical birds.

Lacquer Cup. This 6 inch long lacquer cup is decorated in red, black, and yellow colors. It was one of many eating vessels found in a tomb in Hubei dating to the early third century B.C.E. (*Jingzhou Prefecture Museum, Hubei Province*)

It has been estimated that 70 percent of known Eastern Zhou tombs are in the Chu area. Much more in the way of lacquer and silk survives from tombs in this region than elsewhere in China for this period—a function of the high water tables in many places—giving us a remarkably full picture of the material life of the elite of Chu. Flowing, curvilinear lines, sometimes incorporating birds, dragons, snakes, and other creatures, are found on embroidered silks, inlaid bronzes, and painted lacquer (see **Material Culture: Lacquer**).

One of the most interesting of the Chu tombs, excavated in 1986–1987, was for an official who died in 316 B.C.E. The tomb had four chambers, filled with ritual vessels, furniture, and other objects of daily life such as fans, mirrors, boxes, weapons and chariot fittings, and books. The books include reports by the local government,

texts on divination, and an inventory of the tomb's contents. Although the calligraphy of the books is elegant, many of the characters are in obsolete forms that have not yet been deciphered.

The distinctiveness of Chu culture can also be seen in the masterpiece of Chu literature, the *Songs of Chu* (Chu ci). The fantastic poems in this work are worlds apart from the poems in the *Book of Poetry*. The principal poem in this collection, titled *Encountering Sorrows*, is the lament of Qu Yuan (ca. 340–278 B.C.E.), an anti-Qin minister who lost the favor of the Chu kings and was sent into exile. Distraught that his loyalty to his ruler was not appreciated, he finally threw himself into a river. In the poem Qu Yuan describes his misfortunes, declares his virtue, maligns those who have defamed him, and goes on a cosmic quest for a lord worthy of his devotion. On that venture, he imagines him-

Bells of the Marquis of Yi. The tomb of a minor ruler who died in 433 B.C.E. contained 124 musical instruments, including drums, flutes, mouth organs, pan pipes, zithers, a set of 32 chime stones, and this 64-piece bell set. Five men, using poles and mallets, and standing on either side of the set of bells, would have played the bells by hitting them from outside. *(Henan Museum, Zhengzhou/Cultural Relics Publishing House)*

self wandering on the clouds and looking down on the earth. The structure of this lengthy poem (almost four hundred lines) corresponds to shamanic spirit quests in which the shaman declares his worth and goes to heaven to seek the god or goddess who had spurned him. Several of the shorter poems in the *Songs of Chu* fall into this tradition as well. The one that follows is titled the "Lord of the Yellow River":

> With you I will roam to the river's nine
> channels,
> when blasts of wind rise driving waves
> across stream,
> we will ride my coach of waters, its
> canopy, lotus,
> hitched to paired dragons, by basilisks
> flanked.
>
> I climbed Mount Kun-lun, I gazed all
> around,
> the heart flew aloft, it went sweeping off
> free.
> soon the sun was to set, I, transfixed,
> forgot going,
> and then to the far shore I looked back
> with care.

> My roofs are of fish scales, halls of the
> dragon,
> turrets of purple cowries, palaces of
> carmine—
> why is the holy one here, down in the
> water?
> We will ride on white turtles, goldfish
> attend us,
> with you I will roam by the river's isles,
> where the current is rushing, there we'll go
> down.
>
> You clasp your hands, journeying
> eastward;
> you go with the Fairest to the southern
> shores
> where the swell of the waves is coming to
> meet us,
> and the schools of fishes, will send off my
> bride.[3]

---

3. Stephen Owen, *An Anthology of Chinese Literature* (New York: Norton, 1996), p. 160.

SUMMARY

How did China change during the five centuries of the Eastern Zhou period? The Chinese world had grown by absorbing previously peripheral areas like Chu in the south and Zhongshan in the north. The economy had changed from one that was essentially manorial to one in which coinage was in use, trade was much more extensive, and iron was widely used for tools. The social structure had similarly been transformed from one in which membership in the elite depended almost entirely on birth to one in which there was con-siderable opportunity for advancement for talented *shi*. City-states had become territorial states, with rulers making use of officials to draw on the resources of their entire population. Conscription was nearly universal. Warfare was no longer hemmed in by notions of chivalry and as a consequence had become much more deadly. Intellectual discourse was much richer, with a great many texts in circulation that sought to persuade through argument and example. Distinct schools of thought had emerged. The writing of history had advanced, with much more in the way of extended narratives.

SUGGESTED READING

For both the history and the archaeology of Zhou China, the most authoritative volume is M. Loewe and E. Shaughnessey, *The Cambridge History of Ancient China: From the Origins of Civilization to 221 B.C.E.* (1999). On material history, see also X. Li, *Eastern Zhou and Qin Civilizations* (1985). On the texts surviving from this period, see M. Loewe, *Early Chinese Texts: A Bibliographical Guide* (1993). On the cultural and ethnic diversity of the Chinese subcontinent in this period, see W. Watson, *Cultural Frontiers in Ancient East Asia* (1971); C. Cook and J. Major, *Defining Chu* (1999); and N. de Cosmo, *Ancient China and Its Enemies* (2002).

Good overviews of the intellectual flowering of the Warring States period include A. C. Graham, *Disputers of the Tao: Philosophical Argument in Ancient China* (1989); Benjamin Schwartz, *The World of Thought in Ancient China* (1985); M. Lewis, *Writing and Authority in Early China* (1999); and, more briefly, F. W. Mote, *Intellectual Foundations of China* (1989).

J. Legge did a complete translation of *The Chinese Classics*, 5 vols. (1960) in the nineteenth century. More recent translators include A. Waley, D. C. Lau, and B. Watson. For Waley, see the *Analects of Confucius* (1938) and the *Book of Songs* (1937). Lao translated *Confucius: The Analects* (1979), the *Tao Te Ching: Chinese Classics* (1982), and *Mencius* (1970). Watson has published *The Tso Chuan: Selections from China's Oldest Narrative History* (1989); *The Complete Works of Chuang Tzu* (1968); and *Basic Writings of Mo Tzu, Hsun Tzu, and Han Fei Tzu* (1967). For military thinking, see *Sun-tzu: The Art of War,* translated by R. Ames (1993). For shorter selections of important Chinese texts, see W. de Bary and I. Bloom, eds., *Sources of Chinese Tradition* (1999), and P. Ebrey, ed., *Chinese Civilization: A Sourcebook* (1993).

3

The Founding of the Bureaucratic Empire: Qin-Han China (256 B.C.E.–200 C.E.)

Qin's battle-hardened armies destroyed the Zhou royal domain in 256 B.C.E. and the last of the independent states in 221 B.C.E., thus unifying the Chinese realm. Although Qin rule did not last long, the succeeding Han Dynasty retained its centralized bureaucratic monarchy. Both Qin and Han mobilized huge armies to confront the emergence of a powerful enemy to the north, the Xiongnu tribal confederation. In part to deal with the Xiongnu threat, the Han government extended its territories to the east, west, and south.

In contrast to the Qin government, which favored Legalism, the Han government preferred that its officials be learned in the Confucian classics. With these officials, the Han government proved remarkably successful in coordinating administrative control of a population of about 59 million people. Still, the imperial institution proved vulnerable to manipulation by the families of empresses and by palace eunuchs.

The Han Dynasty is the first of the five major dynasties that lasted more than two and a half centuries (Han, Tang, Song, Ming, and Qing), and scholars often look at the Han with these later dynasties in mind. The structure and operation of the government have been major concerns: What enabled Han to succeed where Qin had failed? What was the impact of the centralized state on ordinary people's lives? What were the consequences of the support the government gave to Confucianism? What type of Confucianism did the government support? Later dynasties had difficulties on their northern borders reminiscent of the Han-Xiongnu confrontation, drawing

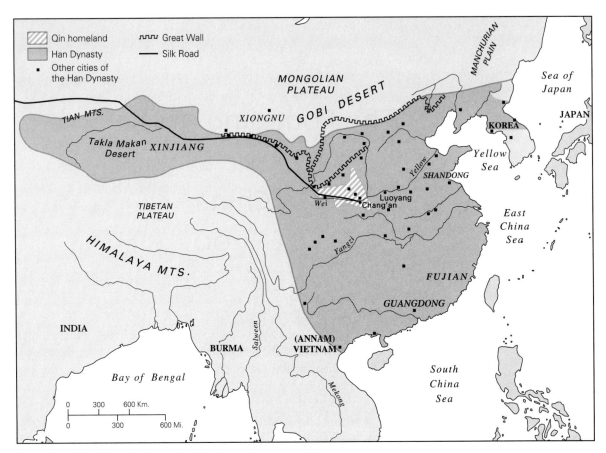

Map **3.1**   **The Han Empire at Its Maximum Extent, ca. 50 B.C.E.**

scholars' attention to this initial stage. Was conflict between China and its northern neighbors inevitable, given the differences in the economies of the two regions, or could different policies have led to different outcomes? Did the Han Dynasty's great territorial expansion aid it in any way, or was it costly overextension?

THE QIN UNIFICATION (256–206 B.C.E.)

The year 221 B.C.E., one of the most important dates in Chinese history, marks the beginning of the Chinese empire. That year, the state of Qin, which had adopted Legalist policies, succeeded in defeating the last of its rivals, thus creating a unified China. (See Map 3.1.) As discussed in the last chapter, following the counsel of Legalist advisers, Qin had restructured itself in the fourth century B.C.E. The power of the old nobility and the patriarchal family were curtailed to create instead a direct relationship between the ruler and his subjects, based on uniformly enforced laws and punishments, administered by officials appointed by the king.

One of the most influential men in Qin in the decades before the conquest was a rich merchant, Lü Buwei. That a merchant could use his wealth to gain political favor is evidence of the high social mobility of the age. Lü was said to have decided that gaining control of a state offered more opportunities to grow rich than commerce did, and to have come up with a scheme to accomplish that by favoring a potential heir to the throne, then helping him succeed to it. Once Lü's protégé became king, Lü became chancellor. There followed a string of stunning victories over other states, allowing Qin to increase its territories steadily. This king died after only three years on the throne, and in 247 thirteen-year-old King Cheng came to the throne, with Lü as regent. One of the orders he issued was that common people who had amassed riches through their own enterprise be granted noble ranks. Those so honored included a man who traded silk for animals with the Rong barbarians and a widow who managed the family cinnabar mines.

Lü recruited scholars to come to Qin, where he put them to work on a book that would present a unified philosophy for the unified realm he envisioned. The resulting book, *The Annals of Mr. Lü*, combines cosmological correlative thinking using the five phases/agents and yin and yang with political philosophy from all the major schools. The ruler should be tranquil and unassertive, as *Laozi* had advised, but select wise ministers and trust their advice, an essentially Confucian attitude. The state should aid farmers, keep taxes low, and encourage merchants. Filial piety is extolled, as is learning.

After King Cheng began to rule on his own, he sent Lü Buwei away. Lü, seeing that he was losing favor, committed suicide. King Cheng's next chancellor was Li Si, a fully committed Legalist who, like Han Feizi, had studied under the Confucian scholar Xunzi. With Li Si's astute advice, Qin was able to reorganize each territory as it took it over. By 230 the tide of war had shifted in Qin's favor, and the final six states—Han, Zhao, Wei, Chu, Yan, and Qi—were defeated in rapid succession. All of a sudden Qin had to rule millions of people who had until then been desperately battling to avoid such a fate.

The First Emperor (r. 221–210 B.C.E.)

Once Qin ruled all of China, King Cheng decided that the title "king" was not grand enough and invented the title "emperor" (literarily, "august theocrat," *huangdi*), using words

Character					
Qi					
Chu					
Yan					
Han					
Zhao					
Wei					
Qin					
Translation	peace	horse	positive	level	city

Figure 3.1   **Standardizing the Writing System**

that linked him to the sage rulers of the mythical past. He called himself the First Emperor in anticipation of a long line of successors.

The First Emperor initiated a sweeping program of centralization that touched the lives of nearly everyone in China. To cripple the nobility of the defunct states, the First Emperor ordered nobles to leave their lands and move to the capital, Xianyang (near modern Xi'an). To administer the territory that had been seized, he dispatched officials whom he controlled through a mass of regulations, reporting requirements, and penalties for inadequate performance. These officials owed their power and positions entirely to the favor of the emperor and had no hereditary rights to their offices. To make it easier to administer all regions uniformly, writing systems were standardized, as were weights, measures, coinage, and even the axle lengths of carts. Private possession of arms was outlawed in order to make it more difficult for subjects to rebel. Thousands of miles of roads were built to enable Qin armies to move rapidly. Investment was also made in canals linking rivers, making it possible to travel long distances by boat. Most of the labor on these projects came from farmers performing required labor service or convicts working off their sentences.

The First Emperor shared the Legalist suspicion of intellectual diversity. In 213 B.C.E., after Li Si complained that scholars used records of the past to denigrate the emperor's achievements and undermine popular support, the emperor ordered the collection and burning of all useless writings. The only works excepted were manuals on topics such as agriculture, medicine, and divination. As a result of this massive book burning, many ancient texts were lost.

Some twentieth-century Chinese historians have glorified the First Emperor as a bold conqueror who let no obstacle impede him, but the traditional evaluation of him was almost entirely negative. For centuries, Chinese historians castigated him as a monster: cruel, arbitrary, impetuous, suspicious, and superstitious.

Qin Law

The Qin was always thought to have had a particularly harsh legal system, but little was known about its exact provisions until 1975 when 625 bamboo strips inscribed with Qin laws and legal texts were found in a tomb in Hubei province. The tomb was for a man who served the Qin government as a prefectural official. Some of the texts reconstructed from the strips contain statutes related to management of government granaries and labor service. One book explains legal terminology in question-and-answer format.

The penalties imposed by Qin law were hard labor, physical mutilation, banishment, slavery, or death. Labor could last from one to six years. Mutilation included shaving of the beard; shaving of the head; branding the forehead; cutting off the nose or left foot; or castration. Death also came in several forms, the most severe of which was being torn apart by horse-drawn chariots. To make sure that criminals were caught and offenses reported, Qin set up mutual responsibility units of five households, whose members were required to inform on each other or suffer the same penalty as the criminal. For particularly heinous crimes, even distant relatives could be enslaved.

Penal labor was a common punishment. Those guilty of theft or homicide were sentenced to long terms, but even those sentenced to pay fines often had to work the sentence off as labor, credited at the rate of eight coins a day (six if one received food rations). Those who owned slaves, oxen, or horses could receive credit for the work they did, or they could hire others to work in their place. Men and women were treated differently. Men had heavier work assignments but received larger rations. A man could volunteer for service on the frontier for five years to redeem his mother or sister but not his father or brother.

Government officials had to take similar responsibility for the performance of their department. Every year in the tenth month, officials had to send in detailed reports to be used for the evaluation of their performance. If they did more or less than expected, they were punished by fines calculated in sets of armor and shields.

The First Emperor's Tomb

The First Emperor started work on his tomb soon after he came to the throne. In 231 B.C.E. the area around the tomb was made a separate administrative district and the people of the district were made responsible for the construction and maintenance of the imperial tomb. Twenty years later, thirty thousand families were resettled to the district, and several hundred thousand forced laborers were sent there as temporary workers.

In 1974, about a kilometer from the tomb, a pit was discovered filled with life-sized terracotta figures of soldiers. Since then, as archaeologists have probed the region around the First Emperor's tomb, they have found more and more pits filled with burial goods of one sort or another. Sometimes actual objects were used, in other cases replicas. One pit had two finely made half-size bronze chariots, each drawn by four bronze horses. In another pit were thirty-

The First Emperor's Army. The thousands of life-sized terra-cotta soldiers placed in pits near the First Emperor's tomb were originally painted in bright colors and they held real bronze weapons. They testify both to the emperor's concern with the afterlife and the ability of his government to organize production on a large scale. *(Laurent Lecat/AKG-Images)*

one rare birds and animals that had been buried alive in clay coffins laid in rows. Although these were real birds and animals (probably from the huge imperial hunting park), they are guarded by a terra-cotta warden. Actual horses were buried in other pits. In many cases a small pit had a single horse and a terra-cotta groom. In one pit, however, were bones of three hundred horses. There is also a pit where more than a hundred human skeletons have been found; according to inscribed shards, these were conscript and penal laborers who died on the job.

By far the most spectacular of the pits discovered in the vicinity of the First Emperor's tomb are the three that contain the terra-cotta army.

Historians had no knowledge of this army, so its discovery was a complete surprise. Pit 1 has more than six thousand figures of warriors arrayed in columns, most of them infantry, but with some chariots near the front. Pit 2 has cavalry plus more infantry and chariots and may represent a guard unit. Pit 3 seems to be the command post, with fewer soldiers. The floor of these pits had been made of rammed earth, covered by ceramic tiles (some 256,000 for pit 1). Wooden supports held up roof beams, strong enough to keep the roof from caving in from the weight of the earth above.

The soldiers were made of simple clay formed with molds. Although viewers often described the soldiers as individualized, in reality they were made of interchangeable parts. For instance, there were two basic forms for hands, with fingers straight or curved, but they could appear quite different depending on how they were attached to the sleeves and the angle at which the thumb was attached. Hand finishing, for instance of the hair, could make figures seem more distinct as well. After the soldiers were molded, they were painted with lacquer, which both preserved them and made them seem more lifelike. These figures carried real weapons, such as spears, halberds, swords, and bows and arrows. These weapons were of high quality (some of the blades are still razor sharp) and were mass-produced in state factories. To ensure quality control, each weapon was inscribed with the names of the worker who made it and the person who supervised him. Each also had a serial number.

Why did the First Emperor want so many replicas of soldiers buried near him? For several centuries, there had been a trend in Chinese burial practice to bury representations rather than real objects in graves. To some extent, this could have been a cost-saving measure: if replicas were just as good as the real thing in the afterlife, why take so much wealth out of circulation by placing it underground? But possibly replicas were considered in some way superior because they caught the unchanging universal aspect of the thing, not one particular manifestation. It is perhaps hard to believe that a ceramic representation of a bronze ritual vessel could be as useful in the afterlife as a real bronze one, but one can imagine that a ceramic guard, which will never decay, could be preferable to a mortal one.

The First Emperor's personal fears and beliefs undoubtedly also contributed to his decision to construct such an elaborate underground world. Three times assassins tried to kill him, and perhaps as a consequence he became obsessed with finding ways to avoid death. He sent a group of young men and women to search for Penglai, the famed isles of immortality in the Eastern Sea. He listened to seers and magicians who claimed to know other techniques for achieving immortality. Was his huge tomb a fallback plan—a way to reduce the sting of death if he couldn't escape it altogether?

Although the First Emperor filled the pits near his tomb with terra-cotta replicas of his minions, his successor saw to it that some human beings were buried there as well. According to Sima Qian, writing in about 100 B.C.E.:

> *The Second Emperor said, "Of the women in the harem of the former ruler, it would be unfitting to have those who bore no sons sent elsewhere." All were accordingly ordered to accompany the dead man, which resulted in the death of many women. After the interment had been completed, someone pointed out that the artisans and craftsmen who had built the tomb knew what was buried there, and if they should leak word of the treasures, it would be a serious affair. Therefore, after the articles had been placed in the tomb, the inner gate was closed off and the outer gate lowered, so that all the artisans and craftsmen were shut in the tomb and were unable to get out.*[1]

Presumably when the archaeologists excavate the tomb itself, they will find the bones not only of the First Emperor, but also those who accompanied him in death.

THE HAN DYNASTY (206 B.C.E.–220 C.E.)

The First Emperor died in 210 B.C.E. while traveling. He had trusted no one, and at this juncture no one proved trustworthy. The chief eunuch plotted with a younger son to send orders to the heir apparent and General Meng Tian to commit suicide. The younger son became the Second Emperor and had several of his brothers executed. The chief eunuch was elevated to chancellor after he got the Second

---

1. Burton Watson, trans., *Records of the Grand Historian: Qin Dynasty* (New York: Columbia University Press, 1993), p. 65.

Emperor to execute Li Si. By this time, the Qin state was unraveling. The Legalist institutions designed to concentrate power in the hands of the ruler made the stability of the government dependent on the strength and character of a single person.

In the ensuing uprisings, many of the rebels called for the restoration of the old states, but this was not what happened. The eventual victor was Liu Bang (known in history as Emperor Gao, r. 202–195 B.C.E.). The First Emperor of Qin was from the old Zhou aristocracy. Liu Bang, by contrast, was from a modest family of commoners, so his elevation to emperor is evidence of how thoroughly the Qin Dynasty had destroyed the old order.

Emperor Gao did not disband the centralized government created by Qin, but he did remove its most unpopular features. He set up his capital at Chang'an, not far from the old Qin capital. He eliminated some laws, cut taxes, and otherwise lessened the burdens on the people. After a century of almost constant war and huge labor mobilizations, China was given several decades to recover. Responding to the desire to restore the old order, Emperor Gao gave out large and nearly autonomous fiefs to his relatives and chief generals. Very soon he recognized that giving followers independent resources was a mistake, and he spent much of his reign eliminating the fief holders who were not relatives. After his death, the fiefs of imperial relatives were also gradually reduced in size.

The Han emperor in theory was all powerful but in actuality depended on his chancellor and other high officials for information and advice. Nine ministries were established to handle matters ranging from state ritual to public works. Officials, graded by rank and salary, were appointed by the central government for their merit, not their birth, and were subject to dismissal, demotion, or transfer, much in the way Qin officials had been. Local officials—magistrates and grand administrators—had broad responsibilities: they collected taxes, judged lawsuits, commanded troops to suppress uprisings, undertook public works such as flood control, chose their own subordinates, and recommended local men to the central government for appointments. The main tax was a poll tax of 120 cash (coins) on adults (less for children). Adults also owed a month of labor service each year. Land tax, largely retained by the county and commandery governments, was set at the low rate of one-thirtieth of the harvest.

When Emperor Gao died, his heir was a child, and the empress dowager (the widow of the former emperor) took control until her death, fifteen years later. This Empress Lü is described in the histories as a vicious, spiteful person, and after her fall her entire family was wiped out. For centuries to come, she would provide an example of the dangers of letting a woman take power, even if she was the mother of the emperor.

The Han emperor who had the greatest impact on Chinese culture and society was Emperor Wu, who came to the throne as a teenager in 141 B.C.E. and reigned for fifty-four years. Unafraid of innovation, Emperor Wu initiated many of the most significant developments in Han culture and government. He took an interest in the arts and patronized both music and poetry. Like many other men of his age, Emperor Wu was fascinated with omens, portents, spirits, immortals, and occult forces, yet he wanted his officials to study Confucian texts.

Emperor Wu expanded the empire through military means. To pay for his military campaigns, he took over the minting of coins, confiscated the land of nobles, sold offices and titles, and increased taxes on private businesses. A widespread suspicion of commerce—from both moral and political perspectives—made it easy to levy especially heavy assessments on merchants. Boats, carts, shops, and other facilities were made subject to property taxes. The worst blow to merchants, however, was the government's decision to enter into market competition with them by selling the commodities that had been collected as taxes. In 119 B.C.E. government monopolies were established on the production of iron, salt, and liquor, enterprises that previously had been sources of great profit for private entrepreneurs. Large-scale grain dealing also had been a profitable business, which the government now took over under the guise of stabilizing prices. Grain was to be bought where it was plentiful and its price low; it would either be stored in granaries until prices rose or transported to areas of scarcity. This policy was supposed to eliminate speculation in grain, provide more constant prices, and bring profit to the government.

The relative success of the Han form of government validated the imperial system, which drew from both Confucian rhetoric and Legalist bureaucratic methods. To put this another way, the Zhou notion of All-Under-Heaven ruled by the paramount Son of Heaven, an idea fully supported by Confucian thinkers, now had attached to it the structures of the centralized bureaucratic empire, indebted though these were to Legalist ideas.

Official Support for Confucianism

Emperor Wu was the first Han emperor to privilege Confucian scholars within the government. He listened to the Confucian scholar Dong Zhongshu, who gave him advice much like Li Si's to the First Emperor. "Because the various schools of thought differ," he said, "the people do not know what to honor," and he advised that "anything not encompassed by the Six Disciplines and the arts of Confucius be suppressed and not allowed to continue further, and evil and vain theories be stamped out."[2] Emperor Wu soon decreed that officials should be selected on the basis of Confucian virtues and established a national university to train officials in the Confucian classics.

The Han government's decision to recruit men trained in the Confucian classics marks the beginning of the Confucian scholar-official system, one of the most distinctive features of imperial China. Since one of the highest duties

of the Confucian scholar was to admonish the ruler against misguided policies, officials whose educations imbued them with Confucian values did not comply automatically with the emperor's wishes. Still, emperors found employing Confucian scholars as officials efficient; because of their ingrained sense of duty, they did not have to be supervised as closely as the Legalist model required. That did not mean that emperors took all aspects of the Confucian model of governing to heart themselves or always treated their Confucian officials with respect. Emperor Wu was so averse to criticism that he once had an official executed on the charge that a wry twist of his lips showed that he disapproved in his heart, and his temper led him to put five of his last seven chancellors to death.

The Xiongnu and the Northern Frontier

As far back as written records allow us to see, the Chinese had shared the Chinese subcontinent with other ethnic groups. To the north were groups that the Shang and Zhou called Rong and Di. At that time, the economy of these northerners was similar to the Chinese settlements, with millet agriculture, animal husbandry, and hunting. Many of these groups were eventually incorporated into the northern Zhou states, which gradually expanded north. Over time, those not incorporated into China seem to have come to depend more and more on animal husbandry, perhaps because the climate grew colder or drier. They took to riding horses before the Chinese did, and by the seventh century B.C.E., many of these groups were making the move to nomadic pastoralism. Families lived in tents that could be taken down and moved north in summer and south in winter as they moved in search of fresh pasture. Herds were tended on horseback, and everyone learned to ride from a young age. Especially awesome from the Chinese perspective was the ability of nomad horsemen to shoot arrows while riding horseback. Their social organization was tribal,

2. William Theodore de Bary and Irene Bloom, eds., *Sources of Chinese Tradition*, rev. ed. (New York: Columbia University Press, 1999), p. 311.

with family and clan units held together through loyalty to chiefs selected for their military prowess. At the end of the Zhou period, there were three main groups of nomads in the Northern Zone: the Eastern Hu in the east (northern Hebei-Liaoning region), the Xiongnu in the Ordos (northern Shaanxi-Shanxi), and the Yuezhi to their west.

In 215 B.C.E. one of Qin's most successful generals, Meng Tian, led a huge army (said variously to be 100,000 or 300,000 strong) to attack the Xiongnu and drive them out of the Ordos region. Once he had succeeded, he built forty-four fortified towns along the river and moved people sentenced to guard the borders to settle them. He also built roads to the region and extended the defensive walls, projects that required tens of thousands of laborers. By connecting these walls, Meng Tian created the first version of the Great Wall.

At this time, the chief of the Xiongnu was Touman. The Xiongnu's failure to defend its territory against the Qin armies naturally weakened his authority, since Xiongnu chiefs were above all military leaders. Touman's own son Maodun soon challenged him. Maodun first trained his bodyguards to kill on command, executing anyone who failed instantly to obey his commands that they shoot his favorite horse and favorite concubine. When he was satisfied that they would do what he said, he ordered them to shoot his father and declared himself the Xiongnu chief.

During the next few years, Maodun led the Xiongnu to defeat both the Eastern Hu and the Yuezhi. Some of the Yuezhi simply moved west, but the Eastern Hu were incorporated into the Xiongnu tribal confederation. Maodun also campaigned north of the Gobi, uniting the tribes in modern Mongolia. His quick military victories made him a charismatic leader whom others wanted to follow. Some of the tribes he defeated were incorporated as tribute-paying vassals and other as slaves. By this time, the Qin Dynasty was falling apart, and Maodun was able to reclaim the Ordos region that Qin had taken from the Xiongnu only a few years earlier.

At the beginning of the Han, even before Emperor Gao had completed the consolidation of the empire, he came to realize the threat posed by the Xiongnu. In 200 B.C.E. the Xiongnu under Maodun attacked one of the recently appointed kings, who decided to go over to the Xiongnu. With his help, the Xiongnu then attacked the major city of Taiyuan. Emperor Gao personally led an army to retake the region, but his army suffered terribly from the cold. Maodun led a huge army of horsemen to surround the Han army. Given little choice, Emperor Gao agreed to make yearly gifts of silk, grain, and other foodstuffs to the Xiongnu. The Xiongnu considered this tribute, but the Han naturally preferred to consider it an expression of friendship.

After Emperor Gao's debacle, the early Han emperors had concentrated on pacifying the Xiongnu, supplying them not only with material goods but also with princesses as brides (which they hoped in time would lead to rulers with Chinese mothers). These policies were controversial, since critics thought they merely strengthened the enemy. Moreover, as they pointed out, no matter how much wealth the Han sent to the Xiongnu, they kept raiding the borders.

Emperor Wu decided to take a tougher stand. To push the Xiongnu back, he sent several armies of 100,000 to 300,000 troops deep into Xiongnu territory. These costly campaigns were of limited value since the Xiongnu were a moving target: fighting nomads was not like attacking walled cities. If the Xiongnu did not want to fight the Chinese troops, they simply decamped. Moreover, it was very difficult for Chinese troops to carry enough food to stay long in Xiongnu territory. What they could do was consolidate the land the Xiongnu had vacated by the same methods Qin had used: building forts, appointing officials, and dispatching settlers.

Wang Mang

The Han practice of hereditary succession to the throne from father to son meant that the heir might be a young child. During the last decades of the first century B.C.E., several children succeeded to the throne. Adult men of the imperial lineage did not serve as regents; they were regularly sent out of the capital to keep them from interfering in court politics. That left the mothers and grandmothers of the new rulers, along with the women's male relatives, as the main contenders for power during regencies. Wang Mang came to power as a relative of Empress Wang (d. 13 C.E.), who for forty years had been influential at court as the widow of one emperor, mother of a second, and grandmother of a third. After serving as regent for two infant emperors, Wang Mang deposed the second and declared himself emperor of the Xin (New) Dynasty (9 C.E.–23 C.E.).

Although he was condemned as a usurper, Wang Mang was a learned Confucian scholar who wished to implement policies described in the classics. He renamed offices, asserted state ownership of forests and swamps, built ritual halls, revived public granaries, outlawed slavery, limited private landholdings, and cut court expenses. Some of his policies, such as issuing new coins and nationalizing gold, led to economic turmoil. Matters were made worse when the Yellow River broke through its dikes and shifted course from north to south, driving millions of farmers from their homes as huge regions were flooded. Rebellion broke out, and in the ensuing warfare a Han imperial clansman succeeded in reestablishing the Han Dynasty. The capital was moved from Chang'an to Luoyang, leading to the references to the first half of the Han as the Western or Former Han and the second half as the Eastern or Later Han (reminiscent of the Western and Eastern Zhou).

Palace Eunuchs

During the second century C.E., Han court politics deteriorated as the eunuchs (castrated men) who served as palace servants vied with relatives of the empresses for control of the court. For centuries, eunuchs had been a part of palace life, charged with managing the women's quarters.

Eunuchs were in essence slaves; a common source seems to have been boys captured from the "southern barbarians." Court officials looked on palace eunuchs with contempt. Emperors who had grown up with them, however, often saw them as more reliable than officials since they had no outside base of power.

During the Eastern Han period, eunuchs were able to build a base of power within the palace, with the result that weak emperors became the captives rather than the masters of the eunuchs. In 124 C.E., a group of eunuchs placed on the throne a child they could manipulate. They gained even more power after 159, when an emperor turned to them to help him oust a consort family faction. In 166 and 169, officials staged protests against eunuch power, but the eunuchs retaliated. In the purges that followed, the protestors were put in jail, banned from office, and even in a few cases killed.

INTELLECTUAL, LITERARY, AND RELIGIOUS CURRENTS

Perhaps stimulated by the Qin destruction of books, learning and literature of all sorts flourished in Han times. At the end of the Western Han period, the imperial library had some 596 titles, divided into six categories: classics, philosophy, poetry, military treatises, mathematics and natural science (including astronomy, the calendar, and divination), and medicine. Also important to the history of books in China is the development of paper. Over the course of the Han, a variety of plant fibers was tested, and by the end of the period, paper was produced that had a good, absorbent writing surface. Books were of course much less cumbersome when written on rolls of paper than on strips of wood or bamboo.

Early in the Han period, a form of Daoism called Huang-Lao Daoism became particularly influential; *Huang* (yellow) refers to the Yellow Emperor, *Lao* to Laozi, both of whom were treated as deities of vast powers. Emperor Wu was attracted to these teachings and tried to make contact with the world of gods and immortals through elaborate sacrifices. He marveled at stories of the paradise of the Queen Mother of the West and the exploits of the Yellow Emperor, who had taken his entire court with him when he ascended to the realm of the immortals. He inaugurated state cults to the Earth Queen in 114 B.C.E. and Grand Unity in 113. In 110 he traveled to Mount Tai to perform a sacrifice to heaven at the peak and a sacrifice to earth at the base. Although claims were made that these sacrifices were of ancient origin, in fact they were designed for him by court ritualists steeped in Huang-Lao ideas. Religious practices among ordinary people were influenced by Huang-Lao ideas, but also by a great variety of other ideas about spiritual beings and the forces of the cosmos (see **Documents: Lucky and Unlucky Days**).

Han Confucianism

> ### The Five Classics
> *Book of Changes*
> *Book of Documents*
> *Book of Poetry*
> *Spring and Autumn Annals*
> *Book of Rites*

Confucianism made a comeback during the Han Dynasty, but in a new form. Although Confucian texts had fed the First Emperor's bonfires, some dedicated scholars had hidden their books, and others could recite entire books from memory. The ancient books recovered in these ways came to be regarded as classics containing the wisdom of the past. Scholars studied them with piety and attempted to make them more useful as sources of moral guidance by writing commentaries to them that explained archaic words and obscure passages. Confucian scholars often specialized in a single classic, a teacher passing on to his disciples his understanding of each sentence in the work.

Perhaps inspired by the political unification of the realm, some Han Confucians attempted to develop comprehensive understandings of phenomena, drawing on ideas of diverse origins. Their cosmological theories explained all phenomena in terms of cyclical flows of yin and yang and the five phases (fire, water, earth, metal, and wood). This cosmos was a fundamentally moral one: natural disasters such as floods or earthquakes were viewed as portents indicating that the emperor had failed in his responsibility to maintain the proper balance in heaven and earth.

The emperor was of unique importance in this cosmology because he alone had the capacity to link the realms of heaven, earth, and man. The leading Han Confucian scholar Dong Zhongshu (195?–105 B.C.E.) wanted a ruler who would serve as high priest and fount of wisdom, who would be all-powerful but also deferential to learned scholars. Dong drew on ideas from earlier Confucian, Daoist, and Legalist texts to describe the ruler as the "pivot of all living

Correspondences of the Five Phases					
	wood	**fire**	**earth**	**metal**	**water**
seasons	spring	summer		autumn	winter
directions	east	south	center	west	north
weather	wind	heat	thunder	cold	rain
colors	green	red	yellow	white	black
emotions	anger	joy	desire	sorrow	fear
organs	eyes	tongue	mouth	nose	ears

DOCUMENTS

Lucky and Unlucky Days

Some of our best evidence of common beliefs in Han China is found in the writings of critics, such as Wang Chong (27–ca. 100 C.E.). Wang's lengthy Balanced Discourses *includes refutations of a wide range of beliefs and practices, from the idea that people could become immortals and fly high above the earth, to the notion that ghosts could come back to harm people. In the passage here, he attempts to refute the idea that taking action on an unlucky day can cause people harm.*

People today commonly believe in evil influences. They think that when people fall ill or die, or there are repeated calamities, executions, or humiliations, some offense has been committed. If inauspicious days and months are not avoided when starting a project, moving, sacrificing, burying, taking up office, or marrying, then the demons and spirits that one encounters at these ill-fated times will work their harm. Thus illness, disaster, legal penalties, death, even the extermination of a family are all thought to be brought about by not taking care to avoid ill-fated times. In truth, however, this is wild talk. . . .

Rulers anxious about their office and commoners concerned about their bodies believe in this theory and do not raise doubts. Thus when a ruler is about to embark on an enterprise, diviners throng his halls, and when ordinary people have work to be done, they inquire into the best time. As a consequence deceptive books and false texts have appeared in large numbers. . . .

Rare are the diseases not caused by wind, moisture, or food and drink. After people have gone out in the wind or slept in a damp place, they spend money to find out which noxious influence [has attacked them]. When they overeat, they should practice abstinence, but if their illness does not improve, they say the noxious force has not been identified. If the person dies, they say the diviner was not careful. Among ordinary people, such talk is considered wisdom.

Among the 360 animals, man ranks first. Man is a living creature, but among the ten thousand creatures, man is the most intelligent. But he obtains his lifespan from Heaven and his *qi* from the origin in the same way as the other creatures. . . . It makes no sense that the misfortune caused by demons and spirits would fall on man alone, and not on other creatures. In man the minds of Heaven and Earth reach their highest development. Why do heavenly disasters strike the noblest creature and not the mean ones? . . .

If I commit a crime and am arrested by the magistrate and sentenced to punishment, no one says I did something wrong. Instead they say that someone in my family was negligent. If I have not been careful where I lodge or go overboard in food or drink, they do not say I have been immoderate, but that I have disregarded an unlucky time. When people die one after the other and dozens of coffins await burial, they do not say the air is contaminated but that the day of a burial was inauspicious. . . .

The city of Liyang one night was flooded and became a lake. Its residents cannot all have violated taboos on years and months. When Emperor Gao rose, Feng and Pei were recovered, but surely its residents had not all been careful in their choice of hours and days. When Xiang Yu attacked Xiangan, no one survived, but surely its residents had not all failed to pray. The army of Zhao was buried alive by Qin at Changping; 400,000 men died together at the same time. It is hardly likely that when they left home not one of them divined for a propitious time.

Source: Wang Chong, *Lunheng jiaoshi*, ed. Huang Hui (Taibei: Commercial Press, 1964), 24.1004–12. Translated by Patricia Ebrey.

things," who is "quiet and nonactive" yet "deliberates with his numerous worthies" and knows how to tell if they are loyal or treacherous.[3]

Sima Qian and the *Records of the Grand Historian*

History writing began early in China. In the early Zhou period, court chroniclers kept track of astronomical matters and advised rulers on the lessons of the past. Two of the Five Classics, the *Book of Documents* and the *Spring and Autumn Annals,* are historical works, the former a collection of documents and the latter a chronicle. By the Warring States period, not only did each of the states compile historical records, but citing examples from the past had become a common way to support an argument.

The art of history writing took a major step forward in the Han period. During Emperor Wu's reign, two historians, father and son, undertook to write a comprehensive history of the entire past. Sima Tan (d. 110 B.C.E.) served as the court astronomer under Emperor Wu and had access to the government archives. His son Sima Qian (145–ca. 85 B.C.E.) carried on his work and brought it to completion.

Before Sima Qian was able to complete his history, he angered Emperor Wu by defending a general who had surrendered to the Xiongnu. As a consequence, he was sentenced to castration and service as a palace eunuch. This punishment was so humiliating that it was expected that he would choose the honorable alternative of suicide. Sima Qian explained in a letter to a friend why he decided to accept his humiliating sentence: he could not bear the thought that the history would not be completed. "I have compiled neglected knowledge of former times from all over the world; I have examined these for veracity and have given an account of the principles behind success and defeat, rise and fall." His ambitions were large: "I also wanted to fully explore the interaction between Heaven and Man, and to show the continuity of transformations of past and present."[4] Only by finishing the work could he make up for the dishonor he had suffered.

Like the Greek historian Thucydides, Sima Qian believed fervently in examining artifacts and documents, visiting the sites where history was made, and questioning people about events. He was also interested in China's geographical variations, local customs, and local history. As an official of the emperor, he had access to important people and documents and to the imperial library. He quoted documents when they were available, and in their absence invented dialogues to bring events to life. The result of his efforts, ten years in the making, was a massive work of literary and historical genius, the 130-chapter *Records of the Grand Historian.*

The *Records* presents several perspectives on the past. A political narrative begins with the Yellow Emperor and continues through the Xia, Shang, and Zhou dynasties, down to Sima Qian's own day. It is supplemented by chronological charts with genealogical data and information on the organization of governments. Key institutions are given their own histories in topical chapters on state ritual, court music, the calendar, waterworks, finance, and other matters of concern to the government. Thirty chapters give the separate histories of each of the ruling houses of the states of the Zhou period. Biographies of individuals take up more than half the book. Although many of those portrayed played important political or military roles, Sima Qian also singled out other notable men, including philosophers, poets, merchants, magicians, rebels, assassins, and foreign groups like the Xiongnu. At the end of each chapter of biographies Sima Qian offered his own comments. Sima Qian's experiences with Emperor Wu did not incline him to flatter rulers. Not only did he give ample evidence of Emperor Wu's arbitrariness and policy errors, but he also found many ways to draw attention to those whose merit went unrecognized in their day.

3. Ibid., pp. 298–299.

4. Stephen Owen, *An Anthology of Chinese Literature: Beginnings to 1911* (New York: Norton, 1996), p. 141.

Reeling and Weaving. Many Han tombs had scenes of daily life depicted on their walls. In this example, seated below a finely-drawn tile roof are three women reeling, twisting, and weaving silk. The weaver is using a treadle-operated loom. *(National Museum of Chinese History, Beijing)*

By writing so well, Sima Qian had a profound impact on Chinese conceptions of history and personal achievement. In the centuries that followed, the *Records of the Grand Historian* was read as much for the pleasure of the narrative as for historical data. The composite style, with political narratives supplemented by treatises and biographies, became standard for government-sponsored histories. Subsequent histories, however, usually covered only a single dynasty. The first of these, *History of the Former Han Dynasty,* was the work of three members of the Ban family in the first century C.E. (see **Biography: The Ban Family**).

CHINESE SOCIETY IN HAN TIMES

During the Western Han, with the establishment of peace and the extension of the empire's fron-

tiers, the Chinese population grew rapidly. The census of 2 C.E. recorded a population of 59 million, the earliest indication of the large size of China's population. These people shared status as subjects of the Han, but their daily lives varied enormously, depending on their social status and where they lived.

Common Farmers

The bulk of the population in Han times (and even into the twentieth century) were farmers living in villages of a few dozen or a few hundred households. At the technical level, agriculture continued to make advances. The new and more effective plow introduced during the Han period was fitted with two plowshares, guided by a pair of handles, and typically pulled by a pair of oxen. Farmers used fans to blow the chaff from kernels of grain, and they used either

BIOGRAPHY The Ban Family

Ban Biao (3–54 C.E.), a successful official from a family with an envied library, had three highly accomplished children: his twin sons, the general Ban Chao (32–102) and the historian Ban Gu (32–92); and his daughter, Ban Zhao (ca. 45–120).

After distinguishing himself as a junior officer in campaigns against the Xiongnu, Ban Chao was sent in 73 C.E. to the Western Regions to see about the possibility of restoring Chinese overlordship there, lost since Wang Mang's time. Ban Chao spent most of the next three decades in Central Asia. Through patient diplomacy and a show of force, he reestablished Chinese control over the oasis cities of Central Asia, and in 92 he was appointed protector general of the area.

Ban Gu was one of the most accomplished writers of his age, excelling in a distinctive literary form known as the rhapsody (*fu*). His "Rhapsody on the Two Capitals" is in the form of a dialogue between a guest from Chang'an and his host in Luoyang. It describes the palaces, spectacles, scenic spots, local products, and customs of the two great cities. Emperor Zhang (r. 76–88) was fond of literature and often had Ban Gu accompany him on hunts or travels. He also had him edit a record of the court debates he held on issues concerning the Confucian classics.

Ban Biao had been working on a history of the Western Han Dynasty when he died in 54. Ban Gu took over this project, modeling it on Sima Qian's *Records of the Grand Historian.* He added treatises on law, geography, and bibliography, the last a classified list of books in the imperial library.

Because of his connection to a general out of favor, Ban Gu was sent to prison in 92, where he soon died. At that time the *History of the Former Han Dynasty* was still incomplete. The emperor called on Ban Gu's widowed sister, Ban Zhao, to finish it. She came to the palace, where she not only worked on the history but also became a teacher of the women of the palace. According to the *History of the Later Han,* she taught them the classics, history, astronomy, and mathematics. In 106 an infant succeeded to the throne, and Empress Deng became regent. The empress frequently turned to Ban Zhao for advice on government policies.

Ban Zhao credited her own education to her learned father and cultured mother and became an advocate of the education of girls. In her *Admonitions for Women,* Ban Zhao objected that many families taught their sons to read but not their daughters. She did not claim they should have the same education; after all, "just as yin and yang differ, men and women have different characteristics." Women, she wrote, will do well if they cultivate the womanly virtues such as humility. "Humility means yielding and acting respectful, putting others first and oneself last, never mentioning one's own good deeds or denying one's own faults, enduring insults and bearing with mistreatment, all with due trepidation."[1] In subsequent centuries, Ban Zhao's *Admonitions* became one of the most commonly used texts for the education of girls.

[1]Patricia Buckley Ebrey, ed., *Chinese Civilization: A Sourcebook,* rev. ed. (New York: Free Press, 1993), p. 75.

mortars and pestles or hand mills to grind grain into flour. Irrigation of farmland was aided by brick-faced wells and pumping devices ranging from a simple pole with an attached bucket and counterweight to a sophisticated machine worked by foot pedals.

Because the Han Empire depended on free farmers to pay taxes and provide labor services, the government tried to keep farmers independent and productive. To fight peasant poverty, the government kept land taxes low, provided relief during famines, aided migration to areas where there was vacant land to be opened, and promoted agricultural advancements, such as planting two crops in alternate rows and planting a succession of carefully timed crops. Still, many farmers fell into debt and had to sell their land. Those who did not migrate in search of new opportunities usually became tenant farmers, often accepting quasi-servile status as the dependent of a magnate. Poverty also contributed to the supply of slaves, as men could sell their wives or children into slavery to pay debts.

Elite Groups

The old nobility of Zhou times did not survive Qin's destruction of the Zhou states and its determinedly anti-aristocratic policies. Still, Han historical sources are full of references to people who outranked ordinary farmers in wealth and power. Some of these gained power through proximity to the throne. Liang Ji, whose power derived from his position as father of the empress, was said to have had huge properties and mansions, forced commoners to become his slaves, used commoners doing labor service to work on his own properties, let his retainers extort property and favors, and so on. Members of the imperial clan and the adopted relatives of eunuchs could similarly take advantage of their position to accumulate wealth and power.

Other groups whose great wealth outraged observers were merchants and manufacturers. Zhao Cuo in 178 B.C.E. complained that merchants suffered none of the hardships of farmers and got the best food and clothing, associated with the nobility, and had more power than officials. Sima Qian spoke of how great merchants commanded the services of the poor. If a man's wealth was ten times their own, they would behave humbly toward him. If it was a hundred times their own, they would fear him. If it was a thousand times their own, they would work for him. And if it was ten thousand times their own, they would become his servants. Even those with noble titles, he added, depended on these rich merchants for loans.

Government officials had high standing in Han times, though rarely did they have the great wealth of the richest merchants or imperial relatives. In the Western Han, some men rose to high office from modest backgrounds. Kuang Heng, for instance, came from a farming family and hired himself out to get the money to study; he eventually became a respected classical scholar and high government official. Yet most of the time those who could afford to get the education needed to become officials came from families of means, most often landholders.

Access to office was largely through recommendations. At the local level, the county magistrate or commandery grand administrators appointed their own subordinates from among the local educated elite. The grand administrators also made recommendations to the central government of men who were "filial and incorrupt," who then became eligible for higher office. Another route to office was to study with a well-known teacher. Patron-client ties were very important in linking members of the elite, especially in the Eastern Han, when former subordinates and students could be counted on to come to one's assistance in political conflicts.

At the local level, better-off families were expected to act as the leaders of their communities and offer assistance to their neighbors and relatives in need. In the second century C.E., leading families in communities often erected stones inscribed with accounts of their good works, such as building or repairing bridges or shrines. Tombs and funerary monuments of the Eastern Han offer further evidence of the self-perception of such families. By decorating funerary architecture with pictures of famous filial sons, dutiful women, or loyal ministers, they were portraying their families as steeped in Confucian traditions. Not all those with power at the local level were Confucian scholars. Han sources are full of complaints of the "great families" or "powerful men" of local communities who intimidated their neighbors and built up their property by taking advantage of families in debt.

During the course of the Han, the educated elite (called the *shi*, the same term used in Zhou times for the lower level of the aristocracy) came to see themselves as participants, even if indirectly, in national literary, scholarly, and political affairs. The agitation against the eunuchs and consort families in the second century C.E. helped strengthen these feelings. The persecution of the leaders of the movement protesting eunuch power, which took place between 166 and 184, created a large group of articulate, energetic, concerned men excluded from office. Their prestige showed that social honor was something the elite conferred on itself rather than something the government controlled through its appointment of men to office.

The Family

During Han times, both the administrative structure of the centralized state and the success of Confucianism helped shape the Chinese family system. Since Shang times, at least at the highest social levels, patrilineal ancestors had been a central feature of the family. By the time of the registration of the population in Qin and Han times, everyone had patrilineal family names. Han laws supported the authority of family heads over the other members of their families. The state preferred to deal only with the family head and recognized this person's right to represent the family. The family head was generally the senior male, but if a man died before his sons were grown, his widow would serve as family head until they were of age. Family members were also held responsible for each other, and for serious crimes, relatives of a criminal were made slaves.

During the Zhou period, inheritance had favored the eldest son, who succeeded to both aristocratic titles and responsibility to maintain ancestral rites. By Han times primogeniture in ordinary families applied only to ancestral rites. Family property such as land was divided among all sons. Daughters did not get shares of the family property, though well-to-do families might provide a daughter with substantial goods as her dowry when she married. Because the family farm had to be divided every generation (at least when there was more than one son), a family with several sons risked rapid downward social mobility.

Marriages were arranged by family heads, generally with the bride joining the husband's family. Men could divorce their wives on any of seven grounds, which included barrenness, jealousy, and talkativeness, but could do so only if there was a family for her to return to. There were no grounds on which a woman could divorce her husband, but divorce by mutual agreement was possible.

The legal underpinnings of the family were closely connected to Confucian teachings. It was one of the Confucian ritual texts that first defined the seven grounds for divorce. Confucian ritual texts compiled in Han times also give elaborate descriptions of the proper deference that sons and daughters-in-law should show to parents. The *Book of Rites,* for instance, told daughters-in-law to rise at the cock's crow, wash and dress, and then call on their parents-in-law: "Getting to where they [the parents-in-law] are, with bated breath and gentle voice, they [the daughters-in-law] should ask if their clothes are too warm or too cold, whether they are ill or pained, or uncomfortable in any part; and if they be so, they should proceed reverently to stroke and scratch the place."[5] Male-female differentiation was much stressed in this book. For instance, in explaining why the man goes to fetch his bride in person, it says, "This is the same principle by which Heaven takes precedence over earth and rulers over their subjects."[6]

In Han times filial piety was extolled in both texts and art. Pictures of famous filial sons were used to decorate not only the walls of tombs but even everyday objects like boxes. The brief *Classic of Filial Piety* argued that at each level of society, sincere filial devotion leads people to perform their social duties conscientiously and prudently, creating peace and harmony.

Other Han texts addressed the virtues women should cultivate. The *Biographies of Exemplary Women,* compiled by Liu Xiang, told the stories of women from China's past who had given their husbands good advice, sacrificed themselves when forced to choose between their fathers and husbands, or performed other heroic

---

5. James Legge, trans., *Li Ki: Book of Rites* (Oxford: Oxford University Press, 1885), 1:450, modified.
6. Ibid., p. 440.

Painted Basket. Unearthed in the Han colony at Lolang, northern Korea, this basket provides excellent evidence of Han figure painting. The three-inch high figures that decorate the basket are all labeled and represent famous figures from history. Note that they are seated on the floor, not on chairs, not yet introduced. *(Central History Museum, Pyong-Yang, North Korea/ Werner Forman/Art Resource, NY)*

deeds. It also contained cautionary tales about scheming, jealous, and manipulative women who brought destruction to all around them. Another notable text on women's education was written by the scholar Ban Zhao. Her *Admonitions for Women* urged girls to master the seven virtues appropriate to women: humility, resignation, subservience, self-abasement, obedience, cleanliness, and industry (see **Biography: The Ban Family**).

CENTRAL ASIA AND THE SILK ROAD

It was during the Han period that the Chinese first learned that theirs was not the only civilization with cities and writing, and also that these

distant civilizations had been obtaining silk from China from merchants who crossed Eurasia.

This discovery was made when Emperor Wu decided to send Zhang Qian as an envoy to look for the Yuezhi, a group that had moved west after defeat by the Xiongnu several decades earlier and which Emperor Wu hoped would return to fight the Xiongnu for him. Despite being captured by the Xiongnu and delayed several years, Zhang eventually reached Bactria, Parthia, and Ferghana (in the region of modern Afghanistan). However, the Yuezhi, once found, had no interest in returning to help out the Han. In 115 B.C.E. Zhang was sent again, this time to look for another group, who proved just as unwilling to return. Zhang's travels, however, were not totally in vain. From the reports he made of these two trips, the Chinese learned firsthand of

MATERIAL CULTURE

Silk from the Silk Road

The Chinese product most in demand outside China was silk. The silkworm had been domesticated in China by the Shang period, and the excellence of Chinese silk technology in Zhou times is well documented through excavations of tombs. Silk is very strong and amazingly fine. A single silkworm can spin a filament 3,000 feet long but a minuscule .025 millimeters thick. Several of these filaments have to be twisted together to make the yarns used for weaving. Besides basic flat weaves and light gauzes, Chinese weavers also made patterned weaves, including multi-colored ones that required the use of a draw loom to separate the warp threads.

Many fragments of Han period textiles have survived in the arid climate of Chinese Central Asia, at sites along the Silk Road. The piece illustrated here was excavated from tomb 8 at Niya, along the southern arm of the Silk Road. The weave is exceptionally fine, with 220 warp threads per centimeter. The five-color woven design shows clouds, birds, a single-horned beast, and a tiger, along with Chinese characters. The inscription, which is the command of a Han emperor to a general

Silk Arm Cover. Excavated at Niya, along the Silk Road, this small piece (12.5 by 18.5 cm) is finely woven in five colors: blue, green, red, yellow, and white (the colors of the five planets). *(Xinjian Institute of Archaeology)*

leading troops to bring order to the north-west frontier, reads: "The Five Planets appear in the east. This is very auspicious for China. The barbarians will be defeated."

---

the countries of Central Asia and heard about the trade in silk with other ones farther out, such as Rome.

In 104 and 102 B.C.E. a Han general led Chinese armies across the Pamir Mountains to subdue Ferghana. Recognition of Chinese overlordship followed, giving China control over the trade routes across Central Asia, commonly called the Silk Road (see Map 3.1). The city-states along this route did not resist the Chinese presence, since they could carry out the trade on which they depended more conveniently with Chinese garrisons to protect them. (See **Material Culture: Silk from the Silk Road.**)

Much of the trade was in the hands of Sogdian, Parthian, and Indian merchants who carried silk and other goods by caravans all the way to Rome. There was a market for both skeins of silk thread and for silk cloth woven in Chinese or Syrian workshops. Caravans returning to China carried gold, horses, and occasionally handicrafts of West Asian origin, such as glass beads and cups (see Color Plate 4). Through the trade along the Silk Road, the Chinese learned of new foodstuffs, including walnuts, pomegranates, sesame, and coriander, all of which came to be grown in China. This trade was largely carried by the two-humped Bactrian camel, which had been bred in Central Asia since the first century B.C.E. With a heavy coat of hair to withstand the bitter cold of winter, each camel could carry about five hundred pounds of cargo.

BORDERLANDS

During the Qin and Han periods, the Chinese empire was extended by both armies and by migrants. Emperor Wu sent armies not only into Central Asia but also into northern Korea, where military districts were established to flank the Xiongnu on their eastern border (see Chapter 6). Armies were also sent south, extending the frontiers into what is now northern Vietnam.

In the south, migrants in search of land to till often were the first to penetrate an area. They moved south along the rivers, displacing the indigenous populations, who retreated farther south or up into marginal hillsides. A comparison of the censuses of 2 and 140 C.E. shows that between 5 and 10 million people left the north China plain for the Yangzi Valley or farther south between those dates.

The government fostered migration by building garrisons on the frontiers to protect settlers, merchants, and adventurers. Once enough settlers had arrived, the government created counties and sent officials to administer them and collect taxes. Often officials sent to the frontier counties tried to encourage the assimilation of the local population by setting up schools to train local young men in Chinese texts. The products of Chinese industry—iron tools, lacquerware, silks, and so on—were generally in demand and helped make Chinese merchants welcome.

Nevertheless, Chinese expansion often ran into active resistance. In the region of modern Yunnan, the Dian state was dominated by horse-riding aristocrats who made captured enemies into slaves. They drew wealth from trade conducted in both Chinese coins and in cowrie shells. Although the Dian did not have a written language, they were skilled metalworkers whose bronze drums often were decorated with images of people and animals. In 109 B.C.E. Emperor Wu sent an army that conquered Dian and made it a tributary state. Although the Dian repeatedly rebelled, the Han government was able each time to reestablish its overlordship.

The Case of Vietnam

To the north and west of China proper, there were natural boundaries to the Chinese way of life, as crop agriculture was not suited to the desserts, grasslands, and high mountains in those regions. The southern boundaries of China proper were not so clear and took centuries to become established. Crops that could be grown in modern Guangdong province could also be grown farther south, especially along the coast in what is today Vietnam. The rivers that are central to this region—both the Red River, which empties into the ocean near modern Hanoi, and the Mekong River, which empties near modern Saigon—start in the highlands of southwest China, and migrants following these rivers would end up in what is today Vietnam. Travel along the coast was also easy, even in early times.

Vietnam is today classed with the countries to its west as part of Southeast Asia, but its ties are at least as strong to China. The Vietnamese appear in Chinese sources as a people of south China called the Yue who gradually migrated farther south as the Chinese state expanded. In the Red River valley in northern Vietnam, they mixed with local people who had bronze technology, could kill elephants with poisoned bronze arrowheads, and knew how to irrigate their rice fields by using the tides that backed up the rivers.

The collapse of the Qin Dynasty in 206 B.C.E. had an impact on this area because a former Qin general, Zhao Tuo (Trieu Da in Vietnamese), finding himself in modern Guangdong province, set up his own kingdom of Nam Viet (Nan Yue in Chinese) that extended as far south as modern-day Da Nang. Trieu Da/Zhao Tuo called himself the Great Chief of the Southern Barbarians, incorporated local warriors into his army, encouraged the adoption of Chinese material culture, and supported intermarriage between Chinese settlers and the local population. Through these measures, he gained the support of the local population and was able to rule to the age of ninety-three, all the while resisting Han efforts to make him accept vassal status.

After almost a hundred years of diplomatic and military duels between the Han Dynasty and Nam Viet, Emperor Wu sent armies that conquered it in 111 B.C.E. As in Korea, Chinese political institutions were imposed, and Confucianism became the official ideology. The Chinese language was introduced as the medium of official and literary expression. The Chinese built roads, waterways, and harbors to facilitate communication within the region and to ensure that they maintained administrative and military control over it. Over time, Chinese art, architecture, and music had a powerful impact on their Vietnamese counterparts.

Chinese innovations that were beneficial to the Vietnamese were readily integrated into the indigenous culture, but the local elite were not reconciled to Chinese political domination. The most famous early revolt took place in 39 C.E., when two widows of local aristocrats, the Trung sisters, led an uprising against foreign rule. They gathered together the tribal chiefs and their armed followers, attacked and overwhelmed the Chinese strongholds, and had themselves proclaimed queens of an independent Vietnamese kingdom. Three years later, a powerful Chinese army reestablished Chinese rule.

China retained at least nominal control over northern Vietnam until the tenth century, and there were no real borders between China proper and Vietnam during this time. Many Chinese settled in the area, and the local elite became culturally dual, serving as brokers between the Chinese governors and the native people.

MAINTAINING THE EMPIRE

Maintaining the Han Empire's extended borders required a huge military investment. To man the northern defense stations along the Great Wall took about ten thousand men. Another fifty to sixty thousand soldier-farmers were moved to the frontiers to reduce the cost of transporting provisions to distant outposts. Drafted farmers from the interior did not make good cavalry troops, and as a consequence, a de facto professional army emerged on the frontiers, composed of Chinese from the northern reaches of the empire hired as mercenaries, reprieved convicts, and surrendered Xiongnu. In 31 C.E. the Han abolished universal military service, which it had inherited from the Warring States.

In the middle of the first century C.E., a succession struggle among the Xiongnu brought one of the rival claimants and his followers to the Chinese border seeking protection. These "Southern Xiongnu" were permitted to live in Chinese territory, primarily in the Ordos region in the great bend of the Yellow River. In 90 C.E. Chinese officials counted 237,300 Xiongnu living in China, of whom 50,170 were adult males able to serve in the army, and substantial numbers of other non-Han groups were also settled in Chinese territory. With the collapse of the Xiongnu confederation, a group from Manchuria, the Xianbei, rose to prominence and absorbed many Xiongnu into their tribal structure. The expeditionary armies of the Eastern Han included soldiers from all of these groups; in some campaigns, Han Chinese formed a tiny minority of the soldiers.

During the Han period, China developed a system of diplomacy to regulate contact with foreign powers. States and tribes beyond its borders sent envoys bearing gifts, which the Han emperor responded to with even more lavish gifts for them to bring back. Over the course of the dynasty, the Han government's outlay on these gifts was huge, perhaps as much as 10 percent of state revenue. In 25 B.C.E., for instance, the government gave tributary states twenty thousand rolls of silk cloth and about twenty thousand pounds of silk floss. But although the diplomacy system was a financial burden to the Chinese, it reduced the cost of defense and offered the Han imperial court confirmation that it was the center of the civilized world.

SUMMARY

What changed over the four centuries of the Han Dynasty? The area that could be called China was greatly expanded. Confucianism had become much more closely identified with the state and with the social elite. A canon of classics had been established, as well as a way of writing the history of a complex empire. The effects of the destruction of books by Qin had been largely overcome, and a great many books were in circulation. Paper was coming into common use. By 200 C.E. Chinese officials were much more knowledgeable about the military threats of China's northern neighbors and had much experience with all sorts of stratagems for dealing with them, such as setting up military colonies and recruiting auxiliary forces. China had knowledge of countries far to its west and knew that trade with them could be advantageous. Perhaps above all, by the end of the Han period, the centralized bureaucratic monarchy had proved that it could govern well; it could maintain peace and stability and allow the population to grow and thrive.

SUGGESTED READING

For solid scholarly studies of both the Qin and Han periods, see D. Twitchett and M. Loewe, eds., *Cambridge History of China*, vol. 1 (1986). On the political and military success of the Qin, see D. Bodde, *China's First Unifier: A Study of the Ch'in Dynasty as Seen in the Life of Li Ssu (280?–208 B.C.)* (1958). For Han material culture, see M. Perazzoli-t'Serstevens, *The Han Dynasty* (1982), and M. Loewe, *Everyday Life in Early Imperial China* (1968).

For China's relations with the Xiongnu, Xianbei, Turks, and other neighbors, see T. Barfield, *Perilous Frontier: Nomadic Empires and China, 221 B.C.–A.D. 1757* (1989); N. DiCosmo, *Ancient China and Its Enemies: The Rise of Nomadic Power in East Asia* (2002); Y. Yu, *Trade and Expansion in Han China: A Study in the Structure of Sino-Barbarian Economic Relations* (1967); and M. Elvin, *The Pattern of the Chinese Past* (1973).

Han view of their own history can be sampled in B. Watson's translations: *Records of the Grand Historian of China*, 2 vols. (1961), *Courtier and Commoner in Ancient China: Selections from the "History of the Former Han"* (1974), and *Records of the Grand Historian: Qin Dynasty* (1993). See also G. Hardy, *Worlds of Bronze and Bamboo: Sima Qian's Conquest of History* (1999). China's most important woman scholar is the subject of N. L. Swann, *Pan Chao: Foremost Woman Scholar of China* (1950).

For religion, see Mu-chou Poo, *In Search of Personal Welfare: A View of Ancient Chinese Religion* (1998); R. Yates, trans., *Five Lost Classics: Tao, Huang-Lao and Yin-Yang in Han China* (1997); and M. Loewe, *Chinese Ideas of Life and Death: Faith, Myth, and Reason in the Han Period (202 B.C.–A.D. 220)* (1982). Many of the works that deal with the intellectual history of the Warring States also cover the Qin and Han. On Qin thought, see in particular J. Knoblock and J. Riegel, trans., *The Annals of Lü Buwei* (2000). W. de Bary and I. Bloom, *Sources of Chinese Tradition*, rev. ed. (1999), has more than 150 pages on the Qin-Han period. Other aspects of social and cultural life can be found in T. Ch'ü, *Han Social Structure* (1972), and C. Hsu, *Han Agriculture: The Formation of the Early Chinese Agrarian Economy (206 B.C.–A.D. 220)* (1980). On Han funerary art, see H. Wu, *The Wu Liang Shrine: The Ideology of Early Chinese Pictorial Art* (1989), and M. Powers, *Art and Political Expression in Early China* (1991).

Buddhism in India and Its Spread Along the Silk Road

EAST ASIAN CIVILIZATION WAS NEVER completely isolated from the rest of Eurasia. Wheat and the chariot arrived in China from west Asia in Shang times. Animal art spread across the steppe in late Zhou times. Nevertheless, ancient China had less contact with other early centers of civilization such as Mesopotamia, India, Egypt, and Greece than they had with each other. India was geographically the closest of those civilizations and therefore it is not surprising that it was the first to have a major impact on East Asia. The vehicle of its impact was one of its religions, Buddhism.

Early India differed from early China in a great many ways. Much farther south, most areas of the Indian subcontinent were warm all year. In the region of the Indus River there had been an ancient literate civilization that was already in decline by 1800 B.C.E. The Aryans, in India by 1000 B.C.E. if not earlier, were Indo-European speaking people who became the dominant group in north India. The culture of the early Aryans is known from the *Rigveda,* a collection of hymns, ritual texts, and philosophical texts composed between 1500 and 500 B.C.E., but transmitted orally for centuries. The *Rigveda* portrays the Aryans as warrior tribes who glorified military skill and heroism; loved to drink, hunt, race, and dance; and counted their wealth in cattle. It presents the struggle between the Aryans and indigenous peoples in religious terms: their chiefs were godlike heroes, their opponents irreligious savages.

Early Aryan society had distinguished between the warrior elite, the priests, ordinary tribesmen, and conquered subjects. These distinctions gradually evolved into the caste system. Society was conceived in terms of four hierarchical strata that did not eat with each other or marry each other: priests (Brahman), warriors or officials (Kshatriya), merchants and landowners (Vaishya), and workers (Shudra). The gods of the Aryans shared some features of the gods of other early Indo-European societies such as the Persians and the Greeks. The *Upanishads,* composed between 750 and 500 B.C.E., record speculations about the mystical meaning of sacrificial rites and about cosmological questions of man's relationship to the universe. They document a gradual shift from the mythical world-view of the early Vedic age to a deeply philosophical one. Associated with this shift was a movement toward asceticism. In search of a richer and more mystical faith, some men retreated to the forests.

Ancient Indian cosmology imagined endlessly repeating cycles. Central concepts were *samsara,* the transmigration of souls by a continual process of rebirth, and *karma,* the tally of good and bad deeds that determined the status of an individual's next life. Good deeds lead to better future lives, evil deeds to worse future lives—even to reincarnation as an animal. The wheel of life included human beings, animals, and even gods. Reward and punishment worked automatically; there was no all-knowing god who judged people and could be petitioned to forgive a sin, and each individual was responsible for his or her own destiny in a just and impartial world. The optimistic interpretation of samsara was that people could improve their lot in the next life by living righteously. The pessimistic view was that life is a treadmill, a relentless cycle of birth and death. Brahmanic mystics sought release from the wheel of life through realization that life in the world was actually an illusion.

The founder of Buddhism was Siddhartha Gautama (fl. ca. 500 B.C.E.), also called Shakya-muni ("sage of the Shakya tribe"), but best known as the Buddha ("enlightened one"). Our knowledge of his life is filtered through later Buddhist texts, which tell us that he was born the son of a ruler of one of the chiefdoms in the Himalayan foothills in what is now Nepal. Within the Indian caste system he was in the warrior, not the priest (Brahman) caste. At age twenty-nine, unsatisfied with his life of comfort and troubled by the suffering he saw around him, he left home to become a wandering ascetic. He traveled south to the kingdom of Magadha, where he studied with yoga masters. Later he took up extreme asceticism. According to tradition, he reached enlightenment while meditating under a bo tree at Bodh Gaya. After several weeks of meditation, he preached his first sermon, urging a "middle way" between asceticism and worldly life. For the next forty-five years, the Buddha traveled through the Ganges Valley, propounding his ideas, refuting his adversaries, making converts, and attracting followers.

In his first sermon, the Buddha outlined his main message, summed up in the Four Noble Truths and the Eightfold Path. The truths are as follows: (1) pain and suffering, frustration and anxiety, are ugly but inescapable parts of human life; (2) suffering and anxiety are caused by human desires and attachments; (3) people can understand these weaknesses and triumph over them; and (4) this triumph is made possible by following a simple code of conduct, the Eightfold Path. The basic insight of Buddhism is thus psychological. The deepest human longings can never be satisfied, and even those things that seem to give pleasure cause anxiety because we are afraid of losing them. Attachment to people and things leads to sorrow at their loss.

The Buddha offered an optimistic message, however, because people can all set out on the Eightfold Path toward liberation. All they have to do is take steps such as recognizing the universal-

ity of suffering, deciding to free themselves from it, and choosing "right conduct," "right speech," "right livelihood," and "right endeavor." For instance, they should abstain from taking life and thus follow a vegetarian diet. The seventh step is "right awareness," constant contemplation of one's deeds and words, giving full thought to their importance and whether they lead to enlightenment. "Right contemplation," the last step, entails meditation on the impermanence of everything in the world. Those who achieve liberation are freed from the cycle of birth and death and enter the blissful state called *nirvana*.

Although he accepted the Indian idea of reincarnation, the Buddha denied the integrity of the individual self or soul. He saw human beings as a collection of parts, physical and mental. As long as the parts remain combined, that combination can be called "I." When that combination changes, as at death, the various parts remain in existence, ready to become the building blocks of different combinations. According to Buddhist teaching, life is passed from person to person as a flame is passed from candle to candle.

The success of Buddhism was aided by the Buddha's teaching that everyone, noble and peasant, educated and ignorant, male and female, could follow the Eightfold Path. Within India this marked a challenge to the caste system, central to early Brahmanism and later Hinduism. Moreover, the Buddha was extraordinarily undogmatic. Convinced that each person must achieve enlightenment on his or her own, he emphasized that the path was important only because it led the traveler to enlightenment, not for its own sake. He compared religious practices to a raft, needed to get across a river but useless once on the far shore. Thus, there was no harm in honoring local gods or observing traditional ceremonies, as long as one kept in mind the ultimate goal of enlightenment.

In his lifetime the Buddha formed a circle of disciples, primarily men but including some women as well. The Buddha's followers transmitted his teachings orally for several centuries until they were written down in the second or first century B.C.E. The form of monasticism that developed among the Buddhists was less strict than that of some other contemporary groups in India, such as the Jains. Buddhist monks moved about for eight months of the year (staying inside only during the rainy season) and consumed only one meal a day obtained by begging. Within a few centuries, Buddhist monks began to overlook the rule that they should travel. They set up permanent monasteries, generally on land donated by kings or other patrons. Orders of nuns also appeared, giving women the opportunity to seek truth in ways men had traditionally done. The main ritual that monks and nuns performed in their monastic establishments was the communal recitation of the sutras. Lay Buddhists could aid the spread of the Buddhist teachings by providing food for monks and support for their monasteries, and could pursue their own spiritual progress by adopting practices such as abstaining from meat and alcohol.

Within India the spread of Buddhism was greatly aided in the third century B.C.E. by King Ashoka. As a young prince, Ashoka served as governor of two prosperous provinces where Buddhism flourished. At the death of his father about 274 B.C.E., Ashoka rebelled against his older brother, the rightful king, and after four years of fighting succeeded in his bloody bid for the throne. In 261 B.C.E., early in his reign, Ashoka conquered Kalinga, on the east coast of India. Instead of exulting like a conqueror, however, Ashoka was consumed with remorse for all the deaths inflicted. In this mood, he embraced Buddhism.

Ashoka used the machinery of his empire to spread Buddhist teachings throughout India. He banned animal sacrifices and in place of hunting expeditions, he took pilgrimages. Two years after his conversion, he undertook a 256-day pilgrimage to all the holy sites of Buddhism and on his return he began sending missionaries to all known countries. Buddhist tradition also credits him with erecting throughout India 84,000 stupas (Buddhist reliquary mounds), among which the ashes of the Buddha were distributed, beginning the association of Buddhism

Gate at the Great Stupa at Sanchi. King Ashoka began the stupa at Sanchi in central India as a site for the preservation of the ashes of the Buddha. Each of its four gates, dating from the first century C.E., is decorated with Buddhist imagery. Note the depiction of a stupa on the horizontal support. *(Borromeo/Art Resource, NY)*

with monumental art and architecture. Also according to Buddhist tradition, Ashoka convened a great council of Buddhist monks at which the earliest canon of Buddhist texts was codified.

Under Ashoka, Buddhism began to spread to Central Asia. This continued under the Kushan empire (ca. 50–250 C.E.), especially under their greatest king, Kanishka I (ca. 100 C.E.). In this region, where the influence of Greek art was strong, artists began to depict the Buddha in human form. By this period Buddhist communities were developing divergent traditions and came to stress different sutras. One of the most important of these, associated with the monk-philosopher Nagarjuna (ca. 150–250), is called Mahayana, or "Great Vehicle," because it is a

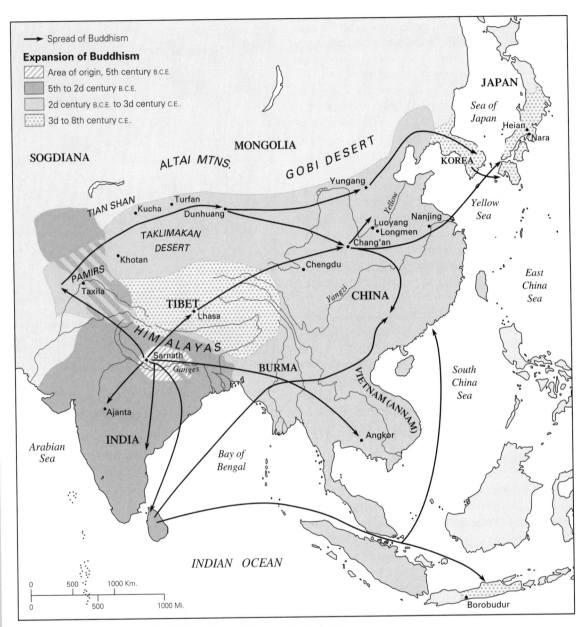

Map C2.1   **Expansion of Buddhism from 500 B.C.E. to 800 C.E.**

more inclusive form of the religion. It drew on a set of discourses allegedly preached by the Buddha and kept hidden by his followers for centuries. One branch of Mahayana taught that reality is "empty" (that is, nothing exists independently of itself). Emptiness was seen as an absolute, underlying all phenomena, which are themselves transient and illusory. Another branch held that ultimate reality is consciousness, that everything is produced by the mind.

Just as important as the metaphysical literature of Mahayana Buddhism was its devotional side, influenced by the Iranian religions then prevalent in Central Asia. The Buddha became deified and placed at the head of an expanding pantheon of other Buddhas and bodhisattvas (Buddhas-to-be who had stayed in the world to help others on the path to salvation). These Buddhas and bodhisattvas became objects of veneration, especially the Buddha Amitabha and the bodhisattva Avalokitesvara (Guanyin in Chinese, Kannon in Japanese, Kwanŭm in Korean). With the growth of Mahayana, Buddhism became as much a religion for laypeople as for monks and nuns.

Buddhism remained an important religion in India until about 1200 C.E., but thereafter it declined, and the number of Buddhists in India today is small. Long before it declined in India, however, it spread too much of the rest of Asia. One route was east to Sri Lanka and most of Southeast Asia, including Indonesia. Another was northeast to Nepal and Tibet. More important for the history of East Asia, however, was the route northwest through Central Asia. During the first few centuries C.E., most of the city-states of Central Asia became centers of Buddhism, from Bamiyan, northwest of Kabul, to Kucha, Khotan, Loulan, Turfan, and Dunhuang. The first translators of Buddhist texts into Chinese were not Indians but Parthians, Sogdians, and Kushans from Central Asia.

Central Asia in the centuries in which Buddhism was spreading east was ethnically diverse, though Indian and Persian languages were the most commonly used for administrative purposes. The economy of these city-states was dependent on the East-West trade. In Han times, the Chinese had become the overlords in the area, wanting both access to the fabled horses of Ferghana and to keep the area out of the hands of its foes, such as the Xiongnu. After the fall of the Han, most of these cities became independent and trade continued unabated. Buddhism thus reached China first as a religion of foreign merchants. Missionaries soon followed, however, and the hugely complex process of translating Buddhist sutras from Sanskrit or other Indian languages into classical Chinese was accomplished through the collaboration of Central Asian and Chinese monks.

Monk Contemplating a Skull. The painting is from the wall of a cave temple in Kizil, along the Silk Road in Central Asia, and dates from about 500 C.E. *(Museum of Indian Art, Berlin/Art Resource, NY)*

Kumarajiva (350–413 C.E.) was one of the most important of these translators. His father, from a high-ranking family in India, had moved to the Silk Road oasis city of Kucha, attracted by the quality of the Buddhist scholarship there, and he married the younger sister of the king of Kucha. At this time, Kucha reportedly had a population of 100,000, of whom 10,000 were monks. Already in this period spectacular cave temples were being constructed in the nearby small town of Kizil. At home Kumarajiva spoke Tokharian, an Indo-European language. He may also have learned some Chinese from merchants who came regularly to Kucha. From age seven he studied Buddhist texts in Sanskrit as part of his Buddhist training. By age twenty he had established himself as a brilliant Buddhist scholar, and the ruler of a small state in the modern Chinese province of Gansu sent a general to abduct him. He stayed in Gansu seventeen years, becoming fluent in Chinese. In 401 he was able to move to Chang'an where another ruler gave financial support to his plan to translate Buddhist sutras into Chinese. Kumarajiva recruited a large group of learned monks and set up a systematic procedure for checking draft translations. Rather than borrowing terms from Daoism, which often proved misleading, Sanskrit terms were retained, represented by Chinese words borrowed for their sound. About thirty-five sutras were translated, including some of the most famous and popular, such as the *Lotus Sutra* and the *Vimalakirti Sutra*. An exponent of Mahayana, Kumarajiva also translated treatises by Nagarjuna and lectured on their content.

Translating Buddhist texts into Chinese helped Buddhism spread throughout East Asia. Not only did these texts come to circulate throughout China (discussed in Chapters 4 and 5), but they also became the basis for Korean and Japanese schools of Buddhism. The Buddhism that reached Japan, for instance, was filtered through Central Asian, Chinese, and Korean lenses.

SUGGESTED READING

On early India, see L. Basham, *The Wonder that Was India* (1954) or R. Thapar, *History of India* (1966). A. Embree, ed., *Sources of Indian Tradition*, 2nd ed. (1988) has translations of central texts of all Indian religions. On Indian Buddhism, see A. Hirakawa, *A History of Indian Buddhism* (1990) and D. Lopez, *The Story of the Buddha* (2001).

CHAPTER FOUR

Political Division in China and the Spread of Buddhism (200–580)

China's four centuries of unification under the Han Dynasty were followed by four centuries when division prevailed. This Period of Division began with a stalemate among the rivals to succeed the Han, resulting in the Three Kingdoms. In 280 China was reunited by the (Western) Jin Dynasty, but peace was short-lived. After 300, Jin degenerated into civil war. For the next two and a half centuries, north China was ruled by non-Chinese dynasties (the Northern Dynasties), while the south was ruled by a sequence of four short-lived Chinese dynasties, all of which were centered in the area of the present-day city of Nanjing (the Southern Dynasties). Although Buddhism gained a remarkable hold in both north and south, the two regions developed in different directions in other ways. In the north, despite frequent ethnic conflict, a hybrid culture emerged that drew from Chinese traditions of government administration and the military traditions of the non-Chinese rulers. In the south, although military men repeatedly seized the throne, high culture thrived among the émigré aristocrats, especially the literary and visual arts.

The Northern Dynasties mark the first period in Chinese history when a large part of China proper was ruled by non-Chinese. Thus, scholars of this period have been particularly interested in issues of ethnicity and sinification (the process of absorbing Chinese culture). In what contexts did the Xianbei rulers promote or discourage adoption of Chinese ways? How was conflict between Chinese and Xianbei handled? How did these experiences shape Chinese notions of cultural and ethnic identity? One by-product of warfare in this period was enormous movements of peoples, voluntary and involuntary. What was the impact of these movements on Chinese civilization? Did they promote cultural integration, countering the effects of political division? In both north and south, birth meant more in this period than it had in the Han. Did the decline in the power of the central government foster growth in hereditary status? Another central issue in the understanding of this period is the success of Buddhism. If earlier philosophies laid the foundation for Chinese government and society, what was the effect of the spread of fundamentally different ideas?

THE THREE KINGDOMS (220–265) AND THE WESTERN JIN DYNASTY (265–316)

The Han Dynasty began to fall apart in 184 C.E. when the followers of a Daoist religious cult called the Way of Great Peace staged a major insurrection. In their efforts to seize power, hundreds of thousands of followers across the country simultaneously attacked local government offices. Although the original uprising was suppressed within a year, other groups preaching similar doctrines rose up elsewhere in the country. To respond to these uprisings, the Han court gave generals and local officials considerable autonomy to raise their own armies. In these unsettled conditions, they found no shortage of willing recruits from among refugees and the destitute. Larger armies were formed by absorbing smaller armies and their leaders. The top generals, once they no longer had rebels to suppress, turned to fighting each other, ushering in several decades of civil war. In 189 the warlord who gained control of the capital slaughtered more than two thousand eunuchs and took the emperor prisoner. Luoyang was sacked and burned, destroying the government libraries and archives.

By 205 Cao Cao had made himself the dominant figure in north China, even though he retained the Han emperor as a puppet. After Cao Cao's death in 220, his son Cao Pei forced the last Han emperor to abdicate and proclaimed the Wei Dynasty. The old Han capital of Luoyang was retained as the Wei capital.

Cao Cao and Cao Pei wanted to reconstruct an empire comparable to the Han, but never gained control over all the territory the Han had once held. In the central and lower Yangzi valley and farther south, the brothers Sun Ce and Sun Quan established the state of Wu. A third kingdom, Shu, was established in the west, in Sichuan province, by a distant member of the Han imperial clan named Liu Bei (see Map 4.1). Although Liu Bei's resources could not compare to those controlled by Cao Pei in the north, he was aided by one of China's most famous military strategists, Zhuge Liang.

Wei was the largest and strongest of these three kingdoms, and several of the institutional measures Wei adopted remained important for the next several centuries. Wei made the status of soldier hereditary: when a commander or a soldier was killed or unable to fight any longer, a son or brother would take his place. Soldiers' families were classified as "military households" and treated as a group separate from ordinary commoners. Their families were assigned land to farm, and their children were required to marry into other military households. These farmers-turned-professional soldiers made good infantrymen, but Wei also needed cavalry. For that purpose, like the Han before them, they recruited Xiongnu in large numbers and settled them in southern Shanxi. To raise revenues to supply his armies, Cao Cao carved out huge state farms from land laid waste by war. He settled defeated rebels and landless poor as tenants on these farms, and had them pay their rent directly to state coffers. In other words, rather than trying to raise revenues by increasing tax collection on local magnates, who had many ways to resist tax collection, he made the state itself an enormous landlord.

Wei also introduced a new system of civil service recruitment, known as the Nine Rank System. Although intended to select men with local reputations for talent and character, this

**Color Plate 1
Bronze Mask.** Larger
than life size, this
bronze mask from
Sanxingdui in Sichuan is
60 centimeters wide and
weighs 13.4 kilograms.
Note the prominent eyes
and wide mouth, found
on all of the masks.

(Cultural Relics Publishing
House)

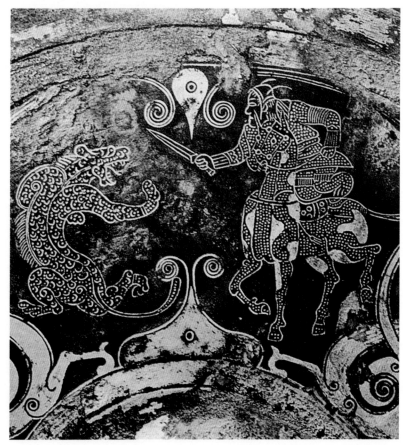

**Color Plate 2
Fighting from
Horseback.** This
depiction of a warrior
fighting a leopard is
from an inlaid bronze
mirror of Warring
States date.

(Gugong Yuekan)

Color Plate 3
Lacquer Coffin from Chu. This coffin, the innermost of three
nested coffins, is a fine example of fourth century B.C.E. lacquer
art. The top and sides are decorated with seventy-two interlaced
serpentine dragons and an equal number of mythical birds.
(Hubei Provincial Museum, Wuhan/Cultural Relics Publishing House)

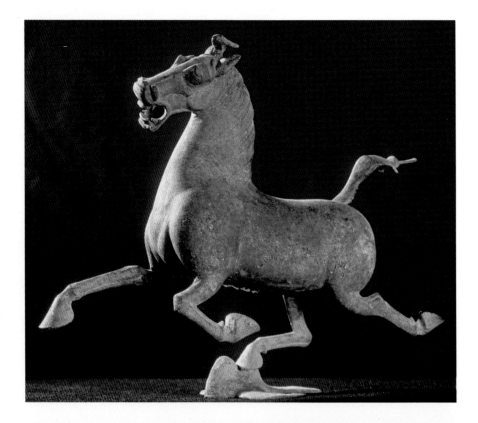

Color Plate 4
Galloping Horse.
Appreciation for fine
horses is evident in this
13.5 inch tall bronze
horse, found in a
second century C.E.
tomb in Gansu
province.
(Robert Harding)

Color Plate 5
Interior of Cave 285 at Dunhuang. Completed in 539, Cave 285 shows
the Buddha surrounded by other deities, meditating monks, and donors.
On the ceiling are celestial musicians and other flying spirits.

(Cultural Relics Publishing House)

Color Plate 6
Women Musicians. Note the range of instruments played by the women on this tenth
century tomb wall. Note also that the Tang appreciation of full-figured women has
continued into the subsequent Five Dynasties period.

(Hebei Provincial Cultural Relics Institute, Shijiazhang/Cultural Relics Publishing House)

Color Plate 7
An Elegant Party. A Song court artist, perhaps copying an earlier Tang painting, depicts an elegant gathering of literary men, hosted by the emperor. Note the array of dishes and cups on the table.
(National Palace Museum, Taipei/The Art Archive)

Map 4.1   Rise and Fall of States During the Period of Division

system rapidly degenerated into a means for leading families to secure the best posts. Men whose families were ranked high did not have to start at the bottom of the bureaucratic ladder, making it considerably more likely that they would eventually rise to the highest posts.

Because Wei had more than twice the population of Shu or Wu, it was able to field a much larger army and eventually prevailed. The Wei general Sima Zhao defeated Shu in 263. Two years later, however, the general's son Sima Yan

forced the Wei emperor to abdicate in his favor, and he established the Jin Dynasty. This was the first of many dynastic transitions in this period that began with a military coup. In 279, the Jin government sent a fleet of ships down the Yangzi River from Sichuan to overwhelm Wu forces and reunify China.

Hope that Jin would be able to restore the glories of the Han Dynasty did not last long. Although Jin held almost all the territory Han had, it did not have the Han government's administrative reach. The census of 280 recorded only 16 million people, evidence that many of those who had fled war, famine, or poverty had not been registered where they settled.

In Luoyang, the Jin Dynasty suffered from strife among the families of empresses. The powerful Jia family was suspected of arranging the assassination of an empress and more than one potential heir to the throne. Another threat came from princes of the Sima family. The Jin founder, wanting to make sure that no general could overthrow his dynasty the way he had overthrown Wei, parceled out the armies and enormous tracts of land to his own relatives. By the time he died in 290, more than half the regional armies were controlled by eight princes. Before long, their bloody struggles for dominance degenerated into general civil war. In 300 one prince marched his army to Luoyang, deposed the emperor, and took his place. One prince after another controlled the capital, but only as long as his army was able to withstand the armies of his opponents. By the end of 304, governors leading locally raised militia forces had been drawn into the fray. By this point, the princes with fiefs in the north were incorporating more and more non-Chinese into their armies. When an army of Xianbei warriors took Chang'an in 306, they pillaged the city, reportedly slaughtering twenty thousand residents. By 307 only one of the original princes still survived, and little was left of the state. With the collapse of control from the center, people everywhere began building fortifications, taking up arms to defend themselves, or fleeing in search of safer places to live. With banditry endemic, both disease and famine spread.

These decades of warfare shaped the intellectual outlook of the educated elite. The late Han had marked a high point in political activism, when many risked their lives and careers to oppose the domination of the court by eunuchs or consort families. When politics took a turn for the worse after 184, many educated men gave up the effort to participate in government.

Armored Horse and Rider. From a Northern Wei tomb near Xi'an, this earthenware model is 15.6 inches tall. *(Nanjing Museum)*

The philosophically inclined turned to Daoist-inspired "Study of the Mysterious," which concerned such topics as the meaning of "being" and its relation to "nonbeing," subjects they discussed in new commentaries on the *Book of Changes, Laozi,* or *Zhuangzi.* Witty repartee, especially apt characterizations of prominent individuals, was much admired (see **Documents: Tales of the Current Age**). Sophisticated aesthetes espoused "naturalness" and "spontaneity" and expressed disdain for mastery of established forms. In this environment, poetry flourished. Cao Cao and his two sons, Cao Pei and Cao Zhi, were all gifted poets. Another group of poets, known as the Seven Sages of the Bamboo Grove, gained fame for shocking their contemporaries. When someone rebuked Ruan Ji for talking to his sister-in-law, he replied, "Surely you do not mean to suggest that the rules of propriety apply to me?"

Seven Sages of the Bamboo Grove. Several tombs near the Eastern Jin capital at modern Nanjing have pictures of the eccentric "seven sages" depicted in the brick walls. In the example shown here, each of the figures is labeled and shown drinking, writing, or playing a musical instrument. *(Shaanxi Provincial Museum, Shaanxi China)*

NON-CHINESE DOMINANCE IN THE NORTH

After the breakdown of Jin, non-Chinese seized power in north China. Why did this happen? One answer is military technology. The invention of the stirrup in about 300 C.E. made cavalry more crucial in warfare. The stirrup gave heavily armored riders greater stability and freedom of motion. From this time on, horses and their riders began wearing heavy armor, giving them more striking power and the ability to engage in shock combat. By the fourth century, sources mention the capture of thousands of armored horses in a single battle.

Another reason is that Xiongnu and other northern auxiliary troops had been settled within China proper ever since Han times. Most of these groups retained their tribal social structure and pastoral way of life, but settled into a specific territory. After Cao Cao defeated the Wuhuan in 207, he moved many of them to interior counties and incorporated many of their men into his armies. Jin followed similar policies, in 284–285 moving about 130,000 surrendered Xiongnu to the interior. The non-Chinese soldiers were often dissatisfied with their conditions, and ethnic friction was not uncommon. In some areas of north China, the non-Chinese came to outnumber the Han Chinese. One Chinese writer claimed that in the region around Chang'an, the Chinese had become the minority.

Although many of these ethnic groups had been part of the Xiongnu confederation, they reasserted their distinct identities (such as Wuhuan, Xianbei, and Di) after it collapsed. But these identities continued to be flexible. Xiongnu who settled among the Xianbei, for instance, would in time call themselves Xianbei. As disorder worsened in the first years of the fourth century, uprisings of Xiongnu, Di, and Qiang occurred in scattered sites. The most threatening of these was the uprising of the Xiongnu chieftain Liu Yuan in 304. Liu Yuan was literate in Chinese and had spent part of his youth at the court in Luoyang. His familiarity with Chinese culture only made him resent Chinese policies toward the Xiongnu more strongly. When a prince sought his help in the civil war, Liu declared himself king of Han and made a bid for the throne as an heir to the Han Dynasty (from which his ancestors had received the Han imperial surname). On his campaigns, he incorporated bands of bandits, including both

DOCUMENTS

Tales of the Current Age

During the Period of Division, as society became more aristocratic, members of the upper reaches of society regularly told stories of each others' clever repartee, slips of the tongue, embarrassing moments, and other situations that they thought revealed character or breeding. The largest collection of such anecdotes was put together by Liu Yiqing in 430 and titled Tales of the Current Age (Shishuo xinyu).

The anecdotes given below from this collection all concern Wang Xizhi (309–ca. 365). Wang came from the most eminent family of the time and was the nephew of the powerful Wang Dao (276–339), a key figure in the reestablishment of the Jin Dynasty in Nanjing after the fall of the north. Wang was later ranked as one of China's greatest calligraphers. In his own day, as these anecdotes attest, he was just one of many witty and cultivated men.

Liu classified his stories under thirty-six topics, many of them virtues or vices. Here the category is listed before the story.

Speech and Conversation

Wang Xizhi and Xie An were traveling together to Yecheng. Xie's thoughts were far away, his mind made up to leave the world. Wang admonished Xie, "[The sage-king] Yu worked so hard at ruling that his hands and feet were worn and calloused. King Wen of Zhou did not even pause for his evening meal. Today, with military danger close at hand, everyone should be doing his part. This is hardly the time for people to neglect their duties for empty talk and let frivolous writing get in the way of essential work."

Xie replied, "Qin adopted the [Legalist] ideas of Lord Shang and lasted only to the Second Emperor. Did 'empty talk' bring them down?" (2.70)

Learning

When Wang Xizhi arrived to take up the post of governor of Kuaiji, [the monk] Zhi Dun was still living there. Sun Chuo told Wang, "Zhi Dun is refreshing and unusual and excels in anything he sets his mind to. Would you like to meet him?"

Wang himself was straightforward and uncompromising and felt only contempt

---

Chinese and non-Chinese. His armies, plundering as they went, moved south through Shanxi to the gates of Luoyang in 308–309.

Another important non-Chinese leader in this period was a much less sinified Jie tribesman named Shi Le. Shi Le had been sold into slavery by a Jin official. After gaining his freedom, he led a group of mounted brigands made up of escaped slaves and others on the margins of society, some of whom were Chinese. Early in these wars, Shi Le allied with Liu Yuan, and it was Shi Le's troops who captured and plundered Luoyang in

311. In 319 Shi Le broke with the Liu family and proclaimed himself king of Zhao. Within a decade, he had destroyed the Liu forces.

The regimes set up in the fourth century by various non-Chinese contenders did not have the institutional infrastructure to administer large territories. When they defeated a Chinese fortress, they normally gave the local strongman the title of governor and claimed him as part of their government. This was a fragile system, since the recently incorporated governor could easily change sides again.

for Zhi. One time when Sun brought Zhi to Wang's home, Wang was very reserved and did not say anything to Zhi, who then withdrew.

Later, when Wang was about to leave, his carriage ready at the gate, Zhi said to him, "Don't leave yet. This poor monk would like to discuss something with you." He then launched into a several-thousand word discourse on the "Free Wandering" chapter of the *Zhuangzi*. His language was fresh and insightful, like the blooming of flowers or a burst of sunlight. Wang settled in to listen, loosening his lapels and untying his belt, unable to leave. (4.36)

Elegant Tolerance

When Chi Jian was in Jingkou, he sent a retainer with a letter to Chancellor Wang Dao, asking for a husband for Chi's daughter. The chancellor told him to go to the eastern apartments and make his own choice.

When the retainer returned, he told Chi, "Each of the Wang boys is admirable in his own way. When they heard that someone had come to choose a son-in-law, they all acted circumspectly. There was only one who lay sprawled out on the eastern bed eating as though he had not heard anything."

Chi said, "He would be perfect." When he went to call himself, he learned the young man was Wang Xizhi, and married his daughter to him. (6.19)

Appreciation

Wang Xizhi said to Liu Tan, "We both ought to recommend Xie An for office."

Liu Tan replied, "As long as Xie An sticks to his determination to live in reclusion in the Eastern Mountains, we should definitely join everyone else in recommending him." (8.77)

Appearance and Deportment

When Wang Xizhi saw Du Yi, he sighed, "His face is as smooth as ointment, his eyes as bright as lacquer. He comes from the realm of the gods and immortals."

When contemporaries praised Wang Meng's looks, Cai Mo told them, "It is just that you never saw Du Yi." (14.26)

Wise Beauties

Wang Xizhi's wife, Miss Chi, told her two younger brothers, Chi Yin and Chi Tan, "In the Wang house, whenever the two Xies [Xie An and Xie Wang] come, people [rush about so much] that they overturn baskets and put their sandals on backwards. But when they see you two coming, everyone is as calm as can be. You need not go to the trouble of visiting anymore." (19.25)

Translated by Patricia Ebrey from Liu Yiqing, *Shishuo xinyu jiaojian* (Hong Kong: Dazhong shuju, 1969), pp. 100, 172–173, 277, 349, 369, 474, 475, 525. For a full translation of this text, see Richard B. Mather, trans., *A New Account of Tales of the World* (Minneapolis: University of Minnesota Press, 1976).

The regimes established by Liu Yuan and Shi Le drew sharp distinctions between Chinese and non-Chinese. In essence, the non-Chinese were the rulers and the soldiers, while the Chinese were the subjects, who were expected to grow grain, pay taxes, and provide labor service. Enemy generals who surrendered were incorporated into the tribally organized military structure, still leading their old troops. Chinese soldiers were often incorporated into these armies, but usually as porters or infantry, not cavalry. Because much of north China had been depopulated, securing labor was more important than gaining land. Many campaigns were essentially slave raids, with those captured sent back to the victor's capital. Not surprising, most of the Chinese population saw none of these regimes as legitimate. Ethnic conflict flared from time to time. Different groups of refugees on the roads often robbed and murdered each other. When an adopted son succeeded to the Shi line in 350, he reverted to his Chinese identity and called for the slaughter of non-Chinese, which his Chinese subjects carried out with a vengeance.

During these decades, Chinese in the north faced a leadership crisis. Some scholars estimate that 60 percent of the elite of government officials and landowners fled south between 311 and 325, most of them taking relatives, retainers, and neighbors with them. Those who did not move south often took their followers to nearby hilltops, which they fortified in order to defend against marauders.

The Northern Wei and Hybrid Xianbei-Chinese Culture

By 400, the rising power in the north was the Northern Wei state founded by the Tuoba clan of the Xianbei. From its base in northern Shanxi, Northern Wei established dominance on the steppe to the north, which gave it the advantage of access to the horses and horsemen of the steppe. Gradually Wei defeated the other states set up by other Xianbei clans, and in 439 reunified north China after more than a century of constant conflict.

Like their rivals, the Xianbei sent out raiding parties to seize captives, horses, cattle, and sheep from other tribes or from Chinese settlements. Wei forced the relocation of thousands of Chinese to populate their capital and bring deserted land into cultivation. To avoid being overwhelmed by the numerically dominant Chinese, the early Wei rulers kept their capital at Pingcheng in north Shanxi. Xianbei warriors were settled nearby and made their living as herdsmen rather than farmers. The army remained a north Asian preserve, with Chinese usually playing only support roles.

As the fifth century progressed, the Xianbei learned how to draw wealth from Chinese farmers. To collect taxes, the Xianbei rulers turned to educated Chinese, whom they employed as officials. They put into place the institutions these Chinese advisers proposed based on Chinese experience. In the late fifth century, the Northern Wei rulers adopted an "equal-field" system to distribute land to farmers and increase production. The state claimed exclusive right to distribute land. Allotments were made to families based primarily on their labor power, with extra for officials and nobles based on rank.

Dynasties of the Period of Division			
Period	**North**	**West**	**South**
Three Kingdoms, 220–265	Wei 220–265	Shu 221–264	Wu 222–280
Western Jin, 265–316			
	16 Kingdoms 304–439		Eastern Jin 317–420
			Song 420–479
Northern and Southern Dynasties, 317–589	Northern Wei 386–534		Qi 479–502
	Eastern Wei 534–550	Western Wei 535–556	Liang 502–557
	Northern Qi 551–577	Northern Zhou 557–581	Chen 557–589
Sui 581–618			

The policy of keeping Chinese and Xianbei separate was abandoned by Emperor Xiaowen (r. 471–499). Born to a Chinese mother, Xiaowen wanted to unite the Chinese and Xianbei elites, and beginning in 493, he initiated a radical program of sinification. He banned the wearing of Xianbei clothes at court, required all Xianbei officials below the age of thirty to speak Chinese at court, and encouraged intermarriage between the highest-ranking families of the Chinese and Xianbei elites. He gave Xianbei new single-character surnames, which made them sound less foreign. The imperial house itself took the name *Yuan* ("primal").

The court itself was moved three hundred miles south to the site of the Han and Jin capital of Luoyang. This transfer was accomplished by subterfuge. Emperor Xiaowen mobilized his army for an invasion of the south, but he halted at Luoyang and announced the plan to build his capital there. By 495, about 150,000 Xianbei and other northern warriors had been moved south to fill the ranks of the imperial guards in Luoyang. Xiaowen also welcomed refugees or defectors from the south, such as Wang Su of the aristocratic Langye Wang family, who was put to work on the reorganization of the

Filial Grandson Yuan Gu. This scene, from an incised Northern Wei stone sarcophagus, depicts the story of a boy who saved his grandfather from being abandoned in the woods. Note the depiction of landscape—rocks, trees, water, wind, and mountains. *(The Nelson-Atkins Museum of Art, Kansas City, Missouri [Purchase: Nelson Trust] 33-1543/1)*

bureaucracy. To make southerners feel at home, at the palace they were served tea, newly popular in the south, rather than the yogurt-like drinks consumed in the north.

Within twenty-five years, Luoyang became a magnificent city again, with a half-million residents, vast palaces, elegant mansions, and more than a thousand Buddhist temples. It had a district where foreign traders lived and another occupied by rich merchants and craftsmen. Many members of the Xianbei nobility became culturally dual, fully proficient in Chinese cultural traditions and comfortable interacting with the leading Chinese families. So many southerners had been welcomed at Luoyang that there was a district known as Wu quarter, where more than three thousand families lived, complete with their own fish and turtle market.

The Revolt of the Garrisons and the Division of the North

This period of prosperity was cut short in 523, only a generation after the relocation, when the

Xianbei who remained in the north rebelled. In the wars that ensued, hostility based on ethnicity repeatedly added to the violence. With the transfer of the Xianbei elite to Luoyang, the garrison forces saw their status plummet to hardly better than that of hereditary military households. When a shortage of food at the garrisons sparked rebellion, the government moved two hundred thousand surrendered garrison rebels to Hebei, where food supplies were more plentiful. This course of action proved to be a colossal mistake. In 526–527, a former garrison officer organized the displaced rebels into a much more potent force.

The Wei court then turned to one of its generals to deal with the new uprising, but he soon turned on the court. The thousand-plus officials who came out of the city to tender their submission were slaughtered by this general, who had the empress dowager and her new child emperor thrown in the Yellow River. He then installed his own puppet Wei emperor.

Struggles of this sort continued for years. In the east, power was seized by Gao Huan. Gao's grandfather was a Han Chinese official who had been exiled to the northern garrisons, and Gao had grown up in poverty, not even owning a horse until he married into a Xianbei family. He was one of the two hundred thousand frontiersmen relocated to Hebei because of the famine, and he took charge of this group in 531. Because of his dual background, he could appeal to both Chinese and Xianbei.

Luoyang soon fell to Gao Huan, but the region of Chang'an was in the hands of rival forces. The central figure there was Yuwen Tai, not yet thirty years old. Yuwen Tai too came from the garrisons, but his father had organized a loyalist militia to resist the rebels. The struggle between Gao Huan and Yuwen Tai and their successors lasted forty years: neither could dislodge the other, even though they set off with armies of one hundred thousand or more troops. The Gao regime maintained a Tuoba prince on the throne until 550 (thus leading to the dynastic name Eastern Wei, 534–550), then declared a new dynasty, known as the Northern Qi (551–577). The Yuwen regime kept a Wei prince a little longer (Western Wei, 535–556), but eventually declared itself the founders of a new dynasty, called the Northern Zhou (557–580).

Gao Huan tried to convince both Chinese and Xianbei that it made sense for the Xianbei to do the fighting and the Chinese the farming. To the Xianbei he would say, "The Han are your slaves. The men till for you; the women weave for you. They provide you with grain and silk so that you are warm and well fed. For what reason do you bully them?" To Han Chinese he would say, "The Xianbei are your retainers. For a single measure of your grain and a single length of your silk they attack the bandits so that you are safe. For what reason do you regard them as a scourge?"[1] Ethnic strife continued, however, and there were several bloody purges of Chinese officials.

In the west, the Xianbei were not so numerous, and Yuwen Tai had to find ways to incorporate Chinese into his armies and his government. He encouraged intermarriage and bestowed Xianbei surnames on his leading Chinese officials, making them honorary Xianbei. The Chinese who joined him were mostly men of action who loved to hunt and take the lead in military ventures.

It was in this environment that the multiethnic militia system called the divisional militia (*fubing*) was created. The households of the soldiers enrolled in it were removed from the regular tax registers and put on the army registers. Such registration carried honorable status. Soldiers of these armies served in rotation as guards at the imperial palace, helping them identify with the dynasty.

With this army, Northern Zhou began expanding, taking Sichuan away from the south in 553 and parts of the middle Yangzi about the same time. In 577, this army defeated Northern Qi, reunifying the north.

THE SOUTHERN DYNASTIES AND ARISTOCRATIC CULTURE

Among those who fled the confusion that followed the sacking of Luoyang in 311 and Chang'an in 316 were members of the Jin royal house and its high officials. At Nanjing (then called Jiankang), these refugees created a government in exile after putting a Jin prince on the throne. Because Nanjing is east of Luoyang, the second phase of the Jin Dynasty is called the Eastern Jin (317–420) (reminiscent of the Western and Eastern Zhou and the Western and Eastern Han). It was followed by four short dynasties that ruled from Nanjing (the Song, Qi, Liang, and Chen, collectively termed the Southern Dynasties, 420–589). The Yangzi River was the great battlefield of the south, with flotillas of ships sailing from the middle Yangzi to attack forces holding Nanjing, or vice versa. None of the successive Southern Dynasties was fully able to keep its military commanders under control, even when

1. From Sima Guang's *Zizhi tongjian*, cited in David A. Graff, *Medieval Chinese Warfare, 300–900* (London: Routledge, 2002), p. 107.

they were imperial relatives. One dynasty after another was founded when a general seized the capital and installed himself as emperor. These generals were strong enough to hold their governments together during their lifetimes but not able to concentrate power in ways that would ensure successful transfers of power to their heirs.

Maintaining an adequate supply of soldiers was a constant challenge for the Southern Dynasties. The Jin tried to continue its earlier practice of designating certain households as military households, but the status of military households fell precipitously, until they were looked on as little better than state slaves, making desertion a constant problem. Generals sometimes resorted to campaigns against the southern non-Chinese to capture men to make into soldiers (analogous to the slave raids of the north, this time with the Chinese as the raiders).

The south experienced considerable economic development during the Southern Dynasties, as new lands were opened and trade networks extended. Trade with countries in the South Seas expanded, especially Funan and Champa (in today's Cambodia and Vietnam), where Chinese came into contact with merchants from India and even farther west.

Social cleavages were pronounced in the south, with deep divisions between the northern émigrés and the local elite; between the aristocrats, who preferred to stay at court, and the generals given the task of defending against the north and maintaining the peace; and between Han Chinese, living in the river valleys, and various indigenous peoples, who largely retreated to upland areas. The aristocracy dominated the upper ranks of officialdom. These families saw themselves as maintaining the high culture of the Han but judged themselves and others on the basis of their ancestors. They married only with families of equivalent pedigree and compiled lists and genealogies of the most eminent families. At court they often looked down on the emperors of the successive dynasties as military upstarts. They dominated the Nine Rank System and used it to appoint men from their families to government service. One of the sharpest critics of the southern aristocrats was Yan Zhitui (see **Biogra-**

phy: Yan Zhitui). As he saw it, because life was easy for the southern aristocrats, they saw no need to study. When important affairs were discussed, "they sit with foolish looks and widely-opened mouths as if sitting in a cloud or fog." When conversation turned to history or they were asked to compose poems, "they silently hang their heads, yawning and stretching, unable to say anything."[2] Members of the Liang royal family were even worse, he charged, perfuming their garments, shaving their faces, using powder and rouge, sitting on cushions and leaning on soft silk bolsters, and getting others to compose their poems for them. Once their dynasty fell, they had no skills to fall back on.

The most outstanding emperor in the south was Emperor Wu of Liang (r. 502–549). He was not only a major patron of Buddhism but also a patron of literature and the arts. A prolific poet himself, he summoned learned men to court and would order his courtiers to compose and recite poems, rewarding the most successful with gifts of gold or silk. His sons were also ardent patrons, several establishing literary salons of their own. The eldest son, Xiao Tong, was an avid book collector and compiled an anthology of 761 great writings organized by genre, the *Selections of Literature (Wen xuan)*.

Not long after Emperor Wu's death, the southern court was hard hit by the rebellion of Hou Jing, a would-be warlord from the north who had gathered a huge army and set siege to Nanjing. The siege lasted four months, by which time many members of the great families had starved to death in their mansions. A general declared a new dynasty, Chen, but he could do little more than confirm local strongmen as his governors.

Poetry, Calligraphy, and Painting as Arts of Men of Letters

During the Period of Division, men of letters developed poetry, calligraphy, and painting into arts through which they could express their

---

2. Ssu-yu Teng, trans., *Family Instructions of the Yen Clan* (Leiden: Brill, 1968), pp. 52–53.

BIOGRAPHY Yan Zhitui (531–591+)

Many people were dislocated during the Period of Division, but few as many times as Yan Zhitui. The Yan family was one of the émigré families that had left north China in 317, and thereafter it continuously supplied officials for the Southern Dynasties. Yan's grandfather, out of loyalty to the Qi Dynasty, starved himself to death when Emperor Wu of Liang usurped the throne in 502. Yan's father, however, served at Emperor Wu's court. When he died, Yan Zhitui was only nine, so his elder brother was responsible for much of his education. Yan himself in his teens became a court attendant of one of the Liang princes. When Yan was eighteen years old, the rebel Hou Jing captured him and the prince he served, and they narrowly escaped execution.

In 552 Yan went with this prince to Jiangling in Hubei, where the prince set up a rival court. In 554, however, the northern state of Western Wei captured Jiangling, and Yan at age twenty-four was one of the 100,000 people enslaved and brought north to Chang'an. Two years later, he and his family managed to escape and make their way east, hoping to return to Liang. By this point, however, Liang had been overthrown. Unwilling to serve the successor state of Chen, Yan Zhitui stayed in the northeast, where the Northern Qi rulers gave him court appointments for the next two decades. In 577 Northern Qi was defeated by the Northern Zhou, and Yan, now forty-six years old, was again forced to move, this time back to Chang'an. He apparently did not serve at court for the next couple of years and seems to have faced poverty in this period. After the Sui Dynasty was founded in 581, Yan was given scholarly posts, working on a new dictionary and related projects.

In the twenty-chapter book of advice Yan wrote for his sons, he frequently commented on his experiences. He said his elder brother had not been strict enough with him, letting him develop bad habits that took years to overcome. He stressed to his sons the importance of a solid literary education; it was because he had skills that he had gained court posts under the Northern Qi. Less literate men who had faced the same dislocations had ended up working on farms or tending horses, even though their ancestors had been officials for centuries.

Yan Zhitui also recommended mastering calligraphy, painting, and lute playing, though he warned that those who became too good might be humiliated by being forced by those of higher rank to produce on demand. He said he had spent many hours copying model pieces of calligraphy, including the ten scrolls in his family's collection done by the fourth-century masters Wang Xizhi and his son Wang Xianzhi.

Although Yan Zhitui's advice to his sons shows him committed to the study of the Confucian classics and the Confucian ideal of service to the ruler, he also had strong faith in Buddhism and included a chapter defending Buddhism against its critics. He wanted Buddhist services after his death and told his sons to omit meat from the traditional ancestral offerings. Since he expected his sons to marry and have children, he did not urge them to become monks, but he did encourage them to "attend to the chanting and reading of the sacred books and thereby provide for passage to your future state of existence. Incarnation as a human is difficult to attain. Do not pass through yours in vain!"

———

Source: Ssu-yu Teng, trans., *Family Instructions of the Yen Clan* (Leiden: Brill, 1968), p. 148.

thoughts and feelings. Poets came to play a distinctive cultural role as exemplars of the complex individual, moved by conflicting but powerful emotions. Cao Cao's son Cao Zhi (192–232) was one of the first poets to create such a persona. Chafing at the restrictions his brother the emperor placed on him, he poured out his feelings into his verse.

Another poet whose persona is as important as his poems is Tao Qian (or Tao Yuanming, 365–427). At times Tao expressed high ambitions, at other times the desire to be left alone. Once when holding a minor post, he quit rather than entertain a visiting inspector, explaining, "How could I bend my waist to this village buffoon for five pecks of rice!" Many of Tao's poems express Daoist sentiments such as "excessive thinking harms life," or "propriety and conventions, what folly to follow them too earnestly." By the age of forty, Tao gave up office altogether and supported himself by farming. He was not a hermit, however, and continued to enjoy friends and family. His poems often express his enjoyment of wine, books, and music:

> I try a cup and all my concerns become
> remote.
> Another cup and suddenly I forget even
> Heaven.
> But is Heaven really far from this state?
> Nothing is better than to trust your true
> self.[3]

In the somewhat rarefied atmosphere of the aristocracy in Nanjing, calligraphy came to be recognized as an art almost on a par with poetry. Because calligraphy was believed to reflect the writer's character and mood, the calligraphy of men of refinement and education was assumed to be superior to that of technically proficient clerks. Calligraphy was written with a highly pliable hairbrush, and the strength, balance, and flow of the strokes were believed to convey the writer's inner self. To attain a good hand took discipline, since one had to copy works by established masters for years before even thinking of developing a distinctive style. Pieces of calligraphy by former masters thus came to be treasured as works of art. With collecting also came forgeries and debates about authenticity. Works by Wang Xizhi (307–365) were highly prized even in his own day. Admirers would borrow pieces of his calligraphy to make tracing copies, so before long, copies were much more numerous than original products of his hand.

Once calligraphy came to be considered an appropriate art for the educated class, painting gained a similar status. Paintings came to be associated with known, named painters, whose talents were compared and ranked. The most famous of these painters was Gu Kaizhi (344–406), who painted portraits of many of the notable men of his day. It was also in this period that works that criticized and ranked individual poets, calligraphers, and painters began to appear.

THE BUDDHIST CONQUEST OF CHINA

Why did Buddhism find so many adherents in China during the three centuries after the fall of the Han Dynasty in 220? There were no forced conversions. China's initial contact with Central Asia in Western Han times did not lead to significant spread of earlier religions of the region such as Zoroastrianism. Moreover, several basic Buddhist teachings ran up against long-established Chinese customs. In particular, becoming a monk involved giving up one's surname and the chance to have descendants, thus cutting oneself off from the ancestral cult.

On the positive side, Buddhism benefited from the dedication of missionaries who traveled east from Central Asia along the Silk Road (see **Connections: Buddhism in India and Its Spread Along the Silk Road**). Buddhism also had something to

---

3. From "Drinking Alone in the Rainy Season," in William H. Nienhauser, Jr., ed., *The Indiana Companion to Traditional Chinese Literature* (Bloomington: Indiana University Press, 1986), p. 768.

offer almost everyone. It offered learned Chinese the intellectual stimulus of subtle cosmologies, and rulers a source of magical power and a political tool to unite Chinese and non-Chinese. In a rough and tumultuous age, Buddhism offered everyone an appealing emphasis on kindness, charity, the preservation of life, and the prospect of salvation.

The monastic establishment grew rapidly after 300, with generous patronage by rulers, their relatives, and other members of the elite. By 477 there were said to be 6,478 Buddhist temples and 77,258 monks and nuns in the north. Some decades later, south China had 2,846 temples and 82,700 clerics. Those not ready to become monks or nuns could pursue Buddhist goals as pious laypeople by performing devotional acts and making contributions toward the construction or beautification of temples. Devotional groups were often organized around particular scriptures, such as the *Lotus Sutra,* the *Pure Land Sutra,* or the *Holy Teachings of Vimalakirti.* Maitreya, the Buddha of the Future, was frequently a central image in Buddhist temples.

In China, women turned to Buddhism as readily as men did. Although incarnation as a female was considered lower than incarnation as a male, it was also viewed as temporary, and women were encouraged to pursue salvation on terms nearly equal to men. Joining a nunnery became an alternative for women who did not want to marry or did not want to stay with their husband's families in widowhood. In 516 the first set of biographies of Buddhist nuns was compiled. Most of the nuns described in it came from upper-class families, but they entered the convent for varied reasons. Huiyao, who entered the convent as a child, had herself immolated as an offering to the Three Treasures (the Buddha, the sanga or body of monks and nuns, and the teachings). Miaoxiang, with her father's approval, left her unfilial husband to enter a convent. Tanhui, after study with a foreign meditation master beginning at age eleven, threatened suicide if forced to marry her fiancé.

After her fiancé tried to abduct her, the foreign meditation master solicited funds to compensate him. The nun Xuanzao entered the convent after a miraculous cure at age ten. A monk had told her father that the illness was probably caused by deeds done in a former life, making medicine useless. They should instead single-mindedly turn to the bodhisattva Guanyin. After seven days of devotions, she had a vision of a golden image and then recovered.

Buddhism had an enormous impact on the visual arts in China, especially sculpture and painting. Earlier Chinese had rarely depicted gods in human form, but now Buddhist temples were furnished with a profusion of images. The great cave temples at Yungang, sponsored by the Northern Wei rulers in the fifth century, contain huge Buddha figures in stone, the tallest a standing Buddha about seventy feet high (see **Material Culture: Cave 285 at Dunhuang**). Temples became sites of dazzling ceremonies. For the Great Blessing ceremony held in Luoyang on the seventh day of the fourth month, all the Buddhist statues in the city, more than a thousand altogether, were brought to the largest monastery, where music and incense filled the air and entertainers performed to amuse the crowds.

Buddhism also provided the Chinese with a new reason to travel. Chinese monks made pilgrimages to India to see the holy places of Buddhism and seek out learned teachers. The first pilgrim to leave a record of his journey is Faxian, who left Chang'an in 399, when he was already over sixty years old. His trip west was overland, through Kucha, Khotan, and Kashgar, into the Indus Valley, and then the cities of the Ganges valley. On his return, he took ship in the Bay of Bengal, stopped in Sri Lanka and then in Sumatra (then the Srivijaya kingdom), reaching Guangzhou in 412. By 414 he was back in Nanjing, where he set to work translating the sutras he had carried back with him.

One of the greatest royal patrons of Buddhism in this period was Emperor Wu of Liang (r. 502–549). Although as a young man he had studied Daoism, in 504 he urged his family and

MATERIAL CULTURE

Cave 285 at Dunhuang

In 523 Prince Dongyang, a member of the Northern Wei royal house, was sent to Dunhuang to serve as its governor. During his fifteen-year tenure there, he and a group of wealthy local families commissioned a new cave to be dug and decorated at the temple complex outside town where the Buddhist faithful had been constructing and decorating caves along a cliff face for a century.

The cave the prince sponsored, cave 285, has as its central figure a statue of the historical Buddha seated (see Color Plate 5). He is flanked by figures of crossed-legged meditating monks who wear the traditional monk's robe made of patchwork, symbolizing their indifference to material goods. Other monks are depicted on the walls. Temple guardians fill the lower reaches of the walls, heavenly beings the upper reaches.

Meditating Monk. On either side of the main image is a side niche with a statue of a cross-legged monk. *(Lois Conner, 1995. Courtesy of the Dunhuang Academy)*

officials to give it up. Out of Buddhist faith he banished meat and wine from palace banquets. He also found a new way to divert court funds to Buddhism: in 527 he entered a monastery and refused to return to the throne until his officials paid a large "ransom" to the monastery. Two years later, Emperor Wu repeated this pious act, hoping that it would help save his people from a deadly plague then spreading.

Not everyone was won over by Buddhist teachings. Its critics labeled it immoral because it severed family ties and posed a threat to the state since monastery land was not taxed and monks performed neither labor service nor military duty. Twice in the north, orders were issued to close monasteries and force monks and nuns to return to lay life, but these suppressions did not last long, and no attempt was made to suppress private Buddhist belief.

DAOIST RELIGION

At the same time that Buddhism was gaining converts, the Daoist religion was undergoing extraordinary growth. This religion had many roots: popular religious movements; the elite pursuit of immortality; and, after the third century, the model of Buddhism with its sacred scriptures and celibate clergy. Although some Daoist masters became influential at court, most governments maintained a cautious reserve toward the Daoist religion, aware of the connection between Daoism and uprisings at the end of the Han. Daoism thus was never the recipient of government patronage on the lavish scale of Buddhism.

The Daoism of elite devotees was generally an individual practice aimed at bodily immortality in a kind of indestructible "astral body." One strove for this through dietary control, gymnastics, good deeds, mystic self-identification with the all-embracing Dao, and visualization of the innumerable gods and spirits that dwelled inside the microcosm of the body. Many of the most famous men of letters of the period were devoted to such practices. Ge Hong (283–343), for instance, tried to convince his readers that immortality could be achieved and wrote on alchemy, breathing and meditation exercises, exorcism, sexual hygiene, herbalism, and talismanic charms. Ge gave a recipe for an elixir called gold cinnabar and described methods for walking on water and raising the dead.

The fall of Luoyang and the retreat of so many members of the northern elite to the south had a major impact on the development of Daoism. Priests from the north came into contact with local traditions of esoteric learning in the south. A series of revelations led to the writing down of a large number of scriptures. These texts formed the core first of the Supreme Purity sect and later of the rival Numinous Treasure sect. By the end of the Period of Division, Daoism had its own canons of scriptural writings, much influenced by Buddhist models but constituting an independent religious tradition.

At the local level, popular collective forms of Daoism continued to thrive. Local masters would organize communal ceremonies for their parishioners. Incantations, music, fasting, and the display of penance and remorse would bring about the collective elimination of sins, which were seen as the main cause of sickness and premature death. According to the indignant reports of their Buddhist adversaries, Daoist ceremonies lasted days and nights and were ecstatic, sometimes even orgiastic. The participation of both men and women may explain the common allegation of sexual excesses at these ceremonies.

In the early centuries, Daoist priests usually married, and the office of Daoist master was hereditary. With the great success of Buddhism,

some Daoist leaders introduced celibacy and monastic life in the sixth century. Daoist monasteries, however, never acquired the economic power of Buddhist ones.

Daoist borrowings from Buddhism did not lead to reconciliation of the two religions. To the contrary, each engaged in bitter polemics against the other throughout this period. Moreover, Daoist masters helped instigate some of the anti-Buddhist persecutions. As an answer to Buddhist claims of superiority, Daoist masters asserted that the Buddha had been merely a manifestation of Laozi, who had preached to the Indians a debased form of Daoism, which naturally China did not need to reimport.

SUMMARY

Between the third and the sixth centuries, China did not become more populous or larger, but it changed in other fundamental ways. Buddhism gained wide acceptance among people of all social levels and was transforming the landscape with its temples and monuments. Because of the popularity of Buddhism, Chinese civilization became much more closely tied to other parts of Asia. Daoism responded to Buddhism's challenge and acquired a large body of texts and monastic institutions. Although warfare disrupted many people's lives, this was an era marked in many ways by advances. The capacity of poetry, calligraphy, and painting to express personal feelings was expanded by a series of highly creative masters. The great migrations from north to south also meant that more and more land in the south was cultivated by Han Chinese farmers, putting pressure on non-Han indigenous peoples to withdraw or assimilate. The north absorbed a huge influx of non-Chinese peoples, leading to both sporadic ethnic conflict and more complicated notions of Chinese identity. Non-Chinese rule did not dim the memory of the greatness of the Han Dynasty, but it showed that non-Chinese rulers could build strong states.

SUGGESTED READING

Current scholarship on the turbulent Age of Division after the fall of the Han can be sampled in S. Pearce et al., *Culture and Power in the Reconstitution of the Chinese Realm, 200–600* (2001), and A. Dien, ed., *State and Society in Early Medieval China* (1990). The early phase of this period is treated in R. de Crespigny, *Generals of the South: The Foundation and Early History of the Three Kingdoms State of Wu* (1990); the final phase is covered in A. Wright, *The Sui Dynasty* (1978). On the militarization of society in this period, see D. Graff, *Medieval Chinese Warfare, 300–900* (2002), which is especially good on the Northern Dynasties.

On the cultural history of this period, see C. Holcombe, *In the Shadow of the Han: Literati Thought and Society at the Beginning of the Southern Dynasties* (1994); S. Teng, trans., *Family Instructions of the Yen Clan* (1968); W. Jenner, *Memories of Lo Yang: Yang Hsuan-chih and the Lost Capital (493–534)* (1981); D. Holzman, *Poetry and Politics: The Life and Works of Juan Chi (210–263)* (1976); J. Frodsham, *The Murmuring Stream: The Life and Works of the Chinese Poet Hsieh Ling-yün (385–433);* and R. Campany, *Strange Writing: Anomaly Accounts in Early Medieval China* (1996).

On the introduction of Buddhism, see the brief A. Wright, *Buddhism in Chinese History* (1959), or the thorough E. Zurcher, *The Buddhist Conquest of China: The Spread and Adaptation of Buddhism in Early Medieval China* (1959). See also K. A. Tsai, trans., *Lives of the Nuns: Biographies of Chinese Buddhist Nuns from the Fourth to the Sixth Centuries* (1994). On Daoism, see L. Kohn, *Daoism and Chinese Culture* (2001); I. Robinet, *Taoism: Growth of a Religion* (1997); and S. Bokenkamp, *Early Daoist Scriptures* (1997).

5

The Cosmopolitan Empires of Sui and Tang China (581–960)

North and south China were politically reunited in 589 when the Sui Dynasty (581–618) defeated the last of the Southern Dynasties. After only two generations, the Sui was itself replaced by the Tang Dynasty (618–907), but progress toward cultural, economic, and political reunification continued, especially under three forceful rulers: Taizong, Empress Wu, and Xuanzong. The capital cities of Chang'an and Luoyang attracted people not only from all parts of China but also from all parts of Asia. The arts, and above all poetry, thrived in this environment. After the massive rebellion of the general An Lushan wracked China in the mid-eighth century, many of the centralizing features of the government were abandoned, and power fell more and more to regional military governors. Yet late Tang should not be viewed simply in terms of dynastic decline, as art and culture continued to flourish.

Historians of the Sui-Tang period have devoted much of their energy to understanding the processes of unification and the military, political, and cultural strength of the early Tang. How did the Tang solve the problems that had kept dynasties short for the preceding four centuries? Did the strength of the early Tang government owe anything to the mixed ethnic background of its founders? What happened to the aristocracies of the north and south? To understand the changes from early to late Tang, scholars have addressed other questions: Why did trade thrive as the government withdrew from active involvement in managing the economy? What were the connections between China's changing military posture and cultural trends? Were late Tang trends in literature, Buddhism, Confucian learning, and other fields of culture linked to each other?

THE NORTHWEST MILITARY ARISTOCRACY AND THE SUI REUNIFICATION OF CHINA

That reunification came about from the north is not surprising, since by the fifth century the south had largely abandoned hope of reconquering the north. Reunification was delayed, however, by the civil war in the north after 523. This changed in 577 when the Northern Zhou Dynasty defeated the Northern Qi, which freed up its battle-hardened armies to take on the south.

The rulers of the Northern Zhou were non-Chinese, like the rulers of the Northern Wei before them, though in this period ethnicity was fluid and intermarriage among ethnic groups common. Generally ethnicity was considered to be passed down with family names on the father's side, but family names could be changed. Yang Jian, the founder of the Sui Dynasty, offers a good example. He claimed descent from Han Chinese, but since *Yang* was one of the names given to Xianbei in the late fifth century, his ancestors may well have been Xianbei. His wife had the non-Chinese surname Dugu, but her mother was Chinese. Yang Jian's daughter married into the non-Chinese Yuwen family, the Northern Zhou royal house.

Yang Jian usurped the throne from his daughter's young son and proclaimed himself emperor of the Sui Dynasty. He quickly eliminated the possibility of Zhou Dynasty loyalists' ousting him in return by killing fifty-nine princes of the Zhou royal house. Nevertheless, he is known as Wendi, the "Cultured Emperor" (r. 581–604).

Wendi presided over the reunification of China. He built thousands of boats to compete for control of the Yangzi River. The largest of these had five decks, could hold eight hundred men, and was outfitted with six 50-foot-long booms that could be swung to damage an enemy vessel or pin it down. Some of these ships were manned by aborigines from southeastern Sichuan, recently conquered by the Sui. By late in 588, Sui had 518,000 troops deployed along the north bank of the Yangzi River, from Sichuan to the ocean. Within three months, Sui had captured Nanjing, and the rest of the south soon submitted.

After capturing Nanjing, the Sui commanders had it razed and forced the nobles and officials resident there to move to the new Sui capital at Chang'an. This influx of southerners into the northern capital stimulated fascination with things southern on the part of the old Northwest aristocracy.

Both Wendi and his empress were pious Buddhists and drew on Buddhism to legitimate the Sui Dynasty. Wendi presented himself as a Cakravartin king, a Buddhist monarch who uses military force to defend the Buddhist faith. In 601, in imitation of the Indian king Ashoka, he had relics of the Buddha distributed to temples throughout the country and issued an edict expressing his goal that "all the people within the four seas may, without exception, develop enlightenment and together cultivate fortunate karma, bringing it to pass that present existences will lead to happy future lives, that the sustained creation of good causation will carry us one and all up to wondrous enlightenment."[1]

Both Wendi and his successor, Yangdi (r. 604–617), had grand ambitions to rebuild an empire comparable to the Han. The Sui tried to strengthen central control of the government by denying local officials the power to appoint their own subordinates. They abolished the Nine Rank System and returned to the Han practice of each prefecture's nominating a few men for office based on their character and talents. Once in the capital, these nominees were given written examinations, an important step in the development of the civil service examination system. The

---

1. Arthur F. Wright, "The Sui Dynasty (581–617)," in *The Cambridge History of China* vol. 3, ed. Denis Twitchett (Cambridge: Cambridge University Press, 1979), p. 77.

Sui helped tie north and south China together by a major feat of construction: the Grand Canal. Built by conscripted laborers, the canal linked the Yellow and Yangzi rivers. (In later dynasties, the canal was extended to the northeast as far as modern Beijing and to the south as far as Hangzhou.) The Sui canal was 130 feet wide and had a road running alongside it, with occasional relay posts and granaries. Easy water transport made it much easier to ship tax grain from the south to the centers of political and military power in north China.

Both Sui emperors viewed their empire building as incomplete because they had not recovered the parts of modern Korea and Vietnam that the Han Dynasty had held. The Hanoi area was easily recovered from the local ruler in 602, and a few years later the Sui army pushed farther south. When the army was attacked by troops on war elephants from Champa (in southern Vietnam), Sui feigned retreat and dug pits to trap the elephants. The Sui army lured the Champan troops to attack, then used crossbows against the elephants, causing them to turn around and trample their own army. Although Sui troops were victorious, many succumbed to disease, as northern soldiers did not have immunity to tropical diseases such as malaria.

Recovering northern Korea proved an elusive goal. The Korean state of Koguryŏ had its capital near modern Pyongyang and also held southern Manchuria as far as the Liao River. When in 598 Koguryŏ troops joined a raid into Sui territory, Wendi ordered three hundred thousand troops to retaliate. However, the Sui army had to turn back when food supplies ran short. Sui then sent a fleet from Shandong, but it lost many of its vessels in storms and accomplished nothing. Another attempt was made in 611. Three hundred seagoing ships were built in Shandong, manned by ten thousand sailors and carrying thirty thousand crossbowmen and thirty thousand javelin men. Yangdi himself traveled to the region of modern Beijing to oversee preparations. Fifty thousand carts were built to carry clothing, armor, and tents. Reportedly six hundred thousand men were conscripted to

transport supplies in wheelbarrows. The *History of the Sui Dynasty* gives the undoubtedly inflated figure of 1,133,800 combat troops summoned for the expedition. Some went overland, weighed down with shields, armor, clothing, tents, and one hundred days' supply of grain. Because the ships failed to resupply them, they had to turn back, hungry and exhausted. The vast majority of the soldiers sent across the Yalu River did not make it back to China.

The cost to the Sui Dynasty of this military debacle was enormous. When floods, droughts, and epidemics reached areas that had been hard pressed by mobilization for war, bandits were joined by deserters. Nevertheless, Yangdi was determined to try a third time to take Korea. The 613 expedition crossed the Liao River and set siege to Koguryŏ strongholds, but the campaign was cut short when word reached the emperor of a major rebellion in central China. Still, in 614 Yangdi ordered the Korea campaign continued. This time the naval force made enough progress that the Koguryŏ king sued for peace and Yangdi could claim victory. When the Korean king failed to appear at the Sui court as he had been commanded, Yangdi began mobilizing for a fourth campaign in 615. Unrest was growing so serious, however, that nothing came of it. Yangdi, by leading the Korean campaigns himself, was personally humiliated by their failures. The imperial dreams of the Sui emperors had resulted in exhaustion and unrest.

THE FOUNDING OF THE TANG DYNASTY (618–907)

With the Sui government unraveling, power was seized at the local level by several kinds of actors: bandit leaders, local officials trying to defend against them, and local elites trying to organize defense on their own. The contender who eventually founded the Tang Dynasty was Li Yuan, the Sui governor of Taiyuan, and his general son, Li Shimin, known respectively as Gaozu (r. 618–626) and Taizong (r. 626–649). Their family belonged to the same northwest military aristocracy as the Sui emperors (Yangdi's and Taizong's mothers were in fact sisters, making them first cousins). *Li* was a Chinese name, and the Tang imperial family presented themselves as Chinese by descent, much as the Sui imperial family had.

Taizong was commanding troops from the age of eighteen and proved a highly talented general. Skilled with bow, sword, and lance, he enjoyed the rough-and-tumble of combat and placed himself at the head of crucial cavalry charges. He later claimed to have killed over a thousand men by his own hand. Taizong was also an astute strategist, able to outmaneuver his opponents. As he defeated one opponent after another from 618 to 621, he began to look like the probable winner, which led local leaders to join him in order to end up on the winning side.

In 626 Taizong ambushed two of his brothers, one of whom was the heir apparent. (He later had the histories record that he was forced to take this step because they were plotting against him.) Taizong then saw to the execution of all ten of their sons and demanded that his father abdicate in his favor. Despite these violent beginnings, Taizong proved a capable monarch who selected wise advisers and listened to their advice. He issued a new legal code and ordered it to be regularly revised. This code, the earliest to survive, had great influence on the codes adopted not only by later Chinese dynasties but also by neighboring countries, including Vietnam, Korea, and Japan.

In the early Tang the Xianbei presence rapidly faded as Xianbei assimilated and their language fell out of use. Many men of Xianbei descent used the Chinese surnames that had been given to them at the end of the fifth century and served as civil rather than military officials.

Although the Sui and Tang founders evoked the memory of the Han Dynasty, they relied on the groundwork laid by the Northern Dynasties. The Sui and Tang governments retained the Northern Zhou divisional militia (*fubing*). Its volunteer farmer-soldiers served in rotation in armies at the capital or on the frontier in return

Soldier and Horse. Taizong, a successful military commander, had his tomb decorated with bas-reliefs of soldiers and horses. Notice the elaborate saddle and the stirrups, which made it easier for soldiers to rise in the saddle to shoot arrows or attack with lances. (*University Museum, University of Pennsylvania*)

for their allocations of farmland. Both Sui and Tang also retained modified forms of the equal-field system introduced by the Northern Wei and regularly redistributed land. They set the taxes in grain and cloth on each household relatively low, making it easier to enroll households on the tax registers. In the census of 609, the registered population reached about 9 million households (for a total population of about 46 million people). Even if considerable numbers of people escaped tax registration, it seems that the population of China had not grown since Han times (when the high point in 2 C.E. was about 59 million).

Both Sui and Tang turned away from the military culture of the Northern Dynasties and sought officials steeped in Confucian learning. Government schools were founded to prepare the sons of officials and other young men for service in the government. Recruitment through examinations grew in importance. In the mature Tang system, there were two principal examinations. One tested knowledge of the Confucian classics (the *mingjing,* or illuminating the classics

Figure 5.1   Layout of Chang'an and One of the Cities Modeled on It Outside China

examination). The other (the *jinshi*, or presented scholar examination) required less memorization of the classics but more literary skill. It tested the ability to compose formal styles of poetry as well as essays on political questions. Preparation for the *jinshi* examination was more demanding, but passing it brought more prestige. Even sons of officials who could have entered the government by grace of their father's rank often would attempt the *jinshi* examinations.

During the sixth century, a new ethnic group, the Turks, emerged as the dominant group on the Inner Asian frontier. To keep them in check, Sui and Tang governments used all the old diplomatic and military strategies. They repaired fortifications; they received trade and tribute missions; they sent princesses as brides; they instigated conflict between different ethnic groups; they recruited non-Chinese into their armies. In 630, the Tang wrested northern Shaanxi and southern Mongolia from the Turks, winning for Taizong the title of Great Khan of the Turks. For the next half-century, Tang China dominated the steppe. Turks were settled in the Ordos region (as the Xiongnu had been in Han times), and several thousand families of Turks came to live in Chang'an. Joint Chinese-Turkish

campaigns into the cities of Central Asia in the 640s and 650s resulted in China's regaining overlordship in the region much as it had during the Han Dynasty. (See Map 5.1.)

The early Tang rulers also embraced Sui ambitions with respect to Koguryŏ. In 644 Taizong began preparations for an invasion. A fleet of five hundred ships was built to transport forty thousand soldiers to the Korean coast while an army of sixty thousand prepared to march. Despite impressive early victories, this army too had to retreat, and the retreat again proved an ordeal. It would not be until 668, when China allied itself with the southern Korean state of Silla, that Koguryŏ was finally subjugated. Eight years later, however, it was Silla, not Tang China, that controlled the area, and China had little to show for the effort put in over the course of eight decades to regain the borders staked out by the Han Dynasty so many centuries earlier.

THE TANG AT ITS HEIGHT

The Tang capital, Chang'an, was built by the Sui Dynasty near the site of the Han capital of the same name. It was the largest capital yet seen, nearly six miles east-west and more than five miles north-south. In the center against the north wall was the walled palace city, with the residence halls to the north and administrative offices to the south. From the south gate of the palace city stretched a wide avenue leading to the main south gate of the city wall. The rest of the city was divided by eleven north-south streets and fourteen east-west ones, making 108 rectangular walled wards, each with four gates. Two of the wards were government-supervised markets. Prime space was also reserved for temples.

Tang retained this city as its capital and made Luoyang a secondary capital. Both cities became great metropolises, with Chang'an and its suburbs growing to more than 2 million inhabitants. At these cosmopolitan cities, knowledge of the outside world was stimulated by the presence of envoys, merchants, and pilgrims from Central Asia, Japan, Korea, Vietnam, and Tibet, among other places. (See **Connections: Cultural Contact Across Eurasia, 600–900,** and **Material Culture: Tea.**) Because of the presence of foreign merchants, many religions were practiced, including Nestorian Christianity, Manichaeism, Zoroastrianism, Judaism, and Islam, although none of them spread into the Chinese population the way Buddhism had a few centuries earlier. Foreign fashions in hair and clothing were often copied, however, and foreign amusements such as polo found followings among the well-to-do. The introduction of new instruments and tunes from India, Iran, and Central Asia brought about a major transformation in Chinese music. (See Color Plate 6.)

In Tang times Buddhism fully penetrated Chinese daily life. In 628 Taizong held a Buddhist memorial service for all of those who had died in the wars, and the next year he had monasteries built at the site of major battles, so that monks could pray for the fallen of both sides. Buddhist monasteries ran schools for children, provided lodging for travelers, and offered scholars and officials places to gather for social occasions such as going-away parties. Merchants entrusted their money and wares to

Monk. This portrait of a monk in ink on paper was among the documents found at Dunhuang. Notice the shaved head, the meditation position, the rosary hanging on the bush, and the patchwork of the robe. *(© The Trustees of the British Museum)*

monasteries for safekeeping, in effect transforming the monasteries into banks and warehouses. The wealthy often donated money or land to monasteries, making them large landlords.

In the Tang period, stories of Buddhist origin were spread by monks who would show pictures and tell stories to illiterate audiences. One of the best loved of these stories concerned a man named Mulian who journeyed to the netherworld to save his mother from her suffering there. The popularity of this story gave rise to the ghost festival on the fifteenth day of the seventh month. On that day, Buddhists and non-Buddhists alike would put out food to feed hungry ghosts suffering in purgatory. Popular

Map 5.1 Map of Asian Trade and Communication Routes in the Sixth–Tenth Centuries

Silk Route
- Silk Route
- - - - Indian Ocean trade routes

MATERIAL CULTURE

Tea

Tea is made from the young leaves and leaf buds of *Camellia sinensis,* a plant native to the hills of southwest China. By Han times tea was already being grown and drunk in the southwest, and for several centuries after, it was looked on as a local product with useful pharmacological properties, such as countering the effects of wine and preventing drowsiness.

Tea was common enough in Tang life that poets often mentioned it in their poems (see Color Plate 7). Perhaps the most famous tea poem was by the eighth-century author of a treatise on the art of drinking tea, Lu Yu. Written to express his thanks for a gift of freshly picked tea, it reads in part:

> To honour the tea, I shut my brushwood
>   gate,
> Lest common folk intrude,
> And donned my gauze cap
> To brew and taste it on my own.
> The first bowl sleekly moistened throat
>   and lips;
> The second banished all my loneliness;
> The third expelled the dullness from my
>   mind,
> Sharpening inspiration gained from all
>   the books I've read.
> The fourth brought forth light
>   perspiration,
> Dispersing a lifetime's troubles through
>   my pores.
> The fifth bowl cleansed ev'ry atom of
>   my being.
> The sixth has made me kin to the
>   Immortals.
> This seventh is the utmost I can drink—
> A light breeze issues from my armpits.[1]

By Tang times tea had become a major commercial crop, especially in the southeast. The most intensive time for tea production was the harvest season, since young leaves were of much more value than mature ones.

Tea Jar. The spread of tea drinking served as a stimulus to the ceramic industry, as tea aficionados carefully selected the containers for storing tea leaves, and mixing, steeping, or drinking tea. This tea jar, made in south China, was exported to Japan, where it came to be treasured as an art object, eventually coming into the possession of the Tokugawa shoguns. *(The Tokugawa Art Museum)*

Women would come out to help pick tea, mobilized for about a month each year. Not only were tea merchants among the wealthiest merchants, but from the late eighth century on taxes on tea became a major item of government revenue.

Tea reached Korea and Japan as a part of Buddhist culture, as a drink preferred by Buddhist monks since it helped them stay awake during long hours of recitation or meditation. The Japanese priest Saichō, patriarch of Tendai Buddhism, visited China in 802–803 and reportedly brought back tea seeds.

---

1. John Blofeld, *The Chinese Art of Tea* (Boston: Shambhala, 1985), p. 12.

elaborations of the Mulian story emphasized the centrality of filial devotion and reinforced the Buddhists' message that the truly filial draw on Buddhism to aid their deceased parents.

During the Tang period, a new sacred geography for East Asia developed, with a network of pilgrimage sites in China. The manifestation of the bodhisattva Manjusri on Mount Wutai became so renowned that it attracted pilgrims from India. The Japanese Buddhist monk Ennin, who spent the years 838 to 847 in China, set his sights on a visit to Mount Wutai.

At the intellectual level, Buddhism was developing in distinctly Chinese directions. New sutras were written, "apocryphal" ones that masked their Chinese authorship by purporting to be translations of Indian works. Some of these texts were incorporated into the Buddhist canon; others were suppressed by the state and the Buddhist establishment as subversive. Among the educated elite the Chan school (known in Japan as Zen) gained popularity. Chan teachings reject the authority of the sutras and extol mind-to-mind transmission of Buddhist truths. Chan claimed as its First Patriarch the Indian monk Bodhidharma, said to have come to China in the early sixth century C.E. The Sixth Patriarch, Huineng, was just as important to Chan traditions. The illiteracy of Huineng at the time of his enlightenment was taken as proof that enlightenment could be achieved suddenly through insight into one's own Buddha nature. The "northern" tradition of Chan emphasized meditation and monastic discipline. The "southern" tradition was even more iconoclastic, holding that enlightenment could be achieved suddenly through a flash of insight, even without prolonged meditation.

In the late Tang period, opposition to Buddhism resurfaced, in large part because its tax-exempt status aggravated the state's fiscal problems. In 845 a Tang emperor ordered more than 4,600 monasteries and 40,000 temples and shrines closed and more than 260,000 Buddhist monks and nuns returned to secular life. Although this ban was lifted after a few years, the monastic establishment never fully recovered. Buddhism retained a strong hold among laypeople, and basic Buddhist ideas like karma and reincarnation had become ingrained, but Buddhism was never again as central to Chinese life as it was in Tang times.

The Tang Elite

The aristocracies of the Northern and Southern Dynasties suffered several blows with the reunification of China. The Sui abolished the Nine Rank System for recruiting men for office, ending nearly automatic access to office and its benefits for men from aristocratic families. Moreover, many of the highest-ranking families in the south were devastated by the wars of the sixth century, especially the rebellion of Hou Jing, which resulted in the death of thousands of members of elite families living in Nanjing. Nevertheless, throughout the Tang period, men from the thirty or so most famous families held an amazingly high share of the most prominent positions in the government. Moreover, the Tang elite remained avidly interested in questions of birth and relative family ranking.

Why did old families remain so prominent? One reason seems to be that their pretensions annoyed the early Tang rulers. In the early Tang the new ruling house and its closest allies (largely from the northwest military aristocracy) resented continued admiration for old families from the east and south whose scions often held only midlevel positions in the Tang government and who, even in earlier eras, had never been associated with a dynasty as glorious as the Tang. The aristocratic families further annoyed the court by preferring to marry within their own circle, scorning proposals from the imperial house and its close allies. Taizong retaliated in 632 by ordering a thorough investigation of the genealogies of leading families and the compilation of a new genealogical compendium. When the work was completed, Taizong found that his own researchers supported the claims to eminence of the aristocratic families, and he demanded a revision to give more weight to official position under the Tang. Twenty years later

Gaozong ordered yet another genealogical compendium, again wanting more emphasis on current offices. When it was completed, Gaozong went so far as to prohibit intermarriage by members of the seven old families whose pretensions rankled most. The effect of this ban was to greatly add to the prestige of the seven named family lines, who from then on knew exactly whom they should marry.

At the same time, an unplanned accommodation was being worked out between the old families and the Tang court. Members of aristocratic families used their many resources to prepare carefully for office, and the government allowed them to occupy a disproportionate share of ministerial posts. With the greatness of the Tang established, the court stopped worrying about whether people also admired the old aristocratic families, who, after all, posed no military threat.

During the Tang many of the old aristocratic families moved permanently to the region of Luoyang or Chang'an, the better to concentrate on political careers. By the eighth century they were justifying their marital exclusiveness not by reference to the glory of their ancestors, but to their superiority in education, manners, and family morality. By bringing attention to characteristics that were largely a product of upbringing, it was easy for the old families to exclude outsiders and retain a common identity. Even if the examinations were becoming an avenue for people from modest backgrounds to rise, a surprising proportion of those who passed in Tang times came from eminent families. Moreover, when it was time for assignments to be made, candidates were judged on their deportment, appearance, speech, and calligraphy, all of which were subjective criteria, making it easy for the responsible officials to favor young men from families like their own. Certainly the elite became broader during the Tang, but at no time did the presence of new families pose much of a threat to the continued eminence of the old ones.

If the Tang elite is compared to the elite of the Han period, several differences stand out.

Within the broad elite of those with the education that could qualify them for official appointment, three levels are clearly distinguishable: a very small elite of famous old families who were conspicuous in high office, below them a broader group of families that had produced officials since before Sui times, and below them families considered eminent in their own prefecture. Those in the two highest levels spent more time in the capitals than their Han counterparts did. Much more than in Han times, they took pride in their ancestry and discussed the ancestry of their peers and marriage prospects. At the same time, the Tang elite was, if anything, better educated than the Han elite, and its members did not disdain competing in the examinations.

Empress Wu

The mid-Tang Dynasty saw several women rise to positions of great political power through their hold on rulers, the first of whom, Empress Wu (ca. 625–705), went so far as to take the throne herself. How could a woman become ruler? Historians of the time, who viewed her as an evil seductress and usurper, attributed her success to her lack of scruples and her skill at manipulation. A brief review of her career shows that luck and political acumen also played a role.

Although Wu entered Gaozong's palace in 651 as a lesser consort, within a few years she convinced him to demote his empress and promote herself in her place. The histories record a chilling story of how Wu accomplished this. One day after the empress had been playing with Wu's baby girl, Wu came in and smothered the baby. When Gaozong later found the baby dead, Wu became hysterical, saying the empress must have killed her. Gaozong's top officials could not calm his rage or keep him from deposing the empress. Wu was made empress and her son made heir apparent.

Four years later Gaozong suffered a stroke, and Empress Wu began to make decisions in his place. Following the customary propriety of "ruling from behind a screen," the councilors could not see her when they talked to her. Wu nevertheless proved a hard-working ruler. In 665 she and Gaozong traveled with a large entourage of princes and high officials to Mount Tai in Shandong province to perform the sacred *feng* and *shan* sacrifices to Heaven and Earth, not performed since Western Han times. She argued that while it was appropriate for the emperor to perform the sacrifice to heaven at the top of the mountain, since it was a yang sacrifice, she and her palace ladies should perform the sacrifice to earth at the bottom of the mountain, since it was a yin sacrifice, thus demonstrating the true complementarity of yin and yang.

By the 670s, Empress Wu's oldest son, the heir apparent, was beginning to take stands on issues, even sometimes opposing his mother's ideas. When he died in 675, many suspected that she had poisoned him. The next heir, not surprisingly, kept a lower profile. However, in 680 Wu accused him of plotting a rebellion; he was banished and later forced to commit suicide.

One of the ways Empress Wu was able to keep the government operating smoothly despite her questionable standing was by bringing new people to court through the civil service examinations. Many of those who had felt left out during the early Tang, when the court was dominated by the northwest aristocracy, were happy to take advantage of new opportunities to become officials.

After more than twenty years as an invalid, Gaozong finally died in 683. The seventeen-year-old heir apparent, posthumously known as Zhongzong, took the throne. After six weeks, Empress Wu had him deposed because he tried to appoint his wife's father as chancellor. Another one of her sons, known as Ruizong, was then placed on the throne, but he was kept in a separate palace and rarely consulted. Now nearly sixty years old, Empress Wu no longer concealed herself behind a screen, and began using the Chinese term for the royal "we." She even ordered the construction of imperial-style ancestral temples for her own Wu ancestors.

In 684 a group of Tang princes and their allies staged a rebellion against Empress Wu. They captured the major city of Yangzhou and issued a proclamation detailing her crimes, ranging from killing her own children to favoring sycophants. The army remained loyal to Empress Wu, however, and within two months had suppressed the rebellion. Wu now was even more confident of her position and moved rapidly to rid herself of opponents. On the advice of new favorites, she undertook another Confucian ritual project based on the Classics, the construction of a Bright Hall for the performance of key rituals. Her Bright Hall was huge—about 300 feet square and 300 feet tall. It had three stories, the bottom two square and the top one round. When the Tang princes outside the capital refused to attend ceremonies marking the hall's completion, Wu took it as a pretext to eliminate much of the Tang imperial clan.

Until 690 Empress Wu had been content to be the power behind the throne. That year, however, when she was about sixty-five years old, she accepted her son's abdication and declared herself emperor of a new dynasty, the Zhou Dynasty. She became China's first and only female emperor.

Although Empress Wu employed Confucian language and diligently performed Confucian state rituals, she was personally deeply drawn to Buddhism. She was the major patron for the great cave temples carved at Longmen outside Luoyang. She found support for her political position in the *Great Cloud Sutra*, which prophesied that the Maitreya Buddha would be reincarnated as a female monarch and bring about an age free of illness, worry, and disaster. One of Wu's followers in 689 wrote a commentary to the sutra pointing out that the female monarch must be Empress Wu. When Empress Wu declared her own dynasty the next year, she had this sutra circulated throughout the country and ordered every prefecture to establish a Great Cloud temple.

When Wu made herself emperor, she did not designate an heir, apparently unsure whether she should let one of her own sons succeed her or have succession go to a member of her natal Wu family. In 697, when she was over seventy, she had her eldest surviving son, Zhongzong, brought back from exile and made heir apparent. Still, all through her seventies she retained power. It was not until 705, when she was about eighty and too ill to get out of bed, that the high officials successfully pressured her to abdicate.

Emperor Xuanzong

The removal of Empress Wu did not end the influence of women at court. Zhongzong was dominated by his wife, Empress Wei, who wanted their daughter to be made heir apparent. Her main rival was Zhongzong's sister, the Taiping Princess. After Empress Wei poisoned her husband, Zhongzong, in 710, she put his last remaining son, a boy of fifteen, on the throne. Two weeks later, probably with the encouragement of the Taiping Princess, another grandson of Empress Wu, the future emperor Xuanzong (r. 713–756), entered the palace with a few followers and slew Empress Wei and her daughter as well as other members of their faction. He installed his father, Ruizong, as emperor, but the Taiping Princess acted as the power behind the throne.

It was over the protests of the Taiping Princess that in 712 Ruizong abdicated in favor of Xuanzong. The princess's attempted coup failed, and she was permitted to commit suicide, ending more than a half-century of women dominating court politics.

Xuanzong, still in his twenties, began his reign as an activist. He curbed the power of monasteries, which had gained strength under Empress Wu. He ordered a new census to shore up the equal-field system. As a result of population growth, individual allotment holders in many areas received only a fraction of the land they were due but still had to pay the standard per household tax. Their only recourse was to flee, which reduced government revenue further. To deal with the threats of the Turks, Uighurs, and Tibetans, Xuanzong set up a ring of military provinces along the frontier from Manchuria to Sichuan. The military governors, often non-Chinese, were given great authority to deal with crises without waiting for central authorization.

Their armies were professional ones, manned by costly long-service veterans rather than inexpensive part-time farmer-soldiers like the divisional militia.

Xuanzong appreciated poetry, painting, and music and presided over a brilliant court. The great horse painter Han Gan served at his court, as did the poet Li Bai. Although many of his leading officials had been selected for office through the examination system, family pedigree was still a great asset. He commissioned a two-hundred-chapter genealogical work that provided him with up-to-date assessments of the relative ranking of the elite families of his realm. After 736 Xuanzong allowed Li Linfu (d. 752), an aristocrat proud of his family background, to run the government for him as his chancellor.

Xuanzong took an interest in both Daoism and Buddhism and invited clerics of both religions to his court. Laozi, as the putative ancestor of the Tang imperial family (both had the family name Li), was granted grand titles. Xuanzong wrote a commentary on the *Laozi* and set up a special school to prepare candidates for a new examination on Daoist scriptures. Among Buddhist teachings, he was especially attracted to the newly introduced Tantric school, which made much use of magical spells and incantations. In 726 Xuanzong called on the Javanese monk Vajrabodhi to perform Tantric rites to avert drought. In 742 he held the incense burner while the Ceylonese Amoghavajra recited mystical incantations to secure the victory of Tang forces.

Some have blamed Xuanzong's growing interest in Daoism and Tantric Buddhism for his declining interest in administrative matters. He was also growing older and wearier. By 742 he was fifty-seven and had spent thirty years on the throne. More and more of his time he spent with his beloved consort Yang Guifei, a full-figured beauty in an age that admired rounded proportions. To keep her happy, Xuanzong allowed her to place friends and relatives in important positions in the government. One of her favorites was the able general An Lushan, who spent more and more time at court. Eventually An got into a quarrel with Yang's cousin over control of the government, which led to open warfare.

THE REBELLION OF AN LUSHAN AND ITS AFTERMATH

An Lushan had commanded the frontier army in northern Hebei since 744. Half Sogdian (Central Asian) and half Turk, he was a professional soldier from a family of soldiers, with experience fighting the Khitans, the dominant group in northern Manchuria at the time. When An rebelled, he had an army of more than a hundred thousand veteran troops. They struck southward, headed toward Luoyang. The court, on getting news of the advance, began raising an army, but the newly recruited troops were no match for the veterans. With the fall of the capital imminent, the heir apparent left to raise troops in western Shaanxi, and Xuanzong fled west toward Sichuan. The troops accompanying Xuanzong mutinied and would not continue until Yang Guifei and her relatives had been killed. The heir apparent, in the meantime, was convinced by his followers to enthrone himself, which Xuanzong did not contest.

How did the Tang Dynasty manage to recover from this disaster? They had to make many compromises. To recover the capital, the Tang called on the Uighurs, a Turkish people allied with the Tang. After the Uighurs took Chang'an from the rebels, they looted it and would not leave until they were paid off with huge quantities of silk. Thereafter, to keep the Uighurs from raiding, the Tang had to trade them silk for horses at extortionate rates.

To get rebel leaders to submit, the Tang offered pardons and even appointed many as military governors of the regions they held. In key areas military governors acted like warlords, paying no taxes to the central government and appointing their own subordinates. They even passed down their positions to their heirs. Posts that once had been held by civil officials were increasingly filled with military men, often non-Chinese or semi-sinified.

The Uighurs were only one of China's troublesome neighbors in this period. Antagonistic states were consolidating themselves all along Tang's borders, from Parhae on the northeast, to Tibet on the west, and Nanzhao on the southwest (Yunnan area). When Tang had to withdraw troops from the western frontier to fight An Lushan's forces, the Tibetans took advantage of the opportunity to claim overlordship of the Silk Road cities themselves. Although the Tibetan empire collapsed in 842 and the Uighur empire broke up soon after, the Tang court no longer had the ambition to dominate Central Asia. Tang did respond when Nanzhao attacked the Tang prefectures in northern Vietnam, and though Tang sent an army to reassert control, the Vietnamese declared their independence in the tenth century.

Because the central government no longer had the local infrastructure needed to enforce the equal-field system, the system was finally abandoned and people were once more allowed to buy and sell land. In place of a one-tax-fits-all system, taxes were based on actual landholding and paid in semiannual installments. Each region was assigned a quota of taxes to submit to the central government and given leeway on how to fill it. With the return of free buying and selling of land, the poor who fell into debt sold their land to the rich, leading to the proliferation of great estates.

Besides reforming land taxes, the late Tang central government learned how to raise revenue through control of the production and distribution of salt, returning to a policy of the Han government. By adding a surcharge to the salt it sold to licensed salt merchants, the government was able to collect taxes indirectly, even from regions where it had minimal authority. By 779 over half the central government revenue came from the salt monopoly. The Salt Commission became a powerful agency, run by officials who specialized in finance.

Although control of salt production and distribution could be seen as a major intervention into the economy, on balance the post-rebellion government was withdrawing from attempts to control the economy. Not only did it give up control of land, it gave up supervision of urban markets and the prices charged for goods. This retreat from government management of the economy had the unintended effect of stimulating trade. Markets were opened in more and more towns, and the provincial capitals became new centers of trade. By the ninth century a new economic hierarchy of markets, towns, and cities had begun to emerge parallel to the government's administrative hierarchy of counties and prefectures. Merchants, no longer as burdened by government regulation, found ways to solve the perennial problem of shortages of copper coins by circulating silver bullion and notes of exchange, allowing trade to proceed without the use of coins.

The economic advance of the late eighth and ninth centuries was particularly evident in the south. During the rebellion, refugees from hard-hit areas sought safety and new opportunities in the south, much as they had in the fourth century. The late Tang was a time of prosperity for the cities of the Jiangnan region, such as Yangzhou, Suzhou, and Hangzhou, and many of those who came to these cities on official assignments or business decided to stay permanently.

Post-rebellion officials and emperors did not give up the goal of strong central control. They created a palace army to counter the power of the regional commanders. Unfortunately, the palace eunuchs placed in charge of this army soon became as troublesome as the regional commanders. In the early ninth century, eunuchs dominated court affairs much as they had in late Han times. High officials had to ally with one faction of eunuchs or another to have any hope of influencing policy. After 820, factions of officials and eunuchs plotted and counterplotted to enthrone, manipulate, or murder one emperor after another. In 835 the emperor plotted with a group of officials to purge the eunuchs, but when their plan was discovered, the eunuchs ordered the slaughter of over a thousand officials. Three chancellors and their families were publicly executed in Chang'an's western marketplace.

THE ACHIEVEMENTS OF TANG MEN OF LETTERS

The Tang Dynasty was the great age of Chinese poetry—the *Complete Tang Poems* includes more than forty-eight thousand poems by some twenty-two hundred poets. Men who wanted to be recognized as members of the educated elite had to be able to recognize lines quoted from earlier poets' works and write technically proficient poems at social occasions. Skill in composing poetry was so highly respected that it was tested in the civil service examinations. The greatness of Tang poetry, however, lies not in its ubiquity but in the achievements of a handful of great poets who brought the art of poetry to new heights.

Prolific Tang Poets	
	number of poems
Bai Juyi	2972
Du Fu	1500
Li Bo	1120
Liu Yuxi	884
Yuan Zhen	856
Li Shangyin	628
Meng Jiao	559
Wang Wei	426

In Tang poems, the pain of parting, the joys of nature, and the pleasures of wine and friendship were all common topics. Subtlety, ambiguity, and allusion were used to good effect. Wang Wei (701–761), a successful official strongly drawn to Buddhism, is known especially for his poetic evocations of nature. His "Villa on Zhongnan Mountain" uses simple, natural language:

> In my middle years I came to love the Way.
> And late made my home by South
>   Mountain's edge.
> When the mood comes upon me, I go off
>   alone,

And have glorious moments to myself.
I walk to the point where a stream ends,
Then sit and watch when the clouds rise.
By chance I meet old men in the woods.
We laugh and chat, no fixed time to turn
    home.[2]

Wang Wei's contemporary Li Bai (701–762) had a brief but brilliant career at the court of Emperor Xuanzong. One of his most famous poems describes an evening of drinking, with only the moon and his shadow for company:

Beneath the blossoms with a pot of wine,
No friends at hand, so I poured alone;
I raised my cup to invite the moon,
Turned to my shadow, and we become
    three.
Now the moon has never learned about
    my drinking,
And my shadow had merely followed my
    form,
But I quickly made friends with the moon
    and my shadow;
To find pleasure in life, make the most of
    the spring.
Whenever I sang, the moon swayed with
    me;
Whenever I danced, my shadow went wild.
Drinking, we shared our enjoyment
    together;
Drunk, then each went off on his own.
But forever agreed on dispassionate revels,
We promised to meet in the far Milky
    Way.[3]

The forms of poetry favored in the Tang were eight-line stanzas of five or seven characters per line. This form, called *regulated verse,* had fixed patterns of tones and required that the second and third couplets be antithetical. The strict antithesis is often lost in translation, but can be seen when lines are translated word for word. For instance, in the first stanza of Li Bai's poem in the previous paragraph, the antithetical couplets read word for word: "Lift cup, invite bright moon/Face shadow, become three men," and "Moon since not understand drinking/Shadow only follow my body."

A younger contemporary of Li Bai, Du Fu (712–770), is often paired with him, the two representing the two sides of Tang poetry: its more light-hearted and its more solemn (see **Biography: Du Fu, Confucian Poet**). In the next generation Bai Juyi (772–846) encompassed both sides. When sent out to regional posts, he took his responsibilities seriously and sympathized with the people whom he governed. At times he worried about whether he was doing his job justly and well:

From my high castle I look at the town
    below
Where the natives of Ba cluster like a
    swarm of flies.
How can I govern these people and lead
    them aright?
I cannot even understand what they say.
But at least I am glad, now that the taxes
    are in,
To learn that in my province there is no
    discontent.[4]

Besides producing a huge volume of poetry, Tang writers wrote in many other genres, some humorous (see **Documents: Poking Fun**). They greatly advanced the art of fiction. Tang tales were short and written in the classical language (in contrast to the longer vernacular language fiction and drama that became important in later periods). Bai Juyi's brother Bai Xingjian

---

2. Stephen Owen, *An Anthology of Chinese Literature* (New York: Norton, 1996), p. 390.

3. Trans. by Elling Eide in Victor Mair, ed., *The Columbia Anthology of Traditional Chinese Literature* (New York: Columbia University Press, 1994), p. 203.

4. Arthur Waley, trans., *More Translations from the Chinese* (New York: Knopf, 1919), p. 71.

BIOGRAPHY Du Fu (712–777), Confucian Poet

Although the civil service examinations in Tang times tested candidates on their ability to write poetry, the man widely considered the greatest of all Chinese poets repeatedly failed the examinations. Du Fu wanted to follow in the path of his grandfather, who had passed the *jinshi* examination in 670 and held prestigious posts in the capital. Instead, he spent much of his adult life wandering through China, returning from time to time to the capital to try once more for a political career. In 751 he even tried presenting some of his literary works to the emperor directly. Emperor Xuanzong had a special examination set for him, and he was passed but still spent the next two years waiting for an appointment. Just when it seemed Du Fu would get his chance, one catastrophe after another befell him. In 754 Du Fu had to move his family because of a famine brought on by floods, and not long afterward he had to move them again during the disorder caused by the An Lushan rebellion.

Nearly fifteen hundred of Du Fu's poems, some quite long, have come down to us. Du Fu's greatness as a poet lies in his poetic inventiveness and creation of the voice of the moral man protesting injustice. In a long poem written in 755, Du Fu began by making fun of his grand ambitions, none of them fulfilled, then described the sights he saw on his journey from the capital. As he approached the place where his family was staying, he heard wailing, which he soon learned was in response to the death of his youngest child. Rather than dwell on his own family's sorrows, however, he turned his thoughts to others:

All my life I've been exempt from taxes,
And my name is not registered for
 conscription.

Brooding on what I have lived through, if
 even I know such suffering,
The common man must surely be rattled
 by the winds;
Then thoughts silently turn to those who
 have lost all livelihood
And to the troops in far garrisons.
Sorrow's source is as huge as South
 Mountain,
A formless, whirling chaos that the hand
 cannot grasp.[1]

After the rebellion, Du Fu gave up hopes of an official career and devoted himself entirely to his poetry. In 760 he arrived in Chengdu (Sichuan) and for the next few years lived happily in a thatched hut outside the city. As Du Fu grew older, his poetry became richer and more complex. His eight "Autumn Meditation" poems, considered among the masterpieces of Chinese poetry, ponder the forces of order and disorder in both the natural and human worlds. One reads:

I have been told that Changan looks like a
 chessboard.
A hundred years, a lifetime's troubles, grief
 beyond enduring.
Mansions of counts and princes all have
 new masters,
The civil and army uniforms differ from
 olden times.
Straight north past the fortified mountains
 kettledrums are thundering
From wagon and horse on the western
 campaign winged dispatches rush.
Fish and dragons grow silent now, autumn
 rivers grow cold.
The life I used to have at home is the
 longing in my heart.[2]

---

1. Stephen Owen, *The Great Age of Chinese Poetry: The High T'ang* (New Haven: Yale University Press, 1981), p. 196.

2. Stephen Owen, *An Anthology of Chinese Literature* (New York: Norton, 1996), p. 436.

DOCUMENTS

Poking Fun

Among the texts surviving from the Tang is a set of four hundred sayings grouped under forty-two headings, a small part of which is given below. By making fun of situations and types of people, these witty sayings provide an amusing glimpse of Tang social life. They have traditionally been attributed to the late Tang poet Li Shangyin (ca. 813–858), but they are not included in his collected works and may well have been written by someone else.

INCONGRUITIES

1. A poor Persian.
2. A sick physician.
3. A (Buddhist) disciple not addicted to drink.
4. Keepers of granaries coming to blows.
5. A great fat bride.
6. An illiterate teacher.
7. A pork-butcher reciting sutras.
8. A village elder riding in an open chair.
9. A grandfather visiting courtesans.

RELUCTANT

1. A new wife to see strangers.
2. A poor devil to contribute to a feast.
3. A poor family to make marriages.
4. To visit retired officials.
5. A pregnant woman to go afoot.

VEXATIONS

1. Happening upon a tasty dish when one's liver is out of order.
2. Making a night of it and the drinks giving out.
3. For one's back to itch when calling upon a superior.
4. For the lights to fail just when the luck begins to favor one at cards.
5. Inability to get rid of a worthless poor relation.
6. A man cleaning out a well who has to go to the toilet in a hurry.

AMBIGUITY

1. Only of a poor gift does one say, "Can it be repaid?"
2. Only of an ugly bride does one say, "She is my fate."

(775–826) wrote a story about an examination candidate who on arrival in Chang'an fell instantly in love with the beautiful prostitute Li Wa. Over the course of the next year, Li Wa and her owner gradually squeezed him of all his money and then disappeared. Bewildered and desperate, the young man was reduced to supporting himself as a funeral singer. When his father discovered this, he beat him nearly to death. Reduced further to begging, he was in the end saved by Li Wa, who took pity on him, nursed him back to health, and convinced him to resume his studies. When he passed the examinations and obtained an official post, his father accepted Li Wa as his daughter-in-law.

Popular stories like these circulated widely and sometimes became the basis for later dramas. The most successful story in terms of its later incarnations was written by the eminent man of letters Yuan Zhen (779–831). In this case the examination candidate, surnamed Zhang, fell in love with a woman of his own class, a distant cousin named Cui Yingying. She is first introduced to him by her mother, who wishes to

3. Only of a nobody does one say, "Tai Gong met King Wen at eighty."[1]

4. Only of a poor appointment does one say, "It's a place to make a living."

5. Only to be rude to a guest does one say, "Make yourself at home."

6. Only of a poor dwelling does one say, "It's quite all right to live in."

7. Only those incapable of making a living for themselves rail at their ancestors.

BAD FORM

1. To wrangle with one's fellow guests.

2. To fall from one's polo pony.

3. To smoke in the presence of superiors.

4. Priests and nuns lately returned to ordinary life.

5. To vociferate orders at a banquet.

6. To cut into the conversation.

7. To fall asleep in somebody's bed with one's boots on.

8. To preface remarks with a giggle.

9. To kick over the table when a guest.

10. To sing love songs in the presence of one's father- or mother-in-law.

11. To reject distasteful food and put it back on the dish.

12. To lay chopsticks across a soup-bowl.

LAPSES

1. Talking to people with one's hat off.

2. Scolding another's servants.

3. Boring a hole in the wall to spy upon neighbors.

4. Entering a house without knocking.

5. Being careless about dripping snot or spitting on the mat.

6. Going into the room and sitting down uninvited.

7. Opening other people's boxes and letters.

8. Lifting chopsticks before the host's signal.

9. Laying down chopsticks before all have finished eating.

10. Stretching across the table to reach things.

_____

Source: From E. D. Edwards, *Chinese Prose Literature of the T'ang Period*, A.D. *618–906* (London: Probsthain, 1937–1938), pp. 128–144.

_____

1. It was not until he was eighty years old that King Wen invited Tai Gong to be his chief adviser.

thank him for coming to their aid during a bandit attack. Yingying is reluctant to greet him and refuses to be drawn into conversation. Zhang, however, is overwhelmed by her beauty and attracted by her shyness. He turns to Yingying's maid for advice, and she suggests that he propose marriage. He counters that the pain of separation from her is so great that he could not wait for a proper engagement. The maid then tells him to try to win her over by sending her poems. Although Yingying at first rebukes Zhang for making advances, eventually she decides to go to his room one night. Although taking the initiative, she still appears weak, leaning on her maid's arm. The ensuing affair is interrupted when Zhang has to go to the capital to take the examinations. When Zhang does not return, Yingying writes him a long letter protesting his faithlessness. Unlike most other love stories, this one does not end happily in a marriage. Zhang decides that beautiful women spell disaster for men and lets his parents arrange a marriage for him to someone else. Yingying, too, in the end marries someone chosen by her mother.

Tang men of letters kept Confucian learning alive in an age when the pull of Buddhism and Daoism was strong. Confucian scholars worked out the ritual programs of the early Tang emperors, served as teachers in the state schools, and wrote commentaries to the classics. State support for Confucian activities coexisted with state patronage of Buddhism and Daoism and private commitment to either religion on the part of many Confucian officials. Neither the state nor the scholarly community felt compelled to sustain exclusive positions.

With the restructuring of the Tang state after the rebellion of An Lushan, the state agencies that had provided the focus for Confucian scholarly activities deteriorated, forcing the scholarly community to reappraise its political and cultural responsibilities. A small group of scholars turned away from an emphasis on preserving inherited traditions in favor of looking directly to the classics to find the "Way of the Sages."

Han Yu (768–824) was perhaps the most important of these politically engaged writers and thinkers. Even though he passed the *jinshi* examinations (on his fourth try), Han Yu found political advancement frustratingly difficult. He was a strong supporter of efforts to strengthen the central government's control over the provinces, and deplored the political and cultural fragmentation that had been tolerated in order to hold together the Tang state. He offended the emperor when he wrote "On the Buddha Bone," a memorial intimating that the emperor was risking his own life by letting something so inauspicious as the bone of a dead person into the palace. As a writer, Han Yu advocated the use of a plainer prose style, labeled "ancient style" as it aimed for the ancient virtues of clarity and concision. This style, he contended, offered the best way to convey the truths of the Confucian tradition. In an essay on the origin of the Confucian Way, Han Yu argued that the Confucian tradition had been passed down in a single line of transmission from the duke of Zhou to Confucius and Mencius, but that the transmission had afterward been disrupted. He proposed that to revive the Way of the Sages, scholars had to go back to the *Analects* and *Mencius*.

THE DUNHUANG DOCUMENTS

The historical sources historians can use to reconstruct what life was like in the Tang period are richer than for earlier periods. There are fuller sources for the workings of the government, including the first surviving legal code, the first surviving court ritual code, and several compendiums of government documents. Much more survives from writers' collected works by way of personal letters, epitaphs for friends and relatives, prefaces to poems, and the like, from which historians can reconstruct social circles, trace marriage patterns, and infer attitudes toward marriage, children, friendship, and other nonpolitical subjects. For the Tang period there is also a substantial body of short fiction, which provides scenes of life in the cities among merchants, beggars, and shop owners in addition to the elite.

An even greater boon to recovering everyday social and economic relations was the discovery of thousands of original documents sealed in a Buddhist cave temple at Dunhuang, at the far northwestern corner of China proper, about 700 miles from Chang'an. The cave was sealed up soon after 1000 C.E., when the region was threatened by invasion, and not discovered again until 1900, when a Daoist monk living there investigated a gap in the plaster. In 1907 and 1908 he sold the bulk of the 13,500 paper scrolls to the British explorer Aurel Stein (1862–1943) and the French sinologist Paul Pelliot (1878–1945). The majority of the scrolls were Buddhist sutras, including numerous copies of the same texts, but there were also everyday documents such as bills of sale or contracts for services; calendars; primers for beginning students; sample forms for arranging divorce, adoption, or family division; circulars for lay religious societies; lists of eminent families; and government documents of all sorts.

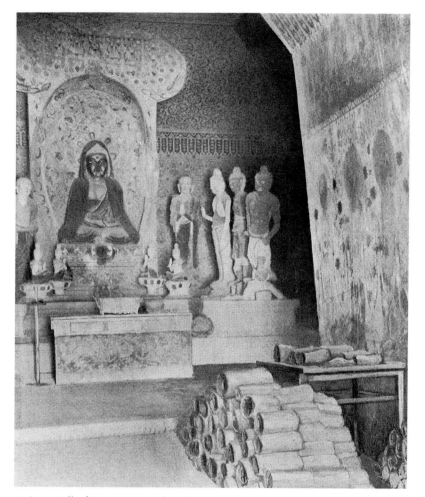

A Cave Full of Documents. This photograph was taken after the documents had been removed from the side chamber of Cave 16 at Dunhuang. *(British Library)*

From these documents, we can see that through the early eighth century, local officials kept the detailed registers of each household needed for the equal-field system. Although there was not enough land available to give everyone his or her full quota, the government did make reassignments every three years, as required by the law. Tenancy was also very common. Some people who found it inconvenient to work the land allotted to them by the government rented it to tenants while working as tenants themselves on other people's land.

Monasteries were among the largest landowners, and monastery tenants had a serf-like status, unfree to move elsewhere or marry outside their group. They could, however, hire others to help them work their land, as well as purchase their own land.

Among the more interesting documents found at Dunhuang were fifty or so charters for lay associations. Usually a literate Buddhist monk helped the group organize Buddhist devotional activities, such as meals for monks or offerings for ceremonies. Wealthier groups might sponsor the construction or decoration of a new cave. Other groups were more concerned with sudden large expenses, such as funerals, with each member making small monthly contributions to what was, in effect, an insurance pool. One association was limited to women, who promised to contribute oil, wine, and flour for a monthly meal.

Many of those who belonged to these associations were illiterate and drew marks besides their names instead of signing. Temples did their best to reduce illiteracy by offering elementary education. Numerous primers have survived, as well as multiplication tables, vocabulary lists, and etiquette books with rules on the language to use when addressing superiors, peers, and inferiors and the steps to follow for weddings and funerals.

Some of China's earliest printed works were found among the Dunhuang documents, including a calendar for the year 877 and a copy of the *Diamond Sutra* dated 868. It is not surprising that the Chinese discovered how to print so early, since China had a long history of mass production by use of molds. Moreover, people were familiar with ways to reproduce words on paper through the use of seals or rubbings taken from inscribed bronze or stone. The method of printing developed in Tang times involved craftsmen carving words and pictures into wooden blocks, inking them, and then pressing paper onto the blocks. Each block consisted of an entire page of text.

THE TANG DYNASTY'S FINAL DECADES AND THE FIVE DYNASTIES

After the rebellion of An Lushan, the Tang central government shared political and military power with the military governors. After 860, this system no longer worked to maintain order. Bandit gangs, some as large as small armies, roamed the countryside and set siege to walled cities. These gangs smuggled illicit salt, ambushed merchants and tax convoys, and went on wild rampages through the countryside. Huang Chao, the leader of the most successful of these bands, was a frustrated examination candidate who had become a salt merchant. His army crossed the country several times. In 879 it took Guangzhou and slaughtered thousands of foreign merchants. Just two years later his army captured Chang'an, where they set up a government. When someone posted on a government building a poem that ridiculed the new regime, the order was given to kill all those able to compose poems. Three thousand people are said to have died as a result.

Five Dynasties	Ten Kingdoms
	Wu (902–937)
	Southern Tang (937–975)
	Wu Yue (907–978)
Later Liang (907–923)	Former Shu (903–925)
Later Tang (923–936)	Later Shu (934–965)
Later Jin (936–946)	Min (909–945)
Later Han (946–950)	Northern Han (951–979)
Later Zhou (950–960)	Southern Han (917–971)
	Jingnan (907–963)
	Chu (927–951)

During the century from 860 to 960 (when the Song Dynasty was founded), political and military power devolved to the local level. Any local strongman able to organize defense against rebels and bandits could declare himself king or even emperor. Many of these local rulers rose from very humble origins; one had started as a merchant's slave. In the south, no self-proclaimed king ever consolidated much more than the equivalent of one or two modern provinces (a situation labeled the Ten Kingdoms). Political fragmentation did not impair the economy of the south. In fact, in their eagerness to expand their tax bases, rulers of the southern kingdoms did their best to promote trade and tax it.

In the north the effects of political fragmentation were less benign. Many of the regional warlords were not Chinese, but Turks from the old garrison armies. Both Chang'an and Luoyang had been devastated by the fighting of the late Tang period, and Kaifeng, located in Henan province at the mouth of the Grand Canal, became the leading city in north China. None of the Five Dynasties that in succession held Kaifeng was able to build a stable government before being ousted by rivals.

SUMMARY

How did China change over the course of the three centuries of Sui and Tang rule? The late Tang did not dominate East Asia the way the early Tang had, as all along its borders powerful states had established themselves. Nor was the late Tang as eager to adopt music, craft, and art styles from distant lands. Although military men held much of the power in both periods, China had not returned to the hybrid Xianbei-Chinese military culture of the Northern Dynasties. The late Tang official elite was oriented toward the civil arts, and more and more welcomed into their midst men of literary talent from undistinguished families. During Tang times, the Chinese economy grew much larger, first stimulated by the reunification of north and south and later by the abandonment of the equal-field system. The government found new ways to raise revenue, notably through control of salt production and distribution. In both the sixth and the ninth centuries, Buddhism was a major force within China, but much had changed about China's engagement with Buddhism. By late Tang, foreign monks were much less of a presence and Chan and Tantric monks much more of one. Confucianism was stronger at the end of the Tang, thanks to the intellectual flowering of the ninth century.

SUGGESTED READING

The Cambridge History of China, vol. 6, covers the political history of the Tang period in some detail. On Sui and Tang military institutions and wars, see D. Graff, *Medieval Chinese Warfare, 300–900* (2002). For other aspects of Tang society and culture, see two collections of essays: A. Wright and D. Twitchett, eds., *Perspectives on the T'ang* (1973), and J. Perry and B. Smith, eds., *Essays on T'ang Society: The Interplay of Social, Political, and Economic Forces* (1976). On Tang rulership, see H. Wechsler, *Mirror to the Son of Heaven: Wei Cheng at the Court of T'ang T'ai-tsung* (1974); Y. Pan, *Son of Heaven and Heavenly Qaghan* (1997); and R. Guisso, *Wu Tse-t'ien and the Politics of Legitimization in T'ang China* (1978). For other aspects of the Tang government, see E. Pulleyblank, *The Background of the Rebellion of An Lu-shan* (1955); D. Twitchett, *Financial Administration Under the T'ang Dynasty* (1970) and *The Writing of Official History Under the T'ang* (1992); and D. Mc Mullen, *State and Scholars in T'ang China* (1988).

On religion in Tang, see E. Reischauer, *Ennin's Diary: The Record of a Pilgrimage to China in Search of the Law,* and the companion volume, *Ennin's Travels in T'ang China* (both 1955); J. Gernet, *Buddhism in Chinese Society: An Economic History of the Fifth to the Tenth Centuries* (1995); S. Teiser, *The Ghost Festival in Medieval China* (1988); and S. Cahill, *Transcendence and Divine Passion: The Queen Mother of the West in Medieval China* (1993).

For an introduction to Tang poetry, see S. Owen, *The Great Age of Chinese Poetry: The High T'ang* (1981), and V. Mair, ed., *The Columbia History of Chinese Literature* (2002). A good selection of Tang literature in translation can be found in C. Birch, ed., *Anthology of*

Chinese Literature, 2 vols. (1965, 1972); V. Mair, ed., *The Columbia Anthology of Traditional Chinese Literature* (1994); and S. Owen, *An Anthology of Chinese Literature* (1996). Still well worth reading are the biographies of two major poets: W. Hung, *Tu Fu: China's Greatest Poet* (1952), and A. Waley, *The Life and Times of Po Chu-i, 772–846 A.D.* (1949).

On late Tang literary and intellectual culture, see S. Owen, *The End of the Chinese "Middle Ages"* (1996); J. Chen, *Liu Tsung-yuan and Intellectual Change in T'ang China, 773–819* (1992); and C. Hartman, *Han Yü and the T'ang Search for Unity* (1985). E. Schafer has written extensively on Tang culture, including material culture. See *The Golden Peaches of Samarkand* (1963), *The Vermilion Bird: T'ang Images of the South* (1967), and *Pacing the Void: T'ang Approaches to the Stars* (1977). On women and gender in the Tang, see J. Tung, *Fables for the Patriarchs: Gender Politics in Tang Discourse* (2000). On the Tang capital, see V. Xiong, *Sui-Tang Chang'an: A Study in the Urban History of Medieval China* (2000).

PART TWO

The Emergence of East Asian Civilization

Cultural Contact Across Eurasia (600–900)

IN 735, WHEN TAJIHINO MABITO Hironari returned to Japan after completing his mission to the Tang court at Chang'an, he was accompanied by a Chinese Buddhist monk, an Indian Brahman, a Persian musician, and another musician from Champa (southern Vietnam). This was an era when Korea and Japan turned to China as a model for everything from architecture to ceramics, music, and medicine. But the China they turned to was a cosmopolitan one that had absorbed much from the rest of Asia. (See Map 5.1.)

During the seventh, eighth, and ninth centuries, the major countries of Asia exchanged ideas, music, technology, art, and commodities. The Chinese avidly adopted Persian musical instruments and the game of polo. The Abbasid caliphs were connoisseurs of Chinese silk and porcelain. Persian seamen carried goods on ships that stopped at India, Sri Lanka, Malaysia, and China. Buddhist monks from India and Java performed ceremonies at the Chinese court. Chang'an hosted as many as 25,000 foreigners, the majority of whom had arrived by the overland route through Central Asia. In Guangzhou there were even more foreigners active in the seaborne trade. In the eighth century a monk described the port as full of "uncountable" Indians, Persians, and Malays, who brought aromatics, drugs, precious stones, and other goods. A century later, in 878, the Persian Abu Zayd was willing to put a number on the foreign community of Muslims, Christians, Jews, and Zoroastrians in the city, but his number— 120,000—is too high to be believable.

Although many more merchants than monks traveled the trade routes of Asia, most surviving records of journeys were written by monks. The monk Xuanzang, who left Chang'an in 629, took the northern arm of the Silk Road. His account testifies to the strictness of Chinese checkpoints, where travel permits were examined, and to the hardship of crossing the deserts. He stopped at the oasis towns of Turfan and Kucha. Next he had to climb the Tianshan Mountains where, he wrote, glaciers "rise mingling with the clouds." A third of those in his party died crossing these passes. At Tolmak he was entertained by a Turkish khan, and from there he went to Samarkand, which he described as a rich entrepot. He stopped at Balk and Bamiyan before turning south toward India. On his return trip, fifteen years later, after Samarkand Xuanzang took the southern route through the city-state of Khotan. After it, however, he had to pass the Taklamakan desert, where drifting sands obscured the path, and travelers were advised to look for bones of those who had not survived to find their way. More than once on his trip, his group was attacked by bandits.

The stories of those who crossed the deserts and mountains of Central Asia by foot and camel are full of romance and adventure. More goods and more people, however, went by the easier sea route. Ships regularly sailed from the Persian Gulf to India and from India to Southeast Asia and China, following the monsoons. A full round trip of the entire route would take about a year and a half. Traders would leave Persia or Mesopotamia in September to catch the northeast monsoon that would take them to the southern tip of India. After trading there, they would sail in December with the southwest

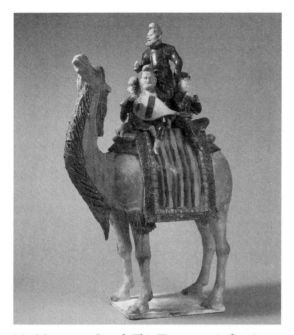

Musicians on a Camel. This Tang ceramic figurine, twenty-three inches tall, depicts Persian or Central Asian entertainers, a popular part of life in Tang cities. *(National Museum of China/Cultural Relics Publishing House)*

monsoon across the Bay of Bengal, through the Straits of Malacca, reaching Guangzhou in south China by April or May. They would spend several months there, buying Chinese goods, before beginning the return trip in the fall.

China, Japan, and Korea in these centuries were part of a larger world that encompassed all of Asia from Persia east. These were the regions of Asia where Buddhism had spread. These parts of the world were themselves undergoing major changes in this period and looked quite different in 900 than they had in 600. In 600 Turks were dominant on the Inner Asian steppe. The major oasis cities, such as Kotan, Kucha, and Turfan, were largely autonomous and devotedly Buddhist. Sogdians dominated the region of Samarkand and Bukhara, and in Persia the Sassainian dynasty ruled. In Persia Zoroastrianism was the state-supported religion, but Manicheanism also had a substantial following, as it did in Sogdia as well. Christian-

ity was to be found in both these regions, but it was Nestorian Christianity, an offshoot originating with the teachings of Nestorius, the fifth-century patriarch of Constantinople, who argued that Jesus had two distinct natures, human and divine.

By far the most momentous development in Persia and Sogdia during the Tang period was the coming of Islam. By the time Muhammad died in 632, his followers had formed a highly disciplined community in Arabia, and within a generation not only had they conquered the Arabian peninsula and Mesopotamia, but they had taken over the Sassanian empire in Persia. By the early eighth century, they had added Bukara and Samarkand in Central Asia. Although populations were not forced to convert, political and economic incentives steadily led to more and more conversions. Zoroastrians, Manicheans, and Nestorians who did not want to convert often chose to move, creating substantial diasporas, especially in India and China. Even before the arrival of Islam, Manicheanism had been spreading to the Uighur Turks of Chinese Turkestan, and the Sogdian Manicheans often moved east to the lands dominated by the Uighurs or farther east to China. Quite a few Manichean texts survived at Dunhuang. The influx of Nestorian Christians into Tang China began before Islam came to Central Asia but probably was stimulated by it. Zoroastrians, by contrast, mostly moved to India, where they were able to maintain their traditions into modern times.

India in these centuries was a land of petty kingdoms where regional cultures flourished. By this point Hinduism was in the ascendancy and had more adherents than Buddhism, but there were still many major Buddhist monasteries. Tantric Buddhism was particularly popular and was spreading to Tibet. In these centuries India came into contact with Islam. The northwest part of India, the Sind, was conquered in 711 by the Ummayad governor of Iraq, who sent a force with six thousand horses and six thousand camels, but Islam did not spread much beyond this foothold until several centuries later.

Tang China maintained sway in northern Vietnam, but elsewhere in Southeast Asia, traders from India were establishing a significant presence. Traders established many coastal settlements. Local rulers often adopted Indian customs and values, embraced Hinduism and Buddhism, and learned Sanskrit, which became the lingua franca of the region, much as Chinese became in East Asia. The most important mainland Southeast Asian state was the Khmer Empire of Cambodia, founded in 802. Indian influence was pervasive; the impressive temple complex at Angkor Wat was dedicated to the Hindu god Vishnu. Just as impressive was the maritime empire of Srivijaya, which from the sixth century on held the important Strait of Malacca, through which most of the sea traffic between China and India passed. Based on the island of Sumatra, the Srivijayan navy ruled the waters around Sumatra, Borneo, and Java and controlled the southern part of the Malay Peninsula as well. Sanskrit was used for government documents, and Indians were often employed as priests, scribes, and administrators. Indian mythology took hold, as did Indian architecture and sculpture. Kings and their courts, the first to embrace Indian culture, consciously spread it to their subjects. The Chinese Buddhist monk Yixing stopped at Shrivijaya for six months in 671 on his way to India and for four years on his return journey. He found a thousand Buddhist monks there, some of whom helped him translate Sanskrit texts. Borobudur, a stone monument depicting the ten tiers of Buddhist cosmology, was begun around 780.

Music and dance offers one of the most interesting cases of East Asia adopting elements of culture from other parts of Asia. In Tang times, no tavern in Chang'an could compete without a troop of foreign musicians and a Western dancing or singing girl. Popular tunes included "South India," "The Three Platforms of the Turks," and "Watching the Moon in Brahman Land." One set of dancing girls from Sogdia who won the favor of Emperor Xuanzong (r. 712–756) were known as the Western Twirling Girls. They wore crimson robes with brocaded sleeves, green pants, and red

Five-Stringed Pipa/Biwa. This musical instrument, decorated with fine wooden marquetry, was probably presented by the Tang court to a Japanese envoy. It was among the objects placed in the Shōsōin. *(Shosoin Treasure House/DNPArchives.com)*

deerskin boots and skipped and twirled on top of balls rolling around the dance floor. The poet Bai Juyi wrote about the dances of girls from modern Tashkent who began their act by emerging from artificial lotuses and ended it by pulling down their blouses to show their shoulders. Countries throughout Asia sent musicians as part of their tribute to Xuanzong's court. Court music was categorized into ten regional styles, including those of Samarkand, Bukhara, Kashgar, Kucha, India, and Korea. Among the instruments that entered the Chinese repertoire in this period is the pear-shaped plucked lute (*pipa* in Chinese, *biwa* in Japanese), originally of West Asian origins. From Kucha came oboes and flutes and a small lacquered drum. Percussion instruments from India, including gongs and cymbals, also came to be part of orchestras and are often illustrated in Buddhist paintings of celestial orchestras.

Imported musical instruments were among the treasures the Japanese Empress Kōmyō placed in the Shōsōin repository at the Buddhist temple Tōdaiji in Nara in 756. These instruments included both four- and five-string *pipa/biwa* of Chinese manufacture. There also was a harp (*konghou/kugo*), another instrument that originated in West Asia. These instruments were greatly outnumbered by the 171 masks for use in dance performances. Masked dances were very popular in the Central Asian city of Kucha, and Kuchan dancers probably helped them gain popularity in China, Korea, and Japan. One mask is for a comic drama, *Drunken Persians,* about a Persian king and his attendant. "As the languid dance, punctuated with slow leaps, picked up tempo, the actors shed their inhibitions and behaved in a thoroughly uproarious manner, probably drawing enthusiastic cheers from the delighted spectators."[1] Central Asia thus provided not only some of the material trappings of this performance, but also its content.

SUGGESTED READING

On contact among China, Japan, and Korea during this period, see C. Holcombe, *The Genesis of East Asia: 221 B.C.–A.D. 907* (2001). On the larger issue of east-west exchanges in this period, see P. Curtin, *Cross-Cultural Trade in World History* (1984), and J. Bentley, *Old World Encounters: Cross-Cultural Contacts and Exchanges in Pre-Modern Times* (1993). On Chinese and Japanese importation of goods and cultural practices from farther west, see E. Schafer, *The Golden Peaches of Samarkand* (1963), and R. Hayashi, *The Silk Road and the Shoso-in* (1975). On other parts of Eurasia in the age of the Islamic expansion, see D. Sinor, ed., *The Cambridge History of Early Inner Asia* (1990), and P. Golden, *An Introduction to the History of the Turkic Peoples* (1992). On Xuanzang and his journey, see S. Wriggins, *Xuanzang: A Buddhist Pilgrim on the Silk Road* (1996).

---

1. Ryoichi Hayashi, *The Silk Road and the Shoso-in,* trans. Robert Ricketts (New York: Weatherhill, 1975), p. 102.

Early Korea: Chosŏn, Three Kingdoms, Silla, and Parhae

Human habitation in the Korean peninsula originated about thirty thousand years ago. The Bronze Age developed during the late Shang Dynasty period in China around 1300 B.C.E. and continued after the introduction of iron during the Warring States period (403–221 B.C.E.) of the late Zhou Dynasty in China. The archaeological artifacts from that period indicate clearly that the inhabitants of areas where the earliest ancestors of the modern Koreans are presumed to have lived—Manchuria and the Korean peninsula—did not share in the cultural developments of the Chinese continent. Their bronze implements lacked the sophisticated animal patterns and fine incisions of the magnificent ritual bronze pieces of the Shang and Zhou dynasties of China. Their different narrow and broad swords, knives, and tools reflected a simpler hunting and gathering culture similar to those found in the Scythian culture of Siberia.

Neolithic pottery was quite distinct, marked mainly by unglazed earthenware with parallel incisions on the lip, like the teeth of a comb. Later, in the Bronze Age of the middle of the first millennium, plain pottery seems to have replaced comb pottery.

The state of Chosŏn, the first state of the progenitors of the Korean people, was mentioned in Chinese records for the first time around 190 B.C.E. In 108 B.C.E. it fell under Chinese control until 313 C.E. Prior to that date, petty chiefdoms existed in Manchuria and the Korean peninsula around Chinese territory, and at the end of the fourth century, the three kingdoms of Koguryŏ, Paekche, and Silla emerged from the earlier chiefdoms and began to expand in a period when China was no longer unified. Koguryŏ, the strongest of the three, and Paekche lost out in their quest for control of the peninsula in 668 to Silla, which allied with a reunified China under the Tang Dynasty to defeat its rivals. Silla, however, lost any claim to Koguryŏ's territory in Manchuria. In 698, Parhae, a Malgal kingdom with a minority ex-Koguryŏ population, was founded in eastern Manchuria, the Maritime Province of Russia, and the northeast portion of the Korean peninsula. Silla and Parhae lasted for another two centuries, during which Silla spread its culture throughout the peninsula but began a steady decline in power.

There are a number of important problems in this period. How were states created from relatively small and weak political units? What were the differences between the Three Kingdoms, and what were the reasons for Silla's eventual victory over its enemies in 668? How were these states able to survive in the face of Chinese power? How much influence did Chinese culture exert over the peninsula? How much interaction was there with other cultures during this period? What was the nature of relations with early Japan? How did the growth of Buddhism affect the art and culture of the region, and what was the relationship between Buddhism, Confucianism, and native religious beliefs? Finally, what were the causes and results of Silla's eventual decline?

GEOGRAPHY OF THE KOREAN PENINSULA

The Korean peninsula includes two ranges, the Taebaek (which runs north to south along the eastern shore) and Sobaek (running northeast from Kangwŏn Province southwest to Chŏlla Province), as well as many hills and small mountains. There were no major rivers like the Yellow and Yangzi rivers in China that could form the foci of major centers of agrarian civilization.

The Yalu River (Amnok in Korean) and the Tumen (Tuman) River, the current boundary between North Korea and Manchuria, did not function as a state boundary, and most of the other rivers flowed short distances from the mountain range that ran from north to south along the eastern half of the peninsula to the East Sea (Yellow Sea). From north to south, the main rivers were the Ch'ŏngch'ŏn, Taedong (through Pyongyang), Yesŏng (through Kaesŏng), Imjin, Han (through Seoul), Kŭm (through Kongju), Yongsan (through Naju) along the west coast, the Sŏmjin (through Kurye), and the Naktong River (through Pusan) that flowed south into the Tsushima Straits.

The weather is cold in the winter, with heavy snowfall in the north from cool continental air flowing south from Manchuria, and warm and humid in the summer from monsoon winds moving north from south and depositing torrential rains in July and August. Most of the fertile land is located in the south, where the double cropping of rice was possible in historical times. Moving up the hills, land was terraced for rice cultivation to allow water to flow down the hills through the paddies, but most upland areas were cultivated in dry crops like barley, millet, and ramie (later cotton). In the mid-region of the peninsula, there is more dry land, and in the north, the wet rice land is sparse.

BRONZE AGE CULTURE

Bronze Age settlements were limited to small communities of one or two dozen households located along rivers or the coast. Some residences were larger than others, suggesting some kind of group or communal life. Individual habitations usually consisted of pit dwellings, with a hearth in the middle and thatching around all sides. Toward the end of the first millennium, at about the same time that rice cultivation appeared, residences were using the ondol household heating system in which flues underneath the floor provided warmth. Religious symbols included dolmens, huge slabs of

Map 6.1   **Korea, 200 B.C.E.–100 B.C.E.**

stone quarried from nearby mountains and transported to the lowlands. In the north, they are usually propped up on two large support stones, but in the south they lie flat on the ground. There are also menhirs, or large stone monuments, that are not decorated with either pictures or writing. Little is known about any religious significance of these large stones.

The main flow of migration came from Inner Asia, Mongolia, and Siberia into Manchuria and the Korean peninsula, and then across the Tsushima Strait to the islands of Japan. These people spoke languages that modern linguists call the Ural-Altaic language group, which were quite different from Chinese. Verbs were placed at the end of sentences, and relative clauses preceded the nouns they modified. *Tungusic* is the term that has been assigned to the languages of the prehistoric inhabitants of Manchuria and Korea, but there is no proof that they all spoke the same language or were able to understand each other.

When these nomadic migrants reached Manchuria and Korea, they settled down to become hunters and gatherers. They may have believed in animal totems and worshipped bears. They had animistic beliefs in the spirits in mountains and large trees, and they probably used shamans to communicate with evil spirits of the dead to avert harm to the living, traditions that remain alive to this day.

The archaeological evidence differs markedly from a powerful traditional Korean myth of later times that a single "Korean people" were born when Tangun was born from the union of a spirit named Hwan'ŭng, who descended from heaven, and had relations with a bear-woman, who gave birth to Tangun in 2333 B.C.E. It is unlikely, however, that there was anything like a single Korean people at the time.

A story in the early Zhou Dynasty *Book of Documents* tells of a Chinese nobleman and sage, Kija (Qizi in Chinese), who advised King Wen of the Chinese Zhou Dynasty around the mid-twelfth century B.C.E. and was rewarded by the grant of a fief called Chosŏn (Chaoxian in Chinese). Koreans in later times used this tale to assume that Kija brought the "Korean people" up to the advanced level of early Zhou civilization, but the absence of Zhou bronzes and examples of Chinese ideographic writing belies that conclusion.

THE EARLY HISTORICAL PERIOD (200 B.C.E.–313 C.E.)

The early historical period was marked by a division between north and south because of a more advanced level of political organization and a greater degree of influence from Chinese culture in the north than in the south. In the north, the states of Puyŏ, Koguryŏ, and Chosŏn were situated in the area from central Manchuria to an area just north of present-day Seoul in the Korean peninsula. In the south, the Samhan confederations of chiefdoms were located in the area from Seoul to the southern tip of the peninsula.

The North: Chosŏn, Puyŏ, Koguryŏ

The *Records of the Grand Historian*, written around 100 B.C.E. by China's first historian, Sima Qian, mentions a state of Chosŏn around 190 B.C.E., but the boundaries of Chosŏn and the site of its capital are under dispute. Pyongyang, south of the Yalu River, is the most likely place, but recently Korean scholars have argued for a capital near the Liao River in Manchuria. For centuries, many Koreans have believed that this Chosŏn state was the same Chosŏn granted to Kija about eight hundred years before, but there is no evidence to justify this assumption. Elements of Chinese culture must have been introduced by Chinese refugees who migrated east to escape the warfare that broke out in north China during the Warring States period in the fourth century B.C.E.

In the early second century B.C.E., a Chinese refugee named Weiman (Wiman in Korean) from the feudal state of Yan fled to Chosŏn with a large group of Chinese followers. The Chosŏn king put him in charge of guarding the frontier, but he seized control of the country. Either he or earlier Chinese refugees may have brought with him the Chinese ideographic writing system and knowledge of Chinese Confucianism, Daoism, Legalism, and Mohism, but there is no evidence to confirm that.

In 108 B.C.E. the Martial Emperor (Wudi) of the Chinese Han Dynasty conquered Chosŏn and incorporated its territory from the Liao River in southwestern Manchuria down to the area just north of present-day Seoul on the Korean peninsula. This territory was divided into four commanderies, part of the Han centralized bureaucratic administration. Lelang commandery (Nangnang in Korean), with its seat in modern Pyongyang, was the most important of the four and the recipient of much of the advanced culture of the Han. Tombs in its magistrate's capital at Pyongyang have yielded significant objects of Han Dynasty culture, architecture, tomb construction, and the famous lacquerware basket with images of Confucian worthies painted around the sides (see page 60). It remained under Chinese control to 313 C.E. and must have influenced a small educated elite with Chinese culture.

Puyŏ, located in central Manchuria around the Sungari River, and Koguryŏ, which straddled the middle Yalu River region, possessed a more advanced social and political structure than Okchŏ, the Eastern Ye along the northeastern coast of Korea, and the Samhan confederations in the south. They had separate foundation myths, but the founder of Koguryŏ was supposedly a Puyŏ native who ran away to found Koguryŏ. They consisted of chiefdoms with populations varying from several hundred to fifty thousand, and the chieftains, collectively called Chega, were named after animals; they belonged to a council that advised and limited the kings and maintained autonomous control of districts. They each had a few officials under them, and they led their forces on horseback in time of war. Society was organized hierarchically with an elite class of what Chinese sources called "great families" (*hojok*), who dominated ordinary commoners and the "lower households" (*haho*), which in Puyŏ were slaves and in Koguryŏ commoners responsible for supplying rice, grain, fish, and salt to the ruling class and serving as baggage carriers during wartime.

Their favorite weapons were bows and arrows, swords, and halberds, and each family had to supply its own weapons. In wartime, the Puyŏ held a sacrifice to heaven and then examined the hooves of a sacrificial ox to divine the outcome of upcoming battles. Both groups had a severe system of discipline and punishment that included execution and reduction to slavery of the family members of criminals. They had practices that deviated from Chinese norms: levirate (the marriage of widows to brothers of their deceased husbands) in Puyŏ just like the Xiongnu tribes north of China, and uxorilocal

marriage (where the husband moves in with the bride's family) in Koguryŏ.

The population of Puyŏ in the third century C.E. was about 400,000, and both Puyŏ and Koguryŏ had adopted some marks of Chinese civilization like the use of ceremonial wine cups, status distinctions, New Year ceremonies, and sacrifices to heaven. They enjoyed drinking, eating, singing, and dancing, and preferred wearing white clothes. The Koguryŏ people constantly trained for war and loved plunder, but they coexisted peacefully with Puyŏ until Puyŏ attacked Koguryŏ around the time of the birth of Christ. Koguryŏ raided Lelang but was able to survive because of its distance from Chinese concerns.

The Okchŏ and Eastern Ye people in northeastern Korea were protected from predatory invaders by a mountain range that ran along the coast, but they were also kept small and less advanced politically and culturally. They retained elements of Siberian customs, specialized in infantry tactics and archery, and were famous for their bows.

When Wang Mang, the Chinese usurper, overthrew the former Han Dynasty in 9 C.E., he decapitated the Koguryŏ king and reduced Koguryŏ to a marquisate under his command, but Koguryŏ's fortunes were revived in 32 C.E. when Emperor Kuangwu overthrew Wang Mang and founded the Later Han Dynasty. Kuangwu restored the title of king to the Koguryŏ ruler and accepted tribute from him, but he abandoned direct control over Okchŏ and let Koguryŏ exert hegemony over it. In the early second century, however, when Koguryŏ launched a number of attacks against the Han commanderies, Han forces forced them to submit.

Even before the Han Dynasty fell in 220, central control lapsed and the Gongsun family took over the Liaodong commandery. The Gongsun attacked the Koguryŏ capital, took over the Lelang commandery, and in 205 established the new Daifang (Taebang in Korean) commandery south of Lelang in modern Hwanghae province to deal with the Samhan confederation states to the south.

In 220 the Han Dynasty fell and was replaced by the Three Kingdoms in China. The northeastern Chinese state of Wei invaded Koguryŏ territory in 244, captured the Koguryŏ capital, and forced King Tongch'ŏn to take refuge in Okchŏ. Koguryŏ recovered when Wei shifted its attention south to the takeover of Lelang and Daifang.

Wei was replaced by the Jin Dynasty in 265, but when Jin was busy conquering the Wu state in southeast China in 280, the non-Chinese Murong branch of the Xianbei tribes in Manchuria invaded Puyŏ in 286. It resettled thousands of Puyŏ captives in its own territory but shifted its attention elsewhere, enabling the Puyŏ king to move back to his capital.

At the beginning of the fourth century, non-Chinese peoples took over north China. While China was in confusion, King Mich'ŏn of Koguryŏ seized Lelang and Daifang in 313 and 314, respectively, but he made no move to shift his capital south of the Yalu River or consolidate his control over that area. Despite four hundred years of Chinese habitation and culture in those commanderies, the area was stripped of population and left devoid of Chinese influence, but the educated elite either moved south to the Samhan confederation or were absorbed by Koguryŏ.

The South: The Samhan

The three Han confederacies (Samhan) located south of present-day Seoul consisted of seventy-four chiefdoms with a population of about 700,000 in the third century C.E. Mahan was located in the southwest, Chinhan in the southeast, and Pyŏnhan along the southern coast in between the other two. Mahan had a total population of about 500,000 people in the third century and consisted of fifty chiefdoms, and Chinhan and Pyŏnhan had a dozen chiefdoms each. Mahan had the largest chiefdoms, but Chinhan in the southeast remained a cultural backwater except for pockets of educated refugees. The land in the south was extremely fertile, and the economy was based on rice and other grains, supplemented by hunting, gathering, fishing, sericulture, and the weaving of ramie cloth.

Chinese sources in the mid-third century stressed the backwardness of the Samhan region compared to Puyŏ and Koguryŏ because it failed to emphasize Chinese values of status distinctions, respect for age, and male domination of women in marriage and control of the family. Dwellings had thatched roofs and earthen floors, and the people did not understand the value of precious metals like gold and silver or appreciate brocade. Some of the men tattooed their bodies, and the men living in the islands of offshore Mahan wore their hair like the Xianbei tribesmen of Manchuria and ran about half-naked. None of their towns were surrounded by walls as in China.

The Mahan conducted planting and harvest rituals in the fifth and tenth lunar months, and each chiefdom had a religious specialist called the lord of heaven (Ch'ŏn'gun), who offered sacrifice to the spirit of heaven. A special holy place called a *sodo* functioned as a safe refuge for people fleeing punishment. In Chinhan, the people flattened the heads of their babies and tattooed their bodies like the Wa people (in Japan). Warriors fought on foot because there were no horses. The Chinhan used a plucked string instrument like the modern *kayagŭm*. Chinese observers did have a few good things to say about Chinhan, however, because its people observed etiquette and were known for their production of iron and their use of iron currency. Pyŏnhan's customs were similar to those of Chinhan.

Early Chinese accounts claimed that the inhabitants of Japan known as the Wa ("dwarf barbarians") were also living somewhere in the Pyŏnhan confederation along the southern coast, but modern Korean scholars believe that view is inaccurate. Chinese envoys sent from Wei to Japan in 240 reported the existence of a queen named Himiko, and early Japanese accounts claimed she had control of territory in Koya Han (Kaya, modern Kimhae). The early Japanese history, *Nihon shoki* (720), also mentioned that the Japanese empress Jingū, who controlled the Yamato court in Nara, invaded southern Korea in the third century and established a colonial regime over Mimana or Kaya. Modern scholars, however, have rejected that possibility because prior to 645 there was no Yamato state powerful enough on the Japanese islands to have done that.

Within the Mahan and Chinhan confederations were two chiefdoms that later developed into two of the Three Kingdoms: Paekche, located along the Han River where Seoul is today, and Saro (modern Kyŏngju) in the southeast. The Paekche foundation myth claimed that two men named Piryu and Onjo, sons of Chumong, the legendary founder of Koguryŏ, led their people from Koguryŏ to the Han River area, but some modern scholars reject the story and insist that the founders of Paekche around Seoul were the indigenous Yemaek.

Saro was organized around a six-village group around modern Kyŏngju that later became Silla. The mythical founder, Pak Hyŏkkŏse, was supposedly born in 57 C.E., and the villagers made him their *Kŏsŏgan* (king). Each of the six villages had mythical founders with different surnames, indicating that local loyalties to ancestors and place obviated any possible sense of affiliation to a larger "Korean" people and its mythical founder, Tangun.

The first chieftains of Saro were supplied by members of the Pak family, and after that line ran out, members of the Sŏk and Kim families. The term for these secular rulers also changed from *Kŏsŏgan*, to *Nisagŭm*, to *Maripkan*. They were assisted by a shaman or spiritual chief. The descendants of the three royal clans became the ruling class of Silla society, referred to as the True Bones (*chingol*) after 645 C.E., and they married only females of other royal families. No member of the *chingol* could drop to commoner status, except as punishment for criminal action. The status system itself was called the *kolp'um*, or bone rank system of inherited status, which resembled the *kabane* of early Japan, both of which obviously had their roots in Inner Asian or Scytho-Siberian social organization. In the third century, the first signs of bureaucracy

appeared along with a deliberative body called the Namdang (Southern Hall), the formal name for the Hwabaek council of minor chieftains from the six villages that exerted a check on the development of royal power.

THE THREE KINGDOMS (KOGURYŎ, PAEKCHE, AND SILLA) (313–698)

After Koguryŏ took control of Lelang in 313, educated refugees fled south to the Mahan confederation and stimulated the development of the Paekche chiefdom around modern Seoul. The Murong tribes of the former Yan state in north China carried out a devastating invasion and defeat of Koguryŏ in 342. After they withdrew, King Kogugwŏn of Koguryŏ in 352 became a Yan tributary, but he switched his allegiance to the former Qin state (357–385) when its ruler, the proto-Tibetan general Fu Jian, conquered Yan in 370. Puyŏ, unfortunately, did not fare as well and was conquered by the Murong in 356. Blocked by the former Qin in the north, King Sosurim of Koguryŏ launched an attack against Paekche in 371 but suffered a major defeat at Pyongyang and lost his life in the battle.

In the late fourth century Paekche society was dominated by five aristocratic lineages, of which the Chin and Hae were the most influential. King Koi began to incorporate the Mahan chiefs into the Paekche aristocracy, but he left them in control of local districts. To centralize authority, he established the post of chief minister and head of the aristocratic assembly and set up a system of sixteen official ranks.

In 353 King Kŭnch'ogo dispatched district magistrates from the capital to replace some of the fifty local aristocrats called Tamno. He promoted Confucian ideas, ordered the compilation of a historical record, and defeated Koguryŏ in 371, but he did not secure control of the area around Pyongyang. Instead he captured some Silla towns to the east. Paekche lost Pyongyang and fifty-eight districts south of that city to Koguryŏ in 396, but it joined the Wa people living along the southern coast to attack Silla in 399.

In the late fourth century, Paekche and Silla were mentioned for the first time in Chinese records, which also noted that Paekche had established a base just west of the Liao River in southwest Manchuria. Paekche was probably the most important maritime nation in the late fourth century, in contact by sea with both the Chinese Eastern Jin (317–420) and the Song (420–479) dynasties in south China. In 394 King Asin also sent his crown prince as a hostage to Japan to gain military support against pressure from Koguryŏ. Paekche developed a triangular trading, cultural, and military relationship by transmitting Chinese culture and Buddhism to Japan in return for Japanese weapons and military support.

The Introduction of Buddhism

Buddhism was probably introduced to Koguryŏ in the 360s and perhaps a decade later to Paekche. Fu Jian in the former Qin state was an active patron of Buddhism and dispatched two monks to Koguryŏ. Paekche was introduced to Buddhism when a monk arrived by sea from the Chinese Eastern Jin state. In the late fourth century Paekche sent Buddhist monks and two specialists in Confucian learning to Japan with the *Analects* and the *Thousand Character Classic*.

Buddhism addressed the suffering of people in times of distress and offered them the hope of spiritual salvation in the afterlife, as opposed to the more mundane appeals of ethical Confucianism. Koguryŏ and Paekche kings sponsored this transcendent and universal religion as a means of gaining a political edge over the dominant aristocratic families. Silla, isolated to the southeast, did not do so until 150 years later.

Buddhist temples and monasteries located in the mountains provided respite from the bustle and complexity of everyday life. Buddhism appealed to those from all walks of life, regardless of status. It preached commiseration and peace instead of violence and war, although Buddhist monks were mobilized for war to defend the nation despite the admonition against the taking of life and they acted as diplo-

mats in the service of the state. Buddhism also had little effect in breaking down the barriers of inherited status or opposing slavery because slave-owning aristocrats became monks and managers of monasteries. The aristocratic monks were educated in classical Chinese, the Chinese classics and histories, Confucianism, Daoism, and other early Chinese thinkers. Their monasteries welcomed Confucian scholars, who provided an ethical system for individual behavior in this world. Even King Sosurim of Koguryŏ established a school for Confucian studies and adopted a law code modeled after one promulgated by the Chinese state of Jin.

The Mahayana sects of Buddhism asserted that there were people of utmost purity called bodhisattvas who postponed their attainment of nirvana to assist others in their quest for salvation. Some sects held that one might be able to achieve nirvana by faith alone. The worship of the Maitreya Buddha of Mercy (Kwan'ŭm) was established from the outset in Koguryŏ and Paekche, but Buddhism never displaced native beliefs and practices like shamanism, geomancy, the worship of animistic spirits and village guardian deities, fortunetelling, and prophecy.

Koguryŏ Expansion (399–493)

After King Kwanggaet'o (The King Who Expands the Territory) of Koguryŏ defeated Paekche in 396, he attacked the Khitan tribes in northwest Manchuria and the Sukchin (Sushen) in the present-day Russian Maritime Province to the east. He sent an expeditionary force to Silla in the southeast in 399 to drive out invading Paekche and Wa forces, stationed his army in Silla, and enrolled King Namul of Silla as his vassal. Koguryŏ culture also had an increased effect on Japan around 450. (See Chapter 7.)

In 406 King Kwanggaet'o ended his long campaign against the Murong Later Yan state with a peace agreement that required him to provide military aid against the powerful Tuoba Northern Wei state in north China. After 410 he conquered most of the territory in Manchuria and the Maritime Province of Russia. Four years

Map 6.2   **Koguryŏ at Its Largest Extent, Late Fifth Century** C.E.

later his successor erected a famous inscribed stele that recorded all his exploits.

Paekche maintained its alliance with the Wa in the peninsula and on the Japanese islands, but by the mid-fifth century, it lost its base in Manchuria and suffered a Koguryŏ blockade of its ports. It was defeated by Koguryŏ in 475 and withdrew from the Han River south to a new capital at Ungjin on the Kŭm River (modern Kongju). Plagued by internal rivalry between the aristocratic Hae and Chin families, Paekche forged an alliance with Silla against Koguryŏ in

493 that protected both states for over half a century.

Silla and Paekche in the Sixth Century

Silla kings began to expand territory and increase their power over the *chingol* or true bone aristocrats—all men descended from kings. King Chijung (r. 500–513) was the first king to adopt the Chinese-style title of *wang*, and his military commander, Isabu, captured territory north to modern Kangnŭng (east of Seoul) on

Pottery Figure of a Silla Mounted Warrior, Fifth–Sixth century C.E. *(National Museum of Korea)*

Map 6.3 **Silla After Conquest of Han River Region in 552 C.E.**

the eastern shore. The king established the first of what later was to become five small capitals and sent aristocrats and commoners there to populate them and spread Silla culture. King Pŏphŭng (r. 514–540) set up a ministry of war and issued a Chinese-style law code. His general, Sadaham, conquered the chiefdom of Kŭmgwan (modern Kimhae) in the Kaya confederation in 532, and the king incorporated its ruling family into the Silla aristocracy at a low rank. Finally, he established Buddhism as a state-sponsored religion in 527 despite great opposition from the old aristocrats.

King Chinhŭng joined forces with Paekche in 552 to recapture the area around the old Paekche capital on the Han River from Koguryŏ, but he betrayed Paekche by ordering Isabu to take over control of the Han River basin once the fighting started. This gave Silla access to the Yellow Sea and direct maritime contact with China for the first time. This conquest was crucial for Silla because it laid the groundwork for a decisive alliance with China a hundred years later. A decade later, in 562, King Chinhŭng took over the Kaya confederation and

built a number of stone-walled forts on strategic mountains (*sansŏng*) throughout his territory. He placed his conquests under military lords, who ruled over local village lords (*ch'onju*), but in the 570s he began to replace them with commissioners dispatched from the capital.

Chinhŭng engaged in a variety of cultural activities, including the compilation of a history of the Three Kingdoms, construction of Buddhist temples, and initiation of the P'algwanhoe ceremonies of the Eight Vows and the Yŏndŭnghoe Festival of Light, which combined the worship of local deities with Buddhism. He also supported the *hwarang* or flower youth group (*hwarangdo*), which engaged in a number of cultural activities, like poetry and Daoistic nature appreciation for young men. Some of its members later became leading commanders of Silla forces. By 625 several kings created more central government agencies, but local justice was handled by clan chiefs and local magnates.

In Paekche, King Muryŏng (r. 501–523) tried to remedy the loss of the Han River basin by expanding central control over local areas. He established relations with the Liang Dynasty in south China, and took over the state of Tamna on Cheju Island and chiefdoms in the Kaya region. In 538, King Sŏng moved the capital from the hills at Ungjin fifteen miles away to Sabi (Puyŏ city), a central trading center in the alluvial floodplain. He increased the number of local magistrates assigned from the capital and registered households for labor service and tax collection. Nevertheless, he was still restrained by the aristocrats, the "eight great surnames," and his effort to expand eastward was stymied when Silla took over the Kaya confederation in 562.

The Final Struggle and Silla's Victory (581–668)

After the Sui Dynasty reunified China in 589, King Yŏngyang (r. 598–617) of Koguryŏ attacked Sui territory in 598. The first Sui emperor, Wendi, invaded Koguryŏ by land and sea, but he was forced to call off the invasion because of Koguryŏ resistance and bad weather conditions. Wendi's successor, Yangdi, again sent an expedition against Koguryŏ in 612, but that invasion was foiled by the Koguryŏ general, Ŭlchi Mundŏk, in a brilliant victory at the Sal (Ch'ŏngch'ŏn) River. After two more unsuccessful invasions in 613 and 614, Yangdi attempted his last invasion in 617, but this too was abandoned when he was pressed hard in the west by the Turks. Yangdi was assassinated by a courtier in 618, bringing his dynasty to a crashing end, due in part to Koguryŏ resistance.

Koguryŏ earned a fragile reprieve for thirty years after the Tang Dynasty was established in 618 because Tang armies were busy reducing the Turks in the north and west and opening up

China to trade and contact with Inner Asia. During this period the Tang court permitted pilgrimages to India by Buddhist monks from Korea. In 642, however, the powerful Koguryŏ aristocrat, Yŏn Kaesomun, massacred his rivals, killed the king, enthroned the young King Pojang, and secured appointment as *Mangniji* (prime minister). He created a virtual dictatorship that allowed him to prepare the country for the oncoming crisis with Tang power.

Silla underwent a similar process of centralization. Hard pressed by Paekche, Queen Sŏndŏk dispatched Kim Ch'unch'u to Koguryŏ to ask for aid, but King Pojang of Koguryŏ detained him and did not release him until Silla threatened to attack. The queen then asked the Tang emperor, Taizong, to pressure Koguryŏ to cease its attacks against Silla, and Taizong responded by launching an unsuccessful campaign against Koguryŏ in 644. When he also suggested that Silla strengthen itself by replacing Queen Sŏndŏk with a king, Kim Pidam, the *Sangdaedŭng* (chairman) of the Hwabaek council rebelled in 647 to seize power. The queen was saved when the *chingol* Kim Ch'unch'u, his brother-in-law from Kaya, General Kim Yusin, and members of the lesser aristocracy repressed the rebellion. Although Queen Sŏndŏk died during the rebellion, Kim Ch'unch'u helped her successor, Queen Chindŏk, strengthen the centralized bureaucracy against the old aristocrats.

Tang Taizong was still convinced that he could defeat Koguryŏ on his own and dispatched two more unsuccessful expeditions against it in 647 and 648. Kim Ch'unch'u went to China in 648 and asked Emperor Taizong to join with Silla in a joint attack against Paekche as the best method for eliminating Koguryŏ, but Taizong died and his successor, Emperor Gaozong, ignored the advice.

When Queen Chindŏk of Silla died in 654, Kim Ch'unch'u pressured the Hwabaek council to select him as king (King Muyŏl, r. 654–661), and he appointed Kim Yusin Sangdaedŭng of the Hwabaek council. After Emperor Gaozong tried and failed to defeat Koguryŏ in 658, he finally agreed to King Muyŏl's strategy and joined Silla forces to defeat Paekche in 660.

Gaozong set up five military commands to administer Paekche territory rather than turn the area over to Silla, but Muyŏl's successor, King Munmu, swallowed the insult to Silla's interests to pursue the greater goal of eliminating Koguryŏ. Fate turned in Silla's favor when Yŏn Kaesomun of Koguryŏ passed away in 666, and a struggle for succession broke out among his sons. Weakened by internal strife, Koguryŏ finally fell to the invading Tang and Silla forces in 668.

Curiously, the Chinese government has recently claimed (in 2004) that Koguryŏ was part of Chinese, not Korean, history. The account provided here should demonstrate that although Koguryŏ borrowed a number of elements of Chinese culture, it was a powerful and independent state that had hostile relations with China for most of its history.

Despite Koguryŏ's reputation for pugnacity, the fascinating paintings on many of its tombs, absent from the tombs of Silla and Paekche, revealed the development of a high culture. Kings lived in wooden palaces, and aristocrats lived in sumptuous houses built of wood in Chinese style with vaulted roofs and elaborate multicolored decorations on support posts. They and their wives were garbed in elaborate and colorful clothing and were served by slaves and servants. The men were mounted warriors and skilled archers. They rode their horses to hunting expeditions for deer and tigers. Their kings conducted colorful progresses (formal visits with full entourage to the countryside) with a full panoply of mounted guards and chariots with military banners waving in the breeze. Commoners lived in single- or double-storied houses with partly covered kitchens with big pots on stoves that led to ondol flues under the internal rooms. The commoner men engaged in wrestling matches, while women entertained kings and nobles in dance troupes wearing polka-dotted robes with elongated sleeves that they waved in circles in the air. Their artists used Tang conventions for landscapes. They painted polychrome pictures of figures and animals and magnificent examples of phoenixes and inter-

twined snakes and turtles that were symbolic of the four points of the compass associated with the five phases (*wuxing*) theory of the Chinese Han Dynasty. (See Color Plates 8 and 9.) The fall of that dynasty was as serious a loss to the cultural heritage of the Korean people as the fall of Paekche.

Modern Korean nationalists have bemoaned the defeat of Koguryŏ because it was the most militant and independent of all the three kingdoms. They argued that had Koguryŏ been victorious against Silla, its hostility to China would have meant the preservation of a native culture against the onslaught of Chinese thought and institutions for the next fifteen hundred years. In the mid-seventh century, however, Silla's diplomacy trumped Koguryŏ's militant independence as the way for a small nation to survive in the face of a huge and powerful neighbor.

Silla's policy, however, was not confined to subservience because King Munmu organized a coalition of forces from his defeated enemies from Paekche and Koguryŏ to help drive the Chinese from the peninsula by 676. Of course, Tang ambitions might not have been thwarted had it desired to conquer Silla outright rather than shift its attention elsewhere. Relations with Tang were severed until the beginning of the eighth century, and after that time Silla was protected from foreign invasion by the Tang Empire.

PARHAE

The foundation of the state of Parhae (Bohai in Chinese) in eastern Manchuria after the fall of Koguryŏ has given rise to much debate over whether it was a Malgal (Mohe in Chinese) or Koguryŏ state. When Koguryŏ fell in 668, it had a population of about 3.5 million people, but after 668 the Chinese forced about 200,000 people, including the Malgal minority, to migrate westward from Koguryŏ to Tang territory, and many others took refuge in Silla and elsewhere. Tae Choyŏng, a third-generation Malgal commander in the old Koguryŏ army, then led a group of Malgal back to a relatively uninhabited

Map 6.4   **Parhae, Silla, and Tang China, Eighth–Ninth Centuries**

ety because his father and grandfather had also served in the Koguryŏ army, but it is doubtful that they lost their ethnic identity because they were probably commanders of a Malgal contingent. About half of the 211 Parhae leaders known to history were members of the Tae family, and most of the rest were from the Ko (Gao in Chinese) family, which meant they could have been either relatives of the Koguryŏ royal house or ordinary Chinese. Other ethnic groups in the population were Wuji, Khitan, and Turks. The cultural artifacts and wall paintings of Parhae tombs do indicate a continuation of Koguryŏ styles in some cases, but most pictures of formal dress appear closer to Tang styles.

After 698, the Jin rulers used the name Koguryŏ (or Koryŏ) in its relations with foreign countries, but they kept Jin as the name of the dynasty. The Tang court adopted a conciliatory policy toward the Jin Dynasty in 705 to prevent it from allying with the Turks, recognized Tae Choyŏng as "king of the commandery of Parhae," and referred to Parhae as a Malgal state. Tae Choyŏng changed the name of his kingdom to Parhae in 706 and began a very active diplomatic relationship with Tang, a significant departure from Koguryŏ's hostility against Tang China.

Parhae territory extended south of the Sungari River and included the present Maritime Province in Siberia and territory in northeast Korea slightly north of Hamhŭng. Parhae relations with Tang turned sour in 719 when it abandoned the Tang year period. When Emperor Xuanzong of Tang challenged Parhae in 726 by granting a title to the chief of the Amur River Malgal, a tribe that resisted Parhae rule, King Mu (Wu in Chinese) of Parhae concluded a defensive alliance with Japan and attacked Tang territory on the Shandong peninsula in 732. Silla assisted the Chinese by attacking Parhae territory in northeast Korea in 733, but that expedition failed miserably and fouled Silla's relations with Parhae until the latter's relations with Tang improved in 764. (For more about Parhae, which lasted until 926, see Chapter 9.) In short, Parhae seems to have been a

area in central Manchuria, where the Wuji, other ethnic groups, and Koguryŏ survivors lived. He defeated pursuing Tang forces and moved his people eastward to the territory of the old Ilou people near the modern Russian Maritime Province in Siberia and established the state of Jin in 698. At that time the population of Jin was only 400,000 because of the exodus of the old Koguryŏ population. Jin formed ties with the eastern Turks and obtained Silla's promise not to join Tang forces in an attack against it.

Some Korean scholars suggest that Tae had become a naturalized member of Koguryŏ socimultiethnic Malgal Dynasty with a large ex-Koguryŏ minority population and a culture that owed much to both Koguryŏ and Tang.

SILLA DOMINATION OF THE PENINSULA (668–892)

After Silla drove out Tang forces in 676, the government had to consolidate its power over opposition from malcontents. It repressed an uprising by Koguryŏ refugees led by one of the clansmen of the Koguryŏ nobility, Ko Ansŭng, in 684 and took back the territory granted to them for their residence. It established a national academy (Kukhak) for training men for appointment to office. It also granted prebendal "feeding areas (sig'ŭp)" and "salary areas (nog'ŭp)" to war heroes and important civil and military officials. Prebends differed from feudal fiefs: the recipients, rather than the state, had the right to collect the land tax but without controlling the population, but in 689 the state cancelled the nog'ŭp and replaced them with outright salaries to officials.

New Bureaucratic Developments

Influenced partly by the Tang bureaucratic model, Silla kings expanded the centralized bureaucracy by establishing agencies to control Buddhist temples and monasteries, the National Academy devoted to Confucian learning, rites, music, and post stations with horses to speed the transportation of officials and communication of official messages. They also created a board of academicians to promote Confucian learning and appointed specialists in medicine, law, mathematics or calculations, astronomy, and water clocks (a mechanical device to measure time by controlling the flow of water).

The kings contributed funds to Buddhist monks and monasteries. One of the greatest monks in Korean history is Ŭich'ŏn whose writings attempted to explain Buddhist works and teachings (see **Documents: The Buddhist Monk Ŭich'ŏn**). Silla monks traveled to China and

India, Silla military officers enrolled in Tang armies, and Silla scholars competed successfully in the Tang examination system and were appointed to civil office in China (see **Biography: Ch'oe Ch'iwŏn**). Yet when they returned home, they found it difficult to crack the upper ranks of the bureaucracy.

The capital at Kyŏngju was laid out in checkerboard fashion like a miniature of the Tang capital at Chang'an. In 685 King Sinmun divided the country into nine prefectures that were subdivided into two hundred superior districts with control over three hundred ordinary districts. Magistrates were now dispatched from the capital, but all were members of the chingol aristocracy. Reluctant to move the capital to a more central area because of the resistance of the Kyŏngju aristocrats, the government established five small capitals in addition to the main one at Kyŏngju by 680, and sent members of the aristocracy there to reside and spread Silla culture throughout the conquered territories. The small capitals, however, did not flourish as expected because of the extraordinary attachment of the Silla elite to the cultural and political attractions of the capital at Kyŏngju. Silla also required powerful local clerks (hyangni) to send a family member to the capital as a hostage (sangsuri) to guarantee their loyalty, a method that would not have been necessary had Silla been able to establish control through central magistrates.

The Silla army consisted of nine units called "oath banners" (sŏdang), only three of which were Silla soldiers. The other banners included one for Paekche men, one for Paekche rebels against the Tang, one for Koguryŏ troops, and two separate ones for the followers of the Koguryŏ prince, Ko Ansŭng. Enrolling ethnic groups separately was a sign of the difficulties of assimilation. Compulsory military service was required for the common peasants from the age of sixteen to sixty, but they served in village military units (pŏptang) under the command of the ch'ŏnju or village lord rather than commanders dispatched from the capital. In any case, a strong national army was no longer necessary under the umbrella of Tang military force.

DOCUMENTS

The Buddhist Monk Ŭich'ŏn

The following text is Ŭich'ŏn of Silla's explication of the "Adamantine Absorption Scripture" (late seventh century).

Ŭich'ŏn was one of the greatest monks of Korean history, and his brief discussion here illustrates two important points about Buddhism. The first is that "the mind that contemplates" will hinder the Buddhist adept's ability to achieve nirvana because a contemplating mind will think that riches and fame are real and have value when, in fact, both are ephemeral, temporary, and unreal. The second point is that not everyone can afford the time to retreat to mountain monasteries to practice contemplation in silence to clear their minds of attachments to achieve nirvana. In such a case, they should still live in the world and do their best to live a moral life to build good karma (a favorable balance sheet of good deeds) in this life to achieve a higher level of existence in the next life.

The beginningless churnings of all deluded thoughts ordinarily result from nothing more than the affliction of discrimination, which derives from clinging to signs. Now, wishing to reverse this churning in order to return to the fountainhead, one must first negate all these signs. It is for this reason that the scripture first explains the contemplation of the signless dharma.

But while all these signs may have been annihilated, if one conserves the mind that contemplates, then the mind that contemplates will continue to arise, and one will not experience original enlightenment. Consequently, one must annihilate the arising of the mind. . . . Once one's practice produces nothing, one then experiences original enlightenment. Drawing from this experi-ence, one transforms beings and prompts them to gain the original inspiration. . . .

Who among human beings would not wish to enter the mountains and cultivate the path? But fettered by lust and desires, no one proceeds. But even though people do not return to mountain fastnesses to cultivate the mind, as far as they are able they should not abandon wholesome practices. Those who can abandon their own sensual pleasures will be venerated like the saints. Those who practice what is difficult to practice will be revered like buddhas.

Source: Robert Buswell, trans., in Peter Lee, ed., *Sources of Korean Tradition* (New York: Columbia University Press, 1997), p. 86.

Social Conventions

Despite the strong influence of Tang culture, Silla culture remained independent in many ways. There is little evidence to indicate that Silla borrowed the Tang equal-field system based on state ownership of land and distribution of land to peasant families on a rotating basis according to the age and sex of each member of the family. Extant household registers indicated that parcels of land were "received" by households, but that term could have been a formality indicating the king's eminent domain over private property rather than state owner-

BIOGRAPHY Ch'oe Ch'iwŏn

Ch'oe Ch'iwŏn was one of the most celebrated scholar-officials of the Silla Dynasty. Born in the Silla capital Kyŏngju in 857 C.E., a period of confusion and decline in Silla, he received an extensive education in classical Chinese, the Confucian classics, Chinese histories, and Chinese poetry during his youth. When he was twelve, his father shipped him off to Tang China with a half-threat: "If you cannot pass the examination in ten years, you are not a worthy son of mine. Go and study hard!" Once in China, he took his father's words to heart.

At the relatively young age of eighteen (873), he passed the guest tribute examination for foreigners in the Tang civil service examinations on his first attempt, one of fifty-eight Koreans who were able to do that. He was also one of the dozen of that group appointed to a post in China, chief of personnel in Liaoxui county. Later he was granted the title of Gentleman for Rendering Service and General Purpose Censor, Auxiliary, a fancy title for someone waiting for an official appointment but performing duties on the job without receiving all the benefits. In 879 he was secretary for Gao Pian, who led an army to suppress the great Huang Chao rebellion. He drafted manifestos pasted on walls condemning the rebels, for which he gained a reputation of great literary skill by stirring up the emotions of the people. While in China, he also submitted an important memorial to the court describing the founding of the Parhae Dynasty in 698.

At the age of twenty-eight, in 885, he expressed a desire to return to Silla. When Emperor Xizong heard of it, he honored him by sending him to the Silla capital as an envoy with an imperial edict. After his return, he was appointed reader in attendance, Hallim academician, and vice minister of war. He was also appointed envoy to China in 893 but was unable to go because Kyŏn Hwŏn and Kungye had risen in rebellion against the Silla throne, and bandits and rebels were overrunning the roads.

In 894 he submitted a famous memorial to Queen Chinsŏng with recommendations for saving the country from disaster, but it was a vain effort in a hopeless situation. He became magistrate of Taesan prefecture in Ch'ungch'ŏng province, but gave up his official position and spent his time wandering around the countryside and devoting his time to poetry. He finally ended up in the Haeinsa monastery in Hyŏnch'ŏn in South Chŏlla province, where he ended his days. Only a few of his writings remain extant.

---

ship. Because there were also parcels of public or state-owned land and prebendal allotments to local and central government officials in every village, it appears that the state did not own all the land in the kingdom.

Some of the *chingol* aristocrats in the capital at Kyŏngju possessed several thousand slaves each, thanks to prisoners of war captured in Silla's victories over rivals. Nevertheless, the few extant village registers indicate that slaves were only about 5 percent of the village population, a situation that changed in the next dynasty. Silla also had special districts called either *hyang*, *pugok*, *so*, or *sŏng*, that were populated by people of inferior social status—below that of commoners but above that of slaves.

Silla had a system of marriage that differed markedly from Koguryŏ and Paekche, but it changed over time. Because information about commoner marriages is sparse, what we know is based on royal marriages. The first eight kings (the dating of which is unreliable) came from the Pak lineage and all queens from the Kim lineage, and the ninth through sixteenth kings to 356 C.E. came from the Sŏk family with queens supplied mostly by the Kim family and some from the Pak. This marriage practice has been labeled the double-descent system.

From 356 through Queen Chindŏk's reign to 654, all kings were members of the Kim lineage, and all the queens came from the Pak family. There was a special feature by which Kim and Pak families exchanged daughters when marriages were contracted, a system of cross-cousin marriage. On a couple of occasions, men ended up marrying their nieces or aunts.

Since King Chinp'yŏng had no sons, one of his daughters became Queen Sŏndŏk (r. 632–647), and the next ruler was a cousin of Queen Sŏndŏk, Queen Chindŏk (r. 647–654), the daughter of King Chinp'yŏng's brother. King Muryŏl (Kim Ch'unch'u, r. 654–661), the man responsible for the conquest of Paekche, was the cousin of these two queens and the son of King Chinp'yŏng's daughter who had been given in marriage to Chinp'yŏng's cousin, and he succeeded Queen Chindŏk. These two women became queens not just because there were no princes available, but because of the high status of the matrilineal line of descent among the wives and daughters of the Kim family kings.

King Muryŏl broke this pattern by marrying the daughter of Kim Yusin, the minor nobleman from the conquered Kŭmgwan Kaya state and leading warrior of the time. Thereafter, the royal succession followed the patrilineal descent pattern in the Kim family. Only in the last stage of the dynasty after 780 was this pattern interrupted by struggles for power within the royal family. When a king died without an heir, there were occasions when a son-in-law or the son of a princess was chosen to be king, reflecting a vestige of the high status shown to elite women in Silla. Cross-cousin marriage that cut across generations violated Chinese taboos, but it also served to bind the consort families closely with the royal line as well as separating their other relatives (the *chin'gol* aristocrats) from the rest of the population.

The Silla aristocrats were far more exclusive than the great families of Tang. The examination system based on the Chinese classics and histories had been established in the Sui Dynasty and was carried over into Tang times to provide an impersonal system of recruitment, but the examinations did not destroy the Tang aristocratic families because they devoted their resources to educating their sons. The introduction of examinations based on the Confucian classics in Silla in 788, however, was only a minor reform and had no effect on weakening the restriction of office-holding to the aristocrats. The state also established strict sumptuary regulations graded by the rank and status of individuals over the size of homes, the type of dress worn, and the right to ride a horse or travel in a palanquin.

New Sects of Buddhism and Culture

After 668 Silla monks traveled to China and brought back many Buddhist sects, including the Vinaya, Nirvana, Dharma Nature (Pŏpsŏng), and Yogacara (Pŏpsang) sects, but the most popular was the Hwaŏm (Huayan in Chinese) sect based on the Avatamsaka or Flower Garland sutra founded by the monk Ŭisang (625–702). Ŭisang had studied in Tang China and wrote a famous exposition of the creed in 661 that became the foundation for the scholastic or textual wing of Buddhism in Korea. Hwaŏm's main doctrine was that all noumena (dharmas, or ideas in the mind) and all phenomena (objects of sense experience) were mutually interrelated and yet transitory and unreal. If one could only realize this, it would be possible to free oneself from the desire for wealth, power, and sex that kept one bound to the world of suffering and attain salvation (nirvana). Hwaŏm Buddhism was also tolerant of other teachings and incorporated elements of the Samnon (Three Treatise), Ch'ŏndae (Tiantai), and meditation or Sŏn (Chan in Chinese, Zen in Japanese) sects, but it also proclaimed that it represented the highest level of enlightenment of all the schools.

The monk Wŏnhyo (617–686) founded the Dharma-nature (Pŏpsŏng) sect. He traveled to Tang in 650 and influenced the Tang monk Fazang and the Chinese Flower Garland sect. He struggled to bring all sects together in ecumenical unity to counter the divisiveness that had occurred in China. He also spread the Buddhist message to the people of the lowest status to alleviate their suffering under the Silla aristocrats. These people lacked the wealth, leisure, and education for the pursuit of esoteric knowledge and meditation, but they could appeal to the panoply of Buddhist images for solace and support against the hardships of life.

The Sŏn or meditation sect of Buddhism was supposedly introduced by the monk Pŏmnang after his return from China in the mid-seventh century. The sect stressed the importance of intuitive enlightenment through meditation over textual or scriptural learning, and by the ninth century nine mountain sects of Sŏn had been established. The Silla Sŏn sect followed the gradual enlightenment approach of the Chinese Northern school until the monk Toŭi introduced the sudden enlightenment doctrine of the Chinese Southern school. That sect launched an attack against the textual and intellectual approaches to enlightenment of Hwaŏm and the other schools. When the curtain was lowered on the Silla Dynasty, the split between the textual and intuitional orientation in Silla Buddhism remained unresolved. Nonetheless, Buddhism contributed to self-effacing and tolerant ideals that transcended the narrowness of national interest and the self-righteousness of the Confucian revival in the subsequent Chosŏn Dynasty.

Buddhist iconography inspired much representational art in painting and sculpture. In addition to the rock-cut temple of Sŏkkuram and the monastery of Pulguksa built in 751 (see **Material Culture: Buddhist Sculpture**), Buddhist images of bronze and gold, magnificent crowns, earrings, necklaces, bracelets, belts, and other gold paraphernalia left in the many earthen tomb mounds in Kyŏngju, and the ruins of palaces, palisades, and artificial ponds created for the indulgence of the leisured Kyŏngju aristocracy testified to the wealth, luxury, and culture that was both the glory and the bane of the Silla Dynasty. The dazzling gold crowns of Silla kings were one sign of the splendor of the capital. (See Color Plate 10.)

In the secular realm, Silla underwent three outside cultural influences in order. The first was Koguryŏ culture as a result of the Koguryŏ military occupation in the early fifth century. After relations turned hostile, Silla was influenced by the culture of the Chinese dynasties in south China transmitted through Paekche. In the sixth century, direct contact with China was reflected in the compilation of a Silla history in 545 (no longer extant), and expansion of the use of Chinese ideographs and *idu*, a language with a special vocabulary that was systematized by the scholar Sŏl Ch'ŏng around 694. *Idu* was written with ideographs for their pronunciation value rather than their meaning (a system called *hyangch'al*), and *idu* words were inserted among the ideographs to indicate particles and conjugations of verbs in Korean to ease comprehension. *Idu* was continued by clerks through the Chosŏn Dynasty as a convenient transcription system.

Poetry was a favorite pastime of the Silla elite from early times. Two of the few early poems remaining were addressed to a turtle, perhaps a spirit or totem, warning it to remain hidden. One type of poem was called "native songs" (*Saenaennorae*). They are short poems in which one author laments the neglect of his master or ruler, a cuckolded husband is shocked when he returns home to find two pairs of legs in his bed, one monk prays to the Amida Buddha that he might be reborn in the Pure Land, and Master Wŏlmyŏng laments the end of autumn (written ca. 763 C.E.):

> We know not where we go,
> Leaves blown, scattered,
> Though fallen from the same tree,
> By the first winds of autumn.[1]

---

1. Peter Lee, *Korean Literature: Topics and Themes*, p. 9.

MATERIAL CULTURE

Buddhist Sculpture

In 751 the famous rock-cut temple of Sŏkkuram near Kyŏngju and the monastery of Pulguksa (Monastery of the Buddhist State) were built. The Sŏkkuram was a cave carved out of a mountain in Kyŏngju with the sculpture of a seated Sakyamuni Buddha surrounded by bas-reliefs of eleven Maitreya Buddhas (*kwan'ŭm*), eleven Lohan (disciples of Buddha), four bodhisattvas, and four guardian deities at the entrance. The organization was inspired by the stupa mound in India around a central axis that connected heaven and earth. The Buddhist devotee would walk around the mound from left to right as part of his devotion. Rock-cut temples with stone pillars resembling wood in central Asia and northwest China had a circular pathway around a seated Buddha. The Sŏkkuram was much smaller than the Chinese examples, but the sculpture of the enlightened Buddha and the bas-reliefs of bodhisattvas surrounding him are refined examples of the sculptor's art.

The Pulguksa was a magnificent edifice of stone and wood containing a lecture hall, places of worship, a pagoda, and quarters for the monks. The pagodas in Korea, modeled after early Chinese military turrets and usually used as reliquaries of bones of enlightened ones of the past, were mostly made of stone rather than wood. Pulguksa was only one of many temples built in the area.

Stone Pagoda at Pulguksa. Silla dynasty, 8th century. *(Corbis)*

Seated Stone Buddha with Bas-Relief Figures. Silla Dynasty, 8th century, Sŏkkuram rock-cut temple near Kyŏngju. *(Han of Han Yong'u, Tasi ch'annuin uri yoksa [Our History, Rediscovered, Volume 5, Buddhist images, p. 6])*

Silla's Decline (700–892)

The *chingol* aristocrats who traced their ancestry to earlier kings were potential rivals for the throne; they were kept in check only by their reluctance to usurp the throne by violence. The bureaucracy was headed by a prime minister (*sijung*), but he was also a *chingol* aristocrat. The Sangdaedŭng, the chairman of the aristocratic Hwabaek council, was selected by the aristocrats in the council, and he held his position for the life of the king. As a sign of their power, the aristocrats forced King Kyŏngdŏk in 745 to restore the *nog'ŭp* system of prebends to high-ranking officials in addition to their salaries.

Beginning in 780 political stability spiraled downward almost without interruption as the *chingol* turned against the royal family in a series of murders, attempted coups d'état, and usurpations. The first of four rebellions led by *chingol* broke out in the reign of the child king Hyegong (r. 765–780), and the last one in 777 put an end to the line descended from King Muyŏl (d. 661). Kim Yangsang, the Sangdaedŭng, took over the throne himself as King Sŏndŏk (r. 780–785) in defiance of the will of the Hwabaek council. The throne was now a football for any aristocrat with the will and fortitude to grab it.

The weakening of local control was made manifest when Kim Hŏnch'ang, a local prefect, rebelled in 822, proclaimed a new Ch'ang'an (Long Life) Dynasty, and seized four of the nine prefectures and three of the five small capitals before he was defeated and executed along with 239 aristocrats who had joined the rebellion. This rebellion was a result of the fascination of the *chingol* with the cultural attractions of the lavish culture of the capital at Kyŏngju in the southeast and the officials' resentment at being posted to the nether regions. In 828 King Hŭngdŏk tried to remedy the situation by appointing an outsider, Chang Pogo, to take charge of a new naval garrison at Ch'ŏnghae (Wando, or Wan Island) to eliminate pirates.

Chang was a commoner merchant prince who became a virtual tsar of the seas for Silla, dominating the trade and transportation routes between Japan, Korea, and China. He made the mistake of shocking the capital aristocrats in 845 when he offered his daughter to King Munsŏng for his second queen. They were so incensed at the prospect of a marriage between the king and a commoner that they blocked the marriage. He rebelled in 846 as the only way to save himself from his enemies in Kyŏngju, but he was murdered by an assassin sent by King Munsŏng. His base at Ch'ŏnghae was destroyed in 851, marking the end of Silla maritime predominance.

A precarious domestic peace was maintained for the next forty years, but the security afforded Silla by Tang power began to evaporate after the An Lushan rebellion of 756 in China. In 819 Silla's relations with Parhae were disrupted when King Hŏndŏk responded to a Tang request to dispatch thirty thousand troops to attack Parhae. When the expedition failed, he had to build a long wall along the border in the northeast in 826. In China the Huang Chao rebellion from 874 to 884 initiated a rapid decline there that led to the collapse of the Tang Dynasty in 907.

Sometime in the ninth century, the bone rank system was expanded in Silla by instituting new head ranks (*tup'um*) as a sop to lower aristocrats, but because only men assigned the sixth and highest head rank (*yuktup'um*) were allowed to hold lower-ranking posts without a chance for further promotion, the reform caused much discontent among them. Many of them were the first to move to the new Koryŏ Dynasty capital in Kaesŏng after Silla's collapse in 935 to seek higher posts in the new regime.

The death knell of the Silla Dynasty was sounded in the reign of Queen Chinsŏng (r. 887–897), whose heavy taxes spawned an uprising in the northwest in 891. That rebellion began a forty-four year struggle for power in the provinces that brought the Silla Dynasty to an end.

SUMMARY

Politically the ancestors of the Korean people had come a long way from the small chiefdoms to the larger Three Kingdoms with kings and centralized bureaucracies, but absolute kingship was blocked by aristocratic power in each of them, yet they were able to maintain their own independence. By the seventh century, all of them had adopted Buddhism, Confucianism, and other teachings from China, which they fused with native religious beliefs. The reestablishment of empire in China in that century seriously disturbed the balance of power in Korea, and Silla, the country that lagged behind culturally, was able to succeed in defeating its enemies because its diplomatic alliance with Tang China overcame Koguryŏ's military superiority.

Under the Tang peace, Silla gradually absorbed its former enemies and flourished culturally, perhaps too much so since the cultural center at Kyŏngju detracted from the maintenance of local control and the rigid concentration of power in the Kyŏngju aristocracy left the majority of the population uncared for. When the solidarity of the aristocrats began to crack because of internal strife, it proved impossible to correct, and yet Silla had survived for nine hundred years.

SUGGESTED READING

The following titles offer good coverage of Korea's prehistory: G. L. Barnes, *China Korea and Japan: The Rise of Civilization in East Asia* (1993); J.-J. H. Kim, *The Prehistory of Korea* (1978); S. M. Nelson, *The Archaeology of Korea* (1993); and H. I. Pai, *Constructing "Korean" Origins* (2000).

R. A. Miller, "Some Old Paekche Fragments," *Journal of Korean Studies* (1979), is a major study of Paekche language by the rigorous use of linguistic methods.

For early relations with Japan, see W. T. Hong, *Paekche of Korea and the Origin of Yamato Japan* (1995); G. Ledyard, "Galloping Along with the Horseriders: Looking for the Founders of Japan," *Journal of Japanese Studies* 1, no. 2 (1975); and W. Edwards, "Event and Process in the Founding of Japan: The Horserider Theory in Archaeological Perspective," *Journal of Japanese Studies* 9, no. 2 (1983).

For valuable studies of the Three Kingdoms, see J. W. Best, "Diplomatic and Cultural Contacts Between Paekche and China," *Harvard Journal of Asiatic Studies* 42, no. 2 (1982); K. J. H. Gardiner, *The Early History of Korea* (1969); J. Jamieson, "The Samguk Sagi and the Unification Wars," Ph.D. dissertation, University of California; E. Reischauer, *Ennin's Travels in T'ang China* (1955); and R. Rutt, "The Flower Boys of Silla," *Transactions of the Korea Branch of the Royal Asiatic Society* 38 (1963).

R. E. Buswell, Jr., is a world-class scholar of Buddhism. See his valuable *The Formation of Ch'an Ideology* (1989). Also see P. H. Lee. "Fa-tsang and Uisang," *Journal of the American Oriental Society* 82, no. 1 (1962).

P. Lee, ed., *Sourcebook of Korean Civilization*, vol. 1 (1993), and *Sources of Korean Tradition*, vol. 1 (1997), are excellent sources for cultural topics.

Early State and Society in Japan (to 794)

The earliest human inhabitants of the seven thousand islands now known as Japan probably arrived from Micronesia or Southeast Asia over twenty thousand years ago. They would have moved up the Ryukyu island chain in the East China Sea to subtropical Kyushu and then to the more temperate zones of Shikoku and Honshu. In shallow bays, they collected shellfish and seaweed. Only a few hunters penetrated the volcanic mountains covered with forests that comprise over 80 percent of Japan's landmass in search of monkeys, deer, birds, and wild boar. The severe winters in northern Honshu and Hokkaido limited access to bear and otter hunters and salmon fishers. Archaeologists estimate the population at between 120,000 and 350,000. They have labeled the decorated clay pots that appeared around 10,000 B.C.E. and the culture that produced them Jōmon. (See **Connections: The Prehistory of East Asia.**) Starting around 500 B.C.E., the Jōmon hunter-gatherers had to compete with new arrivals from northeast Asia who introduced rice growing and metallurgy in river basins. Jōmon people disappeared from western Honshu around 200 B.C.E., replaced by the agriculturally based Yayoi culture that maintained prolonged contact with the continent. By the end of the Yayoi era in approximately 300 C.E., the population had risen to between 1.5 and 4.5 million. Agriculture demanded complex social organization and generated a surplus that could be used to differentiate soldiers, rulers, artisans, and priests from full-time cultivators. Role specialization led to hereditary social classes and inequality.

Archaeologists and historians debate the stages in the process of state formation. What role did connections from the continent play? Where were the early states located, what kind of leadership did they have, and how did they expand and coalesce? What kind of impact did Chinese civilization have on elite life, and how did the introduction of Buddhism change religious beliefs and practices?

THE GEOGRAPHY OF THE JAPANESE ARCHIPELAGO

Geographic features shaped the development of Japanese civilization. The earliest centers of human habitation arose on the fertile plains of southwestern Japan bordering on the relatively placid Inland Sea that later facilitated communications and trade. Protected by a spine of mountains, the Inland Sea basin usually enjoys mild winters, monsoon rains at the height of the growing season, and hot, dry days before the harvests. Later in the fall, typhoons provide moisture for winter crops. Occasionally the monsoon does not arrive, or typhoons come too early and devastate nearly ripe crops.

Other regions suffer more extreme conditions. Winter winds from Siberia blow across the Japan Sea, depositing snow six feet or deeper on plains and mountains. Melted snow cascades down short, fast-flowing streams. Although alluvial deltas acquired the fine soil necessary for agriculture, floods carry rocks and other debris tumbling down the mountains to damage fields. Rapids make navigating rivers treacherous, and only a few could support rafts and small boats for any distance. River mouths and innumerable small bays provide harbor for coastal vessels manned by fishers, smugglers, or pirates. Even whalers tended to stick close to shore.

The islands of what is now called Japan lost their land bridge to the Asian continent some fifteen thousand years ago, but the sea continued to permit access. Although visitors from across the vast Pacific had to wait until the sixteenth century, contact with Asia came via the Tsushima Strait, across the Japan Sea, and down the Kamchatka Peninsula, the Kurile islands and Sakhalin to Hokkaido. Each route had its own

character. The northern route brought pelts and marine products; the Tsushima Straits provided a bridge for agriculture and civilization. (See Map 7.1.)

EARLY KINGSHIP

The earliest written records of rule are found in Chinese sources. The Han court received emissaries from small kingdoms, probably in Kyushu, in 57 and 107 C.E. In 239, a queen called Himiko sent a tribute mission to the kingdom of Wei. She dominated an alliance of thirty chieftains and lived in a palace fortified by walls with watchtowers and guardhouses. She rarely appeared in public; instead her brother, the only person to see her except for servants, conveyed her commands and prophesies to the people outside the gates. Her subjects trembled before her because they believed she had the power to communicate directly with the gods. When she died, over one hundred attendants of both sexes were buried with her in a giant tomb. Archaeologists debate whether her kingdom of Yamatai existed in Kyushu or in western Japan near present-day Kyoto. Equally problematic is the relationship between brother and sister. Should Himiko be seen not as a queen but as a priestess or shaman whose brother did the work of rule?

During this time, rulers frequently came in male-female pairs. As on the Korean peninsula, kinship was reckoned bilaterally. Important men had four or five wives. Children stayed with their mothers for an indefinite period before moving in with their father, and they relied on both their mothers' and fathers' kin for aid and support. Husbands and wives maintained their own establishments, held property separately, and decided how to divide it among their heirs independently. Sibling rivalry made succession disputes inevitable.

Chinese sources note that warfare was endemic. We can suppose that Himiko sent her tribute mission to China to acquire advanced military technology and the prestige of validation by the Wei court. After her death, the chief-

Map 7.1 **Islands of Japan**

tains who had supported her refused to accept a male as their ruler and fought among themselves until they agreed on a young girl to become queen. The remains of fortified hamlets perched high above agricultural plains and the discovery of a formidable array of weaponry indicate that the struggle for paramountcy was more military than political. There must have been several confederacies of chieftains, of whom the Chinese knew but one.

Pseudo-kinship relations structured hamlet life. Each had a chieftain in charge of communication with the gods and relations with the out-side world. Members of his extended family all claimed descent from a common ancestor, no matter how distant. Their economic foundation rested on dependents who performed the work of cultivation, weaving, pottery, and fishing. When one hamlet fought another, warriors seized goods and turned the vanquished into slaves. Slaves could be traded between houses as a form of currency; tribute missions sometimes carried slaves to China.

The first Japanese historians writing five centuries later struggled to fit early Japanese rulers such as Himiko into a single patrilineage. They claimed that Japan had but one ruling family descended from the sun goddess, Amaterasu, who decreed that her descendant Jimmu was to rule over the land. Aided by his divine ancestress, Jimmu led an expedition eastward to Yamato on the Kinai plain. The histories incorporate a number of myth cycles, suggesting that in addition to the Yamato line that claimed the sun goddess as its tutelary deity, other lineages had deities who at one time had rivaled Amaterasu in importance. Historians today have identified at least four breaks in the Yamato line. When the current emperor recently acknowledged a special feeling of closeness with the Korean people because the mother of his ancestor Kanmu (736–806) was Korean, he alluded to a connection with the Korean peninsula that modern historians have only recently appreciated.

The Korea Connection

Twentieth-century Japanese nationalists preferred to stress the sinitic origins of the cultural artifacts from agriculture to written language that came from the Asian continent, rather than the role by people on the Korean peninsula who modified and transmitted them. Chinese military expansion pushed refugees into the peninsula now known as Korea. Conflicts between polities there, some of which allied with polities in Japan, sent migrants across the Tsushima Strait in three waves that began in the early fifth century and ended in the seventh. Seafarers plied the coasts of Korea and Japan, sometimes launching pirate raids into the interior. The immigrants first settled along the western coast of Honshu and the northern end of Kyushu, then accepted the Yamato ruler's invitation to colonize the Kinai heartland. Historians debate whether the immigrants became assimilated into the indigenous population or whether they took over.

The immigrants brought an Altaic language from northeast Asia that is the ancestor of modern Japanese. In addition to rice, they brought bronze bells, swords, and halberds for rituals as well as wheel-thrown, kiln-fired pottery and stoves. The crossbow and iron used for swords, armor, helmets, and plows originated on the Korean peninsula. The Jōmon people had used horses as beasts of burden; the immigrants had bridles, saddles, and stirrups for warriors to ride them into battle. Immigrants irrigated their fields and brought stone-fitting technology used to build walls and burial chambers in tombs. Goldsmiths crafted crowns and jewelry for rulers; metal casters worked bronze. The first scribes and accountants came from the peninsula before 400. The Hata lineage settled west of what is now Kyoto. It introduced sericulture and silk weaving; it founded a number of temples, among them Kōryūji, which still treasures a sixth-century statue of Maitreya, the Buddha of the future. Items that originated in China but were imported through the peninsula included bronze mirrors, ornaments, and coins.

The immigrants brought techniques of rule that contributed to the process of state building in the Japanese islands. The first system of court titles bore a striking similarity to the Silla bone-rank system. Chieftains acquired surnames that they could then use to denote aristocratic status. Territorial divisions from the district (Korean in origin) to the province (Chinese in origin) achieved an administrative cast. Peninsular burial mounds probably provided the model for the giant tumuli that characterized the fifth to seventh centuries. The peninsular experience with Chinese-style civil and criminal law codes foreshadowed the Japanese adoption in the seventh century. Buddhism as taught in Paekche and Silla had a lasting impact on Japanese society and politics.

Ancient Religion

In Himiko's time, religious beliefs held society together. One of her tasks was to perform rituals that propitiated the deities, leading to the argument that politics and religion in ancient Japan were one and the same. When chieftains had to make decisions, they baked deer bones in a fire and examined the cracks to determine what the future might bring. They supervised the agricultural calendar, performed fertility rites, and prayed for victory in war. Female shamans warded off misfortune and communicated with the deities. Because rituals had to be performed by men and women together, priestesses were idealized as sisters helped by brothers. Women and men held secular and sacred authority.

Early Japanese believed that important people became gods, and the gods ordered the conditions for their existence. Gods had created the natural world; gods vitalized mountains and rocks; gods constituted the energy that made rice grow. Human reproduction recapitulated and stimulated the deeds of the creator deities that brought life to the world. This kind of belief system is called animism because it assumes that spiritual forces animate even inanimate objects. The gods abhorred pollution, especially the pollution of death. The death of a chieftain required the destruction of his residence. By the late fourth century C.E., large tombs filled with ritual objects pacified an otherwise threatening departed spirit; moats and clay figurines (*haniwa*) marked the periphery. (See **Material Culture: Haniwa.**) Sacred texts from the seventh and eighth centuries connected gods and mortals, celebrated sex and procreation, and venerated the natural world. Myths propagated by the Yamato court personified the spiritual forces, giving them names, associating them with local lineages, and ranking them in a hierarchy of kinship with the sun goddess at the top. This system of beliefs is now called Shinto, a term created out of Chinese characters, that means the way of the gods.

Excavations of hamlet burial grounds and giant tumuli show that the early Japanese honored the dead by burying them with items that they had used in life. Clothing, cosmetics, and pottery can be found with pots holding human bones. Equal numbers of men and women were buried one to a tomb that contained armor, swords, and arrowheads, considered valuable because they came from Korea. Since the heavy iron swords forged in Japan with ore from abroad were used less for fighting than for ceremony, they suggest a stratified society in which funeral practices reflected disparities in ranks. Between 425 and 500, the number of iron items buried in tombs multiplied, and the objects themselves became more standardized as political authority became increasingly centered in the Kinai region.

THE FORMATION OF A CENTERED POLITY

Beginning about 350 C.E., rulers in the Yamato basin of the Kinai region began to consolidate their power. By the fifth century, they had organized the manufacture of iron implements and taken control of their distribution. Warriors on horseback improved the speed at which armies could travel and the distances they could cover. Five kings sent tribute missions to China to gain Chinese confirmation of their hegemony and acquire the accouterments of kingship with which to entice the chieftains of other lineages into alliance. They provided military support to their ally Paekche against Koguryŏ. When Paekche fell, many of its best-educated and highly skilled supporters fled to Yamato. They brought with them political and administrative talents that the local rulers put to good use.

Yūryaku (late fifth century), the most notable of these early monarchs, placed immigrant and indigenous chieftains into a ranking system. Each chieftain was deemed a lineage head and received lavish gifts such as mirrors from China and permission to build grand tombs. The lineage received a hereditary title derived from Korean nomenclature that defined its position in a new court hierarchy. The chieftains claimed descent from a lineage deity or from a person who had a special relationship with the lineage deity. They acknowledged Yūryaku's suzerainty with tribute and family members sent to serve at his court in return for the right to administer and tax the territories he allotted them, often those they already controlled. Occupational groups that took responsibility for goods and

MATERIAL CULTURE

Haniwa

Clay figurines from the fifth to seventh centuries illustrate how people lived in ancient Japan. Shamanesses wear swirling headdresses; shamans hold mirrors; a falconer lifts his hawk; warriors ride horses with elaborate saddle trappings and carry bows and arrows; one musician plucks a zither and another strikes a drum; a cultivator carries a hoe. Women balance jugs on their heads with babies on their backs. A bowler-type hat with a broad brim and side curls signifies court rank. Sheep, deer, birds, monkeys, dogs, and rabbits abound. Trading ships carry goods between Japan and the continent. Figurines provide evidence that chieftains sat on chairs and slept in beds, customs that later died out.

Clay figurines and cylinders are called *haniwa,* literally clay rings, because the vast majority are hollow tubes standing 3 to 5 feet high. They are found outside the giant tumuli that dot the Japanese landscape from Kyushu to northern Japan, with most clustered in the Kinai region near Osaka and Nara. Why *haniwa* were placed outside rather than inside the tomb is a matter for speculation. According to *Nihon shoki,* they substituted for the chieftain's attendants. Archaeologists debate whether they served to demarcate the sacred space of the tomb and to protect the deceased, much like the stone sculptures of the twelve animal signs that encircled Silla Dynasty burial mounds, or whether they guarded the living against the dangerously powerful spirit of a deceased chieftain.

Haniwa. Haniwa stand 3 to 5 feet tall. The photo on the right shows a warrior with helmet, side curls and armor. The horse in the photo on the left is likewise equipped for war with studded chest band, saddle, and bridle. *(Christie's/Corbis)*

services were also organized into lineages. One provided weapons and the men to use them; another supplied Yūryaku's kitchens; others performed the ritual work that earlier rulers such as Himiko had done themselves. As Yūryaku expanded his dominion, he balanced the territories bestowed on titled lineages with those reserved for the crown. Men appointed to administer crown lands did not have the hereditary powers of the lineage chieftains; they were dependent on the court.

Yūryaku also used marital alliances to bolster his legitimacy and extend his power. His senior consort came from the lineage of an earlier king. Chieftains contributed other consorts to gain status as royal relatives and to exert influence at court. Combined with the court ranking system and gift giving, these connections placed the king above his mightiest supporters in a hierarchy of wealth and privilege that served to distinguish them from untitled, unconnected commoners.

Yūryaku's successors built on and fought over the state he had created in southwestern Honshu and northern Kyushu. Within twenty-five years of his death, his line had been replaced following power struggles between royal relatives aided and abetted by disgruntled chieftains. Rulers in the sixth century defined the royal regalia as mirror, sword, and jewel and selected a princess to serve the royal family's tutelary deity at the sun goddess's shrine at Ise. By the middle of the 500s, the immigrant Soga lineage had entrenched itself as principal consort givers. In 592 a Soga niece named Suiko became head of the Yamato house on the death of her husband, her half-brother, and ruled until 628, the longest reign for the next twelve centuries. Her capital at Asuka is famous for Japan's first flowering of Buddhist art.

The China Connection

Between 592 and 756, the Yamato kings, male and female, transformed themselves from chieftains of confederacies into Chinese-style monarchs. The efforts to expand the functions and reach of the state arose in part in reaction to the

Prince Shōtoku is the subject of innumerable posthumous portraits. Painted in the eighteenth century, the one shown here features him dressed in the courtly attire of eighth century China. *(Private Collection, Paris/Dagli Orti/The Art Archive)*

resurgence of the Chinese empire under the Sui and Tang Dynasties. Kings also saw the need to overcome the violent factional and succession disputes that had weakened ties between center and periphery and led to regicide and the assassination of chief ministers. Suiko and Prince Shōtoku (574–622), her nephew and adviser, opened relations with the Sui Dynasty in China, paving the way for later study missions and the immersion of elite Japanese men in Chinese culture. They promoted Buddhism as much for its magical efficacy as for its religious teachings. They reorganized the court by instituting a ladder of twelve official ranks bestowed on individuals to correspond to Sui rather than Silla practice.

In the Seventeen Injunctions promulgated in 604, Prince Shōtoku announced a new ideology of rule based on Confucian and Buddhist thought. He put a new distance between the ruling Yamato line and all other lineages by proclaiming, "The Lord is Heaven, the vassal is earth." This relationship was to be expressed in ritual and governed by propriety: "Harmony is to be valued and an avoidance of wanton opposition to be honored." Ministers were to put public duties, their duty to the throne, above the private interests of lineage and self. Only the ruler was to levy taxes because, "in a country there are not two lords; the people have not two masters."[1] Suiko and Shōtoku's successors continued these efforts to distinguish the monarch from his ministers and the court from commoners by drawing on the rituals and regulations of Chinese kingship.

The reform of 645, later heralded as marking the start of monarchical rule, incorporated continental culture in the midst of conflict. It followed a bloody coup in which Nakatomi no Kamatari, founder of the Fujiwara lineage, brought down the Soga. The court appointed provincial governors and abolished private land ownership. It instituted a population census, a centralized tax system, a legal code, and a civil service examination. It tried to curtail the ability of local magnates to harass the people and protected the right of women to remarry. It provided a municipal government for the capital. It inaugurated the use of Chinese-style era names, and as in China at the time, the names worked magic. Just as people changed their names to change their luck, so did era names change when they had lost their potency to ward off disaster. The Great Reform era called *Taika* (645–650) did so little to mitigate bloody factional strife that it was changed to *Hakuchi* (White Pheasant, a lucky omen; 650–654). Monarchs had to rely on powerful lineages in implementing these reforms. The Fujiwara consolidated their position by giving their daughters to rulers,

a tradition they had some success in maintaining down to 1924.

The Fujiwara supported monarchs in promoting Chinese models for administration. Following a large-scale and bloody factional dispute called the Jinshin incident (671–672), Tenmu and his wife, Jitō, daughter of the previous monarch, eliminated collateral claimants to the throne in order to preserve it for their descendants. Tenmu reorganized the bureaucracy and filled it with men he had appointed rather than the former chieftains, now titled aristocrats. In 685 he prohibited the private possession of weapons. Through the creation of a conscript army based on Chinese models, the state was to have a monopoly on the use of force. Tenmu tried to abolish the aristocrats' private economic basis by experimenting with the state allocation of land. He enticed the new aristocrats to court to participate in grand ceremonies of state that drew on Buddhist and Chinese models; he also sent envoys to coordinate worship at the regional shrines for lineage tutelary deities. Jitō claimed the sun goddess as Tenmu's ancestor, thereby projecting his dynasty into the mythic past. When she became ruler, she was styled *tennō,* a combination of two Chinese characters meaning "heaven" and "monarch." This title fell into abeyance in the tenth century as monarchical power declined relative to that of ministers. Rulers were called "lord" (*shujō*) in life and "temple" (*in*) in death. Revived in 1841, the official English translation of *tennō* became "emperor" in 1868.

Jitō and her successors oversaw notable advances in state formation. Tenmu started construction on a Chinese-style palace and capital city at Fujiwara, which Jitō occupied in 694. It marked a decision to use architecture in bolstering the ruler's authority. No longer would palaces be destroyed on the death of a monarch or would the ruler's consorts enjoy separate residences. Three generations of rulers lived at Fujiwara before the capital moved to the more central location of Nara in 710, where it remained until 794. (See Map 7.2.) The eighth

---

1. W. G. Aston, trans., *Nihongi: Chronicles of Japan from the Earliest Times to* A.D. *697* (London: Kegan, Paul, Trench, Trübner, 1896), 2:129–133.

century is now called the Nara period. Modeled on the Tang capital at Chang'an, Fujiwara and Nara were laid out on a grid with the palace centered at the north and facing south, because in Chinese cosmology, the ruler's place was fixed like the pole star. By dominating his capital, he brought heaven to earth. The central boulevard divided the city into symmetrical halves just as the Chinese-style bureaucratic structure balanced the minister of the left with the minister of the right lest either one monopolize power that rightfully belonged to the ruler. The physical layout mirrored social relations. Ministers in the Chinese-style bureaucracy took up residence in the capital on assigned building lots in accordance with their rank. Aristocrats and rulers vied in building Buddhist temples. District officials were encouraged to use coins for traveling expenses and land sales. In line with Chinese models and to learn about the realm in order to control it, monarchs had provincial gazetteers compiled that described local customs, places and their deities, specialties, and resources.

During Jitō's reign, officials started to compile official histories and create a set of written administrative statutes and law codes. Modified and expanded during successive reigns, this system became known as the regime of codes. The penal code set out punishments for rebels and robbers as well as for breaching the taboos that conferred sacral status on the king. The administrative code specified relations between the ruler and aristocrats in an effort to freeze the status quo and brought the ruler's jurisdiction down to the level of district magnates. It established political and religious hierarchies of public offices, temples, and shrines that reached from the center to the provinces. Just as district offices fell under the jurisdiction of administrators at the capital, so too were provincial temples subordinated to temple headquarters. The Yamato line's shrines at Ise and Nara ranked above lineage shrines in the provinces. Chief priests appointed by the ruler supervised the conduct of monks and nuns and coordinated ritual while ministers of state ran the bureaucracy.

Map 7.2   Kinai Area of Japan

The codes also dealt extensively with land rights. All land belonged to the ruler, for him to allot to cultivators, except in the case of new fields. Opening them to cultivation was such an expensive undertaking that the person responsible, whether an individual or a temple, received permanent ownership.

The promulgation of these codes had long-lasting effects. Even chieftains resident in the provinces competed for official appointments and titles as local magnates. County, district, and provincial offices and temples spread across the landscape. Each of the sixty-five provinces had a headquarters supervised by a governor. His official mission was to promote agriculture and register the population. In fact, he concentrated on adjudicating land disputes and collecting taxes in kind—cloth, rice, iron, and other goods produced locally and needed by the court. Officials appointed by the court and local magnates worked in tandem on the governor's staff, which numbered in the hundreds. Despite these achievements, the polity remained more centered than centralized, with each segment of the population—aristocrat, bureaucrat, cleric, cultivator—claiming different rights and privileges relative to the throne.

During the reign of Shōmu from 724 to 756 (he officially retired in 749 but did not relinquish power), the ancient system of Japanese kingship reached its zenith. Over seven thousand men staffed the central bureaucracy. Shōmu rebuilt the palace at Nara to include halls for ceremonies, offices for officials, and private quarters for his family. He lavishly supported the Buddhist establishment with the construction of Tōdaiji as the Yamato lineage temple. It contained the world's largest bronze Buddhist statue. Monks came from China and Champa (Vietnam) for the inauguration ceremony. Shōmu sent armies to expand his sway across the Japanese islands and used diplomatic ritual to assert Japan's precedence over Korea.

Shōmu's successors had to deal with the consequences of his success. As power became more centered at the court, struggles for status and influence intensified. Except for a few families that enjoyed adequate access to economic resources, most aristocrats lived precariously close to poverty. Restive local magnates disobeyed directives and rebelled against the center, as did cultivators unhappy at tax collection efforts. Officials at the county and district levels jealously preserved their autonomy while accepting court rank and office. Despite a history of female monarchs, the spread of Confucian philosophy justified the aristocrats' resentment at being ruled by a woman: Shōmu's daughter who reigned twice, first as Kōken (r. 749–758) and then as Shōtoku (r. 764–770). Deposed in a palace coup, Shōtoku was the last female monarch until 1630. Conflict between the ruler and the aristocratic bureaucracy was repeated in the 780s when two retired monarchs sponsored factional intrigue. Buddhist priests, collateral lines of Fujiwara, and other lineages competed for influence, while disgruntled members of the ruling family plotted against their

chief. A decrease in tax revenues forced rulers to scale back building projects and reduce the size of ceremonies. In 794, frustrated at the endless demands for favor that bedeviled him in Nara, the ruler Kanmu moved the capital to Heian-kyō. There it was to remain until 1868.

The Conquest of Emishi and Hayato

In the early eighth century, aristocrats developed a sense of a Japanese ethnic identity that excluded peoples on the islands beyond the court's control. Many inhabitants in the northeast still practiced late Jōmon-style slash-and-burn agriculture. Since being Japanese was associated with rice-based settled communities, they were deemed barbarians (*Emishi*). The court encouraged the spread of settlements ever farther north, sent emissaries to set up district offices and collect taxes, and dispatched military expeditions to remove or enslave the *Emishi*. By 725, the first year of Shōmu's reign, these expeditions had pacified the region up to today's Sendai. Subsequent waves of soldiers and settlers spread agricultural settlements as far as Morioka.

Shōmu also expanded Yamato rule in Kyushu. In 740 the exiled Fujiwara Hirotsugu raised an army of ten thousand conscript troops against the throne. He gained the support of some district chiefs and members of the Hayato minority from southern Kyushu who, like the *Emishi*, resisted the civilization offered by the Yamato rulers. He even made overtures to Silla in search of allies. According to the official history, *Nihon shoki*, Shōmu dispatched an army of seventeen thousand, the largest royal army raised in the eighth century. Within two months, it had scattered the rebel army and executed Hirotsugu. The Hayato had no choice but to submit. The immigration of people from the Korean peninsula and the development of a stratified state in the Kinai basin divided the Japanese islands into three cultural and ethnic zones. By the end of Shōmu's reign, the central zone centered on Nara had squeezed the southern zone onto the Ryukyu island chain, while the northern zone, which extended up through Hokkaido, was shrinking on Honshu.

The Introduction of Buddhism

Buddhism played a major role in the development of the early Japanese state. First sponsored by the Soga and other immigrants from Paekche, it had to overcome opposition by Shinto ritualists before receiving official government support in 587. Enhanced by scribes, metallurgists, painters, and other artisans, it became the faith of rulers in a symbiotic relationship that strengthened both. Buddhism had a rich textual tradition; its monks paraded in majestic processions and held thunderous sutra recitations. From Paekche rulers the Japanese learned that worshipping the Buddha would bring their realm the protection of the Four Guardian Kings of the Buddhist law. In the Seventeen Injunctions, Prince Shōtoku urged the court to revere the Buddha, Buddhist law, and the monastic order. Tenmu and Jitō recognized the value of Buddhism in providing faith in a universal deity at the same time that they sent offerings to the Ise shrine of the sun goddess and regional shrines and read omens to divine heaven's will. By asserting their leadership in all dimensions of the religious realm, they sought to bolster their authority in secular affairs.

Tenmu and Jitō took advantage of Buddhism's appeal to spread their rule across Japan. They built temples in the capital and provinces and used them as storehouses for population and tax records. They oversaw the copying of sutras, held Buddhist ceremonies, and habitually performed Buddhist purificatory rituals. By restricting hunting, fishing, and the eating of meat, they promoted Buddhist beliefs that valued the lives of all sentient beings. The number of monks and nuns increased, their behavior minutely regulated. During Tenmu and Jitō's reigns, Buddhism became a core component of courtly life and practice.

Shōmu did even more to promote Buddhism and harness its power to the court. In line with the ideology of his day that deemed the natural order a reflection of the social order, he saw in natural disasters and rebellion his own lack of virtue. To compensate, he ordered sutra readings at temples, austerities such as cold water baths at Shinto shrines, and the construction of religious structures. Following the Hayato rebellion in 741, he ordered each province to build a seven-storied pagoda, a guardian temple, and a nunnery and to provide adequate rice land to support the monks and nuns. In a thanksgiving service for his victory, he presented brocade, prayers, and Buddhist sutra readings to the shrine for Hachiman, the god of war. The giant Buddhist statue at Tōdaiji was cast in the image of Vairocana, the cosmic Buddha who encompasses the thousands of Buddhas and millions of enlightened beings just as Shōmu saw himself as ruling over all aristocrats and commoners. It was enshrined in a hall larger than the royal palace. The temple complex contained Japan's first ordination platform as well as libraries and schools. There, monks translated texts and sutras for the so-called Six Sects. Rather than go to Tang China or Silla Korea, Japanese monks could now study and receive licenses at Tōdaiji under kingly sponsorship and supervision. After Shōmu passed the throne to his daughter, he established the precedent for abdicated rulers to enter the Buddhist priesthood.

Shōmu saw Buddhism primarily as a state religion, leaving it to monks and nuns such as Gyōki to proselytize among the populace. Through his sermons, Gyōki, the descendant of an immigrant Confucian scholar, propagated the Buddhist notions of causality and retribution and the humanistic promise that following the way of the universal Buddha can bring enlightenment to any person at any time or place. His followers built irrigation works, roads, bridges, and inns for commoners delivering tax payments to the capital, a material demonstration that the Buddhist law can benefit everyone, not just kings and aristocrats. In 717 the government accused Gyōki of violating the regulations that restricted nuns and monks to monasteries, collecting an inordinate amount in alms, and confusing the masses by claiming the power to heal, cast spells, and tell fortunes. Gyōki ignored the accusations, and other monks and nuns followed his example of good works and public preaching. The government then tried to co-opt his appeal. In 741 Gyōki received an official appointment to supervise the building of a bridge near the capital. In this way, the government acknowledged that he was indeed the bodhisattva his followers claimed him to be and brought belief in the saving power of the Buddha into line with official policy.

By the eighth century, Buddhism had become so naturalized in Japan that it had started to blend with native beliefs. Mountain ascetics joined the ancient belief in the sacrality of mountains with esoteric forms of Buddhism that emphasized occult practices. They promised to heal the sick and performed rituals to eliminate pollution and evil. The Mahayana Buddhism that entered Japan offered numerous paths to salvation through the pantheon of Buddhas and bodhisattvas (see **Connections: Buddhism in India and Its Spread Along the Silk Road**). Because the Buddha appeared in so many guises, perhaps he had also appeared as local deities. In what would later be known as Ryōbu Shintō, the deities received Buddhist names. Although an edict from 764 placed Buddhism above Shinto, the reverse was as often the case. In the countryside, the style of worshipping the Buddha reflected beliefs associated with Shinto regarding the importance of fertility and worldly benefits rather than eliminating worldly attachments to achieve enlightenment. In place of large tombs surrounded by *haniwa*, provincial chieftains built Buddhist temples to hold memorial services for the dead and replicate the benefits they hoped to acquire when propitiating the deities: good harvests, health, prosperity, and progeny. People learned that deities and Buddhas supported each other, and both needed festivals and ceremonies. Important Shinto shrines acquired Buddhist temples so that the deities might hear sutra recitations, and deities protected Buddhist temples. In this way particular deities (*kami*) and the universal Buddha entered into an enduring symbiotic relationship.

Elite Culture

The Yamato court attracted followers with its access to Chinese elite culture including a written language, Daoism, Confucianism, the literary arts, sculpture (particularly Buddhist icons), painting, and music. The Chinese writing system arrived in Japan at the end of the Yayoi period, in the late fourth century, brought by immigrants from the Korean peninsula who served as a closed occupational group of scribes for the Yamato court. They left traces of their work in sword inscriptions. Not until the unification of China under the Sui and the introduction of Buddhism did Japanese rulers realize the importance of literacy. Pilgrims to China brought back quantities of Buddhist sutras and Chinese books. In addition to his Seventeen Injunctions of 604, Prince Shōtoku sponsored the writing of a history of Japan based on Chinese models. It later disappeared. The earliest examples of Japanese writing Chinese come from over 150,000 wooden tablets, the vast majority dating from the seventh and eighth centuries. Inscribed on the tablets were official documents, including directives to and reports by local officials, summons, transit passes, and labels attached to tax goods. They prove that women joined men as conscripts on public works projects.

After the wooden tablets came Japan's earliest extant histories. The *Kojiki* (Record of Ancient Matters) of 712 and *Nihon shoki* (Chronicles of Japan) completed in 720 relate histories of Japan from the creation of the cosmos to the establishment of the centered state in the seventh century. *Kojiki,* which details the age of the gods, can be read as an attempt by the Yamato court to justify its preeminence over other lineages. *Nihon shoki* opens with a passage that draws on Chinese yin-yang theory and cosmology. It narrates the history of the Yamato rulers in a straight line of descent from the sun goddess. Both histories exaggerate the antiquity of the early Japanese state and its control over local political arrangements.

Poetry had magical properties in the eyes of ancient Japanese. It both summoned and soothed the gods, and the words had spirits of their own. The earliest extant poetry collection, the *Kaifūsō* (Fond Recollections of Poetry) compiled in 751, contains the biographies of Japanese poets who wrote in Chinese. It is overshadowed by the *Man'yōshū* (Collection of Ten Thousand Leaves) compiled in 759, the first anthology of Japanese verse. (See **Documents: Poems from *Nihon shoki* and *Man'yōshū***). Its poems had the public function of attesting to the process of state building. They expressed the emotions of courtiers and frontier guards who forsook family and homeland to serve their monarch. They lamented the death of wives and lovers as well as rulers and other powerful personages.

Etiquette, ceremony, dance, and music introduced from China transformed provincial chieftains into court aristocrats. Played on flutes and stringed instruments punctuated by gongs and drums, continental music is said to have entered Japan when the king of Silla sent eighty musicians to attend funeral services for King Ingyō in 453. Stately dance performed by men wearing masks came from Silla in 612. The Court Music Bureau established in 702 and staffed chiefly by immigrants had charge of performing a repertoire of Chinese and Korean music and dance called elegant music (*gagaku*) at court ceremonies. Gagaku incorporated indigenous songs that retold tales of victory in battle, accompanied offerings from remote and hence quaint outposts, pleaded for aid from the gods, and celebrated the sexual union of men and women in fertility rites. The court thus appropriated elements of popular culture into an elite culture characterized by massive infusions from the continent. Viewing and participating in music and dance and learning the correct codes for conduct in ceremonies set ever higher standards for civilized behavior.

A Stagnant Agrarian Base

The spread of rice cultivation in the Yayoi period that had transformed western agricultural regions from slash and burn to settled farming soon reached its ecological limit. In contrast to the intensive agriculture that boosted yields in later centuries, cultivators during the eighth century continued to use extensive methods. They cleared fields and planted crops for a few years, and then repeated the process when a lack of proper irrigation and fertilizer depleted the soil in continuous cycles of cultivation and abandonment. Although an edict from 723 noted that a recent increase in population had led to rural overcrowding, the eighth-century regime of codes made much more elaborate provision for returning fallow fields to cultivation than it did for opening new fields. Fragments of census surveys suggest that a population of from 3 to 5.5 million in 700 had changed little by 800. Population gains at the turn of the century were wiped out by an epidemic of smallpox or some similar disease in 733–737 that killed approximately 25 to 35 percent of the population. It was followed by repeated famines and epidemics later in the century. The state's demand for revenue to fund building projects and ceremonies was not matched by an increase in population or an enlarged economic base.

Rural villages tended to be large in area but small in population. Because depleted fields had to lie fallow for years before they could be returned to production, the earlier pattern of fortified hilltop hamlets gave way to dispersed dwellings, each containing a large household of extended family members along with servants and slaves. Each cultivator received an official allotment of land in return for paying taxes, but it did not suffice for survival. To make up the difference, cultivators planted fields hidden from the tax collector, worked as tenants, or foraged for supplies. To the dismay of officials, cultivators felt little connection to their land. Many simply absconded when times were bad, swelling the population of vagrants and weakening the tax base. Infant mortality was so high that a plan to give each child an allotment of land at birth had to be changed to allotments at age five, raised to age twelve in the case of a slave. The average life expectancy at birth was twenty-eight to thirty-three years, approximately the same as in Europe at that time.

DOCUMENTS

Poems from *Nihon shoki* and *Man'yōshū*

Compiled in the early eighth century, these documents include poems first composed centuries before. Here we see depicted fifth- to seventh-century rulers in the process of consolidating power by performing rituals to take possession of the land through viewing and naming, building magnificent palaces, and making excursions. In these circumstances, even poems expressing personal feelings had a public dimension because the poet's relationship with the ruler explains the poem's creation.

6th year [462 C.E.], Spring, 2nd month, 4th day. The ruler [Yūryaku] made an excursion to the small moor of Hatsuse. There, viewing the aspect of the hills and moors, in an outburst of feeling, he made a song, saying:

> The mountain of Hatsuse
> Of the hidden country
> Is a mountain
> Standing beautifully,
> Is a mountain
> Projecting beautifully
> The mountain of Hatsuse
> Of the hidden country
> Is truly lovely,
> Is truly lovely.

Thereupon he gave a name to the small moor, and called it Michi no Ono.

Poems by Kakinomoto Hitomaro at the time of the procession [by the divine monarch Jitō] to the palace at Yoshino.

> Many are the lands under heaven
> And the sway of our Lord,
> Sovereign of the earth's eight corners,
> But among them her heart
> Finds Yoshino good
> For its crystal riverland
> Among the mountains,
> And on the blossom-strewn
> Fields of Akitsu
> She drives the firm pillars of her palace

> And so the courtiers of the great palace,
> Its ramparts thick with stone,
> Line their boats
> To cross the morning river,
> Race their boats
> Across the evening river.
> Like this river
> Never ending,
> Like these mountains
> Commanding ever greater heights,
> The palace by the surging rapids—
> Though I gaze on it, I do not tire.

> Envoy
> Like the eternal moss
> Slick by the Yoshino river
> On which I do not tire to gaze,
> May I never cease to return
> And gaze on it again.

> Our lord
> Who rules in peace,
> A very god,
> Manifests her divine will
> And raises towering halls
> Above the Yoshino riverland
> Where waters surge,
> And climbs to the top
> To view the land.
> On the mountains
> Folding upward around her
> Like a sheer hedge of green
> The mountain gods present their
>   offerings.

They bring her blossoms in springtime
To decorate her hair
And, when autumn comes,
They garland her with yellow leaves
And the gods of the river
That runs alongside the mountains
Make offerings for her royal feast.

They send cormorants forth
Over the upper shoals,
They cast dipper nets
Across the lower shoals,
Mountain and river
Draw together to serve her—
A god's reign indeed!

A very god
Whom mountain and river
Draw together to serve,
She sets her boat to sail
Over pools where waters surge.

Poem by Kakinomoto Hitomaro when he parted from his wife in the land of Iwami and came up to the capital.

At Cape Kara
On the sea of Iwami,
Where the vines
Crawl on the rocks,
Rockweed of the deep
Grows on the reefs
And sleek seaweed
Grows on the desolate shore.
As deeply do I
Think of my wife
Who swayed toward me in sleep
Like the lithe seaweed.
Yet few were the nights
We had slept together
Before we parted
Like crawling vines uncurled.
And so I look back,
Still thinking of her
With painful heart,

This clench of inner flesh,
But in the storm
Of fallen scarlet leaves
On Mount Watari,
Crossed as on
A great ship,
I cannot make out the sleeves
She waves in farewell.
For she, alas,
Is slowly hidden
Like the moon
In its crossing
Between the clouds
Over Yagami Mountain
Just as the evening sun
Coursing through the heavens
Has begun to glow,
And even I
Who thought I was a brave man
Find the sleeves of my well-worn robe
Drenched with tears.

Poem upon the death of the Sovereign by one of his concubines (her name is yet unclear).

As the living are unfit
For commune with the gods
So I am separated from you
Lord whom I grieve for in the morning,
So I am kept from you,
Lord whom I long for.
If you were a jewel,
I would wrap you around my wrist.
If you were a robe,
I would never take you off.
Lord whom I long for,
Last night I saw you
In a dream.

———
Source: Gary L. Ebersole, *Ritual Poetry and the Politics of Death in Early Japan* (Princeton, N.J.: Princeton University Press, 1989), pp. 27, 30–32, 50–52, 175, modified.

Quarrelling Worker. Scribbled on the margin of a record regarding sutra copying in 740, this sketch of a quarrelling worker provides a glimpse of the garb worn by commoners of the time. *(Shosoin Treasure House/DNPArchives.com)*

In addition to paying taxes for the use of state land, cultivators had to meet service requirements and participate in the state's military adventures. In 713, for example, "For the first time Yamashiro-no-kuni was ordered to establish fifty households in charge of milking cows."[2] In this type of corvée (required labor) system, the culti-

vators' obligation to provide services did not mean they would be paid for them. The corvée built the enormous tombs demanded by fifth-century rulers; it built the capitals, palaces, and temples of the later centuries. The court fielded conscript armies and marched them from Kyushu to Tohoku. Many men caught in this system could expect to be ill treated, malnourished, and abandoned once the project for which they had been pressed into service was completed. Although the centered monarchical structure created through the regime of codes provided relief from marauders and bandits as well as some security of landholding, its benefits for cultivators were decidedly mixed.

SUMMARY

By the end of the eighth century, interactions with the continent had radically modified agriculture, material culture, and religion on the Japanese islands. A centered state spread over Shikoku, Kyushu, and most of Honshu, gradually becoming attenuated as it reached the frontiers. Although historians disagree on the extent to which it enforced its decrees, it became a model for kingly rule for centuries to come.

SUGGESTED READING

For an excellent overview of Japan's place in northeast Asia, see B. L. Batten, *To the Ends of Japan: Premodern Frontiers, Boundaries, and Interactions* (2003). W. H. Coldrake, *Architecture and Authority in Japan* (1996) begins with grand shrines and Nara buildings. J. W. Hall et al., general eds., *The Cambridge History of Japan*, 6 vols. (1988–1999), covers the entire history.

For more specific studies, see M. J. Hudson, *Ruins of Identity: Ethnogenesis in the Japanese*

Islands (1999); G. Barnes, *Protohistoric Yamato: Archaeology of the First Japanese State* (1988); K. Imamura, *Prehistoric Japan: New Perspectives on Insular East Asia* (1996); J. R. Piggott, *The Emergence of Japanese Kingship* (1997); W. W. Farris, *Sacred Texts and Buried Treasures: Issues in the Historical Archaeology of Ancient Japan* (1998); and W. W. Farris, *Population, Disease, and Land in Early Japan, 645–900* (1985).

---

2. Robert Karl Reischauer, *Early Japanese History (c. 40 B.C.–A.D. 1167)* (Gloucester, Mass.: Peter Smith, 1967), p. 173.

China Among Equals: Song, Liao, Xia, and Jin

The Song Dynasty did not dominate East Asia the way the Tang Dynasty had, or even rule all areas occupied largely by Chinese speakers. Northern Vietnam defended its independence. The Khitan Liao Dynasty held territory in the northeast down to modern Datong and Beijing, and the Tangut Xia Dynasty held a smaller territory in the northwest. In the twelfth and the thirteenth centuries, Song had new northern rivals, the Jurchens and then the Mongols, who took even larger parts of China proper. The Song period is, as a result, conventionally divided into the Northern Song (960–1127), when the Song capital was in Kaifeng and Liao was its chief rival, and the Southern Song (1127–1276), when the capital had been moved to Hangzhou and it confronted Jin on its northern border.

Modern historians have been fascinated by the evidence that Song China was the most advanced society in the world in its day, and many have drawn attention to all that seems progressive in this period: the introduction of paper money, the spread of printing and increases in literacy, the growth of cities, the expansion of the examination system, the decline of aristocratic attitudes, and so on. These successes naturally raise questions. Why couldn't Song China turn its economic might into military might? How did the increasing importance of the examination system in elite lives affect the operation of the bureaucracy? Why was factionalism such a problem? Because printing led to many more works surviving from the Song than earlier periods, historians have also been able to ask questions they could not ask for earlier periods for lack of sources. What can we learn of daily life among different groups—elite and commoner, men and women, peasants and townsmen? How does Song society, economy, or culture look from the local level?

153

THE FOUNDING OF THE SONG DYNASTY

The founder of the Song Dynasty, Zhao Kuangyin, was a general whose troops put him on the throne when their previous ruler was succeeded by a child. Known as Taizu (r. 960–976), he set himself the task of making sure that no army would ever again be in a position to oust the rightful heir. He retired or rotated his own generals and assigned civil officials to supervise them, thus subordinating the armed forces to the civil bureaucracy.

Curbing generals ended warlordism but did not solve the problem of defending against the Khitans' Liao Dynasty to the north. During the Five Dynasties, Liao was able to gain control of a strip of land in north China (the northern parts of Shanxi and Hebei) that had long been considered part of China proper (and was referred to by Song as the Sixteen Prefectures). Taizu and his younger brother Taizong made every effort to defeat Liao. They wanted to reclaim the Sixteen Prefectures because this area included the line of the Great Wall, the mountains and mountain passes that had been central to Chinese defense against northerners since before the Han Dynasty. However, although the Liao ruled over a population tiny by Chinese standards, their horsemen were more than a match for the Chinese armies. After a Liao invasion of 1004 came within a hundred miles of Kaifeng, the Song settled with Liao, agreeing to pay tribute to Liao in exchange for Liao's maintaining the peace. Each year Song was to send Liao 100,000 ounces of silver and 200,000 bolts of silk. In 1042 this sum was increased to 500,000 units.

The payments to the Liao and Xia probably did not damage the overall Chinese economy. Even after the tribute to Liao was raised to 500,000 units, it did not result in an increase in Liao's bullion holdings since Song exports to Liao normally exceeded their imports by a large margin, which meant that the silver sent to Liao found its way back into China as payment for Chinese goods, a little like foreign aid today. At the time, however, the pro-war irrendentists felt humiliated by these treaties and thought it only common sense that payments to Liao and Xia helped them and harmed Song.

The pro-peace accommodationists, however, could justly point out that tribute was much less costly than war. During the reigns of the first three emperors, the size of the armed forces increased rapidly, to almost 1 million by 1022. By that time the military was consuming three-quarters of the tax revenues. By contrast, even counting the expenses of the exchange of embassies, the cost of maintaining peaceful relations with the Liao consumed no more than 2 or 3 percent of the state's annual revenues.

SONG'S RIVALS: LIAO AND XIA

The Khitan were a proto-Mongol people originally from the eastern slopes of the mountains that separate Mongolia and Manchuria. There they raised cattle and horses, moving their herds in nomadic fashion. They had been in regular contact with the Tang and with other sedentary societies, such as the multi-ethnic kingdom of Parhae (Bohai) in southern Manchuria. They knew of the wealth of cities to the south and the strategies used by the Uighurs and others to extract some of it by exerting military pressure.

In the early tenth century, Abaoji (d. 926), of the Yelü clan, united eight to ten Khitan tribes into a federation and secured control of the steppe. The political institutions he set up drew on both Chinese traditions and tribal customs. Abaoji set aside the traditional Khitan practice of tribal councils' electing chiefs for limited terms and in its place instituted hereditary succession on the Chinese model to ensure that his son would succeed him. The ruling Yelü clan married exclusively with the Xiao clan, and these two clans dominated the higher reaches of the government. In 926 Abaoji advanced southward toward Hebei and destroyed the kingdom of Parhae (see Chapter 6).

The Liao administered their Chinese territories differently from their Khitan territories. The

1000

MONGOLIAN PLATEAU

GOBI DESERT

MANCHURIAN PLAIN

JURCHENS

Sea of Japan

HEIAN JAPAN

Kyoto • Nara

LIAO

Beijing •

KORYO KOREA

Seoul •

Yellow Sea

UIGHURS

XIA

Kaifeng •

East China Sea

TIBET

Chang'an • (Xi'an)

Hangzhou •

SONG CHINA

NANZHAO

Xi • Guangzhou

South China Sea

ANNAM

Bay of Bengal

CHAMPA

Мар **8.1**   **Northern Song, Liao, and Xia ca. 1050**

southern section was governed on the basis of Chinese traditions, using a civil bureaucracy modeled on the Tang, complete with a civil service examination system. In contrast to the Tang, however, counties and even prefectures were granted to Khitan imperial relatives and high-ranking officials as fiefs over which they had full jurisdiction. The central city of the southern region was the Southern Capital, Yanjing, located at modern Beijing, thus beginning the history of that city as a capital. (See Map 8.1.) The southern section generated the bulk of Liao tax revenue.

The northern section of Liao was huge but sparsely settled. The government there was mobile, the ruler and his chief officials moving from place to place in different seasons. To keep records in the Khitan language, a script was created with characters resembling Chinese charac-

ters (a language still not deciphered). This dual form of administration allowed the Khitan to maintain their tribal organization and resist sinification. Although the ruling elite became culturally dual, adept in both Khitan and Chinese languages and customs, the ordinary Khitans in the north maintained their traditional social and military organization.

To the west of the Liao territories another non-Chinese state established itself in this period, the Xia, or Xi-Xia (Western Xia). It was founded by Tanguts, who spoke a language related to Tibetan. In Tang times, under pressure from the expanding Tibetan kingdom, the Tanguts had moved north and east from the Qingtang region into northern Shaanxi and Gansu. In 881 the Tang court appointed a Tangut chief as military governor of the region, and this office became essentially hereditary. By the end of the ninth century, after the collapse of the Tibetan and Uighur empires, the Tanguts gained control over the important trade in horses with the Chinese.

During the tenth century, the Tanguts were largely outside the struggle for power in north China and were able to consolidate their state. Under Yuanhao (r. 1032–1048), a script was adopted for writing the Tangut language and the dynastic name Xia was adopted. When Yuan-hao demanded that the Song Dynasty recognize Xia as a sovereign state, the Chinese sent an army. The fighting went poorly for the Chinese, however, and in 1044 a treaty was reached in which the Song agreed to make payments to Xia much as it did to Liao, though in lesser amounts (200,000 units altogether).

The political institutions of Xia drew on Tang, Song, Liao, Tibetan, and Uighur models. There was a perennial tension between the imperial clan and the ministerial-consort clans, who often were able to dominate the court. Elements of Confucian statecraft were adopted, but Buddhism was firmly entrenched as the state religion. Xia was sometimes at war with Liao but also concluded treaties with it, recognizing Liao as the superior party.

A NEW ERA

The pace of change was rapid from the late Tang into the early Song period, and by the mid-eleventh century, China in many ways was a much more modern society, with cities and commerce transforming its economy and printing and examinations transforming elite culture.

The Medieval Chinese Economic Revolution

In 742 China's population was approximately 50 million, very close to what it had been in 2 C.E. Over the next three centuries, with the expansion of rice cultivation in central and south China, the country's food supply steadily increased, and so did its population. Song popu-lation reached about 100 million in 1102. China was certainly the largest country in the world at the time; its population undoubtedly exceeded that of all of Europe (as it has ever since).

How did China's economy sustain such growth? Agricultural prosperity and denser settlement patterns fostered commercialization of the economy. In many regions farmers found that producing for the market made possible a better life, and therefore they no longer aimed at self-sufficiency. Peasants in more densely populated regions with numerous markets sold their surpluses and bought charcoal, tea, oil, and wine. In many places, farmers purchased grain and grew commercial crops, such as sugar, oranges, cotton, silk, and tea. The need to transport these products stimulated the inland and coastal shipping industries, creating jobs for shipbuilders and sailors. Marco Polo, the Venetian merchant who wrote of his visit to China in the late thirteenth century, was astounded at the boat traffic on the Yangzi River. He claimed to have seen no fewer than fifteen thousand vessels docked at a single city on the river.

As more goods were bought and sold, demand for money grew enormously, leading eventually to the creation of the world's first paper money. The late Tang government had abandoned the use of bolts of silk as supplementary currency, which increased the demand for copper coins. By 1085 the output of currency had increased tenfold since Tang times to more than 6 billion coins a year. To avoid the weight and bulk of coins for large transactions, local merchants in late Tang times started trading receipts from deposit shops where they had left money or goods. The early Song authorities awarded a small set of shops a monopoly on the issuance of these certificates of deposit, and in the 1120s the government took over the system, producing the world's first government-issued paper money.

Marco Polo wrote one of the earliest descriptions of how Chinese paper money was issued:

The coinage of this paper money is authenticated with as much form and ceremony as if it were actually of pure gold or silver; for to each

City Life. Song cities were centers of commerce and government. This 17-foot long painting of the capital, Kaifeng, shows shops, inns, boats, and people engaged in a wide variety of pursuits. Note the gate to the city wall and the sedan chairs. *(Palace Museum, Beijing)*

note a number of officers, specially appointed, not only subscribe their names, but affix their signets also; and when this has been regularly done by the whole of them, the principal officer . . . having dipped into vermilion the royal seal committed to his custody, stamps with it the piece of paper, so that the form of the seal tinged with the vermilion remains impressed upon it.[1]

With the intensification of trade, merchants became progressively more specialized and organized. They set up partnerships and joint stock companies, with a separation of owners (shareholders) and managers. In the large cities, merchants were organized into guilds according to the type of product sold; they periodically set prices and arranged sales from wholesalers to shop owners. When the government requisitioned goods or assessed taxes, it dealt with the guild heads.

The Song also witnessed many advances in industrial techniques. Papermaking flourished

1. *The Travels of Marco Polo, the Venetian,* ed. Manuel Komroff (New York: Boni and Liveright, 1926), p. 159.

with the demand for paper for books, documents, money, and wrapping paper. Heavy industry, especially iron, also grew at an astounding pace. With advances in metallurgy, iron production reached around 125,000 tons per year in 1078, a sixfold increase over the output in 800. At first charcoal was used in the production process, leading to deforestation of parts of north China. By the end of the eleventh century, however, bituminous coke had largely taken the place of charcoal.

Much of this iron was put to military purposes. Mass production methods were used to make iron armor in small, medium, and large sizes. High-quality steel for swords was made through high-temperature metallurgy. Huge bellows, often driven by water wheels, were used to superheat the molten ore. The needs of the army also brought Chinese engineers to experiment with the use of gunpowder. In the wars against the Jurchens in the twelfth century, those defending a besieged city used gunpowder to propel projectiles at the enemy.

The quickening of the economy fueled the growth of great cities, especially the two capitals, Kaifeng and Hangzhou. The Song broke all earlier precedents and did not select either Chang'an or Luoyang as its capital, but a city that had prospered because of its location near the northern end of the Grand Canal. The Tang capital, Chang'an, had been a planned city, laid out on a rectangular grid, with the walls built far out to allow expansion. Kaifeng, by contrast, grew over time as its economy developed. The city did not have the clearly demarcated wards of the Tang capital, and officials found themselves in frequent contact with ordinary city residents. The curfew was abolished in 1063, and from then on, many businesses in the entertainment quarters stayed open all night.

The medieval economic revolution shifted the economic center of China south to the Yangzi River drainage area. Rice, which grew there, provides more calories per unit of land than wheat or millet does and therefore allows denser settlements. Moreover, the milder temperatures of the south often allowed two crops to be grown on the same plot of land. The abundance of rivers and streams in the south facilitated shipping, which reduced the cost of transportation and thus made regional specialization economically more feasible.

International Trade

During the tenth through thirteenth centuries, trade connected all of the states we now classify under China (Song, Liao, Xia, Jin), the less politically important Dali state in the region of modern Yunnan, the oasis city-states of Central Asia, and the other major countries of East Asia, notably Korea and Japan. Maritime trade routes also connected all of these places to Southeast Asia and the societies of the Indian Ocean.

Trade between Song and its northern neighbors was stimulated by the indemnities Song paid to them. These states were given the means to buy Song products, and the Song set up supervised markets along the border to encourage this trade. The Song government collected tariffs on this trade, and the trade itself helped sustain Song China's economic growth. Chinese goods that flowed north in large quantities included tea, silk, copper coin (widely used as a currency outside of China), paper and printed books, porcelain, lacquerware, jewelry, rice and other grains, and ginger and other spices. The return flow included some of the silver that had originated with the Song and the horses that Song desperately needed for its armies, but also other animals such as camels and sheep, as well as goods that had traveled across the Silk Road, including fine Indian and Persian cotton cloth, precious gems, incense, and perfumes.

During Song times, maritime trade for the first time exceeded overland foreign trade. The Song government sent missions to Southeast Asian countries to encourage their traders to come to China. Chinese junks were seen throughout the Indian Ocean and began to displace Indian and Arab merchants in the South Seas. Shards of Song Chinese porcelain have been found as far away as East Africa. Chinese junks were larger than the ships of most of their competitors, such as the Indians or Arabs, and had many technical advances, including waterproofing with tong oil, watertight bulkheads, sounding lines to determine depth, and stern-mounted rudders for improved steering. Some of these ships were powered by both oars and sails and were large enough to hold several hundred men. Also important to oceangoing transport was the perfection of the compass. The way a magnetic needle would point north had been known for centuries, but in Song times the needle was reduced in size and attached to a fixed stem (rather than floating in water). In some cases it was put in a small protective case with a glass top, making it suitable for navigation at sea. The first reports of a compass used in this way date to 1119. An early twelfth-century Chinese writer gave two reasons that the ships engaged in maritime trade had to be large and carry several hundred sailors. First, they had to be ready to fight off pirates. Second, high volume was needed so that there would still be a profit after giving substantial "gifts" to the authorities at every port they visited. The most common product carried by the ships, this author reported, was Chinese ceramics.

In 1225 the superintendent of customs at Quanzhou, named Zhao Rukua, wrote an account of the countries with which Chinese merchants traded and the goods they offered for sale. It includes sketches of major trading cities from Srivijaya (modern Indonesia) to Malabar, Cairo, and Baghdad. Pearls were said to come from the Persian Gulf, ivory from Aden, myrrh from Somalia, pepper from Java and Sumatra, cotton from the various kingdoms of India, and so on. Marco Polo a few decades later wrote glowingly of the Chinese pepper trade, saying that for each load of pepper sent to Christendom, a hundred were sent to China. On his own travels home via the sea route, he reported seeing many merchants from southern China plying a thriving trade.

Much money could be made from the sea trade, but there were also great risks, so investors usually divided their investment among many ships, and each ship had many investors behind it. One observer thought eagerness to invest in overseas trade was leading to an outflow of copper cash. He wrote, "People along the coast are on intimate terms with the merchants who engage in overseas trade, either because they are fellow-countrymen or personal acquaintances. . . . [They give the merchants] money to take with them on their ships for the purchase and return conveyance of foreign goods. They invest from ten to a hundred strings of cash, and regularly make profits of several hundred per cent."[2]

In 1973 a Song ship that had been shipwrecked in 1277 was excavated off the south China coast. It was 78 feet long and 29 feet wide and had twelve bulkheads. Inside them were the luxury objects that the Song imported: over five thousand pounds of fragrant wood from Southeast Asia, pepper, betel nut, cowries, tortoiseshell, cinnabar, and ambergris from Somalia.

The Song Scholar-Official Class

The Song period saw the full flowering of one of the most distinctive features of Chinese civilization: the scholar-official class certified through highly competitive civil service examinations. Compared to its Tang counterpart, the Song Chinese scholar-official class was larger, better educated, and less aristocratic in its habits. The legitimacy of the power of this class was enhanced by its Confucian commitment to public service and by the ostensibly fair and objective ways through which its members gained access to ranks and honors.

The spread of printing aided the expansion of the educated class. In China, as in Europe centuries later, the introduction of printing dramatically lowered the price of books. Song scholars could afford to buy many more books than their counterparts in earlier dynasties. Song publishers printed the classics in huge editions. Works on philosophy, science, and medicine were

---

2. Cited in Shiba Yoshinobu, *Commerce and Society in Sung China*, trans. Mark Elvin (Ann Arbor: Center for Chinese Studies, University of Michigan, 1970), p. 33.

The Scholarly Life. This detail of a long handscroll by the court painter Ma Yuan (active 1189–1225) depicts a scholar writing a poem as others watch. Behind him is a monk; nearby are female attendants and a few children. *(The Nelson-Atkins Museum of Art, Kansas City, Missouri [Purchase: Nelson Trust] 63–19)*

avidly consumed, as were Buddhist texts. Han and Tang poetry and historical works were used as models by Song writers.

The demand for books was fueled in part by eagerness to compete in the civil service examinations. From the point of view of the early Song emperors, the purpose of written examinations was to identify capable men. So long as the successful candidates were literate, intelligent, and willing to work hard and obey the rules, the rulers had reason to be satisfied with the results, even if some able man were overlooked. From the point of view of those aspiring to office, however, issues of equity loomed large. Was everyone given an equal chance? Did examiners favor those they knew? Why should skill in poetry be tested when officials did not have to compose poems as part of their jobs? To increase confidence in the objectivity of the examiners, the names of the test takers were replaced with numbers and clerks recopied each exam so that the handwriting could not be recognized.

The Song examination system recruited four to five times more *jinshi* ("presented scholars," the highest examination degree) per year than the Tang system had. Yet increasing the number of *jinshi* did not lower the prestige of the degree. Rather, it encouraged more men to enter the competition. Early in the eleventh century, fewer than 30,000 men took the prefectural exams, which increased to nearly 80,000 by the end of that century and to about 400,000 by the dynasty's end. Because the number of available posts did not change, each candidate's chances of passing plummeted, reaching as low as 1 in 333 in some prefectures. Men often took the examinations several times and were on average a little over thirty years old when they succeeded.

Young men whose fathers or grandfathers had risen to high rank in the government did not have to take the examinations to get a government post; they could instead take advantage of the privilege higher officials had of nominating sons and grandsons for civil service appointment. Around 40 percent or more of posts in Song times were filled in this way. Men who started their careers through privilege usually had to begin at the very bottom, serving as sheriffs in remote places, and they might well spend their entire careers in county-level posts, never rising above magistrate. They may have spent much of their career collecting taxes and hearing legal cases (see **Documents: A Judge's Ruling**). It is no wonder then that most sons of officials were willing to at least try the civil service examinations.

In the 1950s and 1960s, western historians stressed the meritocratic side of the Chinese

A Judge's Ruling

In 1980 a Ming Dynasty copy of a long-lost Song collection of judicial decisions, titled Enlightened Judgments, *was discovered. This book offers evidence not only of Song judicial procedures, but also of the cast of characters who ended up in Song courts. The Song Dynasty largely took over the law code first issued by the Tang Dynasty, but the administration of justice involved much more than knowing the law. Magistrates and prefects were called on to promote morality, punish the wicked, and recognize which party was at fault when relatives fought over inheritances and merchants accused each other of cheating.*

In the case below, two fishmongers had gotten into a brawl, and the magistrate used his understanding of townsmen and farmers to decide which one was more at fault. The two are both called by numbers, the usual practice among common people in the period. The numbers reflect their sequence among the men of their generation in their family or lineage.

Competition in Selling Fish Resulted in Assaults

A proclamation: In the markets of the city the profits from commerce are monopolized by itinerant loiterers, while the little people from the rural villages are not allowed to sell their wares. There is not a single necessity of our clothing or food that is not the product of the fields of these old rustics. The men plow and the women weave. Their toil is extremely wearisome, yet what they gain from it is negligible, while manifold interest returns to these lazy idlers. This sort, in tens and hundreds, come together to form gangs. When the villagers come to sell things in the marketplace, before the goods have even left their hands, this crowd of idlers arrives and attacks them, assaulting them as a group. These idlers call this "the boxing of the community family." They are not at all afraid to act outrageously. I have myself seen that it is like this.

Have they not given thought to the foodstuffs they require and the clothing they wear? Is it produced by these people of the marketplaces? Or is it produced by the rural farmers? When they recognize that these goods are produced by the farming people of the rural villages, how can they look at them in anger? How can they bully and insult them?

Now, Pan Fifty-two and Li Seven are both fishmongers, but Pan lives in the city and fishmongering is his source of livelihood. Li Seven is a farmer, who does fishmongering between busy times. Pan Fifty-two at the end of the year has his profit, without having had the labor of raising the fish, but simply earning it from the selling of the fish. He hated Li and fought with him at the fish market. His lack of humanity is extreme! Li Seven is a village rustic. How could he fight with the itinerant armed loiterers who hang around the marketplace? Although no injuries resulted from the fight, we still must mete out some slight punishments. Pan Fifty-two is to be beaten fifteen blows with the heavy rod. In addition, Li Seven, although he is a village farmer, was still verbally abusive while the two men were stubbornly arguing. He clearly is not a man of simple and pure character. He must have done something to provoke this dispute. Li Seven is to be given a suspended sentence of a beating of ten blows, to be carried out if hereafter there are further violations.

Source: Brian Ed. McKnight and James T. C. Liu, trans., *The Enlightened Judgements. Ch'ing-ming chi* (Albany: State University of New York Press), pp. 471–472, slightly modified.

examination system and the social mobility it fostered. Lists of examination graduates showed that only about half had a father, grandfather, or great-grandfather who had served as an official. In recent decades, it has been more common to stress the advantages official families had in placing their sons in government posts and that even those who did not have a recent patrilineal ancestor who had served in office might have an uncle or a maternal grandfather who had done so. If the comparison is to other premodern societies, including Korea and Japan, Song China was exceptional in the opportunities it offered to intelligent, hard-working young men without powerful relatives. However, no one should assume that mobility through education occurred with the frequency it does in modern society.

Families able to educate their sons were generally landholders. When the Song elite is looked at from the perspective of the local community, families prominent for generations are more striking than new men. In a county with twenty thousand households, a dozen or so family lines might account for nearly all those who gained national notice. Still, because property had to be divided among sons every generation, downward social mobility was always a possibility if nothing was done to add to the family's income or property every generation. Yuan Cai, writing in the late twelfth century, stressed the importance of finding ways to increase the family's property. When one brother had private funds from office, he should not convert it into gold and silver in order to hide it, but should invest it so that it would grow:

> For instance, if he had 100,000 strings worth of gold and silver and used this money to buy productive property, in a year he would gain 10,000 strings; after ten years or so, he would have regained the 100,000 strings and what would be divided among the family would be interest. If it were invested in a pawn broking business, in three years the interest would equal the capital. He would still have the 100,000 strings, and the rest, being interest, could be

> divided. Moreover, it could be doubled again in another three years, ad infinitum.[3]

Members of the Song scholar-official class would rarely have spent their entire lives in their home counties or prefectures. Many traveled considerable distances to study with well-known teachers. If they succeeded in the first stage of the examinations, they had to travel to the capital for the next stage, held every three years. A large proportion of those who succeeded began their careers in county or prefectural posts, and over the next ten or twenty years might criss-cross the empire several times, returning to the capital between assignments. Travel to a new post might take a month or more, during which time the official would call on his colleagues in the places he passed. When Lu You left his home county in 1170 to take up an assignment in Sichuan, he spent 157 days on the road and called on dozens of officials, retired officials, and Buddhist and Daoist clergy along the way. He also had the chance to visit many sites made famous by earlier visitors who had written poems or essays about them.

Many Song men of letters were adept at a wide range of arts and sciences. One of the most versatile was Shen Gua, who tried his hand at everything from mathematics, geography, economics, engineering, medicine, divination, and archaeology to military strategy and diplomacy. On an assignment to inspect the frontier, he made a relief map of wood and glue-soaked sawdust to show the mountains, roads, rivers, and passes. He once computed the total number of possible situations on a game board and another time the longest possible military campaign given the limits of human carriers who had to carry their own food as well as food for the soldiers. Interest in the natural world, of the sort Shen Gua displayed, was not as common among the educated elite in Song times as interest in art and art collecting. The remarkable poet and states-

---

3. Patricia Buckley Ebrey, trans., *Family and Property in Sung China: Yuan Ts'ai's Precepts for Social Life* (Princeton, N.J.: Princeton University Press, 1984), pp. 199–200.

man Su Shi wrote glowingly of paintings done by scholars, who could imbue their paintings with ideas, making them much better than paintings that merely conveyed outward appearance, the sort of paintings that professional painters made. His friend Mi Fu, a passionate collector, would call on collectors to view and discuss their treasures. Often he would borrow pieces to study and copy. When he came across something that excited him, he made every effort to acquire it, generally by offering a trade.

Reformers and Anti-Reformers

How was the operation of the Song government affected by recruiting a large proportion of its staff through the examination system? Such men entered government service at older ages and after longer periods of study than men who entered other ways. Did the preponderance of such men alter the dynamics of political life?

One might have thought that *jinshi*, having been through much the same experience, would demonstrate remarkable solidarity with each other. But this did not happen. Exam graduates did not defend each other's qualifications or insist that every *jinshi* was fully qualified to practice government. The examination system did not lead to scholar-officials' thinking alike or looking out for each other's interests. To the contrary, they seem to have fought among themselves more viciously than the officials of earlier dynasties.

One explanation for their divisiveness might be that even after passing the examinations, competition continued unabated. Promotions in responsibility, honor, and pay did not come automatically. There were more men qualified for office than posts, so often after finishing one assignment, officials had to wait months or even years before getting their next one. Moreover, to get choice assignments, they often needed high officials to recommend them, adding to the uncertainty they faced.

What did officials fight about? Ostensibly, at least, how best to run the government. It was very common for younger officials, especially ones who had done well in the examinations, to be disappointed in the performance of the average official, whom they viewed as morally lazy, unwilling to make any exertion for the dynasty or the common people. Idealistic officials criticized the examination system for selecting such mediocre men. Other areas of tension were military and fiscal policy. If one wanted to push the Khitan out of the Sixteen Prefectures, as many did, one had to be willing to raise revenue somehow, but no one liked to see taxes raised.

Those with proposals to make had to find a way to get the emperor's ear and convince other officials to support their ideas. This meant lining up allies and maligning opponents. From the emperor's point of view, such activities were obstructionist. Rather, officials should speak candidly to the emperor about the realms of government they knew. It should be up to the emperor and his chancellors to weigh advice from diverse perspectives.

During the first phase of factional strife in the 1040s, a reform program was initiated by Fan Zhongyan, an idealistic Confucian best known for describing the duty of the Confucian scholar-official as "to be first in worrying about the world's troubles and last in enjoying its pleasures." Fan was an experienced official who had served as prefect of Kaifeng and had managed a successful military assignment against the Tanguts. Once appointed chancellor, he submitted a ten-point memorial, calling for reforms of the recruitment system, higher pay for local officials to discourage corruption, more use of sponsorship to base promotions more on competence and character, and the like. His proposals evoked strong resistance from those who were comfortable with the existing system and did not want to see the rules changed in the middle of their career. Within a year, the program was canceled and Fan replaced as chancellor. Fan's example, however, inspired many idealistic officials who hoped to take up where he had left off.

The one who managed to accomplish this was Wang Anshi (1021–1086). After a career largely in the provinces, he submitted a long memorial criticizing the examination system and the state schools. Shenzong, who had just succeeded to the throne at the age of nineteen, made Wang a chancellor and supported his program, called the New Policies.

Wang Anshi was intelligent and hard working and had original ideas. Realizing that government income was ultimately linked to the prosperity of farming families, he instituted measures he thought would help them, such as low-cost loans and replacing labor service with a tax. To raise revenues, he expanded state monopolies on tea, salt, and wine. He also had land resurveyed to make land taxes more equitable. He introduced a local militia to reduce the cost of maintaining a large standing army. To speed up introduction of reforms, a Finance Planning Commission was established to bypass the existing bureaucracy. The poetry component of the civil service examination was dropped in the hope of recruiting men with a more practical bent. Wang Anshi's own commentaries on the classics became required reading for candidates hoping to do well on the examinations.

The resistance these reforms evoked has led historians to suspect that interests were at stake. Wang and many of the reformers came from the south, but the split was not a simple north-south one or an old elite versus a newly rising one. Personal antagonisms certainly played a role, as did philosophical differences. In the vocabulary of the time, however, the struggle was portrayed as one between men of principle motivated by concern for the common good and misguided or nefarious inferior men who could not or would not see the larger picture. Each side, of course, considered themselves the men of principle and their opponents the inferior men.

From the perspective of Wang Anshi and Shenzong, opposition amounted to obstruction. To put their program into place, they wanted officials who supported it, not ones dead set against it. Yet dismissing all critics would make it difficult for the emperor to learn of unforeseen problems. Usually officials deemed obstructive were assigned offices outside the capital, but when the court wanted to be particularly harsh, it could send them to the far south, the regions where malaria and other tropical diseases were sometimes fatal to officials from the north.

One of the most egregious cases of persecution occurred in 1079. Su Shi, then serving in the provinces, was arrested on a charge that his writings defamed the emperor. He was brought to the capital under guard, like a criminal. After about five weeks of interrogation he decided to "tell all" and explained the indirect criticisms in his poems. To give an example, he had earlier written a poem that read:

> An old man of seventy, sickle at his waist,
> Feels guilty the spring mountain bamboo
>   and bracken are sweet.
> It's not that the music of Shao has made
>   him lose his sense of taste,
> It's just that he's eaten his food for three
>   months without salt.[4]

Su Shi explained that in this poem, by saying the hard-working impoverished old man had no appetite for food without salt, he was criticizing the severity of the laws governing the salt monopoly. Su Shi was found guilty and banished to Hubei province. More than thirty other individuals were implicated for such crimes as not reporting his slanderous poems.

The reform program came to an abrupt halt when Shenzong died in his mid-thirties in 1085. His heir, Zhezong, was only ten years old, so his grandmother served as regent. She had never approved the reforms and quickly set about bringing to court opponents of them, led by the senior statesman Sima Guang. Once the anti-reformers were in power, they quickly made sure that the reformers suffered the same treatment they had, sending them out of the capital as prefectural officials or worse. The New Policies were canceled wholesale, even measures that many had appreciated, such as the substitution of a tax for often onerous labor service.

---

4. Charles Hartman, "Poetry and Politics in 1079: The Crow Terrace Poetry Case of Su Shih," *Chinese Literature: Essays, Articles, and Reviews* 12 (1990): 23.

When his grandmother died in 1093, Zhezong began ruling on his own. He reversed his grandmother's policies and brought the reformers back to power. The cycles of revenge and retaliation continued as the reformers banished the anti-reformers. Zhezong succumbed to an illness while still in his twenties and was succeeded by his younger brother Huizong (r. 1100–1125), who also sided with the reformers. His government banned the writings of key opponents of reform including Sima Guang and Su Shi and elevated Wang Anshi. A statue of Wang Anshi was placed in the Confucian temple next to Mencius, and pictures of him were distributed throughout the country.

THE FALL OF THE NORTHERN SONG AND THE JIN DYNASTY

Huizong's interests extended well beyond the reform program. Committed to the cultural side of rulership, he collected paintings, calligraphies, and antiquities on a huge scale and had catalogues compiled of his collections. He took a personal interest in the training of court artists and instituted examinations for their selection. He wrote poetry as well as treatises on medicine and Daoism. He initiated an ambitious reform of court music and court rituals. He took a personal interest in architecture and garden design, created his own distinctive calligraphy style, and produced exquisite paintings.

While Huizong was busy with these projects, the balance of power among Song, Liao, and Xia was radically altered by the rise of a new tribal group in the northeast, the Jurchens. The Jurchens, just one of many tribal groups subordinate to the Liao, lived in villages and small walled towns in the forests and river valleys of the Liao and Sungari rivers, their economy based on fishing, hunting, animal husbandry, and some farming. Jurchens who lived near Chinese, Khitan, Parhae, or Koryŏ cities adopted practices and technologies from these neighbors, leading to a distinction between the "civilized"

Jurchens and their "wild" counterparts in more remote areas. The lands the Jurchens occupied were ideal for horse raising, and by the mid-eleventh century, the Jurchens were selling the Khitans about ten thousand horses per year. During the mid- to late eleventh century, the Wanyan clan gradually gained the dominant position among the Jurchens. In the early twelfth century, under the leadership of Wanyan Aguda (1068–1123), the Jurchens began challenging Liao authority. In 1115 their repudiation of Liao overlordship was made explicit by the proclamation of their own dynasty, the Jin (Golden).

States North of Song	
Dynasty name	**Ethnic group**
Liao	Khitan
Xia	Tangut
Jin	Jurchen
Yuan	Mongol

The Song heard rumors of what was happening from Chinese defectors from Liao. Huizong's leading general, Tong Guan (1054–1126), by then a member of the Council of State (see **Biography: Tong Guan, Eunuch General**), urged making a secret alliance with Jin. After a series of envoys had been exchanged, it was decided that Jin and Song would cooperate to defeat Liao, then divide its territory, with Song promised the recovery of the Sixteen Prefectures.

In the process of defeating Liao, Jin discovered that the Song was not much of a military threat, and attacked it next. Kaifeng was besieged, an enormous ransom paid to escape slaughter, and thousands taken captive, including Huizong, the imperial clan, craftsmen, and female entertainers.

Jin went on to establish a stable government in north China and Manchuria. In the beginning, Jin continued the dual government of Liao and employed former Liao officials, both Chinese and Khitan. Jin ruled a much larger Chinese

BIOGRAPHY Tong Guan, Eunuch General

The eunuch Tong Guan (1054–1126) was the favorite general of the Song emperor, Huizong (r. 1100–1125). In Song times, it was not unusual to have eunuchs serve as military commanders, and Tong Guan began his military career as a protégé of the leading eunuch general of the 1080s.

According to contemporaries, Tong Guan was a striking-looking man, with a strong body, penetrating stare, and more beard than the typical eunuch. Soon after Huizong took the throne, he sent Tong Guan to Hangzhou to acquire old books and paintings for the palace. Not long afterward, Tong Guan was given a military assignment on the northwestern borders, where he had a string of victories and developed a reputation as an excellent commander. In 1111 he accompanied a mission to Liao, and from then on his rank and influence steadily increased. In 1112 he reached the top of the military command structure, and in 1116 he became the first eunuch in Song times to be a member of the highest policy-forming organ in the government.

Huizong treated Tong Guan much as he would have a high civil official, to the annoyance of other high officials. In 1104, after Tong Guan achieved his first notable victory, Huizong conferred on him a piece of his calligraphy in his own distinctive "Slender Gold" style. Accounts of parties Huizong organized for his top officials in 1113 and 1119 list Tong Guan as a guest. When Huizong had the catalogue of his painting collection compiled, Tong Guan was one of ten palace eunuchs given biographies as talented painters. In it he is described as solemn and slow to show his feelings.

In 1118 Tong Guan proposed allying with the Jurchens against Liao as a way to recover the Sixteen Prefectures. Although many officials opposed this plan, Huizong approved it, and Tong Guan played a leading role in negotiations with envoys from Jin. In 1120, by then sixty-six years old, Tong Guan was sent out with his army to attack the Liao southern capital, Yanjing. But when he got his troops in place, he was ordered to turn his army around and march several hundred miles south to Zhejiang province, where the Fang La rebellion had broken out. He quelled the rebellion in a matter of months, then returned to the northern border. There his army was routed. The Jurchens took the city, looted it, and turned it over to Song in exchange for substantial payments. When Tong Guan returned to Kaifeng, he was forced to retire. Yet, in 1124, at age seventy-one, Tong Guan was recalled and sent back to the northern border. Huizong apparently had no other general he trusted as much as Tong Guan.

It was Tong Guan himself who arrived in Kaifeng in the last month of 1125 to tell Huizong that the Jurchens had invaded. Tong Guan took charge of the bodyguards who accompanied Huizong on his flight from the capital after abdicating. Once out of Kaifeng, Tong Guan, like Huizong's other top officials, had calumny heaped on him for his part in the military disaster, and before long Huizong's successor had him executed. Perhaps that was a better fate for a military man than to have remained with Huizong and been carried into captivity by the Jurchens.

population than Liao had and had to distribute Jurchens throughout north China to maintain control. Gradually more and more Chinese political institutions were adopted and more Chinese officials employed. Jin moved its capital from central Manchuria to Beijing in 1153 and to Kaifeng in 1161. Like other non-Chinese rulers before them, the Jurchens found that Chinese political institutions such as hereditary succession were a potent weapon in their competition with their own nobles. The Jurchen rulers did not adopt Chinese traditions of respect for the dignity of officials, however. Jin emperors had high officials flogged in open court, a brutal violation of the Confucian dictum that officials are to be treated according to ritual and not subjected to physical punishments.

Because they lived surrounded by Chinese, many Jurchens adopted Chinese customs in language, dress, and rituals. Jurchen generals opposed to sinification assassinated the Jin emperor in 1161, and the succeeding emperor did his best to raise the prestige of Jurchen as a written language. He ordered Jurchens to attend special Jurchen-language schools, had Chinese texts translated into Jurchen, and instituted Jurchen-language civil service examinations. Later Jin emperors largely accepted sinification, viewing the Chinese classics, for instance, as universal texts, not exclusively Chinese ones. In 1191 an emperor even outlawed referring to the Jurchens as "border people," a relatively polite Chinese term, seeing no reason that their country should not be viewed as the Central Kingdom (the common Chinese term for China).

HANGZHOU AND THE SOUTHERN SONG

One of Huizong's sons was out of Kaifeng when the Jurchens occupied Kaifeng, and after his father and brothers were transported north, Song forces rallied around him and had him installed as emperor (Gaozong, r. 1127–1162). The south had never been held by forces from the steppe, and Gaozong wisely retreated to that region. Still the military situation remained precarious: the Jurchens not only pursued Gaozong across the Yangzi River, but even out into the sea. To get far from the Jurchens, the Song ended up making its capital Hangzhou, a beautiful city well south of the Yangzi River (see Map 8.2).

Gaozong disavowed the New Policies reform program, but this did not end factional strife, as other issues emerged around which officials divided, above all how aggressively to pursue recovery of the north. Efforts to drive the Jurchens out of north China were largely abandoned in 1141, when a peace treaty was concluded with Jin. Song agreed to heavy payments of silk and silver to Jin, much as the Northern Song had made payments to Liao.

Because the economic center of the country had already shifted south, loss of the north did not ruin the Song economy. Sixty percent of the population was still under Song control, along with much of the most productive agricultural land. The government still had to devote a large part of its revenues to defense, but it was able to raise much of its revenue through taxes on commerce. The government's monetary policies in time, however, produced rampant inflation.

Hangzhou itself grew to 1 million or more residents. At the southern end of the Grand Canal, it was a natural center for trade. Fortunetellers, acrobats, puppeteers, storytellers, tea houses, and restaurants were all to be found in the entertainment quarters. There were brokers who had girls and young women available for purchase or hire as rough or refined maids, concubines, singers, or prostitutes. Schools were found throughout the city, which also had many Buddhist and Daoist temples. For banquets and other parties, there were catering companies that provided all of the food, tents, tables, chairs, and even decorations. To combat fire, the government stationed two thousand soldiers at fourteen fire stations within the city and more outside it. Poverty was more of a problem in crowded cities than in the countryside, and the government not only distributed alms but operated public clinics and old age homes as well as paupers' graveyards. The better-off residents in the city often formed clubs; a text written in 1235 mentions the West Lake Poetry Club, the Buddhist Tea Society, the Physical Fitness Club, the Anglers' Club, the Occult Club, the Young Girls' Chorus, the Exotic Foods Club, the Plants and Fruits Club, the Antique Collectors' Club, the Horse-Lovers' Club, and the Refined Music Society.

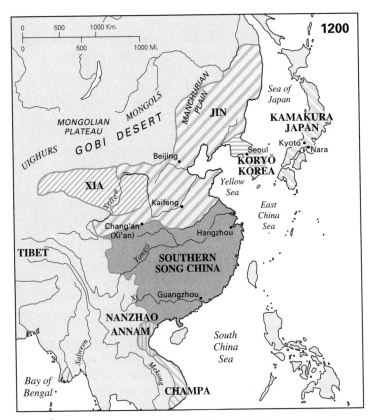

Map 8.2   Southern Song, Jin, and Xia ca. 1200

SONG CULTURE AND SOCIETY

The Song period was one of advance in many facets of culture, ranging from scientific discoveries to landscape paintings. In addition, because of the spread of printing, more books and more types of books survive from the Song than from earlier periods, providing more glimpses of ordinary people's lives.

The Revival of Confucianism and the Learning of the Way

The scholar-statesmen of the eleventh century, such as Fan Zhongyan, Wang Anshi, Sima Guang, and Su Shi, believed that they were pursuing Confucian agendas of advising the ruler and aiding the common people. Other influential Confucian teachers of the period, notably

the Cheng brothers, Cheng Hao and Cheng Yi, were more interested in metaphysics and ethics and argued that moral self-cultivation was more fundamental than service to the ruler. Their explanations of the workings of principle (*li*) and vital energy (*qi*) can be seen as a response to the sophisticated metaphysics of Buddhism. The principle for something could be moral or physical; for example, the principle for wives is essentially moral in nature, that for trees, physical. For either to exist, however, there must also be the energy and substance that constitute things. The theory of principle and vital energy allowed Song thinkers to validate Mencius's claim of the goodness of human nature and still explain human wrongdoing: principle underlying human beings is good, but their endowment of vital energy is more or less impure, giving rise to selfish impulses. Followers of the Cheng brothers referred to their school as the Learning

Color Plate 8
Hunting Scene. This image of a hunting scene appears on the wall of the Dancing Tomb at Tongkou near the Koguryŏ capital of Kungnae, north of the Yalu River, sixth century.

(Kim Wonyong, ed. *Han'guk misul chonjip [the complete collection of Korean Art] vol. 4, Pyokhwa [wall paintings].* Seoul: Tonghwa ch'ulp'an kongsa, 1974, plate 56, p. 68.)

Color Plate 9
Women Dancers. Women dancers performing before an audience on the wall of the Dancing Tomb at Tongkou near the Koguryŏ capital of Kungnae, sixth century.

(Kim Wonyong, ed. *Han'guk misul chonjip [the complete collection of Korean Art] vol. 4 Pyokhwa [wall paintings].* Seoul: Tonghwa ch'ulp'an kongsa, 1974, plate 55, p. 76)

Color Plate 11
Respecting the Elders. This scene from the handscroll *Women's Classic of Filial Piety Illustrated* shows a man kneeling before his parents as his wife and a maid wait for orders.

(National Palace Museum, Taipei, Taiwan, Republic of China)

Color Plate 10
Silla Gold Crown. This is the largest example of Silla gold crowns from the Tomb of the Heavenly Horse, early sixth century.

(Kyongju National Museum, Kyongju)

Color Plate 12
Liao Sculpture of a Luohan. Buddhist art flourished under the Liao, as can be seen from this 30-inch tall ceramic sculpture of one of the Buddha's leading disciples.

(The Metropolitan Museum of Art, Frederick C. Hewitt Fund, 1921 [21.76]. Photograph by Lynton Gardiner. Photograph ©1989 The Metropolitan Museum of Art.)

Color Plate 13
Celadon vase with inlaid cloud and cranes. This is an example of the beautiful celadon vases for which the Koryŏ Dynasty is known. It dates back to the late twelfth century.

(National Treasure No. 68, Kansong Museum of Fine Arts, Seoul. Plate 87 on p. 83 of Choi Sunu, *5000 Years of Korean Art* [Soeul: Hyonam Publishing Co., 1970].)

Color Plate 14
The Tale of Genji. This picture scroll contains text interspersed with illustrations. Both men and women blackened their teeth and painted eyebrows high on their foreheads. Men wore hats, women let their hair trail down their backs.

(Goshima Art Museum in Tokyo/Corbis)

Color Plate 15 Persian View of the Mongols. This fourteenth-century illustration of Rashid ad-Din's *History of the World* shows the Mongols attacking Chengdu. Chinese sources report that the entire population of the city was slaughtered, something one would never guess from the Persian depiction.

(Bibliotheque Nationale, Paris/The Art Archive)

Color Plate 16 Receiving Medical Attention. The fourteenth century wall paintings at the Daoist temple Yongle gong survive in remarkably good condition. Depictions of the miracles performed by Daoist Perfected Ones often show scenes of daily life, such as this one of a woman receiving medical attention.

(Cultural Relics Publishing House)

of the Way (Daoxue). In English this movement is often termed neo-Confucianism to stress how different it was from early Confucianism.

After the loss of the north to the Jurchens, the elite lost confidence in the possibility of reform from above and began proposing ways to build a more ideal society by starting from the bottom, reforming families and local communities, establishing schools and academies, and spreading their message through publishing works for diverse audiences. The greatest of these Southern Song Confucian masters was Zhu Xi (1130–1200). Although he passed the *jinshi* examination at the young age of eighteen, he spent very little of the next fifty-two years in government service. (The government in essence supported his teaching career by regularly appointing him to sinecures with few or no duties.) Zhu Xi taught groups of disciples and led the way in establishing private academies as the institutional basis for the revived Confucianism. These gathering places for teachers and their disciples were often located on mountains, much like monasteries, and like them allowed a retreat from the world.

Zhu Xi extended the Cheng brothers' ideas in many directions. Confucius and Mencius had just said to be good, apparently assuming that anyone who desired to be good could do so. Zhu Xi's letters and conversations show that many of his contemporaries wanted a path toward goodness, with steps to follow and ways to judge their progress. He encouraged his students to master the Four Books—the *Analects, Mencius, Doctrine of the Mean,* and the *Great Learning.* The last two, each a chapter in the canonical *Book of Rites,* stress that improvement of the world starts by improvement of the mind. As the *Great Learning* puts it:

Those in antiquity who wished to illuminate luminous virtue throughout the world would first govern their states; wishing to govern their states, they would first bring order to their families; wishing to bring order to their families they would first cultivate their own persons; wishing to cultivate their own persons, they would first rectify their minds; wishing to rectify their minds, they would first make their thoughts sincere; wishing to make their thoughts sincere, they would first extend their knowledge. The extension of knowledge lies in the investigation of things.[5]

Zhu Xi and his disciples frequently discussed what was entailed in this "investigation of things." Study, Zhu argued, should be intensive rather than extensive:

Zhengchun said, "I'd like to survey a great many books."

"Don't do that," Zhu Xi said. "Read one book thoroughly, then read another one. If you confusedly try to advance on several fronts, you will end up with difficulties. It's like archery. If you are strong enough for a five-pint bow, use a four-pint one. You will be able to draw it all the way and still have strength left over. Students today do not measure their own strength when reading books. I worry that we cannot manage what we already have set ourselves."[6]

Even if he urged his disciples to focus their energies, Zhu Xi's own interests were very broad. He discussed with his disciples everything from geomancy to the nature of fossils, the political events of the past century, and perplexing passages in the classics.

However much his disciples admired him, many of Zhu Xi's contemporaries found him offensively self-righteous. Near the end of his life, his teachings were condemned as "spurious learning," and candidates for the examinations were forbidden to cite them. Yet within decades of his death, this judgment was reversed. In 1241 an emperor credited Zhu Xi with "illuminating the Way," and government students had to study his commentaries to the Four Books.

---

5. William Theodore de Bary and Irene Bloom, eds., *Sources of Chinese Tradition,* rev. ed. (New York: Columbia University Press, 1999), pp. 330–331.

6. Patricia Buckley Ebrey, ed., *Chinese Civilization: A Sourcebook* (New York: The Free Press, 1993), p. 173.

Gender Roles and Family Life

By Song times, sources are diverse enough to see that the old principles that men belong outside the house and women in it, or that men plow and women weave, should not be taken too literally. Song stories, documents, and legal cases show women doing a wide range of activities never prescribed in Confucian didactic texts. There were widows who ran inns, midwives delivering babies, pious women who spent their days chanting sutras, nuns who called on such women to explain Buddhist doctrine, girls who learned to read with their brothers, farmers' daughters who made money by weaving mats, childless widows who accused their nephews of seizing their property, wives who were jealous of the concubines their husbands brought home, and women who drew from their dowries to help their husband's sisters marry well.

Families who could afford it tried to keep their wives and daughters at home, where there was plenty for them to do. Not only was there the work of tending children and preparing meals, but spinning, weaving, and sewing took a great deal of time. Women in silk-producing families were very busy during the silkworm growing period. Women had to coddle the worms, feeding them chopped mulberry tree leaves and keeping them warm, in order to get them to spin their cocoons. (See Color Plate 11.)

Women tended to marry between the ages of sixteen and twenty. Their husbands were, on average, a couple of years older than they were. Their marriages were arranged by their parents, who called on a professional matchmaker (usually an older woman) or turned to a friend or relative for suggestions. Before the wedding took place, written agreements were exchanged that listed the prospective bride's and groom's birthdates, parents' and grandparents' names, and the gifts that would be exchanged, as well as the dowry the bride would bring. The idea was to match families of approximately equal status, but a young man who had just passed the civil service exams would be considered a good prospect even if his family had little wealth or rank.

A few days before the wedding, the bride's family sent her dowry, which at a minimum contained boxes full of clothes and bedding. In better-off families, it also included items of substantial value, such as gold jewelry or deeds for land. On the day of the wedding, the groom and some of his friends and relatives went to the bride's home to get her. Dressed in elaborate finery, she tearfully bid farewell to everyone in her family and then stepped into the fancy sedan chair that carried her to her new home. Musicians were an important part of the procession, alerting everyone on the street that a wedding was taking place. Meanwhile, the groom's family's friends and relatives gathered at his home so they would be there to greet the bridal party. The bride knelt and bowed to her new parents-in-law and later the tablets representing the family's ancestors. Her husband, whom she was meeting for the first time, shared a cup of wine with her, a classical ritual still in practice. Later the young couple were shown to their new bedroom, where the bride's dowry had already been placed, and people would toss beans or rice on the bed, symbolizing the desired fertility. After teasing them, the guests would finally leave them alone and go out to the courtyard for the wedding feast.

After the guests had all departed, the young bride's first priority was to try to win over her mother-in-law, since everyone knew that mothers-in-law were hard to please. One way to do this was to bear a son for the family quickly. Within the patrilineal system, a woman fully secured her position in the family only by becoming the mother of one of the men. Every community had older women skilled in midwifery who could be called to help when she went into labor. If the family was well-to-do, they might also arrange for a wet nurse to help her take care of the newborn, though some Song scholars disapproved of depriving another child of milk for the sake of one's own child.

Families frequently had four, five, or six children, but likely one or more would die in infancy or early childhood. Within the home, women generally had considerable voice and took an active interest in issues such as the selection of marriage partners for their children. If a son reached adulthood and married before his mother was widowed, she was considered fortunate, for she would always have had an adult man who could take care of business for her—first her husband, then her grown son. But in the days when infectious diseases killed many people in their twenties and thirties, it was not uncommon for a woman to be widowed before her children were grown. If her husband had brothers and they had not yet divided their household, she would stay with them, assuming they were not so poor that they could not afford a few more mouths to feed. Otherwise she could return to her natal family. Taking another husband was also a possibility, though it was considered an inferior alternative from a moral point of view.

Women with healthy and prosperous husbands faced another challenge in middle age: their husbands could bring home a concubine (or more than one, if the family was rich enough). Moralists insisted that it was wrong for a wife to be jealous of her husband's concubines, but many women could not get used to their husband's paying attention to another woman. Wives outranked concubines and could give them orders in the house, but concubines had their own ways of getting back, especially when they were twenty and the wife was forty and no longer so attractive. The children born to a concubine were considered just as much children of the family as the wife's children, and if the wife had no sons, she would often raise a concubine's sons herself, since she would be dependent on them in her old age.

As a woman's children grew up, she would start thinking of suitable marriage partners. Women whose sons and daughters were all married could take it easy: they had daughters-in-law to do the cooking and cleaning and could enjoy their grandchildren and help with their education. Many found more time for religious devotions at this stage of their life. Their sons, still living with them, were often devoted to

them and did their best to make their late years comfortable.

The social and economic changes associated with the Tang-Song transition brought changes to gender roles. With the expansion of the educated class, more women learned to read. In the scholar-official class, many women were literate enough to serve as their children's first teachers. One of the most accomplished poets of Song times, Li Qingzhao (1084–ca. 1151), was a woman from a scholar-official family. After her husband's death, she wrote of the evenings she and he had spent poring over his recent purchases of paintings, calligraphy, or ancient bronze vessels. Many of her poems have been interpreted as expressions of her longing for him when he was away or her sorrow at his loss:

> Lovely in my inner chamber.
> My tender heart, a wisp; my sorrow
>   tangled in a thousand skeins.
> I'm fond of spring, but spring is gone,
> And rain urges the petals to fall.
>
> I lean on the balustrade;
> Only loose ends left, and no feeling.
> Where is he?
> Withered grasses stretch to the heavens;
> I can't make out the path that leads him
>   home to me.[7]

The Learning of the Way is sometimes blamed for a decline in the status of women in Song times, largely because Cheng Yi once told a follower that it would be better for a widow to die of starvation than to lose her virtue by remarrying. In later centuries, this saying was often quoted to justify pressuring widows, even very young ones, to stay with their husband's family and not marry someone else. In Song times, however, widows commonly remarried.

---

7. Trans. by Eugene Eoyang in Kang-i Sun Chang and Haun Saussy, eds., *Women Writers of Traditional China: An Anthology of Poetry and Criticism* (Stanford, Calif.: Stanford University Press, 1999), pp. 95–96.

It is true that foot binding began during the Song Dynasty, but it was not recommended by Confucian teachers; rather, it was associated with the pleasure quarters and with women's efforts to beautify themselves. Mothers bound the feet of girls aged five to eight, using long strips of cloth. The goal was to keep their feet from growing and to bend the four smaller toes under to make the foot narrow and arched. Women with feet shaped these ways were considered elegant and lovely. Foot binding spread gradually during Song times but probably remained largely an elite practice. (See **Material Culture: Huang Sheng's Clothing** for an upper-class woman who had bound feet in the late Song.) In later centuries, it became extremely common in north and central China, eventually spreading to all classes. Women with bound feet were less mobile than women with natural feet, but only those who could afford servants bound their feet so tight that walking was difficult.

Religion in Song Life

The religious activities of laypeople are much better known for the Song than earlier periods. The text that has attracted the most attention from historians of the Song is *The Record of the Listener*, a huge book of more than two hundred chapters, written by Hong Mai (1123–1202). Hong came from a prominent official family in the south (Jiangxi), and his book recorded events that he learned about firsthand or from friends, relatives, and colleagues. Many of these anecdotes dealt in one way or another with the spirit realm and people's interaction with it.

How did people conceive of the spirit realm? They understood that both blessings and misfortunes could be caused by all sorts of gods and spirits. The gods included the nationally recognized gods of Buddhism and Daoism as well as gods and demons particular to their locality. As was true in much earlier times, dissatisfied ancestors were seen as possible causes of illness in their descendants. Like ancestors, gods and demons were thought to feel the same sorts of emotions as people. Demons and other malevolent spirits might extort offerings, acting much like local bullies. Gods were seen as parts of complex hierarchies, much like those in the human world. Some were seen as the rulers of small territories—local kings and lords. Others were seen as part of an otherworldly government, where gods held specific offices and transmitted paperwork from those below them to those above. Gods were not conceived as omnipotent, and a god might inform a petitioner that he would have to seek the approval of a higher god. (See Color Plate 12.)

One way people learned whether particular spirits were responsible for their problems was through divination. Another was through dreams or visions. Hong Mai told of an official named Lu Zao who dreamed of meeting an imposing man at an impressive temple. The man introduced himself as the King of Opportune Aid and asked the official to compose an account of him and told him what it should say. Two years later, local people saw an apparition that they concluded must be the same god. Consequently they built a temple for this god, and Lu composed the account that the god had earlier requested.

How did people intervene in the spirit realm? There were steps they could do themselves, such as trying to gain spirits' favor by making offerings, beseeching them in prayers, or discovering their wishes by tossing blocks to see which side they landed on (a form of divination). But people also often turned to religious experts ranging from ordained Buddhist and Daoist clerics, unordained practitioners of these traditions, to professional fortunetellers, and to the wardens of temples to local gods who acted as spirit mediums or exorcists. In one instance, a man pestered by a ghost first employed a local exorcist. When that failed to solve his problem, he called on a visiting Daoist priest to perform an offering ceremony. He then called on Buddhist monks from the local monastery to recite incantations and conduct an exorcism, which finally brought results.

MATERIAL CULTURE

Huang Sheng's Clothing

In 1242, at the age of fourteen or fifteen Huang Sheng married an imperial clansman distantly related to the throne. Her father was a high-ranking official who had earlier served as superintendent of foreign trade in the major seaport of Quanzhou. Her husband's grandfather had recently been administrator of the imperial clan in Quanzhou. Both families hailed from Fuzhou, Fujian, and her father and her husband's grandfather had become acquainted when they both were studying with a disciple of Zhu Xi.

The year after her marriage, Huang Sheng died, possibly in childbirth. Buried with her was a profusion of items that must have constituted her splendid and costly dowry. Altogether there were 201 pieces of women's clothing and 153 lengths of cloth, all finely made. Among the objects were several sets of shoes for bound feet. There were also long robes, jackets, vests, wrap-around skirts, and various sorts of underwear. Patterned gauzes were very common, perhaps because of the warm climate of Fuzhou. From these items we can imagine not only how elegantly upper-class women dressed, but also see how families passed property to their daughters.

Floral Patterns. Many of Huang Sheng's garments were trimmed with ribbons decorated with floral designs, four of which are illustrated here.

Gauze Vest. The light-weight, transparent silk gauze of this vest has woven-in decoration of peonies. *(Cultural Relics Publishing House)*

When doctors failed to cure them, people regularly called on religious experts. Hong Mai recorded a case of a medium known as Pan Who Sees Demons who was called on to help an ill woman. After making offerings to a spirit he served, Pan had a vision of a woman and a cat, which he described to the ill woman. She realized the woman had to be a maidservant who had died years earlier in her home. Pan then had the boy who worked with him become possessed by the maid's spirit. The boy spoke in her voice, letting all see that she blamed her mistress for her accidental death. After the boy awakened, Pan wrote out a dispatch to send to the City God, who in turn had the spirit of the dead maid sent to purgatory. In this instance, the City God acted much like a government official in the human world, receiving and dispatching orders.

In Hong Mai's accounts, educated men were sometimes skeptics. When Liu Zai (1166–1239) served in a low county post, we are told, he was the only official there to ignore a prominent local shrine. In fact, he raised his sleeve every time he went by in order to avoid having to look at the shrine. Before he had been there long, his wife's younger brother died. Then his pregnant wife had an ominous dream: the enshrined god told her that he had taken her brother because of her husband's impudence and would take her next if Liu did not repent. When she too died, Liu went to the shrine to beg forgiveness.

The Song state claimed the power to approve and disapprove local shrines. Occasionally the court ordered the destruction of illicit or excessive shrines, such as shrines whose divinities resembled demons, making extortionate demands on people. Much more common was the government's bestowal of titles on local gods. Local supporters of shrines regularly petitioned the government to confer titles of king, duke, or lord on their gods, recounting the miracles their god had performed.

SUMMARY

In what ways was the China of the late thirteenth century different from the China of the mid-tenth century? Its population had nearly doubled. More of the population lived in the south, which had become the undisputed economic center of China. China had become a more commercialized society, with a higher proportion of its farmers engaged in producing for the market. The scholar-official elite of the late Song was very different from the elite of the Five Dynasties or early Song. With the expansion of education, the size of the educated class had grown much larger, and the *jinshi* examinations had become a defining element in its culture. The Confucian revival was shifting the focus of literati learning from literature toward the Four Books and Zhu Xi's commentaries on the classics. The Song Dynasty began with a powerful neighbor to the north, but over the course of the next three centuries, the balance of power continued to shift in favor of the north. Jin held more of China proper than Liao had, and the Mongols were a more formidable foe in the mid-thirteenth century than the Jurchens had been in the mid-twelfth. The concept of the Mandate of Heaven—that heaven recognizes a single Son of Heaven ruling over the civilized world—was more and more difficult to sustain. During Song times more than one ruler called himself "Son of Heaven."

SUGGESTED READING

Until the Cambridge History volume on the Song appears, the fullest general history on the Song Dynasty is F. Mote, *Imperial China, 900–1800* (1999). Liao, Xia, and Jin, however, are treated in depth in H. Franke and D. Twitchett, eds., *The Cambridge History of China*, vol. 6: *Alien Regimes and Border States* (1994). On Liao, see also K. Wittfogel and C. Feng, *History of Chinese Society: Liao (907–1125)* (1946); J. Tao, *Two Sons of Heaven: Studies in Sung-Liao Relations* (1988); and N. Steinhardt, *Liao Architecture* (1997). On the Jurchens, see J. Tao, *The Jurchen in Twelfth-Century China: A Study of Sinicization* (1976), and H. Tillman and S. West, eds., *China Under Jurchen Rule* (1995). Relations among these states and Song are treated in M. Rossabi, ed., *China Among Equals: The Middle Kingdom and Its Neighbors* (1983).

A lively introduction to the culture of the Song period is J. Gernet, *Daily Life in China on the Eve of the Mongol Invasion, 1250–76* (1962). On the economy, see Y. Shiba, *Commerce and Society in Sung China* (1970), and B. So, *Prosperity, Region, and Institutions in Maritime China: The South Fukien Pattern, 946–1368* (2000). On Song government, see J. Chaffee, *The Thorny Gates of Learning in Sung China: A Social History of Examinations* (1985); J. Liu, *Reform in Sung China: Wang An-Shih (1021–1086) and His New Policies* (1957); P. Smith, *Taxing Heaven's Storehouse: Bureaucratic Entrepreneurship and the Sichuan Tea and Horse Trade, 1074–1224* (1991); E. Kracke, *Civil Service in Sung China: 960–1076* (1953); R. Hymes and C. Schirokauer, eds., *Ordering the World: Approaches to State and Society in Sung Dynasty China* (1993); and B. McKnight, *Law and Order in Sung China* (1992).

For Song men of letters, see J. Liu, *Ou-yang Hsiu* (1967); R. Egan, *Word, Image, and Deed in the Life of Su Shi* (1994); and J. Chaves, *Mei Yao-ch'en and the Development of Early Sung Poetry* (1976). On Song scholar-painters, see S. Bush and H. Shih, *Early Chinese Texts on Painting* (1985), and A. Murck, *Poetry and Painting in Song China: The Subtle Art of Dissent* (2000). On scholar-officials as an elite, see R. Hymes, *Statesmen and Gentlemen: The Elite of Fu-chou, Chiang-hsi, in Northern and Southern Sung* (1986); P. Ebrey, *Family and Property in Sung China: Yuan Ts'ai's Precepts for Social Life* (1984); and B. Bossler, *Powerful Relations: Kinship, Status, and the State in Sung China (960–1279)* (1998).

On the Confucian revival, see A. C. Graham, *Two Chinese Philosophers: Ch'eng Ming-tao and Ch'eng Yi-ch'uan* (1958); P. Bol, *"This Culture of Ours": Intellectual Transitions in T'ang and Sung China* (1992); H. Tillman, *Confucian Discourse and Chu His's Ascendancy* (1992); and D. Gardner, trans., *Learning to Be a Sage: Selections from Conversations of Master Chu, Arranged Topically* (1990).

On religion in the Song period, see V. Hansen, *Changing the Gods in Medieval China, 1127–1276* (1990); P. Ebrey and P. Gregory, eds., *Religion and Society in Tang and Sung China* (1993); P. Gregory and D. Getz, eds., *Buddhism in the Sung* (1999); E. Davis, *Society and the Supernatural in Song China* (2001); and R. Hymes, *Way and Byway: Taoism, Local Religion, and Models of Divinity in Sung and Modern China* (2002). On women's lives, see P. Ebrey, *The Inner Quarters: Marriage and the Lives of Chinese Women in the Sung Period* (1993), and B. Birge, *Women, Property, and Confucian Reaction in Sung and Yuan China (960–1368)* (2002).

CHAPTER NINE

The Koryŏ Dynasty (889–1259)

The last phase of Silla (889–935) is known as the Later Three Kingdoms period during which Korea was divided into three separate dynasties. Power was unified under Koryŏ in 935, and Korea came close to a kind of near-feudal disintegration after a military takeover of the government in 1170, but that process was not carried to completion because of the Mongol conquest of Koryŏ in 1258.

A number of problems that emerged in the period are covered in this chapter. From early Koryŏ to 1170, a series of kings attempted to create a more centralized bureaucracy under civil rule in the face of unprecedented military challenges from the north. What were the obstructions facing both centralized and civil rule? How successful was the Koryŏ military in defending the nation? How successful was Koryŏ diplomacy in meeting foreign challenges? Did early Koryŏ society represent a transformation of the Silla bone rank system? After 1170, did the period of military rule eliminate both aristocrats and Confucian thought from Koryŏ society and protect the nation against the Mongols?

THE LATER THREE KINGDOMS (889–935)

In 889 the son of a Silla general, Kyŏn Hwŏn, rebelled in the southwest. Two years later, a bandit named Yanggil rebelled where modern Kangwŏn province is today, and he was joined by the son of King Hŏn'an by a concubine, Kim Kungye. The two rebels became rivals for the takeover of Silla territory. Kyŏn Hwŏn won Yanggil to his side, but Kungye enlisted Wang Kŏn, a member of a powerful merchant family in Song'ak (modern Kaesŏng), and Kungye moved his base there in 898.

Kyŏn Hwŏn established the Later Paekche Dynasty at Wansan in 900, and Kungye founded the Later Koguryŏ Dynasty in 901. By 905 he had changed the dynasty's name to Majin and moved its capital to Chŏrwŏn, east of modern Seoul. His armies captured most of the territory from Pyongyang south to Ch'ungch'ŏng Province, and he sent Wang Kŏn to capture the port of Naju south of Chŏnju in Kyŏn Hwŏn's rear to control the shipping lanes around Later Paekche.

In 911 Kungye again changed the dynastic name, this time to T'aebong, proclaimed himself a Maitreya Buddha and his two sons boddhisattvas, and personally conducted the P'algwanhoe ceremony (see Chapter 6) to gain spiritual protection for his realm. His behavior was so erratic and cruel, however, that four dozen of his commanders rebelled against him, and Kungye was killed by a peasant. Wang Kŏn ascended the T'aebong throne in 918, changed the name of the dynasty to Koryŏ (a name derived from Koguryŏ and the origin of the modern name of "Korea"), and moved the capital to Song'ak. He immediately began the construction of a dozen Buddhist temples and set up the Western Capital at Pyongyang with a separate complex administration there because he was convinced that the geomantic forces in the Western Capital had to be propitiated. He consolidated his power not by centralizing his civil bureaucracy, but by seeking alliances through intermarriage with the daughters of local magnates called commanders (*changgun*) or lords of walled towns (*sŏngju*), who had their own military forces.

Kyŏn Hwŏn of Later Paekche, however, seized a dozen Silla towns and forced the Silla king to commit suicide in 927. He then put the *chingol* Kim Pu on the Silla throne (King Kyŏngsun, r. 927–935), but soon after, two of Kyŏn Hwŏn's sons began a struggle to replace him. Disheartened, he retired to a Buddhist monastery and then fled to Koryŏ in 935, where Wang Kŏn welcomed him with open arms. Kim Pu, the last king of Silla, then abdicated his throne, bringing the Silla Dynasty to a silent end, but Later Paekche was not defeated by Koryŏ until 936.

KORYŎ DYNASTY: THE RECENTRALIZED BUREAUCRACY AND ITS PROBLEMS (935–1171)

Politically, Wang Kŏn (henceforth, King T'aejo) was neither willing nor able to attempt a radical return to a strong, centralized, bureaucratic system. Instead, he maintained the system of control he had created in the Later Paekche period based on marriage alliances with local leaders. He made no attempt to replace them with members of a central bureaucracy, but he controlled them by establishing a hostage system (*sangsuri*) in which some of their relatives were required to reside in the capital. By contrast with the Silla Dynasty, he chose men to staff his central bureaucracy from a much wider range of families and regions than the *chingol* aristocrats from Kyŏngju by including his military allies, many of whom came from the southwest. He also welcomed the Confucian-educated elite of Kyŏngju into the new elite of Koryŏ, granted the last Silla king a prebend over Kyŏngju with the exalted title of Sasimgwan, and paid homage to the late Silla scholar Ch'oe Ch'iwŏn to assuage any feelings of animosity in the southeast.

To gain legitimacy, T'aejo patronized Buddhism, supported the monks, and built many Buddhist temples in the capital. He also tried to alleviate the conflict between the Buddhist scriptural (*Kyo*) and meditational (*Sŏn*) sects. He continued the Silla procession of light (*yŏndŭnghoe*) every year on the fifteenth day of the first lunar month to celebrate the Buddha and pray for peace and prosperity for the state and royal house. He supported Confucianism as well.

Early Koryŏ Society

T'aejo's ostensibly bureaucratic and centralized administration was compromised by the political and material interests of his allies, who soon developed into a hereditary elite known as the *pon'gwan* aristocracy identified by the place name of the residence of the founder of a person's lineage. The material interests of these families were the land and slaves they either owned or captured in battle during the Later Three Kingdoms period. Although some of T'aejo's officials had suggested that he manumit such slaves, he shied from doing so because it would challenge their owners' property interests.

His failure to manumit slaves created the basis for hereditary slavery. There is no decree from any king in the historical records establishing hereditary slavery, but a decree was issued in 1037 providing that the children of mixed marriages between commoners and slaves would adopt the social status of the mother (*chongmobŏp*). Obviously, if both parents were slaves, the children would automatically become slaves, indicating that hereditary slavery had become an established practice. Since the slave owners soon violated the *chongmobŏp* by taking over the offspring of all mixed marriages, hereditary slavery set the stage for the expansion of the slave population that most likely reached 30 percent of the population or more by the eleventh or twelfth centuries, creating the basis for calling Koryŏ a slave society.

The nature of the family and kinship groups and the role of women in early Koryŏ differed markedly with the Chinese systems based on patrilineal descent and patrilocal marriage. In contrast to the Chinese family, the Koryŏ family traced its ancestry back through the female as well as the male line and conducted mourning ceremonies to both lines. Wives might move into the homes of their husband's family, but husbands more frequently moved into the home of their wife, and their children grew up in the association of the wife's parents, uncles, and brothers. When the head of a family died, all siblings, including the sisters, shared equally in the inheritance of property. When a sister married, she carried her own property with her. She could divorce her husband virtually at will and move back to her birth family or support herself on her inherited property. After divorce, she retained possession of her children. Many aspects of this system were similar to the Heian/Fujiwara period (see Chapter 10) in Japan.

Males found themselves in a family group (the *chok*) that involved eight lines of descent by ancestors of their fathers and mothers. Their connections with the wife's family meant that their marriage relations were as important to them as their own relatives, and the close kin relations became the basis for political groups. Furthermore, the choice of a marriage partner was quite fluid. King T'aejo married twenty-nine queens and had twenty sons and nine daughters. He made those alliances even more secure by marrying some of his daughters to their own half-brothers, a practice that was anathema to the Chinese. Consanguinity, including cross marriage between cousins, occurred not only within the royal family but among the elite as well. Because succession in both the royal house and the aristocracy was not subject to descent in the male line, brothers, cousins, and even relatives of wives could inherit the headship of a family.

Koryŏ society as a whole, of course, was divided into more than two levels. Between the elite, who sometime in the eleventh century or earlier became known as *yangban* (the western file of civil officials and eastern file of military officials who faced north toward the king in audience[1]), and the slaves there were several intermediate levels. The commoners, referred to as the good people (*yangmin*), consisted mainly of peasants, with a small segment of merchants and artisans. Some have referred to them as free, but only in contrast to the slaves, who were the private property of their masters. Obviously,

---

[1]The Chinese emperors and Korean kings always faced south when conducting court audiences. "File" refers to officials lined up in nine files by the nine official ranks. The Koreans adopted this practice from the Chinese.

they were "free" only to pay taxes to the state and rent to landlords, and perform uncompensated labor service or corvée for the state to build roads and palaces, or perform military service to defend the country.

Other types of people lesser in status than commoners, but perhaps higher than slaves, included the *paekchŏng*, who were a nonspecialized group somewhat beneath commoners (in the subsequent Chosŏn Dynasty, the term referred to a hereditary low-born class of butchers and willow-basket weavers). In addition, there were low-status communities called *so, chang,* and *pugok,* perhaps because they had been prisoners-of-war.

Military Threats

In 907 Abaoji, a chieftain of the Yelü branch of the Khitan people in Manchuria, conquered his tribal rivals and formed a tribal confederation. When he conquered Parhae's neighbor, the state of Xi, Parhae sought and obtained aid from Silla. After Abaoji became emperor (posthumous title, Taizu) of the Khitan in 916, he asked King T'aejo of Koryŏ in 922 for military aid against Parhae. T'aejo did not comply, but Parhae refugees migrated en masse into Silla territory just before Abaoji conquered Parhae in 926. Abaoji converted Parhae to the state of Dongtan and made his son ruler, but he soon abandoned Parhae's territory to scattered Malgal tribes and former Koguryŏ residents to prepare for an attack against China. Abaoji was doing battle with the Later Jin (936–946) Dynasty in China (one of the Five Dynasties) when King T'aejo decided to ally with the Later Jin in 938 against Abaoji. Abaoji sent an envoy with a gift of fifty camels to T'aejo in 942 to seek an alliance, but T'aejo exiled the envoy and starved the camels to death, a rash act that caused much trouble for Koryŏ.

A succession struggle followed King T'aejo's death in 943, after which King Chŏngjong (r. 945–949) came to power. As a sign of the weakness of royal authority and the need for support

from close relations and the military to defeat political challenges, he was able to defeat a rebellion in 945 by Wang Kyu, the father of the second king's queen, only by summoning his cousin, Wang Singnyŏm, the commander of the Western Capital garrison, to defeat Wang Kyu's forces. No sooner was this done than King Chŏngjong faced a threat from Abaoji, who had defeated the Later Jin army in 947. Since Koryŏ had enrolled as a tributary of the Later Jin, King Chŏngjong built forts along the northern frontier and the garrison at the Western Capital, and created a new thirty-thousand-man Army of Light for defense. Silla was not forced to build up its military after 700, but in early Koryŏ, the military became a significant force in politics.

Taming and Rewarding Aristocrats

In 956 King Kwangjong (r. 949–975, the younger brother of King Chŏngjong), began to increase his own power and that of his civil bureaucracy. He challenged the new elite by setting up a commission to investigate slaves who had been acquired illegally to convert them back to commoner status and make them available for taxation and labor service for the state, an act that earned him the enmity of the slave owners. In the same year, he used a Chinese refugee from the Later Zhou Dynasty in China, Shuang Ji, to help introduce the Chinese-style civil service examination system to provide an impersonal measure of talent for the recruitment of officials. Nevertheless, the examinations were not held frequently enough to produce enough officials to replace the *pon'gwan* hereditary aristocrats. When a centralized school system was established some time later (in 992) by King Sŏngjong, admission to the best schools was restricted to families of high rank. This action restricted the chance for upward mobility for sons of commoners, let alone slaves.

After the Song Dynasty reunified China in 960, Kwangjong shifted his tributary relationship to Song, once again in the hope of creating an alliance against the Khitan. He carried out a purge of his officer corps and began to discriminate against military commanders in favor of civil officials. This was in emulation of Song policy to prevent powerful regional military commanders from rebelling against the throne, as they had done at the end of the Tang Dynasty.

As a means of increasing compensation to aristocrats, King Kyŏngjong (r. 975–981) began the *chŏnsikwa* system. In this system, "land" allotments of arable and wood land of varying size was granted to men according to the level of their personal rank, and not on the basis of their office rank. These "land" grants were really prebends, or rights to collect taxes in lieu of central government officials. Such prebends were also granted to men who functioned as servants of the state in some capacity, such as local aristocrats called "local clerks" (*hyangni*), who could be appointed district magistrate, and to those peasants who were assigned military service as soldiers (*kunin*). These prebendal grants, which began in 976 and continued to 1076, constituted income over and above any salaries they received as officials. Presumably if a prebend was granted on land that the recipient already owned, it meant that he was being granted a tax exemption on his own land. In any case, the prebends either supplemented incomes of aristocratic officials or guaranteed incomes of aristocrats who held no office.

Despite the *History of Koryŏ* (*Koryŏsa*), compiled in 1454 in the next dynasty, which claimed that the *chŏnsikwa* system was copied from the Tang equal-field system, that information is patently false. There is no notice in the Koryŏ records of a decree nationalizing all private property and granting land to peasant families on a rotating basis according to the age and sex of family members. The Tang term for such a rotating land grant (*koufentian*) was used in Koryŏ (*kubunjŏn*) but only to indicate a prebendal grant to the widows of soldiers. In the Nara period in Japan, by contrast, the *kubunden* grants functioned like the Tang system.

In addition to prebends, there was also state-owned land, from which grants of land (possi-bly also prebends) were made outright to Buddhist monasteries, palace estates for princes and princesses, prestigious individuals in the form of prebends called "feeding areas" (*sig'ŭp*), foreign settlers, degree holders, *yamen* or state offices for expenses, schools, and military colonies cultivated by duty soldiers.

Incomplete Bureaucratic Centralization

A serious centralization of authority under civil bureaucratic rule was carried out in the late tenth century by Kings Kyŏngjong and Sŏngjong. One of the chief advisors to the kings during this period of reform was the Koryŏ official Ch'oe Sŭngno (see **Biography: Ch'oe Sŭngno**). The kings adopted the excessively elaborate centralized bureaucratic system of the Tang with a few Song Dynasty accretions. That reform was completed in 1018, but local government was never as centralized as the Chinese system because officials from the center were dispatched to only one-third of the three hundred or so districts. The other two-thirds were headed by magistrates recruited from local magnates called *hyangni* (literally, local clerks), who were allowed to move up the bureaucratic ladder even into posts in the capital.

Aristocratic Politics, Eleventh and Twelfth Centuries

The tenth century ended with both domestic and foreign crises. A succession dispute occurred just prior to the death of King Mukchong (r. 997–1009). Because the king lacked an heir, a struggle ensued between powerful supporters of two young princes who were the sons of two queens of the deceased King Kyŏngjong (r. 975–981). Powerless to enforce his choice of Prince Taeryang on his own, King Mukchong did what King Chŏngjong had done in 945: summoned Kang Cho, the military commander for the Western Capital, to help him. Unfortunately

BIOGRAPHY Ch'oe Sŭngno

Ch'oe Sŭngno was a high Koryŏ official under King Sŏngjong and his chief adviser on policy. He was born in the town of Kŭmsŏng (later Kyŏngju) in the southeast to a family descended from the famous Silla scholar-official Ch'oe Ch'iwŏn of the late ninth century. The Ch'oe family had been members of the Silla sixth head rank, which chafed at the obstacles to their promotion to higher rank.

Three months after Ch'oe Sŭngno's birth, Kyŏn Hwŏn's Later Paekche army occupied Kyŏngju. His father turned him over to a Buddhist temple for his safekeeping, and fled into the hills until the Later Paekche army departed the city. When the last Silla king abdicated to King T'aejo of Koryŏ in 935, his father took the family north to the Koryŏ capital at Kaegyŏng. Three years later, at the age of eleven, Ch'oe Sŭngno recited the Confucian *Analects* before the king, and in his twenties, during the reign of King Kwangjong (r. 945–975), he was appointed to offices that tapped his literary skills in drafting diplomatic documents.

King Kwangjong's reforms aimed at curtailing the power of King T'aejo's merit subjects and taking away some of their land and slaves, and he purged those merit subjects and replaced them with new men. King Sŏngjong (r. 981–997) appointed Ch'oe chief personnel officer, and at the age of fifty-five he set about filling vacant slots with his own choices.

In 982 Ch'oe replied to King Sŏngjong's request for advice with a detailed proposal on how to achieve stability by building up the authority of the king. Since King T'aejo was unwilling and unable to challenge the authority of local magnates, Ch'oe advised King Sŏngjong to replace them with magistrates dispatched from the central bureaucracy, preferably to every district in the country. If that were impossible, then he should assign at least one magistrate to oversee several districts. The king accepted this plan but sent out only twelve officials.

Ch'oe advised the king to adopt Confucian standards for kingly rule, many of which had been violated by the previous five kings since T'aejo. He advised him to be modest and frugal, refrain from arrogance, treat his inferiors well, give priority to caring for the common people, listen to his teachers, and accept remonstrance from his officials.

Ch'oe, however, advocated the elevation not of talented men from the people but of members of aristocratic families educated in Confucianism. He also advocated strict sumptuary regulations to allow more elegant uniforms, clothing, and houses than those of ordinary commoners. He never questioned slavery as a possible violation of Confucian norms, but instead insisted on maintaining a strict separation between masters and their slaves. His ideal society was only a partial modification of the rigid hereditary bone rank system of Silla in which educated aristocrats would support a virtuous king and yet restrain him by their sage advice.

Although Ch'oe was a Buddhist, he believed in the strict separation of religion from government. Buddhism was concerned with personal salvation and the afterlife, but Confucianism dealt with governance of the state in the here-and-now. He condemned King Kwangjong, who murdered scores of innocent people along with his political enemies but then offered useless and costly prayer ceremonies to the Buddha in atonement for his acts. To counter the superficial aspects of Buddhism, Ch'oe advised the king to ban construction of more temples, donations to temples, loans at interest issued by Buddhist monasteries, and costly expenditures for copying Buddhist sutras.

for Mukchong, Kang Cho persuaded him to abdicate in favor of Prince Taeryang (King Hyŏnjong, r. 1009–1031). He then killed the relatives of the other candidate and had Mukchong killed in 1009. Kang Cho's machinations only provided the Khitan Liao state with a pretext for an invasion of Koryŏ.

From 991 to 1020, Koryŏ was challenged by the expanding power of the Khitan Liao Dynasty, which took over territory in north China and forced the Chinese Song Dynasty to pay tribute. The Koryŏ military was able to win a stalemate and force a peaceful conclusion to that rivalry. After 1020 Koryŏ politics was dominated by an oligarchy of powerful *pon'gwan* clans or lineages. The *chŏnsikwa* system of prebendal allotments began to break down as aristocrats took over prebends for themselves, and in the twelfth century, they began to form estates and either force indebted peasants into commendation of their lands or induce them to become their private slaves to escape the depredations of the government clerks and tax collectors. This concentration of land and slaves in the hands of powerful aristocrats increased their wealth and power significantly. The three most prominent *pon'gwan* clans were the Kyŏngju Ch'oe, the Haeju Ch'oe, and the Kyŏngwŏn (or Inju) Yi. The Kyŏngwŏn Yi became the most prominent political family and solidified its power by supplying queens to the royal family and marrying into other leading clans.

The flourishing reign of King Munjong (r. 1046–1083) was followed by a bloody succession struggle in 1095 between the candidates of Yi Chaŭi of the Kyŏngwŏn Yi clan and So T'aebo, who was backed by Wang Kŭngmo, the brevet minister of war. So and Wang forced King Hŏnjong to abdicate to his uncle (King Sukchong, r. 1095–1105), and Wang's private soldiers killed Yi Chaŭi, his sons, and seventeen officials who supported him, and exiled fifty others. Despite this debacle, the clan survived under the leadership of Yi Chaŭi's cousin, Yi Chagyŏm, who dominated the censorate and the court after 1109.

CONFUCIAN EDUCATION

Culture flourished under King Munjong, who was a devoted believer in Buddhism and a supporter of Confucian learning. His own son, Wang Hu, became the famous monk Ŭich'ŏn. A number of officials traveled to Song China and learned of the development of the Song Confucian school called the Learning of the Way (*tohak*), but the new trend did not spread until two centuries later.

Back at home, the average annual number of passers of the examinations was only eleven in the 1050s but increased to twenty-two by 1120, but the texts of the *tohak* scholars were not part of the required curriculum. King Munjong supported Confucian studies in the state schools, but when the state schools declined in quality, Ch'oe Ch'ung established the first of twelve prestigious private academies for educating the sons of the aristocracy in 1055. It is doubtful, however, that many commoners benefited from private education because they were kept on the farm to support the ruling class and pay taxes to the state.

KORYŎ RELATIONS WITH SONG AND LIAO (943–1071)

The history of Koryŏ's foreign relations represented a major change from the peace and tranquility Silla had enjoyed under the powerful Tang Dynasty. The Song Dynasty, founded in 960, chose to keep its military under control to prevent it from usurping central power in the late Tang Dynasty. That occurred in a period when non-Chinese tribes in Manchuria and Mongolia began to coalesce into powerful military forces that invaded Song territory. The first challenge came from the Khitan in the late tenth and early eleventh centuries, the second from the Jurchen in the twelfth century, and the last from the Mongols in the thirteenth century. As a result of the decline of Song military power, the Khitan took over part of north China, the

Jurchen took over all of north China, and the Mongols took over all of China. Chinese rule was not restored until the founding of the Ming Dynasty in 1368.

Koryŏ was also challenged by these powerful non-Chinese tribes that demanded either capitulation or enrollment as their tributary even though Koryŏ had enrolled as a Song tributary in 963. Faced with powerful foreign forces, Koryŏ had to abandon any notion of moral obligation to China and adopt a more practical foreign policy based on a calculation of the relative power of the foreign states. As a result, Koryŏ ended up switching its tributary relations from Song to the Khitan Liao state, then to the Jurchen Jin state, and finally to the Mongol Yuan state. These decisions were always opposed by Confucian moralists in Koryŏ because they felt that Koryŏ belonged to the superior Chinese civilized world and disdained the horse-riding barbarians. The decision of what policy to pursue varied from military resistance to diplomatic negotiation, depending on domestic politics in each instance.

In the case of the Khitan Liao, two decades of military confrontation resulted in a negotiated settlement to transfer tribute from the Song to the Liao in 1020. In the case of the Jurchen Jin, the choice was made to transfer tribute from the Liao to Jin before serious violence broke out. In the case of the Mongol Yuan, the Koryŏ military leadership refused to negotiate and suffered almost three decades of repeated and destructive invasions that laid waste the country, while the court and its military rulers took refuge on Kanghwa Island. What is amazing is that destruction inside Koryŏ was kept to a minimum until the Mongol invasions, but even after capitulation to the Mongols in 1258, the Mongols chose to rule indirectly for the next century without taking over Koryŏ completely.

In the 960s the Khitan moved into Manchuria, and in 985 Emperor Taizong of Song asked Koryŏ to join Song in an attack against Liao, but Liao forces blocked Koryŏ reinforcements and cut off Koryŏ's land contact with Song. King Sŏngjong of Koryŏ defied the Khitan by building forts along the south bank of the Yalu River in 991, but Liao forces invaded Koryŏ territory in 993. Instead of pushing for total victory, the Khitan negotiated a peace, and King Sŏngjong was forced to adopt the Liao calendar in 994 and end tributary relations with Song, a violation of King T'aejo's testamentary injunction never to make peace with the Khitan. King Sŏngjong's decision proved wise because the Song Dynasty was unable to defeat Khitan forces and decided not only to sign a peace agreement with Liao in 1005 but also to pay heavy tribute to it.

A pretext for breaking the peace was afforded the Khitan in 1009 when Kang Cho deposed King Mukchong without seeking approval from the Emperor Shengzong. Shengzong personally led an invasion force in 1010, defeated Kang Cho's army in battle, and executed him. After setting fire to Kaegyŏng, he withdrew his troops to prepare for more important engagements against the Song Dynasty.

When Emperor Shengzong raided the six Koryŏ forts south of the Yalu River in 1014 and 1015, King Hyŏnjong of Koryŏ offered to resume tributary relations with Song, but Song rejected the request because it preferred to maintain peace with Liao. In 1018 Shengzong sent an army to invade Koryŏ, but the Koryŏ army under Kang Kamch'an won a decisive battle at Kwiju, one of the greatest military victories of Korean history. As a result, Liao pursued diplomacy, and in 1020 Koryŏ agreed to sever relations with Song and shift its tributary relationship to Liao. Liao abandoned its demand for the six forts south of the Yalu River. Later, the Song court debated the possibility of a military alliance with Koryŏ against Liao twice, in 1042 and 1071, but both proposals were blocked by opposition.

Nevertheless, Koryŏ continued trade and cultural exchange with Song by avoiding overland trade and opening a new trade route from the mouth of the Yesŏng River below Kaegyŏng to Zhejiang Province. Trade was spurred by Koryŏ enthusiasm for Song cultural goods like silks, ceramics, and books, which included copies of the Chinese classics and a 983 woodblock edition of the Buddhist Tripitika. Arab merchants attracted to China's coastal seaports also traveled on to trade with Koryŏ. Song cultural influence was important in painting styles, particularly the monumental monochrome landscape paintings, and pottery, especially the celadon, the most outstanding examples of which were produced in the Koryŏ period. (See **Material Culture: The Koryŏ Celadon** and Color Plate 13.)

RISE OF THE JURCHEN (JIN) DYNASTY

The Jurchen people had been living as small, isolated tribes in a region that included modern Manchuria, where the Parhae kingdom used to be, and northeast Korea around modern Hamhŭng, just north of the Koryŏ boundary. They made their first contacts with Koryŏ in the 980s and began to launch pirate raids on Koryŏ's east coast in 997. In 1012, two Jurchen chiefs paid tribute to Koryŏ, but friction rose in 1019 just before Koryŏ enrolled as a tributary of the Liao Dynasty. Koryŏ extended the long wall it had built in the northeast in the 1030s to block Jurchen raids, but it adopted a policy of conciliation and induced some Jurchen chiefs to pay tribute to the Koryŏ court.

The Wanyan branch of the Jurchen in central Manchuria became more powerful in the late eleventh century, and their leader, Yingge, attacked Koryŏ territory in 1103 and defeated a Koryŏ army under Yun Kwan the next year. King Sukchong of Koryŏ reorganized the army as the Special Army Corps (*Pyŏlmuban*), added a new cavalry unit to counter the Jurchen cavalry, and recruited men from all social statuses, including Buddhist monks and slaves. Yun Kwan won a major victory against the Jurchen in 1107 but suffered a serious defeat in 1109.

The Jurchen became more powerful under Aguda (posthumous name, Emperor Taizu). They attacked Liao territory and established the Jin Dynasty in 1115. When Aguda asked Koryŏ

for aid against Liao, Koryŏ agreed in 1119 to an elder brother–younger brother relationship with Jin without severing Koryŏ's suzerain-subject relationship with Liao. A serious policy debate at court ensued between Yi Chagyŏm of the Kyŏngwŏn Yi clan, who favored peace with the Jurchen, and the hawkish supporters of King Yejong led by Han Anin. Yi Chagyŏm purged Han and his group in 1122. When King Yejong died and was succeeded by his thirteen-year-old son, King Injong (r. 1122–1146), Yi Chagyŏm purged more rivals and married two of his daughters to the king. When the king's supporters plotted to remove Yi Chagyŏm, Yi foiled the plot. The king offered to abdicate to him, but Yi declined and moved the king into his home to rubber-stamp his appointments of his friends to high office.

In 1122, the Song government made a fateful decision to ally with Jin for a joint attack against Liao. Jin defeated Liao on their own with little aid from Song forces, and then betrayed their pact with Song by capturing Beijing in 1126 and taking over north China down to the Yangzi River in 1127. It was in 1126 that the new Emperor Taizong of Jin demanded full suzerain status over Koryŏ and control. All Koryŏ officials opposed this except for Yi Chagyŏm and Ch'ŏk Chun'gyŏng, who argued that the Jin forces were too strong to resist. They overcame their opponents and pressured King Injo to enroll as a Jin tributary (see Map 9.1). In the twentieth century, Korean nationalists have condemned Yi Chagyŏm for his capitulation to foreign power, but had Koryŏ defied Taizong, it would have been conquered outright by Jin forces. Yi Chagyŏm, however, was not to enjoy his power for long because Ch'ŏk Ch'un'gyŏng turned against him and forced King Injong to exile him and his entire family and return all his ill-gotten lands and slaves to their original owners. The aristocrat Yi controlled the throne and foreign policy, but the soldier Ch'ŏk trumped his play.

No sooner had King Injong reclaimed a modicum of power than he was won over by a Buddhist monk named Myoch'ŏng, practitioner of

MATERIAL CULTURE

The Koryŏ Celadon

Perhaps the greatest contribution of the Koryŏ Dynasty was the perfection of a type of pottery—the grayish-green celadon—that has become known the world over. Similar pieces were produced in Song China, but in many cases the Koryŏ versions surpass the Chinese in incisions under the glaze, pieces with filled cavities, and designs. The variety of forms include flasks, vases, ewers, cauldrons, teapots, wine bowls, pitchers, bottles, jars, headrests, water pots, boxes, incense burners, bowls, cups, and plates. In addition to plain and undecorated pieces, the most impressive include bas-relief ornaments in the shape of clouds, lotus leaves, and waves, colors that are not found on Chinese pieces, and incised designs on the surface filled with white kaolin or black clay. Many pieces have the famous crackled surface achieved by interrupting the firing of the vessel. In late Koryŏ, designs were painted with ferro-manganese date-plum juice to produce dark-brown or black lines or petals.

The main kilns that produce these pieces were located in the Kangjin area of modern South Chŏlla Province, and they were shipped to Kaegyŏng for distribution by the famous merchants of the capital to the rest of the country and China in the Song and Yuan dynasties. Original pieces are found in museums around the world, and kilns in Korea have been turning out hundreds of copies of Koryŏ archetypes, so proud have Koreans been for centuries for these magnificent pieces.

Celadon, Koryŏ Dynasty, Tenth–Fourteenth centuries. See also Color Plate 13. *(Kansong Museum of Fine Arts, Seoul)*

the occult arts and anti-Confucian nationalist. Myoch'ŏng was as much a powerful political figure as he was a monk because he launched a challenge to three major institutions of the dynasty: the entrenched power of the aristocracy at Kaegyŏng, the tributary relationship with foreign powers, and the policies of the Confucians. These institutions were related in Myoch'ŏng's mind because he detested the Jurchen and insisted that King Injong declare his independence, assume the title of emperor, and launch a campaign against Jin. He knew that the aristocrats surrounded and controlled the king in the capital and that the king's Confucian

Map 9.1   **Koryŏ Dynasty After 1126**

the establishment of the Great Deed (Taewi) Dynasty at the Western Capital, and established a new army. Kim Pusik led the government force against him and crushed the rebellion in 1136. Myoch'ŏng was reviled by the Confucian scholars who wrote the *History of Koryŏ* (*Koryŏsa*) in 1454, but adored by modern nationalists who have portrayed him as one of the few truly nationalist heroes of the traditional era and denounced Kim Pusik for his supine submission to Chinese culture and foreign power. Had Myoch'ŏng succeeded and attacked Jin, however, Koryŏ would have suffered a disastrous reprisal from the Jurchen. The Confucians held sway, and peace with Jin was preserved for close to a century more.

THE DECLINE AND FALL OF CIVILIAN RULE

King Ŭijong (r. 1146–1170) presided over a reign in which government institutions began a serious decline as a result of bureaucratic corruption, domestic rebellions, piracy, and the king's neglect of business. The *chŏnsikwa* prebendal allotment system disappeared as prominent aristocratic families and Buddhist monasteries accumulated large landed estates and tax exemptions. They increased the number of their slaves by offering commoner peasants smallholders' protection from taxes, labor service, and illegal exactions by clerks in return for the commendation of their lands. The king ignored his responsibilities and enjoyed himself in making the rounds of his various palaces, and he immersed himself in spiritualism. He left business in the hands of Chŏng Ham, perhaps the most powerful eunuch in Korean history, and neglected the protests of his Confucian ministers until 1158, when he stripped Chŏng of office.

King Ŭijong also antagonized the ascetic Sŏn meditation sect of Buddhism by shifting his favor to the temples and monasteries of the scriptural Kyo sects that favored numerous and ornate icons to attract the masses. Maybe he

advisers, headed by Kim Pusik, supported tributary subservience over an independent and assertive foreign policy.

He believed that if he could persuade Injong to move the capital to the Western Capital, he would be free to declare independence. To do this, he played on Injong's belief in geomancy by arguing that spiritual forces in the ground under the Western Capital were particularly strong and a move there would prolong and strengthen his reign. Injong did build both a palace and the Hall of the Eight Sages to honor the Buddha at the Western Capital. He visited it frequently to show respect to the spirits there, but he did not move the capital because of the opposition of the aristocrats and Confucians.

Outflanked by his enemies in Kaegyŏng, Myoch'ŏng chose to rebel in 1135, proclaimed could have weathered growing resentment against him had it not been for the growth of contempt for military officers among his aristocratic *yangban* officials. King Ŭijong's reign marked the apogee of the attempt launched by King Kwangjong in 945 to curtail the military in a fashion similar to the Song Dynasty. The growth of civil authority reinforced by Confucian learning did not mature into military acceptance of the new situation, especially in view of the growing arrogance of civil contempt for soldiers that reached its limit when Kim Tonjung, the son of Kim Pusik, playfully set fire to the beard of a royal guard company commander, Chŏng Chungbu. Hardly a fellow to tolerate such an insult, Chŏng tied up Kim and administered a tongue lashing. Kim Pusik demanded that Chŏng be tortured, but King Ŭijong refused, an act of toleration that he was soon to regret. Dynastic fortunes had reached such a low ebb that it appeared that it might come to an end in some sort of cataclysm.

BUDDHISM AND SYNCRETISM IN THE KORYŎ PERIOD

A significant development occurred in Buddhism in the Koryŏ period when a number of erudite monks began an effort, underway in China for some time, to reconcile the doctrinal differences that had occurred in Buddhism. Centuries earlier, the Buddhist monk and geomancer Tosŏn had traveled to China and returned with information on geomancy and occult teachings along with Buddhism. Koryŏ kings honored him posthumously and his teachings gained respect throughout the land (see **Documents: Tosŏn, the Monk and Geomancer**). The monk Ŭich'ŏn (1055–1101), the fourth son of King Munjong (r. 1046–1083), returned from a year's visit to China and attempted to merge the meditative Sŏn sect with the textual Ch'ŏndae (Tiantai, Tendai) sect, especially because the Ch'ŏndae school also laid stress on meditation and intuition.

The monk Chinul (b. 1158) was distressed because many monks had become too concerned with wealth, finery, and administrative management. He abandoned ties with established sects by establishing a separate Sŏn Cultivation Community of monks and laypeople in 1190. Not only did he attempt a reconciliation of Sŏn with Hwaŏm (the Flower-Garland Sect), but he also tried to combine the gradual and sudden enlightenment approaches of the northern and southern Chan schools in China. He admired the Tang monk Zongmi, who argued for gradual cultivation even after enlightenment to make sure that such individuals would continue to cultivate the mind to distinguish good from evil and act accordingly in society. Chinul also supported the Avatamsaka Sutra of the Hwaŏm school because it promoted the use of the intellect in the early stages of self-cultivation together with the possibility of sudden, intuitive enlightenment. Chinul devoted his life to transcending doctrinal division to achieve a better way to nirvana.

In Confucianism the dominant concerns were with ethical governance and skill in poetry and composition rather than the study of the classics or the relations of the functions of the mind to self-rectification. In poetry, Tang Dynasty styles, rhyme prose, and parallel prose were the main genres, but very few poetry anthologies have been preserved. In the twelfth century, some scholars were won over to the advocates of Ancient Text Learning (*guwen*)[2] in China and began to criticize the emphasis on ornate prose as detracting from the study of Confucian ethics and governance. As a result, in 1154 the civil service examinations were changed to place priority on policy questions and essays. When the military took over power in 1170, however, that reform was reversed in favor of poetry. Advocates of the Ancient Style reemerged only in the

---

[2]Ancient Text Learning is the term for what Confucian scholars thought represented the true texts of antiquity as transmitted by Confucius and rediscovered after those texts were burned by the Qin Dynasty. Later in the eighteenth-century Qing Dynasty, some scholars claimed the Old Texts were forgeries and reinterpreted Confucius and classical texts in a New Text movement.

DOCUMENTS

Tosŏn, the Monk and Geomancer

Tosŏn (827–898) began Buddhist studies in a Flower Garland Temple (Hwaŏmsa) around 840 and by 846 was revered by a number of Buddhists as an enlightened man. Around 850 he traveled to China and studied with Tang monks, who taught him certain secret methods. He returned to expound doctrines on yin and yang and geomancy. He served as spiritual adviser to King Hŏn'gang, after which he returned to a mountain monastery to end his days. He was later honored posthumously by late Silla and Koryŏ kings and was important for spreading respect for geomancy and occult teachings along with Buddhism in those two kingdoms.

The master's taboo name was Tosŏn. His secular surname was Kim; he was a man of Yŏngam in Silla. . . . His mother, born Kang, dreamed that someone gave her a beautiful pearl and had her swallow it. Accordingly she became pregnant and for a full month abstained from strong-smelling vegetables and rank meats, devoting herself entirely to chanting the Buddha's name with scriptures in hand. When in due course she suckled and cared for the infant, he was incomparably superior to ordinary children. Even while laughing or crying as a babe in arms, his intention seemed to be to express his reverence and awe for the Buddha's vehicle. . . .

On White Chicken Mountain in Hŭiyang county there is an ancient monastery called Jade Dragon. Stopping here . . . the master loved the secluded beauty of the place and proceeded to repair and refurbish the halls. . . . Students from all the four quarters converged upon him like clouds and adhered to him like shadows, . . . those who became his disciples numbered several hundreds. . . . [Later Tosŏn met a strange man who revealed to him the secrets of geomancy.] Thereafter the master, with a breakthrough of understanding, polished more than ever this knowledge of yin and yang and the five-phases techniques: occult secrets, however recondite, of golden tabernacle or jade cask were all as if imprinted on his heart. [In 874, Tosŏn told Wang Yung, the father of Wang Kŏn, that he would have a son who would be a king, and he entrusted a message to be given to Wang Kŏn after he reached maturity.]

[Wang Kŏn as an adult] proceeded to exterminate the bandit rabble and undertook the creation of his realm . . . . It was in the Source of Transformation that he inaugurated the holy era, and it was in Fate's hidden numbers that he fixed the fulfillment of his destiny. All these achievements have their origin in our master's instigation.

Source: From an inscription dated 1150 by Ch'oe Yuch'ong, in *Tong munsŏn* 117:18b–22b, in Michael Rogers, trans., *Sources of Korean Tradition* (New York: Columbia University Press, 1997), 1:132–135.

mid-thirteenth century. A very important development occurred in 1145 with the compilation of the earliest history of Korea that is extant, the *History of the Three Kingdoms (Samguk sagi)*, compiled under the direction of the versatile Kim Pusik. Earlier histories, including ones used to compile this text, have been destroyed or lost. Kim borrowed the format of Sima Qian's *Shiji* (see Chapter 3) and did his best to be objective, but he was not always successful. Although he was the director of ten other editors, he left his personal imprint on the book by authoring all of the explicit historian's comments.

One of his favorite themes was that despite the division of the Korean people into three kingdoms, they were all part of a single nation. In this spirit he lauded Ulchi Mundŏk of Koguryŏ for his victory over Chinese invaders at the Sal River, and he praised all Three Kingdoms for having strong kings even though he was born into a Kyŏngju Kim family from the previous Silla Dynasty. Nonetheless, he defended the Silla conquests over Paekche and Koguryŏ because their rulers were cruel to their own people, and Silla provided stability to replace the confusion of those two states. Possibly because Silla's relations with Parhae were bad, he failed to take note of the Parhae kingdom with its Koguryŏ population, let alone argue it was part of Korean history, as many Korean scholars today believe.

The text was heavily influenced by Confucian values and didactic historiography. The biographies were designed to praise good and blame evil to guide future generations about the proper way to behave. Stress was placed on those who were loyal and subordinated their own interests to serve the public good, particularly those who died in battle in defense of their country. He also defended the tributary system as the proper way to conduct relations with powerful neighbors, in sharp contrast to Myoch'ŏng's independent stance.

Despite his belief in the validity and universality of Chinese ethical standards, he justified the Silla practice of marriage between close relatives as a legitimate local custom. He also criticized Chinese stories of self-mutilation by filial sons to express their ultimate devotion to their parents as a rather poor substitute for the use of medicine.

On balance, the *Samguk sagi* made an important contribution to a sense of nationhood for the Korean people even though it supported the priority of Silla culture over Paekche and Koguryŏ.

PRAETORIAN RULE AND THE MONGOL INVASIONS (1170–1259)

Koryŏ suffered a sudden and immense disruption in 1170. Chŏng Chungbu had been promoted to superior general, and he and his fellow officers had become enraged by King Ŭijong's frequent pleasure trips, overnight poetry competitions, and drinking sessions with his refined aristocratic friends. They carried out a coup d'état in which they slaughtered a number of civil officials and eunuchs, deposed King Ŭijong (who was assassinated shortly after) and his crown prince, and put the king's younger brother on the throne (King Myŏngjong, r. 1170–1197).

Fearing a possible invasion by the Jurchen Jin in reprisal for their usurpation, they concocted a story to conceal the true facts. They then appointed military officers to civil posts as concurrencies and converted the supreme military council into the highest council of state. The military takeover of the civil government was a major turning point in Koryŏ government and society.

The coup was accompanied by serious disorder as challengers for power emerged in rapid succession. Military commanders, civil officials, monks, pirates, and low-status communities attacked the authorities and each other in the 1170s. The most dangerous uprising lasted from 1174 to 1176 and was led by the minister of war and concurrent magistrate of the Western Capital, Cho Wich'ong. Chŏng Chungbu was barely able to maintain order and was killed by Kyŏng Taesŭng, the son of a high Koryŏ official who began his career as a merchant and then joined the army and rose through the ranks. Kyŏng was one of the few military leaders in this period to die a natural death in 1183.

King Myŏngjong then recalled Yi Ŭimin, the assassin of his own father (King Ŭijong), to the capital in 1183 to run the government. Yi Ŭimin inherited his slave status from his mother, a monastery slave; his father was a commoner salt and liquor merchant. He too worked his way up the ranks in the capital guards to the post of superior general, a prime example of a complete overturning of the social order that characterized the period of military rule. Because his rule was marked by extreme corruption, domination of the court by eunuchs, peasant unrest, and a Silla restoration rebellion in 1193, it is no surprise that another commander, Ch'oe Ch'unghŏn, brought his rule to an end in 1196 by executing Yi, his whole family, and thirty-six high civil officials and military commanders.

Ch'oe demanded that King Myŏngjong dismiss superfluous officials, confiscate illegally acquired land, carry out tax reform, and eliminate Buddhist influence and monastic moneylending. When the king failed to respond to his directives, he replaced him with Myŏngjong's younger brother, King Sinjong, who obediently replaced incumbent officials with Ch'oe's men.

Ch'oe's rule was also punctuated by turmoil, including two slave uprisings, two popular revolts on the eastern coast—one on T'amna (Cheju Island), two by the Specially Selected Guard (Pyŏlch'ogun) and the Special Night Watch (Yabyŏlch'o) in Kyŏngju—a Silla restoration revolt, a Koguryŏ restoration movement in the Western Capital in 1217, and the revolt of a Paekche "generalissimo" in 1237. All were put down successfully, securing Ch'oe family rule over Koryŏ for four generations to 1258, but that security was limited to the king's court and the Ch'oe family after 1216. Pressed by the Mongols to the north, a Khitan army invaded Koryŏ in 1216, and the Mongols followed up in 1231, initiating the worst destruction the Korean people had suffered to date. (For details, see Chapter 12.)

Ch'oe Ch'unghŏn ruled until his death in 1220 and was succeeded by his direct heirs in order: Ch'oe I (originally, Ch'oe U), Ch'oe Hang, and Ch'oe Ŭi. While in power they deposed two kings and enthroned four. Ch'oe I reversed some of Ch'oe Ch'unghŏn's policies by returning the crown jewels to the king and returning all lands and slaves seized from their owners. He exiled his father's sycophants and summoned Confucian scholars to fill posts in his new administrative agencies.

The Ch'oe family regime created a new structure to govern the country. The supreme agency, the Hŭngyŏngbu (later the Chin'gangbu), became

its military headquarters. Ch'oe I revived the Tobang personal guard with three thousand private retainers. The Directorate General of Policy Formulation (Kyojŏng-dogam) handled security, and the Ch'oe family sent its own tax-collecting agents to the provinces. Ch'oe I's Government Chamber (Chŏngbang) took charge of personnel appointments, and his Chamber of Scholarly Advisers (Sŏbang) was staffed by civil officials on rotation.

The Ch'oe family maintained the civil service examinations for the *yangban,* many of whom intermarried with members of the Ch'oe family. Ch'oe Ch'unghŏn held writing and poetry contests for all, and the famed writer and poet Yi Kyubo participated. Yet some scholar-officials refused to serve, particularly the Seven Worthies of the Bamboo Grove, in emulation of the Seven Masters of the Chinese Western Jin Dynasty, and they wrote escapist poems as an outlet for their frustrations.

Unfortunately, these developments were overshadowed by the greatest challenge to the survivability of the Korean people when Temujin (Chinggis Khan), the leader of all Mongol tribes after 1206, and perhaps the greatest conqueror in world history, turned his attention to Koryŏ.

SUMMARY

The Koryŏ Dynasty achieved consolidation of most of the Korean peninsula in 935, but based its control on a decentralized pattern of royal control. King Kwangjong began to strengthen royal and central control and elevate the civil bureaucracy over the military, but it was interrupted by foreign invasion. A new aristocracy emerged to dominate the bureaucracy, and it became corrupted and arrogant and forced a military coup and military domination of both king and government. That regime was similar to the Kamakura regime in Japan in 1185 except that it emerged from the capital guards rather than provincial forces. While it worked out an accommodation with civil bureaucrats under them, it changed the political system drastically and disrupted society.

SUGGESTED READING

For early Koryŏ history, see J. Duncan, *The Origins of the Chosŏn Dynasty* (2000), and P. H. Lee, ed., *Sources of Korean Tradition,* vol. 1 (1997). For a discussion of the early Koryŏ land system and the Koryŏ foundation legend, see the articles by J. B. Palais and M. C. Rogers in the *Journal of Korean Studies,* 4 (1982–1983). For a study of the military rule from 1170 to 1258, see E. J. Shultz, *Generals and Scholars* (2000). For foreign relations, see chapters by M. Rogers, "National Consciousness in Medieval Korea," and Gari Ledyard, "Yin and Yang in the China-Manchuria-Korea Triangle," in M. Rossabi, ed., *China Among Equals* (1983). For an excellent study of Koryŏ Buddhism, see R. J. Buswell, Jr.'s translation and commentary in *The Korean Approach to Zen* (1983). For Koryŏ social history, see M. Deuchler's outstanding study, *The Confucian Transformation of Korea* (1992); E. Salem, "Slavery in Medieval Korea," Ph.D. dissertation, Columbia University (1978); and J. B. Palais, "Slavery and Slave Society in the Koryŏ Period," *Journal of Korean Studies,* 5 (1984).

Heian Japan (794–ca. 1180)

When Kanmu moved the court to Heian-kyō ("capital of peace and stability," now called Kyoto) in 794, he modeled his city on the Chinese imperial layout just as the Nara rulers had. For the next century, the regime of codes continued to provide the basic framework for a bureaucratic-style government. The period from approximately 900 to 1050 marks the apogee of classical refinement during the golden age of the Fujiwara. Rebellions in the provinces suggest that its benefits did not accrue to all. During both periods, political life at the capital remained largely free from violence. The final phase, from 1050 to 1180, saw retired monarchs wrest political power from the Fujiwara while trying to take advantage of the private landholding system. Beginning in the 900s, an outpouring of literary texts ranged in writing styles from royally commissioned poetry anthologies to diaries, memoirs, and the novel *Tale of Genji*. Buddhist thought pervaded the way aristocrats saw the world; Buddhist institutions became a powerful political and economic force.

Scholars debate issues concerning the degree of central control, the naturalization of Chinese civilization, and gender. What changed in relations between state, periphery, and the continent? Why do we see this age as so important for poetry and fiction by women? What kind of impact did the state have on commoners' lives?

THE AGE OF KINGLY RULE

Kanmu continued the bureaucratic and ceremonial practices that had been instituted while the court was at Nara. Men qualified by birth and talent climbed administrative ladders. Commanders of imperial guards rose to generals leading armies against the Emishi in the northeast. Kanmu relied on officials on the Board of Divination to interpret heavenly portents and omens in line with Daoist teachings. Following a factional dispute after his enthronement in 781, he ordered the era name changed to *Enryaku* (prolonged succession) to ensure a long and prosperous reign. Despite assassinations, pestilence, and famine, it remained until his death. Codifying the annual round of celebrations and ceremonies conducted by the Board of Divination began in 823, but the procedures had been in place for over a century.

Despite continuing the fascination with Chinese culture that had characterized the Nara period, Kanmu intended moving the capital to be a break with the past. Perhaps he wanted to free his administration from political interference by Buddhist clergy whose temples encircled Nara. Although he forbade Nara clergy to follow him to Heian-kyō, the court continued to support them financially and send representatives to ceremonies. Kanmu tried to control what was to become the great temple complex of Enryakuji that had opened on Mount Hiei northeast of Heian-kyō in 785 by appointing its abbots and restricting monks to monasteries. Another reason for the move may have been political. Taking advantage of a momentary decline in Fujiwara influence, Kanmu abandoned what had become their stronghold. Finally there was the question of prognostics. Violent factional and succession disputes had tainted Nara. If Kanmu was to launch a new initiative in righteous governance, he needed a fresh venue, one that the diviners promised would be auspicious.

Kanmu retained the formal structure of government defined in the regime of codes, but he also bypassed it in the interest of bureaucratic efficiency. Rather than rely on the large and unwieldy Council of State, he chose a small group of court councilors to advise him. As a necessary retrenchment measure given the limits to government revenues, he and his successors eliminated offices and reduced the number of officials. The Fujiwara having made a comeback, this left fewer positions for other lineages. In 792, Kanmu ended the Chinese-style system of conscripting commoners for the provincial militia. Cultivators made ineffective fighting

men, militia commanders had abused their power by ordering conscripts to labor on private projects, and depopulation caused by repeated famines and epidemics threatened the manpower and tax base. Instead of conscripts, the court relied on hired warriors to resist piracy and push back the frontier. To guard the palace and prosecute crimes in the capital, the Office of Police assumed military and juridical responsibilities. In 894 the court ceased formal relations with China, although private trade and religious traffic continued.

The court gradually relinquished direct supervision over the countryside. It set tax quotas by province and appointed inspectors to audit provincial accounts and prevent provincial governors from returning to the capital until all taxes had been paid. Appointed to four-year terms, the governors selected their own assistants, but they delegated tax collection and ongoing administrative responsibilities to registered lineages of local magnates who staffed the district and county offices. The governors essentially became tax farmers because they kept any revenues collected beyond their quotas. Below the officials were the cultivators, hardly an undifferentiated mass. The "rich and powerful" (*fugō*) acted as middlemen in collecting taxes. They too overcollected so as to keep a share for themselves. They owned livestock and slaves whom they employed on large plots of land. Most cultivators barely scraped by on what they could squeeze from marginal plots and work for others. When harvests failed and provincial governors became too rapacious, they abandoned their fields to try their luck in another location.

Commoners in the countryside managed their own affairs. At most the Office of Police might attack an army of bandits that terrorized a community near Heian-kyō. To handle ordinary thieves, the cultivators defined crimes and meted out punishments. In their eyes, the most heinous crime was theft of their food supply. Anyone caught stealing it was killed. In eastern Japan, people supplemented agriculture with hunting and fishing, woodcutting and charcoal burning, and horse breeding. They too punished theft of their livelihood with death. Cultivators also devised trials to determine if a suspect was telling the truth, placing the suspect's hand in boiling water being a typical ploy. Whereas the Heian court exiled criminals in line with Buddhist teachings forbidding the taking of life, cultivators had no such scruples.

The rebellion by Taira no Masakado from 935 to 940 in the Kanto region of eastern Japan dramatizes the connection between court politics and local issues. Under the regime of codes, the ruler's descendants not in the direct line to rule received family names and gradually fell in rank for six generations. Losing royal status allowed them to fill civilian or military positions in the state bureaucracy closed to members of the royal family. Some chose the clerical route and became temple abbots. Since branches of the Fujiwara lineage monopolized the highest central offices, most royal scions went to the provinces where their exalted lineage gave them prestige unobtainable in Heian-kyō. Kanmu's descendants took the name Taira. By the early tenth century, they and cadet branches of powerful aristocratic lineages dominated provincial headquarters staffs as clients of the governors.

Masakado's rebellion began as a family quarrel with his uncle that expanded into an attack on provincial headquarters. The court also had to contend with another revolt closer to Heian-kyō when Fujiwara no Sumitomo (?–941), an erstwhile official in Iyo province on Shikoku and the leader of a pirate band, began attacking granaries and administrative offices. By deputizing rivals of these rebels to fight in its name, the court managed to have both suppressed. Following his death, Masakado became a hero to the cultivators in the Kanto because he had sided with them against the provincial governor's staff. (His uncle had been vice governor.) They erected a shrine to his spirit that still receives offerings in Tokyo today.

Masakado's attack on his uncle and other relatives exemplifies the rivalry that divided kin and undermined the state adapted from Tang models. Because relatives had the same progenitor, they vied for the same slots in the social and administrative hierarchy. Rival branches challenged the titled chieftain's authority to control the lineage's temples and shrines, educational institutions for the lineage's youth, and appointments for lineage members at court. Like the Fujiwara, the Taira became too unwieldy to function as an effective power bloc. Instead the heads of houses (*ie*) based on residence locations competed among themselves for court honors and position regardless of whomever happened to be the chieftain. In eastern Japan the connection between the *ie* and location was especially strong. There, family compounds (*yashiki*) tended to be dispersed. Each contained many members because in the frontier setting, there was a chronic labor shortage. According to the convention of the time, when Masakado married his uncle's daughter, he should have gone to live in his uncle's compound and worked for him. When Masakado refused, he challenged his uncle's dominance in the lineage and threatened his economic base. This type of kin-based struggle over hierarchy and dominance far removed from the court and the treachery, arson, and pitched battles that ensued mark the beginning of a new stage in Japan's history of violence.

Early Heian Culture

Both luxury and privation characterized the Heian court. Aristocrats wore layer upon layer of beautifully dyed silks and Chinese brocades, especially in winter because they lacked any but primitive heating systems. They hosted elaborate banquets with drinking, dancing, and musical entertainment but kept to a meager diet. Their mansions overlooked landscaped gardens and contained almost nothing by way of furniture except for free-standing armrests, bedding, and screens.

Aristocrats refined their understanding of classical Chinese and took the literary arts in new directions. The monarchy sponsored three anthologies of Chinese poetry. The monk Kūkai, who had studied in China, and Sugawara no Michizane, the preeminent scholar of Chinese learning until the seventeenth century, penned some of the best Chinese poetry ever produced by Japanese. For centuries to come, intellectuals in Japan would employ Chinese categories of thought in the Chinese language. By the end of the ninth century, Japanese scribes had sufficiently modified Chinese characters that they had developed a syllabary (*kana*) in which to write Japanese poetry and prose. Such was the prestige of Chinese that men continued to use it for official documents and personal reflections. Being native to Japan and hence of less cultural value, the syllabary was largely though not entirely relegated to women.

Transformations in Religious Practice

In the early 800s two monks, Kūkai and Saichō, returned from China with texts and practices that transformed the teachings of the earlier Nara sects and entrenched Buddhism ever more firmly in Japan's political, economic, and spiritual life. Kūkai's visit to China from 804 to 806 led him to esoteric rites, symbols, and scriptures. Challenging what he saw as an overdependence on Confucianism in political ideology, he developed rituals and wrote texts based on a philosophy of ideal leadership derived from the great cosmic Buddha Mahavairocana that was to be transmitted to the ruler through an esoteric initiation rite during enthronement ceremonies. In Kūkai's vision of the world, the ruler ranked below priests and nuns in the political hierarchy. He built a retreat for the Shingon (True Word) School on Mount Kōya far from Heian-kyō, where he and his disciples prayed for protection of the state and prosperity for the people in rites that invoked the mystical power of prayer. His headquarters at Tōji in Heian-kyō put art to the service of religion. Rather than spend years studying sutras, aristocrats might find enlightenment in viewing the mandala (a stylized representation of Buddhist teachings) and achieve Buddhahood in their own body, without having to die first.

Saichō is often contrasted with Kūkai, but they shared an interest in esoteric teachings and practice. Saichō performed the first officially sanctioned esoteric initiation rite in Japan because he believed it to be the fastest route to attain Buddhahood. He founded the eclectic Tendai school of Buddhism in Japan and made the temple complex of Enryakuji on Mount Hiei its headquarters. From 804 to 805 he studied four schools of Buddhism in China, including Zen (Chan in Chinese), and brought them back to Japan along with the Tendai sect's central text, the *Lotus Sutra*. One of the most important Buddhist sutras, it contains a rich repository of stories and parables for explaining Buddhism to the uninitiated. It teaches that all Buddhist texts have merit because many are the ways that lead to enlightenment, and it promises that under extraordinary circumstances even women may attain Buddhahood.

The court's fascination with new Buddhist sects neither displaced the native deities nor eroded their assimilation to Buddhas. Daughters and sisters of rulers continued to serve as high priestesses at the family's Ise shrine. Geographic, not doctrinal, boundaries differentiated institutions and beliefs. Buddhist and Shinto deities brought prosperity; they also brought misfortune. In the ninth century, the belief was widespread that powerful spirits caused disease and epidemics. *Goryō*, either a cosmic force or the spirit of an aristocrat who had died unjustly, required cults to be appeased. The most famous cult originated at the Gion temple-shrine complex in 876. It climaxed in a midsummer festival performed when epidemics ran rampant. Angry spirits (*onryō*) resulted from an excess of strong emotion, usually after a well-born person had died unhappy. The conjunction of such a death with epidemics, earthquakes, and drought led the living to believe that the dead person's passion prevented his rebirth by trapping him in limbo. Pacifying his spirit required exorcism performed by mountain ascetics, whose knowledge of the realms of the dead and experiences of hell gave them powers unavailable to ordinary monks. The prayers of ritualists and ordinary people also proved efficacious in transforming angry spirits into guardian deities.

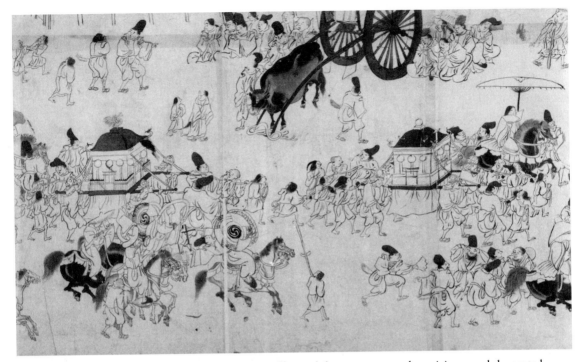

Gion Festival. By 1013 the Gion festival procession featured dancers, mounted musicians, and decorated floats pulled by oxen or carried by men. *(Private collection [Tanaka family]. Photo: Chuokoron-Shinsha, Inc./DNP Archives.com)*

Onryō cults culminated with Sugawara no Michizane in 947. (See **Biography: Sugawara no Michizane.**)

THE FUJIWARA ERA

The heyday for the Fujiwara lineage came between approximately 900 and 1050, idealized retrospectively as a peaceful, golden age of court culture. During these years, a small number of aristocratic women and men produced what are universally deemed to be literary classics. They accomplished this feat despite a lack of growth in either the population or the economy. A population of perhaps 5 million in 700 grew by only 500,000 by 900, and it took another three centuries for it to reach at most 7 million in 1200. The lack of economic growth meant competition for scarce resources between ruler, aristocrats, and temples and a miserable existence for commoners.

The Fujiwara helped hollow out the institutions created by the regime of codes. Approximately twenty thousand men and women constituted the aristocracy, and by 900 they formed three distinct groups in a nine-rank system. The highest three ranks had great wealth derived from office lands and private estates, the prestige of the Fujiwara lineage, and the power to set policy. Approximately twenty houses qualified. Ranks four and five consisted of provincial governors and junior officials, who with the right background might advance to higher ranks. The people who filled ranks six through nine possessed specialized skills in scholarship, astronomy, medicine, and law. They had no hope of advancement and suffered under their inferior status. In 1030, for example, they were forbidden to roof their dwellings with cedar-bark shingles or surround them with earthen walls. As the functions of the court came to center increasingly on performing a yearly round of ceremonial observances, the

BIOGRAPHY   Sugawara no Michizane

Scholar and bureaucrat, Sugawara no Michizane (845–903) rose unseemly high for a man of his modest birth, but he owes his fame to deeds done after he died.

A child prodigy, Michizane wrote his first poem in Chinese at age ten. In 867 he began his career at the junior sixth rank. He assisted in the reception of emissaries from the Manchurian kingdom of Parhae. When offered the post of ambassador to China, he recommended that missions to the Tang court be halted. He served a term as a provincial governor. He helped compile two histories of Japan and taught at the family school and the court university.

Michizane's reputation for scholarship and astute advice brought him to the attention of the monarch Uda, who ascended the throne in 887. Through Uda's patronage, he rose far beyond the rank normally permitted a man from a scholarly family. In 893 he became a court councilor. In 895 his daughter became one of Uda's consorts. Two years later, when Uda decided to abdicate and rule through his son Daigo, he had Michizane and the head of the Fujiwara lineage, Tokihira, share the highest positions in government. When Uda's son Tokiyo came of age in 898, he married yet another of Michizane's daughters, giving Michizane the intimate marital relations with the royal family customarily enjoyed by the Fujiwara. In 899 Michizane became Minister of the Right. Promotion to junior second rank soon followed. These promotions marked him as the retired monarch's favorite, whom everyone else despised. In 901 Tokihira found a man to accuse Michizane of plotting with Uda to force Daigo to abdicate and place Prince Tokiyo on the throne. Daigo promptly exiled Michizane and made Tokiyo a monk. Michizane died in exile, of grief, it was said, at having to leave his beloved plum trees, the urban amenities, and his cultivated friends for the wilds of Kyushu.

When men who had plotted Michizane's fall died in following years, people whispered that his angry spirit was responsible. Tokihira died mysteriously in 909. In 923 the crown prince, Tokihira's nephew, died. In an act of propitiation, the charges against Michizane were burned, the decree of exile was revoked, and he was restored to his previous court rank. In 930 a lightning bolt killed the man who had accused him of treason. Fearing that heaven had turned against him, Daigo died. Speaking through shamans, Michizane demanded that a shrine be built to transform him from a vengeful spirit to the protector of the nation. In 947 he and his literary works were enshrined at the Kitano shrine-temple complex north of Heian-kyō. Forty years later he officially became a god when the reigning monarch bestowed on him the title of Tenjin (heavenly deity). Over the centuries he became identified as the god of literature. Today children pray to him for help in passing their school entrance examinations.

Source: Based on Robert Borgen, *Sugawara no Michizane and the Early Heian Court* (Cambridge, Mass.: Harvard University Press, 1985).

---

task of everyday administration devolved to household officials.

High-ranked houses required large staffs to manage their economic, social, and legal affairs. Staff members served the house as private officials. They received appointments from the ruler at the behest of the house they served that came with court rank for which they were qualified by birth, normally the fourth through the sixth ranks. Even royal scions who had become military men in the provinces or former provincial governors of the fourth or fifth rank might take service in a Fujiwara household, and they too requested appointments for their servants. Reciprocal relations rather than office in a bureaucratic hierarchy mediated the bond between the head of a house and his court-ranked attendant. Household personnel granted fictive kin ties participated in important family ceremonies along with family members. They accompanied their patrons on outings to the family temples and shrines, to the palace, and on visits to other aristocrats. They served as messengers, prepared documents, and supervised the procurement of supplies. Reward came as protection in disputes and advancement in the court bureaucracy at the recommendation of their patron.

The state soon lost control over the extensive networks of patron-client relationships. Each aristocratic house had numerous helpers, military men as well as personal servants, all of whom were clients in that they worked for the house in the expectation that they would receive a benefit from the state. Even admission to an aristocratic house as a toilet cleaner freed a man and his family from conscript labor demanded by the state. Clientage tended to become hereditary and continue for generations.

Marriage and Politics

Marriage bonds reinforced patron-client relations and integrated different levels of society. Because men could use familial ties to advance, they continued the ancient pattern of visiting a wife in her father's household when the father was of higher rank and could serve as their patron. Since no one outranked the ruler, his women lived with him at court. They returned to their natal family to give birth. Aristocratic women could inherit property from their parents. Not bearing an heir did not constitute grounds for divorce. A man might have additional wives of nondescript background who lived with him and managed his household. A man and woman might also consider themselves to be husband and wife even if she lived alone and he visited her only on occasion. A fourth less common practice was for the wife to move into her husband's parental household.

The Fujiwara dominated political life through their mastery of marriage politics. During the peak of their influence, between 967 and 1068, eight rulers occupied the throne for average reigns of thirteen years. Politically, each functioned primarily as a spouse for Fujiwara women. As soon as a Fujiwara consort with a powerful father or brother bore a son to the ruler, the child was appointed crown prince. When he attained puberty, he received Fujiwara women as consorts. Once he had proven capable of siring sons, his father would be encouraged to abdicate, shave his head, and seek enlightenment. The average ruler ascended the throne at age eighteen and abdicated at age thirty-one. Some took the throne as toddlers and abdicated as teenagers. An under-age ruler needed a regent to advise him, and who better than his maternal grandfather in whose house he had been born and raised? Even adult rulers needed regents to make policy decisions; they too were either Fujiwara grandfathers or fathers-in-law. Fujiwara no Michinaga made himself grandfather to two rulers and father-in-law to three. His son served as regent for three monarchs. The original Fujiwara lineage had already split into four branch houses when the court moved to Heian-kyō. In Michinaga's day, all but his house, the northern branch, disappeared in power struggles. By the middle of the eleventh century, Michinaga's descendants monopolized the positions of regent. They later split into five sublineages that competed for political power and forced the few remaining non-Fujiwara houses from the court.

Even during their days of greatest glory, the Fujiwara always had to contend with the possibility that a non-Fujiwara woman would bear the ruler a son. Women too received court rank, and the ruler's officially designated wife enjoyed a status far above that of concubines. Fujiwara women in the houses of high-ranking Fujiwara men started with significant advantages, but to maintain their position over the generations required a finely honed consciousness of status exclusivity. For the monarch, only a wife of the Fujiwara or royal lineage would do; for the Fujiwara, only a wife from another Fujiwara branch or the ruling family sufficed. Monarchs and Fujiwara men married aunts, nieces, and first cousins. They continued to father children with concubines and serving women lest their official wife prove barren.

The Heyday of Aristocratic Culture

The florescence of female literary triumphs during the Fujiwara era is inseparable from political intrigue. When Fujiwara no Michinaga made his daughter Shōshi the monarch Ichijō's wife in 999, he selected a bevy of educated and engaging women to help her compete for Ichijō's attention. Guaranteeing her success in this regard was crucial because his rival and elder brother had a daughter who was already Ichijō's official wife. In Teishi's retinue was Sei Shonagon, famous for her brilliant wit. She is the author of *The Pillow Book*, a collection of essays on taste. "A preacher ought to be good-looking. For, if we are properly to understand his worthy sentiments, we must keep our eyes on him while he speaks." "A good lover will behave as elegantly at dawn as at any other time."[1] A consummate snob, Sei Shonagon hardly considered commoners to be the same species as herself. "Good people," by contrast, had impeccable lineage, taste, and spiritual virtue. Her contemporary and rival Murasaki Shikibu, who served in Shōshi's retinue, chided Sei Shonagon: "She thought herself so clever, and littered her writings with Chinese characters, but if you examined them closely, they left a great deal to be desired."[2] In addition to poetry and a diary, Murasaki Shikibu wrote *Tale of Genji,* a novel of court intrigue, life, and manners about a royal scion who exemplifies masculine perfection in physical appearance and behavior.

The tenth and eleventh centuries marked the pinnacle of classical women's literature. In the 970s a woman known to us only as the mother of Fujiwara no Michitsuna wrote *Kagerō nikki,* a poetic memoir of her unhappy twenty-year marriage to a high-ranking court official who seldom visited her. *Izumi Shikibu Diary* is another memoir that recounts the life of a low-ranking court woman (also in Shōshi's service) who married a man of her own station, had affairs with two princes, and wrote poetry famous for its passion. *A Tale of Flowering Fortunes,* composed during the 1030s by Akazome Emon, Japan's first vernacular historian, begins in 887 and concludes with a triumphal biography of Michinaga. A daughter of Sugawara no Takasue wrote *Hamamatsu Chūnagon monogatari* (A Tale of Hamamatsu Chūnagon) around 1070, which sets a love story in the travels of the eponymous hero who goes to China and returns. She also wrote *Sarashina nikki,* an autobiography notable for her recollections of her childhood with her father who left eastern Japan to try his luck at court. Steeped in the aesthetic sensibility of their day, these women wrote in the Japanese syllabary. (See **Material Culture: Writing Japanese.**) Encapsulated in the phrase *mono no aware* (beauty, evanescence, and pathos), this sensibility derived from the Buddhist view that the material world is transitory.

Men too wrote in Japanese. The poet and aspiring bureaucrat Ki no Tsurayuki edited the first of the royally commissioned Japanese poetry collections, the *Kokinshū* (Collection of the Past and Present), in 905. Female and male poets contributed approximately eleven hundred poems to this anthology, famous for its polished, elegant, intellectual tone. "The seeds of Japanese poetry lie in the human heart," Tsurayuki claimed, and poetry "moves heaven and earth."[3] He also wrote *Tosa nikki,* an account of a two-month trip to the capital across the Inland Sea by the provincial governor and his retinue. In his Preface he pretended to be a woman so as to justify his use of the syllabary

1. Ivan Morris, trans., *The Pillow Book of Sei Shonagon* (New York: Columbia University Press, 1967), 1:29, 33.

2. Robert Bowring, trans. and ed., *Murasaki Shikibu: Her Diary and Poetic Memoirs* (Princeton, N.J.: Princeton University Press, 1982), p. 131.

3. Laurel Rasplica Rodd with Mary Catherine Henkenius, trans., *Kokinshū: A Collection of Poems Ancient and Modern* (Princeton, N.J.: Princeton University Press, 1984), p. 35.

MATERIAL CULTURE

Writing Japanese

When the Japanese first learned to read and write, they did so in Chinese, the only writing system available to them. Chinese is a tonal, monosyllabic language. Japanese is polysyllabic with a dissimilar grammatical structure. Fortunately for the Japanese, the Chinese had already created a system for reproducing the sound of foreign words, primarily Buddhist terms, by using characters for their phonetic value alone. The author of *Kojiki* adopted this method for the names of places, gods, and people. The editor of the *Man'yōshū* also used characters for their phonetic value—twenty-nine of them for the sound *shi* alone. Thanks to the regularity of the poetic meter, it is usually clear when the editor expected characters to be sounded using their Japanese pronunciation—*uma* (horse) instead of *ma* for 馬, for example.

The introduction of calligraphy spurred the development of the Japanese syllabary. The so-called grass style brought from China by Kūkai became a favorite of poets. By the second half of the ninth century, it led writers to streamline commonly used characters, and by the eleventh century these streamlined characters were being used for their sound alone, although each syllable could be written in a number of ways. Called *kana* (borrowed names), the syllables continue to be used for grammatical markers and to soften the appearance of a text by writing out what might also be expressed in visually dense Chinese characters.

Two forms of the syllabary appeared. *Katakana,* angular *kana,* developed from pieces of characters. It was used to transcribe prayers and indicate the Japanese reading of Chinese texts. *Hiragana* has a smooth, round look. Known also as the woman's hand, it was

Preface to Kokinshū. *Kokinshū* was the first poetry anthology commissioned by the monarch in 905. Except for the title, the text is written in the cursive syllabary with calligraphy by Ki no Tsurayuki. *(Tokyo National Museum/ DNPArchives.com)*

used for poetry, essays, novels, and diaries. To show off the elegance of their hand, men and women linked individual *kana* in a cursive style that flowed down the page. The aim was to combine calligraphy, text, and paper into a harmonious and attractive whole.

and enhance the pathos of having lost a child while away. Other men wrote anonymously in Japanese, compiling a history, *Ōkagami* (Great Mirror), to supplement and correct Akazome's portrait of Michinaga; the first military tales; a poetic tale titled *Tale of Ise;* and miscellanies of anecdotes and observations. Along with women, they also produced folding screens, wall panels, and handscrolls in what is known as *Yamato-e,* Japanese art. (See Color Plate 14.)

Men such as Ki no Tsurayuki wrote in both Japanese and Chinese, but until recently, modern scholars of Japan's national literature have slighted Chinese works and the activities they portrayed. *Tale of Genji* shows men with women or performing music, dance, and kick-ball at which women were spectators. But courtiers had another life apart from women. They practiced the martial arts of archery, hawking, and horseback riding. They compiled anthologies of Chinese poetry, copied examinations held in Chinese, made vows to the Buddha in Chinese, and wrote edicts, wills, petitions, and litigation settlements in Chinese. Michinaga's diary records his activities to serve as precedents for his descendants. Like other male officials, he spent three-fourths of his time performing the annual cycle of ceremonial observances designed to arouse respect in subordinates and commoners while influencing supernatural powers to work on the court's behalf. He also fulfilled the duties associated with his position in the bureaucracy. Both ceremony and administration required knowledge of Chinese, from which women were excluded by virtue of their sex. In contrast to prehistoric rites and rituals in which men and women participated together, the Heian court differentiated between a man's world and a woman's. Because men could cross back and forth whereas women could not, gender asymmetry characterized social relations and language.

For women from the middle to lower ranks of the aristocracy, an education in the arts and letters helped them advance at court without ensuring their future. Despite having written great works of literature, Sei Shonagon, Murasaki Shikibu, and Akazome Emon ended their lives in obscurity and probable poverty. Female attendants thronged the court and the mansions of the Fujiwara. When their patron died, they might, if they were lucky, be given a small stipend and paid to recite Buddhist prayers for their master or mistress's salvation. Otherwise, lacking bequests from parents, they might join a group of mendicant nuns.

In the tenth century, female entertainers called players (*asobi*), who lived outside the court but made themselves available for casual relationships, posed a new threat to court women's monopoly over the male courtiers' attentions. They specialized in amusing travelers at river ports and provided song and dance entertainment at banquets. A few *asobi* came from declining aristocratic families and possessed as much education and refinement as any court lady. Some became the consorts of courtiers or even monarchs. The gifts of rice and cloth they received for sexual favors differed only in scale from those received by women who enjoyed longer liaisons with a man, suggesting a continuum of male-female relationships from lifelong to a single evening. In the eleventh century, *asobi* who marketed their skills as entertainers and sex partners had become well established. By the twelfth, *asobi* had been joined by *shirabyōshi* (Masters of the White Clappers) who sang popular songs, danced in male clothing, and brandished swords. They too attracted the patronage of high officials and a retired monarch.

Buddhism and the Fujiwara

During the degenerate last days of the Buddhist law (*mappō*) said to begin in 1052, people had fallen so far from the true teachings of the Buddha that only reliance on the power of the Other could save them from hell. According to the Mahayana tradition, the merciful and compassionate Amida had vowed to take every person who believed in him to the Pure Land of the Western Paradise at death. There they would become buddhas and continue to enjoy their accustomed luxuries in a spiritual realm. Michinaga built an Amida Hall in 1020. He died clutching a silk cord attached to nine statues of Amida who were to pull him to the Pure Land. In 1053 the Fujiwara regent built a graceful building called the *Hōōdō* (Phoenix Hall) at his retirement villa of Byōdōin for the worship of Amida. At this and the other ninety-five Amida halls built before 1192, monks dressed as the Buddha and wearing golden masks ceremoniously welcomed high-ranking patrons to Amida's paradise.

The Amida cult spread widely in the tenth to eleventh centuries. Scriptures describing the Pure Land in the Western Paradise had entered Japan during the Nara period, and monks on Mount Hiei had introduced the practice of chanting Amida's name in the ninth century. By 970, monks who had once spent twelve years studying the entire corpus of Tendai teachings spent ninety days in meditation during which they concentrated their thoughts on Amida, invoked his name, and circumambulated his statue. Holy men (*hijiri*) who shunned monasteries brought the promise of salvation through faith in Amida to the common people along with simple esoteric rites and devotion to the *Lotus Sutra* in one eclectic package. Kūya (903–972) spent his youth in the mountains, where he practiced spiritual exercises to eradicate bodily desires. He ordained himself and then walked all over Japan chanting the name of Amida with sutras and holy images carried on his back. He reached out to people through good works—building roads, burying corpses, and digging wells—because he believed that Buddhism had to be made available to everyone in terms they could understand. His message and that of other *hijiri* appealed to people who had to break the Buddhist precepts against the taking of life, in particular warriors, farmers, hunters, and fishermen.

Buddhist eclecticism coexisted with other teachings and beliefs. Aristocrats chanted Buddha's name, invoked the gods, and followed Daoist teachings regarding auspicious days, directions, and omens. Brushing teeth, washing hands, combing hair, and cutting fingernails and toenails had a ritual dimension that tied them to the worship of gods and Buddhas and protected the doer from malignant forces. Some doctrines preached that deity and Buddha existed as one body, others that deities manifested the essence of the Buddha. In the tenth century, a doctrine developed that whereas the Buddhas truly existed, deities did not; what appeared to be a deity was in reality the manifestation of a Buddha in deity form. This combination of Buddhism and native belief infused the edifying and didactic tales told to commoners, who learned that personal responsibility for their actions had to take into account the desires of the gods and the compassion of the Buddha. The search for salvation and help in coping with the tribulations of disease and famine demanded pilgrimages to numerous temples and shrines in the hope that one might prove efficacious.

Men enjoyed a more diverse range of religious practices than did women. The Enryakuji monastery and the rituals it performed on behalf of the court were closed to women. Monks ordained men; they also ordained women and supervised the nunneries to ensure that nuns obeyed the precepts. Being prone to sin and to arousing sinful thoughts in men, women suffered greater obstacles and hindrances to achieving Buddhahood. In *The Three Jewels* compiled in 984 for the edification of Princess Sonshi (?–985), the scholar-bureaucrat who was its author set forth the teachings that promised to help her overcome these obstacles and described services held on Mount Hiei that she would never be allowed to see. (See **Documents:** *Sanbōe* **(The Three Jewels).**)

RULE BY RETIRED MONARCHS

The last days of the Buddhist law coincided with political turmoil. In 1068 political and marital miscalculations on the part of the Fujiwara regent led to the enthronement of a ruler, Go-Sanjō, whose mother was not Fujiwara and who was already a mature adult. His chief advisers came from the Murakami Genji (the character for Gen can also be read as Minamoto) line of royal scions, and his youngest sons were born to Minamoto mothers. His son, Shirakawa, also exercised considerable authority by manipulating personnel practices in the bureaucracy to promote his supporters. Officials entrusted with provincial administration and tax collection on behalf of provincial governors paid Shirakawa

Heiji War. In the Heiji War of 1159, mounted warriors armed with bows and arrows attacked the retired monarch's residence and set it on fire. *(Museum of Fine Arts, Boston. Fenollosa-Weld Collection, 11.4000)*

enormous kickbacks. Boys in their teens received appointment in provincial offices, and three or four members of one family served simultaneously. None actually ventured to the provinces; they too deputized tax collection. In 1086 Shirakawa abdicated in favor of his son and became the dominant power at court. This initiated the rule by retired monarchs that added another institutional layer to the system already developed under the regime of codes and manipulated by the Fujiwara.

The retired monarchs had even more trouble than the Fujiwara in dealing with lawlessness. For years the local magnate Taira no Tadatsune refused to pay taxes and attacked provincial offices in eastern Japan. When the court delegated a cousin and rival to subdue him, both sides engaged in scorched-earth tactics that left less than 1 percent of the arable land in Tadatsune's home province under cultivation. His revolt of 1031 preceded three major conflicts between 1051 and 1135: two wars in the northeast and piracy on the Inland Sea. In 1051, the

court appointed Minamoto no Yoriyoshi to tackle the Abe family of Mutsu, tax evaders and chiefs of the Emishi. It took Yoriyoshi twelve years to subdue the Abe. The next war, from 1083 to 1087, erupted when Yoriyoshi's son got drawn into an inheritance dispute involving his erstwhile allies, the Kiyowara family of Mutsu; also Emishi. Closer to Heian-kyō on the Inland Sea, provincial soldiers sent after pirates were often pirates themselves. In 1129 and again in 1135, the court dispatched Taira no Tadamori to suppress them. Royal scions figured prominently in all of these incidents, designated either law breakers or court-appointed commanders, and sometimes both. The court also had to deal with obstreperous monks who wielded sacred symbols to gain political demands. Warrior monks from Tōdaiji launched the first violent confrontation when they marched on Heian-kyō in 949. The Fujiwara temple of Kōfukuji repeatedly terrorized the Fujiwara by dispatching monks armed with branches from the sacred sakaki tree prepared by the Kasuga shrine under

DOCUMENTS

Sanbōe (The Three Jewels)

Sponsored by Princess Sonshi and written by Minamoto Tamenori, this was the first Buddhist instruction book to be written in Japan. The first volume explains the essential nature of the Buddha, the second contains biographies of Buddhist monks, and the third describes the monthly round of Buddhist services. The selection here illustrates the wondrous power of the Buddha and Buddhist teachings through stories about ordinary people.

Preface to the Second Volume: The Teachings

Behold, the Buddha's teachings have spread to the east and have come to rest here in our land where they now flourish! Many sages have appeared here and left their marks, and our sovereigns have continuously fostered the spread of Buddhism. . . . The sound of the Law is as efficacious as a "poison drum": even if you hear it just once, your enemy—ignorance—will be destroyed immediately. The names of the sutras are just like medicinal trees: you have only to utter them for the illness—the cycle of birth, death, and rebirth—to be cured. If, in one day, three times as many people as all the sand in the Ganges were to sacrifice themselves, they would not even begin to repay our debt for a single verse in the Buddha's teachings.

A Woman of Yamato Province

There was a woman who lived in the village of Yamamura in Sōkami District in Yamato Province. Her name is unknown. This woman had a daughter who married and had two children. Her husband was appointed governor of another province. He took his wife and children with him and had been living in that province for two years

when his wife's mother, back home in their native village, had an inauspicious dream about her daughter. When she awoke, she was full of dread and grief. She wanted to sponsor readings of the sutras, but she was poor and had no property. She took off her own clothes and washed and purified them and gave them as a fee for the readings.

Her daughter lived in the governor's mansion with her husband. Her two children, who had been playing out in the courtyard, called inside to her: "There are seven monks on our roof, chanting sutras! Come out quickly and see!" Indeed, when she listened for sounds from the roof, she could hear voices chanting, just like a crowd of droning bees. Incredulous, she went out into the yard to have a look. In the next instant, the house collapsed. Just as suddenly, the seven monks had disappeared. In fright and alarm, she thought to herself, "Heaven has come to my aid and kept me from being crushed to death beneath the falling house!"

Later her mother sent a courier who reported the inauspicious dream and how she had sponsored the sutra readings. Hearing this, her daughter's reverence for the Three Jewels [the Buddha, his teachings, and the clergy] was many times increased.

its control. The monks from Mount Hiei expressed grievances by carrying portable shrines through the streets of Heian-kyō. It was popularly believed that any damage done to the shrines or to the monks who carried them

would incur the wrath of the gods. An ongoing dispute between rival Tendai sects at Enryakuji and nearby Onjōji that began in 980 erupted into violence in 1039 when, furious at an ecclesiastical appointment that favored Onjōji, the

Thus it was known: the power generated by the chanting of the sutras brought her the protection of the Three Jewels.

A Miner of Mimasaka Province

In Agata District in Mimasaka Province there was a mine from which the government took ore. In the reign of Empress Kōken [749–758] the governor of the province ordered ten men to go up to the mine and bring out some of the ore. While they were inside, the entrance suddenly crumbled and collapsed. The men were frightened, and they scrambled out. Nine of them managed to escape, but just as the tenth and last man was about to come out, the entrance caved in and was completely closed.

The governor of the province was terribly upset, and the man's wife and children grieved. Images of the Buddha were painted, sutras were copied, and a forty-nine-day period of memorial rites was observed.

The man inside the mine made a vow: "Long ago I planned to offer a copy of the *Lotus Sutra,* but I have not copied or presented it. If am saved, I swear that I will complete the project without delay."

Just then a crack about as wide as his finger opened between the rocks, and a tiny beam of sunlight shone through. A monk appeared and passed through the crack, gave him some food and said, "This was given to me by your wife and children. I have come to you because you are suffering." Then he disappeared through the crack.

Scarcely a moment after his departure, a crack opened immediately over the miner's head, through which he could see the sky. This opening was more than three feet wide and about five feet long.

Just then, thirty villagers had come to the mountain to cut vines. They happened to pass close to this opening. The man inside heard them draw near and shouted "Help!" The villagers heard him, though his voice seemed no louder than a mosquito's buzz. But the sound made them curious, so they tied a vine to a rock and lowered the end down through the opening, and the man inside pulled on it. Then they knew there was a man inside, so they tied vines together and made a basket, and they twisted more vines together to make a rope and lowered them through the opening. The man inside got into the basket, and the men above pulled him out.

They took him to his parents' house, and when his family saw him, there was no limit to their joy. The governor of the province was amazed, and when he made inquiry, the miner told him all about it. The miner, full of respect and awe, gathered together all the faithful of the province, and following his lead, they all contributed to the preparation of a copy of the *Lotus Sutra* and a grand offertory service.

He survived that which is difficult to survive: This was made possible through the power of his faith in the *Lotus Sutra.*

———
Source: Edward Kamens, *The Three Jewels: A Study and Translation of Minamoto Tamenori's Sanbōe* (Ann Arbor: Center for Japanese Studies, University of Michigan, 1988), pp. 166–167, 220, 232–233, modified.

Enryakuji monks set the regent's residence on fire. In 1075 they fought Onjōji's request for an ordination platform. In 1081 they burned the Onjōji temple complex, an act repeated in 1121, 1140, and 1163. These incidents and many others marked the militarization of the clergy.

While abbots and their disciples continued to accept the precepts that forbade monks to carry weapons or take life, they allowed low-ranking and minimally educated monks to fight for them and summoned soldiers from temple estates to attack their enemies.

THE ESTATE SYSTEM

A backdrop to the wars and political turmoil of the eleventh century was a set of decrees by the monarch Go-Sanjō to regulate tax-exempt estates (*shōen*). Starting in 743 the court had decreed that temples and aristocrats who sponsored land reclamation projects would be allowed to hold the land in perpetuity, albeit subject to taxation. All other land belonged to the state. In this agrarian society, officials and holders of court rank received salaries in the form of land assignments that generated income. The same was provided for temple upkeep. In theory these assignments changed when rank or office changed, but as offices became hereditary, land assignments tended to be seen not as the temporary and revocable grant of state land but as constituting a type of ownership. The labor force came largely from cultivators working state lands who rented the land grants on an annual basis. Occasionally influential aristocrats and temples were able to get tax immunities for their land assignments that turned them into estates. What changed with Go-Sanjō's decree of 1068 and an earlier decree in 1045 was the recognition of a distinction between tax-exempt estates and government land (*kokugaryō*, literally, provincial land) that resulted in making the ownership hierarchy of estates more complicated and estates more permanent. Go-Sanjō tried to restrict the growth of estates by voiding estates created after an earlier decree of 1045 and threatening to confiscate those created before if they were improperly documented. The bureau he set up for this purpose certified each proprietor's claims to income and gave him or her de facto legitimacy. Confiscated estates became not government land but monarchical land, its revenues destined for use by Go-Sanjō and his family. Go-Sanjō took this step because in the late tenth and early eleventh centuries, drought, armed conflict, and epidemics of killer diseases left too few cultivators to work the land and pay taxes. To bring land back into production, he gave institutions and individuals with political power incentive to sponsor land reclamation projects by permitting them to receive a guaranteed income from tax-exempt estates.

Although tax-exempt estates placed limits on the state's ability to tax and control landholdings, they did not replace government lands. Approximately 50 to 60 percent of the land remained subject to taxation by the state. This state land included ports, transportation routes on land and sea, and agricultural plots. Provincial governors or their deputies collected taxes on it, kept a portion for themselves and their staffs, and sent the rest to Heian-kyō.

Tax-exempt estates had political, social, and economic functions. In place of a unified bureaucratic framework, multiple quasi-independent centers of power—temples, high-ranking aristocrats, the retired monarchs, and the monarch—had the authority to levy taxes, conduct censuses, and police the inhabitants on their estates. Local magnates who had amassed extensive taxed holdings through clearance, purchase, or extortion in the tenth century petitioned the court for tax immunity through an aristocratic sponsor, who became the formal proprietor and received a share of the produce. That aristocrat in turn sought protection from temples or higher-ranking families. The local magnate remained in charge of the estate as its manager. The process of commendation from lower to higher levels increased the number and size of estates and complicated the levels of proprietorship without increasing the amount of land under cultivation. Each estate encompassed a broad, though not necessarily contiguous, territory divided into a welter of smallholdings of cultivated wet and dry fields, fallow fields, mountains, forests, swamps, huts for the cultivators, and a residence-office block for the manager. The offices (*shiki*) for everyone from titled cultivators to resident manager and his guards to the urban-based legal proprietor and protector all came with rights to income in recompense for fulfilling their documented responsibilities toward the estate. This income included food, clothing, and items of daily use. By the late Heian period, *shiki* became less associated with the duties of office than with income from and authority over estate residents.

SUMMARY

The last hundred years of the Heian period closely resemble the century that followed. Warrior monks, pirates, and confrontations in the northeast were the harbingers of military conflict that would bring warriors to new prominence. Political and factional strife at court took an increasingly militarized hue as aristocrats, monarchs, and retired monarchs called on warriors in the provinces to come to their aid or saw court nobles take to the profession of arms. The leaders of warrior bands, some of whom were royal scions, competed for the domination, not the elimination, of the court. Infected by the esoteric teachings that Kūkai and Saichō had brought back from China, the court performed ever more elaborate rituals that suffocated the monarch as a political player while individuals both high and low sought salvation in the teachings of the *Lotus Sutra* or faith in Amida. The dual system of estate and provincial lands accommodated military, ecclesiastical, and aristocratic demands for income and power. These three power blocs were to dominate Japanese history for centuries to come.

SUGGESTED READING

The general readings listed at the end of Chapter 7 also apply to this period. Two collections of essays that span the years up to the twentieth century are H. Tonomura, A. Walthall, and H. Wakita, eds., *Women and Class in Japanese History* (1999), and B. Ruch, *Engendering Faith: Women and Buddhism in Premodern Japan* (2002).

Few English-language monographs deal with the Heian period. See I. Morris, *The World of the Shining Prince* (1964); G. C. Hurst, III, *Insei: Abdicated Sovereigns in the Politics of Late Heian Japan, 1086–1185* (1976); and K. Friday, *Hired Swords: The Rise of Private Warrior Power in Early Japan* (1992). See also C. J. Kiley, "Estate and Property in the Late Heian Period," in *Medieval Japan: Essays in Institutional History,* ed. J. W. Hall and J. P. Mass (1974).

For Buddhism, see R. Abe, *The Weaving of Mantra: Kūkai and the Construction of Esoteric Buddhist Discourse* (1999). For entertainers, see J. R. Goodwin, "Shadows of Transgression: Heian and Kamakura Constructions of Prostitution," *Monumenta Nipponica* 55, no. 3 (2000). For literature, see works mentioned in the text and footnotes. A good recent book on art is M. H. Yiengpruksawan, *Hiraizumi: Buddhist Art and Regional Politics in Twelfth-Century Japan* (1998).

Kamakura Japan (1180–1333)

The Kamakura period takes its name from the military government established in the seacoast town by that name. (See Map 7.1.) Located a week's journey northeast of Kyoto and tucked into the mountains of the Miura Peninsula, Kamakura exhibited none of the spacious grandeur of the capital. Instead it provided housing, offices, and places of worship for a military regime. The task of awing visitors was delegated to the colossal statue of Amida and the Tsurugaoka Hachiman shrine to the god of war, tutelary deity of the Minamoto. The Kamakura regime sought not to displace Kyoto but to keep the peace and dispense justice while the royal court continued to perform essential rituals and ceremonies.

During the Kamakura period, new forms of literature and religion began to supplement the courtly tradition. By the middle of the thirteenth century, improved agricultural technologies had overcome the stagnation of the previous centuries. Economic growth made the practice of partible inheritance feasible until the defense against the Mongol invasions of 1274 and 1281 exposed fault lines in warrior society. When they fissured some fifty years later, they brought down the regime.

Where did samurai come from and what was the nature of the relationship between the Kyoto court and the military regime? What kind of roles did women play in samurai families and how did Buddhism enhance its appeal?

RISE OF THE WARRIOR

The samurai plays such a central role in Japanese history from the twelfth to the nineteenth centuries that he appears almost timeless. Where he came from is a matter of debate. His connections with

Map 11.1   Major Provinces, Regions, and Cities in Japan

monarchy and court, and what it meant to be a samurai, changed over time. Historians once thought that the aristocracy reneged its responsibility for maintaining peace early in the Heian period when it stopped executing criminals, allowed the conscript army to deteriorate, and permitted provincial governors to hire deputies rather than forsake the capital. By the tenth century, the countryside had fallen into disorder. Men in the provinces active in land reclamation projects armed themselves in local disputes and turned to warfare to protect their interests. A substantial warrior class arose, and in the twelfth century it turned on an effete and ineffectual monarchy.

A number of historians today argue that the monarchy was a dynamic success, functional at least to the beginning of the fourteenth century and capable of manipulating the samurai for its own ends. According to one interpretation, the monarchy deliberately encouraged new forms of military organization after the killer epidemic of smallpox or a similar disease in 733–737. Rather than support a large, ill-trained army, it hired professional mercenaries for police work and military protection.[1] Another interpretation

---

1. See Karl F. Friday, *Hired Swords: The Rise of Private Warrior Power in Early Japan* (Stanford, Calif.: Stanford University Press, 1992).

is more evolutionary: it claims that conscript armies never completely replaced Yayoi period fighters (300 B.C.E.–300 C.E.) and military men of later times were descendants of these professional warriors. Under the regime of codes, they found a niche in offices at provincial headquarters.[2] By retaining the right to sanction military force, even when it could not control how or when it would be used, the monarchy continued to play a crucial role in legitimizing its use down to the end of World War II. The monarchy also retained the privilege of granting rank and office.

A third argument emphasizes the distinction in culture and values between aristocrats and warriors. Warriors originated as hunters in eastern Japan and seamen along the Inland Sea whose occupations and values contrasted with cultivators, who abhorred killing. Rather than initiate land reclamation, they appropriated fields opened by others through forged documentation or force. Instead of releasing captured animals in Buddhist rites that sought merit through freeing sentient beings, they hunted them for the meat, for recreation, and to test their martial skills. In eastern Japan they raised horses and practiced shamanism. They dressed in iron armor and animal skins rather than silk, and many were illiterate. In the eyes of the Kyoto aristocrats, they were rustic boors, hardly more civilized than the Emishi they were called to fight.[3]

The verb *samurau* means to serve; the first samurai were warriors who held the sixth court rank along with scholars, scribes, and artisans. Other terms for fighting men did not carry the connotation of service to the court. By acquiring court rank and offices, such as guard at the left gate, samurai distinguished themselves from commoners. Warriors either sought rank themselves or accepted the leadership of someone who did. When royal scions or Fujiwara descendants moved to the provinces in search of careers that eluded them at court, their qualifications for rank based on their distinguished lineage helped them attract followers. In political terms, the need to have success at arms legitimized by court approbation, rank, and title always limited warrior autonomy.

Samurai fought with bow and arrows on horseback. Their preferred tactic was to catch the enemy off guard, often in night attacks. They violated promises and truces if that would gain them an advantage. Honor lay in winning. Being of lowly rank, samurai felt none of the compassion a superior exhibits toward inferiors. They did not hesitate to burn villages and kill the inhabitants. The fighting season lasted from the fall harvest to the spring planting, and men stayed with the army only so long as they received rewards. They fought for personal glory and social advancement. There was no point in engaging the enemy if the commander was not watching or in risking one's life against a lowly opponent. Samurai sanctioned by the court engaged not in conquest but in police actions. The goal was to eliminate rivals, not seize territory.

PRELUDE TO KAMAKURA RULE

Competition between and within the Taira and Minamoto lineages epitomized political conflicts of the twelfth century. Royal scions with followers in provincial governors' offices used their military credentials to gain access to power holders at the center. The Minamoto became the retired monarch's clients by serving as the leader of his personal bodyguard, but rival claimants to this position fought each other so viciously in 1106 that they left an opening for Taira no Tadamori, victor against Inland Sea pirates, to replace them. Access to the throne enabled Tadamori to obtain lucrative positions in the

2. See Wayne W. Farris, *Heavenly Warriors: The Evolution of Japan's Military, 500–1300* (Cambridge, Mass.: Harvard University Press, 1992).
3. See Eiko Ikegami, *The Taming of the Samurai: Honorific Individualism and the Making of Modern Japan* (Cambridge, Mass.: Harvard University Press, 1995).

provincial governors' offices in western Japan and to promote Taira interests at court. His son Kiyomori was to take the Taira to such preeminence that he rivaled the Fujiwara.

In the middle of the twelfth century, factional disputes in the Heian court merged with warfare, pitting family members against each other in the countryside. The death of the retired monarch in 1156 turned his sons against each other. The retired head of the Fujiwara house wanted his second son to succeed him as chieftain and regent, to the dismay of his first son, who already held these positions. The Minamoto too were divided between father and son. Only Taira no Kiyomori led a unified house. When rival claimants to the throne and the Fujiwara headship called on samurai to aid their cause, Kiyomori and the Minamoto obliged in the Hōgen Incident of 1156. Marked by patricide and fratricide, it brought warfare to the streets of Kyoto for the first time. Kiyomori won and received the fourth rank under the new ruler, Go-Shirakawa. In the 1159 Heiji Incident provoked by renewed conflict within the Fujiwara house, Kiyomori eliminated his chief Minamoto rivals.

Kiyomori's rise from obscure branch of the Taira family to grandfather of ruler followed by the Taira's rapid collapse after his death is the stuff of legend. Kiyomori intended to use his dominance in military affairs to replace the Fujiwara as the monarch's controller. In 1167 he became prime minister and the proud possessor of the first rank, an unprecedented achievement for a samurai. One daughter bore the monarch Antoku. The others married Fujiwara. Kiyomori's kinsmen monopolized the bureaucracy, holding governorships for over thirty provinces, managing over five hundred tax-exempt estates, and amassing a fortune in trade with Koryǒ Korea and Song China. Even before Kiyomori's death, resentment at his usurpation of aristocratic privilege had brought his henchmen under attack.

In 1180, one of Go-Shirakawa's sons issued a proclamation ordering the samurai to punish Kiyomori. Although the hapless prince was immediately forced to commit suicide, this edict provided the justification for samurai, and the warrior-monks of Kōfukuji, to initiate a five-year struggle celebrated in legend as the Genpei War (1180–1185). Minamoto no Yoritomo amassed an army in the Kanto region of eastern Japan and proclaimed himself Minamoto chieftain at a shrine to Hachiman. Other aspiring Minamoto chieftains also revolted against the Taira. Following Kiyomori's death in 1181, the Taira still held the Kinai region around Kyoto and western Japan, but Minamoto forces dominated the Japan Sea coast and the east. Yoritomo's cousin and rival chased the Taira out of Kyoto and installed himself as what the court saw as the boorish leader of a band of hooligans. Go-Shirakawa appealed to Yoritomo for help. Yoritomo dispatched his brothers Noriyori and Yoshitsune to fight under Go-Shirakawa's banner while he stayed in the Kanto to consolidate his control.

Decisive battles in the Genpei War were few; most conflict erupted between close kin in skirmishes that degenerated into endemic lawlessness. Weakened by years of drought in western Japan, the Taira forces melted away. When the first Minamoto forces ventured too far west and remained too long, they too ran out of supplies. Yoshitsune, by contrast, proved to be a brilliant tactician. He quickly defeated rival Minamoto troops and immediately marched west against the Taira who had reassembled around the child monarch Antoku. Yoshitsune's string of naval and land victories against the Taira climaxed at Dannoura at the lower end of the Inland Sea in 1185. The Taira chieftains were annihilated, and Antoku's nurse threw herself into the sea with the child clasped in her arms.

MILITARY GOVERNMENT AT KAMAKURA

While Yoshitsune was fighting battles, Yoritomo was putting together a power base in the east. In

Minamoto Yoritomo. This wooden sculpture of Minamoto Yoritomo depicts the warrior in the robes and hat of a court noble. Realistic portraits and sculptures of Buddhist deities characterize art of the Kamakura Age. *(Tokyo National Museum/DNPArchives.com)*

1180 he summoned housemen and supporters to his residence to witness his claim to jurisdiction over the east as lord of Kamakura by virtue of his distinguished lineage and the call to arms he had received from the now-deceased prince. Each then signed his name to an oath of allegiance under the scrutiny of the head of Yoritomo's Bureau of Samurai. In return, Yoritomo promised to protect each claim to land and office. This oath began the process of differentiating the samurai as a self-conscious class. The estates and offices confiscated from men who might be expected to oppose Yoritomo, in particular the provincial governors' deputies and Taira supporters, were used to reward achievements on Yoritomo's behalf. Although Yoritomo usurped the monarchy's authority to confirm landholdings and office, he did so only

in terms of military personnel. Court officials and temples that had not sided with the Taira retained the rights to income they already enjoyed.

Yoritomo's nascent regime gained new legitimacy in the autumn of 1183. Years of poor harvests, a virtual blockade between eastern and western Japan, and countless refusals to fulfill financial obligations had reduced the revenue owed the government, aristocrats, and temples by provincial headquarters and private estates. After negotiation, Go-Shirakawa bestowed the fifth court rank on Yoritomo, and Yoritomo guaranteed the flow of income from eastern Japan. This official recognition of Yoritomo's de facto jurisdiction in the east proved the springboard for him to assert it across the country, but always as a delegate of the monarchy.

Once Yoritomo received formal recognition of his control over eastern Japan, he exercised it in ways that amassed power to himself while benefiting Go-Shirakawa and the aristocracy. He intervened in land disputes, suppressed outlawry, and issued orders for payments to be made to Kyoto all across Japan, not just in the east. Several weeks after Yoshitsune's first major victory against the Taira in 1184, Yoritomo informed Go-Shirakawa that he was now the emergency protector for the entire country. He claimed the sole right to raise armies, giving him a hold over the entire warrior class. He forbade the monarchy to reward any Minamoto man without his approval. He urged it to restore virtuous rule and to be judicious in its appointments of provincial governors. To assist the operations of provincial headquarters, Yoritomo appointed military governors (*shugo*) who had the power to arrest bandits and pirates, punish traitors, and summon Minamoto housemen to serve their lord. While exercising his authority vis-à-vis the monarchy, he dispatched deputies to western Japan to identify and recruit military men to accept his rule in return for confirmation of their holdings and rewards for defeating his enemies. The monarchy retained its prestige; Yoritomo ended up with a military regime.

Once the Taira had been defeated, Yoritomo found new ways to perpetuate his claim to govern Japan. The defeat had not brought an end to disorder; across Japan, local warriors raided tax-exempt estates and interfered with the collection of taxes by provincial headquarters. To rein in lawlessness and reward his followers, Yoritomo began to appoint estate stewards (*jitō*) to replace Taira supporters on estates with the responsibility to keep the peace and continue to forward the income owed Kyoto. Just as estate personnel remained administratively distinct from provincial governors, so did *jitō* remain independent of military governors. Each *jitō* received his own rights to income (*shiki*), and these *shiki* guaranteed by Kamakura, not by Kyoto, became the means by which Yoritomo

rewarded his followers and demonstrated the necessity for his rule. In 1189 he defeated a family calling itself Fujiwara that had ruled a semi-autonomous state in northern Honshu for a century. This victory enabled him to reward a substantial number of followers with the position of estate steward and its attendant rights to income and to infiltrate his men into the provincial government. Although aristocrats and temples continued to be the protectors and proprietors of estates, the monarchy's sovereignty had been compromised. Yoritomo had taken over the policing of the entire country, and he had created a new office, the *jitō*, that under his control became the backbone for his military.

Family Politics

After the Taira defeat at Dannoura, Yoritomo's kin became his chief adversaries. By executing Yoritomo's elder brothers along with their father, Kiyomori had rid Yoritomo of some rival claimants to the Minamoto chieftaincy. As architect of the Taira's military defeat, Yoshitsune lacked only birth to qualify to head the Minamoto lineage; Yoritomo's mother was the daughter of a shrine official, whereas Yoshitsune's was a menial. When Go-Shirakawa offered Yoshitsune the position of provincial governor and Yoshitsune accepted without waiting for Yoritomo's approval, Yoritomo hounded his brother to his death. Yoritomo dispatched his uncle and his uncle's children in 1186. He had his youngest brother, Noriyori, killed despite the latter's protestations of loyalty. Having eliminated his kinsmen, nothing should have prevented his sons from succeeding him.

In the competition not to overthrow social superiors but to displace kin, a man's staunchest ally became his in-laws. Following his father's execution, Yoritomo had been placed as a hostage in the Hōjō family, followers of the Taira in eastern Japan. There he married his host's daughter, Masako. While Yoritomo was consolidating his power base, the Hōjō proved loyal supporters. His father-in-law even went to

Kyoto in 1184 to get the court's permission for Yoritomo to appoint estate stewards.

As Yoritomo's wife, Masako exercised authority in his name, but she also promoted Hōjō interests. She drove away Yoritomo's mistresses, lest their relatives replace hers. After Yoritomo died, Masako held together the coalition of housemen and allies who had pledged loyalty to him. Their first son, Yoriie, succeeded Yoritomo. In less than five years, Yoriie so preferred his wife's family that Masako and her father killed them all and forced Yoriie to abdicate. He died a few months later. The second son, Sanetomo, then became lord of Kamakura with Masako's father as regent. In 1205 Masako had her father arrested because he favored the children born of his second wife over Masako's full brother. Masako and her brother made the Hōjō not only the dominant power in Kamakura, but also the wealthiest of the Minamoto supporters. When Yoriie's son killed Sanetomo in 1219 and was then summarily executed, Yoritomo's line became extinct. Only Masako provided continuity. As her husband's representative, she adopted a courtier infant to become titular head of the Kamakura regime. When the retired monarch Go-Toba declared Masako's brother an outlaw in 1221, Masako rallied Yoritomo's supporters by presenting herself as the incarnation of his ideals. Despite occasional attempts at coups d'état by the disgruntled descendants of Yoritomo's supporters, successive generations of Hōjō regents governed the samurai through children summoned from Kyoto. Although Masako preserved her husband's legacy, she did so in ways that enriched the Hōjō.

Masako's dual roles as wife and daughter suggest that women played a crucial role in military households. Marriage remained a private matter between a man and a woman, often marked with scant or no ceremony. The Kamakura regime never insisted that marriages be registered nor did it try to prevent marriages across classes. Sanetomo married not a warrior woman but a princess. The property women received or inherited from their mothers and fathers remained theirs and continued to link them to their natal families; it went with them in marriage, left with them at divorce, and was theirs to bestow on their children. Like their brothers, daughters competed for shares in the family estate and frowned when the sibling set grew uncomfortably large. Given the ubiquity of sibling rivalry, people without heirs turned to adoption rather than enrich a brother or sister. Adoption needed no ratification by the state. When a husband died without heirs, his wife, not his siblings, arranged for his successor.

Kamakura Shogunate

The office of *sei-i-tai shōgun* meant little to Yoritomo because it designated a general with only temporary powers to raise troops and suppress barbarians. Yoritomo used it for three years following his investiture in 1192; thereafter, he preferred a title that instantiated higher court rank. Yoriie succeeded his father as lord of Kamakura in 1199; he became shogun in 1202 when his relatives discovered the advantage of an office that could be inherited and thus controlled by one of them. The Hōjō used the title of shogun for the series of figureheads for whom they acted as regents and applied it retroactively to Yoritomo to legitimize their stratagem. Historians often use the term *bakufu* to designate the military dynasties between 1180 and 1867, but it is a nineteenth-century anachronism that elides the substantial differences between regimes.

In 1221 the retired monarch Go-Toba misjudged samurai support for the Hōjō and tried to rally military men in western Japan to crush the Kamakura regime. Following his defeat and exile, the Hōjō extended their reach into western Japan. They confiscated estates belonging to Go-Toba's supporters and apportioned them to estate stewards who fought for Kamakura. They stationed two members of their family in Kyoto to oversee relations with the court and ensure that no future monarch followed Go-Toba's example. They followed the precedent set by Yoritomo in guaranteeing local land rights. All over Japan, estate managers proclaimed themselves loyal followers of Kamakura. They used this stratagem to attack proprietor land rights and appropriate the office of estate steward. As the leaders of the samurai, the Hōjō wanted to have samurai declare themselves for Kamakura. They also had to prevent the fighting that their new followers provoked to gain income. Although the Hōjō and their chief supporters became provincial governors, neither they nor the estate stewards tried to seize territory. Final authority over land rested with the monarchy, and the provincial headquarters continued to administer large portions of it. The hierarchical estate structure remained dominated by Kyoto and defended by Kamakura in a system of dual governance.

Neither Yoritomo nor the Hōjō instituted what would be considered a fully fledged government today. Yoritomo ruled through a chancellery similar to the administrative offices in provincial headquarters, aristocratic households, and temple complexes. In 1225 Masako's nephew Yasutoki established a thirteen-member council composed of the senior Hōjō and the heads of allied families. It made policy decisions and appointments and served as a court of last appeal. There was no public treasury. The thirteen councilors had their own sources of income as the stewards for numerous estates and as Kyoto-appointed officials holding court rank and office. Litigants paid court costs for the judicial system, the residents of Kamakura paid fees for city administration, Minamoto housemen provided the upkeep for the Tsurugaoka Hachiman shrine, and compensation for Yoritomo's followers came out of the revenues generated by the tax-exempt estates.

Legal disputes over land generated the most paperwork (see **Documents: The Estate Stewards in Legal Documents**). Conflict between siblings was common, and women as well as men brought suit. Newly appointed estate stewards wanted clarity in the extent of their authority over the cultivators, their relations with the staff already in place, and the collection of rents. When a steward appropriated too much income

for himself or interfered in the activities of the estate staff, the injured party in Kyoto appealed to Kamakura to restore its rights. For over 150 years, judges in Kamakura made a serious effort to maintain the status quo by adjudicating these cases more or less fairly.

The Hōjō soon realized that disciplining the stewards required clear guidelines. In 1232, Yasutoki published a new code, the *Goseibai shikimoku* (a list of rules for making judgments), the first step in the evolution of juridical procedures passed on contemporary norms. Steeped in the Chinese classics, Yasutoki believed that government had to be just in order to be legitimate. Stewards had to be held accountable for unlawful acts. A steward convicted of starting a brawl, for example, would lose his estates. Adultery and rape were to be punished by exiling the man and woman involved and confiscating their estates. Unlike previous codes based on Chinese models, this code was based on precedent: the decisions made by Yoritomo and Masako cited in the text. When no precedent fit a particular situation, the judges were to rely on reason. In its provisions dealing with inheritance rights, the code made legal what had been customary, including women's legal prerogatives. Women had the right to inherit property and the office that went with it. A woman could become the family head, and a widow could become a steward. The code protected the rights of the monarchy to its income and added legal protection to the land grants made to stewards. The steward in effect owned his or her land rights and could do what he or she liked with them: buy, sell, or divide them among his or her heirs.

Toward Intensive Agriculture and Economic Growth

As an unintended consequence of the tax-exempt estate system, farmers who held permanent title to cultivation rights as *myōshu* had an incentive to cultivate land more intensively. In Kyushu and western Japan they tried growing two crops a

DOCUMENTS

The Estate Stewards in Legal Documents

Underpinning the rise of the samurai was the office of estate steward (jitō shiki), a position central to understanding the nature of Kamakura rule. With it came rights to income that supported a martial lifestyle in return for loyal service. The documents below enumerate the estate steward's responsibilities, adjudicate disputes, recognize women's rights to hold office and receive income, and promote land reclamation. Several are the results of lawsuits over what this office entailed for the steward, his descendants, and previous estate personnel.

Ordered to Shiota Estate, Shinano Province concerning appointment to a *jitō shiki* of Koremune Tadahisa:

The aforesaid person, as *jitō* is to administer estate affairs. Regarding the annual tax and other levies, he shall perform those duties in accordance with precedent. It is commanded thus [by Yoritomo]. Wherefore, this order.

1186, 1st month, 8th day.

Ordered to the residents of paddy and upland areas in Ryūzōji village, Ozu-Higashi Gō, Hizen Province that Fujiwara Sueie shall henceforth be *jitō*.

Concerning the aforesaid place, and owing to Fujiwara Sueie's hereditary claim, an order by the government-general for the island of Kyushu authorizing him to administer it was granted. However, a local chief of Kanzaki district, Shigezane, has reportedly been obstructive. Sueie did not join the Heike rebellion and served loyally, honoring imperial authority. Shigezane plotted rebellion as a Heike partisan, in itself a great crime. Worst of all, his failure to submit formally before the Kamakura lord is evidence of a continuing sympathy for the Heike

rebels. The import of this is outrageous. Accordingly, Shigezane's disturbances are to cease permanently, and Sueie is to hold the *jitō shiki*. Regarding the stipulated taxes and annual rice levy, the orders of the proprietor are to be obeyed and duty discharged in accordance with precedence. It is commanded thus. Wherefore, this order.

1186, 8th month, 9th day.

The chancellery of the shogun's house orders to the residents of three districts—Iwamatsu, Shimo Imai, Tanaka—within Nitta estate, Kōzuke Province that in accord with the last will of the husband, Yoshikane, his widow shall forthwith be *jitō*.

The aforesaid person, in accordance with the will, is appointed to this *shiki*. As to the fixed annual tax and other services, these shall be paid in accordance with precedent. It is commanded thus. Wherefore, this order.

1215, 3rd month, 22nd day.

Concerning the estate manager *shiki* of Tarumi estate, Settsu province:

Regarding the above, the former estate manager Shigetsune had his lands confis-

year, one of rice and one of a lesser grain such as barley. Toward the end of the twelfth century, a hardier rice variety arrived from China that could be grown on previously marginal fields and proved resistant to drought and cold weather.

Cultivators expanded their acreage by using upland areas for dry fields and orchards, and they stopped allowing fields to lie fallow. To keep land in continuous production, they spread processed fertilizer—ashes, mulch, and manure. The dis-

cated because of his Heike affiliation [and bestowed on a *jitō*]. However, the palace woman Izumo-no-tsubone has stated: This estate is a land first opened by my ancestors with a estate managership that is hereditary. Given this original-holder status, we request that the *shiki* be reconferred. Since it is difficult to ignore a suit lodged by a court person, the reappointment will be made to this *shiki*. By command of the Kamakura lord it is decreed thus.
1204, 9th month, 6th day.

Ordered to the *jitō* headquarters of Fukunaga Myō in Matsuura estate in Hizen province that forthwith undeveloped areas shall be opened and taxes paid from them.

Regarding this, a petition from the *jitō* and others states: "this estate is populous, but has too few paddy and upland fields. Accordingly, new fields should be opened and taxes produced." In essence, the restoration of smoke from every house will mean prosperity for the village, and will also ensure the peace. You may open new land, as requested. During the first year of development, taxes will be waived. For the next year the rate will be one-half bushel per .294 acre of whatever the commodity being grown, with an increase of one-half bushel the following year, and ultimately a rate of one and one-half bushels. As regards the miscellaneous obligations, a similar exemption will be in force. Should the newly opened fields become a pretext for the desolation of established ones, payment quotas will conform to those of the old fields, even in newly cultivated areas. As for the stipulated regular taxes, these will be paid, without fail, into the estate warehouse. Also, the number of workers engaged in developing the new land is to be reported each year when the proprietor's agents conduct their annual survey. In response to the petition, it is so decreed.
1229, 2nd month, 21st day.

Concerning a dispute of Ōeda village, a holding of Kashima shrine, between the Kashima priest Tomochika and Nomoto Shirō Gyōshin.

Although both plaintiff and defense have submitted many details regarding the above, it is evident that the land of this village was divided in 1237 by mutual agreement. Nevertheless, Gyōshin now argues that because the 1237 compromise was effected through negotiations with an uninformed deputy *jitō,* the land should be totally controlled by the *jitō,* with rents paid to the shrine. Relative to the original compromise document, the statute of limitations has passed, with dual possession dating from 1237; it is thus very difficult to attempt to disrupt things now. Therefore, authority will be exercised in accordance with the 1237 document. By command of the Kamakura lord, it is so decreed.
1298, 2nd month, 3rd day.

——

Source: Jeffrey P. Mass, *The Kamakura Bakufu: A Study in Documents* (Stanford, Calif.: Stanford University Press, 1976), pp. 38–39, 41, 48, 55, 101, 151 (modified).

semination and improvement in iron smelting technology to make armor and weapons also produced better plows and harrows. Pulled by draft animals, these tools allowed laborers to till more fields more thoroughly. Irrigation canals regulated the flow of water to paddy fields, and human-powered water wheels lifted water from streams to canals. The result was higher agricultural productivity that more than compensated for population growth.

Intensive agricultural practices did not spread uniformly. In the east, only the northern lowlands of the Kanto plain grew wet rice. Mulberry leaves raised on dry fields provided the fodder for silkworms. Alluvial terraces supplied pasturage for horses. The central Kanto plain sheltered deer, boars, and bandits. Areas separated by mountains from the core agricultural regions such as southern Shikoku, southwestern Kyushu, and the regions along the Japan Sea had lower populations and fewer cultivators.

Cultivators included *myōshu*, responsible for paying taxes to the state and rents to proprietors, and the *myōshu's* dependents. Although squeezed by estate managers and stewards, the *myōshu's* cultivation rights made them wealthy. The dependents ranged from slaves to serfs to small holders. The Kamakura shogunate issued bans on trade in human beings several times in the thirteenth century, but professional slave traders continued to kidnap women and children or people voluntarily sold themselves when they were destitute. A type of serf called *shojū* (those who obey) had their own parcels of land and huts for their families. They were not free in that their masters disposed of them as though they were property in wills and legal testaments. Small holders leased fields from the *myōshu* and tilled dry field plots that they had cleared from marginal land. Since these were less likely to be taxed than rice-bearing paddies, they gave their cultivator a measure of independence and a tiny income.

Although regional crop failures owing to drought or unseasonal cold continued to cause famines, demographic crises had been relegated to the past. Major contagious diseases had become endemic, mostly killing children rather than adult workers. After 1189 warfare ceased to be a problem. A population of perhaps 7 million at the beginning of the Kamakura period had grown to roughly 8.2 million by its end, more densely concentrated in western Japan than in other regions. The roads built by the state in the seventh and eighth centuries still centered on Kyoto.

Shinran. The illustrated scroll of Shinran's life portrays him expounding on his teachings as he traveled around Japan. *(Bukkoji, Kyoto/ DNPArchives.com)*

In addition to aristocrats, clerics, warriors, and cultivators, there was a large unsettled population. It included entertainers, itinerant artisans and traders, traveling proselytizers, prostitutes, fishermen, pirates, hunters, bandits, and an amorphous category of outcasts deemed polluted or unclean for reasons of disease, work with dead animals, or ill fortune. Fishermen and people of the forest enjoyed longstanding ties to the court expressed in tribute of fish, game, seaweed, and wild vegetables. Between the eleventh and thirteenth centuries, they received privileges from aristocrats, temples, shrines, and retired monarchs that enabled them to travel freely and avoid taxes. Artisans who traveled in search of the raw materials and markets for their products also sought the court's protection. Female entertainers and prostitutes received licenses to travel and organized themselves into fictive kin groups under the control of influential female chiefs. Buddhist monks castigated entertainers for leading men astray and practiced same-sex relations to satisfy their sexual needs. Some didactic tales told of prostitutes who became nuns; in others they were depicted as bodhisattvas who led men to salvation. Most outcastes enjoyed the protection of religious establishments or the court. They performed police work for warriors. They ran inns where they offered hot baths to travelers. Even beggars performed a useful function because they enabled the wealthy to perform acts of charity.

Buddhism

The six Nara sects as well as the Tendai and Shingon sects dominated mainstream Buddhism and religious life during the Kamakura period, and they attracted some of the greatest minds of the age. A cult grew up around Prince Shōtoku for having propagated Buddhism. Zenkōji in the mountains of central Japan had what was reputed to be a living icon that attracted pilgrims from all walks of life, as did the bronze statue of Amida at Kamakura completed in 1252. Simplified practices and doctrines plus hope for salvation in the latter days of the Buddhist law contributed to Buddhism's mass appeal. In 1245 a group of aristocratic nuns received the precepts for novices at the Hokkeji nunnery in Nara, reviving an order that had died out in the ninth century. Mendicant nuns raised money for the shrine-temple complex at Kumano. Ceremonies that pointed to the mysteries of esoteric Buddhism spread to provincial temples; their audience contained commoners as well as nobles. Aristocrats drew on esoteric initiation rites in formulating secret traditions for the transmission of poetic styles and explained the hidden meaning of poetry collections in terms of Tantric Buddhism. Samurai modeled themselves on aristocrats in patronizing and building shrines and temples. In the history titled *Gukanshō* (*Humble Interpretations*), the

Tendai priest Jien explained the court's lack of virtue and the warrior's rise to power in the context of the latter days of the Buddhist law. Temple-shrine complexes constituted one of the three power blocs, along with the Kyoto court and Kamakura regime. The relations between them were never stable and the distinctions between aristocrats, warriors, and clerics easily blurred.

Outside the mainstream appeared teacher-monks who reformulated doctrines taught at the Tendai headquarters on Mount Hiei and instituted new practices. They criticized the established temples for their superficial ceremonies and monastic decadence. They reached out to new constituents, including women, and addressed female concerns, especially the issue of whether women could be reborn after death in the Buddhist paradise called the Pure Land.

Faith in Amida was already prevalent when Hōnen and Shinran started preaching. Hōnen told crowds of listeners that Buddhism was available to all through absolute faith in the saving power of Amida. The best way to achieve faith was not through pious deeds or religious study but by reciting "praise to Amida Buddha." In 1207 Hōnen was exiled when some of his disciples overstepped the bounds of propriety in taking his message to the ladies-in-waiting at Go-Toba's court. Following his death in 1212, his disciples created the Jōdo (Pure Land) sect. Shinran took Hōnen's teachings to low-ranking warriors, the poor, and criminals. He preached that Amida had vowed to save everyone, sinners, murderers, thieves, the humble, and evil alike, even people who did not know he would save them. All that was required was faith. "At the moment that faith is established, birth in the Pure Land is also established."[4] He rejected monasticism because cutting oneself off

---

4. Quoted in Endō Hajime, "The Original Bōmori: Husband and Wife Congregations in Early Shin Buddhism," in *Engendering Faith: Women and Buddhism in Premodern Japan*, ed. B. Ruch (Ann Arbor: Center for Japanese Studies, University of Michigan, 2002), p. 513.

from the world in order to study and pray was meaningless. He married, begot children, and encouraged his disciples to do the same. He had not planned to start a new sect, but after his death in 1262, his children and disciples founded *Jōdo shinshū* (True Pure Land sect).

Hōnen and Shinran taught people to rely on Amida for salvation; Zen taught reliance on the self. Its teachers had such close ties with China and knowledge of the Chinese language that the shogunate used them as envoys to the Yuan court. Following his training on Mount Hiei, Eisai went twice to China and then settled in Kamakura, where he founded the Rinzai school that uses riddles (*kōan*) to concentrate the mind during meditation. By exposing the limits to rational thought, riddles helped achieve enlightenment. Eisai became the shogunate's master of religious ceremonies when he developed close ties with Hōjō Masako that brought the Rinzai school wealth and power. Dōgen went to China for five years, where he studied Zen in what is now popular in Japan as the Sōtō school. Upon his return, he taught that the essence of Buddha is in everyone, but it is concealed under layers of desire. To remove these layers, the practitioner has to achieve an inner awakening through sitting meditation (*zazen*). Chanting sutras, reciting the Buddha's name, were secondary. During his lifetime, Dōgen's austere search for absolute truth attracted few disciples.

Nichiren opposed all forms of Buddhism that did not center on the *Lotus Sutra*. Only it offered a sure way to salvation. He taught his followers to beat drums and chant, "Praise to the glorious teachings of the *Lotus Sutra*," because the sutra's title contained the essence of the sutra and the sutra contained the summation of Buddhist teaching. Performing the chant enabled the achievement of buddhahood in this very body or at least access to the Pure Land. Salvation came through faith, not doctrinal study or meditation. Calling on the *Lotus Sutra* could bring wealth and good luck for individuals and protection for the state. At the end of his life, when he had been exiled to Sado for having

provoked religious dissension with his intolerant views, Nichiren taught that he was the reincarnation of the bodhisattva to whom the original Buddha Sakyamuni had entrusted the *Lotus Sutra*. Buddhism had arisen in India, but it reached its ultimate moment of truth in Japan. In the name he chose for himself, the character for *nichi* represents the sun and alludes to the Japanese word for Japan, Nihon, the origin of the sun. *Ren* means lotus.

Literature and Popular Arts

Buddhist beliefs permeated Kamakura period literature and the visual arts. A section in the seventh royally commissioned poetry anthology, the *Shinkokinshū* (*New Collection of Ancient and Modern Poems*), completed in 1206, was devoted to Buddhist poetry. The court-poet-turned-priest Kamo no Chōmei wrote an account of his life as a recluse in *Hōjōki* (*An Account of My Hut*) that explored the tension between his pleasure in artistic pursuits and his desire to renounce the world to seek salvation. The realism of portrait sculptures took on meaning only in the context of Buddhist images that served as a focus for religious devotion. Picture scrolls (*emakimono*) depicted the battles that ushered in the Kamakura period and the Mongol invasions; they also brought to life the torments that await the unbeliever in hell. (See **Material Culture: The Mongol Scroll and Mongol Combat.**) The classic war tale, *Tale of the Heike*, began with an evocation of the transience of existence expressed in the tolling of a temple bell. Didactic tales recounted miraculous stories of the Buddha's power. Even the chronicle *Azuma kagami* (*Mirror of the East*), a major source of information on the day-to-day affairs of the Kamakura regime, dwells on Yoritomo's and his successors' pilgrimages to and support for temples.

War tales recounted the course of major conflicts. *Tale of Masakado* (*Shōmonki*) contained imaginative reconstructions of battles and traced Taira no Masakado's defeat in 940 to

MATERIAL CULTURE

The Mongol Scroll and Mongol Combat

In 1293 or thereabouts, the samurai Takezaki Suenaga commissioned scrolls of the Mongol invasions to commemorate his achievements. He had just succeeded in getting the Kamakura shogunate to recognize his merit in having been the first to engage the enemy in 1274. His aim in acquiring the scrolls may have been to provide a pictorial record for his descendants or to present them as an offering to the shrine of his tutelary deity in gratitude for having survived the conflict.

With a troop of five mounted men, Suenaga galloped into battle. The Mongols let fly a withering hail of arrows. Suenaga's standard-bearer fell when his horse was hit. Suenaga was hit in the left chest and left knee.

His horse too was wounded, and a Mongol arrow made a direct hit on his helmet. At this critical juncture, a troop of mounted samurai arrived to rescue him.

The Mongols sent masses of cavalry into battle. They received orders via gongs that launched attacks and drums that signaled retreats. The Mongol infantry followed the cavalry lined up behind tall shields. They used crossbows that fired heavy arrows capable of piercing armor, and the arrows were tipped with poison. Their catapults hurled cannonballs filled with gunpowder that exploded with a roar and gushed fire. Samurai picked off Mongol soldiers with their longbows.

Mongol Scroll. Commissioned by Takezaki Suenaga, the Mongol Scroll shows him in the vanguard of the attack, his horse frightened by an exploding shell. On the left stand the Mongols in long coats, their faces covered with whiskers. *(Laurie Platt Winfrey, Inc.)*

arrogance. It reproduced historical documents supplemented by stories created decades after the event. Yoshitsune was a particular favorite of storytellers, from his youth in Kyoto where he challenged the Herculean warrior monk Benkei to his death in the mountains of northern Japan. Accounts of the Genpei War portrayed it as an epic struggle between the Taira and the Minamoto for control of Japan. Political intrigue and fierce battles filled these tales, as they did *Tale of the Heike.*

Tale of the Heike began as stories recited by blind storytellers to assuage the souls of the Taira who had fallen in battle. Accompanied by the lute, storytellers traveled across Japan to bring people to an understanding of the Buddha by crafting miraculous and edifying tales. Each generation of storytellers enriched the story, adding embellishments and anecdotes before it was written down in the fourteenth century. Their accounts featured Kiyomori, entertainers, guards, widows, and a host of warriors. By speaking their names, storytellers summoned the departed. By recounting their exploits, storytellers pacified the spirits of the dead and sought to save them from hell. *Heike* is permeated with examples of the relationship between humankind and unseen forces and the importance of karma in deciding one's fate.

Another category of tale is *setsuwa* (popular tales). The most famous, *Tales of Times Now Past*, compiled in the early twelfth century, contains more than a thousand short stories set in India, China, and Japan. The Japanese corpus encompasses Buddhist tales, stories about aristocratic and warrior families, and anecdotes, many humorous, about ordinary people such as artisans, criminals, unhappy wives, and abducted ladies, as well as animals and the supernatural. A later collection contains stories that trace the appearance of the supernatural in everyday life. *Kokonchomonjū* (*Stories Heard from Writers Old and New*), compiled in 1254, contains folk stories, stories about the gods, and stories illustrating the Buddha's teachings. There, Yoritomo's pilgrimage to the mountain temple of Zenkōji reveals that its central icon was alive.

War tales and popular tales brought new classes of people into literature, but they did not displace the aristocrats who continued to compile poetry collections, keep diaries, and write essays in the manner of their Heian forebears. Fujiwara no Teika set high standards for poetic diction and kept a diary of distinction. His niece wrote *Mumyōzōshi* (*Anonymous Writing*), which critiqued the classical literary tradition. In 1307 Lady Nijō wrote an autobiography that illustrates how the court continued to model its ceremonies on the past, albeit with considerable

attention to drinking and fornication. The Hōjō and their supporters at Kamakura avidly sought training in the civilizing arts. They hired teachers from Kyoto, studied poetry, and immersed themselves in Buddhist texts.

THE MONGOL INVASIONS

Under threat of Mongol invasion, Kamakura summoned the samurai to defend Japan starting in 1271 after the fall of Korea. (See **Connections: The Mongols.**) Fierce fighting in 1274 proved that the Japanese enjoyed near military parity and numerical superiority. Unable to prevail, the Mongols retreated. The samurai strengthened their fortifications before the second onslaught in 1281. Stone walls on the landing beaches hedged in the Mongol troops and ships harassed their fleet. Fighting raged for almost a month before an epidemic ravaged the tightly packed attacking forces and a typhoon sank Mongol ships. The samurai then killed the thirty thousand troops left stranded. In later centuries, the shrine-temple complexes that had prayed for supernatural intervention claimed that a divine wind (*kamikaze*) had destroyed the Mongols.

The invasions extended Kamakura's reach into Kyushu and made the shogunate a truly national government. It came at a cost. Preparations for the second invasion curtailed food production. The Hōjō made promises of rewards they could not keep and pressured temples for money. They appointed new provincial governors in the west, all of them from the Hōjō family or its allies. Many of the warriors from Kyushu who fought against the Mongols had not previously been subject to Kamakura rule. Their only recompense was confirmation of their rights to the income from estates they already held. For warriors from western Japan who joined the battle, Kamakura announced debt amnesties, a tactic it also used to placate the shrines and temples that had prayed for victory. Since warriors fought not for glory or love of country but for reward, these returns were paltry indeed.

FALL OF THE KAMAKURA REGIME

The growing sophistication of the Hōjō underscored the gulf developing between them and the majority of provincial warriors. Every aristocratic or royal child brought to Kamakura to serve as the figurehead shogun had a retinue of highly cultivated female and male attendants. Yoritomo had emphasized austerity and simplicity; his successors led lives of luxury. They were also growing more despotic. In 1293 the Hōjō regent abolished the councilor form of government. He and his successors exiled opponents, seized governorships, and had their housemen fill positions in the shogunate. In 1297 the regent announced an "edict for virtuous government" aimed at restoring land to impoverished samurai, especially the stewards who had been forced to sell or mortgage their land over the preceding twenty years. It was based on the notion that the sale of land did not mean the original owner lost all claim to it; rather, a family that had worked land for generations possessed it by inalienable right. Under this ruling, former owners retrieved ancestral land. Any satisfaction they obtained was only temporary, because it did not alleviate their poverty and made it more difficult to sell their land in the future. The former buyers were naturally disgruntled. The result of the edict was to lose friends for the regime and narrow its support base.

Partible inheritance was a major cause of the stewards' impoverishment. When every child received a portion of the patrimony, the result was an expansion in the size of the warrior class without a concomitant growth in the income at its disposal. Bequeathed an inadequate inheritance, stewards easily fell into debt and had to mortgage their rights to income. Although the patrimony could be divided, the obligation to fulfill the duties of military service to Kamakura was not divisible. Even women had to field a warrior on horseback should the need arise.

Generations had passed since Yoritomo had rewarded loyal followers by making them estate stewards. Diffused by time and space, the stewards' descendants stayed on their land save when a lawsuit called them to Kamakura. In 1285, the Hōjō regent decided that the shogunate would no longer intervene in disputes between its retainers and Kyoto aristocrats. Instead litigants had to seek redress from Kyoto, a move that heightened conflict between supporters of the two centers. This decision estranged Kamakura from its followers in the provinces. With Kamakura now reluctant to guarantee land rights, loyalty attenuated.

Challenges to the shogunate multiplied in the early fourteenth century. Stone-throwing brawls had long erupted in Kyoto on festival days, but in Kamakura in the early 1300s, they turned into deadly gang warfare. Bands of mounted bandits ravaged the provinces of central Japan, sometimes in league with estate stewards who refused to send income to protectors and proprietors. Pirates ranged as far as Korea, attacking coastal settlements, carrying off goods, and enslaving the inhabitants. The swell of disorder suggested to people both high and low that they could act with impunity.

SUMMARY

Changes during the Kamakura period heralded trends that would continue for centuries. Samurai attained new prominence in governance with the establishment of a military regime. New sects brought new practices to Buddhism. Increases in agricultural production laid the foundation for an increase in trade and manufacturing. One practice that did not carry forward was the division of family assets among all children and female economic autonomy.

SUGGESTED READING

No study of this period would be complete without the works by J. P. Mass, *Antiquity and Anachronism in Japanese History* (1992), *Lordship and Inheritance in Early Medieval Japan* (1989), *Yoritomo and the Founding of the first Bakufu: The Origins of Dual Government in Japan* (1999), and many others.

For a social and economic history of the first military regimes, see P. F. Souyri, *The World Turned Upside Down: Medieval Japanese Society* (2001). For the Mongol invasions, see T. Conlon, *In Little Need of Divine Intervention: Takezaki Suenaga's Scrolls of the Mongol Invasions of Japan* (2001).

A sampling of books on Kamakura Buddhism includes R. K. Payne, *Re-Visioning Kamakura Buddhism* (1998); B. D. Ruppert, *Jewel in the Ashes: Buddha Relics and Power in Early Medieval Japan* (2000); and J. C. Dobbins, *Jōdō Shinshu: Shin Buddhism in Medieval Japan* (1989). For the connection between literature, theater, and religion, see S. B. Klein, *Allegories of Desire: Esoteric Literary Commentaries of Medieval Japan* (2002).

PART THREE

Meeting New Challenges (1200–1600)

The Mongols

BY THE THIRTEENTH CENTURY, CHINA and Korea had had many centuries of experience with northern nomadic pastoralists who from time to time formed wide-ranging confederations that threatened and occasionally conquered parts of their territory. To China and Korea, these neighbors may have seemed a local problem, but in fact settled societies across Eurasia had to cope with horse-riding herders skilled at warfare and raiding.

The grasslands that supported nomadic pastoralists stretched from eastern Europe to Mongolia and Manchuria. Twice before, confederations that rose in the East led to vast movement of peoples and armies across the grasslands. The rise of the Xiongnu in the East beginning in the third century B.C.E. caused rival groups to move west, indirectly precipitating the arrival of the Shakas and Kushans in Afghanistan and northern India and later the Huns in Europe. The Turks, after their heyday as a power in the East in the seventh century C.E., broke up into several rival groups, some of whom moved west into Persia and India. By the twelfth century, separate groups of Turks controlled much of Central Asia and the adjoining lands from Syria to northern India and into Chinese Turkestan, then occupied by Uighur Turks. It was not until the Mongols, however, that the military power of pastoralists created a unified empire linking most of Asia.

In Mongolia in the twelfth century, ambitious Mongols aspired not to match nomads who had migrated west but those who had stayed in the East and mastered ways to extract resources from China. In the tenth and eleventh centuries, the Khitans had accomplished this; in the

twelfth century, the Jurchens had overthrown the Khitans and extended their reach even deeper into China. Both the Khitans and the Jurchens formed hybrid nomadic-urban states, with northern sections where tribesmen continued to live in the traditional way and southern sections politically controlled by the non-Chinese rulers but populated largely by Chinese. Both the Khitans and Jurchens had scripts created to record their languages, and both adopted many Chinese governing practices. They built cities in pastoral areas as centers of consumption and trade. In both cases, their elite became culturally dual, adept in Chinese ways as well as their own traditions.

Chinese, Persian, and European observers have all left descriptions of the daily life of the Mongols in the thirteenth century, which they found strikingly different from their own. Before their great conquests, the Mongols did not have cities, towns, or villages. Rather, they moved with their animals between winter and summer pastures. To make them portable, their belongings had to be kept to a minimum. Mongols lived in tents (called yurts), about 12 to 15 feet in diameter, constructed of light wooden frames covered by layers of wool felt, greased to make them waterproof. A group of families traveling together would set up their yurts in a circle open to the south and draw up their wagons in a circle around the yurts for protection. The Mongols' herds provided both meat and milk, with the milk used to make butter, cheese, and fermented alcoholic drinks. Wood was scarce, so the common fuel for the cook fires was dried animal dung or grasses. Without granaries to store food for years of famine, the Mongols' survival was threatened whenever weather or diseases of their animals endangered their food supply.

Because of the intense cold of the grasslands in the winter, Mongols needed warm clothing. Both men and women usually wore undergarments made of silk obtained from China. Over them they wore robes of fur, for the very coldest times of the year, in two layers: an inner layer with the hair on the inside and an outer layer with the hair on the outside. Hats were of felt or fur, boots of felt or leather.

Mongol women had to be able to care for the animals when the men were away hunting or fighting. They normally drove the carts and set up and dismantled the yurts. They were also the ones who milked the sheep, goats, and cows and made the butter and cheese. In addition, they made the felt, prepared the skins, and sewed the clothes. Because water was scarce, clothes were not washed with water, nor were dishes. Women, like men, had to be expert riders, and many also learned to shoot. Women participated actively in family decisions, especially as wives and mothers. *The Secret History of the Mongols*, a book written in Mongolian a few decades after Chinggis's death, portrayed his mother and wife as actively involved in family affairs and frequently making impassioned speeches on the importance of family loyalty.

Mongol men made the carts and wagons and the frames for the yurts. They also made the harnesses for the horses and oxen, the leather saddles, and the equipment needed for hunting and war, such as bows and arrows. Men also had charge of the horses, and they, rather than the women, milked the mares. Young horses were allowed to run wild until it was time to break them. Catching them took great skill in the use of a long springy pole with a noose at the end. One specialty occupation among the nomads was the blacksmith, who made stirrups, knives, and other metal tools. Another common specialist was the shaman, a religious expert able to communicate with the gods. Some groups of Mongols, especially those closer to settled communities, converted to Buddhism, Nestorian Christianity, or Manichaeism.

Kinship underlay most social relationships among the Mongols. Normally each family occupied a yurt, and groups of families camping together were usually related along the male line (brothers, uncles and nephews, and so on). More distant patrilineal relatives were recognized as members of the same clan and could call on each other for aid. People from the same clan could not marry each other, so clans had to cooperate to provide brides for each other. A woman whose husband had died would be inherited by another male in the family, such as her husband's younger brother or his son by another woman.

Tribes were groups of clans, often distantly related. Both clans and tribes had recognized chiefs who would make decisions on where to graze and when to retaliate against another tribe that had stolen animals or people. Women were sometimes abducted for brides. When tribes stole men from each other, they normally made them into slaves, and slaves were forced to do much of the heavy work. They would not necessarily remain slaves their entire life, however, as their original tribe might be able to recapture them, make an exchange for them, or their masters might free them.

Although population was sparse in the regions where the Mongols lived, conflict over resources was endemic, and each camp had to be on the alert for attacks. Defending against attack and retaliating against raids was as much a part of the Mongols' daily life as caring for their herds and trading with nearby settlements.

In the mid-twelfth century, the Mongols were just one of many tribes in the eastern grasslands, neither particularly numerous nor especially advanced. Their rise had much to do with the leadership of a single individual, the brilliant but utterly ruthless Temujin (ca. 1162–1227), later called Chinggis. Chinggis's early career was recounted in *The Secret History of the Mongols*. When Chinggis was young, the Mongol tribes were in competition with the Tatar tribes. Chinggis's father had built up a modest following and had arranged for Chinggis's future marriage to the daughter of a more powerful

Nomads' Portable Housing. This painting by a Chinese artist illustrates an event that took place in Han times, but it reflects the conditions on the grassland in Song times, when it was painted. *(The Metropolitan Museum of Art, Gift of the Dillon Fund, 1973 [1973.120.3])*

Mongol leader. When Chinggis's father was poisoned by a rival, his followers, not ready to follow a boy of twelve, drifted away, leaving Chinggis and his mother and brothers in a vulnerable position. In 1182 Chinggis himself was captured and carried to the camp of a rival in a cage. After a daring midnight escape, he led his followers to join a stronger chieftain who had once been aided by his father. With his help, Chinggis began avenging the insults he had received.

As he subdued the Tatars, Kereyids, Naimans, Merkids, and other Mongol and Turkic tribes, Chinggis built up an army of loyal followers. He mastered the art of winning allies through displays of personal courage in battle and generosity to his followers. He also proved willing to turn against former allies who proved troublesome. To those who opposed him, he could be merciless. He once asserted that nothing surpassed massacring one's enemies, seizing their horses and cattle, and ravishing their women. Sometimes Chinggis would kill all the men in a defeated tribe to prevent any later vendettas. At other times he would take them on as soldiers in his own armies. Courage impressed him. One of his leading generals, Jebe, had first attracted his attention when he held his ground against overwhelming opposition and shot Chinggis's horse out from under him.

In 1206 at a great gathering of tribal leaders Chinggis was proclaimed the Great Khan. Chinggis decreed that Mongol, until then an unwritten language, be written down in a script used by the Uighur Turks. With this script, a record was made of Mongol laws and customs, ranging from the rules for the annual hunt to punishments of death for robbery and adultery. Another measure adopted at this assembly was a postal relay system to send messages rapidly by mounted courier.

With the tribes of Mongolia united, the energies previously devoted to infighting and vendetta were redirected to exacting tribute from the settled populations nearby, starting with the Jurchen state that extended into north China (the Jin Dynasty). After Chinggis subjugated a city, he sent envoys to cities farther out to demand submission and threaten destruction. Those who opened their city gates and submitted without fighting could become allies and retain local power, but those who resisted faced the prospect of mass slaughter. Chinggis despised city dwellers and sometimes used them as living shields in the next battle. After the Mongol armies swept across north China in 1212–1213, ninety-odd cities lay in rubble. Beijing, captured in 1215, burned for more than a month. Not surprisingly many governors of cities and rulers of small states hastened to offer submission when the Mongol armies approached.

Chinggis preferred conquest to administration and left ruling north China to subordinates while he turned his own attention westward to Afghanistan and Persia, then in the hands of Turks (see Map C4.1). In 1218 Chinggis proposed to the Khwarazm shah of Persia that he accept Mongol overlordship and establish trade relations. The shah, to show his determination to resist, ordered the envoy and the merchants who had accompanied him killed. The next year Chinggis led an army of one hundred thousand soldiers west to retaliate. Mongol forces not only destroyed the shah's army, but pursued the shah to an island in the Caspian Sea, where he died. To complete the conquest, Chinggis sacked one Persian city after another, demolishing buildings and massacring hundreds of thousands of people. The irrigation systems that were needed for agriculture in this dry region were destroyed.

On his return from Central Asia in 1226, Chinggis turned his attention to the Tanguts who ruled the Xia state in northwest China. They had earlier accepted vassal status, but Chinggis thought they had not lived up to their agreements. During the siege of their capital, Chinggis died of illness.

Before he died, Chinggis instructed his sons not to fall out among themselves but to divide the spoils. Although Mongol tribal leaders traditionally had had to win their positions, after Chinggis died the empire was divided into four

khanates, with one of the lines of his descendants taking charge of each. Chinggis's third son, Ögödei, became great khan, and he directed the next round of invasions.

In 1237 representatives of all four lines led 150,000 Mongol, Turkic, and Persian troops into Europe. During the next five years, they gained control of Moscow and Kievan Russia and looted cities in Poland and Hungary. They were poised to attack deeper into Europe when they learned of the death of Ögödei in 1241. In order to participate in the election of a new khan, the army returned to the Mongols' newly built capital city, Karakorum.

Once Ögödei's son was certified as his successor, the Mongols turned their attention to Persia and the Middle East. When the Abbasid capital of Baghdad fell in 1258, the last Abbasid caliph was murdered and much of the population was put to the sword.

Under Chinggis's grandson Khubilai (r. 1260–1294), the Mongols completed their conquest of Korea and China. Not all campaigns succeeded, however. Perhaps because after the fall of the Song surrendered Chinese soldiers and sailors came to make up a large share of the invasion forces, the attempts to conquer Japan, Vietnam, and Java in the 1270s–1290s all failed.

Chinggis and His Descendants

Why were the Mongols so successful against so many different types of enemies? Although their population was tiny compared to that of the large agricultural societies they conquered, their tactics, weapons, and organization all gave them advantages. Like nomadic herdsmen

Map C4.1   **Map of Mongol Conquests**

before them, they were superb horsemen and excellent archers. Their horses were short and stocky, almost like ponies, and able to endure long journeys and bitter cold. Even in the winter they survived by grazing, foraging beneath the snow. Their horses were extremely nimble, able to turn direction quickly, enabling the Mongols to maneuver easily and ride through infantry forces armed with swords, lances, and javelins. On military campaigns Mongol soldiers had to be able to ride for days without stopping to cook food; they would carry a supply of dried milk curd and cured meat, which could be supplemented by blood let from the neck of their horses. When time permitted, the soldiers would pause to hunt, adding to their food dogs, wolves, foxes, mice, and rats.

Marco Polo left a vivid description of the Mongol soldiers' endurance and military skill:

They are brave in battle, almost to desperation, setting little value upon their lives, and exposing themselves without hesitation to all manner of danger. Their disposition is cruel. They are capable of supporting every kind of privation, and when there is a necessity for it, can live for a month on the milk of their mares, and upon such wild animals as they may chance to catch. The men are habituated to remain on horseback during two days and two nights, without dismounting, sleeping in that situation whilst their horses graze. No people on earth can surpass them in fortitude under difficulties, nor show greater patience under wants of every kind.[1]

The Mongols were also open to new military technologies and did not insist on fighting in their traditional ways. To attack walled cities, they learned how to make use of catapults and other engines of war. At first they used Chinese catapults, but when they learned that those used by the Turks in Afghanistan were more powerful, they quickly adopted the better model. The Mongols made use of exploding arrows and gunpowder projectiles developed by the Chinese. Mongols made good use of intelligence and tried to exploit internal divisions in the countries they attacked. Thus, when attacking the Jurchens in north China, they reminded the Khitans of their bitter defeat by the Jurchens a century earlier. In Syria, they exploited the resentment of Christians against their Muslim rulers.

Because of his early experiences with intertribal feuding, Chinggis mistrusted traditional Mongol tribal loyalties, and as he fashioned a new army, he gave it a nontribal structure. Chinggis also created an elite bodyguard of ten thousand sons and brothers of commanders, which served directly under him. Chinggis allowed commanders to pass their posts to their sons, but he could remove them at will.

Since, in Mongol eyes, the purpose of warfare was to gain riches, they regularly looted the settlements they conquered, taking whatever they wanted, including the residents. Land would be granted to military commanders, nobles, and army units, to be governed and exploited as the recipients wished. Those who had worked on the land would be distributed as serfs. To bring Karakorum up to the level of the cities the Mongols conquered, they transported skilled workers there. For instance, after Bukhara and Samarkand were captured, some thirty thousand artisans were seized and transported to Mongolia. Sometimes these slaves gradually improved their status. A French goldsmith working in Budapest named Guillame Boucher was captured by the Mongols in 1242 and taken to Karakorum, where he lived for at least the next fifteen years. He gradually won favor and was put in charge of fifty workers making gold and silver vessels for the Mongol court.

How the Mongols ruled China and Korea is addressed in Chapter 12. In Central Asia, Persia, and Russia, the Mongols tended to merge with the Turkish nomads already there and converted to Islam. Russia in the thirteenth century was not a strongly centralized state, and the Mongols were satisfied to see Russian princes and lords continue to rule their territories as

---

1. *The Travels of Marco Polo, the Venetian*, ed. Manuel Komroff (New York: Boni and Liveright, 1926), p. 93.

long as they paid adequate tribute. The city of Moscow became the center of Mongol tribute collection and grew in importance at the expense of Kiev. In the Middle East, the Mongol Ilkhans were more active as rulers, continuing the traditions of the caliphate.

Mongol control in each of the khanates lasted about a century. In the mid-fourteenth century, the Mongol dynasty in China deteriorated into civil war, and in the 1360s the Mongols withdrew back to Mongolia. There was a similar loss of Mongol power in Persia and Central Asia. Only on the south Russian steppe was the Golden Horde able to maintain its hold for another century.

The Mongol empire did more to encourage the movement of people and goods across Eurasia than any earlier political entity. The Mongols had never looked down on merchants as the elites of many traditional states did, and they welcomed the arrival of merchants from distant lands. Even when different groups of Mongols were fighting among themselves, they usually allowed caravans to pass unharassed.

Once they had conquered a territory, the Mongols were willing to incorporate those they had conquered into their armies and governments. Chinese helped breach the walls of Baghdad in the 1250s, and Muslims operated the catapults that helped reduce Chinese cities in the 1270s. Chinese, Persians, and Arabs in the service of the Mongols were often sent far from home. Especially prominent were the Uighur Turks of Chinese Central Asia, whose familiarity with Chinese civilization and fluency in Turkish were extremely valuable in facilitating communication. Literate Uighurs provided many of the clerks and administrators running the Mongol administration.

One of the most interesting of those who served the Mongols was Rashid al-Din (ca. 1247–1318). A Jew from Persia, the son of an apothecary, Rashid al-Din converted to Islam at the age of thirty and entered the service of the Mongol khan of Persia as a physician. He rose in government service, traveling widely, and eventually became prime minister. Rashid al-Din became friends with the ambassador from China, and together they arranged for translations of Chinese works on medicine, agronomy, and statecraft. He had ideas on economic management that he communicated to Mongol officials in Central Asia and China. Aware of the great differences between cultures, he believed that the Mongols should try to rule in accord with the moral principles of the majority in each land. On that basis, he convinced the Mongol khan of Persia to convert to Islam. Rashid al-Din undertook to explain the great variety of cultures by writing a history of the world that was much more comprehensive than any previously written. The parts on Europe were based on information he obtained from European monks. The sections on China were based on Chinese informants and perhaps Chinese Buddhist narratives. This book was richly illustrated, with depictions of Europeans based on European paintings and depictions of Chinese based on Chinese paintings, leading to the spread of artistic styles as well. (See Color Plate 15.)

The Mongols were remarkably open to religious experts from all the lands they encountered. Khubilai, for instance, welcomed Buddhist, Daoist, Islamic, and Christian clergymen to his court and gave tax exemptions to clerics of all religions. More Europeans made their way as far as Mongolia and China in the Mongol period than ever before. This was the age of the Crusades, and European popes and kings sent envoys to the Mongol court in the hope of enlisting the Mongols on their side in their long-standing conflict with the Muslim forces over the Holy Land. These and other European visitors were especially interested in finding Christians who had been cut off from the West by the spread of Islam, and in fact there were considerable numbers of Nestorian Christians in Central Asia. Those who left written records of their trips often mention meeting other Europeans in China or Mongolia. There were enough Europeans in Beijing to build a cathedral and appoint a bishop.

The most famous European visitor to the Mongol lands was Marco Polo, who was enormously impressed with Khubilai and awed by the wealth and splendor of Chinese cities. There have always been skeptics who do not believe Marco Polo's tale, and some scholars think that he may have learned about China from Persian merchants he met in the Middle East. But most of what he wrote about China tallies well with Chinese sources. The great popularity of his book in Europe contributed greatly to familiarizing Europeans with the notion of Asia as a land of riches.

The more rapid transfer of people and goods across Central Asia in the thirteenth century spread more than ideas and inventions: it also spread diseases, the most deadly of which was a plague called the Black Death in Europe (long thought to be the modern bubonic plague, though some recent scholars have argued that it more closely resembles Ebola-like viral diseases). Europe had not had an outbreak of the plague since about 700 and the Middle East since 1200. There was a pocket of active plague in the southwestern mountains of modern Yunnan province in China, the area that had been the relatively isolated Nanzhao kingdom of Thai speakers. Once the Mongols established a garrison there, plague was carried to central China, then northwestern China, and from there to Central Asia and beyond. By the time the Mongols were assaulting the city of Kaffa in the Crimea in 1346, they themselves were infected by the plague and had to withdraw. But the disease did not retreat and was spread throughout the Mediterranean by ship. The Black Death of Europe thus was initiated through breaching the isolation of a remote region in southwestern China. The confusion of the mid-fourteenth century that led to the loss of Mongol power in China, Iran, and Central Asia probably owes something to the effect of the spread of this plague and other diseases.

Traditionally, the historians of each of the countries conquered by the Mongols portrayed them as a scourge. Russian historians, for instance, saw this as a period of bondage that set Russia back and cut it off from Western Europe. Today it is more common to celebrate the genius of the Mongol military machine and treat the spread of ideas and inventions as an obvious good, probably because we see global communication as a good in our own world. There is no reason to assume, however, that every person or every society benefited equally from the improved communications and the new political institutions of the Mongol era. Merchants involved in long-distance trade prospered, but those enslaved and transported hundreds or thousands of miles from home would have seen themselves as the most pitiable of victims, not the beneficiaries of opportunities to encounter cultures different from their own.

In terms of the spread of technological and scientific ideas, Europe seems to have been by far the main beneficiary of increased communication, largely because in 1200 it lagged far behind the other areas. Chinese inventions such as printing, gunpowder, and the compass and Persian expertise in astronomy and mathematics spread widely. In terms of the spread of religions, Islam probably gained the most. It spread into Chinese Central Asia, which had previously been Buddhist, and into Anatolia as Turks pushed out by the Mongols moved west, putting pressure on the Byzantine Empire.

Perhaps because it was not invaded itself, Europe also seems to have been energized by the Pax Mongolica in ways that the other major civilizations were not. The goods from the East brought to Europe whetted the appetites of Europeans for increased contact with the East, and the demand for Asian goods eventually culminated in the great age of European exploration and expansion. By comparison, in areas the Mongols had conquered, protecting their own civilization became a higher priority for elites than drawing from the outside to enrich or enlarge it.

SUGGESTED READING

On Inner Asia in world history, see D. Simon, ed., *The Cambridge History of Early Inner Asia* (1990); S. Adshead, *Central Asia in World History* (1993); and J. L. Abu-Lughod, *Before European Hegemony: The World System* A.D. *1250–1350* (1989). On the Mongols more specifically, see E. D. Phillips, *The Mongols* (1969). The Mongol conquest is treated in H. D. Martin, *The Rise of Chinghis Khan and His Conquest of North China* (1950); P. Ratchnevsky, *Genghis Khan: His Life and Legacy* (1992); J. Saunders, *The History of the Mongol Conquests* (2001); and T. Allsen, *Culture and Conquest in Mongol Eurasia* (2001). P. Kahn, trans., *The Secret History of the Mongols* (1984), is a readable translation of the best source for Mongol values and way of life.

For Marco Polo, see L. Olschki, *Marco Polo's Asia* (1960), and F. Wood, *Did Marco Polo Go to China?* (1995), which assembles the evidence against believing that Marco Polo saw everything he said he did, and J. Larner, *Marco Polo and the Discovery of the World* (1999), which takes the opposite stance. Many translations of Marco Polo are available; the most authoritative is A. Moule and P. Pelliot, *Marco Polo: The Description of the World* (1938). On other East–West travelers during the period of Mongol domination, see I. de Rachewiltz, *Papal Envoys to the Great Khans* (1971). On the links between the Mongols' conquest and the spread of bubonic plague, see W. McNeill, *Plagues and Peoples* (1976). Juivaini's Persian account of the Mongols has been translated by J. A. Boyle, *The History of the World Conqueror* (1958).

China and Korea Under Mongol Rule (1215–1368)

The Mongols conquered China and Korea in successive campaigns stretching over seven decades. Even the non-Chinese rulers of north China, the Tanguts and Jurchens, themselves horsemen proud of their reputations as fierce fighters, had to submit to the superior striking force of the Mongols. Although the Mongols brought massive destruction in their early campaigns, by the time of Khubilai (r. 1360–1394), they had become more sophisticated administrators. Since Mongols and people from elsewhere in Asia occupied a large share of administrative posts, the traditional elite of Confucian-educated men generally had to turn to other occupations.

Scholars of this period have devoted much of their energy to working out the political and military history of this period. How did Jin, Koryŏ, and Song officials organize resistance, and why did it fail? What policies did the Mongols put in place? Why did the Yuan Dynasty in China fail to last even two centuries? Another set of questions revolves around how Chinese and Koreans coped with the Mongol presence. Did the experience of bitter defeat have any long-term effects on Chinese or Korean culture? What was going on in society at local levels, beyond the purview of Mongol rulers?

THE MONGOL CONQUEST OF THE JIN AND XIA DYNASTIES

North China fell to the Mongols early in Chinggis's campaigns. Chinggis had raided Jin territory in 1205 and 1209 and in 1211 launched a major campaign. He led an army of about fifty thousand bowmen, and his three sons led another of similar size. The Jin, with one hundred fifty thousand cavalry, mostly Jurchen, and more than three hundred thousand Chinese infantrymen, thought they had the strongest army known to history. Yet Mongol tactics frustrated them. The Mongols would take a city, plunder it, and then withdraw, letting Jin take it back and deal with the food shortages and destruction. Both the Jin Western Capital (modern Datong) and their Central Capital (Beijing) were taken in this way more than once.

Jin did not have stable leadership during this crisis. In 1213 a Jurchen general murdered the Jin emperor and put another on the throne, only to be murdered himself two months later. In 1214 Jin negotiated a humiliating peace with Chinggis, who then withdrew his armies from the Central Capital. The new Jin emperor decided the Central Capital was too vulnerable, so he moved the court to the Southern Capital, Kaifeng, bringing thirty thousand carts of documents and treasures (reversing the journey north of 1126). Since Chinggis thought Jin had agreed to vassal status, he interpreted the transfer of the capital as revolt. When the Central Capital fell in 1215, it was sacked and burned. From then on, Jin controlled little more than a province-sized territory around Kaifeng.

The rump Jin state, hoping to expand to the south, attacked Song from 1216 to 1223. The next Jin emperor concentrated on defending against the Mongols, but in 1229 when the new khan, Ögödei, sent the main Mongol army to destroy Jin, Jin could barely slow their advance and succumbed by 1234.

As the Mongols captured Jin territory, Chinggis recruited more and more Chinese and Khitans into his armies, arguing that they had little reason to be loyal to the Jurchen. Chinese soldiers and generals were incorporated into Mongol armies, and literate Chinese were given clerical jobs. Chinese also were put to work as catapult operators during sieges. In 1218 the Mongol commander leading the north China campaigns recommended to Chinggis a well-educated and highly sinicized Khitan named Yelü Qucai. Chinggis is said to have addressed him, "Liao and Jin have been enemies for generations; I have taken revenge for you." Yelü had

the courage to disagree: "My father and grandfather have both served Jin respectfully. How can I, as a subject and son, be so insincere in my heart as to consider my sovereign and my father as enemies?"[1] Chinggis, admiring his forthrightness, took him into his entourage. Yelü served the Mongols for the next twenty-five years, patiently trying to get them to see the benefits of ruling their Chinese subjects in Chinese ways.

The Tangut Xia Dynasty suffered much the same fate as Jin. Early on, in 1209, Xia submitted to Chinggis and agreed to help the Mongols attack Jin, but during the next dozen years also tried to secure alliances with Jin and Song. Chinggis eventually decided that Xia had failed to live up to the terms of its submission to the Mongols and personally led a large force into Xia territory in 1226. It only enraged Chinggis when Xia soldiers fought well; in response, he had his generals systematically destroy Xia city by city. Chinggis himself led the final siege of the capital, which valiantly held out for five months. Chinggis died during the siege, but his death was kept secret. When the Xia ruler offered to surrender, he was persuaded to walk out of the capital with a small entourage. Perhaps because he was held in some way responsible for Chinggis's death, he was promptly hacked to death, and the Mongol troops, on entering the city, did their best to slaughter every living being in it.

North China in this period suffered enormous destruction. Mongol armies did not try to control territory; they only plundered it. Sometimes they slaughtered the entire population of a town, and even when people were not slaughtered, they were frequently seized like their cattle and enslaved. The Mongols began by giving out large chunks of land as fiefs to generals, both Mongols and allies. This did not lead to orderly government, however, as the fief holders were generals on campaigns elsewhere. With no one maintaining order, farmers suffered the depredations not only of Mongol soldiers but also of bandits, rebels, and local defense forces.

---

1. Igor de Rachelwiltz et al., eds., *In the Service of the Khan: Eminent Personalities of the Early Mongol-Yuan Period (1200–1300)* (Wiesbaden: Harrossowitz, 1993), p. xx.

Ögödei's Mongol advisers proposed turning much of north China into pastureland. Yelü Qucai offered the counterargument that the Mongols should leave the Chinese farmers in place because great wealth could be extracted from them through equitably collected taxation. He calculated that the Mongols could raise revenues of 500,000 ounces of silver, 80,000 bolts of silk, and over 20,000 tons of grain by direct taxation of subjects. He was given authorization to put his tax plan into effect, but before it had much of a chance to show its benefits, Yelü's rivals convinced Ögödei that an even more lucrative way to raise revenue was to let Central Asian Muslim merchants bid against each other for licenses to collect taxes. To the Chinese, these Central Asian tax farmers were even more oppressive than the Mongol lords.

Some Chinese who had served the Jurchen refused to serve the Mongols out of loyalty to the defeated dynasty. Yuan Haowen (1190–1257) passed the examinations in 1221 and served in Kaifeng during Jin's final struggle. When Kaifeng fell, he wrote a letter to Yelü Qucai asking that fifty-four men of letters be spared by the Mongols. He himself was interned for two years and on his release devoted himself to collecting materials for a history of the Jin Dynasty. A poet, he also wrote poems on the fall of the Jin. He viewed continuing to write as a way to preserve Chinese civilization. The following poem, "Crossing the Yellow River, June 12," describes what he saw around the time Kaifeng fell:

> White bones scattered
> like tangled hemp,
> how soon before mulberry and catalpa
> turn to dragon-sands?
> I only know north of the river
> there is no life:
> crumbled houses, scattered chimney smoke
> from a few homes.[2]

2. Translated by Stephen West in Wu-chi Liu and Irving Yucheng Lo, *Sunflower Splendor: Three Thousand Years of Chinese Poetry* (Garden City, N.Y.: Anchor Books, 1975), p. 407.

Other Chinese subjects of the Jin took a different attitude. From experience with the Jin, they knew that the Chinese would fare better if Chinese were the administrators and could shield Chinese society from the most brutal effects of Mongol rule. Therefore, many Jin officials willingly served the Mongols. Some dedicated Confucian scholars such as Xu Heng devoted themselves to the task of teaching Mongol rulers the principles of Confucian government.

THE MONGOL CONQUEST OF KOREA

While the Mongols were attacking Jin territory in China, a Khitan rebellion broke out with some aid from the Mongols in 1212 against Jin rule in modern Manchuria. The Mongols took over several districts and defeated a Jin army. When a Mongol force moved into Liaodong in Manchuria, the Jin commander decided not to challenge the Khitan and moved east to the area around the Tumen River in northeast Korea and established an independent Eastern Xia state (also known as the Eastern Jin).

Disruption broke out in the Khitan ranks, and the leader of the Khitan fled to the Mongols, but the remaining Khitan army moved south across the Yalu River to the Korean peninsula in 1216 to evade Mongol forces. Many of the local population in northern Koryŏ cooperated with the Khitan; they were young men called *yangsuch'ŏk*, who earned their living by hunting, weaving willow baskets, and sending their daughters out to become *kisaeng* (female entertainers and courtesans). The Koryŏ government never bothered to tax them or register them for labor and military service, but when Ch'oe Ch'unghŏn imposed taxes on them for the first time, they decided to act as guides for the Khitan. Ch'oe, meanwhile, overestimated the strength of his army and hated to be bothered by all the frequent reports of small-scale attacks and uprisings on the northern frontier. He ordered the border commanders not to inform him of attacks until at least two or three walled towns had been captured.

As a result, government forces were defeated on several occasions. Some Khitan forces made it to the gates of the capital at Kaesŏng, and other units pushed southeast toward the Eastern Capital at Kyŏngju before they were driven off. The serious fighting lasted from 1217 through 1219 because the best troops had been absorbed into the private armies of the Ch'oe family and other military commanders during this period of military rule, leaving only untrained troops in government forces.

In 1218, three years after the Mongols had taken over the Jin Central Capital, they sent units in pursuit of the Khitan south across the Yalu River in an alliance against the Khitan with their previous opponents, the Eastern Xia (Jurchen Eastern). The local Koryŏ commander, Cho Ch'ung, also joined in the operation in 1219 to mop up the Khitan force. The Mongol commander became friends with Cho and promised him that the Mongol-Koryŏ alliance was so firm that it would last forever. A Mongol envoy arrived at the Koryŏ court and also requested a peace agreement, but the court officials were offended by the envoy's arrogant attitude and wary of the Mongols' reputation for cruelty elsewhere.

The Mongols severed relations with Koryŏ in 1225 after their envoy was murdered by bandits on his return from Kaegyŏng. They assumed that Koryŏ was responsible even though the Koryŏ court reported its belief that the Jurchen Eastern Xia commander had his men dress up in either Mongol clothes before attacking Koryŏ towns or in Koryŏ clothes when attacking Mongols to stir up trouble against their two enemies. The Mongols now demanded that Koryŏ sign a peace treaty and pay tribute. When Ch'oe I, the military ruler of Koryŏ, failed to respond, Mongol forces invaded Koryŏ almost to Kaegyŏng (modern Kaesŏng) in 1231 before Koryŏ sued for peace, disbanded the army, paid heavy tribute, and sent five hundred young men and five hundred young women to the Mongols as hostages. The Mongols withdrew but left a number of residence commissioners (*darughachi*) at the Western Capital in 1232. Because some of

Wood-Blocks of Buddhist Tripitika at Haeinsa. Carved 1237–1253, Koryŏ Dynasty. (Korean Buddhism *published by Korean Buddhist Chogye Order, 45, Kyonji-dong, Chongno-gu, Seoul, Korea, May 1996, p. 57; photos by Lee Hone Bae Slide Bank*)

the Mongol commissioners were murdered later that year, Mongol forces again invaded Koryŏ, but Ch'oe I, the king, and his court escaped and took refuge on Kanghwa Island, where they remained for the next two decades.

A year after their conquest of the Jin Dynasty in 1234, the Mongols again invaded Koryŏ and penetrated all the way to the southern provinces by 1238. They wreaked tremendous destruction, but they were unable to capture Kanghwa Island. King Kojong did send hostages to them, but he left individual commanders on the peninsula to hold out against Mongols on their own until 1241, when a succession dispute among Mongol leaders interrupted the fighting until 1247.

The Koreans led the world in inventing metal, movable-type printing in 1234, but they preferred to carve the entire Buddhist canon (*Tripitika*) in Chinese ideographs in wood blocks as an act of piety to gain the aid of the cosmic Buddha in resisting the Mongol armies. Although the effort failed to achieve its goal, many texts otherwise lost have been preserved on those blocks. The project was a herculean effort that took the years from 1237 to 1251, and the wood blocks have been preserved to this day in the Haeinsa monastery near Taegu.

After Möngke became the great khan of the Mongols, he pressed King Kojong to leave Kanghwa Island, return to the old capital at Kaegyŏng, and proceed to the Mongol capital to offer obeisance. After stalling for two years, Möngke sent an army in 1253 to enforce the demand, and Mongol forces captured several mountain forts and slaughtered the inhabitants. Kojong was inclined to surrender, but the new Ch'oe family head, Ch'oe Hang, prevented him from doing so. Finally King Kojong crossed over to the mainland from Kanghwa Island in 1254 and sent his second son to pay court to Möngke, before he returned to the island. Nevertheless, the Mongols charged Kojong with duplicity because Ch'oe Hang and other officials had still not left Kanghwa and Kojong had punished officials who had surrendered to the Mongols.

Because of Ch'oe Hang's refusal to quit the island, the Mongol commander, Jalayir, showed up with another army and over the next six years caused even more destruction. In 1254 alone, about 207,000 Korean prisoners were captured, and the number of deaths reached new heights as starvation and famine spread throughout the country.

Ch'oe Hang was assassinated by a cabal of military and civil officials and some Ch'oe family slaves in 1257. When his successor, Ch'oe Ŭi, was also murdered by two officials in 1258, Ch'oe family rule collapsed, and King Kojong sent the crown prince to the Mongol court as a hostage, tore down the fortifications on Kanghwa Island, and submitted to the Mongols, but he refused to leave the island until his death and died there in 1259. His crown prince returned from the Mongol capital to assume the throne as King Wŏnjong, but he too stayed on Kanghwa Island and sent his crown prince back as a hostage. Peace was restored, and military rule ended.

THE MONGOL CONQUEST OF THE SOUTHERN SONG

The Song Dynasty had plenty of time to get ready to fight the Mongols. They knew of the Mongols' conquests of both Xia and Jin. In the 1230s, the Mongols had also attacked Sichuan, under Song control, and refugees from Sichuan brought stories of the horror of the Mongol advance. Song knew it had to raise revenues and prepare its armies for a fearsome enemy. In a desperate attempt to raise revenues, an activist chancellor confiscated parts of the lands of the rich, leading to the disaffection of important segments of the population. But the attack did not come when expected in the 1240s or 1250s, a period when the Mongols were busy extending their conquests into Central Asia, Persia, and Russia. Song therefore had more time to prepare and the Mongols more time to learn how to deal with south China.

Khubilai

The man behind the final conquest of the Song was Khubilai (b. 1215), a grandson of Chinggis, son of his youngest son, Tolui. In Khubilai's youth, his uncle Ögödei was great khan (r. 1229–1241), and succession went to Ögödei's descendants until 1251, when Khubilai's elder brother Möngke became great khan.

In the 1240s Khubilai spent much of his time in Mongolia. One of the Chinese who came to call on him there was Liu Bingzhong (1216–1274), a believer in Three Teachings syncretism (which drew from Confucianism, Buddhism, and Daoism). Khubilai appointed Liu as a major adviser, and Liu in turn introduced Khubilai to many other Chinese, both generals and scholars. From them, Khubilai came to understand that the repeated plundering of north China had greatly reduced its worth and that letting Mongol lords make the residents of their lands slaves had impoverished the society and made it practically ungovernable.

In 1251, Khubilai was assigned control of all north China and put in place a much more Chinese style of government. Khubilai never learned to read Chinese and did not identify with Chinese culture, but he did come to appreciate that China could be exploited most effectively through Chinese methods. In 1254, Möngke sent Khubilai to lead a campaign south from Sichuan into Yunnan, where he defeated the independent country of Dali, incorporating this region into China for the first time. (See **Documents: The Luoluo.**) When Khubilai was enraged at the resistance of the king of Dali, a Chinese adviser convinced him not to slaughter the population for the faults of their ruler by reminding him of a passage in which Mencius asserted that only someone "who takes no pleasure in killing people" would be able to unify the realm (*Mencius* 1A6).

Möngke died in 1259 during a campaign against Song. His death brought the campaign to a close, as the Mongols headed north to select a new khan. Before a full assembly met, however, Khubilai declared himself the successor. Elsewhere his younger brother Arigh Böke did the same thing. It took a four-year civil war to end this dispute in Khubilai's favor.

In 1264 Khubilai constructed a new capital at the site of the Liao and Jin capitals. This capital, Dadu (modern Beijing), became the main capital of the khanate of the Great Khan (which stretched from Mongolia through north China and Korea). In the 1270s Khubilai began more concerted efforts to gain legitimacy in the eyes of the Chinese. In 1271 he adopted the Chinese name Yuan ("primal") for the Mongols' state in China, casting it as a dynasty to the Chinese. He explained the choice of the word *Yuan* by reference to a passage from the ancient *Book of Changes*. Although the Yuan retained the traditional Chinese county and prefectural governments, it added a new higher level, the province, which had the authority to handle much of government business on its own, without seeking approval from the central government.

Crossing the Yangzi River

Many non-Chinese groups had gained control of north China in the past, from the Xianbei of the Northern Wei to the recent Khitans and Jurchens. None of them, however, had been able to secure control of any territory south of the Yangzi River, in no small part because cavalry were of little advantage in a land crisscrossed with streams and canals. Moreover, controlling the Yangzi required a navy. When Jin had conquered Shu in the third century and Sui had conquered the last of the Southern Dynasties in the sixth century, the first step to conquest of the south had been the construction of a fleet of ships large enough to contest control of the Yangzi River. By the 1260s, the Mongols had plenty of Chinese advisers to explain this to them. They soon put Chinese shipbuilders to work building a fleet.

In 1268 the Mongols set siege to Xiangyang, a major city on a northern tributary leading into the Yangzi River. Both sides saw this city as the key to control of the river, and as a consequence the siege lasted five years. Each side had thousands of boats and tens of thousands of troops. The Mongols' force was multiethnic, with Chinese, Uighur, Persian, Jurchen, and Korean experts in siege warfare and naval tactics. Muslim engineers demonstrated their superior catapults, which could throw rocks weighing up to a hundred pounds each. To keep the residents of the city from starving, the Chinese fleet regularly ran the blockade to ferry food supplies into the city.

Once Xiangyang fell to the Mongols in 1273, the Mongol general Bayan (1237–1295) was put in charge of the invasion of the south. He led an army of two hundred thousand, mainly Chinese. Victory was often achieved without fighting: generals who had already gone over to the Mongols were sent ahead to persuade Song commanders of the wisdom of surrender. At one point the Song chancellor, Jia Sidao, personally led an army of one hundred thirty thousand and a navy of twenty-five hundred ships to keep the Mongols from entering the lower Yangzi region. The Mongols, landing their cavalry on both sides of the river and using catapults to destroy Song ships, still prevailed. Jia was dismissed from office and soon killed by angry local officials.

Although by the 1260s many Chinese in the north were working for the Mongols, Song officials and the educated class more generally tended to see in the Mongols the greatest threat Chinese civilization had ever faced. As Song officials readied themselves for the inevitable onslaught, many committed themselves to an all-out effort. That China had survived rule by non-Chinese before did not allay their fears. The Mongols seemed more savage and less likely to protect key features of Chinese culture and tradition than any previous foe.

Although Song had generals willing to resist to the bitter end, it lacked adequate leadership. The emperor at the time was a child, and the advisers to the empress dowager spent much of their energy opposing each other's plans. By the time the Mongol armies crossed the Yangzi in 1275, the empress dowager was reduced to calling on the people to rise up and fight the invading barbarians. Although some two hundred thousand recruits responded to the call, they were no match for the battle-hardened Mongols. The Mongols also had the advantage of scare tactics. To frighten Hangzhou into submitting without a fight, on the way there the Mongols ordered the total slaughter of the city of Changzhou. The ploy worked. The empress dowager, wanting to spare the people of the capital, surrendered. She, the child emperor, and other members of the Song imperial family were taken north to Beijing as hostages. Song loyalists, however, held out for three more years, placing young children from the Song imperial family on the throne. The final battle occurred off the coast of Guangdong province. Many Chinese fled into Vietnam, which the Mongols soon unsuccessfully attacked with an army of recently defeated Chinese soldiers.

Prominent among the Song loyalists was Wen Tianxiang, a poet and official who took up arms. Long after there was any real chance of driving the Mongols out, Wen kept fighting, withdrawing farther and farther south. Even after he was captured, he resisted all inducements to serve in the Yuan government, preferring execution to serving the Mongols.

LIFE IN CHINA UNDER THE MONGOLS

Life in China under the Mongols was much like life in China under earlier alien rulers. Once order was restored, people did their best to get on with their lives. Some suffered real hardship. Many farmers had their lands expropriated; others were forced into slavery or serfdom, perhaps transported to a distant city, never to see their family again. Yet people still spoke Chinese, followed Chinese customary practices in arranging their children's marriages or dividing their family property, made offerings at local temples, celebrated New Year and other customary festivals, and turned to local landowners when in need. Teachers still taught students the classics, scholars continued to write books, and books continued to be printed. (See Color Plate 16.)

The Mongols, like the Khitans and Jurchens before them, did not see anything particularly desirable in the openness of Chinese society, with opportunities for people to rise in status through hard work or education. They aimed instead at stability and placed people in hereditary occupational categories: farmer, Confucian scholar, physician, astrologer, soldier, artisan, salt producer, miner, Buddhist monk, and others. Many occupational groups had to provide unpaid services according to a rotational schedule and earn their living the rest of the year. Often the only alternative for those whose obligations threatened to bankrupt them was to abscond.

Besides these occupational categories, the Mongols classified the population into four grades, apparently as a way to keep the Chinese from using their numbers to gain a dominant position. Not surprisingly, the Mongols put themselves in the top grade. Next came various non-Chinese, such as the Uighurs and Central Asians. Below them were the former subjects of Jin, called the Han. And at the bottom were the former subjects of the Song, called southerners. These classifications affected methods of taxation, judicial process, and appointment to office. The Han, for instance, were taxed by household according to Jin practice, whereas the southerners were taxed by acreage, following Song precedent. In legal cases, each group was tried and sentenced according to its own legal tradition, which meant, for instance, that Chinese were the only ones tattooed if convicted of theft.

DOCUMENTS

The Luoluo

The region of modern Yunnan province in southwest China became part of China for the first time during the Yuan period, after the Mongols conquered it in the mid-thirteenth century. During Tang and Song times, this region was ruled by the independent kingdoms of Nanzhao and Dali. In 1301 the Chinese official Li Jing was given the post of deputy pacification commissioner for the northwest corner of Yunnan and neighboring Guizhou. After two years there, he wrote a treatise on the many different ethnic groups of the area, with particular attention to where they stood on a continuum from "raw" to "cooked," that is, how civilized they were. In the passage below, he describes the Luoluo. Also called the Yi, the Luoluo remain a major ethnic group in the area.

The Luoluo [Yi] are also known as the Wu Man, or Black Barbarians.

The men put their hair up in a coil and pluck their facial hair, or shave their heads. They carry two knives, one at each side, and enjoy fighting and killing. When a disagreement arises among fathers and sons and among brothers, they are known to attack each other with military weapons. Killing is taken lightly, and they consider it a sign of valor. They prize horses with cropped tails, their saddles have no trappings, and their stirrups are carved from wood in the shape of a fish's mouth to accommodate the toes.

The women wear their hair down and wear cotton clothing, and the wealthy wear jewelry and embroidered clothes; the humble are garbed in sheepskin. They ride horses side-saddle. Unmarried girls wear large earrings and cut their hair level with their eyebrows, and their skirts do not even cover their knees. Men and women, rich and poor, all wear felt wraps and go barefoot, and they can go as long as one year without washing face or hands.

It is the custom of husbands and wives not to see each other during the day, but only to sleep together at night. Children as old as ten *sui* most likely have never seen their father. Wives and concubines are not jealous of each other. Even the well-to-do do not use padding on their beds, but just spread pine needles on the ground with only a layer of felt and mat. Marriages are arranged with the maternal uncle's family, but if a suitable partner cannot be found

---

The reason for codifying ethnic differences in this way was to preserve the Mongols' privileges as conquerors. Chinese were not allowed to take Mongol names, and great efforts were made to keep them from passing as Mongols. Intermarriage was discouraged, though it did occur. Many of the differences in how the Chinese were treated, however, came from the Mongol fear that they would rebel or attempt sabotage. The Chinese were forbidden to own weapons or congregate in public. Khubilai even prohibited Chinese from dealing in bamboo because it could be used to make bows and arrows. Chinese were subject to severe penalties if they fought back when attacked by a Mongol. Mongols, however, merely had to pay a fine if found guilty of murdering a Chinese.

Since the Mongols wanted to extract wealth from China, they had every incentive to develop the economy. They encouraged trade both within China and beyond its borders. The Mon-they can look elsewhere for a match. When someone falls ill they do not use medicine, but instead call in a male shaman, who is known as the *daxipo.* He uses chicken bones to divine good and evil fortunes. The tribal leader always has the shaman at his side, and he must consult the shaman to make a final decision in all matters great and small.

A woman who is about to get married must first have relations with the shaman, and then "dance" with all the groom's brothers. This custom is known as "making harmony." Only after that can she be married to her husband. If any one of the brothers refuses to go along with this custom, he will be regarded as unrighteous and everyone will be disgusted with him.

The first wife is known as the *naide,* and it is only her children who can inherit their father's position. If the *naide* has a son who dies before marrying, she will go ahead and arrange a wife for him anyway. Anyone can then have relations with the deceased son's wife, and any child born is considered the child of the deceased. If the tribal leader does not leave a male heir, his wife's [the *naide's*] daughter then becomes the leader. However, she then has no female attendants—only ten or more young male attendants, with whom she can have relations.

When the tribal leader dies, they wrap his body in a leopard skin, cremate him, and then bury his bones on a mountain at a loca- tion known only to his closest relatives. After the burial they take images of the Seven Precious Things and place them on a high platform. They then go steal the head of a neighboring nobleman and offer it as a sacrifice. If they are not able to obtain one, they cannot make the sacrifice. At the time of the sacrificial ceremony all the relatives arrive, and they sacrifice more than a thousand cattle and sheep, or at least several hundred. Every year when they celebrate the spring festival during the twelfth month, they take a long vertical pole and a horizontal piece of wood, [and arranging a seesaw] with one person on each side, they go up and down together playing.

They support many soldiers, who are called *juke,* and they generously provide for them. When they go off to battle they view death as "returning home." They expertly craft armor and swords that are worth dozens of horses. On their javelins and crossbow arrow tips they put a poison that kills instantly.

They are found in Shunyuan [near Guiyang, Guizhou], Qujing, Wumeng [Zhao-tong], Wusa [near Weining, Guizhou], and Yuexi [north of Xichang, Sichuan].

Source: Translated by Jacqueline M Armijo-Hussein, in *Under Confucian Eyes: Writings on Gender in Chinese History,* ed. Susan Mann and Yu-yin Cheng (Berkeley: University of California Press, 2001), pp. 91–92.

gols allowed the conversion of Song paper money into Yuan currency and tried to keep paper money in circulation. They repaired the Grand Canal, which had been ruined during the initial conquest of north China. Chinese industries with strong foreign markets, such as porcelain, thrived during the Yuan period. A recently excavated vessel headed from Ningbo to Japan that was wrecked off the coast of Korea in 1323 contained about seventeen thousand pieces of ceramics, such as bowls and cups. More than half were green celadon from a kiln complex not far from Ningbo; the next largest group came from the Jingdezhen kilns in Jiangxi. In Yuan times, these kilns invented a new style of decoration using underglaze blue drawing that was widely exported throughout Asia (see **Material Culture: Blue-and-White Porcelain**).

Despite Mongol desire to see China rich, the economy of north China, in particular, was hard

MATERIAL CULTURE

Blue-and-White Porcelain

Porcelain is distinguished from other types of ceramics by its smoothness, whiteness, and translucence. Only certain types of clays can be used to make porcelain, and the wares must be fired at very high temperatures (1280–1400°C, 2336–2552°F). During Song times, Jingdezhen in Jiangxi became a major center for making porcelain.

The development of the highly popular blue-and-white style of porcelain owes much to the circumstances created by the Mongol Empire. The Yuan rulers established an official agency to supervise ceramic production at Jingdezhen. Artists at these kilns invented a new style of decoration, with underglaze-painted decoration using cobalt blue. West Asia was the best source for cobalt, so Chinese production depended on stable trade relations across Asia. Moreover, the designs of this type of porcelain seem to have been stimulated by Arab clients who wanted ceramics that would be more durable and refined than the ones they were used to, but with designs of the sort common in their region. Some Yuan-period blue-and-white wares exported to the Middle East are kept today in the Topkapi Museum in Istanbul. They have dense, busy designs reminiscent of the textiles and carpets of the region.

Blue-and-White Dish. This fourteenth century dish eventually entered the Ottoman collection and is today in the Topkapi Museum in Istanbul. Note how it combines Chinese imagery, such as the auspicious, imaginary *qilin* in the center, with dense floral patterns highly appreciated in the Islamic world. *(Hadlye Cangokce/Topkapi Saray Museum, Istanbul)*

hit by the Mongols and began a downward spiral that took centuries to reverse. First came the devastation of the initial conquest. Restoring production was impeded by widespread scattering of the population, much of it forced by the conquerors. Taxation, once it was in the hands of tax farmers, was often ruinous. The Mongols had difficulty regulating the paper currency, and by the fourteenth century inflation was rampant.

After the death of Khubilai in 1294, Mongol administration began to decline. Cliques of

Mongol nobles fought over the place of China within the khanate of the great khan. Should traditional steppe strategies of expansion remain central to the Mongol state? Or was there too much to be gained from exploiting China that they should give up steppe-based expansion? Unlike the Jurchen, who had largely moved into north China, most of the Mongols remained in Mongolia. Renzong, who came to the throne in 1311, was the first Mongol emperor able to both read and speak Chinese, and he shifted the emphasis toward China. In 1313 he reestablished a limited civil service exam system. His son Yingzong succeeded him in 1320, but when he continued the China-centered policies, he was assassinated by opposing factions. Civil wars and factional violence marred the next several reigns. The last Mongol emperor, who came to the throne in 1333 at age thirteen, was bright and well educated in Chinese but not a strong ruler. By his reign, the central government was failing to keep order in China or even maintain a stable currency. A colder than average climate and the spread of deadly diseases added to the hardship. Power devolved to the local level, to anyone who could organize an area well enough to suppress banditry.

The Chinese Educated Elite During the Mongol Era

Government service, which had long been central to the identity and income of the educated elite in China, was not as widely available during the Yuan Dynasty. Since the Mongols employed Mongols, Tibetans, Uighurs, Persians, Jurchens, and others in their government in China, there were fewer positions for the Chinese educated elite than there had been under either Jin or Song. Moreover, the large majority of Chinese who gained government positions came from clerk, not from scholar-official, families. The Mongols had no interest in doing their own paperwork and employed clerks to keep the records that made government possible. Clerks without classical educations had always been looked down on by Chinese scholars. To

the Mongols, however, they seemed perfectly suited to doing their bidding.

The Mongols reinstituted the civil service examinations in 1315, but opportunities for scholars were still very limited. There were quotas to ensure that no more than a quarter of those who passed would be southerners, no more than a quarter would be Han, and half would be Mongols and other non-Chinese. In addition, there were regional quotas, which had the effect of limiting opportunities for those from the southeast, where educational traditions were strongest. On top of that, only about 2 percent of the positions in the bureaucracy were filled through the examination system anyway.

In the south, the generation that had devoted themselves to resisting the Mongols rarely also served them, but their sons, growing up under Mongol rule, frequently did. The Mongols were tolerant of all religions but tended to favor Buddhists over Confucians. Khubilai gave the Tibetan cleric Yang Lianjianjia wide powers in postwar Hangzhou. He not only converted the Song palaces to Buddhist temples but excavated the Song imperial tombs to extract valuables from them to cover the cost of building more Buddhist temples. Defeated Song loyalists gave meaning to their survival by secretly searching for the bones of the Song emperors and respectfully reburying them.

Zhao Mengfu (1254–1322) is a good example of a southern literatus who decided to serve the Mongols. Descended from the first Song emperor, Zhao had grown up as a member of the privileged imperial clan. He had enrolled in the imperial academy in Hangzhou before the fall of the Southern Song, but he had not yet held office. For the first five years after the Song surrender, he kept to his circle of friends interested in poetry, painting, and calligraphy. Several of them had lost their property during the wars and were dependent on patrons to survive. This group looked on painting in archaic styles as a way to express longing for the past and dissatisfaction with the present.

When Khubilai in 1286 dispatched a southerner to recruit prominent southern literati to

松書多病贏 ... 行跡碌
珊 ... 清陰滿庭戶寒來溜崖
石向雲集朝暮 ... 如盦玉周
子犬無廢退息景以消愶安咚言
思與悟退學觀文私暑辭
親摭事丁役目夢幽珊寒松并
題五言以贈公茶招隱之寬 ... 卒
月十有 ... 倪瓉

Wintry Landscape. Ni Zan (1301–1374) was known for his sketchy monochrome
landscapes. In his inscribed poem, he states that he did this painting as a present
for a friend departing to take up an official post, to remind him of the joys of
peaceful retirement. *(The National Palace Museum, Beijing)*

serve the Mongols, Zhao Mengfu decided to
accept the call. Not all of his friends and relatives approved; some refused to speak to him
after they learned of his decision. Once in the
north, Zhao used Khubilai's favor to work for
Chinese interests. He pressed for better treatment of officials, arguing that literati should
be exempt from corporal punishment. He proposed major currency reforms and did his best

to cause the downfall of the notoriously corrupt
Tibetan chancellor Sangha. By 1316, he had
risen to president of the Hanlin Academy, the
prestigious government organ that supplied literary men to assist the emperor.

Southern literati who did not serve the Mongols found other ways to support themselves.
Some could live off the income from their lands;
others worked as physicians, fortune-tellers,

children's teachers, Daoist priests, publishers, booksellers, or playwrights. Many took on leadership roles at the local level, such as founding academies for Confucian learning, organizing their kinsmen into lineages, and promoting local charitable ventures. Through such activities, scholars out of office could assert the importance of civil over military values and see themselves as trustees of the Confucian tradition.

One art that benefited from the political frustrations of Chinese literati in the Yuan period was painting. Scholars like Su Shi in the Northern Song period had written of the superiority of paintings done by scholars who imbued their paintings with ideas. Still, through the Southern Song period, court painters and professional painters were at the center of stylistic developments, and even of marrying painting and poetry. During the Yuan period, however, men of letters were in the forefront. Some of these painters held office, like Zhao Mengfu. Others, like Huang Gongwang and Wu Zhen, supported themselves as clerks or diviners. Ni Can had enough family wealth to live comfortably without working. All of them painted for a restricted audience of like-minded individuals and often used the allusive side of paintings to make political statements.

Drama

The literary art of drama was given a boost in Yuan times by literati who wrote for the theater. Performing arts had flourished in earlier eras, with plays and performing styles passed down orally from master to disciple among hereditary groups of singers and actors, who were treated as a demeaned caste. Plays generally alternated prose passages and songs. Because women who performed in public were looked on as little better than prostitutes, female roles were often taken by boys or young men impersonating women. The presence of female impersonators, however, only added to the association of the theater with sexual laxity.

With the diminished career prospects of educated men in Yuan times, some talented writers began writing scripts for impresarios, and their scripts began to circulate as texts. About 160 Yuan plays survive, some of which can be read as covert protest against the Mongols. The best known of the Yuan dramatists is Guan Hanqing (ca. 1240–ca. 1320), author of sixty plays, fifteen of which survive complete. The leading characters of most of his plays were virtuous women who act forcefully in a wide variety of social situations, such as a courtesan who befriends a poor examination candidate, a widow who protects her husband's honor, a daughter-in-law who lets herself be executed to spare her mother-in-law from judicial torture, and a mother who is so strict in her education of her sons that all three place first in the civil service examinations in successive years.

There is even a Yuan play in which writing plays is treated as superior to studying the classics. Set in Jin period Kaifeng, *Grandee's Son Takes the Wrong Career* has as its protagonist the son of a Jurchen official who has fallen in love with a girl whose parents are itinerant performers. When she chides him for studying too much, he distracts her by reading a recent collection of plays, and the two learn the songs in them. The play ends with the young man giving up his studies and joining the troupe. When her father hears of his proposal, he responds, "The only man I want for my son-in-law is a writer of play books."[3] Only after the young man has shown that he can write speeches and will carry their costumes does the father consent to the marriage.

MONGOL RULE OVER KORYŎ (1260–1351)

As the khan of the Mongols, Khubilai did not attempt direct government administration over Koryŏ. Instead, he chose to rule indirectly and was lenient in allowing Koreans to abide by

---

3. William Dolby, *Eight Chinese Plays from the Thirteenth Century to the Present* (New York: Columbia University Press, 1978), p. 48.

their own customs. He sent the crown prince back to Koryŏ to take the throne (as King Wŏnjong, r. 1260–1274).

Khubilai promised King Wŏnjong that he would withdraw Mongol forces and the *darughachi* or special administrative officers stationed in Koryŏ, but only if he sent troops and rations to reinforce Mongol armies in return. King Wŏnjong objected because of the tremendous loss of both population and tax revenue as a result of the Mongol invasions, but Khubilai ignored his protest. In 1270, Khubilai took over the territory north of the Chabiryŏng pass (in Hwanghae province) in Korea, and it remained under Mongol control until it was returned in 1290.

King Wŏnjong evacuated the capital on Kanghwa Island and returned to the old capital at Kaegyŏng, but the Sambyŏlch'o guards, who had fought fiercely against the Mongols for years, rebelled against the government in 1270. They evacuated everyone left on Kanghwa Island by ship to Chindo (Chin Island) off the southwestern tip of the peninsula. Although they fought a stiff battle against Mongol and Koryŏ troops, they were defeated in 1273. While that campaign was proceeding, Khubilai established the Yuan Dynasty over China (1272) and made preparations for an invasion of Japan. He ordered twenty-five thousand Mongol and Chinese troops and another eight thousand Korean troops and sixty-seven hundred sailors to begin the invasion of Japan on November 4, but after meeting up with forces from China, a huge typhoon the Japanese referred to as the "divine wind" (*kamikaze*) wrecked over half the ships at anchor off Kyushu and forced the return of the expedition.

King Wŏnjong was succeeded by his son, King Ch'ungnyŏl (r. 1274–1308), who had married the Mongol Qiguo Dazhang princess in 1272, the first of several marriages of a Korean crown prince to a Mongol princess. Because King Ch'ungnyŏl had established close connections with important Mongol leaders, he surrounded himself with his aides and servants in China, many of them men of lower rank: interpreters of the Mongol language, eunuchs, inner palace

functionaries, military officers with little education, scribes, petty clerks, and slaves. He established the Falconry Office (*Ŭngbang*) in emulation of the Mongols' favorite sport and used it as a personal guard. These actions antagonized important aristocratic families and prestigious rural scholars, but when Khubilai began preparations for his second invasion of Japan, Ch'ungnyŏl was much more cooperative than his father had been before the first invasion in 1274.

In 1279 Khubilai established ten branch secretariats throughout China as an intermediate level of Mongol military control over existing Chinese local districts. He also established one in Koryŏ, the branch secretariat for the chastisement of Japan (BSCJ), but only to manage the second invasion, and not to take over local control in place of the king and the Koryŏ magistrates. The second invasion force left Korea on May 21, 1281, with forty thousand soldiers, of whom ten thousand were Koreans, and an additional eighteen thousand Korean sailors manned the ships. They were joined by forces from China, but the expedition suffered the same disaster as before: on July 5 a typhoon destroyed the ships, and rendered the army vulnerable to Japanese counterattacks. About one hundred thousand Chinese and Mongol troops and seven thousand Korean soldiers were lost, and the survivors were recalled.

After the failed invasion, Khubilai vacillated in abandoning and restoring the BSCJ because he could not decide whether to renew the invasion of Japan. He finally left it in place in 1285 with authority only to run the few Mongol military colonies in south Korea for defense in case of a Japanese counterattack. King Ch'ungnyŏl held a sinecure in the BSCJ, but Khubilai adopted a more direct method of control by issuing decrees from China and sending envoys to arrest suspects in criminal cases and bring them back to China for punishment. He also sent a Mongol named Körgüz in 1291 to monitor King Ch'ungnyŏl's actions. After Khubilai's death in 1294, subsequent emperors wavered between some toleration of Koryŏ autonomy and more direct intervention, but they all rejected several requests to convert the BSCJ into an administrative agency to replace Koryŏ kings and incorporate Koryŏ into the Mongol regime in China.

Perhaps the most interesting case occurred in 1300 when Körgüz tried to force King Ch'ungnyŏl to change the system of slavery in Koryŏ to conform to Yuan Dynasty rules by making all children of mixed slave-commoner marriages commoners, presumably to increase the population under the state's control for taxation and labor service. King Ch'ungnyŏl objected because the Korean custom of hereditary slavery was so firmly entrenched that any attempt to change it might cause serious political resistance from *yangban* slave owners. When Emperor Temür demurred and withdrew Körgüz's request, Körgüz returned home, and the BSCJ remained only as a symbol of Mongol dominance.

Nonetheless, many Koreans vying for office and power gravitated to the Mongol capital at Dadu (Beijing), established connections, or passed the examinations to hold office in China while others who remained in Korea collaborated with the Mongols. Even independent Koreans had no choice but to work with the Mongols. There were even two requests from Korean officials in Koryŏ in 1323 and 1343 to abandon the Koryŏ king and dynasty and transfer authority to the BSCJ, but the emperors rejected those requests as well.

Mongol emperors deposed Koryŏ kings who failed to serve their interests in 1298, 1313, 1321, 1330, 1332, 1343, and 1351. Some deposed kings were even restored to the throne and sometimes held in detention in Dadu to issue decrees in absentia. Insult was added to injury in 1343 when Mongol envoys arrested King Ch'unghye for initiating reforms detrimental to Mongol interests. They kicked him around, tied him up, and exiled him to China, but he died on the way, a blatant act of maltreatment that energized the anti-Yuan Dynasty group in Koryŏ.

The rise of anti-Yuan sentiment in Koryŏ led the emperors to realize that their interventionist policy had proved counterproductive. In the brief reign of the Koryŏ child king, Ch'ungmok (r. 1344–1348), the Mongols tolerated the establishment of a reform agency by Koryŏ officials that targeted the pro-Yuan officials in Koryŏ, especially Ki Samman of the prominent Ki family, who died in jail. He was a relative of Emperor Toghŏn Temür's Korean concubine, who gave birth to his heir apparent. When the emperor's second empress died childless in 1365, he made her his legal consort and changed her surname to the Mongol name for the Koreans, Sulangqa. Her powerful elder brother, Ki Ch'ŏl, was an influential pro-Yuan official at the Koryŏ court.

When King Ch'ungmok died a natural death in 1348, Emperor Toghŏn Temür reversed policy, dismantled his reforms, and reinstated pro-Yuan officials. In 1351, however, he decided to curtail Ki family power by enthroning King Kongmin without realizing that Kongmin was determined to free Koryŏ from Mongol domination just at the time that rebellions against Mongol rule broke out in China.

One of the most significant developments during the period of Mongol overlordship was the introduction of the Song Dynasty version of Confucianism, called the Learning of the Way (*tohak*). An Hyang was the first Korean to introduce this school to Koryŏ in 1286. The Yuan Dynasty court adopted Zhu Xi's commentaries on the *Four Books* for the civil service examinations in 1315, and several dozen Koryŏ men were able to go to China and pass the examinations and then return to Korea. Although Mongol support for Confucianism flagged, Koreans adopted the *Four Books* as a subject for study in Koryŏ in 1344, and King Kongmin established the National Academy (Sŏnggyun'gwan) in 1367. Eminent scholars like Yi Chehyŏn, Yi Saek, Chŏng Mongju, and Kwŏn Kŭn admired Zhu Xi's teachings because of its emphasis on the cultivation of virtue, but other scholars, like Chŏng Tojŏn and Cho Hun (see Chapter 15), were more interested in institutional reform and contributed significantly to the centralization of government authority in the Chosŏn Dynasty after 1392. (See **Biography: Yi Chehyŏn.**)

BIOGRAPHY Yi Chehyŏn

Yi Chehyŏn (1287–1367) was a member of the Kyŏngju Yi family who were originally *hyangni* (local clerks) but became *yangban* in the late thirteenth century. The son of a high-level official, he passed the examinations at the National Academy in first place in 1301 and later passed the highest civil service examination, the *munkwa*. A close associate of King Ch'ungsŏn (r. 1308–1313), he accompanied him to the Yuan court, where he held posts in the literary and historical offices. In 1320, Yi was instrumental in replacing the poetry and rhyme-prose sections of the civil service examinations with policy treatises. This was only seven years after Zhu Xi's work was adopted in the Yuan examinations, but Zhu Xi's commentaries on the *Four Books* were not mentioned in Korea at this time.

In 1323 Yi submitted a protest to the Yuan Executive Office of the Department of State Affairs to protest a plan proposed by two Koryŏ officials to incorporate Koryŏ into the Yuan Empire as a province, and he succeeded in blocking the idea. When King Ch'unghye (r. 1339–1344) was summoned to the Yuan court, Yi Chehyŏn accompanied him and acted as an intermediary to assuage Mongol concerns. During this reign, Yi Chehyŏn complained that the selection of personnel had been tainted. Although the assassination of Ch'oe Ŭi had brought an end to the domination of the court by the Ch'oe family, the personnel agency of the family was carried over even after nominal authority was supposedly returned to the king after 1260. Yi's ideal was to transfer personnel authority not to an absolute king but to the civil bureaucracy.

In King Ch'ungmok's reign (r. 1344–1348), Yi Chehyŏn submitted an important memorial calling for the abolition of the personnel office in the palace to return that responsibility to the outer bureaucracy. He was successful, but in 1347 that office was restored because of pressure from the queen mother. Nonetheless, Yi and the reformers succeeded in establishing a special Directorate for Ordering Politics, which was charged with restoring order in the localities, but they also carried out a purge of opponents of the *yangban*. Those opponents were men of lower social status like slaves who had risen to office through patronage. Unfortunately, the directorate was abolished by the Mongols because of the appeal of Kim Samman, brother of Palace Lady Ki, just before she became the consort of the last emperor of the Yuan dynasty, Toghōn Temür.

Yi also played a major role in pushing the adoption of Zhu Xi's thought. In 1344 he praised the king for reading the *Classic of Filial Piety* and the *Four Books* that Zhu Xi had selected for serious study, and the same year his disciple and relative sponsored the introduction of the Six Classics and Zhu Xi's *Four Books* into the civil service examinations along with the traditional question on the composition of rhyme prose in the Ancient Style. Yi also criticized the Buddhists for emphasizing poetry over the true learning (*sirhak*) of the Confucian moral message.

When Yi became acting prime minister under King Kongmin in 1351, he purged a number of palace favorites and helped to abolish the Personnel Authority. He was stymied when the Mongols intervened, restored the Personnel Authority, and pardoned some of those who had been purged. Yi Chehyŏn, however, was able to assist King Kongmin in 1356 in purging Korean in-laws of the Yuan emperor and dissolving the Branch Secretariat for the Chastisement of Japan.

By the time of his death in 1367, Yi had become one of the outstanding leaders of the reform that removed the vestiges of Ch'oe family institutions and transferred authority to civil agencies.

SUMMARY

How different were China and Korea in the 1360s than they had been before the Mongols took control? The more destructive side of this period helped reinforce in China a preference for things Chinese and a wariness about things from outside. Some innovations can be attributed to this period, most notably the province as a political unit with a full array of administrative functions. The elite were given even more incentives than they had had in Song times to find ways to maintain their standing without participation in the government. Population had declined, but population records are not good enough to be certain by how much. The gap between north and south China had been reinforced, though it also had very deep roots, leaving the north further behind economically.

In the case of Korea, the Mongol conquest crushed the military domination of Koryŏ society by removing the Ch'oe family dictatorship. It restored nominal authority to the king but robbed him of real power. What was more important was that it restored the civil bureaucracy to prominence and laid the groundwork for Zhu Xi orthodoxy. Socially, it had little effect on the slave-holding *yangban* aristocracy, which continued into the next dynasty with little change. In material life, cotton was introduced to Korea in 1361 and began to replace ramie as the main textile fiber. Gunpowder was introduced in late fourteenth century and was used for cannon, but not yet for small arms.

Despite the enormous destruction of the invasions and the heavy tribute demands, the Koreans were given far more autonomy in running their own affairs than the Chinese in China, who suffered much discrimination at the hands of Mongols and their many foreign officials. Nevertheless, the threat of total absorption into the Yuan Empire was strong enough to divide society into collaborators and defenders of autonomy, if not total independence, a conflict that was not ended until just before the Koryŏ Dynasty collapsed.

SUGGESTED READING

H. Franke and D. Twitchett, eds., *The Cambridge History of China*, vol. 6: *Alien Regimes and Border States* (1994), devotes several chapters to the Yuan period and also covers the Mongol conquest of Jin and Xia. On the Mongol conquest of Jin, see H. Chan, *The Fall of Jurchen Chin: Wang E's Memoir on Ts'ai-chou Under the Mongol Siege* (1993). On Chinese resistance to the Mongols, see R. Davis, *Wind Against the Mountain* (1996), and F. Mote, *The Poet Kao Ch'i, 1336–1374* (1962). One of the most important Yuan rulers is treated in M. Rossabi, *Khubilai Khan: His Life and Times* (1988). A. Waley, trans., *The Travels of an Alchemist* (1931), is the account of a Chinese traveler to Chinggis Khan's camp. Studies of social, cultural, and political aspects of Yuan history can be found in J. Langois, Jr., *China Under Mongol Rule* (1981); H. Chan and W. T. de Bary, eds., *Yuan Thought: Chinese Thought and Religion Under the Mongols* (1982); and J. Dardess, *Conquerors and Confucians: Aspects of Political Change in Late Yuan China* (1973). On the development of drama in this period, see J. Crump, *Chinese Theater in the Days of Kublai Khan* (1980), and W. Idema and S. West, *Chinese Theater from 1100–1450: A Source Book* (1982).

For Korea in the Mongol period, see W. E. Henthorn, *Korea: The Mongol Invasions* (1963); J. Duncan, *The Origins of the Chosŏn Dynasty* (2000); and K.-B. Lee, *A New History of Korea* (1984).

Japan's Middle Ages (1330–1600)

Historians today see the fourteenth century as marking a decisive break between ancient Japan and its middle ages. Political power became increasingly fragmented among contending military configurations, the court, ecclesiastical establishments, urban residents, and cultivator leagues. Trade networks expanded, carrying a greater variety of goods over longer distances than ever before, while urban markets supplied the needs of social and political elites as well as ordinary residents. Women exchanged economic autonomy for domestic authority. Samurai became moralists and poets. The fourteenth century began with conflict between samurai and the court. The fifteenth and sixteenth centuries saw civil war. Europeans brought new weapons and a new religion in the middle of the sixteenth century. At its end, the world turned upside down: a commoner ruled Japan and sent his armies to invade Korea.

Historians disagree over who were significant political actors, the losers such as Go-Daigo, the religious establishment, and commoner leagues, or the winners among the samurai. Much of the dynamism in this period came from its unsettled margins. What impact did they have on the center? How did men and women protect their interests? How did the arts manage to flourish in the midst of unrest?

NEW POLITICAL ALIGNMENTS

The monarch Go-Daigo's plan to restore power to the monarchy provided the catalyst for the Kamakura shogunate's fall. In 1321 Go-Daigo got his father to agree to renounce the political power held by the retired monarch. Go-Daigo revived the monarchical records office and attracted able administrators who reasserted the royal prerogative of adjudicating lawsuits. Three years later the shogunate learned of his plots against it and arrested his accomplices. Go-Daigo continued to insist on monarchical privilege. When the shogunate tried to force him to abdicate in favor of his cousin's line in 1331, he called on loyalists across Japan to revolt.

Although the shogunate exiled Go-Daigo to the remote island of Oki, men all over Japan rallied to the monarchical cause. Some believed in it; others saw an opportunity to gain wealth and power. Ashikaga Takauji first led Kamakura's legions against Kyoto and then switched sides. In 1333 his forces set fire to Kamakura. The Hōjō family and its retainers, over eight hundred men, women, and children, committed suicide. Takauji brought Go-Daigo back from exile, only to turn on him when forced to share spoils of war with members of the aristocracy. Having overcome a string of reversals, Takauji drove Go-Daigo out of Kyoto and placed his cousin on the throne. Takauji built his headquarters in the Muromachi section of Kyoto where he could supervise the new monarch and oversee his followers. Claiming descent from Minamoto Yoritomo to legitimize his rule, he had himself named shogun in 1338. Despite this title, the administrative structure that he and his successors put together over the next sixty years owed nothing to the Kamakura regime and everything to the exigencies of the moment.

Takauji's victories over Go-Daigo did not bring peace to an increasingly militarized Japan. Go-Daigo's sons established a rival southern court in the mountains of Yoshino that held out until 1392. The coexistence of two courts, northern and southern, allowed men to fight in the name of rival claimants to the throne, depending on which suited their interests. Takauji's grandson Yoshimitsu brought an end to the rival courts by promising to alternate rule between their descendants. He later broke this promise. He brought recalcitrant fighters in Kyushu under his control, but he had less success with military leaders under a rival Ashikaga branch in eastern Japan. In 1402 he received the title "king of Japan" from the Ming emperor (a title not heretofore used in Japan although analogous to the Yi Dynasty's ruler being titled "king of Korea") and appeared poised to replace the monarchy with his son. His reign marked the high point of Ashikaga power. It declined thereafter, although the shogunate remained in Ashikaga hands to 1578.

The Ashikaga shoguns tried to rule Japan through a combination of family ties and marriage politics. As a gesture at institutional continuity with the Kamakura shogunate, they used the title of *shugo* (military governor). The *shugo* appropriated the administrative functions of the provincial governors appointed by the court. By the end of the fourteenth century, they had also taken over the responsibilities and the income of the estate stewards (*jitō*). Fourteen *shugo* were branches of the Ashikaga family; the remaining seven, such as the Shimazu of Satsuma in Kyushu, lived far from Kyoto and supported the Ashikaga in return for a free hand at home. *Shugo* served as high officials, military governors, and the Ashikaga's chief retainers. Takauji and his heirs exchanged women with *shugo* to maintain their allegiance and solidify alliances. Each ruled large, unwieldy territories defined in patents of appointment made by the shogun. The Ashikaga shoguns were the chief of the *shugo* and derived some of their income from being *shugo* of two provinces. They also controlled some sixty estates scattered across Japan.

The most important office under the shogun was the deputy shogun (*kanrei*), normally filled by the Shiba, Hatakeyama, or Hosokawa. They had prestige as the shogun's close relatives, governing Japan's richest provinces as *shugo* made them wealthy, and their office gave them authority. By combining these three constituents of power, they formed an inner bastion of support for the shogun. When they acted together on his behalf, they made it possible for him to dominate the other *shugo* and his retainers. When they quarreled, they tore the country apart.

The *shugo* normally supported the shogun because they also had weaknesses. Although they had jurisdictional authority over entire provinces, they did not control land. Even when a military man had managed to expropriate the aristocrats' claims to income from estates, he still had to contend with temples, other *shugo*, or even the shogun. Not all military families within a *shugo*'s province were his direct retainers. With increasing frequency, rustic warriors (*kokujin*) accepted no one as their overlord. The longer the *shugo* resided in Kyoto with the shogun, the more they relied on deputies to manage provincial administration. To intimidate their underlings, they needed the prestige bestowed by the shogun. The crucial problem left unsolved by both the Kamakura and Ashikaga regimes was how to maintain the connection between center and periphery. Unlike China, where a bureaucracy marinated in a common ideology was first gathered to the center, then dispatched to the provinces, Japan remained in danger of fragmentation.

Apologists for the Ashikaga wrote the history of the Kamakura regime in such a way as to provide precedents for the new relationship between the Ashikaga shoguns, the *shugo*, and the monarch. The *shugo* had much broader power than any single office at Kamakura. The monarchy had lost so much of its income and autonomy that one ruler had to put off his enthronement ceremony for twenty years because the shogun refused to fund it. The Kamakura regime had subsisted on a relatively small income generated from land. The Ashikaga shoguns cast their net more broadly, collecting fees to license both foreign and domestic trade, demanding kickbacks from temples, dunning the populace in the name of the monarch, and erecting toll barriers to tax commerce. Whereas during Kamakura times, monarch and shogun had ruled Japan together, if not to the same ends, during the Muromachi period, neither can be said to have exercised effective governance.

Changes in Roles for Women

Nothing better marks the break between ancient and medieval Japan than the changes that took place in the relationships between men and women, especially at the higher reaches of society. Even before the Mongol invasions, it had become clear that dividing property among all children, men and women alike, seriously weakened a family's viability. At the same time, the fluidity in marriage arrangements that had characterized the Heian period largely disappeared. Women increasingly moved to their husband's residence. If they took property with them, less was left for their brothers. Loath to bestow property on daughters or too many sons, powerful families selected a single heir. With women and their husbands out of the picture, brothers and cousins competed to inherit the family estate. Property rights in cultivator households evolved differently. Increases in agricultural productivity plus new commercial opportunities left more income in cultivator hands. Women as well as men traded in land and other goods. Women continued to manage their own property even when they moved into their husband's household.

Marriages became more durable and of greater consequence. When seen as a way to ally two families, the exchange of betrothal gifts and the bride's entry into her husband's residence became ceremonies. Once ensconced in her new home, the bride served her parents-in-law as well as her husband. Her trousseau supplied her with what she needed for daily life, but she lost the autonomy that had come from owning real property. She became her husband's property. No legal distinction was made between adultery and rape because both constituted crimes against the husband. On the other hand, the woman's position as wife became much more secure. The elaboration of the marriage ceremony and its public character meant that only compelling political reasons justified divorce. If a man fathered children on a concubine, his wife became their official mother. A wife became the person primarily responsible for domestic affairs. When her husband was off at war, she managed the household economy and dispatched his supplies. A mark of her responsibilities was her title: *midaidokoro* (the lady of the kitchen).

Women at the Kyoto court had always participated in public ceremonies; during the medieval period, they assumed administrative functions

BIOGRAPHY Hino Meishi

Aristocrat, official, mother, and writer, Hino Meishi (?–1358) lived through a time of high political intrigue and learned what it meant to be a wife while the family structure was in transition.

Meishi was the daughter of Hino Sukena who served the monarch Kōgon (r. 1331–1333). When she was about ten years old, she became a maid to Kōgon's mother, Kōgimonin. Meishi developed an expertise in court ceremonies at Kōgon's coming-of-age ceremony. When he was enthroned by the Kamakura shogunate as a replacement for Go-Daigo, she stood directly behind the new monarch.

While Meishi was fulfilling official public functions, sometime before 1331 she started a romance with Kōgimonin's nephew, Kinmune, from the powerful Saionji branch of the Fujiwara lineage. They continued to see each other while Kyoto was thrown into turmoil by Go-Daigo's return, Kōgon's dethronement, and her father's involuntary decision to shave his head and become a monk. For a while they met at hideaways far from the eyes of their parents or their employers. In 1333 Meishi became Kinmune's recognized consort when he wrote her a poem pledging his fidelity. He then visited her publicly at her father's home and stayed the night. A few months later, the Saionji family summoned Meishi to its main residence at Kitayama as Kinmune's official wife, in a move that united two aristocratic opponents to Go-Daigo's rule.

In 1335 Kinmune and Sukena were both arrested for having plotted against Go-Daigo. The night before Kinmune was to be exiled to Izumo, Meishi visited him at the mansion where he had been confined. They exchanged a tearful farewell, and Kinmune handed over several mementos. Before Meishi left, a messenger arrived with the news that Kinmune was to be transferred to another residence. As he was bending down to enter a palanquin, the messenger cut off his head. The pregnant Meishi fled to the Saionji mansion, where she gave birth to her son, Sanetoshi. A messenger from Go-Daigo's court arrived with an offer to find a wet nurse for the child. Kinmune's mother told him that Meishi had miscarried to protect her grandson from his enemies. When the northern court was restored in 1337, Meishi used her connection with the now retired monarch Kōgon to promote her son and restore the Saionji family to its former glory.

Meishi wrote a two-volume memoir. The first volume covers the period of her romance with Kinmune from 1329 to 1333; the second takes up the restoration of the northern court in 1337 and the revival of the Saionji family fortunes. She thus omitted the years of turmoil that exposed the political calculations behind her marriage.

Source: Based on Hitomi Tonomura, "Re-Envisioning Women in the Post Kamakura Age," in *The Origins of Japan's Medieval World: Courtiers, Clerics, Warriors, and Peasants in the Fourteenth Century,* ed. Jeffrey P. Mass (Stanford, Calif.: Stanford University Press, 1997).

---

as the circle around the monarch shrank. (See **Biography: Hino Meishi.**) Only the highest-ranking aristocrats managed to survive the turmoil of the age; others rusticated to keep close to their sources of income. Women replaced them in running the monarch's household, a transformation in female function seen espe-cially in their writing. Earlier women's diaries and memoirs had been subjective and recorded their lives and thoughts. Those from the fourteenth century and later recorded men's deeds. Women also served as secretaries, writing letters and transmitting orders on behalf of monarch, regent, and shogun.

Trade in Town and Country

The fourteenth century saw a series of transformations in rural Japan. The conversion of dry fields to paddy, the growing of two crops per year, and the extensive use of irrigation made possible by water wheels brought increased yields, population growth, and commercial expansion. Estates split into corporate villages. On estates, each cultivator manager (*myōshu*) had his own distinct legal relationship with multiple overlords. In villages, former *myōshu*, who might also be warriors, plus smallholders dealt with overlords as a unit. They presented petitions for reductions in taxes and corvée labor, and they asserted corporate control over common land and irrigation systems. This process was hastened by the development of self-governing organizations encouraged by overlords as a way to replace the Kamakura-sanctioned estate stewards. Land rights became transferable commodities rather than being associated with office and status. During times of endemic social disorder when overlords were far away, cultivators banded together in nucleated villages, constructed walls and moats, and defended themselves. They met in committee to handle village administration—irrigation procedures and tax payments, for example—and deal with judicial issues. In central Japan these village assemblies took the form of shrine associations that discriminated between members according to status and gender. Many of today's hamlets trace their names back to this century, suggesting the creation of a village identity that excluded outsiders and regulated the behavior of insiders.

Trade had spread in Kamakura times, but the early fourteenth century saw new developments. First was the monetization of commerce by relying on coins imported from Ming China. Although cultivators continued to present taxes in kind and bartering never disappeared, large and small transactions came to be denominated in cash. Second, commercial centers evolved out of places where people congregated: at toll barriers, river crossings, harbors, post houses, and the entrances to shrines and temples. Men and women from nearby villages brought their wares for sale, primarily vegetables, but also processed food such as bricks of tofu. As in earlier ages, proselytizers followed the crowds; some used pictures to teach faith in Amida or to warn of the torments of hell. Nuns solicited donations for the Kumano temple complex. The authorities tried to keep people tied to a specific place and required that travelers carry a passport. Markets received a dispensation from such regulation, making them a zone where people could mingle and exchange goods and information.

The third development centered on the spread of guilds (*za*). They first appeared in the twelfth century and reached their peak in the fourteenth to fifteenth centuries. The idea behind a guild was that the traders or artisans dealing in a specific product would pay a fee to a patron (court noble, religious establishment, shogun) and receive two privileges in exchange: a monopoly on the sale or production of their product and the right to travel in pursuit of trade. Comb makers, sesame oil producers, metal casters, and potters all joined guilds. Many of them lived in the countryside, where they were listed in land records as *hyakushō* (the hundred names). Although this term came to specify cultivators in the seventeenth century, in the fourteenth century it simply meant anyone who was not an aristocrat or warrior. It thus included fishermen, salt makers, and other people who did not grow crops. Horse traders from central Japan relied for centuries on a monarchical decree that gave them exclusive rights to trade in horses. They expanded their monopoly to everything carried by horses from the Pacific to the Japan Sea. Not until modern times did researchers discover that the decree was a forgery.

Kyoto functioned as both the political and economic center of Japan. The court, shogunate, and religious establishments competed as well as cooperated to control and tax commoners in cross-cutting systems of overlord authority that made for interdependence, exploitation, and tax evasion. During the Kamakura period, low-ranking monks from Enryakuji on Mount Hiei had begun to brew and sell sake and lend

Female Moneylender. This segment from a twelfth-thirteenth century scroll of diseases (*yamai no sōshi*) depicts a female moneylender so suffering from obesity brought on by her wealth that she needs help to walk. (*Fukuoka Art Museum*)

and Chinese coasts. Communities of foreign traders thrived in all the port cities of East Asia, including Japan. The Ming Dynasty closed China to foreign commerce after 1368, with the only exception being official trade carried on between states under the rubric of tribute. In 1402, the Chinese emperor agreed to provide two ships a year with the official seal that allowed them to trade in China. By 1465, two *shugo* had taken over the trade, although the shogunate continued to assess a fee of 10 percent on private merchandise. Late-fourteenth-century state formation in the Ryukyu Islands led three principalities to merge into one under King Sho Hashi in 1429. The Ryukyuans sent tribute missions to China and received official permission to pursue trade. As a maritime nation, they sailed their ships from Southeast Asia to Japan and Korea. Through their delegations to the shogunate, piracy, and legitimate trade, Japan participated in economic networks stretching across the East Asia seas and established a community in Vietnam's Hoi An. In the sixteenth century, these networks brought Europeans in search of trade and Christian converts. (See **Connections: Europe Enters the Scene.**)

Life on the Margins

Trade did not alleviate the disruptions caused by crop failures. Famines forced desperate people to sell themselves into bondage, a form of slavery that could last for generations. Disease was another scourge. Leprosy terrorized people in Japan as it did in Europe. The afflicted suffered increasing disfigurement as their flesh rotted away. How could it be other than a punishment for evil committed in a previous life? Lest they contaminate the healthy with their pollution, lepers had to leave their families and join groups of paupers, the infirm, and entertainers, referred to as the people of the riverbank (*kawaramono*).

The *kawaramono* were outcasts. They included people whose occupations brought them into contact with things deemed to be polluting, death in particular. Tanners, butchers, policemen, and undertakers were excluded from

money. By the fourteenth century, wealthy moneylenders provided cash loans to aristocrats, warriors, townspeople, and cultivators at annual interest rates of up to 300 percent. Enryakuji issued business licenses and ran a protection racket, fending off attempts by other overlords to tax the moneylenders and helping to collect debts. As lobbyist for its clients, Enryakuji paid stipends to shogunal officials to protect their interests, and moneylenders bribed them to grant tax exemptions. The shoguns made prominent moneylenders their storehouse keepers and later their tax agents in return for 10 percent of the take and the prestige of an official appointment, although the relationship was more ad hoc than bureaucratic. The shogunate's income shrank while individual officials grew rich.

The shogunate strove mightily to control and profit from the maritime trade that flourished regardless of political boundaries. Seafarers of mixed ethnicities pursued trade and piracy with equal aplomb, ravaging the Korean, Japanese, ordinary society. For them, the only fit habitation was on untaxed land that nobody wanted. Occasionally riverbank people were hired to cleanse a shrine after it had been desecrated by fire or the loss of life in a fight. Purifying the shrine involved the dirty work of removing dead bodies. Such rites performed by outcasts suggest a social imagination in which two negatives become a positive and the power to purify lies with the impure.

Other people used marginal spaces carved out of ordinary life as temporary refuges. Markets, river crossings, the entrances to temples and shrines, and graveyards offered sanctuary to unfree people fleeing bondage. Mountains provided shelter for entire villages that absconded to protest unjust taxes or forced labor. Another form of protest was for groups of warriors or cultivators to dress in the persimmon-colored robes reserved for lepers. It was a desperate measure because it cut them off from normal human interaction. It worked because spaces set apart from ordinary life were under the inviolable protection of the deities and Buddhas.

Changes in Religious Practice

An important characteristic of Japan's Middle Ages was the power of the Buddhist establishment. Although Ashikaga shoguns dominated the court, they had to conciliate the temples that largely controlled the urban economy and had their own police force as well as deep roots in the lives of Japanese people. The major temples that had received support from the Heian court continued to flourish; the popular sects that originated in the Kamakura period attracted sometimes vehement converts. Zen Buddhism made major contributions to Japanese aesthetics and played an important political role.

Rather than patronize the temples already entrenched in the Kyoto court, Ashikaga shoguns preferred the Rinzai Zen sect. At the suggestion of a Zen monk, Takauji and his son set up official temples named Ankokuji (temples for national peace) in each province to console Go-Daigo's spirit and raise the shogun's prestige. They also had pagodas built in the precincts of temples belonging to other sects for the same purpose. Later shoguns promoted and ranked Zen temples in Kyoto and Kamakura in loose accord with the system already developed for Zen (Chan) temples in China. Priests jockeying for position and shogunal preference meant that the ranking shifted considerably. By 1410, ten temples enjoyed the top rank of "five mountains" (*gozan*), and all the Kyoto temples ranked above their Kamakura counterparts. Next in importance were the sixty-odd "ten temples" (*jissetsu*). At the bottom were the "multitude of temples," patronized by powerful provincial families. Many had originally been temples of other sects that changed their affiliation to Zen to become part of this ranking system that bestowed prestige and connections to the center on its affiliates.

The Ashikaga established a hierarchy of priests that aligned the Rinzai sect even more closely with its fortunes. When Yoshimitsu built Shōkokuji next to his palace on Muromachi Street in 1382, he had the chief Rinzai priest reside there. This priest decided appointments to the heads of the Rinzai temples, recommended promotions, and determined ceremonial procedures. Owing to his prowess in the Chinese language, he prepared documents related to maritime trade and foreign affairs. In the fifteenth century, the shogunate appointed men from aristocratic families to this position, with the result that the chief priest often had little interest in routine administration or religious observances.

As the Rinzai school became increasingly associated with the dominant power structure, its teachings and practice moved further from what is conventionally associated with Zen. Instead of seeking the path to enlightenment through meditation, Rinzai became syncretic. It absorbed secret teachings and incantations from esoteric Buddhism that had proved popular with the aristocracy. Even in provincial temples, question-and-answer sessions between master and disciple took a fixed form based on oral tradition handed down in secret. In Kyoto the chief priests participated with the military and civilian aristocracy in literary and artistic pursuits.

Yoshida Shinto (also called Yuiitsu Shinto—"one and only") opposed Zen Buddhism and Buddhist-Shinto syncretism by insisting on the worship of deities only as deities rather than as bodhisattvas. Based on his claim to a tradition stretching back to the creation of Japan through his Urabe lineage of court diviners, Yoshida Kanetono (1435–1511) invented Shinto rituals that spread across Japan. Some had an open, exoteric dimension accessible to ordinary worshipers. Secret esoteric rituals for initiates surprisingly similar to Buddhist rites drew on Buddhist hand gestures called *mudras* and used quotations from *Nihon shoki* in place of mantras. Yoshida Shinto dogma and practice reasserted the centrality of the monarch in indigenous terms and rescued Shinto from complete submersion in Buddhism.

Muromachi Culture

The cult of sensibility (*aware*) from the Heian period and the Kamakura aesthetic characterized by austerity were combined in the fifteenth century into a notion of beauty and elegance modified by stern simplicity. The key term was *yūgen,* used to describe the profound, the remote, the mysterious—a term taken from Nō, the quintessential dramatic form of the day. (See **Material Culture: Nō.**) In Nō every gesture must be refined, the dance graceful, and the language elevated. The most meaningful moments are those when the actor's unspoken, unmoving spiritual presence allows the audience a glimpse of the inexpressible. The same search for the presence behind the form can be seen in monochrome ink brush painting wherein the spaces left blank give shape to the composition, flower arranging based on the asymmetrical placement of a blossom or two, and the tea ceremony.

Zen permeated the arts and architecture of the time. Natural settings depicted in ink brush paintings became allegories to doctrinal points just as did the late-fifteenth-century rock garden

at Ryōanji. Raked white sand surrounds fifteen rocks, only fourteen of which are visible from any one perspective. It takes the experience of enlightenment to grasp all fifteen at once. Partly inspired by Song Dynasty architecture, the Golden Pavilion (Kinkakuji) and its pond built in 1398 were designed to model paradise. Ashikaga Yoshimasa built the Silver Pavilion (Ginkakuji), a more modestly refined building, seventy-five years later. A truncated cone of white sand designed to reflect moonlight on the pavilion dominates its Zen garden.

Literary arts also reflected Buddhist influence. Between 1310 and 1331, the poet and recluse Yoshida Kenkō wrote *Essays in Idleness,* a collection of reflections on his time, didactic statements, and meditations, all suffused with longing for the past. In the late fourteenth century, stories about the conflict between the northern and southern courts coalesced in *Taiheiki* (*Records of Great Pacification*). Castigating Ashikaga Takauji as a traitor and emphasizing the legitimacy of the southern court, this late military history became a favorite of storytellers. Ghost stories, didactic tales, folktales, testimonials to the saving power of the Buddha, and sermons were sold in booklets later called *otogi zōshi* (chapbooks).

The tea ceremony, from which women were excluded, assimilated warriors and priests to aristocratic standards of taste. In the first century of Ashikaga rule, imbibing bitter green tea provided the occasion for parties at which the host displayed his finest art treasures in a beautifully appointed sitting room overlooking a garden. With the coming of warfare in the late fifteenth century, this florid style gave way to a simpler, more ritualized and disciplined ceremony performed in a modest hut. Instead of richly decorated Chinese vessels, the emphasis shifted to plain, often misshapen pots because the aesthetic of the time expressed in the combination of *wabi* and *sabi* (elegant simplicity) celebrated the beauty of imperfect objects. The practitioners included provincial samurai and merchants from Kyoto and Sakai who found the tea ceremony an excellent excuse to mingle with

MATERIAL CULTURE

Nō

Combining music, dance, and story, Nō drew on rural dances that appealed to the gods for good harvests, comical skits, popular songs, and tales told by jongleurs. The early spectacles were vulgar and exuberant, attracting crowds of people from all walks of life. At a performance in 1349, monks solicited donations, princes and the Fujiwara regent were among the spectators, and thieves tried to steal the actors' costumes.

Protégé and lover of Ashikaga Yoshimitsu, Zeami transformed Nō into art. In some plays he took themes from *The Tale of Genji,* and in others he used the elevated diction of the court to recast *The Tale of the Heike.* He crafted stories about ghosts, condemned by jealous passion or murderous deed to wander the netherworld between death and salvation. Not content to remain spectators, the shoguns and daimyo performed Nō and made it a state ceremony.

The accouterments of Nō are simple yet elegant. The wooden stage is bare, with a pine tree painted across the backdrop. The musicians and chorus perform on drums and flute for one or two performers. Men in black arrange costumes and provide the occasional prop. One performer wears a mask denoting men and women of various ages, gods, the possessed, and demons. Subtle movements of the head combined with skillful carving lend these masks great expressive power. In contrast to the stern simplicity of the set, the robes are of brilliant brocade, their glitter designed to catch the light from the torches that light the stage.

Nō Performance. One detail on a folding screen showing scenes in and around Kyoto depicts a Nō performance in the early sixteenth century. *(National Museum of Japanese History/DNPArchives.com)*

aristocrats. Linked verse (*renga*), a collaborative form of poetry writing, provided a venue for the talented but lowborn to attract attention. Traveling priests such as Sōchō carried the practices of poetry and tea to provincial strongmen across Japan. (See **Documents:** *The Journal of Sōchō.*)

In contrast to the Zen-influenced arts of earlier times, exuberant color characterized the Momoyama period at the end of the sixteenth century. Epitomized in Toyotomi Hideyoshi's golden tearoom, parvenu extravagance marked lacquer boxes dusted with gold, and wall paintings with gold leaf background. Vividly painted screens depicted European traders and missionaries and celebrated local customs. (See Color Plate 17.) Artistic triumphs based on technological innovation led to elaborate textile designs and towering castle keeps.

CIVIL WAR

The hundred years of civil war that began with the Ōnin conflict of 1467–1477 diffused elite cultural practices across the country. The breakdown of unified public authority spurred innovations from military organization to village life. Estates vanished. Buddhist temples lost power and income when they were not simply destroyed. Without their protection, the Kyoto moneylenders and other guild organizations disappeared. Territorial units of domains and villages replaced the former patchwork of competing jurisdictions.

Succession disputes provided the pretext for retainers and overlords to push their own interests. In the Hatakeyama case, the aging *shugo* first appointed a nephew to be his heir, but when a son was born to his concubine, he tried to have his decision reversed. In the 1450s, powerful retainers and the shogunal deputy backed the nephew and got the shogun to censure the son. Son and nephew fought on the political front, each being censured three times and forgiven three times, and on the military front where their retainers demanded rewards after each battle. This conflict foreshadowed the dispute in the

Ashikaga house when Yoshimasa appointed his younger brother his successor, only to be forced to change his mind when his wife, Hino Tomiko, gave birth to Yoshihisa in 1465. Her dedication to her son's future shows how family loyalties had changed from Hōjō Masako's day. Already at odds over the Hatakeyama dispute, the two chief *shugo* each picked a rival claimant.

The *shugo* fought their first battles in and around Kyoto in 1467. Their chief weapon was arson, used to punish and exorcise enemies. Temples, aristocratic mansions, and the treasures of the ages burned. Commanders marched armies through the streets to intimidate their opponents. When they fought, they did so during the day, and seldom did they pursue a fleeing adversary. In the early years, a defeated opponent might be sent into exile or allowed to retire to a monastery. Later, a demand for retribution led to the slaughter of hostages and prisoners, the mutilation of corpses, the lacquering of an enemy's skull for use as a drinking cup. By the end of the Ōnin war, Kyoto's palaces had become fields, the *shugo* had become pawns of their erstwhile retainers when they had not disappeared, and Yoshihisa had inherited an empty office. He died in 1489 while trying to subdue a recalcitrant retainer who had organized rustic warriors in Ōmi to expropriate estates that paid tithes to nobles and temples.

The shogunate became irrelevant to power struggles that rent Japan. *Shugo* families split in fratricidal disputes over titles and the power to control land holdings that they conferred. Retainers embroiled themselves in factional disputes or betrayed one lord for another. Believing their honor to be at stake in every encounter, they fought bloody duels over imagined slights. Fortunately for the residents of Kyoto, even before the Ōnin war drew to an inconclusive close in 1477, battlefields had shifted to the provinces, closer to the spoils of war.

Local Leagues

The power vacuum at the top provided an opportunity for locally based leagues (*ikki*—literally,

DOCUMENTS

The Journal of Sōchō

Written by Saiokuken Sōchō, an acclaimed master of linked verse and a Zen monk, these entries show how the poet received commissions to write poetry from a high shogunal official amid the ravages of civil war. During his travels around central Japan in search of patrons and poetic inspiration, Sōchō turned a critical eye on his society in describing people on the margins, merchants, sake brewers, impoverished samurai, and lazy priests.

1522: We crossed to Ōminato harbor in Ise and proceeded to Yamada, where we visited Ise shrine. The matter had been raised earlier of a thousand-verse sequence to be presented to the shrine, and I had invited the priest Sōseki down for that purpose. He arrived near the end of the seventh month, and we began composing the sequence soon thereafter, on the fourth of the eighth month. Two hundred verses a day for five days. The work was commissioned as a votive sequence by the present shogunal deputy, Hosokawa Takakuni, when he returned to the capital from Ōmi. His opening verse (*hokku*) for the first hundred verses was sent from Kyoto:

> Everywhere aglow
> in the morning sunlight—
> the haze!
>> Takakuni
> Plum trees blossom,
> willows bend, and even
> the wind abates!
>> Sōchō

Sōseki then left for Owari. Knowing it was likely to snow before long, I decided to set out for the north on the sixteenth. There has been fighting in this province beyond Kumozu river and Anonotsu, making it difficult to get from place to place.

Anonotsu has been desolate for more than ten years, and nothing but ruins remains of its four or five thousand villages and temples. Stands of reeds and mugwort, no chickens or dogs, rare even to hear the cawing of a crow.

1525: Asahina Tokishige came to visit. We had a pleasant conversation by the hearth about frustrations at year's end, the repayment of loans, the allotment of rice stipends, and the lack of enough of anything, during the course of which I rambled on in my dotage as follows:

Item. There is nothing like going into business for profit. People who do so never speak of gods or Buddhas, give no thought to the world's prosperity or decline, know nothing of the elegant pursuits of snow, moon, and blossoms, grow distant from friends, reject appeals from their near and dear, and spend every waking moment thinking of making money. But that is how to get on in the world. Note, though, that those with even nominal lands, and monks with temple properties, should not take an interest in business. But note too that the sake dealers in the capital, Sakai, the Southern Capital, Sakamoto, and also in this part of the country do very well.

Item. Consider the low-ranking samurai, starving with no land to call his own. There is no help for him. He obviously cannot part from his wife and children. Their food runs

union of minds) to escape from the vertical hierarchies that had tied them to aristocratic, ecclesiastical, and military patrons. In 1487 rustic warriors in Yamashiro united province-wide to resist the incursions of overlords. Theirs was a horizontal alliance of self-reliant men of no particular pedigree. They developed tactics of mass demonstrations organized village by village. On out, and the woman must draw water and the man must gather brushwood. Their children are taken away before their eyes to slave for others. Their bowing and scraping is pitiful. Driven to that pass, those with self-respect may even do away with themselves. Someone said that to such unfortunates one should give a little something. That is the essence of charity. Of course one must give as well to those who beg by the roadside and wait by houses and gates.

Item. Lion dancers, monkey trainers, bell ringers, bowl beaters, and the like have something they can do for a living. People somehow provide for them, though their need is no greater than that of those I have just mentioned. It is the latter, for whom there is no help at all, who are the world's true unfortunates, even more than lepers and beggars. They are truly wretched.

Item. People who pursue the study of Zen are embarked on a difficult and estimable course. But those who are perfunctory in their Zen practice, even highly placed samurai in the capital and provinces, easily fall into error.

Item. Where today can one find an inspirational teacher of the doctrines of "separate transmission outside the teachings" and "nonverbalization"? Some call today's Zen practitioners a pack of devils, of the lowest guttersnipe sort. Abbots, monks, and novices these days consort with the high and mighty, curry donations from provincial gentry, pursue their austerities only when it suits them, run hither and yon all day, and dally with other practitioners. But who are the masters they practice with themselves? Some say it is far better to repeat the Holy Name [of Amida]. I am more attracted to those who follow a simple and ignorant practice, as I do.

Item. Acquiring bows, horses, and armor and maintaining good retainers—that is the way of the samurai. But there is no need to run out and buy things for which one has no specific purpose. Constant spending and extravagance must be avoided, I am told.

1526, fourth month: We crossed the Mountain of Meeting and entered the capital at Awataguchi without meeting a soul. This route used to be filled with horses and palanquins, everyone bumping shoulders and tilting hats to squeeze by. As I looked out over the city, I saw not one in ten of the houses that had been there formerly, either rich or poor. The sight of tilled fields around farmhouses, with the Imperial Palace in the midst of summer barley, was too much for words.

1527: On the fourth of the third month I left Yashima. A village called Minakuchi [Water's mouth] in Kōga continued for about ten chō, and I recalled the old palace built here once for an imperial pilgrimage to Ise. There are many toll gates in these parts, and as we went along people would shout "Stop! Toll!" at every one, whereupon I composed the following:

I must have appeared
at the water's mouth,
for at every gate
"Stop! Toll!" is what
they cry together.

Source: H. Mack Horton, trans. and anno., *The Journal of Sōchō* (Stanford, Calif.: Stanford University Press, 2002), pp. 15–16, 84–86, 104, 143.

occasion they looted, burned, and killed. Between 1428 and 1526, twenty-four *ikki* demanding debt amnesty from moneylenders erupted in Kyoto and its environs. Many were at least partially suc- cessful; indeed they ceased to be a threat only when moneylenders mobilized Kyoto towns- people to go on the offensive in 1536. They took the lead in consolidating the cityscape into two

Map **13.1**   **Kyoto in the Tenth–Eleventh Centuries and Its Transformation in the Sixteenth Century**

sectors—for defense and in building fortifications. (See Map 13.1.) They had already organized neighborhood associations for crime prevention, mutual protection, and firefighting. When the shogun proved unable to defend the city, the associations hired mercenaries. Many moneylenders helped build the temple fortresses belonging to the Lotus sect that dominated the commoners' religious life.

The Lotus League (*hokke ikki*) attracted adherents in urban areas with its exclusive faith in the saving power of the *Lotus Sutra*. In teaching that this world can be the Buddhist paradise, it encouraged worldly success. It provided institutional support independent of traditional elites, thus making it feasible for moneylenders to end their subordination to Enryakuji. It supported a paramilitary organization useful in times of disorder. With the shogun on the run

after 1521, believers in the *Lotus Sutra* massed in tens of thousands not only to defend the city but to attack military commanders and adherents of different Buddhist sects. They withheld some rents, collected taxes, and settled disputes, in effect setting up a commoner-run city government, though the merchants in Sakai went further in developing the instruments of self-rule. Enryakuji was the first to organize opposition to the league, soon joined by a military commander in Ōmi. In eight days of fighting in 1536, the attackers destroyed all the Lotus temples, burned the entire lower city and one-third of the upper, and slaughtered men, women, and children suspected of being true believers. Kyoto suffered worse damage than it had during the Ōnin war. From a military point of view, suppression had to be brutal because the Hokke teachings placed commoners on the same level as their masters.

The most radical renunciation of allegiance to overlords came in the One-Mind Leagues (*Ikkō ikki*) that flourished in central Japan after the Ōnin war. Adherents to the True Pure Land school of Buddhism believed that Amida offered salvation to all who accepted his gift of faith. Since everyone was equal in Amida's eyes, the One-Mind Leagues rejected both religious and secular hierarchies. Although their adherents lived in largely autonomous communities organized around a lay teacher and temple, they were linked to a nationwide organization through the sect's headquarters situated in the fortified temple complex called Ishiyama Honganji built in Osaka in 1532. The most militant and long lasting of the One-Mind Leagues on the Noto peninsula held out against warlords from 1488 to 1578.

Rise of Warlords

Out of the same crucible of lawlessness and disorder that produced *ikki* appeared military men determined to create a new vertical hierarchy. Unlike the *shugo* who depended on the shogun for patents of rule, the new leaders, called *daimyo,* relied on nothing other than military force. Daimyo constructed domains from the inside out. They ignored provincial boundaries in favor of natural defenses—rivers, mountains, and seas. Their domains were much smaller than those held by the former *shugo,* but they were more secure. To the impoverishment of the Kyoto aristocrats and temples, they tolerated no absentee proprietors. In order to survive, monarch and court sold themselves as arbiters of taste and erected toll barriers to tax goods in transit.

Warlords acquired territory through conquest, alliance, or marriage. Territory came with fighting men, the samurai, and cultivators, often one and the same. Samurai were incorporated into the warlord's retainer band through an oath of loyalty in return for land or perhaps a stipend. Sometimes this meant confirming a samurai's hold over the land he brought with him, though when possible warlords preferred to move retainers to a different area, often with the promise of a raise, in order to break their ties with former supporters. Even village headmen swore allegiance to a warlord in return for protection. They were expected to fight in time of war in addition to cultivating their land, maintaining order, and collecting taxes.

Warlords tried to mold their territories and retainer bands into a cohesive unit. They surveyed land to find out how much it produced and who was responsible for its taxes. They promoted irrigation works to open new land. They forbade cultivators to move away. They relaxed restrictions on commerce. They issued laws to maintain order and tame the samurai. They suppressed private feuds by announcing that in cases of quarrels, both sides would be judged equally guilty and punished accordingly. They wrote house codes that warned against fomenting factions or indulging in luxury. Income and responsibility rewarded dedication to duty, loyalty, and obedience. In this way, warlords created competing power blocs, centered on castle towns, each based on the principle of vertical hierarchy.

The most notable warlords of the sixteenth century were self-made men who rose from obscurity to become mighty conquerors, a process summarized in the term *gekokujō* (the overthrow of those above by those below). Maeda Toshiie of Kaga started his career as a low-ranking retainer. He initiated land surveys and reorganized his retainer band to reduce its autonomy. Takeda Shingen fought nearly constantly from age twenty to his death. Realizing that military force legitimizes nothing, he claimed that his quest for personal gain was done in the name of public authority (*kōgi*). The political experiments tried by Maeda, Takeda, and others laid the groundwork for Japan's unification through military conquest.

The Conquerors

The earliest conqueror was Oda Nobunaga, born to a junior branch of an obscure lineage. His first accomplishment was to wipe out his kin. He brought masterless samurai who had been living by robbery and extortion into his retainer band and demanded that they swear loyalty to him personally. Although Nobunaga commanded fewer troops than his opponents, he used them more effectively. He marched on Kyoto in 1568 on the pretext of installing Ashikaga Yoshiaki as shogun. There he provided sorely needed material assistance to the impoverished court. When Yoshiaki proved recalcitrant, Nobunaga drove him out of Kyoto in 1573, bringing the Ashikaga Dynasty to an ignominious end.

Nobunaga's signal achievement was to destroy the Buddhist temples' military, economic, and political power. He began with Enryakuji, which had allied with his enemies after he seized some of its land. In 1571 he burned three thousand buildings in its temple complex on Mount Hiei and massacred the monks. By threat or force, he expropriated the holdings of several other monasteries and ordered them to reduce their personnel. Between 1570 and 1580 he waged war against the *Ikkō ikki,* showing no mercy to its adherents and slaughtering tens of thousands. To destroy the fortified headquarters at Ishiyama Honganji, he built armored ships outfitted with cannon. As a result of his efforts, the power of the Buddhist establishment, which had characterized Japan's Middle Ages, was permanently eliminated.

As befit a man who aspired to bring the entire realm under one military regime, Nobunaga designed new economic and social policies. He freed merchants from having to seek the protection of guilds in return for monetary contributions called "thank-you money." He eliminated toll barriers within the areas he controlled. He tried to stabilize the exchange rates between different types of coins, and he minted his own, the first time since 958 that a Japanese government had issued currency. He collected tax registers to gauge how much his land was worth and assert his authority over its disposal. In this way, he could argue that his retainers held their ancestral lands only at his pleasure. They had to be willing to move from place to place as he deemed fit; otherwise they would be marked as traitors and

destroyed. Fearing Nobunaga's growing power, one of his generals, Akechi Mitsuhide, launched a surprise attack on Nobunaga in 1562. Nobunaga and his son committed suicide.

Nobunaga's avenger, Toyotomi Hideyoshi, exemplified the social turbulence of the time. He came from little more than cultivator stock, rising through his own efforts to become hegemon of Japan. Although Nobunaga had pacified central Japan, independent warlords still controlled northern Japan and most of the western reaches of Honshu, Kyushu, and Shikoku. Hideyoshi either subdued them or so intimidated them that they acknowledged him as overlord. When he defeated the Shimazu of Satsuma in 1586, he allowed them to keep a portion of their domain, and he did the same for the Mōri of Chōshū. Preferring the security of subordination to the vicissitudes of battle, the northern warlords surrendered without a fight after he defeated the Hōjō (no relation to the Kamakura Hōjō) at Odawara in 1590. For the first time in over 250 years, Japan had a single ruler.

Although Hideyoshi epitomized the self-made man and created a new government structure, he looked to the monarchy to validate his rule. He rebuilt the Kyoto palace and paid for court ceremonies. He took the name Fujiwara and had himself appointed retired regent (*taikō*). He allowed his chief supporters and even his rivals to remain as daimyo of domains, though he carefully interspersed them to prevent collusion. He rewarded his faithful supporter Tokugawa Ieyasu with the eight Kantō provinces after the defeat of the Hōjō in a move that shifted Ieyasu from his homeland in Mikawa to an unfamiliar region swarming with rustic warriors. Hideyoshi commanded enormous resources through the land he controlled and his taxes on commerce in Osaka and Sakai. Rather than spend his own money, he had the daimyo pay for construction projects and provide military service on demand. He created an ideological basis for his rule by claiming descent from the sun god who had entered his mother's womb, a drama he enacted on the Nō stage for the benefit of aristocrats, daimyo, and foreign visitors.

Korean invasion. This detail from a scroll painted by a Chinese participant shows a Japanese ship set on fire by Ming pursuers. Samurai armed with swords leap into the waves. *(Laurie Platt Winfrey, Inc.)*

Desiring order and stability above all, Hideyoshi tried to ensure that no one would be able to rise as he had. Building on the work of his rivals, he instituted a nationwide land survey to determine the extent of arable land and to fix a name to every plot. Hideyoshi's land survey marked the beginning of efforts to quantify landholdings and estimate tax revenues. By eliminating intermediary claims to landed income, the land survey marked the end of the largely defunct estates. He ordered subsidiary castles torn down and destroyed the remaining fortified neighborhoods in Kyoto. In 1588, he also tried to insist on a rigid status distinction between samurai and commoners by forbidding all but samurai from wearing two swords, one long and one short. Thereafter, commoners might own swords, but they could not put them on display. Hideyoshi issued a series of decrees prohibiting samurai from leaving their lord's service to become merchants or cultivators and preventing farmers from deserting their fields to become city folk. Although it proved impossible to make clear distinctions between various statuses and some domains such as Satsuma or Tosa continued to recognize rustic samurai (*gōshi*), Hideyoshi's intent remained the law of the land until 1871.

In 1592, Hideyoshi turned his attention to an invasion of Korea. He mobilized 158,000 samurai supported by 9,200 sailors and kept 100,000 men as a backup force, one indication of how heavily militarized Japanese society had become. In his most grandiloquent pronouncements, Hideyoshi promised to conquer both Korea and China and put the Japanese monarch on the Chinese throne with Hideyoshi's adopted heir as regent. (He later withdrew the adoption when his concubine bore a son.) The first invasion went as far as Pyongyang. It drove the

Korean king from Seoul, decimated the regular Korean army, and devastated the countryside. It was forced to retreat when supplies ran low, the Ming came to Korean aid, and the Korea admiral Yi Sunsin won a major sea battle with armor-plated ships and cannon. Hideyoshi tried again in 1597. When he died the next year, the Japanese troops in Korea decamped to participate in the succession dispute to come.

Hideyoshi had hoped to pass his dominion to his son by establishing a balance of power in the five-man advisory council created shortly before his death. Its most powerful member was Tokugawa Ieyasu, who like Nobunaga and Hideyoshi came from an obscure background in central Japan. Ieyasu strengthened his retainers' devotion and loyalty by making them completely dependent on him for their rewards. Rather than kill his kin, he left them with the original Matsudaira name when he took the Tokugawa name in 1566. He honored them as his relatives while he relied on men he had made to be his advisers and generals. Upon moving from central Japan to the Kantō plain, he turned the village of Edo into his castle town and started to build an administrative and personnel system based on the initiatives of his peers. He fought only those battles he knew he could win. By the time the advisory council fell apart in 1600, he had neutralized, compromised, or won over most of his rivals.

The battle of Sekigahara in 1600 brought the civil wars to a close. Although Hideyoshi's son remained ensconced in Osaka castle, his supporters were samurai who had lost their masters (*rōnin*) and other warriors who found that peace left little outlet for their talents. When Ieyasu decided to move against the castle in two campaigns in 1615 and 1616, the resistance was fierce but futile. Another threat to peace was the Shimabara Christian rebellion of 1637 in Kyushu, the last of the religiously based *ikki*. Like its predecessors, it was suppressed with the slaughter of approximately ten thousand men, women, and children. Its end marked the last military conflict Japan was to suffer for over two hundred years.

SUMMARY

The warfare of the middle ages destroyed Japan's estate system and forged new political institutions from the ground up. Although religion continued to be important in people's lives, religious institutions lost economic and political power. Shifting patterns in marriage and inheritance practices affirmed patriarchal authority in the ruling class. The popularity of the tea ceremony among merchants prefigured the spread of popular culture centered on townspeople.

SUGGESTED READING

For political histories, see M. S. Adolphson, *The Gates of Power: Monks, Courtiers, and Warriors in Premodern Japan* (2000), and A. Goble, *Kenmu: Go-Daigo's Revolution* (1996). For the fourteenth-century transformation, see J. P. Mass, ed. *The Origins of Japan's Medieval World: Courtiers, Clerics, Warriors, and Peasants in the Fourteenth Century* (1997). For villages, see H. Tonomura, *Community and Commerce in Late Medieval Japan: The Corporate Villages of Tokuchin-ho* (1992). For an imaginative exploration of the late fifteenth and sixteenth centuries, see M. B. Berry, *The Culture of Civil War in Kyoto* (1994). For trade and commerce, see S. Gay, *The Moneylenders of Late Medieval Kyoto* (2001). For culture, see D. Keene, *Yoshimasa and the Silver Pavilion: The Creation of the Soul of Japan* (2003). An innovative study of the estate system is in T. Keirstead, *The Geography of Power in Medieval Japan* (1992). See also J. W. Hall and T. Toyoda, *Japan in the Muromachi Age* (1977).

The Ming Empire in China (1368–1600)

The Ming Dynasty was founded by a man who lived through the disorder of the late Yuan and knew poverty firsthand. His efforts to impose order on Chinese society sometimes took draconian forms, but his thirty-year reign brought China peace and stability. Although he and some of his successors treated officials cruelly, in time competition to join officaldom surpassed Song levels. Literati culture was especially vibrant in the economically well-developed Jiangnan region, south of the lower Yangzi River. As population increased, both rural and urban areas took on distinctive traits. Rural areas differed greatly by region, with powerful lineages, tenantry, and absentee landlords much more common in some areas than others. The merchant-centered culture of cities found expression in vernacular fiction and drama, published in increasing quantity and accessible even to those with rudimentary educations.

Since the Ming Dynasty was succeeded by a non-Chinese conquest dynasty (the Qing Dynasty of the Manchus, 1644–1911), the Ming was the last of the native dynasties. Historians have therefore often turned to it for a baseline against which modern change has been judged. How did China compare to western Europe in the fifteenth and sixteenth centuries? Had China already begun to fall behind western Europe in technology, standard of living, or pace of change? At the local level, were communities becoming more integrated into the realm as standardizing policies and economic linkages spread? Or were they becoming more diverse as the economy developed in different directions in different places? A related set of questions concerns the government and the educated elite. How effective and how adaptable was the government? Why did educated men continue to seek office when the government so often treated them poorly? What was the impact on the educated class of the changes in the examination system and the explosion of printing?

THE FOUNDING OF THE MING DYNASTY

The founder of the Ming Dynasty, Zhu Yuanzhang (1328–1398), started life at the bottom of society. His parents often moved to look for work or evade rent collectors. His home region in Anhui province was hit by drought and then plague in the 1340s, and when he was only sixteen years old, his father, oldest brother, and brother's wife all died, leaving two penniless boys with three bodies to bury. A neighbor let them bury them in his field, but they had no way to provide coffins or anything to eat. With no relatives to turn to, Zhu Yuanzhang asked a monastery to take him on as a novice. The monastery was short of funds itself, as its tenants could not pay their rent, and in less than two months, Zhu was sent out to beg for food. For the next three to four years, he traveled widely through central China. Not until he returned to the monastery did he learn to read.

A few years later, in 1351, a millenarian sect known as the Red Turbans rose in rebellion. The Red Turbans were affiliated with the White Lotus Society, whose teachings drew on Manichean ideas of the incompatibility of the forces of good and evil and the cult of the Maitreya Buddha, who would in the future bring his paradise to earth to relieve human suffering. The Red Turbans met with considerable success, even defeating Mongol cavalry. In the course of fighting the rebels, the Yuan government troops burned down Zhu Yuanzhang's temple. Zhu, then twenty-four, joined the rebels. The leaders of the Red Turbans were men of modest origins, and Zhu Yuanzhang rose quickly among them. One of the commanders let Zhu marry his daughter. Within a couple of years, Zhu had between twenty thousand and thirty thousand men fighting under him.

At this time there were strongmen all over China—some rebels, some loyal to the Yuan, but all trying to maintain control of a local base. Zhu quickly attracted some literati advisers who thought he had a chance to be the final victor and hoped to help shape his government. They encouraged him to gradually distance himself from the Red Turbans, whose millenarian beliefs did not appeal to the educated elite. In 1356 Zhu took Nanjing, made it his base, and tried to win over the local population by disciplining his soldiers.

Many of Zhu's followers developed into brilliant generals, and gradually they defeated one rival after another. In 1368 his armies took the Yuan capital (which the Yuan emperor and his closest followers had vacated just days before). Then forty years old, Zhu Yuanzhang declared himself emperor of the Ming Dynasty. The word *ming,* meaning bright, resonated with the Manichean strain in Red Turban ideology. His first reign period he called Hongwu ("abundantly martial"), and since he did not change the name of his reign period for the rest of his thirty-year reign, he is often referred to as the Hongwu emperor. It became the custom from this point on for emperors not to change their reign period names. Zhu Yuanzhang's posthumous temple name (the name used in the sacrifices to him after his death) is Taizu, so he is also called Ming Taizu.

Ming Taizu

In the milieu in which Taizu grew up, the deities in Daoist temples labeled "emperors," such as the Yellow Emperor and the Emperor of the Eastern Peak, provided a folk image of imperial rule. Taizu seems to have taken these divine autocrats as his model and did everything he could to elevate the position of emperor to their level. He required his officials to kneel when addressing him, and he did not hesitate to have them beaten in open court. He issued instructions to be read aloud to villagers, telling them to be filial to their parents, live in harmony with their neighbors, work contentedly at their occupations, and refrain from evil.

Taizu wanted a world in which everyone obeyed their superiors and those who committed evil acts were promptly punished. In order to lighten the weight of government exactions on the poor, he ordered a full-scale registration of cultivated land and population so that labor service and tax obligations could be assessed more fairly. Taizu called for the drafting of a new law code and took it through five revisions. He had legal experts compare every statute in it to the Tang code in his presence, but he made the final decisions.

Some Yuan practices Taizu retained. One was the strengthening of the provinces as the administrative layer between the central government and the prefectures. The creation of provinces should not be viewed as a decentralization of power, but a way for the central government to increase its supervision of the prefectures and counties. Another Yuan practice that Taizu retained was use of hereditary service obligations for artisan households that had to supply the palace or government as their tax obligation. The army too made use of hereditary households. Centuries earlier, during the Northern and Southern Dynasties, armies composed of men with inherited obligations to serve had been common. Among the non-Chinese in the north, the status was an honorable one, but in the south, the status became despised. In the Tang, the divisional militia, with its hereditary obligations, had worked well for a half-century, but then it was supplanted by recruited professional armies, a practice the Song retained. The Mongols, however, made military service a hereditary obligation as they did so much else, and the Ming took over this practice.

Under Taizu, the Ming army reached 1 million soldiers, drawn from the armies that had fought for control of China as well as some conscripts and some convicts. Once their families had been classed as military households, the family was responsible for supplying one soldier in succession, replacing ones who were injured, died, or deserted. Garrisons were concentrated

along the northern border and near the capital, each garrison allocated a tract of land that the soldiers took turns cultivating to supply their own food, a system that had been repeatedly tried since the Han Dynasty. Although in theory this system should have supplied the Ming with a large but inexpensive army, the reality was less satisfactory. Just as in earlier dynasties, garrisons were rarely self-sufficient, men compelled to become soldiers did not necessarily make good fighting men, and desertion was difficult to prevent.

Many of the soldiers in the Ming army were Mongols in Mongol units. Although anti-Mongol sentiment was strong among the rebels, Taizu recognized that the Yuan Dynasty had had the Mandate of Heaven and told Mongols that they would be welcome in his dynasty: "Those Mongols and Inner Asians who live on our land also are our children, and those among them who possess talent and ability also shall be selected and appointed to office by us."[1] Taizu did not try to conquer the Mongols, and Ming China did not extend into modern Inner Mongolia. Where it did expand was to the southwest. In the 1380s Ming took control of modern Yunnan and created the new province of Guizhou east of it.

Taizu had twenty-six sons, several in their teens by the time he became emperor, and he took measures to see that they and their descendants would not interfere in the government. The princes were sent out of the capital to fiefs, and Taizu issued rules that they and their descendants were not to take examinations, serve in office, or follow any sort of career other than specified military assignments. They were to live outside the capital, supported by government stipends.

Taizu had deeply ambivalent feelings about men of education and sometimes brutally humiliated them in open court. His behavior was so erratic that most likely he suffered from some

---

1. Cited in F. W. Mote, *Imperial China, 900–1800* (Cambridge, Mass.: Harvard University Press, 1999), p. 560.

form of mental illness. In 1376 Taizu had thousands of officials killed because they were found to have taken a shortcut in their handling of paperwork related to the grain tax. In 1380 Taizu concluded that his chancellor, Hu Wei-yong, was plotting to assassinate him. Anyone remotely connected to him was executed, the investigations taking nearly a decade, with as many as fifteen thousand people losing their lives. From 1380 on, Taizu acted as his own chancellor, dealing directly with the heads of departments and ministries.

As Taizu became more literate, he realized that scholars could criticize him in covert ways, using phrases that had double meanings or that sounded like words for "bandit," "monk," or the like. Even poems in private circulation could be used as evidence of subversive intent. When literary men began to avoid official life, Taizu made it illegal to turn down appointments or resign from office. He began falling into rages only his wife, Empress Ma, could stop. After her death in 1382, no one could calm him.

Chengzu

Taizu lived a long life, to seventy-one *sui*, outliving his eldest son, who had been his heir apparent. He made that son's eldest son the next heir, and this grandson succeeded to the throne at the age of twenty-one. (He is known as Huidi, or the Jianwen emperor.) Almost immediately, however, the eldest of Taizu's surviving sons by the empress, a man known then as the Prince of Yan, launched a military campaign to take the throne himself. After a three year civil war, he prevailed. He is known as Chengzu, or the Yongle emperor (r. 1403–1425).

Chengzu was a military man, like his father, and he was married to the daughter of a leading general, who encouraged his military interests. He directed the civil war himself and often led troops into battle, leading to victories over the Mongols. In 1406 he authorized a major expedition into Vietnam, which had been independent for over four centuries. Although the campaign was a success, the region was held

only two decades. Also like his father, Chengzu was willing to use terror to keep government officials in line. Quite a few officials serving Huidi resisted his usurpation. When the leading Confucian scholar, Fang Xiaoru, refused to draft the proclamation of his accession, Chengzu not only had him executed by dismemberment, but had his relatives and associates to the tenth degree executed as well, including all those who had been passed when he conducted the civil service examinations. Tens of thousands were killed.

Yet Chengzu also had impressive accomplishments. He put two thousand scholars to work making a 50-million word (22,938-chapter) compendium of knowledge, drawn from seven thousand books (the *Yongle Encyclopedia*). To assist those studying for the civil service examinations, he had a selection of texts from the Cheng-Zhu school of Confucianism compiled. He expanded and regularized the court diplomatic system.

Early in his reign, Chengzu decided to move the capital from Nanjing to Beijing, which had been his own base as a prince, as well as the capital during Yuan times. Construction employed hundreds of thousands of workers and lasted from 1407 to 1420. Although little of the original city walls and gates survives today, the palace complex remains, its layout and architecture still reflecting the fifteenth-century design. The city was a planned city, like Chang'an in Sui-Tang times, built near the site of the Yuan capital, but starting afresh. Like Chang'an, it was built on a north-south axis and consisted of boxes within boxes. The main outer walls were forty feet high and nearly fifteen miles around, pierced by nine gates. Inside it was the Imperial City, with government offices, and within that the Forbidden City, the palace itself, with close to ten thousand rooms. The main audience halls were arranged along the central axis, with vast courtyards between them where attending officials would stand or kneel. The design, as intended, awes all who enter.

The areas surrounding Beijing were not nearly as agriculturally productive as those around

Nanjing. To supply Beijing with grain, the Grand Canal was extensively renovated, broadening and deepening it and supplying it with more locks and dams. The fifteen thousand boats and one hundred sixty thousand soldiers of the transport army, who pulled loaded barges from the tow paths along the canal, became the lifeline of the capital.

Weaknesses of the Imperial Institution

Ming Taizu had decreed that succession should go to the eldest son of the empress, or the latter's eldest son if he predeceased his father, the system generally, but not inflexibly, followed by earlier dynasties. In Ming times, the flaws in this system became apparent as one mediocre, obtuse, or erratic emperor followed another. Yingzong (r. 1436–1450), who came to the throne at age eight, liked to play soldier; with the encouragement of his favorite eunuch, he led an army against the Mongols when he was twenty-one years old, leading to the destruction of his fifty-thousand-man army and his own capture. The Mongols found him so useless that they returned him the next year, after his brother had been enthroned. Xianzong (r. 1465–1488), after coming to the throne at age sixteen, let himself be manipulated by a palace lady almost twenty years his senior; she had his children born to other women systematically killed. Wuzong (r. 1505–1521) willfully defied established practices and spent much of his time drunk. Shizong (r. 1522–1567) refused to treat his predecessor as his adoptive father. Subject to fits of rage, he was so cruel to his palace ladies that a group of them tried to murder him in 1542. In 1565 the brave official Hai Rui submitted a memorial saying the emperor had failed as a man, a father, and a ruler and had been a disaster for the country. Shenzong, the Wanli emperor (r. 1573–1620), was intelligent but refused to hold court for years at a time and allowed memorials to pile up unopened and vacancies to go unfilled.

Because Ming Taizu had abolished the position of chancellor, the emperor had to turn to members of the inner court to help him. At first, relatively junior men in the Hanlin Academy served as secretaries, a practice that became regularized as a kind of cabinet of grand secretaries. Although they were given concurrent titles as vice ministers to enhance their standing, their lack of actual administrative experience hampered their dealings with the outer court. Added to this, they had to work with the eunuchs to manage the flow of paperwork, and some of the stigma attached to eunuchs spilled over to them.

Eunuchs became as serious a problem in Ming times as they had in late Han and late Tang. From the time of Ming Taizu on, eunuchs were employed in the palace, their numbers gradually growing. As in earlier dynasties, emperors often preferred the always compliant eunuchs to high-minded, moralizing civil service officials. A eunuch bureaucracy developed, headed by the director of ceremonial, who was responsible for seeing that the emperor was attended at all times, that security was maintained, and that documents were properly handled. When the emperor allowed it, the director of ceremonial became a kind of chief of staff who could impose his will on the civil service. In 1420 Chengzu set up the Eastern Depot, headed by a eunuch, which acted as a secret service and investigated cases of suspected corruption and sedition. During the late fifteenth century, the eunuch bureaucracy grew as large as the civil service, each with roughly twelve thousand positions. After 1500, the eunuch bureaucracy grew much more rapidly and by the mid-sixteenth century, seventy thousand eunuchs were in service throughout the country, with ten thousand in the capital. Eunuch control over vital government processes, such as appointments, was especially a problem during the long reign of the derelict Shenzong (1573–1620).

Confucian writers generally vilified eunuchs, as though they were by nature evil, and rarely showed sympathy for their unfortunate circumstances. Eunuchs were essentially slaves. Many were acquired by dubious means as children, often from non-Chinese areas in the south, and once they were castrated, they had no option but to serve the imperial family. Zheng He, for instance, was taken from Yunnan as a boy of ten by a Ming general assigned the task of securing boys to be castrated. Society considered eunuchs the basest of servants and heaped scorn on them.

What was a conscientious official to do, given the flaws in the Ming government? Officials serving in local posts could do their best to make the government work, even when they knew that needed reforms would not be made. Some, discouraged, left office after a few years. If they had enough property to live on, they could enjoy the status of retired official and concentrate on matters more within their control, such as writing local histories or collecting works of calligraphy.

Although the educated public complained about the performance of emperors, no one proposed or even imagined alternatives to imperial rule. High officials were forced to find ways to work around uncooperative emperors but were not able to put in place institutions that would limit the damage an emperor could do. They came to prefer weak emperors who let them take care of the government, knowing that strong emperors often acted erratically. Probably one of the reasons so many Ming emperors resisted their officials' efforts to manage them was that the officials were indeed trying to keep emperors engaged in tasks where they could do relatively little harm.

Many officials did in fact risk their careers, and sometimes their lives, trying to admonish emperors. The tradition of protesting against evil officials, harmful policies, and wrong-headed imperial decisions was strong throughout the Ming, though it rarely led to the results the protesters sought. In 1376 when Taizu asked for criticism, Ye Boju submitted a memorial objecting to harsh punishment of officials for minor lapses. In it he noted that many officials considered themselves fortunate to be out of office. Taizu, incensed, had Ye brought to the capital in chains and let him starve to death in prison. A few decades later, many of Huidi's top officials

protested Chengzu's usurpation, with dire consequences to themselves and their families. In 1519 when Emperor Wuzong announced plans to make a tour to the southern provinces, he was flooded with memorials objecting to his decision. Over a hundred officials staged a protest by kneeling in front of the palace. Wuzong was outraged and ordered the officials to remain kneeling for three days, after which he had them flogged; eleven died. A few years later, in 1524, during the crisis over Shizong's refusal to treat the previous emperor as his adopted father, hundreds of officials again gathered at the palace gate. The emperor had 134 of them imprisoned, and 16 died of the floggings they received. The Confucian tradition celebrated these acts of political protest as heroic. Rarely, however, did they succeed in moving an emperor to change his mind; more often they exacerbated factional tensions within the government.

DIPLOMACY AND DEFENSE

The Ming government faced both new and old challenges along its borders. Until 1600 and the rise of the Manchus, the Ming looked on the Mongols as their primary military threat. The coast at this time was presenting new challenges. Ming China was being drawn more deeply into maritime trading networks, which brought both piracy and new sources of wealth.

Early in the Ming, the government expanded and regularized the court diplomatic system, trying to make it conform to the idealized view of how it had functioned in the Han and Tang dynasties, when China had dominated East Asia, rather than in Song times, when a multistate system had operated and Song had paid tribute to its northern neighbors. To the Ming court, the arrival of envoys from dozens of countries, bringing their strange or valuable goods with them, served to confirm China's moral centrality. As in earlier dynasties, countries that sent missions had their own agendas and were as eager to benefit from the trade that the missions made possible as to stay on China's good side. Vietnam, for instance, regularly sent missions to the Ming court after it expelled the Ming invaders.

Zheng He's Voyages

It was in order to invite more countries to send missions that Emperor Chengzu authorized an extraordinary series of voyages to the Indian Ocean under the command of the Muslim eunuch Zheng He (1371–1433). Zheng He's father had made the Hajj to Mecca, and the voyages followed old Arab trade routes. The first of the seven voyages was made by a fleet of 317 ships, of which 62 were huge "treasure ships," 440 feet long. Each expedition involved from twenty thousand to thirty-two thousand men. Their itineraries included stops in Vietnam, Malaysia, islands of Indonesia, Sri Lanka, India, and, in the later voyages, Hormuz on the coast of Persia and east Africa (see Map 14.1). At each stop, Zheng He would go ashore to visit rulers, transmit messages of China's peaceful intentions, and bestow lavish gifts. Rulers were invited to come to China or send envoys, many of whom were accommodated on the return voyages. Chengzu was delighted in the exotic things the fleet brought back, such as giraffes and lions from Africa, fine cotton cloth from India, and gems and spices from Southeast Asia. These expeditions were not voyages of discovery; they followed established routes and pursued diplomatic, not commercial, goals.

Why were these voyages abandoned? Officials complained of their cost and modest return. As a consequence, after 1474, all of the remaining ships with three or more masts were broken up and used for lumber. Not long after that, the more modest expeditions of Vasco de Gama and Christopher Columbus changed the course of world history.

The Mongols and the Great Wall

The early Ming emperors held Mongol fighting men in awe and saw in them the potential for another great military machine of the sort Chinggis had put together. Both Taizu and Chengzu were determined to avoid the fate of the Song Dynasty, which had to pay off its powerful northern neighbors. Both emperors personally led armies into Mongolia. Chengzu, in fact, died on his fifth campaign in 1424, at age sixty-four.

As it turned out, the Mongols in Ming times never formed the sort of federation that could have seriously threatened China. After the last Yuan emperor retreated to Mongolia, he did not find it easy to keep the Mongols united under his leadership, since his loss of China discredited him. Ensuing Mongol civil wars weakened Mongolia and led to division. Through much of the Ming, the 3 million or so Mongols were loosely divided into six groups, located in today's Inner Mongolia, Manchuria, Mongolia, or north of those areas. Under Taizu and Chengzu, the Ming sent large and well-provisioned armies into Mongol territory, with as many as two hundred fifty thousand troops. Such campaigns were extremely expensive and did not accomplish much, given the Mongols' mobility. Later in the dynasty, the Ming was less inclined to send armies into Mongolia and concentrated on defending its borders against attack.

Although in Ming times, the Mongols were never united in a pan-Mongol federation, groups of Mongols could and did raid, and twice they threatened the dynasty: in 1449, when Esen, the khan of the Western Mongols, captured the emperor, and in 1550, when Beijing was surrounded by the forces of Altan Khan, khan of the Mongols in Inner Mongolia. The Ming was very reluctant to grant any privileges to Mongol leaders, such as trading posts along the borders, and wanted the different groups of Mongols to trade only through the envoy system. Repeatedly Mongol envoys said friction could be reduced if regularized trade could be introduced, but until 1570, when an agreement was reached with Altan Khan, the Ming court refused.

Two important developments shaped later Ming-Mongol relations: the building of the Great Wall and the Mongols' forging of close ties

THE VOYAGES OF ZHENG HE, 1405–1433

Map 14.1   **Ming Empire**

with Tibetan Buddhism. Work on the wall began by the mid-fifteenth century, when administrators of the western sections of the border began connecting principal garrison points and had some successes in trapping contingents of Mongol cavalry. Extending the wall was later seen as a solution to the deadlock between officials who argued that the Mongols could be managed by allowing more trade and those who insisted that no concessions be made to them.

Much of the Ming Great Wall survives today. It is about 1,500 miles long, from northeast of Beijing into Gansu province. In the eastern 500 miles, the walls average about 35 feet high and 20 feet across, with towers every half-mile for lookouts. The wall itself is faced with brick much of the way, giving it an imposing appearance that greatly impressed the first westerners who saw it.

Although there was considerable trade between Tibet and China through Sichuan and

Yunnan, Ming China did not have close diplomatic ties to Tibet, then largely ruled by the major monasteries. When Tibetan monasteries needed military assistance, they called for help from competing Mongol leaders, and many struggles were decided by Mongol military intervention. Tsong-kha-pa (1357–1419) founded the Yellow Hat or Gelug-pa sect, whose heads later became known as the Dalai Lamas. In 1577 the third Dalai Lama accepted the invitation of Altan Khan to visit Mongolia, and the khan declared Tibetan Buddhism to be the official religion of all the Mongols. The Dalai Lama gave the khan the title "King of Religion" and the khan swore that the Mongols would renounce blood sacrifice. When the third Dalai Lama's reincarnation was found to be the great-grandson of Altan Khan, the ties between Tibet and Mongol, not surprisingly, became even stronger.

Trade and Piracy Along China's Coasts

The Ming court's obsession with defending against the Mongols was not because its other borders posed no problems. The court wanted trade subordinated to diplomacy and stipulated that envoys from the Philippines were supposed to enter only through the port of Fuzhou, those from Japan only through Ningbo, those from Indonesia only through Guangzhou, and so on. Moreover, the size and frequency of missions was restricted; Japanese embassies, for instance, were not to call more than once in ten years or bring more than two ships with three hundred men. In the sixteenth century, this formal system proved unable to contain the emergence of an international East Asian maritime trading community composed of Japanese, Portuguese, Spanish, Dutch, and Chinese merchants and adventurers. Because the profits to be had from maritime trade were high, both open and clandestine trade took place all along the coast.

Boats leaving China carried silk and porcelains; those entering it brought silver from Peruvian and Mexican mines, transported via Manila, to pay for the Chinese goods. Boats laden with goods attracted pirates. Pirates grew so strong that they took to raiding the coast from Shandong to Guangzhou. Instead of trying to suppress the pirates by expanding its navy, the Ming government forced people to move away from the coast, hoping to starve out the pirates. Anti-pirate efforts did not have much success until maritime trade restrictions were eased in the late sixteenth century. Under the new policies, Portugal was permitted to set up a trading base at Macao in 1557, a base it held until 1999.

Besides stimulating the Ming economy, the expansion of maritime trade brought New World crops to China. Sweet potatoes, maize, peanuts, tomatoes, chili peppers, tobacco, and other crops were quickly introduced into China. Sweet potatoes and maize in particular facilitated population growth because they could be grown on land that had not been cultivated because it was too sandy or too steep. Spanish and Portuguese ships also began to bring missionaries, with radically different sets of ideas about the nature of the world (see **Connections: Europe Enters the Scene**).

SOCIAL AND CULTURAL TRENDS

From the founding of the Ming until about 1500, China recovered from the wars and dislocations of the Yuan period, and attempts were made to stabilize society. By the sixteenth century, however, Chinese society and culture were breaking free of many of the restraints that the early Ming government had tried to impose on them, and social and cultural change sped up.

The Educated Class and the Examination Life

Despite the harsh and arbitrary ways in which Ming emperors treated their civil servants, educated men were as eager to enter the bureaucracy as in earlier ages. As discussed in Chapter 12, civil service examinations played only a very small part in the recruitment of officials during the Yuan period. In Ming times, the examinations more than regained their significance as the most prestigious way to enter government service. To a greater degree than in Tang or Song times, the Ming examination system created a nationwide culture for all those who participated. All had to learn to write in the approved "eight-legged" style, which emphasized reasoning by analogy and pairing statements. The orthodoxy of Zhu Xi's teachings was an integral part of the Ming system. All had to study the Four Books and Zhu Xi's interpretations of them. Since Zhu Xi considered writing poetry of no value to moral cultivation, the poetic composition component of the examinations was dropped.

Another new feature of the Ming examination system was a screening test taken at the province level, adding to the number of tests a successful candidate would eventually have to pass. There were thus three principal degrees: the *shengyuan,* at the county or prefectural level; the *juren,* at the province level; and the *jinshi,* those selected at the final capital examination. Surprisingly, fewer men made it to the top in Ming times than in Song times. In contrast to the 135 *jinshi* per year in Southern Song plus the 149 per year given at the same time by the Jin, the Ming average was only 89 per year.

Another difference between the Song and Ming systems was that the Ming made a more concerted effort to ensure that the wealthy and cultured Jiangnan area did not dominate the examination results. Quotas were established for the number of candidates each province could send on to the capital. In 1397 all of those passed at the palace examination were southerners, leading Taizu to execute two of the examiners. Taizu retested everyone and passed only northerners. Thereafter, the examiners considered regional origin and tried for a balance. After 1427, northern candidates were ensured 35 percent of the places.

The lowest degree holders, the *shengyuan,* had to pass tests periodically to retain their status and compete for the privilege of traveling to the provincial capital to take the *juren* examination. By 1500, there were about thirty thousand *shengyuan* in the country (about one in three thousand people, counting women and children). Since only a small number of the *shengyuan* became *juren* in each triennial exam, taking exams became a way of life for most degree holders.

Preparation for the examinations required, in essence, learning a different language—the classical written language, which was quite different from everyday spoken language. Education thus was best started young. Moreover, the young are usually more adept at memorizing long texts, a necessary part of examination preparation. Calligraphy counted at this level, since tests were not recopied by clerks until the provincial level. Literati families who started to teach their sons at age four or five had a significant advantage.

As in earlier periods, well-off families hired tutors for their boys, but schools became more

Ming Examination Degrees

Degree	How Attained	Benefits	Likely Age	Likely Percentage Passed
Shengyuan	Pass test to enter county or prefecture school	Exempt from labor service; may take test to qualify for provincial exams; need to recertify regularly	17–30	Highly variable
Juren	Pass provincial examinations	Permanently qualified to take capital examinations; may receive less desired appointments	20–30	2–4%
Jinshi	Pass capital and palace examinations	Qualified for entry-level official appointment	30–40	7–9%

Figure 14.1 **Examination Cells.** The spare cells that candidates occupied during the three days of the examination were furnished only with two boards, which could be arranged to make a bed or a desk and seat.

and more available in Ming times. Families that for generations had pursued other careers, such as physician or merchant, had more opportunities than ever before to attain success through the exams (see **Biography: Tan Yunxian, Woman Doctor**). Lineages were especially active in setting up and sometimes endowing schools for their members. Because the lineage as a whole would enjoy the prestige that came with examination success, lineage leaders were willing to invest in the education of any talented boy in the lineage.

The provincial and capital examinations had three sessions spread out over a week, and involved a series of essays. In the first session, the essays were on passages from the Four Books and the classic of the candidate's choice. In the second and third sessions, candidates had to write essays on practical policy issues and a passage from the *Classic of Filial Piety.* In addition, they had to show that they could draft state papers such as edicts, decrees, and judicial rulings. Reading the dynastic histories was the best way to prepare for the policy issue and state paper questions.

Examinations themselves were major events not only for the candidates but for the officials serving in the locality and for nearby residents. At the county or prefectural level, the tests lasted a day and drew hundreds or thousands of candidates. The government compound was taken over to give all candidates a place to sit and write. Outside were stalls selling supplies, friends and relatives pressing gifts on those entering, and the curious, eager to watch the examiners and the candidates file in.

Even more elaborate were the week-long affairs of the provincial examinations. From five thousand to ten thousand candidates descended on the city and filled up its hostels. Candidates would show up a week in advance to present their credentials and gather the needed paper, ink, brushes, candles, blankets, and food they would need to survive in their small exam cells. Each cell was open in the front, to allow guards to watch the candidate, and was bare except for two shelves, which could be arranged together to make a bed, or at different levels to form a seat and a table to write on.

BIOGRAPHY   Tan Yunxian, Woman Doctor

The grandmother of Tan Yunxian (1461–1554) was the daughter of a physician, and her husband had married into her home to learn medicine himself. At least two of their sons passed the *jinshi* examination and became officials—including Tan Yunxian's father—raising the standing of the family considerably. The grandparents found Yunxian very bright and therefore decided to pass on their medical knowledge to her.

Tan Yunxian married and raised four children but also practiced medicine, confining her practice to women. At age fifty she wrote an autobiographical account, *Sayings of a Female Doctor*. In the preface she described how, under her grandmother's tutelage, she had first memorized the *Canon of Problems* and *Canon of the Pulse*. Then when her grandmother had time, she asked her granddaughter to explain particular passages in these classic medical treatises.

Yunxian began the practice of medicine by treating her own children, asking her grandmother to check her diagnoses. When her grandmother was old and ill, she gave Yunxian her notebook of prescriptions and her equipment for making medicines, telling her to study them carefully. Later, Yunxian became seriously ill herself and dreamed of her grandmother telling her on what page of which book to find the prescription that would cure her. When she recovered, she began her medical career in earnest.

Tan's book records the cases of thirty-one patients she treated. She treated only women, and mostly women with chronic complaints rather than critical illnesses. Many of the women had what the Chinese classed as women's complaints, such as menstrual irregularities, repeated miscarriages, barrenness, and postpartum fatigue. Others had ailments men could also suffer, such as coughs, nausea, insomnia, diarrhea, rashes, and swellings. Like other literati physicians, she regularly prescribed herbal medications. She also practiced moxibustion. The theory behind burning moxa (dried artemisia) at specified points on the body was similar to acupuncture: it stimulated the circulation of *qi*. Because the physician applying the moxa has to touch the patient, it was not something male physicians could perform on women.

Tan's patients included working women, and she seems to have often thought their problems sprang from overwork. One woman came to her because she had had vaginal bleeding for three years. When questioned, the woman told her that she worked all day with her husband at their kiln making bricks and tiles. Tan Yunxian's diagnosis was overwork, and she gave her pills to replenish her yin. When a boatman's wife came to her complaining of numbness in her hands, Tan found out on questioning that the woman worked in the wind and rain plying the boat and advised a respite. Tan Yunxian explained to a servant girl that she had gone back to work too quickly after suffering a wind damage fever. By contrast, when her patient came from an upper-class family, Tan saw negative emotions as the root of her problems, particularly if she reported that her mother-in-law had scolded her or that her husband had recently brought a concubine home. Two women who had miscarried were told that they had hidden their anger, causing fire to turn inward and destabilize the fetus.

Tan Yunxian herself lived a long life, dying at the age of ninety-three.

Source: Based on Charlotte Furth, *A Flourishing Yin: Gender in China's Medical History, 960–1665* (Berkeley and Los Angeles: University of California Press, 1999), pp. 285–295.

Candidates were searched before being admitted, as no written material could be taken into the cells. Anyone caught wearing a cheat-sheet (an inner gown covered with the classics in minuscule script) was thrown out of the exams and banned from the next session; he might also lose his status as *shengyuan*. Each exam had three sessions, each session lasting two days. Clerks used horns and gongs to begin and end each session. Candidates had time to write rough drafts of their essays, correct them, then copy final versions in neat, regular script. Tension was high. Sometimes rumors that the examiners had been bribed to leak the questions led to riots in the exam quarters, and knocked-over candles occasionally led to fires.

After the papers were handed in, clerks recopied them and assigned them numbers to preserve anonymity. Proofreaders checked the copying before handing them on to the assembled examiners, who divided them up to read. The grading generally took about twenty days. Most candidates stayed in the provincial capital to await the results. Those few who became the new *juren* would be invited to the governor's compound for a celebration. By the time they reached home, most of their friends, neighbors, and relatives would have already heard their good news.

Wang Yangming's Challenge to Confucian Orthodoxy

One might have thought that the intellectual conformity encouraged by the examination system would stifle thought or channel it narrowly. But the government's ability to channel the intellectual and literary pursuits of the elite should not be overestimated. The educated class did not lose their love of poetry, even though it was no longer tested, and examiners were not immune to new intellectual trends. Moreover, although the government continued to use Zhu Xi's teachings as the standard for the civil service examinations, during the sixteenth century Confucian thought developed in new directions, with a remarkable official and teacher, Wang Yangming, leading the way.

Wang Yangming (1472–1529) grew up in the Jiangnan region in a literati family that had not had an official in a century. When he was ten, however, his father passed the examinations in first place, guaranteeing him a prominent career in the capital. Wang Yangming went with him to Beijing, where as a youth he met court officials, poets, writers, and thinkers and pursued interests in military strategy, horsemanship, and archery. Like so many others, he failed the *jinshi* examinations the first two times he took them, but passed in 1499. During his first term in office, he fell ill and had to return to Zhejiang, where he became more interested in philosophy. After he returned to the capital in 1504, he fell afoul of the eunuch dictator Liu Jin by defending two officials who had submitted memorials condemning Liu. Wang was arrested, sent to the eunuch-controlled secret service prison, and severely beaten. On his release, he was assigned a banishment post in an aboriginal region of Guizhou province in the far southwest. He took this post seriously, however, doing his best to understand the problems of the Miao tribesmen. It was in Guizhou that he had his spiritual and intellectual breakthrough.

Wang had been struggling with Zhu Xi's concept of "the extension of knowledge," that is, gaining understanding through careful and rational investigation of things and events, usually through study of the classics and other books. Wang came to realize that universal principles existed in every person's mind. People could discover them by clearing their minds of obstructions such as selfish desires and allowing their inborn knowledge to surface. The teachings of others, even those of Confucius and Mencius, are mere aids; they are not the source of truth. According to Wang, "If words are examined in the mind and found to be wrong, although they have come from the mouth of Confucius, I dare not accept them as correct."[2] Since everyone has a mind with similar capacity, common people have just as much potential to become sages

2. Wing-tsit Chan, trans., *Instructions for Practical Living and Other Neo-Confucian Writings* (New York: Columbia University Press, 1963), p. 81.

Portrait of an Official. The man depicted here in official dress, Jiang Shunfu, lived from 1453 to 1504. The front of his robe had a panel with the two cranes, a "rank badge" that indicated he was a civil official of the first rank. *(Nanjing Museum)*

lowers to concentrate on the basic moral truths that everyone could understand. He once asserted that what was truly heterodox was not Buddhism but ideas incomprehensible to average people. Critics of Wang, however, saw his teachings as dangerously contaminated with Chan Buddhist ideas.

Wang Yangming lived up to his own ideals. Even after he attracted dozens of disciples, he did not give up his official career. After the eunuch Liu Jin was executed in 1510, Wang accepted high-ranking appointments in Nanjing and Beijing while still lecturing to his growing circle of disciples. Conservative officials, disturbed by his message, got him out of the capital by arranging an assignment as governor of a special military district in southern Jiangxi, an area with many non-Chinese aboriginal people. Once there, he had to lead the regional armies into battle and set up a governing structure for the local people. He was a successful military commander, and when a prince rebelled nearby, it was he who led troops to capture him. On Wang Yangming's way back to the capital, his father died, which necessitated his retiring from office to mourn him. In 1527 he was called out of retirement because of uprisings among the non-Chinese in Guangxi. He spent a year there, directing campaigns, winning victories, and negotiating surrenders, but his health was failing, and he died on his way home in 1529.

In the century after Wang Yangming's death, his followers extended his ideas in many directions. Some took a new interest in both Daoism and Buddhism. Some questioned the traditional social hierarchy, such as the elevation of the scholar above the farmer. One of Wang's most enthusiastic followers, Wang Gen, came from a plebeian family of salt workers. He gave lectures to crowds of ordinary people, focusing on issues important in their lives and encouraging them to pursue education to improve their lots. In the next generation, He Xinyin was more radical in that he challenged the age-old elevation of the family. To He, the family was a restrictive, selfish, and exclusive institution, and loyalty to family was inferior to loyalty to friends. His

as those who have pored over the classics their entire lives. Wang also argued against distinguishing knowledge and action. Moral action results spontaneously from true understanding. One does not truly understand filial piety if one does not practice it, any more than one understands taste, smell, or pain without experiencing them. True knowledge compels action.

Wang believed firmly that people could pursue sagehood in the midst of everyday activities. When an official told him that his official duties left him no time to study, Wang urged him not to abandon his work: "Real learning can be found in every aspect of record-keeping and legal cases. What is empty is study that is detached from things."[3] Wang wanted his fol-

3. Patricia Buckley, ed., *Chinese Civilization: A Source-book,* rev. ed. (New York: Simon & Schuster, 1993), p. 258.

contemporary Li Zhi championed the validity of feelings and passion and ridiculed conforming to conventional patterns of behavior. He contended that women were the intellectual equals of men and should be given fuller educations. Li Zhi also reinterpreted history to present some of the great villains as heroes.

Only a small minority of late Ming literati were ready to hear these messages. Both He Xinyin and Li Zhi died in prison, having been arrested on charges of spreading dangerous ideas.

Local Society

As best historians can reconstruct, China's population more than doubled over the course of the Ming Dynasty, from between 60 and 80 million to between 150 and 200 million. Small market towns appeared all over the country. Regional specialization increased as communities took advantage of the availability of cheap water transport to take up cash cropping. By the end of the sixteenth century, the Yangzi River delta area had become a center of cotton and silk production, coastal Fujian was known for tobacco and sugar cane, and porcelain manufacture at Jingdezhen in Jiangxi had achieved unprecedented levels of output. All of this occurred despite continued government suspicion of those who pursued profit.

Ming Taizu had grown up in a family that lived in fear of rapacious tax collectors, and he redesigned tax collection at the village level in the hope that future families would not have to suffer as his had. In each village, the better-off families were identified and assigned the obligation to perform low-level judicial, police, and tax-collecting services without pay as part of what was called the *lijia* system. In other words, villagers themselves, not underlings of the magistrate, would be responsible for assessing, collecting, and transporting taxes, paid mostly in grain.

Taizu's efforts to organize his government around unpaid service created many headaches for later Ming administrators. Local officials found that legal sources of revenue were so limited that they had had no choice but to levy extralegal ones to continue basic services, leading to just the sort of abuses Taizu had wanted to prevent. Ordinary households, for their part, often were devastated by the burden of uncompensated responsibility for delivering taxes or maintaining local hostels for government travelers. Reforms eventually had to be introduced, which converted most obligations into a monetary tax.

The *lijia* system and subsequent tax reforms were supposed to be enforced uniformly around the country. Much of local social organization, however, was highly variable from place to place, depending on the crops grown, whether there were significant non-Han populations, when migrants had arrived, and the like.

During the Ming Dynasty, voluntary associations that included both educated men and ordinary villagers became a common feature of local society. Religious associations were formed to support a temple and its ceremonies. Lineages were formed to promote cooperation among relatives descended from a common ancestor. Often the lineage held land in common to support joint ancestral rites. When income was sufficient, a lineage might also build an ancestral temple or school. Generally lineages were more common in the south than in the north, perhaps a reflection of migration patterns. In Fujian large lineages were evident in Song times and continued to play prominent roles through the Ming. In Huizhou in Anhui province, lineages were flourishing in the mid-Ming, their strength owing much to the wealth of local merchant families. In Taichang in Jiangxi province, most of the lineages were deliberately formed in the early Ming by educated men to enhance their own status at a time of intense competition for social prestige. In Guangdong, by contrast, most of the major lineages date back only to the seventeenth century or later. In some areas, lineages seem to have been initiated by members of the educated class—in other places, by ordinary people who saw advantages in banding together.

By the mid-Ming, lineages in some parts of the country were setting up systems to discipline and control members, complete with long lists of rules and ways to handle disputes. In this they resembled community compacts, a form of local organization Zhu Xi had praised, believing it could promote moral renewal. Members of the compact had to agree to correct each other's faults, offer assistance to those in need, and expel those who failed to cooperate. Wang Yangming used the term community compact for the organizations he set up as part of a rebel pacification program. His followers made even broader use of the plan, urging villagers to form compacts in which they all encouraged each other to strive for goodness.

One reason scholars encouraged this form of voluntary social organization was the common fear that the moral fabric of society was unraveling. Many complained that the rich and poor no longer helped each other but looked on each other as enemies. Some educated men turned to charitable works as a way to try to lessen social tensions. At the end of the sixteenth century, for instance, one man set up the Society for Sharing Goodness, whose members paid monthly dues to support projects such as repairing roads and bridges or offering assistance to families unable to cover funeral expenses.

Urban Culture

Many literati, especially those with ample means, lived in cities where they could pursue the elegant life (see **Material Culture: Gardens of Suzhou**). But literati were not the only cultural force in the cities. As cities grew and the commercial economy thrived, a distinctive urban culture emerged, a culture of those with money to spend in the cities, centered on entertainment of many sorts.

Books accessible to the urban middle classes were now published in large numbers, including reference books of all sorts and popular religious tracts, such as ledgers for calculating the moral value of one's good deeds and subtracting the demerits from bad ones. To make their books attractive in the marketplace, entrepreneurial book publishers commissioned artists to illustrate them. By the sixteenth century, more and more books were being published in the vernacular language, the language people spoke. Writing in the vernacular had begun on a small scale in Tang and Song times, when it was used to record the oral teachings of Buddhist and Confucian teachers. By mid-Ming it was widely used for short stories, novels, and plays. Ming short stories written in the vernacular depicted a world much like that of their readers, full of shop clerks and merchants, monks and prostitutes, students and matchmakers.

It was during the Ming period that the full-length novel appeared. The plots of the early novels were heavily indebted to story cycles developed by oral storytellers over the course of several centuries. *Water Margin* is the episodic story of a band of bandits, set at the end of the Northern Song period. *The Romance of the Three Kingdoms* is a work of historical fiction based on the exploits of the generals and statesmen contending for power at the end of the Han Dynasty. *The Journey to the West* is a fantastic account of the Tang monk Xuanzang's travels to India; in this book he is accompanied by a monkey with supernatural powers as well as a pig. *Plum in the Golden Vase* is a novel of manners about a lustful merchant with a wife and five concubines, full of details of daily life as well as the quarrels and scheming of the women. In none of these cases is much known about the author. Competing publishers brought out their own editions, sometimes adding new illustrations or commentaries.

Musical drama was also a major element in Ming urban culture. The Jesuit missionary Matteo Ricci, who lived in China from 1583 to 1610, described resident troupes in large cities and traveling troupes that "journey everywhere throughout the length and breadth of the country" putting on operas. The leaders of the troupes

MATERIAL CULTURE

Gardens of Suzhou

Well-to-do families in the Jiangnan region often constructed gardens within the walls enclosing their homes. The gardens of Suzhou became particularly famous for their sophisticated beauty. These gardens were places to entertain friends and pass leisure hours. They were considered works of art in progress. Like landscape painters, garden designers tried to capture essential features of nature and made use of objects laden with metaphorical meaning, such as bamboo, gnarled pine trees, and craggy rocks.

Architecture was integral to garden design, and Suzhou gardens had walkways, pavilions, bridges over ponds, and other features. Views were appreciated, but they were intimate in scale, not broad vistas. The spaces within a garden were often visually linked by views glimpsed through open doorways and lattice windows.

About twenty Ming gardens still survive in Suzhou. (See Color Plate 18.)

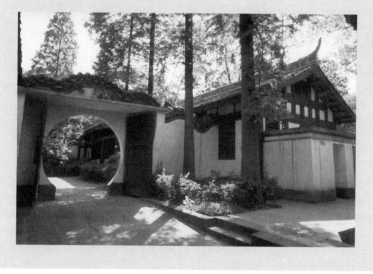

Entrance Gate to the Garden of the Humble Administrator. The round entry way serves to frame the view of those approaching the garden. (*Corbis*)

would purchase young children and train them to sing and perform. Ricci thought too many people were addicted to these performances:

> *These groups of actors are employed at all imposing banquets, and when they are called they come prepared to enact any of the ordinary plays. The host at the banquet is usually presented with a volume of plays and he selects the one or several he may like. The guests, between eating and drinking, follow the plays with so much satisfaction that the banquet at times may last for ten hours.*[4]

People not only enjoyed listening to plays; they also avidly read the scripts for them. Perhaps because so much of a dramatic script was composed of poetry, authors of plays were less likely to conceal their identity than the authors of novels. The greatest of the Ming playwrights was Tang Xianzu, whose love stories and social satires were very popular. His *Dream of Han Tan* tells

---

4. Louis J. Gallagher, trans., *China in the Sixteenth Century: The Journals of Matthew Ricci: 1583–1610* (New York: Random House, 1953), p. 23.

DOCUMENTS

Scene from *The Peony Pavilion*

The Peony Pavilion, written in 1598, is probably Tang Xianzu's best-loved play. Its main characters are a young woman from an official family who falls in love with a young man she encounters in a dream, then pines away for him. Before she dies, she buries a portrait of herself in the garden. Her family moves, the young man moves into the garden, discovers the portrait, and falls in love with her from her picture. His love is so strong it revives her.

With fifty-five scenes, this play was rarely performed in its entirety, but people knew the play and would ask for specific scenes. Minor characters provide much of the humor of the play. In the early scene below, the young woman's maid, Fragrance, talks to herself and then with the recently hired tutor.

The parts that are sung are here indented.

Scene 9: Sweeping the Garden
FRAGRANCE:

> Little Spring Fragrance
> favored among the servants,
> used to pampered ways within the
>   painted chambers
> waiting on the young mistress,
> I mix her powder, match her rouge,
> set her feather adornments, arrange
>   her flowers,
> ever waiting beside the boudoir mirror
> ready to smoothe the brocaded quilt,
> ready to light the fragrant nighttime
>   incense,
> urged on by Madam's stick on my puny
>   shoulders.
> Bondmaid with petaled cheeks just
>   into my teens,
> sweet and charming, wide awake to
>   the spring's arrival.
> A real "passion flower" is what we need
>   now
> to follow our every step with admiring
>   glances.

Day and night you will find me, Fragrance, by the side of my mistress. She, though she might win fame above all others for her beauty, is more concerned with jealous guarding of the family reputation. Maiden modesty composes her gentle features, and it is her nature to be serious and reverent. The master having engaged a tutor to instruct her, she commenced the study of the *Book of Songs*; but, when she reached the lines "So delicate the virtuous maiden, a fit mate for our Prince," she quietly put the book down and sighed, "Here we may observe the full extent of love to the true sage. As men felt in ancient times, so they feel today, and how should it be other than this?" So then I suggested, "Miss, you are tired from your studies, why don't you think of some way to amuse yourself?" She hesitated and thought for a moment. Then she got to her feet. "And how would you have me amuse myself, Fragrance?" she asked me. So I said, "Why, miss, nothing special, just to take a walk in that garden behind the house." "Stupid creature," says the young mistress, "what would happen if my father found out?" But I said, "His Honor has been out visiting the country districts for several days now." Then for ages the young mistress walked up and down thinking, not saying a word, until at last she began to consult the calendar. She said tomorrow was a bad day, and the day after not very good, but the day after that is a propitious day because the God of Pleasure Trips is on duty for the day. I was to tell the gardener to sweep the paths to ready for her visit. I said I would. I'm scared of Madam's finding out, but there's nothing we can do about that. So let me go give the gardener his instructions. Hello, there's Tutor Chen at the end of the verandah. Truly,

> on every side the glory of the spring
> and what does this old fool see?—Not a thing.

TUTOR CHEN (*enters*):

> Aging book lover
> now for a while "within the green gauze tent"
> where once the learned Ma Rong gave instruction
> curtain flaps against hook in warmth of sun.
> Ha, there on the verandah
> young girl with hair in double coil
> seeming to speak, but wordless, closer now, who can it be?
> Oh, it's Fragrance. Tell me,
> where is your gracious lord
> and where his lady?
> And why is my pupil absent from her lessons?

FRAGRANCE: Oh, it's you, Tutor Chen. I'm afraid the young mistress has not had time for classes these last few days.
CHEN: And why is that?
FRAGRANCE: I'll tell you:

> Spring in its splendor
> cruel to a sensitive nature
> —everything's gone wrong?

CHEN: Why, what has gone wrong?
FRAGRANCE: Ah, you've no idea how angry the governor is going to be with you.
CHEN: For what reason?
FRAGRANCE: Why, that *Book of Songs* of yours, you've been singing a bit too sweetly, my poor young mistress—

> your classical exegesis
> has torn her heart to pieces.

CHEN: All I did was explicate the "*Guanguan* cry the ospreys."
FRAGRANCE: That was the one. *Guan* means "shut in," doesn't it? My young mistress said, "Even though the ospreys were shut in, they still had the freedom of the island: why should a human being be treated worse than a bird?"

> In books the head must be buried,
> but it lifts itself to gaze on a scene of beauty.

Now she has ordered me to take her in a day or two to stroll in the garden behind the house.
CHEN: What will be the purpose of this stroll?
FRAGRANCE:

> Unsuspected the spring has struck
> and before it hastens past
> she must cast off there in the garden spring's disquiet.

CHEN: She should not do this.

> When woman walks abroad
> lest eyes should light upon her
> at every step she should be screened from view.

Fragrance, by the grace of Heaven I, your tutor, have enjoyed some sixty years of life, yet never have I felt such thing as "spring-struck," nor have I ever strolled in any garden.

———

Source: From Tang Xianzu, *The Peony Pavilion*, trans. Cyril Birch (Bloomington: Indiana University Press, 1980), pp. 38–40.

Painting a Self Portrait. Popular editions of Ming novels and plays were frequently illustrated with wood block prints. In the scene shown here the heroine of *The Peony Pavilion* uses a mirror to paint a self portrait. *(Beijing Library)*

the story of a young man who falls asleep while his meal is cooking. In his dream he sees his whole life: he comes in first in the *jinshi* examinations, rises to high office, is unfairly slandered and condemned to death, then cleared and promoted. At the point of death, he wakes up and sees that his dinner is nearly done. He then realizes that life passes as quickly as a dream. (For a passage from Tang's most popular play, a love story, see **Documents: Scene from *The Peony Pavilion*.**)

Fiction and plays were so avidly consumed in Ming times that the values and attitudes expressed in them began to have an impact on the culture of the literati. Educated men and women often seem to have judged themselves and others on the standards of purity of feelings that they had come to expect in literary characters. Headstrong attachments—verging on obsessions—came to be admired. Courtesan culture flourished in this environment, and writers wrote of the romantic liaisons between well-known writers and famous courtesans. Because they associated courtesans with high aspirations and disappointed hopes, writers saw parallels between the frustrated official and the talented but powerless woman waiting for her lover to appreciate her full worth.

SUMMARY

How different was China in 1600 than China in 1368? China was more populous, with a population in the vicinity of 175 million by 1600. Some of this increase was made possible by the Chinese pushing deeper into the southwest, but much of it occurred in long-occupied areas that became more densely populated, with more towns and larger cities. Many more books were in circulation, and more of these books were aimed at an audience looking to be entertained rather than educated. Regional disparities may well have increased, as the Jiangnan area stayed several steps ahead of other regions. At the intellectual level, China was much more lively in 1600, with writers and thinkers offering much more sustained critiques of inherited ideas. The fear of the Mongols had largely abated, but those fears had left their trace in the Great Wall. The civil service was discouraged by failures of leadership at the top, but with the expansion of education, the number of those aspiring for civil service careers was much larger in 1600 than it had been in the first generation of the Ming.

SUGGESTED READING

D. Twitchett and F. Mote, eds., *The Cambridge History of China,* vols. 7 and 8 (1988, 1997), cover the Ming Dynasty in rich detail. See also F. Mote, *Imperial China* (1999). For biographies of important individuals, see L. C. Goodrich and C. Fang, eds., *Dictionary of Ming Biography, 1368–1644* (1976). On the Ming government in social context, see R. Huang, *1587, A Year of No Significance: The Ming Dynasty in Decline* (1981); J. Dardess, *Confucianism and Autocracy: Professional Elites and the Founding of the Ming Dynasty* (1983) and *Blood and History: The Donglin Faction and Its Repression 1620–1627* (2002); C. Fisher, *The Chosen One: Succession and Adoption in the Court of Ming Shizong* (1990); J. McDermott, *State and Court Ritual in China* (1999); S. Tsai, *The Eunuchs of the Ming Dynasty* (1995); A. Waldron, *The Great Wall of China: From History to Myth* (1990); and L. Levathes, *When China Ruled the Seas: The Treasure Fleet of the Dragon Throne, 1405–33* (1994).

For early western accounts of China in this period, see C. Boxer, ed., *South China in the Sixteenth Century* (1953), and L. Gallagher, trans., *China in the Sixteenth Century: The Journals of Matthew Ricci, 1583–1610* (1953).

For Ming local elites and lineages, see J. Dardess, *A Ming Society: T'ai-ho County, Kiangsi, Fourteenth to Seventeenth Centuries* (1996); M. Szonyi, *Practicing Kinship: Lineage and Descent in Late Imperial China* (2002); H. Beattie, *Land and Lineage in China: A Study of T'ung-ch'eng County, Anhwei, in the Ming and Ch'ing Dynasties* (1979); H. Zurndorfer, *Change and Continuity in Chinese Local History: The Development of Hui-Chou Prefecture, 800–1800* (1989); P. Ebrey and J. Watson, eds., *Kinship Organization in Late Imperial China, 1000–1940* (1986); and T. Brook, *Praying for Power: Buddhism and the Formation of Gentry Society in Late-Ming China* (1993). On the Ming examination system and how it differed from the earlier system, see B. Elman, *A Cultural History of Civil Examinations in Late Imperial China* (2000), and P. Ho's classic, *The Ladder of Success in Imperial China* (1962).

Recommended studies of Ming culture include C. Clunas, *Superfluous Things: Material Culture and Social Status in Early Modern China* (1992); T. Brook, *The Confusions of Pleasure: Commerce and Culture in Ming China* (1998); D. Johnson, A. Nathan, and E. Rawski, eds., *Popular Culture in Late Imperial China* (1985); P. Wu, *The Confucian's Progress: Autobiographical Writings in Traditional China* (1990); W. deBary, ed., *Self and Society in Ming Thought* (1970); K. Chow, *Publishing, Culture, and Power in Early Modern China* (2004).

For Ming vernacular short stories, see S. Yang and Y. Yang, trans., *Stories Old and New: A Ming Dynasty Collection* (2000). On the Ming novel, see A. Plaks, *The Four Masterworks of the Ming Novel* (1987). For translations, see M. Roberts, trans., *Three Kingdoms: A Historical Novel* (1991); S. Shapiro, trans., *Outlaws of the Marsh* (1981); and D. Roy, trans., *The Plum in the Golden Vase or, Chin P'ing Mei* (2 vols. to date) (1993, 2001).

Centralization in Early Chosŏn (1351–1598)

After almost one hundred years under Mongol domination, Koryŏ began to regain control of its affairs in the reign of King Kongmin (1351–1374). Kongmin attempted to restore authority to the king and created the basis for a stronger central government run by civil officials chosen primarily through success in the civil service examinations. He expanded central control over local districts through the dispatch of magistrates from the capital and increased land tax revenues by taking away tax exemptions from aristocratic landlords. In the cultural sphere, Buddhism was replaced with *tohak*, or neo-Confucianism, as the primary ethical-philosophical core of Korean belief and practice.

Despite the progress that he made, King Kongmin was limited in his success by the influence that the Mongols exerted from afar and by the pro-Yuan contingent in the bureaucracy. Nevertheless, his reign laid the groundwork for the completion of many objectives in 1391, a year before the collapse of the Koryŏ Dynasty.

King Kongmin provided the first step in the strengthening of royal power, the complete centralization of government in the Chinese style, strengthening of the military, expansion of tax revenue, and the replacement of Buddhism with Zhu Xi orthodoxy. Zhu Xi orthodoxy became the basis for the civil-service examinations, passage of which in turn became the only means for advancement into the highest ranks of government office. In addition, Zhu Xi Confucianism had serious effects on the family and women. The hereditary *yangban* had to devote themselves to education to gain office, but they were able to maintain their control over slaves. Flaws began to appear in many institutions already by 1450, and by 1592 those flaws had become serious and weakened considerably Korea's ability to resist Hideyoshi's invasion from Japan (1592–1598).

Questions that have concerned many scholars are the reasons for the fall of Koryŏ and the rise of Chosŏn—whether or not the dynastic transformation signified a social revolution; whether *tohak* Confucianism strengthened the king, state, and national defense or had limiting and contrary effects; whether the tributary relationship with Ming China was beneficial or deleterious; whether the economy showed signs of growth with deleterious effects on the taxation system; why the leading scholars of the sixteenth century made the ideas of Zhu Xi the unshakable center of Confucian thought; and whether they succeeded in establishing enlightened rule by contrast with the period before 1550, or contrarily, created the basis for the beginning of hereditary factionalism in 1575. Finally, what were the reasons for the weakness of the military in 1592 during the Hideyoshi invasion?

RECENTRALIZATION AND ZHU XI CONFUCIANISM (1351–1392)

After King Kongmin ascended the throne in 1351, the relatives of Empress Ki in Koryŏ realized that they were in danger from anti-Yuan forces. In November 1352, one of the king's pro-Yuan supporters, Cho Ilsin, tried to justify a rebellion by claiming that he wanted to wipe out the Ki family, but he killed only one family member before he was captured and beheaded. The emperor tried to restore balance by removing Ki Ch'ŏl and pro-Yuan officials from office in 1355, executing him for plotting a rebellion the next year. He also abolished the use of the pigtail and Mongol-style clothing, abolished the branch secretariat for the chastisement of Japan, abandoned the Yuan year period, and restored civil agencies that had existed prior to military rule and the Mongol conquest.

King Kongmin's reform efforts were interrupted by frequent attacks from the Wakō (*Waegu*, in Korean) pirates based on Tsushima and other islands in Japan and by two major invasions by the Red Turban rebels from China

between 1359 and 1361. Kongmin survived a failed Mongol plot to overthrow him, and Koryŏ forces under Northeast Army commander Yi Sŏnggye, who eventually established the Chosŏn Dynasty in 1392, drove out another invasion by Nahachu, a Yuan official who took advantage of Yuan weakness to establish his own satrapy in Manchuria. The king was now constrained by military commanders, but because both military and civil officials remained divided between pro- and anti-Yuan groups, he was not free to pursue his anti-Yuan policy completely.

The capital was occupied for months by the invaders. When they burned the national slave registers in the capital and the household registers of Kyŏnggi province, they weakened the government's hold over the population for taxation and labor service. After King Kongmin returned to the capital, he survived another coup in 1363 thanks to aid from a pro-Yuan commander, Ch'oe Yŏng. Ch'oe and Yi Sŏnggye also defeated a division-sized force dispatched from Mongol territory by Empress Ki in 1363 to unseat King Kongmin.

King Kongmin's Reforms

To overcome resistance to reform from his military protectors and officials of the aristocratic *yangban* families, Kongmin tried to train officials in *tohak* in new schools, increase the number of classics licentiate degrees (*saengwŏn*), and appoint more degree holders to office, especially in the censorate. The censorate was in charge of surveillance of official malfeasance, and they held the poorly educated military in low esteem. Most of them came from either aristocratic families in the capital or the *hyangni* local aristocrats in the countryside, in contrast to the conventional view that they were a new class of rising scholar-officials (*sadaebu*) from small- to medium-size landowners. Most supported government reform and opposed Mongol intervention.

These men did not always agree with each other. Some like Chŏng Tojŏn viciously attacked the Buddhists, but others believed in Buddhism, donated to Buddhist temples, and had relatives who had become monks. Many of them were won over to Zhu Xi's emphasis on moral self-cultivation, policy essays in the examinations, and a more straightforward and unadorned style of writing, but others preferred the belles-lettres tradition of the Chinese Han and Tang Dynasties. Since Kongmin could not always rely on the new *tohak* officials to support his policies, he chose people for office he knew well, including his mother's relatives (who happened to be large landlords), merit subjects, and even pro-Yuan officials who were unsympathetic to his reforms. He even chose a Buddhist monk who was the son of a slave woman, Sin Ton, to take charge of his reform program in 1356. He appointed Sin Ton to a special position of leader (*Yongdosa*) of his administrative council, higher than the prime minister, and he also put him in charge of the monk registers, the office of yin/yang and geomancy, the Royal Guards, and the personnel bureau. Since Sin Ton had no landed estates and no independent economic base, he was totally dependent on the king's favor.

The neo-Confucian officials despised the idea of taking orders from a slave-monk. A century later, the Confucians who wrote the history of the Koryŏ dynasty, the *Koryŏsa*, portrayed Sin Ton as a corrupt tyrant and womanizer who had his own armed guards and acted as the king's equal by taking his place at official occasions. If that were not enough, he was not on good terms with the Buddhist establishment or the main palace eunuch, Yi Kangdal, either. In 1366 King Kongmin appointed Sin Ton director of the General Directorate for the Investigation of Land and Slaves to convert everyone who had illegally been made a slave during the period of turmoil to tax-paying commoners and to register and tax all the land that the landlords had been reclaiming, stealing, and hiding from the central government for decades. These measures drove the *yangban* land and slave owners to intense antipathy.

When the Chinese rebel Zhu Yuanzhang established the Ming Dynasty in China in 1368, the Mongols fled north to Shangdu in 1369.

King Kongmin abandoned the Yuan year period that year and accepted a patent of investiture as king of Koryŏ from Ming emperor Taizu in 1370. The Yuan emperor died that year and was succeeded by his half-Korean son by Empress Ki, but the Yuan was in rapid decline and Ming Taizu was suspicious of pro-Mongol elements in the Koryŏ court.

Meanwhile, the political tide in Koryŏ had turned against Sin Ton. There was intense rural suffering from intermittent drought and famine after 1358 and three plots against him. When trumped-up charges were leveled against him in 1371, Kongmin withdrew his support, executed him, and purged about fifty officials. Sin Ton had been placed in the impossible situation of leading a frontal attack against the interests of the most powerful families without a political base of his own. Three years later, King Kongmin himself was assassinated. Although his reforms had failed, he had set in motion a process that reached fruition in the next dynasty.

The Rise of Yi Sŏnggye

For the next fourteen years, the Koryŏ throne was in the hands of Yi Inim, a vice minister who acted as de facto regent over the next king, King Kongmin's nine-year-old son by a concubine, King U. Yi Inim wanted to support the Mongol Northern Yuan Dynasty, but because he was opposed by Confucian scholar-officials at court and needed support from the Chinese Ming Dynasty against the Wakō pirates, he had to adopt the Ming year period in 1378 as a sign of subservience to China. Wakō pirate raids had became more frequent and ferocious in the 1370s. In 1377 Ch'oe Musŏn learned about nitrates from Chinese merchants and established an arsenal to manufacture gunpowder. Korean forces under Yi Sŏnggye used gunpowder and cannon in two campaigns in 1380 and 1383, and in 1389 Koryŏ forces successfully raided the Wakō base on Tsushima Island.

When a Ming envoy was murdered in Koryŏ territory, Emperor Taizu increased Koryŏ's tribute burden in 1385, demanded the return of thousands of Chinese refugees, and closed the border with Liaodong, even to Koryŏ envoys. Finally, the Koryŏ generals Ch'oe Yŏng and Yi Sŏnggye toppled Yi Inim in a coup d'état in 1388. By this time Taizu had completed the conquest of the Northern Yuan, but Ch'oe Yŏng was angered by Ming Taizu's demands for more tribute, cession of the area north of Ch'ŏllyŏng pass that Khubilai had once annexed, and the establishment of a Wei (border unit) with a thousand troops and a string of guard stations in the area north of the Yalu River. Ch'oe Yŏng killed about a dozen Ming envoys sent to negotiate a border agreement, and then induced King U to order an attack on Liaodong. Unfortunately for him, he chose Yi Sŏnggye, generalissimo for the northeast, to lead the force despite Yi's opposition to an attack against superior Ming forces. As Yi led his army north, he stopped his army on Wihwa Island in the middle of the Yalu River and decided that his mission would be disastrous for his country. Since failure to obey orders was an act of treason, he had no choice but to return with his troops and seize power. He exiled Ch'oe Yŏng and forced the king to appoint him and Cho Minsu vice ministers of state, and then to adopt the Ming year period. Cho Minsu, however, deposed the young king for another puppet king, a child in the Wang royal family.

Yi took the lead in domestic reform. He took over all prebendal grants of land taxes on privately owned land, cancelled all tax-free exemptions to favored *yangban,* and carried out a national land survey to increase central land tax revenue. He was supported by many of the *tohak* Confucians, but he rejected the radical proposal of Chŏng Tojŏn to nationalize all privately owned land and adopt a system of rotating distribution of cultivated land to peasant families in emulation of the famous equal-field system of the Chinese Northern Wei and Tang Dynasties. Instead, he chose Cho Chun's alternate plan to preserve private ownership and adopt the *kwajŏn* prebendal system, except that tax collection prebends were limited to only about two-thirds of the land in Kyŏnggi province that surrounded the capital. Prebends were granted to men who held high official rank (not official posts), government institutions, post stations, Buddhist monasteries, shrines, and Confucian schools. In the next several decades, the central government gradually recaptured as many of these taxes as it could, and finally took it all back and ended prebendal grants in the late fifteenth century. In 1389, Yi eliminated Cho Minsu, paving the way for his decision to establish a new dynasty in 1392.

THE CHOSŎN DYNASTY AND CONFUCIANIZATION (1392–1450)

Yi Sŏnggye decided to enroll as a tributary of the Ming Dynasty for purely practical reasons, but his neo-Confucian supporters insisted on making the tributary relationship a moral and ethical one. The establishment of the Chosŏn Dynasty was not accompanied by any social revolution, however. The vast majority of new officials in the Chosŏn Dynasty belonged to the *yangban* aristocratic families of the late Koryŏ period. As members of the elite, they were part of the land- and slave-owning class. Late Koryŏ was probably a slave society in which slaves constituted more than 30 percent of the population, and there was no attempt by any of the early Chosŏn kings to manumit slaves and challenge the property rights of the *yangban* aristocrats. Only *yangban* who opposed the new dynasty ran the risk of punishment and loss of their property.

In government and politics, however, the early kings completed the adoption of the Chinese model of bureaucratic centralization by dispatching bureaucrats at the capital to become magistrates in all of the 330 or so local districts. In contrast with the Koryŏ Dynasty, it became virtually impossible for anyone to advance to high official rank without passing the civil service examinations. In fact, slaves and merchants were banned from taking the examinations in the Chosŏn Dynasty (merchants had not been banned in China since the Ming Dynasty, and

Map 15.1   **Chosŏn Dynasty, 1392–1910**

maybe earlier). Commoner peasants were not, but few of their families had the economic means to support and educate an idle son until adulthood.

Once in a position of dominance, however, the *yangban* of Chosŏn took measures to make the path to high office even more exclusive. They banned the Koryŏ practice of allowing *hyangni* (local prominent families who held local magistrate's posts) to be promoted to the central bureaucracy. To preserve their narrow notion of the purity of the male blood line in the

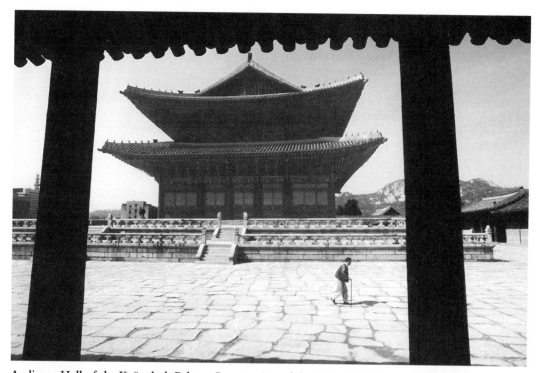

Audience Hall of the Kyŏngbok Palace. Construction of the Kyŏngbok Palace was begun by King T'aejo in the 1390s and continued through the end of the fifteenth century. A fire in 1553 wiped out part of the palace compound, but it was repaired. The palace was burned down by Hideyoshi's army in the 1590s, and the country was too poor to finance its reconstruction for over a hundred years. The Taewongun repaired the palace between 1865 and 1872 as a symbol of his attempt to restore power to the king after a half-century of consort clan domination over the royal house. *(Peter Gutman/Corbis)*

family, they relegated the *nothoi,* or sons of concubines of the family head, to inferior status and banned them from taking the examinations. The neo-Confucian ideologues diminished the status and property rights of women. In Koryŏ women had inherited equal shares of their parents' patrimony with their brothers, took it with them when they married, and retained it if a husband died without a male heir. These rights were gradually eliminated as women who married out of the family became totally absorbed in the husband's family, which took over her property. These debilities were the result of strict limitation of succession rights to family headship and performance of ancestral rituals to the eldest son of the father, and property rights in large part to the eldest son as well.

Koryŏ men could have several wives, and they were all treated equally, but the Confucian moralists insisted that a man could only have a single primary wife, a few secondary wives, and concubines, who usually were commoners or slaves. That rule caused friction from the loss of status by all but the primary wife. Even the primary wife was subordinated to her husband's father, her husband, and her mother-in-law; was unable to obtain a divorce except in rare circumstances; was confined to the inner quarters and restricted from venturing outside; and on those rare occasions when she did go outside publicly was required to wear a veil. These developments were carried out gradually over a period of a couple of centuries or more, and even then some vestiges of Koryŏ custom remained in some cases, like cross-cousin marriages by men with maternal cousins, the husband's residence in the wife's family's household, and an occasional grant of property to a daughter in her father's will.

In addition, the new regime began a long-term, top-down movement to replace Buddhist and other native customs involving adulthood, marriage, and funerals with Confucian practices. It took about three hundred years before Buddhist burial practices and beliefs were replaced at the lowest level of society.

The majority of the neo-Confucian scholars supported the overthrow of the Koryŏ Dynasty, and men like Kwŏn Kŭn and Chŏng Tojŏn led in proselytizing Zhu Xi's teachings rather than supporting the free and open exchange of ideas. They inherited the Chinese *tohak* arguments against Buddhism not only because of the corrupt practices that had infected the Buddhist temples, but also because they felt that the Buddhist emphasis on the individual attainment of enlightenment by separation from the family interfered with the Confucian obligation of filial piety. As a result, most Buddhist monasteries were disbanded and stripped of their land, and eighty thousand of their slaves were converted to official slaves in the employ of the state.

The early Chosŏn adepts of Confucian *tohak* adopted the Chinese Song Dynasty notion that individual moral self-rectification required not only thorough education in the Chinese classics to understand the nature of Confucian ethics, but also meditation, or "quiet sitting," as an important method of achieving an intuitive unity with pure goodness conferred on the mind by heaven. They were, wittingly or unwittingly, borrowing a Mahayana Buddhist notion that meditation would lead to an intuitive unity with the cosmic Buddha nature that was found within the minds of every sentient being. The difference from Buddhism, however, was that Zhu Xi learning involved accepting the world of sense experience and society as real, not transitory, and perfecting individual Confucian morality to create a well-ordered society, not as a means of escaping a world of suffering and frustration.

The ethical obligation of filial piety and loyalty to the ruler was useful to the Chosŏn kings in gaining conformity to their authority. On the other hand, the Confucians viewed themselves as men schooled in Confucian morality with the obligation to guide the ruler toward moral perfection, and they insisted that the ruler was obliged to heed their remonstrance. At the same time, they used remonstrance to hamstring the king's authority and protect their *yangban* class interests.

During the early Chosŏn period, Korea had a basically agrarian economy with limited commercial activity. All taxes were paid in kind or physical labor. Handicrafts were limited mostly to slave artisans, who served the needs of the *yangban* and the royal house; commerce in the capital was restricted to monopoly merchants and in the countryside to itinerant peddlers and five-day markets, with only a few commercial towns and permanent shopkeepers. National defense was based on military service for all adult males except for merchants, slaves, and men in official schools; sons of *yangban* with official rank (not necessarily office) were allowed to serve in special guard units set aside for them. Slaves were exempt to preserve the labor power of the *yangban* elite.

Various aspects of these systems began to deteriorate, however. In politics, the civil service examinations were designed as an objective system based on knowledge and literary accomplishment, but this objective was blocked by the hereditary *yangban* families who adjusted to the new situation by educating their sons and thus dominating success in the examinations. Kings found it difficult to exercise their theoretically absolute power because of the obstruction and remonstrance of the civil officials, almost all of whom came from *yangban* families with longer histories and more prestige than the Chŏnju Yi royal family. The neo-Confucians began to limit royal power and prevented the development of the imperial despotism that characterized the Ming and Qing Dynasties in China.

Members of the royal family itself failed to remain loyal to kings, and the system of succession was often irregular. The third king, T'aejong (r. 1400–1418), manipulated the succession against the wishes of his father, King T'aejo (Yi Sŏnggye); King Sejo was originally the uncle of

King Tanjong, and he usurped the throne from his nephew in 1455; King Yŏnsan'gun was deposed by his officials for his tyrannical behavior in 1506. And in the sixteenth century, Kings Injong and Myŏngjong were subjected to the control of the relatives of their mothers.

Nonetheless, many successes were achieved in the reigns of kings in the fifteenth century. King T'aejong moved the capital from Kaesŏng to Hanyang (Seoul), established a strong military, confiscated Buddhist temple and monastery property, and created a sound fiscal base for the state. His son, King Sejong (r. 1418–1450), established a record of accomplishment that far outshone any of his successors. He improved both the army and navy, extended Chosŏn's territory north to the Yalu and Tumen rivers, and defeated the Wakō pirates on Tsushima Island. He promoted improvements in crop yields such as continuous cultivation by the application of night soil fertilizer, and improved productivity by the irrigation of wet fields. He established a complicated system of land registration to eliminate inequities in the land tax by adjusting for differences in fertility and weather conditions. He published books on agriculture and sericulture to promote better yields. He reinstituted state-sponsored grain loans to peasants to tide them over the spring planting season and famine periods. He prohibited cruel punishments, allowed appeals on death penalty cases, and punished masters who beat their slaves without first obtaining official permission. He introduced metallic and paper currency to improve the circulation of goods, but the public was too unused to cash to trust the new money, and the effort failed.

One of his most important achievements was the establishment of the Hall of Worthies (*Chiphyŏnjŏn*) in 1420. It was an institute to which scholars were appointed to publish books and organize collections of documents. Sejong put it in charge of inventing an alphabet in 1443—the first and only one of its kind in all of East Asia—to spread learning beyond the elite *yangban,* but they opposed its use lest it break their stranglehold on knowledge (see Figure

15.1). He sponsored the publication of books and cast movable type to expand their availability. These publications included *Episodes from the Life of the Buddha (Sŏkpo sangjŏl),* eulogies of his ancestors, *The Songs of the Flying Dragons (Yongbi ŏch'ŏnga),* and *Illustrated Guide to the Three Moral Relationships (Samgang haengsil).*

Other texts on scientific subjects were published, including three pharmacopeias of Chinese and Korean herbal medicines, *Straight Talk on Farming (Nongsa chiksol,* 1429) on agricultural methods, and *Calculations of the Movements of the Sun, Moon, and Five Planets (Ch'ilchŏngsan)* in 1444. The most advanced scientific accomplishments of his reign were a rain gauge invented in 1442, two centuries before Europe's first; musical bronze bells; water clocks; sundials; and an astronomical chart. In short, he produced an unmatched record of accomplishment. (See **Material Culture: King Sejong's Clepsydra.**)

THE SEJO USURPATION AND THE LITERATI PURGES (1450–1519)

Despite the great accomplishments of King Sejong, he was unable to bequeath political stability to his heirs. His son who succeeded him died early, and his twelve-year-old grandson, King Tanjong, was robbed of his throne by his uncle, King Sejo (r. 1455–1468), an act that sowed the seeds of political discord for the rest of the century. He also repressed two serious rebellions by Yi Ching'ok in 1453 and Yi Siae in 1467.

Sejo was devoted to military strategy and published three studies about it. He authorized an attack against the Jurchen tribes in 1460 and 1467, established military colonies to support troop units, and established the Five Guards Command in 1466 to function as a supreme national defense council. He adopted the famous Chinese ever-normal granaries to stabilize the

Vowel pairs	ㅏ a	ㅑ ya,	ㅓ ŏ	ㅕ yŏ,	ㅗ o	ㅛ yo, ㅜ u ㅠ yu, ㅡ ŭ ㅣ i.

Some consonant pairs   ㄱ k ㅋ k', ㄷ t ㅌ t', ㅂ p ㅍ p', ㅈ ch ㅊ ch'.

Some other consonants   ㅅ s, ㄴ n, ㅁ m, ㅇ ng.

Syllables*	Chosŏn	조선	Taedong	대동
	ch'ŏnmin	천민	T'aejong	태종
	Puyŏ	부여	*yangban*	양반
	Pyongyang	평양		

*K, t, p and ch are voiced (g, d, b, and j) when occurring between vowels. The symbol ㅇ is used both for a final ng and to indicate the absence of an initial consonant. Ae is written ㅐ (ai).

Figure 15.1   **Han'gul Chart**

price of grain by buying or selling grain on the market, and he tried, but failed, to put iron cash into circulation to promote commerce.

Sejo antagonized the Confucian officials by neglecting the state council and ordering the six ministries to send all their communications directly to him. He abolished King Sejong's Hall of Worthies because he was annoyed by remonstrance against some of his decisions. His admiration for Buddhism was one such case. He studied Buddhist scripture, established an agency for the publication of Buddhist texts, and built the Wŏn'gaksa (Buddhist temple) in 1464 on Bell Street (Chongno) in the capital (Seoul). On the other hand, he also promoted neo-Confucian culture by publishing an edition of the Four Books and an annotated edition of the *Book of Changes*. He also sponsored two chronological histories: the *Treasured Mirror of the National Dynasty (Kukcho-bogam)* and the *Comprehensive Mirror of the Eastern Country (Tongguk t'onggam)*. He ordered the compila-

tion of a major law code, the Grand Institutes for Governing the State *(Kyŏngguk taejŏn)*, completed in 1461 but not published until after his death in 1469.

Despite Sejo's accomplishments, his legitimacy was tarnished, and the civil Confucian officials regained their power under subsequent kings. Their domination was brief when Yŏnsan'gun came to the throne in 1494. Yŏnsan'gun never received a posthumous kingly title because he was deposed in 1506. After he came to the throne, he began compilation of the *Veritable Record (Sillok)* of the previous reign and discovered a critical condemnation of King Sejo's usurpation in the private account of the deceased Kim Chongjik. Since Kim's criticism questioned Yŏnsan'gun's legitimacy as well, he desecrated his tomb and executed his disciples for lese majesty in 1498.

He continued to act in ever more arbitrary fashion against real and supposed insults to his authority, ordering the execution of people for

MATERIAL CULTURE

King Sejong's Clepsydra

King Sejong (r. 1418–1450) was a truly unique king with an unmatched curiosity, and one area of his interest was astronomy. He had his officials set up a royal observatory and prodded them to produce a number of astronomical instruments. These included a striking clepsydra or water clock that operated by the use of flues that dropped brass balls on bells to announce the hours throughout the day. The description of this device was recorded in minute detail in the *Veritable Record (Sillok)* of King Sejong's reign, in more detail than descriptions of Chinese water clocks. Because water clocks of similar type were introduced into China in the early thirteenth century and two similar clepsydras were built in the Yuan Dynasty around the 1260s, it is possible that Korean envoys may have learned something of its construction. Nonetheless, Sejong's clepsydra was a major accomplishment for Korea.

Other instruments associated with astronomical observation included an instrument that was both a sundial and a star-dial, a hundred-interval ring that was a simplified version of the former, a variety of other sundial types, an armillary sphere to track the movement of the stars in the heavens, and a celestial globe. The striking clepsydra was destroyed during Hideyoshi's invasions in the 1590s. In 1651 the technology of King Sejong's era was replaced by new astronomical knowledge and instruments developed in Beijing by Christian missionaries and Chinese astronomers.

Striking Clepsydra (Water Clock). King Sejong's reign, 1418–1450. Chosŏn Dynasty. *(The Hall of Heavenly Records: Korean Astronomical Instruments and Clocks 1380–1780 by Joseph Needham, Lu Gwei-Djen, John Combridge, John Major, Cambridge University Press, 1986, p. 32)*

minor offenses to his person. His critics (the *sarimp'a,* or neglected moral scholars in the countryside) believed that their cause was a moral crusade against a usurper and his political appointees (the *hun'gup'a,* or merit subjects), but he thought he was defending his rights as an absolute monarch. He carried out a second

purge of the literati in 1504, cancelled the royal lectures because young officials were aggressive in criticizing his actions, and neglected the National Academy. His wrath became so extreme that he was overcome with paranoia about perceived threats to his power. Yŏnsan'gun represented the epitome of despotic behavior in the Chosŏn dynasty, but he had carried his tyranny too far and was overthrown by a cabal of high officials in 1506.

Under Yŏnsan'gun's replacement, King Chungjong, the political tide turned in the opposite direction when the new king went out of his way to tolerate remonstrance from his Confucian officials. Because King Chungjong had to reward the men who had overthrown Yŏnsan'gun and put him on the throne, his high officials now became the butt of criticism from younger officials who had passed the civil service examinations and received appointments to the censorate. These censors were led by Cho Kwangjo, who styled himself a moral man with better qualifications than the new political appointees at the top. He persuaded King Chungjong to allow a new "recommendation" examination to provide an opportunity for neglected outstanding scholars and men of virtue in the countryside to gain appointment to office. When the examination was held in 1515, it turned out that Cho's friends and supporters passed the examinations and obtained posts, and immediately joined in his efforts to topple what they thought were political appointees.

The high officials (*hun'gup'a*), however, did not think of themselves as immoral men at all. King Chungjong lost patience with his critics, purged the young censors, and executed Cho in 1519. To those outside the locus of power at the time, like the students of the National Academy, Cho Kwangjo became a martyr to the cause of pure Confucian government, a representative of the *sarimp'a* ethical purists. Cho and his associates were, however, skillful politicians playing the moral card to gain political power. By the middle of the sixteenth century, a rivalry for the throne developed between two cousins related to the king. When one of them acceded to the throne in 1545 as King Myŏngjong, his mother, Queen Munjŏng, became regent, and the leader of the Little Yun faction purged the leader of his rival, the Big Yun group. Once again, neo-Confucian morality had failed to eliminate political rivalry over the royal succession.

CONFUCIAN DISPUTATION

After the death of Queen Munjŏng in 1565, more scholars with mighty reputations for virtue were appointed to high office, and they began to explore the ethical and metaphysical arguments of Zhu Xi. Zhu Xi and his predecessors had argued that everything in the cosmos consists of two inseparable factors: pattern (or principle, *i*; *li* in Chinese) and psychophysical force (*ki*; *qi* in Chinese). The pattern (*i*) that existed in the mind was human inborn nature (*sŏng*), which contained all the fundamental factors of human ethics, but that nature was obstructed or beclouded by the imperfect psychophysical force in the mind, providing a metaphysical explanation for the existence of both good and evil in Confucian society.

A debate began over which of the two elements was primary even though most of the debaters agreed that they were both inseparable. Yi Hwang (pen name, T'oegye) held that the nonphysical pattern in the mind took priority because it contained all the elements of pure virtue, while the younger Yi I (pen name, Yulgok) took the view that psychophysical force was prior because without it, the mind would not exist at all. Zhu Xi himself had allowed space for different interpretations, and the debate was carried on without rancor at the time. The followers of these two men became rivals, however, and used their ideas to bolster the political rivalries that emerged after they died and split into the opposing views of *i*-monism and *ki*-monism, a development that went far beyond Chinese thought on that issue (see **Documents: Excerpts from T'oegye**).

This new mood of philosophical inquiry in Chosŏn coincided with the emergence in Ming China of the meditational wing of neo-Confucian thought led by Wang Yangming. Wang posed a challenge to Zhu Xi's stress on the need for both textual study and meditation as the proper means for attaining perfect virtue, but T'oegye defended Zhu Xi's formula and condemned

Wang as a heterodox thinker who had rejected the study of the classics and relegated the judgment of Confucian virtue to the whims of the imperfect vagaries of the emotions beclouded by *ki*.

T'oegye's rejection of Wang Yangming set the tone for Korean Confucianism for the rest of the Chosŏn Dynasty by rejecting not only the meditational but also the utilitarian (or practical statecraft) wings of Song Dynasty thought to concentrate only on individual self-rectification. T'oegye's reputation was so powerful at the time that his opinion had the force of stigmatizing Wang Yangming's ideas so that anyone interested in them had to keep his fascination secret lest he be condemned for apostasy. When the Japanese became interested in *tohak* in the late sixteenth century, they admired T'oegye's work as a guide to a new system, but they tired of his apparent rigid adherence to Zhu Xi and opted for Wang Yangming instead because he seemed to justify emotional and intuitive spontaneity.

INSTITUTIONAL DETERIORATION

Unfortunately, the presence of some Confucian moralists in the government served to effect neither the elimination of corruption or the reform of institutions that had been in decline for some time. The institutions in need of reform in the late sixteenth century were the tribute tax on local products, the maldistribution of landownership and the land tax burden, and the military system. The local products tribute tax originated as a fixed and unchanging assessment on local villages that specialized in the production of certain goods, but when many villages ceased producing those products, they had to pay fees to so-called tribute merchants to procure those products elsewhere for remittance to the government or the royal palace. This practice of tribute contracting (*pangnap*) was regarded by the authorities as illegal, and those caught doing it were subject to punishment and fines, but there was no other way for villagers to meet their

tribute tax quotas, and they suffered from the fees and scams of the tribute merchants. Yet although tribute contracting was illegal, it contributed to the expansion of commercial activities by private merchants in the countryside.

By the sixteenth century rich landlords, most of whom came from *yangban* families, expanded their holdings by legal and illegal means at the expense of smallholding commoner peasants. The *yangban* landlords became financiers of peasant debt and foreclosed when the smallholders could not repay their debts. As they accumulated "estates" (*nongjang*) consisting primarily of an accumulation of scattered parcels, indebted poor peasants often commended their land to such landlords and became their slaves to escape both the tax collector and military service. The state failed to remedy this situation by conducting timely cadastral surveys to record landownership and maintain the tax base. It also failed to provide relief loans to peasant smallholders to tide them over the planting season or relieve them of accumulated debts.

There was a strong trend for most *yangban* without office and some commoners to escape military service by bribing clerks to register them falsely as students in school (*haksaeng*) or young students (*yuhak*) to qualify them for an exemption from either military duty or the payment of a military cloth tax to pay for the upkeep of duty soldiers. Local commanders conspired with them by letting them off actual duty in return for bribes or military cloth tax payments. As a result, there was a serious decline in the number of troops on duty in the army and the local garrisons. Although a new national security agency, the Border Defense Command (*Pibyŏnsa*), had been created in 1522 to deal specifically with defense against Japanese pirate raids, the government failed to remedy the hollowing out of the military. In 1582 Yulgok (Yi I) recommended the creation of an armed force of one hundred thousand men to be distributed around the country in anticipation of military threats. Other officials called for the establishment of naval bases on

DOCUMENTS

Excerpts from T'oegye

Yi Hwang (pen name, T'oegye) was a leading neo-Confucian thinker who speculated on the operations of the human mind and its relationship to good and evil in human behavior. He accepted the definitions handed down from Cheng Yi and Zhu Xi of the Song Dynasty on the definition of i (the pattern on the surface of a piece of jade, or principle), and its inseparable coalition with ki (psychophysical force) in the human mind. He believed that the imperfection of ki was tantamount to a cloud that prevented the mind's eye from seeing and understanding one's inborn goodness in i, and he insisted that intense study of the classics was necessary to learn the fundamental Confucian moral principles of humaneness or compassion, modesty, subordination of the self, filial piety to parents, and respect for elders. But he also insisted on deep meditation to make contact with one's inner goodness. He rejected the thought of Wang Yangming and kept Confucian thought within the confines of Zhu Xi orthodoxy. The following excerpts from T'oegye's writings explain his views of i and ki.

Tŏkhong asked [T'oegye] about the meaning of pattern. The master replied: "It seems difficult to understand, but it is really easy. If you think closely about what the early Confucians meant when they said that you make a boat to travel on the water, and you make a cart to travel on land, then you can extend this to other matters as well. In general, a boat ought to go on the water and a cart ought to go on land. That is what pattern is. The ruler ought to be humane. The subject ought to be respectful. The father ought to be compassionate. The son ought to be filial. That is what pattern is."

Whence do the feelings of commiseration, shame and dislike [for evil], yielding and deference, and right and wrong issue? They

---

strategic islands off the coast and a major army base at Pusan to block any attack from Japan. The court of King Sŏnjo, however, failed to adopt any of those suggestions, leaving three walled towns—Pusan, Tongnae, and Kimhae—as the only defense against invasion.

FACTIONALISM AND THE JAPANESE INVASION

The emergence of factionalism among the *yangban* officials also played a key role in the weakness of defense. Factionalism began in 1575 over competition between two men for appointment to a key post in the ministry of personnel. They and their followers became known as easterners and westerners, terms related to the location of their homes in the capital, not regional discrimination. To be sure, personal relations based on blood ties, marriage alliances, schoolboy friendships, and master-disciple relations affected political group formation for centuries, but no permanent factional groups had been created until 1575. After 1575, the factions tended to become hereditary and created issue from the nature that is composed of humanity, righteousness, propriety, and wisdom. And whence do feelings of joy, anger, sorrow, fear, love, hatred and desire issue? They are occasioned by circumstantial conditions when external things contact one's form and cause a movement internally. As for the issuance of the Four Beginnings, since Mencius has already referred to them in terms of the mind-and-heart, and since the mind-and-heart is the combination of principle and material force, then why do we say that what is referred to in speaking of them has principle as its predominant factor . . . ? That is because the nature composed of humanity, righteousness, propriety, and wisdom exists in its pure condition within us, and these four are the commencements [of its active manifestation]. . . .

But then why is what is referred to in speaking of [the seven feelings, human emotions] a matter of material force [*ki,* or psychophysical force]? When external things arrive [i.e., make contact on the mind], that which is most susceptible to stimulus and the first to move is our physical form, and the Seven Feelings are its systematic outgrowth. It does not make sense to say that the Four Beginnings are within us as pure

principle, but at the moment they issue they are mixed with material force. . . .

The Four Beginnings are all good. Therefore, it is said, "Without these four dispositions, one is no longer human." And it is also said, "As for the feelings, it is possible for them to be good." In the case of the Seven Feelings, then, good and evil are not yet fixed. Therefore, as soon as we have them but are not able to exercise discernment, the mind-and-heart will not attain its proper condition. And only after they have issued with proper measure can they be called harmonious.

From this perspective, although neither of the two is separable from principle and material force, on the basis of their point of origin, each points to a predominant factor and emphasis, so there is no reason why we cannot say that the one is a matter of principle and the other a matter of material force.

Sources: First excerpt: *T'oegye chŏnsŏ,* T'oedo sŏnsaeng ŏnhaeng t'ongnok 5:1a-b. Vol. 2 (Seoul: Taedong munhwa yŏn'guwon, Sŏnggyun'gwan University, 1958), p. 702, translation, Palais. Second excerpt: *The Four-Seven Debate,* trans. Michael C. Kalton et al. (Albany: State University of New York Press, 1994), pp. 10–11. From the *Kobong chŏnjip* [The complete and collected works of Ki Taesŭng].

internecine strife and frequent purges that restricted the Confucian ideal of open access to office based on individual morality and blocked unity in times of crisis.

Although factionalism was disesteemed traditionally because it represented the formation of groups of officials to protect their own interests against the superior interest of the king, Korean officials justified their own factions because they represented moral superiority over rival factions, an argument that had been made in the Song Dynasty in China. King Sŏnjo (r. 1567–1608) disliked the factions but failed to

eliminate the problem. Instead, he encouraged it by shifting his favor from one faction to another and back again.

When the Chŏng Yŏrip rebellion broke out in Chŏlla province in the southwest in 1589, King Sŏnjo accepted the unjustifiable charge of the westerners that the rebellion was an easterner plot, and he executed over seventy easterner officials. He then sent a delegation to Japan in 1591 to assess the intentions of the Japanese leader, Toyotomi Hideyoshi. When it returned, Sŏnjo rejected the warning of the westerner ambassador that Hideyoshi was preparing an invasion of Korea and adopted the opinion of the easterner vice envoy that Hideyoshi was not. As a result, King Sŏnjo took no action to prepare the nation for war.

Japan, by contrast, had been engaged in almost constant internal warfare among powerful war lords (daimyo) since the outbreak of the Ōnin War in 1467. The victor in this long struggle was Toyotomi Hideyoshi, an uneducated peasant who had risen from the ranks and now could mobilize the mounted samurai warriors and archers and the commoner foot soldiers from all domains of Japan. His armies were also equipped with muskets and cannon, which had been introduced into Japan in the sixteenth century by the Portuguese but which Korea lacked. Hideyoshi decided to conquer all of Ming China and asked King Sŏnjo of Chosŏn for free passage through Korea. The king refused. Hideyoshi then sent his army to invade Korea in 1592, overwhelmed the Korean defenders, and occupied Seoul in three weeks and Pyongyang in two months before settling in for the winter. The only major military success of Chosŏn forces was by Admiral Yi Sunsin, whose naval forces succeeded in blocking Japanese ships from landing men off Chŏlla province on Korea's west coast (see **Biography: Admiral Yi Sunsin**). Regular Chosŏn military forces were overrun, and most of the fighting was done by guerrillas who attacked Japanese lines.

Under the tributary system, the Ming emperor had a moral obligation to send forces to defend Chosŏn as well as Chinese territory, but the Ming government was plagued by the raids of Mongol tribesmen, internal conflict between powerful eunuchs and orthodox Confucian reformers, fiscal shortages, and the decline in the number and quality of soldiers. Because Chinese officials initially thought that the Koreans were acting in complicity with the Japanese, Ming forces did not arrive in Korea until January 1593, seven months after the Japanese invasion. Although they succeeded in defeating Japanese forces at Pyongyang in February, they suffered a stunning defeat just north

of Seoul at the battle of Pyŏkchegwan late that month. Ming generals became much more cautious after that and in 1593 negotiated a truce with the Japanese commander, Katō Kiyomasa, that lasted until 1597.

Hideyoshi renewed the fighting in 1597 because he was angered by the terms that the Chinese offered. This time Japanese ground forces were blocked by the Ming army and forced to retreat to the southern littoral while Yi Sunsin's naval forces won major victories against enormous odds until he was killed at the end of the war. When Hideyoshi died in 1598, Japanese forces withdrew from the peninsula. Ming military intervention had saved Chosŏn from destruction, but Korea was left devastated by the massive loss of about 2 million lives. Agricultural production was not restored to pre-1592 levels until the beginning of the eighteenth century.

SUMMARY

The reforms initiated by King Kongmin of Koryŏ and completed by Yi Sŏnggye (King T'aejo) of Chosŏn reestablished the authority of the king and the central civil bureaucracy, established a firm fiscal basis for state government, secured stable foreign relations with the Ming Dynasty, and eliminated the challenge of the Wakō pirates in the Japanese islands. Three of the most successful kings in Korean history—T'aejong, Sejong, and Sejo—achieved tremendous achievements in culture, science, and military defense. The Confucian transformation of society at the expense of Buddhism was well underway, and family organization was shifted from Koryŏ patterns to emphasize the paterfamilias as the owner of family property and reduce the status and property rights of women. Although the *yangban* elite were now required to pass the civil service examinations to hold high office, those who did pass still came from the most prestigious aristocratic families, and

BIOGRAPHY Admiral Yi Sunsin

One of the greatest military heroes of Korean history was Admiral Yi Sunsin (1545–1598), who successfully led his small fleet against Hideyoshi's invasions between 1592 and 1598. In the first phase of the war (1592–1593) he won a major contest with his unprecedented use of an iron-clad flat-bottomed command ship in the shape of a turtle with a dragon's head at the bow, and other smaller ships of the same type along with wooden vessels with hulls and cabins made of thick boards. Ten oars on each side of the ship allowed it to escape enemy pursuit. The surface had long iron spikes camouflaged with straw mats to prevent enemy sailors from jumping on board. The ship had a lower deck with six gun ports and an upper deck with twenty-two gun ports on each side. The cannons inside shot shells of gunpowder and iron splinters. The ships were first used at the battle of Sach'ŏn on July 7, 1592. From August through October Yi won major battles at Yulp'o, Hansan Island, and Angolp'o and destroyed an additional four hundred Japanese ships in ten battles in December alone, preventing Japanese forces from entering the Chŏlla province area in the southeast. In the battle at Angolp'o, the Japanese beached their ships rather than challenge the turtle boat.

After a brief imprisonment on false charges in 1597, during which Yi Sunsin's replacement, Wŏn Kyun, suffered the loss of all but twelve Korean ships, Yi was recalled to service. He won one of his greatest victories at Myŏngnyang on October 26, 1597, where he defeated three hundred Japanese ships with those dozen ships. He won victories in seventeen of the eighteen naval battles he fought. Tragically, he died in his last battle in 1598, but he ordered his aides to keep his impending death secret and maintain the attack against the enemy.

the commoners and slaves had little chance of upward mobility. The hierarchical status pattern was maintained without excessive hardship or disruption.

Nevertheless, in the fifteenth century, chinks in the armor of the dynasty began to appear. The extra privileges of the merit subjects of several kings and King Sejo's usurpation of the throne created animosity among new scholars left out of the government. As a result, three bloody purges occurred between 1498 and 1519 and another major succession struggle occurred in 1545. *Yangban* landowners took over more land from tenants and added to the number of their slaves with bankrupt peasants. At the point when Confucian scholarship began to show some originality in the development of fundamental principles, it also became the tool of Confucian bureaucrats, who divided into political factions in 1575.

Finally, the institutions of taxation and labor service were so rigid that they proved incapable of changing with the times, and corrupt officials diverted revenues into their pockets rather than state coffers. More serious, both *yangban* and commoners evaded military service, leaving the garrisons empty just when Hideyoshi launched his invasion of Korea in 1592. All the signs of dynastic collapse were now present.

SUGGESTED READING

There are several valuable sources on Confucianism. See W. T. de Bary and J. Haboush, eds., *Neo-Confucianism and Culture: The Rise of Neo-Confucianism in Korea* (1985); E. Y. J. Chung, *The Korean Neo-Confucianism of Yi T'oegye and Yi Yulgok* (1995); M. Deuchler, *The Confucian Transformation of Korea* (1992); P. H. Lee, ed., *Sourcebook of Korean Civilization,* vol. 1 (1993) (paperback, *Sources of Korean Tradition,* Vol. 1, 1997); M. C. Kalton, trans. and ed., *To Become a Sage* (1988); M. C. Kalton et al., *The Four-Seven Debate* (1994); and Y.-C. Ro, *The Korean Neo-Confucianism of Yulgok* (1989).

For coverage of the early Chosŏn dynasty, see J. Duncan, *The Origins of the Chosŏn Dynasty* (2000); E. W. Wagner, *The Literati Purges* (1974); and J. B. Palais, *Confucian Statecraft and Korean Institutions* (1996).

For discussion of women and the family, see Deuchler, *The Confucian Transformation of Korea;* S. Mattielli, ed., *Virtues in Conflict* (1977); L. Kendall and M. Peterson, eds., *Korean Women: View from the Inner Room* (1983); and M. Peterson, *Korean Adoption and Inheritance* (1996).

PART FOUR

Growth and Stability (1600–1800)

Europe Enters the Scene

TRADE ROUTES FLOURISHED BETWEEN Northeast and Southeast Asia long before European merchants and Catholic missionaries entered the South China Sea. Lured by Asian silks, ceramics, and spices, ships under the Portuguese flag were the first to risk the voyage in the early sixteenth century. The Spanish, British, and Dutch followed. In early seventeenth-century Japan, early eighteenth-century China, and early nineteenth-century Korea, rulers put a stop to missionary activities, albeit for different reasons. Trade between Europe and East Asia continued, but it was confined to Guangzhou in China and Nagasaki in Japan.

Hemmed in by Spain, Portugal relied on trade to fill royal coffers. At the beginning of the fifteenth century, Portuguese ships started exploring the west coast of Africa in search of gold. African gold then financed a voyage around the Cape of Good Hope in 1488. From there, the Portuguese established a colony at Goa on the west coast of India and followed Muslim and Indian trade routes to the Spice Islands of Indonesia. Once Queen Isabella and her husband, Ferdinand, captured Grenada, the last Muslim emirate in Spain, in 1492, they funded Christopher Columbus's voyage across the Atlantic in hopes of finding an alternative route to China. In 1494, the pope divided the world beyond Europe between Spain and Portugal. Spain's sphere included most of the western hemisphere except Brazil; Portugal went east.

China's contact with Portugal began in 1511 when Admiral Alfonso de Albuquerque captured the Chinese entrepôt of Malacca near the tip of the Malay Peninsula. With this as a base, the first official Portuguese embassy followed traders to China in 1517. It behaved badly by refusing to conform to Chinese customs. Ship captains acted more like pirates than traders. Few Portuguese were willing to risk the long voyage in tiny ships around the Horn of Africa, across the wide expanse of the Indian Ocean and through the Strait of Malacca to Macao. Most were neither officials dispatched from the Portuguese court nor explorers seeking glory and territory. What they had in limited resources and manpower had to go toward making a profit in an already thriving commercial milieu (see Map C5.1).

Periodic prohibitions on maritime travel by Ming emperors at Beijing did not stop the Portuguese or seafaring people on the south China coast who made little distinction between trade, smuggling, and piracy. In 1521 the Ming tried to ban the Portuguese from China. Two years later an expeditionary force commissioned by the Portuguese king and charged with negotiating a friendship treaty defeated its mission by firing on Chinese warships near Guangzhou. In 1557, without informing Beijing, local Chinese officials decided that the way to regulate trade was to allow the Portuguese to build a trading post on an uninhabited bit of land near the mouth of the Pearl River. This the Portuguese called Macao. It became the first destination for all Europeans going to China until the nineteenth century, and it remained a Portuguese settlement until 1999.

The only significant new products Portuguese traders brought to networks that had already developed in East Asia were firearms and New World crops such as corn, sweet potatoes, and tobacco. They reached Japan by accident in 1543 when a typhoon blew three ships with a mixed crew of Southeast Asians to a small island called Tanegashima. The islanders helped repair their ship and bought their cargo. Among the goods exchanged for Japanese silver was the harquebus, a clumsy ancestor of the musket. The island's ruler ordered his retainers to study its operation and manufacture and distributed samples to more powerful mainland warlords. In 1570, Japanese troops deployed the Tanegashima harquebus in battle. In the meantime, Portuguese traders profited from the Ming ban on Japanese ships because they had raided the coast. The Portuguese carried 20 metric tons of Japanese silver a year to China in exchange for silk, sugar, medicine, and dye.

Trade between China and Europe increased in the late sixteenth century through an economic conjuncture that included the Americas. China needed silver because its monetary system depended on it and domestic production had declined after 1430. Chinese merchants bought Japanese silver carried on Portuguese ships. China also absorbed 50 percent of silver mined in Mexico and Bolivia and carried in Spanish ships to Manila, founded in 1571 when Spain made the Philippines a colony. Disruptions in the flow of silver from Japan and the western hemisphere in 1639 contributed to the fall of the Ming. Spanish silver bought manufactured goods—Chinese silk, porcelain, and lacquer—that dominated the luxury trade in Europe and funded Spain's wars against multiple enemies for generations.

Portuguese merchants seeking profits in East Asia faced competition from their government when the Portuguese viceroy at Goa made the Japan trade a royal monopoly in 1550. The Ming approved because their officials also wanted to see trade regularized. Each year a captain major appointed by the crown sent ships to Japan where warlords competed to attract the ships to their ports. (See Color Plate 19.) The governor of Macao forbade the sending of goods to Japan on private ships via third countries, especially the Philippines. His directives were futile; Portuguese and Spanish traders with crews drawn from all over East and Southeast Asia found Manila too convenient to abandon.

Catholic missionaries seeking converts who followed the traders hoped to keep the religious wars that undermined the pope's spiritual hegemony secret from Asia. The first were Jesuits, from the order founded by Ignatius Loyola in 1534 to promote Catholic scholarship and combat the Protestant Reformation initiated by Martin Luther in 1517. Jesuits insisted that Christianizing China and Japan was not to be done with the intent to conquer, as had been the case in the western hemisphere. As individuals, they displayed a rare sensitivity to other cultures. They were willing to find universal principles of belief outside a European context, but they served an institution that refused to compromise with indigenous beliefs and practices. Despite the efforts of charismatic missionaries, the Catholic church never gained the ascendancy in East Asia enjoyed by that other foreign religion, Buddhism.

The Jesuit priest Francis Xavier had worked in India and the Indies before China and Japan attracted his attention. After many misadventures, he landed on Satsuma in 1549. The Satsuma lord hoped that by treating Xavier well, he would attract the official Portuguese trading ships the next year. When the ships went instead to the island of Hirado, the lord expelled Xavier's party. Xavier traveled throughout western Japan as far as Kyoto, proselytizing wherever warlords gave permission. Asked why the Chinese knew nothing of Christianity if it was indeed an ancient and true religion, Xavier decided that Japan would become Christian only if China led the way. His efforts to enter China ended when he died on an uninhabited island off the China coast in December 1552.

Jesuits and Dominicans soon joined the missionaries and converts Xavier left behind in Japan. In 1565 Louis Frois met Oda Nobunaga who befriended the Jesuits to discomfort his Buddhist enemies. In 1580 Jesuits acquired Nagasaki from a warlord interested in promoting trade with Portuguese ships. In 1582, four young Kyushu samurai left Nagasaki for Lisbon and Rome, where they helped Jesuits get a papal bull that put Japan off limits to other orders. It proved to be ineffective, and quarrels between the Catholic orders over how best to present Christianity to East Asia damaged the missionaries' credibility in the eyes of Asian rulers.

Map C5.1 Seaborne Trading Empires in the Sixteenth and Seventeenth Centuries

Warlords trying to unite Japan under secular authority became increasingly suspicious of Christianity. If an absolute god demanded absolute loyalty, where did that leave the bonds between lord and retainer? Repression began in 1587 and intensified nine years later when the pilot of a ship wrecked on the Japanese coast allegedly pointed out that soldiers had followed Spanish missionaries to the Philippines. In 1614 Tokugawa Ieyasu decided that missionaries undermined the social order and were not essential to foreign trade. He ordered them expelled under threat of execution. He also tortured and killed Christian converts who refused to apostatize. Among the martyrs were Koreans who had been brought to Japan as slaves during Toyotomi Hideyoshi's invasions in the 1590s. The shogunate broke off relations with Catholic countries in 1624. The remaining Christians practiced their religion in secret by crafting statues of the Virgin Mary in the guise of Kannon, the Buddhist goddess of mercy.

Christianity arrived later in China. Not until 1583 did the Jesuit Matteo Ricci receive permission to move farther inland than Macao. Once he had educated himself in the style of Chinese literati, he set himself up in Nanjing. In 1601 he received tacit imperial permission to reside in Beijing. From him the Chinese learned western-style geography, astronomy, and Euclidean mathematics. In the years after Ricci's death in 1611, Jesuits regulated the Chinese lunar calendar. They suffered occasional harassment from xenophobic officials, but they retained their standing with Chinese literati during the turmoil that led to the collapse of the Ming Dynasty and the founding of the Qing in 1644. Catholic mendicant orders allowed into China in 1633 criticized Jesuits for aiming their efforts at the ruling class and trying to fit Christian ideas into the Chinese world-view rather than remaining European in approach and appealing to the masses.

Ricci and his Jesuit successors believed that Confucianism as a philosophy could be assimilated to monotheism. Confucianists and Christians shared similar concerns for morality and virtue. Rites of filial piety performed for the ancestors did not constitute a form of worship,

Matteo Ricci. Matteo Ricci is shown here in a French lithograph holding a map of the world to which he offers the crucified Christ. *(The Granger Collection)*

which made them compatible with Christianity. Mendicant orders disagreed. In 1715, religious and political quarrels in Europe exacerbated by longstanding antagonism to the Jesuits resulted in Ricci's accommodation with Chinese practices being deemed heretical. Angry at this insult, the Kangxi emperor forbade all Christian missionary work in China, although he allowed Jesuits to remain in Beijing to assist with the calendar. A Jesuit portrait painter later proved popular at the courts of his son and grandson. The outcome of the rites controversy over whether converts should be allowed to maintain ancestral altars, exacerbated by accusations that missionaries had meddled in the imperial succession, led the Qing to view all Europeans with suspicion.

China's rulers also tried to limit trade for strategic reasons. Between 1655 and 1675 the Qing banned maritime trade and travel to isolate Ming loyalists on Taiwan. In addition to official trade at the state level, the Qing permitted merchants to trade with foreigners, but only under tight control. After 1759, all maritime trade, whether with Southeast Asia or Europe, was confined to Guangzhou. Merchants put up with burdensome restrictions because in exchange for silver, China provided luxury items and tea, a bulk ware, introduced to Europe in 1607.

The profits to be made in East and Southeast Asia lured traders from Protestant countries following the religious wars of the latter half of the sixteenth century. Determined not to allow their Catholic rivals to dominate the world, Protestant nations sent explorers across the oceans. Britain's defeat of the Spanish Armada in 1588 began Spain's long decline. Early in the seventeenth century, the Dutch started their assault on Portuguese trade and colonies, especially in what is now Indonesia. Both nations established East India Companies in 1600 whose ability to capitalize trade far exceeded that of the merchants of Spain and Portugal.

Like Qing emperors, seventeenth-century Japanese shoguns tried to regulate foreign trade by confining it to specific harbors. In contrast to the sixteenth century, they also tried to prevent the increasingly short supply of precious metals from leaving the country by practicing import substitution for silk and sugar. A Dutch ship carrying a mixed crew of men from Europe and the western hemisphere arrived in 1600. (Of five ships with a crew of 461 men, only one ship and twenty-five men survived to reach Japan.) The next ships that arrived in 1609 received permission to set up quarters on Hirado, as did the British, who arrived in 1613. Both the Dutch and British arrived as representatives of trading companies, not their governments. Disappointed with scant profits, the British soon shut down their quarters. Unhappy with what it deemed smuggling, in 1635 the shogunate issued a maritime ban that forbade all Japanese from sailing overseas and ordered those who had migrated to Southeast Asia to return home or face permanent exile. The thriving Japanese community at Hoi An in Vietnam disappeared. In a further attempt to control unregulated trade and piracy, the shogunate later banned the building of ocean-going ships. In 1641 it ordered the Dutch to move from Hirado to the artificial island called Dejima in Nagasaki bay originally constructed for the Portuguese. The annual visits by Dutch ships allowed an exchange of information, continued Japan's connections with Southeast Asia, and opened the door to western science and medicine.

Korea proved inhospitable to merchants and missionaries alike. In the early seventeenth century British and Dutch traders made several attempts to insert their goods into the Japanese trade route through the islands of Tsushima, but memories of piracy, fear of unregulated trade that smacked of smuggling, and suspicion of European intentions led the government to refuse entry to their goods. Korean scholars in residence at the Chinese court read the Jesuits' religious, scientific, and mathematical treatises and took them back to Korea, where they attracted a small following for Catholic Christianity. The converts soon became embroiled in the factional infighting that characterized politics in eighteenth century Korea. No European missionary or merchant tried to visit Korea until three French priests landed illegally in 1836–1837. The Korean court had them and their converts executed in 1839 for spreading the "evil teaching" that ran counter to the dictates of filial piety.

SUGGESTED READING

For Southeast Asian networks, see A. Reid, *Southeast Asia in the Age of Commerce: 1450–1680*, vols. 1 and 2 (1988, 1993). For a recent book that compares trade in Europe and Asia, see K. L. Pomeranz, *The Great Divergence: China, Europe, and the Making of the Modern World* (2000). For the Jesuits in China, see J. Spence, *The Memory Palace of Matteo Ricci* (1984). For Japan see M. J. Cooper, *They Came to Japan: An Anthology of European Reports on Japan, 1543–1640* (1965); G. Elison, *Deus Destroyed* (1974); and D. Massarella, *A World Elsewhere: Europe's Encounter with Japan in the Sixteenth and Seventeenth Centuries* (1990).

The Creation of the Manchu Empire (1600–1800)

The seventeenth and eighteenth centuries were the age of the Manchus. As the Ming Dynasty fell into disorder, the Jurchens put together an efficient state beyond Ming's northeastern border and adopted the name *Manchu* for themselves. After they were called in to help suppress peasant rebellions, the Manchus took the throne themselves, founding the Qing Dynasty (1644–1911). Many Chinese did all they could to resist the Manchus out of loyalty to the Ming, but by the eighteenth century, Chinese and Manchus had learned to accommodate each other. In many ways the eighteenth century was the high point of traditional Chinese civilization. The Manchus created a multiethnic empire, adding Taiwan, Mongolia, Tibet, and Xinjiang to their realm, making the Qing Empire comparable to the other multinational empires of the early modern world, such as the Ottoman, Russian, and Habsburg Empires.

Many historians have been attracted to research on the seventeenth and eighteenth centuries because it provides a baseline of traditional China before the rapid changes of the modern era. Besides the usual questions of why the Ming fell and the Qing succeeded, scholars have recently been asking questions about the Manchus themselves. Who were they, and how did their history shape how they ruled China? How did they compel the allegiance of peoples of different backgrounds? How did they manage to give traditional Chinese political forms a new lease on life? Other historians have focused more on what was going on among the Chinese during these two crucial centuries. Was population growth a sign of prosperity? Or was it beginning to cause problems? How did scholars respond to Manchu rule?

THE MING DYNASTY LAPSES INTO DISORDER

After 1600 the Ming government was beset by fiscal, military, and political problems. The government was nearly bankrupt. It had spent heavily to help defend Korea against a Japanese invasion (see Chapters 13 and 15), had to support an ever-increasing imperial clan, and now had to provide relief for a series of natural disasters.

The bureaucracy did not pull together to meet these challenges. Officials diagnosed the problems confronting the dynasty in moral terms and saw removing the immoral from power as the solution, which led to fierce factionalism. Accusations and counteraccusations crossed so often that emperors wearied of officials and their infighting. Frustrated former officials who gathered at the Donglin Academy in Jiangsu province called for a revival of orthodox Confucian ethics. They blamed Wang Yangming for urging people to follow their innate knowledge, which seemed to the critics as equivalent to urging them to pursue their personal advantage.

At this time a "little ice age" brought a drop in average temperatures that shortened the growing season and reduced harvests. When food shortages became critical in northern Shaanxi in 1627–1628, army deserters and laid-off soldiers began forming gangs and scouring the countryside in search of food. By 1632 they had moved east and south into the central regions of Shanxi, Hebei, Henan, and Anhui provinces. Once the gangs had stolen all their grain, hard-pressed farmers joined them just to survive. Li Zicheng, a former shepherd and postal relay worker, became the paramount rebel leader in the north. The ex-soldier Zhang Xianzhong became the main leader in the central region between the Yellow and Yangzi rivers. The Ming government had little choice but to try to increase taxes to deal with these threats, but the last thing people needed was heavier exactions. Floods, droughts, locusts, and epidemics ravaged one region after another. In the Jiangnan area tenants rose up against landlords, and urban workers rioted. Meanwhile, the two main rebel leaders were in a race to see which of them could topple the Ming and found a new dynasty.

Part of the reason people rioted over rents was that real rents had risen due to deflation, itself brought on by a sudden drop in the supply of silver. In 1639 the Japanese authorities refused to let traders from Macao into Nagasaki, disrupting trade that had brought large quantities of silver to China. Another major source of silver was cut off a few months later when Chinese trade with the Spanish in the Philippines came to a standstill after a slaughter of Chinese residents. For China the drop in silver imports led to hoarding of both silver and grain, creating artificial shortages.

In 1642 a group of rebels cut the dikes on the Yellow River, leading to massive flooding. A smallpox epidemic soon added to the death toll. In 1644 Li Zicheng moved through Hebei into Beijing, where the last Ming emperor, in despair, took his own life. Zhang Xianzhong had moved in the opposite direction, into Sichuan, where his attacks on Chongqing and Chengdu led to widespread slaughter. Both Li and Zhang announced that they had founded new dynasties, and they appointed officials and minted coins. Neither, however, succeeded in pacifying a sizable region or ending looting and violence.

THE MANCHUS

The Manchus were descended from the Jurchens who had ruled north China during the Jin Dynasty (1127–1234). Although they had not maintained the written language that the Jin had created, they had maintained their hairstyle. Manchu men shaved the front of their head and wore the rest of their hair in a long braid (called a queue). The language they spoke belongs to the Tungus family, making it close to some of the languages spoken in nearby Siberia and distantly related to Korean and Japanese.

During the Ming Dynasty the Manchus had lived in dispersed communities in what is

Map 16.1 **Manchu Empire at Its Height**

loosely called Manchuria (the modern provinces of Liaoning, Jilin, and Heilongjiang). In the more densely populated southern part of Manchuria, Manchus lived in close contact with Mongols, Koreans, and Chinese, the latter especially in the Ming prefecture of Liaodong (see Map 16.1). The Manchus were not nomads, but rather hunters, fishermen, and farmers. Like the Mongols, they had a tribal social structure and were excellent horsemen and archers. Also like the Mongols, their society was strongly hierarchical, with elites and slaves. Slaves, often Korean or Chinese, were generally acquired through capture. From the Mongols, the Manchus had adopted Lamaist Buddhism, originally from Tibet, and it coexisted with their native shamanistic religion. Manchu shamans were men or women who had experienced a

spiritual death and rebirth and as a consequence could travel to and influence the world of the spirits.

Both the Chosŏn Dynasty in Korea and the Ming Dynasty in China welcomed diplomatic missions from Manchu chieftains, seeing them as a counterbalance to the Mongols. Written communication was frequently in Mongolian, the lingua franca of the region. Along the border with the Ming were officially approved markets where Manchus brought horses, furs, honey, and ginseng to exchange for Chinese tea, cotton, silk, rice, salt, and tools. By the 1580s there were five such markets that convened monthly, and unofficial trade occurred as well.

The Manchus credited their own rise to Nurhaci (1559–1626), who in 1583 at age twenty-four became the leader of one group of

Manchus. Over the next few decades, he was able to expand his territories, in the process not only uniting the Manchus but also creating a social-political-military organization that brought together Manchus, Mongols, and Chinese. When the Korean Sin Chung-il traveled to Nurhaci's headquarters in 1595–1596, he encountered many small Jurchen settlements, most no larger than twenty households, supported by fishing, hunting for pelts, collecting pine nuts or ginseng, or growing crops such as wheat, millet, and barley. Villages were often at odds with each other over resources, and men did not leave their villages without arming themselves with bows and arrows or swords. Interspersed among these Manchu settlements were groups of nomadic Mongols who lived in yurts in the open areas. Sin observed that Nurhaci had in his employ men from the Ming territory of Liaodong who could speak both Chinese and Manchu and could write in Chinese. Nurhaci's knowledge of China and Chinese ways was not entirely second-hand, however. In 1590 he had led an embassy to Beijing, and the next year he offered to join the Ming effort to repel the Japanese invasion of Korea. Nurhaci and his children married Mongols as well as Manchus, these marriages cementing alliances.

Early Manchu Rulers and Their Reigns

Nurhaci (Tianming)	1616–1626
Hong Taiji (Tiancong)	1627–1635
(Chongde)	1636–1643
Fulin (Shunzhi)	1644–1661
Xuanye (Kangxi)	1662–1722
Yinzhen (Yongzheng)	1723–1735
Hongli (Qianlong)	1736–1795

Like Chinggis, who had reorganized his armies to reduce the importance of tribal affiliations, Nurhaci created a new social basis for his armies in units called *banners*. Each banner was made up of a set of military companies, but included the families and slaves of the soldiers as well. Each company had a captain, whose position was hereditary. Many of the commanding officers were drawn from Nurhaci's own lineage. Over time new companies and new banners were formed, and by 1644 there were twenty-four banners (eight each of Manchu, Mongol, and Chinese banners). When new groups of Manchus were defeated, they were distributed among several banners to lessen their potential for subversion.

In 1616 Nurhaci declared war on the Ming Empire by calling himself khan of the revived Jin Dynasty and listing his grievances against the Ming. In 1621 his forces overran Liaodong and incorporated it into his state. After Nurhaci died in 1626, his son Hong Taiji succeeded him. In consolidating the Jin state, then centered on Mukden, Hong Taiji grudgingly made use of Chinese bureaucrats, but his goal was to replace them with a multiethnic elite equally competent in warfare and documents. In 1636 Hong Taiji renamed his state Qing ("pure"). When he died in 1643 at age forty-six, his brother Dorgon was made regent for his five-year-old son, Fulin, the Shunzhi emperor (r. 1643–1661).

The distinguished Ming general Wu Sangui (1612–1678), a native of Liaodong, was near the eastern end of the Great Wall when he heard that the rebel Li Zicheng had captured Beijing. Dorgon proposed to Wu that they join forces and liberate Beijing. Wu opened the gates of the Great Wall to let the Manchus in, and within a couple of weeks they had occupied Beijing. When the Manchus made clear that they intended to conquer the rest of the country and take the throne themselves, Wu joined forces with them, as did many other Chinese generals.

MING LOYALISM

When word reached the Yangzi valley of the fall of Beijing to the Manchus, Ming officials selected a Ming prince to succeed to the throne and shifted the capital to Nanjing, the Ming secondary capital. They were thus following the strategy that had allowed the Song Dynasty to continue to flourish after it had lost the north in 1126. The Ming court offered to buy off the Manchus, as the Song had bought off the Jurchens. Dorgon, however, saw no need to check his ambitions. He sent Wu Sangui and several Manchu generals to pursue the rebel forces across north China. Li Zicheng was eliminated in 1645, Zhang Xianzhong in 1647.

At the same time, Qing forces set about trying to defeat the Ming forces in the south. Quite a few able officials joined the Ming cause, but leadership was not well coordinated. Shi Kefa, a scholar-official who had risen to minister of war in Nanjing, took charge of defense and stationed his army at Yangzhou. Many other generals, however, defected to the Manchu side, and their soldiers were incorporated into the Qing armies. As the Qing forces moved south, many local officials opened the gates of their cities and surrendered. Shi Kefa refused to surrender Yangzhou, and a five-day battle ensued. The Manchu general was so angered at Shi's resistance that he unleashed his army to take revenge on the city, slaughtering hundreds of thousands. As cities in the south fell, large numbers of Ming loyalists committed suicide, their wives, mothers, and daughters frequently joining them.

In the summer of 1645, the Manchu command ordered that all Chinese serving in its armies shave the front of their heads in the Manchu fashion, presumably to make it easier to recognize whose side they were on. Soon this order was extended to all Chinese men, a measure that aroused deep resentment and made it easier for the Ming loyalists to organize resistance. When those newly conquered by the Qing refused to shave their hair, Manchu commanders felt justified in ordering the slaughter of defiant cities such as Jiading, Changshu, and Jiangyin. Still, Ming loyalist resistance continued long after little hope remained. The Manchus did not defeat the two main camps until 1661–1662, and even then Zheng Chenggong (Koxinga) was able to hold out in Taiwan until 1683.

Ming loyalism also took less militant forms (see **Biography: Printer Yu Xiangdou and His Family**). Several leading thinkers of this period had time to think and write because they refused to serve the Qing. Their critiques of the Ming and its failings led to searching inquiries into China's heritage of dynastic rule. Huang Zongxi (1610–1695) served the Ming resistance court at Nanjing, and followed it when it had to retreat, but after 1649 he lived in retirement at his home in Zhejiang province. The Manchu conquest was so traumatic an event that he reconsidered many of the basic tenets of Chinese political order. He came to the conclusion that the Ming's problems were not minor ones like inadequate supervision of eunuchs, but much more major ones, such as the imperial institution itself. Gu Yanwu (1613–1682) participated in the defense of his native city, then watched his mother starve herself rather than live under Manchu rule. He traveled across north China in search of a better understanding of Ming weaknesses, looking into economic topics Confucian scholars had rarely studied in depth, such as banking, mining, and farming. He had only disdain for scholars who wasted their time on empty speculation or literary elegance when there were so many practical problems awaiting solution. He thought that the Ming had suffered from overcentralization and advocated greater local autonomy. Wang Fuzhi (1619–1692) had passed the provincial exams under the Ming, but marauding rebels made it impossible for him to get to Beijing to take the *jinshi* exams in 1642. After Beijing fell to the Manchus two years later, Wang joined the resistance. He raised troops in his native Hunan province and for a while held a minor post at the court of the Ming pretender, but fell victim to factional strife and in 1650 withdrew to live as a retired scholar. Wang saw an urgent need not only to return Confucianism to its roots, but to protect Chinese civilization from the "barbarians." He insisted that it was as important to distinguish Chinese from barbarians as it was to distinguish superior men from petty men. It is natural for rulers to protect their followers from intruders:

BIOGRAPHY Printer Yu Xiangdou and His Family

The Qing conquest impinged on the lives of people of all walks of life, though in different ways. The printers in Jianyang in western Fujian province supported the Ming loyalist cause and published books with Ming dates well after 1644, which not surprisingly turned the Qing authorities against them, leading to the decline of their industry.

The Yu family of Jianyang in western Fujian began publishing books in the Song Dynasty, and the town where they lived eventually came to be called "Book Market." By late Ming there were several related Yus who operated publishing companies. One of the most successful of them was Yu Xiangdou. His grandfather had established a family school, and there had been hopes that Xiangdou would become an official, but by 1591 he gave up trying to pass the civil service examinations and concentrated on making money in the book business.

Yu did not merely solicit manuscripts and hire carvers for the wood blocks; he also wrote, annotated, and edited books himself. He compiled two collections of Daoist stories and another three of court-case fiction. He published versions of major novels, sometimes abridged, sometimes with commentaries. Sometimes he claimed that he had written or compiled a work that now we can see he merely copied, as there was nothing like copyright protection in his day.

Yu did not hide his presence in his books. At least three times, he included a portrait of himself in the book. In these portraits, he presents himself much as scholars were presented in the illustrated fiction he published: writing at a desk with servants in attendance or standing in a pavilion looking at the reflection of the moon on the water.

For twenty or more of his books, Yu wrote the preface himself. In a 1628 book on geomancy, which he published jointly with his son and nephew, he included a diagram of the burial sites of his parents and earlier ancestors. He also claimed that one of his ancestors, after recognizing the geomantic advantages of the place, encouraged his family to take up printing.

Yu published all sorts of books he thought would sell well. As aids to examination candidates, he published simplified histories and collections of selected literary pieces. Other reference works were explicitly addressed to the "four classes of people" and included information on farming, weaving, strange countries, medicine, music, chess, and the like, all with illustrations. Yu also published morality books by Yuan Huang, a well-known advocate of the Three Teachings (Confucianism, Buddhism, and Daoism). Yu was particularly active in publishing illustrated fiction, especially historical novels. The format he popularized had the illustrations run across the top of the page, with captions beside it, and the text below, allowing one to glance at the picture while reading the story. One of his historical novels proved so popular that the wood blocks wore out after several reprintings and he had to have them totally recarved.

Although Yu Xiangdou's son and grandson followed him in the book trade, Qing government efforts to eliminate Ming loyalism hurt their business and Jianyang rapidly declined as a book center.

"Now even the ants have rulers who preside over the territory of their nests, and when red ants or flying white ants penetrate their gates, the ruler organizes all his own kind into troops to bite and kill the intruders, drive them far away from the anthill, and prevent foreign interference."[1] The Ming rulers had failed in this basic responsibility.

THE QING AT ITS HEIGHT

For more than a century, China was ruled by just three rulers, each of whom was hard working, talented, and committed to making the Qing Dynasty a success. The policies and institutions they put into place gave China a respite from war and disorder, and the Chinese population seems to have nearly doubled during this period, from between 150 and 175 million to between 300 and 325 million. Population growth during the course of the eighteenth century has been attributed to many factors: global warming that extended the growing season; expanded use of New World crops; slowing of the spread of new diseases that had accompanied the sixteenth-century expansion of global traffic; and the efficiency of the Qing government in providing relief in times of famine. Some scholars have recently argued that China's overall standard of living in the mid-eighteenth century was comparable to Europe's and that the standards of China's most developed regions, such as the Jiangnan region, compared favorably to the most developed regions of Europe at the time, such as England and the Netherlands. Life expectancy, food consumption, and even facilities for transportation were at similar levels. The government in this period had the resources to respond to famines and disasters; indeed, during the eighteenth century, the treasury was so full that four times the annual land tax was cancelled.

Kangxi

After the Shunzhi emperor died of smallpox (which struck many Manchus after they settled in Beijing), one of his sons who had already sur-

vived the disease was selected to succeed. Known as the Kangxi emperor (r. 1661–1722), he lived to see the Qing Empire firmly established.

The Kangxi emperor proved adept at meeting the expectations of both the Chinese and Manchu elites. At age fourteen, he announced that he would begin ruling on his own and had his regent imprisoned. He could speak, read, and write Chinese and appreciated the value of persuading educated Chinese that the Manchus had a legitimate claim to the Mandate of Heaven. Most of the political institutions of the Ming Dynasty had been taken over relatively unchanged, including the examination system, and the Kangxi emperor worked to attract Ming loyalists who had been unwilling to serve the Qing. He undertook a series of tours of the south, where resistance had been strongest, and held a special exam to select men to compile the official history of the Ming Dynasty.

The main military challenge the Kangxi emperor faced was the revolt of Wu Sangui and two other Chinese generals who in the early years of the conquest had been given vast tracts of land in the south as rewards for joining the Qing. Wu was made, in effect, satrap of Yunnan and Guizhou, and it was his armies that had pursued the last Ming pretender into Burma. When the Qing began to curb the power of these generals in 1673, Wu declared himself the ruler of an independent state, and the other two "feudatories" joined him. Although the south was not yet fully reconciled to Qing rule, Wu, as a turncoat himself, did not attract a large following. Although it took eight years, the military structure that the Qing had put together proved strong enough to defeat this challenge. At the conclusion of these campaigns, Taiwan, where the last of the Ming loyalists had held out, was made part of Fujian province, fully incorporating it into China proper.

By annexing Mongolia, the Kangxi emperor made sure the Qing Dynasty would not have the northern border problems the Ming had had (see Map 16.1). In 1696 he led an army of eighty thousand men into Mongolia, and within a few years Manchu supremacy was accepted

---

1. W. Theodore de Bary and Richard Lufrano, *Sources of Chinese Tradition: From 1600 Through the Twentieth Century* (New York: Columbia University Press, 2000), p. 35.

there. Qing forces were equipped with cannons and muskets, giving them military superiority over the Mongols, who were armed only with bows and arrows. They thus could dominate the steppe cheaply, effectively ending two thousand years of northern border defense problems.

The Qing also asserted its presence in Tibet. This came about after a group of Western Mongols tried to find a new place for themselves in Tibet. The army the Qing sent after them occupied Lhasa in 1718. In the 1720s, the Qing presence in Tibet was made firm with the establishment of a permanent garrison of banner soldiers. By this time, the Qing Empire was coming into proximity of the expanding Russian Empire. In 1689 the Manchu and the Russian rulers approved a treaty—written in Russian, Manchu, Chinese, and Latin—defining their borders in Manchuria and regulating trade. Another treaty in 1727 allowed a Russian ecclesiastical mission to reside in Beijing and a caravan to make a trip from Russia to Beijing once every three years.

The Kangxi emperor took a personal interest in the European Jesuit priests who served at court as astronomers and cartographers and translated many European works into Chinese. However, when the pope sided with the Dominican and Franciscan orders in China who opposed allowing converts to maintain ancestral altars (known as the "rites controversy"), he objected strongly to the pope's issuing directives about how Chinese should behave. He outlawed Christian missionaries, though he did allow Jesuit scientists and painters to remain in Beijing.

Qianlong

The Kangxi emperor's heir, Yinzheng, who ruled as the Yongzheng emperor (r. 1723–1735), was forty-five years old when he took the throne. A hard-working ruler, he tightened central control over the government. He oversaw a rationalization of the tax structure, substituting new levies for a patchwork of taxes and fees. The Yongzheng emperor's heir, Hongli, the Qianlong emperor (r. 1736–1795), benefited from his

father's fiscal reforms, and during his reign, the Qing government regularly ran surpluses.

It was during the Qianlong reign that the Qing Empire was expanded to its maximum extent, with the addition of Chinese Turkestan (the modern province of Xinjiang). Both the Han and Tang Dynasties had stationed troops in the region, exercising a loose suzerainty, but neither Song nor Ming had tried to control the area. The Qing won the region in the 1750s through a series of campaigns against Uighur and Dzungar Mongol forces. Like Tibet, loosely annexed a few decades earlier, this region was ruled lightly. The local population kept their own religious leaders and did not have to wear the queue.

The Qianlong emperor put much of his energy into impressing his subjects with his magnificence. He understood that the Qing capacity to hold their empire together rested on their ability to speak in the political and religious idioms of those they ruled. Besides Manchu and Chinese, he learned to converse in Mongolian, Uighur, Tibetan, and Tangut and addressed envoys in their own languages. He was as much a patron of Lamaist Buddhism as of Chinese Confucianism. He initiated a massive project to translate the Tibetan Buddhist canon into Mongolian and Manchu. He also had huge multilingual dictionaries compiled. He had the child Dalai Lamas raised and educated in Beijing. He made much of the Buddhist notion of the "wheel-turning king" (cakravartin), the ruler who through his conquests moves the world toward the next stage in universal salvation (see Color Plate 20).

To demonstrate to the Chinese scholar-official elite that he was a sage emperor, Qianlong worked on affairs of state from dawn until early afternoon, when he turned to reading, painting, and calligraphy. He took credit for writing over forty-two thousand poems and ninety-two books of prose. He inscribed his own poetry on hundreds of masterpieces of Chinese painting and calligraphy that he had gathered into the palace collections. He especially liked works of fine craftsmanship, and his taste influenced artistic styles of the day. The Qianlong emperor was ostentatiously devoted to his mother, visiting her daily and tending to her comfort with all the devotion of the most filial Chinese son. He took several tours down the Grand Canal to the Jiangnan area, in part to emulate his grandfather, in part to entertain his mother. Many of his gestures were costly. His southern tours cost ten times what the Kangxi emperor's had and included the construction of temporary palaces and triumphal arches.

For all of these displays of Chinese virtues, the Qianlong emperor still was not fully confident that the Chinese supported his rule, and he was quick to act on any suspicion of anti-Manchu thoughts or actions (see **Documents: Fang Bao's "Random Notes from Prison"**). When he first took the throne, he reversed the verdict on the case of a Chinese named Zeng Jing who had been persuaded by an anti-Manchu tract to try to start an uprising. His father, the Yongzheng emperor, had treated Zeng leniently, preferring to persuade him of Manchu legitimacy than to punish him. The Qianlong emperor had him dragged back to Beijing, retried, and executed. More than thirty years later, when rumors reached the Qianlong emperor that sorcerers were "stealing souls" by clipping the ends of men's queues, he suspected a seditious plot and had his officials interrogate men under torture until they found more and more evidence of a nonexistent plot. A few years after that episode, the Qianlong emperor carried out a huge literary inquisition. During the compilation of the *Complete Books of the Four Treasuries*, an effort to catalogue nearly all books in China, he began to suspect that some governors were holding back books with seditious content. He ordered full searches for books with disparaging references to the Manchus or previous alien conquerors. Sometimes passages were omitted or rewritten, but when the entire book was offensive, it was destroyed. So thorough was the proscription that no copies survive of more than two thousand titles.

The Qianlong emperor lived into his eighties, but his political judgment began to decline in his sixties when he began to favor a handsome and intelligent young imperial bodyguard named Heshen. Heshen was rapidly promoted to posts normally held by experienced civil officials, including ones with power over revenue and civil service appointments. When the emperor did nothing to stop Heshen's blatant corruption, officials began to worry that he was becoming senile. By this time, uprisings were breaking out, especially in the southwest, where the indigenous Miao were being pushed out of the river valleys by Han Chinese migrants. Heshen supplied the Qianlong emperor with rosy reports of the progress in suppressing the rebellions, all the while pocketing much of the military appropriations himself.

The Qianlong emperor abdicated in 1795 in order not to rule longer than his grandfather, the Kangxi emperor, but he continued to dominate court until he died in 1799 at age eighty-nine.

The Banner System

The Kangxi, Yongzheng, and Qianlong emperors used the banner system to maintain military control and preserve the Manchus' privileges. In the first few decades of the Qing, as the country was pacified, banner forces were settled across China in garrisons, usually within the walls of a city. All of the Chinese who lived in the northern half of Beijing were forced out to clear the area for bannermen, and Beijing became very much a Manchu city. In other major cities, such as Hangzhou, Nanjing, Xi'an, and Taiyuan, large sections of the cities were cleared for the banners' use. The bannermen became in a sense a hereditary occupational caste, ranked above others in society, whose members were expected to devote themselves to service to the state. They were also expected to live apart from nonbanner Chinese and were not allowed to intermarry with them.

Outside the cities, lands were expropriated to provide support for the garrisons, some 2 million acres altogether, with the densest area in the region around Beijing. In China proper bannermen did not cultivate the fields (as they had in Manchuria), but rather lived off stipends from

DOCUMENTS

Fang Bao's "Random Notes from Prison"

As more and more varied types of sources survive, it becomes possible to get better glimpses of the less pleasant sides of life. The ordeal of judicial confinement was hardly new to the eighteenth century, but it was not until then that we have so vivid a depiction of it as that provided by Fang Bao (1668–1749). In 1711 he and his family members were arrested because he had written a preface for the collected works of one of his friends whose works had just been condemned for language implying support for revival of the Ming Dynasty. After Fang spent two years in prison, he was pardoned and went on to hold a series of literary posts. Despite this brush with imperial censorship, Fang was willing in his account of his time in prison to point to the inhumane way people not yet found guilty of a crime were treated and the corruption of prison personnel, who demanded cash in exchange for better treatment.

In the prison there were four old cells. Each cell had five rooms. The jail guards lived in the center with a window in the front of their quarters for light. At the end of this room there was another opening for ventilation. There were no such windows for the other four rooms and yet more than two hundred prisoners were always confined there. Each day toward dusk, the cells were locked and the odor of the urine and excrement would mingle with that of the food and drink. Moreover, in the coldest months of the winter, the poor prisoners had to sleep on the ground and when the spring breezes came everyone got sick. The established rule in the prison was that the door would be unlocked only at dawn. During the night, the living and the dead slept side by side with no room to turn their bodies and this is why so many people became infected. Even more terrible was that robbers, veteran criminals and murderers who were imprisoned for serious offenses had strong constitutions and only one or two out of ten would be infected and even so they would recover immediately. Those who died from the malady were all light offenders or sequestered witnesses who would not normally be subjected to legal penalties.

I said: "In the capital there are the metropolitan prefectural prison and the censorial prisons of the five wards. How is it then that the Board of Punishment's prison has so

the rents, paid part in silver and part in grain. The dynasty supported banner soldiers and their families from cradle to grave, with special allocations for travel, weddings, and funerals. Once the conquest was complete, the banner population grew faster than the need for soldiers, so within a couple of generations, there were not enough positions in the banner armies for all adult males in the banners. Yet bannermen were not allowed to pursue occupations other than soldier or official. As a consequence, many led lives of forced idleness, surviving on stipends paid to a relative. By the time of the Qianlong emperor, this had become enough of a problem that he had most of the Chinese bannermen removed from the banner system and reclassified as commoners, increasing the Manchu dominance of the banner population.

Bannermen had facilitated entry into government service. Special quotas for Manchus allowed many prisoners?" [My fellow prisoner, the magistrate] Mr. Du answered: ". . . The chiefs and deputy heads of the Fourteen Bureaus like to get new prisoners; the clerks, prison officials, and guards all benefit from having so many prisoners. If there is the slightest pretext or connection they use every method to trap new prisoners. Once someone is put into the prison his guilt or innocence does not matter. The prisoner's hands and feet are shackled and he is put in one of the old cells until he can bear the suffering no more. Then he is led to obtain bail and permitted to live outside the jail. His family's property is assessed to decide the payment and the officials and clerks all split it. Middling households and those just above exhaust their wealth to get bail. Those families somewhat less wealthy seek to have the shackles removed and to obtain lodging [for the prisoner relative] in the custody sheds outside the jail. This also costs tens of silver taels. As for the poorest prisoners or those with no one to rely on, their shackles are not loosened at all and they are used as examples to warn others. Sometimes cellmates guilty of serious crimes are bailed out but those guilty of small crimes and the innocent suffer the most poisonous abuse. They store up their anger and indignation, fail to eat or sleep normally, are not treated with medicine, and when they get sick they often die.

"I have humbly witnessed our Emperor's virtuous love for all beings which is as great as that of the sages of the past ages. Whenever he examines the documents related to a case, he tries to find life for those who should die. But now it has come to this [state of affairs] for the innocent. A virtuous gentleman might save many lives if he were to speak to the Emperor saying: 'Leaving aside those prisoners sentenced to death or exiled to border regions for great crimes, should not small offenders and those involved in a case but not convicted be placed in a separate place without chaining their hands and feet?'" . . .

My cellmate Old Zhu, Young Yu, and a certain government official named Seng who all died of illness in prison should not have been heavily punished. There was also a certain person who accused his own son of unfiliality. The [father's] neighbors [involved in the case only as witnesses] were all chained and imprisoned in the old cells. They cried all night long. I was moved by this and so I made inquiries. Everyone corroborated this account and so I am writing this document.

Source: From Pei-kai Cheng, Michael Lestz, and Jonathon D. Spence, *The Search for Modern China: A Documentary Collection* (New York: Norton, 1999), pp. 55–58, slightly modified.

them to gain more than 5 percent of the *jinshi* degrees, even though they never exceeded 1 percent of the population. Advancement was also easier for bannermen, since many posts, especially in Beijing, were reserved for them, including half of all the top posts. In the middle and lower ranks of the Beijing bureaucracy, Manchus greatly outnumbered Chinese. One study suggests that about 70 percent of the metropolitan agencies' positions were reserved for bannermen and less then 20 per-

cent for Chinese (the rest were unspecified). In the provinces, Manchus did not dominate in the same way, except at the top level of governors and governors-general, where they held about half the posts.

Bannermen had legal privileges as well. They fell under the jurisdiction of imperial commissioners, not the local magistrate or prefect. If both a Chinese and a Manchu were brought into court to testify, the Chinese was required

Imperial Bodyguard Zhanyinbao. Dated 1760, this life-size portrait was done by a court artist in the European-influenced style favored by the Qianlong emperor. *(The Metropolitan Museum of Art, The Dillon Fund, 1986 [1986.206])*

to kneel before the magistrate but the Manchu could stand. If each was found guilty of the same crime, the Manchu would receive a lighter punishment—for instance, wearing the cangue (a large wooden collar) for sixty days instead of exile for life.

Despite the many privileges given to Manchu bannermen, impoverishment of the banner population quickly became a problem. Although the government from time to time forgave all bannermen's debts, many went bankrupt. Company commanders sometimes sold off banner land to provide stipends, which made it more difficult to provide support thereafter. The Qianlong

emperor also tried resettling Manchus back in Manchuria, but those used to urban life in China rarely were willing to return to farming, and most sneaked back as soon as possible.

Within a generation of settling in China proper, the Chinese dialect of the Beijing area became the common language of the banner population. The Qing emperors repeatedly called on the Manchus to study both spoken and written Manchu, but it became a second language learned at school rather than a primary language. Other features of Manchu culture were more easily preserved, such as the use of personal names alone to refer to people. (Manchus had names for families and clans but did not use them as part of their personal names.)

The elements of Manchu culture most important to the state were their martial traditions and their skill as horsemen and archers. Life in the cities and long stretches of peace took a toll on these skills, despite the best efforts of the emperors to inspire martial spirit. The Qianlong emperor himself was fully literate in Chinese, but he discouraged the Manchu bannermen from developing interests in Chinese culture. He knew the history of the Jin Dynasty and the problems the Jurchens had faced with soldiers living in China taking up Chinese ways, and he did everything he could think of to prevent this. Although the Qing court was as sumptuous as any other in Chinese history, the emperor tried to convince the bannermen that frugality was a Manchu characteristic, to be maintained if they were not to lose their ethnic identity.

Perhaps because they were favored in so many ways, the bannermen proved a very loyal service elite. Unlike their counterparts in other large empires, the banner armies never turned on the ruling house or used the resources that had been assigned to them to challenge central authority.

CONTACTS WITH EUROPE

The Qing regulated its relations with countries beyond its borders through a diplomatic system modeled on the Ming one. Countries like Korea, Ryukyu, Japan, Vietnam, and many of the other states of Southeast Asia sent envoys to the court at Beijing. Europeans were not full players in this system, but they had a marginal presence.

Trading contacts with Europe were concentrated at Guangzhou in the far south (see **Connections: Europe Enters the Scene**). Soon after 1600, the Dutch East India Company had largely dislodged the Spanish and Portuguese from the trade with China, Japan, and the East Indies. Before long, the British East India Company began to compete with the Dutch for the spice trade. In the seventeenth century the British and Dutch sought primarily porcelains and silk, but in the eighteenth century, tea became the commodity in most demand. By the end of the century, tea made up 80 percent of Chinese exports to Europe.

In the early eighteenth century, China enjoyed a positive reputation among the educated in Europe. China was the source of prized luxuries: tea, silk, porcelain, cloisonné, wallpaper, and folding fans. The Manchu emperors were seen as wise and benevolent rulers. Voltaire wrote of the rationalism of Confucianism and saw advantages to the Chinese political system as rulers did not put up with parasitical aristocrats or hypocritical priests.

By the end of the eighteenth century, British merchants were dissatisfied with the restrictions imposed on trade by the Qing government. The Qing, like the Ming before it, specified where merchants of particular countries could trade, and the Europeans were to trade only in Guangzhou, even though tea was grown mostly in the Yangzi valley, adding the cost of transporting it south to the price the foreign merchants had to pay. The merchants in Guangzhou who dealt with western merchants formed their own guild, and the Qing government made them guarantee that the European merchants obeyed Qing rules. In the system as it evolved, the Europeans had to pay cash for goods purchased and were forbidden to enter the walled city of Guangzhou, ride in sedan chairs, bring women or weapons into their quarters, and learn Chinese.

Great Pagoda at Kew Gardens. A taste for things Chinese led to the construction of a ten-story, 162-foot tall octagonal pagoda in Kew Gardens in London in 1762. It was originally very colorful and had eighty dragons decorating its roofs. *(The Art Archive)*

As British purchases of tea escalated, the balance of trade became more lopsided, but British merchants could not find goods Chinese merchants would buy from them. The British government also was dissatisfied. It was becoming suspicious of the British East India Company, which had made great fortunes from its trade with China, and wanted to open direct diplomatic relations with China in part as a way to curb the company. To accomplish all this, King George III sent Lord George Macartney, the former ambassador to Russia and former governor of Madras. Macartney was instructed to secure a place for British traders near the tea-producing areas, negotiate a commercial treaty, create a desire for British products, arrange for diplomatic representation in Beijing, and open Japan and Southeast Asia to British commerce as well. He traveled with an entourage of eighty-four and six hundred cases packed with British goods that he hoped would impress the Chinese court and attract trade: clocks, telescopes, knives, globes, plate glass, Wedgwood pottery, landscape paintings, woolen cloth, and carpets. The only one of the British party able to speak Chinese, however, was a twelve-year-old boy who had learned some Chinese by talking with Chinese on the long voyage.

After Lord Macartney arrived in Guangzhou in 1793, he requested permission to see the emperor in order to present a letter to him from George III. Although the letter had been written in Chinese, its language was not appropriate for addressing an emperor. Still, the British party was eventually allowed to proceed to Beijing. Once there, another obstacle emerged: when instructed on how to behave on seeing the emperor, Macartney objected to having to perform the kowtow (kneeling on both knees and bowing one's head to the ground).

Finally Macartney was permitted to meet more informally with the Qianlong emperor at his summer retreat. No negotiations followed this meeting, however, as the Qing court saw no merit in Macartney's requests. It was as interested in maintaining its existing system of regulated trade as Britain was interested in doing away with it.

Several of the members of the Macartney mission wrote books about China on their return. These books, often illustrated, contained descriptions of many elements of Chinese culture and social customs, less rosy than the reports of the Jesuits a century or two earlier. The official account of the embassy, prepared by George Staunton, depicted Chinese women as subjugated: "Women, especially in the lower walks of life, are bred with little other principle than that of implicit obedience to their fathers or their husbands." Although the wives of the peasantry worked very hard at domestic tasks and did all the weaving in the country, they were treated badly: "Not withstanding all the merit of these helpmates to their husbands, the latter arrogate an extraordinary dominion over them, and hold them at such distance, as not always to allow them to sit at table, behind which, in such case, they attend as hand-maids."[2] From books like these, Europeans began to see more of the complexity of China. The Chinese, by contrast, did not learn much about Europe or Britain from this encounter.

SOCIAL AND CULTURAL CROSS CURRENTS

During the late Ming, Chinese culture had been remarkably open and fluid. Especially in the cities of Jiangnan, new books of all sorts were being published; the theater flourished; and intellectuals took an interest in ideas of Buddhist, Daoist, or even European origin and, encouraged by Wang Yangming's teachings, pursued truth in individualistic ways.

With the collapse of the social order in the early seventeenth century and the conquest by the Manchus, many in the educated class turned against what had come to seem like a lack of standards and commitments. Early Qing Confucian scholars often concluded that the Ming fell as a result of moral laxity. Wang Yangming and his followers, by validating emotion and spontaneity, had undermined commitment to duty and respect for authority. The solution, many thought, was to return to Zhu Xi's teachings, with their emphasis on objective standards outside the individual.

This conservative turn was manifested in several ways. Laws against homosexuality were made harsher. Because literati argued that drama and fiction were socially subversive, theaters were closed and novels banned. Qian Daxian, a highly learned scholar, went so far as to argue that the vernacular novel was the main

---

2. George Staunton, *An Authentic Account of an Embassy from the King of Great Britain to the Emperor of China* (London: W. Bulmer, 1798), 2:109.

threat to Confucian orthodoxy. The cult of widow chastity reached new heights, with local histories recording more and more widows who refused to remarry, including those who lived their entire lives as the celibate "widows" of men to whom they had been engaged but who had died before they had even met.

The conservative turn in scholarship fostered a new interest in rigorous textual analysis. Some Confucian scholars turned back to the Han commentaries on the classics, hoping that they could free their understandings of the texts from the contamination of Buddhist and Daoist ideas that had infiltrated Tang and Song commentaries. Others wanted to rely solely on the classics themselves and to concentrate on verifiable facts. Yan Ruoju compiled a guide to the place names in the Four Books and proved that the "old text" version of the *Book of Documents* could not be genuine. Research of this sort required access to large libraries, and it thrived primarily in Jiangnan, with its high densities of both books and scholars.

There are always those who resist calls for decorum and strenuous moral effort, and in the eighteenth century, both the Manchu rulers and the Chinese intellectual elite provided room for the less conventional to contribute in creative ways. Exploration of the potential of ink painting for self-expression reached a high point in the eighteenth century with a closely affiliated group of painters known as the Eight Eccentrics of Yangzhou (see **Material Culture: Jin Nong's Inscribed Portrait of a Buddhist Monk**). These painters had no difficulty finding patrons, even among social and cultural conservatives. Similarly, Yuan Mei, on familiar terms with the great classicists and philologists of his day, was willing to risk their censure by taking on women as poetry students. One of his female poetry students, Luo Qilan, wrote in 1797 to defend him from charges of impropriety, arguing that if Confucius had believed in the principle that words spoken inside a chamber must stay indoors, he would have removed poems by women from the *Book of Poetry*.

The Dream of Red Mansions

Women with poetic talents figure prominently in an eighteenth-century novel, *The Dream of Red Mansions* (also called *Story of the Stone*), considered by many the most successful of all works of Chinese fiction. Concerned with the grand themes of love and desire, money and power, life and death, and truth and illusion, it is at the same time a psychologically sensitive novel of manners. The author of the first eighty chapters was Cao Xueqin (1715–1764). He died before it was completed, but another writer added forty chapters to complete it before it was published in 1791. Cao Xueqin came from a Chinese family that had risen with the Manchus. Bondservants of the ruling house, they were in a position to gain great wealth and power managing enterprises for the rulers. In the eighteenth century, however, the family lost favor and went bankrupt.

The *Dream* portrays in magnificent detail the affairs of the comparably wealthy Jia family. The central characters of the novel are three adolescents: Jia Baoyu and his two female cousins of other surnames who come to live with his family. One of the cousins, Lin Daiyu, is sickly and difficult; the other, Xue Baochai, is capable and cheerful. A magnificent garden is built in the family compound in order to receive a visit from Baoyu's sister, who had become an imperial consort. After the visit Baoyu and his cousins and their personal servants move into the garden, an idyllic world of youth and beauty. This magical period comes to an end when Baoyu is tricked into marrying Baochai (thinking he is marrying Daiyu). While the wedding is taking place, Daiyu is on her sickbed, dying of consumption. The novel ends with Baoyu passing the *jinshi* examinations, only to leave his wife and family to pursue religious goals.

Much of the power of *Dream* comes from the many subplots and the host of minor characters from all walks of life—officials, aristocrats, monks and nuns, pageboys, gardeners, country relatives, princes, gamblers, prostitutes, actors,

MATERIAL CULTURE

Jin Nong's Inscribed Portrait of a Buddhist Monk

Chinese painters often combined words and images, sometimes inscribing poems or explanations of the occasion that gave rise to the painting on the painting itself. The highly individualistic painters of the eighteenth century known as the Eight Eccentrics of Yangzhou sometimes carried this practice to its limit, filling all the space on a painting with their writing. The painting shown here, by Jin Nong (1687–1764), is dated 1760. Writing in his highly distinctive calligraphy, Jin Nong fills the space around the Buddha with a history of the painting of images of Buddhas followed by personal remarks:

> I am now a man beyond seventy years of age who has no false ideas and desires. Though physically I am in the dusty world, I earnestly try to live cleanly. I wash my ten fingers, burn incense, and hold the brush to record the dignity and seriousness of humanity. What I do is not far from the ancient tradition. I offer good wishes to all men on earth.
>
> In the second lunar month, 1760, on the date when Buddha achieved enlightenment, I painted several Buddha images, four Bodhisattvas, sixteen Lohans, and distributed these sacred materials. These works are the product of my deep conviction, not in the style of famous masters of the Jin and Tang. My inspiration came from the Longmen caves that were carved a thousand years ago. When my priest friend, Defeng commented, "These paintings found [a new school] and will be followed by the coming generations," I roared with laughter.[1]

––––––

1. Tseng Yuho, trans., *A History of Chinese Calligraphy* (Hong Kong: University of Hong Kong Press, 1993), p. 94, slightly modified.

Portrait of a Monk. This hanging scroll, painted by Jin Nong in 1760 in ink and colors on paper, measures 133 by 62.5 cm. *(Collection of the Tianjin History Museum)*

Color Plate 17
Rice Planting. This sixteenth-century painting of *Rice Planting* depicts it as a fertility festival with men providing the music while women work.

Color Plate 18
The Garden of the Master of Nets. A large pond is the central feature of the *Garden of the Master of Nets* in Suzhou. Notice the use of plants, rocks, and walkways.

Color Plate 19
Arrival of the Portuguese. This six-panel folding screen depicts the *Arrival of the Portuguese*—soldiers in short pants, merchants in balloon pants, and priests in black robes accompanied by African servants.

(Musee des Arts Asiatiques-Guimet, Paris, France/RMN/Art Resource, NY)

Color Plate 20
The Qianlong Emperor Receiving Tribute Horses. This detail from a 1757 painting by the Italian court painter Giuseppe Castiglione (1688–1768) shows the reception of envoys from the Kazakhs. Note how the envoy, presenting a pure white horse, is kneeling to the ground (performing the kowtow).

(Musee Guimet, Paris/The Art Archive)

Color Plate 21
Dry Goods Store in Surugacho. In this painting entitled *Dry Goods Store in Surugacho, Edo,* customers take off their shoes to enter the shop. Male clerks serve female customers while others gather around the manager. The owner is at the back of the store.
(Corbis)

Color Plate 22
Women at the Tano Festival, by Sin Yunbok (1758–?), Chosŏn Dynasty. This painting captures the eroticism that is frequently associated with Sin Yunbok's depiction of women. Notice the two boy monks stealing a glance at the women from behind the rocks.
(Kansong Museum of Fine Arts, Seoul)

Color Plate 23
Procession for Crown Prince Sado. Procession returning from a visit to Hwasŏng (modern Suwŏn) to Seoul in 1795 led by King Chŏngjo with his mother, Lady Hyegyŏng, to honor the 60th birthday of his father, Crown Prince Sado, who had been murdered by his own father, King Yŏngjo, in 1762.
(Han Yong'u, *Tasi ch'annuin uri yoksa [Our History, Rediscovered]*, p. 11 left)

Color Plate 24
The Foreign Quarter in Guangzhou. Before the Opium War, foreign traders in Guangzhou were not to leave the small strip of land outside the city where their "factories" were located. They could live there only while arranging shipments and had to return to Macao once their ships were loaded.

(Winterthur Museum)

and innkeepers. The seamier side of political life is portrayed through memorable cases of abuse of power. The machinations of family politics are just as vividly captured through numerous incidents in which family members compete for advantage. The maids in the family are often unable to keep the lustful men away, in the process attracting the anger of their wives. A concubine of Baoyu's father plots demon possession against both Baoyu and his sister-in-law, the household manager Xifeng. One of Baoyu's mother's maids commits suicide after Baoyu flirts with her. This incident, coupled with Baoyu's dalliance with an actor, provokes his father into administering a severe beating.

At one point Baochai notices that Daiyu has unconsciously quoted a line from a play. She then confesses that since she was seven or eight, she and the other children in her family had read plays:

> *All of us younger people hated serious books but liked reading poetry and plays. The boys had got lots and lots of plays:* The Western Chamber, The Lute-Player, A Hundred Yuan Plays—*just about everything you could think of. They used to read them behind our backs, and we girls used to read them behind theirs. Eventually the grown-ups got to know about it and then there were beatings and lectures and burnings of books—and that was the end of that.*[3]

SUMMARY

How different was China in 1800 than it had been in 1600? China was part of a much larger empire—the largest since the Mongol Empire. For the first time, China was administered as part of the same polity as Tibet and Xinjiang. It was the most populous and economically dominant part of the empire, but politically the Manchus were in control. The Manchus depended on Chinese officials and soldiers to help administer their empire, but they perfected ways to ensure that the Manchus would maintain their dominance.

Although a large segment of the educated elite alive during the conquest did everything in their power to resist the Manchus, in deep dread of another "barbarian" dynasty, the Manchus proved to be very different sorts of rulers than the Mongols had been, and by 1800 Chinese of all social levels had gotten used to Manchu rule. The Manchu rulers made a point to patronize Chinese culture, and many facets of Chinese culture thrived during this period, ranging from historical research to manufacturing technology. The standard of living in the mid-eighteenth century was high, and the population was growing. The Manchu rulers were highly sensitive to ethnic slights, however, which may have made Chinese in high office especially cautious.

SUGGESTED READING

W. Peterson, ed., *The Cambridge History of China*, vol. 9, part 1, covers the early Qing. A. Hummel, ed., *Eminent Chinese of the Ch'ing Period (1644–1912)*, 2 vols. (1943), is a useful reference work. Good overviews of Qing history are found in F. Wakeman, *The Fall of Imperial China* (1975), and J. Spence, *The Search for Modern China* (1990). On the Ming-Qing transition, see F. Wakeman, *The Great Enterprise* (1985); J. Spence and J. Wills, eds., *From Ming to Ch'ing: Conquest, Region, and Continuity in Seventeenth-Century China* (1979); and L. Struve, *The Southern Ming, 1644–1662* (1984). On the Manchus, see P. Crossley, *The Manchus* (1997) and *A Translucent Mirror: History and Identity in Qing Imperial Ideology* (1999); M. Elliott, *The*

---

3. Cao Xueqin, *The Story of the Stone*, vol. 2, trans. David Hawkes (New York: Penguin Books, 1977), p. 333.

Manchu Way: The Eight Banners and Ethnic Identity in Late Imperial China (2001); and E. Rawski, *The Last Emperors* (1998).

On how China fits into global change in the seventeenth and eighteenth centuries, see K. Pomeranz, *The Great Divergence: China, Europe, and the Making of the Modern World Economy* (2000); R. Wong, *China Transformed: Historical Change and the Limits of European Experience* (1997); and J. Waley-Cohen, *The Sextants of Beijing: Global Currents in Chinese History* (1999). China's population growth is reexamined in J. Lee, *One Quarter of Humanity: Malthusian Mythology and Chinese Realities* (2000).

On the Qing court and government, see J. Spence, *Emperor of China: Self Portrait of K'ang Hsi* (1974); H. Kahn, *Monarchy in the Emperor's Eyes: Image and Reality in the Ch'ien-lung Reign* (1971); A. Zito, *Of Body and Brush: Grand Sacrifice as Text/Performance in Eighteenth-Century China* (1997); and J. Hevia, *Cherishing Men from Afar: Qing Guest Ritual and the Macartney Embassy of 1793* (1995). On the Qing fears of anti-Manchu sentiments, see L. C. Goodrich, *The Literary Inquisition of Ch'ien-lung* (1935); K. Guy, *The Emperor's Four Treasuries: Scholars and the State in the Late Ch'ien-lung Era* (1987); P. Kuhn, *Soulstealers: The Chinese Sorcery Scare of 1768* (1990); and J. Spence, *Treason by the Book* (2001).

For Early Qing social history, see J. Spence, *The Death of Woman Wang* (1978); S. Naquin and E. Rawski, *Chinese Society in the Eighteenth Century* (1987); B. Elman and A. Woodside, eds., *Education and Society in Late Imperial China, 1600–1900* (1994); G. W. Skin-

ner, ed., *The City in Late Imperial China* (1977); and S. Naquin, *Peking: Temples and City Life, 1400–1900* (2000). Biographies offer excellent insight into the life of the elite. See A. Waley, *Yuan Mei, Eighteenth Century Chinese Poet* (1956); D. Nivison, *The Life and Thought of Chang Hsüeh-ch'eng (1738–1801)* (1966); and W. Rowe, *Saving the World: Chen Hongmou and Elite Consciousness in Eighteenth-Century China* (2001).

For Qing intellectual and cultural history, see B. Elman, *From Philosophy to Philology: Intellectual and Social Aspects of Change in Late Imperial China* (1984), and K. Chow, *The Rise of Confucian Ritualism in Late Imperial China: Ethics, Classics, and Lineage Discourse* (1994). Contact with European ideas and religion is treated in J. Gernet, *China and the Christian Impact: A Conflict of Cultures* (1985), and D. Mungello, *The Great Encounter of China and the West, 1500–1800* (1999).

China's greatest novel is available in an excellent translation by D. Hawkes and J. Minford, *The Story of the Stone*, 5 vols. (1973–1982). Another important and entertaining eighteenth-century novel is *The Scholars*, trans. H. Yang and G. Yang (1973). On women in the seventeenth and eighteenth centuries, see D. Ko, *Teachers of the Inner Chambers: Women and Culture in Seventeenth-Century China* (1994); S. Mann, *Precious Records* (1997); F. Bray, *Technology and Gender: Fabrics of Power in Late Imperial China* (1997); E. Widmer and K. Chang, eds, *Writing Women in Late Imperial China* (1997); and K. Chang and H. Saussy, eds., *Women Writers of Traditional China: An Anthology of Poetry and Criticism* (1999).

CHAPTER SEVENTEEN

Edo Japan (1603–1800)

Tokugawa Settlement

Material Culture: Night Soil

Documents: Ihara Saikaku's "Sensible Advice on Domestic Economy"

Biography: Tadano Makuzu

Maturation and Decay

The social and political order imposed under the Tokugawa shoguns consolidated trends long in the making. The demarcation of villages as corporate communities, the separation of samurai from commoners, the creation of bounded domains, and the growth of and restrictions on commerce all had antecedents in the late sixteenth century. The structure of family life, in particular the emphasis on primogeniture and the custom of brides serving their husbands' families, continued practices already apparent in the fourteenth century. Yet peace also made possible economic developments that some historians deem proto-industrialization, unprecedented urbanization, and a flourishing of theater, fiction, poetry, and intellectual life.

What distinguished the Tokugawa shogunate from previous military regimes? What were the consequences of the political settlement for economic and demographic growth? To what extent did shogunal efforts to restrict foreign contact isolate Japan? What did samurai do without battles to fight? How did urban and rural commoners make their presence felt?

TOKUGAWA SETTLEMENT

The cadastral surveys and separation of warriors from the land begun under Hideyoshi and continued in the seventeenth century aimed at ordering society according to unchanging criteria. The Tokugawa brought an end to the conflicts caused by sibling rivalry by insisting on strict primogeniture for the military ruling class and confiscating domains rived by succession disputes. As a result, a ruler's personality and level of competence mattered less than his office, and the retainers' loyalty focused on the position, not the individual. The monarch and his court lived, according to popular parlance, "above the clouds" in Kyoto. Samurai stood at the top of the official status order, followed by commoners in order of their contributions to society. In principle no one was to change residence or status, nor was marriage permitted across status lines. In reality, status boundaries were fluid. Since changing names changed identity, a commoner woman took an aristocratic name when serving a military household. Individual actors and prostitutes became celebrities, and the exclusive right to work with animal skins made some outcasts wealthy.

Tokugawa Social Hierarchy

Core Social Statuses	Other Social Groups (Between Statuses)	Outcasts
Samurai	Priests	Blind Female Entertainers
Cultivators	Doctors	Beggars
Artisans	Monks	Prostitutes
Merchants		Actors
		Non-Humans *(Hinin)*
		Polluted Ones *(Kawata)*

This status order restricted rural communities to cultivators. In the seventeenth century, most villages had at least one dominant family, often descended from a rusticated warrior, which monopolized the position of headman. A council of elders comprising landholding cultivators known as *honbyakushō* provided a sounding board for matters pertaining to village affairs. The *honbyakushō* households included family members, house servants, and fieldworkers. In central and eastern Japan, villages contained complex lineage systems with multiple branches. Across Japan social, economic, and political inequality structured village life. The men who claimed descent from village founders expected to be treated with deference, they claimed the largest and best fields, and they dominated village politics. Their wives shared their prestige; a male of lesser standing had to treat such women with respect.

Villages divided up the countryside. A village contained residential plots, rice paddies, and dry fields, each assigned to households. In some regions the agricultural lands periodically rotated from family to family. These households cooperated in doing the heavy work of leveling rice paddies and building dikes, managing irrigation networks, and transplanting rice seedlings into the paddies. Women performed this last backbreaking task in a carryover of medieval religious beliefs that sanctified it as a fertility ritual. Beyond this basic level, each household was on its own to prosper or to fail. Village boundaries also enclosed wastelands and forests with access to their products carefully regulated by the village council. As a corporate entity embodied by the headman, the village was collectively responsible for paying taxes, both the yearly tribute measured in units of rice (*koku*—1 koku equals 5.1 bushels of rice, the amount needed to feed one man for a year) and various ancillary exactions, for example, fees for the privilege of exploiting forest resources.

Bounded, contiguous villages constituted the building blocks of domains ruled by daimyo that typically were bounded and contiguous. The shogun had the largest domain concentrated chiefly in eastern and central Japan totaling approximately one-fourth of the total agricultural base. Vassal daimyo (*fudai*) were hereditary retainers. They governed domains; they also served as the shogun's chief advisers and his first line of defense against potential foes. According to a decree of 1634, only vassals whose domains contained over 10,000 *koku* enjoyed the status of daimyo. The shogun's retainers with smaller fiefs, often made up of parcels in several villages, were called *hatamoto* ("beneath the banner"). In addition the shogun commanded the services of thousands of housemen who received stipends from the shogun's warehouses. Daimyo who had been shogun Tokugawa Ieyasu's rivals or peers were deemed outside lords (*tozama*). Fewer in number than the vassal daimyo, the mightiest controlled large domains that functioned almost as nations. Some of the shogun's collateral relatives also

numbered among the daimyo. They were neither wealthy nor politically powerful, but they
enjoyed great prestige. All daimyo, who numbered between two hundred fifty and two hundred eighty, had retainer bands to be supported
and employed.

Government

The government pieced together by the Tokugawa shoguns over some forty years developed
an elaborate bureaucratic structure (later called
a *bakufu*—tent government). The senior councilors—four to five men who rotated on a
monthly basis, each of them a vassal daimyo
worth at least 30,000 *koku*—took responsibility
for policy decisions, personnel matters, and
supervising the daimyo. Their assistants, also
vassal daimyo, handled matters relating to the
shogun's retainers. The *hatamoto* staffed the
administrative positions, beginning with the magistrates in charge of finances, cities, and temples
and shrines. Finance magistrates supervised
the intendants responsible for seeing that the
villagers paid their taxes and general agrarian
affairs. They also managed the increasingly futile
task of balancing expenditures with income.
Their staff, and those of the other magistrates,
included an array of functionaries, guards, and
servants. Although the shogun tried to reduce
the size of his army in the seventeenth century, he
was never able to provide more than part-time
employment to his retainer: 42 percent of *hatamoto* (1,676 in 1829) served in the fatigue regi-
ment, the default category for men without
office. Each daimyo likewise had an overly abundant staff of advisers, accountants, liaison officers, attendants, tax collectors, doctors, teachers,
guards, servants, and placeholders.

The shogunal and domainal governments
developed the most complex, sophisticated, and
coherent administrative systems Japan had ever
seen. Retainers learned to wield a brush as well
as a sword, understand high finance, and accus-
tom themselves to routinized office jobs.
Administrative systems also retained distinctly
unmodern bureaucratic elements. The shogun

bestowed his former family name of Matsudaira
on important *fudai* and *tozama* daimyo, both
as an honor and as a reminder that rulers were
kin. Opportunities for promotion depended on
hereditary rank; men born of guards stayed
guards. The senior councilors may have been
policy experts, but they were also the shogun's
vassals. Their duties included watching him perform ancestral rites, lecture on the Chinese classics, and dance in Nō. When he left the castle to
go hawking or visit one of their number, they
and their subordinates had to attend him. The
shogun maintained a large staff of palace women
ordered in a female bureaucracy to serve him, his
wife, and his mother in the great interior (*ōoku*).
Their responsibilities included a yearly round of
ceremonies and managing gift exchanges with
the Kyoto court and daimyo families.

Although the daimyo ran their domains as
they saw fit, the shogunate started to issue
decrees to regulate their behavior in 1615. It
limited the number of guns allowed per castle
and restricted castle repairs. The daimyo could
not harbor criminals, collude against the shogun, or marry without the shogun's permission. All daimyo had the responsibility of con-
tributing men and money to the shogun's
building projects, and they could be relocated
from one region to another at the shogun's
pleasure. Most important, the shogunate issued
increasingly stringent guidelines governing the
daimyo's attendance on the shogun. Known as
sankin kōtai and formalized in 1635, this system
stipulated that each daimyo spend half of his
time in his domain and half in the shogun's capital at Edo. Each daimyo's wife and heir had to
reside in Edo as hostages. Designed to keep the
daimyo both loyal to the shogun and effective in
local administration, the system balanced the
centrifugal forces that had weakened the
Kamakura regime and the centripetal tendencies
that had destroyed the Ashikaga. *Sankin kōtai*
also had the inadvertent consequence of stimulating trade, encouraging travel, and spreading
urban culture to the hinterland.

The shogunate appropriated certain national
responsibilities to itself. It refurbished the highway

system with post stations and checkpoints to keep guns out of Edo and female hostages in. For its own defense, it forbade the building of bridges over major rivers. It oversaw the development of coastal shipping routes, took over the mines for precious metals, and minted copper, silver, and gold coins. It initiated an official handwriting style for documents. It forbade the practice of Christianity and set up a nationwide system of temple registration to ensure compliance. In 1635 it forbade Japanese to travel overseas and banned foreign books. In 1639 it regulated relations with the West by allowing only the Dutch to trade at Nagasaki. It delegated the oversight of trade and diplomacy with neighboring countries to three domains: Satsuma for the Ryukyus, Tsushima for Korea, and Matsumae for the Ainu and the north. The shogunate supervised trade with China that took place at Nagasaki; it had less control over the Chinese goods that arrived indirectly through the Ryukyus and Hokkaido.

Under the Tokugawa regime, people inhabiting the Ryukyu Islands found themselves forced into much closer proximity to Japan. An independent kingdom with tributary ties to China as well as Japan in the sixteenth century, the Ryukyus suffered invasion by Satsuma in 1609. Although the king survived and trade with China continued, he had to surrender control over his islands' diplomatic and economic affairs, to the detriment of the islanders' well-being. Intellectuals in the Ryukyus tried to craft a new identity by claiming that although they were politically subservient to Japan, they achieved moral parity with both Japan and China by cultivating the way of the Confucian sage.

Relations with the Ainu in Hokkaido evolved differently. There the shogunate had the Matsumae family with longstanding ties to the region establish a domain on the island's southern tip. The Matsumae received the privilege of monopolizing trade with the Ainu in exchange for a pledge of loyalty. In 1669, conflict between Ainu tribes over access to game and fish escalated into a war to rid Hokkaido of the Japan-

Ainu Feeding a Hawk. This mid-nineteenth century drawing of an Ainu feeding a hawk depicts the bird as almost as large as its captor. The Ainu is stereotypically hairy with full beard and heavy eyebrows. *(Brett Walker/Collection for Northern Studies, Hokkaido University Library)*

ese. Following its bloody suppression, the Ainu and the Japanese solidified distinct ethnic identities that incorporated elements of the other— eagle feathers and otter pelts for the Japanese ruling class and ironware, rice, and sake for the Ainu. Between 1590 and 1800, the Ainu became increasingly dependent on trade with the Japanese for their subsistence, while periodic epidemics brought by traders ravaged their population. Many ended up working as contract laborers in fisheries that shipped food and fertilizer to Japan.

The Tokugawa shogunate survived for over 250 years not simply because it dominated Japan militarily but because, like Oda Nobunaga and Toyotomi Hideyoshi, Ieyasu and his heirs recognized the importance of ideology in transforming power into authority. Nobunaga claimed that he acted on behalf of the realm (*tenka*), not his private, selfish interests. Governance of his domain became public administration (*kōgi*). He also built a shrine to himself; Hideyoshi actively promoted a cult to his own divinity.

Map 17.1   Tokugawa Japan, 1600–1868

Ieyasu's posthumous title apotheosized him as *Tōshō daigongen*—the Buddha incarnate as the sun god of the east. Enshrined at Nikkō, he protected the shogunate from malignant spirits and worked for the good of all people. (See Map 17.1.) The third shogun Iemitsu claimed that the shogunate manifested a just social order that followed the way of heaven (*tendō*). This way is natural, unchanging, eternal, and hierarchical. The ruler displays the benevolence of the Buddha, the warrior preserves the peace, and the commoners are obedient. The fifth shogun, Tsunayoshi, tried to domesticate the warriors by codifying mourning rituals, lecturing on Confucian classics, and forbidding the killing of animals, especially dogs (used for target practice). His successor reversed the last stricture, and the eighth shogun Yoshimune sought to revive the martial arts. One aim of later reforms between 1787 and 1793 was to redress the balance between brush and sword, suggesting that for samurai, how to follow the way of heaven was not self-evident.

Agricultural Transformations and the Commercial Revolution

Cultivators, merchants, artisans, and rulers quickly exploited the peace dividend. Large- and small-scale reclamation projects, often funded

Artisans. Cottage industries relied on families. Both the pattern dyers depicted on the screen to the right and the weavers shown on the screen to the left employed men and women, children and grandparents. *(LEFT: Werner Forman/Corbis; RIGHT: Sakamoto Photo Research Laboratory/Corbis)*

by merchants at a daimyo's behest, opened rice paddies and expanded arable land by 45 percent. Rivers were diked and new channels dug to bring irrigation water to fields. Countless building projects, partly to repair the ravages of war in Kyoto but mainly to build the plethora of daimyo mansions, shogunal palaces, and merchant quarters in the new capital at Edo and the castle towns, seriously depleted forests. By the end of the seventeenth century, floods sweeping down denuded mountains threatened hard-won fields. The shogunate led the way in regulating the use of forestry products, but the agricultural base continued to press against ecological limits. (See **Material Culture: Night Soil.**)

The introduction of better seeds and new crops intensified the use of land and labor. The accumulation of small innovations based on observations of soil types and climatic condi-

tions led to the development of rice varieties suited for specific local conditions. Fast-ripening rice spread cultivation into the marginal lands of the northeast. Farther south, it allowed the sowing of a second crop, often wheat, although some paddies in Kyushu supported two rice crops a year. Corn, tobacco, and sweet potato, products of the western hemisphere, became dry field staples along with barley and millet. In a trend that continued throughout the Tokugawa period, seventeenth-century agronomy experts traveled Japan building social networks of like-minded experimenters, seeking the most advanced methods for increasing crop yields, and disseminating their findings in books.

Cultivators also grew cash crops and developed products based on Chinese technology. The spread of cotton growing in western Japan beginning in the sixteenth century reduced the

MATERIAL CULTURE

Night Soil

The Edo city government left waste disposal in the hands of individual landlords. Daimyo and *hatamoto* contracted with nearby villages to bring fresh vegetables to their compounds and remove waste. Communal toilet facilities in each commoner ward also had to be cleaned.

In the eighteenth century, cultivators planted crops where they had once foraged for green fertilizer. The more intensive use of land forced them to look outside their communities for soil amendments. Vegetable farmers near Edo carted away night soil and other organic wastes to supplement the manure they produced themselves. Separated into solids and liquid and cooked in its own heat to kill harmful organisms, night soil became a valuable commodity.

In the late eighteenth century, townspeople expected cultivators to pay for the privilege of collecting night soil. Landlords insisted that tenants use their toilet facilities and tried to sell their product to the highest bidder. Transactions between subcontractors, wholesalers, and middlemen raised costs. Regional alliances of cultivators petitioned the shogunate to keep prices down.

The value placed on night soil reflected status inequality. Landlords segregated toilets by sex because men's excrement was valued more highly than women's. Samurai received more for their waste than did commoners. An eighteenth-century farmhouse had a toilet for samurai made of polished wood. The tenant farmers and family members used an open pit.

Toilets. The photo on the left depicts a toilet for the use of samurai officials next to the formal reception room at a village headman's house. On the opposite side behind the stable is the pit for family and servants to use (right). *(Photos courtesy of Anne Walthall)*

hours women had to spend preparing cloth for their families while revolutionizing clothing and bedding. During the seventeenth century, Japan imported Chinese silk and sugar. By the 1730s for silk and the 1830s for sugar, domestic production provided substitutes. The daimyo competed in developing products for export to fund

their mandated trips to Edo. They hired teachers to show cultivators how to harvest lacquer, make paper, and raise silkworms. They promoted distinctive styles of wooden combs, paper hair ties, and ceramics. Merchants supplied the capital, and cultivators supplied the labor, although a few rural entrepreneurs managed to profit from the distribution of raw materials and the transportation of goods. Lights fueled by rapeseed oil enabled work to continue into the night. Increases in agricultural productivity spurred demand for nonagricultural goods produced by rural households. The growth of cottage industries diversified income sources and led to a virtuous cycle of interaction between agriculture and manufacturing. Neither entrepreneurs nor domains tried to set up large-scale production units. Instead they emphasized quality and variety, trying to beat the competition by producing regional specialties found nowhere else.

The agricultural and commercial revolutions meant higher per capita productivity and a trend toward smaller families. After almost a threefold increase in the seventeenth century, Japan's population remained surprisingly stagnant. In villages the extended families characteristic of earlier times broke down by the end of the seventeenth century into main families and branches or landlords and tenants. Most households cultivated parcels just big enough to support a stem family of grandparents, parents, and children. There was not enough to bestow on more than one heir. Historians have supposed that cultivators practiced abortion and infanticide lest they have more children than they could afford. Even if the heir died, the ease of adoption meant that a family could usually find someone to carry on the family line. Other factors were also at work. Men often left their homes for months at a time to work in towns and cities, especially during the winter. The female age at marriage went up in central Japan because women increasingly worked to gain experience before settling down. Disease mattered: smallpox, for example, can reduce male fertility by 50 percent. Syphilis struck urban populations. Periodic famines hit some regions harder than others. In the early nineteenth century, population decline in the impoverished northeast offset growth in the more commercially developed and prosperous west.

One characteristic of Japan's early modern growth was that while labor remained in the countryside, capital largely concentrated in the cities. Not until the late eighteenth century did rural entrepreneurs amass significant amounts of capital, and they often depended on urban merchants for financial backing. Daimyo traveling on *sankin kōtai* marketed rice they collected in taxes to merchants in Osaka who advanced them currency and letters of credit. These promissory notes, redeemable at the merchant's branch in Edo, served as Japan's first paper money. Domains later printed their own currency, modeled on religious talismans to gain users' trust. Merchants either advanced the money to make specialty products or bought them at a discount to sell to urban consumers. Some merchants acted as purveyors to daimyo and their women, stimulating the desire for high-quality labor-intensive goods. Others catered to the broader market by selling cotton cloth, lamp oil, and soy sauce. At the end of the seventeenth century, a few Osaka and Edo merchants had become extremely wealthy, and a number of daimyo found themselves deeply in debt.

Urban Life and Culture

Edo's spatial layout mirrored the shogun's strategic concerns. Taking advantage of technological advancements in fortifications, the shogun's castle was enclosed behind multiple stone walls surrounded by moats. The shogunate drained the swamp on which the city was built through canals that provided transportation for goods and people. Bridges over the moats were faced with guardhouses, forcing the traveler to make a sharp turn, and no roads led directly to the castle. Vassal daimyo and the shogun's retainers lived in its immediate vicinity, providing another ring of protection. The wealthy *tozama* daimyo had large compounds containing barracks for their retainers, storehouses, mansions, and gardens. None was allowed moats and stone walls, and quarters for the vassal daimyo surrounded them. Each daimyo maintained multiple compounds; the total number was over one thousand. The ruling class took the salubrious highlands for itself, leaving the lowlands directly east and south of the castle for commoners. Scattered throughout the city were shrines and temples. Daimyo castle towns followed a similar pattern of segregating people according to status and occupation.

The seventeenth century saw an unprecedented increase in urban growth, from little more than 1 percent of Japan's population to almost 15 percent after 1700. In addition to the castle towns were three metropolises: Kyoto became a manufacturing center of luxury goods, Osaka served as Japan's chief market, and Edo's swollen population of daimyo and bureaucrats made it a consumption center. Urbanization stimulated the growth of commercial publishing that created and fed a reading public hungry for knowledge and entertainment. It provided space for exhibitions from religious icons to botanical specimens and for private salons where scholars, artists, and writers met patrons. Urban residents paid for services—hairdressing, amusements—that had once been provided by servants. They bought processed food and cloth that their ancestors had made themselves. Labor and leisure were oriented toward the market, and purchasing finished products saved time. This transformation stimulated a consumption revolution—the increased demand for a greater variety of goods from durable luxury items such as elaborately carved transoms to drug foods such as sake and tobacco.

Unprecedented urban prosperity culminated in the Genroku era (1688–1704), the heyday of townsman (*chōnin*) culture, justly celebrated in art and literature. Ihara Saikaku wrote stories about the samurai passion for boys, but most of his works focused on the foibles of the townspeople in books such as *Five Women Who Loved Love* and *The Life of an Amorous Man*. He also wrote books on how to make and keep money. (See **Documents: Ihara Saikaku's "Sensible Advice on Domestic Economy."**) Matsuo Bashō raised the seventeen-syllable verse form known as haiku to a fine art, in the process making poetry accessible to commoners in town and country. Chikamatsu Monzaemon wrote librettos for the puppet theater that explored the complex interplay between social obligations and human feeling, as when a young man in love with a prostitute wants to buy the contract that indentures her to the brothel owner but lacks the resources to do so without causing irreparable harm to his family's business. Caught between love and duty, the couple resolves the dilemma by committing double suicide. Although Chikamatsu wrote for puppets, the literary artistry of his scripts endeared them to amateur performers and raised the quality of theatrical performances.

Two pleasure zones are associated with the Genroku era: the brothel district and the theaters, often located in close proximity to each other on the margins of respectable society. These constituted the "floating world" (*ukiyo*), celebrated in woodblock prints of courtesans and actors along with pornography. In the early seventeenth century, entrepreneurs in the three metropolises petitioned the shogunate to establish districts for prostitution where it could be regulated and controlled. A moat and walls surrounded Edo's Yoshiwara with a main gate where guards noted the men who entered and prevented women from leaving. The earliest customers were daimyo and samurai. Merchants whose lavish spending brought them great renown soon eclipsed them. In this status-conscious society, courtesans too were ranked.

Kabuki began in the early seventeenth century on a riverbank in Kyoto where a prostitute erected a stage on which to sing and dance to attract customers. Fights over her charms led the shogunate to forbid women to appear on stage in 1629. Boys then replaced them as actors and prostitutes. Again the shogunate stepped in to quell disorder, banning all but mature men from performing in public. To make up for what they lacked in sex appeal, actors developed the techniques of acting, singing, and dancing performed on elaborate and frequently changing sets that made kabuki the spectacle known today. It became enormously popular, with the highest acclaim reserved for the men who specialized in playing women. It staged reenactments of the scandals arising in

DOCUMENTS

Ihara Saikaku's "Sensible Advice on Domestic Economy"

Ihara Saikaku (1642–1693) is often considered Japan's first professional author because he lived by his pen, writing haiku, short stories, novels, and essays that described life in Osaka during the heyday of the townspeople. Here he feeds the merchants' obsession with the making and saving of money by focusing on the details of daily life and the qualities desired in a wife.

"The immutable rule in regard to the division of family property at the time of marriage," said the experienced go-between from Kyoto, "is as follows: Let us suppose that a certain man is worth a thousand *kan*. To the eldest son at his marriage will go four hundred *kan*, together with the family residence. The second son's share will be three hundred *kan*, and he too is entitled to a house of his own. The third son will be adopted into another family, requiring a portion of one hundred *kan*. If there is a daughter, her dowry will be thirty *kan*, in addition to a bridal trousseau worth twenty *kan*. It is advisable to marry her off to the son of a family of lower financial status. Formerly it was not unusual to spend forty *kan* on the trousseau and allot ten *kan* for the dowry, but because people today are more interested in cash, it is now customary to give the daughter silver in the lacquered chest and copper in the extra one. Even if the girl is so ugly that she can't afford to sit near the candle at night, that dowry of thirty *kan* will make her bloom into a very flowery bride!"

"In matchmaking, money is a very important consideration. If thirty *kan* of silver is deposited with a trustworthy merchant at six-tenths percent interest per month, the income will total one hundred and eighty *momme* monthly, which will more than suffice to support four women: the bride, her personal maid, a second maid, and a seamstress. How unselfish must be the disposition of a bride who will not only look after the household faithfully, meantime taking care never to displease her husband's family, but also at the same time will actually pay for the food she eats! If you are looking merely for beauty, then go where women are made up solely to that end, to the licensed quarters. You are free to visit them any time of night you may wish, and thoroughly enjoy it, but next morning you will have to pay out seventy-one *momme*—which is not in the least enjoyable!"

"It is better on the whole to give up dissipation in good time, for a roué is seldom happy in later life. So even if life at home seems dry and tasteless, you'd better have patience with a supper of cold rice, potluck

townspeople's society, but it became best known for swashbuckling melodramas set in the past, for the shogunate forbade any discussion of its own affairs or those of contemporary samurai society.

Intellectual Trends

The Edo period saw an explosion in intellectual life. Deprived of the opportunity to gain fame in

battle, some samurai turned to scholarship and made serious efforts to understand society. In the seventeenth century, Hayashi Razan formulated the Tokugawa ideology in neo-Confucian terms that saw the social order as a reflection of the visible natural order in that both realized an underlying metaphysical principle. Among his students was Yamaga Sokō, famous for defining a way for samurai to survive during a time of peace: "The bean curd, and dried fish. You may lie down whenever you like, at perfect ease, and have a maid massage you down to the very tips of your toes. If you want tea, you may sip it while your wife holds the cup for you. A man in his own household is the commander supreme, whose authority none will dare to question, and there is none to condemn you. There's no need to seek further for genuine pleasure."

"Then, too, there are certain business advantages to staying home. Your clerks will stop their imprudent visits to the Yasaka quarters and their clandestine meetings at that rendezvous in Oike. And when in the shop, since they can't appear to be completely idle, maybe they'll look over those reports from the Edo branch office, or do some other work that they have been putting off doing—all to the profit of you, the master! The apprentice boys will diligently twist wastepaper into string, and in order to impress you, the master, sitting in the inner room, they will practice penmanship to their profit. Kyushichi, whose habit it is to retire early, will take the straw packing from around the yellowtail and make rope on which to string coins; while Take, in order to make things go more smoothly tomorrow, will prepare the vegetables for breakfast. The seamstress during the time you're at home will take off as many knots of Hino silk as she ordinarily does in a whole day. Even the cat keeps a wary watch in the kitchen and when she hears the least sound in the vicinity of the fish hanger she will

mew to scare away the rats. If such unmeasured profit as this results from the master's remaining at home just one night, think how vast will be the benefits that will accrue within the space of a whole year! So even if you are not entirely satisfied with your wife, you have to exercise discretion and realize that in the gay quarters all is but vanity. For a young master to be well aware of this is the secret of the successful running of his household."

Such was the counsel offered by the veteran go-between.

Be that as it may, let me say that the women of today, under the influence of the styles of the gay quarters, dress exactly like professional entertainers. Prominent drapers' wives, who in public are addressed as mesdames, are so attired as to be mistaken for high-class courtesans; while the wives of small shopkeepers, who once served as clerks of the drapers, look exactly like courtesans one grade lower. Again, the kimono worn by wives of tailors and embroiderers who live on the side streets bear a startling resemblance to those of the women employed in teahouses. It is fun to spot them in a crowd dressed in conformity with their respective degrees of fortune.

Source: Saikaku Ihara, *This Scheming World,* trans. Masanori Takatsuka and David C. Stubbs (Rutland, Vt.: Charles E. Tuttle Company, 1965), pp. 54–57 (modified).

business of the samurai consists in reflecting on his own station in life, in discharging loyal service to his master . . . in deepening his fidelity in associations with friends, and . . . in devoting himself to duty above all."[1] Kyoto scholar Itō Jinsai likewise began as a neo-Confucianist, only to reject the notion of metaphysical principle in favor of studying Confucius himself. For him, the purpose of scholarship was to show how to put morality based on benevolence and love into practice, a goal achievable by commoners as well as samurai. Such was the cachet of Chinese philosophy that any man who had pretensions of becoming

1. Ryusaku Tsunoda et al., eds., *Sources of the Japanese Tradition* (New York: Columbia University Press, 1959), 1:390.

learned had to employ Chinese categories of thought. Women were not subject to this restriction, but for that reason, they had no formal access to scholarship beyond the study of Japanese poetry. (See **Biography: Tadano Makuzu**.)

Ogyū Sorai gained influence by attacking the neo-Confucian Hayashi school and Itō Jinsai. He argued that only the most ancient Chinese texts, those that predated Confucius, were worthy of study because they contained the teachings of the sage kings, the creators of civilization. The social order did not reflect the unchanging natural order of beasts; instead it was an artificial construct, made in history, and that was a good thing. Men needed rules lest their passions run away with them. Japan was fortunate that its own sage king Ieyasu had created the shogunate, and his deeds were not for mere mortals to challenge. Sorai's rational bureaucratic view of government called on the samurai to devote themselves to public duty. In 1703 forty-seven retainers from the Akō domain assassinated their dead lord's enemy (an incident dramatized as "The Treasury of Loyal Retainers," *Chūshingura*) because, they claimed, their honor as samurai left them no choice. Sorai applauded the deed but acceded to the official position that since they had broken the law against private vendettas, they had to atone by committing suicide. As long as people obeyed the law, government had no business interfering in their private lives.

The eighteenth century saw a proliferation of schools and thinkers. Dazai Shundai explored the ramifications of political economy. He urged daimyo to supplement the flat revenues derived from an agrarian tax base by promoting the production of goods for export. Kaiho Seiryō took Shundai's ideas a step further by arguing that all social relationships are predicated on the measured exchange of goods and services, a principle understood by merchants but not, unfortunately, by samurai. Andō Shōeki claimed that Sorai's sage kings were thieves and liars who created governments to deceive and cheat the cultivators. In his eyes, the samurai were no better than parasites.

Merchants pondered business ethics. Troubled by the excesses of the Genroku period when some financiers had gone bankrupt through lavish spending and making too many bad loans to the daimyo, Ishida Baigan founded the Shingaku school (literally, study of the heart). He argued that merchants deserved to make a just profit because their profit was equivalent to the samurai's stipend. They should devote themselves to their enterprises with the same devotion a samurai showed to his lord, and like the samurai they should strive for moral perfection. Texts and teachers could guide this quest, but it could be completed only through meditation and the practice of diligence, thrift, and fortitude. Baigan and his followers had no political agenda; the idea that merchants might have something to say to samurai was left to the merchant academy in Osaka, the Kaitokudō, founded in 1724. Its teachers denied that merchants caused the ills of famine and indebtedness through their pursuit of profit. Merchants, they argued, played a crucial role in society by facilitating the circulation of goods based on objective and accurate calculations. When they applied this principle to domain finances, their advice regarding fiscal policy ought to be followed. A number of them gained coveted positions as advisers to daimyo and shogun.

Other thinkers found inspiration in the Japanese past. The greatest of them was Motoori Norinaga, whose prodigious memory enabled him to decipher the patterns of Chinese characters used to write *Kojiki*, Japan's most ancient history. Through the study of history and literary classics, he affirmed Japan's unique position in the world as the sole country ruled by descendants of the sun goddess, and he celebrated the private world of the individual. Based as they were on the spontaneity of human feeling, Japanese values were superior to those of other peoples. "In foreign countries, they place logic first, even when it comes to revering the gods . . . all this is but shallow human reasoning." The Chinese had introduced rules that while they might be necessary in China where people were naturally inclined toward error, were entirely unsuited to Japan, where people were intrinsically perfect in their possession of the "true

BIOGRAPHY   Tadano Makuzu

Male intellectuals focused on morality, politics, and economics; Tadano Makuzu (1763–1825) drew on her observations and experience as a daughter of the samurai to analyze human relations.

Born Kudō Ayako, she grew up in a lively and prosperous family of parents, her father's mother, and seven siblings. At age nine she insisted that her mother teach her classical Japanese poetry. Ayako enjoyed her grandmother's company because she was a cheerful and attractive woman who loved kabuki. To complete her education, at fifteen Ayako became an attendant to the lord of Sendai's daughter, a position she held for ten years.

Ayako's father, Heisuke, had many friends who shared his interests in medicine, botany, foreign trade, and western countries. He hoped to arrange a good marriage for Ayako should his proposal of 1780 for the colonization of Hokkaido and trade with Russia lead to a position with the shogunate. The fall of his patron in 1786 stymied his career and his plans for his daughter.

When Ayako left service, she was too old to make a good match. In 1789 she was married to a man so decrepit that she cried until she was returned to her parents. In 1797 her father found her a husband in a widower with three sons, Tadano Iga Tsurayoshi, a high-ranking Sendai retainer with an income four times that of the Kudō family. Marrying Iga meant that Ayako had to leave the city of her birth for Sendai, a move she likened to "the journey to hell." There she spent the remainder of her life visited only occasionally by her husband, who remained on duty in Edo.

Signed with the pen name Makuzu, "Solitary Thoughts" (*Hitori kangae*) encapsulates Ayako's views on her society distilled during her years of isolation in Sendai. She bemoans her ignorance of Confucianism because her father thought it inappropriate knowledge for a woman. It was of little use even for men, she believed, because it was too clumsy to regulate the niceties of Japanese behavior. Like other intellectuals of her day, she pitied the samurai for not understanding the principle of money. Instead of a well-ordered harmonious society, she saw competition, hatred, and strife: "Each person in our country strives to enrich him or herself alone without thinking of the foreign threat or begrudging the cost to the country." Townspeople despised warriors: "They take secret delight in the warriors' descent into poverty, hating them like sworn enemies." Antagonism governed even relations between the sexes: "When men and women make love, they battle for superiority by rubbing their genitals together."

Source: Janet R. Goodwin, Bettina Gramlich-Oka, Elizabeth A. Leicester, Yuki Terazawa, and Anne Walthall, "Solitary Thoughts: A Translation of Tadano Makuzu's *Hitori Kangae*," *Monumenta Nipponica* 56 (Spring 2001): 21, 25, 36; 56 (Summer 2001): 179.

heart" (*magokoro*).[2] Even when he was asked by a daimyo to comment on the conditions of his day, Norinaga took a resolutely apolitical position, claiming that rulers should live in accordance with the way of the gods discernable in the study of history and poetry.

Official interest in western studies began in 1720 when Shogun Yoshimune lifted the ban on western books so long as they did not promote Christianity. Japanese doctors and scientists

---

2. Sey Nakamura, "The Way of the Gods: Motoori Norinaga's Naobi no Mitama," *Monumenta Nipponica* 46 (Spring 1991): 39.

attracted to what was called "Dutch studies" paid little attention to western philosophy; their enthusiasm was for practical matters, in particular the study of human anatomy, astronomy, geography, and military science. Sugita Genpaku discovered that a Dutch human anatomy book provided names for body parts not found in Chinese medical texts. In 1771 he watched the dissection of a criminal's corpse, a fifty-year-old woman, performed by an outcast. Although this was not the first dissection performed in Japan, the evidence of his own eyes plus the Dutch text led him to invent Japanese terms for pancreas, nerve, and other body parts; these terms were later exported to China. The belief in empirical reason and the efficacy of experiment promoted by the Chinese "practical learning" school already constituted one strand of Japanese intellectual life; the opportunity to engage with western scientific texts developed it further. Sugita spread his ideas through his writing and salons, whose members ranged from merchants to daimyo. Western instruments such as the telescope and microscope fascinated intellectuals. The insights they gained into the natural world percolated into popular culture when Utagawa Kunisada drew pictures of greatly magnified insects to illustrate a story about monsters.

MATURATION AND DECAY

Following the excesses of the Genroku period, shogunal and domainal officials fretted over the state of government finances and their retainers' morale. The miserly Ieyasu had left stores of gold bullion, but his heirs spent them so freely that by the 1690s, the shogunate had to devalue the currency. Creeping inflation eroded the value of tax revenues and samurai stipends, while the growing availability of consumer products stimulated demand. Shogun Yoshimune responded by instituting reforms in the 1720s. To aid the samurai who received their stipends in rice, he supported rice prices even though urban consumers complained. He assessed a "voluntary contribution"

from all daimyo of a rice donation in proportion to their domain's size in return for spending less time in Edo on *sankin kōtai*. Instead of basing taxes on each year's harvest, he tried to eliminate fluctuations in revenues by establishing a fixed tax rate. He allowed villages to open new fields in regions previously set aside to provide forage and fertilizer and encouraged the cultivation of cash crops. To reduce expenditures, he issued sumptuary legislation and cut the staff of palace women. He inaugurated a petition box, already tried in some domains, to allow commoners' suggestions and complaints to reach his ear. A famine caused by a plague of locusts in western Japan in 1732 brought the reform period to an end.

Popular Culture

In contrast to the ruling class, urban commoners generally enjoyed the benefits of the consumption revolution. By 1750 Edo's population had reached well over 1 million inhabitants, making it perhaps the largest city in the world at the time. A fish market dominated the hub of the city at Nihonbashi; the surrounding streets were lined with shops selling goods of every sort. Restaurants catered to people for whom dining out had become a pleasure. Innkeepers who specialized in accommodating plaintiffs became proto-lawyers in an increasingly litigious society. The draper Echigoya innovated a fixed price system for cash (see Color Plate 21). The world's first commodity futures market opened in Osaka. Kabuki actors incorporated advertisements into their routines starting in 1715. In 1774 a popular actor affixed his name to cosmetics sold in his store, mentioned his products on stage, and placed them in woodblock prints. Best-selling authors accepted money to praise products such as toothpaste and pipes.

The spread of commerce made education both possible and necessary. In thousands of villages across Japan, priests, village officials, and rural entrepreneurs opened schools to provide the rudiments of reading and mathematics. Coupled with the private academies in castle towns and cities for samurai and merchants, their

School Children and Teacher. In this early nineteenth cartoon by Hokusai, the teacher listens to three boys recite. Another student counts on his toes; rough housing turns into a fight. *(Corbis)*

efforts led to impressive rates of literacy by the mid-nineteenth century: approximately 40 percent for men and between 10 and 15 percent for women. Students studied didactic texts; those for women emphasized docility, modesty, and self-restraint lest the young working woman slip from seamstress to prostitute. Publishers supplied a growing market with one-page almanacs and Buddhist mandalas as well as pamphlets giving advice on agriculture and etiquette. Some students learned to read well enough to enjoy multivolume works of historical fiction, but for many, the aim was more practical: to learn when to plant crops and calculate profit and loss.

The national road system designed to bring daimyo to Edo began to attract increasing numbers of commoners in the eighteenth century. Although the shogunate prohibited travel in the interests of preserving order, it allowed pilgrimages, visits to relatives, and trips to medicinal hot springs. With a passport issued by a local official giving name, physical description, and destination, travelers set off, usually on foot, always in groups, accompanied by neighbors to see them to the community border. Many traveled in confraternities that raised money to send a few members on pilgrimage each year. The most popular destination was Ise, with its outer shrine to the god of agriculture. Since few trav-

elers were likely to repeat the pilgrimage experience, they were determined to see as much as possible. They took enormous detours through temple circuits and stopped in Edo and Osaka for sightseeing and theater. Men traveled in the prime of life; women traveled either before they were married or after they had a daughter-in-law to raise the children and run the household. Rather than suffer the invasive inspection procedures required at checkpoints, women hired guides to show them byways. Men and women bought quantities of souvenirs to ship back home and distribute to those who had given them money before they left. They kept diaries of their trip; some were little more than expense accounts, and others were lengthy descriptions of things seen and heard.

Not every pilgrim was literate or had the permission of his or her local official. Fired, they said, with the imperative to make a pilgrimage to Ise or some other sacred spot, they escaped from parents or employers with nothing but the clothes on their backs. They depended on the charity of strangers who hoped to accrue some of the merit of making the pilgrimage by giving alms. They also fell prey to bandits and procurers. At approximately sixty-year intervals, thousands of people, men and women alike, left towns and villages to make a thanksgiving pilgrimage (*okage mairi*) to the inner shrine of the sun goddess at Ise. Many never returned home. Instead they found their way to cities, where they joined a floating population of day laborers and prostitutes.

Hard Times and Peasant Uprisings

The underside to prosperity, continuing inequities, and injustice gave rise to thousands of incidents of rural protest. The corporate structure of the village meant that protest was organized collectively. When cultivators lodged complaints against unjust officials or pleas that the tax burden be reduced following a crop failure, they petitioned the lord to show compassion to the honorable cultivators because their hardships threatened their survival. As the village's representative, the headman was supposed to take the responsibility for seeking redress from samurai officials dealing with rural affairs. If officials deemed the matter worthy of consideration, they passed it up the chain of command. If at any point an official decided not to trouble his superiors, those below had no legal recourse. According to rural lore, in the seventeenth century a few brave headmen, epitomized by Sakura Sōgorō, made a direct appeal to the daimyo, or, in Sōgorō's case, to the shogun. Sōgorō paid for his audacity by suffering crucifixion along with his wife and saw his sons executed before his eyes. Although historians doubt his existence, he became Japan's most famous peasant martyr.

Few headmen in the eighteenth century were willing to risk their families to help their neighbors. Instead of an individual groveling before his superiors, cultivators marched together to assert their grievances en masse. They called their deeds *ikki*, harking back to the leagues that had bedeviled political authorities in the sixteenth century. In 1764, approximately two hundred thousand cultivators marched toward Edo to protest new demands for forced labor to transport officials and their goods on the national roads. Smaller outbursts roiled domains, peaking at times of economic hardship. Seldom did any district erupt more than once, and protestors wanted redress, not revolution. Yet fear that rural protest would expose such weaknesses in domainal administration that the shogun would transfer the daimyo or simply dispossess him limited efforts to expropriate the products of cultivators' labor.

The 1780s brought hard times to Japan. Mount Asama erupted in 1783, spewing ash that blocked sunlight all summer. Widespread crop failures exacerbated by misguided governmental policies led to famine, a catastrophe repeated in 1787. It is said that the population declined by nine hundred twenty thousand. In the eyes of many sufferers, the cause of their plight was not so much natural disaster as human failing. Unlike earlier rural protests that had demanded tax relief and government aid, the majority of incidents in the 1780s focused on commercial issues and the perfidy of merchants accused of hoarding grain while people starved. Commoners rioted for five days in Edo, punishing merchants by smashing their stores, trampling rice in the mud, and pouring sake in the street.

The famine exposed problems at all levels of society. The shogunate had struggled for years with an inadequate tax base and the increasing competition between daimyo, merchants, and cultivators for access to commercial income. Under the aegis of senior councilor Tanuma Okitsugu, it had proposed schemes to force merchants to buy shares in guilds granted a monopoly over trade in a specified item. The guild then paid regular fees in "thank you" money to the shogun. These monopolies angered those excluded, manufacturers forced to accept lower prices for their products, and daimyo who had their own schemes for profiting from trade. Following the Edo riot, the shogunate launched a second reform led by essayist, novelist, and staunch neo-Confucian Matsudaira Sadanobu to rectify finances and morals. He established new standards for bureaucratic conduct that endured to modern times. His "Edo first" policy ensured that the city remained quiescent for almost eighty years.

Sadanobu's reforms also had a darker side. A floating population of men without families or property worked as day laborers in fields and cities. Sadanobu had those in Edo rounded up and confined to an island in the bay. From there they were transported to the gold mine on Sado in the Japan Sea, where most of them died within two or three years. The harshness of this measure brought universal condemnation, and it was not repeated. Instead governments encouraged urban wards and rural villages to police themselves.

SUMMARY

By the beginning of the nineteenth century, the Japanese people had enjoyed almost two centuries of peace. Most cultivators seldom saw samurai officials. Despite the village and ward notice boards hung with placards admonishing commoners to refrain from luxuries, people let their pocketbooks regulate their behavior. To be sure, cultivators suffered under heavy taxes. Merchants had to accept arbitrary restrictions on commerce and pay ad hoc forced loans to meet the governments' endemic financial crises.

Sankin kōtai kept the daimyo coming to Edo to pay homage to the shogun and scheming to enhance their domain's prosperity. Many samurai could not afford the pleasure districts nor did their offices keep them occupied. Rather than concentrate on the public performance of duty, they retreated to the private world of intellectual stimulation and the pursuit of pleasure.

SUGGESTED READING

For the best overview, see C. Totman, *Early Modern Japan* (1993). The most recent book on relations between the shogunate and domains and domainal institutions is M. Ravina, *Land and Lordship in Early Modern Japan* (1999). For foreign relations, see R. P. Toby, *State and Diplomacy in Early Modern Japan: Asia in the Development of the Tokugawa Bakufu* (1984).

For intellectual history, see H. Ooms, *Tokugawa Ideology: Early Constructs, 1570–1680* (1985); T. Najita, *Visions of Virtue in Tokugawa Japan: The Kaitokudō Merchant Academy of Osaka* (1987); P. Nosco, *Remembering Paradise: Nativism and Nostalgia in Eighteenth Century Japan* (1990); and D. L. Keene, *The Japanese Discovery of Europe: Honda Toshiaki and Other Discoverers, 1720–1798* (1954).

For recent work on proto-industrialization, see D. L. Howell, *Capitalism from Within: Economy, Society, and the State in a Japanese Fishery* (1995); T. Morris-Suzuki, *The Technological Transformation of Japan: From the Seventeenth to the Twenty-First Century* (1994); and K. Wigen, *The Making of a Japanese Periphery, 1750–1920* (1995). For transformations in village life, see H. Ooms, *Tokugawa Village Practice: Class, Status, Power, Law* (1996). An excellent summary of demographic issues is

by L. L. Cornell, "Infanticide in Early Modern Japan? Demography, Culture, and Population Growth," *Journal of Asian Studies* 55 (Feb. 1996): 22–50. For disease, see A. Jannetta, *Epidemics and Mortality in Early Modern Japan* (1987). The most recent book on social protest is J. W. White, *Ikki: Social Conflict and Political Protest in Early Modern Japan* (1995).

For popular culture, see S. Hanley, *Everyday Things in Premodern Japan: The Hidden Legacy of Material Culture* (1997); M. Nishiyama, *Edo Culture: Daily Life and Diversion in Urban Japan, 1600–1868* (1997); P. F. Kornicki, *The Book in Japan: A Cultural History from the Beginnings to the Nineteenth Century* (1998); and C. N. Vaporis, *Breaking Barriers: Travel and The State in Early Modern Japan* (1994).

For peripheries, see G. Smits, *Visions of Ryukyu: Identity and Ideology in Early Modern Thought and Politics* (1999), and B. L. Walker, *The Conquest of Ainu Lands: Ecology and Culture in Japanese Expansion, 1590–1800* (2001).

For sexuality, see G. M. Pflugfelder, *Cartographies of Desire: Male-Male Sexuality in Japanese Discourse, 1600–1950* (2000), and C. S. Seigle, *Yoshiwara: The Glittering World of the Japanese Courtesan* (1993).

Late Chosŏn Korea (1598–1800)

The end of the Hideyoshi invasion in 1598 was marked by a period of continued difficulty in foreign relations as a result of the challenge to the Chinese Ming Dynasty by the increasing power of the Manchus. After succumbing to the Manchus in 1637, the Chosŏn government made efforts at political, economic, and military recovery. It endured severe fiscal shortages, and agricultural production did not recover to prewar levels until 1700. The local tribute taxes were reformed, and cash entered the economy again.

The poor showing of the army made necessary reorganization of the military, but that ran up against strict Manchu surveillance. Everyone recognized that military weakness had been caused by evasion of military service, and so attention was turned to requiring military duty from slaves. Nevertheless, evasion by the *yangban* persisted, possibly because the powerful Manchu Qing Dynasty protected Korea from invasion and lessened the need for a strong defense.

Political tranquility was achieved after 1728, but it was shaken once again by an act of filicide by King Yŏngjo in 1762 and the introduction of western astronomy and Roman Catholic religious knowledge, which shocked the Confucian literati into a defensive posture. A new intellectual movement arose in the late eighteenth century, challenging conventional economic thinking and prejudiced attitudes toward the Manchu Qing Dynasty.

Women were faced with the reduction of their position and status in society as Confucian principles changed the organization of the family. Confucian thought seemed to get more restrictive in controlling the thought of men as well. Yet the end of the eighteenth century witnessed an outburst of literary activity, culture, and entertainment that appealed to the common people and called into question the repressed position of women and the ordinary peasantry. A potential for radical cultural change was emerging along with the crises in policy and

**Landscape of the Diamond Mountains
(Kŭmgangsan).** This painting, by Chŏng Sŏn
(1676–1759), depicts the landscape of the Diamond
Mountains (Kŭmgangsan) with a touch of animistic
spirits in the swaying mountains. Chosŏn Dynasty.
(Hoam Museum of Fine Arts, Yong'in; Koreana:
Korean Cultural Heritage, Volume 1, Fine Arts. *Korea
Foundation, 1994, p. 56)*

MANCHUS AND FACTIONAL DISPUTES

Korea severed all relations with Japan after
Japanese withdrawal from the peninsula in
1598. Hideyoshi's successor, Tokugawa Ieyasu,
had no interest in invading Korea, however, and
Korea reestablished relations in a 1609 treaty.
The treaty restricted trade to Tongnae, near
Pusan, where a Japanese office called the *Waeg-
wan* (Japanese Hall) was established behind a
palisade fence, and the Japanese were left to
administer it. Trade with Japan was regulated
through tallies that were issued to the head of
the Sŏ family on Tsushima Island, and then distributed to various daimyo throughout Japan.
The trade was limited to a certain number of
ships per year. On the continent, however,
Korea found itself embroiled in a conflict
between a declining Ming Dynasty and the rising Jurchen tribes in Manchuria.

Relations with the Manchus

While the Japanese invasion was going on in the
1590s, the Jurchen tribes in Manchuria, previously divided into a number of independent
small units, began to coalesce under Nurhaci,
who changed the name of the Jurchen to
Manchu. Nurhaci attacked Ming territory and
demanded military aid from Chosŏn at the same
time that the Ming court demanded Korean
reinforcements. Caught in a difficult spot
between the two rivals, the Chosŏn king,
Kwanghaegun (Lord Kwanghae, who never
received a posthumous title because he was
deposed in 1623), tried to maintain neutrality,
but the vast majority of his own officials
opposed him for failing to meet his moral obligation to support the Ming, whose armies had
saved Chosŏn from Hideyoshi.

Kwanghaegun also faced domestic opposition
to his rule. Kwanghaegun was the son of one of
King Sŏnjo's concubines and was elected crown
prince by the king during the Imjin War. Once
Sŏnjo's second queen gave birth to a son, the

administration. Some of the scholarly issues surrounding this period include the following: Did
Chosŏn handle relations with the Manchus well?
How successful were the reforms of these two
centuries? Why did political factionalism become
so bloody after 1659, and was King Yŏngjo able
to end it during his reign? Did the Chosŏn economy remain stagnant, or did it progress? How
radical were the social changes in the late eighteenth century? How did Korea react to western
learning and Christianity?

Great Lord Yŏngch'ang, however, many officials of the small northerner, southerner, and westerner factions wanted to depose Kwanghaegun, as the son of a queen took ritual precedence over the son of a concubine. With the support of the great northern faction, Kwanghaegun had Grand Prince Yŏngch'ang and his younger brother assassinated for plotting against him.

In 1623 the westerner faction led a coup to depose Kwanghaegun and replaced him with King Sŏnjo's grandson, Lord Nŭngnyang, known posthumously as King Injo. All the Northerners who had supported Kwanghaegun were executed or banished, and they remained out of high office for the next two centuries. Upon seizing power, the westerners reversed Kwanghaegun's controversial foreign policy and supported the Ming against the Manchus.

Unfortunately, military defense in the northeast was wrecked when Yi Kwal, one of the coup leaders, rebelled with two-thirds of the seventeen thousand men in the area and occupied the capital in Seoul before the rebellion was put down. Instead of rethinking his anti-Manchu policy, Injo prepared for war but made the error of stationing more soldiers around the capital to guard against potential rebels than on the northern frontier. When the Manchus invaded Korea in 1627 with a force of thirty thousand, they overran the opposition and imposed a peace treaty on King Injo. Fortunately for him, the Manchus withdrew rather than commit troops to occupy Korea.

King Injo stubbornly continued with his anti-Manchu policy. When he refused a demand from the new Manchu Qing Dynasty in 1636 to send anti-Manchu officials to the Qing court for punishment along with a hostage from the Chosŏn royal family, the Qing emperor, Taizong, led a Manchu force of one hundred twenty thousand men in an invasion of Korea in February 1637. The Chosŏn border commander failed to transmit the war beacon signals to the capital on time, causing King Injo to receive word of the invasion in Seoul only two days before Manchu troops arrived. He took refuge in the fort on top of the North Han Mountain (*Pukhansansŏng*) but was surrounded and

forced to submit to the Qing demand that he sever relations with the Ming Dynasty and enroll as a Qing tributary, seven years before the Manchu conquered most of China in 1644.

The Manchus levied heavy tribute demands on Chosŏn, and King Injo turned his anger against those who had favored accommodation with the Manchus. He even suspected his own son, Crown Prince Sohyŏn, of cooperating with the Manchu regent, Prince Dorgon. It was rumored that Injo poisoned his son and then executed Sohyŏn's widow, her family, and two of Sohyŏn's three sons in 1646. He then chose his second son to be crown prince, and he became King Hyojong in 1649.

King Hyojong, who also tried to form an army to avenge Chosŏn's defeat, was frustrated by close Manchu surveillance. By the end of the seventeenth century, Chosŏn kings abandoned that policy, and the Qing court reduced its tribute demands. Most Korean *yangban*, however, still held the Manchus in contempt and remained loyal to the memory of the Wanli Emperor of the Ming for saving Korea from Hideyoshi.

Economic and Institutional Reforms

Once the foreign issue was settled, the Chosŏn government began a program of recovery. Korean kings reformed the system of tribute levies in kind on the villages by legalizing the illegal contracting system by which villagers paid fees to merchants to supply special goods that they no longer produced to the king and government agencies. Under the *taedong* reform, the government replaced local product payments in kind by imposing an extra land tax in grain, which it used to purchase the special goods it needed from the merchants. The new *taedong* tax was adopted gradually, but by 1708 the new system covered the whole country and more than doubled the land tax and the burden on landowners. The law stimulated increased commercial activity, particularly among private, unlicensed merchants.

The government reorganized the army and extended military service to private slaves for the first time. In 1650, the official Kim Yuk returned from a trip to China with large amounts of cash he had purchased with funds saved from his expenses. He received King Hyojong's approval to put it into circulation, and in 1654 persuaded the king to order that the cash be accepted in payment of the *taedong* tax. This marked the first use of cash in about a hundred years.

The devastation of war stimulated some scholars to shift their attention to statecraft and utilitarian problems. Yu Hyŏngwŏn, a reclusive scholar of the northerner faction, spent twenty years between 1650 and 1672 writing a comprehensive analysis of contemporary institutional problems and making recommendations for reform. He derived inspiration for reform from the ancient Chinese classics and the statecraft writings of the Song scholars and active officials. He criticized the hereditary nature of both the *yangban* and the slaves and argued that according to Confucian principles, neither of those two social strata should be determined by birth. He also opposed the examination system because it tested only rote memorization and literary skill. He insisted on eliminating hereditary slavery because passing the sins of the father on to the sons was contrary to Confucian teaching and ancient precedent. Only the enslavement of prisoners of war or criminals was proper. His reforms were rational and radical, but not to the point where he ever questioned the legitimacy and propriety of Confucian values, classical wisdom, and an agricultural economy. Unknown in his own time, his ideas were transmitted through disciples to men like Yi Ik (pen name, Sŏngho) in the early eighteenth century.

The Resumption of Factional Disputes (1659–1730)

Factional disputes subsided after 1623 as officials were consumed primarily with recovery from devastation. In 1659, however, factionalism reemerged when Song Siyŏl of the westerner faction insisted that a member of the royal family should perform a lesser degree of mourning for the deceased King Hyojong because he was the second son of King Injo. The southerner faction, led by Yun Hyu, accused Song Siyŏl and the westerners of impugning the legitimacy of King Hyojong and his heirs. The southerners eventually persuaded King Hyŏnjong to adopt their position and dismiss Song. Westerners led by Yun Ch'ung, who disliked Song's uncompromising and arrogant leadership of the westerner faction, also split to form their own Disciples faction (Soron), leaving Song and his supporters to form their own Patriarchs faction (Noron).

Ostensibly an issue of ritual that should have been resolved without trouble led to a series of major purges and executions. King Sukchong (r. 1674–1720) contributed to the conflict by switching his support almost whimsically back to the Patriarchs and Disciples. He replaced them with southerners in 1689 because they opposed his decision to replace his first queen with a palace concubine and then turned around and purged the southerners in 1694 after he lost interest in her. When the Patriarchs regained power, they excluded the descendants of southerners from office until the late eighteenth century.

The Patriarchs and Disciples factions now turned against each other over the choice between two of King Sukchong's sons for crown prince: the Disciples favored Yi Kyun and the Patriarchs favored Lord Yŏnning. King Sukchong chose the childless and sickly Yi Kyun, but he appointed Lord Yŏnning as crown prince. When Yi Kyun became King Kyŏngjong in 1724, his Disciple supporters persuaded him to execute the four leading Patriarchs for supporting Lord Yŏnning, but Yŏnning remained crown prince. King Kyŏngjong died an early death in 1727, at which time Lord Yŏnning became King Yŏngjo, and his Patriarch supporters exacted revenge on the Disciples (see **Biography: King Yŏngjo**). King Yŏngjo, however, decided that the time had come to put an end to factional strife by announcing his "equal opportunity" policy (*tangp'yŏngch'aek*). In practice, however, King Yŏngjo appointed officials from moderate members of both the Disciples and Patriarchs' factions and excluded not only radical members of those two factions who still

BIOGRAPHY King Yŏngjo

King Yŏngjo (1694–1776, r. 1724–1776) was a complex and strong ruler whose reign lasted a half-century. He came to the throne as part of bloody conflict over the succession and is famed for calling a halt to factionalism. He was a student of Confucianism and began his reign by attending daily the lectures on the Chinese classics by his officials, but he began to challenge their views and to write his own commentaries, contrary to the Confucian admonition to learn from rather than teach his mentors. He sponsored the publication of Confucian texts like *The Five Rituals, Continued* (*Sok Oryeŭi*), the compilation of the first institutional encyclopedia, the *Taedong munhŏnbigo* modeled after the Chinese *Wenxian tongkao*, a new edition of the law code (*Soktaejŏn*), and a manual on classical music (*Akhak kwebŏm*), but did he always live up to those values?

He began his domestic policy with laudable motives, to reinstitute military service for *yangban* and convert some slaves to commoner status, but he backed down in the face of landlord and slave owner opposition. He fought against the expansion of currency because of the traditional fear of the evil effects of inflation, but he finally yielded to entreaties from officials who had a greater understanding of economic matters.

His decision to commit filicide against Crown Prince Sado in 1762 created the basis for continued factional controversy that lasted into the beginning of the next century. As a father, he was aloof and thoughtless, not unusual for many Korean fathers then and now. His incompetent fatherhood was a function of the protocol of the palace, which kept royal children separate from kings and made him dependent on infrequent reports of fact and rumor, all of which was beyond his power to control. Then he chose to kill his son, but only when it was rumored that his son was participating in a conspiracy, not when he murdered a eunuch and his palace paramour in fits of anger. It was theoretically possible for a Confucian gentlemen to pursue filicide in an extreme case, but was that King Yŏngjo's only alternative? Prince Sado's wife, Lady Hyegyŏng, tried to raise these issues long after his death, but she never accused him of a violation of Confucian standards, only laxity in showing care and concern for his son's welfare. Open discussion was, of course, banned lest any aspersions be cast on the reputation of Yŏngjo and his royal line, but to this day he retains a reputation for being one of the greatest kings in the dynasty. Although Yŏngjo could not be expected to appreciate his son's psychosis in a pre-Freudian time, he could have chosen to depose or exile his son instead of starving him to death in a box.

sought to take revenge on their opponents but northerners and southerners as well.

The radical Disciples, however, rose up in rebellion under Yi Injwa in 1728 in Ch'ungch'ŏng province. King Yŏngjo put the rebellion down and maintained his coalition cabinet, but the rebellion alerted King Yŏngjo to serious danger in the future if he damaged *yangban* interests.

THE DECLINE OF THE MILITARY SERVICE AND RURAL CREDIT SYSTEMS

By the eighteenth century most *yangban* had succeeded in evading military service, because they regarded it as an embarrassing reduction to com-

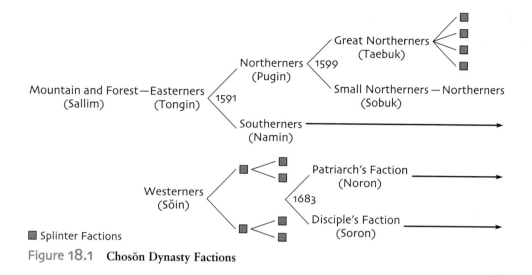

Figure 18.1   **Choson Dynasty Factions**

moner status. Military service now was called commoner service (*yangyŏk*) because *yangban* had escaped military service and regarded it as demeaning, but even commoners were evading it by bribing registration clerks to register them as students. The reduction of eligible commoners to pay the military cloth tax increased the tax burden on registered adult males and weakened the army. The Qing peace was Choson's main defense against foreign invasion.

Since the 1680s, reformers had been proposing the reform of military service by imposing the military cloth support tax on *yangban* households. King Yŏngjo favored the idea, but the resistance to it was so extreme that he refrained from a direct attack against *yangban* interests. When he proclaimed his equal service law (*kyunyŏkbŏp*) of 1750, he abandoned the challenge to the *yangban* and merely reduced the military cloth tax rate on commoners by half.

By the end of the dynasty, the system of rural credit and relief administered by local magistrates also fell apart as corrupt officials robbed the funds or superimposed them on peasants unable to repay loans. Instead of driving impoverished smallholding commoner peasants into bankruptcy, however, local officials chose not to collect payments on principal. Instead they turned the payment of interest on loans into an annual collection that was equivalent to an

additional tax. King Yŏngjo did not address this issue, leaving an unresolved problem that exacerbated peasant resentment against the state.

LATE CHOSON SOCIETY: SLAVES AND *YANGBAN*

Between 1750 and 1790 there was a sharp reduction in the slave population: from about 30 percent to less than 10 percent of the population. King Yŏngjo had contributed a little to this reduction by approving the readoption of the matrilineal rule governing the inheritance of slave status by offspring of mixed slave-commoner marriages in 1730. The main cause of the decline, however, was the increase in the number of runaway slaves. Instead of paying the cost of chasing after them, *yangban* and rich landlords took advantage of the recent increase in indebted peasants who had lost their land for failure to repay loans. They simply rented land to the army of landless peasants. Escaped slaves did not necessarily see a rise in income and standards of living because now they had to pay rackrents to landlords, interest on grain loans from the state or private lenders, and payment of the commoner military cloth tax.

Another factor in the decline in the slave population was that the government had begun to replace official slaves with hired commoner labor, further reducing the number of official slaves from three hundred fifty thousand in 1590 to sixty thousand by 1801. King Chŏngjo (r. 1776–1800) entertained several proposals to abolish official slavery, but in the end he failed to take action and paid no attention at all to abolishing private slavery.

The *yangban* preserved their elite position during this period and kept a near monopoly of access to high office. The percentage of successful examination passers from the top two dozen *yangban* families increased as well. While the government had begun to sell rank titles in this period, the purchase of such titles did not confer official posts and did not elevate purchasers into the ranks of *yangban*. Since an average of only thirty men per year passed the examinations, many *yangban* who studied for the examinations were deprived of the chance for office and were left in the countryside to make their way there.

Some were able to form single-family villages and further strengthen their power. In other villages, *yangban* power declined because magistrates unified the variety of taxes previously collected separately in a new single tax called *togyŏl* as a more efficient form of tax collection. In order to alleviate the tax burden, village associations called *tonggye* were formed of all households regardless of status to divide the tax burden equally among all families. Finally, *chung'in,* or middle people, who staffed clerks' posts as well as legal specialists, accountants, and interpreters, gave up any hope of holding regular office and followed their *yangban* superiors to form another hereditary class that excluded ordinary commoners from easy access to their positions.

ECONOMIC DEVELOPMENT IN THE EIGHTEENTH CENTURY

The Chosŏn population grew to 14 million by the year 1810, a 40 percent increase over 1650. Connected to this growth was an increase in agricultural productivity and market activity.

From the late fourteenth century, the use of fertilizer spread throughout the country to provide annual cultivation; it replaced the fallow system, under which land was left alone for a year or two to recover fertility. The conversion of dry to wet, irrigated rice fields also increased, and the adoption of transplantation instead of broadcast seeding improved weeding and achieved higher yields.[1] But by the late seventeenth century transplantation was followed by serious crop failures if weather conditions were bad. By around 1900, average production per acre in Korea was about 15 bushels, about the same as China in 1400 and about one-third less than production in Japan and China around 1880.

The eighteenth century witnessed the development of warehousing and wholesale merchants, and the number of periodic five-day markets increased (see **Material Culture: Five-Day Markets**). The number of commercial towns remained small, however; Seoul was the biggest of these, with only two hundred thousand people. Market growth was slowed when King Sukchong decided to stop minting cash in 1697 because of inflation from excessive minting. That policy continued for thirty-three years and produced deflation. King Yŏngjo reluctantly agreed to mint more cash in 1731, and minting continued for the rest of the dynasty, but no multiple-denomination cash (the equivalent of nickels, dimes, and quarters) was minted until the 1860s because of the fear of inflation. The restriction to penny cash along with the absence of paper money, bills of exchange, or banks was another obstacle to rapid commercial expansion.

Nonetheless, private, unlicensed merchants began to compete with the licensed merchants in the capital. In the 1740s the government capitulated and stopped prosecuting unlicensed merchants trading in certain goods. King Chŏngjong in 1791 adopted a compromise solution, the joint-sales policy, which protected monopoly privileges

---

1. Broadcast seeding is done by throwing out the seed on the field by hand. Transplantation means planting the rice seeds in a small seed bed to make it easier to weed the early sprouts and then transplanting them to the growing field after the rice plants have matured.

MATERIAL CULTURE

Five-Day Markets

The most important material development in this period was the spread of market activity and the use of currency, indicating that Korea was able to move forward economically despite the powerful anticommercial prejudice of Confucian thought in Korea. That development, however, has been exaggerated to the point where it has been perceived as constituting the beginning of capitalism.

One of the best types of evidence to demonstrate that market development was quite sluggish in creating commercial towns with permanent shops was to see what a typical market looked like in the eighteenth century. Rather than a commercial town, it was a five-day market that opened only once every five days. Market development meant that residents of villages were now surrounded by a number of five-day markets that allowed an individual to travel to one of them every day of the ten-day week, a trip that took no more than a day's walk back and forth. Even some of the larger towns, which were more administrative than commercial centers, housed only one of the five-day markets instead of permanent shops, as in Seoul.

Typical Five-Day Market. Chosŏn Dynasty, late nineteenth century. *(Sajinuro ponun Choson sidae: Saenghwal kwa p'ungsok [The Choson period in Pictures: Life and Customs] [Seoul: Somundang, 1986], p. 7)*

only for six shops (*Yug'ŭijon*) in Seoul and allowed private merchants to manufacture or sell all other products. Beyond this, there was no development toward a completely free market system.

POLITICS, IDEOLOGY, AND REFORM AFTER 1762

Despite King Yŏngjo's efforts to end factionalism, he made politics more complicated in 1762 when he decided to lock Crown Prince Sado in a small rice box in the palace courtyard and left him to starve to death; he died eight days later. King Yŏngjo was an absentee father whose neglect of Sado was compounded by stern expectations of excellence, but the boy had already displayed severe neurotic tendencies. Yŏngjo had given Sado responsibility as prince regent at the age of fifteen in 1749 to take over many of the king's tasks, but Sado was obviously mentally disturbed because of his fear of his father, and his father's ridicule pushed the prince over the edge of sanity. He released his pent-up frustrations in paroxysms of rage in which he murdered ladies of the palace who offended him.

A-Frame Carrier. Chosŏn Dynasty, nineteenth century. *(Sajinuro ponun Choson sidae: Saeghwal kwa p'ungsok* [The Choson Period in Pictures: Life and Customs] *[Seoul: Somundang, 1986], p. 47)*

ordered him not to do so to prevent the reemergence of factional strife, however. Chŏngjo was also beholden to those factions for protecting him against seven assassination plots.

Chŏngjo chastised his officials for their devotion to their own private interests and their failure to master the moral teachings of the Chinese classics. To rectify this problem, he ordered that Chinese classical texts be imported and housed them in a new Kyujanggak Royal Library staffed by his favorite officials. He turned that staff into his own private cabinet for advising him on state affairs. Nevertheless, he banned the free importation of books from China because he disliked the subversive nature of Chinese thought, particularly Wang Yangming's meditational approach to Confucianism, the rising trend of popular genres in literature and art, the writing of sardonic novels, the useless concern with prose and poetry styles, and the influence of Christian theology. He remarked that Korea already possessed more than enough editions of the Chinese classics, a curious position for a king whose reign was marked by a blossoming of popular genres in literature.

Chŏngjo wanted to rule Chosŏn as an active ruler like the ancient Chinese sages, but the Patriarch and *pyŏkp'a* factions believed that a sage king should turn over the administration to men who passed the civil service examinations. They also insisted that their factions represented the morally good men while their opponents were either immoral or amoral, an argument made famous by Ouyang Xiu of the Chinese Song Dynasty. King Chŏngjo told the Patriarchs that he was a better judge than they of good and ethical government and reminded them that the sage kings of ancient China allowed no factions.

Chŏngjo frequently made demonstrations of his ardent devotion to his deceased father. In 1795 he led a procession of six thousand men to Hwasŏng (Suwŏn) with his mother, Princess Hyegyŏng, ostensibly to honor her seventieth birthday, but the underlying goal was to honor his father, who was buried there (see Color Plate 23). He also ordered construction of a new commercial city in his father's honor, but he had to abandon the project because of four crop disasters in the 1790s.

King Yŏngjo appears to have decided to commit filicide when it was reported to him that Prince Sado was overheard praying for his own father's death. This action immediately split the bureaucrats into the *pyŏkp'a* (mostly Patriarchs), who agreed with Yŏngjo's decision, and the *sip'a* (mostly Southerners), who sympathized with the deceased crown prince, laying the groundwork for another round of purges. When King Chŏngjo, the son of the deceased Sado, came to the throne in 1776, he ardently desired to find some means to honor his father, restore his reputation, and take out vengeance against the Patriarch and *pyŏkp'a* factions. His grandfather, King Yŏngjo, had explicitly

The bad harvests in 1792, 1794, 1797, and 1798 prompted Chŏngjo to put out a call for advice to the nation for reform proposals. The leading private statecraft scholars of that period, including Pak Chiwŏn and Chŏng Yagyong (Tasan), recommended limiting land holdings, but their limits were far too high to be effective because they feared fierce opposition from landlords. King Chŏngjo rejected the idea because land limitation had not been tried in China since the Han Dynasty. Since Chŏngjo also failed to manumit official slaves, his reform project ended in dismal failure. The only policy that apparently did succeed was strengthening central control over district magistrates to clean up corruption, but after his death when corruption resumed, the magistrates had greater power to harass the local population.

NEW MOVEMENTS IN SCHOLARSHIP AND LEARNING

The economic and material devastation caused by the Japanese and Manchu invasions created a crisis that caused some scholars to turn their attention to statecraft problems. Following in the footsteps of Yu Hyŏngwŏn, the Southerner Yi Ik wanted to save the peasants from suffering and poverty, but he opposed the idea of confiscating land from landowners by force lest social order be disrupted. He preferred that limits be placed on the amount of land owned according to the rank and status of the individual. Sŏ Yugu, who wrote in the 1820s, also feared confiscation. He wanted the state to purchase land to establish colonies that would be organized around the well-fields (a large square divided into nine small squares) of the ancient Zhou Dynasty and to recruit skilled managers to increase efficiency.

Northern Learning

In the late eighteenth century a group of reform scholars and officials dubbed the Northern Learning group challenged the conventional prejudice against the Manchus. They urged that Korea learn from the Qing Dynasty to improve the economy and the material aspects of life. Most came from the minority Southerner or Northerner factions.

Hong Taeyong was attracted to the statecraft writings of Yulgok (Yi I) and Yu Hyŏngwŏn. When he accompanied his uncle on a mission to the Qing capital in 1765, he became interested in western astronomy and mathematics, but he confined his speculations to analogical reasoning rather than astronomical observation. He also rejected the idea that China was either at the center of the earth or the only enlightened country on earth, and he criticized his fellow *yangban* for focusing only on China and neglecting the history and culture of their own country. He criticized the disdain for manual labor by the *yangban* aristocracy and the backwardness and poverty of the economy, but he did not propose any revolutionary social change.

Pak Chiwŏn studied with Hong Taeyong. After accompanying a tribute mission to China in 1780, he left a detailed record of his trip in his *Jehol Diary* (*Yŏlha ilgi*), and was appointed to office in 1786. He attacked the *yangban* monopoly of the examination system and satirized them in stories like *Master Hŏ* (*Hŏsaengjŏn*) and *The Yangban* (*Yangbanjŏn*). He condemned scholars for ignoring practical subjects, and he demanded a ban on discrimination against *nothoi* (sons of concubines), manumission of official slaves, and adoption of a land-limitation scheme.[2] He encouraged everyone to engage in commerce and industry and recommended improving transportation by copying the better carts and boats in Qing China.

Pak Chega was a Southerner who studied with Pak Chiwŏn. In 1786 he proposed that the king invite Christian missionaries from China to Korea to teach western astronomy and mathematics. In 1788 he wrote a book entitled *Northern Learning* (*Puhag'ŭi*) that expanded on

---

2. The Greek term *nothos* (pl., *nothoi*) is very close to the Korean term *sŏŏl*, because they do not convey any notion of illegitimacy to children of concubines. "Secondary sons" has also been used to describe *sŏŏl*, but I prefer the Greek term because it was coined explicitly to fit sons of concubines.

themes introduced by Hong Taeyong and Pak Chiwŏn, and he urged the king to appoint the best merchants to office and expand trade with Qing China.

Northern Learning represented a liberalization of interest and thought among intellectuals in this period, but it had a very limited effect on government policy because anti-Manchu prejudice and the Confucian bias against merchants were too powerful to overcome.

Christianity and Western Learning

After the Jesuit Francis Xavier arrived in Japan in 1549, many Japanese were converted to Christianity. Some Korean captives who were taken to Japan during Hideyoshi's invasions converted, but they had a negligible effect on Korea. Many of Matteo Ricci's works on Catholic theology and western mathematics, astronomy, and geography were brought into Korea from China in the early seventeenth century. The Koreans lumped Christian theology and western science together in a single term, *Western Learning (Sŏhak)*. Koreans were won over to western astronomical ideas and adopted the western calendar in 1653, nine years after the Qing Dynasty had done so.

A few scholars became curious about Christianity in the 1720s. Yi Ik was greatly impressed by "Seven Victories" (*Jige*) by Diego Pontoja (1571–1618) because it praised self-denial, frugality, and other virtues compatible with Confucianism, but otherwise he rejected Christian theology. Yet he urged his disciples to study it. Yi Imyŏng in 1720, however, rejected the Catholic notion of heaven and hell, and Yi Ik's disciple, Sin Hudam, in 1724 condemned Christianity for its resemblance to the selfish aspect of Buddhism (leaving the family to become a mendicant monk in the search for individual salvation) and its concern with life after death. Another disciple, An Chŏngbok, became tutor to King Chŏngjo when he was crown prince and wrote refutations of Catholic dogma.

The Jesuit emphasis on the truth of Catholic dogma as a means of proving the validity of the Christian message in the manner of St. Thomas Aquinas passed over the heads of most of these Confucian scholars, who were interested only in whether Catholic doctrines would aid or hinder adherence to Confucian social morality.[3] Meanwhile, in 1715, the pope's condemnation of Chinese ancestral ceremonial practices as idolatry was followed in 1724 by Emperor Yongzheng's condemnation of Christianity and his ban against Christian proselytization. The papal ban influenced mainstream attitudes in Korea and helped turn the tide later from scholarly criticism to violent repression.

Toleration and Persecution of Christians

King Chŏngjo went much beyond King Yŏngjo in opening opportunities for office to members of the Southerner and Northerner factions, including those who had previously been exiled. This proved to be a risky strategy. One of Yi Ik's disciples, Hong Yuhan, in 1770 began to observe the Sabbath, not to convert to Christianity but to meditate to eliminate selfishness from his mind. In 1779, however, a group of men including some of Yi's disciples participated in a retreat for ten days at the Chuŏ Temple (Chuŏsa) near Kwangju in Kyŏnggi province to explore the available literature on Christianity.

In 1784, Tasan concluded that because virtue could be attained only after a much longer period of arduous practice than even Zhu Xi had imagined, reverence for God was the best way to nourish a feeling of awe and apprehension before the external moral power. Tasan's God (Matteo Ricci's *Sangje*), however, was the Confucian ruler of the universe, not the Christian creator of the universe.

That same year Yi Sŭnghun traveled to Yanjing in China to be baptized, but the Catholic missionaries refused because of his inadequate knowledge of Catholic doctrine. He brought back Christian texts to proselytize among acquain-

3. Don Baker, "Confucians Confront Catholicism in Eighteenth-Century Korea," Ph.D. diss., University of Washington, 1983, p. 150.

tances like Tasan and his two brothers and members of the *chung'in* hereditary specialists and clerks. Several dozen men formed the first Christian congregation and worshipped at the home of the *chung'in* Kim Pŏm'u in Seoul in the spring of 1785. When the meetings were discovered, Kim Pŏm'u was beaten and died of his wounds in 1786, becoming Korea's first Christian martyr.

In 1787, however, two students of the National Academy (*Sŏnggyun'gwan*) in Seoul, Yi Sŭnghun and Tasan, were attacked for studying Christian texts, and the next year, two high officials asked the king to ban European books. The southerner Councilor of the Right, Ch'ae Chegong, who was not Christian but a relative of many Catholic southerners, pleaded with King Chŏngjo not to punish the Christians because their knowledge of Confucian doctrine was still insufficient. Chŏngjo agreed, but he also ordered the destruction of all Christian books.

In 1790 Bishop Alexandre de Bouvea in Yanjing sent a letter to the Korean Catholics informing them of the papal ban on the *chesa* ancestral worship ceremony, understood by the pope as idolatry. The ban drove some sympathizers like Tasan from Christianity, but in 1791 two Catholics who were also Southerners from Chŏlla province, Paul Yun Chich'ung and his cousin, James Kwŏn Sangyŏn, burned the ancestral tablets for Yun's mother. When they refused to recant, King Chŏngjo ordered their decapitation, interrogated several others under torture, and forced them to commit apostasy.

In 1794, however, the first Christian missionary to Korea, the Chinese Zhou Wenmo, was discovered. King Chŏngjo executed him and demoted or exiled southerners, and two years later he dismissed Ch'ae Chegong. King Chŏngjo's attempt at toleration had backfired, and he adopted a hard line against southerners and Christians.

THE FAMILY AND WOMEN IN THE CONFUCIAN AGE

By the eighteenth century Confucian ancestor worship had completely replaced Buddhist ceremonies for the deceased, and the Confucian pattern of patriarchal domination of the family reached its zenith. Succession to family headship was restricted where possible to the eldest son, and if there were no sons, adoption was restricted to sons of close relatives in the male line.

At the age of seven, sons and daughters were separated from each other, and daughters were educated in accordance with Confucian manuals to learn the rule of modesty and subordination to men. Their training was confined to female chores, with minimal attention to education unless the child's parents defied convention. Upon marriage, women had to move to their husband's home and lost their right of inheritance to property from their parents. They were subordinated to their mothers-in-law, had to remain silent unless spoken to, and were often treated as little more than household maids. Women were kept in the inner quarters (*nanbang*) of the house for the most part and had to wear a head covering when going out. They had to remain chaste while their husbands were free to chase after women and *kisaeng* (female entertainers), even bringing them into the house as concubines. Wives were subject to expulsion if they failed to produce a male heir or were deemed insubordinate to any member of their husband's household, and they were banned from remarriage after the death of the husband.

A wife who bore a son immediately gained status, but on her husband's death, she had to remain subordinated to her son's decisions. Her only respite came when her son married and she could lord her authority over her daughter-in-law. Since her husband spent his time in study or association with male friends in the *sarangbang*, or outer guest room, she managed the household. She participated in ancestor worship for her husband's parents but not for her own, and she was not allowed to lead the service if there were any male survivors.

At the beginning of the dynasty, women were listed in the family genealogy (*chokpo*) along with their brothers in the order of birth. By the eighteenth century, however, they were all listed after their brothers, and when they married, they were expunged from it and were listed instead in their husband's genealogy as the daughter of their father. Their names were not even recorded.

Female Clothing. Outdoor garb, as depicted in this photo, was required attire for *yangban* women to keep them hidden from the gaze of men. Chosŏn Dynasty, nineteenth century. *(Sajinuro ponun Choson sidae: Saeghwal kwa p'ungsok [The Choson Period in Pictures: Life and Customs] [Seoul: Somundang, 1986], p. 162)*

Marriages among the *yangban* in Chosŏn were the result of an agreement between two families, and they were usually contracted when the partners were quite young. (See Chapter 15.) Commoner women had fewer of these restrictions on them, but *kisaeng* were free to dispense with husbands, choose them, or leave them to find another.

In the home, the woman managed popular religious practices usually frowned on by men. They prayed to mountains, trees, and household gods. They regarded their dreams as predictive of the sex and capacity of a new child, and they had to take care to defend the family against bad omens around the home. A special ceremony might be held for cutting the umbilical cord, and unusual burials were practiced for women who died in labor or committed suicide to prevent their spirits from plaguing surviving members of the family. Women also attended religious festivals, such as the Tano Festival (see Color Plate 22).

The wife took charge of hiring shamans, usually female ones (*mudang*), to go into a trance and communicate with the angry spirits of her own dead parents and grandparents, who were believed to cause sickness and other problems among family members. For that matter, even kings used shamans. They taxed them, used them for *kut* in the palace to pray for rain or cure illness, and set up an office to control official shamans. Women, as well as many men, continued to believe in Buddhist ideas despite Confucian condemnation, particularly transmigration, karma, and punishment in Buddhist hell, especially in facing illness or impending death.

THE GROWTH OF LITERATURE

In the seventeenth and eighteenth centuries, there was a burgeoning of literary production, including about a hundred tales usually written by men in classical Chinese and women in the *han'gŭl* alphabet. About one-third of them (twenty-five such tales) are about women, and the other two-thirds deal with women at some length. Many of the stories of women portray them defending their womanly virtues, but suffering is usually the main theme. In other tales, *kisaeng* exert their independence despite their low status by demanding or stealing their lovers' money or humiliating them in public.

The most popular of all tales was about Ch'unhyang. It evolved from the troubadour tradition of *p'ansori* singers, which began around 1800 and was written down in several versions. The most complete version includes many references and allusions to Chinese emperors, officials, and poets, obviously to appeal to *yangban* as well as commoners. It was both a didactic tale of the triumph of womanly virtue over evil and a romantic tale between the daughter of a *kisaeng* who chose not to adopt her mother's occupation and the son of a *yangban* official. In defiance of

Shaman Attire. Male (*paksu*) and female (*mudang*) shamans dressed as civil or military officials. Late Chosŏn Dynasty. *(Sajinuro ponun Choson sidae: Saeghwal kwa p'ungsok [The Choson Period in Pictures: Life and Customs] [Seoul: Somundang, 1986], p. 122)*

convention, the two wed secretly at the age of fifteen, but the husband left for Seoul to prepare for the civil service examinations and passed in first place. Meanwhile, a cruel governor arrived in Ch'unhyang's town and demanded that the young woman become his concubine. When she refused, he ordered her beaten unmercifully and threw her in jail to die. The husband then returned as a secret inspector to cashier the governor, and the two lived happily ever after. The story contains many dream sequences, constant reminders of unexpected dangers, and Buddhist awareness of karma, life after death, and resignation to fate. The erotic description of the two lovers affirms the priority of love over stifling convention, undoubtedly the reason that the story has remained so popular.

The *Nine Cloud Dream* was written by Kim Manjung (1637–1692), a high official and member of the Patriarch faction who was dismissed twice, in 1674 and 1689, when the Patriarchs were purged. Despite his deep Confucian training, the story's main message is Buddhist: the glories of a Confucian education, promotion to high office, and unrestricted access to sex with two wives and seven concubines was no more meaningful than a dream. It was better to realize that a humble life devoted to Buddhist devotion was the way to live. In this story, the wives and concubines are all independent, resourceful women who stand out as more vivid characters than the supposed hero.

Two other famous literary works of the period are more political in nature. *The True*

DOCUMENTS

Lady Hyegyŏng's Memoirs

Most outstanding as a literary work was Memoirs of Lady Hyegyŏng (Hanjungnok or Records Written in Silence), *written in* han'gŭl *by the wife of Crown Prince Sado, who was starved to death by his father, King Yŏngjo, in 1762. The book consists of four separate accounts written in 1795, 1801, 1802, and 1805. No other source provides a better introduction to the vicissitudes of palace life, particularly at a time when the slightest slip could mean death. In fact, her uncle and younger brother were executed, in 1776 and 1801, respectively. Probably the most interesting of her narratives was in her Memoir of 1805, in which she relates Sado's psychosis to the deficiencies of King Yŏngjo as a father and a relentless taskmaster.*

His Majesty's [King Yŏngjo] sagacious heart became irritated with small things at the Prince's quarters, mostly imperceptible and of an unspecified nature. Consequently, without really knowing why, he visited his son less frequently. This happened just as the Prince began to grow; that is just when a child, suffering some inattention or relaxation of control, might easily fall under other influences. As the Prince was often left to himself at this stage, he began to get into trouble. . . .

In his study sessions with tutors, however, Prince Sado was a serious and attentive student. . . . Thus it is all the more sad that, in his father's presence, the prince grew inarticulate and hesitant out of fear and nervousness. His Majesty became more and more exasperated with him during these encounters in which the Prince was hopelessly tongue-tied. He was alternately angry and concerned about his son. Nonetheless, he never sought a closer relationship with his son, never sought to spend more time with him or to teach him himself. He continued to keep the Prince at a distance, hoping that his son would become on his own the heir he dreamed of. How could this not lead to trouble? . . .

Sometime around the *ŭlch'uk* year (1745) [at the age of ten], the Prince's behavior became strange indeed. It was not just the behavior of a child playing excitedly or loudly. Something was definitely wrong with him. The ladies-in-waiting became quite concerned, whispering to each other

History of Queen Inhyŏn (*Inhyŏn wanghujŏn*), written by an unknown author though presumably a member of the Patriarch faction, was a biased account aimed at justifying the defense of Queen Inhyŏn of the Min family, who was deposed by King Sukchong for Palace Lady Chang in 1689 and then later reinstated. The other was Lady Hyegyŏng's brilliant memoirs, which provide a glimpse into palace life (see **Documents: Lady Hyegyŏng's Memoirs**).

As part of the emergence of popular culture, *p'ansori* was an oral tradition that became part of culture in the countryside in the eighteenth century. It was performed by the singer (*kwangdae*) as a chant, usually in a guttural tone accompanied by a drummer who accelerated or slowed the beat according to the mood of piece as it went through different segments. Famous *kwangdae* had much license in the songs themselves. As time passed, classical Chinese phrases of their fears. In the ninth month of that year, the Prince fell gravely ill, often losing consciousness. . . .

[In 1749, when Sado was fifteen, King Yŏngjo appointed him Prince-Regent to sit in court and conduct business.] There was nothing that the Prince-Regent did that His Majesty found satisfactory. He was constantly discontented and angry with his son. It reached a point where the occurrence of cold spells, droughts, poor harvests, strange natural omens, or calamities caused His Majesty to denounce "the Prince-Regent's insufficient virtue" and to reproach the Prince most severely. . . .

In the sixth month of *chŏngch'uk* (1757) . . . Prince Sado began to kill. The first person he killed was Kim Hanch'ae, the eunuch who happened to be on duty that day. The Prince came in with the severed head and displayed it to the ladies-in-waiting. The bloody head, the first I ever saw, was simply a horrifying sight. As if he had to kill to release his rage, the Prince harmed many ladies-in-waiting. . . .

In the ninth month of that year, Prince Sado took in Pingae, a lady-in-waiting . . . . Before this, he had been intimate with many ladies-in-waiting. Whoever resisted him in any way he beat until he rent her flesh and consummated the act afterwards. Needless to say, no one welcomed his advances. Despite the many women he had

been intimate with, he neither cared for anyone for long nor showed any particular fondness while it lasted. This was true even of the secondary consort who had borne him children. It was different with Pingae. He was mad about her. . . . His Majesty learned of Pingae. He was highly provoked. He summoned the Prince to question him. "How dare you do that?"

By this time [1761], whenever he was seized by his illness the Prince invariably hurt people. For some time now, Pingae [Prince Sado's concubine who bore him two children] had been the only one to attend the prince when he dressed. Hopelessly in the grip of the disease, he grew oblivious even of his beloved. One day, for one of his outings incognito, he was suddenly overwhelmed by a fit of rage and beat her senseless. No sooner had he left than Pingae drew her last breath there where he left her. How pitiful her end was! . . . Upon his return, Prince Sado heard of what had happened, but he said nothing. He was not in his senses.

———
Source: JaHyon Kim Haboush, trans., *The Memoirs of Lady Hyegyŏng* (Berkeley: University of California Press, 1996), pp. 247, 250–251, 252, 258, 283–285, 301.

were inserted into the songs to appeal to *yangban* as well as commoners, but the tradition remained part of the popular genre. Many of the songs mocked the *yangban*, but rural dances (*talch'um*) and local masked plays (*t'allorum*) were more biting in their sarcasm.

Poetry also remained a favorite pastime of both men (in Chinese) and women (in *han'gŭl*), and the favorite forms in this period were the short *sijo* poems, their longer versions (*sasŏl sijo*), and the still longer lyrical *kasa*.

SUMMARY

The seventeenth and eighteenth centuries began in the aftermath of the destructive Hideyoshi invasions, and the humiliation was compounded by two invasions by the Manchus, in 1627 and 1637. The recovery of agricultural production took a century, but the shock of war acted as a spur to market activity, due to the reintroduction of metal currency and the replacement of the in-kind tribute tax with a land surtax to finance government purchases of goods from the market. After a monetary retrenchment between 1696 and 1729, the state resumed the minting of cash permanently.

In the eighteenth century, technological improvement in agriculture led to a surplus that stimulated market activity and a challenge by private merchants to government-licensed monopoly shops. Those developments nevertheless fell short of the level of commerce and urbanization in either Japan or China.

Internecine political struggle among factions marked both centuries, particularly between 1659 and 1728. That struggle declined between 1728 and 1762, but King Yŏngjo's filicide of Crown Prince Sado reopened factional dispute, and the introduction of Christianity created the basis for more conflict, which was constrained by King Chŏngjo until his death in 1800.

The *yangban* maintained its control over official posts in the capital, but the significant slave population dropped off sharply after 1750, not because the state manumitted them or slaves were buying their freedom, but because they deserted their homes and were replaced by an increase in peasants who had lost their land to creditors.

Intellectual and cultural life flourished in the late eighteenth century because of the Northern Learning school, the introduction of western learning, King Chŏngjo's requests for advice on governance, and the greater use of *han'gŭl* as well as classical Chinese in literature by women as well as men.

There was great promise for greater developments in economy, society, and culture by 1800, but that promise was not fulfilled in the next century.

SUGGESTED READING

For political history and institutional studies, see J. B. Palais, *Confucian Statecraft and Korean Institutions* (1996); J. K. Haboush, *A Heritage of Kings: One Man's Monarchy in the Confucian World* (1988); and M. Deuchler and J. K. Haboush, eds., *Culture and the State in Late Chosŏn Korea* (1999).

For a summary survey of Korean society, see E. W. Wagner, "Social Stratification in Seventeenth Century Korea: Some Observations from a 1663 Seoul Census Register," *Occasional Papers on Korea*, no. 1 (1979): 36–54.

See G. Ledyard, *The Dutch Come to Korea* (1971) for an account of Hendrik Hamel's captivity in the mid-seventeenth century in Korea. Hamel came from Holland and was shipwrecked off the Korean coast.

For Confucian and other modes of thought, see W. T. de Bary and J. Haboush, eds., *The Rise of Neo-Confucianism in Korea* (1985), and M. Kalton et al., *The Four-Seven Debate* (1994).

For studies of women and shamans, see L. Kendall and M. Peterson, eds., *Korean Women: View from the Inner Room* (1983), and L. Kendall, *Shamans, Housewives and Other Restless Spirits* (1985).

For two masterful translations of literature, see J. K. Haboush, *The Memoirs of Lady Hyegyŏng* (1996), and R. Rutt and K. Chong'un, trans. and comm., *Virtuous Women: Three Classic Korean Novels* (1974). For literary analysis, see D. Cho, *Korean Literature in Cultural Context and Comparative Perspective* (1997).

WESTERN IMPERIALISM (1800–1900)

Western Imperialism (1800–1900)

IN CONTRAST TO THE FRAIL WOODEN-hulled sailing ships that carried Europeans to the Pacific Ocean in the sixteenth century, nineteenth-century vessels were increasingly powered by coal-fueled steam engines. The industrial revolution that rescued Europe from the ecological trap of reliance on agrarian products propelled technological innovations in weaponry and an expansion in the state's ability to command men and resources. Following in the wake of trading companies, government officials began to regulate and tax commerce, then administer territories, and finally recruit natives into tightly disciplined, uniformed battalions capable of projecting force thousands of miles from European homelands. No longer mere participants in maritime trade, Europeans transformed their trading posts from India to Indonesia into colonies.

During the eighteenth century, European states had established trading posts throughout the Indian Ocean and the Pacific, the only colony being Spain's in the Philippines. Under Catherine the Great, Russia extended its reach across Siberia to Alaska and sent teams of explorers down the Kamchatka peninsula, along the coast of Sakhalin, and into Hokkaido. Confrontations with Japanese officials led to sporadic efforts to open diplomatic relations. Having defeated French efforts to challenge its forays into India in the middle of the eighteenth century, the British East India Company spearheaded the battle for markets that brought administrators and troops to protect mercantile interests and made Britain the greatest of the European powers. While France was embroiled in revolution, Britain sent an official mission to

China in 1793. Headed by Lord George Macartney, its aim was to eliminate what the British saw as frivolous restrictions on trade that limited the number, destination, and schedules for their ships. Since controlling trade helped stabilize the social order, reduced smuggling, and reaffirmed the Qing emperor's superiority over all other monarchs, the mission failed.

The Napoleonic Wars following the French Revolution remade the map of Europe and contributed to a new sense of nationalism. In Asia Britain took over the Dutch colony at Batavia because Napoleon had tried to make his brother king of the Netherlands. The Dutch never told the Japanese that the only place flying the Dutch flag was Dejima in Nagasaki harbor. The Napoleonic Wars had spilled over into European colonial possessions in Latin America. There, wars of liberation starting in 1809 resulted in the establishment of independent nations in the 1820s. The heightened focus on nationhood required a clear demarcation of sovereignty and a clear delineation of boundaries. No longer would small states such as Vietnam, the Ryukyus, and Korea be permitted to claim quasi-autonomy under China's mantle, and every inch of land had to belong to a nation. Regardless of whether peasants saw themselves as Frenchmen, their rulers and the educated classes imagined communities in which everyone spoke the same language, professed similar beliefs, and despised foreigners. The cosmopolitan Enlightenment admiration for Chinese civilization and Confucian rationality gave way to disdain for godless heathens who failed to appreciate the superiority of western technol-

Timeline: Western Advances in Asia

1793: Earl of Macartney travels to Beijing seeking diplomatic recognition; Russians seek same in Japan.

1797: Broughton, a British captain, surveys east coast of Korea.

1804: Russian advances in Siberia and Sea of Okhotsk culminate in emissary to Japan.

1805–1812: Russia builds forts in Alaska and northern California.

1808: British warship enters Nagasaki harbor.

1811: Britain captures Java from the Dutch; returned in 1816.

1816: Anglo-Nepalese War.

1819: Raffles, a British official, occupies Singapore for Britain.

1820: Vietnam bans Christianity and expels missionaries.

1824–1826: First Anglo-Burmese War.

1837: U.S. ship *Morrison* tries and fails to establish relations with Japan.

1839–1840: Opium War and First Anglo-Afghan War.

1842: Treaty of Nanjing.

1846: U.S. Commodore Biddle seeks trade with Japan; refused.

1852: Second Anglo-Burmese War.

1853–1854: U.S. Commodore Perry forces unequal treaty on Japan.

1856–1857: Arrow War between Britain, France, and China.

1858: Treaties of Tianjin; Japan signs commercial treaty with United States.

1857–1858: Great "Indian Mutiny"; British East India Company abolished.

1860: British and French troops occupy Beijing.

1862: Treaty of Saigon: France occupies three provinces in south Vietnam.

1863: France gains protectorate over Cambodia.

1866: France sends punitive expedition to Korea.

1871: United States sends ships to open Korea to foreign trade by force; repulsed.

1874: France acquires control over all of south Vietnam; Japan sends expeditionary force to Taiwan.

1876: Japan signs unequal treaty with Korea.

1877: Queen Victoria proclaimed empress of India.

1882: Korea signs unequal treaties with United States and other Great Powers.

1884–1885: France makes Vietnam a colony.

1885–1886: Third Anglo-Burmese War.

1893: France gains protectorate over Laos.

1894–1895: Sino-Japanese War.

1898: Scramble for concessions in China by European powers.

1898: United States seizes the Philippines from Spain; annexes Hawai'i.

1900: Boxer Rebellion.

ogy. In contrast to older empires that allowed natives the opportunity to participate in running their affairs, new empires discriminated between the white man and everyone else.

By bringing decades of peace to Europe, Napoleon's defeat at Waterloo in 1815 freed nations to concentrate on expanding trade net-works while competing for Great Power status. Great Power status required colonies, and competition with other nations spurred imperialism. France reestablished its preeminence in North Africa, contended with Britain for ports in Burma, and tried to force a commercial treaty on Vietnam. In 1816 Britain was at war with Nepal when it dispatched a second mission to the Qing court. Because the envoy refused to participate in the customary rituals that regulated relations between tribute nations and the Son of Heaven, including the kowtow, the emperor refused to see him. Britain had already established ports on the Malay Peninsula; adding Singapore gave it a harbor to protect and provision British ships sailing between India and China. British ships started appearing off the coast of Japan, sometimes threatening the natives in their quest for food and fuel. Britain and France clashed over Burmese ports while Burmese troops threatened Bengal. The first Anglo-Burmese War ended in victory for Britain, a large indemnity extracted from the Burmese, a British diplomat stationed at the Burmese court, and British hegemony over the Bay of Bengal.

Bengal supplied the opium that Britain used to buy tea. By 1750, Britain was importing well over 2 million pounds of tea from China a year, and demand was rising. Having little that the Chinese found of value, the British at first had to pay for tea with silver, thus leading to a negative trade balance. After 1761, the balance began to shift in Britain's favor. The East India Company allowed the illegal export of Bengali opium into China, bought tea for homeland consumption, and used the silver accruing as a result of the trade surplus to finance its operation and the British administration of Bengal. From the British point of view, that drug addicts multiplied as the price went down and the supply went up, that bribes to allow drug trafficking corrupted local officials, simply demonstrated Chinese racial inferiority.

British merchants remained unhappy with trading conditions in China. Textile manufacturers wanted to sell machine-made cloth, and private traders resented the East India Company monopoly. When the monopoly was abolished in 1834, the government named Lord Napier to be superintendent of trade in Guangzhou. He tried to bypass the Cohong, the merchant guild responsible to the Qing court for managing foreign trade, and negotiate directly with the provincial governor-general, who saw no reason to sully his dignity by dealing with barbarians. Diplomatic incident led to a confrontation between British warships and Chinese defenses. Napier was forced to withdraw. Trade continued, albeit with British merchants calling for more warships to enforce their demands for the elimination of the Cohong monopoly over foreign trade and the opening of ports farther north.

The Opium War tested Chinese morality against British technology. In 1839, Imperial Commissioner Lin Zexu arrived in Guangzhou with orders to suppress the drug trade. He moved swiftly against dealers and users and demanded that opium under foreign control be turned over. When the British merchants proved recalcitrant, he stopped trade altogether. He appealed to Queen Victoria to allow him the same right to regulate trade and suppress drugs that administrators enjoyed in Britain. When the traders reluctantly relinquished their stocks, he allowed them to flee to the Portuguese city of Macao and thence to Hong Kong while he washed twenty thousand chests of opium out to sea. Indignant at the expropriation of their property without compensation, the traders appealed to Parliament. A fleet that included four armed steamships carrying Indian troops under British officers refused to contest the defenses Lin had built upstream to protect Guangzhou. Four ships blockaded the river mouth while the rest of the fleet sailed north to harass Chinese shipping along the coast. By the time it reached Tianjin, the closest port to Beijing, the Qing court realized that it had to negotiate. In the first round of negotiations, China agreed to pay an indemnity to compensate British merchants for their destroyed property and allow expanded trade in Guangzhou, direct access to Qing officials, and British possession of Hong Kong. When these terms proved unsatisfactory to the British home government, another round of fighting forced additional concessions.

China's defeat in the Opium War forced it to open to the West and inaugurated a new era in western imperialism. (See Color Plate 24.) It marked the first time a western power had emerged victorious in battle in East Asia, a debacle that sent shock waves through Japan and Korea. The Treaty of Nanjing opened five ports to British residency and trade, abolished the Cohong, and ceded Hong Kong to Britain. A supplementary treaty signed a year later fixed low tariffs on British imports and included the most-favored-nation clause whereby any privilege granted any western power automatically accrued to Britain. In 1844, Americans signed a treaty with China that gave them the right to build churches and hospitals and to protect American nationals from the Chinese judicial system. "Extraterritoriality" meant that with the exception of opium traders, Americans in China were subject to American laws, judges, courts, and prisons. The British automatically participated in this infringement on Chinese sovereignty, as did the other western powers that signed treaties with China. Historian Akira Iriye has termed this "multilateral imperialism."[1] Because China and its subjects did not enjoy the same privileges abroad, most favored nation and extraterritoriality became the hallmarks of the unequal treaty system.

Following in the British wake, American traders, whalers, and missionaries lured their government into engagement across the Pacific. During the 1840s, swift clipper ships with clouds of sail dominated trade routes. In 1846, an American ship shelled what is now Danang in central Vietnam to win the release of an American missionary who had ignored proscriptions on proselytizing. That same year, Commodore James Biddle tried to open negotiations with Japan, only to suffer a humiliating rejection. The United States completed its westward continental expansion in 1848 when it wrested California from Mexico. (It acquired Alaska by purchase from Russia in 1867.) In developing steamer routes across the Pacific to Shanghai, it saw Japan's coal fields as playing an important role. Whalers too needed access to fuel and fresh

water. In 1853, Commodore Matthew Perry sailed four ships, two of them steamers, into Uraga Bay near Edo. He forced shogunal authorities to accept a letter proposing a friendship treaty and promised to return the next year for their response. Despite Japanese efforts to fend him off, Perry obtained the Kanagawa treaty of friendship that opened two small ports to American ships, allowed an American consul to reside on Japanese soil, and provided for most-favored-nation treatment.

The Americans led in imposing modern diplomatic relations on Japan because Britain was busy elsewhere. Angry at what it considered unwarranted obstruction of trade and the exploitation of Burma's magnificent teak forests, Britain launched two more wars against Burma that resulted in Burma's becoming a British colony. Allied with France, Austria, Prussia, and the Ottoman Empire, Britain also fought the Crimean War of 1853–1856 against Russia for control over the mouth of the Danube and the Black Sea. Britain's rule in India suffered a temporary setback with the 1857 revolt, but the result was to strengthen Britain's hand in dealing with the remaining principalities, many of which had to accept British advisers and the protection of British troops.

Determined to open markets, western powers soon imposed fresh demands on China and Japan. After suppressing the 1857 revolt, Britain joined with France to attack Guangzhou and capture its governor-general who had refused to pass their demands on to Beijing. Again the menace of foreign ships at Tianjin compelled the emperor to sign new treaties. Eleven new treaty ports, foreign vessels on the Yangzi, freedom of travel for foreigners in the interior, tolerance for missionaries and their converts, low tariffs, foreign ambassadors resident in Beijing, and the legalization of opium imports accrued to Britain, France, the United States, and Russia. When the Qing court tried to postpone the ambassadors' arrival and had the temerity to fire on British ships from new fortifications at Tianjin, the British and French retaliated by marching twenty thousand troops, many from

---

1. A. Iriye, "Imperialism in East Asia," in *Modern East Asia: Essays in Interpretation,* ed. J. B. Crowley (New York: Harcourt, Brace & World, 1970), p. 129.

A Factory at Guangzhou. Supervised by a merchant, Chinese workers prepare tea and porcelain for export. *(Bridgeman Art Library)*

India, to Beijing, where they destroyed the summer palace outside the city. In 1858, Townsend Harris, the American consul resident in Japan, pointed to what the European powers had achieved with their gunboats in China to convince the shogun's government to sign a commercial treaty with the United States. In addition to setting low tariffs on American goods, it extended the principle of extraterritoriality to westerners in Japan. Angry at the murder of missionaries, a combined French and Spanish fleet attacked Vietnam in 1858. France went on to acquire most of southern Vietnam, a large indemnity, and a commercial treaty.

Western encroachment on East Asia waxed and waned in consort with conflicts elsewhere. In 1861, Russian sailors occupied Tsushima, an island in the strait between Japan and Korea, for

six months, in part to forestall a similar action by the British, in part to gain a warm water port. Unable to win official backing for this maneuver, they eventually withdrew. During the American Civil War, 1861–1865, the United States managed only one military initiative: support for reopening the straits of Shimonoseki after the Japanese tried to close them. France, by contrast, made considerable gains. In 1863, it forced the Cambodian king to accept its protection. Two years later, it annexed two more provinces in south Vietnam and attacked Korea in retaliation for the execution of Catholic priests who had entered the country illegally. France's defeat in the Franco-Prussian War in 1871 put a temporary halt to its ambitions in Asia. In the meantime, a small American squadron tried to replicate Perry's success in

Korea. When the Koreans refused to negotiate, it raided Korean forts guarding the entrance to Seoul and withdrew.

Western imperialism demanded new countermeasures from China and Japan. Both nations started sending diplomatic missions abroad in the 1860s, in part to try to revise the unequal treaties or at least mitigate their effects, in part to study their opponents. Korea too sent study missions to China, Japan, and the United States in the early 1880s. Trade increased, especially after the completion of the Suez Canal in 1869 halved travel time. The laying of telegraphic cables made communication between East and West practically instantaneous. To the north, China resolved its boundary disputes with Russia. Chinese laborers migrated to Southeast Asia, the United States, Hawai'i, Cuba, and Peru, where they were brutally exploited because their government was perceived as too weak to protect them.

Japan soon began to mimic the western claim that imperialism was necessary to civilize the savages by acquainting them with the material and spiritual benefits of modern technology and mechanisms of social control. In 1871, it proposed an unequal treaty with China, only to be rejected. Three years later, it dispatched a military expedition to Taiwan to retaliate for the murder of Ryukyuan fishermen. After the Qing court agreed to pay an indemnity, Japan withdrew. A similar plan to invade Korea did not materialize only because Japan's leaders did not think they were ready. Instead, Japan imposed a treaty on Korea that gave it the same privileges of most-favored-nation status and extraterritoriality that westerners enjoyed in Japan. It also solidified its northern boundary by agreeing with Russia that while Sakhalin would become part of Russia, the Kuril Islands belonged to Japan.

Rivalries between the Great Powers brought a fresh wave of western imperialism across Asia and Africa. In 1882, the United States became the first western power to sign a commercial treaty with Korea. Thanks to the most-favored-nation clause, the European powers and Japan immediately gained the same privileges. Follow-

ing Vietnam's appeals for help from China, its nominal overlord, the French attacked a new naval base in China. China had to grant that Vietnam existed as a separate country and watch it be combined with Cambodia and, later, Laos into a French colony. Sandwiched between British Burma and French Indochina, Thailand remained independent by acquiescing to a series of unequal treaties. Russia and Britain tried to outbid each other for influence in Korea, while one faction at the Korean court sought American intervention to preserve Korean independence. Following decades of European exploratory trips through Africa, King Leopold II of Belgium in 1876 fostered the founding of the International Association for the Exploration and Civilization of Africa while the British and French took over Egyptian finances to manage that country's debt to its European creditors. Britain performed a similar role in China when it undertook to collect customs duties for the Qing court. Belgium, Germany, Italy, Portugal, and Spain joined Britain and France in carving up Africa into protectorates and colonies notable in varying degrees for the exploitation of natural resources and the brutal treatment of natives. (See Map C6.1.)

Imperialism in Asia entered a new phase when China and Japan fought over Korea in 1894–1895. When the Korean king requested help from China in suppressing rebellion, Japan responded first, lest China gain what it saw as unacceptable influence over the Korean court. After Japan sank a British ship transporting Chinese troops, China and Japan declared war on each other. Japan's victories on land and sea enabled it to claim Taiwan, the Pescadores islands, the Liaodong peninsula in Manchuria, forts on the Shandong peninsula, commercial concessions, and the usual bank-breaking indemnity. Russia opposed the Japanese land grab because of its own designs on Manchuria and Korea. Germany had growing commercial interests in China and wanted to divert Russia away from central Europe. France had an alliance with Russia. The three nations launched the Triple Intervention to make Japan restore

Map C6.1 Western Imperialism, Late Nineteenth Century

The colonial powers and their possessions

Germany
France
Great Britain
Russia

United States
Japan
Belgium
Netherlands

Portugal
Italy
Spain
Major shipping routes

PACIFIC OCEAN

ALASKA

CANADA

UNITED STATES

GREENLAND
(Denmark)

ATLANTIC OCEAN

BAHAMA IS.
(Gr. Br.)

BR. HONDURAS

PACIFIC OCEAN

BRITISH GUIANA
DUTCH GUIANA
FRENCH GUIANA

GREAT BRITAIN

NETHER.
BELG.
FRANCE
PORTUGAL
SPAIN

GERMANY
AUSTRIA-HUNGARY
ITALY

OTTOMAN EMPIRE
CYPRUS (Gr. Br.)

MOROCCO
RIO DE ORO
GAMBIA (Gr. Br.)
PORT. GUINEA

TUNISIA
ALGERIA
LIBYA
EGYPT
ANGLO-EGYPTIAN SUDAN
ERITREA
FR. SOMALILAND
BR. SOMALILAND
HADHRAMAUT

FRENCH WEST AFRICA
TOGO (Ger.)
GOLD COAST (Gr. Br.)
NIGERIA
SIERRA LEONE (Gr. Br.)
KAMERUN
SP. GUINEA

FR. EQUA. AFRICA

BELGIAN CONGO
UGANDA
BRITISH EAST AFRICA
GERMAN EAST AFRICA

ANGOLA
NORTHERN RHODESIA
GERMAN SOUTHWEST AFRICA
SOUTHERN RHODESIA
BECHUANALAND
MOZAMBIQUE
NYASALAND (Gr. Br.)
MADAGASCAR
SWAZILAND
LESOTHO
UNION OF SOUTH AFRICA

RUSSIA

MANCHURIA
KARAFUTO
Sakhalin
KOREA
JAPAN
Formosa (Japan)

INDIA
BURMA
FRENCH INDOCHINA
CEYLON
MALAY STATES

PHILIPPINE IS. (U.S.)
BR. NORTH BORNEO (Gr. Br.)
SARAWAK (Gr. Br.)
DUTCH EAST INDIES

Mariana Is.
Caroline Is. (Germany)
Marshall Is.
Solomon Is.
New Hebrides (Gr. Br. and France)
Papua
New Caledonia (France)

AUSTRALIA

NEW ZEALAND

INDIAN OCEAN

the Liaodong and Shandong peninsulas to China. In a move that the Japanese public saw as blatant hypocrisy, the French then gained concessions in southern China for railroads and mines, and Russia got an eighty-year lease over the Liaodong peninsula from China that was later expanded to include Port Arthur. When the Germans built forts on portions of the Shandong peninsula, Britain took a naval base across from Port Arthur. Competition between the European powers precluded any of them from making China its colony. Instead they scrambled for concessions by carving out spheres of influence dominated by their officials and traders, primarily along the coast and up the Yangzi River. Uneasy at the prospect of being shut out of the market for Chinese goods and souls, American merchants and missionaries called on their government to act. Secretary of State John Hay urged the European powers and Japan to adopt an "open door" policy that would preclude the spheres of influence from excluding Americans. The other powers agreed, albeit with reservations that protected their interests.

Even beyond the spheres of influence, missionaries brought change to northern and eastern China. They built hospitals, schools, and orphanages where none had existed before. They educated women and tried to prevent foot binding. They taught western science and political philosophy, opening a window on the West used to advantage by Chinese reformers. Their letters to parishes back home heightened awareness of and interest in Chinese affairs. The missionaries also proved disruptive. When they forbade the rituals associated with ancestor worship, they seemingly threatened the fabric of family life. Since converts often came from the lower rungs of society, missionary efforts to protect them against the gentry or to rescue them from district magistrates' courts provoked outrage by entrenched local interests. When the missionary presence provoked violence, the western powers dispatched gunboats and troops to intimidate local officials. Worst of all, Christian teachings subverted the Confucian doctrines that fostered loyalty to the state.

Although attacks on missionaries often roiled relations between the western powers and China, none matched the consequences of the so-called Boxer Rebellion. It began in Shandong in 1898 as an antiforeign movement that combined martial arts with rituals promising invulnerability to weapons, somewhat similar to the Ghost Dance that rallied the Sioux against American encroachment in the Dakotas in the late 1880s. Boxers attacked converts and missionaries, sometimes with the quiet approbation of Qing officials. They routed western troops sent to reinforce the defenses for the diplomatic community in Beijing and tore up railroad tracks between Tianjin and the capital. The court ordered the massacre of all foreigners on Chinese soil and declared war on the foreign powers.

Faced with a common threat, the western powers and Japan united against China. Efforts by Chinese generals in central and south China to suppress antiforeign elements in their areas helped Americans to convince the other powers not to expand the scale of conflict beyond an expeditionary force sent to liberate the diplomatic community besieged in Beijing. When it reached the city in August 1900, the Qing court fled to Xi'an. Japanese soldiers watched with amazement as western troops ran amok for three days in an orgy of looting, rape, and murder. Negotiations over the size of the indemnity to be extracted from China and its distribution among the powers dragged on for a year. The indemnity imposed a crushing financial burden on the Chinese government and absorbed funds needed for economic development. Only rivalry among the powers, and particularly distrust of Russia, precluded proposals for China's dismemberment.

The nineteenth century marked the heyday of western imperialism as practice and ideology. Following the spread of Darwin's revolutionary ideas on evolution and the survival of the fittest, Herbert Spencer and others developed the notion of social Darwinism. They thought that not just species but nations stood in danger of extinction unless they emerged victorious in the ceaseless competition between them. States that did not understand this principle or found themselves too weak to resist modern military technology naturally fell prey to conquerors from afar. Social Darwinism provided new justification for the westerners' sense of racial superiority. Some used this notion to justify brutal exploitation of native populations. Others felt it their duty to bring civilization to the heathens. After the American colonization of the Philippines and annexation of Hawai'i, Rudyard Kipling wrote, "Take up the White Man's burden/Send forth the best ye breed/Go bind your sons to exile/To serve your captives' need; . . . /Your new-caught, sullen peoples,/Half-devil and half-child."[2]

Western imperialism in East Asia took a different form than in the rest of the world. Rather than establish colonies (Hong Kong and Macao being the exception), the western powers imposed unequal treaties. Although they sought Asian labor for difficult, dangerous jobs such as building the transcontinental railroad, they issued various discriminatory exclusion laws to prevent first Chinese and then Japanese from residing permanently in their countries or becoming citizens. By dint of a vast westernization project that included the enactment of western-style commercial, civil, and criminal legal codes plus the creation of a modern army, Japan managed to gain abolition of most-favored-nation treatment and extraterritoriality in 1899. Its victory in war with Russia to win control of the Liaodong peninsula in 1904–1905 gave hope to people all over Asia that western dominance might pass.

SUGGESTED READING

For the long view of relations between Asia and the rest of the world, see W. I. Cohen, *Asia at the Center: Four Thousand Years of Engagement with the World* (2000). Studies include P. Chatterjee, *Nationalist Thought and the Colonial World: A Derivative Discourse* (1993), and R. Eskildsen, "Of Civilization and Savages: The Mimetic Imperialism of Japan's 1874 Expedition to Taiwan," *American Historical Review* 107 (2002): 388–418.

---

2. R. Kipling, "The White Man's Burden," *McClure's Magazine* 12:4 (February 1899): 0-004.

CHAPTER NINETEEN

China in Decline (1800–1900)

During the early nineteenth century, the Qing Dynasty seemed to be slipping into dynastic decline. Revenues were no longer adequate to cover the costs of administration. Rural poverty was worsening. Then in midcentury, some of the bloodiest rebellions in Chinese history broke out. On top of this, a new enemy had appeared on China's shores, one able to land its ships where it liked and destroy Chinese defenses with its cannons.

Yet the Qing Dynasty did not fall. The generals who suppressed the rebellions did not take to fighting among themselves to see which of them could found the next dynasty, as had happened so many times before in Chinese history. Some credit should go to the Qing elite who in the 1860s and 1870s took on the task of self-strengthening. Yet progress, though real, was never rapid enough, and late in the century China suffered further blows to its pride: first its defeat by Japan in 1894–1895, then in 1900 by the allied occupation of Beijing as a consequence of the Boxer Rebellion.

These internal and external threats and how the Qing responded to them have preoccupied most historians who study nineteenth century China. What made China's encounter with the West so different in the nineteenth century than the eighteenth? How many of China's problems came from within and how many from outside forces? Does putting stress on the new challenges of western imperialism distort understanding of this period, making the West into the actor and China merely a reactor? How did the Chinese elite understand the challenges they faced? Did it matter that China's rulers in this period were Manchu? Could the Qing have fared better if they had adopted different policies? Or were the forces of global capitalism and imperialism so skewed against China at the time that different policies would have made little difference?

ECONOMIC AND FISCAL PROBLEMS

The peace that the Qing Dynasty brought to China allowed the population to grow rapidly. Although scholars have not come to a consensus on the details of China's population growth, there is wide agreement that by the beginning of the nineteenth century, China had a population in the vicinity of 300 million and was continuing to grow, reaching about 400 million by 1850. The traditional Chinese view of population increase was positive: growth was a sign of peace and prosperity. Through the eighteenth century, most still accepted that view. As developed areas became more crowded, farmers tried cultivating more intensively, making more use of irrigation and fertilizer and weeding more regularly, allowing denser population in the richest areas. Others moved to less crowded regions, both at the peripheries of the long-settled areas and the thinly populated southwest, previously occupied largely by minority peoples. The only lands suited to agriculture that were out of bounds were those in Manchuria, which the Qing maintained as a preserve for the Manchus.

China's standard of living fell behind Europe's. From the early nineteenth century on, Britain had benefited from its access to the resources and markets of the New World as well as the first stages of its industrialization. China, in contrast, was feeling the negative effects of its population growth on both its economic productivity and its social fabric. As farms grew smaller and surplus labor depressed wages, the average standard of living suffered. When the best lands were all occupied, conflicts over rights to water or tenancy increased. Hard times also led to increased female infanticide, as families felt they could not afford to raise more than two or three children, but they saw sons as necessities. A shortage of marriageable women resulted, reducing the incentive for young men to stay near home and do as their elders told

them. Many of those who took to the road in hope of finding better opportunities elsewhere never found a permanent home; instead they became part of a floating population of the unemployed, moving around in search of work. They would take seasonal farm work or work as boatmen, charcoal burners, night soil collectors, and the like. In cities they might become sedan chair carriers, beggars, or thieves. Women, even poor ones, had an easier time finding a place in a home because of the demand for maids and concubines. But poverty fed the traffic in women, as poor families sold their daughters for cash, perhaps expecting them to become rich men's concubines, though many ended up as prostitutes. Population growth also added to the burdens placed on local governments. Although the population doubled and tripled, the number of counties and county officials stayed the same. Magistrates often found that they had to turn to the local elite for help, even turning tax collection over to them.

During the Qianlong reign, the government had resources to try to improve the lot of the poor. But in the nineteenth century, even determined emperors like the Daoguang emperor (r. 1821–1850) were chronically short of revenue for crucial public works and relief measures. The Daoguang emperor set an example of frugality at court and encouraged his officials to cut every possible cost, but the fiscal situation steadily worsened. He ordered repairs to the Grand Canal (see **Material Culture: The Grand Canal**), yet the years of neglect meant that more and more tax grain had to be sent by sea, exacerbating unemployment in north China.

Another problem the emperor faced was supporting the hereditary military force, the banners, which in a manner reminiscent of the decline of the Ming hereditary soldiers was no longer effective in war. To suppress the rebellions of the late eighteenth century, the government had had to turn to local militias and the professional (as opposed to hereditary) army of Chinese recruits called the Army of the Green

MATERIAL CULTURE

The Grand Canal

Transport canals were dug in China from ancient times. The first Grand Canal connecting Luoyang to the Yangzi River was completed during the Sui Dynasty. During Song times, the canal extended south to Hangzhou, and in Yuan times, it reached north to Beijing. During the Ming period, the government invested a lot of effort in maintaining the Grand Canal as it carried a large share of the tax grain.

The canal that the Qing inherited was 1,747 kilometers long and crossed five major rivers. It had to rise to 138 feet above sea level to get over the mountains of western Shandong. This necessitated an elaborate system of locks, dams, sluice gates, and slipways. Pulleys driven by animal or human labor pulled boats through sluice gates and skips. Because the canal crossed the Yellow River, maintaining the dikes on the river was crucial to keep floods with their heavy deposits of silt from clogging the canal.

By the early nineteenth century, more than fifty thousand hereditary boatmen and migrant laborers worked moving the tax grain up the canal from the southeast to the capital. In 1824 the grain ships en route to Beijing became mired in silt because the canal had not been properly maintained. Boatmen were put to work making repairs, but more and more grain tax had to be sent by the sea route. By 1850 the canal was largely abandoned. Unemployed boatmen were prominent among those who joined the Nian rebellion in the 1850s.

Map 19.1 **Grand Canal During the Ming and Qing Dynasties**

Standard. Because the banners were so tied to Manchu identity and privileges, the emperor could not simply disband them, as the Ming had its hereditary military households. The best the Daoguang emperor could hope for was to keep bannermen from becoming beggars, bandits, opium smugglers, or opium addicts.

MIDCENTURY CRISES

The decline of the Qing military forces was made evident to all in the 1840s and 1850s when the dynasty had to cope with military crises along its coastlines and throughout its interior.

The Opium War

As discussed in Chapter 16, the Qing Dynasty dealt with foreign countries according to a set of rules it had largely taken over from the Ming Dynasty. Europeans were permitted to trade only at the port of Guangzhou and only through licensed Chinese merchants. In the eighteenth century, the balance of trade was in China's favor, as Great Britain and other western nations used silver to pay for steadily increasing purchases of tea. British traders found few buyers when they brought British and Indian goods to Guangzhou to sell. When Macartney asked the Qianlong emperor to alter the way trade was conducted, the emperor saw no reason to approve his request.

As discussed in **Connections: Western Imperialism (1800–1900)**, all this soon changed. By the late eighteenth century, the British had found something the Chinese would buy: opium. Made from poppy plants, opium had been used in China for medicinal purposes for several centuries. Once a way was found to smoke pure opium sap in pipes, opium became a recreational drug, which people took to relieve pain and boredom and to make tedious or taxing work more bearable. The drawback was that it was addictive; those who stopped taking it suffered chills, nausea, and muscle cramps. The Daoguang emperor was outraged when an 1831 investigation showed that members of the imperial clan, high officials, and bannermen were among those addicted to the drug. Once addicted, people would do almost anything to keep up the supply of the drug, even pawning their clothing and selling their children. To fight addiction, the Chinese government banned both the production and the importation of opium in 1800. In 1813 it went further and outlawed the smoking of opium, punishing it with a beating of a hundred blows.

The opium that the British brought to China was grown in India. Following the British acquisition of large parts of India, the East India Company invested heavily in planting and processing opium, over which it had a profitable

Physic Street, Guangzhou. The English photographer who took this picture in the 1860s described the street as one of the finest in the city, not nearly as narrow as others nearby. The shop signs announce the sale of such things as drugs, cushions, seals, and ink. *(Photo by John Thomson/George Eastman House/Getty Images)*

monopoly. Once China made trade in opium illegal, the company did not distribute opium itself; rather, licensed private traders, Americans as well as British, carried the drug to China. Chinese smugglers bought opium from British and American traders anchored off the coast, then distributed it through a series of middlemen, making it difficult for the Qing government to catch the major dealers.

By 1831 there were between one hundred and two hundred Chinese smugglers' boats plying the Guangdong coastal waters. The competition among private traders led to a price war in China that drove the price of opium down and thus spread addiction. Imports increased rapidly, from forty-five hundred chests smuggled into China in 1810 to forty thousand chests in

1838, enough to supply 2 million addicts. By this point, it was China that suffered a drain of silver. The outflow increased from about 2 million ounces of silver per year in the 1820s to about 9 million in the 1830s. This silver drain hurt farmers because their taxes were assessed in silver. A tax obligation of 1 ounce of silver took about 1,500 cash to pay in 1800, but 2,700 cash in 1830.

The Daoguang emperor called for debate on how to deal with this crisis. Some court officials advocated legalizing the sale of opium and taxing it, which would help alleviate the government revenue shortfalls and perhaps make the drug expensive enough to deter some people from trying it. Other officials strongly disagreed, believing that an evil like opium had to be stopped. The governor-general, Lin Zexu, argued that rather than concentrate on the users, the government should go after those who imported or sold the drug. Unless trade in the drug was suppressed, he argued, the Qing would have no soldiers to fight the enemy and no funds to support an army. Lin's impassioned stand and his reputation as incorruptible led the Daoguang emperor in late 1838 to assign him the task of suppressing the opium trade. Once Lin arrived at Guangzhou, he made rapid progress, arresting some seventeen hundred Chinese dealers and seizing seventy thousand opium pipes. He demanded that foreign firms turn over their opium stores as well, offering tea in exchange. When his appeals failed, Lin stopped all trade and placed a siege on the western merchants' enclave. After six weeks the merchants relented and turned over their opium, some 2.6 million pounds. Lin set five hundred laborers to work for twenty-two days to destroy the opium by mixing it with salt and lime and washing it into the sea. He pressured the Portuguese to expel the uncooperative British from Macao, as a consequence of which they settled on the barren island of Hong Kong.

To the British superintendent of trade, Lin's act was an affront to British dignity and cause enough for war. The British saw China as out of step with the modern world in which all "civilized" nations practiced free trade and maintained "normal" international relations through envoys and treaties. With the encouragement of their merchants in China, the British sent from India a small, mobile expeditionary force of forty-two ships, many of them leased from the major opium trader Jardine, Matheson, and Company. Because Lin had strengthened defenses at Guangzhou, the British sailed north and shut down the major ports of Ningbo and Tianjin, forcing the Qing to negotiate (see Map 19.2). A preliminary agreement called for ceding Hong Kong, repaying the British the cost of their expedition, and allowing direct diplomatic intercourse between the new countries.

In both countries, the response was outrage. The Daoguang emperor had withdrawn his support for Lin as soon as the war broke out and had sent him into exile in the far northwest; now the official who negotiated the treaty was also treated like a criminal. The English sent a second, larger force, which attacked Guangzhou, occupied other ports as it proceeded up the coast, including Shanghai, and finally sailed up the Yangzi River to Nanjing. Dozens of Qing officers, both Manchu and Chinese, committed suicide when they saw that they could not repel the British (see **Biography: Manchu Bannerman Guancheng**).

At this point the Qing government had no choice but to capitulate, and its representatives signed a treaty on board a British naval vessel. The 1842 Treaty of Nanjing, which settled the Opium War, was concluded at gunpoint and provided benefits for Britain but not China, making it "unequal." It was soon followed by an amended agreement and treaties with the United States and France. This set of treaties mandated ambassadors in Beijing, opened five ports to international trade, fixed the tariff on imported goods at 5 percent, imposed an indemnity of 21 million silver dollars on China to cover Britain's war costs, and ceded the island of Hong Kong to Britain. Through the clause on extraterritoriality, British subjects in China were answerable only to British law, even in disputes with Chinese. The most-favored-nation clause

Map **19.2**   **Internal and External Conflicts During the Nineteenth Century**

meant that whenever one nation extracted a new privilege from China, it was extended automatically to Britain. Western imperialism had had its first victory in China.

At the Daoguang court, the aftermath of this debacle was a bitter struggle between war and peace factions, reminiscent of the similar disputes during the Song Dynasty. Those who had favored compromising with the "sea barbarians" to avoid further hostilities included the Manchu chancellor Mujangga; those opposed were mostly Chinese degree holders who had supported Lin Zexu and believed the Qing should have put up stronger resistance. After the Daoguang emperor died in 1850, his successor announced his determination to make no more concessions by dismissing Mujangga and bringing back Lin Zexu. The court kept finding excuses not to accept foreign diplomats at its capital in Beijing, and its compliance with the commercial clauses fell far short of western expectations.

BIOGRAPHY Manchu Bannerman Guancheng

Guancheng (ca. 1790–1843) was born the son of a Manchu bannerman of the Hangzhou garrisons, stationed at the nearby port of Zhapu. Although he would be considered Manchu through descent on the male line, both his mother and his father's mother were daughters of Chinese bannermen in the same garrisons. His father died when he was an infant, and he was raised by his mother and his deceased elder brother's widow. In his youth the banner garrisons were chronically short of funds for bannerman stipends and payments for widows and orphans; therefore, he most likely grew up in straitened circumstances. Still, he attended banner schools, where he studied both Chinese and Manchu. By the age of twenty he was working as a tutor himself, and at age twenty-seven he attained the *juren* degree, availing himself of the special quota for Manchu bannermen. By then he also had a Chinese name, Guan Weitong, which used part of his personal name as a Chinese family name. (In Manchu, his clan name was Gūwalgiya, but Manchu clan names were not used as terms of address.) To supplement his family's income, in this period Guancheng took on some publishing jobs.

In the late 1820s Guancheng traveled to Beijing to take the *jinshi* examinations. Beijing was the great center of Manchu life, home to perhaps one hundred fifty thousand Manchus. Opium addiction had already become a major problem among the under-employed bannermen, something Guancheng would undoubtedly have noticed. But it was also home to Manchu nobles who lived a highly cultivated life. The highest-ranking member of his clan had a mansion in the city and welcomed Guancheng to his social circle. There he met descendants of Qing emperors and heard much lore about Manchu court life. The language in which they discussed these subjects was, however, Chinese.

Although Guancheng did not pass the *jinshi* exam, he was given an honorary degree and in 1833 appointed a probationary magistrate of a county in Sichuan. He took two of his sons, ages nine and eleven, with him to Sichuan but sent his wife and two youngest sons back to Zhapu. At first he was rapidly transferred from one county to another, then from 1834 to 1842 had a long stint as magistrate of Nanchuan county, a tea-producing region 30 miles south of the Yangzi River. Local non-Chinese rebelled during his tenure, adding to hardships caused by locusts. Still, his son remembered the time in Sichuan as a very enjoyable one.

When Guancheng returned to Zhapu in 1842 at age fifty-three, he was something of a celebrity—a local bannerman who had succeeded in the outside world. His home community, meanwhile, had suffered a devastating blow. In 1840, at the start of the Opium War, British ships had shelled the Zhapu ports but had not stayed long. Despite attempts to reinforce the garrisons for a possible return of the British, when they did in fact return in the spring of 1842, Zhapu's defenses proved sorely lacking. Many of those who did not die defending it took their own lives afterward, often first killing their wives and children. On his return, Guancheng, though ill himself, took on the task of writing and printing an account of the heroism of the bannermen in the defense of Zhapu, to be submitted to the court. He wanted help for those who had survived and honor for those who had died. "The officers, soldiers, men and women of our garrison were ill-prepared for this, the corpses having been found piled against buildings and even suspended from the battlements. In mourning our nation's dead, how could we bear to allow these loyal clansmen to be buried without benefit of ceremony?"[1] After Guancheng died in early 1843, his son issued a revised "Record of Martyrs."

---

1. Translated in Pamela Kyle Crossley, *Orphan Warriors: Three Manchu Generations and the End of the Qing World* (Princeton, N.J.: Princeton University Press, 1990), p. 115.

The Opium War exposed the fact that Qing military technology was hopelessly obsolete. The Qing had no navy. Britain had not only large men-of-war but also new shallow-draft steamships that could sail up rivers. Thus, the British could land troops wherever they liked. Troops would pillage, then return to their ships to attack a new target. On a single day in 1841, a British steam-powered warship with long-distance artillery destroyed nine war junks, five forts, two military stations, and a shore battery. Even when Qing forces fought on land, they were no match for the British troops. To fight British soldiers armed with rifles, the Chinese and Manchu soldiers used swords, spears, clubs, and arrows. The minority with firearms had only matchlock muskets that required soldiers to ignite each load of gunpowder by hand.

Taiping Rebellion

Beginning less than a decade after the Opium War, the Qing Dynasty faced some of the most destructive rebellions in world history. The bloodiest was the Taiping Rebellion (1851–1864), in which some 20 to 30 million people lost their lives.

Like many of China's earlier insurrections, this one had its organizational base in an unorthodox religious sect. The founder of this sect was Hong Xiuquan (1814–1864). Hong was a Hakka, a large Han Chinese ethnic group that spoke a distinct dialect and lived predominantly in the far south. Although from humble background, Hong had spent years attempting the civil service examinations. His career as a religious leader began with visions of a golden-bearded old man and a middle-aged man who addressed him as younger brother and told him to annihilate devils. After reading a Christian tract given him by a missionary in Guangzhou, Hong interpreted his visions to mean that he was Jesus's younger brother. He began preaching, calling on people to destroy idols and ancestral temples, give up opium and alcohol, and renounce foot binding and prostitution. Hong spent two months studying with a Christian preacher and adopted the Ten Commandments, monotheism, and the practice of communal

prayer and hymns. He called his group the God Worshipping Society and soon attracted many followers, especially among the Hakkas.

Hong was a visionary, not an organizer, and other leaders emerged who learned how to manipulate him. In 1848, while Hong and his closest associate were away from their headquarters, an illiterate charcoal maker and local bully named Yang Xiuqing elevated himself and three others to top posts within the God Worshippers. To claim superiority over Hong, Yang announced that when he spoke, it was the voice of God the Father, putting him above Hong, the mere younger brother.

In 1850 the Taiping leaders told all God Worshippers to leave their homes, pool their money into a common treasury, and move to Thistle Mountain in Guangxi province, a site that soon became a huge military camp. In 1851 Hong declared himself king of the Heavenly Kingdom of Great Peace (Taiping), an act of open insurrection. Men were to abandon the Manchu queue and let their hair grow long. Hong's true believers were brave in battle, maintained strict discipline, and seized large stores of government weapons as they campaigned. Their religious zeal propelled them to destroy local temples, even though this alienated many commoners. They regularly forced those whose villages they captured to join their movement, enrolling men and women into separate work and military teams. Some brigades of women soldiers fought Qing forces.

Once news of the progress of the rebellion reached the court, Qing troops were dispatched to disperse the Taipings and arrest their leaders (see Map 19.2). To the shock of the court, the Qing troops were soundly defeated. A rebel proclamation of 1852 made use of resentment of the Manchus, who, it said, "stole China's empire, appropriated China's food and clothing, and ravished China's sons and daughters."[1] Manchu bannermen and their families were often slaughtered after Taiping forces took a city.

---

1. Franz Michael, *The Taiping Rebellion: History and Documents* (Seattle: University of Washington Press, 1971), 2:145–147.

After making Nanjing their capital, the Taipings announced plans for a utopian society based on the equalization of land holdings and the equality of men and women. Women could take the civil service examinations, which were based on Hong Xiuquan's teachings and translations of the Bible. Christian missionaries at first were excited about the prospect of revolutionaries spreading Christianity, but quickly concluded that the Christian elements in Taiping doctrines were heretical and did nothing to help them. In fact, when the Taipings tried to take Shanghai in 1860 and 1862, the western residents organized counterattacks.

In time the Taipings were weakened by internal dissension. The group of leaders called Kings gave themselves all sorts of privileges, including well-stocked harems, while they made their followers live in sex-segregated housing. Hong and Yang turned on each other. When Yang claimed that God the Father insisted Hong should be beaten for kicking one of Yang's concubines, Hong arranged to have Yang executed. The king entrusted with this task killed not only Yang and his family but twenty thousand followers, leading to another round of revenge killings.

The Chinese elite were horrified by the Taiping movement, with its bizarre foreign gods and women soldiers. In many places local officials and landlords organized their own defense, repairing city walls, gathering food to withstand a siege, and arming and drilling recruits. The Qing government soon realized that it would have to turn to such locally raised armies if it wished to make progress against the Taipings.

The man they turned to, Zeng Guofan (1811–1872), was back at home in Hunan province to mourn his mother. Since passing the *jinshi* exam in 1838, Zeng had risen in the government and had served in Beijing in high positions in the ministries of justice and personnel. Although a man devoted to his family, he was persuaded that his duty to his country superseded his duty as a filial son to mourn his mother.

Zeng knew the failings of the Qing armies and organized his army in a new way. He recruited officers from among the Confucian-educated elite and had them recruit their own soldiers from among farmers in their region. Zeng was given permission to draw on local tax receipts and so could pay the soldiers and officers well. Soldiers were loyal to their officers and the officers to Zeng, creating an essentially private army. After Zeng constructed two hundred forty war junks so that he could attack by river and gathered some modern western weapons such as artillery, he set about recovering Hunan province bit by bit. The Taipings, however, also made advances, and Zeng needed twelve years and one hundred twenty thousand troops before he had fully defeated the Taipings. Generals under him, including close relatives and his protégés Li Hongzhang and Zuo Zongtang, played major roles in the slow stranglehold placed over the Taiping capital at Nanjing. When Nanjing fell, none of the Taipings survived. Elsewhere in south China, the Taipings held out longer, with some armies relocating to Taiwan or Vietnam. In Vietnam, where they were known as the Black Flags, they took an active part in resistance to French colonial expansion.

The devastation wreaked both by the Taipings' campaigns and the Qing campaigns to suppress them was horrendous. One western observer wrote in 1865 that China's plains were "strewn with human skeletons," its rivers "polluted with floating carcasses."[2] Much of the productive power of the lower Yangzi region was ruined for a generation.

Other Rebellions

The Taipings were turned back when they took their campaign into north China, but that region soon found itself torn apart by homegrown insurrections. Along the route of the Grand Canal, poverty and unemployment had driven many villagers into banditry. These groups of the disaffected, called Nian gangs,

2. Cited in R. Keith Schoppa, *Revolution and Its Past: Identities and Change in Modern Chinese History* (Upper Saddle River, N.J.: Prentice Hall, 2002), p. 64.

engaged in a variety of predatory practices. Riding horseback, they would seize villagers' crops, rob traveling merchants, and kidnap the wealthy to hold them for ransom. Severe flooding in 1851 weakened the dikes of the Yellow River, which gave way in 1855, leading to a devastating shift in the Yellow River from south of the Shandong peninsula to north of it. Those made homeless by the floods joined the Nian bands simply to survive. Many of those who joined did so on a seasonal basis, staying home in the summer and winter but raiding and plundering in the autumn and spring. After the Taipings fell in 1864, some of their soldiers joined the Nian rebellion. In 1865, when it was clear that the Qing regular armies had failed to suppress the Nian, Zeng Guofan and Li Hongzhang were assigned the long and difficult task.

With the transfer of armies to the interior to fight the Taipings and Nian rebels, uprisings also got out of hand in the northwest and southwest. These rebellions drew from and also exacerbated ethnic tensions and hatreds. In Yunnan, the large Muslim population had grievances based on Han Chinese settlers moving into their territory and seizing resources such as copper, gold, and silver mines. As tensions escalated, so did feuds and violence. Han Chinese formed militias to kill Muslims, who in retaliation assassinated Chinese officials. Rebels captured the city of Dali and announced the sultanate of Panthay. The remote location of Yunnan and its mountainous topography made it difficult for the Qing to send troops there. The Qing was able to regain control in 1873 only because it learned to play off opposing factions of Muslims.

The Muslim rebellion in the northwest was rooted in the spread of a mystical school of Islam known as Sufism, but much of the violence came from long-standing antagonism between the Han Chinese and the Muslims. By 1867 all of Gansu was in Muslim hands. Preoccupied with its problems elsewhere, the Qing did not send Zuo Zongtang (1812–1885) to retake the region until 1866. Zuo classed Sufis as heterodox, like White Lotus or Taiping sectarians, and ordered their slaughter. The campaign took five years and consisted largely of sieges during which the population slowly starved. Zuo Zongtang marched his troops into Xinjiang, which might well have broken away from Qing control otherwise.

The Second Opium War

While the Qing court was struggling to suppress the Taiping, Nian, and Muslim rebellions, it had to face demands from foreign powers as well. Russia, seeing China's weakness, penetrated the Amur River valley, violating the borders agreed to in 1689. In new treaties of 1858–1860, Russia gained the maritime provinces of eastern Manchuria down to Vladivostok. A large part of the reason the Qing decided to march an army into Xinjiang was fear of Russian expansion there.

Britain and France were pressing China as well. Both sides wanted the trade agreement reached after the Opium War renegotiated, though for different reasons. On the grounds that China had failed to implement all of the provisions agreed to a decade earlier, the British and French decided to make swift, brutal coastal attacks, a repeat of the Opium War. (They called it the Arrow War, from the name of a ship that gave the British a pretext for war.) Guangzhou was easily captured at the end of 1857 and held for three years. By mid-1858 the French and British ships were in the north and took the forts at Tianjin. At this point, the court in Beijing sent senior officials to negotiate. When the British threatened to march on Beijing unless they were allowed permanent diplomatic representation in Beijing, the hard-pressed Manchu negotiator conceded. Also secured in these treaties were the opening of ten new ports; permission for westerners, including missionaries, to travel through China; a fixed transit tariff for foreign goods within China of no more than 2.5 percent; and an indemnity of 4 million ounces of silver for the British and 2 million for the French. Each side was to have its rulers ratify the treaties and return in a year for the signing.

The Qing emperor was strongly opposed to allowing ambassadors to reside in Beijing, viewing them as little better than spies. When the British returned and insisted on taking their ships up the Beihe River toward Beijing instead of going overland, as the Qing wanted them to, Qing forces withstood them. A new expedition was then dispatched with eleven thousand British soldiers and sixty-seven hundred French ones. When Qing authorities did not let them have their way on all matters, they charged into Beijing. The Russian ambassador, already in residence in Beijing, talked the British out of burning the palace in retaliation. The British and French then marched to the summer palace located northwest of the city, a complex of two hundred or so buildings. They looted the buildings of furniture, porcelains, robes, and whatever else attracted them and then torched the entire 10-square-mile complex. The Russian ambassador this time approached the Qing court and talked them into accepting the offered terms, which included having to pay a larger indemnity of 16 million ounces of silver and transfer of the Kowloon peninsula opposite Hong Kong island to Britain.

Because the western powers gained many advantages through these unequal treaties, after 1860 they increasingly saw propping up the faltering Qing Dynasty as in their interest.

SELF-STRENGTHENING

In 1861 the Xianfeng emperor died and was succeeded by a young son. The child's uncle, Prince Gong, and his mother, Empress Dowager Cixi, served as regents. A change in emperor normally meant a change in chancellors and other high officials, making it easier for the court to take new directions. Certainly new policies were needed: much of the most productive parts of the country had been laid waste by the rebellions, none of which was yet suppressed, and the British and French had only recently left Beijing after extracting new concessions.

In that same year a scholar named Feng Guifen (1809–1874) wrote a set of essays presenting the case for wide-ranging reforms. He had taken refuge in Shanghai during the Taiping War and there had seen how the westerners defended the city. In his essays he pointed out that China was a hundred times bigger than France and two hundred times bigger than Great Britain. "Why are western nations small and yet strong? Why are we large and yet weak?" He called for hiring a few "barbarians" to help set up shipyards and arsenals in each major port. To get ambitious men to take on the task of managing these enterprises, he proposed rewarding them with examination degrees if the ships and weapons produced were as good as the foreigners'. He also proposed setting up translation bureaus to translate western books on mathematics and the sciences. Westerners should be hired to teach groups of boys western languages. "China has many brilliant people. There must be some who can learn from the barbarians and surpass them."[3] He pointed out that many westerners had learned the Chinese language and much about the country; surely there should be Chinese people just as capable. To improve the morale of officials, he proposed subjecting high officials to election by lower-ranking officials. Local elites would be given the power to nominate local officials, thus broadening political participation considerably. Undoubtedly influenced by what he had learned of foreign election practices, he specified that the votes were to be counted.

An important minority of officials, including Zeng Guofan and Li Hongzhang, were more and more persuaded by these sorts of arguments. Prince Gong sided with them, and changes were made not only in how soldiers were trained and weapons produced, but also in the conduct of foreign affairs. Arsenals and

3. W. Theodore de Bary and Richard Lufrano, *Sources of Chinese Tradition: From 1600 Through the Twentieth Century* (New York: Columbia University Press, 2000), pp. 236, 237.

dockyards were established, schools opened to teach European languages and international law, and a foreign office established to manage diplomatic affairs, with Prince Gong in charge. By 1880 China had embassies in London, Paris, Berlin, Madrid, Washington, Tokyo, and St. Petersburg.

Li Hongzhang's Self-Strengthening Projects, 1862–1893

1862 Created gun factories at Shanghai with British and German instructors

1863 Established a foreign language school in Shanghai

1864 Created a gun factory at Suzhou

1865 Established Jiangnan Arsenal at Shanghai with a translation bureau attached, jointly with Zeng Guofan

1867 Established Nanjing Arsenal

1870 Expanded machine factory in Tianjin

1872 Sent officers to study in Germany. Made request to open coal and iron mines. Jointly with Zeng recommended sending teenagers to study in the U.S. Supported China Merchants' Steam Navigation Company as a "government-supervised merchant enterprise"

1876 Sent seven officers to Germany

1877 Created the Bureau for the Kaiping Coal Mines in Tianjin

1878 Established the Shanghai Cotton Mill

1880 Established a naval academy in Tianjin. Requested permission to build a railroad.

1882 Began construction of a harbor and shipyard at Port Arthur

1884 Sent naval students and apprentices to Europe to learn shipbuilding and navigation

1885 Established a military academy in Tianjin with German teachers

1887 Established a mint at Tianjin. Began gold mining operation in Heilongjiang

1888 Established the Beiyang fleet

1891 Established a paper mill in Shanghai

1893 Set up a general office for mechanized textile manufacturing

---

the governor-general of Zhili province (modern Hebei) and headed one of the most important of the new armies. As the Chinese learned more about western ways, Li and other modernizers came to recognize that guns and ships were merely the surface manifestation of the western powers' economic strength. To catch up with the West, they argued, China would have to initiate new industries, which in the 1870s and 1880s included railway lines, steam navigation companies, coal mines, telegraph lines, and cotton spinning and weaving factories. By the 1890s, knowledge of the West had improved considerably. Newspapers covering world affairs had begun publication in Shanghai and Hong Kong, and more and more western works were being translated.

For a while China seemed to be taking the same direction as Meiji Japan (see Chapter 21), but in China resistance proved much stronger. Conservatives thought copying western practices compounded defeat. The high official Woren objected to the establishment of an interpreters' college on the grounds that "from ancient down to modern times" there had never been "anyone who could use mathematics to raise a nation from a state of decline or to strengthen it in times of weakness."[4] Even men like Zeng Guofan, who saw the need to modernize the military, had little respect for merchants and profit seeking.

Although to the Qing court new policies were being introduced at a rapid rate, the court never became enthusiastic about the prospect of fundamental change. Most of those in power were apprehensive about the ways changes in education or military organization would undermine inherited values and the existing power structure. Repeated humiliations by foreigners from the 1840s on fostered political rancor and denunciations of men in power. Both the court and much of the population remained opposed to doing anything that smacked of giving in to

After Zeng Guofan's death in 1872, Li Hongzhang emerged as the leading Chinese political figure. From 1872 to 1901 he served as

---

4. Ssu-yü Teng and John K. Fairbank, *China's Response to the West* (Cambridge: Harvard University Press, 1979), p. 76, modified.

the arrogant and uncouth foreigners. As a consequence, the reforms were never fundamental enough to solve China's problems. Guo Songtao, China's first ambassador to Britain (1877–1879) sent letters from London to Li Hongzhang praising both the British parliamentary government and its industries. On his return he became a persona non grata, and the court ordered that the printing blocks carved to publish his diary be seized and destroyed.

Empress Dowager Cixi

During the self-strengthening period, the most powerful person at court was Empress Dowager Cixi. In 1875, when her son, the Tongzhi emperor, was nineteen, he died of smallpox, barely having had a chance to rule on his own. Cixi chose his cousin to succeed him, who is known as the Guangxu emperor (r. 1875–1908). By selecting a boy of four, Cixi could continue in power as regent for many years to come.

Cixi was a skillful political operator. She recognized the fears of the Manchu establishment that they were being sidelined and presented herself to them as a staunch defender of Manchu privileges. Cixi knew how to use traditional concepts of filial piety and loyalty to control members of the imperial family and officials at her court. She needed modernizers like Li Hongzhang and cajoled them with titles and honors, but she kept them in check by also encouraging their conservative critics.

It was under Cixi's watch that the old tribute system was finally dismantled. Three neighboring countries—Korea, the Ryukyu Islands, and Vietnam—had been regular, loyal tributaries, making them seem to westerners not fully independent countries. Japan forced the Ryukyus away from China in the 1870s. In the 1880s France forced Vietnam away.

Although no part of Vietnam had been under direct Chinese rule since Tang times, Chinese influence there had remained strong. The Vietnamese government was closely modeled on the Chinese, supported Zhu Xi's Confucian teachings, and used examinations to recruit officials.

Empress Dowager Cixi. Cixi spent more than half a century in the palace. She entered in 1852, became Empress Dowager in 1861, and had her nephew the Guangxu emperor put under house arrest in 1898. *(Free Gallery of Art and Arthur M. Sackler Gallery Archives, Smithsonian Institution, Washington, D.C. Purchase. Photographer: Xunling.)*

Chinese was used for official documents and histories. By the mid-nineteenth century, France was eying "Indochina" as the best target for imperialist expansion, given Britain's strength in India. This brought France into conflict with the Qing, which viewed Vietnam as one of its most loyal vassal states, next only to Korea. In 1874 France gained privileges in Vietnam through treaties and in 1882 seized Hanoi. When the Vietnamese ruler requested Chinese help, realists like Prince Gong and Li Hongzhang urged avoiding war, but a shrill group of conservative critics insisted that China had to stop giving in, since appeasement only encouraged the bullying of the powers. Cixi hesitated, called on Li Hongzhang to negotiate, and then scuttled the draft treaty when she was flooded with protests about its terms. When the French issued an ultimatum that China withdraw its forces from Vietnam or they would attack China, Cixi sided with the conservative critics. Skirmishes between the Qing and the French quickly escalated into war. The French sailed their fleet 20 miles up the Min River to Fuzhou, home port of a quarter of the new Chinese navy and the site of the main shipyard. In just 15 minutes on August 23, the French fleet destroyed the shipyard and all but two of the twenty-three Chinese warships. About three thousand Chinese were killed in the action. Cixi had adopted the conservative position and stood firm; the result was not only humiliating but a fiscal disaster. The only consolation, a bittersweet one, was that Li Hongzhang had disobeyed her order to send his northern fleet to Fuzhou to help.

Reparations Imposed on China (or, the Loser Pays)

1842 21 million ounces of silver to Great Britain at conclusion of the Opium War

1858 4 million ounces of silver to Britain and 2 million to France at conclusion of the Second Opium War

1860 16 million ounces of silver, divided evenly between Britain and France after attack on Beijing

1862–1869 400,000 ounces of silver to compensate for violence against missionaries

1870 490,000 ounces of silver to France after the Tianjin massacre

1873 500,000 ounces of silver to Japan after the Japanese incursion into Taiwan

1881 5 million ounces to Russia for Qing reoccupation of the Ili valley in Xinjiang

1895 200 million ounces of silver to Japan after the Sino-Japanese War

1897 30 million ounces of silver to Japan for its withdrawal of troops from Liaodong

1901 450 million silver dollars to the countries that invaded to relieve the legation quarters

---

Cixi officially retired in 1889 when the Guangxu emperor was nineteen *sui* and she was fifty-five. She insisted, however, on reading all memorials and approving key appointments. Since the court was filled with her supporters, the emperor had little room to go his own way, even after he began to form his own views about reform.

FOREIGNERS IN CHINA

After 1860, the number of westerners in China grew steadily, and a distinct treaty port culture evolved. The foreign concessions at treaty ports were areas carved out of existing Chinese cities. They had foreign police and foreign law courts and collected their own taxes, a situation the Qing accepted with little protest, even though most of the population within the concessions continued to be Chinese. At the treaty ports, the presence of the British and Indians was especially strong, and the habits of the British Empire tended to spill over into these cities. Foreign warships anchored at the docks of the treaty ports, ready to make a show of force when called on. Although missionaries and merchants often had little love for each other, they had similar tendencies to turn to their consuls for support when they got into conflicts with Chinese. When missionaries or their converts were attacked or killed, gunboats were often sent to the nearest port to threaten retaliation, a practice termed *gunboat diplomacy*.

When the disorder of the Taiping Rebellion disrupted tariff collection in Shanghai and Amoy, the British and American consuls there collected the tariffs themselves, a practice later regularized into a permanent Imperial Maritime Customs, staffed at its higher level by westerners. In addition to recording and collecting tariffs, the customs published annual reports on the outlook for trade at each port and undertook projects to improve communications, such as telegraph and postal systems.

By 1900 there were a hundred treaty ports, but only Shanghai, Tianjin, Hankou, Guangzhou, and Dalian (at the southern tip of Manchuria) became major centers of foreign residence. (Hong Kong was counted not as a treaty port but as a colony.) The western-dominated parts of these cities showed Chinese what western "progress" was all about, with their street lights and tall buildings. The Chinese in these cities also felt the disdain of the westerners towards China and the Chinese. To westerners, the Chinese educated class seemed too obtuse to understand progress. Couldn't they see that the world outside China had changed drastically in the last century and that China's response to it was disastrously out-of-date?

Away from the treaty ports, missionaries were the westerners the Chinese were most likely to encounter. Once China agreed in the treaty of 1860 to allow missionaries to travel through China, they came in large numbers. Unlike merchants in the treaty ports, missionaries had no choice but to mix with the local population, and they spent much of their time with ordinary, poor Chinese, finding the best opportunities for conversion among them.

Missionaries often ran orphanages, a "good work" that also helped produce converts, but the Chinese suspected that they were buying babies for nefarious purposes. Widely circulated antimissionary tracts were often filled with inflammatory charges of this sort. The volatility of relations between Chinese and foreign missionaries led to tragedy in Tianjin on a June day in 1870. French troops had been based there from 1860 to 1863, the French had taken over a former palace for their consulate, and they had built a cathedral at the site of a former Chinese temple, all reasons for the local population to resent them. At the cathedral, nuns ran an orphanage. They welcomed (and even paid small sums to receive) sick and dying children, wanting to baptize them before they died. When an epidemic swept through the orphanage in June 1870, so many orphans died that rumors spread that they were being killed for their body parts. Scandalous purposes seemed confirmed when the nuns would not let parents retrieve their children. When a local official came to search the premises, a fight broke out between converts and

onlookers. The official ordered soldiers to put a stop to the disturbance. Meanwhile, the French consul, carrying two pistols, charged into the official's office and shot at him. After the consul was restrained, the official, unhurt, advised him not to go back on the street, where an angry crowd had formed. Claiming he was afraid of no Chinese, the consul went out anyway. On the street, he recognized the city magistrate, whom he shot at, again missing. The crowd then killed the consul and the officer with him, as well as twelve priests and nuns, seven other foreigners, and several dozen Chinese converts. The French victims were mutilated and the cathedral and four American and British churches burned. Although the French consul had incited the violence, it was the Chinese who had to pay reparations, as well as punish members of the mob and send a mission of apology to France.

By 1900 there were 886 Catholic and about 3,000 Protestant missionaries in China, more than half of them women. Although the majority of missionaries devoted themselves to preaching, over the course of the nineteenth century, more and more concentrated on medicine or education, which were better received by the Chinese. By 1905 there were about three hundred fully qualified physicians doing medical missionary work, and the two hundred fifty mission hospitals and dispensaries treated about 2 million patients. Missionary hospitals in Hong Kong also ran a medical school that trained hundreds of Chinese as physicians. At their schools, missionaries helped spread western learning. For their elementary schools, missionaries produced textbooks in Chinese on a full range of subjects. They translated dozens of standard works into Chinese, especially in the natural sciences, mathematics, history, and international law. By 1906 there were nearly sixty thousand students attending twenty-four hundred Christian schools. Most of this activity was supported by contributions sent from the United States and Britain. Missionaries in China had more success in spreading western learning than in gaining converts: by 1900 fewer than 1 million Chinese were Christians.

THE FAILURES OF REFORM

Despite the enormous efforts it put into trying to catch up, the end of the nineteenth century brought China more humiliation. First came the discovery that Japan had so successfully modernized that it posed a threat to China. Japan had not been much of a concern to China since Hideoyoshi's invasion of Korea in the late Ming period. In the 1870s, Japan began making demands on China and in the 1890s seemed to be looking for a pretext for war.

As discussed in Chapter 21, Korea provided the pretext. When an insurrection broke out in Korea in 1894, both China and Japan rushed to send troops. After Japan sank a steamship carrying Chinese troops, both countries declared war. The results proved that the past decade of accelerated efforts to upgrade the military were still not enough. In the climatic naval battle off the Yalu River, four of the twelve Chinese ships involved were sunk, four were seriously damaged, and the others fled. By contrast none of the twelve Japanese ships was seriously damaged. An even worse loss came when the Japanese went overland to take the Chinese port city of Weihaiwei in Shandong province, then turned the Chinese guns on the Chinese fleet in the bay. This was a defeat not of Chinese weapons but of Chinese organization and strategy.

China sued for peace and sent Li Hongzhang to Japan to negotiate a settlement. Besides a huge indemnity, China agreed to cede Taiwan and Liaodong (the southern tip of Manchuria) to Japan and allow Japan to open factories in China. (Liaodong was returned to the Qing for an additional indemnity after pressure from the European powers.) China had to borrow from consortiums of banks in Russia, France, Britain, and Germany to pay the indemnity, securing the loans with future customs revenue. From this point until 1949, China was continually in debt to foreign banks, which made reform all the more difficult.

European imperialism was at a high point in the 1890s, with countries scrambling to get territories in Africa and Southeast Asia. China's helplessness in the face of aggression led to a scramble among the European powers for concessions and protectorates in China. At the high point of this rush in 1898, it appeared that the European powers might divide China among themselves the way they had recently divided Africa. Russia obtained permission to extend the Trans-Siberian railway across Manchuria to Vladivostok and secured a leasehold over the Liaodong Peninsula. Germany seized the port of Qingdao in Shandong province, and the British stepped in to keep them in check by taking a port (Weihaiwei) that lay between Russia's and Germany's concessions. France concentrated on concessions in the south and southwest, near its colonies in Southeast Asia.

The mixture of fear and outrage that many of the educated class felt as China suffered blow after blow began to give rise to attitudes that can be labeled nationalism. The two most important intellectual leaders to give shape to these feelings were Kang Youwei (1858–1927) and Liang Qichao (1873–1929), both from Guangdong province. Kang was a committed Confucian, dedicated to the ideals of personal virtue and service to society. He reinterpreted the classics to justify reform, arguing that Confucius had been a reformer, not a mere transmitter as he had portrayed himself in the *Analects*. Liang, fifteen years younger, was Kang's most brilliant follower and went even further than Kang in advocating political change. Liang contended that self-strengthening efforts had focused too narrowly on technology and ignored the need for cultural and political change. The examination system should be scrapped and a national school system instituted. China needed a stronger sense of national solidarity and a new type of state in which the people participated in rule. Kang, Liang, and like-minded men began setting up study societies in 1895 in several large cities. In Hunan province, for instance, fourteen study societies were founded in 1897 and 1898, the largest with over twelve hundred members. Some of these societies started publishing newspapers (see **Documents: Comparing the Power of China and Western Nations**). Worrisome to the court was that some of these societies expressed anti-Manchu sentiments, seeming to imply that many of China's problems could be solved if only the Chinese were ruling China.

The reformers called for an end to distinctions between Manchus and Han Chinese. Some implied that the bannermen's status as a hereditary military caste should be discontinued, the way the special status of the samurai had been ended in Japan. Others proposed that banner families and Han Chinese families intermarry to break down the separation between the two groups. Many bannermen became alarmed, not seeing how the banner population could survive without government handouts. In Japan, samurai had not only joined the new armies in large numbers as officers, but many had successfully switched to other occupations requiring skill or learning. The hereditary military caste of the Qing did not fare as well. Although banner garrisons had schools for banner children, many were illiterate and unprepared to step forward as the country modernized.

In the spring of 1895, provincial graduates in Beijing for the triennial *jinshi* examinations submitted petitions on how to respond to the crisis caused by the war with Japan. Some twelve hundred signed the "ten-thousand word petition" written by Kang Youwei. Kang called for an assembly elected by the general populace. Such an assembly would solve China's most pressing problems:

> Above, they are to broaden His Majesty's sage-like understanding, so that he can sit in one hall and know the four seas. Below, they are to bring together the minds and wills of the empire, so that all can share cares and pleasures, forgetting the distinction between public and private. . . . Sovereign and people will be of one body, and China will be as one family. . . . So when funds are to be raised, what sums cannot be raised? When soldiers are to be trained, what numbers cannot be trained? With 400 million minds as one mind: how could the empire be stronger?[5]

One of the tutors to the Guangxu emperor joined one of these societies in Beijing and introduced its ideas to the emperor. In January 1898, the emperor let Kang Youwei discuss his ideas with the high officials at court. Afterward Kang sent the emperor three memorials on constitutions, national assemblies, and political reform. Kang even implied that the Qing rulers should abandon the queue, noting that in Japan, western dress had been adopted and the Japanese emperor had cut his hair short. In June the emperor gave Kang a five-hour audience. Over the next hundred days, the emperor issued over a hundred decrees on everything from revamping the examination system to setting up national school, banking, postal, and patent systems. He was redesigning the Qing as a constitutional monarchy with modern financial and educational infrastructures.

After three months, Empress Dowager Cixi had had enough and staged a coup with the help of Yuan Shikai's army. She had the Guangxu emperor locked up and executed those of the reformers she could capture. All of the reform edicts were revoked. Kang and Liang, safely out of Beijing at the time, managed to flee to Japan, where each lived for years.

THE BOXER REBELLION

In the summer of 1898, while the Guangxu emperor was issuing reform edicts, Shandong province was suffering from a break in the dikes on the Yellow River, which flooded some two thousand villages and made millions of people refugees. Not only was that year's crop ruined, but in many places the land could not be planted even the next spring. When the government failed to provide effective relief, antigovernment resentment began to stir. Another local grievance concerned the high-handed behavior of Christian missionaries, especially a group of German missionaries who actively interfered in their converts' lawsuits, claiming the privileges of extraterritoriality for their converts. They

5. Translated in Philip A. Kuhn, *Origins of the Modern Chinese State* (Stanford, Calif.: Stanford University Press, 2002), p. 123.

DOCUMENTS

Comparing the Power of China and Western Nations

This essay was written in 1898 by Mai Menghua (1874–1915), a twenty-four-year-old follower of Kang Youwei. It responds to conservative critics who saw Kang's program as weakening the ruler's hand. Mai argues that modern western governments are in fact much stronger than the Chinese government.

Nowadays, men of broad learning all say China is weak because the power of the ruler is mighty while the power of the people is slight. Those who like to map out plans for the nation say that the western nations are strong because their way is exactly the opposite of this. Mai Menghua says: This is not so. China's misfortunes arise not because the people have no power but because the ruler has no power. Hence, over all five continents and throughout all past ages, no ruler has had less power than in present-day China, and no rulers have had more power than in present-day European nations. There are far too many points for me to compare them all here, but permit me to say something about a few.

In western countries, the age, birth, and death of every person in every household is reported to the officials, who record and investigate it. An omission in a report is punished as a criminal offense. In China, birth, death, and taking care of oneself are all personal matters, beyond state intervention. In western countries, when property is inherited by descendants, the amount of the property and its location must be reported and registered with the authorities. An inheritance tax must be paid before the property is transmitted to the inheritors. In China, people give and take as they please, and the state is unable to investigate. In western countries, when children reach the age of eight [*sui*], they all go to elementary school. Doting parents who neglect their children's studies are punished. In China, 70 to 80 per cent of the population is indolent, worthless, uncouth and illiterate, and the state can do nothing to encourage them to improve themselves. In western countries, one must go through school to become an official, and unless one does adequately, one cannot make his own way. In China, one can be a slave in the market place in the morning, and bedecked in the robes of high office by evening, and this is beyond the capacity of the state to control. In western countries, the currency system is fixed by the court; one country has the pound, another the ruble, and another the franc, but each cur-

also irritated people by forbidding their converts to contribute to traditional village festivals that involved parading statues of the local gods.

Not surprisingly, this region soon exploded into violence. Small groups began pillaging the property of missionaries and their converts. They were dubbed by foreigners "Boxers" because of their martial arts practices, but these Boxers also practiced spirit possession, which allowed individuals to achieve direct communication with their gods and gain a sense of personal power. The governor of Shandong suppressed them by 1899, but they began drifting into other provinces, even into the capital, where they recruited new members with placards urging the Chinese to kill all foreigners as well as Chinese contaminated by their influence. They blamed the drought on the anger of the gods at the foreign intrusion.

rency is uniform throughout the entire country, and no one dares to differ. In China, each of the 18 provinces has a different currency, and the shape of the money is different. The people are satisfied with what they are accustomed to, and the state is unable to enforce uniformity.

In western countries, only the government may print and distribute paper money within its borders. In China, banks in every province and money changers in every port make and circulate their own money, and the state is unable to audit and prohibit them. In western countries, all new buildings are inspected by officials, who examine the quality of the construction materials as a precaution against collapse causing injuries. Older houses are periodically inspected, and ordered demolished or repaired. In China, one can construct as one pleases. Even if there are cracks and flaws, the state cannot supervise and reprove the builder. In western countries, roads and highways must be broad and spacious, neat and clean. There are legal penalties for discarding trash [on the roads]. Broad roads in Chinese cities are swamped in urine and litter, filled with beggars and corpses, and the state is unable to clean them up. In western countries, all doctors must be graduates of medical schools and be certified before they can practice medicine. In China, those who fail to do well academically switch to the medical profession; quack doctors, who casually kill patients, are everywhere, and the state is

unable to punish them. In western countries, the postal service is controlled by the government. In China, post offices run by private persons are everywhere, and the government is unable to unify them.

In western countries, there is an official for commerce. Inferior goods cannot be sold in the market. New inventions are patented, and other merchants are forbidden to manufacture imitations. In China, dishonest merchants are everywhere, devising illicit means to make imitation products, and everything is of inferior quality, and yet the state has no control. In western countries, wherever railroads pass, homes, temples, huts, or gravestones must be demolished. No one dares obstruct the opening up of new mineral resources in mountains. In China, conservatives raise an outcry and block every major project, and the state is unable to punish them. In western countries, foresters are appointed to superintend mountains and forests, and there are officials to oversee the fishing industry. Trees are felled only at the proper time, and large numbers of fishing nets are not permitted [in order to protect the stock of fish]. In China, no one is master of the woods and waters; the people can despoil them as they please, and the state has no way to know about it.

Source: From J. Mason Gentzler, ed., *Changing China: Readings in the History of China from the Opium War to the Present* (New York: Praeger, 1977), pp. 90–91, slightly modified.

The foreign powers demanded that the Qing government suppress the attacks on foreigners. Cixi, apparently hoping that the Chinese people if aroused could solve her foreign problem for her, did little to stop the Boxers. Eight foreign powers announced that they would send troops to protect missionaries. Then, on June 20, 1900, the German minister was shot dead in the street. Cixi, having been told by pro-Boxer Manchus that the European powers wanted her to retire and restore the emperor to the throne, declared war on the eight powers. Although she had repeatedly seen China defeated when it was fighting only one of these powers, she deluded herself into thinking that if the people became sufficiently enraged, they could drive all eight out and solve the foreign problem once and for all. (See Color Plate 25.)

Foreign Troops. Many of the troops brought in by the eight powers to suppress the Boxer Rebellion were native troops in colonial armies, like the ones seen here. *(War Office Records of Military Headquarters, Public Records Office/HIP/The Image Works)*

Foreigners in the capital, including missionaries who had recently moved into the capital for safety, barricaded themselves in the Northern Cathedral and the legation quarter, two miles away. After the Boxers laid siege to the legation quarter, an eight-nation force (including Japan) sent twenty thousand troops to lift the siege. Cixi and the emperor fled by cart hundreds of miles away to Xi'an. By the end of the year, there were forty-five thousand foreign troops in north China. Most of the Boxers tried to disappear into the north China countryside, but the foreign troops spent six months hunting them down, making raids on Chinese towns and villages.

Antiforeign violence also occurred elsewhere in the country, especially in Shanxi, where the governor sided with the Boxers and had missionaries and their converts executed. Most of the governors-general, however, including Li Hongzhang and Yuan Shikai, simply ignored the empress dowager's declaration of war.

In the negotiations that led to the Boxer Protocol, China had to accept a long list of penalties, including canceling the examinations for five years (punishment for gentry collaboration), execution of the officials involved, destruction of forts and railway posts, and a staggering indemnity of 450 million silver dollars.

THE DECLINE OF THE QING EMPIRE IN COMPARATIVE PERSPECTIVE

Late Qing reformers often urged the court to follow in the footsteps of Japan, which had adopted not merely western technology but also western ideas about political organization and even western dress. Ever since, it has been common to compare the fates of Qing China and Tokugawa Japan and ask why Japan was so much more successful at modernizing its government and economy.

The main arguments for lumping together China and Japan are that they were geographically close (both were "the Far East" to Europeans), and some significant features of Japanese culture had been derived from China, such as Confucianism and the use of Chinese characters in writing. The differences, however, should not be minimized. China in the nineteenth century was not an independent country, but part of the multiethnic empire of the Manchus, making it more similar to other large multiethnic empires, like the Mughals in India, the Ottomans in the Middle East, the Romanovs in Russia, and even the Hapsburgs in eastern Europe. Even if only the China proper part of the Qing is considered, it was a much larger country than Japan in both territory and population, with all that that implied in terms of political structure.

Another common way to frame the experiences of China in this period is to compare it to other countries where western imperialism was felt. Those Chinese who urged the court to follow Japan's example also warned of being carved up like Africa or taken over like India. But only small pieces of the Qing Empire were directly ruled by foreign powers in China, giving its history a different trajectory.

Better comparisons for the Qing Dynasty in this period are probably the Ottoman and Russian Empires. All three were multiethnic, land-based Eurasian empires, with long experience with mounted horsemen of the steppe—and in the case of both the Ottomans and the Qing, currently ruled by groups that claimed this tradition themselves. All three knew how to deal with problems of defending long land borders but were not naval powers. During the eighteenth century all had experienced rapid population growth that was reducing the standard of living for much of the population by the mid-nineteenth century. In each place, by then the military pressure put on them both by internal unrest and foreign pressure forced them to spend more on military preparedness at the cost of deficit financing. As the importance of cavalry declined in warfare, each lost its military advantages. In this period western sea powers sought to profit from trade with them, forcing them to accept their terms, but not trying to take over management of their empires. The sea powers gained more by making loans to them that kept them in a type of debt bondage, securing their advantage through treaties without any of the responsibilities of direct rule.

In each of these empires, during the mid- and late nineteenth centuries, the elites were divided between westernizers and traditionalists, each looking for ways to strengthen the government. Urban merchants were usually more willing to see changes made than the imperial elite, who had the most stake in the existing power structure. Even when modernizers won out, improvements were generally too little or too late to make much of a difference when the next confrontation with western powers came. Reform programs could not outpace the destructive effect of economic decline, social turmoil, and the intrusion of the West. Foreign powers did not encourage domestic challenges to the dynastic rulers, perhaps fearing that they would lose the privileges they had gained through treaties. Thus, many of those who sought radical change came to oppose both the foreign powers and the ruling dynasty, giving rise to modern nationalism.

SUMMARY

How different was China in 1900 than it had been in 1800? At the beginning of the nineteenth century, most Chinese had no reason to question the long-held belief that China was the central kingdom: no other country had so many people, Chinese products were in great demand in foreign countries, and the borders had recently been expanded. True, an alien dynasty occupied the throne, but the Manchus administered the country through institutions much like those earlier Chinese dynasties had employed, and even proved generous patrons of strictly Chinese forms of culture, such as publications in Chinese. Chinese civilization thus seemed in no danger. By 1900, this confidence was gone. Besides traditional evidence of dynastic decline—peasant poverty, social unrest, government bankruptcy—new foreign adversaries had emerged. China had been humiliated repeatedly in military encounters with western nations and more recently Japan and was deeply in debt to these countries because of imposed indemnities. Most of the educated class had come to feel that drastic measures needed to be taken. Chinese civilization—not just the Qing Dynasty—was at stake.

SUGGESTED READING

Volumes 10 and 11 of the *Cambridge History of China* cover the nineteenth century. Briefer narrative overviews can be found in the works cited in Chapter 16, plus J. Fairbank, *The Great Chinese Revolution* (1986). Primary sources can be found in W. de Bary and R. Lufrano, eds., *Sources of Chinese Tradition: From 1600 Through the Twentieth Century* (2000), and S. Teng and J. Fairbank, *China's Response to the West: A Documentary Survey* (1971).

On the Daoguang emperor and efforts to strengthen the Qing, see J. Leonard, *Controlling from Afar: The DaoGuang Emperor's Handling of the Grand Canal Crisis, 1824–26* (1996). The relevance of dissatisfaction with the government in this period and later changes in the constitution of the Chinese state are a theme of P. Kuhn, *Origins of the Modern Chinese State* (2002).

On the many nineteenth-century rebellions and their suppression, see J. Chesneaux, *Peasant Revolts in China, 1840–1949* (1973); P. Kuhn, *Rebellion and Its Enemies in Late Imperial China* (1970); E. Perry, *Rebels and Revolutionaries in North China, 1845–1945* (1980); and J. Spence, *God's Chinese Son: The Taiping Heavenly Kingdom of Hong Xiuquan* (1996). On the Boxers, see J. Esherick, *The Origins of the Boxer Uprising* (1987), and P. Cohen, *History in Three Keys* (1997).

On the Opium War, see H. Chang, *Commissioner Lin and the Opium War* (1964); P. Fay, *The Opium War, 1840–1842* (1975); J. Polacheck, *The Inner Opium War* (1992); and A. Waley, *The Opium War Through Chinese Eyes* (1968). For Chinese who went abroad, see D. Arkush and L. Lee, *Land Without Ghosts* (1989). On Christian missionaries, see P. Cohen, *China and Christianity: The Missionary Movement and Growth of Chinese Anti-Foreignism, 1860–1870* (1963), and J. Hunter, *The Gospel of Gentility: American Missionary Women in Turn of the Century China* (1984).

On the Chinese economy as it became more involved in global trade, see S. Mazumdar, *Sugar and Society in China: Peasants, Technology, and the World Market* (1998), and R. Marks, *Tigers, Rice, Silk, and Silt: Environment and Economy in Late Imperial South China* (1998).

On the concerns of intellectuals, see H. Chang, *Chinese Intellectuals in Crisis: Search for Order and Meaning (1890–1911)* (1987); B. Schwartz, *In Search of Wealth and Power: Yen Fu and the West* (1964); and K. Hsiao, *A Modern China and a New World: K'ang Yu-wei, Reformer and Utopian, 1858–1927* (1975). Insight into Chinese society and the culture of the time can be gleaned from D. Cohn, ed., *Vignettes from the Chinese: Lithographs from Shanghai in the Late Nineteenth Century* (1987), and I. Pruitt, *A Daughter of Han: the Autobiography of a Chinese Working Woman* (1967).

Japan in Turmoil (1800–1867)

Many commoners in Japan's cities and villages prospered during the first three decades of the nineteenth century, but the same could not be said for the laboring poor, low-status samurai, or daimyo wrestling with shortfalls in domainal finances. Belying prosperity were problems such as vagrancy, gambling, and prostitution that threatened the social order propped up by administrators and wealthy entrepreneurs. Added to these signs of domestic distress was an increasing fear of threats from abroad. The shogunate's ineffectual and inconsistent attempts to deal with these problems weakened it in the eyes of the military ruling class. Its decision to seek approval for foreign treaties from the monarch opened the door for wide-ranging debate that enabled commoners as well as officials to participate in a new political public realm. Beset on all sides, the shogunate collapsed at the end of 1867, ushering in a regime headed by the newly named emperor.

Historians have long searched the early nineteenth century for clues as to what brought about the Meiji Restoration. Those who emphasize domestic factors point to how the social and political order came unglued in the early nineteenth century. But that begs the question of whether the fall of the Tokugawa shogunate should be seen as a coup d'état or a revolution. Was it primarily the effect of domestic changes or a reaction to foreign pressure?

DOMESTIC SECESSIONS

Early nineteenth-century villages had to deal with internal conflict. Outcasts deemed polluted by their association with dead animals protested discrimination and the indignities they had to suffer. Long accustomed to apportioning the village tax assessment, headmen tended to treat expenses for family business and village administration as one and the same. The walls around their houses had gates; the roofs had eaves that marked their superior status. Complaints against headmen perceived to be unjust in dividing the tax burden, efforts to clarify the costs of village administration, and demands that the headman cease to lord it over his neighbors led to lawsuits that sometimes dragged on for decades. A recalcitrant headman might be subjected to ostracism. Sometimes disputes resulted in the village council's being expanded to include a cultivator's representative to verify the tax assessment. In villages where the position of headman had once been hereditary, it might instead rotate among a group of families. Some villages started a system of having the heads of household elect the headman. When a woman was the house head, she too voted.

In eastern Japan, village leaders agonized over fields gone to waste because of population decline. Worse, gamblers and bandits disrupted the social order. Village officials organized regional leagues, inserting a new level of administration between the village and ruling authority. In the region around Osaka, these leagues launched province-wide appeals beginning in the 1780s to eliminate restrictions on commerce and regulate the price of herring meal fertilizer from Hokkaido. In 1827 the shogunate started sending security patrols through the Edo hinterland, where villages might be fragmented among several domains. Some headmen organized militia; others hired unemployed swordsmen, some running protection rackets, to keep the peace. Longer-term solutions came in the teachings of the peasant sage Ninomiya Sontoku. Sontoku revitalized villages, increasing their population and bringing fields back into production by preaching an ethic of diligence, fortitude, and frugality to repay the bounty of the gods while instituting mutual aid associations to give villagers who had fallen into dire straits access to low-interest loans. His emphasis on rational planning to wring the most from land and labor demanded steady work habits instilled in men and women alike.

Hirata Atsutane and his followers offered a vision of a just social order that largely ignored existing political arrangements. Although they acknowledged shogunal authority and the Confucian principles of social inequality, they sought the wellspring of human virtue in Japan's ancient past and looked to the monarch as a manifest god who linked the divine and human worlds. Atsutane claimed to be a disciple of Motoori Norinaga, thus putting him in the mainstream of nativist thought. Unlike his teacher, he did not envision the afterlife as a filthy, polluted realm but rather as an invisible world that parallels the visible world. From that vantage, the deceased watch over and protect their descendants. Atsutane's teachings placed primacy on agricultural practices that brought people into close communion with the gods and each other. Village officials and rural entrepreneurs were his most numerous disciples because they believed his message to contain the secret for revitalizing the village community without threatening their role either socially or economically (see **Biography: Kitahara Inao**).

Domainal Reforms

Faced with challenges from below, rural entrepreneurs sought new ways to bolster their prestige. Rather than marry within the village, they sought marriage partners of similar background a day's walk or more away. They educated themselves; they also educated their daughters to standards beyond what could be achieved by an ordinary cultivator. They studied Chinese philosophy and classical poetry as well as western science and geography. They took up swordsmanship. In the 1830s and 1840s, their quest for ways to enhance their dignity meshed with the ruling authorities' need for funds. In return for loans, wealthy commoners received permission to wear swords on official business and use a surname, privileges supposedly reserved for the samurai.

The willingness of daimyo to sell markers of prestige to commoners was but one sign that their governments verged on bankruptcy. Owing to rural opposition, tax revenues had long since ceased to cover the expenses of carrying redundant personnel on the books, supporting the

BIOGRAPHY Kitahara Inao

In the early nineteenth century, rural entrepreneurs dominated their villages politically, socially, and economically. A representative figure was Kitahara Inao (1825–1881), who had wide-ranging interests and an abiding concern with national affairs.

Based in the mountains of central Japan, Inao's family claimed warrior connections through an ancestor who died in battle in 1575 and through him to the Minamoto lineage. His father received permission to wear swords and use a surname for his work on water control projects; he also served as one of the village's headmen, managed the family's land, and sold the silk produced by Inao's mother. He educated himself, his children, and his neighbors in western geography and Japanese poetry. When his eldest son wished to learn a musical instrument called the *samisen,* he sent him to Kyoto. The boy was murdered en route. Thus did Inao become his father's heir.

The short-tempered Inao had a short career as village headman. In 1852, cultivators from the village's upper elevations complained that they had to pay for flood control that benefited only their wealthier neighbors on the plain. Four years later, they questioned the way costs had been assessed. A meeting with Inao turned into a shouting match. One man called Inao a liar, and Inao slugged him.

The cultivators announced that to strike one was to strike them all. Inao had to resign his office and concentrate his efforts on teaching village boys and girls.

Inao helped found the Hirata school in the Ina valley by hosting study groups, proselytizing, and publishing Atsutane's works. He used his own capital to publish a chronology composed by Atsutane that traced the monarchy back to the creator gods and raised money to publish Atsutane's magnum opus, the multivolume *Koshiden* (Lectures on Ancient History). In 1867 he helped build a shrine to the four great nativist teachers ending with Atsutane. Through these efforts, his valley acquired the largest population of Hirata disciples outside Edo.

Following the Meiji Restoration, Inao organized a development fund to promote new agricultural products and bring mechanized filatures to the Ina valley. Conditions for loans were so strict and interest rates so high that only landlord families could benefit, to the resentment of poor folk who had contributed to it. Despite his promotion of industrialization, Inao continued to castigate westernizers who did not understand the fundamental principle of respecting Japanese ways and despising the foreign. At the end of his life, he wrote a set of precepts for his descendants that emphasized harmony, diligence, and frugality. He urged them to be modest in dress, eat simple food, and marry plain but intelligent women.

daimyo's women and children in the style to which life in Edo had accustomed them, and paying for the trips made by the daimyo and his retinue back and forth to Edo. Daimyo borrowed money from merchants with the promise of repayment out of future tax receipts. In the 1830s, domains across Japan launched administrative and financial reforms. Those that tried to increase exports and restrict imports disrupted markets and created shortages. Some instituted monopolies by strengthening existing controls: Satsuma doubled its profits in sugar. Most domains sought to reduce expenditures by cutting costs. Concerned that luxury-loving commoners both threatened samurai privilege and encouraged samurai extravagance, governments issued sumptuary legislation forbidding socially inferior people to wear silk garments, ornamental hairpins, and other products of the commercial revolution.

The samurai, especially those in the lower ranks, saw themselves beset on all sides. Wealthy commoners in crested kimono carrying swords challenged their sense of status superiority. Educated, capable samurai were frustrated by the system of hereditary ranks that relegated them to dead-end menial tasks. During domainal reforms, low-ranking samurai proposed that men of talent and ability be promoted to decision-making positions. Satsuma heeded this call, allowing Saigō Takamori to rise from rural administrator to the daimyo's adviser in 1854. Efforts to promote men from below often led to factional disputes when upper-status samurai fought to preserve their hereditary privileges. "Borrowing" stipends posed the most ubiquitous threat to samurai welfare. While some domains tried to confine the practice to samurai without regular bureaucratic appointments and pretended that cuts were temporary, others insisted that everyone must make sacrifices. In one case, guards assigned to escort a daimyo to his regular audience with the shogun protested the arrears in their salary by going on strike.

Conditions reached a crisis when poor harvests in the 1830s recalled the famines of the 1780s. Commoners assumed that food shortages owed more to greedy merchants than to crop failures. They turned on village leaders for not offering prompt relief, and they called on the gods of world renewal (*yonaoshi*) for salvation from economic hardship and political ineptitude. Women played an active role, marching with men to protest arbitrary government policies and complaining to rice merchants that hoarding grain threatened the poor with starvation. A retired shogunal policeman named Ōshio Heihachirō decided that government and merchants had become morally bankrupt. Raised in the Confucian tradition that deemed bureaucratic work a service to the people, Ōshio had also studied Wang Yangming, who argued that at time of crisis, a man had to use his intuition, not institutional norms, to guide his behavior. In 1836 Ōshio petitioned the Osaka city magistrate to save the starving. When he

refused, Ōshio sold his books to buy food. In a last desperate effort, he issued a manifesto that charged shogunal officials with corruption and led a rural army against the city. A quarter of Osaka burned before shogunal troops caught up with him, and he committed suicide.

Religion and Play

One secessionist response to economic dislocation and political ineptitude came in the form of new religions. In 1838 a long-suffering rural woman named Nakayama Miki was possessed by a spirit who deemed her to be the "shogun of heaven" and the mouthpiece for the true and original god of salvation. She insisted that her family sell its property, the proceeds of which were used to succor the poor. According to the god's divine wisdom (*tenri*), the shogun and daimyo were far too removed from daily life to aid the people; instead, the people should trust in the god of world renewal and work together, offering mutual assistance in time of need. Like other new religions of the time, Tenri-kyō envisioned a world opposed to the hierarchical and socially stratified system of the past and present. In a renewed world saturated with divine goodness, the poor would receive relief, and everyone, men and women, would be equal.

An alternative to the secessionist impulse found in the new religions came in the form of play. Dominated by the theater, urban culture celebrated bodily pleasures. Townspeople employed the possibilities presented by multiple identities—merchant, poet, sword-wearing samurai—to escape from the rigidities of the status system (see **Documents: Kohei's Lawsuit**). By the 1830s, readers of popular literature had alternatives to didactic tracts that bolstered the official status order. They indulged in novels that depicted the immediate world of human feelings such as Jippensha Ikku's travelogues featuring an irreverent pair, Kita and Yaji, who poked fun at self-important samurai, stole when they could, seduced serving maids, and laughed at farts. Woodblock prints and kabuki, in particular ghost stories staged by Tsuruya Namboku and his successors, portrayed bloodshed and gruesome murders. In 1850 the story of Sakura Sōgorō appeared on stage with scenes of his crucifixion and reincarnation as an angry spirit. Although these dramas went to extraordinary lengths to rivet their audience's attention, they remained linked to social mores. Dramas might be set in the daimyo's domestic quarters, but the subjects of action were commoners who acted according to the logic of everyday life.

Japanese commoners played hard. Festivals in town and country became increasingly elaborate, and laborers demanded ever more of them. Kabuki troupes discovered the money to be made in touring the countryside. In prosperous regions, villages built kabuki stages and competed in presenting plays to their neighbors. City folk flocked to entertainment districts. The shops with female clerks, theaters, and variety shows surrounding Asakusa temple in Edo combined appeals to prayer and play. Play constituted one way to appeal to the gods, and the pursuit of pleasure had a spiritual dimension.

Another sign that the practices of everyday life had escaped governmental control can be seen in prostitution. Unlicensed prostitutes, both men and women, plied their trade in informal entertainment districts that had sprung up across Edo and in castle towns. Post stations employed maids to lure customers to inns and teahouses, where singers, dancers, and servants often doubled as prostitutes. The development of a commercial economy contributed to the spread of prostitution in two ways: it put more money in the pockets of potential customers and stimulated the monetization of female labor. When families' expectations that their women supplement the family income by raising silkworms or working for wages went unmet, prostitution became the logical alternative.

As part of a far-reaching reform effort in 1841, the shogunate tried to curtail what it saw as the excesses of urban culture. It clamped down on unlicensed prostitution by closing teahouses and other venues where women sold their bodies. It forbade women to dress men's hair, teach them music, serve as attendants at archery ranges, or perform onstage in public. It even outlawed men and women sharing public baths in an effort to promote public morality. Gambling, lotteries, and full-body tattoos were forbidden. The shogunate tightened censorship over the publishing industry, refusing to permit romantic novels or erotica, including the serial best-seller, *The False Murasaki and the Rustic Genji,* produced by Ryūtei Tanehiko between 1829 and 1842. Theaters and entertainment districts received undesired attention. The shogunate condemned extravagance and ordered commoners not to dress, eat, or house themselves above their station. It tried to enforce these strictures by making an example of egregious violators in hopes of intimidating the rest. These measures had but a temporary effect.

FOREIGN AFFAIRS

The Russians were the first foreigners to encroach on Japan. During the eighteenth century, they started to trade with the Ainu in the Kuril Islands and Kamchatka. In 1793 Adam Laxman, a delegate to Catherine II, tried to open relations between Russia and Japan. He got as far as Nagasaki, only to be rebuffed by Matsudaira Sadanobu, who insisted that respect for his ancestors required that he not initiate new foreign relations. In 1798 the shogunate sent an expedition to Hokkaido to assess the Russian threat. Based on its report, the shogunate decided to annex Hokkaido and Sakhalin. Its reach exceeded its grasp; it did not have the forces to defend either. Russians again asked for permission to trade at Nagasaki in 1804. When that was not forthcoming, officers attacked trading posts on Sakhalin and the Kurils in 1806 and 1807. In 1811 the Japanese captured Vasilii Golovnin, the captain of a Russian surveying crew, and held him at Hakodate for two years before Russia secured his release. His captivity narrative intrigued readers across Europe.

DOCUMENTS

Kohei's Lawsuit

In a litigious society, people turned to the shogun's court to decide disputes. The summation of a conflict over inheritance that follows, titled "Action by Kohei of Haruki-chō, Hongō, against Heisuke of Sugamo-chō and Kurōbei of Fujimae-chō, Komagome as to the succession and division of personality of Sawamura Gisaburō, Master Carpenter," exposes a particularly complex set of family relations and the permeability of supposedly strict occupational and status boundaries. Note that the people involved in the suit, including the deceased, took different names depending on the occupation of the moment. Why is the conflict over Gisaburō's personality, not simply his possessions?

5th month, 1849, Inquiry by the city magistrate to the engineering magistrates:

Kohei demanded succession and division of personality of Sawamura Gisaburō, master-carpenter, subject to your lordships' authority, producing for evidence Gisaburō's will written by a person other than the testator; the defendants, on the other hand, deny the validity of the will, and the parties are at issue.

Kohei alleges that his sister's husband Sawamura Gisaburō made a will so that his personality may be divided according to the will, and that Gisaburō's adopted son Kosuke may be made to succeed Gisaburō.

Rubric: This Kosuke was one who, calling himself Utazō, tenanted the land of Ichibei in Yanaka, and was engaged in the management of a public bath-house. Four years ago, in 1845, he was adopted by Gisaburō, and in the 11th month of the same year, his petition to be a master-carpenter on probation was granted. It has been found that he is still living in a separate house on Ichibei's land and is working as a master-carpenter on probation.

What Heisuke alleges is as follows: His adoptive father Sawamura Gisaburō was a master carpenter in service of the shogunate.

Gisaburō was formerly called Heisuke and was engaged in the management of a tavern at Sugamo-chō. About that time this person [Heisuke] was adopted by Gisaburō and in 1835 he succeeded to Gisaburō's family name. Gisaburō served as a master-carpenter from 1810, and from 1812 to 1834 he was also registered in the census book of Sugamo-chō under the name of Heisuke. Therefore it seems that he was entered in two different census registers.

Gisaburō bought two years ago in 1846 a piece of land at the market in front of Yushima Tenjin Shrine, and on this occasion Heisuke advanced part of the purchase money. On the deed of sale, the land was entered as the property of Sei, daughter of Saku, Gisaburō's concubine. Gisaburō had a house on this land repaired for Saku to occupy. Lately he himself moved into this concubine's house, and because of old age, he called in one Kosuke, who is more in the relation of a servant to him, to wait on him, and had this Kosuke, by nominally adopting him, serve as a master carpenter on probation. Besides the above piece of land, some other lots in Gisaburō's possession have been nominally the property of Gisaburō's grandson Chōsuke, for whom Heisuke has acted as guardian. The deeds of sale of these lands were kept by Gisaburō, as they were often used, by agreement of Gisaburō and Heisuke, for financing the business when Gisaburō engaged in various contracts, government and otherwise. When in 1847 Gisaburō married Sei, Saku's daughter [by her former husband] to one Mohachi and had Mohachi inherit the family name of Yoshikawa, palanquin-maker for the Shogunate, Heisuke on Gisaburō's request, advanced 500 *ryō* to Gisaburō to cover the expenses. Since Heisuke had advanced Gisaburō great sums of money for the latter's contract business, government, and otherwise, Heisuke should be given the right to decide on the succession and other matters.

Yasuda Chōsuke is son to Hanzaemon and grandson to Gisaburō and was formerly called Toraichirō. He is registered as a house-owner of Fujimae-chō. He has served, under the guardianship of the defendant Heisuke, as purveyor and contractor of commodities and laborers for the Fukiage Garden [in the shogun's palace] and is living with his father.

Nakamura Hanzaemon is adopted husband to Hisa born to Gisaburō by Gin, his former wife, since divorced. He was formerly called Shōgorō, and while tenant of a shop belonging to Kanbei, Fujimae-chō, Komagome, was engaged in dealing in socks. He is said to have become a guard in service of the Banner Magistrates for the Shogunate.

The defendant Kurōbei is nephew to Sawamura Gisaburō and head of Gisaburō's original family. Because of this relationship, Gisaburō, repairing a house on his land, had Kurōbei and his wife Chiyo, whose other name is Shige, live there. Even now Gisaburō's domicile is registered at the office of the Engineering Department as at this house on Kurōbei's land. So it was rumored that the boxes containing Gisaburō's papers and books etc. are kept in the above Kurōbei's godown [storehouse], including the instruments pertaining to the various money transactions which Gisaburō mentioned in his will.

The plaintiff says that when, during this autumn, he went to negotiate with Heisuke and Kurōbei, Kurōbei together with the ward officers admitted plainly that he had in his care the papers in question. The plaintiff continues that it seems possible, however, that Heisuke, taking advantage of his having access to the household of the Lord of Kaga through his business in contracting for transport horses, may have here done something tricky; that there is no box containing instruments kept now at Kurōbei's house in Fujimae-chō. It is suspected that it has since been taken to Heisuke's house. Heisuke has for several years past been in the habit of advancing loans to the household of the Lord of Kaga out of money belonging to Sawamura Gisaburō.

Instrument of Settlement to be filed: Both parties have agreed that we should petition for Gisaburō's adopted son Sawamura Kosuke to succeed Gisaburō, and should agree that neither party has grounds on which to dispute further about the deposit instruments said to be entrusted by Gisaburō with Heisuke and Kurōbei and about the money which Heisuke claims to have advanced Gisaburō, since the issue utterly lacks proof. Therefore we have come to a compromise, and will never in future resort to action or dispute.

———
Source: John Henry Wigmore, ed., *Law and Justice in Tokugawa Japan, Pt. VIII-A: Persons: Legal Precedents* (Tokyo: University of Tokyo Press, 1982), pp. 214–242 (modified).

The Closing of Japan

The British posed a more serious threat. In 1808 their warship *Phaeton* barged into Nagasaki bay in search of Dutch ships. Despite orders from the Nagasaki city magistrate to destroy it, the *Phaeton* left with food and supplies. In two separate incidents in 1824, British whaling ships raided villages on the coast north of Edo and southern Kyushu. The first village belonged to the Mito domain, home to one of the shogun's relatives and a leading xenophobe, Tokugawa Nariaki. The second was located in Satsuma, the powerful outside (*tozama*) domain that dominated the Ryukyus. The next year, the shogunate issued new instructions for dealing with westerners. With the exception of the Dutch ships allowed at Nagasaki, all foreign ships, regardless of the circumstances, were to be driven off without hesitation. This order announced that the shogunate was closing the country (*sakoku*) to the West, its first truly isolationist policy.

The decision to close the country came as a result not only of foreign intimidation but also of information gathered by scholars and officials. The head of the shogunate's translation bureau established in 1811 argued that foreigners must be kept away from Japan lest they subvert the credulous masses with Christian teachings. In 1825, an adviser to Tokugawa Nariaki named Aizawa Seishisai wrote his "New Theses" (*Shinron*). Mito scholars believed that loyalty to their lord had to be predicated on his loyalty to the monarch. Although they based their arguments on neo-Confucian principles, their ideas were readily assimilated to the nativist belief that Japan was superior to all other countries, including China, because the monarch was descended from the sun goddess. Aizawa had studied writings about the West, and he interrogated the British sailors who had landed on the Mito coast in 1824. *Shinron* argued that Japan had to beware of foreigners, even if they said they came only to trade. Trade would weaken Japan because Japan would lose precious metals, and the pursuit of novelty and luxury items would erode the people's moral fiber. But traders brought something more pernicious than goods: Christianity. They hoped to beguile the foolish commoners with their religion, turn them against their rightful leaders, and "conquer from within by recruiting the local inhabitants into their ranks." To counter the threat of "barbarian teachings," Aizawa urged his lord to convince the shogunate to launch educational, religious, and military initiatives that would reform the armed forces by allowing daimyo to recruit cultivators as soldiers and educate the masses in Japan's unique spiritual essence (*kokutai*).[1] *Shinron* had a lasting impact on nationalist thought.

Despite domainal penury, the Mito reform movement of the 1830s largely involved strengthening coastal defenses, a policy followed by a handful of other domains. Domains ignored shogunal restrictions on the number of guns permitted each castle. Mito built a reverberatory furnace to cast cannon, and Saga in Kyushu did the same. *Tozama* domains in southwestern Japan—Satsuma, Fukuoka, Kumamoto, and Chōshū—bought mortars, howitzers, and field guns from weapons dealers in Nagasaki and tried to manufacture their own. Fear of foreigners spurred a renewed emphasis on military training. Domains also mobilized militia to man coastal lookout points and serve as a first line of defense. They competed for access to military technology, and they refused to cooperate in developing systems to warn of approaching foreign ships. They saw themselves as defending not an entity known as Japan but rather their own territory. Building coastal fortifications increased their isolation from each other while weakening the shogun's authority in matters of defense.

The shogunate too tried to bolster its military preparedness, spurred by reports of the British victory over China in the Opium War. (See **Connections: Western Imperialism [1800–1900]**.) In the 1841–1842 reform, it began to adopt western military technology and trained a small contingent of foot soldiers in the use of guns. It also tried

---

1. Bob Tadashi Wakabayashi, *Anti-Foreignism and Western Learning in Early Modern Japan* (Cambridge, Mass.: Harvard University Press, 1986), p. 211.

to reassert its dominance by ordering an end to domain monopolies that interfered in commerce, seeking to transfer daimyo from one domain to another, and threatening to suppress copper coins and paper money minted in the domains. In 1843 the shogun went to Nikkō to worship at the shrine for his ancestors, escorted by one hundred fifty thousand men provided by the daimyo, who had to serve as his retinue in an affirmation of Tokugawa supremacy. At the same time, the shogunate announced a more conciliatory policy toward foreigners: shipwrecked sailors succored, Japanese castaways allowed to return home, and ships in need to receive supplies before being sent on their way.

Unequal Treaties with the United States

When Commodore Matthew C. Perry sailed four ships into Edo Bay on July 8, 1853, he had been preceded by the 1846 expedition under Commodore James Biddle, and the Dutch had warned of his arrival. Perry treated the shogunate's exclusion order with disdain, and he refused to shift anchorage until he had handed over a letter from President Millard Fillmore addressed to the monarch. He paraded his men, opened his gunports to expose his weaponry, and announced that he would return the next year for a reply. This time he had six ships under his command, having commandeered two more in Hong Kong. Confronted with this display of force, the shogunate reluctantly signed a friendship treaty with the United States. Japan made all the concessions: American ships were to be allowed to call at Shimoda and Hakodate and to obtain coal and other supplies. Shipwrecked sailors were to be treated fairly, and the United States had the right to station a consul at Shimoda.

Perry brought gifts that displayed the wonders of the industrial revolution—a telegraph using Morse code and a quarter-size steam locomotive with carriages and track. Sailors put on a minstrel show in blackface. Men and women flocked to see the strange black ships with their steam stacks and cannon.

Portrait of American Official. This image depicts an American official who landed with Perry at Uraga bay. This woodblock print emphasizes facial features most like those of demons—large nose, red mouth with gaping teeth. *(Peabody Essex Museum, Salem, MA/Bridgeman Art Library)*

The shogunate soon found itself making further concessions. In 1856, Townsend Harris arrived as the first U.S. consul at Shimoda, to the consternation of shogunal officials, who had never expected a barbarian to live on Japan's sacred soil. A failed businessman in the China trade, Harris was determined to sign a commercial treaty with Japan. Realizing Shimoda's isolation, he bullied Japanese officials to allow him to negotiate in Edo. Fearing that delay might bring the same gunboats to Japan that had devastated China's coast, shogunal officials signed the treaty Harris wanted on July 29, 1858. According to its provisions, the two countries were to exchange diplomatic representatives.

Japan was to open six cities—Edo, Osaka, Kanagawa (later Yokohama), Hyōgo (Kōbe), Nagasaki, and Niigata—to foreign residence and trade just as the Chinese treaty ports had earlier been opened. Japan had to accept low tariffs on imported goods, whereas its own exports faced steep tariffs in the United States. Finally, Japan had to allow foreign residents and visitors the privilege of extraterritoriality. Japan soon signed similar treaties with the Netherlands, Britain, France, and Russia.

Debates on the Foreign Threat

Unnerved by the unprecedented responsibility of signing treaties with western powers, the shogunate revoked its two hundred fifty-year-old monopoly over foreign policy. In 1854 it asked leading daimyo for their opinions; in 1858 it asked the monarch Kōmei to endorse the Harris commercial treaty. In neither case was a consensus forthcoming. Worse, Kōmei rejected the treaty, urged the shogun to consult the leading daimyo, and demanded the foreigners' expulsion. When the shogunate signed the treaty against Kōmei's wishes, it was considered treasonous. People from many walks of life began to collect and debate information on political affairs. By ignoring prohibitions on discussion of contemporary events and creating a new public political realm, they helped bring about what hindsight has deemed as the last days of the shogunate.

Some voices supported engagement with the West. Sakuma Shōzan argued for a proactive policy of seeking advanced western military technology in order to strengthen Japan and of fusing western science to Japan's Confucian ethical base. Only by opening Japan to trade could it achieve the knowledge and tools it needed to compete in the emerging world order. His ideas found supporters among advisors to important daimyo such as Yokoi Shōnan, who popularized the slogan *fukoku kyōhei* (rich country, strong army), taken from a line in the Chinese classics. Both Sakuma and Yokoi died at the hands of xenophobic assassins.

The men who opposed signing treaties with the West had a rational basis for their stance. Tokugawa Nariaki believed that allowing trade with the West would weaken Japan both materially, in that Japan would lose precious metals in exchange for fripperies, and spiritually, because it would be infected by Christianity. The only way to revive Japan's martial spirit was to fight, even though it meant certain defeat. Yoshida Shōin had studied military science in Chōshū. In 1854, he opened a small school where he taught public policy under the rubric *sonnō jōi* (revere the monarch and expel the barbarian). By this he meant that the monarch should participate in policy decisions and the foreigners must be driven off. He was furious that by spinelessly signing the treaties, the shogunate had made Japan look weak in the eyes of the world.

The social networks that had previously transmitted information on agricultural innovation and the rice market now disseminated news of current events. Doctors, merchants, and samurai in Edo told friends and relatives in the countryside about Perry's arrival and the shogun's response. Their letters circulated widely, and their recipients copied their contents into diaries to discuss with like-minded neighbors. Proselytizers for the Hirata school and experts in swordsmanship linked people across domainal boundaries. Broadsheets (*kawaraban*) reported gossip on the treaty negotiations. They circulated primarily in urban areas, where they could be easily and anonymously sold, but travelers also took them back to villages. A few commoners presented plans for coastal defense to their daimyo for forwarding to the shogun. They traveled to Edo and Kyoto to see for themselves the changes taking place (see **Material Culture: Foot Traffic**).

POLITICAL TURMOIL

The shogunate found itself stymied by Kōmei's disapproval of the Harris treaty and a dispute over shogunal succession. Prodded by Satsuma,

MATERIAL CULTURE

Foot Traffic

Before the coming of the railroad, feet provided the means of locomotion for most Japanese travelers. Arising at 4:00 A.M. and moving briskly on straw sandals, they generally covered thirty miles a day before seeking an inn for the night. Occasionally a traveler rented a horse for a day's journey, but most horses carried merchandise. Boats plied the Inland Sea and Lake Biwa, carrying travelers as well as goods. Given their reputation for capsizing, many travelers preferred to walk.

The chief alternative to feet was the palanquin. These came in several sizes and styles, depending on their function and the status of the user. Most travelers rode in a wicker basket seated on a cushion, grasping a strap to keep their balance. Rural entrepreneurs transported their brides in enclosed palanquins; in cities these were reserved for the daimyo and high-ranking samurai. Most palanquins were carried by two men, with relays running in front and back.

The rickshaw superseded the palanquin. Invented in 1869 by Izumi Yōsuke, a restaurateur in Tokyo, it substituted human-powered carriages for horse-drawn coaches. Built in various sizes to carry up to four people and various designs depending on whether strength or speed was the object, rickshaws spread from Japan to China and the rest of Asia. They made unmerciful demands on human labor, but they were cheap, simple to make and repair, and nonpolluting. Nothing could beat them for short distances until the taxi arrived in 1912.

Fifty-Three Stations on the Tōkaidō. At Kusatsu, one of the fifty-three stations on the Tōkaidō depicted in woodblock prints by Hiroshige, travelers rest their weary feet. Three types of palanquins are featured in this scene. *(Tokyo National Museum/TNM Image Archives/DNPArchives.com)*

Mito, and other activist daimyo, Kōmei urged shogunal officials to appoint Nariaki's son, Hitotsubashi Yoshinobu, perceived as more capable than the man who had the strongest claim by blood, Tokugawa Iemochi. The senior councilors rejected interference in the decision that was theirs alone to make. They appointed a vassal daimyo, Ii Naosuke, regent for Iemochi and chief senior councilor. Ii purged his daimyo opponents and arrested, exiled, or executed over one hundred men employed as agents by daimyo and court nobles. In 1859, the shogunate executed Yoshida Shōin for plotting to assassinate the shogun's emissary to Kyoto. The daimyo cowed, opponents silenced, Ii asserted that the shogunate had sole responsibility for foreign affairs.

On a snowy morning in the third month of 1860, young samurai from Mito and Satsuma assassinated Ii outside Edo castle. Angry at the execution of men they revered, they believed passionately in the politics of direct action. Their deed galvanized public opinion against Ii by deeming him a traitor for having executed men of high purpose (*shishi*) whose only aim was to serve the monarch. Equally alarming, the assassins had overcome the antipathy that distanced *tozama* domains such as Satsuma from Mito, home to the shogun's relative. The shogunate abandoned its authoritarian stance for a more conciliatory posture. It proposed a union of court and military (*kōbu gattai*) that would give important *tozama* and collateral daimyo advisory positions on foreign affairs and reinstated daimyo purged by Ii. It sealed the deal by having Shogun Iemochi wed Kōmei's younger half-sister, Kazunomiya, in return for a promise to expel the barbarians.

Within this framework of cooperation, a number of self-styled able daimyo called for national reforms to match the military reforms they had carried out at home. They urged the shogunate to employ men of talent and ability, regardless of their domainal affiliation, promote the study of western technology, and strengthen the nation's defenses. To fund these goals, the shogunate agreed to cut its expenses, reduce the daimyo's attendance in Edo to one hundred days every three years, and permit the daimyo to take their families held hostage in Edo to their domains. Women and servants had to abandon the only city they had ever known for life in provincial backwaters.

The *shishi* demanded immediate expulsion of the barbarians in accordance with Kōmei's wishes. Young and reckless, they absconded from their domains to study swordsmanship in Edo and Kyoto and imbibe the ideas of Aizawa Seishisai and Yoshida Shōin. Filled with the Japanese spirit (*Yamato damashii*), they swaggered through the streets, less concerned with personal grooming than with purity of purpose. As soon as Yokohama opened as a treaty port in 1859, they launched a reign of terror against foreign merchants, sailors, and officials. (See Color Plate 26.) Following Kazunomiya's marriage, *shishi* in Kyoto assassinated advisers to the daimyo and nobles they held responsible.

Monarch, shogun, and daimyo feared that the *shishi*'s antics would so weaken the established political order as to invite foreign invasion. Satsuma forced its radicals to return home in disgrace. When *shishi* tried to capture the palace in the eighth month of 1863, planning to place Kōmei at the head of an army to unite western Japan under the slogan of "Restore monarchical rule," Satsuma allied with shogunal forces to drive them from Kyoto. Many fled to Chōshū. The daimyo of Tosa forced *shishi* in his domain to leave or commit suicide. *Shishi*-led uprisings in the foothills of Yamato and at Ikuno near the Japan Sea were brutally suppressed. Conflict between radical expulsionists and conservatives in Mito erupted in civil war. In the seventh month of 1864, Chōshū *shishi* returned to Kyoto with supporters from other domains and rural militia in tow. Once again, the shogunate routed them.

The exploits performed by *shishi* had less impact on policy than on public opinion. They dramatized the monarchy's cause and ruptured the alliance between shogun and court. But how significant was the expansion of a public political sphere based on the discussion and exchange of information given that 60 percent of the population was illiterate? Most commoners remained bystanders because they lacked an organizational structure to mobilize effectively. Historians who claim that commoners remained quiescent during the years leading to the Meiji Restoration and therefore it cannot be deemed a revolution from below overlook a similar inertia in the ruling class. Most daimyo did nothing, either because they sided with the shogun out of loyalty and self-interest, he being the ultimate guarantor of their office, or because opposing factions had gridlocked domainal administration. Most samurai remained embedded in the vertical hierarchy predicated on loyalty and obedience to their lord. They had less to do with the eventual outcome than rural entrepreneurs who provided supplies to traveling *shishi,* enlisted their tenants in rural militia, and supported the monarchical cause or the shogunate with their pocketbooks.

THE FALL OF THE SHOGUNATE

The *shishi's* attacks on foreigners and shogunal forces had unforeseen consequences. The British demanded that the men from Satsuma responsible for killing a British merchant be turned over to them and an indemnity paid. When Satsuma refused, British ships bombarded Kagoshima in the seventh month of 1863. For all its military reforms, Satsuma was still no match for foreign gunboats. In the eleventh month, it signed a peace treaty, acceding to British demands. In compliance with Kōmei's decree that the barbarians be expelled in the fifth month of 1863, Chōshū gunners fired on French and American ships in the straits of Shimonoseki. In the eighth month of 1864, the foreigners retaliated. These salutary lessons were not lost on their victims. Both Satsuma and Chōshū began to rebuild their military along western lines. Just days before foreign ships attacked Chōshū, the shogunate had it branded an enemy of the court for harboring *shishi* and sent a coalition of daimyo troops to its borders. Chōshū backed down. It

apologized for its misdeeds, expelled radical court nobles who had sought refuge there in 1863, and executed three high-ranking officials. The shogunate declared victory and withdrew its forces.

The shogunate had less success controlling the consequences of foreign trade. Beginning in 1859, foreign merchants in the treaty ports at Nagasaki and Yokohama discovered that the silver-to-gold ratio in Japan was one-third what it was in the West, meaning that any man with silver in his pockets could buy gold at ludicrously low prices. The gold rush ended only when the shogunate recoined and devalued gold, silver, and copper. When it granted daimyo permission to mint money, counterfeiters flooded the market, and inflation soared. Foreign merchants bought tea and silk in exchange for weapons, making gunrunning a lucrative enterprise, but also leading to a sudden expansion in cash crops on rice paddies. Weavers lost work because they could not compete with foreigners for silk thread. In the summer of 1866, rising unemployment, crop failures, inflation, and shogunal efforts to tax trade created the conditions for the most widespread riots in Edo history, particularly in the shogun's stronghold of eastern Japan.

The shogunate hoped to use new taxes levied on foreign trade to subsidize its military modernization program. It imported thousands of weapons through Yokohama and drilled its retainer band in rifle companies supplemented by rural recruits. It sent missions abroad. The first in 1860 signed a friendship treaty with the United States; subsequent envoys emphasized the study of foreign technology. In 1861 it opened a naval training school at Hyōgo. In 1865 it started an ironworks at Yokohama and a shipyard at Yokosuka. It also received Kōmei's sanction for signing foreign treaties, and it marginalized the *tozama* daimyo by excluding them from policy making circles.

The shogunate's revitalization campaign destabilized the balance of power with the daimyo. When it announced a second punitive campaign against Chōshū because *shishi* had returned to

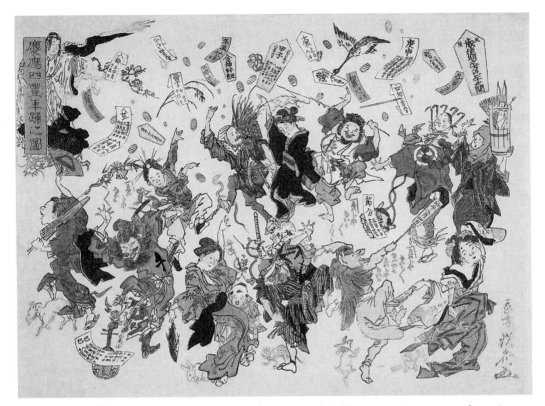

Ee ja nai ka. As amulets fall from the sky, men, women, and children, some in costume, dance in thanksgiving, shouting, "ain't it great" (*Ee ja nai ka*). *(National Diet Library, Tokyo, Japan)*

positions of power, it pushed former enemies together. Chōshū and Satsuma formed an alliance in the first month of 1866. Both had launched self-strengthening programs, using emergency funds to buy arms through Nagasaki, sending retainers on fact-finding missions abroad, and organizing western-style armies. Now they argued that the shogunate ought not move against Chōshū when pressing domestic and foreign problems remained to be solved. Few domains responded to the shogun's call, riots in Edo and Osaka tied down garrisons, and the attack on Chōshū ended in ignominious defeat. Iemochi's death at just that juncture provided the shogunate with a face-saving out. But when Kōmei died unexpectedly just five months later, the shogunate lost its strongest supporter at court. Unlike the shogun's opponents who had come to believe that Japan should have but a sin-

gle monarch, Kōmei supported the division of powers that left administrative and foreign affairs in the shogun's hands.

Hitotsubashi Yoshinobu reigned as shogun for less than a year. At first he moved vigorously to reassert shogunal authority and continue military reforms. His efforts stirred up turmoil and strengthened the alliance against him. In the eighth month of 1867, a new popular movement swept the coast from the inland sea to Edo. Claiming that amulets inscribed with the name of the sun goddess that portended a prosperous future had fallen from heaven, men and women danced in the streets chanting, "Ain't it great" (*ee ja nai ka*). When the movement reached eastern Japan, dancers threw stones at foreigners to drive out the barbarian demons and rehearsed a mock funeral for the shogunate. In the tenth month, the court issued a secret decree to Satsuma and Chōshū to overthrow the Tokugawa. Realizing he could no longer fulfill the duties of shogun, Yoshinobu returned his patent of office to the monarch. The restoration of monarchical rule was at hand.

In the name of the Meiji emperor, Kōmei's fifteen-year old son, leaders of the Sat-chō forces abolished the offices of shogun and regent and replaced them with new advisory positions open to daimyo, court nobles, and "men of talent." They declared Yoshinobu a traitor to the emperor, revoked his court rank, and confiscated his family lands. When the shogunate fought back, it was defeated after four days of heavy fighting outside Kyoto in the first days of 1868. The imperial armies moved slowly north, hamstrung for lack of cash, which they tried to ameliorate by demanding loans from wealthy commoners. The long-standing animosity between eastern and western Japan prolonged the fighting until Aizu fell in the ninth month, after suffering heavy casualties of men and women. The last stronghold of shogunal support at Hakodate did not surrender until the middle of 1869, supported to the last by the American envoy. Both official and popular opinion feared that prolonged civil war might give foreign troops an excuse to invade Japan. A better alternative was to unite around the new emperor. Although many retainers died, Yoshinobu and the daimyo of Aizu survived to take their places in the new imperial peerage and join their efforts to the task of strengthening state and economy to compete in the new world order. Hirata disciples and other imperial loyalists rushed to offer their services to the new government; people in Edo watched warily as their old masters were replaced with new.

SUMMARY

Long before the Meiji Restoration, the social and political order crafted in the seventeenth century had ceased to fit everyday practice. The commercial economy, opportunities for travel, and information networks eroded the status and geographical divisions that kept people in their place. Reforms by shogun and daimyo to shore up their authority and fill government coffers could not rectify the gap between reality and their ideal of the proper relations between rulers and commoners. Debates over how to deal with the foreign threat added further strain to the system. When it collapsed in 1867, it left behind a dynamic economy, a large pool of able administrators, and a population well educated for its time.

SUGGESTED READING

Many books have been written on the fall of the shogunate. The most recent include G. M. Wilson, *Patriots and Redeemers in Japan: Motives in the Meiji Restoration* (1992), and A. Walthall, *The Weak Body of a Useless Woman: Matsuo Taseko and the Meiji Restoration* (1998). For a collection of essays focused on the nineteenth century, see M. B. Jansen, ed., *Cambridge History of Japan*, vol. 5 (1989).

For nativism see H. D. Harootunian, *Things Seen and Unseen: Discourse and Ideology in Tokugawa Nativism* (1988). For popular culture, see N.-L. Hur, *Prayer and Play in Late Tokugawa Japan: Asakusa Sensōji and Edo Society* (2000). For Mito, see J. Victor Koschmann, *The Mito Ideology: Discourse, Reform and Insurrection in Late Tokugawa Japan, 1790–1864* (1987), and K. Yamakawa, *Women of the Mito Domain: Recollections of Samurai Family Life,* trans. K. W. Nakai (1992). For an entertaining look at samurai life, see K. Katsu, *Musui's Story: The Autobiography of a Tokugawa Samurai,* trans. T. Craig (1988).

Meiji Transformation (1868–1900)

The restoration of the Meiji emperor as head of state marked the beginning of profound changes in Japanese politics, culture, and society. A small group of self-selected men, who had led the drive to overthrow the shogun, implemented programs to abolish status distinctions that had compartmentalized social groups and to centralize government. Fearful of the West, they acknowledged the necessity of importing western military technology, industry, legal norms, constitutional thought, science, dress, and food. (See **Material Culture: New Food for a New Nation.**) They built railroads, shipyards, and schools. They propounded a new ideology to rally the citizens. They colonized the Ryukyu Islands and Hokkaido. They projected Japan's power abroad in Taiwan and Korea and renegotiated treaties. They faced considerable opposition, often from within their own ranks. Farmers rioted against new state policies that threatened their livelihood; samurai rebelled at the loss of their traditional identity. Local notables promoted democracy. Intellectuals, novelists, and essayists hammered out new identities that refused to fit a single pattern. By the end of the century, modernity had arrived.

To what extent did changes in the latter half of the nineteenth century build on what had gone before? Did the Meiji Restoration herald a revolution in politics and society, or simply a transition? Did modernization mean westernization?

THE MEIJI STATE

The oligarchs who created the institutions for a centralized government had little idea of what they hoped to accomplish and disagreed on what

MATERIAL CULTURE

New Food for a New Nation

Although rice had been grown in Japan since the third century B.C.E., it did not become a staple of the average Japanese diet until imported from Korea and China starting in 1873. Before that, most people ate wheat, barley, and millet. Between 1869 and 1900, the per capita consumption of rice went from 3.5 bushels a year to 5.0 bushels a year. Rice balls became ubiquitous in lunch boxes, and except for the poor, steamed rice replaced rice gruel for breakfast.

The Meiji government officially promoted the eating of meat because it was thought to produce stronger workers and soldiers. In 1869 it established the Tsukiji beef company. In 1871, a butcher shop in Tokyo's Asakusa district became popular selling beef for sukiyaki, a Meiji period invention, as well as milk, cheese, and butter. In the 1880s, butcher shops started selling horse meat. It was cheaper than beef or pork and redder than chicken.

Vegetables, fruits, and breads had a harder sell. Asparagus, cabbage, cauliflower, and tomatoes did not blend easily into Japanese cuisine. Importing apples, peaches, and grapes stimulated the cultivation and spread of indigenous fruits such as persimmon, Satsuma tangerine, and Asian pear. Bread and cakes became popular only after they were modified to suit Japanese taste.

Aguranabe. This flyer advertising Aguranabe, a butcher show, linked eating beef to "civilization and enlightenment." *(Tokyo Metropolitan Foundation for History and Culture/ DNPArchives.com)*

By selectively adapting western foods, Japanese people developed a much more varied diet than they had had in the past. They ate more, and what they ate was more nutritious. An improved diet made them stronger and healthier. It increased life expectancy and childbearing rates. A population of approximately 33 million at midcentury had grown to 45 million by the end of the nineteenth century.

to do. An amorphous group of samurai from Satsuma and Chōshū, plus a few activist Kyoto aristocrats and imperial loyalists from other domains, they had diverse interests and goals. Their first pronouncement came in the Oath of 1868, offered by the emperor in the company of court nobles and daimyo to the gods of heaven and earth. In it he promised that everyone was to unite in promoting the nation's well-being, government policy was to be decided through public discussion, all would be allowed to fulfill their just aspirations, "the uncivilized customs of former times shall be broken through," and "intellect and learning shall be sought throughout the world in order to establish the foundations of the Empire."[1] The Five Injunctions issued to commoners the next day had a different message. It ordered them to practice the Confucian virtues of

---

1. Donald L. Keene, *Emperor of Japan: Meiji and His World, 1852–1912* (New York: Columbia University Press, 2002), p. 139.

loyalty, filial piety, chastity, obedience, and harmony; to desist demonstrations and protests; to abjure Christianity; to conform to international public law; and to stay in Japan. Emigration to the United States began almost immediately.

Ambiguities in the oath speak to the lack of agreement on national goals. The nation's well-being could justify a national land tax and universal military conscription; it could require promoting entrepreneurship and compulsory education. None of the men present envisioned public discussion of national affairs to include anyone but themselves. In the context of the past, in which each daimyo had set policy for his domain, it meant that decisions and power were to be centralized. It did not mean parliamentary democracy, although it was later interpreted that way. The third clause implied that hereditary status distinctions would be abolished and held out the promise of social mobility. Abolishing old customs acknowledged the reality of cultural imperialism inherent in international law and unequal treaties. The purpose of gaining knowledge was to serve the state.

At first, the oligarchs looked to eighth-century models for a new government. The Council of State became the highest deliberative body. It was assisted by a board of 106 advisers, the activists in the Meiji Restoration, who made the real decisions. The Council of Shinto Affairs enjoyed a brief existence equal to the Council of State. This structure was reorganized four times in the next four months. Most daimyo remained in control of their domains, leaving the oligarchs who spoke in the emperor's name only the former shogun's lands. Monetary proof of support for the emperor from daimyo, former shogunal retainers, merchants, and rural entrepreneurs staved off fiscal crisis in the short run. The necessity of finding sufficient tax revenues to fund the government forced the oligarchs to take hesitant steps toward centralization.

Centralization required convincing the daimyo to give up their domains. Some daimyo hoped to play a larger role in national affairs; some concentrated their efforts on self-strengthening. Most stayed aloof from the court and isolated from each other. In 1869, the daimyo of Satsuma and Chōshū agreed to make a formal declaration of returning their land and population registers to the emperor, with the understanding that he would then confirm their holdings as governors. The government put all domainal retainers above the level of foot soldiers into one general category called former samurai (*shizoku*). To eliminate the redundancies of two hundred seventy independent domain administrations and centralize tax collection, the oligarchs in 1871 abolished the domains and established prefectures (see Map 21.1). They started the process of consolidating one hundred seventy thousand towns and villages into larger administrative units with a new hierarchy of local officials and inaugurated a household registration system whereby each household head had to establish a place of legal residence and inform the government of births, deaths, marriages, and divorces in his family.

The daimyo accepted the loss of their hereditary lands with equanimity. The most important became prefectural governors. Since the number of prefectures was seventy-two, later reduced to fifty, the area under their control expanded. All daimyo benefited by no longer having responsibility for their domains' debts and being guaranteed a substantial income for their personal use. They did not have to support standing armies of retainers. In place of their former titles, they received court rank. In return for giving up their already circumscribed autonomy, they received wealth and prestige.

Abolishing domains disinherited roughly 2 million *shizoku*. All they received were small stipends later commuted to government bonds. The oligarchs urged them to find another line of work, in agriculture, forestry, business, and the colonization of Hokkaido. Some succeeded; many did not. Former shogunal bureaucrats staffed the new government offices, but most domain samurai remained in castle towns. Political power had become sufficiently bureaucratized over the course of the Edo period that neither samurai nor daimyo became landed gentry.

Having taken the first steps toward a more centralized state, in 1871 one faction of the oli-

Map 21.1   Modern Japan

garchs left for the United States and Europe. Forty-nine officials and fifty-eight students, including five girls, made up the delegation. Headed by Iwakura Tomomi, a former court noble, their goal was to convince the western powers to revise the unequal treaties that infringed on Japanese sovereignty. Informed by President Ulysses S. Grant that western powers would never consent to treaty revision unless Japan reformed its laws and institutions along western lines, the diplomatic mission became a study mission. Wealth and power that the West had created through industrialization and centralized political institutions came as a shock. Officials inspected prisons, schools, factories, and government agencies. They expected their absence to preclude any initiatives by the leaders left behind; in 1873 when Saigō Takamori proposed to invade Korea for having insulted the emperor in the first diplomatic exchange following the restoration, they rushed home to stop him. They opposed not the use of force but its timing. Domestic reform had to precede military engagements abroad.

Reforms and Opposition

The abolition of domains took place in the context of social reforms that did not suit everyone. For many farmers, the emperor's progress from Kyoto to Edo (renamed Tokyo in 1869) in 1868 symbolized the Meiji Restoration. This, they felt, would usher in new prosperity and social justice. Instead, village officials continued to collect taxes, rents remained the same, and moneylenders charged exorbitant interest. Disappointment fueled the rage with which rural and urban people punished what they saw as wrongdoing. When the new government replaced familiar faces in domain administrations with men from foreign parts, this too led to protest, as did the official end to discrimination against outcasts when status distinctions were erased and the outcasts became "new commoners." The first ten years of the Meiji period saw more protest and more violence than at any time during the Edo period.

Bureaucrats initiated reforms and technological innovations to strengthen the state against its domestic and foreign enemies. They hired western experts to transform government, economy, infrastructure, and education. Drawing on western models, they issued civil and criminal codes that replaced different regulations for different statuses with rule by law that considered only the nature of the crime. They built telegraph lines and railroads to improve communications and foster unity. On January 1, 1873, they replaced the lunar calendar that farmers had used as a guide to planting and harvesting with the western calendar. They outlawed traditional hairstyles for men and suppressed village festivals. They issued these laws and directives without warning or explanation. In defense of time-honored custom, farmers rioted.

Religious practices also provoked controversy. In the third month of 1868, the oligarchs ordered the separation of Shinto and Buddhism and the conversion of what had been shrine-temple complexes into shrines by eliminating Buddhist icons, rituals, and priests. In some regions officials infected with Hirata Atsutane's doctrines destroyed Buddhist temples where the farmers' ancestral tablets were kept. The establishment of Yasukuni shrine to the war dead in 1869 used Shinto to promote national goals. The development of State Shinto in the 1870s consolidated local shrines and brought them into a hierarchy with the Ise shrine to the sun goddess at the top. Rather than shrines containing only deities particular to their region, they had to accept deities of national significance in addition. New religions founded in the Edo period received official recognition as Sect Shinto. Meiji period new religions were viewed with suspicion, if not proscribed outright. (See **Biography: Deguchi Nao.**) Farmers protested the destruction of their familiar temples, and Buddhist priests fought back by associating Buddhism with anti-Christian sentiment, recalling ties to the imperial house, and helping immigrants in Hokkaido.

The directives that had immediate effects and aroused the strongest opposition dealt with education, the military, and taxes. In 1872, the government decreed eight years of compulsory education for all children (shortened to four in 1879 and then increased to six in 1907) to fit them for their responsibilities as productive citizens in a modern nation. Communities had to pay for schools themselves. Enraged at the cost, farmers destroyed or damaged nearly two hundred schools between 1873 and 1877. Pre-Meiji teachers continued their unlicensed schools and dissuaded parents from sending their children to new ones. Needing their child's labor or unable to afford tuition, many parents never enrolled daughters or even sons or allowed them to attend only a few months. Over time, compliance increased until it reached 90 percent in the twentieth century.

The slogan of the day was "Rich Country, Strong Army." In January 1873 the government issued the conscription ordinance that summoned all males over the age of twenty to serve three years on active duty in the armed forces,

BIOGRAPHY Deguchi Nao

Women have played a major role in the founding of Japan's new religions; Deguchi Nao (1836–1918), an illiterate commoner, became a prophet.

Nao was born in a castle town near Kyoto to a family in declining circumstances. Her grandfather had the privilege of wearing a sword and using a surname as an official carpenter. Her father squandered his life on drink; he died when she was nine. Nao went to work for a merchant who provided her with room and board. Her earnings went to her mother. Nao helped with the cooking and cleaning; she spun thread and strung coins, thereby gaining a reputation for diligence and hard work. In her third year of service, the domain awarded her a prize for being a filial daughter.

Nao hoped to marry the man she loved, but her widowed aunt Yuri insisted that she accept an arranged marriage and be adopted into the Deguchi family as Yuri herself had done. Yuri drowned herself after Nao repeatedly rejected her offer. A few days later Nao developed a high fever and lost consciousness. Upon her recovery, she attributed her illness to Yuri's vengeful spirit. To placate it and care for the Deguchi ancestral tablets, Nao agreed to marry the man Yuri had selected for her and continue the Deguchi house.

Nao's husband was no better than her father. By 1872 she had borne five children and was living in a rented house in Ayabe. She opened a small restaurant, and when it failed she sold sweet-bean buns. She continued to have children—eleven in all, three of whom died in infancy. When her husband became paralyzed from a fall off a roof in 1885, Nao collected rags to support her family. His death in 1887 freed her to work in a filature as well.

One winter morning in 1892 as she was out collecting rags, Nao became possessed by a god. The experience transformed her personality and her outlook on the world. Instead of being gentle and deferential, she became dignified, filled with divinely inspired authority. She rejected the social order because it rewarded vice and valued money. Since the oligarchs and the emperor were responsible for these conditions, they exemplified absolute evil. They would soon be destroyed and replaced by a divine order of harmony and equality. Under the spell of her god, this formerly illiterate woman wrote hundreds of texts that spelled out what was wrong with the world and what was to come. She also became a faith healer. In 1899, her adopted son Deguchi Onisaburō organized a sect called Ōmoto-kyō based on her revelations. Under his leadership, the group grew rapidly and suffered repeated government persecutions. Nao quarreled with him over his interpretation of her writings and his refusal to reject all that was modern. She died frustrated that she had not been able to reconstruct the world in accordance with her beliefs.

Source: Based on Emily Groszos Ooms, *Women and Millenarian Protest in Meiji Japan: Deguchi Nao and Ōmoto-kyō* (Ithaca, N.Y.: East Asia Program Cornell University, 1993).

followed by four years in the reserves. In accord with the French system, heads and heirs of family farms and businesses received exemptions, and exemptions could be purchased. Its architect was Yamagata Aritomo from Chōshū, who had spent 1869–1870 in Europe studying French and German conscript armies. The conscription ordinance put Japan's defense on the shoulders of the masses. It provided a way to educate conscripts and their families in the goals of government leaders. By revoking the samurai's monopoly of force, it did more than any other reform to eliminate status distinctions and create equality of opportunity.

Both farmers and *shizoku* opposed conscription. The ordinance used the term "blood tax," meaning that all citizens should willingly sacrifice themselves for their country. Farmers who took it literally assumed that the government wanted their blood. Even those who understood the message believed that farmers could best contribute to the nation by growing crops. Commoners opposed to conscription rose up in sixteen localities in the months after the ordinance's promulgation. Samurai opposition took longer to develop but cost more lives. Conservative oligarchs such as Saigō Takamori had already insisted that the national army be composed of the men bred to military service. When Iwakura and his faction outvoted Saigō on whether to invade Korea, he left the government. In 1876, the government ordered *shizoku* to stop wearing the two swords that distinguished them from the rest of the population. Between 1874 and 1877, over thirty rebellions erupted in defense of samurai privilege. The largest and last, in Satsuma, led by Saigō, required the mobilization of sixty-five thousand troops and took eight months to suppress. Saigō committed suicide. In 1878 samurai counterrevolution ended with the assassination of the oligarch Ōkubo Toshimichi, also from Satsuma, because he had opposed invading Korea and arbitrarily initiated reforms.

The Satsuma rebels had had reason to oppose the 1873 tax law. Applied nationwide to agricultural land, its aim was to provide a steady flow of income for the government by replacing the old hodgepodge of domain taxes on fluctuating harvests with a single, uniform property tax. In most regions of Japan, the land surveys that accompanied the new tax simply confirmed de facto proprietary rights farmers already enjoyed. Satsuma domain had allowed *gōshi* (rustic warriors) to assign land to the cultivators and treat them like tenant farmers. Faced with the loss of income as well as hereditary status and privilege, *gōshi* became the shock troops for the Satsuma rebellion.

Even though the Meiji oligarchs tried to promote industry and demanded loans from merchants, they had an agrarian mind-set. Nearly 80 percent of the government's revenues came from tax on agricultural land through the 1880s. Farmers with market access for their products benefited; those who misjudged the market or suffered a crop failure had to sell their land to pay taxes. In some areas, officials imposed the new tax while requiring farmers to continue to pay ancillary taxes it was supposed

Composition of Tax Revenues, 1872–1940 (%)									
Fiscal Year	Land Tax	Liquor Tax	Customs Duties	Income Tax	Corporation Tax	Business Tax	Sugar Excise	Inheritance Tax	Other
1872	90.1	1.5	3.3	—	—	—	—	—	5.1
1880	72.3	14.9	4.4	—	—	—	—	—	8.4
1890	58.1	22.9	6.9	1.6	—	—	—	—	10.5
1900	34.6	38.0	10.9	4.3	1.2	3.9	1.3	—	5.8
1910	23.8	26.2	15.3	10.0	2.9	7.0	5.1	0.9	8.8
1920	10.2	22.6	11.1	23.5	11.8	6.6	6.8	1.1	6.3
1930	7.9	26.4	15.1	22.1	6.6	6.2	9.6	3.5	2.6
1940	0.9	8.9	2.9	34.0	11.7	2.6	3.2	1.6	33.9

Source: Based on Minami Ryōshin, *The Economic Development of Japan: A Quantitative Study,* trans. Ralph Thompson and Minami with assistance from David Merriman (New York: St. Martin's Press, 1986), p. 340.

to replace. Farmers petitioned for redress; they killed officials suspected of being corrupt. In 1876 widespread, if uncoordinated, opposition to the tax forced the government to reduce it from 3 percent of assessed value to 2.5 percent.

While dealing with opposition from outside the government, oligarchs also quarreled among themselves. They created and abolished ministries to consolidate their power or deny a rival and disputed what kind of government Japan was to have. In the early 1870s, Kido Takayoshi and Ōkubo advocated some measure of popular representation in government lest arbitrary rule generate unrest. Their proposal contained a veiled attack on Itō Hirobumi and Yamagata. Disgruntled at having been shut out of power, Itagaki Taisuke left the government in 1874, joined with disaffected *shizoku* from his home domain of Tosa to form the Patriotic Party, and petitioned the government to establish an elected national assembly. He disbanded the party when he was invited back into the government in 1875 at the Osaka Conference. There, the oligarchs agreed to establish prefectural assemblies (done in 1878) and plan for a national assembly. Four months later, the emperor announced that he would promulgate a constitution after due deliberation.

Constitution and National Assembly

The publicity attracted by the promise of a national assembly and a constitution stimulated responses that coalesced into the Popular Rights Movement. *Shizoku,* village officials, rural entrepreneurs, journalists, intellectuals, and prefectural assemblymen held lengthy meetings and circulated petitions for an immediate national assembly that collected hundreds of thousands of signatures. Radicals and impoverished farmers rioted and planned attacks on the government in the name of human rights. A woman who held property demanded she be allowed to vote in prefectural elections (she was denied). Kishida Toshiko and Fukuda Hideko gave public lectures at which they demanded rights, liberty, education, and equality for women. Baba Tatsui drew on social Darwinism to argue that since democracy based on an egalitarian society was the most advanced form of government, it should be established forthwith. Local notables drafted model constitutions. Activists criticized the oligarchs for blocking communication between emperor and people. They argued that a representative government would harmonize imperial and popular will by providing a forum for the free expression of popular opinion, thereby strengthening the nation. Drawing on the natural rights theories propounded by French and British philosophers, Ueki Emori propounded a theory of popular sovereignty and right of revolution.

The oligarchs responded to the Popular Rights Movement by issuing increasingly draconian peace preservation laws. Press censorship began in 1875; the 1880 Ordinance on Public Meetings stationed policemen at assemblies to ensure that the speakers did not deviate from texts that had been approved beforehand. Excluded from audiences were soldiers, off-duty police, teachers, and students. Demonstrations in Fukushima opposed to a particularly arbitrary governor in 1882, the Chichibu uprising of 1884 that mobilized tenant farmers in demanding debt relief, and other violent incidents met with mass arrests and executions. Having learned the cost of direct action, local notables turned to organizing political parties in anticipation of the first election for the national assembly promised in 1890.

The Meiji Constitution defined institutions established before its promulgation. In 1878 the military General Staff was made directly responsible to the emperor, bypassing the War Ministry run by bureaucrats. A new peerage destined to fill the upper house of the bicameral national assembly known as the Diet was announced in 1884. It included oligarchs, former daimyo, and Kyoto nobility. Over time it expanded to include entrepreneurs and academics. The lower house was to be elected by commoners. The highest policymaking institution, the cabinet, replaced the Council of State in 1885. It was composed of ministers in charge of education, finance, foreign affairs, and other bureaucracies under the prime minister appointed by the emperor.

Itō Hirobumi drafted the constitution in great secrecy. He traveled to Europe in 1882 where he studied nine months in Berlin under the most respected constitutional theorists of his day. Itō and his brain trust then created a document that defined the emperor in terms of his descent from the gods and employed western notions regarding the rights and obligations of citizens. Once they had finished, a new institution, the Privy Council, headed by Itō, met to discuss it. On February 11, 1889, the date chosen to be the anniversary of Jimmu's accession 2,349 years earlier, the Meiji emperor bestowed the constitution on the prime minister. Three days of festivities announced to people across the nation that they were now citizens of a state founded on principles enshrined in a constitution.

The oligarchs wanted a constitution that secured the governing bodies and protected the imperial house through which they exercised power, and they mistrusted the "ignorant" masses. After its promulgation, they designated themselves *genrō*, elder statesmen, charged with picking cabinet ministers for the emperor. The constitution defined the emperor as sovereign and sacred. The emperor:

- exercises executive power through the cabinet
- exercises legislative power with the consent of the Imperial Diet
- has supreme command of the army and navy
- declares war, makes peace, and concludes treaties
- determines the organization of the government
- convokes the Diet and dissolves the lower house

Subjects had these rights and duties:

- present petitions, provided that they observe the proper form of respect

- within limits not prejudicial to peace and order, and not antagonistic to their duties as subjects, enjoy freedom of religious belief
- enjoy freedom of speech, within the limits set by law[2]

Subjects had to serve in the military, a clause that excluded women from the category of subject.

Japan's first experiment with parliamentary democracy nearly did not work. Although Itō and Yamagata had assumed that party politics had no place in an institution directly responsible to the emperor, they had to deal with opposition parties headed by Itagaki and other men who had been ejected from the oligarch's inner circle. Suffrage was limited to men paying at least 15 yen a year in property taxes, a qualification met by only 1.1 percent of the population, most of them in rural areas. Once elected, members discovered that the Diet had more power than the oligarchs had intended. Diet members could criticize the cabinet in memorials to the emperor; they could make speeches, published in newspapers, that outside the Diet might have landed them in jail. They had the power to approve the budget. If they refused, the previous year's budget remained in effect, but it seldom sufficed for the government's needs. When the Diet stood up to the cabinet, the prime minister dissolved it, forcing members into costly reelection campaigns. Campaign finance scandals and vote buying tarnished the reputations of politicians and oligarchs alike. Twenty-five men died during the 1892 election, most at the hands of the police.

Divided by personality, political preference, and self-interest, the oligarchs had to seek political support outside their narrow circle. In so doing, they enlarged the realm of political actors to include bureaucrats, military officers, and politicians. In 1898 Itō had the quasi-oligarchs, Ōkuma Shigenobu, head of the Progressive Party, and Itagaki Taisuke, leader of the Liberal Party,

---

2. Hugh Borton, *Japan's Modern Century* (New York: Ronald Press Co., 1955), pp. 490–507.

Triptych Showing Inauguration of the First Diet. Members of the upper house dressed in uniform are in the foreground; lower house members sit farther back. The emperor is in the box at upper left. *(Museum of Fine Arts, Boston. Jean S. and Frederic A. Sharf Collection, 2000.535)*

participate in a coalition cabinet as prime minister and home minister, respectively. Aghast at this concession to politicians, Yamagata Aritomo sabotaged their cabinet by having the army minister refuse to accept cuts in the military budget. A few months later, Yamagata became prime minister for the second time. To increase military autonomy, he made it a requirement that all army and navy ministers be active-duty officers. To dilute the power of political parties and their resistance to higher taxes, he expanded the suffrage to 2.2 percent of the population and gave more representation to urban districts. In 1900 Itō responded by forming and becoming president of a new political party, the Friends of Government (*Seiyūkai*). His compromise with politicians dramatized the oligarchs' difficulty in controlling the institutions they had created.

Industrialization

The oligarchs promoted economic reform and industrialization. They appropriated the arms-related industries already established by the domains and the shogunate. Some came under state control to supply the military; others were sold at favorable terms to cronies. Iwasaki Yatarō founded Mitsubishi enterprises on the maritime shipping line he acquired from Tosa and expanded it with low-interest government loans. The oligarchs had foreign experts write banking laws; they set up banks and issued paper currency. Their initial investments were in advanced and expensive technologies, the kind needed to build railroads and shipyards. Although building support industries for the military constituted their first priority, they also worried about the effects of unequal treaties on the balance of payments and unemployment. To maintain social stability and to compete with foreign products, they built cotton spinning and weaving factories to make cloth for domestic consumption and imported French silk spinning technology to produce thread for export. They founded a sugar refinery to help growers market their crop and compete with Chinese sugar. By bringing the state's resources to bear on industry, the oligarchs squeezed out private capital.

Agriculture supported industrial growth. Agricultural development groups, seed exchange

Steam Engine. The steam engine epitomized the industrial age. Its use on the railroad that paralleled the Tōkaidō eliminated palanquins and most foot traffic. *(Yokohama Archives of History)*

societies, journals, and lecture circuits taught farmers about new seed varieties, commercial fertilizers, and equipment. Without expanding the amount of arable land, annual agricultural productivity rose between 1.5 and 1.7 percent in the late nineteenth century. Since the land tax remained fixed, the increase put more income into the hands of rural entrepreneurs for use in promoting small-scale industry. Farmers were already accustomed to producing handicrafts; the elimination of internal restrictions on trade made it easier for them to market their goods.

Entrepreneurs and artisans developed intermediate technologies that adapted western machines to Japanese circumstances. They modified the manufacture of new daily necessities such as matches to suit the domestic and Asian markets and undersold western brands. The metric system, the new calendar, and western timepieces brought the standardization and regularization modeled by military organization to ordinary work practices. Local clubs tried to preserve handicrafts in the face of foreign imports and sought national and international markets for specialty products. They pooled capital to upgrade indigenous skills, brought in foreign

technology when it fit their needs, and hosted industrial exhibitions to diffuse technological knowledge and stimulate competition. In the mid-1870s, small water-powered filatures spread throughout the mountain valleys of central Japan, close to the silk-producing regions and a work force of young women. By 1900 silk thread accounted for one-third of the value of Japan's commodity exports and textiles totaled over half.

Another model for private enterprise was Shibusawa Eiichi. The son of a rural entrepreneur, he used his connections with oligarchs to become president of the First National Bank. In that capacity he provided capital for the construction of a privately owned shipyard at the mouth of Tokyo Bay. In 1880 he started the Osaka Spinning Mill and went on to found more than one hundred companies. Thanks to investments like his, Japan's imports by the beginning of the twentieth century were of raw materials; it exported manufactured goods. Other entrepreneurs built equipment for railroads, mines, and factories. Many thrived with the government as their biggest customer. They justified their immense wealth by insisting that they worked for the good of the nation.

In 1880 the government faced financial disaster. It had printed money recklessly during the 1870s to finance its projects, and private banks issued their own notes. It spent heavily suppressing *shizoku* rebellions and other police actions; most of the industries it built operated at a loss. Inflation that doubled the price of rice in Tokyo between 1877 and 1880 reduced the value of property tax revenues, and taxes did not cover expenditures. The negative balance of payments sucked gold and silver out of the country. From an economic point of view, Japan faced the most serious crisis of the Meiji period.

After acrimonious debate, the oligarchs decided on a deflationary policy of retrenchment. Finance Minister Matsukata Masayoshi balanced the budget, reduced government expenditures until they fell within revenues, and established a sound currency backed by gold and silver. Except for railroad, telegraph, and military-related industries, he sold at a loss all industries that the government had tried to develop. He recalled students sent abroad on government scholarships, fired foreign experts, enacted sin taxes on tobacco and sake, and increased old taxes. Between 1881 and 1885, he reduced the quantity of currency by 20 percent and stifled commerce. Farmers who saw the price of rice fall 50 percent while taxes remained the same worked longer hours to increase production. Bad loans bankrupted banks started with samurai capital. Small businesses collapsed. The ranks of tenant farmers and factory workers swelled. By 1886 key industries had become concentrated in the hands of a few wealthy capitalists with excellent government connections. The government had rid itself of drains on its income, the budget was balanced, and prices were stable.

By the 1890s Japan had a substantial work force in light and heavy industry. Filatures employed single farm women who worked eighteen-hour days when demand was high. When they contracted tuberculosis, as many did, they were returned to their families. Spreading of the disease made it modern Japan's most severe epidemic. The women who worked twelve-hour shifts in cotton mills were often married. Factory owners assumed that since women did not maintain households independent of fathers or husbands, they had no need to pay a living wage. The first strike in Japan's industrial history occurred at a filature in Kōfu in 1885 where women protested a proposed increase in hours and decrease in pay. Women unable to find factory work turned to prostitution. Poor women from Kyushu were lured to brothels in Southeast Asia. Money remitted to their families helped Japan's balance of payments.

Male factory workers in heavy industry earned up to five times the wages of women. They worked under bosses called *oyakata* who contracted for specific jobs. Because workers ran the factory floor, they were able to retain a measure of autonomy that gave them pride in their work. They moved at will from one factory to another because they possessed skills in high demand. Despite these advantages, wages barely covered the rent for a shack in the slums and a dismal diet of rice and vegetables. In 1898 railroad workers launched the largest strike of the nineteenth century. They demanded respect, higher status, and an increase in overtime pay.

Conditions for miners were worse. The low wages, dangerous work, and prison-like barracks made it so difficult to attract workers that the owner of the Ashio copper mine contracted for convict labor. By the end of the nineteenth century, the mine's demand for timber had stripped surrounding hills, leading to deadly floods. Effluent from the mine had killed the marine life in the Watarase River, devastated farmland, and caused premature deaths. Responses to environmental damage pitted proponents of "Rich Country, Strong Army" against the well-being of ordinary citizens in a conflict that was to play out repeatedly in Japan's modern history.

Civilization and Enlightenment

The local notables who had responded enthusiastically to the Popular Rights Movement wanted to bring a cultural revolution to their villages. In place of the hidebound customs of the past, they wanted "Civilization and Enlightenment," a slogan promoted by urban intellectuals and by oligarchs bent on modernizing communications, hairstyles, and education. The Meiji 6 Society founded in Tokyo in 1873 published a journal in which the members debated representative government, foreign affairs, modernizing the Japanese language, ethics and religion, and roles for women. That same year, local notable Ida Bunzō bought a copy of Samuel Smiles's *Self Help*. In a local magazine, he explained the virtues of perseverance and frugality, competition and progress, moral responsibility and the national interest. Other local notables used informal discussion groups to promote better hygiene and social improvement through hospitals, new foods, better roads, and technological innovation based on western models. They tried to overcome their neighbors' antipathy to the government-mandated schools that they saw as the best hope for improving conditions for rural people and for raising Japan's standing in the world.

The man who coined the phrase "Civilization and Enlightenment" was Fukuzawa Yukichi, a leading member of the Meiji 6 Society. In 1868 he founded Keiō University for the study of western science and business. His multivolume *Seiyō jijō* (*Western Matters*) described modern institutions—schools, hospitals, newspapers, libraries, and museums and western ideas regarding the importance of entrepreneurship and achievement. In the best-seller *Encouragement of Learning*, he indicted Japan for its backwardness and urged citizens to seek learning for its practical value in the modern world. He also served as adviser to Mitsubishi and Mitsui, destined to become the largest conglomerates in Japan. Although he advocated equality, freedom, and education for women, he kept his daughters ignorant and arranged their marriages.

Civilization and enlightenment also pertained to personal appearance. To use western technology, it was more efficient to wear western-style clothes. Replacing distinctive styles of samurai armor with standardized military uniforms submerged the individual in the ranks. Uniforms distinguished policemen from civilians. Changing appearances might help Japan gain the respect of foreigners who flaunted their cultural superiority. The government issued directives to men to stop shaving their pates and to women to stop blackening their teeth and shaving their eyebrows. Emperor and empress led the way. At his first public performance, the Meiji emperor had dressed in the court robes of his ancestors. He wore cosmetics and powder and had false eyebrows smudged on his forehead. Within two years he had changed to western-style uniforms, cut his hair, and grown a beard. The empress too appeared in western-style clothing and hairstyles.

The new nobility and educated elite followed the imperial family's example. In 1883 the foreign minister built a modern two-story brick building called *Rokumeikan* (Deer-Cry Pavilion) that contained a restaurant, billiard room, and ballroom. Invitations to garden parties, charity balls, and receptions included Japanese and foreigners, husbands and wives, a startling innovation because samurai women had not previously socialized with their husbands. Western-style dance by couples was de rigueur, even at parties far from Tokyo sponsored by prefectural governments. The late 1880s government became known as the "dancing cabinet."

Newspapers, journals, and other mass media exemplified and promoted civilization and enlightenment. Woodblock prints used chemical dyes to depict the marvels of westernization. Prints of horse-drawn carriages, steam locomotives, imposing new schools, and red brick buildings illuminated by gaslight in Tokyo's downtown Ginza district inspired progressive youths to seek modernity. (See Color Plate 27.) Magazines for women urged them to become educated in modern modes of thought to help them fulfill their roles as "good wives and wise mothers" (*ryōsai kenbo*). Fukuchi Gen'ichirō epitomized the professional journalist. He covered Saigō's rebellion in 1877 and later became chief editor of the influential *Tōkyō nichinichi shinbun* (Tokyo Daily Newspaper). It was a so-called big paper written in a style only the highly educated could read, with a focus on politics and serious editorials. Founded in 1874, the *Yomiuri Newspaper* aimed at the barely literate. Like other "small papers," it covered scandals and titillating stories of sex and murder. Hawked on street corners, it exploited the growing market for information and entertainment.

Modern newspapers serialized modern novels. In 1885 the aficionado of kabuki and student of English literature Tsubouchi Shōyō wrote *Essence of the Novel,* which tried to define a new realistic literature. Japan's first modern novel is deemed *Floating Clouds* (1887–1889) by Futabatei Shimei, because it tried to get inside the protagonist's head and used language close to the colloquial. Perhaps the most subtle and gifted writer was Higuchi Ichiyō, who garnered recognition in the male world of letters only at the end of her short life. Dominated at the end of the century by the medical doctor Mori Ōgai who had studied in Germany, and Natsume Sōseki who had studied in Britain, this world embraced modernity while questioning the superiority of western civilization.

CONSERVATIVE RESURGENCE

By the middle of the 1880s, many people thought that aping western customs had gone too far. They tried to retain traditional values while accepting the need for western rationalism in scientific inquiry and western technology. In 1882 Kanō Jigorō began the transformation of martial arts into judo and other forms through the scientific selection of techniques from earlier jujitsu schools. He emphasized that judo built character in a way that complemented developments in the study of ethics by religious figures and western-trained philosophers. By establishing an absolute standard for "the good," they sought to promote community suppression of socially disruptive thought. The head of the Hygiene Bureau, Gotō Shimpei, claimed that the

only way to get people to respond to public health initiatives was to work through established community structures and appeal to community values. Bureaucrats argued the need for the state to promote social welfare and a collectivist ethic through factory laws, tenancy laws, and agricultural cooperatives lest a social revolution undo their efforts to build a strong state. In 1890 the revised Police Security Regulations forbade women to participate in politics. The intent was to eliminate the need for selfish and unpatriotic competition and conflict.

The educational system bore the brunt of the conservative resurgence. In the 1870s, it imparted strictly utilitarian and materialistic knowledge; in the mid-1880s it focused more on Confucian ethics, Shinto mythology, and civic rituals. For the few who could afford to go beyond compulsory schooling, the Educational Code of 1872 had specified that a rigorous examination system would qualify students for middle schools, and the best would then take examinations for university. Founded in 1877, Tokyo University remained the only public institution at that level until 1897. Private universities such as Keiō and missionary schools provided lesser avenues for educational advancement. In 1886 the Ministry of Education established specialized higher schools above the middle schools. The First Higher School funneled students into Tokyo University for positions in the most prestigious ministries. Some higher schools offered degrees in liberal arts for students going to universities and then to careers in the bureaucracy or business world. Others consisted of vocational schools, military schools, teachers' colleges, and women's colleges. Each socialized the students by crafting character suitable to their station in life.

Education prepared citizens to serve the nation; it also provided the opportunity for personal advancement. The oligarchs opened the ranks of government service to men who had demonstrated talent and ability. The way they measured these qualifications was through academic achievement, but only men from families affluent enough to support them through years of schooling had any chance of success. Women were to serve the state as wives and mothers. Class and gender thus placed limits on equality, and the promise of social mobility concealed an economically stratified society.

Education trained citizens in the civic virtues personified by the emperor. In the 1870s and 1880s he toured Japan to unite the people under his gaze. Newspaper reports of his diligent work habits and concern for his subjects' welfare made him into a symbol of national unity and progress. He moved his headquarters to Hiroshima during the Sino-Japanese War (1894–1895), celebrated war victories, and appeared at imperial funerals, weddings, and wedding anniversaries. Hung in every school and public building, his portrait had to be treated with utmost respect. In 1890 he issued the Imperial Rescript on Education. It urged students to practice filial piety, harmony, sincerity, and benevolence; to respect the constitution; to obey the laws; and to be loyal to the *kokutai* (national polity).

The 1898 Civil Code adjusted the norms of western jurisprudence to the conservative concern for civic morality. Unless the primacy of the house and the patriarchal authority of the household head were maintained in law, the legal scholar Hozumi Yatsuka warned, reverence for the ancestors, loyalty, and filial piety would perish. The Civil Code affirmed legal equality, individual choice, and personal ownership of property for all men and single women, regardless of their former social status. Succession was to follow the male line, with all assets to go to the eldest son. A husband had authority to dispose of his wife's real property, though not her personal property (her trousseau); he decided when and whether to register a marriage and their children. Divorce by mutual consent freed both partners for remarriage in a continuation of Edo period practice. The Civil Code thus balanced a concern for social stability and modern, western norms with an understanding of customary mores.

IMPERIALISM AND MODERNITY

When Japan appropriated and adapted western industrial technology, juridical institutions, constitutional theory, and culture, it also imbibed western imperialism. Gaining colonies compensated for the humiliation suffered in accepting unequal treaties, put Japan on the side of the civilized world by exporting enlightenment to the backward peoples of Asia, and demonstrated Great Power status. A sense of national identity that could unite factory owners with factory workers demanded imperialist enterprises to divert attention from their differences. Social Darwinism taught that nations had to conquer or be conquered. Seeing what had happened to China and India, Fukuzawa Yukichi urged Japan to "escape from Asia" lest it too be conquered. (See **Documents: Fukuzawa Yukichi's "Escape from Asia."**)

The connection between modernity and colonization appeared early in the Meiji period. Japan's overtures to China in 1870 included an effort to extract an unequal treaty because having taken steps toward a modern centralized state made it the more civilized. A treaty negotiated in 1871 granted mutual extraterritoriality. In 1874, Japan used the murder of Ryukyuan fishermen by Taiwanese three years earlier as an excuse to send an expeditionary force to Taiwan. The ostensible purpose was to punish the Taiwanese; a covert aim was to bring civilization to the natives by establishing a colony. The war dragged on for five months before a settlement reached in Beijing acknowledged China's claims to Taiwan and Japan's claims to the Ryukyus. The expeditionary force withdrew, though not before Japanese newspapers had celebrated its victory over barbarism.

The Ryukyus and Hokkaido became internal colonies. In 1871 the Ryukyus were incorporated into Kagoshima prefecture. In 1879, the king was invited to reside in Tokyo and become a member of the new Japanese nobility while a Japanese governor took his place. Japanese fishermen and settlers had already spread north as far as Sakhalin and the Kuril Islands, territory that Russia claimed. In 1874 Japan evacuated Sakhalin and negotiated a treaty ceding it to Russia in exchange for Japanese control of the Kurils. It turned Hokkaido into a Japanese prefecture and established a modern definition of property ownership under which it sold off land the Ainu had customarily used for hunting and fishing to Japanese developers. Without material support, Ainu culture lost its meaning.

Japan's relations with Korea illustrate the relationship between modernity and imperialism. The oligarchs sent a diplomatic mission to "open" Korea in 1875–1876 that mimicked Perry's tactics in 1853–1854. The treaty forced on Korea replicated the unequal treaties Japan had been forced to sign in the 1850s. The following years saw successive incidents as factions at the Korean court abetted by Japan and China collided over the country's future course. In Japanese eyes, Korea was a weak, backward nation, easy prey for aggressive western powers. A German military adviser warned that were Korea to be controlled by any other power, it would become a dagger pointing at the heart of Japan. In 1890 Yamagata Aritomo linked parliamentary political participation with a militant international stance by telling the first Diet that for Japan to maintain its independence, it had to protect its territorial boundary, the line of sovereignty, and an outer perimeter of neighboring territory, a line of interest. Korea fell within Japan's line of interest.

The pressure brought by domestic public opinion to revise the unequal treaties affected Japan's diplomatic relations with its Asian neighbors. When negotiations for revision stalled in the face of western intransigence, clamor intensified for an aggressive stance toward China and Korea on the part of patriotic Popular Rights advocates as much as conservatives. In 1886 Britain and Germany proposed the partial abolition of extraterritoriality in exchange for allowing unrestricted travel by foreigners. The strength of domestic opposition to this compromise was so strong that the foreign minister had to resign. Finally, in 1894, western powers promised to abolish extraterritoriality and give Japan tariff autonomy in 1899.

Treaty negotiations took place in the context of the first Sino-Japanese War of 1894–1895. Fought over Korea, it lasted nine months. Japanese troops expelled the Chinese army from Korea, defeated the north Chinese navy, captured Port Arthur and the Liaodong peninsula in south Manchuria, and seized a port on the Shandong peninsula. The Treaty of Shimonoseki in April 1895 gave Japan Taiwan and the Pescadores, Port Arthur and the Liaodong peninsula, an indemnity, and a promise by China to respect Korea's autonomy. Japan's victory took western powers by surprise. In their eyes, it threatened peace and stability in East Asia. A week after the treaty was signed, Russia (with its own designs on Manchuria), France (Russia's ally), and Germany (hoping to steer Russian expansion toward what was now referred to as the Far East) collectively advised Japan to surrender its claim to territories in China. Despite popular outcry at the "Triple Intervention," the government had no choice but to obey. Russia then grabbed control of Port Arthur and the Liaodong peninsula.

SUMMARY

By the end of the nineteenth century, Japan had been transformed from a decentralized, largely agrarian regime into a centralized industrializing nation. Molded by schools and the military, informed by newspapers and journals, the peoples of Japan had become citizens. They had learned to ride on trains, wear western-style clothes, work in factories, and be self-reliant in striving for success. In dealing with the outside world, they had discovered that economic development and national defense required expansion abroad.

DOCUMENTS

Fukuzawa Yukichi's "Escape from Asia"

The most prominent intellectual and promoter of westernization of Meiji Japan, whose views on domestic policy were decidedly liberal, here Fukuzawa takes a hard-line approach to foreign affairs. His ruthless criticism of Korea and China, published on March 16, 1885, can be read as justifying colonialism, while at the same time he urges his readers to reject the civilization they had to offer. In 1895, ten years after writing this call to action, he rejoiced at Japan's victory over China.

Civilization is like an epidemic of measles. The current measles in Tokyo, which has advanced eastwards from Nagasaki in western Japan, seems to have begun to claim more victims with the arrival of springtime. Will we be able now to find a means of checking this epidemic? It is obvious that we have no way to do so. We cannot put up effective resistance, even against an epidemic that carries with it only harm; much less against civilization, which is always accompanied by both harm and good, but by more good than harm.

Though our land of Japan is situated on the Eastern edge of Asia, the spirit of its people has already shaken off the backwardness of Asia to accept the civilization of the West. Unfortunately, however, we have two neighboring countries, one being called China, the other called Korea. The people of these two countries are no different from us Japanese people in having been brought up since olden times in the Asian culture and customs, and yet, whether because they are of another racial origin, or because, while similar in culture and customs, differ from us in the main lines of their traditional education, a comparison of the three countries, Japan, China, and Korea, reveals that the latter two resemble each other more closely than they do Japan. The people of those two countries do not know how to go about reforming and making progress, whether individually or as a country. It is not that they have not seen or heard of civilized things in the present world of facile communication; yet what their eyes and ears perceive have failed to stimulate their minds, and their emotional attachment to ancient manners and customs has changed little for the past hundreds and thousands of years. In this lively theater of civilization, where things change daily, they still speak of education in terms of Confucianism, cite humanity, justice, civility, and wisdom as their principles of school education, are completely obsessed only with outward appearance, are in reality not only ignorant of truths and principles but so extreme in their cruelty and shamelessness that for them morality is completely non-existent, and yet are as arrogant as if they never gave a thought to self-examination.

In our view, these countries have no likelihood of maintaining their independence in the current tide of civilization's eastward advance. Let there not be the slightest doubt that, unless they are fortunate enough to have motivated men appear in their lands who, as a first step to improve the condition of their countries will plan such a great enterprise of overall reform of their governments as our Restoration was, and succeed in altering their people's minds through political reforms, those countries will meet their doom in but a few years, with their territories divided among the civilized countries of the world. The reason is that China and Korea, confronted by an epidemic of civilization comparable to measles, are impossibly trying to ward it off, despite its inevitability, by shutting themselves up in a room, with the result being that they are cutting off their supply of fresh air and asphyxiating themselves. Though mutual help between neighboring countries has been likened to the relationship between the lips and the teeth, China and Korea of today cannot be of any assistance at all to our country of Japan.

Civilized western man is not without a tendency to regard all three countries as identical because of their geographic proximity and to apply his evaluation of China and Korea to Japan also. For example, when he finds that the governments of China and Korea are old-fashioned autocracies without abiding laws, the western man will suppose Japan too to be a lawless country. When he finds that the gentlemen of China and Korea are too deeply infatuated to know what science is, the western scholar will think that Japan too is a land of Yin-Yang and the Five Elements. When the Chinese display their servility and shamelessness, they obscure the chivalrous spirit of the Japanese. When the Koreans employ cruel means of physical punishment, the Japanese too are surmised to be just as inhuman. Such examples are too numerous to count. This may be compared to the case in which most of those in a string of houses within a village or town are foolish, lawless, cruel, and inhuman; an occasional family that heeds what is just and right will be eclipsed by the other's evil and its virtue will never be noticed. It is indeed not infrequent that something similar happens in our foreign relations and indirectly interferes with them. This should be regarded a great misfortune for our country of Japan.

To plan our course now, therefore, our country cannot afford to wait for the enlightenment of our neighbors and to cooperate in building Asia up. Rather, we should leave their ranks to join the camp of the civilized countries of the West. Even when dealing with China and Korea, we need not have special scruples simply because they are our neighbors, but should behave toward them as the westerners do. One who befriends an evil person cannot avoid being involved in his notoriety. In spirit, then, we break with our evil friends of Eastern Asia.

Source: Centre for East Asian Cultural Studies, comp., *Meiji Japan through Contemporary Sources, Vol. 3, 1869–1894* (Tokyo: Centre for East Asian Cultural Studies, 1972), pp. 129–133, modified.

SUGGESTED READING

The transformation of the Meiji state has attracted numerous scholars. Works include J. M. Ramseyer and F. M. Rosenbluth, *The Politics of Oligarchy: Institutional Change in Imperial Japan* (1995); C. Gluck, *Japan's Modern Myths: Ideology in the Late Meiji Period* (1985); and T. Fujitani, *Splendid Monarchy: Power and Pageantry in Modern Japan* (1996).

For contrasting perspectives on foreign affairs, see W. G. Beasley, *Japanese Imperialism, 1894–1945* (1991), and S. Tanaka, *Japan's Orient: Rendering Pasts as History* (1998).

For economic development, see S. J. Ericson, *The Sound of the Whistle: Railroads and the State in Meiji Japan* (1996), and E. D. Westney, *Imitation and Innovation: The Transfer of Western Organizational Patterns to Meiji Japan* (1987).

Two excellent books on education are D. T. Roden, *School Days in Imperial Japan: A Study in Adolescence and Student Culture* (1975), and B. Platt, *Burning and Building: Schooling and State Formation in Japan, 1750–1890* (2004).

For social history, see M. Hane, *Peasants, Rebels, Women and Outcastes: The Underside of Modern Japan* (2003), and H. Fuess, *Divorce in Japan: Family, Gender, and the State, 1600–2000* (2004). For the media, see J. L. Huffman, *Creating a Public: People and Press in Meiji Japan* (1997). For "Civilization and Enlightenment," see D. Irokawa, *The Culture of the Meiji Period* (1985). For disease, see W. Johnston, *The Modern Epidemic: A History of Tuberculosis in Japan* (1995). For religious change, see J. E. Ketelaar, *Of Heretics and Martyrs in Meiji Japan: Buddhism and Its Persecution* (1990), and H. Hardacre, *Shinto and the State, 1868–1988* (1989).

For views from the periphery, see N. L. Waters, *Japan's Local Pragmatists: The Transition from Bakumatsu to Meiji in the Kawasaki Region* (1983), and M. W. Steele, *Alternative Narratives in Modern Japanese History* (2003).

The Final Years of Chosŏn Korea (1800–1895)

The nineteenth-century decline of Chosŏn Dynasty fortune was marked by three rebellions caused primarily by the failure of government to solve long-standing institutional problems, intermittent persecution of Catholics, domination of the throne and government by consort relatives of mostly minor kings, and the threat to national survival by foreign imperialism. Korea was also faced with demands from foreign powers to open its doors to trade. Despite stubborn resistance, it was forced out of seclusion by Japan in 1876, but attempts to modernize the country were obstructed by conservative Confucian antiforeignism at home. That conflict reached a crisis in 1884, and the conservatives won the day. While reformers retreated abroad, the Chinese asserted themselves in unprecedented ways to block any reforms that would weaken their control over Korea, but domestic rebellion and a strengthened Japan brought Chinese interference to an end in the Sino-Japanese War of 1894–1895 and seemed to open a path for serious reform.

Scholars have concerned themselves with the following questions: What were the reasons behind the rebellions and the resulting obstructions to active response to rebellion and foreign aggression? What influenced the Taewongun's policies, including the anti-Catholic persecution? How should the nature of Chinese and Japanese interference in Korean affairs after 1882 be categorized? What capacity existed for reform and independent action from 1876 to 1895? And finally, what were the causes of the Sino-Japanese War?

THE NATURE OF CONSORT RULE

After the death of King Chŏngjo in 1800, his second queen, the dowager regent, Queen Chŏng-sun of the Kyŏngju Kim family, rose to power. She ruled over the minor king, Sunjo (about eleven years old), until 1804 and died the following year. During that four-year period, the queen elevated the king's father-in-law, Kim Chosun of the Andong Kim clan, to a position of power and influence and chose his daughter for Sunjo's queen. This marked the beginning of consort clan domination of the royal house, which lasted to the end of the century. One important cause of this was that a number of nineteenth-century kings came to the throne as minors under regencies established by the eldest living dowager queen or were selected by such dowager regents when there was no crown prince. The dowager regent remained as such until she resigned voluntarily or the king decided that it was time for him to rule on his own.

The male relatives of the dowager regents and queens benefited the most from this situation because they were appointed to high office. Regencies were established for all four kings of the nineteenth century; everything depended on who the eldest living dowager happened to be. The dominant Andong Kim were challenged by the P'ungyang Cho relatives of King Hŏnjong's queen in 1834. The Andong Kim dowager regent was forced by the P'ungyang Cho to relinquish her regency in 1840, two years after the leader of the Andong Kim died. After King Hŏnjong died in 1849 without a male heir, the Andong Kim dowager queen selected the twenty-year-old King Ch'ŏlchong, declared a regency from 1849 to 1852, chose another Andong Kim for his queen, and replaced many of the top officials with members of the Andong Kim. When King Ch'ŏlchong died without an heir in 1863, however, Queen Sinjŏng of the P'ungyang Cho clan was now the eldest living queen. She selected the twelve-year-old second son of King Ch'ŏlchong's second cousin, Yi Haŭng, as the new king, King Kojong.

The P'ungyang Cho and Yi Haŭng shared something in common: both had been demeaned by the dominant Andong Kim family and hungered for a chance at power. Yi Haŭng was then given the title of Taewongun, or grand prince, a title reserved only for a father of a king who had never been king. He was only the second in the dynasty with that title. The dowager became regent and held the position for only two years, to 1866, but the young King Kojong was oblivious to his right to assert his rule. Instead, the Taewongun continued as de facto regent from 1863 to 1874 even though he had no formal title or position. He then carried out a major reform program.

NEW SOCIAL POLICIES

In 1801, one year after King Sunjo came to the throne, Dowager Regent Chŏngsun manumitted most of the sixty-seven thousand official slaves, while retaining those slaves working in select offices. This constituted an important liberalization of the slave system, but hereditary slavery for several million private slaves remained until 1886, and slavery itself lasted until 1894. The power of the mostly *yangban* slave masters was not broken until the dynasty itself was near its end.

This act of liberalization, however, was followed by a bloody reaction to Catholics and other minority factions. In 1801 Dowager Regent Chŏngsun, supported by the Patriarch and *pyŏkp'a* factions, ordered the institution of a five-family mutual surveillance system (*oga chakt'ong*) to ferret out Christians in the southerner faction. Tasan and his brother, Chŏng Yakchŏn, were among those exiled. The next month, the dowager exiled the Chinese missionary Zhou Wenmo, King Chŏngjo's half-brother, the Ŭnŏn'-gun (Lord Ŭnŏn), his wife, and daughter-in-law.

The situation for Christians took a drastic turn for the worse when officials intercepted a silk letter from the Christian Hong Sayong to the papal court in Rome requesting a military expedition from France to protect Korean Christians from persecution. Outraged by this act of treason, the dowager purged over three hundred Christians that year alone and persecuted members of the southerner and *sip'a* factions. Those factions were kept out of office for another half-century.

The Christian issue would emerge once again in 1839 when the government arrested ten Christian missionaries. Among them was the prominent Korean Christian Kim Taegŏn, who had been proselytizing the faith in secret since the missionaries' arrival in Korea at the beginning of the decade.

FOREIGN INCURSIONS AND REBELLION

In 1842, Korea received news of the defeat of Qing forces by the British in the Opium War (1839–1842) and the imposition of an unequal treaty on China that allowed Britain trading privileges, extraterritoriality, consular jurisdiction, and limitation on import taxes to remove domestic obstacles to imported British goods (see Chapter 19). Two years later, Wei Yuan wrote a book, *An Illustrated Essay of the Maritime Nations* (*Haiguo tuzhi*), which was brought back to Korea in 1845 by a member of a Korean diplomatic mission. The *Haiguo tuzhi* included recommendations for manufacturing advanced western weapons and equipment or hiring foreign technicians to build a better defense, along with descriptions of the western nations. Despite having many admirers, the recommendations made in the book were not followed.

Admiral Perry arrived on the Japanese coast in 1853 with a flotilla of U.S. ships and forced an unequal treaty on Japan the next year. War between China and the British and French occurred after 1856, resulting in the foreign occupation of Beijing and the flight of the emperor to Jehol in 1860. When the British and French imposed another unequal treaty on China, China gave Russia a lease on the Liaodong peninsula and territory east of Manchuria contiguous to Korea for a few miles. News of these events created a crisis atmosphere in Korea.

A major rebellion led by a professional geomancer, Hong Kyŏngnae, broke out in P'yŏng'an province in the northwest in 1812. Part of the cause was the breakdown of the taxation and service systems, but general discontent in that province with the central administration and resentment against blocking promotion to high office among its examination passers were also important factors.

Inside Korea, the failure of the government to solve the problems of maladministration in the land tax, military cloth tax, and grain relief and loan system provided the main cause for a series of rebellions in 1862 throughout the country, but primarily in the three southern provinces. As mentioned before (Chapter 18), taxes due from these three institutions had been combined into a single land tax (*togyŏl*), but corruption by clerks and magistrates more than offset the reductions gained from distributing the taxes equally among all residents.

This rebellion was more massive and widespread than the rebellion of 1812, but it lacked central organization. Despite a few attacks against *yangban* landlords, it was aimed mainly at corrupt clerks and magistrates, not at the overthrow of the dynasty or the overthrow of either the *yangban* or the landlords as a class. The largest uprising occurred in Chinju on the southern coast, and the influence of it spread elsewhere. Although *yangban* participated in the planning of some protests, they usually withdrew when the protests became violent. Commoners provided most of the leadership in the dozens of spontaneous uprisings, but rebellious enthusiasm declined shortly after the release of pent-up animosity in acts of violence against local clerks and magistrates. The government under King Ch'ŏlchong attempted to respond by considering serious reforms, but he died before any action could be taken.

Partly as a result of rebellion, population growth was checked in the nineteenth century. An increase in flood, drought, and disease further reduced the overall population to 12.4 million by 1816. Thereafter, population fluctuated between 12.2 and 12.7 million to 1876, a major contrast with the significant population increase that was taking place in China in the Qing Dynasty.

CH'OE CHEU AND THE TONGHAK RELIGION

Around 1860 Ch'oe Cheu, a member of a déclassé *yangban* family, established a new religion in Korea. Discontented with his own life and the sorry situation of his country, Ch'oe Cheu experienced a vision in which he believed Hanŭnim (the Lord of Heaven) spoke to him and entrusted him with the task of spreading a new faith to the Korean people. He called the faith Tonghak (Eastern Learning, or "Korean National Teaching"). It combined Confucian ethics with Buddhist faith, Taoist naturalism and longevity, geomancy, and the use of talismans, imprecations, and shamanistic appeals to spirits in an amalgam that was supposed to represent Korean thought as a counterpoise to the Western Learning (*Sŏhak*) (see **Biography: Ch'oe Cheu, Founder of the Tonghak Religion,** and **Documents: Tonghak Beliefs**).

Korean Confucians regarded Ch'oe Cheu's teachings as a threat to both the stability of the dynasty and the purity of Confucian belief. Authorities decapitated him even though he was not a participant in that rebellion. The movement went underground and did not remerge (except for one minor rising in 1879) until 1893, but it was a sign that popular discontent with affairs was calling into question the power of Confucian orthodoxy to solve the problems Korea was facing at the time.

Taewongun. The Taewongun (Yi Haŭng), father of King Kojong and de facto regent (1864–1873) and rival of the Yŏhŭng Min faction and Queen Myŏngsŏng (the Min family queen). *(B. Cummings, Korea's Place in the Sun, Norton, 1997, p. 74)*

THE TAEWONGUN'S DE FACTO REGENCY (1864–1874)

At the beginning of the reign of the Taewongun's second son, King Kojong (r. 1864–1907), the dowager queen of the P'ungyang Cho clan was formal regent from 1863 to 1866. When she retired, a formal declaration was issued in King Kojong's name that he had assumed "personal rule" over the state, but the fourteen-year-old king was kept unaware that he was now in charge. His father, the Taewongun, simply continued his control behind the scenes from 1864 to 1874.

There were several aspects to the Taewongun's policies: an active reform program to address the causes of the 1862 rebellions; palace construction to elevate the prestige and power of the king; abolition of the majority of private academies in the provinces (they had become centers of *yangban* factional interest); persecution of Korean Catholics for suspected treasonous collaboration with foreigners; minting of

BIOGRAPHY Ch'oe Cheu, Founder of the Tonghak Religion

Ch'oe Cheu (1824–1864) was born to a remarried widow of a *yangban* family; by the age of fifteen, he had lost both parents. He received a Confucian education but was barred from the civil service examinations because his mother had remarried. He became interested in religion through his study of Buddhism, Taoism, and Christianity. Restless in his home village, he took to the road as a peddler but squandered his patrimony, was abandoned by his wife and children, and suffered depression.

He built a thatched hut in the mountains where he meditated, and in 1855 he began to believe that he had superhuman powers to heal the sick. He returned to his home town of Kumi, near Taegu, and changed his given name to Cheu (saving the ignorant). In 1860, Cheu had a revelatory experience in which God (Ch'ŏnju, the Lord of Heaven) spoke to him and entrusted him with the task of saving mankind on earth. He also created a potion for curing illness.

By 1861 he began to preach and developed incantations for his congregation. He left Kumi and moved to Namwŏn in South Chŏlla province to preach, but moved east to Kyŏngju in Kyŏngsang province in 1862, where he created an organization and converted hundreds. His religion became known as Tonghak (Eastern Learning) or Ch'ŏndo (Heavenly Way). It was a syncretic attempt to fuse the religious traditions of Korea as a counterpoise to western learning or Christianity. Cheu's followers were mostly commoners and slaves because the *yangban* regarded his departure from Confucian orthodoxy as unacceptable. Although he was not involved in the many local rebellions that began in the south in 1862, he was arrested by the authorities in 1863 for fomenting rebellion by his heterodox teachings and was executed in March 1864.

the first multiple-denomination coin in Korean history, the 100-cash (*tangbaekchŏn*), to pay for expenses; and total resistance to western and foreign demands for treaties and trade. The reform program resulted in a partial land survey to register land hidden from the tax collectors, the imposition of the military cloth tax on *yangban* households for the first time in three centuries (but in the name of their slaves to save them embarrassment), and the cancellation of past unrecoverable loans in the official grain loan system administered by district magistrates. Indebted peasants no longer had to pay permanent interest on loans they were unable to pay, and the Taewongun shifted the administration of grain loans from corrupt district magistrates and their clerks to local elders.

These reforms were perhaps less radical than they seemed because the land survey was not completed for the whole country, and village *yangban* had already been included among villagers to pay the combined *togyŏl* tax. Nonetheless, imposition of the military cloth tax was particularly galling to *yangban* because it was a direct affront to their status. The abolition of all but forty-seven private academies dedicated to Confucian worthies of the dominant factions was an insult to both hereditary factions and past titans of Confucian scholarship. And government spending and the inflation that resulted from the 100-cash was a violation of conservative Confucian attitudes toward profligacy.

Reaction to the Reforms

The Taewongun's opponents were led by conservative Confucians Yi Hangno and his disciple, Ch'oe Ikhyŏn. Yi opposed institutional tinkering

DOCUMENTS

Tonghak Beliefs

The following sources shed light on some of the fundamental ideas of the Tonghak religion and movement. Ch'oe Cheu illustrates differences between Tonghak and Christianity; the instructions for women of the second patriarch, Ch'oe Sihyŏng, combine Confucian precepts with acceptance of slavery modified with compassion. Kim Ku, a Tonghak and later ardent nationalist, shows how the egalitarian bent of Tonghak attracted him to the religion.

CH'OE CHEU ON THE DIFFERENCE BETWEEN TONGHAK (EASTERN LEARNING) AND SŎHAK (WESTERN LEARNING OR CHRISTIANITY)

Many scholars and gentlemen . . . asked me, "Is it any different from the western way, from Christianity?" I replied, "The [w]estern religion is similar to our religion but also different. They worship a God who is not real. The forms of the truth may be similar, but their doctrines are really different. . . . Our way emphasizes accomplishing things through natural action. . . . But the [w]esterners have no order in their words and no pure concern for God. They pray really for their flesh, and they have no effective God. . . . I was born in the East and received the truth in the East. Therefore, the way is the Heavenly Way and the doctrine is the Eastern Learning (Tonghak).

CH'OE SIHYŎNG (PEN NAME, HAEWŎL) ON TONGHAK PRECEPTS FOR WOMEN (1888), SUGGESTING LIMITATIONS ON TONGHAK SOCIAL EQUALITY

Be a filial daughter to your parents; cherish and respect the head of the house, love your brothers and sisters, cherish your son and daughter-in-law, be cordial to your neighbors. Treat your slaves as though they were your offspring, and do not mistreat domestic animals. If you violate these teachings, God will be angry.

KIM KU'S INTRODUCTION TO A TONGHAK MASTER AT THE AGE OF SEVENTEEN (ABOUT 1892)

As I bowed politely to him [O Ŭngsŏn], he bowed in return. Taken aback [by an adult's bow to a mere teenager], I told him my name and clan and protested, "Even if I were a mature man, you as a noble should not bow to me, but since I am only a child of the commoner class, you are treating me [with too much respect]." The noble appeared moved and said, "According to the Master's counsel, there is no distinction between rich and poor, noble and lowborn, and everyone should be treated equally, so there is no need to apologize."

————

Sources: For Ch'oe Cheu: *Ch'ŏndogyo kyŏngjŏn*, pp. 1–5, trans. Yong Choon Kim in Peter Lee, ed., *Sourcebook of Korean Civilization*, vol. 2 (New York: Columbia University Press, 2000), pp. 316–317. For Ch'oe Sihyŏng: Pak Inho, *Ch'ŏndogyo sŏ* (1921), pp. 86ff., trans. Susan S. Shin, "The Tonghak Movement," *Korean Studies Forum* 6 (1980): 34. For Kim Ku: Kim Ku, *Paekpŏm ilchi* (Seoul: 1947), p. 26, trans. S. Shin, "The Tonghak Movement," p. 33.

and believed that frugality, the reduction of taxes, and the cultivation of Confucian virtue were all that was needed for good government. After Yi died in 1868, Ch'oe Ikhyŏn in 1873 took the lead in impeaching the Taewongun for destroying moral standards throughout the nation.

For their part, almost all Confucian scholars, including Yi and Ch'oe, supported his foreign policy. Their antiforeign slogan was, "Defend

Confucian correctness against foreign perversity" (*wijŏng ch'ŏksa*). The Taewongun rejected all requests from foreigners for treaties because he was determined to avoid imposition of the unequal treaty system imposed on China and Japan by the foreign powers.

In 1866, when some Korean Catholics offered to mediate with the Russians in their demands for trade, the Taewongun suspected collusion to undermine Korean security and ordered a nationwide persecution of Korean Catholics that lasted all the way to 1871 and reduced their ranks from twenty thousand to eight thousand believers. The French landed troops on Kanghwa Island to chastise the Koreans for their refusal to tolerate Christianity, but Korean troops were able to force the small French force to abandon the island.

Military Pressure from the West

In 1866, a ship of U.S. registration, the *General Sherman,* with an English captain and a crew of Malays and Chinese, had run aground in the Taedong River near Pyongyang and demanded trade. The irate local residents attacked the ship, burned it to ashes, and killed all its crew. Pak Kyusu, the governor of P'yŏng'an Province during the *General Sherman* incident, submitted a plan for strengthening coastal defenses by building new forts along the coast, particularly one at the mouth of the Taedong River, recruiting more soldiers skilled in the use of firearms, and instituting a special examination for them. The Taewongun approved this.

About this time, Pak's disciple, Kim Yunsik, submitted a memorial based on Wei Yuan's *Haiguo tuzhi.* Since Wei had written that the secret of western strength was their domination of the seas by a small number of skilled troops with superior cannon, not superior numbers, Kim recommended that Korea concentrate on building advanced cannon and sea mines and distribute them to coastal garrisons. The Taewongun ordered the construction of three new warships and a cannon for laying mines. He even ordered construction of the first steamboat in 1867, although it failed its trial on the water and had to be broken up for scrap metal.

In 1868, the German adventurer Ernst Oppert landed on Korean soil and tried to disinter the bones of the Taewongun's father to hold them as ransom before Korean troops forced his withdrawal. Finally, in 1871, the United States landed marines on Kanghwa Island to teach the Koreans a lesson for their obduracy and to force a treaty of trade and amity (!). They did this by killing dozens of Korean defenders in the process. There is no evidence in either of these two incidents, however, that the new warships, cannon, and mine-laying cannon played any role at all in the fighting. Despite Korean losses from these attacks, the Taewongun declared victories for Korean arms and issued a manifesto that anyone who advocated peace with the foreigner was a traitor to the state.

One of the reasons for the use of violence by the French and Americans was the frustration caused by the ambiguity over who was responsible for the conduct of Korean foreign relations under the tributary system. The foreigners wanted to know whether Korea was a sovereign nation and if its king had the power and right to sign treaties. If not, they would negotiate with China as the suzerain power. Not only did the Taewongun refuse to negotiate with them, but the Qing government also avoided responsibility because it knew that if the Koreans violated any codicil in a treaty with a foreign power, that power would demand reparations from China.

Pressure on Korea from abroad was increased in 1868, when the Japanese overturned their previous system of military rule under the Tokugawa shogunate, restored the Meiji emperor from obscurity to the formal head of a centralized state, and created an oligarchy headed by a few samurai from four domains to change customs and modernize the country. When they sent a note in the Japanese emperor's name to the king of Korea asking for a treaty of trade and amity, the Taewongun refused even to accept the note on the grounds that there was only one legitimate emperor in the world, the emperor of the Qing Dynasty in China. Prior to that, the Korean king had maintained equal relations with a fictitious Japanese "king," a pretense the Japanese were willing to maintain since the emperor had declined to near obscurity. Japanese resentment over what radical samurai perceived to constitute an insult to the restored Japanese emperor almost resulted in a Japanese invasion of Korea in 1873 under Saigō Takamori, the acting prime minister. When Prime Minister Iwakura Tomomi returned from an investigation trip to Europe, he canceled Saigō's invasion plan and decided that Japan could not afford a debilitating and costly war just when it was embarking on a forced march to self-strengthening and industrialization.

KING KOJONG AND THE KANGHWA TREATY OF 1876

In 1874, King Kojong decided that he was old enough to rule on his own, leaving the Taewongun no choice but to give up power. King Kojong then adopted the advice of officials who advocated accepting communications from the Japanese emperor on the grounds that existence of the Japanese emperor was a domestic Japanese problem that had no effect on Korea, and that eliminating animosity and restoring friendship with Japan would result merely in a continuation of trade relations and friendship that had prevailed from 1609 to 1868. He adopted the advice but avoided signing a treaty until the Japanese found out about his new attitude toward Japan. The Japanese government created an excuse for hostile action by sending a survey ship off the Korean coast in 1875 in the expectation that Korean shore batteries would fire on it. When the Koreans obliged by doing so, the Japanese landed a battalion of troops on Kanghwa Island and threatened military action unless King Kojong signed the Kanghwa Treaty with Japan in 1876.

With encouragement from Qing authorities to avoid a confrontation with Japan, King Kojong signed the Kanghwa Treaty, which had most of the provisions of the unequal treaty system. He agreed to open up three ports to trade with Japan—two more to be selected in the future in addition to Tongnae near Pusan—and limited Japanese traders under the treaty to a small radius around the three ports. Under the long

tradition of extraterritoriality, the Japanese in the treaty ports were allowed to run their own affairs inside the radius. King Kojong assumed that the situation would return to normal and that the Japanese would be content to trade without invading Korean space elsewhere or making further demands. In fact, he had opened the door not only to trade but to foreign interference and a world of trouble.

FOREIGN INTERFERENCE AND QING CONTROL

The Taewongun had erred in making provision for King Kojong's queen when he chose the niece of his wife from the Yŏhŭng Min clan to become Queen Min (literally, the Min family queen; her formal title was Queen Hyoja). She began to influence her husband, and her male relatives, who began to move into office after the Taewongun was forced into retirement in 1874, remained in power to 1894.

King Kojong had resisted many of the Kanghwa Treaty's provisions at first, including the opening of two new ports and the demands for a Japanese legation in Seoul. However, a recommendation entitled "Strategy for Korea" sent to him in 1880 by Huang Zunxian, the Chinese minister to Tokyo, persuaded him to reconsider his position. Huang argued that Korea should negotiate treaties with all the western powers as a means of self-protection.

Huang Zunxian's recommendation was in line with the policy for Korea of Li Hongzhang, the governor of Zhili province and commissioner for the Five Northern Ports in China and the chief of Qing Dynasty relations with Chosŏn. Li sought to maintain China's suzerainty over Korea by capitalizing on the rivalries among the imperialist powers to check any attempt by Russia and Japan to strip China of its tributary control of Korea. He realized that China was militarily too weak to maintain its control over Korea by military force, but the policy depended on the willingness of foreign powers with little interest in trade with Korea to intervene militarily to check their imperialist rivals. The policy allowed China to maintain control until the Sino-Japanese War of 1894 but only by changing the very nature of the tributary system itself.

By 1881 Korea had agreed to open two additional ports to Japan at Inch'ŏn and Wŏnsan and allow the first Japanese minister to Korea to set up a legation in Seoul. That same year, King Kojong set up a new agency, the T'ongnigimu amun, to handle diplomacy and trade with foreign states, and he welcomed the first Japanese ambassador. He also hired a Japanese officer to train a small unit of troops in the capital in western military tactics and weapons. He dispatched an investigation mission to Japan that year (the *sinsa yuramdan*) to report on developments there, but he did so secretly to avoid conservative opposition. Some of the people on the trip were inspired by Japan's foremost westernizer, Fukuzawa Yukichi, but when they returned to Korea, they found a very inhospitable situation for the kind of reform that Japan had already begun. A conservative protest movement against Huang Zunxian's advice reached its culmination in the fall of 1881, when a plot to overthrow the king and abolish the T'ongnigimu amun was uncovered and the plotters arrested and executed.

King Kojong continued with his reform policy but decided to consult with China on how to make modern weapons and conduct negotiations with the United States and other western powers. In 1881, Li Hongzhang undertook negotiations with Commodore Robert W. Shufeldt of the U.S. Navy to conclude a treaty of amity and trade between the United States and Korea. A draft of the treaty was sent to Korea and signed by King Kojong and Shufeldt in May 1882, a sure sign that the Korean king had by no means ended his inferior status to Chinese suzerainty.

The treaty contained several elements of the unequal treaty system like extraterritoriality and the most-favored-nation clause, which guaranteed the United States any advantages concluded by other foreign powers in future treaties with Korea. During the negotiations Li Hongzhang had tried to insert a clause in the treaty indicating that Korea was a tributary of China. Shufeldt refused to accept it because the United States would never agree to sign a treaty with a dependency, but he finally agreed to compromise by allowing King Kojong to send a letter to President Chester A. Arthur declaring that Korea was both "self-governing" and a Chinese tributary at the same time, a description that fit tributary relations since the Qing regime never interfered with either Korea's domestic problems or its relations with Japan. The U.S. side ignored the contradiction and acted as if Korea was a sovereign state, but the ambiguity was not really resolved because both Korea and China still regarded the tributary relationship as undamaged.

Soon after the signing of treaties with the United States, England, and Germany in 1882, an uprising occurred, led by members of the old capital guard units who were incensed at the favorable treatment afforded the new Japanese-trained unit in the capital and the delay in the payment of their own salaries. Possibly goaded on by the Taewongun, who opposed the treaties with Japan and the United States and hated Queen Min and her relatives in the Yŏhǔng Min clan, the rebel soldiers attacked the Japanese legation and drove the ambassador and his party from Seoul and from Korea. At the same time, they invaded the palace to murder the Yŏhǔng Min officials and the queen as well, but she was able to make her escape. The rebels forced King Kojong to recall his father, the Taewongun, to the capital and appoint him chief of administration.

In China, Kim Yunsik and Ŏ Yunjung warned the Chinese that the Taewongun's hostility to Japan might bring on a Japanese invasion of Korea. The Qing emperor dispatched a few thousand troops on ships, where they landed and pitched camp. They invited the Taewongun to what was supposed to be an amicable meeting, but they hustled him off to one of their ships, transported him to China, and kept him under close surveillance for three years. After the Taewongun's departure, Chinese troops attacked the rebel troops and wiped them out unmercifully.

Although the tributary system with China had involved no written treaties and specifications, the kidnapping of the de facto head of state and father of the king marked a major departure from the long tradition of noninterference in Korean affairs and transformed China's relations with Korea to behavior quite similar to the western imperialists. China negotiated a commercial treaty with Korea for the first time that provided to Chinese merchants trading in Korea privileges denied to other states and instructed King Kojong to pay reparations to Japan to prevent any hostilities. The Chinese restored the king, queen, and her Yŏhŭng Min clan relatives to power and allowed them to repress the Taewongun's supporters.

Late in 1882 King Kojong put out a request to the nation for everyone to submit memorials recommending policy in the current situation. One hundred private memorials were received, of which one-fifth advocated reform, and many of those cited the *Iyan* (*Simple Talk*) by Zheng Guanying. Zheng, a Chinese comprador merchant for a western company, wrote the book in 1862 to alert China to the need to manufacture western-style weapons by hiring western experts. Many Korean reformers traveled to China to meet Zheng, and his book exerted a greater influence in Korea than in China. His main theme was the need to adopt western technology while still maintaining Chinese fundamental Confucian values (*sŏgi tongdo*). Kojong republished the book in *han'gŭl* in 1883 and urged everyone to read it, but this formula was to prove as inadequate for meaningful reform in Korea as it did in China because western culture included more than machines and tools.

The 1884 Coup

King Kojong instituted a number of reforms in 1883 by establishing a modern post office and the Ministry of Culture and allowing publication of the first newspaper, the *Hansŏng sunbo* (Seoul Weekly), supervised by Inoue Kakugorō, a disciple of Fukuzawa Yukichi. Nevertheless,

Koreans who had visited Japan and were eager for more radical reforms began to feel that they were under a serious threat to their lives because of conservative opposition. In 1884, Kim Okkyun with Pak Yŏnghyo, Sŏ Chaep'il, Sŏ Kwangbŏm (Philip Jaisohn), and Yun Ch'iho organized a coup to seize power and carry out the kind of reforms that Japan had undertaken. Most were disciples of Pak Kyusu, who had died in 1877, and Pak's friend, the *chung'in* interpreter Yu Taech'i, had taken over as the intellectual leader of the young reformers.

Because the conspirators had no support inside Korea, Kim Okkyun turned instead to Takezoe Shinichirō, the head of the Japanese legation, to use the Japanese legation guards as the main military force to carry out a coup in 1884 known as the *kapsin* coup. The coup leaders seized the palace, held King Kojong captive as their symbol of legitimacy, and summoned a half-dozen high officials to court, where they decapitated them on the spot. Before they had time to issue any orders, however, Chinese legation guards with some regular Korean troops led by Yuan Shikai (later the first president of the Chinese Republic in 1912) attacked the palace, killed a half-dozen leaders, and drove the rest of the plotters, along with the Japanese ambassador and his entourage, out of the country. Once again, Chinese intervention restored the political situation to the status quo ante and scotched the chance for a significant reversal of policy. Of course, the actions of Kim Okkyun's party had aroused the ire of many conservative Koreans because they had used the hated Japanese as the chief agent of their politics.

China, then bogged down in a dispute with France over Indochina, was powerless to resist Japan. It forced Korea to pay Japan reparations for the murder of Japanese victims and property damage even though the damage was the result of a coup in which the Japanese ambassador, Takezoe, and his troops were part of the plot. Because Takezoe had authorized the use of Japanese troops to aid the plotters without prior authorization from Tokyo, he was tried in the

Kim Okkyun (1851–1894). The leader of the failed reformist coup d'état of 1884. *(Sajinuro ponun tongni undong: Oech 'im kwa t'ujaeng, sang, p. 26)*

Japanese courts but let off for lack of evidence. No further action was taken against him.

The Tianjin Treaty

To settle any potential conflict between Japan and China, the Japanese prime minister, Itō Hirobumi, negotiated the Tianjin Treaty with Li Hongzhang in 1885 by which both sides withdrew their troops and agreed that neither side would supply officers to train Korean soldiers. Furthermore, if either Japan or China should feel it necessary to send troops, it would inform the other side in advance, so that presumably the other side could dispatch an equal number of troops to maintain the military bal-

ance between them. Unfortunately, this apparently peaceful settlement had the potential for escalating any conflict that might occur in the future, but the worst did not come to pass until a decade later.

That same year, Li Hongzhang appointed Yuan Shikai resident commissioner for Korea, the first such case of a Chinese foreign overseer on Korean territory since the departure of the Mongols in the mid-fourteenth century. For the next decade, Yuan sat at the side of King Kojong and prevented him from doing anything that might interfere with China's control over Korea and lead to true national independence. Li had also dispatched P. G. von Moellendorff, a German official in the employ of the Chinese Maritime Customs administration in China, to Korea to oversee the Korean customs agency. Von Moellendorff, however, sympathized with the Koreans against Chinese domination, and in 1884 he induced Min Yŏng'ik of the Min clan to negotiate secretly with the Russians for aid and troop instructors. When Li Hongzhang discovered Von Moellendorff's activities, he recalled him.

Yuan Shikai also succeeded in scotching King Kojong's attempt to dispatch an ambassador to the United States and other foreign countries to conduct diplomacy as an independent state. When the British navy temporarily seized Kŏmun Island (Port Hamilton) off the southern coast of Korea in 1885 as a feint to block the Russians from any attempt to obtain a leasehold at Wŏnsan and expand their influence into Korea, the Chinese took no action to force the British to retreat. Russia, which both China and Japan had perceived as a threat to their interests, also decided to accept the continuation of China's traditional relationship with Korea. By mid-1885, the Chinese decided to send the Taewongun back to Korea because King Kojong, Queen Min, and her relatives were defying Qing interests, but the king kept his father under close surveillance.

When a provincial Korean official blocked the export of rice and beans to Japan in 1888 to preserve food stocks during famine conditions after they had been purchased by Japanese merchants, Yuan delayed negotiations but finally pushed Korea to pay. He obstructed Japanese efforts to build a telegraph line from Pusan to Seoul and to reform Korean coinage with Japanese assistance despite the agreement of the Korean court to do so. He also blocked Korean attempts to obtain foreign loans and foreign military advisers. All of Yuan's actions merely demonstrated that Chinese direct intervention in Korea's foreign and domestic affairs had become part of the new relationship. Japan, by contrast, acquiesced in China's domination as long as Korea observed all its treaty obligations to Japan.

WESTERN INFLUENCES

The 1880s brought western influences in education and medicine from Protestant missionaries from the United States. In the 1890s Japanese and other businessmen stimulated interest in trade, modern transportation projects, and the exploitation of natural resources as well. The first streetcar arrived in 1898, demonstrating to the populace its advantage over the hand-carried palanquins for female *yangban*, donkeys and horses for male *yangban*, and ox-drawn carts for commoners. The laying of tracks for streetcars and trains preceded cobblestones or paved streets, overcoming one of the most important obstacles to rapid transportation of goods and people, the unpaved streets and roads that turned to impassable mud in the rainy season (see **Material Culture: Streetcars**).

Protestant Christianity

The first Protestant missionaries arrived in Korea from the United States in 1884. Most were Presbyterians and Methodists who strove to attract reluctant Koreans to the faith by the demonstration of good works, such as the construction of hospitals and schools. The Presbyterian Horace Allen, a twenty-six-year-old

doctor, gained immediate acceptance by King Kojong and Queen Min by saving the life of Min Yŏng'ik during the *kapsin* coup of December 4, 1884. Kojong made him physician to the royal court and allowed him to establish the first western hospital, the Kwanghyewŏn, the next year. Allen later gave up his status as missionary, became a secretary to the Korean legation in Washington, D.C., U.S. minister to Korea and consul-general in 1890, and ambassador plenipotentiary from 1901 to 1905.

Allen was followed in 1885 by the Methodists Horace G. Underwood, Henry G. Appenzeller, and Dr. William B. Scranton and his wife, Mary Fitch Scranton. Scranton founded the first Methodist Hospital, Underwood the *Paejae haktang* (School for Training Men of Talent), and Mary Scranton the first school for women, which Queen Min dubbed the *Ehwa haktang* (Pear Blossom School). The hospital evolved into Severance Hospital, and the two schools became Yonsei and Ehwa universities in the twentieth century. Other important missionaries were educators Homer B. Hulbert and James Gale, who wrote the first histories of Korea in English. Their efforts were not easy because propagating heterodox beliefs was still punishable by death, and the population had strong prejudices against Christians.

Efforts to Modernize

The first efforts to modernize included reorganization of the bureaucracy and the establishment of a western-style post office in 1884. The Protestant missionaries introduced the first western hospitals and medical techniques. Japanese currency and banks and telegraph lines made their appearance. Brick buildings, automobiles, and electricity arrived in the 1890s to power streetcars, and they wended their way through the main streets of Seoul in tandem with oxen and hand-pulled carts.

Most of these developments occurred in Seoul, Pyongyang, and a few border towns, and a small segment of the urban population was

MATERIAL CULTURE

Streetcars

The late nineteenth century was a period of rapid modernization in Korea. The first material signs of western culture came with the modern post office in 1884. By the 1890s, new forms of transportation arose, including streetcars, the first train between Inch'ŏn and Seoul, and a railroad bridge between Seoul and Noryangjin over the Han River in 1900. Pictured here is a streetcar wending its way through Namdaemun (South Gate) in 1904, but the streetcar tracks here and on Chongno (Bell Street) had been laid a decade before.

Streetcars. One of the first streetcars in Seoul, heading toward Namdaemun (Great South Gate), ca. 1900. *(Kim Wonmo and Chong Songgil, Korea 100 Years Ago in Photographs, p. 70, Collection of Chung Sung)*

most affected by education. Housing for the general population did not change much, but modern, public buildings provided models for the future.

THE TONGHAK REBELLION AND THE SINO-JAPANESE WAR (1894–1895)

Peace was finally interrupted by the Tonghak Rebellion, the biggest rebellion in Korean history. Contrary to popular belief that Japan had been planning a war to take over Korea, there is no evidence in the Japanese archives to prove it, but when the Tonghak Rebellion broke out in 1894, the Japanese cabinet seized the opportunity to eliminate the Chinese from Korean affairs. The Tonghak under its second patriarch, Ch'oe Sihyŏng, had been petitioning the govern-

ment repeatedly for an end to persecution by the government and toleration of their religion. It was also fueled by its antiforeign reaction to the presence of Japanese and other foreigners on Korean soil. The Tonghak made a powerful appeal to followers based on their religious declaration of the equality of all people before Hanŭnim (God), its rejection of Christianity, and a powerful organization based on a network of Netrope Coordinating Centers (Chipkangso) to administer captured territory.

In one of his more foolish actions, King Kojong lost confidence in his own army to control or repress the Tonghak rebels and asked the Chinese to dispatch troops to Korea. Even before the Chinese troops arrived, however, the government reached an agreement with the Tonghak military leader, Chŏn Pongjun, to call off the rebellion in return for toleration of their faith and a turnover of administrative responsibility for their captured territory. The Japanese

Chŏn Pongjun (1854–1895). The leader of the Tonghak rebel army after his capture in 1895. *(Sajinuro ponun tongni undong: Oech 'im kwa t'ujaeng, sang, p. 30)*

government took this opportunity to force a war on China by sending more troops than the Chinese had sent and making unacceptable demands. Japan attacked China without bothering to declare war, surrounded the Korean palace, and kept the king and queen under detention while the war continued.

Kabo Cabinet Reforms

Inoue Kaoru, one of the leading Japanese oligarchs, was sent to Seoul to establish a new cabinet. After failed efforts to recruit the Taewongun, Inoue brought Pak Yŏnghyo and Sŏ Kwangbŏm, the leaders of the *kapsin* coup of 1884, back from Japan and placed them in the Kabo cabinet. They were instrumental in drawing up reform decrees to create a more responsible bureaucracy; end the king's control over the exchequer; abolish slavery, concubinage, and child marriage; provide universal medical care and primary education for both sexes; and put an end to the civil service examinations, status distinctions between *yangban* and commoners, economic controls, and the mistreatment of wives.

Alarmed by the Japanese takeover of the Korean government and the return of men they regarded as the traitors of 1884 as cabinet members, the Tonghak under Chŏn Pongjun rose up again to drive the Japanese out of the country. This time, they had to fight a fierce but hopeless struggle against superior Japanese forces with advanced weapons and units of the Korean army. While this struggle was underway in mid-November 1894, King Kojong opposed Japanese control over himself, but Inoue countered that challenge by threatening to withdraw Japanese troops from the battle against the Tonghak rebels. In January 1895 he finally agreed to exclude the queen and her relatives from decisions and consult with ministers before making them. He then declared the end of Korea's tributary relationship with the Qing Dynasty. Inoue thought he had won a victory, but the Min faction proved just as contrary as the Taewongun and intrigued behind the scenes against Japanese interests.

The Japanese reform program called for rationalizing the bureaucracy, abolishing sinecures, establishing a regular budget and a uniform currency, creating a new judicial structure with professional judges and a modern police and military, initiating a modern universal educational system through high school, expanding railroads and telegraph lines, and beginning a modern postal service. The reforms were not carried to completion because they were attempted during war and the central government had weak control over local officials, but the abolition of slavery and the civil service examination system were preserved. Not all slaves were manumitted immediately, and members of the educated *yangban* elite continued to monopolize admission to government office under the new system of examinations run by individual ministries, but the door to upward mobility had been opened to members of lower-status groups, especially the educated *chung'in* clerks and specialists, who began a trek up the bureaucratic ladder despite their low status, which continued into the colonial period after 1910.

Meanwhile, the reform cabinet was being torn apart by Pak Yŏnghyo's ambition to become prime minister. He sealed his fate when a Japanese legation official leaked his proposal to assassinate the queen, and he barely escaped to Japan in July 1895. Inoue was also recalled by his government because of the Triple Intervention in April 1895. Because Russia could not countenance the Japanese takeover of ports and railroad rights in the Liaodong peninsula in

Manchuria as the fruits of victory, it led a three-nation coalition, with France and Germany, to force Japan to give up these territorial gains. Japan also had to retreat from Korea as well.

Assassination of the Queen

In April 1895, the Japanese government replaced Inoue Kaoru with Miura Gorō as minister to Seoul. When Miura was informed that King Kojong was about to appoint Min Yŏng'ik, who had negotiated with Russia in the past, to take charge of the court, he decided that it was essential to assassinate Queen Min without authorization from Tokyo to eliminate the Min family from politics. In October he sent two dozen Japanese police disguised as Korean guards and Japanese thugs (*sōshi*) into the palace, where they killed the queen and two of her palace ladies and then burned her body on the spot. Miura had a Japanese guard escort the Taewongun to the palace to take charge of the government and then appointed Koreans like Ŏ Yunjung and Yu Kilchun, who were willing to serve despite the queen's death, to the Kim Hongjip cabinet. Yu had studied briefly in Japan while living in Fukuzawa Yukichi's house, and then in the United States for four months, returned to Korea in 1887, and while under house arrest wrote his famous account of conditions in western nations, the *Sŏyu kyŏnmun* (What I Saw and Heard in the West), modeled after Fukuzawa Yukichi's *Seiyō jijō* (Conditions in the West). He was a strong advocate of the adoption of western institutions including the English-style constitutional monarchy, but he opposed the radicalism of Kim Okkyun and Pak Yŏnghyo and any idea of republicanism.

Miura tried to evade condemnation by blaming the Taewongun for the queen's assassination, but when eyewitnesses testified about the Japanese assassins, he was recalled to Japan and arrested. His action was so atrocious that it roused the ire of the Korean people and caused deep embarrassment for the Japanese government. In November, a few hundred armed Koreans loyal to the queen attacked the palace to murder members of the cabinet, but were driven off by Japanese guards. The cabinet then added fuel to the fire by having King Kojong issue a decree for all adult men to cut off their top-knots, a traditional Korean rite of passage to adulthood. That type of decree was the same measure adopted in Meiji Japan to mark the rejection of old customs and a commitment to modernity, but Korean men were not ready for the shock, and local guerrillas responded by attacking the authorities.

The Kabo reform cabinets of 1894 and 1895 had carried out major institutional reforms, but those cabinets were protected against conservative forces by the Japanese army. The Triple Intervention of 1895 orchestrated by Russia and Miura's murder of the queen weakened Japan's position in Korea so severely that the reforms and their Korean supporters were placed in dire jeopardy from conservative retaliation.

The reform movement had made some progress but had been blocked by the Chinese. Now that the tributary system was ended, and Japan was forced to withdraw from Korea, there appeared to be a chance that Korea might be able to push reforms against the conservatives to bolster its independence.

SUMMARY

Faced with internal rebellion and foreign aggression throughout the century, the Taewongun's traditional reform only postponed the inevitable. No sooner had Korea compromised with foreign states by signing trade treaties, when conservative attacks brought China into Korean affairs. The Chinese repressed Kim Okkyun's attempt at modern reform in 1884, and Li Hongzhang imposed Yuan Shikai on King Kojong to prevent any serious liberation from Chinese control. The Tonghak Rebellion sought to drive out foreign influence, but it only sparked Japan's defeat of China and the major Kabo reform, compromised, however, by Japanese sponsorship. The chance for Korean independence was cloudy indeed.

SUGGESTED READING

J. K. Fairbank, ed., *The Chinese World Order* (1968), and M. F. Nelson, *Korea and the Old Orders in Eastern Asia* (1945) provide a theoretical construct of the tributary system. The reign of the Taewongun in the 1860s is covered by C. Y. Choe, *The Rule of the Taewongun, 1864–1873* (1972), and J. B. Palais, *Politics and Policy in Traditional Korea* (1975). The reforms and troubles of the 1880s are covered in M. Deuchler, *Confucian Gentlemen and Barbarian Envoys* (1977); K. Key-Hiuk, *The Last Phase of the East Asian World Order* (1980); and Y.-B. Lee, *Diplomatic Relations Between the United States and Korea: 1866–1887* (1970).

Korea's relations with Japan, Russia, and the powers are covered by H. Conroy, *The Japanese Seizure of Korea, 1868–1910* (1960); P. Duus, *The Abacus and the Sword* (1995); E. Kim and H. Kim, *Korea and the Politics of Imperialism* (1967); and G. A. Lensen, *Balance of Intrigue* (1982). B. Weems, *Reform, Rebellion, and the Heavenly Way* (1964), deals with the Tonghak Rebellion, and V. Chandra, *Imperialism, Resistance, and Reform in Late Nineteenth-Century Korea* (1988), studies the Kabo Reforms of 1894–1895. Chung-shin Park, *Protestantism and Politics in Korea* (2003), concentrates on early Protestantism.

Y. Ch'oe, P. Lee, and W. T. de Bary, eds., *Sources of Korean Tradition*, Vol. 2 (2000), contain primary sources on the period.

PART SIX

EAST ASIA IN THE MODERN WORLD

CHAPTER TWENTY-THREE

Remaking China (1900–1927)

The first decade of the twentieth century was a period of rapid change, especially in cities and among the educated. Chinese cities were being paved, lighted, and policed. The Qing court announced plans for gradual transition to a constitutional monarchy. Voluntary reform societies tackled problems like foot binding and opium smoking. Then, in 1911, the Qing Dynasty was overthrown. Although the dynasty handed over its armies to the republican government under Yuan Shikai, military unity was soon lost, and regional armies and warlords competed to secure bases. In the 1920s, the Nationalist Party under Sun Yatsen built a base in Guangdong, and in 1926 launched the Northern Expedition, which reunified the country.

Nationalism was central to much of the cultural activity of this period. Patriots wanted to reconstitute China as a nation of the Chinese people and make it strong enough to stand up to foreign threats. A new type of intellectual emerged: trained at modern universities or abroad, deeply concerned with China's fate, and attracted to western ideas ranging from science and democracy to anarchism and communism. Young people attacked old social norms, especially filial piety and arranged marriages. The encounters between new and old and East and West stimulated a literary and scholarly renaissance.

Understanding these changes has been the central goal of most of the research on this period. Who led the way in the changes to the Chinese economy, education, and political organization? How was resistance to change overcome? What role did foreign countries play? Did the militarization of society slow down or speed up other changes? Which changes were felt even by farmers in the countryside?

THE END OF MONARCHY

As the twentieth century opened, the Qing Dynasty needed to regain the people's confidence after the debacle brought on by its support of the Boxers and the imperialists' subsequent intervention. It faced a fiscal crisis. The Boxer Protocol of 1901 imposed on China a staggering indemnity of 450 million silver dollars, twice as large as the one exacted by Japan a few years earlier and nearly twice the government's annual revenues. It was to be paid from customs revenue in thirty-nine annual installments, with interest. When interest on existing foreign loans was added in, these debts absorbed all of the customs revenue. Little was left for the ordinary operation of the government, much less investment in modernization.

Local Activism

Forced to look after their own interests, local elites increasingly took on modernization projects. They set up new schools and started periodicals, which by one estimate increased tenfold from 1901 to 1910. Interest in western forms of government was growing as people asked how the European powers and Japan had gained wealth and power. Yan Fu, one of the first to study in England, published translations of books such as J. S. Mill's *On Liberty* (1903) and Montesquieu's *The Spirit of Laws* (1909). Yan Fu argued that the western form of government freed the energy of the individual, which could then be channeled toward national goals. As he saw it, the West had achieved wealth and power through a complex package, a key part of which was a very differently conceived nation-state. Yan Fu once commented that only 30 percent of China's troubles were caused by foreigners; the rest were its own fault and could be remedied by its own actions.

Interest in western forms of government did not translate into positive feelings toward the western powers, which were seen as gaining a stranglehold on the Chinese economy. Activists solicited funds to buy back railroads built by foreign firms. Between 1905 and 1907 there were boycotts of the United States for its immigration restriction law and its mistreatment of Chinese at the 1904 World's Fair in Saint Louis. In treaty ports, protests were staged over westerners' extraterritoriality. Some protesters even talked of waging their own opium war after the British refused to stop shipping opium to China on the grounds that opium cultivation in China had not been fully eradicated.

In this period, Japan served as an incubator of Chinese nationalism. By 1906, of the thirteen thousand students studying abroad, ten thousand were in Tokyo. The experience of living in a foreign country, where they felt humiliated by China's weakness and backwardness, aroused nationalistic feelings in the students, who often formed groups to discuss how Japan had modernized so rapidly and what could be done in China. One student newspaper reported, "Japanese schools are as numerous as our opium dens, Japanese students as numerous as our opium addicts."[1] The two best-known reformers, Kang Youwei and Liang Qichao, had settled in Japan. In Chinese magazines published in Japan, Liang promoted the idea that China could become strong through "democracy," which to him meant a government that drew its strength from the people, but not necessarily a representative government or one that defended individual rights. Liang had traveled in the United States for five months in 1903 and found the American form of populist democracy unsatisfactory. He preferred the statist ideas and constitutional monarchies of Japan and Germany. When Japan defeated Russia in 1905 (see Chapter 24), some reformers drew the inference that it was Japan's constitutional form of government that enabled it to best autocratic Russia.

---

1. Cited in Douglas R. Reynolds, *China, 1898–1912: The Xinzheng Revolution and Japan* (Cambridge, Mass.: Harvard University Press, 1993), p. 62.

The Anti-Manchu Revolutionary Movement

Ever since the late nineteenth century, some people had argued that the root of China's problems lay in its subjugation by a different "race"—the Manchus. In 1903 the nineteen-year-old Zou Rong published an inflammatory tract, calling for the creation of a revolutionary army to "wipe out the five million barbarian Manchus, wash away the shame of two hundred and sixty years of cruelty and oppression, and make China clean once again."[2] He described the "sacred Han race, descendants of the Yellow Emperor," as the slaves of the Manchus and in danger of extermination. The language of social Darwinism, with its talk of countries in desperate competition for survival, seemed to many to describe China's plight accurately.

The anti-Manchu revolutionary who would eventually be mythologized as the founding figure of the Chinese republic was Sun Yatsen (Sun Zhongshan, 1866–1925). Like Hong Xiuquan, Kang Youwei, and Liang Qichao before him, Sun came from Guangdong province. Unlike them, he was neither from a literati family nor trained in the Confucian classics. Several of his close relatives had emigrated, and in 1879 he was sent to join a brother in Hawaii. Later he went to Hong Kong to study western medicine, completing his degree in 1892. In Hong Kong, Sun and his friends began discussing the advantages of a republic. The best way to overthrow the Manchus, they concluded, would be to ally with the secret societies so pervasive in south China. Groups like the Triads were anti-Manchu, had large mass followings, and had an organizational base reaching from one province to another, making them an ideal base for an insurrection, they thought.

In 1894 Sun went to Beijing in the hope of seeing Li Hongzhang, but when that failed, he returned to Hawaii, where he founded a chapter of the Revive China Society. The next year he set up a similar group in Hong Kong. The society's efforts to instigate an uprising with secret society members as the muscle never got very far, however. In 1896 Sun cut off his queue and began wearing western clothes. He spent time in England, where he discovered that many westerners saw flaws in their own institutions and were advocating a variety of socialist solutions. Sun began to think China could skip ahead of the West by going directly to a more progressive form of government. He also spent time in Japan, where he found Japanese eager to help in the regeneration and modernization of China. In 1905 some Japanese helped Sun join forces with the more radical of the student revolutionaries to form the Revolutionary Alliance. Despite the difference in social background, the students from educated families were excited by Sun's promise of quick solutions to China's problems. This alliance sponsored seven or eight attempts at uprisings over the next few years. Sun himself continued to spend most of his time traveling in search of funds and foreign backers, especially overseas Chinese.

In these years Sun worked out his theory of the Three People's Principles: nationalism (which opposed both rule by Manchus and domination by foreign powers), democracy (which meant to Sun elections and a constitution), and the "people's livelihood," a vague sort of socialism with equalization of landholdings and curbs on capital. Sun admitted that the Chinese people were unaccustomed to political participation; nevertheless, he believed that they could be guided toward democracy through a period of political tutelage, during which the revolutionaries would promulgate a provisional constitution and people would begin electing local officials.

The Manchu Reform Movement

Amid all this activism and agitation, the Manchu court began to edge in the direction of parliamentary government. Empress Dowager Cixi in 1901 announced the establishment of a

---

2. Cited in Michael Gasster, "The Republican Revolutionary Movement," in *Cambridge History of China*, vol. 11, pt. 2 (Cambridge: Cambridge University Press, 1980), p. 482.

national school system and called for putting questions about foreign government and science on the civil service examinations. In 1905 she took the momentous step of abolishing the civil service examination system altogether, a system that had set the framework for relations between the government and the elite for a millennium. New military academies were set up and new armies formed, trained by German or Japanese instructors. With the death of Li Hongzhang in 1901, Yuan Shikai emerged as the most powerful general, serving as both commander of the Northern Army and head of the Baoding Military Academy.

In 1905 Cixi approved sending a mission abroad to study constitutional forms of government. On its return the next year, the commission recommended the Japanese model, which retained the monarchy and had it bestow the constitution on the country (rather than a constitution that made the people sovereign). In 1907 plans for national and provincial assemblies were announced, with a full constitution to be in place by 1917. The next year, the seventy-three-year-old Cixi died (the thirty-three-year-old Guangxu emperor died suspiciously the day before). She had arranged for a three year old to succeed. His regents did not prove particularly effective leaders and soon dismissed Yuan Shikai. Hope for a Japanese-style constitutional monarchy looked less and less promising.

Still, in 1909 assemblies met in each province and sent representatives to Beijing. Although less than 1 percent of the population had been allowed to vote, the elections generated excitement about participatory government. The provincial assemblies circulated three petitions calling for the immediate convening of the national assembly, the last reportedly signed by 25 million people. In 1910 the provisional national assembly met, with one hundred members elected by the provincial assemblies and one hundred appointed by the court. Anti-Manchu feelings rose, however, when in May 1911 the court announced the formation of a cabinet with eight Manchu, one Mongol, and only four Chinese members.

Cutting Off a Queue. After the success of the 1911 revolution, soldiers often forced men to cut off their queues. *(Roger Viollet)*

The 1911 Revolution

The Manchu court's efforts to institute reform from above satisfied very few, and in October 1911, a plot by revolutionaries finally triggered the collapse of the Qing Dynasty. In the city of Wuchang on the Yangzi River, a bomb accidentally exploded in the headquarters of a revolutionary group. When the police came to investigate, they found lists of the revolutionaries, including many officers of the new army division located there. Once the police set out to arrest those listed, the army officers, facing certain execution, staged a coup. The local officials fled, and the army took over the city in less than a day. The revolutionaries then telegraphed the other provinces asking them to declare their independence. Within six weeks, fifteen provinces had seceded.

The Qing court did not immediately capitulate. In desperation it turned to Yuan Shikai, whom they had dismissed only a few years before, and asked him to mount a military campaign against the revolutionaries. Yuan went back and forth between the court and the revolutionaries, seeing what he could get from each. The biggest fear of the revolutionaries was foreign intervention, and to avoid that they were willing to compromise. In the end, agreement was reached to establish a republic with Yuan as president; the emperor would abdicate, but he and his entourage would be allowed to remain in the Forbidden City, receive generous allowances, and keep much of their property. Thus, unlike the Bourbons in France or the Romanovs in Russia, the Manchu royal family suffered neither executions nor humiliations when it was deposed.

In February 1912, the last Qing emperor abdicated, and in March Yuan Shikai took over as president. As a mark of solidarity with the revolutionaries, men cut off their queues, the symbol of their subordination to the Manchus.

THE PRESIDENCY OF YUAN SHIKAI AND THE EMERGENCE OF THE WARLORDS

Yuan Shikai had strong credentials as a reformer of the old, self-strengthening type. While governor, he had initiated reforms in education, commerce, and industry, and his army not only was equipped with modern weapons but was trained along lines established by German and Japanese advisors. He believed in careful central planning, of the sort Germany and Japan had shown could be effective. He was committed to a strong China but not a republican one. If local or provincial assemblies were empowered to act as they liked, how could China move rapidly toward a modern nation-state?

Yuan did not prevent parliamentary elections from being held in 1913, but when Sun Yatsen's new Nationalist Party won a plurality of the seats, Yuan was unwilling to accept the outcome. The key Nationalist organizer, Song Jiaoren, was soon assassinated, and the shocked public assumed Yuan was responsible. Then Yuan, without consulting the national assembly, negotiated a $100 million loan from a foreign consortium. By summer the Nationalist Party was organizing open revolt against Yuan, and seven provincial governments declared their independence. This second revolution ended in military rout, and Sun Yatsen and other Nationalist leaders once more fled to Japan. Yuan outlawed the Nationalist Party; in 1914, he abolished all assemblies down to the county level, trying to nip in the bud participatory democracy.

Yuan did undertake some progressive projects, extending elementary education, suppressing opium cultivation, and promoting judicial reform. But he was out of touch with the mood of younger people, especially when he announced that Confucianism would be made the state religion. When in August 1915 he announced that he would become emperor, the educated and politically aware elite were outraged, their protests dying down only after Yuan died unexpectedly in June 1916.

During the decade after Yuan Shikai's death, China was politically fragmented. Without a central strongman, commanders in Yuan's old army, governors of provinces, and even gangsters built their own power bases. The outer regions of the Qing Empire, such as Tibet and Mongolia, declared their independence. Tibet soon fell under British sway and Mongolia under Russia's. Manchuria was more and more dominated by Japan. In the far south Sun Yatsen and his allies tried to build a power base for the Nationalist revolutionaries. A government of sorts was maintained in Beijing, under the domination of whichever warlord held the region. It was hardly stable, however, with six different presidents and twenty-five successive cabinets. For a while, the key struggle seemed to be for control of the north, as the strongest warlords waged highly destructive wars across north China.

Warlords, not surprisingly, did little to maintain infrastructure or advance modernization. They disrupted rail lines and allowed the dikes on the Yellow River to deteriorate, leading to some catastrophic floods. They caused havoc in the countryside because the armies lived off the land, looting wherever they moved. One warlord reported, "My men would surround a village before dawn and fire several shots to intimidate the people. We told them to come out and give up. This was the classic way of raiding a village. Sometimes we killed and carried away little pigs. . . . We took corn, rice, potatoes, taro."[3] Because they also needed money to buy weapons, warlords instituted all sorts of new taxes. Foreign countries were more than willing to sell modern arms to the warlords, often backing their own favorite contender. Opium cultivation had been nearly eradicated in many places until the warlords entered the scene and forced peasants to grow it as a revenue source.

TOWARD A MORE MODERN CHINA

Social, cultural, and political change was rapid in the early decades of the twentieth century, some of it flowing directly from the pens of those advocating change of many sorts, some of it the direct or indirect consequence of changes in China's economy and political situation. Even forms of entertainment changed (see **Material Culture: Shanghai's Great World Pleasure Palace**).

The New Culture Movement

Young people who received a modern education felt that they had inherited the obligation of the literati to advise those in power. Their modern education, they believed, uniquely qualified them to "save" China. They had expected much

of the 1911 revolution and then had had their hopes dashed.

The newly reorganized Beijing University played a central role in this New Culture movement. Chen Duxiu, the founder of the periodical *New Youth,* was appointed dean of letters. Chen had had a traditional education and taken the civil service examinations before studying in Japan and France. A participant in the 1911 revolution, he became a zealous advocate of individual freedom. In the first issue of *New Youth* in 1915 Chen challenged the long-standing Confucian value of deference toward elders. Youth, he asserted, was worth celebrating: "Youth is like early spring, like the rising sun, like the trees and grass in bud, like a newly sharpened blade." He urged his readers not to waste their "fleeting time in arguing with the older generation on this and that, hoping for them to be reborn and remodeled." They should think for themselves and not let the old contaminate them. In other articles, he wrote that Confucianism had to be rejected before China could attain equality and human rights: "We must be thoroughly aware of the incompatibility between Confucianism and the new belief, the new society, and the new state."[4] To him, "loyalty, filial piety, chastity, and righteousness" were nothing but "a slavish morality."[5] Young people responded enthusiastically to his attack on filial piety and began challenging the authority of their parents to make decisions for them about school, work, and marriage. Conflict between parents and their marriage-age children became extremely common as the young insisted on choosing their own spouses.

Soon leaders of the New Culture movement proposed ending use of the classical literary language that had been the mark of the educated person for two thousand years. The leader of

3. Cited in James E. Sheridan, *China in Disintegration* (New York: Free Press, 1975), p. 91.

4. Cited in Chow Tse-tsung, *The May Fourth Movement: Intellectual Revolution in Modern China* (Stanford: Stanford University Press, 1960), p. 482.

5. Ssu-yu Teng and John K. Fairbank, *China's Response to the West: A Documentary Survey* (New York: Atheneum, 1971), p. 241.

MATERIAL CULTURE

Shanghai's Great World Pleasure Palace

Commonplaces of modern life such as malls and window shopping were once new and controversial. In China, they usually appeared first in Shanghai. In 1917 an entrepreneur who had made his fortune in medicine built the Great World, a six-story amusement park touted as the Crystal Palace and Coney Island rolled into one. At the intersection of two major roads in the International District, from the outside it seemed an agglomeration of European building motifs, with columns holding up a decorative tower. Inside, it catered more to Chinese tastes, and its customers were primarily Chinese. On the first floor were gaming tables, slot machines, magicians, acrobats, sing-song girls, and miscellaneous things for sale such as fans, incense, and fireworks. On the next floor were restaurants, as well as acting troupes, midwives, barbers, and earwax extractors. The third floor had photographers, jugglers, ice cream parlors, and girls in high-slit dresses. The fourth floor had masseurs, acupuncturists, and dancers. The fifth floor had storytellers, peep shows, scribes who composed love letters, and a temple. On the top floor were tightrope walkers, places to play mahjong, lottery tickets, and marriage brokers.

Great World Pleasure Palace. The building is seen here in a photo from the 1920s. *(Shanghai Historical Museum)*

the movement to write in the vernacular was Hu Shi, appointed to the faculty of Beijing University by Chen Duxiu after he returned from seven years studying philosophy in the United States at Cornell and Columbia. "A dead language," Hu declared, "can never produce a living literature."[6] Since Chinese civilization had been so closely tied to this language, Hu's assertions came dangerously close to declaring Chinese civilization dead. Hu Shi did recognize that the old written language had allowed speakers of mutually unintelligible dialects to communicate with each other and thus had been a source of unity, but he argued that once a national literature was produced in vernacular Chinese, a standard dialect would establish itself, much as standard vernaculars had gained hold in France and Germany. Chen Duxiu concurred with Hu, and soon *New Youth* was written entirely in vernacular Chinese.

The use of vernacular language had political implications. As Chen Duxiu argued, a modern Chinese nation needed a literate public, and literacy could be achieved more easily when writing reflected speech. The movement to write in the vernacular caught on quickly. In 1921 the Ministry of Education decided that henceforth elementary school textbooks would be written in the vernacular.

One of the first to write well in the vernacular was Lu Xun (1881–1936). In 1902 Lu had gone to Japan to study medicine after traditional doctors had failed to cure his father of tuberculosis. He gave up medicine, however, after watching a newsreel of the Russo-Japanese War that showed a group of Chinese watching apathetically as Japanese in Manchuria executed a Chinese accused of spying for the Russians. From this Lu Xun concluded that it was more important to change the spirit of the Chinese than protect their bodies. He began reading widely in European literature, especially Russian. The May 1918 issue of *New Youth* contained his first vernacular short story, "Diary of a Madman." In it the main character goes mad (or is taken to be mad) after he discovers that what his elders saw as lofty values was nothing more than cannibalism. In his longest story,

"The True Story of Ah Q," the protagonist is a man of low social standing. Always on the lookout for a way to get ahead, he is too cowardly and self-deceiving ever to succeed. No matter how he is humiliated, he claims moral superiority. His ears prick up in 1911 when he hears talk of a revolution, but soon he discovers that the old, classically educated elite and the new, foreign-educated elite are collaborating to take over the revolution for themselves and want him to stay away. In the end, he is executed by representatives of the revolution for a robbery he would have liked to have committed but actually had not managed to pull off. In stories like these, Lu Xun gave voice to those troubled by China's prospects and weary of China's old order but wary of promises of easy solutions. Lu Xun put the blame for China's plight on China's own flaws much more than on foreigners. (See **Documents: Lu Xun's "Sudden Notions."**)

By 1919 *New Youth* had been joined by many other periodicals aimed at young people aspiring for a New China. Magazines were filled with articles on western ideas of all sorts, including socialism, anarchism, democracy, liberalism, Darwinism, pragmatism, and science. The key goals were enlightenment and national survival.

Industrial Development

Despite all of the political and cultural turmoil of the first two decades of the twentieth century, a modern economy began to take off in China. China had opened some modern enterprises as early as 1872, when Li Hongzhang had started the China Merchant Steamship Navigation Company, but those were government-supervised and -supported ventures, not true capitalist ones. In 1895 Japan won the right to open factories in China, and the other imperialist powers leaped at the chance to set up factories as well, since labor costs in China were very low by international standards. By the eve of World War I, China had an emerging bourgeoisie made up of merchants, bankers, industrialists, compradors working for foreign firms,

---

6. Cited in Leo Ou-fan Lee, "Literary Trends I: The Quest for Modernity, 1895–1927," in *Cambridge History of China,* vol. 12, ed. John K. Fairbank (Cambridge: Cambridge University Press, 1983), p. 467.

DOCUMENTS

Lu Xun's "Sudden Notions"

The fiction writer and essayist Lu Xun (1881–1936) disagreed with those who urged preserving China's "national character" or "national essence," as he saw much in China's past and present that could profitably be abandoned. When he considered China's history, he saw the recurrence of undesirable patterns rather than past glories to be remembered with pride. The essay below on these topics was published in February 1925.

I used to believe the statements that the twenty-four dynastic histories were simply "records of mutual slaughter" or "family histories of rulers." Later, when I read them for myself, I realized this was a fallacy.

All these histories portray the soul of China and indicate what the country's future will be, but the truth is buried so deep in flowery phrases and nonsense it is very hard to grasp it; just as, when the moon shines through thick foliage onto moss, only checkered shadows can be seen. If we read unofficial records and anecdotes, though, we can understand more easily, for here at least the writers did not have to put on the airs of official historians.

The Qin and Han Dynasties are too far from us and too different to be worth discussing. Few records were written in the Yuan Dynasty. But most of the annals of the Tang, Song, and Ming Dynasties have come down to us. And if we compare the events recorded during the Five Dynasties period or the Southern Song Dynasty and the end of the Ming Dynasty with modern conditions, it is amazing how alike they are. It seems as if China alone is untouched by the passage of time. The Chinese Republic today is still the China of those earlier ages.

If we compare our era with the end of the Ming Dynasty, our China is not so corrupt, disrupted, cruel or despotic—we have not yet reached the limit.

But neither did the corruption and disruption of the last years of the Ming Dynasty reach the limit, for Li Zicheng and Zhang

---

and overseas Chinese engaged in import-export. Foreign investment grew rapidly, with big increases especially in Japanese investment. In the first decade of the century, more and more chambers of commerce had been established in cities large and small, giving this bourgeoisie more of a voice in politics. With the deterioration of the national government after 1915, it was often the chambers of commerce that took over running cities, seeing to sanitation, education, and police. Many of those who returned from study abroad took jobs in modern enterprises, where their foreign degrees brought prestige and often higher salaries. (See **Biography: Sophia Chen and H. C. Zen, a Modern Couple.**)

Commercial Press Pay Scale by College, Type 1912–1927 (yuan per month)	
Chinese college	80
Japanese college	100–120
Japanese imperial college	150
Western college	200
Harvard, Yale, Oxford, Cambridge	250

World War I gave China's businesses and industries a chance to flourish. Britain, France, Germany, and Russia were preoccupied with what was happening in Europe and no longer

Xianzhong rebelled. And neither did their cruelty and despotism reach the limit, for the Manchu troops entered China.

Can it be that "national character" is so difficult to change? If so, we can more or less guess what our fate will be. As is so often said, "It will be the same old story."

Some people are really clever: they never argue with the ancients, or query ancient rules. Whatever the ancients have done, we modern man can do. And to defend the ancients is to defend ourselves. Besides, as the "glorious descendants of a divine race," how dare we not follow in our forebears' footsteps?

Luckily no one can say for certain that the national character will never change. And though this uncertainty means that we face the threat of annihilation—something we have never experienced—we can also hope for a national revival, which is equally unprecedented. This may be of some comfort to reformers.

But even this slight comfort may be cancelled by the pens of those who boast of the ancient culture, drowned by the words of those who slander the modern culture, or wiped out by the deeds of those who pose as exponents of the modern culture. For "it will be the same old story."

Actually, all these men belong to one type: they are all clever people, who know that even if China collapses they will not suffer, for they can always adapt themselves to circumstances. If anybody doubts this let him read the essays in praise of the Manchus' military prowess written in the Qing Dynasty by Chinese, and filled with such terms as "our great forces" and "our army." Who could imagine that this was the army that had conquered us? One would be led to suppose that the Chinese had marched to wipe out some corrupt barbarians.

But since such men always come out on top, presumably they will never die out. In China, they are the best fitted to survive; and, so long as they survive, China will never cease having repetitions of her former fate.

"Vast territory, abundant resources, and a great population"—with such excellent material, are we able only to go round and round in circles?

___

Source: From *Lu Xun: Selected Works* (Peking: Foreign Languages Press, 1980), 2:125–127.

had spare goods to export. Imports from the West thus dropped dramatically, giving Chinese manufacturers a chance to sell more profitably. At the same time, the demand for products from China increased, helping China's export industries. The number of Chinese textile mills increased from 22 in 1911 to 109 in 1921. Tonnage of coal produced grew from 13 to 20 million tons between 1913 and 1919. Modern banking took off: between 1912 and 1923, the number of modern banks soared from 7 to 131. Telephone and electric companies were formed not only in major cities, but in county seats and even market towns. New fortunes were made. For instance, the Rong brothers, from a family of merchants in Wuxi, built a flour mill in 1901 and another in 1913. As opportunities opened up, they built eight new factories between 1914 and 1920, expanding into textiles.

Industrialization had its predictable costs as well. Conditions in China's factories in the 1910s were as bad as they had been a century earlier in Britain, with twelve-hour days, seven-day weeks, and widespread child labor, especially in textile mills. Labor contractors often recruited in the countryside and kept laborers in conditions of debt slavery, providing the most minimal housing and food. That many of the factories were foreign owned (increasingly Japanese owned) added to management–labor friction.

BIOGRAPHY Sophia Chen and H. C. Zen, a Modern Couple

The first generation to return to China from study abroad found many opportunities to put their new skills to work. Although many men returned to marry wives their families had selected for them, others, like Sophia Chen (1890–1976) and H. C. Zen (1886–1961), found their own marriage partners while abroad.

H.C. Zen is the English name taken by Ren Hongjun. He was born into an educated family in Sichuan and in 1904 graduated from a modern middle school. Although he was reading banned publications by the reformer Liang Qichao, he took the first stage of civil service examinations in 1904. After the exam system was abolished, he left China to study at a technical college in Tokyo, where he joined Sun Yatsen's Revolutionary Alliance. When the revolution broke out in 1911, he returned to China and at age twenty-five was made secretary to the president. Disagreeing with Sun's successor, Yuan Shikai, he resigned and went to the United States to study chemistry at Cornell and Columbia (1912–1917), finishing with a master's degree. While there, he became friends with Hu Shi and courted Chen Hengzhe, studying at Vassar. She took the English name Sophia Chen. While still in China, Zen also helped found the Science Society of China, an organization that sponsored scientific monographs and translations, lectures, and exhibitions. He served as its president from 1914 to 1923.

Sophia Chen, from an official family in Jiangsu, had faced more difficulty getting satisfactory schooling in China, either being tutored at home or studying in mediocre schools. In her teens, she convinced her father to withdraw from a marriage arrangement he had made for her so that she could continue her studies. In 1914, at age twenty-four, she was selected to study in the United States in the examinations held for Boxer Indemnity Fund scholarships. She studied history at Vassar, then went on for a master's degree at the University of Chicago in 1920. That year she returned to China, and became the first woman to be offered a professorship at Peking University. That same year, she and H. C. Zen married.

Since he had returned to China in 1917, Zen had held posts at Peking University and the Ministry of Education. When he became editor of the Commercial Press in 1922, the family moved to Shanghai. Two years later, in 1924, they moved to Nanjing, where Zen became vice chancellor of Nanjing University and Chen taught western history. Chen did not continue teaching after 1925, however, deciding to concentrate instead on writing. Her *History of the West* went through many printings. She also edited the *Independent Critic,* a liberal journal that she cofounded and that flourished in the 1930s. Both she and her husband wrote pieces for it. Most of Zen's time, however, was taken up with a series of prominent posts. From 1935 to 1937, he was head of the National Sichuan University.

After the Japanese invasion, the family moved to Kunming, where Zen, as the secretary general of the Academic Sinica and director of its Institute of Chemistry, tried to keep scientific research going in difficult circumstances. After a few years, they moved to Chongqing, where Zen took up other posts.

Both Chen and Zen made return trips to the United States. Chen attended several international conferences and after a meeting in Canada in 1933 traveled in the United States, which she found much changed since the advent of the automobile age. Zen visited the United States after the war, in 1946–1947.

After 1949, both Zen and Chen, nearing retirement age, stayed in China, living in Shanghai. Of their three children, two settled in the United States and one stayed in China.

Demonstrating at the Gate of Heavenly Peace. For months after May 4, 1919, students continued to gather at the Gate of Heavenly Peace to protest. *(The Sidney D. Gamble Foundation for China Studies)*

The May Fourth Incident

In 1914, Japan as an ally of Britain and France seized German territories in China. In 1915, when the European powers were preoccupied with their war, Japan took steps to strengthen its hand in China. It presented Yuan Shikai's government with the Twenty-One Demands, most of which entailed economic privileges in various regions of China. Others confirmed Japan's position in the former German leasehold in Shandong. The fifth group of demands would have made China in effect a protectorate of Japan by requiring that Japanese advisers be attached to key organs of the Chinese government, even the police. When a wave of anti-Japanese protests swept China, Japan dropped the last group but gave Yuan an ultimatum to

accept the rest. The day he did, May 7, was in later years called National Humiliation Day.

In 1917 the Republic of China joined the allied war effort, and although China sent no combatants, it did send some one hundred forty thousand laborers to France, where they unloaded cargo ships, dug trenches, and otherwise provided manpower of direct use to the war effort. China was thus expecting some gain from the allies' victory, particularly in the light of the stress placed on national self-determination by the U.S. president, Woodrow Wilson. Unfortunately for China, Japan had reached secret agreements with Britain, France, and Italy to support Japan's claim to German rights in Shandong. Japanese diplomats had also won the consent of the warlord government that held Beijing in 1918. At Versailles the Chinese representatives were not even admitted, while those from Japan were seated at the table with the western powers.

On May 4, 1919, when word arrived that the decision had gone in favor of Japan, there was an explosion of popular protest. Some three thousand Beijing students assembled at Tiananmen Square in front of the old palace, where they shouted patriotic slogans and tried to arouse spectators to action. After some students broke through police lines to beat up a pro-Japanese official and set fire to the home of a cabinet minister, the governor cracked down on the demonstrators and arrested their leaders. These actions set off a wave of protests around the country in support of the students and their cause. Everyone, it seemed, was on the students' side: teachers, workers, the press, the merchants, Sun Yatsen, and the warlords. Japanese goods were boycotted. Soon strikes closed schools in more than two hundred cities. The Beijing warlord government finally arrested 1,150 student protesters, turning parts of Beijing University into a jail, but patriotic sympathy strikes, especially in Shanghai, soon forced the government to release them. The cabinet fell, and China refused to sign the Versailles Treaty. The students were ebullient.

The protesters' moral victory set the tone for cultural politics through the 1920s and into the 1930s. The personal and intellectual goals of the New Culture movement were pursued along with and sometimes in competition with the national power goals of the May Fourth movement. Nationalism, patriotism, progress, science, democracy, and freedom were the goals; imperialism, feudalism, warlordism, autocracy, patriarchy, and blind adherence to tradition were the evils to be opposed. Intellectuals struggled with how to be strong and modern and yet Chinese. Some concentrated on the creation of a new literature in the vernacular, others on the study of western science, philosophy, and social and political thought. Among the prominent intellectuals from the West invited to visit China to lecture were Bertrand Russell (in 1920 and 1921), Albert Einstein (in 1922), and Margaret Sanger (in 1922). When the educational reformer John

Dewey visited between 1919 and 1921, he was impressed. "There seems to be no country in the world," he commented, "where students are so unanimously and eagerly interested in what is modern and new in thought, especially about social and economic matters, nor where the arguments which can be brought in favor of the established order and the status quo have so little weight—indeed are so unuttered."[7]

Not all intellectuals saw salvation in modern western culture. Some who for a while had been attracted to things western came to feel western culture was too materialistic. Fear that China was in danger of losing its "national essence" was raised. Liang Qichao, by now a conservative, saw more to admire in China's humanistic culture than in the West's rationalism and hedonism and worried about the threat to China's national character.

The Women's Movement

All of the major political and intellectual revolutionaries of the early twentieth century, from Kang Youwei and Liang Qichao to Sun Yatsen, Chen Duxiu, Lu Xun, and Mao Zedong, spoke out on the need to change ways of thinking about women and their social roles. Early in the century, the key issues were foot binding and women's education. In a short period of time, women's seclusion and tiny feet went from being a source of pride in Chinese refinement to a source of embarrassment at China's backwardness. Anti–foot binding campaigners depicted the custom as standing in the way of modernization by crippling a large part of the Chinese population. The earliest anti–foot binding societies, founded in the 1890s, were composed of men who would agree both to leave their daughters feet natural and to marry their sons to women with natural feet. After 1930 it was only in remote areas that young girls still had their feet bound. (Bound feet continued to be seen on the streets into the 1970s or later, as it was dif-

---

7. Cited in Chow Tse-tung, op. cit., p. 183.

Pilgrims at Taishan. Taishan, one of the sacred peaks of China, attracted many pilgrims, like these women, photographed in the 1920s. Notice that some have made it up the mountain despite their bound feet. *(The Sidney D. Gamble Foundation for China Studies)*

ficult and painful to reverse the process once a girl had reached age ten or twelve.)

As women gained access to modern education, first in missionary schools but then also in the new government schools and abroad, they began to participate in politics. Some revolutionaries appeared, most famously Qiu Jin, a woman who became an ardent nationalist after witnessing the Boxer Rebellion and the imperialist occupation of Beijing. Unhappy in her marriage, in 1904 she left her husband and went to Japan, enrolling in a girls' vocational school. Once there, she devoted most of her time to revolutionary politics, even learning to make bombs. She also took up feminist issues. In her speeches and essays she castigated female infanticide, foot binding, arranged marriages, wife beating, and the cult of widow chastity. She told women that they were complicit in their oppression because they were willing to make pleasing men their goal. In 1906 she returned to Shanghai, where she founded the *Chinese Women's Journal* and taught at a nearby girls' school. In 1907 she died a martyr, executed for her role in an abortive uprising.

Schools for women, like the one Qiu Jin taught at, were becoming more and more common in this period. By 1910, there were over forty thousand girl's schools in the country, with 1.6 million students; by 1919, the figures had reached 134,000 schools and 4.5 million students (though schoolboys still outnumbered schoolgirls seven to one). Schools offered girls much more than literacy: they offered a respectable way for girls to interact with people they were not related to. After 1920, opportunities for higher education also rapidly expanded, leading to a growing number of women working as teachers, nurses, and civil servants in the larger cities. In the countryside, change came much more slowly. A large-scale survey of rural households in the 1930s found that fewer than 2 percent of the women were literate compared to 30 percent of the men.

Young women in middle and high schools became just as avid readers of *New Youth* and other periodicals as their brothers. Lu Xun wrote essays and short stories that targeted old moral standards that constrained women. In an essay on chastity, he noted how a woman who committed suicide to avoid being ravished won great glory, but no man of letters would write a biography of a woman who committed suicide after being forcibly raped. In his short story "The New Year's Sacrifice," a poor widow forced by her parents-in-law to remarry was viewed by herself and others as ill omened after her second husband also died. She ended up surviving by begging, worried that she would have to be split in two after death to serve her two husbands.

Besides attempting to change people's ways of thinking about parental authority and women's proper roles in society, activists fought for changes in women's legal status. Efforts to get the vote were generally unsuccessful. However, in the 1920s, both the Nationalists and Communists organized women's departments and adopted resolutions calling for equal rights for women and freedom of marriage and divorce. Divorce proved the trickiest issue. As Song Qingling, the widow of Sun Yatsen, reported, "If we do not grant the appeals of the women, they lose faith in the union and in the women's freedom we are teaching. But if we grant the divorces, then we have trouble with the peasant's union, since it is very hard for a peasant to get a wife, and he has often paid much for his present unwilling one."[8]

REUNIFICATION BY THE NATIONALISTS

The ease with which Yuan Shikai had pushed the revolutionaries out of power demonstrated to them that they needed their own army. Sun Yatsen in 1917 went to Guangzhou, then controlled by warlords, to try to form a military government there. That year, the Bolshevik Revolution succeeded in Russia, and Sun began to think Russia might offer a better model for political change than Japan. Russia had been a large, backward, despotic monarchy that had fallen behind the West in technology. Both China and Russia were predominantly peasant societies, with only small educated elites. Why shouldn't the sort of revolution that worked in Russia also work in China? The newly established Soviet Union wanted to help build a revolutionary China. In Marxist-Leninist theory, socialist revolution would occur by stages, and since China had not yet gone through a bourgeois, capitalist stage, a victory by the Nationalist revolutionaries who would overthrow the imperialists appeared to be the next stage for China. Besides, a weak China might invite the expansion of Japan, the Soviet Union's main worry to the east.

For help in building a stronger revolutionary party and army, in 1920 Sun turned to the Comintern (short for Communist International, the organization Lenin had founded to promote Communist revolution throughout the world). The Comintern sent advisers to Sun, most notably Michael Borodin, who drafted a constitution for the Nationalist Party, giving it a more hierarchical chain of command. When some party members thought it resembled the Communist model too closely, Sun countered that "the capitalist countries will never be sympathetic to our Party. Sympathy can only be expected from Russia, the oppressed nations, and the oppressed peoples."[9]

By 1925 there were about one thousand Russian military advisers in China helping the Nationalists build a party army. Chinese officers were also sent to the Soviet Union, including Chiang Kaishek, who was sent there for four months' training in 1923. On Chiang's return, Borodin helped him set up the Huangpu (Whampoa) Military Academy, near Guangzhou, and the Soviet Union made a substantial contribution to its costs. The Communist Zhou Enlai, recently returned from France, became deputy head of this academy's political education department. The first class was admitted in 1924 with nearly five hundred cadets ages seventeen to twenty-four. The cadet corps was indoctrinated in Sun's Three Principles of the People and dedicated to the rebuilding of national unity. As they rose within the Nationalist army, the former cadets remained fiercely loyal to Chiang.

At the same time that Comintern advisers were aiding the buildup of the Nationalists' power base, they continued to guide the development of a Chinese Communist Party (discussed in Chapter 26). This party grew slowly, and at no time in the 1920s or 1930s did it have nearly as many members or supporters as the Nationalist Party. In 1922, on Comintern urging, the two parties formed a united front, as a

---

8. Cited in Anna Louise Strong, *China's Millions* (New York: Coward-McCann, 1928), p. 125.

9. Cited in C. Martin Wilbur and Julie Lien-ying How, *Missionaries of Revolution* (Cambridge, Mass.: Harvard University Press, 1989), p. 92.

consequence of which members of the Communist Party joined the Nationalist Party as individuals but continued separate Communist Party activities on the side. Sun Yatsen endorsed this policy, confident that the Nationalist Party would not be threatened by a small number of Communists and eager to tap all possible resources for building a strong state.

Among those the Comintern sent to Guangzhou was Ho Chi Minh, a Vietnamese who had become a Communist in France and gone to Moscow to work at Comintern headquarters. Ho spent much of the next twenty years in China and Hong Kong organizing a Vietnamese Communist movement among Vietnamese patriots in exile in south China.

Nationalism continued to grow during the 1920s, as one incident after another served to remind people of China's subjection to the imperialist powers. On May 30, 1925, police in the foreign-run International Settlement of Shanghai fired on unarmed demonstrators, killing eleven. Three weeks later, a sympathy protest in Guangzhou led foreign troops to open fire, killing fifty-two demonstrators. A fifteen-month boycott of British goods and trade with Hong Kong followed. The time seemed ripe to mobilize patriots across the country to fight the twin evils of warlordism and imperialism.

In 1925, before the planned Northern Expedition to reunify the country could be mounted, Sun Yatsen died of cancer. The recently reorganized Nationalist Party soon suffered strain between the leftists, who shared many of the goals of the Communists, and the rightists, who thought Borodin had too much power and the Communists were acting like a party within the party. Nevertheless, in July 1926, the two-pronged Northern Expedition was finally launched with Chiang Kaishek as military commander and Russian advisers helping with strategy. Communists and members of the left wing of the Nationalist Party formed an advanced guard, organizing peasants and workers along the way to support the revolution. Many warlords joined the cause; others were defeated. By the end of 1926, the Nationalist government was moved from Guangzhou to Wuhan, where the left wing of the party became dominant. By early 1927, the army was ready to attack Shanghai. This would mark the end of the United Front, a topic taken up in Chapter 26.

SUMMARY

How different was China in 1927, compared to 1900? Two thousand years of monarchical government had come to an end. Nationalism had become a powerful force. Political parties had come into existence. Through the spread of modern schools, the outpouring of new publications, and much more extensive study abroad, a much larger proportion of the population knew something of western countries and western ideas. Confucianism was no longer taken to be an obvious good. Radically new ideas such as individualism and democracy were widely discussed and advocated. Young people with modern educations had become important political actors as protesters and agitators. Women had come to play much more public roles in society. An urban proletariat had come into existence with the growth of factories in the major cities.

SUGGESTED READING

An authoritative source for the Republican period is J. Fairbank, ed., *The Cambridge History of China,* vols. 12 and 13 (1983, 1986). Overviews of China in the twentieth century are provided in the texts by Spence, Hsu, Fairbank, and Schoppa, mentioned in earlier chapters. See also J. Sheridan, *China in Disintegration: The Republican Era in Chinese History, 1912–1949*

(1975). A useful reference work is H. Boorman and R. Howard, eds., *Biographical Dictionary of Republican China*, 4 vols. (1967–1977).

The collapse of the monarchical system is treated in M. Wright, ed., *China in Revolution: The First Phase, 1900–1913* (1968); E. Rhoads, *Manchu and Han: Ethnic Relations and Political Power in Late Qing and Early Republican China, 1861–1928* (2000); and H. Schiffrin, *Sun Yat-sen: Reluctant Revolutionary* (1980). For the aftermath of the revolution, see E. McCord, *The Power of the Gun: The Emergence of Modern Chinese Warlordism* (1993).

The intellectual and culture changes of the May Fourth era have attracted many scholars. See T. Chow, *The May Fourth Movement: Intellectual Revolution in Modern China* (1960); L. Lee, *The Romantic Generation of Chinese Writers* (1973); Y. Lin, *The Crisis of Chinese Consciousness: Radical Antitraditionalism in the May Fourth Era* (1979); V. Schwarz, *The Chinese Enlightenment: Intellectuals and the Legacy of the May Fourth Movement of 1919* (1986); W. Yeh, *Provincial Passages* (1996); J. Spence, *The Gate of Heavenly Peace: The Chinese and Their Revolution, 1895–1980* (1981); L. Li, *Student Nationalism in China* (1994); J. Fitzgerald, *Awakening China* (1996);

and M. Goldman and L. Lee, eds., *An Intellectual History of Modern China* (2002).

On women's participation in the movements of the period, see K. Ono, *Chinese Women in a Century of Revolution* (1989); W. Zheng, *Women in the Chinese Enlightenment: Oral and Textual Histories* (1999); and C. Gilmartin, *Engendering the Chinese Revolution: Radical Women, Communist Politics, and Mass Movements in the 1920s* (1995).

Social change is considered in D. Strand, *Rickshaw Beijing: City People and Politics in the 1920s* (1989). The industrial and commercial economy are analyzed in L. Li, *China's Silk Trade: Traditional Industry in the Modern World, 1842–1937* (1981); S. Cochran, *Big Business in China: Sino-Foreign Rivalry in the Cigarette Business, 1890–1930* (1980) and *Encountering Chinese Networks: Western, Japanese, and Chinese Corporations in China, 1880–1937*; and M. Bergere, *The Golden Age of the Chinese Bourgeoisie, 1911–1937* (1990). The lives of urban factory workers are documented in G. Hershatter, *Workers of Tianjin, 1900–1949* (1986), and E. Honig, *Sisters and Strangers: Women in the Shanghai Cotton Mills, 1919–1949* (1986).

CHAPTER TWENTY-FOUR

Rise of Modern Japan (1900–1931)

The early 1900s found Japan ever more deeply entangled in world affairs. Wars on the Asian continent brought it colonies and complicated notions of national identity. Contradictory impulses toward democracy and totalitarianism, modernity and atavism marked the home front. The state impinged more directly than before on the everyday lives of Japanese citizens. The same mechanisms that allowed it to do so—conscription, education, and mass media—provided channels for people to create new organizations at the community level, oppose state policies, and define individual goals. Changes in the economic structure heightened the importance of industrial labor and the fears of social unrest. A new middle class provided a ready market for popular culture. The most visible signs of modern life concentrated in the cities, to the disgust of people who located the preserve of Japanese values in pristine communities of the countryside.

The first decades of the twentieth century are often analyzed to explain what came after. To what extent was Japan's descent into fascism preordained? Why consider countervailing forces, given that they failed? What is this period's legacy for postwar Japan?

A FLUID INTERNATIONAL ORDER

In the 1900s, foreign relations resonated throughout Japan's economy, politics, society, and culture. The imperative to challenge white supremacy by achieving great power status and rising in the hierarchy of nations shaped Japan's national identity. Colonies came to be seen as an economic necessity, both to supply raw materials for Japan's emerging industries and to provide living space for Japan's teeming population.

Japan began the drive for great power status by signing an alliance with Britain in 1902 and going to war against Russia in 1904–1905.

The alliance committed each country to come to the defense of the other should a third party join the enemy in time of war. It functioned as planned against Russia. Russia's leasehold on the Liaodong peninsula and fortification of Port Arthur threatened Japan's interests in Korea. When Russia refused to make concessions, Japan's military launched a surprise attack on Port Arthur. It hoped to win a short war before Russia could mobilize its larger army and bring it to the scene of battle, but the siege dragged on longer than expected. By the time Port Arthur fell, Japan's army was exhausted. U.S. President Theodore Roosevelt offered to negotiate a peace settlement. The Treaty of Portsmouth gave Japan the southern half of Sakhalin, Russia's leasehold on the Liaodong peninsula, the South Manchurian Railway built by the Russians between Port Arthur and Mukden and its associated mining concessions, and Russian acknowledgment of Japan's paramountcy in Korea. In demonstrating that a "yellow race" could beat the "whites," Japan inspired Asians with hopes that they could throw off the colonial yoke.

Japan landed troops in Korea two days before it declared war on Russia. Two weeks later, it forced the Korean king to accept a limited protectorate that made Korea Japan's ally and subject to Japan's lead in administrative matters. The Japanese army then occupied the country. Six months later, Korea had to accept Japanese financial and diplomatic advisers. They reformed the currency and drew up a government budget. They took over the communications system for reasons of national security. The army imposed martial law to prevent sabotage. The Taft-Katsura agreement of 1905 acknowledged Japan's control of Korea in return for Japan's acquiescence in the U.S. colonization of the Philippines. In 1906, Korea became a Japanese protectorate with Itō Hirobumi as resident general. Government offices had to obey Japanese advisers, courts came under the jurisdiction of Japanese judges, the Korean army was disbanded, a Japanese police force maintained order, and Japan took

Cartoon of Amaterasu and Britannia. This cartoon of Amaterasu and Britannia celebrates the 1902 signing of the Anglo-Japanese alliance. The goddesses representing Japan and Great Britain cast their benevolent protection over Korea. *(Saitama Municipal Cartoon Art Museum/DNPArchives.com)*

over Korea's diplomatic relations. When the king complained to the Hague Peace Conference of 1907, Itō forced him to abdicate. In 1909 a Korean nationalist assassinated Itō. In 1910 Japan annexed Korea. At the same time, Japan formalized control over Taiwan. Both remained in the Japanese empire for the next thirty-five years, and Japan had joined the ranks of imperial powers. (See Map 24.1.)

Japan envisioned that its empire would bring not only prestige, but also coal and iron for its factories, food for its people, a market for the export of finished products, and space for its expanding population. Taiwan supplied sugar

Map **24.1** **Japanese Imperial Expansion, 1868–1910**

financed by Japanese capital and, after 1920, rice produced on family farms that inadvertently promoted the island's economic development. The Oriental Development Company bought land in Korea to sell to Japanese settlers, channeled capital to Japanese-owned businesses, and participated in the development of Manchurian mines. The military government improved the infrastructure by building roads, railways, and opening schools. It ruthlessly suppressed all dissent.

Japanese who migrated to Korea enjoyed a higher standard of living than Koreans and special privileges in education and employment.

World War I proved advantageous for Japan both economically and diplomatically. Its alliance with Britain allowed it to absorb Germany's leasehold on China's Shandong province and acquire a mandate over German-held islands in the Pacific. In 1918, Japan invaded Siberia along with Allied forces. Japan also tried to impose the infamous Twenty-One Demands on China. Most of them ratified and prolonged Japan's existing privileges in Manchuria and along the China coast. The last set of "requests" would have turned China into a Japanese protectorate. A public outcry in China and abroad forced Japan to back down. The Chinese complained bitterly about the Twenty-One Demands at the Versailles Peace Conference, but to no avail. Despite the open door policy promoted by the United States, no western power was willing to challenge Japan's interests in China.

Following World War I, Japan collaborated with western powers. It joined the League of Nations. In 1921 it participated in the multilateral Washington Conference designed to preserve the status quo in the Pacific and China and prevent a new naval arms race. A delegation of Japanese businessmen sent abroad in 1921–1922 demonstrated Japan's commitment to participation in the developed world's economy. Japan had been unable to get a clause on racial equality in the Versailles Peace Treaty, and in 1924, the United States offended Japan by passing the Oriental Exclusion Act. Despite this insult, Japan signed the Kellogg-Briand Pact of 1928 that outlawed war in the settlement of international disputes. In 1930 civilian diplomats agreed to additional naval limitations in the London Naval Treaty over the navy's objections and without addressing the military's concerns regarding China. When the army acted on its own to take over Manchuria, it ended the era of cooperation with the West.

ECONOMIC DEVELOPMENT

In the early twentieth century, Japanese corporations took advantage of international technological and managerial innovations often called the "second industrial revolution." Japan's electrical technology became second to none. Electric streetcars appeared in Tokyo in 1904. Of Japanese households, 85 percent had electricity in 1935 compared to 68 percent in the United States. Techniques of mass production required both standardized equipment and scientific management or Taylorism, an American theory of rational labor practice that Japan adapted to make the work force more efficient. Localities hoping to attract businesses developed research centers to find foreign technology, channel it to the factory floor, and modify foreign products for domestic consumption. Large enterprises developed new metallurgical and chemical technologies, often at the prompting of the Japanese military, which promoted the automobile and the airplane.

A dual structure characterized Japan's modern economy. Conglomerates linked through holding and trading companies called *zaibatsu* (financial cliques) dominated the most modern sectors of the economy—mining, shipbuilding, machinery, steel, and chemicals—and produced standardized, high-volume products. Although each company within the *zaibatsu* pursued a single enterprise and remained legally distinct, access to the *zaibatsu's* capital through its bank, a central advisory committee that set policy and long-term goals, and interlocking boards of directors tied them together. In some cases *zaibatsu* cooperated in cartels that divided up raw materials and access to markets as in the textile industry and maritime shipping. *Zaibatsu* chairmen enjoyed access to bureaucrats and cabinet ministers, who steered public investment their way and smoothed the regulatory road. Small firms found niches as makers of specialty items and basic consumer goods such as processed food, housing, and clothing. They produced ceramics and toys for export by the *zaibatsu* and functioned as suppliers and subcontractors to the large enterprises.

Japan's industrial sector was well placed to take advantage of World War I. Coal fueled locomotives, factories, and generators. Steel works had capacity to spare. Mitsubishi both built ships and operated a worldwide shipping line in competition with the Sumitomo-backed OSK shipping company. These and other enterprises profited from the Allies' demand for munitions and war-related material. Japanese textiles and consumer goods filled the vacuum

Real National Income Produced, 1878–1936
(million yen at 1928–1932 prices)

Year	Total	Primary Industry	Secondary Industry	Tertiary Industry
1878	1,117	691	95	331
1890	2,308	1,429	224	655
1900	3,640	1,671	818	1,151
1914	5,665	2,127	1,354	2,184
1920	6,316	2,147	1,686	2,483
1925	9,268	2,779	2,216	4,273
1929	10,962	2,740	2,911	5,311
1930	12,715	2,477	3,550	6,688
1931	13,726	2,372	3,716	7,638
1932	13,843	2,594	3,987	7,262
1936	16,133	3,149	5,096	7,888

Primary industry = agriculture, forestry, fisheries. Secondary industry = mining, manufacturing, construction, transportation, communication, and utilities. Tertiary industry = commerce and services. Source: G. C. Allen, *A Short Economic History of Modern Japan* (New York: St. Martin's Press, 1981), p. 284.

left by the departure of British exports from Asia. Business profits soared, and Japan's gross national product jumped by 40 percent between 1914 and 1918. The percentage of real national income contributed by manufacturing passed that of agriculture.

Imbalances between different sectors of the economy and cycles of contraction and expansion characterized the 1920s. Japanese companies assumed that demand would continue after World War I. When Britain took back markets in China and South Asia and European manufacturing replaced Japanese exports, they found themselves overextended financially and forced to lay off workers. They had just pulled out of the postwar recession when the Great Kanto Earthquake of September 1, 1923, leveled factories and workshops between Tokyo and Yokohama: one hundred forty thousand people died, and five hundred seventy thousand structures (70 percent of Tokyo and 60 percent of Yokohama) were destroyed. Aftershocks ruptured gas and water pipes, snapped electrical lines, and halted transportation and communications. Most companies rebuilt using generous credit

provided through the government to banks, which led to a credit crisis in 1927. Trouble came to the domestic market when silk sales slipped and cotton mills in China cut into Japan's biggest Asian market. In contrast to stagnation and decline in the textile industry and agricultural sector, old *zaibatsu* grew by absorbing existing enterprises and diversifying into new areas. Founded in 1908, the Chisso chemical corporation became Japan's third largest manufacturer as a new *zaibatsu* and industrialized northern Korea. When the Great Depression hit at the end of 1929, Japan's economy was already depressed. Japan joined other industrialized nations in imposing steep tariffs on imports, secure in the knowledge that except for oil and scrap iron used in making steel, its colonies had given it the requirements for an autarchic economy.

CONSTITUTIONAL GOVERNMENT

In the public's eyes, the oligarchs' efforts to control the selection of cabinet ministers demonstrated the persistence of clique government dominated by men from Satsuma and Chōshū. To counter Itō Hirobumi's influence in the lower house, Yamagata Aritomo forged a faction of conservative bureaucrats, members of the Privy Council and the upper house, and prefectural governors. In 1907 he made it possible for the military to issue orders in the emperor's name independent of the prime minister. Itō's protégé among elected politicians, Hara Takashi, had experience in the Foreign Ministry and the business world that helped him to arrange compromises between the oligarchs and the Diet and showed him the way to manipulate the bureaucracy. During the Russo-Japanese War, Hara promised Seiyūkai support for the cabinet, and in return, he convinced Yamagata to trust him with the powerful position of home minister.

Hara used his control over the Home Ministry to make the Seiyūkai the dominant party in the Diet. The home ministry appointed prefectural governors and district chiefs. It ran the police, the health bureau, and the public works bureau. Hara worked with bureaucrats in the Tokyo office and built a following for Seiyūkai in prefectural offices. Since prefectural officials supervised elections and influenced the local economy, a prefecture with a bureaucracy that supported the Seiyūkai was likely to elect Seiyūkai politicians to the Diet. Hara also perfected pork barrel politics. Unlike the early parties that simply opposed government spending and tried to cut taxes, the Seiyūkai followed a "positive policy" of government spending for economic development. Railroad lines spidered across the country, linking cities, towns, and centers of Seiyūkai support in remote mountain villages. Roads, schools, bridges, irrigation works, and harbors blessed the districts that voted Seiyūkai.

Even before Hara became prime minister in 1918, Diet members had mastered manipulating the electorate. Businessmen provided political funds in return for favors. They also offered politicians and bureaucrats positions on their companies' boards of directors. In buying votes,

some Diet members relied on election brokers. Others used prefectural assembly members, tainting them as well with the stench of corruption. Playing on Yamagata's fears of a socialist revolution following the Bolshevik takeover in Russia and nationwide rice riots in Japan in 1918, Hara convinced him that party control of an expanded electorate was the safest way to channel popular unrest. The 1919 expansion of the electorate to 5 percent of the population benefited small landlords, not urban workers. In 1921 an unemployed railroad worker assassinated Hara because of what he saw as Hara's disdain for the military.

Between 1924 and 1932, selection of the cabinet shifted back and forth between the two major parties in the lower house. Former bureaucrats and prefectural governors became politicians and ran for the Diet. Although it was not in Seiyūkai's interest to widen the electorate, the pressure of public opinion, maneuvering by other political parties, and the Privy Council's fear of social upheaval led the Diet to pass a bill for universal suffrage for males over age twenty-five in 1925. In the next election three years later, eight proletarian candidates were elected out of four hundred fifty contested seats.

The politics of compromise developed by Hara continued after party cabinets became the rule. The Privy Council, House of Peers, much of the bureaucracy, and the military remained beyond the parties' control. Despite the efforts of the constitutional scholar Minobe Tatsukichi to devise a theoretical legitimization for party cabinets, they rested on neither law nor precedent but on a pragmatic balance of power.

The crises that bedeviled Japan in the late 1920s and early 1930s tested the limits of constitutionally sanctioned parliamentary democracy. Japan had to deal with the Great Depression and fears of Russian or Chinese threats to Manchuria. Right-wing ultranationalists inside the military and outside the government accused the parties of having traitorously weakened Japan by their corrupt pursuit of self-interest. In 1930, one of their number attacked Prime Minister Hamaguchi Osachi for having signed the controversial

London Naval Treaty. He died nine months later. Convinced that the party cabinet was about to sacrifice Japan's interests in Asia, colonels in the army acted unilaterally in taking over Manchuria. The early months of 1932 saw the assassinations of a former finance minister and an industrialist blamed for hardships brought by the depression. Prime Minister Inukai Tsuyoshi also died at the hands of a group of naval cadets, junior army officers, and civilians. The next prime minister was a military man, as were his successors to 1945 with two exceptions, both of whom supported the military. The parties still dominated the lower house, but they received only minor cabinet appointments. Even during the war, the Diet continued to function. The cabinet continued to decide policy, although the military's right of access to the emperor precluded debate over its actions. The constitution remained the law of the land.

Imperial Democracy

According to critics in Japan before World War II, liberalism's focus on the individual contradicted the notion that all Japanese were part of the same body politic, *kokutai,* also translated as "national essence." Democracy was a foreign import, antithetical to indigenous custom based on harmony, consensus, and service to the emperor. Many Japanese people proved them wrong by striving for a more open government and society. In the early twentieth century, the struggle for democracy engaged academic theorists, journalists, feminists, outcasts, and the working men and women who expressed themselves in riots and efforts to organize unions.

For Japanese intellectuals, liberalism meant representative government, constitutionalism, and rule by law. It meant individual rights and freedom from undue governmental interference in the individual's life. It distinguished between the naturalness of society and the artifice of the state. The problem for liberals was that imperial ideology defined the emperor as present at society's inception. The imperial institution was not to be analyzed as though it were an artificial construct because it united state and society. Liberals were patriots. They approved of the government's efforts to promote industrialization and make Japan the equal of the West, and they never questioned the centrality of the emperor.

Intellectuals who professed liberal views jeopardized their careers. Yoshino Sakuzō had to resign his position at Tokyo University because he had argued that the people are the basis of the state and the aim of the state is to promote their well-being. The public interest, that of people as a whole, has to supersede the private, partial interests of oligarchs, bureaucrats, politicians, and businessmen. Minobe Tatsukichi argued that according to the constitution, the Diet, in particular the lower house, was the organ that represented the people. Sovereignty lay not in the emperor but in the state, and the emperor was one of its organs. In 1935 he was accused of disrespect for the emperor, his writings banned, and his membership in the upper house revoked.

Educated women promoted democracy through their organizations and deeds. Teachers, many of them Christian or influenced by missionaries, hoped to improve and reform society. The Woman's Christian Temperance Union found adherents in Japan because men's drinking wrecked the home. In 1886 the Tokyo Women's Reform Society opposed concubinage and prostitution, both deemed trafficking in women. Since the oligarchs kept concubines and the Meiji emperor fathered the crown prince on a concubine, the notion that civilized behavior included sexual fidelity was a hard sell. More acceptable was the Reform Society's work in aiding earthquake victims and providing financial support for former prostitutes. In 1901 members of the Reform Society joined the Greater Japan Women's Patriotic Association. Under its auspices they could speak in public to women, and they received government support for their activities.

The staging of Henrik Ibsen's *A Doll's House* in 1911 and inauguration of the journal *Bluestocking* marked the arrival of the "new woman" in Japan. The play offered a scandalous alternative to the government-sponsored ideology of "good wife and wise mother" when Nora walked out on husband and children. Matsui Sumako who played Nora gained fame as Japan's first western-style actress. Her tumultuous private life dramatized her rejection of domesticity. *Bluestocking* started as a literary magazine, but it soon became a forum for discussing women's roles and expectations. The feminist activist Hiratsuka Raichō and the poet, translator, and social critic Yosano Akiko debated state support for motherhood, Hiratsuka wanting government protection, Yosano arguing that state support would be degrading and would cost women their independence. They agreed that marriage is not sacrosanct, patriarchy need not go unchallenged, and women ought to have equal legal, educational, and social rights.

In the 1920s, feminists advocated family planning and women's suffrage. Katō Shidzue brought Margaret Sanger to Japan in 1924 to promote birth control as a way to deal with the threat to family budgets and women's health posed by too many children. The government refused Sanger permission to land until she promised to make no public speeches. The examples of Britain and the United States that granted women the vote after World War I and the growing numbers of women who followed politics in mass circulation newspapers and magazines convinced some politicians and bureaucrats that political rights for women marked advanced societies. In 1922 the Diet revoked the law that barred women from political meetings. In 1931 a bill for local women's suffrage passed the lower house but foundered on a conservative coalition in the House of Peers. Give women the right to vote, and they will stop having children, predicted one baron. The end to party cabinets stymied proposals for women's political rights.

Mass Movements

Modern mass movements emerged in the context of Japanese imperialism. In 1905, newspapers and speechmakers informed the public that

the Russo-Japanese War had concluded without the indemnity that a great power deserved from a defeated foe and with slight territorial gain to justify the sacrifices made by Japanese troops. Riots began at Tokyo's Hibiya Park outside the palace and continued for three days, destroying over 70 percent of police boxes that provided shelter for policemen stationed across the city and fifteen trams. (See Map 24.2.) Smaller riots erupted in Kobe and Yokohama. All but two of the forty-four prefectures reported rallies in cities, towns, and villages. Between 1905 and the rice riots of 1918, Tokyo experienced nine serious riots, many part of larger movements that swept the nation. Although rioters attacked police stations and government offices, they did so in the name of the emperor. By conflating imperial and popular will, they differentiated between evil advisers behind the throne and the throne itself.

The rice riots of 1918 protested high prices, degrading work conditions, and governmental ineptitude. They began with fishermen's wives who organized demonstrations along the Toyama coast and grew to include urban rioters who castigated war profiteers and asserted a right to free speech, tenant farmers who demanded lower rents and decent treatment from landlords, and coal miners who demanded higher wages and respect as human beings. Out of them grew the mass movements of the 1920s for *burakumin* (outcast) liberation and labor organization.

Outcasts found that the Meiji transformation did not improve their lot. Losing the monopoly over leather work and other lucrative, if unpleasant, tasks brought poverty. The household registration system made it well nigh impossible for outcasts to escape their past. Schools refused to admit them, employers to hire them, landlords to rent to them, public baths and barbers to serve them, and other Japanese to marry them. When conscripted into the military, they were assigned menial tasks and never promoted. In the early twentieth century, the central government set up advisory committees to deal with the issue of poverty lest

Map **24.2** Modern Tokyo

socialism creep into Japan. Since *burakumin* were among the worst off, they became one focus. In 1908 the cabinet encouraged them to emigrate. In 1911 the Home Ministry started to distribute funds for the improvement of *burakumin* communities, and in 1920 it started the Harmony Movement to mobilize the *burakumin* to work for gradual reform. Private organizations lent support. Both assumed that the reason for discrimination lay in *burakumin* filth, ignorance, and immorality. In 1922, a group of

young *burakumin* organized the Leveller's Society (*Suiheisha*) to protest discrimination and promote the equality of all Japanese subjects before the emperor.

The *burakumin* liberation movement of the 1920s blamed the *burakumin*'s problems on prejudice and discrimination. The goal was to change social attitudes, but Leveller's Society members could not agree on tactics. Some believed in educational programs and nonviolent confrontations that aimed at greater democracy. Others wanted

Women Supporters of the Suiheisha. This nation-wide organization tried to end discrimination against burakumin in the 1920s. These women were from the Fukuoka branch in northern Kyushu. *(50 Years of History of Suiheisha by Buraku Liberation Publishing House/DNP Archives.com)*

a social revolution to overthrow capitalism through challenging institutions and individuals known to oppose fair practices. Denunciation campaigns targeted primary schools that permitted students and staff to insult *burakumin* or public officials and individuals who had uttered derogatory remarks. The offenders would have to offer an apology, sometimes publicized in newspapers. In 1926, the first year of the Shōwa emperor's reign, antimilitarism plus anger at the treatment of conscript *burakumin* led to a movement promoting noncompliance with military organizations. Despite police repression, denunciation campaigns continued into the 1930s. Only after the outbreak of the China war in 1937 did the Leveller's Society agree to support national unity and the war effort.

Tenant farmers and industrial workers tried to gain acceptance for their organizations and legitimacy for their grievances. The 1898 Civil Code gave landlords the right to buy, sell, and lease land without any protection for tenants who might have farmed it for generations. Of Japan's farm families, 28 percent owned no land, while another 41 percent owned some and rented the rest. Tenants and tenant-owners organized unions in the 1910s to demand rent reductions and the right of cultivation, especially in the most economically advanced regions in central and western Japan, where landlords had previously been in the forefront of encouraging agricultural improvements. The tenants established a national federation in 1922 that grew to nearly seven hundred branches. In the 1920s, over eighteen thousand disputes between tenants and landlords filled police dockets.

Agricultural conditions in the 1930s began badly. The economic downturn in the 1920s when synthetic fabrics replaced silk and the government allowed the import of rice from Asia reduced the demand for agricultural products and unskilled labor. Real income for farm families declined by 30 percent. Unseasonably cold weather in the agriculturally backward northeast brought crop failures between 1931 and 1933. Landlords tried to repossess tenanted land, refused to reduce rents, or even tried to raise them. Debt-ridden farmers migrated to Japan's overseas colonies or sold their daughters into prostitution. Tenants petitioned the Agriculture Ministry for rural relief. The ministry responded by organizing cooperatives and providing funds for development. In central and western Japan, where absentee landlords no longer performed ceremonial and support functions, tenants lost their former deference. Their habit of looking on the land they cultivated as theirs led to rent refusals and conflict. By the mid-1930s, being a landlord was more trouble that it was worth. With the coming of war in 1937, agricultural conditions improved when the government moved to limit rice imports, and tenant unions disbanded in the drive for national unity.

Industrial development led to labor activism, though not labor solidarity. Heavy industry employed highly skilled and relatively well-paid male workers sufficiently educated to read newspapers and understand socialist theory. Textile mills continued to hire cheaper and, it was hoped, docile women and girls. Even in 1930, they constituted over 50 percent of the factory work force. Urban women found jobs as teachers, journalists, nurses, clerks, ticket sellers, bus conductors, telephone operators, actresses, and café hostesses. Small firms employed male and female workers at low wages to manufacture parts for other sectors of the economy. Below them were rickshaw pullers and delivery boys. At the bottom were the miners.

Worker grievances and the ability to organize varied across industries and within factories. The 1907 riot at the Ashio mine originated with ore diggers, the most highly paid workers, not copper refinery workers whose wages had recently dropped and who feared being laid off. The expansion in heavy industry and the need to raise productivity prompted factory owners to reduce worker autonomy and eliminate the bosses who contracted for specific jobs. Workers countered with demands that they be treated with respect. (See **Documents: Negotiations Between Strike Group Representatives and Company Directors.**) In 1912 they organized the Friendship Society (Yūaikai) to provide mutual aid, self-improvement classes, and improved relations with employers. If workers worked hard and deferred to foremen, then the factory owners ought to treat them with benevolence. To keep skilled workers, employers instituted a seniority system of raises and offered fringe benefits.

In many cases, implementation of paternalistic benefits came only after workers had launched work stoppages and strikes. Over one hundred labor disputes erupted between 1902 and 1917. In 1919 the Hara cabinet interpreted the Public Order and Police Act of 1900 to mean that workers might organize unions and go on strike so long as they remained nonviolent. In 1921 the Yūaikai became the Japan Federation of Labor. Union membership burgeoned in the 1920s, although it never included more than 8 percent of the industrial work force. Hundreds of strikes a year roiled both heavy and textile industries. Although owners resisted unionization, workers bargained collectively for higher wages, severance pay, a minimum wage, better working conditions, shorter workdays, an end to child labor, and improved housing.

Minorities

Although nationalist propaganda assured Japanese people that they were uniquely homogeneous, the pairing of colonialism and modernity created groups perceived as different. The

DOCUMENTS

Negotiations Between Strike Group Representatives and Company Directors

This confrontation between strike group representatives Itō, Iwasa, and Shiga and company directors for the Yokohama Dock Company Tōjō and Miyanaga on September 28, 1921, exposes conflict between workers and management over work conditions and financial issues such as wages and severance pay. The hyperbole on both sides scarcely conceals fundamentally different attitudes regarding company goals, the value of work, and the treatment of workers.

Itō: Today the three of us have come as worker representatives with this petition.

Miyanaga: Does this demand for a 20 percent daily wage increase mean an average wage increase of 20 percent for all the workers?

Iwasa: Our wages average 1 yen 60 sen. Out of 1,000 people, if there is one getting 3 yen, the rest are getting around 1 yen 40 sen. With days off, one month is 25 days and, with a wife and children, we can't make ends meet. This is why we have asked for a pay raise. With the present severance pay, if one of us is fired, he is reduced to poverty.

Miyanaga: We want you to understand the company's situation. As you are well aware, the economy, especially the shipbuilding industry, is facing a severe depression. The question of how to support the workers in this situation is one that troubles us greatly. Because of the shipbuilding depression there have been many layoffs, and aware of your anxiety about this, the other day we announced that we would not carry out any large-scale layoffs. As for ship repairs, which this company has been engaged in since its founding, in good times we were able to charge the shipowners a good price, but today the situation is so bad that, even if we offer a price below cost, they won't take it.

Shipbuilding revived briefly after the war and we were able to make some profit, but now we are making no profit and are taking orders at a loss. In this depression, we are taking on such orders because we do not want to have to lay off you workers. We understand well your plight, but, even at present pay levels, the situation is as I have described, so we would hope to have your understanding regarding the pay raise. You also raised demands regarding severance and retirement pay. As I have already noted, our policy is to avoid layoffs at all costs in the hopes that this will reduce your anxiety, so we would like to gain your understanding on these points also. As for the fourth demand, you use the term "expel." Does that mean you want us to fire them?

All three: That's right.

Miyanaga: You want us to fire the three factory heads. However, the decision to take action against those who break company regulations does rest with these people. Although we hope to avoid such situations, every day two or three people are fired for breaking company rules, and there was nothing exceptional in the case of these three. Thus it would be difficult to take action [and fire the supervisors who had

government defined the Ainu as "formerly indigenous people" and demanded that they assimilate into the Japanese mainstream by renouncing their peripatetic lifestyle and settling in villages. Officials who supervised their transformation into tenant farmers, laborers, and welfare recipients in the course of selling off their lands and opening Hokkaido to develop-fired three union members.] As for what the company will do in the future, we feel it would be best to work to harmonize your desires with those of the company and work from a position of mutual understanding. We are presently studying ways to promote your welfare. In due time, we are hoping to implement these plans. Thus we would like to gain your understanding regarding both the company's present position and future plans and have you pass this on to your fellow workers.

Itō: Are you saying you will absolutely not lay off any workers?

Miyanaga: I can't promise "absolutely" but . . .

Miyanaga and Itō (together): Insofar as possible.

Itō: In that case wouldn't it be better to decide on severance pay and relieve our anxieties in that way?

Miyanaga: Our thinking is that is would be even kinder to take the policy of avoiding layoffs rather than getting involved in the severance pay issue.

Itō: So you mean to say that there is no necessity to decide on severance pay? If your policy is not to lay off workers, well, this is a bit of an extreme example, but in that case wouldn't it be just as well to set severance pay at 10 to 20 thousand yen?

Miyanaga: I didn't say that there was no need. We are now considering the issue of severance pay.

Itō: You say "insofar as possible," but does that mean that in the eventuality of a layoff, you will handle it as in the past?

Miyanaga: We are now also considering the possibility of increasing the level in the future.

Iwasa: Isn't what you are saying merely that, if you accept our demands, your profit will be narrowed? For us this is a matter of life and death.

Miyanaga: You say "our profits are narrowed," but in fact, not only are we not expecting any profit, but the company is going so far as to operate at a loss.

Itō: We have already heard at length from Mr. Yamaguchi on this point and understand it well. In any case, we regard the fact that the company will not now announce its intention to change the present severance pay as an indication of the company's total lack of sincerity regarding this entire affair. Let's go back and report this to all the others.

Miyanaga: You say that we are insincere, but as I have already explained the company is striving to promote your welfare and guarantee your security, and we'd like you to report this to the others.

Iwasa: The other day a worker named Tsukui, who was working in one of your manufacturing shops, was fired for going to another shop and talking to a worker there. You said that this was a violation of company rules, so he was fired. But this is something which other workers are constantly doing. If you look for such little matters and fire someone everyday, pretty soon you'll have fired all the workers. Therefore, all your kind words are just the attitude of a man who stands laughing after having strangled seven people. We'll go and report this situation to all the other workers.

———
Source: Andrew Gordon, *The Evolution of Labor Relations in Japan: Heavy Industry, 1853–1955* (Cambridge, Mass.: Council on East Asian Studies, Harvard University, 1985), pp. 116–119, modified.

ment saw them as a dying race. Many Ainu accepted the necessity of assimilation despite discrimination at the hands of employers, teachers, and non-Ainu neighbors. Others objected to contradictory policies that made them use the Japanese language and forgo tattooing and earrings while setting them up as tourist attractions and anthropological exhibits. During the 1920s,

Ainu scholars recorded Ainu songs, legends, and customs. Ainu activists created self-help programs to cope with alcoholism and violence. Social critics drew on radical thought to counter prejudice and discrimination. Fearful lest Hokkaido go red with the Soviet Union so close to its border, government officials and assimilationist Ainu founded the Ainu Society in 1930 to improve the individual lot through education and to remind Ainu of the gratitude they owed the emperor.

The government's attitude toward the Ryukyus was more complicated. The land tax was not imposed in the Ryukyus until 1903. Ryukyuans had a social hierarchy topped by a monarch and aristocracy that made sense in the eyes of Japanese accustomed to inherent social inequality. Ryukyuan nobles used their status to gain favors from the prefectural governor's office and insisted on their right to speak for the commoners. To be placed on a par with Ainu was, they felt, an insult to their superior culture.

Nearly three hundred thousand Koreans lived in Japan by 1930. The earliest arrivals in the late nineteenth century were students of Japan's resistance to western imperialism. Next came workers forced from their villages by colonial policies that expropriated land and put Japan's dietary needs first. Enticed by labor contractors who promised employment in factories, mines, and construction, workers ended up in low-paying jobs and substandard housing. Excluded from skilled labor except when used to break strikes, they performed dirty and dangerous jobs shunned by Japanese at wages half that of Japanese workers. Although the government made Koreans citizens of Japan and promoted an ideology of racial brotherhood under the emperor, Koreans in Japan were deemed inherently stupid, lazy, bellicose, and vicious. Accused of having set fires and poisoned wells following the Great Kanto Earthquake, thousands died at the hands of Japanese vigilantes.

Koreans who showed intellectual promise earned the mistrust of Japanese officials, who feared, with reason, that they harbored anti-Japanese sentiment. Korean students in Japan suffered arrest, imprisonment, and death for supporting national resistance movements and joining Japanese students who professed universal brotherhood, socialism, and communism. The Osaka Confederation of Korean Laborers earned official enmity when it called for an end to capitalism. Moderate Korean residents feared that opposition to colonialism would only invite repression. They organized mutual aid societies to help Koreans find work, adequate housing, and health care. Government officials promoted assimilation policies to bring Koreans gradually and peacefully into Japanese society, albeit with the proviso that ethnically they could never become Japanese.

Radicals

The government suppressed ideas it deemed dangerous in socialism and other western theories. In 1901 the Socialist Democratic Party enjoyed mere hours of existence before being outlawed. It advocated public ownership of land, capital, and communications; abolition of the military; education funded by the state; workers' rights to unionize; universal suffrage; and abolition of the House of Peers. It did not reject the emperor system, unlike the anarcho-syndicalists Kōtoku Shūsui and Kanno Suga. He opposed capitalists, militarists, aristocrats, and politicians on behalf of workers and farmers. She advocated overthrow of the government and assassination of the emperor. In what is known as the Great Treason Trial of 1911, Kōtoku and Kanno were convicted and sentenced to death, although they were innocent of the charges brought against them. Ōsugi Sakae believed that society consists of two classes: the conquerors and the suppressed. It was up to workers to abolish the state and destroy capitalism. Following the Great Kanto Earthquake, he and his wife, the feminist and anarchist Itō Noe, were strangled by the police. The nihilist Kaneko Fumiko advocated Korean independence. She died in prison. In 1933, the proletarian writer Kobayashi Takiji, who had graphically depicted the brutal conditions of fishermen in *The Cannery Boat* (1929), died at the hands of the police.

During the 1920s, a few socialists enjoyed a brief opportunity to propagate their views. The Red Wave Society founded in 1921 urged women to join the fight against capitalist society that enslaved them inside and outside the home. Sakai Toshihiko organized a study group to discuss socialist ideas in the late 1890s. In 1922 he participated in the secret founding of the Japanese Communist Party. Inuta Shigeru launched a literary movement that advocated self-rule for farmers through land reform. Kawakami Hajime took a torturous path from religious movements and nationalism to Marxism, revolutionary communism, and the study of historical materialism. Between 1927 and 1937, socialists and Communists debated the nature of Japanese capitalism, seeking to find a balance between universal Marxist categories and the Japanese experience that determined the kinds of political action possible in the present. The Peace Preservation Law of 1925 promised punishment for attacks on the emperor system or capitalism. In the early 1930s, the police arrested over ten thousand people a year for propagating ideas disloyal to the emperor and dangerous to the *kokutai*. Their intent was to induce a repudiation of socialist thought and conversion to a belief in Japan's sacred mission. Men and women who refused to confess and convert remained in prison until after World War II.

MODERN URBAN CULTURE

Industrial growth and expansion of the government bureaucracy created a new middle class of salaried white-collar workers. (See **Material Culture: Houses for the Middle Class.**) In contrast to the old middle class of shopkeepers and landlords, these workers got their jobs through educational achievement and enjoyed the security of lifetime employment with fringe benefits such as subsidized housing and medical care. Income depended on seniority as much as proficiency or accomplishment. In his novels *Sanshirō* (1908) and *Kokoro* (1914), Natsume Sōseki depicted socially mobile young men from the countryside. Sanshirō found himself torn between an academic career, the glittering world of business, and a return to his village. *Kokoro* expressed the sense that the era of great expectations passed with the death of the Meiji emperor in 1912. His son, the Taishō emperor, was universally seen as a lesser figure. In the 1920s the opportunities for becoming extremely rich declined, but the new middle class continued to grow.

The Great Kanto Earthquake of 1923 that brought down brick buildings and wooden houses ushered in modern Japanese culture. The new Tokyo had more ferro-concrete. Even before the earthquake, the new middle class had started moving south and west of the city limits. Private railroads and the real estate developers who owned them intensified this trend. With the exception of the publishing industry, light industry moved east of the city; heavy industry moved south to Kawasaki. The space left behind filled with offices, retail shops, and entertainment arcades.

Modern culture incorporated a second wave of westernization driven not by national goals but individual inclinations. Dry goods stores had already transformed themselves into department stores at the turn of the century. After the earthquake, they added theaters, galleries, exhibition halls, and rooftop arcades. In 1926, vending machines started providing refreshment for travelers at Tokyo and Ueno stations. In 1927, the first subway in Asia connected corporate headquarters in Ginza with movie houses and cafés in Asakusa. Mass transit changed urban patterns of work, family life, leisure, and consumption. Unlike the old middle class that lived behind their business and shopped in the neighborhood, the white-collar worker commuted

MATERIAL CULTURE

Houses for the Middle Class

Houses built after the Great Kanto Earthquake for the new middle class were derived from western architectural styles. Rooms had fewer functions but greater privacy than before. They had walls and doors and were further separated from one another by corridors. Guests were received on the first floor at the front of the house in the parlor, decorated with sofa, chairs, antimacassars, and carpet on a hardwood floor beneath a small chandelier. In line with the changing social etiquette of the time, guests were discouraged from making unexpected calls, and the telephone gave them little excuse for doing so. The family living room overlooked the garden. Although located on the dark north side of the house, the kitchen had a floor. Bedrooms were on the second floor. A modern water supply made it possible for each house to have its own bath.

New middle-class furnishings were designed chiefly for entertainment and the convenience of the family, especially the wife, rather than being objects with which to impress guests. The living room ideally contained a phonograph and radio. Appliances included the gas range for cooking, a gas heater with ceramic grill, an electric fan, and an electric rice cooker. For reasons of etiquette and security, old-style houses had required that someone always be home to greet guests and guard the premises. Western-style front doors made it easy for the housewife to lock the door and go shopping, visit friends, or see a movie.

Modern Living Room. This modern living room was photographed for the journal *Homu raifu* (Home Life). Chairs, tables, potted plants, sofa, and cushions provide a western-style backdrop for the woman wearing kimono.

from his suburban home to his work downtown. The entertainment districts that grew up around train terminals enticed him to spend evenings at coffee shops and cafés.

The new middle class consumed a modern culture removed from politics. Mass literacy spurred the development of mass media. Self-help books and magazines taught the rudiments of popular science, how to be modern, how to succeed in business, and how to create the perfect home environment. (See Color Plate 28.) By 1920, eleven hundred newspapers found 6 to 7 million buyers. Registered magazines were ten times that number. Journals for men appealed to the highbrow, the middlebrow, and the vulgar. Women's journals, calibrated according to class, girls' journals, and boys' journals divided the market into ever more discrete segments. Retail bookstores jumped from three thousand in 1914 to over ten thousand in 1927. They sold complete editions of western authors in translation, serious works of idealist philosophy by the Kyoto School, novels by best-selling authors such as Tanizaki Junichirō (male) and Uno Chiyo (female), and illustrated books given to escapist sensationalism. Cinemas showed films from abroad alongside domestically produced animated cartoons and historical dramas. Movie stars became celebrities. Government-operated radio stations started broadcasting in the mid-1920s. Record companies churned out patriotic songs. Popular music celebrated romantic love and the delights of Tokyo, including hanging out in Ginza. A cheap escape from the workaday world was to watch small balls bounce down a pachinko board, the vertical version of the pinball machine.

Modern mass culture promoted a privatizing world of pleasure and self-expression. Women danced in chorus lines and performed in the Takarazuka Girl's Theater. (See **Biography: Kobayashi Ichizō.**) In the novel *Naomi* (1924–1925), Tanizaki depicted the transformation of a café waitress into a *modan gaaru* (modern girl; *moga* for short) who bobbed her hair, wore revealing dresses, and danced the Charleston. The *moga*'s less flamboyant companion was the *mobo* (modern boy). Together they scandalized onlookers by smoking cigarettes and holding hands in public. The late 1920s are often characterized by the words *ero, guro,* and *nansensu*—eroticism, grotesquerie, and nonsense, referring to both the flood of foreign words in urban vocabularies and the perceived decline in public morals. Materialism, individualism, and decadence had apparently replaced the beautiful Japanese virtues of diligence, decorum, and duty.

ALTERNATIVES TO MODERNITY

People repelled by modern culture found solace in folk traditions of rural Japan, high art of ancient Japan, and communities of the devout created by the new religions. Ethnographer Yanagita Kunio sought a cultural authenticity that had been lost in urban areas. He traveled from Tohoku to the Ryukyus, collecting folk tales and documenting what he viewed as pristine customs of the folk. Industrialist and builder of the Mitsui *zaibatsu* Masuda Takashi tried to preserve Japan's artistic patrimony and supported the government's system for designating cultural artifacts as national treasures. First established in 1897, the designation applied foremost to religious objects from the Kyoto area, declared Japan's sovereignty over its past, magnified differences between Japan and the outside world, and demonstrated that Japan possessed the trappings of world-class culture.

The new religions provided alternative visions of modernity that did not please the state. Deguchi Onisaburō, the organizer of Ōmoto-kyō, criticized government policies that disadvantaged the poor. In the 1920s, he proclaimed that as the Maitreya, he would establish a new order on earth, a message that found believers even among government officials and army officers. In the early 1930s, he founded a semimilitaristic youth group to restore the kingdom of God at the Ōmoto-kyō headquarters. Ōmoto-kyō was suppressed in 1921 and again in 1935. New religions

BIOGRAPHY Kobayashi Ichizō

Entrepreneur, politician, and diplomat, Kobayashi Ichizō (1873–1957) fostered consumer culture by founding a railroad, a department store, a baseball team, and the Takarazuka Girl's Theater.

Kobayashi had wanted to become a writer, but after graduating from Keiō University, he joined the Mitsui Bank in 1893. In 1906 he left the bank to become executive director for a private electrical railroad near Osaka. Through hard work and creative planning in the building of new lines and improving service, he made his company dominant in train travel between Osaka and Kobe. In 1918 he became president of the newly named Hankyū electric railroad. To attract riders he expanded into real estate development by building suburban housing developments for the new middle class.

Kobayashi's interests tended toward popular culture. One of his train lines went to Takarazuka, a fading hot springs resort. To lure customers, he built a zoo and, in 1913, the Takarazuka Girl's Theater. In 1919 he founded the Takarazuka Music Academy to train young women for his productions. The first revue with chorus line and musical spectaculars was *Mon Paris,* staged in 1927. Having watched commuters surge through the Hankyū terminal in Osaka, he opened a market adjacent to the station in 1924. Five years later it became the Hankyū department store with restaurants, an art gallery, and a bookstore. Kobayashi also founded the Tōhō Cinema Company to make and distribute films. He built his movie empire with a mass audience in mind by scheduling show times and setting ticket prices for the benefit of workers. In 1936 he joined other railroad magnates and real estate developers to establish Japan's first professional baseball league to give people another reason to ride trains in search of entertainment. Loyal fans still cheer the Hankyū Braves. In 1940 Kobayashi reached the pinnacle of his career by becoming commerce and industry minister and special ambassador in charge of trade to the Netherlands.

Kobayashi insisted that the performers in the Takarazuka Girl's Theater be of unquestionable virtue; his aim was to provide entertainment for respectable women and to mold his actresses' character so that they could later perform as good wives and wise mothers on their most important stage, the home. The Music Academy provided training in etiquette, ethics, and homemaking as well as singing and dancing. On stage women played male roles; they also played Asians from countries incorporated into the Japanese empire. Lest actresses aspire to make the theater a profession, Kobayashi insisted that they retire at the peak of their popularity while they were still considered young enough to make a good match.

Source: Based on Jennifer E. Robertson, *Takarazuka: Sexual Politics and Popular Culture in Modern Japan* (Berkeley: University of California Press, 1998).

---

founded after 1905 more commonly based their teachings on Nichiren Buddhism and answered the needs of uprooted, underprivileged masses in the cities. Charismatic leaders preached a gospel of social equality and promised either a pure new world or salvation to come. They emphasized faith healing, deliverance from suffering, and a focus on this world's benefits. For recent urban migrants, the new religions provided self-help groups, a sense of identity, and a community that was neither self-righteously traditional nor alienating modern.

Twentieth-century agrarianism exhibited more virulent antimodernism. It identified agriculture as the ethical foundation of the state when agriculture was no longer the country's main source of wealth. Its adherents professed a farm *bushidō* (way of the warrior) that assimilated the farmers' virtues of diligence, frugality, fortitude, and harmony to loyalty and self-sacrifice on behalf of the state. This agrarianism criticized city life for making people selfish and ambitious; it detested capitalism for increasing the corrupting power of money, destroying the farm family economy, and eroding harmony between city and country. It demanded a spiritual alternative to materialism and a national alternative to universal socialism. Its nostalgic search for a return to a primitive rural society that manifested the *kokutai* frequently turned violent in the 1930s.

SUMMARY

By 1931, modern Japan had parliamentary democracy, an educated citizenry, and an industrialized economy. It also contained conflicting visions of what it meant to be Japanese, who should be incorporated into the nation and how, and what should be Japan's role in the world. The relatively peaceful world of the 1920s allowed space for controversy. When the Great Depression struck in 1930, plural and critical voices within Japan appeared as dangerous as threats from abroad to Japan's economic and national security.

SUGGESTED READING

This period is so well researched by scholars that only a sampling of recent works is listed here. For Japan in Asia, see P. Duus, *The Abacus and the Sword: The Japanese Penetration of Korea, 1895–1910* (1995); P. Duus, R. H. Myers, and M. R. Peattie, eds., *The Japanese Informal Empire in China, 1895–1937* (1989); T. Matsusaka, *The Making of Japanese Manchuria, 1904–1932* (2001); and M. R. Peattie, *Nan'yō: The Rise and Fall of the Japanese in Micronesia, 1885–1945* (1988).

For women, see G. L. Bernstein, ed., *Recreating Japanese Women, 1600–1945* (1991); B. Sato, *The New Japanese Women: Modernity, Media, and Women in Interwar Japan* (2003); and M. Hane, *Reflections on the Way to the Gallows: Rebel Women in Prewar Japan* (1988).

For labor, see A. Gordon, *Labor and Imperial Democracy in Japan* (1991); K. Nimura, *The Ashio Riot of 1907: A Social History of Mining in Japan* (1997); and W. M. Tsutsui, *Manufacturing Ideology: Scientific Management in Twentieth-Century Japan* (1998). For agriculture, see K. Smith, *A Time of Crisis: Japan, the Great Depression, and Rural Revitalization* (2001).

For minorities, see R. Siddle, *Race, Resistance and the Ainu of Japan* (1996); I. Neary, *Political Protest and Social Control in Prewar Japan: The Origins of Buraku Liberation* (1989); and M. Weiner, *Race and Migration in Imperial Japan* (1994). For riots, see M. L. Lewis, *Rioters and Citizens: Mass Protest in Imperial Japan* (1990).

For modern life, see S. A. Hastings, *Neighborhood and Nation in Tokyo, 1905–1937* (1995); S. Garon, *Molding Japanese Minds: The State in Everyday Life* (1997); J. Sand, *House and Home in Modern Japan: Architecture, Domestic Space and Bourgeois Culture, 1880–1930* (2003); and E. K. Tipton and J. Clark, eds., *Being Modern in Japan: Culture and Society from the 1910s to the 1930s* (2000).

CHAPTER TWENTY-FIVE

The Loss of Korean Independence and Colonial Rule (1896–1945)

After the Sino-Japanese War ended in 1895, Korea had an all too brief period to save itself from subjugation to Japan. It failed to do so and lost its independence for thirty-five years. That period was disruptive because it involved major social, economic, cultural, and ideological transformations that entailed both much human suffering and possibilities for development. Liberation from colonial rule as a consequence of the U.S. victory over Japan in 1945 should have resulted in the restoration of a healthy independence for Korea, but the development of nationalism and the introduction of communism created the basis for political division that began soon after 1945 and was caught up in the maelstrom of the Cold War conflict between the United States and the Soviet Union.

There are three major issues of contention among scholars. Should attention be focused mainly on the suffering of the Korean people under Japanese oppression or on the progress made in economic development, modern education, the liberation of women, and the introduction of modern culture? A second is should anti-Japanese guerrilla fighters be given greater credit for their patriotic resistance to Japanese imperialism over cultural nationalists, who acquiesced to Japanese control and sought to educate the masses to higher national consciousness over the long term, and expatriate nationalists in the United States, who sought to persuade western nations to liberate Korea? Finally, were the Communists greater patriots than the non-Communists because they fought against the Japanese in China and Manchuria versus the Korean landlords and businessmen who not

Queen Myŏngsŏng. Queen Myŏngsŏng (a.k.a. Queen Min of the Yŏhŭng Min family), 1851–1895, was assassinated by Japanese thugs and soldiers in the palace in 1895. *(5,000 Years of Korean Art, p. 183)*

only prospered under Japan, but supported Japanese efforts in the late 1930s to eliminate Korean language and culture? Should the landlords and businessmen be absolved of the charge of collaboration because they had no choice but to survive under Japanese rule?

THE TRANSITION TO COLONIAL RULE (1896–1905)

In 1896 King Kojong escaped from his palace, where he was under the watch of Japanese

guards, and fled to the Russian embassy. Once there, he dismissed the reform cabinet. The reform ministers were killed by street mobs, and the new, conservative cabinet reversed the topknot edict and many reforms. The Japanese were forced to withdraw from direct involvement in Korean domestic affairs, and Russia gained the upper hand in Korea. Strapped for funds to pay off indemnities and finance his government, King Kojong began to lease rights to the exploitation of natural resources like lumber to the Russians, gold mines to the Americans, and railroad construction to the Japanese and others in return for loans.

Early Nationalist Movements

Popular reaction against the king's sacrifice of national resources gave rise to the first explicitly nationalist movement, the Independence Club, in 1896. The club demanded the dismissal of corrupt officials and strove to educate people on the need to modernize the country. It organized street meetings and education sessions and established a newspaper, *The Independent* (*Tongnip sinmun*), written in the vernacular language instead of classical Chinese. Membership in the group increased as its leaders made public speeches, established branches in small towns, campaigned for the construction of an Independence Gate as a sign of liberation from subservience to China, held mass meetings and demonstrations in Seoul, and demanded and received a couple of dozen seats on the king's council. Its leaders included men like Sŏ Chaep'il (also called Philip Jaisohn), an American citizen who returned to Korea; Syngman Rhee (Yi Sŭngman), who had attended Paejae Christian missionary school; and Yun Ch'iho, who visited Japan and was educated in the United States. All these men were fired with the zeal to create a truly independent nation, and some talked of forming a constitutional monarchy.

King Kojong decided in 1897 to change the title of his kingdom to "The Great Empire of Korea" (*Taehan'jeguk*) and adopt the title of emperor, but he had no inclination to tolerate a

King Kojong. This photo depicts King Kojong (king of the Chosŏn Dynasty from 1864–1897; emperor of the Great Han Empire, *Taehan'jeguk,* from 1897–1907) as emperor wearing a military uniform in 1897. *(Sajinuro ponun tongnip undong, vol. 1, p. 42)*

to demand the abolition of concubinage. Esther Park, the first woman doctor, began practice at the Women's Hospital (Pogu yŏgwan) in 1900 and taught sanitation in addition to clinical work.

Russian Influences

Russia had acquired a narrow boundary with northeastern Korea in 1860 and constructed a trans-Siberian railway across Siberia to Vladivostok. In 1896, Russia began construction of a second railway, the Chinese Eastern Railway, which stretched across Manchuria to shorten the distance to Vladivostok. The next year Russia obtained a twenty-five-year lease on the Guandong area, Port Arthur, and the commercial port of Dalian on the Liaodong peninsula, which it had taken away from Japan in 1895, and it obtained railroad rights from there to Harbin to connect with the Chinese Eastern Railway. After Germany established the first sphere of influence in China involving exclusive privileges over trade and railways in the Shandong peninsula in 1897, Russia did the same in Manchuria. The Japanese could only watch these events in ever-growing frustration.

In 1896, while King Kojong was residing in the Russian legation, Russia and Japan signed two agreements (the Komura-Weber Memorandum and the Protocol of Moscow) that granted Russia equal rights with Japan to station legation guards and grant loans to the Korean government. Korea also signed the secret Min-Lobanov Agreement in which Russia promised to protect King Kojong and provide military and financial aid.

The Russo-Japanese War (1904–1905)

In 1897, the Russian position in Korea was compromised when the Japanese revealed the terms of a secret agreement with Russia for possible partition of the Korean peninsula. Japan then opened negotiations with Russia in 1898 for resolving the balance of power between them in northeast Asia. The Japanese wanted Russia to recognize Japan's sphere of influence

constitutional monarchy or a republic. He banned the Independence Club suddenly in 1898 and imprisoned its members. Yun Ch'iho went into hiding, and Syngman Rhee was jailed from 1898 to 1904.

The Independence Club had inspired women to debate sexual equality and education. They organized the Ch'anyanghoe (Praise the Lord Society) in 1898 to form a school for women and the Yŏuhoe (Friends of Women) the next year in Korea in return for Japanese acknowledgment of Russia's sphere in Manchuria. Neither side agreed because neither was willing to sacrifice all interests in Manchuria and Korea. The Nishi-Rosen Agreement between the two powers in April 1898 recognized Korean independence and the right of Japan to pursue commercial and industrial interests in Korea, but it did not solve the fear of future aggression from the other party.

Both countries fought over concessions inside Korea. In 1901 the Japanese made plans to complete the railway between Pusan and Seoul and build a connection from Seoul to Ŭiju while Russia tried to expand its leasehold around the Yalu River and bring soldiers in to defend it. Because of its growing mistrust of Russia, Japan entered into an alliance with Great Britain in 1902. Great Britain would remain neutral if Japan went to war with another country, but if a third country joined in, Great Britain would intervene on Japan's side. This measure prevented both Germany and France from joining with Russia in a repetition of the Triple Intervention of 1895 and opened the possibility of a war by Japan against Russia alone.

Fruitless negotiations continued, and despite a last-ditch appeal by Korea for neutralization of the Korea peninsula, Japanese-Russian relations broke down in February 1904. Japan sent an invasion force to occupy Seoul, thus beginning the Russo-Japanese War. Japanese land forces won the last land battle at Mukden in Manchuria in March 1905, and the Japanese navy under Admiral Tōgō Heihachirō completely destroyed Russia's Baltic fleet in the Tsushima Strait in May. U.S. President Theodore Roosevelt mediated a peace settlement at the Portsmouth Conference that ended the war on September 8, 1905. Russia withdrew from Korea after the Portsmouth Treaty, and Great Britain extended its alliance with Japan and acknowledged its freedom to take any action it saw fit in Korea. That same year, the United States signed the Taft-Katsura Agreement acknowledging Korea as part of the Japanese sphere of interest in return for a Japanese

guarantee of U.S. domination over the Philippines and Guam, which it had captured from Spain in the Spanish-American War of 1898–1900. The United States, which Koreans had hoped would protect them against a foreign predator, betrayed those hopes.

THE INTRODUCTION OF WESTERN TECHNOLOGY AND INFLUENCES

In the last two years of the century, streetcars, electric lights, foreign buildings, a modern hospital, and a bridge over the Han River were introduced to Seoul. The bridge was the first step toward the modern transportation of goods, the reduction of transportation costs, and the expansion of trade.

Women began the fight for equality. After 1900, the royal mint and private textile companies began to hire women workers for the first time. Women's groups were established to pay back the foreign debts incurred by the regime. Others protested administrative corruption, called for independence, and organized participatory groups. Women founded societies in 1906 and 1907 to campaign for women's education, against separation of the sexes, abolition of the shawl to cover women's faces (*ssŭgech'ima*), establishment of a hospital, and publication of new journal, *A Guide for Women* (*Yŏja chinam*). Two of the prominent leaders were Yi Okkyŏng and Helen Kim. Other women, such as Louise Yim, wrote of their struggles to achieve more independence for women (see **Documents: Louise Yim's Writings on Female Independence**).

In 1905, the Tonghak movement changed its name to the Religion of the Heavenly Way (Ch'ŏndogyo). Son Pyŏnghŭi, a Tonghak leader, took a trip to Japan and returned to form the Progressive Party (Chinbohoe), which then linked up with the Unity and Progress Society (Ilchinhoe). Both went a step further than the Independence Club by seeking members from the rural peasants as well as city dwellers. The Unity and Progress Society, under Song

DOCUMENTS

Louise Yim's Writings on Female Independence

Louise Yim (Im Yŏngsin) was a rare patriot who suffered torture for participating in the resistance against Japanese rule. She earned a B.A. and M.A. from the University of Southern California and served in the Republic of Korea National Assembly after the Korean War. She began her career as a protester against Korean conventions, including the restrictions against women's education and independence and early arranged marriage.

On Grammar School

Often I stood outside the boys' school which my father had started and I would listen to the boys repeating the lessons after their teacher. One day after the boys had gone home I went inside the little, square, mud-walled building.

"May I speak?" I asked Cho Tugy, the teacher.

He was so startled that he dropped a pencil. Then he saw me and smiled.

"If I may have the honor to listen," he replied formally.

"Would it be possible for a girl to learn how to read and write?"

He said nothing for a little while. I was afraid he would laugh and send me home. Then he said:

"If the gods have given you the courage to ask, we can hope they have given you the power to learn, little one. Come to school anytime and I will teach you."

By the time I was twelve [1912], there were rumors that Korean girls were going to be forced to marry Japanese. Therefore, all parents were in a hurry to get their daughters married. My sister was to marry soon and my turn was to be next.

One day, two women came to my room. I knew right away who they were. They were matchmakers. I had never hated anybody as much as I did those two women. I felt as though they were trying to imprison me. Instead of answering their questions, I questioned them and I lectured them. They were shocked and sometimes they put their hands to their faces and moaned as I spoke.

I told them it was a crime to force marriage on a girl too young to know what it was all about. This was almost too much for them to bear. A Korean child was not supposed to speak this way to her elders.

When they left, I heard one say to the other, "We will speak to her mother. She will come to no good, that one. Her blood is wild."

On High School, ca. 1916

I knew then that the masculine belief that females did not have a place in the national life of Korea was the belief of men who knew nothing about women and in their ignorance shut them out of the family's life too. It has always been a great mystery to me why men think that women are different from them intellectually. I wish I could go to every man and tell him that besides certain physical differences and the ability of a woman to bear children, a woman thinks of all the things a man does. Just because she allows herself to be exiled in the kitchen a woman does not give up her feelings as an individual.

_____
Source: Louise Yim, *My Forty Year Fight for Korea* (Seoul: Chungang University, 1964), pp. 27, 39, 56.

Pyŏngjun, however, favored Japanese leadership in achieving reform and volunteered to assist Japanese forces during the Russo-Japanese War, a collaborationist act that drove the Progressive Party from its alliance with the society.

During its war with Russia, Japan appointed advisers in all the Korean ministries, and in November 1905, it established a protectorate over Korea. When Emperor Kojong and several of his ministers refused to sign the protectorate treaty, Itō Hirobumi, who was in charge of the negotiations with the Chosŏn court, ignored the king and declared that a majority of ministers had approved it. Min Yonghwan of the Yŏhŭng Min clan and military aide to the emperor committed suicide in protest.

The Japanese government created a new residency general for Korea and appointed Itō to head it. He was directly responsible to the Japanese emperor instead of the Japanese cabinet, which meant that there were no constitutional limits on his arbitrary exercise of power, a precedent carried over after annexation in 1910. Itō's vision was to maintain an "independent" Korean government that would willingly carry out institutional reforms under Japanese guidance. He opposed other Japanese leaders who preferred outright annexation. Nevertheless, Itō used the Japanese police, gendarmerie, and regular army units to maintain order while Emperor Kojong was left on the throne as a figurehead.

Emperor Kojong secretly sent messages to the heads of foreign states in Europe for help in gaining independence, and the American missionary, Homer Hulbert, led a mission to the Hague Conference to present the Korean case, but it was refused admission because they lacked proper credentials. Itō then appointed the opportunist Yi Wanyong to the post of prime minister and Song Pyŏngjun, an advocate of Kojong's abdication, to the cabinet. In 1907 Yi and Song persuaded Kojong to appoint the crown prince as acting monarch, but then immediately declared erroneously that he had abdicated.

Riots broke out in the street during the accession ceremony for the new emperor, Sunjong,

but Itō ordered the dissolution of the Korean army. The discharged soldiers began a guerrilla war that lasted for four years before it was crushed by superior Japanese forces, resulting in the loss of thousands of lives. The Home Ministry under Song Pyŏngjun took charge of peace preservation, banned freedom of association, and instituted censorship of the press and book publication.

In 1909 Itō Hirobumi resigned from his position as resident general and agreed to a Japanese cabinet decision to annex Korea. His plan to maintain a facade of Japanese paternalism behind a nominally independent Korea failed in the face of Korean opposition. When Itō made a trip to Harbin to gain Russian acquiescence to the annexation, he was assassinated by An Chunggŭn, a Korean patriot. The new resident general, Terauchi Masatake, clamped down on all criticism of Japanese policy and forced the Koreans to sign the treaty of annexation on August 22, 1910, thus ending Korea's national sovereignty.

JAPANESE COLONIAL RULE (1910–1945)

Japanese colonial rule went through three distinct phases. The first was the period of military rule (*budan seiji*) from 1910 to 1919, during which the Japanese created a police state called the Government-General (GG) of Chōsen. The new regime eliminated all Korean political participation, restricted and banned serious business activity, and invested heavily in the promotion of rice cultivation for the export of rice to Japan. It instituted flogging as punishment for minor offenses even though it had been banished in Japan in 1882. In addition, the GG granted extensive authority to the police to use violence on the spot, levy fines, detain suspects for long periods, and use torture in interrogation.

Despite the draconian nature of the regime, the Korean nationalist movement continued its work underground, mainly through religious groups like the Christians, the religion of the

Heavenly Way (Ch'ŏndogyo), and the Buddhists because the Japanese were reluctant to persecute Christianity and offend western nations. The nationalist movement burst forth right under the noses of the Japanese authorities on March 1, 1919, when thirty-three patriots signed a Declaration of Independence and marched peacefully to the Japanese authorities to petition for liberation. They had been inspired by Woodrow Wilson's call for self-determination for people subject to foreign rule, and they expected support from the United States and other western powers. As opposed to the Independence Club, the participants in the March First movement came from all walks of life and from all over the country, marking a significant spread of national consciousness.

Tragically, the Japanese responded to the nonviolent demonstrations with mass arrests and executions. The western powers paid no attention. Nonetheless, the Japanese government in Tokyo under Prime Minister Hara Takashi shifted to a "cultural government" policy (*bunka seiji*) for Korea, which allowed a certain degree of freedom of speech and association and permitted the formation of Korean businesses. That policy marked the second phase of colonial rule and lasted until the Manchurian Incident of 1931, when the Japanese army in Manchuria launched a coup d'état against the Chinese governor and established the puppet state of Manchukuo.

The third phase lasted from the Manchurian Incident to the defeat of Japan by the United States in 1945 (see **Connections: World War II**). During this period Japan invested huge amounts of capital in heavy industry and infrastructure in Korea in support of Japan's expansion into Manchuria in 1931 and China after 1935. Japan initiated the second Sino-Japanese War in 1937, attacked Pearl Harbor before declaring war in 1941, and invaded Singapore, Indochina, and Burma. Japan severely repressed the freedoms of the 1920s in Korea, and after 1937 it instituted military conscription, forced labor, and forced assimilation of Koreans. It forced Koreans to use the Japanese language exclu-

sively, worship the Japanese emperor in Shinto shrines, and adopt Japanese names in an effort to eradicate Korean identity.

Scholars' views of the colonial period in Korea generally fall into two broad categories. The first is a totally negative view of Japanese colonialism, including its cruel and tyrannical behavior, its exploitation of the Korean economy, its reduction of the mass of the population to bare subsistence, its prevention of modern industrial development, and its attempt to obliterate Korean culture without granting equal citizenship rights. The second is a more positive attempt to fit the colonial experience into major trends that lasted to the end of the twentieth century. These trends included abolishing inherited social status as a barrier to advancement; liberating women from male domination; introducing modern mass education for both sexes; creating a modern economy through heavy investment in railroads, bridges, and harbors; establishing a modern financial sector in the 1920s; and industrializing the peninsula in the 1930s. A small middle class of businessmen and shopkeepers was formed, and a half-million peasants were converted to factory wage workers and miners. In retrospect, the most important economic contribution was Japan's use of state-led industrialization involving planning and controls of all kinds in the process of late industrialization to catch up to the advanced economies of the western imperialists. This process, now known as developmentalism, was a far cry from the free-market capitalism of Britain and the United States in the nineteenth century, but it opened the eyes of some Koreans to economic development without liberal democracy.

The Land Survey

Colonial economic policy was based on the expansion of agricultural production in Korea by investment in reclamation, irrigation, chemical fertilizer, and the introduction of new seeds to provide for rice exports to Japan. To create an efficient land tax for raising revenue, the colonial government adopted a land registration program in 1911 to record accurately the owners of all land. Korean nationalists and many scholars have condemned this policy as a sham designed to transfer land from Korean owners to Japanese by force or guile. The Japanese justified it on the grounds that land ownership had not been clearly established in law in the Chosŏn Dynasty. Private landownership had been the economic basis of the Korean elite at least for a thousand years, but the security of tenure was weak because judges in civil cases were district magistrates of *yangban* families who defended landlord interests. Written evidence of land ownership did exist in the form of deeds, inheritance documents, bills of sale, and state registers of land, but not every owner possessed those. Because landowners hoped to avoid registering their land with the state to avoid taxes, the late Chosŏn state lacked the funds to modernize its military and fund development projects.

The Japanese land investigation program did not result in a major transfer of land from Korean to Japanese hands. That took place only because of the world depression of 1929 when indebted smallholding peasants lost their land to creditors. From 1910 to 1925 there was an economic boom in Korea and a rise in the price of rice. The Korean landlords, most of whom were *yangban,* fared far better than the sharecroppers, and the Japanese succeeded in winning *yangban* landlords' compliance to colonial rule by granting them noble titles and guaranteeing their private property rights. As a result, the landlords played very little role in the development of active nationalist resistance to Japanese rule.

The influx of cheap Korean rice into Japan depressed the price of rice there and caused rice riots there in 1918. By 1940 the price of rice dropped continuously to only 39 percent of the 1925 price. Korean peasants who both owned and rented land earned a reasonable living, but pure tenants did not. Rice consumption declined because of exports to Japan, and although the diet was supplemented by millet from Manchuria, Koreans perceived this as a serious deprivation of their favorite staple food.

The Chosŏn Labor-Farmer General Alliance was established in 1924 to address the many tenant disputes of the 1920s and to wage class struggle against the capitalist class. The farmers later split to form their own General Korean Farmer Alliance. Middle peasants, rather than the poorest sharecroppers, led the tenant disputes and demanded sharecropping reduction from 50 to 40 percent or less of the crop. Most tenant disputes ended favorably before 1925, but after 1929 many smallholders went bankrupt. Tenants tried to preserve their sharecropping contracts, but the percentage of tenant households increased from 41 to 50 percent of the farm population in the 1930s, and the number of tenant unions increased from about 30 in 1922 to 1,301 in 1933. When in 1934 the Japanese ended the policy to promote rice production, agricultural production declined continuously to 1945.

Throughout the 1930s sixty-nine radical red peasant unions challenged local officials until the colonial regime banned all such activity. Thereafter, peasants turned to actions of passive resistance like failing to fulfill contracts or hiding crops from the authorities. In 1933 the Japanese government instituted the Tenancy Mediation Law to resolve tenant disputes in the courts, and many were resolved in favor of the tenants. After Pearl Harbor in 1941, however, the GG banned all tenant protest, exacerbating sharecropper resentment.

The Growth of Korean Industry

In the 1920s Korean businesses sprang up overnight on the basis of limited capital resources. Large landlords used their accumulated savings from tenant rents to launch into a number of small-scale enterprises. One of the best examples of this was the Kyŏngbang textile corporation founded by Kim Yŏnsu and Kim Sŏngsu, members of a landlord family with large landholdings in Chŏlla province. The Kim brothers used capital accumulated from tenant rents to establish the company, but when the company was threatened by bankruptcy, they turned to Japanese banks for working capital that saved the company and allowed it to expand. They also received help from Japanese trading companies in marketing products. The GG provided protection by allowing it to carve out a niche in the cheap textile sector for the Korean economy while Japanese textile companies provided more expensive goods. It also summoned the Kims to offer their opinions in economic policy councils.

By 1919 most Korean companies were confined to undercapitalized small-scale operations in dyeing, paper, leather, ceramics, milling, and brewing. Korean-owned breweries grew and supplied half the domestic market demand. The Tong'a Rubber Company was capitalized with 300,000 yen by landlords and rich merchants from Mokp'o in South Chŏlla province, and the Pando Rubber company was founded with 50,000 yen raised by a Korean merchant. By 1930, Korean rubber plants outnumbered Japanese thirty to seventeen. The dominant industry in Korean hands besides cheap textiles was food processing. Most Korean metal factories were no more than blacksmiths' shops, but Japan Steel had a big plant at Kyŏmip'o, and Japan Mining had a smelting plant at Chinnamp'o.

Japanese investment in Korea dwarfed the paid-in capital of Korean firms. Among the major Japanese *zaibatsu,* Mitsui founded the Sansei Mining Company, Mitsubishi the Chōsen Anthracite Company, and Noguchi the Chōsen Nitrogen Company to make fertilizer. Japanese also established chemical, electrical, textile, mining, and railroad companies. The purpose was to provide hydroelectric power, railroad lines from Pusan to Sin'ŭiju on the Manchurian border, and cement, chemicals, and the like for exports to China. Japanese businesses purchased large amounts of forest land and invested in cotton textiles, food processing, brewing, milling, paper, and printing. While some argue that the purpose of Japanese economic interest in Korea was to obtain raw materials and markets for Japanese exports, Japan invested more than it ever received in profits because its strategic and political objectives were more important.

In the 1930s Japan invested heavily to build up both infrastructure and industry to support the Japanese puppet state of Manchukuo and to provide essential equipment to support the military there. By 1941 over 90 percent of the capital invested in Korean industry came from Japan. The railroad system had been constructed on the basis of a south-to-north trunk line into Manchuria that could funnel goods from both Japan and Korea to Manchuria and, after the outbreak of the Sino-Japanese War in 1937, to China. Heavy investment in hydroelectric power plants and power along the Yalu River and elsewhere and power lines throughout the country was accompanied by the establishment of steel, chemical, machinery, metal, chemical, and machine factories to support the war effort elsewhere. Most of the weapons were manufactured in Japan, however, while the Korean machine industry was confined to repairs, vehicles, and shipbuilding. Japan subsidized the Mitsui, Mitsubishi, and Sumitomo *zaibatsu* to mine copper, zinc, manganese, tungsten, molybdenum, and other metals for military purposes. The average annual growth in all industrial production in the 1930s was 15 percent, almost double the rate from 1910 to 1928.

Nevertheless, Koreans were allowed small-scale businesses. They owned about a fifth of metal and machine and tools plants; ceramics, wood and lumber, and chemicals; roughly half of pharmaceutical companies, rice mills, and printing; over 70 percent of beverages; and over 90 percent of textile firms. The large Korean Kyŏngbang textile corporation did not hesitate to take advantage of Japanese expansion by setting up textile plants in Manchuria and buying up a textile plant in Nanjing after the Nanjing massacre there during the second Sino-Japanese War of 1937. When Kyŏngbang had labor problems over wages and working conditions, it summoned the Japanese police to put down strikes. Other Korean businessmen like Min T'aesik, Min Kyusik, and Pak Hŭngsik were also financed by the Japanese Development Bank (Shokusan ginkō). Pak Hŭngsik established the Hwasin Department Store and became one of the wealthiest Korean business-men in the period, and Yi Pyŏngch'ŏl started with a rice mill and then prospered in the liquor business.

Businessmen like Kim Sŏngsu of the Kyŏng-bang Corporation garnered a reputation after liberation in 1945 for being "national capital-ists" because they placed the welfare of the Korean nation above collaboration for profit. He and his brother, Kim Yŏnsu, however, had become a full partner in Japanese imperialism on the continent. Other prosperous Korean businessmen could not have survived unless they collaborated with the Japanese, but recently they have been condemned for collaboration.

Although the Japanese did not aim to improve the welfare of the Korean population, Korea became an industrialized area nonethe-less. The Korean capitalists became the core of a new bourgeoisie, and a miniscule proletariat was expanded in Korea to about five hundred thousand by the time Japan was defeated in 1945, not counting the factory workers, miners, and other forced laborers in Japan and Man-churia during this period. Urbanization was stimulated by the expansion of industry as peas-ants abandoned their homes for higher-paying jobs, and Korea was beginning to take on the lineaments of an advanced industrial economy with most Koreans as the underclass.

Literacy and Education

In the 1920s the colonial government allowed the publication of newspapers, magazines, and books in the Korean language, but it subjected all publications to the sharp eye of the Japanese censors. It expanded primary education beyond what existed in the late Chosŏn Dynasty, but it limited the number of Korean private schools and restricted mass education to a few grades. It founded a single university as part of the impe-rial university system, Keijō (Kyŏngsŏng or Seoul in Korean) Imperial University, but it allowed only a small minority of well-to-do stu-dents to attend it and colleges in Japan.

In the private sector, Kim Sŏngsu, a Korean businessman of the Kyŏngbang Corporation, established the *Tong'a ilbo* (*East Asia Daily*) newspaper and the Posŏng Normal School (later Koryŏ University). Women established educa-tion centers, night schools in churches and rural areas, to educate the illiterate. The Sŏngjukhoe (Pine and Bamboo Society) was founded in 1910 by women to foster national conscious-ness. Helen Kim, a Christian who was later the first person to receive the doctorate in Korean history (from Columbia University in 1929), and other women from the Ewha School took a tour of rural areas to enlighten the public before being shut down by the police. She and Kim Pilye organized the YWCA in 1922, while Bud-dhist women organized the Buddhist Women's Association in 1920. Many women received training in nursing either in Japan or at the Women's Medical College (Pogu yŏgwan) under the missionary nurse Margaret Edmond. The first women's medical school, the Kyŏngsŏng Medical College, was founded in 1928. Women were also hired as workers for the first time by both the Japanese GG and private industry.

The Japanese civil code in 1912 generally con-firmed traditional practices in male succession to family headship, ownership of property, and the sole right of men to initiate divorce. In 1918 women were given the right to petition for divorce, provided they had approval from both their husband and parents. A 1922 ordinance ele-vated the minimal age for marriage for women to fifteen, banned polygamy and concubinage, and allowed a woman to divorce her husband for polygamy or adultery, commission of a crime, insult, and abandonment for three years. Many of the discriminatory practices against women never-theless continued past the end of colonial rule.

In the 1920s two women's journals began publication: Kim Wŏnju's *Sin yŏja* (*The New Woman*) and Na Hyesŏk's *Yŏjagye* (*Women's World*). Socialist women's groups appeared in 1924, and they and the nonsocialists demanded abolition of early marriage, female slavery, licensed prostitution, and wage discrimination.

Korean literature in the vernacular flourished in this period. Yi Kwangsu, whose work was influenced by Tolstoy, published the first modern novel, *Mujŏng* (Heartless) in 1917, followed by *Chaesang* (Rebirth) and *Hŭk* (Earth) by 1933. Hyŏn Chin'gŏn portrayed the suffering of common men and women from traditional customs and colonial rule, but his novel about a Paekche general who resisted Tang armies was banned. Kim Tongin established *Creation* magazine in 1921 and wrote about the denizens of the slums and the life of a shaman. Yi Hyosŏk joined the KAPF (Korean Art Proletarian Federation) literary movement from 1928 to 1932, but he, like almost all other members of KAPF, abandoned socialism to write about itinerant peddlers and the anomie produced by urban life. In 1936 Yi Sang wrote a stream-of-consciousness story, "Wings," about a solipsistic husband who dealt with his wife's prostitution by sealing his mind from the shame of external facts.

Movies first appeared in Korea in the late 1890s, and foreign films were first shown in 1903. After annexation, the Japanese monopolized film production, but the first Korean films appeared: *The Righteous Revenge* (1919) directed by Kim Tosan, and *The Plighted Love under the Moon* (1923), directed by Yun Paengnam. There were close to 9 million moviegoers by 1935. Despite censorship, the movies *Arirang* (1926) and *Searching for Love* (1928), directed by Na Un'gyu, and *Wandering* (1928), by Kim Yuyŏng, produced by the KAPF told stories of oppression of peasants by landlords and the evils of Japanese imperialism. In 1931, however, the Japanese banned Korean films outright.

Radio broadcasting began in 1927 under the Japanese Korean Broadcasting Company. Korean-language programs expanded from one-third to one-half the airtime, and in 1933 the first all-Korean station was allowed. It devoted many programs to Korean history, science, the arts, international affairs, translations of western plays, pop songs with a distinct Korean flavor, and instruction in the use of *han'gŭl* and the standardization of Korean grammar. The Japanese even tolerated Korean language programs after the ban on the use of Korean in 1938. All these programs must have expanded knowledge about Korea and stimulated national consciousness.

The Rise of Communism and Militant Nationalism

The colonial period witnessed the continuing development of nationalism among Koreans. A number of intellectuals looked back on Korea's past and now saw only a sad history of subservience, both political and cultural, to China. Many militant nationalists were attracted to communism after the Russian Revolution of 1917 because Marxist-Leninist theory explained the emergence of western imperialism in economic terms, fit Korea into a universal system of historical development, and promised a chance for modernization and liberation. In addition, the new Soviet state was the only country offering monetary and spiritual support to Koreans for liberation from colonial rule.

Militant nationalists viewed the colonial period in black-and-white terms: one was either a true patriot willing to die for national liberation and independence, or a collaborator who worked with the Japanese and gained riches as a landlord or businessman. Many nationalists expected that a struggle against Japanese rule would kill two birds with one stone by overthrowing the Japanese and Korean capitalists and landlords and achieving Korean independence. They also expected that militancy and struggle were healthy antidotes to Korea's long history of subservience to Chinese power and culture.

Soon after the Russian Revolution of 1917, Yi Tonghwi formed the first Korean Communist Party (KCP) in Siberia. The early Korean Communists were divided geographically by groups in Moscow, Siberia, the Maritime Province of Russia, Manchuria, Shanghai, and Korea proper.

The movement to establish a Korean Provisional Government (KPG) in exile with a provisional national assembly began in April 1919 in Shanghai. The assembly drew up a constitution for a Great Korean People's Republic (Taehan min'guk), and it eventually chose Syngman Rhee (Yi Sŭngman) as president in 1922. Yi Tonghwi, the Communist from Vladivostok and guerrilla commander after 1907, became prime minister. This KPG combined radical left-wing and conservative right-wing elements, but Yi Tonghwi favored military action against Japan while Rhee preferred diplomacy to sway the United States and other powers to intervene on behalf of Korean independence. Yi Tonghwi soon left Shanghai in disdain and returned to Manchuria to resume armed struggle, and Rhee left Shanghai to work in the United States.

Between 1919 and 1924, about fifty Korean anarchists formed a terrorist group, the Ŭiyŏltan (Righteous Heroes), which carried out three hundred acts of violence during the period. After two failed assassination attempts, all three hundred members of the Ŭiyŏltan were exterminated by Japanese police. The patriot and anarchist Sin Ch'aeho founded the Anarchist Black Youth League in 1921, which dissolved in 1924.

Although the colonial government moderated the harsh aspects of the first decade of colonial rule, they increased the number of police and increased surveillance. They also hoped to co-opt potential militants and convert them to the harmless pursuit of educational and cultural projects. Korean nationalists like the author Yi Kwangsu, Yun Ch'iho, and others already believed that the Korean public lacked national consciousness and needed more education to form the basis for a viable nationalist movement. Yi's slogan, *kaejoron* (Reconstruction!), meant just that, but he and the others, known as "cultural nationalists," postponed national independence into the indefinite future.

The Communists and radical non-Communist nationalists, however, claimed that cultural nationalism was tantamount to outright collaboration. This intense nationalism was the product of a new awareness of the long history of Korea's past of supine subordination and subjugation to Chinese dynasties and Chinese culture, particularly to the Confucian ethical justification of tributary relations. Writers like Sin Ch'aeho began a new historiographical tradi-

tion of extolling examples of militancy and resistance in the Koguryŏ Dynasty and the leading military heroes of the Korean past. Inside Korea, the Communists supported strikes and succeeded in establishing a Korean Communist Party (KCP) in Korea in 1925, but the Japanese police broke it up, and the Communists abandoned the attempt in 1928.

Korean nationalists were attracted by Marxist theory and Lenin's economic explanation for the rise of imperialism as the product of monopoly capitalism, the last stage of capitalism, in which core capitalist states had saturated their own domestic markets and were seeking colonies around the globe to provide cheap raw materials and markets for their manufactured products. Korean Communists believed that the struggle against Japan would lead simultaneously to the overthrow of capitalism and national liberation. Furthermore, the Soviet Union was the only country in the world willing to offer aid to Koreans and other national liberation movements in European colonies.

The Comintern in Moscow decided that Korea was still in a "feudal" stage of development without a proletariat, and it pushed the Korean Communists to form a united front with the bourgeois nationalists to achieve a bourgeois-democratic revolution. Although the Korean Communists opposed joining their class enemies in a united front, they capitulated to Comintern pressure and joined the united front Singanhoe (New Root Society) in 1927. That took place only a couple of months before Chiang Kaishek, the leader of the Chinese Nationalist Party (Guomindang, or GMD), launched an extermination attack against his Communist allies. In 1927, women organized the Kŭnuhoe (Friends of the Rose of Sharon), which included some socialists and cooperated with the United Front Singanhoe. The Singanhoe helped to organize strikes and tenancy disputes and planned a nationwide protest demonstration after an anti-Japanese student protest movement broke out in Kwangju in Chŏlla province in 1929, but the police arrested the leaders before it could take place. After that, the Singanhoe headquarters turned more moderate and even decided to support the Korean self-government movement and use the legal system to improve conditions, but the Communist members were disaffected by this and called for the dissolution of the Singanhoe in December 1930. The Kŭnuhoe also closed down.

Manchuria

Active Korean resistance against the Japanese began in Manchuria in 1919, but Korean military units were forced to cross the border into the Maritime Province of the Soviet Union by Japanese forces. There they joined Soviet Red Army forces in battles against Japanese armies that had been dispatched to Siberia in 1918 to fight against the new Soviet regime. This action ended when the Soviet Union reached a peace agreement with Japan in 1921, but by 1925 three separate Korean governments were established in Manchuria to handle the affairs of Korean residents in Manchuria.

In 1931 the Japanese "cultural government" policy of limited toleration in Korea came to an end when the Japanese army in Manchuria established the puppet regime of Manchukuo. Northern Jiandao in south Manchuria just north of the Yalu River, where Koreans composed 76 percent of the population, became the center of anti-Japanese activity. Chu Chin, one of four guerrilla commanders in the area, led the nine hundred men of the Second Division of the Northeast People's Revolutionary Army in 1934 and fought hundreds of engagements against the Japanese that year. Kim Il Sung (Kim Ilsŏng), the future leader of the Democratic People's Republic of Korea, organized a small guerrilla unit of eighteen men in Manchuria in 1932.

In 1934, however, the Korean Communist guerrillas were faced with a serious crisis that occurred after the Japanese in Manchuria created the Minsaengdang (People's Welfare Party) to recruit members of the Korean community ostensibly as a defense against "bandits" but actually to infiltrate anti-Japanese Chinese Communist groups. The Chinese Communists

in Manchuria had incorporated Korean Communists in their ranks but insisted that they had to devote themselves entirely to the Chinese struggle against Japan and not dilute the effort by attacking the Japanese in Korea. Now they distrusted their Korean Communist allies for being Minsaengdang spies and began an extermination campaign that killed anywhere from five hundred to two thousand loyal Korean Communists. The Korean patriot Kim San was sent to Manchuria to help smooth relations between the Chinese and Korean Communists but was himself arrested (see **Biography: Kim San**). The persecution continued until March 1935, when the Chinese General Wei Zhengmin called a halt to the persecution. There is circumstantial evidence that Kim Il Sung, who was fluent in Chinese and close friends with Wei, played a crucial role in persuading the Chinese to abandon the persecution.

The Chinese Communists changed their previous policy and offered Kim Il Sung the choice between forming his own unit of several hundred men to operate independently or keeping his unit with Chinese Communist forces. Kim chose to keep his men with a Chinese unit because it afforded a better chance of survival. Some have criticized Kim for subservience to Chinese interests on this occasion, but his decision did enable his guerrilla unit to survive. He then launched the most successful guerrilla raid against the Japanese in the Korean peninsula on June 4, 1937, at Poch'ŏnbo just south of the Yalu River. He occupied it for a day, retreated, defeated a pursuing Japanese police contingent, and a few days later joined another force under Ch'oe Hyŏn to attack the Yokoyama timber camp. Although the attack was followed by a bloody reprisal by the Japanese against the town, Kim earned a reputation for daring heroism.

After Japan initiated a war with China in 1937, it repressed all signs of opposition to Japanese rule among Koreans. The colonial government required all Koreans to attend services at the Japanese shrines (*jinja*) dedicated to the worship of the Japanese emperor, banned the use of the Korean language in the schools and movies, and

BIOGRAPHY Kim San

Kim San (a pseudonym for Chang Chirak; 1905–?) was one of many Korean patriots who became a Communist to fight for Korean national liberation against Japanese imperialism, but he did it by moving to China and joining the Chinese Communist movement because it was easier to fight Japanese imperialism there than by remaining in Korea. In 1937 he was in Mao Zedong's base in Yan'an in northwest China when Helen Foster Snow, journalist Edgar Snow's wife, interviewed him and transcribed his life story into English.

Born to a poor peasant family in 1905 just south of Pyongyang, he was shocked at the age of seven when two Japanese policemen came to his home in 1912 and slapped and bloodied his mother's face because she had delayed reporting for a vaccination. His mother brought him up as a Christian and provided personal warmth, but his father's detachment and harsh discipline turned him away from Confucianism and caused him to run away to live with a married brother nearby.

In grammar school he admired the anti-Japanese guerrillas. He entered a Christian middle school but left it at the age of fourteen to join the March First movement of 1919. Amazed at the passive reaction of praying Christians to the bloody repression of the unarmed civilians by the Japanese, he abandoned Christianity, belief in God, and trust in nonviolence.

He traveled to Tokyo to attend school and was influenced by Japanese anarchists and Marxists. He dropped out of school and moved to Manchuria to attend a Korean Nationalist military school for three months. In 1920 he moved to Shanghai and then in 1921 to Beijing, where he attended the Union Medical College for over three years. He studied Marxist theory and joined the Korean Communist Youth organization, but he left school to join the Chinese Nationalists when the Canton uprising occurred in 1925. After Chiang Kaishek massacred his Communist allies in Shanghai in 1927, he joined the Communists in the Canton Commune. The Nationalists forced him to flee Canton to Peng Pai's Hailufeng Soviet nearby in 1928, and then to escape from Hailufeng through the mountains, where his health was ruined from exposure, malaria, and tuberculosis.

He returned to Beijing to become secretary of the Beijing Communist Party. He was sent to Manchuria in 1932 to smooth relations between the Chinese and Korean Communists there, but he was arrested by the authorities and subjected to water torture for forty days. Released because he refused to confess membership in the Communist Party, he returned to Beijing only to suffer impeachment by fellow Communists for leftist deviation in 1931 and rightist deviation the next year! In 1933 the Chinese Nationalists arrested him briefly. Depressed and near suicide, he recovered and moved to Mao's headquarters in Yan'an in 1937. After that date, neither he nor his two wives and child were heard of again.

He summarized his career as a revolutionary as follows:

> My whole life has been a series of failures, and the history of my country has been a history of failure. I have had only one victory—over myself. This one small victory, however, is enough to give me confidence to go on. Fortunately, the tragedy and defeat I have experienced have not broken but strengthened me. I have few illusions left, but I have not lost faith in men and in the ability of men to create history.[1]

---

[1]Nym Wales, *Song of Ariran* (San Francisco: Rampart Press, 1941), p. 315.

Comfort Women. Korean "Comfort women (*wianbu*)," who were abducted by the Japanese to serve as prostitutes for Japanese soldiers on the front, demanding an apology and compensation from Japan, 2000. (*Li Jin-Man/AP/Wide World Photos*)

forced all Koreans to adopt Japanese names. The colonial government requisitioned Koreans for forced labor in Japanese and Manchurian mines and factories (see **Material Culture: Korean Gold Miners**), recruited young men into the Japanese army, and abducted or enticed thousands of Korean women with false promises of jobs and then forced them to become "comfort women"—prostitutes—for Japanese troops in active theaters of operations in China, Manchuria, the South Sea islands, and Southeast Asia.

The Japanese left no wiggle room for Koreans who had prospered under Japanese rule to evade responsibility for leadership in carrying out these programs. Many young Korean men took to the hills to evade forced labor and military conscription, but most were unable to avoid it. There were also those, like Park Chung

Hee (Pak Chunghŭi), the dictator of South Korea from 1961 to 1979, who volunteered and became officers in the Kwantung Army in Manchuria to do battle against opponents of Japanese colonialism, including Korean guerrillas. By contrast, Kim Il Sung fought many battles in Manchuria against the Japanese between 1937 and 1940 until Japanese mopping-up forces eliminated the Chinese Communist armies in Manchuria and forced Kim Il Sung to cross into Russian territory west of Vladivostok by March 1941. Kim's men joined Chinese guerrillas under Zhou Baozhong in a Russian training camp near Vladivostok, and Kim was appointed major in the new 88th Division of the Far Eastern Command of the Soviet army.

Other nationalists struggled for independence outside Manchuria. Korean Communists in China included Kim Wŏnbong, who commanded the Korean Volunteer Corps, and Mu Chŏng, Kim Tubong, and Ch'oe Ch'ang'ik, who commanded Chinese units under Mao Zedong in Yan'an. Non-Communist nationalists like Kim Ku fought with Chinese Nationalist forces. An Ch'angho organized the Hŭngsadan (Corps for Promoting Scholars) in Los Angeles in 1911, joined the KPG in Shanghai, and was arrested in 1932 and sent back to jail in Korea. Syngman Rhee spent two decades in the United States to gain support for Korean liberation. In the end, neither Communists nor non-Communists succeeded in obtaining Korea's independence.

SUMMARY

Japanese colonial rule placed the Korean people under the yoke of a harsh, imperialistic regime that eliminated meaningful participation in the political process. On the other hand, by allowing Korean landlords and businessmen to flourish economically, colonial rule established a few models for successful business operations. By exerting a demonstration effect on the Korean population of successful, rapid, economic development under a powerful, centralized police state, it provided a model to future generations of how to catch up with the West. By breaking down

MATERIAL CULTURE

Korean Gold Miners

In the 1930s the colonial government mobilized Korean laborers to mine alluvial gold in South Chŏlla province. This was part of the Japanese government's mobilization effort after the beginning of the second Sino-Japanese War in 1937. It included forcing Koreans to work in mines in Japan and war materiel factories and to sign up as auxiliaries in the armed forces. Wages were lower than those paid to Japanese, and treatment was so harsh that many Koreans went into hiding or took refuge in the hills to avoid it.

Korean Miners. Korean miners mobilized by the Japanese during the Japanese Colonial Period in the 1930s for mining alluvial gold in South Chŏlla Province. *(Sajinuro ponun Choson sidae: Saenghwal kwa p'ungsok [The Choson Period in Pictures: Life and Customs] Seoul: Somundang, 1986, volume on* Independence Movement Through Pictures II, *p. 120)*

hereditary status barriers, it opened opportunities to many people blocked from upward mobility. By introducing a modicum of modern education, it introduced some Koreans to science, foreign languages, and social science—a far cry from the Confucian curriculum of traditional Korea.

Despite the success of the colonial regime in repressing almost all signs of resistance by the

1930s, it created many radical nationalists both Communist and non-Communist who populated the jails or were forced into exile waiting for the chance to return and create some kind of new society. It forced the migration of millions of Koreans from their family farms by removing them from their village communities and subjecting them to the iron discipline of Japanese factories and mines. It created a major contradiction between capitalist industrialists and wealthy landlords versus a new proletariat and a mass of sharecropping tenants. In short, Japanese colonialism had produced both wealth and poverty, contentment and animosity, revolutionary potential and conservative reaction. Whether this mix would lead to peace or disruption depended on whether these contradictions would be resolved peacefully after liberation in 1945.

SUGGESTED READING

For the best work on the period from 1896 to 1910, see E. Kim and H. Kim, *Korea and the Politics of Imperialism* (1967), a political and diplomatic history; Vipin Chandra, *Imperialism, Resistance, and Reform in Late Nineteenth-Century Korea* (1988), a study of the Independence Club; and André Schmid's examination of the reform debate to 1910 in the Korean press in *Korea Between Empires, 1895–1919* (2002). For discussion of Japanese policy in that period, see H. Conroy, *The Japanese Seizure of Korea, 1868–1910* (1960), and P. Duus, *The Abacus and the Sword* (1995). For Russia's relationship with Japan and Korea, see G. Lensen, ed., *Korea and Manchuria Between Russia and Japan 1894–1904* (1966), and A. Malozemoff, *Russian Far Eastern Policy, 1881–1904* (1958).

For the best work on Japanese colonial policy, see Duus, *The Abacus and the Sword*; P. Duus et al., *The Japanese Wartime Empire, 1931–1945* (1996); R. H. Myers and M. R. Peattie, *The Japanese Colonial Empire, 1895–1945* (1984); C. Lee, *Korea, the Politics of Nationalism* (1963); and G. Henderson, *Korea: The Politics of the Vortex* (1968). E. Gragert explored the effects of the Japanese land investigation in *Landownership Under Colonial Rule* (1994).

In economics, C. J. Eckert's *Offspring of Empire* (1991) explored the history of the Kyŏngbang Corporation. S. C. Suh's *Growth and Structural Changes in the Korean Economy* (1978) concentrated on the negative consequences of Japan's economic policy. S. W. Park's *Colonial Industrialization and Labor in Korea* (1999) concentrated on the operations of the Onoda Cement Factory, and G. Shin's *Peasant Protest and Social Change in Colonial Korea* (1996) provides a balanced portrait of tenancy in the 1930s.

The religious history of Protestants is covered by C. Park, *Protestantism and Politics in Korea* (2003), and the political history in K. M. Wells, *New God, New Nation* (1990).

The conflict between cultural nationalists and Communists is handled in M. Robinson's *Cultural Nationalism in Colonial Korea, 1920–1925* (1988), and the best work on Korean communism is found in D. Suh, *The Korean Communist Movement, 1918–1945*, 2 vols. (1981), and *Documents of Korean Communism* (1970); R. Scalapino and C. Lee, *Communism in Korea*, 2 vols. (1972); H. Han, *Wounded Nationalism: The Minsaengdan Incident*, forthcoming; C. Lee, *The Korean Workers' Party: A Short History* (1978); and N. Wales and K. San, *Song of Ariran* (1941).

For a study of comfort women, see G. Hicks, *The Comfort Women* (1994). M. Robinson and G. Shin, eds., *Modernity, Domination, and Identity in Colonial Korea* (1999), contains a variety of articles on the colonial period. B. Cumings includes sharp insights in his general history, *Korea's Place in the Sun* (1997). Translations of literature are found in K. Chong-un and B. Fulton, *A Ready-Made Life* (1998), and P. H. Lee, *Flowers of Fire* (1974).

War and Revolution, China (1927–1949)

During the two decades from 1927 to 1949, China was ruled by the Nationalist Party and its head, Chiang Kaishek. The Nationalist government turned toward the West for help in modernizing the country, but in general was distrustful of intellectuals. In its big cities, above all Shanghai, China took on more of a modern look, with tall buildings, department stores, and western dress. The government had to concentrate most of its energies on military matters, first combating the remaining warlords, then the Communist Party bases, then Japan. The Communist Party attracted a small but highly committed following. Because of the Nationalists' pressure, it was on the run much of the time until a base area was established in Yan'an in 1935, where Mao Zedong emerged as the paramount leader. During the war with Japan (1937–1945), the Communist Party formed itself into a potent revolutionary force, able to mobilize poor peasants into a well-disciplined fighting force. The Civil War of 1947–1949 resulted in the victory of the Communist Party.

The large questions behind much of the scholarly work on this period revolve around the outcome in 1949. Why did May Fourth liberalism decline in significance? Could the economic politics of the Nationalists have brought prosperity to China if Japan had not invaded? How much of a difference did the Comintern's often misguided instructions make to the development of the Communist Party? How crucial was Mao to the way the policies of the party developed? Why did the Nationalist Party and Chiang Kaishek lose the support of the urban middle class?

THE CHINESE COMMUNIST PARTY

With the success of the Bolshevik revolution in Russia in 1917, Chinese intellectuals began to take an interest in Marxism-Leninism, which seemed to provide a blueprint for a world of abundance without exploitation. Communism was scientific, anti-western, anti-imperialist, and successful: it had just proved itself capable of bringing revolution to a backward country. For the May 1919 issue of *New Youth*, Li Dazhao, the librarian at Beijing University, wrote an introduction to Marxist theory, explaining such concepts as class struggle and capitalist exploitation. Soon intellectuals were also looking into the works of Lenin and Trotsky, who predicted an imminent international revolutionary upheaval that would bring an end to imperialism. Although China did not have much of a proletariat to be the vanguard of its revolution, the nation as a whole, Li Dazhao argued, was exploited by the capitalist imperialist countries. In 1920 Li organized a Marxist study group at Beijing University. At much the same time, Chen Duxiu organized one in Shanghai, where he had gone after resigning his university post in Beijing. Another source of knowledge of European Marxism were the thousands of Chinese students, male and female, who had gone to France in 1919 and 1920 to participate in work-study programs. Most worked in factories, where they were introduced to both strikes and Marxism-Leninism.

The early Marxist study groups were offered financial assistance and guidance by the Comintern. In 1920, soon after the Comintern learned of the existence of Marxist study groups in China, agents were sent to help turn the groups into party cells. This entailed teaching "democratic centralism," the secret to party discipline. Each local cell elected delegates to higher levels, up to the national party congress, with its central executive committee and the latter's standing committee. Delegates flowed up, and decisions flowed down. Decisions could be debated within a cell, but once decisions were reached, all were obligated to obey them. This cell structure provided a degree of discipline and centralization beyond anything in the prior repertoire of Chinese organizational behavior.

Following Comintern advice, thirteen delegates met in July 1921 to form the Chinese Communist Party as a secret, exclusive, centralized party. The party broke with the anarchists and guild socialists and asserted the primacy of class struggle. Chen Duxiu was chosen as secretary general. The party agreed to put priority on organizing labor unions and recruiting workers into the party. In Shanghai, the Communist Party oversaw the establishment of a Russian language school, helped organize labor unions, and formed a Socialist Youth Corps.

It was at the insistence of the Comintern, and against the advice of many of the Chinese members, that the decision was made in 1922 to ally with the Nationalists. The United Front between the Nationalist and Communist parties was expedient for both at the time, as they could concentrate on their common foes, the warlords. However, it covered over deep differences. The Nationalist military included many staunch anti-Communists who were appalled by talk of class warfare. One reason the Communists remained in the United Front was that it gave them the opportunity to organize both workers and peasants. Along the route of the Northern Expedition, farmers' associations were established, with membership by the end of 1926 exceeding 1 million people.

The United Front ended in the spring of 1927. On March 21, as the Nationalist army neared Shanghai, the Communist-led General Labor Union called for a general strike. Over six hundred thousand workers responded and seized the city. Flush with victory, they began demanding the return of the foreign concessions. On April 11, the head of the union was invited to the home of the leader of the mafia-like Green Gang, where he was murdered. The next day Green Gang members and soldiers loyal to Chiang attacked union headquarters. Soon soldiers were mowing down civilians with machine guns; an estimated five thousand were killed.

The terror quickly spread to other cities and continued into 1928. The labor union base of the Communist Party was destroyed. Although the party tried to continue working with the left wing of the Nationalist Party in Wuhan, Chiang's show of force carried the day. By July the Soviet advisers had withdrawn from the Nationalist army, and the United Front was over.

That fall, the Communist Party tried to organize uprisings in both cities and the countryside, but none met with much success. A failed uprising in Guangzhou led to the execution of three thousand to four thousand worker revolutionaries. From 1927 through 1930 the hunt was on for Communist organizers all over the country; in some areas, the only evidence that troops needed to conclude that a young woman was a Communist was bobbed hair. What Communist leadership that survived was driven underground and into the countryside. On orders of the Comintern, Chen Duxiu was blamed for these disasters and expelled from the Communist Party. Party membership, which had reached about sixty thousand in April 1927, plummeted to fewer than ten thousand within the year.

Mao Zedong's Emergence as a Party Leader

Through the 1920s, Mao Zedong was just one of hundreds of Communist Party organizers. He ended up playing such an important role in twentieth-century Chinese history that it is useful to begin with his early experiences.

Mao was born in 1893 in a farming village about 30 miles south of Changsha, the capital of Hunan province. He began helping out on his father's 3-acre farm when he was six. At age eight, in 1901, he entered the local primary school, where he studied for six years. Mao then worked full time on the farm for three years, from ages thirteen to sixteen. When he was fourteen years old, he was betrothed to the eighteen-year-old daughter of a neighbor, but she died in 1910, and Mao left the farm to continue his education. One of his teachers was a returned student from Japan, and from him

Mao became fascinated with the writings of Kang Youwei and Liang Qichao. In 1911, at age seventeen, Mao walked the 30 or so miles to Changsha to enter a middle school. Not only was Changsha a large city; the new provincial assembly was then meeting, and all sorts of newspapers were in circulation. Mao joined student demonstrations against the Qing government and cut off his queue. Then, in October, in nearby Wuhan, revolutionary soldiers seized power, and the fall of the Qing Dynasty soon followed. Mao, wanting to be a part of the action, joined the republican army, but after six months of garrison duty in Changsha, he quit to continue his education.

For a year Mao spent his days at the Changsha public library, reading world history and Chinese translations of works by such western writers as Rousseau, Montesquieu, J. S. Mill, Adam Smith, and Charles Darwin. Only when his father refused to support him any longer unless he enrolled in a school that gave degrees did he enter the Hunan Provincial Fourth Normal School, where he studied for five years (1913–1918). The teacher there who had the greatest impact on him was Yang Changji, a social science teacher deeply interested in philosophy, which he had studied during his decade abroad in Japan, Great Britain, and Germany. Mao came to share Yang's dissatisfaction with the physical fitness of Chinese intellectuals, and he wrote an article on physical education that was published in *New Youth* in 1917.

Mao was twenty-four years old when he graduated. When Yang moved to Beijing to take up an appointment at Beijing University, Mao followed him there. Yang helped him get a job as a clerk in the library, which made him a subordinate of Li Dazhao, only four years his senior but already well known in intellectual circles, having studied law for six years in Japan and been offered a position on the editorial board of *New Youth*. That year Li Dazhao wrote about Marxism and the Russian Revolution for *New Youth*.

Before he had been in Beijing a year, Mao had to return home because his mother was ill, but he stopped to visit Shanghai for a couple of weeks on the way. Mao thus missed the excitement of Beijing University during the May Fourth incident. Back in Changsha Mao took a teaching job and started his own magazine, producing four issues with articles on topics such as democracy, unions, and fighting oppression. Mao also turned his hand to organizing, forming the Hunan United Students Association and organizing a strike of thirteen thousand middle school students against the local warlord.

After his mother died, Mao returned to Beijing to find Professor Yang desperately ill. At the beginning of 1920, both Yang and Mao's fathers died. When Mao returned to Hunan a few months later, he was appointed principal of a primary school. That seems to have left him some time, as he also organized a cooperative bookstore that proved a commercial success. Professor Yang's daughter Yang Kaihui also returned to Hunan, and by the end of 1920 she and Mao were living together. Two years later, their first son was born, and they spoke of themselves as married.

It was not until 1920 that Mao showed particular interest in Marxism. Part of this new interest came from letters he received from fellow students who had gone to France. When the first meeting of the Communist Party was held in Shanghai in July 1921, Mao was one of the two delegates from Hunan. He was sent back to Hunan with instructions to build up the party there and develop ties to labor unions. Mao recruited former classmates, his two younger brothers, and others to help him organize unions and strikes. In early 1923, conforming to party policy, Mao joined the Nationalist Party. That June he went to Guangzhou for the third congress of the Chinese Communist Party. In December he sent in a pessimistic report on the situation in Hunan, where peasant organizations had been crushed and many factories had closed.

During much of 1924, Mao was away from home, in Guangzhou or Shanghai, doing United Front work. In 1925 he did the opposite, returning to his home village to work with peasants,

out of the reach of the party authorities. In October 1925 he returned to Guangzhou and took up work for the Nationalist Party's propaganda department, becoming the director of the Peasant Training Institute in 1926. During the Northern Expedition, Mao and those he had trained organized peasants in advance of the army. In February 1927 Mao submitted a highly positive report to the Communist Party on the revolution among the peasants in Hunan who had seized power from landlords and felt the joy of righting ancient wrongs.

In April 1927, when Chiang Kaishek unleashed the terror in Shanghai, Mao was in Hunan. Following party instructions, he tried to ignite peasant insurrection, but found that the terror had crushed the movement that only recently had looked so promising to him. Mao now wrote a report that emphasized the need to back political ideas with military force, contending, in his oft-quoted phrase, that "political power is obtained from the barrel of the gun." In October 1927 he led his remaining peasant followers into a mountain lair used by secret society members on the border between Hunan and Jiangxi, called Jinggangshan. Mao lost contact with Yang Kaihui, who had just given birth to their third son. He also was out of touch with the party hierarchy. He began to draw in other Communists, among whom was nineteen-year-old He Zizhen, from a nearby landlord family, who had joined the party during the Northern Expedition. She and Mao, then thirty-four years old, became lovers and had a child in 1929.

In the mountain area that Mao's forces controlled, he pushed through an extreme form of land reform, redistributing all the land of the rich and requiring all the physically able to work. His troops suffered, however, with little in the way of arms or ammunition, clothes, or medicine.

In January 1929 Mao decided to look for a better-supplied base area that would be less vulnerable to Nationalist attacks. His choice was a border region between Jiangxi and Fujian, where he set up what came to be called the Jiangxi Soviet. The party leadership, which could reach him there, quickly condemned him for his views on rural revolution and the role of military force. Mao fell ill and managed to avoid responding to the party's order that he go to Shanghai. Mao did, however, in 1929–1930 conduct an exhaustive study of rural life in one county in the Jiangxi Soviet, Xunwu County, to learn more about how a party could be built on a peasant base. In his analysis of land ownership, he classified the population into landlords (those who lived off the rents of their lands, subdivided into large, medium, and small landlords), rich peasants (those who rented out some land or made loans but worked the rest themselves), middle peasants (those who worked their own land without borrowing or hiring help), poor peasants (tenants and owners of plots too small to support them), and others, including hired hands, loafers, and those who did such manual labor as boatmen and porters. The vast majority of the population fell into the category of poor peasant or lower. When land was redistributed many more would receive land than would lose it. In his study of Xunwu, Mao also recorded literacy rates, postal service, shops and services, and even the number of prostitutes.

The Communist Party leadership was still trying to ignite urban uprisings and in October 1930 assaulted Changsha. Not only did the attack fail, but the Nationalists arrested Yang Kaihui and had her shot. The three young boys were sent by friends to Shanghai. The youngest died, and Mao did not see the other two until 1946.

THE NATIONALIST GOVERNMENT IN NANJING

The decision of the Nationalist Party to purge itself of Communists did not delay the military unification of the country, and in 1928 the Nationalists gained the allegiance of three key warlords to reunite the country. It established its capital at Nanjing, not used as a capital since the early Ming Dynasty. International recognition quickly followed, and western observers were more optimistic about the prospects for China than they had been for decades. Men who had studied in western countries were appointed to many key government posts, and progressive policies were adopted, such as a new land law limiting rents and a new marriage law outlawing concubinage and allowing women to initiate divorce. (See **Biography: Yuetsim, Servant Girl**). Over the next several years, most of the foreign powers consented to reductions in their special privileges. Tariff autonomy was recovered, as well as control over the Maritime Customs, Salt Administration, and Post Office. Foreign concessions were reduced from thirty-three to thirteen, and extraterritoriality was eliminated for some more minor countries.

From 1928 on, Chiang Kaishek was the leader of the Nationalists. From a landlord-merchant family near Ningbo, Chiang had aspired to take the civil service examinations, but when they were abolished he went to Japan to study military science, joining the precursor of the Nationalist Party while there. His appointment to head the Huangpu Academy in 1924 was a crucial one in his rise because it allowed him to form strong personal ties to young officers in the party's army. Once Chiang, a skillful politician, became fully enmeshed in party and government matters, he proved able to balance different cliques and build personal ties to key power holders. In 1927 he married Soong Meiling, the daughter of a wealthy merchant family and the sister of Sun Yatsen's widow.

To modernize his army, Chiang turned to Germany, attracted by the success the Nazis were having in mobilizing and militarizing Germany. Indeed, Chiang once argued, "Can fascism save China? We answer: yes. Fascism is now what China most needs."[1] German advisers helped Chiang train an elite corps, plan the campaigns

---

1. Cited in Lloyd Eastman, *Abortive Revolution* (Cambridge, Mass.: Harvard University Press, 1974), p. 40.

BIOGRAPHY Yuetsim, Servant Girl

Yuetsim, born around 1910, knew nothing about her natal family. All she knew was that she had been kidnapped when she was about three years old and sold, through intermediaries, as a "slave girl." She thought disbanded soldiers, then roaming the countryside, might have been the ones who kidnapped her.

A Hong Kong family, the Yeos, purchased Yuetsim. Her master's father had been a successful merchant and had three concubines besides his wife. Her master, Mr. Yeo, was the son of the first concubine, and he held a modest government position as a clerk. When his wife had no children, he purchased a prostitute as a concubine, and she gave birth to four children. The wife, with bound feet, rarely left her room. To help the concubine with the housework and care of the children, the family bought little Yuetsim. It is difficult to imagine that a three year old could be of much use to anyone, but by four or five she could at least fetch and carry. Naturally she never learned to read or write.

Since Yuetsim knew no other life, she put up with the way she was treated. Her mistress, the concubine, was often harsh and contemptuous. In this period Hong Kong newspapers were filled with agitation against the custom of selling girls into bondage. Yuetsim, however, never heard anything of the movement or the 1923 law that took the first steps toward outlawing selling girls into service. In December 1929, a further strengthening of the laws against child slav-ery required owners of slave girls to register them with the government, pay them wages, and free them at age eighteen. Since Mr. Yeo worked for the government and was known to have had a slave girl for years, he had to take some action. He might have married her off, as many masters did, but his concubine was so angry at losing Yuetsim's services that she simply ordered Yuetsim out of the house.

In 1930 one of the officials in charge of the registration of slave girls found a place for Yuetsim in a home for women and girls in need of protection, and she stayed there several years. Finally she went back to the Yeos as a maid, knowing no other place to go. Soon after her return, both the wife and the concubine died. Yuetsim continued to take care of the master and his children.

After the death of his wife and concubine, Mr. Yeo wanted to make Yuetsim his concubine. His children, however, were adamantly opposed and threatened to cut off contact with him if he went through with the marriage. They, after all, had known her all their lives as a humble servant. Although their own mother had been a prostitute before becoming their father's concubine, they thought marriage to a former slave girl would disgrace the family. Mr. Yeo gave in to them.

Yuetsim stayed on anyway. In retirement, Mr. Yeo's fortunes declined, but she nursed him in his illnesses and shopped and cooked for him. She was still living with him when she told her story in 1978.

Source: Based on Maria Jaschok, *Concubines and Bondservants: The Social History of a Chinese Custom* (London: Zed Books, 1988), pp. 69–77.

against the communist base in Jiangxi, and import German arms. Young officers became members of the Blue Shirts, an organization devoted to the nation and against such New Culture ideas as individualism. Chiang entrusted political training in the army and schools to the Blue Shirts, who also took on secret service work.

Chiang Kaishek and Soong Meiling. In 1927 Chiang Kaishek married Soong Meiling, the younger sister of Sun Yatsen's widow. Soong came from a wealthy family, had been educated in the United States, and after the Japanese invasion worked hard to gain American support for China. *(Popperfoto/Retrofile)*

Chiang was a patriot, however, and wanted a strong and modern China. Much progress was made in economic modernization. Life in the major cities took on a more modern look. Conveniences like electricity were gradually changing how all major cities functioned. A professional class was gaining influence, composed of scientists, engineers, architects, economists, physicians, and others with technical expertise, often acquired through study abroad.

The primary failing of the Nationalists' modernizing programs was their failure to bring improvements to the countryside (see **Documents: The Peasant Exodus from Western Shandong**). The government and private philanthropic organizations sponsored rural reconstruction projects that tried to raise the level of rural education, create facilities for credit, encourage modern enterprises, and form peasant associations, but gains were usually limited to small areas and short periods. Most peasants had seen no improvement in their standard of living since Qing times. Continued population growth to over 500 million by 1930 relentlessly increased the pressure on available land. The advantages brought by modernization—cheaper transportation by railroads and cheaper manufactured consumer goods—were yet to have a positive impact on the rural economy. China's exports were struggling, silk and tea having lost ground to Japanese and Indian competition, then all exports facing decreased demand due to the worldwide depression of the 1930s. The Nationalist government did little to disturb the local power structure in the countryside. Getting the new land or marriage laws observed in rural areas was never given much priority. The Northern Expedition had succeeded by accepting virtually anyone willing to throw in his lot with the Nationalists, and thus all sorts of local power holders had been incorporated. Villagers thus suffered from local bullies and local elites who put their own survival first.

Chiang was not a political progressive. He made no attempt at elective democracy, as this was to be a period of "political tutelage." The press was heavily censored, and dissenters and suspected Communists were arrested and often executed. To combat the intellectual appeal of the Communists and build support for his government, Chiang in 1934 launched an ideological indoctrination program, the New Life Movement. Its goal, he claimed, was to "militarize the life of the people of the entire nation" and to nourish in them "a capacity to endure hardship and especially a habit and instinct for unified behavior," to make them "willing to sacrifice for the nation at all times."[2]

2. Cited in Jonathan Spence, *The Search for Modern China* (New York: Norton, 1990), p. 415.

DOCUMENTS

The Peasant Exodus from Western Shandong

In the 1930s, those with modern educations were well aware of the problems facing Chinese farmers and discussed at length what could be done to solve them. The article below was published in the magazine Minjian *(Among the People) in 1937. The author, Hao Pensui, describes what he learned by visiting villages and talking to peasants.*

Toward the northwest of Jinan, in western Shandong, is the district of Yuecheng. . . . Deforestation, dumping, and lack of any river conservancy have prevailed for so many years that the main river bed is narrower than either of its branches. Whereas the Dengjin river is now 32 feet wide and the Zhaonui 48 feet wide, the joint stream is only 28 feet wide. No wonder then that since 1930, five out of the seven years have witnessed floods.

The peasants were able to maintain themselves with what little grain store and money savings they had for the first two flood years, but when the fourth and fifth floods came they had absolutely nothing to fall back on. Usurers in the city and at the railway station who were more resourceful than the village usurers, naturally refused to loan at this time, realizing that they had very little chance of being repaid. In such cases the peasants were unable to borrow even at the very high interest rates of four or five per cent per month, and indeed the higher the interest rate the more hesitant was the usurer to loan. . . .

In the winter of 1935 the peasants of Chengnan were reduced to eating the bark from trees and the roots of herbs. . . . Destitute peasants from this large area had no alternative but to rove from one place to another. This further agitated the peasants of Chengnan, who organized themselves to petition the magistrate for relief. The magistrate immediately ordered the shutting of the city gate in order to prevent the entry of over 3,000 peasants into the city. Only a few peasant delegates were permitted to talk to him, resulting in the usual way with the magistrate promising to petition the provincial government for relief from the public granary.

Unending delays and bureaucratic red tape proved once again complete indifference to the acute suffering of the hungry masses. A year's delay meant a year of hunger and it was not until the spring of 1936 that the peasants received from the public granary 6 kg of unhusked rice per person. . . .

The investigations in one village by the writer of the present article may be taken as a typical example. The village in Chengnan that he investigated is named Zhaozhuang and it had a population of 530 people in 76 families. In the winter of 1935, 25 entire families left the village, and from each of 39

Shanghai

During the Nanjing Decade, Shanghai emerged as one of the major cities of the world. Since 1910 it had been China's most populous city, and by the 1930s it had about 4 million residents. It attracted Chinese entrepreneurs, especially ones willing to collaborate with foreigners. It had China's largest port and was the commercial center of China. In the 1920s and 1930s it had half of China's modern industry.

Shanghai attracted more foreigners than any other of the treaty ports, a high of over thirty-six thousand. The largest number were British families one to three persons left, leaving only 12 families intact. In all, 230 people left the village that winter. . . .

The almost annual flood created great confusion among the peasants who were quite unable to effect any organized control. Whatever feeble attempts they did make to turn back the water, such as the building of small mud banks, proved useless in nine cases out of ten. The flood meant the loss of a year's crop, for when the water receded the fields were left in very bad condition, covered with a thick layer of black silt which dried and cracked in a hard crust. Having lost their seed and probably their animals, the peasants had no hope of starting afresh, so after every flood a procession of peasants could be seen from nearly every village abandoning their homes and setting out in search of food. Creaking wheelbarrows, piled high with quilts, clothing and household utensils, were pushed by able-bodied men along narrow paths, each being followed by a group of women and children. Behind them they would leave some houses with the doors sealed with mud, or others with one or two people too old to travel, left to scrape a living as best they could. . . .

The writer himself was in the village of Zhaozhuang in 1936 just two months after the wheat harvest and his own investigation brought to light the fact that out of the total of 76 families, only nine, at that time, had as much as three months food, 11 only had two months, 19 only one month and as many as 37 families had already exhausted their supplies. These figures are all the more significant because it was a year in which there was no flood and a good harvest.

Once the writer met a peasant of sorrowful appearance who said,

> This year our family harvested about 600 kg of wheat out of which 72 kg were paid for rent, 150 for the repayment of loans in kind, about 108 for taxes, about 60 for the purchase of a working animal, and about 60 to repay recent credit purchases. Thus only about 150 kg remained, and of these 108 had already been consumed by the family. How we are to manage to live with less than 50 kg in hand until the next harvest is hard to conceive. Furthermore, there are still some outstanding debts from credit purchases, some $12 worth of things in the pawnshop to be redeemed and school fees for the boys to be met.

Such a budget reveals the almost hopeless condition of the peasantry in this area, for it not only allows of no leeway to meet such emergencies as flood, drought and locusts, but it also shows that even in normal years a moderately well-to-do peasant family is being rapidly reduced in its economic status. This explains why the peasant exodus is more or less continuous, regardless of the harvest or the presence of natural calamities.

———

Source: From *Agrarian China: Selected Source Materials from Chinese Authors* (London: George Allen and Unwin, 1939), pp. 247–251, modified.

or Japanese, as they owned the most foreign companies. Some of Shanghai's foreigners had come in the nineteenth century and stayed; others were there for only a few years. Among the merchant families who amassed huge fortunes were the Sassoons, from a family of Jewish traders active in Baghdad and Bombay. David Sassoon began by trading cotton from Bombay to China in the 1870s, his son Elias Sassoon bought warehouses in Shanghai later in the nineteenth century, and his grandson Victor Sassoon turned to real estate, in the 1930s owning a reported nineteen hundred buildings in Shanghai, including what are now the Peace

The Shanghai Bund. The European character of Shanghai was nowhere more striking than on its main boulevard, the "Bund" along the river, seen here in the 1910s. The domed building in the center is the Hong Kong & Shanghai Bank. *(Ivan D. Yeaton Collection)*

and Cypress hotels. Some of the early employees of the Sassoons also made fortunes, including Silas Hardoon and Elly Kadoorie. Hardoon started as a night watchman in the 1870s. Kadoorie's mansion is now the Shanghai Children's Palace.

Because the international districts admitted anyone, no matter what their passport or visa status, Shanghai became a magnet for international refugees. After the Russian Revolution many of the Russian bourgeoisie fled east via the trans-Siberian railroad. Later they made their way south through Manchuria, many eventually settling in Shanghai, often to find only menial jobs. In the 1930s, thousands of Jews fleeing the Nazis also found refuge in Shanghai, where they were aided by the wealthy Jewish families already there, such as the Sassoons, Hardoons, and Kadoories.

The foreign presence in Shanghai was visible to all in its western-style roads and buildings. Along the river an embankment was built called the bund and made into a park where signs were posted that read, "No dogs" and "No Chinese."

With its gambling parlors and brothels, Shanghai had the reputation as a sin city. Reportedly about fifty thousand women worked in Shanghai as prostitutes in the 1930s. Young women were also drawn into Shanghai to work in textile mills or as servants. In 1930 over one hundred seventy thousand women worked in industry, about half in cotton mills. The typical prostitute or mill hand was a young, unmarried, illiterate woman recruited in the countryside by labor contractors. The contractor would supply a small advance payment, often to the girl's parents, and would make arrangements in the city for employment, housing, and food. The women were often kept in conditions of debt servitude. Some factory workers joined unions and engaged in strikes; others put their hopes on getting married and returning to the country. Women in Shanghai, from factory girls and prostitutes to office workers and the wealthy, commonly wore dresses called *qipao*, a compromise between western and Chinese styles. (See **Material Culture: Qipao.**)

Shanghai also attracted Chinese intellectuals, especially as Nationalist censorship got more severe. If they worked from the International District or French Concession, they were usually safe from the Chinese police. Dissidents, radicals, and revolutionaries chose Shanghai for much the same reasons.

Relocating the Communist Revolution

The Central Committee of the Communist Party in 1932 gave up trying to foment urban insurrections and joined Mao in the Jiangxi Soviet. Mao was the chairman of the soviet, but after their arrival, he was on the sidelines, his recommendations often overruled. In the fall of 1934, with the German-planned fifth "extermination campaign" of the Nationalists encircling them with a million-man force, the Communist Party leadership, without consulting Mao, decided to give up the Jiangxi Soviet. In October, about eighty-six thousand Communist soldiers, cadres, porters, and followers broke out of the encirclement, the start of the much mythologized year-long Long March in search of a new place to set up a base. Most wives and children had to be left behind (only thirty-five women joined the march). To protect them and the thousand or so sick or wounded soldiers left behind, about fifteen thousand troops remained in Jiangxi. Mao's wife, He Zizhen, was allowed to come, although pregnant, but they had to leave their two-year-old child behind with Mao's younger brother. When Mao's brother, like many of those left behind, was killed in 1935, Mao lost track of the child.

Month after month the Red Army kept retreating, often just a step or two ahead of the pursuing Nationalist troops. Casualties were enormous. The farther west they went, the more rugged the terrain; as they skirted Tibet, they also had to deal with bitter cold. By the time they found an area in Shaanxi where they could establish a new base, they had marched almost ten thousand kilometers. Only about eight thousand of those who began the march made it the whole way, though some new recruits and communists from other base areas had joined en route, to bring the total to nearly twenty thousand. (See Map 26.1.)

To the Nationalists in Nanjing, the Long March must have seemed a huge victory. The Communist Party's urban activists had been crushed in 1927–1928, and now the rural activists had suffered just as devastating a blow, their numbers greatly diminished and the survivors driven into remote and poverty-stricken regions. Those who made the Long March, however, saw it as a victory. That they had overcome such daunting odds reinforced their belief that they were men of destiny with a near-sacred mission to remake China.

It was during the Long March that Mao Zedong reached the top ranks of party leadership. When the marchers reached Zunyi in Guizhou province in early 1935, they paused to hold an enlarged meeting of the Politburo and assess their strategy. Seventeen veteran party leaders were present, including Mao, the Comintern representative Otto Braun, and thirty-year old Deng Xiaoping to take notes. Blame was placed on Braun and others who had urged positional warfare to defend against the Nationalist attack. Mao was named to the Standing Committee of the Politburo and given new responsibility for military affairs.

From 1936 to 1946 the Communist Party made its base at Yan'an, a market town in central Shaanxi where homes were often built by cutting caves into the loess soil cliffs. When the American journalist Edgar Snow visited Yan'an in 1936, the survivors of the Long March appeared to him to be an earthy group of committed patriots and egalitarian social reformers, full of optimism and purpose. They lived in

MATERIAL CULTURE

Qipao

In the first decades of the twentieth century, as educated young people came to look on the West as the source of everything modern, they turned to western styles of dress, especially those who had worn this style while studying abroad. Some people adopted full western-style dress, but others tried to develop a style that would be both Chinese and modern at the same time. The so-called Mao suit, first popularized in China by Sun Yatsen, is an example of this sort of hybrid style for men. For women in the early twentieth century the garment that most successfully modernized Chinese dress was the *qipao*.

The *qipao* is a one-piece dress characterized by an upright ("mandarin") collar, an opening from the neck to under the right arm, and a fairly narrow cut, often with a slit, especially if the skirt reached below midcalf. The *qipao* was much more form fitting than anything worn in the nineteenth century, but reflected traditional styles in its collar, its slanted opening, and sometimes its fastenings. It could be made in silk, cotton, or synthetics, for everyday wear or elegant occasions.

Well-Dressed Young Women. These three young women wear *qipao* with short sleeves and high slits. Notice also their high-heel shoes and curled hair. *(Hulton Archive/Getty Images)*

caves, ate simple food, and showed no disdain for the peasants whom they were mobilizing to fight against the Japanese. During the war, too, outside observers were impressed with the commitment to group goals of the Yan'an forces. All through Mao's lifetime the official media promoted this image of the leaders of the Yan'an Soviet as a cohesive group of idealistic revolutionaries.

Mao's standing in Yan'an was high, but he still had rivals. A group of Communists who had gone to Russia for training arrived in late 1935 and provoked debate on the errors that had cost the lives of so many party members.

Mao realized that he would have to improve his grasp of Communist dialectic and began systematic study. His new secretary, Chen Boda, who had studied in Moscow for several years in the late 1920s, began writing of Mao as a theorist. Mao was becoming more set against the claims of the well educated, even if their education was in Marxism. To contrast himself from the urban intellectuals, Mao would act like a peasant, opening his clothes to look for lice with guests present.

Mao was victorious over the Soviet returnees in part because he was the better politician but also because he seems to have become truly con-

SOVIET UNION

OUTER MONGOLIA
(Independent 1924)

Amur

MANCHURIA

• Qiqihar

• Jiamusi

Ussuri

• Harbin

• Baotou

Zhangjiakou
• (Kalgan)

• Jinzhou

• Shenyang
(Mukden)

KOREA
(Japanese 1910–1945)

• Beijing

• Lanzhou

• Tianjin

• Taiyuan

• Yan'an

Yellow

SHANDONG

SHAANXI
Xi'an

• Jinan

• Qingdao

• Luoyang

• Zhengzhou

CHINA

• Chengdu

Yangzi

• Xuzhou

SICHUAN

• Wuhan

• Nanjing

• Chongqing

• Nanchang

• Shanghai

• Hangzhou

Zunyi

• Changsha

Jiangxi Soviet under
Mao Zedong and
Zhu De, 1929–1934

HUNAN

• Guiyang

Ji'an

• Kunming

BURMA

• Shantou

Xiamen
(Amoy)

TAIWAN
(Japanese
1895–1945)

*PACIFIC
OCEAN*

• Guangzhou

Hailufeng Soviet,
1927–1928

Hong
Kong
(British)

**FRENCH
INDOCHINA**

Areas under Communist control before Nov. 1934

Areas under Communist control, 1929–1938

Areas occupied by Japan by end of 1938

Route of the Long March, Oct. 1934–Oct. 1935
Main forces from Ji'an

Other forces

0   250   500 Km.

0   250   500 Mi.

Map **26.1**   **China in 1938**

fident that he was in the right. He began spending more time lecturing party members. He also started to allow or encourage the beginnings of the cult of Mao: in 1937 a portrait of him appeared in the revolutionary newspaper, and a collection of his writings was printed.

It was in this period that Mao took up with Jiang Qing. He Zizhen and Mao's surviving children had gone to the Soviet Union for safety and medical treatment. Jiang Qing, twenty-four years old, had worked as an actress in Shanghai and made her way to Yan'an after the Japanese invasion. Some of the other Communist leaders resented her liaison with Mao, having liked and admired He Zizhen. Mao and Jiang Qing had a daughter in 1940, the last of his four surviving children (six were lost or died).

THE JAPANESE INVASION AND THE RETREAT TO CHONGQING

From the time of the May Fourth protests in 1919, Chinese patriots saw Japan as the gravest threat to China's sovereignty. In 1895 Japan had won Taiwan. In 1905, after an impressive victory over Russia, it gained a dominant position in southern Manchuria. In 1915, by applying pressure on Yuan Shikai, Japan had secured a broad range of economic privileges. The Japanese Army in Manchuria, ostensibly there to protect Japan's railroads and other economic interests, was full of militarists who kept pushing Japanese civil authorities to let the army occupy the entire area. In 1928, Japanese officers assassinated the warlord of Manchuria, Zhang Zuolin, hoping for a crisis that would allow Japan to extend its power base. In 1931 Japanese soldiers set a bomb on the Southern Manchurian Railroad to give themselves an excuse to occupy Shenyang "in self-defense." China did not attempt to resist militarily but did appeal to the League of Nations, which recognized China as being in the right but imposed no real sanctions on Japan. Then in January 1932, Japan attacked Shanghai to retaliate against anti-Japanese protests. Shanghai was by that

point such an international city that the Japanese assault and the bombing of civilian residential areas was widely condemned. After four months, the Japanese withdrew from Shanghai, but in Manchuria they set up a puppet regime, making the last Qing emperor the nominal head of Manchukuo ("Manchu land").

Anger at Japanese aggression heightened Chinese nationalism and led to the formation of national salvation leagues and boycotts of Japanese goods. Still, Chiang, like most other military men of the day, did not see any point in putting up a fight when Japanese firepower was so clearly superior. Chiang was convinced that all Chinese would have to be united under one leader before China could hope to thwart Japan.

In 1936 troops that had been driven out of Manchuria by the Japanese were ordered by Chiang to blockade the Communists in Yan'an. When Chiang came to Xi'an, they kidnapped him and refused to release him until he agreed to form a united front with the Communists against Japan. These troops did not want to be fighting other Chinese when the Japanese had occupied their home towns. The Communists played no part in the kidnapping but joined the negotiations when Stalin urged them to keep Chiang alive and create a nationwide united front against Japan.

The next year, 1937, Chiang did put up a fight when the Japanese staged another incident as an excuse for taking more territory. Chiang was probably hoping to inflict a quick defeat to convince Japan that the Nanjing government was a power to be reckoned with, so that they would negotiate with him rather than continue to move into China as though it was unoccupied. Japan instead launched a full-scale offensive, sweeping south. Chiang had to abandon Beijing and Tianjin, but he used his best troops to hold off the Japanese at Shanghai for three months. He asked for an all-out stand, and his troops courageously persisted despite heavy shelling and bombing, absorbing two hundred fifty thousand casualties, killed or wounded (compared to forty thousand Japanese casualties). When Shanghai fell, the Nationalist troops streamed toward the Nationalist capital, Nanjing. After the Japanese easily took Nanjing in December 1937, they went on a rampage, massacring somewhere between forty thousand and three hundred thousand civilians and fugitive soldiers, raping perhaps twenty thousand women, and laying the city waste. The seven weeks of mayhem was widely reported in the foreign press, where it was labeled the Rape of Nanking. If this violence was intended to speed a Chinese surrender, it did not achieve its goal.

During the course of 1938, the Japanese secured control of the entire eastern seaboard and set up puppet regimes headed by Chinese collaborators (see Map 26.1). Terror tactics continued, including biological and chemical warfare in Zhejiang in 1940, where bubonic plague was spread and poison gas released. Civilian casualties were also inflicted by the Nationalist government. When the Chinese had to retreat from Kaifeng, Chiang ordered his engineers to blow up the dikes on the Yellow River, creating a gigantic flood that engulfed more than four thousand villages, drowned some three hundred thousand people, and left 2 million homeless. It held up the Japanese for only three months.

Japan had assumed that once they captured the capital at Nanjing and inflicted an overwhelming defeat on the Nationalist army, Chiang Kaishek would come to terms. When he refused and moved inland, the war bogged down. Rather than persuading the Chinese to surrender, Japanese terror tactics instead intensified popular hatred for the Japanese. China's great distances spread Japanese forces. In north China, Japan concentrated on holding rail lines, and Chinese guerrilla forces concentrated on blowing them up. Guerrilla soldiers depended on local peasants to feed them and inform them of enemy concentrations and movements. They acquired weapons and ammunition by capturing them from the Japanese. Many resistance fighters worked in the fields during the day and at night acted as guides or scouts to help blow up bridges, rail lines, and roads. Peasant cooperation with the guerrillas provoked savage Japanese reprisals, including killing everyone in villages suspected of harboring resistance fighters, which the Japanese called their "kill all, burn all, loot all" policy. Chinese resistance forced Japan to keep about 40 percent of its troops in China even after the Pacific War had begun in late 1941 (see **Connections: World War II**).

The Nationalists' capital was moved inland first to Wuhan, then to Chongqing, deep in Sichuan. Free China, as it was called in the western press, started with the odds heavily against it. The capital, Chongqing, suffered repeated air raids and faced not only shortages of almost everything, but runaway inflation, as high as 10 percent a month, leading to widespread corruption as government workers' salaries fell to a pittance. The army was in worse shape. China had lost most of the army Chiang had spent a decade training in preparation for war with Japan. From 1939 on, the bulk of China's 5 million soldiers were ill-trained peasant conscripts. Press gangs would enter villages and seize the able-bodied. As many as a third of the conscripts died on the forced marches to their bases because they were not given enough to eat or medical care. Desertion, not surprisingly, was a huge problem. Another serious disability for Free China was the lack of an industrial base inland. Chinese engineers made heroic efforts to build a new industrial base, but constant Japanese bombing, the end of Soviet aid in 1939, and the closing of the route through Burma in 1942 frustrated their efforts. From 1942 on, American advisers and American aid flown over the mountains from Burma enabled Chiang to build a number of modern divisions, but not an army able to drive the Japanese out of China.

During World War II, international alignments began to shift. After Britain proved unable to defend Hong Kong, Singapore, or Burma from Japanese invasions in 1941–1942, it lost its standing in Chinese eyes as the preeminent western power. Its place was taken by the United States, which ended up doing most of the fighting against Japan. The American-educated wife of Chiang, Soong Meiling, was popular with the American press and lobbied effectively for China. President Franklin D. Roosevelt, looking ahead, wished to see China become the dominant power in East Asia after the defeat of Japan, and convinced his allies to include Chiang in major meetings of the allies at Cairo and Yalta (though Churchill referred to making China one of the Big Four as an absolute farce). It was as a result of this sort of geopolitics that China, so long scorned as weak and backward, became one of the five permanent members of the UN's Security Council after the war.

THE CHINESE COMMUNIST PARTY DURING THE WAR

During the first few years of the war, there was some genuine cooperation between the Communists and Nationalists. This largely ended, however, when the Communist divisions of the New Fourth Army were attacked by the Nationalists in January 1941 on the grounds that they had not complied rapidly enough with an order to retreat north of the Yangzi. Not only were around three thousand troops killed in battle, but many were shot after arrest or sent to prison camps. From this point on, the Nationalists imposed an economic blockade on the Communist base area.

Some one hundred thousand people made their way to Yan'an during the war, about half students, teachers, and writers. Party membership swelled from forty thousand in 1937 to about eight hundred thousand in 1940. The fight against Japan helped the Communists build a base of popular support. In areas of north China where the Japanese armies had penetrated, peasants were ready to join forces against the Japanese.

Resistance forces were not exclusively Communist. Patriotic urban students fled to these relatively uncontested rural areas where they helped both Nationalist and Communist resistance forces. The Communists, however, were more successful in gaining control of the social, political, and economic life in villages because they gave peasants what they wanted: an army of friendly troops who not only did not steal their crops but helped them bring in the harvest and implemented popular but gradual economic reforms.

Class struggle was not emphasized during the war against Japan, nor was there much confiscation of land. Still, considerable redistribution was accomplished by imposing graduated taxes that led larger landholders to sell land that was no longer profitable. Landlords were more than welcome to help with forming and supplying militia forces, and educated youth from better-off families were recruited as party members. Party propagandists did their best to stoke patriotic passions, glorify the Soviet Union, and convey the message that the Communist Party could build a better, more egalitarian future. They called so many meetings that rural folk in Hebei quipped, "Under the Nationalists, too many taxes; under the Communists, too many meetings."[3]

The Japanese did not penetrate as far west as Yan'an, and during the war Mao could concentrate on ideological issues. As the party grew rapidly, Mao sought ways to instill a uniform vision. He began giving lectures to party members in which he spelled out his version of Chinese history, the party's history, and Marxist theory. Neither Marx nor Lenin had seen much revolutionary potential in peasants, viewing them as petty capitalist in mentality, and in Russia the party had seized power in an urban setting. Since the Communists in China had failed in the cities, Mao reinterpreted Marxist theory in such a way that the peasants could be seen as the vanguard of the revolution. Indeed Mao came more and more to glorify the peasants as the true masses and elaborate the theory of the mass line: party cadres had to go among and learn from the peasant masses before they could become their teachers. Marx was a materialist who rejected idealist interpretations of history. Ideas did not make history; rather, they reflected the economic base, the mode of production, and the relations of production. Mao's vision of rev-

---

3. Edward Friedman, Paul G. Pickowics, and Mark Selden, *Chinese Village, Socialist State* (New Haven, Conn.: Yale University Press, 1991), p. 41.

The Communist Leadership. Zhou Enlai, Mao Zedong, and Zhu De (left to right) were photographed in the winter of 1944, by which time the Communist Party had gained a foothold behind Japanese lines all across north China. (*Popperfoto/Retrofile*)

olution, by contrast, was voluntaristic: it emphasized the potential for people, once mobilized, to transform both themselves and the world through the power of their wills.

This "Thought of Mao Zedong" did not win out in a free competition of ideas among the survivors of the Long March, but in a power struggle in which Mao proved a master tactician, able to eliminate his rivals one after the other and get the Central Committee to label them deviationists of the right or left. To reform the thinking of both old cadres who had deviated from the correct line and new recruits from bourgeois families, in 1942 Mao launched the first of many rectification campaigns. Cadres had to study documents Mao selected in small groups, analyze their own shortcomings in Maoist terms, listen to criticism of themselves at mass struggle sessions, and confess their errors. Everyone watched the dramatic public humiliations of the principal targets, including

the party theorist Wang Ming and the writer Wang Shiwei. People learned to interpret any deviation from Mao's line as defects in their thinking due to their subjectivism and liberalism, characteristics of their petty bourgeois background. One man, for instance, who confessed to being bothered by the party elite's special privileges (such as getting to ride on horseback while others walked) was taught that liberal ideas elevating the individual over the collective lay behind his feelings. Those who balked were punished; some even died. Many of those invited to overcome their errors truly developed a new collective consciousness that greatly increased their usefulness to the party. Others simply learned to be more circumspect when they talked.

In May 1943 Mao received a new title, chairman of the Central Committee, and began to be treated as the party's paramount leader. The people of China were urged to arm themselves with Mao Zedong's thought. The Seventh Party Congress, the first to be held since the 1920s, was held at Yan'an in the spring of 1945. The preamble of the new constitution recognized Mao's new role as sage of the party: "The Chinese Communist Party takes Mao Zedong's thought—the thought that unites Marxist-Leninist theory and the practices of the Chinese revolution—as the guide for all its work, and opposes all dogmatic or empiricist deviations."[4]

THE CIVIL WAR AND THE COMMUNIST VICTORY

The end of the war with Japan set the stage for the final confrontation between the Nationalists and the Communists. When Japan surrendered in August 1945, there were over 1 million Japanese troops in China proper and nearly another 1 million in Manchuria, as well as about 1.75 million Japanese civilians. Disarming and repatriating them took months, as the

---

4. Cited in Jonathan Spence, *Mao Zedong* (New York: Viking, 1999), p. 101.

Nationalists, the Communists, the Americans, the Russians, and even some warlords jockeyed for position. The United States airlifted one hundred ten thousand Nationalist troops to key coastal cities like Shanghai and Guangzhou, and fifty-three thousand U.S. Marines were sent to help secure Beijing and Tianjin. The Russians had entered Manchuria in early August in fulfillment of their secret promise to the United States and Britain to join the eastern front three months after victory in Europe. They saw to it that large stores of Japanese weapons got into the hands of the Red Army—some seven hundred forty thousand rifles, eighteen thousand machine guns, and four thousand artillery pieces—giving them about as much Japanese equipment as the Nationalists got.

From August 1945 until January 1947, the United States made efforts to avert civil war by trying to convince Chiang to establish a government in which opposition parties could participate. The American ambassador brought Mao and Chiang together for several weeks of meetings in Chongqing, but the agreements reached on cooperation led nowhere. Full-scale civil war ensued.

The civil war itself lasted only about two years. The Red Army (now called the People's Liberation Army, or PLA) began to isolate the cities, starting in Manchuria and working south. It lost battles but built support through moderate land reform. When Nationalist soldiers defected, they took their equipment with them, and the PLA incorporated them into its armies. Within a year the Nationalist forces in Manchuria were routed and the PLA was moving into China proper. In 1948, a two-month battle near the railway center of Xuzhou pitted six hundred thousand of Chiang's troops against an equal number of Communist ones. Although Chiang had air support, his army was smashed and he lost almost half a million men. Thus, although the Nationalists had started with much more in the way of modern armaments and several times the number of troops, they fared poorly on the battlefield. In early 1949 Chiang Kaishek and much of his army and government retreated to Taiwan and reestablished their government there.

The unpopularity of the Nationalists had many roots. Prices in July 1948 were 3 million times higher than they had been in July 1937, and inflation did not let up then. People had to resort to barter, and a tenth of the population became refugees. Nationalist army officers and soldiers were widely seen as seizing whatever they could for themselves rather than working for the common good. Student protests were often put down by violence. When liberals demanded that Chiang widen participation in his government, he had his secret police assassinate them. No amount of American support could make the Chinese want to continue with this government in power.

SUMMARY

What changed between 1927 and 1949? How different was China? More than half a century of struggle against a Japan intent on imperialist expansion was over: Japan had been thoroughly defeated and had turned against war. The Nationalist Party had been defeated by the Communist Party and had withdrawn from the mainland. The Communist Party itself had changed dramatically. The party had broken free from Comintern control and tied itself intimately to the peasantry. Mao had risen to the top position in the party and established his version of Marxism as the correct ideology of the party. The party had grown enormously and acquired extensive experience in redistribution of land, mobilizing peasants, and keeping intellectuals on a tight rein.

SUGGESTED READING

Most of the general works mentioned in Chapter 23 also cover this period. In addition, see D. Klein and A. Clark, eds., *Biographic Dictionary of Chinese Communism, 1921–1965*, 2 vols. (1971). On the first United Front between the Nationalists and the Communists, see H. Issacs, *The Tragedy of the Chinese Revolution*, rev. ed. (1951), and D. Jacobs, *Borodin: Stalin's Man in China* (1981).

On the Nationalists, see L. Eastman, *The Abortive Revolution: China Under Nationalist Rule, 1927–1937*, rev. ed. (1990) and *Seeds of Destruction: Nationalist China in War and Revolution, 1937–1949* (1984); F. Wakeman, *Policing Shanghai, 1927–1937* (1995); and B. Martin, *The Shanghai Green Gang: Politics and Organized Crime, 1919–1937* (1996). On the Chinese economy in this period, see P. Coble, *The Shanghai Capitalists and the Nationalist Government, 1927–1937* (1986), and T. Rawski, *Economic Growth in Prewar China* (1989).

The lively literature of the 1920s and 1930s is treated in C. T. Hsia, *A History of Modern Chinese Fiction* (1971); O. Lee, ed., *Lu Xun and His Legacy* (1985); and O. Lang, *Pa Chin and His Writings: Chinese Youth Between the Two Revolutions* (1967). For translations, see *The Selected Stories of Lu Hsun* (1972); Pa Chin, *Family*, trans. S. Shapiro (1972); and Lao She's *Rickshaw*, trans. J. James (1979). On Shanghai in the culture of the period, see H. Lu, *Beyond the Neon Lights: Everyday Shanghai in the Early Twentieth Century* (1999), and L. Lee, *Shanghai Modern: The Flowering of a New Urban Culture in China, 1930–1945* (1999).

On the war against Japan, see J. Hsiung and S. Levine, *China's Bitter Victory: The War with Japan, 1937–1945* (1992), and J. Fogel, ed., *The Nanjing Massacre in History and Historiography* (2000).

On the Communist victory, see O. Wou, *Mobilizing the Masses: Building Revolution in Henan* (1994); J. Yick, *Making Urban Revolution* (1995); A. Dirlik, *The Origins of Chinese Communism* (1989); M. Selden, *The Yenan Way in Revolutionary China* (1971); and S. Pepper, *Civil War in China: The Political Struggle, 1945–1949* (1978). Early firsthand accounts still of value are E. Snow, *Red Star over China* (1938); J. Belden, *China Shakes the World* (1970); and W. Hinton, *Fanshen: A Documentary of Revolution in a Chinese Village* (1966). For a brief biography of Mao, see J. Spence, *Mao Zedong* (1999); for a long one, see either R. Terrill, *Mao: A Biography* (1999), or R. Short, *Mao: A Life* (2000).

World War II

In both the western and eastern theaters, World War II was characterized by indiscriminate bombing of civilian populations and death tolls in the millions. The aggressors were the Axis: Japan, Germany, and to a lesser extent, Italy. Allied against them were the British Commonwealth (including officially India and Australia), the United States, and the Soviet Union, along with the Chinese government under Chiang Kai-shek. What is known as the fifteen-year war began with Japan's takeover of Manchuria in 1931. In 1937 Japan launched all-out war against China. The war in Europe began in 1939 when Hitler provoked a declaration of war from Britain and France by invading Poland. The United States got involved when Japan bombed Pearl Harbor on December 7, 1941, and Hitler declared war on the United States.

Timeline: The Greater East Asia War

1931–1932	Japan's Kwantung army takes over Manchuria
1932	January 28: Japan bombs Shanghai
1933	May 27: Japan withdraws from the League of Nations
1935	November 24: Puppet government established in Beijing
1936	January 25: United Front against Japan
1937	July 7: Marco Polo Bridge Incident; Japan invades China
	November 20: Chinese capital established at Chongqing
	December 13: Rape of Nanjing begins
1938	United States embargoes war materiel to Japan
1939	May through August: Japanese and Soviet troops fight at Nomonhan
1940	Spring: U.S. Pacific Fleet moves to Pearl Harbor in Hawai'i
	September 26: Japan invades North Vietnam
	September 27: Japan, Italy, and Germany sign Tripartite Mutual Defense Pact
	October 15: United States embargoes scrap iron and steel to Japan
1941	April 13: Japan signs neutrality pact with Soviet Union
	July 26: Britain and United States cut off trade with Japan
	December 7: Japan attacks Pearl Harbor
	December 8: Japan attacks the Philippines, Wake, Guam, Hong Kong, and Malaya
	December 23: Japan bombs Rangoon, Burma
1942	January 23: Japan takes Rabaul north of New Guinea
	January 26: Japan lands on Solomon Islands
	February 15: Japan captures Singapore
	February 27–March 1: Battle of Java Sea
	March 9: Japan conquers Java

	April 9: U.S. Army on Bataan peninsula in the Philippines surrenders
	May 2: Japan captures Mandalay in Burma
	May 7: Battle of Coral Sea
	June 4–7: Battle of Midway
	June 12: Japan occupies Attu in Aleutian Islands
	July 9: Chinese Nationalist forces win a major battle in Jiangxi province
	July 21: Japan captures Buna, New Guinea; drives toward Port Moresby
1943	February 9: Japan retreats from Guadalcanal in Solomons
	July 1: Allied offensive in South Pacific
	July 29: United States drives Japan from Aleutian Islands
	November 22: U.S. troops land on Tarawa in Gilbert Islands
1944	February 2: Invasion of Marshall Islands
	February 17: Battle of Truk lagoon
	June 15–July 7: U.S. forces take Saipan
	August 11: U.S. forces take Guam
	August: Britain retakes Burma
	October 23–25: Battle of Leyte Gulf
1945	March 10: Firebombing of Tokyo
	March 17: United States captures Iwo Jima
	April 1: Invasion of Okinawa begins
	June 22: Okinawa falls
	July 26: Potsdam Declaration
	August 6: Atomic bomb dropped on Hiroshima
	August 8: Soviet Union declares war on Japan
	August 9: Plutonium bomb dropped on Nagasaki
	August 15: Japan surrenders

The belligerents each had reasons for fighting. Still angry at the punitive terms that included a loss of territory imposed on it by the armistice that ended World War I, Germany insisted that it needed living space for its growing population. Hitler's Nazi Party believed Aryans were superior to all other races and destined to rule the world. Many people in Japan believed it was superior to the rest of Asia. Junior officers agreed with the Nazis and the Fascists in Italy that social dislocations in the early twentieth century had resulted from individualistic liberalism expressed in hedonistic urban culture and the compromises and corruption of politicians. They opposed capitalism and the capitalist powers—England, France, and the United States—that dominated the world economically and

militarily. They also feared universal socialism emanating from the Bolshevik revolution that threatened the national polity. Japan's government and many of its citizens believed that Japan needed colonies for its national security. Fear that Soviet expansion threatened Japan's interests in Asia led it to take over Manchuria. It fought in China to protect its interests in Manchuria; once in that quagmire, it was sucked inextricably into conflict with the Allied powers.

Officers in the Japanese army took control of Manchuria to protect Japanese railroads and mines built after victory in the Russo-Japanese War. The army installed a puppet government in what it called Manchukuo headed by Puyi, the last Qing emperor. Treating Manchukuo as a new frontier, it encouraged settlers to displace indigenous people in farming what then became wide-open spaces. By 1945, Manchuria had absorbed approximately two hundred seventy thousand Japanese immigrants.

Japan's conquest of Manchuria sparked a wave of anti-Japanese demonstrations and a boycott of Japanese goods in China's major cities. The Japanese navy retaliated by bombarding civilian quarters in Shanghai before the eyes of the largest international community in China. An explosion of outrage filled foreign newspapers, but foreign governments did little. The League of Nations sent a fact-finding team to China, and when the League Assembly accepted the team's report that castigated Japan's aggression in Manchuria, Japan withdrew from the League.

Japan's attempts to establish a buffer zone in north China fed the growing anti-Japanese nationalist sentiment among Chinese people. A national salvation movement led by student demonstrations demanding national unity and resistance to Japan erupted in Beijing and spread to other cities. The Communists in Yan'an issued a call for all to resist Japanese imperialism. Even warlords in southwest China joined the clamor, though their patriotic fervor was tinged with a self-interested desire to obstruct Chiang Kaishek's nationalist government in Nanjing. The United Front of 1936 allied Communists and Nationalists against Japan. The development of anti-Japanese organizations meant that when the Japanese army invaded north China in July 1937 to protect its interests in Manchuria and seize attractive resources, it met fierce opposition.

The war in China was marked by the first atrocities of World War II committed against civilian populations. Japan did not expect the level of resistance offered by Chinese troops that attacked Japanese forces in and around Shanghai in retaliation for Japan's capture of Beijing and Tianjin. Not until December did the Japanese army capture Nanjing. When the city surrendered, Japanese army spokesmen contended that Chinese troops had taken off their uniforms

Crying Baby. This photograph of a crying baby that appeared in *Life* magazine following the Nanjing Massacre garnered America's sympathy for China in its struggle against Japan. *(Getty Images)*

to mingle with the civilian population, thereby justifying the murder of thousands of Chinese civilians. Frustrated that five months of warfare had not resulted in decisive victory, Japanese officers encouraged their men to loot stores and rape women. The number killed is disputed even today. This horror was dubbed the "Rape of Nanking" by the foreign press. Although this was the worst, it was by no means the last of the atrocities committed by Japanese troops.

Shocked at the international outcry and disturbed by the troops' behavior that they had encouraged, Japanese officers decided that indiscriminate rape threatened Japan's international reputation and military discipline. To provide for what was deemed the soldiers' physical needs and to combat venereal disease, the army developed a system of "comfort stations," already inaugurated in Shanghai in 1932. Japanese prostitutes were primarily reserved for officers in the rear. To find women for soldiers on the front lines, the military turned to its colonies and then to territories conquered after 1940. Koreans composed 80 percent of the "comfort women" who serviced troops as far away as Burma and island Southeast Asia. In some areas they had to service up to fifty men a day for a modest fee per soldier. Only the end of the war brought release from sexual slavery.

The China war demonstrated the importance and limitations of air power. Having few planes of its own, the Chinese nationalist army had to use natural defenses to hold off Japanese troops and delay their advance. When Chiang moved his government to Chongqing in the mountains of Sichuan, nearly perpetual fog protected the city from Japanese bombers. The narrow Yangzi gorges precluded an overland attack. Instead, Japanese troops fanned out along the eastern seaboard and along railroad lines in the interior. By the end of 1938, they occupied cities and major towns from Manchuria to Guangdong. In the days before helicopters, their superior air power had less effect in the countryside.

Although Chinese living under Japanese occupation tried to remain inconspicuous, many had to make a choice between collaboration and resistance. Collaborators set up a provisional government in Beijing in 1937 to administer north China. In 1940, Japan created the Reorganized Government of the Republic of China under Wang Jingwei, a member of Chiang Kaishek's Nationalist Party who hoped to win peace with Japan in the name of Greater East Asianism. In 1943 Japan allowed him to declare war on the United States and Great Britain. In the countryside, persistent guerrilla warfare led Japanese army units to launch indiscriminate punitive missions against villages thought to be harboring Communists. These "rural pacification" campaigns proved ineffective. Although 1 million Japanese troops occupied China's richest regions for eight years, they could not subdue the people or find an exit strategy from a war neither side could win.

Japan expected more than collaboration from its Korean subjects in its war with China. It expanded cotton and wool production at the expense of cereals; it developed hydroelectric power in the north. In 1936, it declared a new policy of forced assimilation: all Korean were to be taught that they too were children of the emperor. Later it banned the use of the Korean language in classrooms and ordered Koreans to adopt Japanese names. Japanese became the only language allowed in public offices and in record keeping by businesses and banks. Koreans had to worship at Shinto shrines and pray for the emperor's good health. Over six hundred thousand Korean men were drafted to work in Japanese and Manchurian mines, harbors, and factories. Although Japan taught that Korea and Japan were one, it did not trust the Koreans to fight its battles. By 1944 upwards of 4 million Koreans worked outside Korea, some as policemen and guards as far away as New Guinea, where they died in battles that made no distinction between combatants and noncombatants.

Japan's aggression in China provoked a response similar to what greeted Italy's conquest of Ethiopia in 1936. Both the League of Nations and the United States (which had not joined the League) officially deplored Japan's action. Neither tried to stop it, even though Japanese forces destroyed American property, sank an American warship, and killed American civilians. Fearful of Japan's intentions north of Manchuria, only the Soviet Union provided significant aid to China. It shipped munitions and airplanes to both Communist and Nationalist forces along with military advisers. Over two hundred Soviet pilots died in China's defense. In May 1939 the Japanese army in western Manchuria confronted Soviet forces at Nomonhan. The fight cost Japan eighteen thousand men and exposed critical weaknesses in the army's tactics and equipment. Japan sued for peace following the Russo-German Non-Aggression Pact signed in August. In 1941 Japan and the Soviet Union signed a neutrality pact. After Germany invaded the Soviet Union at the end of June, the Japanese army both kept alive the possibility of war with the Soviet Union and tried to honor the neutrality pact. Soviet aid to China came to an end with the outbreak of the war in Europe.

The United States relied on sanctions and threats to try to force Japan out of China and check Japan's expansion in Indochina. It placed a series of increasingly stringent embargos on goods to Japan and helped Chiang Kaishek by extending credit with which to buy American arms. When President Roosevelt had the Pacific Fleet move to Pearl Harbor to protect U.S. shipping lanes and intimidate Japan, Japan's navy took it as a threat to its interests in Micronesia and the South Pacific. In September 1940, Japan invaded North Vietnam to secure raw materials for its war machine and cut supply lines running to Chiang Kaishek. When the United States, Britain, and the Netherlands, which controlled the oil fields of Indonesia, cut off trade unless Japan pulled out of China and North Vietnam, Japan felt it had to fight or accept humiliation.

Neither the Allies nor Japan understood the other's motives, and they underestimated their opponents. Japan claimed to be liberating Asia from colonial powers. In 1940 it promoted, though it did not practice, the notion of a Greater East Asia Co-Prosperity Sphere, an economic regional power bloc similar to that envisioned in the western hemisphere under the Monroe Doctrine. In Japan's eyes, the United States and Soviet Union had everything they needed for an autonomous defense, but without colonies, Japan did not. Japanese soldiers saw themselves as spiritually superior to the materialistic West; they were hard and high-minded, whereas British and Americans were soft. Public opinion in the United States saw China as a victim of Japanese totalitarian aggression. Madame Chiang Kaishek gave an impassioned speech before the U.S. Congress in which she contrasted China striving for democracy and Japanese warmongers. Henry Luce, son of missionaries in China and owner of *Time-Life*, flooded his magazines with heart-rending pictures from war-torn China. Editorial cartoons drew on racial stereotypes to mock Japanese for their physical and mental inferiority and portrayed them as vermin to be exterminated.

Japan's desperation to find a solution to its war with China pushed it to open one battlefront after another, many over 3,000 miles from the home islands. To break through what it called the ABCD encirclement (American, British, Chinese, Dutch) and secure the oil crucial for its China campaign, it struck south. It bombed Pearl Harbor in hopes of forcing the

United States to negotiate a settlement. Ten hours later, it launched an invasion of the Philippines, a U.S. colony. Britain had expected attack on Singapore to come from the sea; Japanese troops advanced through the jungle to capture the city. (The same month that saw the fall of Singapore also saw President Roosevelt sign Executive Order 9066 to place one hundred ten thousand Japanese Americans, over half of them U.S. citizens, behind the barbed wire of relocation camps in the western United States.) Within months Japan captured Indonesia, the Philippines, Guam, Wake, and the Solomon Islands. The Japanese army took over the rest of Vietnam, forced an alliance on Thailand, chased Britain out of Burma, closed the Burma Road that had carried to supplies to Chongqing, and threatened India and Australia. Combined with the islands taken from Germany in World War I, this gave the Japanese a vast empire, albeit mostly over water. (See Map C7.1.)

Beset with enemies from within and without, Japan's new empire lasted a scant two years. In some cases, men who were later to lead independence movements against western imperialism began by collaborating with Japan, as did General Aung San of Burma. When British soldiers beat a hasty retreat to India, units left behind formed the Indian National Army to fight for Indian independence. These instances serve as reminders that South and Southeast Asia welcomed Japan's message of liberation from colonial rule, but not the way it was delivered. Japan's arrogant sense of racial superiority soon made it enemies. Resistance to Japanese occupation from China to Indonesia to the Philippines contributed significantly to the Allies' counterattack. The British led Indian troops to reconquer Burma, Australians pushed Japan out of New Guinea, Chiang Kaishek's forces inflicted a major defeat on troops in China, the U.S. Army under General Douglas MacArthur advanced through the South Pacific before returning to the Philippines, and the U.S. Navy island-hopped across the Central Pacific.

Much of the fighting in the Pacific and Southeast Asia took place in jungles hated by both

Map C7.1   **World War II in Asia and the Pacific**

sides. After four months on the Bataan peninsula in the Philippines, one-third of the U.S. troops were in rain-dampened field hospitals suffering from festering wounds, dysentery, and malaria. Although the Japanese army used the jungle to advantage in taking Singapore, its troops too fell victim to disease in Burma and Malaya. Japanese troops tried to cross the spine of New Guinea from Buna to Port Moresby over steep mountain passes covered with rain forest. Thrown back by Australian forces, both sides struggled through knee-deep mud to engage an enemy seen only sporadically. Communications with headquarters broke down, and fighting erupted haphazardly when individual units ran afoul the enemy.

Fighting on so many fronts meant that Japan lacked the ability to provide its troops with adequate supplies. Troops dispatched to far-flung islands and atolls were expected to live off the land. When U.S. submarines sank supply ships, they starved. Because the United States had signed a disarmament pact before the war that abjured submarine warfare as inhumane, Japan did not anticipate attacks on tankers and freighters sailing the western Pacific behind its defensive perimeter. In 1942, Japan received 40 percent of Indonesia's oil. Owing to the war of attrition, it received only 5 percent in 1944, and it received none in 1945. Taxis in Tokyo ran on wood-burning engines, and the air force adulterated scarce fuel with sap from pine roots.

Lacking adequate resources meant that the Japanese army and navy had to rely on men over machines. When Japan built runways on Pacific islands, it used human labor—natives, Koreans, Okinawans, prisoners of war. The Allies used bulldozers. At war's beginning, Japan had well-trained pilots flying the Zero, the most advanced fighter of its day. When those pilots were gone, their barely trained replacements had to fly against American pilots in planes constantly improved through new technology. Japan lost so many planes trying to defend Truk in Micronesia that American pilots called the battle "a turkey shoot." After the Japanese fleet lost six aircraft carriers at the battle of Leyte Gulf, the navy asked its pilots to crash their planes into enemy ships. Designated the Divine Wind Special Attack Corps to recall the typhoon credited with repelling Mongol invaders almost seven hundred years earlier, *kamikaze* pilots struck fear and loathing into Allied hearts. Nearly five thousand young men sacrificed their lives in a futile effort to stem the Allied tide sweeping toward Japan.

Air power made the decisive difference in the major battles on sea and land. From the battle of the Coral Sea, to Midway, to Leyte Gulf, although enemy ships saw each other's planes, the ships themselves never fought. Even before the attack on Pearl Harbor, the Allies had broken Japanese codes, and at the decisive battle of Midway, the United States used its knowledge of Japan's positions and intentions to sink three

of Japan's aircraft carriers and severely damage a fourth. The battle of the Coral Sea ended with Japan thinking it had lost, even though it sank more ships than the Allies. Throughout the war, Japan's admirals sought the decisive sea battle fought with battleships that would turn the tide of war just as Admiral Tōgō's stunning defeat of the Russian navy in 1905 had brought victory then. Little did they realize that aircraft carriers had made battleships irrelevant.

When Japan destroyed U.S. planes on the ground in the Philippines, it left U.S. troops defenseless against aerial attack. Later in the war, Japan's troops, and later cities, suffered the same experience once its air force had been decimated. The fall of Saipan in Micronesia after the navy lost over four hundred planes and every Japanese soldier had died in its defense put Japan's main islands within range of U.S. heavy bombers. The first raids, carried out at high altitudes, did little but psychological damage. Once General Curtis E. LeMay arrived from Europe, pilots in the Pacific perfected the art of carpet bombing, that is, dropping incendiary bombs at low attitudes that decimated Japan's wooden cities. In the largest air offensive in history, U.S. planes destroyed the remnants of the Japanese navy, shattered Japanese industry, and dropped forty thousand tons of bombs on population centers. Approximately ninety thousand civilians died in the firestorm that engulfed Tokyo. The plane that carried the atomic bomb to Hiroshima took off from Tinian, just north of Saipan. Its flight was virtually unimpeded.

Even before the fall of Okinawa that sacrificed one-quarter of the island's population to the defense of the homeland, cabinet members began to call for an end to the war. The army rebuffed them. With 5.5 million men relatively unscathed in China and Manchuria, it demanded that all Japanese prepare to make the ultimate sacrifice, to die like "shattered jewels" in protecting the emperor-centered national polity. Recalling President Theodore Roosevelt's mediation of an end to the Russo-Japanese War in 1905 and hoping to keep the Soviet Union neutral, the army finally agreed to let the Japan-

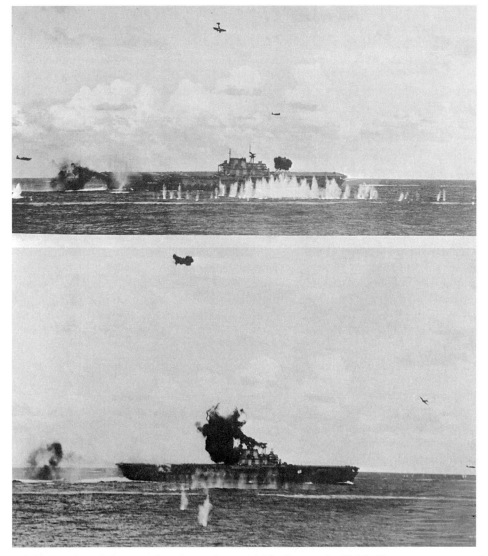

Suicide Bomber. A Japanese bomber makes a suicide dive on the *U.S.S. Hornet* on October 26, 1942, off Santa Cruz in the Solomon Islands. *(Bettmann/Corbis)*

ese ambassador to Moscow ask Foreign Minister Molotov for help. Busy with preparations for the Potsdam Conference, Molotov repeatedly put him off. On July 26, Churchill and Truman issued the Potsdam Declaration (Stalin did not sign it) demanding that Japan submit to unconditional surrender. Japan was to agree to allow occupation by foreign troops and to renounce all claims to territory on the Asian

mainland and Taiwan. Its leaders and soldiers were to be tried for war crimes, and the Japanese people were to choose the form of government they wanted. The alternative was "prompt and utter destruction."

The Potsdam Declaration was both extremely specific and maddeningly vague. Japanese leaders had no way of knowing that destruction was to come via a bomb first tested ten days before.

To the distress of his loyal subjects, the declaration made no mention of the emperor. The cabinet decided to sit tight and hope for mediation by the Soviet Union. For three days in early August, the atomic bomb, the Soviet Union's declaration of war, and the plutonium bomb sent shock waves through the cabinet. At a climatic meeting on August 14, the emperor instructed the cabinet to surrender. Later, he made a recording to tell the Japanese people that they must bear the unbearable. Despite a plot by junior army officers to steal it, it was broadcast at noon on August 15. World War II was over.

After the war, Japanese military personnel were prosecuted for war crimes. In Indonesia, the Dutch convicted Japanese who had forced European women to service Japanese troops; they ignored cases involving Indonesian women. Other war crimes trials made no mention of comfort women. Nor did they include men from Unit 731 who had turned over their data on bestial experiments performed on Chinese in Manchuria to test bacteriological weapons. Instead the trials focused on crimes against humanity broadly defined as the decision to wage war; atrocities such as the Bataan death march in which thousands of American and Filipino soldiers died; the indiscriminate bayoneting of British doctors, nurses, and patients in Singapore; the machine-gunning, decapitation, and drowning of civilians in Southeast Asia; and the massacre of Filipinos in Manila at the end of the war. Japan's treatment of prisoners of war merited special condemnation; soldiers who survived surrender were starved, tortured, and forced to labor for the Japanese war machine in contravention of the Geneva Convention. The war crimes tribunals ignored atrocities committed by Allied forces.

Following World War II, the world split into two camps: the free world dominated by the United States and the Communist bloc led by the Soviet Union. An iron curtain came down in Europe. Forgetting that Japan's early victories had exposed their vulnerabilities, some western powers assumed that their former colonies in South and Southeast Asia would welcome them as liberators. The United States freed the Philippines in 1946. Britain pulled out of Burma and India in 1947. Two years later, the Dutch grudgingly granted independence to Indonesia. France refused to leave Vietnam until defeated in 1954. Civil war in China ended with the establishment of the People's Republic of China and the Nationalist Party's flight to Taiwan. Soviet troops began to enter Korea in August 1945. Hoping to prevent the whole country from falling into their hands, the United States got the Soviet Union to agree to a dividing line just north of Seoul at the 38th parallel. The two nations then sponsored the creation of two separate states on the Korean peninsula. Japan escaped that fate. Under U.S. occupation, it became a bulwark against communism.

SUGGESTED READING

There is a vast array of books on World War II. Some of the most recent include: E. Bergerud, *Touched with Fire: The Land War in the Pacific* (1996); N. Tarling, *A Sudden Rampage: The Japanese Occupation of Southeast Asia* (2001); and J. C. Hsiung and S. I. Levine, *China's Bitter Victory: The War with Japan, 1937–1945* (1992). The classic is J. W. Dower, *War Without Mercy: Race and Power in the Pacific War* (1986). On related topics, see K. Honda, *The Nanjing Massacre: A Japanese Journalist Confronts Japan's National Shame* (1999); Y. Tanaka, *Japan's Comfort Women: Sexual Slavery and Prostitution During World War II and the US Occupation* (2002); and S. H. Harris, *Factories of Death: Japanese Biological Warfare, 1932–1945 and the American Cover-up* (2002).

27

War and Aftermath in Japan (1931–1964)

Japan's war in Asia and the Pacific expanded in response to military imperatives and domestic problems. It spurred institutional and economic development; it caused devastation and loss of life. After surrender, the United States occupied Japan and instituted reforms designed to transform it into a demilitarized democracy. Those that had lasting impact built on trends apparent during the war; others, including Japan's diplomatic relations with the United States, sparked controversy. The despondency of defeat turned into a determination to rebuild. High-speed economic growth began in the 1950s. When the economy reached prewar levels of production in 1956, the government declared the postwar period to be officially over. In 1960 it announced the Income Doubling Plan. The 1964 Tokyo Olympics marked Japan's return to the world order and restored its self-confidence as a nation.

The further World War II recedes into the past, the more historians emphasize continuities across its divide. Although the impact of the war on individual lives is undeniable, its long-term consequences on the economy and society are more problematic. Other questions to consider are: Who was responsible for the war? What kind of impact did the Occupation have on Japan? What enabled the postwar recovery?

ROAD TO WAR

Military actions exacerbated by rural crises dominated politics in the 1930s. The army demanded support for its takeover of Manchuria in 1931; the navy criticized the limitations imposed by the London Naval Treaty. The armed forces transformed Japan into a militaristic state by forcing the Diet to curtail freedom of speech and approve its war budgets. Anger at capitalist *zaibatsu* for sucking the farmers' blood and at corrupt politicians who put their interests ahead of the nation erupted in abortive coups d'état that exposed factions within the military. Mass organizations drew the farmers' support to the military; farmers also participated in self-improvement drives sponsored by bureaucrats and civilian reformers. Only a few intellectuals dared criticize imperialist policies. For the majority of citizens, being Japanese meant taking pride in the slogan, "Asia for the Asiatics," which obfuscated Japan's colonizing project.

Junior Officers and the Citizenry

Radical junior officers drew inspiration from diverse sources. They heard their men's stories of sisters being sold into prostitution to save the family farm from moneylenders. They read in the newspapers of how the *zaibatsu* profited from currency speculation when Japan went off the gold standard in 1931. They studied Kita Ikki's *A Plan for the Reorganization of Japan*. Kita proposed that the "people's emperor" suspend the constitution and have the government confiscate surplus wealth, manage the economy, and provide social welfare and "world knowledge based on the Japanese spirit." When these goals had been accomplished, Japan would liberate Asia and "the Sun Flag of the Land of the Rising Sun will light the darkness of the entire world."[1] Officers modeled their plans for revolution on the Meiji Restoration. Like men of high purpose (*shishi*), they had to act to remove evil advisers who prevented the emperor from making his will known to the people. They credited violence with purifying the state and mistrusted old men who might tarnish their youthful idealism.

The junior officers responded to and exacerbated factions in the military. Their hero, General Araki Sadao, promoted spiritual training to inculcate devotion to the emperor and martial virtues of loyalty and self-sacrifice. The Japanese spirit (*Yamatodamashii*) sufficed to overcome mere material obstacles. His Imperial Way faction opposed the Control faction's arguments that battles could be won only by rational planning using the latest military technology and sophisticated weaponry. In 1935, an Araki supporter assassinated the Control faction's General Nagata Tetsuzan and electrified the nation with his diatribe against military men and their civilian toadies who had corrupted army and *kokutai*. On February 26, 1936, junior officers armed with the slogan, "Revere the Emperor, Destroy Traitors," led fourteen hundred troops to seize the Diet building and army headquarters, kill cabinet ministers, and call on the emperor to announce a Shōwa Restoration. Horrified at the threat of insurrection, the emperor summoned the army to suppress the rebellion. After a four-day standoff, the junior officers surrendered. They were executed along with their mentor Kita Ikki in a victory for the Control faction.

A symbiotic relationship developed between the military and the old middle class of shopkeepers and factory owners as well as teachers, low-ranking officials, and farmers. The army founded the Imperial Military Reserve Association in 1910, the Greater Japan Youth Association in 1915, and the Greater Japan National Defense Women's Association in 1932. Organized at the hamlet, not the amalgamated village level, the Reserve Association took over community functions such as firefighting, police, road and canal repairs, shrine and temple maintenance, emergency relief, and entertainment. It promoted drill practice, "nation-building" group calisthenics, and bayonet competitions. It hosted lectures by military-approved speakers, and it corresponded with battalion adjutants regarding the welfare and conduct of conscripts. The women's association sank roots in urban as well as rural areas. These associations identified the

---

1. George M. Wilson, *Radical Nationalist in Japan: Kita Ikki 1883–1937* (Cambridge, Mass.: Harvard University Press, 1969), pp. 75, 81.

individual with the community, the community with the army, and the army with the emperor.

Social Reform

In the 1930s, bureaucrats and social reformers focused on devastation resulting from crop failures in northeastern Japan. When students dispatched by Hani Motoko, journalist and founder of the magazine *Woman's Friend* (*Fujin no tomo*), reported that farmers knew nothing of modern hygiene and sanitation, spent money foolishly on ceremonies, lazed about, and drank, Hani established settlement houses that taught poor women sewing, cleanliness, etiquette, nutrition, and thrift. The Agriculture Ministry supported similar plans that promoted social education, agricultural cooperatives, economic planning, and moral betterment. The emphasis on thrift and frugality paralleled the nationwide effort by the Home Ministry, social reformers, educators, and women's leaders to increase Japan's savings rate, both to help individuals plan for emergencies and to fund national projects.

WARTIME MOBILIZATION

During eight years of war between 1937 and 1945 (see **Connections: World War II**), government ministries were often poorly informed, disorganized, and overextended. Faced with unexpected challenges, they cobbled together ad hoc measures and made mistakes in prosecuting the war overseas and on the home front. Just as the army and navy competed for resources, the former emphasizing the threat from the Soviet Union while the latter focused on the United States, so did civilian ministries duplicate each other's efforts and fight for control of domestic policy. Like the Germans, the Japanese at first refused to mobilize women, a policy that limited the war effort.

Civilian commitment to the war varied. Businessmen supported military goals so long as they did not threaten survival of their firms. Under pressure to conform, citizens greeted news of the first victories with exultation. Dwindling food supplies, higher taxes, and a black market led to forbearance and despair. Malnutrition increased the incidence of tuberculosis (one hundred sixty thousand deaths in 1942), rickets, and eye disease. First children and then adults fled cities for the countryside. When the flower of Japan's youth was called to make the supreme sacrifice in the Special Attack Forces (*kamikaze*), many did so gladly; others did not. (See **Documents: Excerpts from the Diary of Hayashi Toshimasa**.)

Unlike other belligerents in World War II, Japan's wartime leadership changed repeatedly. Seven prime ministers served between the outbreak of war with China on July 7, 1937, and surrender on August 15, 1945. Executed as a war criminal for having declared war against the United States, General Tōjō Hideki served concurrently as prime minister (1941–1944), army minister, home minister, and munitions minister and filled other posts as he perceived the need. He never directed naval operations nor did the navy inform him when it fought. Even the army general staff challenged his authority. Civilian bureaucrats, especially in the Justice Ministry, maintained their constitutional autonomy. Only the Shōwa emperor received complete information on military policy and operations, including plans for surprise attacks on American, Dutch, and British bases in 1941. For fear of jeopardizing the throne, he sanctioned military decisions as his ancestors had done for centuries.

Government planning of the economy began in 1931 when the Diet passed the Major Industries Control Law. It promoted cartels and required industries to tell the government their plans. In 1937 came the New Economic Order to make the Japanese Empire self-sufficient. Bureaucrats allocated funds to critical industries, nationalized electrical plants, supervised banks, and spun a web of regulation. The National Mobilization law of 1938 focused research on chemicals and machine technology. Large companies had to introduce on-the-job

DOCUMENTS

Excerpts from the Diary of Hayashi Toshimasa

Why do soldiers fight? What do they think about as they wait to die? This diary, written by Hayashi Toshimasa, a graduate of Keiō University who was killed in action on August 9, 1945, affords one answer to these questions and provides glimpses of the camaraderie and resentments that supported members of the Special Attack Forces in their final days.

April 13, 1945

First Lieutenant Kuniyasu was killed in action, as was Second Sub-lieutenant Tanigawa Takao. Everyone is dying away. The lives of plane pilots are short indeed. I just heard today that Second Sub-lieutenant Yatsunami also died the day before yesterday; he dove straight into the sea while participating in night-training, and his dead body was washed ashore yesterday onto the white beach of Kujūkuri-hama. Dear Yatsunami! I enjoyed getting together with him again here—the last time was in Mie. Dressed in his nightclothes, he came to my room rather late on the evening of the day before the accident, and we drank beer together. I wonder whether or not it was some kind of premonition. He was very gentle and quiet. When I said, "What a splendid nightwear," he just chuckled and said that it had been made by his wife, whom he just married in January. His wife too suffered the misfortune on this earth of a typical pilot's wife. How is she going to spend the long life that stretches ahead of her?

Tanigawa has a fiancée too, in Kobe. Those who were left behind may be unlucky, but their sacrifice is an offering for Japan's ultimate victory. So I would ask to please continue to live with strength and pride, and in such a way as not to bring shame to the brave men who courageously and willingly died for their country.

April 23

Nighttime flying began. After our flying operation we drank beer at a welcome party for Kamiōseko. I got a little high. Second Sub-lieutenant Kamiōseko and I were enraged at the current situation. It was all about our position as reserve officers in the Imperial Navy. Now I declare! I will not fight, at least not for the Imperial Navy. I live and die for my fatherland, and, I would go so far as to say that it is for my own pride. I have nothing but a strong antipathy for the Imperial Navy—absolutely no positive feelings at all. From now on I can say in and to my heart, "I can die for my own pride, but I would not die—absolutely not—for the Imperial Navy." How terribly we, the 13th class of pilots to come out of the "students mobilized for war" program, have been oppressed by the Imperial Navy! Who exactly is fighting this war now anyway? A full half of my classmates of the 13th class who were bomber pilots on carriers, and my friends, are now already dead.

I will live and die for my fatherland, my comrades of the 13th class, all those senior fighting men who are members of the "students mobilized for war" program, and, lastly, for my own pride. I shall do so cursing all the while the Imperial Navy, which to me merely means a certain group of officers who graduated from the Etajima Naval Academy.

---

training for workers. Labor was rationed according to production needs. Military requirements prompted the rise of new industries in fields such as optics, determined techniques used in existing industries such as steel, and stimulated technological innovation. Wartime priori-

June 30

It was raining when I woke up this morning, and I was so glad I could sleep some more that I pulled a blanket over me again. I got up a little after seven, took a late breakfast, and at a barracks I went over some slides designed to help us recognize the different types of enemy ships. Now I have finished with the slides. I returned to my own room, and am writing this and playing a record. Next door, on a blanket spread over the floor, Kamiōseko, Yamabe, Tejima, and Nasu are having fun playing bridge. No change outside—the steady rain continues.

I cannot begin to do anything about everything.

Simply because I shall have to leave this world in the very near future.

I should thank the Navy's traditional spirit, or rather their cliquishness, which drove Eguchi to say: "I want to go to the front soon—I want to die soon," and even drove me into that sort of psychological state. It even drove all the rest of us, university students transformed into pilots, into that same state of mind.

July 31

Today is a sortie day. It is the day for the eight planes of our Ryūsei (Falling Star) squad to carry out a special attack. The fog was extremely thick when I got up. It turned into water that dripped from the leaves and treetops on the mountain.

When I arrived at the airport, the items that were to be carried onto our planes were neatly set out in rows.

Last night, I completely changed everything that I was wearing. I also wound tightly around my waist the thousand-stitch cloth my mother sent me. Then there was the brand-new muffler my aunt in Yudate

gave me.—In other words, I put on the very best things I had.

I am all alone and, expecting the sortie command to come along at any moment, I am writing this in an air-raid shelter.

Farewell dear Father, Mother, Brothers and Sisters, and other relatives and friends.

Please continue to live on enjoying very good health.

This time I am going right into Han Christian Andersen's fairyland, and I will become its prince.

And I shall be chatting with little birds, flowers, and trees.

I pray for the eternal prosperity of the great Japanese Empire.

August 9 A clear day

Once again the enemy's mechanized divisions are approaching the home islands.

In one hour and a half I shall leave here for the sortie, as a member of the special attack force. The skies are a breathtakingly deep blue, and there is a sharp touch of autumn.

August 9th!

Today I shall fly one of the very latest in war planes, a Ryūsei, and will slam it into an enemy carrier.

Source: *Listen to the Voices from the Sea: Writings of the Fallen Japanese Students*, comp. Nihon Senbotsu Gakusei Kinen-Kai, trans. Midori Yamanouchi and Joseph L. Quinn (Scranton, Pa.: University of Scranton Press, 2000), pp. 247–250, modified.

ties transformed Japan's industrial structure. Textile industries declined; heavy and chemical industries expanded.

The Home Ministry bent social mores and popular culture to the war effort. Foreign words being considered symptomatic of foreign sympathies, "baseball" became *yakyū*. Martial music replaced jazz. Hair permanents were criticized because they were western and wasted resources. Women had to dress in baggy pants called *monpe*. The Communications Ministry founded the Dōmei News Agency in 1936 to channel national and international news to newspapers. It already controlled radio broadcasts through the national public radio station, NHK. To extend its reach, the ministry distributed free radios to rural villages.

The Education Ministry suppressed academic freedom and promoted patriotism. Professors critical of the war in China and military dominance over politics had to resign. School children performed physical exercises to build bodies for the emperor; after 1940 they volunteered for community service projects. Starting in 1941 they took paramilitary training to identify enemy aircraft and practiced charging with bamboo spears. Published in 1937, the textbook *Cardinal Principles of the National Polity* (*Kokutai no hongi*) taught students that the emperor was the divine head of state and benevolent father to the Japanese people. The Japanese were superior because of their racial homogeneity. They possessed a distinctive culture and history infused by the radiant presence of the imperial house. No sacrifice was too great to protect this unique heritage.

In the name of national unity, the government suppressed all pacifist new religions under the Religious Organizations Law of 1939. Social reformers and feminist activists joined the Greater Japan Women's Society that sent soldiers off to war and disseminated ways to practice frugality. Patriotic Associations united tenant farmers and landlords, workers and businessmen. The ideology of "dedicated work" valorized labor as a public activity in service to the nation. Neighborhood associations organized air raid drills and kept watch for dangerous thought. In 1944 the Home Ministry folded them all into the Imperial Rule Assistance Association.

A dedicated citizenry and long-range planning could not overcome growing shortages. The government struggled to shore up the collapsing economy. Lacking imported technology, companies developed new techniques that took military needs and scarce resources into account. The Zero fighter was crafted with extreme precision and used minimal amounts of steel regardless of the pilot's safety. In addition to the lack of fuel because of disruptions to shipping, the destruction of factories meant fewer manufactured goods such as fertilizer. Food production dropped.

Military conscription created labor shortages in industry and mining. The first to fill the gap were Koreans. In 1943, the government allowed women to volunteer for work in ordnance and aircraft industries. It drafted prisoners of war to work in steel plants and mines. The military ended educational deferments and drafted university students. In 1944 middle school boys started factory work.

The last months of the war brought widespread hardship. Evacuees to the countryside put an extra burden on scarce resources. Nutritional levels declined following the meager harvest of 1944. A few people criticized their leaders in anonymous graffiti and letters to the editor. Worker absenteeism rose, product quality slipped, and work stoppages spread. Although signs of disaffection were slight, they were enough to make politicians and bureaucrats worry about the threat of social revolution. By the time most factions in the government were willing to admit defeat, approximately 3 million Japanese had died. Despite the evidence of destruction, the emperor's announcement on August 15 that the war had been lost came as a shock.

OCCUPATION

Defeat did not bring an end to hardship. The suburban middle class was spared the fate of poor and working-class urban residents who lost everything in the firestorms, but everyone was short of food. Farmers were better off, although stunned by defeat that called into question cherished ideals of loyalty, patriotism, and service to the emperor. Occupation by a

Japanese Women Working in an Ordnance Factory.
With able-bodied men drafted for the war effort, women had to take their place in industry. *(AKG, London)*

labor camps. Soviet soldiers raped and killed women and children. Of Japanese settlers in Manchuria, 50 percent died at the end of the war, many at the hands of Chinese. Japanese settlers in Korea made their way across hostile territory to refugee camps and then on crowded ships to Japan. Seventy thousand Japanese in the Philippines had to wait until the end of 1946 before seeing Japan; the British and Dutch did not return their prisoners of war until 1947. On Pacific islands, pockets of Japanese soldiers resorted to cannibalism or starved. The last soldiers came home in the 1970s.

Repatriated soldiers and civilians met a cold welcome in war-devastated Japan. War widows, homeless orphans, and maimed veterans became social rejects. Most shunned were the victims from Hiroshima and Nagasaki, subject to radiation sickness that turned them into pariahs. With the economy at a standstill, there was little work even for the able-bodied. Competition for jobs depressed already low wages. The winter of 1945–1946 was worse than the winters of wartime. Rationed supplies of coal and food were not enough to stave off freezing and starvation. Urban women traveled to the countryside to trade heirlooms for food and patronized the black market.

For some, defeat meant liberation. If life had no meaning, why not drink, take drugs, and steal? In his 1947 novel *The Setting Sun,* Dazai Osamu mourned the loss of prewar values and presented the only choice left: to live for oneself alone. People who celebrated the end to restrictions on freedom of thought and behavior had an easier time coping with material shortages. Defeat vindicated the beliefs of prewar Marxists and socialists who hoped to build a just society out of the rubble of failed capitalist fortunes. The black market flourished at every train terminal, organized and patrolled by gangsters. Small factory owners made pots instead of helmets, and former soldiers became businessmen. Prostitutes called pan-pan girls who serviced GIs dressed in rayon dresses and nylon hose, curled their hair, and painted their faces in an orgy of self-expression not seen since the 1920s. The

military dictatorship under General Douglas MacArthur began on August 30, 1945. At first the mood was to punish Japan, perhaps by returning it to an agrarian economy. After the beginning of the Cold War with the Soviet Union and the 1949 Communist takeover of China, the emphasis shifted to making Japan a bulwark against communism.

Despair and Liberation

The war left 6.6 million Japanese soldiers and civilians stranded in enemy territory from Manchuria to Southeast Asia. The Soviet Union sent five hundred seventy-five thousand military personnel and adult male civilians to Siberian dominant themes in popular culture were titillation and sex; the carnal body replaced the *kokutai,* the body politic.

Occupation Goals

As Supreme Commander of the Allied Powers (SCAP—also shorthand for the Occupation bureaucracy), MacArthur intended to demilitarize Japan and work through existing governmental institutions to install democracy. The United States kept the Allies out of Japan by putting them on the Far East Commission (FEC) that oversaw SCAP policy. It met in Washington, D.C. The United States bought off the Soviet Union by handing over islands north of Hokkaido. Only judges for the Tokyo war crimes trials represented countries that had suffered under the Japanese war machine. One SCAP faction wanted to restrict Japan's international trade and dispatch the fruits of industrialization to Japan's victims as war reparations. The other consisted of economists and lawyers primed to practice social engineering. By instituting land reform, revising education, promoting labor unions, emancipating women, limiting police powers, and rewriting the constitution, they planned to make Japan fit to rejoin the community of nations.

What was to be done with the Shōwa emperor? He did not sign the instrument of surrender on September 2, 1945; that humiliation was left to a general and a diplomat. Instead, he, the cabinet, and his staff tried to distance him from responsibility for the war, taking a stance of plausible deniability on all decisions save the last that ended it. MacArthur dissuaded him from admitting even moral responsibility. Although the British wanted to try him as a war criminal, MacArthur believed that once the military was gone, the emperor was needed as a bulwark against communism. By refusing to accept responsibility for the war in which so many had died in his name, the emperor also alienated far right militarists. The issue of his responsibility for the war has continued to rankle at home and with Japan's neighbors. On January 1, 1946, the emperor announced that

he was a human being, not a manifest god. Defined by the new constitution as symbol of the state, he continues to embody a national identity predicated on ethnic homogeneity.

Occupation Reforms

On October 13, 1945, the prime minister appointed a committee at SCAP's urging to consider constitutional revision. Political parties, progressive and socialist groups, scholars, and think tanks drafted constitutions ignored by the prime minister's committee. Its recommendations were so minor that in February 1946, MacArthur ordered his Government Section to take over the task lest a grass-roots movement for a constitutional convention lead to too much democracy and an attack on the emperor. His people hid their work from the United States and Japanese governments, the FEC, and other branches of SCAP. After conferences between SCAP officials and cabinet representatives to debate the draft, it was published in early March 1946. SCAP intervened repeatedly in Diet deliberations to limit discussion and prevent substantial revision. The new constitution replaced the Meiji constitution, to which it was offered as an amendment, when the Upper House approved it in October. The emperor promulgated it on November 3, 1946.

Articles in the constitution define the rights to life, liberty, and the pursuit of happiness as the rights to education, health care, police protection, work, and a minimum standard of living. Women received the right to vote. People detained by the police had the right to legal counsel. Freedoms included freedom from arbitrary arrest and unauthorized search and seizure plus freedom of assembly, speech, and religion. The judiciary became separate and independent. The Privy Council was dissolved in accordance with the principle of popular sovereignty. The Diet acquired the sole authority to make laws. Its vote of no confidence sufficed to dissolve the cabinet. Within the Diet, the Lower House of Representatives took precedence over the Upper House of Councilors, which became an elected body.

The new constitution had clauses that MacArthur would have deplored in the U.S. Constitution. Workers obtained the right to organize unions and bargain collectively, professors had the right to academic freedom, and women were guaranteed equal rights with men. Most controversial was Article 9: "The Japanese people forever renounce war as a sovereign right of the nation . . . land, sea, and air forces will never be maintained."[2] This wording was later interpreted to mean that armed forces could be created for self-defense. When the FEC insisted on a clause that limited the cabinet to civilians, this too was interpreted as implying the existence of a military. In 1950, SCAP wanted Japan to create an army to fight in Korea. Prime Minister Yoshida Shigeru refused. He created a Police Reserve, soon transformed into the Self-Defense Force.

Once the constitution had been promulgated, the Justice Ministry reformed the civil code. The new code emphasized the equality of the sexes and the dignity of the individual. It abolished patriarchal authority in the household, reiterated the freedom of marriage promised in the constitution, and required that all children share the family estate. This was not a burden for middle-class families whose assets consisted of their children's education. For shopkeepers, restauranteurs, or farmers, an equal division of property plus heavy inheritance taxes all too often meant selling off the patrimony.

SCAP quickly imposed additional reforms. The most radical forced landlords to sell their holdings to the government for resale to tenants, a measure met with approval by the Agriculture and Forestry Ministry that wanted a class of independent farmers even before the war. Absentee landlords had to relinquish all their land; resident landlords were allowed to keep only land they farmed themselves plus an additional five or so acres depending on the region. Although collecting tenant fees had already

proved so onerous that many landlords welcomed the chance to sell out, they lamented the loss of their ancestral way of life. By 1950, farmer-owners cultivated 90 percent of Japan's agricultural land.

SCAP also intervened in educational reform. With American schools as the model, a new single-track system of primary school, middle school, and high school replaced the specialized higher schools. Compulsory education was extended to nine years. Teachers embraced the new curriculum that stressed the civic virtues of democracy and individual responsibility. Locally elected school boards selected texts, although in later years they did so from a list vetted by the Education Ministry. The Parent-Teacher Association involved mothers in school activities. New junior colleges, colleges, and universities made higher education available to a wider segment of the population than before. None rivaled Tokyo University, and all required that students pass entrance examinations.

SCAP kept itself above the law. Despite the separation of church and state, MacArthur allowed Christian missionaries to use U.S. government equipment and encouraged the emperor and empress to take instruction in Christianity. Censorship of printed materials and movies continued. Left-wing publications that criticized capitalism faced prepublication scrutiny. In movies, sword fighting and criticism of the emperor were out. Instead, SCAP encouraged movie makers to depict romance between men and women. The first mouth-to-mouth kiss made headlines.

Economic Developments

Economic reform took many turns. Trustbusters took aim at the *zaibatsu* because they had contributed to Japan's war effort (Mitsubishi made the Zero fighter) and because their economic dominance appeared inherently undemocratic. SCAP ordered the holding companies for the ten largest *zaibatsu* dissolved, broke up the Mitsui and Mitsubishi trading companies, forced

2. Dale M. Hellegers, *We, the Japanese People: World War II and the Origins of the Japanese Constitution*, 2 vols. (Stanford: Stanford University Press, 2002), p. 576.

family members to sell their stock and resign from boards, and purged fifteen hundred executives accused of aiding the war machine. Japanese bureaucrats allowed government assets, including construction materials and machinery, to disappear into the black market or the hands of business cronies. To cover the deficit and the run on savings deposits at war's end, the Finance Ministry printed reams of money. Official prices soared 539 percent in the first year of the Occupation, with black market prices ranging from fourteen to thirty-four times higher. Fearing the destabilizing effects of inflation, at the end of 1948, Washington dispatched a banker from Detroit named Joseph Dodge. At Dodge's command, the government collected more in taxes than it paid out. It eliminated government subsidies to manufacturers. Public works, welfare, and education suffered cuts. Dodge curbed domestic consumption and promoted exports. He got the United States to agree to an exchange rate of 360 yen to the dollar. Deflation and economic contraction forced small businesses into bankruptcy.

The Korean War rescued Japan from the brink of depression and laid the foundation for future economic growth. The industrial sector gorged on procurement orders for vehicles, uniforms, sandbags, medicines, electrical goods, construction materials, liquor, paper, and food. Despite the prohibition on the manufacture of war materiel, Japanese companies made munitions. Their mechanics repaired tanks and aircraft. Businesses plowed profits into upgrading equipment and buying advanced technology from the United States through licensing agreements and the purchase of patent rights. Industries that looked beyond the war for a way to compete in the expanding world economy incorporated the quality control method that the statistician W. Edwards Deming had introduced to Japan in 1949. By the end of the Korean War, the increase in wages and economic growth had brought food consumption back to pre–World War II levels. Consumers were able to buy household amenities and still put money into savings accounts.

Labor and the Reverse Course

To promote democracy, SCAP had the Trade Union Law issued in December 1945, and workers seized the opportunity to organize. Free to participate in politics, the Japanese Communist Party (JCP) and the Japanese Socialist Party (JSP) fostered trade unions. By the middle of 1948, unions enrolled over half of the nonagricultural work force, including white-collar workers, especially in the public sector. Other workers organized production control movements to take over businesses, factories, and mines that owners were accused of deliberately sabotaging in revenge for democratization. Like unionized workers, they wanted to get back to work and make a living wage.

Labor union activism led to the "reverse course." Workers united around issues including adequate food, support for working mothers, equal pay for equal work, and democratic elections. Before the postwar election of April 10, 1946, in which women voted for the first time, a rally in Tokyo brought together workers, farmers, Koreans, and ordinary citizens to listen to speeches by Communists, Socialists, and liberals demanding a people's constitution and criticizing the cabinet for obstructing democratic reform. On May 1, International Workers' Day, cities nationwide witnessed demonstrations in support of worker unity and democracy. On May 19, women joined demonstrations demanding that the emperor force the government to deliver food. Students held demonstrations a week later to demand self-government at their institutions. Socialist- and Communist-led labor unions formed in August organized strikes in October. In January 1947, the prime minister warned that striking government workers would be fired. A coalition of labor unions announced plans for a general strike on February 1. MacArthur called it off. In 1948 SCAP had the Japanese government issue regulations forbidding public employees to strike.

The reverse course had additional dimensions. The Cold War led the United States to view its erstwhile enemy as an ally against communism. SCAP compiled lists of "reds" to purge first the public sector and later, during the Korean War, the private sector. Approximately twenty-two thousand workers lost their jobs, and most of the JCP leadership went underground. Previously purged politicians, bureaucrats, and business leaders were rehabilitated. In 1948, plans to dismantle the *zaibatsu* came to a halt. The Diet gave the bureaucracy greater control over trade and investment than it had during the war. The Ministry of International Trade and Industry (MITI) had the Japan Development Bank lend money from the government's postal savings system to private companies. MITI also advised the Bank of Japan on its loans to private banks. It approved the transfer of foreign technology to industries it deemed worthy and provided them with administrative guidance. The Finance Ministry regulated currency transactions by restricting the amounts of money individuals and corporations could take or send out of the country.

Before ending the occupation, the U.S. Senate had Japan sign a peace treaty with the Nationalist Chinese on Taiwan that precluded recognition of and trade with the People's Republic of China. The peace treaty and security treaty signed with the United States plus associated agreements signed in 1951 continued the Occupation under a different name. After SCAP was dismantled in 1952, one hundred thousand American personnel plus dependents stayed on at military bases that dotted the islands. The right of extraterritoriality protected them from the Japanese judicial system and removed the bases from oversight by the Japanese government. Okinawa remained under U.S. military jurisdiction until 1972. Under the U.S. security umbrella, Japan was free to pursue economic development, although it had to follow the U.S. lead in international relations. On Bloody May Day 1952, four hundred thousand workers, students, and housewives denounced the Security Treaty, Japanese rearmament, the status of Okinawa, and government plans to pass an "antisubversive" bill that threatened academic freedom. Political positions divided between left-wing support for neutrality, democratization, and demilitarization and the conservative affirmation of alliance with the United States.

POLITICAL SETTLEMENT AND ECONOMIC RECOVERY

A host of political parties contended for Diet seats in the first postwar election of 1946. Yoshida Shigeru pulled together a coalition of conservative parties willing to make him prime minister, but he had to resign when elections the following year gave a significant share of the votes to the JSP. Taking advantage of the JSP's inability to deal with economic crises, Yoshida regained the prime ministership in 1948 and held it until 1954. He recruited former bureaucrats into his party whose administrative experience and skill at in-fighting gave them an edge in faction building. The JSP split over whether to support the U.S.-Japan Peace Treaty; it reunited in October 1955. The next month, the two conservative parties formed the Liberal Democratic Party (LDP). It dominated Diet and cabinet until 1993. During this period of one-party rule, heads of factions within the LDP selected the prime minister, who rewarded his supporters with powerful and lucrative ministerial appointments.

The LDP promoted economic growth as the nation's highest goal, less to enhance state power than to wean workers from socialism by offering them a better life. Starting in the late 1950s, the LDP spread the benefits of the growing economy across all sectors of society through higher wages and a higher standard of living. In 1958, it inaugurated national health insurance. It helped farmers increase productivity by mechanizing production and spreading chemical fertilizers and pesticides. The government paid villages to reorganize land holdings into fewer, bigger plots and individuals to diversify crops. It encouraged companies to locate factories in rural areas and hire farmers. It built roads and sewer systems. It restricted the import of rice and subsidized rice production. Through these programs and the outright purchase of votes, the LDP acquired a lock on rural electoral districts. The appeal of conservative policies to small businessmen and shopkeepers gave it urban votes as well.

The LDP also maintained power by aligning itself with bureaucrats and businessmen. Advisory groups composed of businessmen and bankers, consumers and union officials, consulted with cabinet ministers on policy and proposed legislation. Ex-bureaucrats either ran for office or joined corporations whose fortunes they had helped guide. Undergirding the web of personal connections was a flow of cash from businessmen to politicians to voters.

Political and Social Protest

Opposition parties in the Diet so little impeded the LDP juggernaut that citizens with grievances sought other forms of protest. Demonstrations against American bases and nuclear testing erupted periodically during the 1950s. The Japan Teachers' Union resisted the centralization of educational policy and personnel practices instituted by the Education Ministry in 1955. The General Council of Japanese Trade Unions (Sōhyō) opposed the Japan Productivity Center set up by Japanese businessmen with U.S. assistance because the unions feared it would exploit workers. When the government decided to switch Japan's chief energy source from coal to oil, the Mitsui Mining Company called for the voluntary early retirement of six thousand workers at its Miike mine in Kyushu. The union responded with a strike marked by violence and death that lasted 113 days. Workers learned that radical calls for class struggle undercut job security, and corporate managers learned that it was cheaper to transfer redundant workers to other operations than to fire them.

The largest political demonstrations in Japanese history erupted from late 1959 to June 1960 over revision and extension of the U.S.-Japan Security Treaty. Negotiations removed the clause that permitted the use of U.S. troops to quell internal disturbances, but bases remained off-limits to Japanese scrutiny. Indicted as a war criminal and former minister in Manchuria, Prime Minister Kishi Nobusuke rammed the revised treaty through the lower house with the help of police who evicted the JCP and JSP opposition. Outraged at Kishi's high-handed tactics, masses of demonstrators gathered outside the Diet. Sōhyō had already coordinated strikes and mobilized workers against the treaty. The All Japan Federation of Student Self-government Associations (Zengakuren) organized weeks of agitation. Some 134 groups and organizations including farmers and housewives joined the protest. Kishi had planned to celebrate the revised security treaty by welcoming U.S. President Dwight D. Eisenhower to Japan, but Eisenhower canceled the trip. Daily demonstrations continued at the Diet and in cities across Japan. On June 18, several hundred thousand people surrounded the Diet, but they could not prevent the treaty's automatic ratification at midnight. Kishi resigned five days later. In 1965 Japan signed a peace treaty with South Korea, to the outrage of the left wing, which demonstrated against the exclusion of North Korea and the People's Republic of China. The ideological divide between conservatives and progressives sparked political unrest throughout the 1960s.

The constitution's guarantee of social equality and the Civil Code's emphasis on human dignity spurred the *burakumin* to renew their struggle for equal rights. Founded in 1955, the Buraku Liberation League (BLL) allied itself with the JCP and JSP to publicize unfair treatment by individuals and institutions. It participated in demonstrations against the renewal of the U.S.-Japan Security Treaty that gained it widespread support. Later protest marches focused nationwide attention on the *burakumin*'s plight. A government commission report in 1965 blamed *burakumin* problems on unwarranted social and economic discrimination. The Diet responded in 1969 by passing the Special Measures Law for Assimilation Projects that decried discrimination without instituting measures to stop it. To ameliorate this defect, the BLL resorted to denunciation campaigns sometimes escalating to violence and threats that silenced public discussion of *burakumin* problems.

Women's organizations in the 1950s worked to protect children and encourage respect for

Demonstrations Opposing the U.S.–Japan Security Treaty. During demonstrations opposing the U.S.–Japan Security Treaty, men and women marched on the American Embassy demanding cancellation of President Eisenhower's visit, the prime minister's resignation, and dissolution of the Diet. *(Bettmann/Corbis)*

mothers. Women joined movements to prohibit nuclear testing and to promote world peace for the sake of their children. They demanded clean elections. They elected women to the Diet who pushed for sexual equality and human rights. Women had campaigned for the abolition of state-sanctioned prostitution before the war; their goal became a reality in 1956 when the Diet passed the Prostitution Prevention Law that took effect two years later. While it abolished legal protection for prostitutes, it did not eliminate sex work. Women justified political activism on two grounds: their responsibility for their families and their constitutional rights.

Post-Occupation Economic Development

International and domestic factors promoted economic growth. Under the Potsdam Declara-

tion, Japan was guaranteed access to raw materials it had previously extracted from its colonies. Exchange rates remained stable until 1971. The world market was relatively open. Economic expansion across the free market world stimulated a growing demand for manufactured goods. Japan still had infrastructure developed before and during World War II. The most important prewar legacies were human resources—trained engineers, accountants, and workers—and the commitment to achievement through education. The first postwar generation of workers went into factories on graduation from high school, received on-the-job training, and worked long hours for the sake of their companies. Enterprise unions held demonstrations during the yearly spring offensive but interfered as little as possible in production. Management upped basic wages, promised lifetime employment, and distributed raises based on seniority. Workers came to live middle-class lives.

Heavy industries developed in wartime, and new companies that fashioned products for domestic consumption and export saw the greatest expansion. Steel producers, ship builders, manufacturers of synthetic fibers, and electronics and household appliance makers invested heavily in technologies imported from the United States and in labor-saving mass-production facilities. The government provided low-cost financing that made Japan the largest shipbuilder in the world in the 1950s. MITI protected car and truck manufacturers by forbidding foreign investment in the auto industry and imposing tariffs of up to 40 percent on imported cars. Companies that enjoyed less help from MITI were Matsushita, maker of household appliances, and the electronics innovator Sony. (See **Material Culture: The Transistor.**) Supporting corporate growth were subcontractors that produced quality components for finished products. Between 1947 and 1952, the economy grew at an average annual rate of 11.5 percent. From 1954 to 1971, it grew at over 10 percent a year, to rank second to the United States among free market economies.

Increases in domestic consumption stimulated high-speed economic growth. During the Occupation, SCAP broadcast images of American prosperity in the comic strip *Blondie* and other media to promote American values. Department store exhibitions and magazine advertisements illustrated the material life of the conqueror. Once the quality of food had improved, people wanted fashionable clothes. Every household wanted labor-saving devices such as a washing machine, refrigerator, and vacuum cleaner. Television broadcasts began in 1953 because the owner of the *Yomiuri* newspaper and key bureaucrats believed that national pride required Japan to have the latest technology. The wedding of Crown Prince Akihito to the industrialist's daughter Shōda Michiko in 1959 swept televisions from retailers' shelves as viewers reveled in the democratic dream of a love marriage. Beginning in 1955, a massive exodus

from farms to cities fueled a housing boom of high density apartment buildings in suburbs. In these years, 90 percent of Japan's production went into the domestic market.

Postwar Culture

The consumption of mass culture stimulated growth in the entertainment industries, publishing, and film. Commercial television stations demanded an endless supply of programming. The government-owned NHK had two channels: one devoted to news analysis, dramas, and *sumo* wrestling, the other specializing in education. Magazine and book publishers continued prewar trends without the fear of censorship that had kept them from sensitive political topics. Kurosawa Akira directed *Ikiru* (To Live), which criticized bureaucratic arrogance. His 1951 film *Rashomon*, which questioned the possibility of knowing the truth, brought international recognition to Japanese cinema when it won the grand prize at the Venice Film Festival. A series with wider appeal was *Godzilla*, started in 1954, which drew on Japan's sense of victimhood by depicting a monster roused from the deep by nuclear explosion. Misora Hibari captured hearts with her songs of parting and loss. They spoke to the will to survive that had carried women through the hardships of war and Occupation. Public intellectuals and writers such as Maruyama Masao and Mishima Yukio questioned the ingredients of Japan's national identity. What did it mean to be Japanese if the nation's only goal was economic success? Wherein laid responsibility for wartime aggression?

New religions provided one answer to these questions. Founded in 1930 and suppressed during the war, Sōka Gakkai (value-creating society) was Japan's largest new religion in the 1960s. Its political arm, the Clean Government Party (Kōmeitō), founded in 1964, became Japan's third largest political party. Today its leaders serve as town councilors and school board officers. It owns land, businesses, and shops. It provides a sense of family and community, help in finding marriage partners, jobs, loans, and

MATERIAL CULTURE

The Transistor

Every electronic product today relies on transistors, symbol and product of the technological age. Invented by Bell Laboratories in 1948, the early transistors were too unreliable and delicate for consumer applications, and they could not handle high frequencies for the human voice. It took Sony researchers months of experimentation to find a useable combination of materials.

Sony introduced a transistor radio in January 1955, only to discover that it disintegrated in summer heat. The second version placed on the market in August had poor sound quality, but it sold domestically owing to its battery's long life. Sony could not compete with American transistor radios until 1957 when it started selling a tiny "pocketable" radio. More important than the radio's size was the technological breakthrough based on the high-performance alloy germanium. In 1960 transistor radios became Japan's second biggest earner on the export market after ships. Teenagers loved carrying them to parks, mountains, and beaches to listen to rock and roll.

Sony introduced the world's first all-transistor television in 1960 and successfully miniaturized it two years later. In 1964 Sony displayed a prototype of a transistorized calculator at New York's World Fair. Three years later it introduced a desktop calculator.

The transistors in the early radios, televisions, and calculators were huge compared to the silicon transistors in integrated circuits today that work liquid display calculators and watches. People typically buy electronic goods on impulse, indulging in a plethora of gadgetry that fills purses, pockets, and homes.

The TR-63. Sony's first successful transistor radio, the TR-63, could be called 'pocketable' only because Sony salesmen wore shirts with extra large breast pockets. *(Sony Corporation)*

higher education. The *zadankai,* a type of group therapy, helps followers solve personal problems and gain self-confidence. Sōka Gakkai teaches that the purpose of life is the pursuit of happi-ness; the three virtues of beauty, gain, and goodness bring happiness; following the teachings of Nichiren and having faith in the *Lotus Sutra* bring virtue. The constitutional guarantee of

BIOGRAPHY   Daimatsu Hirobumi

Soldier, prisoner of war, women's volleyball coach, and Diet member, Daimatsu Hirobumi (1921–1978) gained worldwide fame for his draconian coaching methods when his team won the gold medal at the 1964 Tokyo Olympics.

Hirobumi's wartime experience marked him for life. Conscripted into the army after the attack on Pearl Harbor, he attended an officers' preparatory school in China and fought in China and Southeast Asia. The last months of the war found him in Burma with only raw bamboo shoots for food. Many soldiers died; sheer willpower kept him alive. He ended up at a prisoner of war camp run by the British in Rangoon. In revenge for the atrocities that the Japanese army had inflicted on British POWs and the humiliating surrender of Hong Kong and Singapore, British officers subjected Japanese POWs to shameful indignities. Hirobumi later recounted how he cleaned the latrines for British and Indian soldiers with his bare hands. Worse, he had to clean the female officers' rooms and wash the underwear that they removed before his eyes in a gesture calculated to be emasculating.

Repatriated to Japan after twenty-two months as a POW, Hirobumi found work coaching a women's volleyball team at the Nichibō textile factory in Kaizuka. At that time volleyball was a popular sport among factory workers because it could be played with just a ball in whatever space was available. In 1954 Nichibō organized a company team with Hirobumi in charge. In 1958, the team won all of Japan's major titles; in 1962 it won the world championship.

Hirobumi's training methods were brutal. He hurled balls at the players until they collapsed from pain and exhaustion. He insisted that they play regardless of injuries. He allowed them only three and one-half hours of sleep a night before the Olympics and had them practice for four hours the day of the final match. He also emphasized the incremental improvement of technique, relying on methods similar to quality control circles. His players once complained to the factory management that he was an enemy of women because he worked them unmercifully. He expected them to sacrifice everything for the chance to win, first for the company, then for Japan, just as he had sacrificed himself in wartime.

Eight-five percent of Japan's television sets were tuned to the Olympics the night the Japanese team defeated the Soviet Union in three sets. The women's unprecedented success made volleyball a national obsession. Hirobumi's fame swept him to a seat in the Diet's upper house in 1968. He lost his bid for a second term.

Source: Based on Yoshikuni Igarashi, *Bodies of Memory: Narratives of War in Postwar Japan* (Princeton, N.J.: Princeton University Press, 2000).

---

religious freedom and the population shift from country to town led to an explosion in the numbers of new religions and their membership. Although they criticize the excesses of popular culture and consumerism, part of their appeal lies in their promise of material benefits.

The Tokyo Olympics of 1964 marked the climax of high-speed economic growth and a turning point in Japan's postwar history. (See **Biography: Daimatsu Hirobumi**.) The national and Tokyo metropolitan governments cleaned up and paved city streets; rebuilt stores, schools, and government offices; constructed stadiums at Yoyogi Park; dug new subway lines; laid new roads; and renovated Haneda Airport and connected it to the city by monorail. New hotels became Japan's first postwar high rises. The centerpiece of this vast public works project was the Shinkansen (bullet train), which covered the distance between Tokyo and Osaka in three hours and ten minutes. It was the fastest, most reliable, and safest train in the world.

Japan had been allowed to join the United Nations in 1956, and the Olympics marked the culmination of its reentry into the global community. Worldwide coverage of the games focused attention on Japan as a peaceful modern state. When Kawabata Yasunari received the Nobel Prize in Literature in 1968, the international accolade testified to Japan's acceptance by world opinion.

SUMMARY

Between 1931 and 1945, Japan passed through the dark valley of wartime aggression and deprivation. It recovered thanks to the changing international climate of the late 1940s and early 1950s, the reforms initiated by the U.S. Occupation, the protection provided by the security agreement with the United States, and the U.S. recognition that democracy required economic stability. It must not be forgotten that recovery also built on the educational and industrial foundation laid before the war.

SUGGESTED READING

For general coverage of this period, see H. P. Bix, *Hirohito and the Making of Modern Japan* (2000), and T. Nakamura, *A History of Shōwa Japan, 1926–1989* (1998). For prewar Japan, see M. Barnhart, *Japan Prepares for Total War: The Search for Economic Security, 1919–1941* (1987), and S. Vlastos, ed., *Mirror of Modernity: Invented Traditions of Modern Japan* (1998). For wartime, see S. Ienaga, *The Pacific War, 1931–1945* (1978); B. Shillony, *Politics and Culture in Wartime Japan* (1981); and L. Young, *Japan's Total Empire: Manchuria and the Culture of Wartime Imperialism* (1998). For the Occupation, see K. Hirano, *Mr. Smith Goes to Tokyo: Japanese Cinema Under the American Occupation, 1945–1952* (1992), and J. W. Dower, *Embracing Defeat: Japan in the Wake of World War II* (1999).

For the postwar era, see A. Gorden, ed., *Postwar Japan as History* (1993); A. Gordon, *The Wages of Affluence: Labor and Management in Postwar Japan* (1998); L. F. Hein, *Fueling Growth: The Energy Revolution and Economic Policy in Postwar Japan* (1990); J. V. Koschmann, *Revolution and Subjectivity in Postwar Japan* (1996); W. Sasaki-Uemura, *Organizing the Spontaneous: Citizen Protest in Postwar Japan* (2001); and B. Johnstone, *We Were Burning: Japanese Entrepreneurs and the Forging of the Electronics Age* (2000).

China Under
Mao (1949–1976)

By the end of 1949, the Communist Party had gained control of almost the entire country, and Mao Zedong had pronounced the establishment of the People's Republic of China (PRC). The party quickly set about restructuring China. People were mobilized to tackle such tasks as redistributing land, promoting heavy industry, reforming marriage practices, and unmasking counterrevolutionaries. Wealth and power were redistributed on a vast scale. Massive modernization projects created new factories, railroads, schools, hospitals, and reservoirs. Ordinary people were subject to increased political control as the central government set policies that determined what farmers would produce, where and how their children would be educated, what they might read in books and newspapers, where they could live or travel. The most radical phase was during the Cultural Revolution, especially 1966 to 1969, when the party itself was attacked by students and workers mobilized to make permanent revolution.

Until the late 1970s, western scholars had limited access to the PRC and had to rely heavily on analyzing official pronouncements and interviewing refugees. Scholars studied the structure of the government, its policies, its top figures, and their factional struggles. As China has become more open in the past two decades and new sources have become available, research has revealed much more complex pictures of how China fared during the Mao years. Not only can the human dramas be examined with more nuance, but variation from one place to the next can be assessed. Mao still fascinates. Can the excesses of the Great Leap and the Cultural Revolution be fully blamed on Mao's inadequate grasp of reality? How could one person make such a difference? The party is also a subject of renewed interest. How did policies set at the center play out at the local level? What means did local cadres (party functionaries) use to get compliance with policies? What were the consequences of vilifying intellectuals? How did day-to-day life change for ordinary people in villages or towns?

THE PARTY IN POWER

From 1950 on, the Communist Party, under the leadership of Mao Zedong (to use the phrase of the time), set about to fashion a new China, one that would empower peasants and workers and limit the influence of landlords, capitalists, intellectuals, and foreigners. New values were heralded: people were taught that struggle, revolution, and change were to be celebrated; compromise, deference, and tradition were weaknesses. People throughout the country were filled with hope that great things could be achieved.

In terms of formal political organization, the Soviet Union's model was adopted with modifications. Rather than a dictatorship of the proletariat, as the Soviet Union called itself, China was to be a "people's democratic dictatorship," with "the people" including workers, both poor and rich peasants, and the national bourgeoisie, but excluding landlords and certain classes of capitalists. The people so defined were represented by a hierarchy of irregularly scheduled People's Representative Congresses.

Real power, however, lay with the Communist Party. The People's Liberation Army (PLA) was not subordinated to the government but rather to the party, through its Military Affairs Commission. By the end of the 1950s, there were more than 1 million branch party committees in villages, factories, schools, army units, and other organizations. Each committee sent delegates up to higher units, including county and province committees, leading up to the three top tiers: the Central Committee with a few dozen members, the Politburo with around a dozen members, and its Standing Committee, which in 1949 consisted of Mao Zedong, Liu Shaoqi, Zhou Enlai, Zhu De, and Chen Yun and later was expanded to include Deng Xiaoping. Mao Zedong was recognized as the paramount leader and treated almost as though he was an emperor. In 1953, when he was sixty years old, Mao was chairman of the party, chairman of the Military Affairs Commission, and chairman of the PRC. The central government had dozens of ministries, and Mao needed an array of secretaries to handle all of the paperwork he had to process. Expert organizers like Zhou Enlai and Liu Shaoqi, both of whom had been active in the party since the early 1920s, coordinated foreign and economic policy, respectively.

The Communist Party faced enormous challenges. After forty years of fighting in one part of the country or another, the economy was in shambles. Inflation was rampant. Railroad tracks had been torn up and bridges destroyed. Harbors were clogged with sunken ships. People displaced by war numbered in the millions. Many of those manning essential services had been either Japanese collaborators or Nationalist appointees and did not inspire trust. Chiang Kaishek had transferred much of his army to Taiwan and had not given up claim to be the legitimate ruler of China.

In December 1949, Mao went to Moscow to confer with Joseph Stalin. He stayed nine weeks—his first trip abroad—and arranged an agreement on Soviet loans and technical assistance. Soon more than twenty thousand Chinese trainees went to the Soviet Union, and some ten thousand Russian technicians came to China to help set up 156 Soviet-designed heavy industrial plants. To pay for these projects, agriculture was heavily taxed, again on the Soviet model. According to the First Five Year Plan put into effect for the years 1953 to 1957, output of steel was to be quadrupled, power and cement doubled. Consumer goods, however, were to be increased by much smaller increments—cotton piece goods by less than half, grain by less than a fifth.

But China could not create everything from scratch. Ways had to be found to maintain the infrastructure of modern urban life, the factories, railroads, universities, newspapers, law courts, and tax-collecting stations, even as the party took them over. When the Red Army entered cities, its peasant soldiers put an end to looting and rounded up beggars, prostitutes, opium addicts, and petty criminals. They set up street committees, which were told to rid the cities of flashy clothes, provocative hairstyles, and other signs of decadence. But illiterate soldiers were not qualified to run all urban enterprises themselves.

Some enterprises the new state took over outright. By taking over the banks, the government brought inflation under control within a year. The new government took control of key industries, such as the railroads and foreign trade. In other cases, capitalists and managers were left in place but forced to follow party directives. A large-scale campaign was launched in 1951–1952 to weed out the least cooperative of the capitalists still controlling private enterprises. City residents were mobilized to accuse merchants and manufacturers of bribery, tax evasion, theft of state assets, cheating in labor or materials, or stealing state economic secrets. In the single month of April 1952, seventy thousand Shanghai businessmen were investigated and criticized. The targets often felt betrayed when their family members and friends joined in attacking them. Once businessmen confessed, they had to pay restitution, which often meant giving shares of their enterprises to the government, turning them into joint government-private ventures. To keep enterprises running, the former owners were often kept on as government-paid managers, but they had been discredited in the eyes of their former subordinates. Smaller manufacturing plants, stores, and restaurants were gradually dominated by the government through its control of supplies and labor.

As the party took control, it brought the advantages of modern life, such as schools and health care, to wider and wider circles of the urban and rural poor. During the 1950s rapid progress was made in cutting illiteracy and raising life expectancy. Employment was found for all, and housing of some sort was provided for everyone.

Ideology and Social Control

China's new leaders called their victory in the civil war "the liberation." As they saw it, the Chinese people had been freed from the yoke of the past and now could rebuild China as a socialist, egalitarian, forward-looking nation. China would regain its stature as a great nation and demonstrate to the world the potential of socialism to lift the masses out of poverty. Achieving these goals required adherence to correct ideology, identified as "Mao Zedong Thought." Since Mao's ideas changed over time and put emphasis on practice over theory, even those who had studied Mao's writings could never be totally sure they knew how he would view a particular issue. As long as Mao lived, he was the interpreter of his own ideas, the one to rule on what deviated from ideological correctness.

Spreading these ideas was the mission of propaganda departments and teams, which quickly took over the publishing industry. Schools and colleges were also put under party supervision, with a Soviet-style Ministry of Education issuing directives. Numerous mass organizations were set up, including street committees in cities, the Youth League, Women's Federation, and Labor Union Federation. Party workers who organized meetings of these groups were simultaneously to learn from the masses, keep an eye on them, and get them behind new policies. Meeting halls and other buildings were festooned with banners and posters proclaiming party slogans. (See **Material Culture: Political Posters.**)

The pervasive attack on the old led to the condemnation of many features of traditional culture. Traditional religion was labeled feudal superstition. In 1950 the Marriage Reform Law granted young people the right to choose their marriage partners, wives the right to initiate divorce, and wives and daughters rights to property. The provisions of these laws did not go much further than the Nationalists' Civil Code of 1930, but they had a considerably greater impact because campaigns were launched to publicize them and to assure women of party support if they refused a marriage arranged by their parents or left an unbearable husband or mother-in-law. During the first five years of the new law, several million marriages were dissolved, most at the request of the wife. This campaign should not, of course, get full credit for changes in the Chinese family system, as many other forces contributed to undermining patriarchal authority, such as the drastic shrinkage of family property as a result of collectivization of land and appropriation of business assets, the entry of more children into schools and mass organizations like the Youth League,

MATERIAL CULTURE

Political Posters

Under Mao, political posters, reproduced from paintings, woodcuts, and other media, were displayed prominently in classrooms, offices, and homes. The artists who produced these works had to follow the guidelines set by Mao Zedong at the 1942 Yan'an Forum for Literature and Art. Art was to serve politics and further the revolutionary cause. Toward that end, it had to be appealing and accessible to the masses. "Cultural workers" were sent out to villages and factories to study folk art and learn from real life. In addition, workers and peasants were encouraged to attend art schools and create artwork of their own. During the Cultural Revolution, Jiang Qing, Mao's wife, dominated cultural productions during this period, and art showed a new militancy. (See Color Plate 29.)

Mao Among Happy Peasants. The caption for this poster reads "All Living Things Depend on the Sun." Viewers would have understood that Mao is China's sun. *(David King Collection, London, UK)*

the mobilization of women in large numbers into the work force, and the public appearance of more women in positions of authority, ranging from street committees to university faculties and the upper echelons of the party.

Art and architecture were deployed to spread new ideas. The old city of Beijing was given a new look to match its status as capital of New China. The huge walls around Beijing were torn down as outmoded obstacles to traffic. The area south of the old imperial palace was cleared of buildings to create Tiananmen ("Gate of Heavenly Peace") Square. On either side of this square, two huge Soviet-style buildings were erected: the Great Hall of the People and the Museum of Chinese History. In the center was placed a hundred-foot-tall stone Monument to

the People's Heroes, with friezes depicting heroic revolutionaries of the past century in the new international socialist realist art style. When huge May Day and National Day rallies were held, China was visually linked to Communist countries all around the world.

The Communist Party developed an effective means of social and ideological control through the *danwei* (work unit). Most people's *danwei* was their place of work; for students it was their school; for the retired or unemployed, their neighborhood. Each *danwei* assigned housing, supplied ration coupons (for grain, other foodstuffs, cloth, and anything else in short supply), managed birth control programs, and organized mass campaigns. One needed permission of one's *danwei* even to get married or divorced.

The Korean War and the United States as the Chief Enemy

The new government did not have even a year to get its structures and policies in place before it was embroiled in war in Korea. After World War II, with the ensuing Cold War between the United States and the Soviet Union, Korea had ended up with the Soviet Union dominant above the 38th parallel and the United States below it (see Chapter 30). Mao knew that China's development plans hinged on respite from war. Stalin, however, approved North Korea's plan to invade South Korea, which occurred in June 1950. In October U.S. forces, fighting under the United Nations flag in support of the South, crossed the 38th parallel and headed toward the Yalu River, the border between North Korea and China. Later that month, Chinese "volunteers," under the command of Peng Dehuai, began to cross the Yalu secretly, using no lights or radios. In late November they surprised the Americans and soon forced them to retreat south of Seoul. Altogether, more than 2.5 million Chinese troops were sent to Korea, as well as all of China's tanks and over half its artillery and aircraft. A stalemate followed, and peace talks dragged on until 1953, largely because China wanted all prisoners repatriated but fourteen thousand begged not to be sent back.

This war gave the Communist Party legitimacy in China: China had "stood up" and beaten back the imperialists. But the costs were huge. Not only did China suffer an estimated three hundred sixty thousand casualties, but the war eliminated many chances for gradual reconciliation, internal and external. The United States, now viewing China as its enemy, sent the Seventh Fleet to patrol the waters between China and Taiwan and increased aid to Chiang Kaishek on Taiwan. China began to vilify the United States as its prime enemy.

With Taiwan occupying the China seat on the UN Security Council, the United States pushed through the UN a total embargo on trade with China and enforced it by a blockade of China's coast. Of necessity, self-reliance became a chief virtue of the revolution in China. When the United States helped supply the French in their war to regain control of Vietnam, China supplied Ho Chi Minh and the Vietminh. China became more afraid of spies and enemy agents and expelled most of the remaining western missionaries and businessmen. A worse fate awaited those who had served in the Nationalist government or army. A campaign of 1951 against such "counterrevolutionaries" resulted in the execution of tens or hundreds of thousands, with similar numbers sent to harsh labor reform camps. This campaign was also used to disarm the population; over five hundred thousand rifles were collected in Guangdong alone.

Collectivizing Agriculture

The lives of hundreds of millions of China's farmers were radically altered in the 1950s by the progressive collectivization of land and the creation of a new local elite of rural cadres. Ever since the 1930s, when the Communist Party took control of new areas, it taught peasants a new way to look on the old order: social and economic inequalities were not natural but a perversion caused by the institution of private property; the old literati elite were not exemplars of Confucian virtues but the cruelest of exploiters who pressured their tenants to the point where they had to sell their children. That antiquated "feudal" order needed to be replaced with a communal order where all would work together unselfishly for common goals.

The first step was to redistribute land. Typically, the party would send in a small team of cadres and students to a village to cultivate relations with the poor, organize a peasant association, identify potential leaders from among the poorest peasants, compile lists of grievances, and organize struggles against those most resented. Eventually the team would supervise the classification of the inhabitants as landlords, rich peasants, middle peasants, poor peasants, and hired hands. The analysis of class was supposed to be scientific, but moral judgments tended to intrude. How should one classify elderly widows who rented out their meager holdings because they were incapable of working them themselves? Somewhat better-off families of veterans?

Families that had bought land only recently from money earned in urban factories? Or families newly impoverished because the household head was a decadent wastrel or opium addict?

These uncertainties allowed land reform activists to help friends and get back at enemies. In some villages, there was not much of a surplus to redistribute. In others, violence flared, especially when villagers tried to get those labeled landlords or rich peasants to reveal where they had buried their gold. Landlords and rich peasants faced not only loss of their land but also punishment for past offenses; a not insignificant number were executed. Another result of the class struggle stage of land reform was the creation of a caste-like system in the countryside. The descendants of those labeled landlords were excluded from leadership positions while the descendants of former poor and lower-middle peasants gained preference.

Redistribution of land gained peasant support but did not improve productivity. Toward that end, progressive collectivization was promoted. First, farmers were encouraged to join mutual aid teams, sometime later to set up cooperatives. Cooperatives pooled resources but returned compensation based on inputs of land, tools, animals, and labor. In the "old liberated areas" in north China, this was accomplished in the early 1940s; in south China, these measures were extended during the period 1950–1953. From 1954 to 1956 a third stage was pushed: higher-level collectives that amalgamated cooperatives and did away with compensation for anything other than labor. Most of these higher-level cooperatives were old villages or parts of large villages. Once higher-level cooperatives were in place, economic inequality within villages was all but eliminated.

In 1953, the Chinese state took over control of the grain market. After taking 5 to 10 percent of each collective's harvest as a tax, the government allowed the unit to retain a meager subsistence ration per person; then it purchased a share of the "surplus" at prices it set, a hidden form of taxation. Interregional commerce was redefined as criminal speculation, an extreme form of capitalist exploitation. Trade was taken over by the state, and rural markets ceased to function. Many peasants lost crucial sideline income, especially peasants in poorer areas who had previously made ends meet by operating such small enterprises as oil presses, paper mills, or rope factories. Carpenters and craftsmen who used to travel far and wide became chained to the land, unable to practice their trades except in their own localities.

Rural cadres became the new elite in the countryside. How policy shifts were experienced by ordinary people depended on the personal qualities of the lowest level of party functionaries. In some villages, literate middle peasants who knew a lot about farming rose to leadership positions. In other villages, toughs from the poorest families rose because of their zeal in denouncing landlord exploitation. To get ahead, a team leader had to produce a substantial surplus to serve the needs of the revolution without letting too much be taken away and thus losing his team's confidence. As units were urged to consolidate and enlarge, rural cadres had to spend much of their time motivating members and settling squabbles among them. For those with the requisite talents, serving as a rural cadre offered farmers possibilities for social mobility way beyond anything that had existed in imperial China, since local team leaders could rise in the party hierarchy.

Much was accomplished during collectivization to improve the lot of farmers in China. Schools were opened in rural areas, and children everywhere enrolled for at least a few years, cutting the illiteracy rate dramatically. Basic health care was brought to the countryside via clinics and "barefoot doctors," peasants with only a few months of training who could at least give vaccinations and provide antibiotics and other medicines. Collectives took on responsibility for the welfare of widows and orphans with no one to care for them.

Minorities and Autonomous Regions

The new China proclaimed itself to be a multinational state. Officially the old view of China as the civilizing center, gradually attracting, acculturating, and absorbing non-Chinese along its frontiers, was replaced by a vision of distinct ethnic groups joined in a collaborative state. "Han" was promoted as the correct term for the most advanced ethnic group; "Chinese" was stretched to encompass all ethnic groups in the People's Republic.

The policy of multinationality was copied from that of the Soviet Union, which had devised it as the best way to justify retaining all the lands acquired by the czar in the eighteenth and nineteenth centuries. For China the model similarly provided a way to justify reasserting dominion over Tibet and Xinjiang, both acquired by the Qing but independent after 1911. (Mongolia had fallen away as well, but under the domination of the Soviet Union it had established a Communist government in the 1920s, so China did not challenge its independence.)

Identifying and labeling China's minority nationalities became a major state project in the 1950s. Stalin had enunciated a nationalities policy with four criteria for establishing a group as a "nationality": common language, common territory, a common economic life, and a common psychological makeup manifested in common cultural traits. Using these criteria, Chinese linguists and social scientists investigated more than four hundred groups. After classifying most as local subbranches of larger ethnic groups, they ended up with fifty-five recognized minority nationalities making up about 7 percent of the population. Some of these nationalities were clear cases, like the Tibetans and Uighurs, who spoke distinct languages and lived in distinct territories. Others seemed matters of degree, like the Hui, Chinese-speaking Muslims scattered throughout the country, and the Zhuang of Guangxi, who had long been quite sinified. In cases where a particular minority dominated a county or province, the unit would be recognized as autonomous, giving it the prerogative to use its own language in schools and government offices. Tibet, Xinjiang, Ningxia, and Inner Mongolia were all made autonomous provinces, and large parts of Sichuan, Yunnan, and Guizhou were declared autonomous regions of the Zhuang, Miao, Yi, and other minorities. (See Map 28.1.) By 1957, four hundred thousand members of minority groups had been recruited as party members.

Despite the protections given minorities in their autonomous regions, many of them became progressively more Han through migration (see **Biography: Jin Shuyu, Telephone Minder**). Inner Mongolia soon became 90 percent Han Chinese, and the traditional Mongol nomadic culture largely disappeared as ranch-style stock raising replaced moving the herds with the seasons. In Xinjiang too, in-migration of Han Chinese changed the ethnic makeup, especially in the cities. Manchuria, now called the Northeast, had for nearly a century been the destination of millions of Han Chinese, a process that continued as the Communists built on the heavy industry base left by the Japanese.

Tibet was a special case. It had not come under rule of any sort from Beijing until the eighteenth century, and the Manchu rulers had interfered relatively little with the power of the Lamaist Buddhist monasteries. From the 1890s on, Tibet fell more under the sway of the British, but Britain left India in 1947, ending its interest in Tibet. In 1950, when Lhasa would not agree to "peaceful liberation," the PLA invaded. Tibetan appeals to the UN were not considered, on the recommendation of India. Tibet had no choice but to negotiate an agreement with the Chinese Communist Party. Tibet recognized China's sovereignty and in exchange was allowed to maintain its traditional political system, including the Dalai Lama. From 1951 to 1959, this system worked fairly well. By 1959, however, ethnic Tibetans from neighboring provinces were streaming into Tibet, unhappy with agricultural collectivization. When massive protests broke out in Lhasa, the army opened fire. The Dalai Lama and thousands of his followers fled to India, which welcomed them. The aftermath included more pressure on Tibet to conform to the rest of the People's Republic and the sense among Tibetans that theirs was an occupied land.

Intellectuals and the Hundred Flowers Campaign

In the 1920s and 1930s some of the most enthusiastic supporters of socialism were members of the educated elite (now usually called intellectuals). Professors like Chen Duxiu and Li Dazhao

Color Plate 25
Boxer Print. The Boxers spread word of their invincibility through woodblock prints like this one, which shows their attack on the treaty port city of Tianjin.
(British Library)

Color Plate 26
People of the Five Nations: A Sunday. This woodblock triptych published in 1861 showed Japan how westerners dressed and entertained themselves in the foreign settlement at Yokohama.
(Arthur M. Sackler Gallery, Smithsonian Institution, Washington, DC: Gift of Ambassador and Mrs. William Leonhart, S1998.96a–c)

Color Plate 27
Gas Lights. Gas lights illuminating the streets of Tokyo became
a favorite subject for modern woodblock print artists.
(Edo Tokyo Museum/Tokyo Metropolitan Foundation for History and Culture Image
Archives/DNP Archives.com)

Color Plate 28
Magazine covers for *Kagaku chishiki* (Scientific
Knowledge) by Sugiura Hisui from 1931–1935
illustrated the wonders of science and technology
for young readers.
(The National Museum of Modern Art, Tokyo)

Color Plate 29
Raising Mao Zedong's Thought. This 1967 poster is titled "Revolutionary Proletarian Right to Rebel Troops, Unite!" The books they hold are the selected works of Mao Zedong. The woman's armband reads "Red Guard."

(David King Collection, London, UK)

Color Plate 30
Goddess of Democracy. During the 1989 demonstrations in Tiananmen Square, art students provocatively placed a 37-foot tall statue labeled the Goddess of Democracy facing the portrait of Mao Zedong.

(Jeff Widener/AP Wide World Photos)

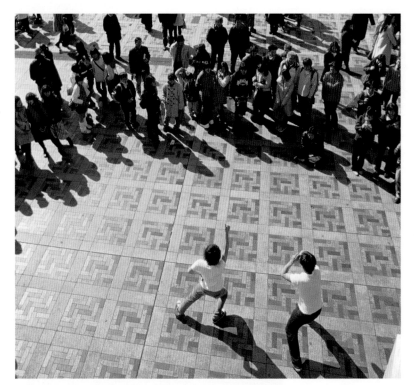

**Color Plate 31
The Takenoko Zoku
(Bamboo Tribe).** Young
people gather each
Sunday on the bridge
between trendy
Harajuku and the
Yoyogi stadiums built
for the 1964 Tokyo
Olympics to dance
and show off.
(Lonely Planet Images)

**Color Plate 32
Industrial Plants.** This photo depicts industrial plants stretching along
Japan's Pacific coast, transforming what had once been scenic views of
mountains and water into a modern landscape.
(Corbis)

Map **28.1**   Ethnic Groups in China

Map Legend:
- Mandarin Chinese
- Southern Chinese dialects
- Tibetan
- Mongolian
- Turkic (including Uighur)
- Other (Kam-Tai, Miao-Yao, Tajik, Mon-Khmer, Korean, Manchu-Tungus)

and writers like Lu Xun and Ding Ling saw socialism as a way to rid China of poverty and injustice. Many intellectuals made their way to Yan'an, where they soon learned that their job was to serve the party, not stand at a critical distance from it (see Chapter 26).

After 1949 the party had to find ways to make use of intellectuals who had not publicly sided with it, but rather had stayed in the eastern cities, working as teachers, journalists, engineers, or government officials. Most members of this small, urban, educated elite were ready and eager to serve the new government, happy that China finally had a government able to drive out imperialists, control inflation, banish unemployment, end corruption, and clean up the streets. Thousands who were studying abroad in 1949 hurried home to see how they could help. China needed

expertise for its modernization projects, and most of the educated were kept in their jobs, whatever their class background.

Mao, however, distrusted intellectuals and since Yan'an days had been devising ways to subordinate them to the party. In the early 1950s the educated men and women who staffed schools, universities, publishing houses, research institutes, and other organizations were "reeducated." This "thought reform" generally entailed confessing one's subservience to capitalists and imperialists or other bourgeois habits of thought and one's gratitude to Chairman Mao for having helped one realize these errors. For some going through it, thought reform was like a conversion experience; they saw themselves in an entirely new way and wanted to dedicate themselves to the socialist cause. For others, it was devastating.

BIOGRAPHY Jin Shuyu, Telephone Minder

Jin Shuyu was born in 1917 to an ethnic Korean family in southern Manchuria near the border with Korea. Her father was a doctor, but when she finished middle school in the early 1930s, Japan had taken over Manchuria, and she, like many of her classmates, ran away into the hills to join the anti-Japanese resistance. They engaged primarily in guerrilla action, trying to blow up storehouses or convoy trucks and the like. To support themselves, they would kidnap rich people and hold them for ransom. Their group accepted advice from Communist organizers but was not a Communist group. Finally, they were hard hit by the Japanese and had to scatter. Her family could not hide her because the Japanese knew she was a "bandit." She therefore decided to try to slip into Korea. She worked first as a servant near the border. After she was able to get forged papers, she went to Seoul, where she got a job teaching middle school. In Seoul she married a Han Chinese eleven years her senior who owned a Chinese restaurant and soon had children. At the end of the war in 1945, the Japanese ransacked their restaurant. Added to that, they lost all their savings when the banks failed. Yet they were able to borrow enough money to start another restaurant.

In 1949, when the Communists won in China, Jin was thirty-two and wanted to return to China, but her husband was against it. Then the Korean War started. Their restaurant did well, as Seoul was swollen with foreign soldiers who liked Chinese food, but she wanted to return home. Her husband said she could go; he would stay behind until she had sized up the situation. In 1953 she took their children with her across the 38th parallel, then made her way through North Korea and back into China. Her husband never followed. They wrote to each other through a cousin in

Japan, and in 1983 they were both able to go to Japan to see each other, the first time in thirty years. Her son tried to convince his father to return with them to China, but he said he still wanted to wait to see how things turned out. She thought he kept on putting off joining them because he was too influenced by the anticommunist propaganda of South Korea, or perhaps because he had taken a new wife and never told them.

Jin's life in China was relatively uneventful. In 1958 she was given a job by her street committee to mind the community telephone. Those who wanted to make a call would pay her the fee and she would let them use it. She also would go get people when a call came in for them. Her salary was very low, but she got half of the fees people paid to make calls. Moreover, as she told her interviewer in 1984, she enjoyed listening to people talk on the phone, especially young people who often grinned through their calls or bowed and scraped when seeking a favor from someone.

During the Cultural Revolution, people accused Jin of having a bad class background. She had to locate some of her old comrades to speak up for her, and they said she had distinguished herself in an unofficial anti-Japanese force and should be getting money from the government. After that things were easier because she was classified as an "Anti-Japanese Alliance Veteran" and a repatriated overseas Chinese. She also had some minor privileges as an ethnic minority. However, she told her interviewer, "I'm no more Korean than you are. I became Han Chinese long ago."[1]

Her son did well, not only graduating from college but becoming a college professor, and by the early 1980s Jin lived comfortably. Her only complaint was that her daughter-in-law thought too highly of herself.

---

1. Zhang Xinxin and Sang Ye, *Chinese Lives: An Oral History of Contemporary China* (New York: Pantheon Books, 1987), p. 20.

Independence on the part of intellectuals was also undermined by curtailing alternative sources of income. There were no more rents or dividends, no more independent presses or private colleges.

In response to de-Stalinization in the Soviet Union, in 1956 Mao called on intellectuals to help him identify problems within the party, such as party members who had lost touch with the people or behaved like tyrants. "Let a hundred flowers bloom" in the field of culture and a "hundred schools of thought contend" in science. As long as criticism was not "antagonistic" or "counterrevolutionary," it would help strengthen the party, he explained. The first to come forward with criticisms were scientists and engineers who wanted party members to interfere less with their work. To encourage more people to come forward, Mao praised those who spoke up. Soon critics lost their inhibitions. By May 1957 college students were putting up wall posters, sometimes with highly inflammatory charges. One poster at Qinghua University in Beijing even dared attack Mao Zedong by name: "When he wants to kill you, he doesn't have to do it himself. He can mobilize your wife and children to denounce you and then kill you with their own hands! Is this a rational society? This is class struggle, Mao Zedong style!"[1]

Did Mao plan this campaign to ferret out dissidents? Or was he shocked by the outpouring of criticism? Whatever the truth of the matter, in June 1957, the party announced a campaign against rightists, orchestrated by the newly appointed secretary general of the party, Deng Xiaoping. In this massive campaign, units were pressed to identify 5 percent of their staff as rightists. Altogether almost 3 million people were labeled rightists, which meant that they would no longer have any real influence at work, even if allowed to keep their jobs. Half a million suffered worse fates, sent to labor in the countryside. Some of those labeled rightists had exposed party weaknesses, like the thirty reporters who had reported on secret shops where officials could buy goods not available to ordinary people. But other "rightists" had hardly said anything, like the railroad engineer relegated to menial labor for twenty years because someone reported hearing him say "how bold" when he read a critique of the party.

By the end of the campaign, the western-influenced elite created in the 1930s was destroyed, condemned as "poisonous weeds." Old China had been dominated, culturally at least, by an elite defined by lengthy education. Mao made sure the educated would know their place in the New China: they were employees of the state, hired to instruct the children of the laboring people or provide technical assistance. They were not to have ideas of their own separate from those of the party or a cultural life distinct from the masses. Most of those labeled rightists in 1957 had to wait until 1979 to be rehabilitated (that is, to have their rightist label removed and their civil rights restored).

DEPARTING FROM THE SOVIET MODEL

By 1957, China had made progress on many fronts. The standard of living was improving, support for the government was strong, and people were optimistic about the future. Still, Mao was not satisfied. Growth was too slow and too dependent on technical experts and capital. As he had found from the Hundred Flowers campaign, people's ways of thinking had not been as quickly transformed as he had hoped. Mao was ready to try more radical measures.

The Great Leap Forward

Why couldn't China find a way to use what it was rich in—labor power—to modernize more rapidly? In 1956 Mao began talking of a Great Leap Forward. Through the coordinated hard work of hundreds of millions of people, China would transform itself from a poor nation into a mighty one. With the latent creative capacity of the Chinese masses unleashed, China would surpass Great Britain in industrial output within fifteen years.

1. Gregor Benton and Alan Hunter, eds., *Wild Lily, Prairie Fire* (Princeton, N.J.: Princeton University Press, 1995), pp. 100–101.

These visions of accelerated industrialization were coupled with a higher level of collectivization in the countryside. In 1958, in a matter of months, agricultural collectives all over the country were amalgamated into gigantic communes. Private garden plots were banned. Peasants were organized into quasi-military production brigades and referred to as fighters on the agricultural front. Peasant men were marched in military style to work on public works projects, while the women took over much of the fieldwork. Those between ages sixteen and thirty were drafted into the militia and spent long hours drilling.

Both party cadres and ordinary working people got caught up in a wave of utopian enthusiasm. During the late summer and fall of 1958, communes, factories, schools, and other units set up "backyard steel furnaces" in order to double steel production. As workers were mobilized to put in long hours on these projects, they had little time at home to cook or eat. Units were encouraged to set up mess halls where food was free, a measure commentators hailed as a step toward communism. Counties claimed 1,000 and even 10,000 percent increases in agriculture production. The Central Committee announced with great fanfare that production had nearly doubled in a single year.

Some Great Leap projects proved of long-term value; bridges, railroads, canals, reservoirs, power stations, mines, and irrigation works were constructed all over the country. All too often, however, projects were undertaken with such haste and with so little technical knowledge that they did more harm than good. With economists and engineers downgraded or removed in the antirightist campaigns of the year before, plans were formulated not by experts but by local cadres eager to show their political zeal. Fields plowed deep were sometimes ruined because the soil became salinized. The quality of most of the steel made in backyard furnaces was too poor to be used. Instead it filled railroad cars and clogged train yards all over the country, disrupting transportation.

It was not just the legacy of the Hundred Flowers campaign that kept cadres from reporting failures. The minister of defense and hero of the Korean War, Peng Dehuai, tried to bring up problems in a private letter he gave to Mao at a party conference in July 1959. In the letter Peng began by saying that the Great Leap was an indisputable success, but pointed to the tendency to exaggerate at all levels, which made it difficult for the leadership to know the real situation. He also noted that people began to think that the food problem was solved and that they could give free meals to all. Peng's language was temperate, but Mao's reaction was not. Mao distributed copies of the letter to the delegates and denounced Peng for "right opportunism." He made the senior cadres choose between him and Peng, and none had the courage to side with Peng, who was soon dismissed from his post. Problems with the Great Leap were now blamed on all those like Peng who lacked faith in its premises.

Mao's faulty economics, coupled with droughts and floods, ended up creating one of the worst famines in world history. The size of the 1958 harvest was wildly exaggerated, and no one attempted to validate reports. Tax grain was removed from the countryside on the basis of the reported harvests, leaving little for local consumption. No one wanted to report what was actually happening in his locality for fear of being labeled a rightist. Grain production dropped from 200 million tons in 1958 to 170 million in 1959 and 144 million in 1960. By 1960 in many places people were left with less than half of what they needed to survive. Rationing was practiced almost everywhere, and soup kitchens serving weak gruel were set up in an attempt to stave off starvation. But peasants in places where grain was exhausted were not allowed to hit the roads, as people had always done in the past during famines. From later census reconstructions, it appears that during the Three Hard Years (1959–1962) there were on the order of 30 million "excess" deaths attributable to the dearth of food. Yet neither Mao nor the Communist Party fell from power.

Producing Steel in Henan Province. During the Great Leap Forward, inexperienced workers labored for long hours to produce steel in makeshift "backyard" furnaces. *(Xinhua News Agency, Beijing/Sovfoto)*

Death Rates in Hard-Hit Provinces, 1957 and 1960			
Province	**1957**	**1960**	**Change**
Anhui	c. 250,000	2,200,000	780%
Gansu	142,041	538,479	279
Guangxi	261,785	644,700	146
Henan	572,000	1,908,000	233
Hunan	370,059	1,068,118	189

Source: Based on Roderick MacFarquar, *The Origins of the Cultural Revolution, vol. 3: The Coming of the Cataclysm, 1961–1966* (New York: Columbia University Press, 1997), pp. 2–3.

The Great Leap destroyed people's faith in their local cadres, who in the crisis put themselves and their families first. Another blow to peasants was new curbs on their mobility. Beginning in 1955 a system of population registration bound rural people to the villages of their birth, or in the case of married women, their husbands' villages. When the hasty expansion of the nation's industrial plant was reversed, millions of unemployed workers were sent back to the countryside. To keep them from returning, or other peasants from sneaking into the cities, a system of urban household registration was introduced. Only those with permission to reside in a city could get the ration coupons needed to purchase grain there. These residence policies had the unintended effect of locking rural communities with unfavorable man-land ratios into dismal poverty.

It is not surprising that the rural poor would want to move to the cities. Those who got jobs in state-run factories had low-cost housing, pensions, and health care, not to mention a reliable supply of subsidized food. Children in the cities could stay in school through middle school, and the brightest could go further. In the countryside, only a tiny proportion of exceptionally wealthy communities could come at all close to providing such benefits. In the poorest regions, farmers, forced by the government to concentrate on growing grain, could do little to improve their situations other than invest more labor by weeding more frequently, leveling and terracing fields, expanding irrigation systems, and so on. Such investment often brought little return, and agricultural productivity (the return for each hour of labor) fell across the country.

The Sino-Soviet Split

In the 1920s and 1930s Stalin, through the Comintern, had done as much to hinder the success of the Chinese Communist Party as to aid it. Still, in 1949, Mao viewed the Soviet Union as China's natural ally and went to Moscow to see Stalin. Mao never had the same respect for Stalin's successor, Khrushchev. The Great Leap Forward put further strain on relations between China and the Soviet Union. China intensified its bellicose anti-imperialist rhetoric and began shelling the islands off the coast of Fujian still held by the Nationalists on Taiwan, and the Russians began to fear that China would drag them into a war with the United States. In 1958 and 1959, Khrushchev visited Beijing and concluded that Mao was a romantic deviationist, particularly wrongheaded in his decision to create communes. All of the assistance the Soviet Union had given to China's industrialization seemed to have been wasted as Mao put his trust in backyard furnaces.

When Mao made light of nuclear weapons—saying that if using them could destroy capitalism, it would not matter that much if China lost half its population—Khrushchev went back on his earlier promise to give China nuclear weapons. There was also friction over India and its support for the Dalai Lama and other refugees from Tibet. Russia wanted India as an ally and would not side with China in its border disputes with India, infuriating Mao. In April 1960 Chinese leaders celebrated the ninetieth anniversary of Lenin's birth by lambasting Soviet foreign policy. In July 1960, just as famine was hitting China, Khrushchev ordered the Soviet experts to return and take their blueprints and spare parts with them. By 1963 Mao was publicly denouncing Khrushchev as a revisionist and capitalist roader and challenging the Soviet Union's leadership of the international Communist movement. Communist parties throughout the world soon divided into pro-Soviet and pro-China factions. As the rhetoric escalated, both sides increased their troops along their long border, which provoked border clashes. China built air raid shelters on a massive scale and devoted enormous resources to constructing a defense establishment in mountainous inland areas far from both the sea and the Soviet border. As the war in Vietnam escalated after 1963, China stayed on the sidelines, not even helping the Soviet Union supply North Vietnam. Meanwhile, China developed its own atomic weapons program, exploding its first nuclear device in 1964.

THE CULTURAL REVOLUTION

After the failure of the Great Leap Forward, Mao, nearly seventy years old, withdrew from active decision making. Liu Shaoqi replaced Mao as head of state in 1959, and he along with Chen Yun, Zhou Enlai, Deng Xiaoping, and other organization men set about reviving the economy. Mao grew more and more isolated. Surrounded by bodyguards, he lived in luxurious guest houses far removed from ordinary folk.

Senior colleagues had not forgotten the fate of Peng Dehuai, and honest debate of party policy was no longer attempted in front of Mao. Any resistance to his ideas had to be done in secret.

By the early 1960s Mao was afraid that revisionism was destroying the party—that Marxism was being undermined by contamination by capitalist methods and ideas. In 1962 he initiated the Socialist Education campaign to try to get rural cadres to focus again on class struggle. When Liu Shaoqi and Deng Xiaoping rewrote the directives to deemphasize class struggle, Mao concluded that the revisionists were taking over the struggle for control of the party.

After gathering allies, Mao set out to recapture revolutionary fervor and avoid slipping in the inegalitarian direction of the Soviet Union by initiating a Great Revolution to Create a Proletarian Culture—or Cultural Revolution for short—a movement that came close to destroying the party he had led for three decades.

Phase 1: 1966–1968

The Cultural Revolution began in the spring of 1966 with a denunciation of the mayor of Beijing for allowing the staging of a play that could be construed as critical of Mao. Mao's wife, Jiang Qing, formed a Cultural Revolution Small Group to look into ways to revolutionize culture. Jiang Qing had not played much of a part in politics before and was widely seen as a stand-in for Mao. Soon radical students at Beijing University were agitating against party officials' "taking the capitalist road." When Liu Shaoqi tried to control what was going on at Beijing University, Mao intervened, had him demoted by a rump session of the Central Committee, and sanctioned the organization of students into Red Guards.

The Cultural Revolution quickly escalated beyond the ability of Mao, Jiang Qing, or anyone else to control or direct. Young people who had grown up in New China responded enthusiastically to calls to help Mao oust revisionists. In June 1966 middle schools and universities throughout the country were closed as students devoted their full time to Red Guard activities.

Millions rode free on railroads to carry the message to the countryside or to make the pilgrimage to Beijing, where they might catch a glimpse of Mao, their "Great Helmsman," at the massive Red Guard rallies held in Tiananmen Square. (See **Documents: Big Character Poster.**)

At these rallies, Mao appeared in military uniform and told the students that "to rebel is justified" and that it was good "to bombard the headquarters." The Red Guards in response waved their little red books, *Quotations from Chairman Mao,* compiled a few years earlier by Lin Biao to indoctrinate soldiers. The cult of Mao became more and more dominant, with his pictures displayed in every household, bus, train, even pedicabs, and his sayings broadcast by loudspeaker at every intersection. From early 1967 on, the *People's Daily* regularly printed on its front page a boxed statement of Mao.

In cities large and small, Red Guards roamed the streets in their battle against things foreign or old. They invaded the homes of those with bad class backgrounds, "bourgeois tendencies," or connections to foreigners. Under the slogan of "destroy the four old things [old customs, habits, culture, and thinking]," they ransacked homes, libraries, and museums to find books and artwork to set on fire. The tensions and antagonisms that had been suppressed by nearly two decades of tight social control broke into the open as Red Guards found opportunities to get back at people. At the countless denunciation meetings they organized, cadres, teachers, or writers were forced to stand with their heads down and their arms raised behind them in the "airplane" position and listen to former friends and colleagues jeer and curse them. Many victims took their own lives; others died of beatings or mistreatment.

Liu Shaoqi, the head of state but now labeled the "chief capitalist roader," became a victim of the Red Guards. In the summer of 1967 Red Guards stormed Zhongnanhai, the well-guarded quarters where the party hierarchy lived, and seized Liu. Then they taunted and beat him before huge crowds. Liu died alone two years later from the abuse he received. His family suffered as well. Liu's wife ended up spending ten years in solitary

DOCUMENTS

Big Character Poster

Red Guards used "big character posters" to declare their political values and revolutionary zeal. The poster below was selected by the journal Red Flag *in November 1966 as exemplary because it used the "invincible thought of Mao Zedong" to launch an offensive against the old ideas and habits of the exploiting classes. It was written by a group of Red Guards at a high school in Beijing.*

Revolution is rebellion, and rebellion is the soul of Mao Zedong's thought. Daring to think, to speak, to act, to break through, and to make revolution—in a word, daring to rebel—is the most fundamental and most precious quality of proletarian revolutionaries; it is fundamental to the Party spirit of the Party of the proletariat! Not to rebel is revisionism, pure and simple! Revisionism has been in control of our school for seventeen years. If today we do not rise up in rebellion, when will we?

Now some of the people who were boldly opposing our rebellion have suddenly turned shy and coy, and have taken to incessant murmuring and nagging that we are too one-sided, too arrogant, too crude and that we are going too far. All this is utter nonsense! If you are against us, please say so. Why be shy about it? Since we are bent on rebelling, the matter is no longer in your hand! Indeed we shall make the air thick with the pungent smell of gunpowder. All this talk about being "humane" and "all-sided" —let's have an end to it.

You say we are too one-sided? What kind of allsideness is it that suits you? It looks to us like a "two combining into one" all-sided-ness, or eclecticism. You say we are too arrogant? "Arrogant" is just what we want to be. Chairman Mao says, "And those in high positions we counted as no more than the dust." We are bent on striking down not only the reactionaries in our school, but the reactionaries all over the world. Revolutionaries take it as their task to transform the world. How can we not be "arrogant"?

You say we are too crude? Crude is just what we want to be. How can we be soft and clinging towards revisionism or go in for great moderation? To be moderate toward the enemy is to be cruel to the revolution! You say we are going too far? Frankly, your "don't go too far" is reformism, it is "peaceful transition." And this is what your daydreams are about! Well, we are going to strike you down to the earth and keep you down!

There are some others who are scared to death of revolution, scared to death of rebellion. You sticklers for convention, you toadies are all curled up inside your revisionist shells. At the first whiff of rebellion, you become scared and nervous. A revolutionary is a "monkey king" whose golden rod is might, whose supernatural powers are far-reaching and whose magic is omnipotent precisely because he has the great and invincible thought of Mao Zedong. We are wielding our "golden rods," "displaying our supernatural powers" and using our "magic" in order to turn the old world upside down, smash it to pieces, create chaos, and make a tremendous mess—and the bigger the better! We must do this to the present revisionist middle school attached to Tsinghua University. Create a big rebellion, rebel to the end! We are bent on creating a tremendous proletarian uproar, and on carving out a new proletarian world!

Long live the revolutionary rebel spirit of the proletariat!

Source: From Patricia Buckley Ebrey, ed., *Chinese Civilization: A Sourcebook*, rev. ed. (New York: Simon and Schuster, 1993), p. 450.

Red Guards. In September 1966 a teenage girl Red Guard humiliates the governor Li Fanwu by forcing him to bow, making him wear a placard saying he is a member of the Black Gang, and clipping his hair. *(Li Zhensheng/Asia-Network.co.jp)*

confinement. Four other members of his family also died either of beatings or mistreatment in prison where interrogators made every effort to get them to reveal evidence that Liu or his wife was a spy. Deng Xiaoping, another target of Mao, fared better, sent off to labor in a factory in Jiangxi after being humiliated at struggle sessions.

By the end of 1966 workers were also being mobilized to participate in the Cultural Revolution. Rebel students went to factories to "learn from the workers" but actually to instigate opposition to party superiors. When party leaders tried to appease discontented workers by raising wages and handing out bonuses, Mao labeled their actions "economism" and instructed students and workers to seize power from such revisionist party leaders. Confusing power struggles ensued. As soon as one group gained the upper hand, another would challenge its takeover as a "sham power seizure" and attempt "counterpower seizure."

As armed conflict spread, Mao turned to the People's Liberation Army to restore order. Told to ensure that industrial and agricultural production continued, the army tended to support conservative mass organizations and disband the rebel organizations as "counterrevolutionary." Radical Red Guard leaders tried to counterattack, accusing the army of supporting the wrong side. In Wuhan in July 1967, when radicals seized trains loaded with weapons en route to Vietnam, the army supplied their opponents. Then a conservative faction in Wuhan kidnapped two of the radical leaders from Beijing, and the Cultural Revolution Small Group responded by calling on the Red Guards to arm themselves and seize military power from the "capitalist roaders" in the army. Thus began the most violent stage of the Cultural Revolution, during which different factions of Red Guards and worker organizations took up armed struggle against each other and

Big Character Posters. Soldiers of the PLA and peasants of the model commune at Dazhai are shown here putting up big character posters in 1970. *(Sovfoto)*

against regional and national military forces. Rebels seized the Foreign Ministry in Beijing for two weeks, and others seized and burned the British diplomatic compound. With communication and transportation at a standstill, consumer goods became scarce in urban areas.

In the first, violent phase of the Cultural Revolution, some 3 million Party and government officials were removed from their jobs, and as many as half a million people were killed or committed suicide.

Phase 2: 1968–1976

By the summer of 1968, Mao had no choice but to moderate the Cultural Revolution in order to prevent full-scale civil war. In July he disbanded the Red Guards and sent them off to work in the countryside. Revolutionary Committees were set up to take the place of the old party structure. Each committee had representatives from

the mass organizations, from revolutionary cadres, and from the army; in most places the army quickly became the dominant force. Culture remained tightly controlled. Foreign music, art, literature, and books (other than works on Marxism, Leninism, and Stalinism) disappeared from stores. Revolutionary works were offered in their place, such as the eight model revolutionary operas Jiang Qing had sponsored. The official line was that it was better to be red than expert, and professionals were hounded out of many fields. High school graduates were sent into the countryside, as the Red Guards had been before them, some 17 million altogether. Although the stated reason for sending them to the countryside was to let them learn from the peasants and give the peasants the advantage of their education, this transfer also saved the government the trouble and expense of putting the graduates on the payroll of urban enterprises or finding them housing when they married.

The dominance of the military declined after the downfall in 1971 of Lin Biao. To the public, Lin Biao was Mao's most devoted disciple, regularly photographed standing next to him. Yet according to the official account, Lin became afraid that Mao had turned against him and decided to assassinate him. When Lin's daughter exposed his plot, Lin decided to flee to the Soviet Union. His plane, however, ran out of fuel and crashed over Mongolia. Whatever the truth of this bizarre story, news of his plot was kept out of the press for a year, the leadership apparently unsure how to tell the people that Lin Biao turned out to be another Liu Shaoqi, a secret traitor who had managed to reach the second highest position in the political hierarchy.

By this point Mao's health was in decline, and he played less and less of a role in day-to-day management. The leading contenders for power were the more radical faction led by Jiang Qing and the more moderate faction led by Zhou Enlai. In this rather fluid situation China softened its antagonistic stance toward the outside world and in 1972 welcomed U.S. president Richard Nixon to visit and pursue improving relations. In 1973 many disgraced leaders, including Deng Xiaoping, were reinstated to important posts.

The Cultural Revolution's massive assault on entrenched ideas and the established order left many victims. Nearly 3 million people were officially rehabilitated after 1978. Urban young people who had been exhilarated when Mao called on them to topple those in power soon found themselves at the bottom of the heap, sent down to the countryside where hostile peasants could make life miserable. Their younger siblings received inferior educations, out of school for long periods, then taught a watered-down curriculum. The cadres, teachers, and intellectuals who were the principal targets of the Cultural Revolution lost much of their trust in others. When they had to continue working with people who had beaten, humiliated, or imprisoned them, the wounds were left to fester for years. Even those who agreed that elitist values and bureaucratic habits were pervasive problems in the party hierarchy found little positive in the outcome of the Cultural Revolution.

THE DEATH OF MAO

Those who in 1976 still believed in portents from heaven would have sensed that heaven was sending warnings. First, Zhou Enlai died in January after a long struggle with cancer. Next, an outpouring of grief for him in April was violently suppressed. Then in July, north China was rocked by a huge earthquake that killed hundreds of thousands. In September Mao Zedong died.

As long as Mao was alive, no one would openly challenge him, but as his health failed, those near the top tried to position themselves for the inevitable. The main struggle, it seems with hindsight, was between the radicals, Jiang Qing and her allies, later labeled the Gang of Four, and the pragmatists, Deng Xiaoping and his allies. In March 1976 a newspaper controlled by the radicals implied that Zhou Enlai was a capitalist roader. In response, on April 4, the traditional day for honoring the dead, an estimated 2 million people flocked to Tiananmen Square to lay wreaths in honor of Zhou. The radicals saw this as an act of opposition to themselves, had it labeled a counterrevolution-

ary incident, and called the militia out. Yet the pragmatists won out in the end. After a month of national mourning for Mao, Jiang Qing and the rest of the Gang of Four were arrested.

Assessing Mao's role in modern Chinese history is ongoing. In 1981 when the party rendered its judgment on Mao, it still gave him high marks for his military leadership and his intellectual contributions to Marxist theory, but assigned him much of the blame for everything that went wrong from 1956 on. Since then, Mao's standing has further eroded as doubts are raised about the impact of his leadership style in the 1940s and early 1950s. Some critics go so far as to portray Mao as a megalomaniac, so absorbed in his project of remaking China to match his vision that he was totally indifferent to others' suffering. Some Chinese intellectuals, however, worry that making Mao a monster relieves everyone else of responsibility and undermines the argument that structural changes are needed to prevent comparable tragedies from recurring.

Mao Zedong has often been compared to Zhu Yuanzhang, the founder of the Ming Dynasty. Both grew up in farming households, though Mao never experienced the desperate poverty of Zhu's childhood. Both were formed by the many years of warfare that preceded gaining military supremacy. Both brooked no opposition and had few scruples when it came to executing perceived opponents. Both tended toward the paranoid, suspecting traitorous intentions others did not perceive. But Zhu Yuanzhang cast a shadow over the rest of the Ming Dynasty. As will be seen in the next chapter, within a short period of Mao's death, much of what he had instituted was undone.

SUMMARY

How different was China in 1976 compared to 1949? Although the Cultural Revolution had brought enormous strain and confusion, China was by many measures better off. It was not dominated by any other countries and held itself up as a model to developing nations. The proportion of the population in school more than doubled between 1950 and 1978. Life expectancy reached age sixty-seven for men and age sixty-nine for women, due in large part to better survival of infants and more accessible health care. Unemployment was no longer a problem, and housing was provided for all. Inflation had been banished.

But life was also much more regimented and controlled. There was no longer anything resembling a free press and not many choices people could make about where they would live or what work they would do. Peasants could not leave their native villages (or in women's cases, the villages of their husbands). Graduates of high schools or universities were given little choice in job assignments. From the experience of repeated campaigns to uncover counterrevolutionaries, people had learned to distrust each other, never sure who might turn on them. Material security, in other words, had been secured at a high cost.

SUGGESTED READING

The first four decades of the PRC are covered in vols. 14 and 15 of *The Cambridge History of China,* ed. R. MacFarquhar and J. K. Fairbank (1987, 1991). For briefer overviews, see C. Dietrich, *People's China* (1994), and M. Meisner, *Mao's China and After* (1986).

After the death of Mao and the opening of China, quite a few Chinese who went abroad wrote revealing memoirs of their time in China. Among the better ones are J. Chang, *Wild Swans* (1991); H. Liang and J. Shapiro, *Son of the Revolution* (1984); N. Cheng, *Life and Death in Shanghai* (1987); X. Zhu, *Thirty Years in a Red House: A Memoir of Childhood and Youth in Communist China* (1999); B. Liu, *A Higher Kind of Loyalty: A Memoir by China's Foremost Journalist* (1990); J. Yang, *Six Chapters from My Life "Downunder"* (1983); and D. Chen, *China's Son: Growing Up in the Cultural Revolution* (2001). Fiction can also be very revealing of ordinary life. Much of the fiction of the 1980s depicts life during Mao's time. See, for instance, J. Zhang, *Love Must Not Be Forgotten* (1986) and *Heavy Wings* (1989); H. Yu, *To Live* (2003) and *The Past and the Punishments: Eight Stories* (1996); H. Bai, *The Remote Country of Women* (1994); H. Siu and Z. Stern, eds., *Mao's Harvest: Voices from China's New Generation* (1983); and P. Link, ed., *Stubborn Weeds: Popular and Controversial Chinese Literature After the Cultural Revolution* (1983).

The social science literature on China under Mao is enormous. On the government, see K. Lieberthal, *Governing China* (1995); R. MacFarquhar, *The Origins of the Cultural Revolution,* 3 vols. (1974, 1983, 1997); and H. Wu, *Laogai: The Chinese Gulag* (1992). On changes in the family and on women's lives, see K. Johnson, *Women, the Family, and Peasant Revolution in China* (1983); M. Wolf, *Revolution Postponed: Women in Contemporary China* (1985); and N. Diamant, *Revolutionizing the Family: Politics, Love, and Divorce, 1949–1968* (2000). On life at the village level, see J. Jing, *The Temple of Memories: History, Power, and Morality in a Chinese Village* (1998); P. Seybolt, *Throwing the Emperor from His Horse: Portrait of a Village Leader in China, 1923–1995* (1996); H. Siu, *Agents and Victims in South China* (1989); and A. Chan, R. Madsen, and J. Unger, *Chen Village Under Mao and Deng* (1992).

On the Cultural Revolution, see E. Perry and X. Li, *Proletarian Power: Shanghai in the Cultural Revolution* (1997), and A. Thurston, *Enemies of the People: The Ordeal of Intellectuals in China's Great Cultural Revolution* (1988). On Mao, besides the biographies of Mao listed in Chapter 26, see Z. Li, *The Private Life of Chairman Mao* (1994).

On literature and the arts, see J. Andrews, *Painters and Politics in the People's Republic of China, 1949–1979* (1994), and P. Link, *The Uses of Literature: Life in the Socialist Chinese Literary System* (2000).

China Since Mao (1976 to the Present)

After the death of Mao in 1976, the Chinese Communist Party turned away from class struggle and made economic growth a top priority. Gradually the intrusion of the government into daily life abated, leaving people more leeway to get on with their lives in their own ways. Not only did the government permit increased market activity and private enterprise, but it began courting foreign investment and sending students abroad. The infiltration of western popular culture and political ideas troubled authorities, but with the spread of technologies like telephones, shortwave radios, satellite television, telephones, fax machines, and the Internet, it became nearly impossible for the government to cordon China off from global cultural trends.

The aggregate figures for China's economic growth in the 1980s and 1990s are very impressive, but not everyone has benefited equally. In broad terms, those in cities have gained more than those in the countryside, those in the coastal provinces more than those in the interior, and those entering the job market during these decades more than their parents and grandparents.

Every facet of China's rapid changes since 1976 has intrigued scholars and journalists who have been able to live in China and observe development firsthand. With the collapse of communism in Russia and eastern Europe, many have speculated on the hold of the Communist Party in China. Can it maintain tight control over political expression when communications with the rest of the world have become so much more open? Can it dampen the unrest that results from unemployment, unpaid pensions, and political corruption? Will the disparities between the rich and the poor in China continue to widen? Is China becoming, as it claims, a country that follows the rule of law? Will China accept the pressure to conform to international standards that comes with its increased participation in international organizations? Is a return to Maoist policies possible any longer?

THE COMMUNIST PARTY AFTER MAO

The pace of change in the quarter-century after the death of Mao was extraordinary. Much of what had been instituted in the 1950s was abolished outright or slowly transformed. The Communist Party, however, maintained its large membership and its political power.

In the immediate aftermath of Mao's death, Hua Guofeng took over as head of the Communist Party. He was a relatively obscure party veteran singled out by Mao only months before his death. Soon after Mao's funeral, Hua sided with the pragmatists and arranged for the arrest of Mao's wife, Jiang Qing, and three of her closest associates. This "Gang of Four" was blamed for all the excesses of the Cultural Revolution. In 1977 Deng Xiaoping was reappointed to his old posts, and in December 1978 he supplanted Hua as the top official.

Like Mao, Deng had an impressive revolutionary pedigree, going back to the early 1920s when he was active with Zhou Enlai in France, and continuing through the Shanghai underground, the Long March, and guerrilla warfare against Japan. In 1956, at age fifty-two, he became a member of the Standing Committee of the Politburo and secretary general of the party. Twice ousted from power during the Cultural Revolution, he labeled absurd the Cultural Revolution slogan that it was "better to be poor under socialism than rich under capitalism," insisting that "poverty is not socialism."

A pragmatist, Deng Xiaoping took as his catchword "the Four Modernizations" (of agriculture, industry, science and technology, and defense). He openly admitted that China was poor and backward and saw no reason not to adopt foreign technology if it would improve the lives of the masses. Thousands of people who had been sent to the countryside were allowed to go home. People everywhere were eager to make up for what they saw as the "wasted years."

Party membership stood at 39 million when Mao died. Deng quickly set about weeding out the leftists recruited during the Cultural Revolution and rehabilitating those who had been persecuted. Deng knew that party members qualified to manage and direct the modernization projects were in short supply. Only 14 percent of party members had finished the equivalent of high school, and only 4 percent had college educations. Moreover, many of those who had gone to high school or college did so during the 1970s when admission was on the basis of political fervor and the curriculum was watered down to conform to the anti-elitist and anti-intellectual ideology of the period. About 15 million party members were sent back to school to learn to read and write. Retirement ages were imposed to reduce the number of elderly party members. Party recruitment was stepped up to bring in younger people with better educations.

Asserting that the influence of the Gang of Four had created "an entire generation of mental cripples," Deng pushed for reform of universities. Intellectuals responded to the more open atmosphere with a spate of new magazines and a new frankness in literature. In 1978 the Democracy Wall in Beijing attracted a wide variety of self-expression until it was shut down the following spring.

Television coverage was extensive in 1979 when Deng Xiaoping visited the United States and discussed deepening commercial and cultural ties between the United States and China. The need to modernize was also brought home that year when the People's Liberation Army did poorly in its invasion of Vietnam (in retaliation for Vietnam's invasion of Cambodia). In 1980, with Deng Xiaoping's sponsorship, the first Special Economic Zone was created at Shenzhen, just across the border from Hong Kong. By the early

1980s China was crowded with foreign visitors. Thousands of western teachers were brought to China especially to teach English and other foreign languages. Christian churches reopened, as did Buddhist and Daoist temples. People began wearing more varied colors, giving the streets a very different look from China in the 1960s.

Economic restructuring placed many party cadres in positions where corruption was easy and tempting—they were the ones to supervise distribution or sale of state and collective assets. Between 1983 and 1986 some forty thousand party members were expelled for corruption, and in 1987 the number reached one hundred nine thousand.

Not everyone in the party was happy with the rapid changes or the new interest young people were taking in the West. In 1983 the party launched a campaign against "spiritual pollution" to warn against overenthusiasm for things western. After political unrest at several universities in 1986, the party revived a campaign from the early 1960s to "learn from Lei Feng," a model of the selfless party member devoted to advancing China's development. Still, an even bigger political protest movement occurred in 1989, with huge demonstrations at Beijing's Tiananmen Square (see Color Plate 30). After its bloody suppression, the 48 million party members had to submit self-evaluations in order to weed out sympathizers. About 1 million were sent to the countryside to learn from the masses.

By the early 1990s, the collapse of communism in eastern Europe and the Soviet Union added to Deng Xiaoping's determination to persist in economic reform. In Deng's view, the Soviet Union broke up because central planning had not produced prosperity. To show his support for market reforms in 1992 Deng went south to visit the Special Economic Zones. He told people not to worry if policies were capitalist or socialist, only whether they would make China more prosperous. Soon the party constitution was rewritten to describe China as a "socialist market economy" and to declare "the essential nature of socialism" to be "to liberate and develop productive forces." Joint ventures grew more and more common in the 1990s, with businessmen from Hong Kong, Taiwan, and South Korea especially active. Local elections that allowed people to elect some of their leaders were changing the nature of political participation.

By the time Deng died in 1997, it was clear that China's rapid economic growth was not a simple success story. In many places, plans had been too ambitious, and new buildings stood vacant. The efforts to privatize the huge state-owned factories had led to massive layoffs and rarely turned the enterprises profitable. Many levels of government were out of money and failed to pay their workers for months. In rural areas, cadres often supported themselves by levying taxes and fees, sparking protests by farmers.

By the year 2000, there were some 63 million party members, about 83 percent of whom were male, half high school graduates or better, and about 6 percent members of minorities. Corruption remained a major problem. In 1998 alone, twenty-two thousand seven hundred cases of abuse of power were brought before the courts. The scale was sometimes staggering. In 2000 fourteen corrupt officials embezzled about $60 million in the funds for resettling those displaced by the Three Gorges Dam. That same year nearly two hundred officials accepted bribes to help a Fujian magnate escape tariffs of nearly $10 billion.

RESTRUCTURING THE ECONOMY

Deng Xiaoping's economic policies set in motion an economic boom that led to the quadrupling of average incomes by 2000. Overall poverty declined sharply. According to the World Bank's statistics, the proportion of the rural population below the poverty line fell from 33 percent in 1976 to 6.5 percent in 1995 (or from 262 million to 65 million). Life expectancy has continued to rise (to sixty-eight for men and seventy-one for women in 2000), as has the average height of Chinese, both reflecting improvements in nutrition.

Encouraging Capitalist Tendencies

In the countryside the most important reform was the dismantling of collective agriculture. In the early 1980s Deng Xiaoping instituted a "responsibility system," under which rural households bid for land and other assets that they could treat as their own (though legally held on leases of up to fifty years). In turn they agreed to provide the team with specified crops in exchange for use of particular fields; whatever the household produced above what it owed the team was its to keep or sell. Sideline enterprises like growing vegetables and raising pigs or chickens were encouraged, as were small businesses of all sorts, ranging from fish farming and equipment repair to small factories producing consumer goods for export. Rural industry boomed. By 1995 township and village enterprises employed 125 million workers. Especially in the coastal provinces, where commercial opportunities were greatest, the income of farmers rapidly increased.

Deng Xiaoping abandoned Mao's insistence on self-sufficiency and began courting foreign investors. Special Economic Zones were created—the best known were Shenzhen on the border with Hong Kong and Pudong, across the Huangpu River from Shanghai. These zones offered incentives to foreign firms, including low taxes, new plants, and a well-trained but cheap labor force. China had to bring its legal system more into line with international standards to court these foreign investors, but the payoff was substantial since joint ventures pumped a lot of capital into the Chinese economy.

Foreign manufacturers were attracted to the low labor costs in China, and both set up factories to produce goods for the Chinese market (such as vehicles) and contracted with Chinese manufacturers to produce consumer goods for western markets (such as clothing, toys, watches, and bicycles). Guangdong, with the best access to the financial giant Hong Kong, did especially well in the new environment. Between 1982 and 1992, 97 percent of Hong Kong's thirty-two hundred toy factories relocated to Guangdong. By 1996 China was the world's largest garment maker, accounting for 16.7 percent of world garment exports. In 1997, it manufactured 1.55 billion shirts. The market for shoes too came to be dominated by China, which in 1998 made 6.3 billion pairs of leather shoes and about 1 billion pairs of sport shoes.

Shrinking the State Sector

During the 1980s and 1990s, those who worked for the state found that reform meant they could lose their jobs. Between 1990 and 2000 some 30 to 35 million workers were shed by state-owned enterprises, under pressure to become profitable. Still, few state enterprises found it easy to compete with private or collective enterprises. The mines run by the Ministry of Coal could not compete with the eighty thousand small mines operated by local governments or private individuals. By 1992 the ministry had a debt of 6 billion yuan and needed to lay off 1 million miners. More jobs had probably been created at the small mines, but those jobs lacked the benefits and pensions of the state jobs.

The province of Liaoning in northeast China can be taken as an example. In the 1990s about half of the 10 million people who worked in state-owned enterprises there lost their jobs. The mayor of Shenyang tried to find buyers for the city's bankrupt factories, but no one wanted to take on their obligations to retirees. The situation was even worse farther north. In the cities of Heilongjiang at the end of the 1990s, up to 60 percent of the urban population was either unemployed or not being paid. Bankrupt companies paid neither salaries nor pensions, but they were not dissolved because the government did not want to take over their obligations.

The military is another part of the state sector that has shrunk considerably. The PLA peaked at 4.75 million troops in 1981. Many were later moved to the People's Armed Police, a domestic force. By 2000, soldiers on active duty were thought to number about 2.5 million. The PLA also divested itself of many of the factories it owned and operated, even many of its military

Map **29.1**   **Population Density in China**

ones. Some factories that once produced tanks have been converted to produce buses or trucks; others have been abandoned.

Regional Disparities and Internal Migration

Deng Xiaoping announced early on that he was willing to tolerate growing inequalities, saying it was acceptable that "some get rich first." Because most of the industrial growth was in the coastal provinces, regional inequalities increased. (See Map 29.1.) Some regions of the country, especially ones far from good roads, remain extremely poor. In Shanxi province, the uplands are occupied by about 9 million people, a third of whom fall below the poverty line. In the late 1990s half the boys and most of the girls in this area did not attend school. About 80 percent of the adult women were illiterate.

When internal controls on migration collapsed in the early 1980s, the coastal regions were flooded with job seekers willing to live in shantytowns or a dozen to a room to get a chance to share in the wealth that the market economy was bringing to the fortunate regions. In the 1980s, about 10 million migrated to the dozen largest cities. In 1992 city authorities estimated that 100 million migrant laborers were working away from home or roaming China in search of work. Crime in cities grew, much of it blamed on migrants. In Guangdong, internal migrants, especially those who cannot speak Cantonese, have become an exploited class, hired for the worst work, kept on the job for ten or twelve hours a day, seven days a week, unable

Migrant Workers. China's rapid economic development has brought not only prosperity to the cities, but also millions of peasants looking for a better life. Those shown here in January 2004 sit beneath a billboard waiting to be hired. *(Agence France Presse/Getty Images)*

to protest without losing their jobs. In the 1990s, as newly unemployed workers from state factories took jobs migrants had previously taken, cities began to deport larger numbers of migrants back to the countryside.

For poorer areas in the countryside, the costs of dismantling the communes have been considerable. Health care has become harder for poor people to obtain. Communes had paid the so-called barefoot doctors. Their replacements, village doctors with little more education, now have to support themselves by charging high prices for the drugs they dispense, making antibiotics beyond the reach of many peasants. Diseases that had been under control, such as hookworm and tuberculosis, have made comebacks. When poor people fall ill, their families usually have to borrow money to put down a deposit before a hospital will admit them.

There has been some trickle-down effect from the booming areas to the poorer ones. The Pearl River Delta in Guangdong imports pigs and rice from Hunan and Sichuan, helping their economies. The millions of migrant laborers from those provinces also help, sending home whatever they can spare from their wages. Yet it is often the poorer areas that are most pressed by cadres. In 1998 and 1999 peasant riots were common in Hunan, protesting the imposition of new fees and taxes by local officials.

Consumer Culture

In the early 1980s, although people began to have more disposable income, there was not yet much to buy, even in city department stores, which were well stocked with thermos bottles and inflatable children's toys but not the TVs and tape recorders customers wanted. By the 1990s all this had changed. Disposable income of urban households steadily increased, and more and more factories were turning out consumer goods. Like people elsewhere in the world, Chinese bought TVs, stereos, clothes, furniture, air conditioners, and washing machines. Shopping streets of major cities abound-

An Evening Out in Shanghai. On a Friday night in February 2002, people flock to the pedestrian-only streets of downtown Shanghai to shop, dine, and enjoy the streets. *(Bob Krist/Corbis)*

ed in well-stocked stores, with imported as well as domestically produced goods. Between 1986 and 1995, the number of refrigerators per hundred households went from 62 to 98 in Beijing, 47 to 98 in Shanghai, and 14 to 83 in Xi'an. Acquisition of washing machines made similar gains. Telephone service lagged, but Chinese responded eagerly when pagers and cellular phones became available. By 2000 there were 26 million cellular phones in China. By then there were also 8 million Internet users, with sales of personal computers ranging around 3 million per year.

In the 1990s many grew rich enough to buy imported cars, build lavish houses, and make generous gifts to all the officials they dealt with. In 1978 there had not been a single privately owned car in China; by 1993 there were over 1 million, and the number was increasing by 12 percent a year. In 1995 the government announced plans to increase car production so that by 2005 every family could own a car.

Consumer culture also came to the countryside, though there it is limited by the much lower level of disposable income. In the 1980s, as farm incomes grew, farmers began building new homes, buying better food, and purchasing consumer goods such as TVs, furniture, and clothing. Villages without electricity built small local generators. With migrant workers bringing home knowledge of city life and with television bringing everyone images of modern living, families in the countryside steadily added to the list of goods they considered essential. Chinese, like people in more developed countries, were identifying more with the goods they consumed than with politics.

SOCIAL AND CULTURAL CHANGES
Education

Education at all levels had deteriorated during the Cultural Revolution, when it was considered more important to be red than expert. An important symbolic reversal of these policies occurred in 1977 with the reinstitution of college entrance examinations. Soon those graduating from college could also apply to study abroad in Europe, the United States, or Japan, which led to a craze for studying foreign languages. In the 1990s there were as many as one hundred thousand studying in the United States at any given time.

Only a tiny proportion of Chinese reached college, however. In the 1980s there was room for only a quarter of the elementary school students to continue to middle schools, and room for only 2 percent to enter college. In the cities, the competition for middle school and college places put children under great pressure.

Educational opportunities had always been better in the cities than in the countryside, and in the 1990s the disparity seemed to grow. During the Cultural Revolution, when the educated were ousted from their jobs, teaching positions were filled by peasant teachers paid like other workers on the commune through workpoints (redeemable largely in shares of the commune's grain). With the dismantling of the communes in the early 1980s, other ways had to be found to pay teachers. The most common method was to charge parents fees, which could run 200 to 300 yuan per year for elementary school and as high as 1,000 yuan per year for middle and high school, too much for most peasants. Sometimes rural schools tried to make ends meet by having the students work, peddling apples on the streets or assembling firecrackers in their classrooms. By the end of the 1990s, universities were also charging fees, generally about 10,000 yuan per year. Like medical care, education came to be priced beyond the means of many people, especially in rural areas.

The Arts

During the decade of the Cultural Revolution, intellectuals learned to keep quiet, and ordinary people were fed a dull and repetitive diet of highly politicized stories, plays, and films. With

Cui Jian in Concert. Chinese rock star Cui Jian performs with his band for an audience of more than three thousand at New York City's Central Park on August 8, 1999. *(Getty Images)*

the downfall of the Gang of Four, people's pent-up desire for more varied and lively cultural expression quickly became apparent. A literature of the "wounded" appeared at the end of the 1970s, once those who had suffered during the Cultural Revolution found it politically possible to write of their experiences. Greater tolerance on the part of the government soon resulted in much livelier media, with everything from investigative reporters exposing corruption of cadres, to philosophers who tried to reexamine the premises of Marxism, to novelists, poets, and filmmakers who experimented with previously taboo treatments of sexuality.

Television as a cultural force expanded enormously as TV sets became a readily available consumer good and programming became diverse enough to capture people's interest. China severely restricted the showing of foreign films in theaters, but people still saw them because VCRs or DVD players became common and the pirating of videotapes and DVDs made them inexpensive. Western music of all sorts found fans, and China developed its own rock bands capable of filling a stadium for their shows. Cinema reached new artistic heights and found a large audience abroad as well as in China (see **Material Culture: China's New Cinema**).

Gender Roles

The Communist Party, from its beginnings in the 1920s, had espoused equality for women, and women were eligible to join the party on the same terms as men. Moreover, the party pushed for reforms in marriage practice that were generally seen as improving women's situations, such as giving them the right to initiate divorce. The reality never came up to the level of the rhetoric, but women did play more active roles in the revolution than they had in earlier eras of Chinese history.

After 1949 official rhetoric encouraged people to think of men and women as equal. With collectivization, women were mobilized to participate in farm work, and efforts were made to get girls enrolled in schools. Images of tough women who could do jobs traditionally done by men were part of everyday propaganda. Women did increase their presence in many jobs; the proportion of elementary school teachers who were women increased from 18 percent in 1951 to 36 percent in 1975, and continued to increase in the reform era to 49 percent in 1998.

When western scholars were first able to do research in China in the early 1980s, it was not the advances women had made that struck them most forcefully, but how far the reality lagged behind the rhetoric. Girls and women were certainly more visible outside their homes than their counterparts had been in the nineteenth century, but men still occupied most positions of power and the better-paid jobs. In rural areas, the work points women earned by working for the collective were given to the family head, not to them as individuals. The reform era seemed at that point to be taking things backward. With

fees charged by elementary schools, poorer families did not send their daughters to school for as long as their sons. New opportunities opened up by the expanding economy favored males. Young men could join construction companies and do relatively well-paid work far from home; young women could work in textile, electronic, and toy factories for lower wages. For those who did not want to leave their hometowns, employment patterns were also skewed by gender. The women often did the fieldwork while the men got the better-paid skilled work.

In the cities girls were more likely to stay in school as long as boys did, but once the state withdrew from the hiring process, their degrees were worth less. New female graduates of high schools or colleges tended not to get jobs that were as good as the ones their male classmates got, something that happened less frequently when state bureaus made job assignments. The decline in the state-owned factories has hurt both men and women, but women complain that they are the first to be laid off.

Population Control and the One-Child Family

From 1957 to 1970 China's population grew from about 630 million to 880 million. Public health measures promoted in the 1950s deserve much of the credit for reducing the death rate and thus improving life expectancy, which increased dramatically from forty years in 1953 to sixty in 1968 and sixty-five in 1984. As a consequence, population growth accelerated, and even the horrible famine of 1959–1962 could make only a temporary dent in its upward course. Mao had opposed the idea that China could have too many people, but by the time Mao died, China's population was approaching 1 billion, and his successors recognized that China could not afford to postpone bringing it under control.

Since the late 1970s, the government has worked hard to promote the one-child family in the cities and the one- or two-child family in the countryside. Targets were set for the total numbers of births in each place and quotas then

MATERIAL CULTURE

China's New Cinema

During the Mao period, feature films were produced by state-run studios under the Ministry of Culture. Particularly during the Cultural Revolution, most movies had predictable plots and stereotyped characterizations, and even within China would not have had much of an audience except for the lack of other forms of entertainment and distribution of free tickets. After the graduation of a new generation of directors from the Beijing Film Academy, beginning in 1982, films of high artistic level began to be made, and by the 1990s Chinese films were regularly screened at international film festivals. Heart-wrenching, visually stunning melodramas like *Ju Dou* (1990), *Raise the Red Lantern* (1991), and *Farewell My Concubine* (1993) often ran afoul of censors at home but found appreciative audiences abroad. Some of these movies dramatized a long sweep of modern Chinese history, as did some quieter, less exoticized movies like *Blue Kite* (1993) and *To Live* (1994). The actress Gong Li starred in enough of these movies to gain fans around the world.

During the 1990s, Chinese filmmakers produced around fifteen hundred films, perhaps a dozen of which were widely circulated abroad. Standards of quality continued to improve, and by the late 1990s, even movies made primarily for Chinese urban audiences were gaining international audiences. *Shower* (1999), a comedy about ordinary people with no exotic past or political turmoil, won both the best picture and best director awards at the Seattle International Film Festival. *Not One Less* (2000) succeeded with children from a remote area as its main characters.

Searching Through the City. The thirteen-year old heroine of the film *Not One Less* had to figure out how to find a ten-year old boy in a large city she had never visited before. *(Kobal/The Picture Desk)*

assigned to smaller units. Young people needed permission from their work units to get married, then permission to have a child. In the early 1980s, women who got pregnant outside the plan faced often unrelenting pressure from birth control workers and local cadres to have abortions. In the 1990s, the campaign was relaxed a little, making it easier for families with only daughters to try again for a son.

The preference for boys remains so strong that China faces a shortage of young women in coming decades as female fetuses are more likely to be aborted (after being identified by ultrasound) and girl babies are more likely to be made available for adoption. In the mid-1990s China quietly began to allow unwanted children, primarily baby girls, to be adopted by foreigners, and by the end of the century, more orphans were adopted from China into the United States than from any other country.

Almost no one questions that China needs to limit population growth. The 2000 census reported a population of 1.27 billion (excluding Taiwan and Hong Kong, or 1.3 billion with them). Population control policies are not without consequences, however. By the 1990s, with increased prosperity, people talked about the pampered only children in the cities, whose parents would take them to western fast food restaurants and pay for all sorts of enrichment experiences. Not only will this generation grow up without siblings, but their children will have no aunts and uncles. Planners are already worrying about how they will take care of their aging parents, since one young couple could well have four elderly parents to support (see **Documents: Supporting the Rural Elderly**).

Family Life

Both changing gender roles and population control policies have had an impact on family organization and family dynamics. So too have many other policies put into effect by the government since 1949. Ancestor worship, lineages, and solidarity with patrilineal kin were all discouraged as feudal practices. The authority of family heads declined as collectives took over property and allocated labor. As both women and children spent much more time away from the home, the family became less central in their lives. Coerced marriages became less common, and in the cities at least, people did in fact choose their own spouses much of the time.

The reform era has not turned the clock back on these changes in family structure and authority. Scholars who have studied families in rural areas have shown that although patrilineal stem families are still quite common—the newly married couple living with or very near the husband's family—the older couple has much less power over the younger one. Even in the countryside the younger couple is likely to have decided to marry on their own and seek a companionate marriage. They may extract a hefty bride price from the husband's family, but use it to purchase things they want for their home. If a new house is built or an extension added, they will work hard to give themselves more privacy. Although the older couple may push for grandsons, the younger couple often are quite comfortable with birth control policies, happy with only one or two children, even if they are daughters. They are more concerned with the happiness of their nuclear family than with family continuity. Although divorce is still very rare in the countryside, women believe that the ability to threaten divorce gives them more voice in family decision making.

CRITICAL VOICES

From early in the reform period, people found ways to express political criticism. The first "big character" posters were pasted on Democracy Wall in Beijing in the fall of 1978. Many of those who participated were blue-collar workers with high school educations, and Deng gave them his blessing. Soon a twenty-eight-year-old electrician named Wei Jingshen courageously pasted up a call for the "fifth modernization":

What is true democracy? Only when the people themselves choose representatives to manage

DOCUMENTS

Supporting the Rural Elderly

Under Mao, scholars at universities and research institutes published relatively little, some finding the required Marxist frameworks too stifling, some wary that in the next campaign, something they wrote could be held against them. In the more open atmosphere of the 1980s and 1990s, social science disciplines were revived, and scholars analyzed Chinese society and its problems in depth.

In 1997 the Chinese journal Population Research *devoted an issue to the problem of caring for the elderly in rural areas, where traditionally people had depended on their sons to provide for them. Not only were people having fewer sons, but in the changing economy, sons were not always able or willing to provide support to their aging parents. Xu Qin, the author of the article excerpted below, stressed that the current problem will only grow worse unless the state intervenes.*

In China, a social security system has been set up only in the cities, and three-fourths of the elderly, who live in the rural areas, are almost entirely dependent on family support. . . . Respecting, loving, and supporting the elderly are traditional virtues of the Chinese nation. Since the recent reforms [1978–], however, the number of disputes over support for the elderly handled by judicial courts at all levels has risen each year, and family eldercare is becoming an increasingly salient social problem. According to a report in the *China Journal for the Elderly,* relevant units in Shanxi province have received and handled more than twenty thousand complaints from the elderly in the last four years, and Shanghai city is handling six thousand such cases every year. . . . Most of

the elderly failing to obtain support were those in the high-age bracket, the sickly, those who had no income and no spouses, and those who lived in the rural areas.

The majority of China's elderly live with their sons, but today most rural households are managed by daughters-in-law, and the relationship between mothers- and daughters-in-law has a direct bearing on eldercare. Since women have begun to participate in the labor force, they now have their own incomes and have become financially independent. Their status in the family has accordingly risen, and the relationship between mothers- and daughters-in-law increasingly favors the latter. But since the current law does not specify that daughters-in-law have the duty to support their par-

affairs in accordance with their will and interests can we speak of democracy. Furthermore, the people must have the power to replace these representatives at any time in order to prevent them from abusing their powers to oppress the people. Is this possible? The citizens of Europe and the United States enjoy just this kind of democracy and could run people like Nixon, de Gaulle, and

Tanaka out of office when they wished and can even reinstate them if they want to, for no one can interfere with their democratic rights. In China, however, if a person so much as comments on the now-deceased "Great Helmsman" or "Great Man peerless in history" Mao Zedong, the mighty prison gates and all kinds of unimaginable misfortunes await him. If we compare the ents-in-law, arbitration is difficult when cases arise of daughters-in-law refusing to support the elderly.

The new generation of young people in rural areas have the advantage of better educations, so that their role in production is greater than that of the older generation. The declining role of the rural elderly in production, plus the fact that they were unable to accumulate any wealth before the rural reforms, has resulted in a lowering of their authority in the family. They have gradually lost control over their children providing for them; they find it increasingly difficult to resolve conflicts among their children, and frequently become scapegoats in fights among them. . . . Village cadres in charge of work related to old-age issues say that family disputes have to be resolved within three days of being reported, otherwise the elderly will have no food on the table. . . .

Currently, the state has taken a number of measures to solve the problem of family eldercare in rural areas: (1) it has launched activities for signing agreements on supporting the elderly; (2) it has promulgated the Protection Law for the Elderly and is implementing family eldercare through social intervention consisting of both ideological work and legal means; and (3) the state has begun to set up an old-age insurance system in the countryside. However, there are limitations to all of these measures. To begin with, there are no departments with authority to implement the "Eldercare Agreements." . . . Second, although the Old-Age Law has been promulgated, substantial limitations exist in the use of legal means to handle problems of family eldercare. Judicial departments have found in the course of practice that investigations and obtaining evidence are difficult, and enforcement is even more difficult when they try to resolve disputes related to family support. Last but not least, the weak economic foundations in the rural areas are a major hindrance to forming a rural old-age insurance system. . . .

On September 25, 1980, the Central Committee of the Chinese Communist Party made public the "Open Letter to All Members of the Communist Party and the Communist Youth League Concerning the Matter of Controlling China's Population Growth" and advocated that each couple should have one child. The "Open Letter" also pointed out: "Forty years after implementing the system of one child per couple, some families may be faced with a lack of persons in the family to take care of the elderly. This problem exists in many countries and we should pay attention to seeking solutions." The birth rate has fallen since then, and, with the coming of an aging society, the state should make good on its promise.

Source: From *Chinese Sociology and Anthropology* 34:2 (2002), 75–80, slightly modified.

---

socialist system of "democratic centralism" with the "exploiting class democracy" of capitalism, the difference is as clear as night and day.[1]

Wei was soon to know those prison gates from personal experience. By April 1979 he had been arrested and Democracy Wall shut down. Wei spent most of his time from then on in prison, with long stretches in solitary confinement, until he was exiled to the United States in 1997.

Wei's fate did not deter intellectuals from speaking up. In 1986 the physicist Fang Lizhi

1. Wm. Theodore De Bary and Richard Lufrano, *Sources of Chinese Tradition: From 1600 Through the Twentieth Century* (New York: Columbia University Press, 2000), p. 498.

told students that the socialist movement "from Marx and Lenin to Stalin and Mao Zedong, has been a failure" and advocated adopting the western political system.[2] That year students at one hundred fifty campuses demanded greater freedom, less corruption, and better living conditions in their dormitories. After the protests were suppressed, Deng had party secretary general Hu Yaobang dismissed from his post because he had been too conciliatory toward the students.

Debate about China's cultural and political form reached a large audience in the spring and summer of 1988 with a six-part TV documentary, *River Elegy*. It traced many of China's problems back to its ancient traditions, especially its persistent inward orientation and disinterest in the outside world. *River Elegy* attacked some of the country's most revered symbols, relabeling the Yellow River, the Great Wall, and the dragon as symbols of backward passivity, not greatness. It argued that China should move toward the outward-looking Blue Ocean civilization and away from the conservative Yellow River one.

The following spring, huge student protests erupted in Beijing. The students' protest began modestly in April with a parade honoring the memory of a recently deceased Hu Yaobang, viewed as the strongest voice in the government for political reform. Buoyed by the positive reaction of the Beijing citizenry, student leaders gradually escalated their activities and their rallying cries. They called for more democratic government: Make officials disclose their income and assets! Renounce the use of mass political campaigns! Abolish prohibitions against street protests! Permit journalists to report protest activities! End corruption! Many evoked the ideas of the May Fourth movement, claiming that China had still not achieved science and democracy. When Deng Xiaoping called the students' actions "counterrevolutionary turmoil,"

they did not tone down their rhetoric. When the momentum seemed to be flagging, a couple of thousand students staged a hunger strike to testify to their sincerity and determination.

On May 17, 1989, with the international press present to cover the visit of the Soviet premier Gorbachev, Tiananmen Square was filled not merely with students from every university in Beijing, but also from other organizations, even government ones like the Foreign Ministry, the Central Television Station, the National Men's Volleyball Team, even the Public Security Bureau Academy. There were workers in their work clothes, holding banners inscribed with the names of their factories. The formation of the Beijing Autonomous Workers Federation was announced with calls for democracy and an end to the "lawlessness and brutality of corrupt officials."

The students themselves had no experience with democracy, and the leaders who emerged often disagreed on the best tactics. Chai Ling, a female student, was one of the most zealous of the leaders. She told an American reporter in late May that she hoped for bloodshed, because the Chinese people would not open their eyes until the government brazenly butchered the people. She complained about other leaders who were talking to government officials in the hope that violence could be avoided. She claimed to feel sad that she could not tell the other students "straight out that we must use our blood and our lives to wake up the people."[3]

The public's support for the students was a humiliation to Deng and the other leaders, who declared martial law as soon as Gorbachev left and dismissed the more conciliatory Zhao Ziyang. Yet when truckloads of troops attempted to enter the city, the citizens in Beijing took to the streets to stop them. Successful against these unarmed soldiers, they were exhilarated by this evidence of "people power." On May 30 demonstrators unveiled a plaster statue of the Goddess of Democracy made by art stu-

2. Richard Baum, *Burying Mao: Chinese Politics in the Age of Deng Xiaoping* (Princeton, N.J.: Princeton University Press, 1994), p. 201.

3. Geremie Barmé, *In the Red* (New York: Columbia University Press, 1999), p. 329.

dents. Just a few days later, on June 3–4, seasoned troops were brought into central Beijing through underground tunnels, and tanks and artillery soon followed. Many unarmed citizens still tried to halt their advance, but the armored vehicles got through the blockades after bloody clashes and successfully ended both the protest and the occupation of the square. At least several hundred people lost their lives that night, many of them ordinary citizens trying to stop the soldiers from entering central Beijing.

Demonstrations against the government suppression of the Tiananmen protestors erupted in several other cities. In Chengdu, rioting led to martial law and dozens of deaths. In Shanghai a train ran into demonstrators trying to stop it. Huge rallies were held in Hong Kong. All around the world people expressed shock and outrage. Yet to party hard-liners, this bloody suppression was essential because the entire power structure was in jeopardy. In their view, allowing nonparty forces to interject themselves into the decision-making process was a greater threat to stability than corruption was. Soon Deng and the hard-liners followed up the initial military seizure of the square with the arrest and sentencing of hundreds of participants and other dissidents. Thousands of party members were expelled from the party for sympathizing with the students.

Suppression of this movement, coupled with compulsory political study classes at universities, kept political discussion subdued within China for the next several years. In the 1990s, no single issue united critics of the government. The plight of workers has prompted some to try to organize workers facing unsafe conditions or not being paid (see **Biography: Li Qiang, Labor Activist**). The government was more alarmed by the political potential of a school of Qigong teachings. Until then, the government had pointed with pride to the elderly who early each morning could be seen in parks practicing the stretching and balancing exercises called Qigong, believed to nurture the practitioners' *qi* (vital energy). Masters of Qigong often attributed all sorts of powers to their techniques. In

the 1990s one such teacher, Li Hongzhi, developed Falun Gong, a form of Qigong that drew on both Buddhist and Daoist ideas and promised practitioners good health and other benefits. Many from the party and PLA, as well as their wives and mothers, were attracted to this system of knowledge beyond the understanding of western science. When in 1999 Li organized fifteen thousand followers to assemble outside the party leaders' residential complex in Beijing to ask for recognition of his teachings, the top leadership became alarmed and not only outlawed the sect but also arrested thousands of members and sent them for reeducation. The potential of Falun Gong to reach the masses and offer an alternative to the party was seen as particularly threatening.

During the 1990s Chinese living abroad raised some of the bluntest critical voices. They publicized abuses in the legal system, such as long detentions without being charged and the use of torture to extract confessions. It is also largely activists outside China who have drawn attention to the looming crisis in China's ecology. Encouraging small rural factories has led to serious pollution problems as paper mills, chemical plants, and tanneries dump their wastes in rivers. The air quality in many large cities is very poor. In the north, so much water has been taken from the Yellow River that it runs dry for longer and longer periods each year. So much water gets brought up from underground that the water table is dropping steadily in many places. In the Yangzi region, floods have gotten worse because of tree cutting and soil erosion in recent years. Development projects of all sorts have led to the paving over of more and more arable land, leading to questions about how China will be able to feed its growing population in the decades to come. Environmentalists have been especially critical of the 600-foot-tall Three Gorges Dam project on the Yangzi River, which has required the displacement of more than 1 million people and will flood nearly 400 square miles (632 square kilometers) with more than a hundred towns.

BIOGRAPHY Li Qiang, Labor Activist

Li Qiang was born in 1973 in a small city in Sichuan. After his father died when he was eleven years old, the family had a hard time surviving on his mother's wages as a worker in the Second Construction Company. He had to quit school at age fourteen, but unable to find a job, spent much of his time reading. Li, at age sixteen, was energized by the 1989 Democracy Movement and even gave a speech in front of the city hall on justice and social inequality.

In his readings, Li had learned how the Communists in the 1920s had organized workers, and he thought workers still needed that sort of organization. In the spring of 1990, he put up unsigned big character posters calling for the right to set up independent unions. Also that spring he wrote a letter to Jiang Zemin, China's president, describing his family's plight with his mother in the hospital with hepatitis. His letter brought results. A provincial party official saw to it that his mother's medical bills were paid and a temporary job was found for Li. At the same time, the local public security office discovered that he was the author of the big character posters. He was questioned and his home searched, but they could find no evidence that he had listened to the Voice of America or had foreign contacts.

From July 1990 to December 1991, Li worked in an office for his mother's company, arranging housing for employees. The unfairness of the system angered him when he discovered that the senior cadres often had two apartments while people like his mother, who had worked there over twenty years, still did not have one. He persuaded many maltreated workers to sign letters of complaint. Not surprisingly, he was soon fired.

By this point Li had studied enough to get admitted to college and for the next two years studied law and political science. After leaving school, Li took a job in sales with a trading company, where he made a lot of money during the next two and a half years. In his spare time, he gave legal assistance to laid-off workers.

In February 1997 Li heard that an unemployed worker was planning to immolate himself in front of the city hall. The worker, over forty years old, had a wife and child and saw no hope for himself or his family. Although the worker was dragged away after pouring gasoline over himself, Li felt compelled to do something and became a full-time labor organizer. Over the next six months, he organized rallies and protests by workers at several factories as well as taxi and pedicab drivers. In December 1997 he was arrested and questioned for hours. When released the next day, he fled to Shanghai.

For the next couple of years, Li worked underground, moving from city to city, organizing strikes, protests, and demonstrations. For a while in 1999 he worked in a joint-venture factory in Shenzhen to document the long hours and inhuman treatment of workers. Fearful of being apprehended, by 2001 he had left China for the United States, where he continued to work for Chinese workers' right to set up independent unions.

TAIWAN

In 1949, when the victory of the Communist Party in the civil war seemed imminent, Chiang Kaishek and large parts of the Nationalist government and army evacuated to the island of Taiwan, less than a hundred miles off the coast of Fujian province. Taiwan had been under Japanese colonial rule from 1895 to 1945 and

Comparisons of China, Taiwan, and Other Countries				
Country	GDP per Capita (in U.S. dollars)	Life Expectancy (years)	Literacy Rate	Fertility Rate
United States	35,831	77.2	97%	2.1
Japan	24,848	80.2	99	1.4
Taiwan	17,255	76.5	94	1.8
China	3,535	71.6	82	1.8
India	2,136	62.8	52	3.0
Vietnam	1,931	69.5	94	2.5

Source: World Factbook, 2002.

had only recently been returned to Chinese rule. The initial encounter between the local population and the Nationalist government had been hostile: in 1947 the government responded to protests against the corruption of its politicians by shooting at protesters and pursuing suspected leaders, killing, it is estimated, eight thousand to ten thousand people, including many local leaders. In part because of the support the United States gave Chiang and his government as the Cold War in Asia intensified, the Nationalists soon stabilized their government and were able to concentrate on economic development. After Chiang Kaishek died in 1975, he was succeeded by his son Chiang Chingkuo (Jiang Jingguo). During his presidency in the late 1980s, Taiwan succeeded in making the transition from one-party rule to parliamentary democracy.

During the 1950s and 1960s, the United States treated Chiang's Republic of China as the legitimate government of China and insisted that it occupy China's seat at the United Nations. When relations between the United States and the PRC were normalized in the 1970s, Taiwan's position became anomalous. The United States and the PRC agreed that there was only one China and Taiwan was a part of China. The United States maintained that any unification of China should come by peaceful means and continued military aid to Taiwan. China insisted that countries that wanted embassies in Beijing had to eliminate their embassies in Taiwan. As China joined more

and more international organizations, Taiwan was frequently forced out.

This loss of political standing has not prevented Taiwan from becoming an economic power. In 2002 Taiwan's per capita income for its 22 million citizens was about $17,000, placing it next after Japan in Asia and way beyond China. Several factors contributed to this extraordinary economic growth. The Nationalists started with the advantage of Japanese land reform and industrial development. They also benefited from considerable foreign investment over the next couple of decades, especially from the United States and Japan. But hard work and thoughtful planning also deserve credit for Taiwan's growth. The Taiwan government gave real authority to those with technical training. Economists and engineers, including many trained abroad, became heads of ministries. Through the 1950s, emphasis was placed on import substitution, especially by building up light industry to produce consumer goods. The 1960s saw a shift toward export-oriented industries, especially electronics, as Taiwan began to try to follow along behind Japan, moving into stereos and televisions as Japan moved into cars. In 1966 the first tax-free export processing zone was set up, attracting foreign capital and technology. By the 1980s, there was adequate wealth in Taiwan to develop capital-intensive industries such as steel and petrochemicals.

Over the past fifteen or more years, there has been increasing contact between Chinese in

Taiwan and the PRC. In 1987, when Taiwan lifted restrictions on travel, thousands of people from Taiwan visited the mainland. In 1992, 24.11 million items of mail passed between the two countries, 14.72 million phone calls were placed, and 62,000 telegrams delivered. The scale of Taiwan's investment in its giant neighbor has been a staggering $70 billion since 1987. In the early 2000s, nearly 1 million Chinese from Taiwan were living on the mainland, roughly 400,000 of them in and around Shanghai. This movement reflects the relocation of Taiwan's semiconductor and personal computer manufacturing plants to the mainland, where wages are much lower. In 2003, for the first time since 1949, charter planes carried Taiwanese home for the Lunar New Year holidays direct from Shanghai or Fujian to Taibei.

In 1996 Taiwan held its first open elections for the presidency and the National Assembly. In 2000, the Nationalist Party lost the general election for the first time, and Chen Shuibian of the Democratic Progressive Party (a party long associated with Taiwan independence) was elected president.

CHINA IN THE WORLD

After China split with the Soviet Union in the early 1960s, China severely limited its contacts with the rest of the world. It provided some assistance to African countries and to Maoist revolutionary groups, but had too great a fear of spies to encourage people to maintain ties with relatives abroad. All of this changed after Mao's death. China sought entry into international organizations, invited overseas Chinese to visit and participate in China's development, and began sending its officials on trips around the world.

It took a while for China to readjust its foreign policy. In the 1970s it supported the murderous Khmer Rouge government in Cambodia and was incensed when Vietnam invaded Cambodia. In February 1979 Deng Xiaoping ordered the army to invade Vietnam to pressure it to withdraw from Cambodia. Despite absorbing large numbers of casualties, China failed in its objectives and soon withdrew.

In the 1980s, China worked to improve its relationship with western countries, partly to reduce the threat from the Soviet Union. After the collapse of the Soviet Union, when the United States emerged as the sole superpower, China was less worried about Russian aggression, but more worried about possible independence movements among the Muslims in Chinese Central Asia. Although the United States remained a key economic partner, importing vast quantities of goods from China, China rarely supported its foreign policies and found its military might threatening.

In 1984 the British government agreed to return Hong Kong to China when the ninety-nine-year lease on the New Territories expired in 1997. China had made no attempt to take Hong Kong in 1949 and had benefited from indirect trade through Hong Kong since then, but as it took a larger role in the world, China was ready to take over Hong Kong, though it promised to let it maintain its own political and economic system for fifty years. During the 1990s, the professional and business elites of Hong Kong tried to make sure that they had alternative places to go if China imposed too draconian an order on Hong Kong, but during the first few years after the transfer, life in Hong Kong continued much as before.

To help expand its economy, China joined the World Bank, the International Monetary Fund, and the Asian Development Bank, which offered both low interest loans and various types of technical and economic advice, but also required that China report its economic situation more openly. In 2001 China was admitted to the World Trade Organization and succeeded in its bid for hosting the 2008 Summer Olympics. China's goal for so long—recognition as one of the great nations of the world—seemed finally within its grasp.

SUMMARY

How different is China early in the twenty-first century than it was at the death of Mao more than a quarter-century earlier? In the more modernized coastal provinces, the standard of living is much higher. Knowledge of the outside world is much more extensive. Inequalities are also more extreme: some Chinese have grown fabulously wealthy, while others have not been able to find work or cannot afford to send their children to school or pay for medical care. The party is no longer as dominated by a single person as forms of collective leadership have been developed, and leaders now can rise as much because of their technical expertise as their political fervor. Nevertheless, the Communist Party still dominates the government and has its hands in much of what goes on in the country. The Chinese state does not interfere in everyday affairs to the extent it used to, but it still has tremendous coercive force.

SUGGESTED READING

Post-Mao changes are considered in R. Baum, *Burying Mao: Chinese Politics in the Age of Deng Xiaoping* (1994). For specific dimensions of the politics and economics of the reform era, see S. Lubman, *Bird in a Cage: Legal Reform in China After Mao* (1999); D. Solinger, *Contesting Citizenship in Urban China: Peasant Migrants, the State and the Logic of the Market* (1999); C. Ikels, *The Return of the God of Wealth* (1996); M. Yang, *Gifts, Favors, and Banquets: The Art of Social Relationships in China* (1994); and V. Smil, *China's Environmental Crisis* (1993). Well-written journalists' accounts of China in the 1980s and 1990s include O. Schell, *Discos and Democracy: China in the Throes of Reform* (1989) and *The Mandate of Heaven* (1994); N. Kristof and S. WuDunn, *China Wakes: The Struggle for the Soul of a Rising Power* (1994); J. Starr, *Understanding China* (1997); and J. Becker, *The Chinese* (2000).

On the 1989 democracy movement, see M. Han, ed., *Cries for Democracy: Writings and Speeches from the 1989 Chinese Democracy Movement* (1990); L. Feigon, *China Rising: The Meaning of Tiananmen* (1990); and J. Wasserstrom and E. Perry, eds., *Popular Protest and Political Culture in Modern China: Learning from 1989* (1992).

On Chinese cinema in the post-Mao period, see J. Silbergeld, *China into Film: Frames of Reference in Contemporary Chinese Cinema* (1999), and S. Lu, ed., *Transnational Chinese Cinemas: Identity, Nationhood, Gender* (1997). Other facets of contemporary culture are treated in J. Lull, *China Turned On: Television, Reform, and Resistance* (1991); J. Zha, *China Pop: How Soap Operas, Tabloids, and Bestsellers Are Transforming a Culture* (1995); G. Barmé. *In the Red: On Contemporary Chinese Culture* (1999); P. Link, *Evening Chats in Beijing* (1992); J. Wang, *High Culture Fever: Politics, Aesthetics and Ideology in Deng's China* (1996); and D. Davis, ed., *The Consumer Revolution in Urban China* (2000).

Changes in the family and women's lives under the CCP are considered in M. Wolf, *Revolution Postponed: Women in Contemporary China* (1985); G. Hershatter and E. Honig, *Personal Voices: Chinese Women in the 1980's* (1988); W. Jankowiak, *Sex, Death, and Hierarchy in a Chinese City* (1993); E. Judd, *Gender and Power in Rural North China* (1994); T. Jacka, *Women's Work in Rural China: Change and Continuity in an Era of Reform* (1997); B. Entwisle and G. Henderson, *Re-Drawing Boundaries: Work, Households, and Gender in China* (2000); and Y. Yan, *Private Life Under Socialism: Love, Intimacy, and Family Change in a Chinese Village, 1949–1999* (2003). S. Brownell and J. Wasserstrom, *Chinese Femininities/Chinese Masculinities* (2002), also covers earlier periods, starting in late imperial.

Korea (1945 to the Present)

The liberation of Korea from Japanese rule was accompanied by an immediate division of the Korean peninsula in two. Stalin declared war against Japan, and Russian forces were the first to enter the Korean peninsula on August 8, 1945, six days before Japan surrendered to the United States. The United States rushed troops to Korea after the war ended on August 15, 1945, and won Soviet acquiescence to divide the peninsula at the 38th parallel to administer the surrender of Japanese forces. After Japan's defeat Soviet forces took over North Korea and U.S. forces South Korea. Korea has remained tragically divided to this day.

Both North and South formed two separate states in 1948, and the division was sealed by the bloody Korean War between 1950 and 1953, which left Korea divided at the demilitarized zone (DMZ) close to the 38th parallel. The race for superiority in military and economic strength began, but the threat of a resumption of hostilities was ever present.

Scholars have been concerned with a number of questions about this period. Was the division of Korea in 1945 simply a matter of foreign interference in Korea's affairs or an internal division? Were the leaders of North and South Korea puppets of the Soviet Union and the United States, respectively? Was the Korean War simply a North Korean act of aggression or the continuation of a civil conflict? What were the strengths and weaknesses of the North and South Korean economies? Did North Korean communism differ in any ways from Stalinist dictatorship? What were the strengths and weaknesses of South Korean developmentalism? What forces created dictatorship in South Korea under U.S. hegemony, and democracy in 1987? How successful was the U.S. role in Korea after 1945? What are the chances for Korean reunification?

LIBERATION AND NATIONAL DIVISION (1945–1949)

After liberation on August 15, 1945, both the Russians and the Americans were greeted by a spontaneous organization of people's committees (PCs) at the local level. These PCs spanned the political spectrum and demonstrated an amazing example of spontaneous democratic self-government after thirty-five years of colonial rule. Unfortunately, neither the United States nor the Soviet Union used them as a basis for an independent government and left the country. Had both sides removed their troops, Korea would most likely have ended up with a left-wing or Communist government, either peacefully or as a result of civil war, but Koreans were not left to work out their own destiny.

The Soviets used the PCs as a basis for reconstructing civilian rule, but General Hodge, who established a U.S. military government for South Korea, refused to accept them. The Soviets recruited the nationalist and socialist Cho Man-sik as an interim leader in the North. In the South, the Americans brought back Syngman Rhee from the United States. Rhee considered himself above politics and parties, but he sought followers from anti-Communist collaborators with the Japanese. Kim Ku, the nationalist leader of the Korean Provisional Government (KPG), hated both the collaborators and Rhee. General Hodge disliked both Rhee and Kim Ku and sought to find the equivalent of a moderate democratic center in South Korea, but the only centrist around was the left-leaning populist, Yŏ Unhyŏng (Lyuh Woon Hyung), and he was later assassinated by the conservative police.

After Liberation, millions of Koreans living abroad in Japan and Manchuria flooded back to the peninsula, most of them radicalized by their experience during the colonial period. In North Korea, former collaborators were excluded from leadership roles, but in South Korea, collaborator businessmen and landlords formed the Korean Democratic Party (KDP). Communists jailed by the Japanese were released, and one of them, Pak Hŏnyŏng, formed the Korean

Syngman Rhee and Kim Ku. Syngman Rhee (Yi Sŭngman) on the left, nationalist leader and later first President of the Republic of Korea (1948–1960), and Kim Ku on the right, anti-Japanese nationalist and terrorist and President of the Korean Provisional Government to 1945, assassinated by one of Rhee's henchmen. *(Sajinuro ponun Choson sidae: Saenghwal kwa p'ungsok* [The Choson Period in Pictures: Life and Customs] *Seoul: Somundang, 1986, p. 202)*

Communist Party (KCP) in Seoul, expecting that Seoul would be the capital of a united Korea.

In North Korea, a variety of Communist groups greeted the Soviet commanders: the domestic Communists, the Yan'an Communists who had fought with Mao Zedong in the Chinese civil war, Koreans of Soviet citizenship, and the Manchurian guerrilla fighters who had fought alongside Kim Il Sung. The thirty-two-year-old Kim Il Sung and a few of his

Manchurian guerrilla fighters arrived in North Korea from Siberia on September 19, 1945. The Soviets established a northern branch bureau of the KCP and introduced Kim at a large public meeting in Pyongyang, where he praised Stalin and supported Cho Mansik. By January 1946, however, the Soviets had removed Cho Mansik from power and replaced him with Kim Il Sung. This occurred because Cho opposed Stalin's agreement with the United States to set up a trusteeship for Korea at the Moscow Conference in December.

In South Korea violent protests by workers and peasants began in late 1945. A railroad strike and mass demonstrations broke out in the autumn of 1946 in Pusan and Taegu, followed by peasant riots against Hodge's grain policies in Chŏlla and Kyŏngsang, leaving two hundred police and a thousand civilians dead. U.S. authorities quickly blamed the Communists, declared martial law, put an end to the PCs, and supported armed repression. Pak Hŏnyŏng and many Communists fled to North Korea in 1946 while landlords, businessmen, and Christians in the North moved to the South. By 1947 Syngman Rhee ruled with U.S. support.

In North Korea, Kim Il Sung became chairman of the Provisional People's Committee (PPC) and eclipsed Pak Hŏnyŏng. The PPC in 1946 carried out a popular land reform program to eliminate the landlord class and redistribute land to sharecroppers. Kim nationalized all industries without much violence because the Japanese factory owners had left the country. He reduced working hours to eight hours per day, banned child labor, created a labor federation, declared equal rights for women, established universal education through the eleventh grade, and founded Kim Il Sung University. He made his guerrilla allies from Manchuria, Kim Ch'aek and Ch'oe Yonggŏn, his chief aides and had Ch'oe create the Korean People's Army (KPA).

By 1948 the United States was locked in the Cold War against the Soviet Union. The United States supported Syngman Rhee's plan to hold national elections, but the Soviets refused to allow elections in the North because its population was only half that of the South. In April a peasant rebellion in South Korea on Cheju Island broke out against a repressive right-wing governor appointed by Rhee. Two regiments of the ROK Army assigned to Cheju also rebelled at Yŏsu on the southern coast and murdered hundreds of police and landlords. U.S. forces helped in the suppression of both rebellions. Forty-five thousand people died in the fighting on Cheju, forty thousand fled to Japan, and seventy thousand were placed in concentration camps.

Finally, a separate election was held in the South alone on May 10, 1948, and the Republic of Korea (ROK) was proclaimed on August 15. A constitution modeled on the U.S. Constitution was adopted; a National Assembly was elected, and it chose Syngman Rhee as its first president. On September 10, 1948, North Korea established the Democratic People's Republic of Korea (DPRK) with Kim Il Sung as chairman of the National People's Assembly. The Soviets withdrew their forces from Korea in December, and the United States withdrew most of its forces in 1949.

KOREAN WAR (1949–1953)

Both Kim Il Sung and Syngman Rhee began conducting cross-border raids in 1949, but the United States prevented Rhee from invading the North lest he drag the United States into a war with the Soviet Union. Kim Il Sung had a new ally in Mao Zedong after he won the Chinese civil war in 1949, but in March Kim met with Stalin in Moscow to seek support for a full-scale invasion of South Korea. Stalin refused to allow it, and Mao said that the timing for an invasion was premature.

In January 1950 U.S. Secretary of State Dean Acheson in his famous Press Club speech left South Korea out of the area that the United States would defend automatically against Communist forces. Many in South Korea and the United States castigated Acheson for inducing a North Korean invasion in June, but Kim Il Sung had already decided to invade the South. Stalin finally approved Kim's invasion plan in 1950, but he promised only to supply weapons, planes, and pilots because he wanted to avoid a direct challenge to the United States. He left Mao with the responsibility of preventing North Korea's defeat.

Mao sent perhaps as many as eighty thousand experienced Korean troops who had fought in the Chinese civil war to North Korea, and on June 25, 1950, Kim launched his invasion with seven divisions and 258 Soviet tanks against the four front-line divisions of the ROK Army, which had no tanks. North Korean forces overran the South Korean military and pushed south all the way to Pusan. Years later, the Korean novelist Sŏnu Hwi would write about the fighting in his story "Flowers of Fire" (see **Documents: "Flowers of Fire" by Sŏnu Hwi**).

President Truman viewed the invasion as a plot by Stalin to spread communism, and he dispatched U.S. forces to Korea as a "police action" rather than declare war. He also used the absence of the Russian delegate from the UN Security Council to win Security Council approval of a UN force under the command of U.S. General Douglas MacArthur.

The initial contingent of U.S. forces with remnants of the ROK Army was barely able to defend the Pusan perimeter until General MacArthur turned the tide of battle completely by launching his amphibious attack at Inch'ŏn on September 15, near Seoul. Kim was forced to withdraw his main forces north across the 38th parallel.

Truman had already signed a policy document early in 1950, NSC 48, which committed the United States to the containment of communism within its present boundaries in Asia and "where feasible" to reduce Communist power in Asia—in other words, containment with the possibility of rollback. Truman did not pause a second before choosing the rollback option and authorizing an advance into North Korea even though that action spurred Mao Zedong to commit Chinese "volunteers" to enter the war. Oblivious to Chinese signals passed through India, General MacArthur ordered his troops north to the Yalu River in his "home by Christmas" campaign on November 24, only to have his forces overrun by invading Chinese forces.

The Chinese recaptured Seoul only to lose it once again, and the fighting stabilized in 1951 along a front that eventually became the Demilitarized Zone (DMZ) near the 38th parallel (see Map 30.1). The battle raged for two more years over a few yards of territory at the cost of many casualties until an armistice was signed in 1953 by all parties except Syngman Rhee. To this day, a peace treaty has never been signed.

During the war both Presidents Truman and Eisenhower contemplated the use of atomic bombs to force the Chinese to sign an armistice. MacArthur had also wanted to bomb Chinese airfields in Manchuria, contrary to Truman's limited-war policy to prevent a third world war. When MacArthur went public with his demands, Truman relieved him of his command, a courageous decision because MacArthur was riding high in U.S. public opinion.

More than 3 million North Koreans, 1 million South Koreans, 1 million Chinese, and fifty-two thousand U.S. soldiers died in the conflict. South Koreans suffered another four hundred thousand casualties and Americans one hundred thousand. North Korean and Chinese casualties are unknown. The North was laid flat by U.S. napalm and carpet bombing and the South was devastated. Numerous atrocities were carried out on both sides, including the recently discovered massacre of Korean refugees at Nogunri by U.S. troops.

While later observers viewed it as Kim Il Sung's naked aggression against another suzerain state, one historian has argued that the Korean War was a civil war that began in 1949.[1] Because the United States stopped Syngman Rhee from invading the North, however, Kim Il Sung bears responsibility for a fruitless war that left millions dead. Many Americans condemned Truman for "losing" the war, but others believe that the United States saved South Korea for freedom and democracy. Unfortunately, it was not freedom and democracy that

---

1. Bruce Cumings, *The Origins of the Korean War*, vol. 2 (Princeton, N.J.: Princeton University Press, 1990).

DOCUMENTS

"Flowers of Fire" by Sŏnu Hwi

Sŏnu Hwi's "Flowers of Fire" was written in 1957. It tells the story of Ko Hyŏn, who was only a child when his father was shot dead by Japanese gendarmes for participating in the March First demonstrations of 1919. When his grandfather condemned his father's stupidity for losing his life and widowing his mother, Hyŏn tried to avoid dangerous commitments to survive under colonial rule. When the Japanese drafted him into the Japanese army in Manchuria, he escaped to the Chinese Communists in Yan'an. Back in Korea in 1950, North Korean troops took over his village, and the leading Communist cadre in charge was of his village was his childhood friend, Yŏnho. Yŏnho demanded he join the KPA to fight against the class enemies in South Korea, but he refused and once again ran away to the mountains. Before he did, he explained to Yŏnho why he refused to get involved.

[Hyŏn] "Capitalists, landowners, pro-Japanese, reactionaries—these are what you hate?"

"And opportunists," Yŏnho's voice rose suddenly.

[Hyŏn] "I'm not an opportunist. The object of hatred is not someone you can point to. This so-called hatred is a hatred that does nothing but produce a vicious circle of hatred."

[Yŏnho] "So?"

[Hyŏn] "The object of hatred is the absurd human condition. The poison that lurks in your breast and mine. The barbarity which oppresses others. Arrogance that pretends to have excelled others. Self-promoting, cheap, heroistic, meddling. Impudence that arrogates the right to kill or let live. . . ."

Yŏnho looked at Hyŏn with a mixture of derision and pity. The retrogression of the confused petit bourgeois grasping at a straw in muddy capitalist society!

———

Source: Peter H. Lee, ed., *Flowers of Fire* (Honolulu: University of Hawaii Press, 1974), pp. 229–230.

was defended in the ROK, but an anti-Communist dictatorship.

THE REPUBLIC OF KOREA (1953–1992): DICTATORSHIP AND ECONOMIC GROWTH

Syngman Rhee and Chang Myŏn (1953–1961)

The ROK constitution guaranteed elections and civil liberties, but Syngman Rhee proceeded to construct a dictatorship based on the police, a new army, and a centralized bureaucracy that appointed all district magistracies throughout the country. In 1949 he passed the infamous National Security Law that allowed imprisonment for treason for anyone who supported, abetted, or praised an "enemy state" (i.e., North Korea), terms so vague that Rhee immediately began to use it as a tool to repress his political rivals. It has not been significantly revised since.

Rhee railroaded bills through the National Assembly over opposition by the Korean Democratic Party. He used officials and police to intimidate voters during elections. He distributed favors to politicians, gagged newspapers,

Map 30.1   Korean War

and jailed critics and subjected them to torture. Whatever he had learned from America about respect for law, democracy, and civil liberties he forgot once he returned to Korea.

Rhee was forced to adopt land reform during the Korean War to compete with the North. The landlord class was eliminated, but the reform created a class of conservative small property owners who henceforth voted in heavy numbers for Rhee and subsequent dictators. Eleven billion dollars of U.S. civil and military aid during the Rhee regime kept the economy above water. Rhee distributed U.S. dollars to favored businessmen in return for political contributions.

His import-substitution policy cut the cost of imported goods, but the country's economic growth rate remained very low. U.S. officials viewed the ROK as a basket case incapable of serious development and planned to turn South Korea into a supplier of agricultural products and raw materials in return for Japan's manufactured goods, but Rhee opposed beggaring South Korea for Japan's benefit.

Rhee refused to negotiate a peace treaty with Japan. He relied heavily on the United States for conventional defense, and in 1958 the United States began placing over two hundred nuclear weapons on South Korean soil, with missiles aimed at China and the Soviet Union as well as North Korea.

Finally, college students took to the streets on April 19, 1960, to protest Rhee's attempt to fix his reelection. The police fired into the crowd and killed student demonstrators, but the death knell sounded on Rhee's regime when the army refused to do likewise. American officials finally persuaded Rhee to retire in tattered dignity to Hawaii.

A revised constitution promised the arrival of democratic government, but the new premier, Chang Myŏn, was faced with anti-Communist conservatives and the old guard in his own KDP, who were incensed when he capitulated to student demands to initiate negotiations with North Korea. The economy did not thrive, and the Americans lost confidence in his leadership. He still might have served a full term had not General Park Chung Hee (Pak Chŏnghŭi) overthrown him in a coup d'état on May 16, 1961. President John F. Kennedy faced the ticklish prospect of either using force to crush the coup to preserve democracy or leave the military in command. Kennedy, fearing another DPRK invasion, chose military dictatorship rather than disrupt political stability.

Park Chung Hee: The First Decade (1961–1972)

Park Chung Hee began another dictatorial regime that began with a supreme council for

Park Chung Hee (Pak Chŏnghŭi). Army general Park Chung Hee led a coup d'état against the Chang Myŏn government in 1961 and ruled South Korea as dictator until his assassination in 1979. *(Park Chung Hee,* Toward Peaceful Unification: Selected Speeches by President Park Chung Hee *[Seoul: Kwangmyong Publishing Company, 1976])*

reconstruction staffed by military men. It lasted two years. He dissolved the National Assembly, barred the old politicians from political activity, and cracked down on civil liberties, but the Kennedy administration induced him to don civilian garb and hold presidential and National Assembly elections in 1963.

His chief deputy, Kim Jong Pil (Kim Chong-p'il), organized the Democratic Republican Party (DRP) for Park and created the Korean Central Intelligence Agency (KCIA), an all-encompassing organization that investigated, kidnapped, and tortured domestic political opponents of the regime as well as North Korean spies. Park held elections to preserve a facade of democratic procedure to please Americans, but he relied on the civil bureaucracy, police, army, and KCIA to maintain power and coerce enough voters to win the presidential elections of 1963 and 1967 and majorities for his DRP in the National Assembly. The massive migration of the rural population to Seoul and other cities, however, expanded the opposition vote until Kim Dae Jung (Kim Taejung) from Chŏlla province came within a hair of winning the presidential election of 1971.

In economic policy, Park ignored the principles of free market capitalism and adopted a developmentalist strategy similar to that of imperial Japan to expand the economy. He controlled the banks to direct foreign exchange and loans at preferential low interest rates to labor-intensive export industries like textiles to take advantage of South Korea's low wages. He allowed the most efficient companies to grow to become huge conglomerates (*chaebŏl*) and protected them from bankruptcy. Park devalued the currency to cut export prices and expand exports to America's open markets, but he also protected the economy with tariffs and nontariff barriers, banned the sale of export items on the domestic market, and prevented foreign investors from 51 percent ownership of businesses. After repressing strikes for higher wages, he created a single national trade union to block labor activism. He maintained subsistence income for the new class of smallholding farmers by buying up their rice crop at artificially inflated prices and distributing it to low-wage urban factory and white-collar workers at artificially low prices, and he socialized the cost by paying for it with tax revenue from the public. He also built multistory apartment houses for squatters and the homeless poor.

Park was able to raise $800 million in grants and loans from Japan in 1965 in return for normalizing relations against violent opposition from students and nationalists. As a result, the economy grew about 9 percent a year for almost two decades. Despite his reduction of investment in agriculture, the small landowners provided him a solid electoral base. In 1971, he established the Saemaŭl (New Village) Movement to mobilize both peasants and workers with mixed results, and factory workers struck against low wages several times between 1968 and 1971. The nation was particularly shocked in 1970 at the self-immolation of Chŏn T'ae'il, a worker in the Peace Market in Seoul, who protested worker repression.

Although close to 80 percent of women finished high school and 25 percent attended college by the 1970s, educated women were limited to secretarial or white-collar jobs. They were separated from men on the job and given lower wages for similar work. These women had no chance for promotion and were usually forced out once they married.

In the late 1960s Park feared that the U.S. commitment to defend the ROK was weakening because the United States was mired down in the Vietnam War. U.S. President Lyndon Johnson refused Park's request for military retaliation after about thirty North Korean commandoes tried to assassinate him in the presidential Blue House on January 21, 1968. Two days later, Johnson again took no action after North Korea captured a U.S. intelligence ship, the *U.S.S. Pueblo,* 15 miles offshore and kept its eighty-two crew members in detention.

Park agreed to President Johnson's request that he dispatch Korean troops to Vietnam to fight alongside U.S. forces. In return, the ROK received $1 billion in compensation for the fifty thousand Korean soldiers on the ground and the equipment supplied by South Korea for the Vietnam war effort. When Johnson decided not to run for reelection that year because of anti–Vietnam War protest, Park was convinced of U.S. weakness.

The U.S. pattern of inaction continued with the presidency of Richard Nixon. In 1969 President Nixon took no retaliatory actions when North Korea shot down a U.S. EC-121 reconnaissance plane. In July, he announced his "Nixon Doctrine," which shifted the main responsibility for self-defense to Asian nations, and in February 1970, he removed twenty thousand of the sixty-two thousand U.S. troops in Korea to cut U.S. costs. Alarmed, Park worked around Nixon by having his agents in Washington, D.C., bribe U.S. congressmen to grant more funds to the ROK—the "Koreagate" scandal. Park perceived Nixon's rapprochement with Mao's China in 1971 as capitulation to the Communist enemy, so he decided to negotiate directly with Kim Il Sung and induced him to sign a joint communiqué on July 4, 1972, for peaceful reunification. Those talks, however, soon collapsed.

Park Chung Hee: The Big Push (1972–1979)

Park now decided to carry out forced industrial development. On October 17, 1972, he proclaimed a *yusin* revitalization movement and revised the constitution to allow the president to appoint one-third of the members of the National Assembly, guaranteeing him a two-thirds majority and the ability to declare martial law at any time. Subsequently his infamous Decree No. 9 banned any criticism of the president, and he also forbade all labor union activity.

In January 1973 Park initiated his heavy and chemical industry (HCI) program to develop heavy industry, petrochemicals, and electronics for weapons production and expanded exports. He put the engineer Oh Won Chul (O Wŏnch'ŏl) in charge of the program to run it under strict military discipline from the Blue House. When the Middle Eastern oil-producing nations raised oil prices in 1973 and 1974, he refused to derail industrialization and borrowed heavily from abroad to keep the factories going. By the end of the decade, South Korea was exporting machinery, chemicals, and ships.

To eliminate his biggest political challenger, Park in 1973 authorized the KCIA to kidnap Kim Dae Jung from his hotel room in Tokyo and dump him overboard in Tokyo Bay, but a sharp U.S. protest forced Park to bring Kim back to Seoul and put him under house arrest. Park, however, regained some public sympathy when an assassin's bullet went awry and killed Park's wife, the popular Yuk Yŏngsu.

In 1974 Park began the secret Yulgok Program to develop an independent nuclear weapons program and obtained a loan for nuclear reactors from France right after South Vietnam fell to the Vietcong on July 16, 1975. President Gerald Ford immediately forced cancellation of the agreement with France, a clear example of direct intervention in ROK domestic affairs. Nonetheless, Park continued to build nuclear power plants and missiles. When Jimmy Carter of the Democratic Party became president in 1976, he was so disturbed by Park's violation of human rights that he tried to reduce the number of U.S. troops in South Korea, but members of his own administration, along with conservatives in the Republican Party, forced him to abandon the plan.

It was not until 1979 that inflation and labor protests in Pusan and the free export zone of Masan brought an end to Park's regime. Park was about to crack down on the demonstrators with military force when the head of the KCIA, Kim Chaegyu, one of the few with direct access to Park, shot and killed him on October 26 in the Blue House compound. Kim acted on his own and was arrested forthwith.

The Chun Doo Hwan Dictatorship (1979–1987)

Public expectations for the beginning of a democratic system were crushed on December 12, 1979, when General Chun Doo Hwan (Chŏn Tuhwan), chief of the Army Security Command, used a contingent of troops to seize power in Seoul. Chun declared martial law and on May 17, 1980, closed all universities, banned political activity, suspended the National Assembly, and arrested hundreds of students and opposition politicians. When students in Kwangju in Chŏlla province protested en masse on May 18 and citizens took over the city, Chun sent in troops who clubbed, bayoneted, and killed people on the streets indiscriminately. When the repression was complete the government announced 191 had died, but census officials recorded a drop of 2,000 in the population the next year. The Kwangju massacre turned a large

Kim Dae Jung (Kim Taejung), Opposition Politician and Later President of South Korea, 1997–2002. Here, on August 14, 1980, Kim Dae Jung appears on trial on the phony charge for fomenting the Kwangju uprising of May, 1980, for which he received the death penalty. *(Han'guksa vol. 19 [Seoul: Han'gilsa, 1994], p. 29)*

segment of the population against the United States for failure to prevent the bloodshed.

Chun Doo Hwan made Kim Dae Jung the scapegoat for Kwangju and had a kangaroo court sentence Kim to death. In 1980 President Ronald Reagan reached a deal with Chun to abrogate Kim's death sentence and abolish the ROK nuclear weapons program in return for a formal invitation to the White House. Kim Dae Jung was saved, but Reagan's invitation legitimized Chun's military usurpation and left many democratic activists in jail.

Chun then revised the constitution to establish a seven-year term for the presidency. He banned 567 past politicians from political activity and won a sham presidential election in February 1981. Meanwhile, Kim Il Sung in North Korea decided in 1983 that assassinating an unpopular dictator like Chun might spark a revolutionary uprising. His agents planted a bomb

in Rangoon while Chun and his cabinet were visiting Burma, and the explosion killed sixteen ROK cabinet members and officials. Kim's terror backfired when Chun was unharmed, and the tragedy only increased sympathy for Chun's regime. By 1985 Chun lifted the ban against most politicians but dismissed a half-dozen dissident professors, expelled 1,363 university students, forcibly conscripted 465 others into military service where several were murdered on duty, and subjected others to brainwashing in concentration camps. Chun took revenge on his critics in the media by dismissing about 820 newspaper and broadcast reporters, banning 172 periodicals, closing down 617 publishing companies, and taking over the Munhwa Broadcasting Corporation (MBC).

In 1987 Chun Doo Hwan gave signs of reneging on his pledge to retire at the end of his seven-year term, but the most massive demonstrations in history broke out to demand direct election of a new president in 1987. Forced to retreat, he nominated his comrade in arms, General Roh Tae Woo (No T'aeu), a commander in the Kwangju massacre, to be his party's nominee for president. He authorized Roh on June 29 to announce direct elections, restoration of freedom of the press, and reinstatement of Kim Dae Jung's right to run. Pressure from President Reagan on Chun was critical for the decision, but the main force for democracy came from the students who had fought against dictatorship for decades and elements of the urban middle class who finally joined the democratic struggle at the end.

Democracy Arrives (1987–1992)

Now that the opposition finally had a chance to replace a military leader at the ballot box, the Three Kims (Kim Dae Jung, Kim Jong P'il, and Kim Young Sam) blew the chance because personal ambition blocked them from uniting behind a single candidate. Roh Tae Woo won the election with only 35.9 percent of the vote. Regional voting was prominent as Kim Dae Jung won heavily in Chŏlla province, Kim Jong P'il in South Ch'ungch'ŏng, Kim Young Sam in Pusan and South Kyŏngsang, and Roh in Taegu and North Kyŏngsang, a pattern that remains strong. Chun had founded his own private Ilhae Foundation to control Roh after the election, but his hopes were dashed when Roh jailed fourteen of Chun's brothers and relatives for embezzlement and corruption. Chun retired in disgrace to a Buddhist monastery.

The National Assembly elections left Roh's new Democratic Liberal Party (DLP) with only a minority of seats, but once again opposition leaders Kim Young Sam and Kim Jong P'il sold out principle for power by joining Roh's DLP. Kim Dae Jung was left alone in opposition, but his reputation suffered too when it was revealed that he had accepted campaign funds from Roh. At least the workers seized the initiative to found a new, independent National Federation of Trade Unions (Chŏnnohyŏp) in defiance of the government-controlled Korean Federation of Trade Unions (KFTU). Roh, however, blocked schoolteachers from unionizing.

Roh's Nordpolitik (Northern Policy) foreign policy succeeded in achieving a breakthrough in relations with the Communist states of the Soviet Union, eastern Europe, and China. In 1988, South Korea hosted the Summer Olympics in Seoul, and Roh invited the Communist states to send athletes to the games. Kim Il Sung sought to intimidate them by sending two agents to blow up South Korean Flight 858 from the Middle East to Seoul. It killed all on board, but those nations defied Kim by sending their athletes to the games anyway.

Instead of retaliating, Roh sent officials to Pyongyang in 1989 to persuade Kim Il Sung to allow Chung Ju Yong (Chŏng Chuyŏng) of the Hyundai Corporation to open a tourist area in the Kŭmgang (Diamond) Mountain area just north of the DMZ (see **Material Culture: The Visitors' Center at the Kŭmgang Mountains**). On the other hand, he punished others under the National Security Law for traveling to North Korea without his permission to discuss peaceful reunification.

Roh induced Prime Minister Kaifu of Japan to apologize publicly for the damage done to Korea by colonial rule. He also gained Soviet and Chinese support to admit South Korea to the United Nations in 1991, forcing Kim Il Sung to abandon its previous opposition and accept admission to the United Nations as well. In short, by using carrots instead of sticks, Roh obtained most of his objectives.

CIVILIAN PRESIDENTS (1992 TO THE PRESENT)

Kim Young Sam's single-term presidency (1992–1997) solved the curse of military interference in politics by purging the high-ranking military officers who had served the dictators and stripping the Agency for National Security (the old KCIA) and the Military Security Command of their power to investigate domestic

MATERIAL CULTURE

The Visitors' Center at the Kŭmgang Mountains

The Kŭmgang (Diamond) Mountains span over 40 kilometers of land and are considered the most beautiful mountain range on the Korean peninsula. Located in North Korean territory, it has been off-limits to visitors until recently. Kim Il Sung began to allow South Korean civilians into North Korean territory in large numbers in the 1990s. Hyundai corporation financed the construction of a visitors' center in 1998, and South Korean tourists can now come directly by land across the DMZ. The project stands as the first step to larger and more peaceful relations, perhaps reunification someday in the future.

Diamond Mountains (Kŭmgangsan). A view of the recently opened tourist center for South Korean tourists to view the Diamond Mountains (Kŭmgangsan), just over the DMZ in North Korea. *(Photonica)*

politicians. In 1995 he held the first local elections for provincial governors, city mayors, county magistrates, and local assemblies in history. Even more courageous, he prosecuted former presidents Chun Doo Hwan and Roh Tae Woo for treason, mutiny, and corruption and sent Chun to jail for life and Roh for seventeen years.

Kim suddenly became an advocate of globalization and the wholesale adoption of liberal, free market principles, but the results were dire. He reduced tariffs, and cheap imports undercut home industries. He encouraged companies to cut costs to increase efficiency, but workers were laid off. He encouraged the inflow of foreign capital, but the *chaebŏl* glutted the market with autos, semiconductors, and steel and doctored their books to hide their indebtedness from the banks. By 1996, South Korea's national debt almost doubled to $109 billion, of which two-thirds was short-term debt.

In 1997 the Asian financial crisis spread from Thailand to South Korea, and the economy crashed. Foreign lenders called in short-term loans overnight and drove a half-dozen *chaebŏl* and their suppliers into bankruptcy. South Korea was saved from defaulting on its national debt only because the International Monetary Fund (IMF) provided a record bailout package of $55 billion. When the IMF imposed a brutal retrenchment policy by raising interest rates from 12 to 27 percent per annum to stabilize the currency, more companies failed, and thousands of workers were laid off. Female workers were often the first to be fired. Kim Young Sam's popularity plummeted, even more so when several cabinet members and his two sons were sent to jail for evading military service and receiving bribes.

Kim Jong P'il split from Young Sam's party to form his own United Liberal Democratic Party, and he joined with Kim Dae Jung to ensure the latter's victory in the 1997 presidential election, the first opposition victory in ROK history. Now it was Kim Dae Jung's turn to deal with the economic crisis. He abandoned his earlier defense of low-wage workers and the unemployed by following IMF demands to allow unrestricted layoffs. The unemployment rate rose from less than 2 percent to 7.6 percent by September 1998, and national per capita income dropped from $10,000 to $7,000. Kim had to sell eleven state-owned industries, including the prized Pohang Iron and Steel Company (Posco), to private owners to raise funds.

Kim finally defied IMF dictates in the fall of 1998 by lowering interest rates to increase business investment, but the *chaebŏl* gobbled up the loan money and left small business in the lurch. When the *chaebŏl* supported unprofitable member companies, Kim Dae Jung induced foreign companies to invest in failing Korean businesses with majority ownership to save them from bankruptcy. By 2000, the economy finally began to recover.

South Korea still suffers from technological gaps and the loss of jobs to low-wage countries like China, exacerbated by *chaebŏl* outsourcing of factories to China. Kim Dae Jung's reputation hit rock bottom because his son and many officials were also prosecuted for taking bribes, and his own party took his party's chairmanship away from him.

Independents and defectors from the major parties formed a new liberal party, Our Open Party (Yŏllin uridang). Roh Moo Hyun of Kim's Millennium Democratic Party was elected president in 2002, thanks to a backlash against President George W. Bush's North Korea policy, but conservatives in his party forced him out. They then joined up with the opposition One Nation Party to impeach him for publicly endorsing Our Open Party for the upcoming April 2004 national assembly elections. Incensed by the pettiness of the impeachment, the electorate proceeded to vote the Our Open Party into a parliamentary majority, leaving the One Nation Party in a minority and the Millennium Democratic Party with only nine seats. The Three Kims were finally removed from politics.

Roh lost some liberal support when he sent troops to Iraq, but in the fall of 2004 he regained support from Our Open Party when he openly demanded abolition of the National Security Law. Possibly the victory of Our Open Party will open the path to stable party politics based on policy positions rather than shifting patron-client groups.

MODERNIZATION: CHANGES IN FAMILY LIFE, CONSUMER CULTURE, AND LITERATURE

Rapid changes have occurred in South Korean society since 1945. Arranged marriages began to decline, as marriage brokers were used for introductions only. College men and women arranged group "meetings" or group dating to enable couples to pair off for dates and "love marriages," but they still sought parental approval for marriage. Wives were still subordinated to men and mothers-in-law in marriage, but middle-class married couples obtained some distance from parents who bankrolled their large rental deposits (*chŏnse*) for individual apartments. Couples put intense pressure on their children to gain entry into the best colleges. Middle-class wives were virtually abandoned by their overworked white-collar husbands who stayed out drinking until midnight, but they took to making money in the real estate or stock markets. As women became conscious of gender discrimination and frustrated by unhappy marriages, books and movies from the 1990s began to portray (and reflect) married women seeking sexual liberation with lovers.

The growth of income and wealth led to a consumer culture and ostentatious consumption in clothing, appliances, pianos, and luxury apartments. South Koreans today continue to have wide access to goods and technology, while residents of North Korea lag significantly behind. The table on this page compares the two countries in terms of their standards of living and access to technology.

Korean poetry and literature in the vernacular came into its own in the postwar period. Many authors were consumed with the Korean War, social justice, and the evils of dictatorship.

Ch'ae Mansik's *Peace Under Heaven* portrayed an evil landlord, and the famous "Five Bandits" poem of Kim Chiha condemned bureaucrats and businessmen. Hwang Sunwŏn wrote of the poor in the 1970s, and Hwang Suk-young (Hwang Sŏgyŏng) wrote about personal problems and Korean soldiers in the Vietnam War in *The Shadow of Arms* (1985). Pak Kyŏngni's lengthy *The Land* (1980) was a best-seller, and short-story writers like Kang Sŏkkyŏng, Kim Chiwŏn, Pak Wansŏ, and O Chŏnghŭi left their mark with descriptive and contemplative stories of anomie under industrialization.

THE DEMOCRATIC PEOPLE'S REPUBLIC OF KOREA (1953 TO THE PRESENT)

The history of the DPRK in this period involves the maximization of political power in the hands of the supreme leader, a military policy based on arming the entire population backed by Soviet support to 1991, periodic terrorist acts, a revolutionary social policy, and a roller-coaster economic ride under a command economy. The collapse of communism in the Soviet Union and eastern Europe in 1991 provided a major shock to North Korea's fortunes.

Economic Growth and Political Consolidation (1953–1959)

After the end of the Korean War in 1953, Kim Il Sung relied heavily on aid from the Soviet Union and China. He invested primarily in heavy and defense industries to create the basis for economic independence and a national arms industry. He postponed the production of consumer goods to the indefinite future, called on the public to accept sacrifice for the greater good of the nation, and compensated by providing cheap housing and food, free education, and free medical treatment.

In the mid-1950s Kim embarked on a rapid farm collectivization plan aimed at converting all farmers to proletarians on wages on state farms,

A Comparison of Living Standards in North and South Korea		
	South Korea	North Korea
Population	47.6 million	22.5 million
Life expectancy (years)	73.9	62.4
Infant mortality rate (per 1,000 live births)	5.0	42.0
Fixed line and mobile telephones (per 1,000 people)	1,168.0	21.1
Internet users	26.3 million	No data available
Paved roads (% of total)	74.5	6.4

Source: World Bank, http://www.worldbank.org/data/countrydata/countrydata.html.

but the plan was never fully achieved and ended with smaller collectives at the village level. Broad fields were created out of small parcels to enable the use of tractors and chemical fertilizer. Originally successful, the drawbacks of this program were not seen until decades later, particularly the shortages of foreign oil, erosion, the replacement of age-old farming experience with bureaucratic managers, and restrictions on the freedom to move or change jobs.

Industrial production in the DPRK surpassed growth in South Korea through the mid-1960s but then began to slow because of the decline in aid from the Soviet Union and China, bottlenecks in the production process, insufficient technological development, and excessive investment in weapons. Kim Il Sung's solution was to use a moral appeal to workers for greater sacrifice and undertake mass mobilization efforts like the Ch'ŏllima (the Thousand-League Horse) campaign of 1958. It was similar to the Great Leap Forward campaign in China, but was not designed to supplement factories with backyard steel furnaces and did not result in massive starvation (see Chapter 28). Workers were required to work extra hours, and students were taken out of classrooms to work.

The new proletarian state banned collective bargaining and created only single state trade and farmers' unions. Kim Il Sung borrowed Mao Zedong's "mass line" strategy in 1960 to force party cadres to consult with the workers and farmers in devising production plans. Faced with a dearth of proletarians, he ignored the Leninist party model by admitting a majority of peasants into the KWP and converting them to proletarian class consciousness by indoctrination and self-criticism. Contrary to Mao, however, he never launched periodic mass mobilization campaigns to purge party cadres and bureaucrats that had lost their revolutionary ideals.

Kim purged only members of the party who challenged his supremacy, starting with Pak Hŏnyong and the domestic Communists after the Korean War. After Stalin died in 1953 and Khrushchev denounced Stalin for creating a cult of personality in 1956, he purged members of the Russian and Yan'an factions who accused him of doing the same thing. He also purged three generals after his military ventures against South Korea and the United States in 1968 and 1969 failed.

Foreign Relations and Expansion of Personal Power (1959–1975)

When the Soviet Union and China finally split in 1959, Kim Il Sung remained neutral and signed mutual defense treaties with both countries in 1961. He was distressed when Mao allowed President Nixon to visit Beijing in 1972 (even more so in 1979 when China normalized relations with the United States). Perhaps that was the reason that in 1972 he allowed members of families separated by the Korean War to meet for the first time since 1953 and signed a joint pledge for peaceful unification with Park Chung Hee.

In 1972 Kim Il Sung introduced a new constitution that created a new office of president, which gave him control of all government agencies. More shocking for Communists, he subordinated the KWP to his command and left it out of many of his policy decisions. As signs of his megalomania, he also built gigantic statues of himself and adopted grandiose titles like "supreme leader," "fatherly leader," "the Great Sun," and "the supreme mind of the nation."

Kim also began to displace Marxism-Leninism with *chuch'e* (self-reliance) as the leading ideology of the country. *Chuch'e* is an untranslatable term that constitutes "a subjective, solipsistic state of mind, the correct thought that will then determine correct action" in almost any imaginable situation.[2] In 1973 Kim borrowed from the dynastic tradition by grooming his son, Kim Jong Il (Kim Chŏng'il), to succeed him. He gave him responsibility for running most state affairs when he appointed him secretary of the KWP and member of the Military Commission in 1980.

Kim Il Sung divided society into a new status hierarchy. The nuclear masses included KWP party members, government officials, military officers, anti-Japanese guerrilla fighters, and

---

2. Bruce Cumings, *Korea's Place in the Sun* (New York: Norton, 1997), pp. 403–404. See also pp. 404–414.

martyrs who died in Korean War. The nonnu-
clear masses included nonparty workers, peasants, and clerical workers. The lowly mixed
masses were outcasts with tainted backgrounds:
descendants of the bourgeoisie, landlords, capitalists, and dissidents. Instead of equal treatment
for all, Kim turned the status structure upside
down, reviving hereditary privilege for the elite
and hereditary stigma for the despised.

Kim locked all individuals into a variety of
state-run mass organizations. Because of the
shortage of labor, he encouraged women to work
and had the state provide child care facilities for
working parents. He replaced the home with
communal mess halls, gave women the right to
divorce, and incorporated them into the military
but gave political responsibilities to only a few.

When the economy began to decline in the
late 1960s, Kim opened trade relations with the
West in 1972 to import advanced machinery
and even fabrication plants from Europe and
Japan on credit. Lacking a serious export industry, however, he defaulted on his international
debt in 1975, and serious trade with the West
evaporated.

After 1973 Kim Il Sung constructed along the
DMZ secret tunnels into South Korea large
enough to accommodate an invasion, but he
attempted no large-scale attacks. The axe murder of a few U.S. troops by North Korean soldiers in the DMZ in 1976 over the petty issue of
cutting down a large tree, however, created
more tension. In the early 1980s President Reagan countered these challenges by shipping
cruise missiles and F-16 fighters to South Korea
and increased the number of troops in the joint
U.S.-ROK Team Spirit military exercise of 1981.

Kim supported the Soviet Union's invasion of
Afghanistan as a means of ensuring military aid.
Possibly in return for that favor, a Soviet inter-
ceptor in August 1983 shot down a South
Korean airliner, KAL Flight 007, that had
strayed into Russian territory over Siberia. The
next year the Soviets shipped more military
equipment in return for docking and overfly
rights, and in 1986 it promised to construct a
nuclear power plant in the North.

Economic Decline After 1987

One sign of economic difficulty came in 1987
when Kim Il Sung was forced to abandon construction in midpoint on what was to be the
tallest building in East Asia, the 105-story
Ryugyŏng Hotel. He decided to shift investment
to light industry and consumer products to
improve living conditions, and he opened talks
with South Korea on economic and humanitar-
ian cooperation and sent food aid to flood victims in South Korea. In 1988 he began informal
talks with U.S. representatives, but his terrorist
downing of the KAL plane interrupted them. In
1990, Kim did agree with the United States to
establish trade offices with consular functions in
both countries.

After the collapse of communism in the Soviet
Union in 1991, oil supplies to Korea dropped
sharply because Russia demanded cash payment, and factories operated at only a fraction
of capacity. North Korea opened a free economic trade zone in the Rajin-Sŏnbong area in
the northeast in 1991, but no foreign investors
responded. The floods of 1995 and 1996 and
the drought of 1997 reduced the country to
near-famine conditions, and perhaps 1 million
people lost their lives. Denizens of Pyongyang
and the army fared well, while the civilian population suffered from malnutrition and disease.
For the first time, the government allowed people to leave their homes without permission to
forage for food, cultivate small private plots,
and sell the products in farmers' markets.

Nonetheless, illegal emigration into China
increased, and refugees jumped the gates of foreign embassies in Beijing to escape to South
Korea, but China cracked down on refugees and
returned them home. Worldwide charitable
organizations, South Korea, China, the United
States, and Japan supplied perhaps a fifth of
North Korea's food consumption in the 1990s.
Despite the hardship, North Korea defied the
prediction of foreign pundits that the regime
would collapse like East Germany.

After Kim Il Sung's death in 1994, Kim Jong
Il took some cautious steps to open society. He

opened the Diamond Mountain tourist center for South Koreans, the Ŭiju free trade zone south of the Yalu River, and the Kaesŏng industrial park, and he permitted construction of rail and road lines across the DMZ from South Korea to Kaesŏng and the Diamond Mountains. He welcomed South Korean *chaebŏl* plans to invest in factories to hire cheap North Korean labor to export abroad, but the nuclear crisis delayed fruition.

The North Korean Nuclear Challenge

Between 1964 and 1986 North Korea received and built several gas-graphite nuclear reactors in the Soviet style at Yŏngbyŏn north of Pyongyang, for research and electrical generation. All produced plutonium as a by-product, which could be used to manufacture hydrogen bombs. In 1985 the Soviet Union induced Kim Il Sung to sign the Nonproliferation Treaty (NPT), which required inspections by the UN International Atomic Energy Agency (IAEA) to prevent military use of fissile material. The IAEA, however, never followed through on the inspections. In 1989 and 1990 North Korean officials informed Tony Namkung (Namgung Kun), an American citizen, of their desire to normalize relations with the United States and Japan, open trade with South Korea, support peaceful coexistence, reduce defense expenditures, and introduce market reforms. They also voiced their objection to the U.S. nuclear weapons on South Korean soil, the joint ROK-U.S. Team Spirit exercises, and the thirty-seven thousand U.S. troops stationed in South Korea.

In 1991, Kim Il Sung signed a denuclearization pact with South Korea, and the United States eased growing tension when it announced withdrawal of all U.S. nuclear weapons from Korean soil and cancelled the joint Team Spirit exercises with South Korea. Nevertheless, fears over the nuclear capabilities of the North continued. U.S. intelligence surmised that enough plutonium from spent reactor fuel at Yŏngbyŏn could have been extracted to make thirty plutonium bombs. That estimate was dropped to two to eight bombs, but with no concrete evidence that a single bomb had been made or tested.

Kim Il Sung offered to replace his gas-graphite reactors with new light-water reactors, which produce less plutonium as a waste product, but the United States ignored the offer and considered taking punitive action unless Kim abandoned his nuclear weapons program. A few American generals warned that a second Korean war would result in three hundred thousand to five hundred thousand military and millions of civilian Korean casualties on both sides, but Kim created a crisis when he threatened to pull out of the NPT. President Bill Clinton sent ex-president Jimmy Carter on a last-ditch effort to Pyongyang to talk directly with Kim. Carter eliminated the crisis when he appeared on CNN and announced his agreement with Kim Il Sung to freeze the processing of nuclear waste to extract plutonium at Yŏngbyŏn in return for new light-water reactors. Kim Il Sung even told Carter he was willing to carry out the North-South denuclearization agreement, pull back forces from the DMZ, match South Korea in reducing troops by 1 million men, and allow U.S. troops to remain in Korea in smaller numbers. Unfortunately, he died that year before negotiations could be expanded.

His son, Kim Jong Il, finally signed the Agreed Framework with the United States in 1994. Under this agreement, South Korea and Japan assumed the cost for the light-water reactors and the United States had to provide only 500,000 tons of heavy oil to replace energy lost from the inactive reactor. A neutral agency, KEDO (Korean Energy and Development Organization), was established to administer construction. North Korea remained a party to the NPT and promised to allow the IAEA to inspect facilities not subject to the freeze when the light-water reactors were completed but before the nuclear components were installed.

Subsequently, the United States delayed delivery of heavy oil, and the economic crash of 1997 rendered the ROK incapable of financing construction. Possibly to spur the United States to action, in 1998 North Korea fired a Taep'odong missile over Japan as a test, but that only shocked the Japanese public into consideration of abandoning the no-war clause of its constitution and American officials into contemplating North Korean nuclear-tipped missiles landing on U.S. territory.

Kim Dae Jung was elected president of the ROK in 1997 and inaugurated a new "sunshine policy (*haetpyŏtch'aek*)" based on peaceful negotiations with North Korea. When he visited President George W. Bush in Washington in March 2001 to gain support, however, Bush gave him the cold shoulder and rejected Kim's policy as appeasement. Undeterred, Kim Dae Jung "persuaded" Kim Jong Il to hold a summit meeting in Pyongyang in June 2000 and agree to solve all problems peacefully. Although Kim Dae Jung won the Nobel Peace Prize for that meeting, it was later revealed in 2002 that that he had paid a bribe of $500 million to Kim Jong Il in advance to enable the talks. When Kim Jong Il took no further measures to ease tension, Kim Dae Jung's reputation was severely damaged at home.

After the destruction of the twin towers in New York City by the Islamic terrorist al-Qaeda organization on September 11, 2001, President Bush declared his hostility to what he called the "axis of evil," a group "rogue states" that included North Korea, and he maligned Kim Jong Il for starving his own people, an obvious sign that Bush was not interested in negotiations. When U.S. intelligence discovered in 2002 the North's clandestine plan to build atomic weapons from enriched uranium (supplied by Pakistan), which the North subsequently denied, Bush cancelled all talks. He declared that the North would have to abandon its nuclear weapons program entirely before the United States offered any material aid, but Kim Jong Il refused to give up North Korea's last line of defense on a promise.

The ROK was split over Bush's policy, but the liberal Roh Moo Hyun, who supported the sunshine policy, was elected president in November 2002. When he expressed reservations about sending Korean troops to support the U.S. invasion of Iraq in 2003, the Bush administration threatened to pull all U.S. troops from South Korea in retaliation. Roh capitulated and sent the troops.

Increased Iraqi resistance to the U.S. occupation forced Bush to retreat from his threat to launch a preemptive strike against North Korea. Instead he brought China and Russia in to join the United States, South Korea, and Japan in six-nation talks with North Korea, but no progress was achieved. After Bush won reelection to the presidency in 2004, his administration resumed its harsh rhetoric.

SUMMARY

The period after 1945 was difficult for Korea: a brief liberation in 1945 followed by superpower domination by the Soviet Union and the United States, division of the country in two, and the Korean War, the worst war in Korean history. Peace was maintained between North and South Korea by a precarious armistice, with both sides heavily armed. Both the Communist North and the bureaucratic capitalist South were dominated by repressive regimes. The North Korean party dictatorship under Marxist-Leninist theory was transformed into a nationalistic, hereditary monarchy under *chuch'e* ideology, while in South Korea, Park's military dictatorship's command economy dragged the country out of poverty while trampling on human rights (see **Biography: Suh Sung and Kang Chol-hwan, Victims of Oppression**).

Students in South Korea, with the help of some intellectuals and opposition politicians, led the way in breaking the yoke of dictatorship and opening the way to democracy. The developmentalist strategy that vaulted the country to the heights of economic power began to show its flaws when the demands of the world market weakened protectionism and burst the bubble economy.

In North Korea, the Stalinist, heavy industrial economy rose initially, but fell because autarchy closed off technological innovation from external stimulation, and the collapse of communism

BIOGRAPHY Suh Sung and Kang Chol-hwan, Victims of Oppression

Both the North and South Korean governments left behind victims of oppression. Suh Sung (Sŏ Sŭng) was a Korean resident living in Japan when he traveled to Korea to complete a master's degree at Seoul National University in March 1971. Upon his arrival, he and his brother Suh Joon-shik (Sŏ Chunsik) were arrested and tortured to force a confession that they were North Korean spies. Unable to stand the torture, Suh Sung tried to commit suicide by self-immolation in April, but he survived, his face horribly disfigured. He was sentenced to death and his brother to fifteen years in prison, but his sentence was reduced to life imprisonment the next year. He was not released until 1990, after twenty-eight years in jail (his brother too, well past the term of incarceration). Suh's account of his horrific experience reveals the names of his torturers and the heroism of committed Communists or innocents who refused to confess to false charges to obtain release. Since his release, he has devoted his life to the promotion of human rights in South Korea.

The grandmother of Kang Chol-hwan (Kang Ch'ŏlhwan) migrated to Japan from Cheju Island in the 1930s at the age of thirteen. At the age of twenty, she joined the Japanese Communist Party and married a man from Cheju, who later made money from his pachinko parlor in Kyoto and became friends with the *yakuza*. Their son, Kang's father, was born in the early 1930s. In the 1960s, the grandmother persuaded her reluctant husband to move the whole family, including her brothers, to Pyongyang. They were treated as celebrities on the ship over, greeted by Kim Il Sung when they arrived, and provided a first-class apartment in the capital. The grandmother was elected to the Supreme People's Assembly, and the grandfa- ther was appointed to the Office of Commercial Affairs. Kang's parents married in 1967, and he was born soon after.

One day in 1977, the grandfather disappeared, never to return, shipped off to a concentration camp for treason without a word to his family. Shortly after, at the age of nine, Kang returned home to find that security agents were sending him, his grandmother, his father, and his uncles to a concentration camp because of his grandfather's crime. His mother was left behind with no way to communicate with the rest of the family. They arrived at a camp where whole families were living in rags and filth, and they were placed in a hut with earthen walls and floor. The camp included two thousand or three thousand people; every year about a hundred died from hunger and disease. Minor violations were punished by a trip to the sweatbox for as long as three months. The prisoner had to crouch on his knees at all times in darkness without moving or speaking or suffer beatings for doing either. Many failed to survive.

Kang spent ten years in the camp and was able to avoid the worst punishments, but he had to carry ore from the mines and hunt rats to survive. One of his uncles attempted suicide twice. Adults worked in the gold mine for thirteen hours a day and many died from cave-ins. Women caught engaging in sex were humiliated in public or physically abused. Any babies born in the camp were taken away.

Finally, after a decade in the camp, Kang and his family were released by an amnesty, only to be subjected to strict surveillance in the countryside. Kang finally left his family behind and bribed his way across the border to China, and then to South Korea. His experiences are still being duplicated in the North.

Sources: See Suh Sung, *Unbroken Spirits* (Lanham, Maryland: Rowman & Littlefield, 2001), and Chol-hwan Kang and Pierre Rigoulot, *The Aquariums of Pyongyang* (New York: Basic Books, 2000).

in the Soviet Union robbed the country of its major material support. Both North and South had transformed their societies in different ways through social leveling and the partial liberation of women. The North turned the social order upside down, while the South created a new society of urban capitalists and white- and blue-collar workers while the farming class declined sharply. Religion was suppressed and replaced by hero worship and intense patriotism in the North, while Christianity, Buddhism, Ch'ŏndogyo, and new religions emerged in the South, along with residual Confucian values and shamanism.

In the North, the loss of Soviet support and the Chinese departure from Marxist purity left nuclear weapons as the only option for defense. This forced a conversion of U.S. policy from the defense of South Korea from northern aggression to a militant policy to dismantle the North's nuclear weapons program. North Korea, however, remained fiercely committed to the kind of pugnacious independence that Korea had not experienced since the fall of Koguryŏ in 668.

SUGGESTED READING

For a general surveys of the period, see B. Cumings, *Korea's Day in the Sun* (1997); D. Oberdorfer, *The Two Koreas* (1997); and M. Noland, *Avoiding the Apocalypse* (2000).

Studies on the Korean war include B. Cumings, *The Origins of the Korean War*, vol. 2 (1990); J. Halliday and B. Cumings, *Korea: The Unknown War* (1988); S. N. Goncharov, J. W. Lewis, and L. Xue, *Uncertain Partners: Stalin, Mao, and the Korean War* (1993); and J. Chen, *China's Road to the Korean War* (1995). For an early study of the fighting, see R. Appleman, *South to the Naktong, North to the Yalu* (1961).

Studies on ROK politics include Cumings, *Origins of the Korean War*, vol. 1 (1981); G. Henderson, *Korea: The Politics of the Vortex* (1968); P. Hayes, *Pacific Powderkeg* (1990); C. K. Armstrong, ed., *Korean Society* (2002); and H.-A Kim, *Korea's Development Under Park Chung Hee* (2004).

For analysis of the ROK economy, see E. S. Mason et al., *The Economic and Social Modernization of the Republic of Korea* (1980); A. Amsden, *Asia's Next Giant* (1989); F. C. Deyo, ed., *The Political Economy of the New Asian Industrialism* (1987); C. Woo, *Race to the Swift* (1991); M. Hart-Landsberg, *The Rush to Development* (1993); R. L. Janelli with D. Yim, *Making Capitalism* (1993); P. Kuznets, *Korean Economic Development* (1994); D. Kirk, *Korean Dynasty: Hyundai and Chung Ju Yung* (1994); and H. Koo, *Korean Workers* (2001).

For South Korean literature, see P. H. Lee, ed., *Flowers of Fire* (1974), and B. and J.-C. Fulton, eds., *Words of Farewell: Stories by Korean Women Writers* (1989).

For studies on North Korea, see R. Scalapino and C. Lee, *Communism in Korea*, 2 vols. (1972); D. Suh, *Kim Il Sung* (1988); E. van Ree, *Socialism in One Zone* (1989); N. Eberstadt and J. Banister, *The Population of North Korea* (1992); B. Myers, *Han Sŏrya and North Korean Literature* (1994); M. J. Mazarr, *North Korea and the Bomb* (1995); L. V. Sigal, *Disarming Strangers* (1998); K. Oh and R. C. Hassig, *North Korea Through the Looking Glass* (2000); C. Armstrong, *The North Korean Revolution, 1945–1950* (2002); E. Cornell, *North Korea Under Communism* (2002); S. S. Harrison, *Korean Endgame* (2002); and A. Lankov, *From Stalin to Kim Il Sung* (2002).

Contemporary Japan (1965 to the Present)

Japan's desire for peace with its neighbors was marked in 1965 by demonstrations against the Vietnam War. The storms of protest provoked by public policy decisions and industrial pollution were also signs that by the late 1960s, the consequences of Liberal Democratic Party (LDP) domination and high-speed economic growth could no longer be ignored. The 1970s brought political scandals, diplomatic crises, and economic opportunities in the midst of setbacks. Minorities and working women demanded political initiatives to ameliorate their condition. Economic adjustments positioned Japanese companies to expand in export markets. In the 1980s, Japan had the world's second largest economy, but the euphoria of seemingly unstoppable growth led to a bubble in overpriced investments. When it burst in 1990, the economy deflated. Although social problems increased, most Japanese people enjoyed low crime rates, clean cities, superb public transportation, and unprecedented prosperity.

Why did the Japanese economy rise so far and fall so fast? Are protest and demonstrations worth discussing given the power of the LDP and bureaucrats? Which social trends will prove enduring, and which will prove beneficial?

POLITICAL PROTEST AND ENVIRONMENTAL POLLUTION

The 1960s saw student movements worldwide, and Japan was no exception. Students joined citizen's movements to protest Japan's support for the American war in Vietnam under the U.S.-Japan Security Treaty at the same time that they attacked educational policies. At some universities, they criticized what they viewed as assembly-line style courses. At Tokyo University, medical students protested a top-down reorganization of the program that ignored their concerns. In January 1968 they went on strike. When the university administration refused to hear their grievances and expelled their leaders, students in other departments struck in sympathy. They wanted curriculum control, amnesty for students arrested in confrontations, and no riot police allowed on campus. To make their point, they barricaded the central building. The administration cancelled entrance examinations for 1969. On campuses across Tokyo, students launched sympathy strikes. On January 19, 1969, eighty-five hundred riot police retook the campus in a two-day battle broadcast live on TV. The Diet passed a University Control Bill giving the Education Ministry enhanced authority to punish students. Radical student groups went underground.

Japan's rise to prominence in world affairs and the increase in air travel led the LDP and the Transportation Ministry to decide on a new international airport for Tokyo in 1965. Farmers who owned land at the proposed site outside Narita protested because expropriating their land destroyed their livelihood, secrecy surrounding the decision demonstrated that popular opinion counted for naught, and the airport might be used to support the American war effort in Vietnam. Farmers petitioned prefectural and national ministries; they rallied support in the Diet among the opposition parties. When these measures failed, they built barricades and fortresses; they dug ditches to trap bulldozers; they chained themselves to fences. The radical student union Zengakuren helped with agricultural work and publicity. Citizens in peace, antinuclear, and environmental movements joined them because they were fighting against government indifference to the social costs of economic growth. Plans called for the airport to be built in six years; it took twelve. The government reduced the number of runways from three to one; a proposal in 1998 to add a second also faced opposition. Having learned its lesson, the government later built

Osaka International Airport on an artificial island in the bay.

At the end of the 1960s, the left and right wings attacked capitalism and materialism. Mishima Yukio created a paramilitary organization and received permission to join Self Defense Force military maneuvers. In 1970 he called on the soldiers at SDF headquarters to remember the sacrifices made in World War II and rally behind nationalist goals by overthrowing the government. When they laughed at him, he committed ritual suicide. Between 1970 and 1972 students in the Red Army robbed banks and post offices, hijacked a plane to North Korea, and machine-gunned travelers in Tel Aviv's Lod airport in support of Maoist revolution and Palestinian rights.

Less dramatic but longer lasting, citizens' movements arose in response to industrial pollution. In the 1950s, local and prefectural governments encouraged industrial development that spread pollution from cities to towns and made Japan the most polluted nation on earth. By the early 1970s about half the population complained of suffering from pollution (see Color Plate 32). Citizens' movements mobilized hundreds of thousands of ordinarily apolitical residents to sign petitions, visit industrial sites, display posters, and launch education drives to rally support in stopping potential polluters from building in their neighborhood. They warned against trusting promises by industry and local government that a proposed factory would not pollute, and they rejected charges that fighting to protect the individual's quality of life is egotistical.

Between 1932 and 1968 at Minamata in southern Kyushu, a Chisso factory produced acetaldehyde, a key ingredient in making plastics through a process that released methyl mercury as a by-product. Dumped into the water, mercury concentrated in shellfish and other marine life and then attacked brain cells in domestic animals and humans. Although mercury can kill in a few weeks, many victims suffered progressive debilitation leading to a vegetative state and death. In 1959, a Kumamoto University research

A Victim of Mercury Poisoning. Held by her mother, this sufferer has a malformed hand along with other physical deformities characteristic of the Minamata disease. *(AP/Wide World Photos)*

team traced the cause to the Chisso factory. The team lost its government funding. With support from the Ministry of International Trade and Industry, Chisso hired researchers that proved mercury was not at fault. Workers at the plant and community leaders blamed the victims' poor diet and unsanitary living conditions for their afflictions. In 1965 another outbreak of the disease in Niigata on the Japan Sea was traced to mercury discharged by a chemical factory. Despite efforts by company officials and government bureaucrats to undermine the investigators' credibility, the Niigata outbreak lent weight to the Minamata case. The victims launched petitions, demonstrations, and sit-ins. They attracted support from doctors, lawyers, filmmakers, journalists, and academics. In 1971 they sued Chisso. The verdict against the company in 1973 brought it to the verge of bankruptcy. The victims then sued the government. The Environmental Agency refused to comply with the court's recommendation to settle. In 1995 the cabinet accepted an out-of-court final settlement that denied governmental responsibility for either the disease or the delay in acknowledging the problem.

Diseases caused by pollution in Minamata and elsewhere exposed the costs of high-speed economic growth and the way politicians and bureaucrats insulated themselves from ordinary citizens. Despite free elections and a free press, pollution victims had to protest outside regular government channels. Owing to their demands, the government instituted stringent pollution controls in the 1970s and began spending a larger portion of the gross national product (GNP) on antipollution measures than any other developed nation. By 1978 air and water pollution had declined, and manufacturers had learned how to profit from measures to keep the environment clean.

STRAINS OF THE 1970S

Having enjoyed the economic benefits of supporting the United States during the Cold War, Japan was unprepared for the international crises that punctuated the 1970s. When President Richard Nixon announced in 1971 that the United States would no longer accept fixed exchange rates that overvalued the dollar, the yen rose 14 percent. Nixon intended to make Japanese exports to the United States more expensive and less competitive. Japanese companies survived by taking advantage of lower costs for imported raw materials. Nixon's second shock came in 1972 when he recognized the People's Republic of China without notifying Japan in advance. Prime Minister Tanaka Kakuei followed Nixon to China seven months later. In 1978 China and Japan signed a peace and friendship treaty. The first oil shock came when the Organization of Petroleum Exporting Countries (OPEC) embargoed oil to countries that had supported Israel in the 1973 war. Dependent on oil for 80 percent of its energy, Japan had to pay premium prices on the world market. Inflation rose, companies reduced energy use by cutting production, and consumers stopped spending. During the remainder of the decade, Japan built nuclear power plants. Companies so rationalized energy use that when

OPEC raised prices again in 1978–1980, they had a competitive advantage over less efficient firms in their prime export markets.

To retain dominance in the Diet and cabinet, the LDP catered to its core constituencies, sometimes to the point of scandal. Tanaka Kakuei had Japan National Railroad (JNR) build a bullet train line through the mountains to his constituents in Niigata, at the cost of $60 million a mile. It provided government contracts for his cronies in the construction business and fattened the purses of real estate developers. Although all Diet members collected money from businesses and individuals for whom they did favors, Tanaka's excesses were so blatant that public outcry drove him from office in 1974. In 1976 an investigation by the U.S. Senate disclosed that President Nixon had arranged for Lockheed Aircraft Corporation to pay Tanaka almost $2 million to have All Nippon Airways buy Lockheed planes. Despite the stench of corruption, LDP politicians held on to power because voters believed that the opposition parties were too ideologically driven and fragmented to be trusted with national policy.

Industry had to make traumatic adjustments. Some arose from increasing protectionist pressures, exemplified in a 1979 report to the European Economic Community Executive Committee that called the Japanese "work maniacs who live in houses little better than rabbit hutches."[1] Nixon demanded that Japan reduce its textile imports through voluntary restraints. The increase in oil prices hurt petrochemical and energy-intensive industries. Shipbuilders saw the market for tankers decline, which hurt steel. The shipbuilding industry survived by consolidating and moving into new fields such as ocean drilling platforms. The government helped workers with wage subsidies, retraining programs, and relocation expenses. To compete with low-labor-cost countries, the steel industry developed specialty high-value-added products. Automobile and electrical manufacturing grew. In 1980, Japan produced more cars than any other country. Big electrical companies made generating plants and electric motors for trains; small firms made office equipment, household appliances, and entertainment items.

Although lifetime employment became a watchword, it covered less than half the work force. Toyota, for example, had permanent workers who received regular salary increases based on seniority and fringe benefits; during good times, it hired temporary workers, who were terminated when necessary. Over two hundred independent contractors made parts and components for cars in accordance with guidelines and timetables established by Toyota. Their workers enjoyed no job security. Women returning to the labor force after raising children typically worked at part-time or temporary jobs in small, often marginally profitable companies.

White-collar workers joined a firm straight after college and expected to stay with it for life. For indoctrination into company culture, first-year recruits lived in dormitories where they learned to maintain constant contact with their coworkers by working together and drinking together after work. Since only family men were deemed suitable for promotion, most workers soon married, perhaps to an "office lady" (OL) who understood that the company came first. Debuted in 1969, a popular movie series, *It's Tough Being a Man* (*Otoko wa tsurai yo*), commented on the conformity engineered by the straitjacket of company life through the eyes of an itinerant peddler who rejected job security for the byways of modern Japan.

Husbands and wives lived in separate worlds. Rural-based factory workers left farm work to parents, wives, and children. Only 2 to 5 percent farmed full time. For the urban middle class, a wife's job was to provide a stress-free environment for her husband. Since he had to devote full attention to his company, she managed the household, raised the children (preferably two), and did household repairs. The husband handed her his paycheck; she gave him an allowance, allocated money for food and other expenses, and saved the rest. Mothers devoted themselves

---

1. "Europe Toughens Stand Against Japan's Exports," *New York Times*, April 2, 1979, D:1, 5.

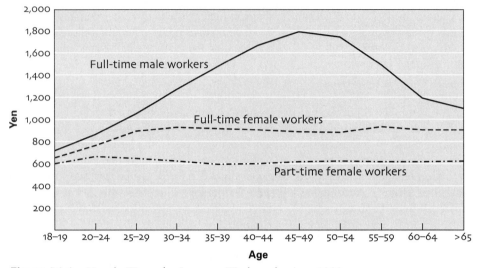

Figure 31.1   Hourly Wages for Japanese Workers, by Age, 1989
(*Mary C. Brinton,* Women and the Economic Miracle: Gender and Work in Postwar Japan
[Berkeley: University of California Press, 1992], p. 47.)

to their children's education, earning the opprobrium of being *kyōiku mama* (education mothers, implying an obsession with their children's educational success). When children needed extra help, mothers sent them to after-school schools. Mother consulted with teachers, attended Parent-Teacher Association meetings, volunteered at school, and supervised their children's nutrition, health, and homework. For the professional housewife, her child was her most important product. (See **Documents: Fujita Mariko, "'It's All Mother's Fault': Childcare and the Socialization of Working Mothers in Japan."**)

Continuing Social Issues

Women's career choices were limited. They typically worked after graduating from high school or junior college; to the mid-1980s almost 90 percent of companies rejected female graduates of four-year colleges because they had to be placed on a management track. Instead, women were hired as clerical or assembly line workers with the understanding they would retire at marriage or when they turned thirty years old. In the late 1960s women got the courts to agree that this practice constituted sex discrimination. In the early 1970s the courts forbade mandatory retirement because of pregnancy or childbirth or at a younger age than men. Women objected to being kept from managerial positions and well-meaning restrictions on the hours they could work and the kinds of work they were allowed to do. In response, the Diet passed the Equal Employment Opportunity Act of 1985. Although it urged employers to put women on the same track as men, it made no provisions for sanctions if they did not. In 1976 women's earnings stood at 56 percent of men's; in 1988 they declined to 50 percent. Companies still refuse to promote women at the same rate as men. Rather than pay women equal wages, some companies do not hire women at all. Full responsibility for home and children makes it hard for women to work past childbirth. Once the children are in school, mothers take part-time jobs. Although the working woman in Japan is imagined to be single, most are married women over age thirty-five.

Despite decades of denunciation tactics, *burakumin* still faced economic hardship and discrimination. Under the Special Measures and Enterprise Law concerning Assimilation of 1969, national and local governments put sewage systems, paved streets, better housing, schools, hospitals, and fire stations in the ghettoes. In 1976, the Justice Ministry agreed to restrict access to family registers that could be used to trace individuals back to the "new commoners" category established in 1871. Private detective agencies then published lists giving addresses for *burakumin* ghettoes. Their customers were companies, especially the largest and most prestigious, individuals, and colleges. In 1977, the overall unemployment rate was around 3 percent, but 28.5 percent of Osaka *burakumin* were unemployed. Those with jobs worked in small enterprises for low wages. Although most *burakumin* lived next to large factories, they never received more than temporary or part-time work.

Ainu and Okinawans launched movements in the 1970s to assert pride in their ethnic identities. Ainu protested that the 1968 celebration for the centenary of Hokkaido's colonization ignored them and their suffering. Kayano Shigeru opened an ethnographic museum in 1972 and wrote on Ainu language, folk tales, and practices of daily life. In 1994 he became the first Ainu elected to the Diet. He and other culturalists sought to restore seasonal ceremonies and protested plans to turn Hokkaido into an energy source for the rest of Japan with an oil-generated power station. The United States returned Okinawa to Japan in 1972, but left its bases on the islands. The local economy depended on servicing them and catering to Japanese tourists in search of a tropical experience at home. Okinawan music, dance, and crafts attracted aficionados on the mainland because they were seen as both a variant on primitive Japanese folk arts and exotic island culture. Although the national government spent lavishly on construction projects, it hired natives only in low-level jobs. *Burakumin,* Ainu, and Okinawan poverty rates and school dropout rates were

higher than the national average. Negative stereotypes abounded, and outsiders tried to avoid marrying or hiring them.

Koreans resident in Japan (six hundred thirty-seven thousand in 1999) faced special disabilities in fighting discrimination. As long as Korea was part of the Japanese Empire, Koreans were Japanese citizens. The postwar constitution defined Japanese citizens as those born of Japanese fathers, and Koreans became permanent resident aliens. Although celebrities and spouses of diplomats found the naturalization process easy, working-class Koreans did not. They also suffered a division between supporters of North Korea, who followed a separatist path, and supporters of the South, who tried to preserve vestiges of Korean identity while sending their children to Japanese schools. Children and grandchildren of Korean residents who grew up in Japan and spoke only Japanese paid taxes, but they could not vote. They had to be fingerprinted for their alien registration cards. After years of protest, that requirement changed in 1991, and resident Koreans were allowed to vote in local elections. Still, Japanese refused to marry Koreans, employers to hire them, landlords to rent to them. Resident Koreans who protested were told they should go back to Korea.

Japanese nationalists ignored all evidence to the contrary in praising the virtues of their uniquely homogeneous race. The debate on Japaneseness (*Nihonjinron*) reacted to the protest movements of the late 1960s, universalizing social science theories that pigeonholed Japan solely in terms of economic development, and Japan bashing by foreigners. The more Japanese people ate, dressed, and lived like people across the developed world, the more they had to be reminded that they possessed a uniquely distinctive culture. According to *Nihonjinron,* "we Japanese" speak a language intrinsically incomprehensible to outsiders, think with both sides of the brain, and have intestines too short to digest Australian beef. "We Japanese" innately prefer consensus and

Fujita Mariko, "'It's All Mother's Fault': Childcare and the Socialization of Working Mothers in Japan"

Various sectors in postwar society have made a fetish of conformity. This essay by a college professor provides a glimpse of how women enforce the standards for being a professional housewife. What are the conflicts between working and being a mother? How do women interact across the work divide? What is the role fathers are expected to play in child rearing?

A woman should recognize herself as the best educator of her child. An excellent race is born from excellent mothers. . . . Only women can bear children and raise them. Therefore mothers should be proud and confident in raising their children. It is also a fundamental right of children to be raised by their own mothers. . . . Employment opportunities should be given to those women who have finished raising their children and who still wish to resume working outside the home.

—1970 Family Charter by the Committee on Family Life Problems

I live in a small-scale *danchi* (apartment block) built for national governmental employees in the southeastern part of Nara City. The complex consists of three four-story buildings which house about 70 families. The occupants are mostly young and early middle-aged couples, though some are *tanshin-funinsha* (husbands who reside away from their families due to the relocation of their jobs). The ages of the children in this complex range from babies to junior-high-school students. There are only a handful of high school students. Therefore, the mothers' ages range roughly between 25 and 45.

Because the rent is substantially lower than in private housing, there is not much economic pressure for the wives to work. This explains the fact that the majority of wives are full-time housewives. The mothers of older children may engage in occasional part-time jobs. As far as I know, those women who work full-time are without children. If a couple has preschool children, the wives most certainly stay at home to raise them.

My contacts with my neighbors, especially the wives, are through the various activities of the *jichikai* (the voluntary association of the housing complex) such as a monthly clean-up of the common area. I also belong to one of the two Nara Citizens' Co-op groups available in the housing complex. Members of each group jointly order groceries, which the Co-op brings to the housing complex once a week. Members together divide the groceries according to each member's order.

As soon as my neighbors found out that I had a toddler, they assumed that I was a full-time housewife and mother. They never thought to ask whether I worked outside the home. Because I did have a job, they often found me walking alone without my son and they would always ask, "Where is

harmony, and we put the interests of the group above the individual.

Despite social problems, by the mid-1970s, most Japanese people enjoyed unprecedented

levels of prosperity. Income and salary disparities remained relatively narrow, and 90 percent of the population considered itself to be middle class. The proportion of total income

Hosaki today?" indicating their expectation that I would always be with my child. The situation was complicated because at the time I was a part-time lecturer at a university and I did most of my work at home. My neighbors found this kind of work pattern very difficult to understand because to them work means regular employment between 8:00 AM and 5:00 PM. Telling them that my son was at day care was tricky because they would wonder what I was doing at home during the day instead of being at work. Only after I took a full-time teaching position, which keeps me away from home most of the time, were my neighbors convinced that I was actually working.

The fact that working mothers and non-working mothers do not belong to the same circle of friends became clear to me when I spent a day with my son instead of sending him to day care. I took him to the neighborhood playground where he played in the sand box by the other children. Since he did not have toys of his own (I did not know the children were supposed to bring their own toys), a mother told her son to let my son use his toys. Several mothers were present; they talked among themselves and politely ignored me. I said a few words to them and they replied, but that was the end of our conversation. I basically watched my son, and later played with him when he wanted to play ball. After half an hour, one of the mothers finally asked me whether I lived in the same apartment complex. The question astonished me because I had frequently seen them in the neighborhood. But, as far as they were concerned, I was a total stranger.

Our son frequently became ill his first year in Japan, perhaps due to lack of immu-

nity to the viruses he was exposed to at day care. He had hardly had even a mild cold while we were in the United States, and we were puzzled and distressed by his frequent fevers, respiratory problems, and even pneumonia. Soon after enrolling our son at Sakura Day Care, we asked the director if she had a list of baby-sitters, or if she would introduce us to people who would be willing, with pay, to take care of our son when he became sick. Her answer made us realize how unusual our request was in Japan: she was truly astonished by our question and replied that she had never heard of such people.

Our neighbors frequently offered the folk belief that "boys are more susceptible to all sorts of illness than girls when they are young" to explain my son's frequent sicknesses. But as soon as they found out that my work required me to spend two nights a week away from home, they started to use my absence to explain my son's illness. They thought Hosaki was lonely and thus became ill. No one openly criticized me for working until they found out about my absence. Then, they were quick to criticize the mother, making her absence the cause of illness, although the times of Hosaki's illness and my absence did not coincide and although his father was with him and took care of him. They sympathized with the father, who was, from their point of view, unduly burdened while the "selfish" mother was neglecting her duty of childcare.

Source: *Journal of Japanese Studies* 15:1 (Winter 1989): 70–71, 72–73, 80, 86, 87, 89, modified.

spent on food declined while quantity, quality, and variety increased. The older generation ate rice, vegetables, and fish. Young people ate meat, dairy products, and spaghetti. Although

Japan maintained the highest savings rate in the industrialized world, people had discretionary income to eat out, go to movies, and take vacations.

THE ROARING 1980S

Japan's recovery from the shocks of the 1970s put it on a collision course with its major trading partner, the United States. Japan adjusted to oil and pollution crises by building fuel-efficient, less-polluting cars. When stricter pollution emission requirements, consumer demand for higher quality, and increased gasoline prices caught Detroit by surprise, Japan's automobile makers seized the American market. To make Japanese goods less competitive, President Ronald Reagan devalued the dollar in 1985. Japan discovered that it was twice as rich as before. The yen bought twice as much oil, and since Japanese manufacturers had already streamlined production techniques, they needed half as much to make their products as their American competitors did. When Honda raised the price of the Accord by a thousand dollars, American manufacturers raised their prices as well.

American negotiators demanded that Japan import more foreign products. Japan had lower tariffs on manufactured goods than other industrialized countries, but it protected farmers by restricting food imports. It also had nontariff structural barriers to trade—regulations to ensure quality and safety, the requirement that car buyers show proof of an off-street parking space, a multilayered distribution system, and zoning that favored shops over supermarkets and discount stores. Despite reluctance to disturb a system that provided employment and political support, the LDP and the bureaucracy gradually reduced restrictions. Australian cheese appeared in supermarkets. Shakey's Pizza, McDonalds, Kentucky Fried Chicken, and family-style restaurants invaded Japan in the late 1970s. Seven-Eleven spawned a boom in convenience stores. In 1983, Disneyland opened its first international venue near Tokyo. In 2000 it welcomed 16.5 million visitors, the largest number for any theme park in the world.

Trade surpluses and a strong currency generated more capital than Japan could absorb domestically. With unemployment rates at about 3 percent and labor costs rising, companies built factories in low-wage countries on the Asian mainland. To get around protective tariffs, antidumping measures, and quotas, they built high-technology factories in developed countries, and Toyota became a multinational corporation. In 1982, industrial plants, equipment, and capital goods constituted 43 percent of Japan's exports. Japanese capital serviced the U.S. debt. Japan became the world's largest supplier of loans to developing countries and the chief donor of foreign aid, and it supplied 50 percent of lendable capital to the World Bank.

The electronics industry had two modes of expanding overseas. In setting up production facilities, first in Southeast Asia in the mid- to late 1970s and then in developed countries in the 1980s, parent companies retained complete control of local subsidiaries. The managerial staff was Japanese; the workers were local. The U.S. Semiconductor Industry Association accused Japan of dumping in 1985; in an agreement a year later, Japan agreed to voluntary quotas. Corporations then instituted cooperative ventures with partners in the United States and Europe to develop new technology or combine specialties. Automobile manufacturers followed suit: Toyota and General Motors, Nissan, Honda, and Ford operate joint ventures and exchange components at factories from Australia to Brazil to Europe and the United States.

Japanese capital investment deepened ties with Asian neighbors, while nationalist sentiment strained diplomatic relations. Japan dominated China's Special Economic Zones and invested heavily in Korea and the Pacific Rim, leading pundits to claim that it had succeeded in creating a Greater East Asia Co-Prosperity Sphere. In 1982, the Education Ministry approved a textbook for middle school and high school students that minimized Japanese aggression in China. This led the PRC, North and South Korea, and other Asian nations to denounce resurgent Japanese nationalism. Japan's aggression and its refusal to acknowledge the suffering it inflicted on Korean women were still issues in the textbooks prepared for 2005. Asians and some Japanese criticized visits by prime ministers to Yasukuni Shrine, where war criminals are enshrined. Textbook revision and Japan's refusal to apologize for waging war roiled popular opinion even as government leaders drew closer together. When the president of South Korea visited Japan for the first time in 1984, demonstrations erupted in Seoul.

The government faced domestic problems as well. The LDP did not want to raise taxes to cover deficit spending that started in 1973. Among the culprits were subsidies for farmers, public corporations—Japan National Railroad (JNR) and Nihon Telephone and Telegraph (NTT)—and national health insurance, which initiated free care for the elderly in 1972. Following the lead of Prime Minister Margaret Thatcher in Britain, a commission set up in 1981 promoted privatizing public corporations to relieve the government of drains on its resources and undermine the strength of the railroad workers' union. Although allowed to bargain collectively, unions in the public service sector did not have the right to strike nor did they have incentive to boost productivity. In 1975, railroad workers shut down the JNR for eight days in a strike to win the right to strike.

The conservative triumvirate of the free market world consisted of Margaret Thatcher, Ronald Reagan, and Nakasone Yasuhiro, Japan's prime minister from 1982 to 1987. Nakasone privatized JNR and NTT and took the government out of the business of selling tobacco and cigarettes. Beginning in 1982, the elderly had to contribute payments for health services. Nakasone urged a return to family values, especially the obligation of the younger generation to care for their elders. He attributed Japan's economic success to its ethnic homogeneity and funded research into the foundation of Japan's distinctive identity. He also called for internationalization so that government leaders would learn how to reduce trade friction and businessmen would feel comfortable with foreigners. His promotion of corporate capitalism made Japan a major player at the Group of 7 conferences of industrialized nations while he lectured the United States on its social and economic failings exemplified in racial diversity and the lack of a work ethic.

The Good Life

For many people, old and young, the good life meant material possessions. It meant automated bread-making machines, three-dimensional TV, and self-heating canned sake. It meant laughing at Itami Jūzō's movies about funeral practices, food, tax evasion, new religions, and gangsters. The good life made it easy to buy books and magazines (1.45 billion and 4.01 billion, respectively, in 1987). (See **Material Culture: *Manga*.**) Whether a meaning for life could be found in a late capitalist society divided Japanese writers. Murakami Haruki captured the absurdity of modernity in his novels *A Wild Sheep Chase, Hardboiled Wonderland,* and *Sputnik Sweetheart.* Yoshimoto Banana's *Kitchen,* a novella popular with college students, depicted a dysfunctional family and individuals alone in a postmodern world. Nostalgia for simpler times under the Occupation sold 4 million copies of *Totto-chan, The Little Girl at the Window* by the fast-talking television celebrity Kuroyanagi Tetsuko.

Rejecting the materialism of the present meant seeking the roots of Japanese identity. A self-styled Kyoto philosopher creatively interpreted the prehistoric Jōmon era as when Japanese lived in harmony with nature and each other in a community of man and gods. Mystically transmitted through the emperor system and buried deep within every Japanese, the national essence could be recapitulated by a visit to the *furusato* (home village). JNR's "Discover Japan" and "Exotic Japan" advertising campaigns promoted visits to thatched roof farmhouses foreign to urban residents. Villages striving to overcome depopulation revived agricultural festivals to attract tourists; castle towns put on daimyo processions. On Yaeyama in the Ryukyu Islands, a new tradition of sash weaving

MATERIAL CULTURE

Manga

Japanese comics called *manga* attained their present form in 1959 when they became a source of entertainment and information for all ages.

Early *manga* were printed on cheap paper and sold at a price that the working poor could afford. The first generation born after World War II grew up reading them and continued the habit through college and into their working lives. *Manga* gave them a chance to laugh at the restrictive conditions that enforced conformity while warning them that failing to work hard and toe the corporate line would lead to mockery. *Manga* and their close cousins, animated films, became the domain of Japan's most creative minds.

From the 1960s to the mid-1990s *manga* offered escapist fantasies, often violently pornographic, for white-collar workers on their daily commute. Science-fiction *manga* appealed to children and teenagers. *Manga* taught history to students studying for entrance exams. *Barefoot Gen* graphically illustrated the horrors of the atomic bomb explosion over Hiroshima. Cookbooks and biography could be found in *manga*. *Manga* explained energy policy, the value-added tax, investment strategies, and the principles of superconductors. *Japan Inc.: An Introduction to Japanese Economics in Manga* (1986) sold over 1 million copies in hardcover.

Manga reached their peak of sales in 1994. Publishing houses devoted one-third of their total output to *manga* and sold 553 million copies a year. Shibuya, the crossroads for youth culture in Tokyo, contained *manga* superstores where the clerks dressed as *manga* characters.

Manga. Manga provided education and entertainment. "The Manga Introduction to Superconductors" explained new technology in 1987 through the eyes of three young salaried workers who visit a research laboratory. *(The Manga Introduction to Supercomputers by Takashi Hashimoto and Fumio Hisamatsu)*

Manga and the Japanese publishing industry are in decline. Their former readers on trains and in coffee shops thumb cell phones with Internet connections or play handheld computer games.

for betrothal gifts became a way to assert a folk identity and sell souvenirs to tourists.

The search for origins scarcely concealed new and to conservative eyes troubling trends among Japanese youth. In 1978 the "bamboo shoot tribe" (*takenokozoku*) of middle and high school students dressed in outlandish and expensive costumes started appearing every Sunday near trendy Harajuku in Tokyo. (See Color Plate 31.) Late at night, gangs of motorcycle riders roared through residential neighborhoods, disrupting the sleep of salary men. In

Opponents of Narita Airport. Waving staves and wearing helmets, opponents of Narita Airport battled riot police protected by heavy shields, helmets, and padded armor. *(Corbis)*

1985 newspapers started reporting an increase in incidents of bullying, some leading to murder or suicide, in elementary through high schools. The "new breed of human beings" rejected the work ethic, harmony, and consensus of their elders. They took part-time jobs that did not require the commitment of a regular position. Since many of them lived with their parents, their income bought luxury items rather than necessities. They splurged on designer clothes, meals and entertainment, and trips abroad. Married couples demanded bigger living spaces and better plumbing. They wanted a shorter work week and longer vacations. Rather than put up with low initial salaries and long hours of after-work socializing, a few workers switched jobs, and some husbands went home to their wives.

Despite these problems, Japan's economy appeared unstoppable. In 1988, its per capita GNP surpassed that of the United States. The United States cited unfair trade practices and Japan's free ride under the American security umbrella. In 1989, Morita Akio, chairman of Sony, and Ishihara Shintarō, mayor of Tokyo in 2002, published *The Japan That Can Say No*. It criticized U.S. business practices and claimed that Japan bashing was the result of racial prejudice. It also castigated the Japanese government for fearing reform and Japanese people for being soft. Banks awash with yen urged capital on borrowers. Japanese art purchases led to an outcry that the cream of western heritage was being shipped to Asia. Mitsubishi bought Rockefeller Center in New York City. Sony bought Columbia Pictures. Real estate rose so high that land in Tokyo was valued at three times the entire United States. The tripling of the stock market inflated a speculative bubble. (See Color Plate 32.)

MALAISE IN THE 1990S

For the LDP, political problems began in 1989. The Shōwa emperor died at the beginning of the year. For having remarked that the emperor bore some responsibility for the military's behavior during World War II, the mayor of Nagasaki was shot by a right-wing fanatic. The new emperor took Heisei, translatable as "achieving peace" or "maintaining equilibrium," for his era name. Prime Minister Takeshita Noboru inaugurated a value-added tax of 3 percent that infuriated consumers. Two months later he resigned because of publicity surrounding 150 million yen he had received from Recruit Cosmo, an employment information firm with investments in real estate and publishing. LDP faction bosses had difficulty identifying an untainted successor. Uno Sōsuke lasted barely six weeks before a palimony suit by his mistress brought him down. In the election that summer, the JSP under the female leadership of Doi Takako ran an unprecedented number of women candidates and gained control of the upper house. It also did well in the more powerful lower house in 1990.

The LDP faced challenges from members of its own party. Frustrated by elderly faction bosses who monopolized the prime ministership, younger politicians split the LDP. In 1993, Hosokawa Morihiro from the Japan New Party became prime minister when the LDP suffered defeat in elections for the lower house. The worst rice harvest in two hundred years forced him to allow rice imports from Asia for the first time since World War II. Farmers were outraged. He too was caught in a financial scandal. Two more non-LDP prime ministers followed him, neither capable of dealing with Japan's economic woes. The government's tardy response to the Kobe earthquake on January 17, 1995, which killed over five thousand two hundred people and left over three hundred thousand homeless, received much criticism. In 1996, a chastened LDP returned to power, and faction bosses picked the next prime minister. In 2001, they chose a third-generation Diet member, Koizumi Jun'ichirō, who promised liberals he would make structural reforms needed to bolster the economy and pleased conservatives by his call to revise the pacifist constitution.

Koizumi inherited a stagnant economy. The speculative bubble of the late 1980s collapsed when a recession in the developed world sent sales tumbling and competition from low-labor-cost countries eroded corporations' market share. The stock market lost nearly 40 percent of its peak value in 1990 and 65 percent by August 1992. When the inflated real estate market vanished, Mitsubishi had to sell Rockefeller Center at a loss. Corporations that had borrowed billions of yen to buy land or expand their businesses discovered that their debts exceeded their rapidly depreciating assets. Banks were reluctant to lend money. The Asian economic turmoil of 1997 caused by speculators dumping Asian currencies caused another recession in Japan. Two brokerage houses and a bank went bankrupt, leading to fears of depression. Economic growth, which had limped along at barely 1 percent per annum between 1992 and 1995, went negative in 1997. In 2002, bad loans ballooned to $1.3 trillion, and government debt climbed to 150 percent of the GDP. Except for an occasional quarter of slight expansion, deflation stalked Japan.

The LDP scrambled to stimulate the economy. In the 1980s it tried to revitalize rural communities by building culture halls and art museums and encouraging production of traditional handicrafts as souvenirs. In the 1990s it poured money into dams, roads, and postmodern public buildings. In 1991 the Tokyo Metropolitan Government moved into massive new headquarters that soared above office buildings and hotels, many half empty. Koizumi halted a project to turn a saltwater swamp into farmland while the government paid farmers not to plant rice. His proposal to privatize the postal savings system threatened the Finance Ministry's control over the $3 trillion in personal savings kept outside government budgets that it used to finance public works projects, prime the stock market, and buy government bonds. Proposals to streamline the bureaucracy, reduce regulatory oversight, and eliminate positions foundered on bureaucratic inertia. Near-zero interest rates and government support for nonperforming loans failed to stimulate business investment. The Education Ministry tried to make universities more responsive to the interests of industry and eliminate irrelevant fields in the humanities and social sciences. In 2004 national universities became independent entities.

Japan faced international criticism regarding its role in world affairs. The United States grumbled when Japan refused to commit troops to the Gulf War in 1991 even though Japan's military spending ranked third below the United States and Russia. Six months after the war, Japan sent six minesweepers to the Persian Gulf amid debate fueled by antiwar sentiment in the postwar generation over whether their dispatch violated constitutional restrictions. Japan also paid $10 billion toward the cost of the war and permitted its troops to participate in peacekeeping missions in Cambodia and East Timor. After the terrorist attacks in the United States on September 11, 2001, the Diet passed an antiterrorism law that allowed Japanese troops to provide rear-echelon support for the war in Iraq in 2004.

Social Problems for the Twenty-First Century

Japan's social problems also defied easy solution. In the 1980s, American social scientists praised Japan's educational system for producing literate students who scored far higher on mathematics tests than Americans. Japanese critics feared that schools were turning out soulless automatons with weak characters and no sense of national identity, unable to think for themselves, and lacking the creativity to put Japan in the lead of technological innovation. Preteenage rebels disrupted classrooms and terrorized teachers. In a series of high-profile crimes, youths killed classmates, tortured the homeless, and murdered elderly neighbors. Labor shortages in the 1980s in the sex trade and the dangerous, dirty, and low-paying work of construction and stevedoring brought men and women from Taiwan, the Philippines, Iran, and other countries to work as prostitutes and day laborers. About half entered illegally because the Labor and Justice ministries refused to acknowledge the need for their services. Immigration of Latin Americans of Japanese ancestry was encouraged because it was thought they would assimilate to the dominant culture. In 1999, 1.56 million foreigners lived legally in Japan out of a total population of 126.6 million. Tokyo became a more cosmopolitan city, but mainstream Japanese were quick to accuse foreigners of robbery, rape, and drug trafficking.

Economic stagnation and rising unemployment had social consequences. Corporations stopped competing to hire college graduates, and unemployment rose to an official rate of 5 percent in 2001. This figure excluded part-time workers who had lost their jobs, most of them women. The government reduced the duration and value of unemployment benefits. Job security guarantees covered just over 15 percent of workers in 2002. "Pay for performance" started to replace the seniority system of merit raises. Tokyo, Yokohama, and Osaka had long had a floating population of farm men from the north who spent the winter working as day laborers and congregated in flophouses. In the late 1980s permanent dropouts started to swell their numbers. Osaka laborers caused the worst rioting in nearly twenty years in 1990 in reaction to police harassment. Homeless people appeared as well. They built cardboard cities in parks and pedestrian tunnels that surrounded train terminals except when police periodically chased them away.

The search for meaning in a materialistic world took new paths. Right-wing militants who rode sound trucks blaring martial music and decorated with posters calling for the return of the northern territories held by Russia attacked the offices of the Asahi publishing company for articles showing disrespect for the emperor. Adherents of new religions such as the Unification Church and Mahikarikyō sought a sense of community and a merging of the individual ego in a larger entity. Aum Shinrikyō attracted students from Japan's elite universities, lawyers, and businessmen. Feeling persecuted by the Justice Ministry, in March 1995 its followers released Sarin, a poison gas, in the Tokyo subway system adjacent to National Police headquarters. It killed twelve people and incapacitated thousands. The LDP tried to revise the 1951 Religious Corporations Law to bring governmental oversight to the fund-raising, educational activities, and business-related income of the 183,970 registered religious organizations. Opposition by Sōka Gakkai's political arm and other religious organizations kept the 1951 law intact.

Starting in the late 1960s, LDP politicians urged women to have more children; thereafter they lamented the selfishness of young women who put consumerism ahead of maternal responsibilities. National health insurance, a 99 percent literacy rate, sanitary housing, and nutritious diets contributed to one of the lowest infant mortality rates in the world at 5 per thousand in 1989 and longevity rates for men reaching into the mid-seventies and for women into the eighties. Women had 1.57 children apiece, well below the 2.2 necessary to maintain the population. Couples who wanted a higher standard of living or worried about the costs of their children's education limited their family size regardless of political propaganda.

In 2000, 16 percent of the population was age sixty-five or older, and Japan had the oldest population in the industrialized world. In 2015 it is projected to be 25 percent, and 25 percent of the national budget will have to be spent on social welfare. Through the 1990s, corporations had plentiful sources of investment capital at low interest rates because Japan had the highest rates of personal savings in the world. With more people retired, the savings rate will drop.

The government wants to limit its costs for hospitals and nursing homes by having children care for parents. Elder sons with the traditional responsibility for parental care have trouble finding marriage partners because women increasingly prefer to take care of their own parents. Some farmers have even sought brides in the Philippines.

Although marriage is still the norm, it too has changed. The average age of marriage for women crept from twenty-two in 1950 to over twenty-six in 2000. Crown Princess Masako delayed marriage for a career in the Foreign Ministry until she was twenty-nine. Her only child is a girl. Since the constitution defines the ruler as male, allowing this child to succeed her father will require a constitutional change, devoutly desired by Japanese feminists. So many women opt for four years of higher education that the former junior colleges have become universities even though the decline in the college age population means that more are having trouble meeting their enrollment targets. In hopes of better futures than they perceive possible in Japan, some women seek academic degrees and employment abroad. Women want careers, and they have become increasingly choosy about whom they will marry and under what conditions. Older women have been known to divorce their retired husbands because they cannot stand having "that oversized garbage" underfoot every day.

SUMMARY

Japan is a mature industrial society. Its cities are among the world's cleanest and safest, and most of its citizens enjoy a comfortable life. Japanese foods are eaten in Europe and the United States; Japanese fashions and popular music are followed in Asia. Introduced in 1980, karaoke is performed around the world. Ōe Kenzaburō won the Nobel Prize in literature in 1994 for his writings that express universal truths regarding the human condition. Japanese politicians infuriate their Asian neighbors by calling the emperor a living god and Japan a divine nation while participating in Asian economic conferences. Lingering memories of the war and Japan's wariness of China's growing economic and military strength has not prevented Japan from trading more with China than with the United States, even as it offers support for the global war on terrorism.

SUGGESTED READING

For protest against Tokyo International Airport, see D. E. Apter and N. Sawa, *Against the State: Politics and Protest in Japan* (1984).

For recent books on pollution, see J. Broadbent, *Environmental Politics in Japan: Networks of Power and Protest* (1998), and T. S. George, *Minamata: Pollution and the Struggle for Democracy in Postwar Japan* (2001).

For politics, see R. J. Hrebenar, *Japan's New Party System* (2000). For legal issues, see F. K. Upham, *Law and Social Change in Postwar Japan* (1987).

For economic issues, see R. M. Uriu, *Troubled Industries: Confronting Economic Change in Japan* (1996). For minorities, see M. Weiner, *Japan's Minorities: The Illusion of Homogeneity* (1997).

For popular culture, see S. Kinsella, *Adult Manga: Culture and Power in Contemporary Japanese Society* (2000).

For recent books on women. see Y. Ogasawara, *Office Ladies and Salaried Men: Power, Gender, and Work in Japanese Companies* (1998); R. M. LeBlanc, *Bicycle Citizens: The Political World of the Japanese Housewife* (1999); and K. Kelsky, *Women on the Verge: Japanese Women, Western Dreams* (2001).

East Asia in the Twenty-First Century

It should come as no surprise that in our increasingly global world, the countries of East Asia are now more connected than ever before. Tens of thousands of Korean, Taiwanese, and Japanese businesspeople now live in China to manage the manufacturing operations they have located there, and they regularly fly back and forth to their home countries. Thousands of Chinese now live in Japan, some as students or businesspeople; others are laborers, who often are there illegally. Huge drops in the cost of international phone calls, as well as the ubiquity of email and the Internet, make it much easier for those living outside their home countries to keep in regular contact with friends and relatives back home, creating diasporas very different from the immigrant communities of earlier times.

For two decades, Japanese, Korean, and Taiwanese tourists have been visiting China, often on package tours, and today Chinese who have prospered during the reform period are reciprocating and visiting nearby countries in increasing numbers. Popular and classical music no longer respects national boundaries, and singers and instrumentalists often have large followings throughout the East Asian countries, adding to the huge popularity of karaoke in the region. Popular TV serials are often dubbed to be shown in other East Asian countries.

Right now in Japan, there's a major Korea boom owing to the popularity of a soap opera, *Winter Sonata,* and its star, Bae Yong-joon (called in Japan Yon-sama). He has such a powerful appeal that when he visited Japan, middle-aged women were throwing themselves in front of his car and swarming his hotel. There are sev-eral Internet sites where young women who are fed up with Japanese men can try to meet Korean men (without realizing that the attitudes of Korean men are quite similar to those of Japanese men). Japan's experimental music is the world's leader in something called "noise." There are global currents in which Japan, Korea, and Taiwan participate. A Japanese wedding company is exporting Japanese-style weddings to Shanghai. In other parts of China, however, Japanese soccer players have been booed by fans still angry at Japan's wartime behavior.

Politically, East Asian countries have changed, but not necessarily toward western liberalism. After the U.S. occupation of 1945, Japan succeeded in establishing free elections and free speech and association, but it did little to reform the prewar bureaucracy, which subsequently played the leading role in devising policy for industrial development. The Liberal Democratic Party (LDP) remains the most powerful political party in Japan. Its leader-follower factions meet behind the scenes to choose prime ministers and operate to stymie initiatives for meaningful reform. The middle class has not been able to change the political system to reflect public demands, the labor movement has remained quiescent, the women's movement has not broken workplace discrimination, and the public has not demanded reform.

After forty years of student and activist struggles against dictatorial repression, South Korea held the first democratic elections for the presidency in 1987. Since 1992 the military has been subordinated to civilian control, mayors and governors and local assemblies are now elected, and two past presidents have been jailed for their crimes. In 1997, the first electoral regime change occurred. Yet the political parties have shown no lasting power and consist of many leader-follower groups that shift allegiance from one party to another. The nefarious national security law still remains on the books. Despair over economic problems since 1997 has created a conservative backlash that pines for the double-digit growth of the dictator Park Chung Hee. The country still has a long way to go before completing the democratic transition and could possibly suffer a reversal.

In Taiwan the repressive politics of Chiang Kaishek and the Nationalist Party have been replaced by democratic elections. Credit for the democratic transition goes largely to Chiang's son, Chiang Chingkuo. As president of the Republic of China he was instrumental in creating that democracy by fiat. An independence movement backed by native Taiwanese was able to elect Chen Shuibian president in 2000, but China's military threats against secession from China mean that the prospect for independence is slim. Democratic processes have gone a long way in Taiwan but for the external constraint against independence.

Although the Tiananmen massacre of 1989 scotched the democratic movement in China, there have been signs of liberal thought among students and intellectuals, who hope that economic development will lead to a larger middle class and democracy, but the regime shows little sign of liberalizing. Dissatisfaction about aspects of the new economic system has materialized in attacks against soldiers and police in several cities, strikes by workers, and rural protests against local officials for corruption. Charismatic leaders revive slogans and symbols of traditional religious beliefs to attract followers, and others appeal to Maoist egalitarianism to critique the materialism and inequality of the Deng era. If the rigid, centralized political system fails to stem corruption and meet the needs of the people, the regime might well collapse in rebellion as most past dynasties did, but not as a result of mass demand for democracy.

Finally, North Korea has maintained central control over the country with hardly a pause. Although restrictions on residence movement and occupations have eased and private plots and small private markets have been allowed under the famine conditions of the 1990s, no evidence of political protest and organization of a serious nature has been revealed. North Korea toys with the idea of adopting Deng's economic policies but is wary of doing so because liberalism and human rights threaten foreign capitalist domination and destruction of the power elite.

The 1990s were a difficult period for East Asian economies. In both Japan and South Korea, state control and protectionism caused severe economic decline. Japan had come close to surpassing the United States in a number of measurements of economic power by the late 1980s. All hopes for that were dashed, however, when the bubble economy in Japan burst in 1990, and the economy plunged into stagnation for over a decade. South Korea had a similar experience when it was the victim of the Asian financial crisis in 1997. It was bailed out eventually by the International Monetary Fund.

Meanwhile, the Chinese economy was blasting ahead at a 6 to 7 percent annual growth rate and using its low wage structure to undercut many of the labor-intensive industries of Japan, South Korea, Taiwan, and Hong Kong. China was able to escape the Asian crisis of 1997 despite an increasing rate of foreign direct investment in Chinese business because its currency is inconvertible and not susceptible to speculation. Because it has to meet foreign competition, it has had to close many state enterprises, eliminate tariff and nontariff protectionism, and admit foreign capital and investment, especially after it joined the World Trade Organization and the World Bank.

China has begun to show many of the problems that Japan and South Korea have experienced: bank loans forced by the state to insolvent companies; collusive and corrupt agreements between bureaucrats and businessmen; maintaining inefficient state enterprises as a substitute for welfare payments to workers.

The gap between rich and poor, between flourishing coastal urban regions and backward rural areas in the interior, and between skilled and unskilled workers is growing. Millions of unemployed and homeless migrant workers from the countryside fill urban slums. Strikes by workers have increased, only to be met by government repression.

North Korea's stubborn insistence on self-sufficiency and economic autarchy to prevent foreign dependency closed the country off from trade with the non-Communist world and blocked the stimulus of foreign competition to develop new technology. When communism in the Soviet Union and eastern Europe collapsed between 1989 and 1991, Russia cut off subsidized oil exports, and North Korea lacked the foreign exchange to pay for it. Without sufficient energy, its factories had to operate at less than full capacity. The country has recovered partially from the massive floods of the mid-1990s, but the population is still malnourished. Attempts at modest liberalization of the economy have been stymied by American hostility.

Despite the despair accompanying the downturn in the business cycle in East Asia, all regions but North Korea have moved away from poverty and will continue their climb toward providing decent livelihoods for their populations. There has been much talk about the possibility of creating a regional free trade bloc in East Asia like the European Community, but there are serious obstacles. The Chinese economy has by far the highest growth rate based on a huge population and low wages and stands to gain the most from unrestrained trade until its wage rates rise. North Korea needs economic assistance from China as long as its economy remains moribund, but its intense nationalism precludes domination by any foreign economy. South Korean business is shipping its factories to China, but the public fears the loss of industry and the resulting economic decline and is wary of recent Japanese hostility to North Korea. Japan has much to gain from exports of high-tech products and investment in factories in China, but lingering Chinese resentment of Japanese atrocities in World War II, official visits to the Yasukuni shrine, Japan's military alliance with the United States, and suspicion of Japanese rearmament could put a brake on further development. All nations except North Korea continue to benefit from exports to the United States and, although maybe on a smaller scale, to Europe. Trade with Southeast Asia and Latin America is growing, and the potential for exports to Russia and surrounding states in return for oil and gas could be enormous if serious political and bureaucratic obstacles to free trade in those states could be removed.

Despite economic development in most East Asian states, they all brought with them fundamental conservative traditions based on familial ties, respect for status, and male domination. Some of these traditions have been weakened by egalitarian Communist ideals, education for men and women, marriage by choice and divorce, and rising incomes, but they remain formidable obstacles against the adoption of western values.

China has undergone significant influence from the worldwide communications revolution. Cell phones and fiber optics have lowered the costs of telephones and electrical transmission. Computers have given access to about 59 million people (3 percent of the Chinese population), and the figure might grow to 250 million by 2008. Microsoft opened a research laboratory in the Haidian District of Beijing, where some eight hundred ten thousand Chinese research scientists and engineers live. Oracle, Motorola, Siemens, IBM, Intel, General Electric, and Nokia (which produces mobile phones) are running research facilities in China to develop new products as well, opening the door to innovative and independent research to young scientists.

Aware that unlimited contact with the outside world poses a political threat to the regime, the Chinese leadership has ordered operators of Internet sites to monitor government bans against rumors, libel, subversion, sabotage of national security, the promotion of cults and feudal superstition, pornography, violence, and gambling.

The movie industry has developed, and foreign movies, popular songs, and chain stores from Japan, South Korea, and the United States have penetrated the country. Whether these influences will lead to the liberalization of centralized political rule in the future remains to be seen.

Culturally, South Korea has leaped to the forefront of modern technology. It seems that everyone (including teenagers) has a cell phone. Computers and access to the Internet are widespread. The movie industry is developing rapidly, producing a generation of directors, producers, and actors. Its movies are gaining popularity abroad. Thousands of young students travel to the United States to get an education, and interest in China, Chinese language study, and tourist trips is growing rapidly. North Korea has tried to insulate itself from the communications revolution and the cultural effects of globalization, but clandestine access to the Internet has already proved subversive to the closed society by slightly opening the window of information from the world outside.

Despite stagnation in the Japanese economy, contemporary Japanese culture in the form of Japanese comics books (*manga*), computer cartoon and video games and animation (*anime*), designer clothing, pop music, new dance steps, and the paraphernalia that accompanies it for sale on the market have become major export industries. In Japan 53 million people are connected to the Internet, and cell phones are ubiquitous. Japan leads the world in new and innovative products and designs in electronics. Most of these innovations mainly affect Japanese youth and create new job opportunities outside the rigid hierarchies of big business, opening up the possibilities of individual creativity and entrepreneurship.

Signs of American culture abound in Japan, including fast food parlors; McDonald's, Burger King, Colonel Sanders, and Starbucks coffee shops are ubiquitous. Designer boutiques from the United States and Europe have taken over floors in major department stores, and Japanese designers have penetrated the West. American teenage clothing and music styles are everywhere, but no more than Japanese Nintendo games, cartoons, and the Hello Kitty fad have overwhelmed American youth. Baseball is now a Japanese national sport, albeit with its own special variations, and Japanese ballplayers have joined several American major league teams.

The tensions between the Japanese and South Korean governments have lessened somewhat over time. After 1945, the Korean government imposed a ban on all cultural imports from Japan, which included music, movies, television shows, and comic books. In October 1998, South Korean president Kim Dae Jung said that his administration would gradually reopen South Korea to Japanese cultural imports. Today, most Japanese products enter the country freely, and remaining bans on some Japanese comic books and movies are expected to be eliminated soon. The two nations agreed in 2002 to cohost the World Cup tournament, the first time that the World Cup was played in Asia and the first time that two countries had split hosting duties.

Nevertheless, suspicions about Japanese attitudes and policies remain strong. The Japanese refuse to correct distortions in Japanese textbooks about mistreatment of Koreans during the colonial period, to apologize publicly and pay reparations to the comfort women (the kidnapped sex slaves of Japanese troops), and to share advanced technology in some industries. Japanese prime ministers continue to pay homage to the war dead of the imperial period at Yasukuni shrine. The Japanese public has showed increased hostility toward North Korea and Korean residents in Japan, and proposals for rearmament are gaining strength. South Korean universities have still failed to expand Japanese language instruction and academic programs in Japanese studies.

The main question for the future of East Asia is whether peace can be maintained and war avoided. China's relations with Tibet remain troubled because of ongoing nationalistic resistance to the Chinese, but Chinese migration there has overwhelmed the smaller Tibetan population. The Chinese Muslim population in the northwest has been a problem but not a major one. Tensions with the Soviet Union and its past allies, Vietnam and India, have been eliminated because of the collapse of communism in the Soviet Union in 1991.

China supported Pakistan throughout the Cold War against India, but hostile relations with India also declined after 1991. China's relations with Indonesia were not close after the military coup in that country in 1965, but they have improved, and China's relations with the military dictators of Myanmar have generally remained close. No serious problems have emerged with other Southeast Asian states.

A major problem for East Asia is whether Japan and South Korea will remain in their dependent military relationship with the United States in the face of U.S. hostility toward North Korea. The public yearning in Japan to create a military force to establish Japan as an independent nation seems to be gaining force, but that has created serious fears in China and the two Koreas and has forced the United States to rethink its relationship to East Asia. How the United States handles the problem of a potential North Korean nuclear weapons program will make a big difference in whether peaceful trade and coexistence continue in East Asia. U.S. demands for complete and total dismantlement of nuclear weapons have been rejected by North Korea, and the United States refuses to offer incentives to the North for a negotiated solution. The possibility of unilateral U.S. military action remains despite the opposition of South Korea and China to that policy. The impasse remains.

The Japanese fear of a serious threat from a possible North Korea weapons arsenal has only served to push public sentiment toward rearmament and nuclear weapons. Six hundred books were published on North Korea in Japan, most of them extremely hostile. Prime Minister Koizumi Jun'ichirō's initial attempt to negotiate with North

Korea to pay reparations for the damage during Japanese colonialism backfired when Kim Jong Il admitted kidnapping Japanese from Japan as a means of recruiting Japanese language instructors. The public, the media, and Japanese nationalists led by Abe Shinzō of the Liberal Democratic Party and Satō Katsumi of the Contemporary Korea Institute have responded with demands for a hard line against North Korea, pushing Koizumi away from a peaceful resolution of differences. While Japan might well choose to remain a junior partner in the U.S.-Japan military alliance as the best means of defense, that kind of unequal partnership cannot last forever, and hard-core nationalists are pushing for rearmament.

Japan has sought accommodation with China's economic growth, but the growth of China's military troubles Japanese leaders. At present, the Chinese military has a large army capable of defending against invasion, but its outmoded weaponry and its weak navy and air force cannot support aggressive expansion abroad as long as the United States is committed to the defense of Japan and Taiwan. Any threat against Japan would undoubtedly trigger Japanese rearmament and a Japanese nuclear weapons program backed up by a vastly superior industrial base. It seems likely that for the near future, Sino-Japanese relations will remain calm as both sides concentrate on peaceful trade and investment.

The U.S. military presence in East Asia has had a strong stabilizing effect by preventing Japanese rearmament, stemming both the growing Taiwanese desire for independence and the Chinese desire to take Taiwan by force. It has blocked both a North Korean invasion of the South and a southern invasion of the North. If it finds a way to reach a negotiated solution of problems with North Korea by not challenging its survival, it might be able to maintain a beneficial presence in East Asia. Otherwise, the United States could spark another disastrous Korean War, or East Asia may decide to solve its own problems without U.S. interference.

SUGGESTED READING

For Chinese foreign relations, see A. J. Nathan and R. S. Ross, *The Great Wall and the Empty Fortress* (1997). For the Chinese economy, see N. R. Lardy, *China's Unfinished Economic Revolution* (1998) and *Integrating China into the Global Economy* (2002). For Chinese politics and disruption, see M. Goldman and R. Mac-Farquhar, eds., *The Paradox of China's Post-Mao Reforms* (1999). For reform and resistance in China, see E. J. Perry and M. Selden, *Chinese Society: Change, Conflict and Resistance* (2003). For Japanese politics, see C. Johnson, *Japan Who Governs?* (1995), and R. W. Bowen, *Japan's Dysfunctional Democracy* (2003). For the Japanese economy, see B. Gao, *Japan's Economic Dilemma* (2001), and for Japan's foreign relations, see K. B. Pyle, *Japan and the Primacy of Foreign Policy: Facing New Orders in Asia* (forthcoming). For Japanese policy toward North Korea, see G. McCormack, *Target North Korea* (2004), esp. pp. 125–148.

For the two Koreas, see D. C. Shin, *Mass Politics and Culture in Democratizing Korea* (1999); B. Cumings, *North Korea, Another Country* (2003); M. O'Hanlon and M. Mochizuki, *Crisis on the Korean Peninsula* (2003); V. D. Cha and D. C. Kang, *Nuclear North Korea* (2003); and G. McCormack, *Target North Korea* (2004).

CREDITS

220, 232–33. Used with permission of the publisher.

Chapter 11

p. 216: Excerpt from Mass, Jeffrey P., *The Kamakura Bakufu, A Study in Documents.* Copyright © 1976 by the Board of Trustees of the Leland Stanford Jr. University.

Chapter 12

p. 237: Reprinted courtesy of Stephen West. p. 242: From *Under Confucian Eyes: Writings on Gender in Chinese History,* ed. Susan Mann and Yu-yin Cheng (Berkeley, CA: University of California Press, 2001), pp. 91–92 [ISBN: 0-520-22274-1]. Reprinted by permission of The University of California Press.

Chapter 13

p. 262: Excerpt from Horton, H. Mack, translator, *The Journal of Sōchō.* Copyright © 2002 by the Board of Trustees of the Leland Stanford Jr. University.

Chapter 14

p. 279: As seen in Benjamin Elman, *A Cultural History of Civil Examinations in Late Imperial China,* University of California Press, 2000, p. 184. p. 286: Reprinted by permission of Indiana University Press.

Chapter 15

p. 298: Reprinted by permission of Houghton Mifflin Company. p. 302: Reprinted courtesy of Michael C. Kalton.

Chapter 16

p. 322: Fang Bao's Random Notes from Prison, from *The Search for Modern China, A Documentary Collection* by Pei Kai Cheng, Michael Lestz and Jonathan Spence. Copyright © 1999 by W. W. Norton & Company, Inc. Used by permission of W. W. Norton & Company, Inc.

Chapter 17

p. 340: Reprinted by permission of Tuttle Publishing.

Chapter 18

p. 353: Reprinted by permission of Houghton Mifflin Company. p. 362: From JaHyun Kim Haboush, transl., *The Memoirs of Lady Hyegyŏng* (University of California Press, 1996), p. 301 [ISBN: 0-520-20054-3]. Reprinted by permission of The University of California Press.

Chapter 19

p. 392: J. Mason Gentzler, ed., *Changing China: Readings in the History of China from the Opium War to the Present.* Copyright © 1977 by Praeger Publishing. Reproduced with permission of Greenwood Publishing Group, Inc., Westport, CT.

Chapter 23

p. 456: Reprinted by permission of Foreign Languages Press.

Chapter 24

p. 476: Reprinted courtesy of The Asia Center.

Chapter 27

p. 532: Reprinted by permission of The University of Scranton Press.

Chapter 29

p. 576: From *Chinese Sociology & Anthropology,* vol. 34, no. 2 (Summer 2002): 75–80. English-language translation copyright © 2002 by M.E. Sharpe, Inc. Reprinted with permission of M.E. Sharpe, Inc.

Chapter 31

p. 608: From Mary C. Brinton, *Women and the Economic Miracle: Gender and Work in Postwar Japan* (Berkeley: University of California Press, 1992), p. 47. Reprinted by permission of The University of California Press. p. 610: Reprinted by permission.

INDEX